Contexts for Criticism

Contexts for Criticism

Third Edition

DONALD KEESEY

San Jose State University

Mayfield Publishing Company
Mountain View, California
London • Toronto

Library of Congress Cataloging-in-Publication Data

Contexts for criticism / [compiled] by Donald Keesey.—3rd ed.
 p. cm.
Includes bibliographical references and index.
ISBN 1-55934-844-5
 1. Criticism. 2. Literature—History and criticism—Theory, etc.
3. English literature—History and criticism—Theory, etc.
I. Keesey, Donald.
PN81.C745 1997
801'.95—dc21

97-16924
CIP

Manufactured in the United States of America
10 9 8 7 6 5 4 3 2 1

Mayfield Publishing Company
1280 Villa Street
Mountain View, California 94041

Sponsoring editor, Renée Deljon; production, Rogue Valley Publications; manuscript editor, Patterson Lamb; art director, Jeanne M. Schreiber; text designer, Susan M. Breitbard; cover designer, Jean Mailander; manufacturing manager, Randy Hurst. The text was set in 9/11 Palatino by ColorType and printed on 50# Buttes des Morts by The Banta Book Group.

Text Credits Page 86: Randall Jarrell, "Eighth Air Force," from *The Complete Poems* by Randall Jarrell. Copyright © 1969 by Mrs. Randall Jarrell. Reprinted by permission of Farrar, Straus & Giroux, Inc. Page 308: William Carlos Williams, "This Is Just to Say," reprinted by permission of New Directions Publishing. Page 400: Reprinted with the permission of Simon & Schuster from *The Poems of W. B. Yeats: A New Edition*, edited by Richard J. Finneran. Copyright © 1928 by Macmillan Publishing Company, renewed © 1956 by Georgie Yeats.

 Printed on acid-free, recycled paper.

PREFACE

This new edition of *Contexts for Criticism* changes two of the "target" texts, with *The Tempest* replacing *Hamlet* and Wordsworth's Intimations Ode replacing Keats's "Ode on a Grecian Urn." Kate Chopin's *The Awakening* remains as the third target text, guaranteeing that this edition continues to give considerable attention to issues of feminist criticism. The two new target texts require fourteen new "application essays." There are also three new theoretical essays: Mark Schorer's "Technique as Discovery," Robert Alter's "Character and the Connection with Reality," and Adena Rosmarin's "Defining a Theory of Genre."

In short, users of the second edition will find much fresh material here, but despite the many changes in content, the book's purpose and the structure that supports it remain the same. That purpose is to help readers focus on the fundamental issues of literary interpretation. The organization supports this end, first, by arranging competing theories in a clear and useful way, and second, by applying these theories to the same literary texts. The book begins with a general introduction setting forth its "contextual" organization. Each chapter then opens with an introductory essay that explains the assumptions and interests of the critics who work in that context, traces briefly the role the context has played in the history of criticism, and offers an assessment of its place in the contemporary scene. The emphasis in these introductory essays is on the general orientation that critics in each context share rather than on matters that divide them, for the first task is to get a clear view of the basic approach. Each chapter next presents three "theoretical" essays representing strong contemporary arguments for this way of looking at literature. The essays are written by well-known critics who are themselves committed to the approach. These writings often exhibit a polemical stance, for I have tried to include essays that state the issues forcefully enough to provoke thought and clearly enough to give that thought some direction.

To further clarify the issues, each chapter concludes with three essays applying some version of the critical approach to the same three texts: *The Tempest*, the Intimations Ode, and *The Awakening*. These widely studied works, representing different periods and genres, are rich enough to have inspired a variety of critical comment and short enough to be read and reread in conjunction with the critical essays. So, as readers see each theory applied to works they know well, they will better understand what that theory can do. Further, as they see the other approaches applied to the same three works, readers can more accurately estimate the strengths and uses of each context. And they will be better equipped to make their own applications of the theories. Criticism, as this book seeks to show, is something one *does*, and when I use the book in classes, I have each student choose yet another target text and develop one more set of applications as we work through the various contexts. In the process, the students discover that they have always been making their own applications in at least one of these contexts, for there are no other ways to read. By systematically comparing the competing theories, readers will come to see what theories inform their own practice and what alternatives are available.

The application essays, then, provide a way to clarify and test the theories. And because the same target texts appear in all chapters, they open a dialogue between the contexts. Helen Vendler, for example, uses Lionel Trilling's mimetic reading of Wordsworth's Ode as the foil for her formal interpretation, and Trilling's essay is at least a reference point for most of the other commentators on this poem. In a similar way, Paul Brown's cultural critique of *The Tempest* serves as a reference point, or even as a starting point, for critics who argue for other ways to read the play. The essays on *The Awakening* are likewise cross-referential; in addition to representing the various contexts, the essays by Gilbert, Yaeger, and Stange insist on the centrality of feminist issues while the essays by Walker, May, and Wolff insist the book transcends such issues.

This dialogue is continued in the theoretical essays as well. E. D. Hirsch, for example, seizes on Cleanth Brooks's reading of a short Wordsworth poem to argue the primacy of authorial meaning; in the next section, Brooks offers that same reading to argue the primacy of textual meaning. And in the following section, Louise Rosenblatt revisits Wordsworth's poem, taking the Hirsch-Brooks debate as a starting point for developing a rationale for her reader-oriented approach. In the same context, Norman Holland defines his position with reference to Wolfgang Iser and other reader-response critics; Bernard Paris argues for the mimetic uses of psychology; and Cynthia Griffin Wolff's essay as well as his own show what some of those uses are. Robert Alter reasserts the claims of mimetic criticism in the face of structural and poststructural challenges; Northrop Frye explains how he developed an intertextual emphasis to remedy the deficiencies of mimetic and formal criticism; Jonathan Culler extends the intertextual argument in overtly structuralist terms; and Jacques Derrida deconstructs structuralism, ushering in what is sometimes called the "poststructural" era. In the final chapter, the insights and assumptions of formalism, structuralism, and poststructuralism are given a historicizing critique and redirection.

In these and other ways, the dialogue is carried on from essay to essay and from context to context. As a result, readers who work through the contexts in sequence will see how the focus of interest in literary theory has shifted from mid-century to the present. We should remember, though, that despite these shifts in theoretical focus, each context remains the ground for much contemporary critical practice. We should remember, too, that while arguments about the fundamental issues of interpretation appear here in modern dress, the issues are indeed fundamental — and perennial. Since every reading is necessarily an interpretation, every reader has an important stake in these arguments. These are contexts *for* criticism, ways of reading, and I hope that users of this book will not merely follow the dialogue but actively join it, adopting each perspective in turn, applying it to particular works, comparing it with other approaches, and deciding what use they can make of it. The book is designed to invite this participation and to enable these operations.

Acknowledgments

A number of people have helped to make this book. Several users of the second edition have offered suggestions, as have my colleagues Balance Chow, Paul Douglass, Jack Haeger, and Scott Hymas. Douglas Keesey again provided advice and encouragement at every stage, and my students in "Modern Approaches to Literature" helped me to see what changes were needed. Other reviewers were Marshall Alcorn,

George Washington University; John Ehrstine, Washington State University; Anne Laskaya, University of Oregon; Mary Libertin, Shippensburg University; Dave Samuelson, California State University, Long Beach; Carol J. Singley, The State University of New Jersey, Rutgers Campus at Camden; John M. Sullivan, California State University, San Bernardino; and Edward M. White, California State University, San Bernardino. I should add that it was once more a pleasure to work with Jim Bull, Renée Deljon, and the always cooperative staff at Mayfield Publishing.

CONTENTS

III. Reader-Response Criticism: Audience as Context

IV. Mimetic Criticism: Reality as Context

V. Intertextual Criticism: Literature as Context

VI. Poststructural Criticism: Language as Context   371

VII. Historical Criticism II: Culture as Context   451

General Introduction

Some are bewilder'd in the Maze of Schools.
　　　　　—Pope, *An Essay on Criticism*

Why study literary criticism? Even to students of literature the answer is not always clear, for I have heard students announce that they make it a principle to ignore "criticism," by which term they mean everything from the popular book review to the scholarly tome, and sometimes this attitude is encouraged by their instructors. No doubt the purpose of this principled ignorance is to keep "interpretation" from coming between the reader and the text. Critics, in this view, are specialists whose concerns are remote from the reader's interests or may even threaten those interests. For the belief is widespread that the reader should confront the work with no pre-conceptions and should achieve thereby an authentic, unmediated response.

But in fact there can be no unmediated response. In the first place, every reader must bring to a text at least a basic understanding of the work's language and there-fore must bring as well an extensive range of cultural experience that "understand-ing the language" presupposes. Only the reader who knew no English at all could have a truly unmediated response to a work in that language. In the second place, every reader must bring not only a knowledge of language but also a set of expecta-tions about "literature" that will cause that reader to emphasize, to value, even to perceive some features of the work rather than others.

In short, we must always read in some way, for every reading is an active process of making sense, an interpretation. And since "literary criticism" may be broadly defined as the art of interpreting literature, every reading is an act of criticism and every reader is a critic. Perhaps the best argument, then, for the study of literary criticism is the realization that critics are not other people. To read literature at all is to practice some type of criticism, to read in some way and not in some other. No reader has a choice about this. The only choice is to decide what kind of critic one will be, a critic who remains unaware of his or her own critical assumptions, or one who has a chosen a way of reading with full knowledge that it is a way of reading and after some careful study of the alternatives.

But how can such a study be most usefully conducted? If every reader is a critic, then the kinds of criticism must be many and various, and certainly the names for the types or "schools" of criticism are bewildering in their number and diversity. We hear of old historians, new historians, and antihistorians, of Freudians, Jungians,

1

and Lacanians, of Marxists and feminists, affectivists and geneticists, structuralists and poststructuralists, old New Critics and new New Critics. The list of labels can be extended to distressing lengths. To confuse matters further, these terms are not all built on the same principle. Some indicate a critic's philosophical assumptions, his or her view of the world or of the mind; some announce allegiance to a particular discipline or to a particular ideology; some suggest an interest or lack of interest in historical background or social concerns or biographical information. Small wonder that books attempting to survey the field of literary criticism offer a perplexing variety of labels and organizing schemes. And any number of these might be valid for descriptive purposes.

But not all are very helpful for systematic study. To devise a usable grammar for this Babel, we need a conceptual scheme that will include the many types of literary criticism and at the same time separate the competing voices in a way that will help us make useful comparisons. Our categories, then, must be parallel and not so multiple that they add to the confusion. The idea of critical contexts offers such a scheme. Consider the different answers that might be given to the deceptively simple question "Why is there a gravedigger's scene in *Hamlet?*" One type of critic will immediately translate this question to a historical context and explain that the stage traditions, or the presence of a similar scene in the source plays, or the audience's demand for a favorite clown would motivate Shakespeare to write the scene, and so sufficiently answer the question. A different critic in the same context will argue that the scene is designed to reveal further Hamlet's melancholy *adust,* especially that form deriving from sanguine humor, since his grave levity, his jesting with death, would be recognized by the Elizabethan playgoer as a standard symptom of that malady.

Operating in a different context, another critic will explain the scene in terms of its effects, pointing out that the comic interlude temporarily relieves, if only finally to heighten, the emotional tension in the audience. This is "why" the scene is in the play. Yet another critic will interpret our question as a call to explain how the scene fits with other parts of the play, how its diction, imagery, and action serve to develop the coherent structure we call *Hamlet.* And still a different critic will understand the question as a request to account for the scene on some imitative principle. Directing our vision to the world of experience, this critic will remind us that the comic and the tragic are often inextricably mixed in life, and will praise the genius of Shakespeare for furnishing richer and truer representations than those found in the more monotonic Greek or French tragedies.

These answers do not exhaust the possibilities, but they reveal an important point about the process of interpretation: the first and crucial step in that process is to decide from what perspective or angle of vision we will view the work. To put it another way, we must decide in what context the work should be placed. Since each answer to our *Hamlet* question involves the choice of a different context, we get the impression — an impression we often get from critical debates — that the respondents are not really answering the same question, are not really debating the issue. This impression is understandable, but it points up the fact that the central issue in criticism is precisely the choice of context. Each of these answers represents an implicit argument that the context the interpreter has selected is the most useful, relevant, or illuminating context.

To study criticism systematically, we need to make these arguments explicit. And we need a conceptual scheme or organizing metaphor that will help us define, ana-

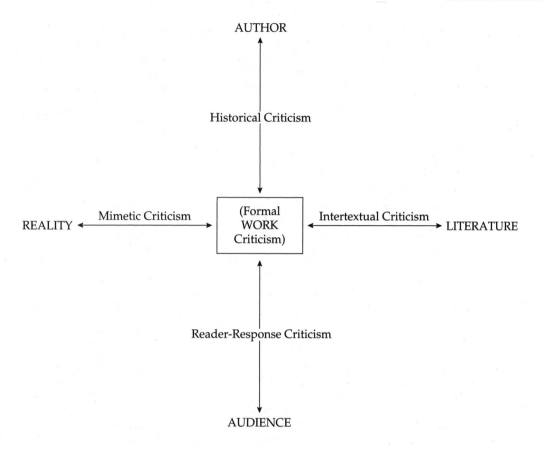

lyze, and compare the various contexts within which all particular interpretations are made. The scheme I use in this book may be visualized in the form of the accompanying diagram.

Because criticism usually involves the interpretation of a particular literary work, it is logical that the work in question should hold the central place in the diagram. The symmetrical arrangement of the various "contexts" around that work is, I should add, perfectly arbitrary and is designed, like the diagram itself, simply to help us think systematically about literary criticism. As presented here, a vertical axis unites the author and the audience and represents the basic communication line. Meanings, some semanticists are fond of saying, are in people, not in words, and many theories of interpretation are based on the belief that we must look either to the author or to the audience if we are to understand the meaning of the literary text. Types of criticism that see the author's conscious and unconscious intentions and, beyond these, his or her entire social, political, and intellectual milieu as the determiners of the poem's meaning are concerned to investigate the causal contexts of the work, and these represent forms of historical criticism. Other forms of criticism pursue the line in the opposite direction and focus on the work's effects rather than on its causes. Critics who adopt these approaches may argue that the study of causes is beyond our reach or merely beside the point, but they agree that the real "meaning" of literature results from the interaction of audience and work. For these critics, then, the reactions of the audience form the important context for the study of literary meaning, and they may be classed together as "reader-response" critics.

In the view of another group of critics, this tendency to look either to the author or to the audience causes us to overlook the very thing that unites them — the literary work itself. In the language of the communication model, these critics urge us to pay less attention to senders and receivers and more attention to poems, for they believe that meanings are, in fact, in words, and especially in the arrangement of words. In practice, their efforts are devoted largely to demonstrating the poem's coherence by showing how its various parts are integrated to create a complex but artistically unified whole. On their assumptions, the primary context for the study of literature is the completed work itself, and the parenthetical placement of "formal criticism" on the diagram represents the attempt of these critics to isolate the work from the other contexts, especially those labeled "historical" and "reader-response." Because they want to show how the various parts interrelate to create the complete poem, these critics are particularly concerned with the "form" of literary works, and "formal criticism" is a widely used label for this context.

The horizontal axis of the diagram cuts across the communication line and locates the work with reference to two very different contexts. One of these is that large, ill-defined, yet very important context we somewhat helplessly call "life," or "truth," or, as here, "reality." None of these terms is entirely satisfactory, and the context not only resists precise definition but also offers notorious philosophical puzzles. Despite these difficulties, forms of criticism that orient the work toward "reality" or "life as experienced outside of art" are at once the most venerable and the most popular. Since they are chiefly concerned with measuring the accuracy or "truth" of the characters and actions presented in literature, these approaches are traditionally labeled "mimetic." Unfortunately, no traditional or widely accepted label exists for those kinds of criticism that direct our attention away from reality and place the work instead in the context of literature as a whole. Because these approaches stress the artifice or conventionality of all literature and argue that any work must be understood by analogy with other works that employ similar conventions, I have called such approaches "intertextual" criticism.

Additional explanations for these and other terms will be developed in the introductions to the separate chapters. But the matter of terminology deserves some further comment here. First, we must face the troublesome fact that English has no synonym for the awkward "literary work"; consequently the word "poem" must do double duty, denoting sometimes a verse composition and sometimes any work of literature in verse or prose. In this book I follow the usual practice and occasionally use "poem" in the general sense. So *The Tempest*, for example, and *The Awakening* are poems as well as the *"Intimations Ode,"* and "poetics" is the theory of "poetry" in this extended meaning. But I use "literary work" or "literary structure" when the situation requires the more cumbersome but less ambiguous term; and often I use "literary text," since in practice most of our concern is with the printed page, although we should remember that some poems have existed for centuries in purely oral form and that recitations or dramatic performances are not quite the same as written texts.

My effort to keep terminology simple is especially apparent in the very general definition I have given of "literary criticism" as "the art of interpreting literary works." Although this fairly bristles with ambiguities, attempts at this point to narrow our terms will only expand our confusions. There is, for example, no leak-proof definition of a "literary" work. The adjective fits most of what we call lyrics, dramas, and fictional narratives in verse or prose, but what else it fits is a matter of endless debate. Similarly, "criticism" is usually thought to have both theoretical and practical aspects, as the arrangement of the essays in this book assumes, but it is often difficult and usually unnecessary to trace the fine line between them, or to assign them different names. So I include under "criticism" all attempts to interpret literature as well as all arguments about how this can best be accomplished, however specific or general, *ad hoc* or theoretical. In the last analysis, clarity and precision may lie down easily together, but in this introductory text, which is far from the last analysis, I have tried to keep the distinctions few and functional. After the basic issues have become clear, further refinements can be made. Provisionally, then, "literary works" will mean what we usually mean by the phrase — that is, plays, lyrics, narratives, and things that resemble them — and attempts to interpret these are forms of "literary criticism."

The diagram of critical contexts and the conceptual map it supplies are also offered provisionally, not as the only valid way to classify types of criticism, but as a way that can help us understand some of the fundamental problems of interpretation. One result of this contextual organization is that critics who are usually classed together because they share a set of beliefs may be separated in this scheme according to the context in which they operate. So a Freudian critic who investigates an author's unconscious motivations is practicing a form of historical criticism, whereas a Freudian critic studying a reader's reactions is, in this plan, a reader-response critic. And since Freudian psychoanalysis claims to interpret human behavior in general, it also provides a mimetic model by which the truth or "realism" of a literary character's behavior can be measured. Feminist criticism, which has seen explosive growth in the last three decades, will pattern in the same way. So although "feminism" is absent from the table of contents, it is by no means absent from the book; on the contrary, feminist critics will be found in nearly every context. Other schools of thought and other psychological approaches could be similarly distributed. By cutting across these kinds of classifications, this book's contextual organization pushes to the background questions about the validity of these larger theories and focuses attention instead on the interpretive problems central to all forms of literary criticism. Whatever the critic's political or philosophical position, he or she will have to decide questions of meaning within one of the contexts we will be exploring.

The neatly symmetrical diagram is designed to aid that exploration. But such a spatial metaphor can be misleading if we forget that the diagram maps only the main terminals and not the often twisty routes that traffic between them. In practice, a single critic, sometimes in a single essay, may operate in two or more of these contexts. Furthermore, the contexts themselves tend to shade into each other as we move from their central to their peripheral concerns. Nevertheless, as the diagram may serve to remind us, the central position of each context represents a particular way of looking at literary meaning. As we try out these different perspectives and come to see what each can and cannot show us, we can learn something important about the art of reading literature. This is our goal; and this simple diagram is useful if it can help us think more clearly about the fundamental issues of interpretation.

This goal has guided my organization in other ways as well. The book is divided into seven chapters, each dealing with a separate critical context. Each chapter opens with an introductory essay that explains the basic assumptions and interests of the critics represented in that section. This essay traces briefly the role the context has played in the history of criticism, and it offers an assessment of its place and strength within the contemporary scene. But the main purpose of each prefatory essay is to show how those who adopt this perspective approach the literary work, what kinds of questions they ask, and what kinds of answers they offer.

After this general orientation, each section presents three "theoretical" essays by well-known critics who are themselves committed to this approach. As readers try to come to terms with these wide-ranging and often polemical discussions, they should find that their understanding of the issues is considerably aided by the three "application" essays that conclude each section. Since we may at least provisionally assume that the proof of a critical theory is its ability to somehow illuminate a literary work, readers must be continually testing any theory against the literature they know. Unfortunately, in most collections of critical essays they will face an accumulation of references to a bewildering number and variety of works, many of which they may not have read well, or recently, or at all. And even readers who manage to sort through the various examples may still complain that the arguments are difficult to compare because the theories are not brought to bear on the same literary texts. The application essays are included here to allow such comparison. So, after the theoretical essays that explain and defend aspects of the general approach, often with references to various examples, each section contains three essays that apply some version of this approach to three famous literary works: *The Tempest,* the *"Intimations Ode,"* and *The Awakening.*

Because these works are widely studied, chances are good that many readers will already be familiar with them. Because they are few and relatively brief, they can be read and reread along with the critical essays. And because they represent different literary forms and were written in different periods, they furnish useful test cases for theories that claim to illuminate literature of all types and times. Finally, each work is extraordinarily rich and complex, and each has inspired a large body of critical commentary representing the different perspectives. So, as readers see each theory applied to works they know well, they will be able to understand more fully what that approach can accomplish. Equally to the point, as they see the different approaches applied to the *same* works, they will be able to estimate more accurately their relative strengths and possible uses.

The arrangement of the chapters is designed to facilitate these comparisons. It is also designed to show how the major theoretical debates have shifted over the last half of the twentieth century. We begin with the formalist challenge to author-centered historical criticism, move on to the reader-response critics' challenge to formalism, pause to examine mimetic theories (these cannot be easily fixed in the sequence), take up the structural and semiotic approaches of the intertextual critics, look next at the poststructuralists' simultaneous continuation and deconstruction of structuralism, and end not quite where we began with a return to historical criticism, but a poststructural historicism very different in many ways from traditional literary history.

We should remember, though, that although the theoretical debates have shifted in this roughly dialectic sequence, critical practice has maintained a more stable heterogeneity. That is to say, theorists may not be arguing much at the moment about authors' intentions, but studies of authors' lives and times, which assume the importance of intentions, continue to be published in large numbers. Formal concepts may not be at the center of today's theoretical controversies, but formal analysis is at the center of much published criticism and much classroom practice. And so with the other contexts. Each may be the focus of theoretical discussion for only a limited time, but all offer approaches that many sophisticated readers find useful, and all continue to be heavily cultivated grounds for practical criticism, as the recent dates for most of the application essays in this book will confirm. In short, while my chapters present a sequence of dialogues that approximates the shifting emphases in contemporary theory, contemporary critical practice might be better characterized as a polyphony—or cacophony—with all the voices still sounding loudly. The essays on *The Tempest* included here offer a clear confirmation on this point. Most of these first appeared in the nineties, after a decade in which "new historical" and cultural materialist approaches had come to dominate criticism of the play, and they show that "old historical" and formalist approaches, for example, are very much alive and very forcefully asserting their own claims against those of the cultural critics.

I should add, too, that I have further simplified matters by staging these debates from an Anglo-American perspective. Continental influences—and these have been very strong in recent decades—are acknowledged primarily as their impact is felt in the English-speaking world. If these dialogues were replayed from a European point of view, the chronology and the emphases would be different. But the basic questions, and the fundamental issues of interpretation, would be the same. These are what we want to get at, and it seems to me that for most readers of this book, the Anglo-American perspective offers the most direct way to get at them.

I have chosen a contemporary focus for the same reason. The "applications" included here are mainly of recent vintage, for I want to stress the point that although each of these contexts has a rich history, none is merely a historical curiosity; on the contrary, each is the basis for some vital contemporary criticism. At the same time, I have sought to include clear and forceful examples of each approach, and I have occasionally selected an earlier essay that met these criteria better than more recent examples. Similar concerns have controlled my choice of the "theoretical" essays. For the most part I have reprinted fairly recent writings, since these can take into account current refinements and objections and reflect more directly the contemporary debate on these perennial issues. But we should always remember that these *are* perennial issues, and I have not hesitated to include an older essay if it seemed to set forth the basic arguments more clearly and more provocatively. Without clarity, we seldom think well; without provocation, we seldom think at all.

In fact, I am convinced that the reader who is provoked enough to enter actively into these debates will gain the most from this book. Throughout this introduction I have talked about "perspectives" and "approaches," and the book itself describes and illustrates different critical "contexts." It will be easy for the reader to assume that each context must have a special but limited validity and that the best literary criticism must be an eclectic combination of all contexts. Such a conclusion has some points to recommend it. It is consistent with the complexity of literature and with the diversity of critical practice; it acknowledges the difficulty of applying "outside" objections in some useful way to internally consistent systems; and it allows the eclectic critic to adopt an inclusive and tolerant, rather than an exclusive and combative, rhetorical stance. Besides, elementary logic suggests that no one of these contexts is likely to offer all the important truths about a literary work.

But by the same logic it is also unlikely that all contexts should offer equally valid or useful insights. To put it another way, though we may agree that there is no complete, definitive, and absolutely correct interpretation of a poem, it does not necessarily follow that there are no better or worse interpretations, interpretations more or less complete, more or less accurate, more or less approximating a "best" reading. At any rate, most of the writers included here will argue that their perspective offers a better way to read, and since all readers must confront the same problems of interpretation, all readers have a real stake in these arguments. If you are to come to an informed decision about them, you will need to analyze them carefully, compare them closely, and test them against specific literary works. This book is designed to make these operations easier. As my title is meant to suggest, these are contexts *for* criticism. Since to read at all is to read from one or another of these perspectives, the informed reader should at least know which he or she has chosen, and why.

Suggestions for Further Reading

Although this book tries to get at some of the perennial issues of literary interpretation through a reading of contemporary criticism, we should remember that these issues are indeed perennial and that discussion of them has a long and rich history. Many of the earlier discussions can be found in Hazard Adams, ed., *Critical Theory Since Plato* (2nd ed., 1992), which also includes a good collection of twentieth-century essays. M. C. Beardsley, *Aesthetics from Classical Greece to the Present: A Short History* (1966), and W. K. Wimsatt and Cleanth Brooks, *Literary Criticism: A Short History* (1957), are useful one-volume surveys, neither especially "short" except by reference to the size of the subject. That size is better gauged and the ground more thoroughly covered in the first four volumes of René Wellek's *A History of Modern Criticism* (1955–1965), which discuss Western criticism from 1750 to 1900. Cambridge University Press is publishing a multivolume *Cambridge History of Literary Criticism,* each volume containing essays by several contributors. So far, Volume 1, *Classical Criticism* (1990), and Volume 8, *From Formalism to Poststructuralism* (1995), have appeared. A very selective list of the many more specialized histories, roughly in order of the period treated, includes G. M. A. Grube, *The Greek and Roman Critics* (1965); D. A. Russell, *Criticism in Antiquity* (1981); B. Weinberg, *A History of Literary Criticism in the Italian Renaissance* (2 vols., 1961); B. Hathaway, *The Age of Criticism: The Late Renaissance in Italy* (1962); E. R. Marks, *The Poetics of Reason* (1968); and M. H. Abrams, *The Mirror and the Lamp* (1953). For the present century, Wellek has continued his monumental history from 1900 to 1950, devoting a volume each to Britain and the United States (1986); a third to Germany, Russia, and Eastern Europe (1991); and a fourth to France, Italy, and Spain (1993). For contemporary criticism, many books will be cited in the suggestions for reading that follow each chapter. But readers should know of two book-length bibliographies of recent critical theory: Leonard Orr, *Research in Critical Theory Since 1965* (1989), and Donald M. Marshall, *Contemporary Critical Theory: A Selective Bibliography* (1993).

CHAPTER ONE

Historical Criticism I: Author as Context

In ev'ry Work regard the Writer's End,
Since none can compass more than they Intend.
　　　　　　　—Pope, *An Essay on Criticism*

Most models of written communication posit an author and an audience. From the author's point of view, the task is to communicate meaning as effectively as possible. From the audience's perspective, the task is to interpret that meaning as accurately as possible. To ask what a poem means is, on this model, to ask what the author meant when he or she created it.

The poem's real meaning, it follows, is always in the past, even if sometimes in the very near past, and the search for that meaning is a search for the author's original intention. So even when we're dealing with contemporary writers, inquiry is seldom a simple matter. Not only are writers notoriously inclined to be reticent, evasive, or even deceptive when discussing the "meaning" of their works, but they are seldom in a position to know what they may have unconsciously intended, and in any case they must always talk about what they may have meant at some point in the past—last week, last year, three decades ago. Frequently, of course, the writers we're interested in are dead, making direct inquiry even less productive. But their works remain, and since it is the task of criticism to discover as fully as possible the meaning of those works, this can best be done by understanding as fully as possible the minds that created them.

The kinds of historical criticism that aim to supply this understanding, since they focus on the author as the cause of meaning, may be conveniently labeled "genetic." As we'll see, there are other kinds of historical criticism, and other places to center meaning. Our concern here is with those historical studies that ground the meaning of the poem in the mind of the poet at the time of creation.

Even with this limited focus, the genetic critic's job is formidable. To understand the author's mind at the time of creation means, in practice, to assemble and interpret all documents that may throw light on that mind, and these documents can be numerous. A writer's letters and library will be relevant certainly, earlier and later works probably, laundry lists possibly. Then there are the recorded comments of all those who knew the author well or casually. As we approach our own time, the number of available documents pertaining to a writer may become very large, and for a contemporary author, the enterprising biographer can supplement the written record with direct interviews.

Conversely, as we move back in time, the amount of information about authors rapidly diminishes; we know little about Marlowe, less about Virgil, nothing at all about "Homer." This state of affairs is naturally lamented by genetic critics who assume if we had more information about, say, Shakespeare's schooling or Chaucer's reading or Sophocles' religious views, we would be better able to understand their writings. But the lack of specifically biographical information does not fatally handicap genetic criticism. We may have no documentary evidence about Shakespeare's school days, but we can find out a good deal about what was studied and how in the schools available to someone of his age and station. We may not know exactly what Chaucer read, but we can discover what most educated people of his time were reading. We can never know with any precision what Sophocles' religious views were, but we can learn something about the forms of worship practiced in his day, what was considered orthodox, what not.

By this logic the inquiry widens to include a great deal more than the strictly biographical. For the genetic critic, after all, is by definition a student of causes, and if a poem is the product of an author and the author is the product of an age, then nothing less than a full understanding of that age—the author's entire political, social, and intellectual milieu—is required if we are to fully understand that author's art. And, paradoxically, the need for this kind of information seems to grow as the author is more distant from us and the biographical information more scant. This explains why, although the known facts of Shakespeare's life will barely fill a page, the books about his life can easily fill a shelf. Add to these the many books treating Elizabethan religion, politics, economics, science, and all the other elements that make up the "life" of the "time," from sweeping generalizations about "world views" to the minutiae of numerology and pneumatology, and you have a sizable library.

And so with every writer and his or her "age." To be sure, not all these studies are examples of genetic criticism strictly defined; some don't even pretend to be. Just as a biography, even of a literary figure, can exist as biography and make no claim to supply interpretations of poems, so a study of Elizabethan psychology or seventeenth-century religious controversy or Victorian legal reforms may be written simply to cast light on that subject, and may use literary texts as part of its evidence, without making any claim to the status of literary criticism. In practice, however, most biographies of writers and most period studies with a literary cast do make such claims, at least implicitly. When we are offered an investigation of the sources of Blake's religious thought, of the background of the Battle of the Books, of the inadequacies of Keats's philosophy or Dryden's wife, we naturally expect that the investigator will get around to telling us something interpretive about poems. Sometimes this expectation is disappointed. Critical procedures using the life to explain the work can easily get entangled with biographical procedures using the work to explain the life, and the result may be a vast tautology. More often, scholars may be content simply to amass information about the writer's life or age on the assumption that somehow it will be critically useful to someone.

But this is merely to observe that not all historical studies manage to keep an unwavering critical focus. This observation does not undercut the historical critic's basic premise that literary meaning must be grounded in the author, and this premise is widely accepted. Inquiries into writers' intimate personal lives and into their social and intellectual backgrounds continue to be the focus of much classroom discussion, continue to be published by both academic and commercial publishers, continue to form the bulk of what is generally called "literary study." This state of affairs is so familiar in the last quarter of the twentieth century we may be a little startled when we reflect that the immense industry devoted to historical study is a relatively recent phenomenon. While the historical context has been the most heavily cultivated one in the past century, in the previous twenty-three it was the least. Aristotle, for instance, showed a lively interest in most of the contexts I have diagrammed, but he saw no reason for criticism to be much concerned with the maker of poems, and with few exceptions critics agreed with him on this point until well into the eighteenth century. So, despite the apparently axiomatic nature of the argument for genetic criticism, and despite its prominence in bibliographies and classroom instruction, the emphasis on the author and the period, on the circumstances of the poem's composition, is distinctly modern.

This emphasis seems to have come about largely as a result of two different but mutually reinforcing influences. The first was a gradual shift in the conception of a poem from something that reflected or imitated nature to something that reflected or expressed an individual, a unique mind. This shift, which had its chronological center somewhere near the beginning of the nineteenth century, was bound to focus attention on the life of the author, a kind of attention, not coincidentally, that some writers of the period seemed to invite. The second influence, which also had its roots in the eighteenth century but which did not become dominant until the nineteenth, was the sense of the *pastness* of the past, the idea that each "age" has different assumptions and different values, and hence that the art of any period can be understood only by someone specially trained to understand those assumptions and values.

These two ideas, then, one stressing the individuality of the poet, the other the individuality of the age, combined in the nineteenth century to turn literary study toward the biographical and the historical. And when, very late in the century, the graduate study of literature came into being, first in Germany, then in the United States and England, that study developed as a variation of the "scientific historicism" that dominated most academic disciplines at the time. Here the poetic value of a work might be assumed, could even occasionally be discussed in a warm "appreciation," but such discussions were "after hours," so to speak, and hopelessly "impressionistic." Real scholarship was concerned with the facts—that is to say, with the historical facts. And again this emphasis meant that at the inception of modern literary study on the academic level, the chief concern was with the circumstances of the poem's composition.

Thus, in the early decades of the twentieth century, various forms of historical criticism—the approach to the poem through the study of the life and times of its author—reigned virtually unchallenged in the universities. This historical criticism dealt in facts and required "research," like any solid academic discipline. It investigated the causes of things—something else that marked it as a legitimate field of study. And if, though few as yet raised the objection, the approach had no way to distinguish a poem from any other verbal construct, this inability was not necessarily a defect; any document could tell us something about the author or the age that produced it, and that knowledge in turn could be reflected back to illuminate any document. For the study of "literature," sometimes defined as anything written, was in its grandest conception nothing less than the study of cultural history. But even when more narrowly conceived as an inquiry whose end was the understanding of poems, the genetic approach had academic respectability: it was concerned with objective data; it employed "scholarship," and—not least important—it provided an easily understood and widely accepted scheme for organizing literary study.

Given the assumptions of genetic criticism, the proper context for such study was clearly the causal context. *Paradise Lost* may be an epic, *Lycidas* a pastoral elegy, and *Samson Agonistes* a drama, but to the genetic critic the fact of overriding importance is that they are all poems by John Milton. So the author, the most obvious cause of poems, becomes the first organizing focus of literary study. As one result, we have hundreds of books describing the lives and works of major and not-so-major writers, and few English curricula are considered complete if they lack separate courses devoted to, at the very least, Chaucer, Shakespeare, and Milton. But the writer, according to these same assumptions, is the product of an age, and that assumption suggests another causal principle: we should study the "Renaissance" writers together, and the "Victorians," the "Romantics," the "Augustans," and so on. The different sources implicit in these labels and the notoriously shifty boundaries between such "ages" may suggest that the problems of periodicity have never been fully resolved. But these difficulties are minor. The logic of historical criticism demands some period arrangement, just as the concern with causes further suggests that, as far as practical, we should study the writers within each period and the periods themselves in chronological order. Causes, after all, work through time and only in one direction.

In fact, despite the powerful and in some ways successful challenges to the dominance of historical criticism, the genetic categories of author, period, nation, and chronological sequence, which are the categories employed by Hippolyte Taine in the nineteenth century, remain nearly the only categories used to organize literary study in American universities. This conservatism shows partly the strength of the genetic position, partly that the other contexts have been unable to supply any alternative schemes. As a consequence, the organization of literary study often shows a historical basis even when some other forms of criticism are being practiced.

But genetic criticism continues to be much more than a framework for other kinds of studies. Many scholars accept all or part of the causal argument, teach comfortably within the period organization, and publish books and essays about the historical backgrounds of poems and authors. Biographical studies flourish, some employing the analytical tools of Freud and his followers and rivals to get at the author's unconscious meanings, others content to concentrate on more conscious and more fully documented intentions. And studies of the writer's "age," of the various aspects of the cultural milieu, continue to be published in large numbers.

Nevertheless, in contrast to the earlier decades of the century, genetic approaches no longer monopolize literary study. Other contexts are also heavily cultivated, and the story of their challenge to historical criticism is the opening chapter in the theoretical debates of the last half-century. It will be enough to sketch a few of the challengers' arguments to provide a context for the essays that follow.

Many of these arguments focus on the central but problematic concept of "cause," a concept especially problematic when causal explanations are offered for "effects" as complicated as poems. On the one hand, it seems reasonable to assume that the crucial experiences in a writer's life must leave some mark on his or her character and thought. On the other hand, it is often difficult to use specific pieces of biographical information to explain the meaning of a literary work. And information about the writer's period is similarly problematic. Even if we could discover what many or most Elizabethans believed about ghosts, and even if it turned out that they believed much the same things, we still wouldn't necessarily know what Shakespeare thought about the subject or what he might have meant in *Hamlet,* unless, that is, we were willing to assume that Shakespeare was a typical Elizabethan or that he expressed only typical beliefs in his plays. Such assumptions do seem to underlie many investigations of the writer's political, social, or intellectual milieu, but the assumptions are seldom clearly stated, and when they are, they look somewhat questionable. If the "age" does in fact make the writer, then we must admit that it sometimes makes him or her very different from their contemporaries. Furthermore, close examination generally shows that a historical "period" is fully as complex, unpredictable, and contradictory as the individuals it comprises. As it happens, different Elizabethans believed wildly different things about ghosts.

So here again we face a dilemma. On the one side, we have the plausible assumption that authors will be affected by the intellectual currents and social conditions that surround them. As we have noted, most literary study is organized on this assumption. On the other side, we have the argument that it is seldom easy in practice to make firm connections between (1) a knowledge of these currents and conditions and (2) the attitudes held by particular authors or — and this is not always the same thing — the attitudes expressed in particular poems.

By such arguments the objectors have sought to show that causal links between the period, the poet, and the poem are much more elusive, much more difficult to establish, than many genetic critics were willing to admit, and that to demonstrate them would require much more rigor and finesse than many historical studies were wont to show, if indeed they could be demonstrated at all. Most genetic critics today would probably admit that their task is more problematic than it had once appeared, that it demands not only wide knowledge but interpretive delicacy and tact. Naturally they would not agree that their difficulties are inherently insoluble or that the causal links can never be plausibly demonstrated.

A more radical challenge to historical criticism does not trouble to deny the possibility of the genetic task but denies instead its relevance. The entire genetic model, so this argument runs, is misleading. Poems are not like other documents. They are special verbal constructs that use language in a special way, and they do not relate to their authors the way other documents do. Formal critics have pursued this line of argument most vigorously, an argument based on a particular conception of a poem. For the formalist, such features as the tensive balance between different parts, the unity controlling a diversity of elements, and the resulting ambiguity, paradox, and irony are the defining features of poems, and it is with these that criticism must deal. Since a study of the circumstances of the poem's composition, no matter how carefully conducted, can never tell us much about these features, it can never lead to *critical* interpretation. The historians' tendency to treat the poem like any other kind of document, their failure to conceive of poetry as a special use of language, deflects attention to nonessential, "unpoetic" factors, and when historians do provide interpretations, they are likely to be reductive. That is, even if we could discover precisely what the poem meant to its author or its original audience, we still would not have discovered the full range of the "legitimate" meanings of the poem. In short, the "real" poem, in this argument, is not the poem in the author's mind at the moment of creation, so there is little point in searching for that mind or that moment.

We will leave to another section the discussion of the ways a poem may be thought to exist independently of its author or period. Here we simply note that such a conception undermines the foundation of all forms of genetic criticism. At the same time, by urging a definition of a poem that is also a description of a "good" poem, the formalist reminds us that it is difficult to develop a convincing theory of poetic value on strictly historical lines. Although values of a kind are apparently implied in many historical studies—this work is worth our attention because it is so thoroughly Jamesian, so typical of the Restoration, so representative of the Victorian concern with evolution—most often such reasons are advanced, if they are directly advanced at all, to justify the study of minor or second-rate works. And obviously a poem might just as easily be valued for the opposite reasons, for its lack of typicality. More to the point, the typicality of acknowledged masterpieces is seldom discussed, and we would think it odd if someone were to try to persuade us that *Oedipus Tyrannus* or *King Lear* was valuable simply because it was, or was not, a "representative" Greek or Elizabethan play.

Closely related to estimates of typicality but more promising as a basis for value is the argument of the historical relativist that our judgment of poems should be guided by period standards. Poets aim to excel under the terms and conditions of their times, and it is unfair to try their works by a different court. To judge accurately a medieval fabliau or an eighteenth-century satire, a Romantic ode or a Victorian novel, we have to condition ourselves to think and feel as their intended audiences did. This position seems defensible, and it has the further advantage of appealing to our sympathetic imagination. In practice, though, the advice may not hold in the crucial cases. We are inclined to say that the "Miller's Tale" or *Gulliver's Travels*, "Ode on a Grecian Urn" or *Middlemarch* are simply great works, and we probably feel little need to add that they were great by the standards of their own periods. Then too, it is easy to find examples of works we value highly, like Melville's novels or Blake's poems, which were largely unappreciated by their first audiences. And, from the other side, a check of publishing records from the eighteenth century to this week's bestseller list indicates that popular taste has rather consistently run toward what most serious students of literature would call the ephemeral. Historical relativists may object that they are really urging us to think like a discriminating Elizabethan playgoer, a perceptive Victorian reader. But this objection seems to beg the question.

The basic communication model suggests yet another value scheme. Every utterance is an attempt to express something, an idea, a feeling, a set of facts, and is successful to the extent that it effectively communicates what it set out to communicate. A poem, then, would be good if it achieved what its author intended. Surely it is pointless to complain about the presence of a chorus in a play by Aeschylus or about the absence of one in a play by Ibsen, to object that Donne's meter lacks the regularity of Pope's or that *Ulysses* is not structured like *Tom Jones*. It is foolish to condemn a work for lacking features the author never intended to supply. But in these and similar instances the argument is not really genetic. The evidence for "intention" is simply our understanding of the work itself. The procedure becomes genetic only when the evidence for what was intended, consciously or otherwise, is sought elsewhere, in letters, diaries, recorded conversations, in assumptions about what the "age" demanded or understood—in other words, only when "intention" is conceivably different from the achieved poem and independently knowable.

In such cases, we could compare what the author did with what he or she intended to do. But even this comparison might not give us a firm basis for judging poetic excellence. For example, if coherence is a value and a poem is judged incoherent, it is a weak defense of the poem to claim that it was meant to be incoherent. For similar reasons, apparent value terms such as "sincerity" or "authenticity," insofar as they refer to an alignment of achievement and intention, are of little help. A mawkish sonnet remains mawkish even if it perfectly expresses the sentiment of its creator, and a puerile satire is none the less puerile for accurately reflecting its author's mind.

Indeed, the more the subject is examined, the clearer it becomes that the study of intention provides little basis for evaluating poems. If the ghost of Chaucer were to appear to us and swear that he saw nothing funny or ironic in the "Nun's Priest's Tale," we would have to revise our estimate, not of the poem, but of the critical sensibility of Chaucer's ghost.

But the fact that historical criticism continues to thrive shows that large numbers of critics do not find these objections overwhelming. For them, the failure to provide a historical ground for evaluating poems is probably the least troublesome charge. Not all critics are convinced that judging poems is a major part of the business of criticism and, in any event, it seems axiomatic that the full understanding of a poem must precede any sound evaluation of it. To the extent historical critics can claim to provide at least part of that understanding, they can concede their lack of value theory with a shrug. As to the inherent difficulty of their task, here again the historians can grant the point. We need, they argue, more and better information, more refined methodology, and more careful application. If psychoanalytical criticism of authors has often been clumsy, the remedy is not to abandon psychoanalysis but to apply it with more care and tact. If generalizations about, say, the "neoclassical" concern with restraint and reason are too simplistic or inaccurate to throw much light on writers such as Swift or Gay, the cure is not to abandon studies of the period but to pursue them with more intensity and rigor.

More radical objections that historical studies, no matter how carefully conducted, are doomed to fail in the nature of the case, are more difficult to address. To answer them directly, critics must step outside their own frame of reference far enough to examine and defend their most basic assumptions. If such defenders were rare when genetic studies were — and perhaps because they were — the only firmly established kinds of literary study, they are more plentiful now that strong rivals have entered the field. On the one side, these defenders stand opposed to the ahistorical view that we *should* read each poem as if it were essentially anonymous and contemporary, a verbal object to be understood by the public norms of language and judged by universal standards. On the other side, paradoxically, they confront the radically historical view that we *must* read each poem as if it were contemporary with us, for no matter how we try to transport ourselves to other places and periods, we inevitably carry our cultural perspective with us and remain twentieth-century readers. The radical historicist, in other words, applies the idea of historical relativism with a vengeance, and in such a way as to undercut the historicist's program. For if we can never lay aside our cultural blinders, then we are forced to read as the ahistorical critics say we should.

Against this odd alliance of forces, genetic theorists continue to maintain that we can, with much care and labor, reach an understanding of other periods that will allow us at least to approximate the perspective of the poem's original and intended audience. On this point they find the radical position simply too sweeping to be logically supportable. And furthermore, they argue, we *should* labor to gain such understanding. For these critics, the communication model remains the fundamental model, and it follows that to speak of meaning in any determinate sense is to speak of an author's meaning. Other contexts, they grant, can tell us what a work *may* mean, but only their own can tell us what it *does* mean. Without the knowledge of an author's character and culture that historical studies supply, there can be no useful check on the often "impressionistic," "anachronistic," "overly ingenious," and otherwise "irresponsible" interpretations that critics operating in other contexts are apt to produce. In short, only the historical context, they claim, can offer a stable meaning for "meaning."

Suggestions for Further Reading

Because this context includes many and diverse approaches, about all one can do is cite representative examples of some of the different kinds of "genetic" criticism. At the center is the very popular "critical biography." The form is discussed in Leon Edel, *Literary Biography* (1957), and it may be sampled in such exemplary works as Edel on Henry James (1953–1972), Edgar Johnson on Charles Dickens (1952), and Richard Ellmann on James Joyce (rev. ed., 1982). See also Ellmann's *Golden Codgers: Biographical Speculations* (1973). Sigmund Freud, *On Creativity and the Unconscious* (1958), shows some of the master's ideas; Frederick Crews, *The Sins of the Fathers: Hawthorne's Psychological Themes* (1966), shows one critic's use of Freud's concepts. If the author's life is the center of genetic studies, the elastic boundaries of his or her "times" or "milieu" form the circumference. The once-popular *Zeitgeist* or "spirit of the age" study is illustrated in E. M. W. Tillyard's *The Elizabethan World Picture* (1943); Eleanor Prosser, *Hamlet and Revenge* (2nd ed., 1971), shows how a scholar's wide reading in one aspect of a period can be focused to challenge our usual interpretations of a literary work. A classic example of source tracing is John L. Lowes, *The Road to Xanadu* (1927); an equally classic instance of the "history of ideas" approach is A. O. Lovejoy, *The Great Chain of Being* (1936). Both of these methods overlap a good deal with intertextual criticism, though they are based on quite different assumptions about the locus of literary meaning. Two attempts to formulate the internal dynamics of literary history are W. J. Bate, *The Burden of the Past and the English Poet* (1970), and Harold Bloom, *The Anxiety of Influence* (1973). E. D. Hirsch, *Validity in Interpretation* (1967), advances arguments for regarding the author as the ultimate source of meaning. Some of these arguments are further developed in P. D. Juhl, *Interpretation: An Essay in the Philosophy of Literary Criticism* (1980). Essays on both sides of this issue have been gathered in D. Newton-DeMolina, ed., *On Literary Intention* (1976).

THEORY

The central purpose of E. D. Hirsch's "Objective Interpretation" is to make the search for the author's meaning once again the main business of literary study, and to provide for that study a closely argued rationale that will allow it to stand as "a corporate enterprise and a progressive discipline." In making his case, Hirsch directly disputes the contention of formal and intertextual critics that the "public norms of language" are sufficient to establish the meaning of a text without reference to the author's probable intentions. Examining the Cleanth Brooks–F. W. Bateson controversy over the meaning of a Wordsworth poem, Hirsch seeks to show that such "public norms" can support different, and even totally opposed, interpretations. While he grants the relevance of most formalist criteria for meaning, including the central criterion of "coherence," Hirsch argues that "coherence" is not an absolute quality. It depends on the context the interpreter has invoked, and for an interpretation to be valid "it is necessary to establish that the context invoked is the most probable context" [author's emphasis]. And to establish this, we need to know all we can about the intender of the meaning. Thus, although Hirsch explicitly distinguishes between the "speaking subject" and the biographical person, he sets forth a clear rationale for intentionalist criticism. Unless we assume an author whose probable meaning we can recover, he claims, "meaning" itself can have no stable sense, "interpretation" cannot be objective, and literary commentary is in danger of becoming a subjective and relativistic babble.

It is worth noting that although the direct targets of Hirsch's arguments are formal critics like Cleanth Brooks and W. K. Wimsatt, the formalists agreed with Hirsch

Objective Interpretation

E. D. Hirsch, Jr.

Reprinted by permission of the Modern Language Association of America from *PMLA* 75 (1960): 463, 470–79. Copyright © 1960 by the Modern Language Association of America. A part of the essay has been omitted, and the notes have been renumbered.

that literary meaning is determinate; they simply disagreed about the context in which it should be determined. In some ways, then, Hirsch's essay may be read as opposing even more directly reader-response critics, poststructural critics, and cultural critics, many of whom are inclined to stress the indeterminacy of meaning and the irrelevance of authorial intention. Yet these approaches had scarcely been developed when Hirsch wrote his essay. Clearly, literary theory in the last forty years has taken not the direction Hirsch wished but the direction he feared.

The fact that the term "criticism" has now come to designate all commentary on textual meaning reflects a general acceptance of the doctrine that description and evaluation are inseparable in literary study. In any serious confrontation of literature it would be futile, of course, to attempt a rigorous banishment of all evaluative judgment, but this fact does not give us the license to misunderstand or misinterpret our texts. It does not entitle us to use the text as the basis for an exercise in "creativity" or to submit as serious textual commentary a disguised argument for a particular ethical, cultural, or aesthetic viewpoint. Nor is criticism's chief concern—the present relevance of a text—a strictly necessary aspect of textual commentary. That same kind of theory which argues the inseparability of description and evaluation also argues that a text's meaning is simply its meaning "to us, today." Both kinds of argument support the idea that interpretation is criticism and vice versa. But there is clearly a sense in which we can neither evaluate a text nor determine what it means "to us, today" until we have correctly apprehended what it means. Understanding (and therefore interpretation, in the strict sense of the word) is both logically and psychologically prior to what is generally called criticism. It is true that this distinction between understanding and evaluation cannot always show itself in the finished work of criticism—nor, perhaps, should it—but a general grasp and acceptance of the distinction might help correct some of the most serious faults of current criticism (its subjectivism and relativism) and might even make it plausible to think of literary study as a corporate enterprise and a progressive discipline.

No one would deny, of course, that the more important issue is not the status of literary study as a discipline but the vitality of literature—especially of older literature—in the world at large. The critic is right to think that the text should speak to *us*. The point which needs to be grasped clearly by the critic is that a text cannot be made to speak to us until what it says has been understood. This is not an argument in favor of historicism as against criticism—it is simply a brute ontological fact. Textual meaning is not a naked given like a physical object. The text is first of all a conventional representation like a musical score, and what the score represents may be construed correctly or incorrectly. The literary text (in spite of semi-mystical claims made for its uniqueness) does not have a special ontological status which somehow absolves the reader from the demands universally imposed by all linguistic texts of every description. Nothing, that is, can give a conventional representation the status of an immediate given. The text of a poem, for example, has to be construed by the critic before it becomes a poem for him. Then it is, no doubt, an artifact with special characteristics. But before the critic construes the poem it is for him no artifact at all, and if he construes it wrongly, he will subsequently be talking about the wrong artifact, not the one represented by the text. If criticism is to be objective in any significant sense, it must be founded on a self-critical construction of textual meaning, which is to say, on objective interpretation.

•　　•　　•

[In the section of the essay omitted here, Hirsch draws a distinction between the "meaning" of a text, "in and for itself," and the "significance" that can be given to that meaning when it is related to something else, like contemporary issues, our present concerns, and so forth. "Meaning," which is relatively stable and unchanging through time, is the object of "interpretation"; "significance," which may change from reader to reader and from period to period, is the object of "criticism." Interpretation of textual meaning, then, is the logically prior task and the foundation for all criticism. But to what extent is "textual meaning" the same thing as "authorial meaning"? On this crucial question, Hirsch parts company with the New Critics. —ED.]

Determinateness of Textual Meaning

In the previous section I defined textual meaning as the "verbal intention" of the author, and this argues implicitly that hermeneutics must stress a reconstruction of the author's aims and attitudes in order to evolve guides and norms for construing the meaning of his text. It is frequently argued, however, that the textual meaning has nothing to do with the author's mind, but only with his verbal achievement, that the object of interpretation is not the author but his text. This plausible argument assumes, of course, that the text automatically has a meaning simply because it represents an unalterable sequence of words. It assumes that the meaning of a word sequence is directly imposed by the public norms of language, that the text as a "piece of language" is a public object whose character is defined by public norms.[1] This view is in one respect sound, since textual meaning must conform to public norms if it is in any sense to be verbal (i.e., sharable) meaning; on no account may the interpreter permit his probing into the author's mind to raise private associations (experience) to the level of public implications (content).

However, this basically sound argument remains one-sided. For even though verbal meaning must conform to public linguistic norms (these are highly tolerant, of course), no mere sequence of words can represent an actual verbal meaning with reference to public norms alone. Referred to these alone, the text's meaning remains indeterminate. This is true even of the simplest declarative sentence like "My car ran out of gas" (did my Pullman dash from a cloud of Argon?). The fact that no one would radically misinterpret such a sentence simply indicates that its frequency is high enough to give its usual meaning the apparent status of an immediate given. But this apparent immediacy obscures a complex process of adjudications among meaning-possibilities. Under the public norms of language alone no such adjudications can occur, since the array of possibilities presents a face of blank indifference. The array of possibilities only begins to become a more selective system of *probabilities* when, instead of confronting merely a word sequence, we also posit a speaker who very likely means something. Then and only then does the most usual sense of the word sequence become the most probable or "obvious" sense. The point holds true a fortiori, of course, when we confront less obvious word sequences like those found in poetry. A careful exposition of this point may be found in the first volume of Cassirer's *Philosophy of Symbolic Forms,* which is largely devoted to a demonstration that verbal meaning arises from the "reciprocal determination" of public linguistic possibilities

and subjective specifications of those possibilities.[2] Just as language constitutes and colors subjectivity, so does subjectivity color language. The author's or speaker's subjective act is *formally* necessary to verbal meaning, and any theory which tries to dispense with the author as specifier of meaning by asserting that textual meaning is purely objectively determined finds itself chasing will-o'-the-wisps. The burden of this section is, then, an attack on the view that a text is a "piece of language" and a defense of the notion that a text represents the determinate verbal meaning of the author.

One of the consequences arising from the view that a text is a piece of language—a purely public object—is the impossibility of defining in principle the nature of a correct interpretation. This is the same impasse which results from the theory that a text leads a life of its own, and indeed, the two notions are corollaries since any "piece of language" must have a changing meaning when the changing public norms of language are viewed as the only ones which determine the sense of the text. It is therefore not surprising to find that Wellek subscribes implicitly to the text-as-language theory. The text is viewed as representing not a determinate meaning, but rather a system of meaning-potentials specified not by a meaner but by the vital potency of language itself. Wellek acutely perceives the danger of the view: "Thus the system of norms is growing and changing and will remain, in some sense, always incompletely and imperfectly realized. But this dynamic conception does not mean mere subjectivism and relativism. All the different points of view are by no means equally right. It will always be possible to determine which point of view grasps the subject most thoroughly and deeply. A hierarchy of viewpoints, a criticism of the grasp of norms, is implied in the concept of the adequacy of interpretation."[3] The danger of the view is, of course, precisely that it opens the door to subjectivism and relativism, since linguistic norms may be invoked to support any verbally possible meaning. Furthermore, it is not clear how one may criticize a grasp of norms which will not stand still.

Wellek's brief comment on the problem involved in defining and testing correctness in interpretation is representative of a widespread conviction among literary critics that the most correct interpretation is the most "inclusive" one. Indeed, the view is so widely accepted that Wellek did not need to defend his version of it (which he calls "Perspectivism") at length. The notion behind the theory is reflected by such phrases as "always incompletely and imperfectly realized" and "grasps the subject most thoroughly." This notion is simply that no single interpretation can exhaust the rich system of meaning-potentialities represented by the text. *Ergo* every plausible reading which remains within public linguistic norms is a correct reading so far as it goes, but each reading is inevitably partial since it cannot realize all the potentialities of the text. The guiding principle in criticism, therefore, is that of the inclusive interpretation. The most "adequate" construction is the one which gives the fullest coherent account of all the text's potential meanings.[4]

Inclusivism is desirable as a position which induces a readiness to consider the results of others, but, aside from promoting an estimable tolerance, it has little theoretical value. For although its aim is to reconcile different plausible readings in an ideal, comprehensive interpretation, it cannot, in fact, either reconcile different readings or choose between them. As a normative ideal, or principle of correctness, it is useless. This point may be illustrated by citing two expert readings of a well-known poem by Wordsworth. I shall first quote the poem and then quote excerpts from two published exegeses in order to demonstrate the kind of impasse which inclusivism always provokes when it attempts to reconcile interpretations, and, incidentally, to demonstrate the very kind of interpretive problem which calls for a guiding principle:

> A slumber did my spirit seal;
>   I had no human fears:
> She seemed a thing that could not feel
>   The touch of earthly years.
>
> No motion has she now, no force;
>   She neither hears nor sees;
> Rolled round in earth's diurnal course,
>   With rocks, and stones, and trees.

Here are excerpts from two commentaries on the final lines of the poem; the first is by Cleanth Brooks, the second by F. W. Bateson:

1. [The poet] attempts to suggest something of the lover's agonized shock at the loved one's present lack of motion—of his response to her utter and horrible inertness.... Part of the effect, of course, resides in the fact that a dead lifelessness is suggested more sharply by an object's being whirled about by something else than by an image of the object in re-

pose. But there are other matters which are at work here: the sense of the girl's falling back into the clutter of things, companioned by things chained like a tree to one particular spot, or by things completely inanimate like rocks and stones.... [She] is caught up helplessly into the empty whirl of the earth which measures and makes time. She is touched by and held by earthly time in its most powerful and horrible image.

2. The final impression the poem leaves is not of two contrasting moods, but of a single mood mounting to a climax in the pantheistic magnificence of the last two lines.... The vague living-Lucy of this poem is opposed to the grander dead-Lucy who has become involved in the sublime processes of nature. We put the poem down satisfied, because its last two lines succeed in effecting a reconciliation between the two philosophies or social attitudes. Lucy is actually more alive now that she is dead, because she is now a part of the life of Nature, and not just a human "thing."[5]

Now, if we grant, as I think we must, that both the cited interpretations are permitted by the text, the problem for the inclusivist is to reconcile the two readings.

Three modes of reconciliation are available to the inclusivist: (1) Brooks's reading includes Bateson's; it shows that any affirmative suggestions in the poem are negated by the bitterly ironical portrayal of the inert girl being whirled around by what Bateson calls the "sublime processes of Nature." (2) Bateson's reading includes Brooks's; the ironic contrast between the active, seemingly immortal girl and the passive, inert and dead girl is overcome by a final unqualified affirmation of immortality. (3) Each of the readings is partially right, but they must be fused to supplement one another. The very fact that the critics differ suggests that the meaning is essentially ambiguous. The emotion expressed is ambivalent, and comprises both bitter regret and affirmation. The third mode of reconciliation is the one most often employed, and is probably, in this case, the most satisfactory. A fourth type of resolution, which would insist that Brooks is right and Bateson wrong (or vice versa) is not available to the inclusivist, since the text, as language, renders both readings plausible.

Close examination, however, reveals that none of the three modes of argument manages to reconcile or fuse the two different readings. Mode (1), for example, insists that Brooks's reading comprehends Bateson's, but although it is conceivable that Brooks implies all the meanings which Bateson has perceived, Brooks also implies a *pattern of emphasis* which cannot be reconciled with Bateson's reading. While Bateson construes a primary emphasis on life and affirmation, Brooks emphasizes deadness and inertness. No amount of manipulation can reconcile these divergent emphases, since one pattern of emphasis irrevocably excludes other patterns, and, since emphasis is always crucial to meaning, the two constructions of meanings rigorously exclude one another. Precisely the same strictures hold, of course, for the argument that Bateson's reading comprehends that of Brooks. Nor can mode (3) escape with impunity. Although it seems to preserve a stress both on negation and on affirmation, thereby coalescing the two readings, it actually excludes both readings, and labels them not simply partial, but wrong. For if the poem gives equal stress to bitter irony and to affirmation, then any construction which places a primary stress on either meaning is simply incorrect.

The general principle implied by my analysis is very simple. The sub-meanings of a text are not blocks which can be brought together additively. Since verbal (and any other) meaning is a *structure* of component meanings, interpretation has not done its job when it simply enumerates what the component meanings are. The interpreter must also determine their probable structure, and particularly their structure of emphases. Relative emphasis is not only crucial to meaning (perhaps it is the most crucial and problematical element of all), it is also highly restrictive; it excludes alternatives. It may be asserted as a general rule that whenever a reader confronts two interpretations which impose different emphases on similar meaning components, at least one of the interpretations must be wrong. They cannot be reconciled.

By insisting that verbal meaning always exhibits a determinate structure of emphases, I do not, however, imply that a poem or any other text must be unambiguous. It is perfectly possible, for example, that Wordsworth's poem ambiguously implies both bitter irony and positive affirmation. Such complex emotions are commonly expressed in poetry, but if that is the kind of meaning the text represents Brooks and Bateson would be wrong to emphasize one emotion at the expense of the other. Ambiguity or, for that matter, vagueness is not the same as indeterminateness. This is the crux of the issue. To say that verbal meaning is determinate is not to exclude complexities of meaning but only to insist that a text's meaning is what it is and not a hundred other things. Taken in this sense, a vague or ambiguous text is just as determinate as a logical proposition; it means what it means and nothing else. This is true even if one argues that a text could display shifting emphases like those Sunday supplement magic squares which first seem to jut out and then to jut in. With texts of this character (if any exist), one need only say that the emphases shift, and must not, therefore, be construed statically. Any static construction would simply be wrong. The fundamental flaw in the "theory of the most inclusive interpretation" is that it overlooks the problem of emphasis. Since different patterns of emphasis *exclude* one another, inclusivism is neither a genuine norm nor an adequate guiding principle for establishing an interpretation.

But aside from the fact that inclusivism cannot do its appointed job, there are more fundamental reasons for rejecting it and all other interpretive ideals based on the conception that a text represents a system of meaning-possibilities. No one would deny that for the interpreter the text is at first the source of numerous possible interpretations. The very nature of language is such that a particular sequence of words can represent several different meanings (that is why public norms alone are insufficient in textual interpretation). But to say that a text *might* represent several structures of meaning does not imply that it does in fact represent all the meanings which a particular word sequence can legally convey. Is there not an obvious distinction between what a text might mean and what it does mean? According to accepted linguistic theory, it is far more accurate to say that a written composition is not a mere locus of verbal possibilities, but, rather, a record (made possible by the invention of writing) of a verbal actuality. The interpreter's job is to reconstruct a determinate actual meaning, not a mere system of possibilities. Indeed, if the text *represented* a system of possibilities, interpretation would be impossible, since no actual reading could correspond to a mere system of possibilities. Furthermore, if the text is conceived to represent all the *actual* structures of meaning permissible within the public norms of language, then no single construction (with its exclusivist pattern of emphases) could be correct, and any legitimate construction would be just as incorrect as any other. When a text is conceived as a piece of language, a familiar and all too common anarchy follows. But, aside from its unfortunate consequences, the theory contradicts a widely accepted principle in linguistics. I refer to Saussure's distinction between *langue* and *parole*.

Saussure defined *langue* as the system of linguistic possibilities shared by a speech community at a given point in time.[6] This system of possibilities contains two distinguishable levels. The first consists of habits, engrams, prohibitions, and the like derived from past linguistic usage; these are the "virtualities" of the *langue*. Based on these virtualities, there are, in addition, sharable meaning-possibilities which have never before been actualized; these are the "potentialities." The two types of meaning-possibilities taken together constitute the *langue* which the speech community draws upon. But this system of possibilities must be distinguished from the actual verbal utterances of individuals who draw upon it. These actual utterances are called *paroles;* but they are *uses* of language, and actualize some (but never all) of the meaning-possibilities constituting the *langue*.

Saussure's distinction pinpoints the issue: does a text represent a segment of *langue* (as modern theorists hold) or a *parole*? A simple test suffices to provide the answer. If the text is composed of sentences it represents *parole*, which is to say the determinate verbal meaning of a member of the speech community. *Langue* contains words and sentence-forming principles, but it contains no sentences. It may be presented in writing only by isolated words in disconnection (*Wörter* as opposed to *Worte*). A *parole*, on the other hand, is always composed of sentences, an assertion corroborated by the firmly established principle that the sentence is the fundamental unit of speech.[7] Of course, there are numerous elliptical and one-word sentences, but wherever it can be correctly inferred that a text represents sentences and not simply isolated words, it may also be inferred that the text represents *parole*, which is to say, actual, determinate verbal meaning.

The point is nicely illustrated in a dictionary definition. The letters in boldface at the head of the definition represent the word as *langue,* with all its rich meaning-possibilities. But under one of the subheadings, in an illustrative sentence, those same letters represent the words as *parole,* as a particular, selective actualization from *langue*. In yet another illustrative sentence, under another sub-heading, the very same word represents a different selective actualization. Of course, many sentences, especially those found in poetry, actualize far more possibilities than

illustrative sentences in a dictionary. Any pun, for example, realizes simultaneously at least two divergent meaning-possibilities. But the pun is nevertheless an actualization from *langue* and not a mere system of meaning-possibilities.

The *langue–parole* distinction, besides affirming the determinateness of textual meaning, also clarifies the special problems posed by revised and interpolated text. With a revised text, composed over a long period of time (*Faust,* for example) how are we to construe the *unrevised* portions? Should we assume that they still mean what they meant originally or that they took on a new meaning when the rest of the text was altered or expanded? With compiled or interpolated texts, like many books of the Bible, should we assume that sentences from varied provenances retain their original meanings, or that these heterogeneous elements have become integral components of a new total meaning? In terms of Saussure's distinction, the question becomes: should we consider the text to represent a compilation of diverse *paroles* or a new unitary *parole* "respoken" by the new author or editor? I submit that there can be no definite answer to the question, except in relation to a specific scholarly or aesthetic purpose, for in reality the question is not, "How are we to interpret the text?" but, "*Which* text are we to interpret?" Is it to be the heterogeneous compilation of past *paroles,* each to be separately considered, or the new, homogeneous *parole*? Both may be presented by the written score. The only problem is to choose, and having chosen, rigorously to refrain from confusing or in any way identifying the two quite different and separate "texts" with one another. Without solving any concrete problems, then, Saussure's distinction nevertheless confirms the critic's right in most cases to regard his text as representing a single *parole*.

Another problem which Saussure's distinction clarifies is that posed by the bungled text, where the author aimed to convey a meaning which his words do not convey to others in the speech community. One sometimes confronts the problem in a freshman essay. In such a case, the question is, does the text mean what the author wanted it to mean or does it mean what the speech community at large takes it to mean? Much attention has been devoted to this problem ever since the publication in 1946 of Wimsatt's and Beardsley's essay on "The Intentional Fallacy."[8] In that essay the position was taken (albeit modified by certain qualifications) that the text, being public, means what the speech community takes it to mean. This position is, in an ethical sense, right (and language, being social, has a strong ethical aspect): if the author has bungled so badly that his utterance will be misconstrued, then it serves him right when folk misunderstand him. However, put in linguistic terms, the position becomes unsatisfactory. It implies that the meaning represented by the text is not the *parole* of an author, but rather the *parole* of "the speech community." But since only individuals utter *paroles*, a *parole* of the speech community is a non-existent, or what the Germans call an *Unding*. A text can represent only the *parole* of a speaker or author, which is another way of saying that meaning requires a meaner.

However, it is not necessary that an author's text represent the *parole* he desired to convey. It is frequently the case, when an author has bungled, that his text represents no *parole* at all. Indeed there are but two alternatives: either the text represents the author's verbal meaning or it represents no *determinate* verbal meaning at all. Sometimes, of course, it is impossible to detect that the author has bungled, and in that case, even though his text does not represent verbal meaning, we shall go on misconstruing the text as though it did, and no one will be the wiser. But with most bungles we are aware of a disjunction between the author's words and his probable meaning. Eliot, for example, chided Poe for saying "My most immemorial year," when Poe "meant" his most *memorable* year.[9] Now we all agree that Poe did not mean what speakers of English generally meant by the word "immemorial"—and so the word cannot have the usual meaning. (An author cannot mean what he does not mean.) The only question, then, is: does the word mean more or less what we convey by "never-to-be-forgotten" or does it mean nothing at all? Has Poe so violated linguistic norms that we must deny his utterance verbal meaning or "content"?

The question probably cannot be answered by fiat. But since Poe's meaning is generally understood, and since the single criteria for verbal meaning is communicability, I am inclined to describe Poe's meaning as verbal.[10] I tend to side with the Poes and Malaprops of the world, for the norms of language remain far more tolerant than dictionaries and critics like Eliot suggest. On the other hand, every member of the speech community, and especially the critic, has a duty to avoid and condemn sloppiness and needless ambiguity in the use of language, simply in order to preserve the effectiveness of the *langue* itself. Moreover, there must be a dividing line between verbal meanings and those meanings which we half-divine by a supra-linguistic exercise of imagination. There must be a dividing line between Poe's successful disregard of normal usage and the incommunicable word sequences of a bad freshman essay. However, that dividing line is not between the author's meaning and the reader's, but rather between the author's *parole* and no *parole* at all.

Of course, theoretical principles cannot directly solve the interpreter's problem. It is one thing to insist that a text represents the determinate verbal meaning of an author, but it is quite another to discover what that meaning is. The very same text could represent numerous different *paroles*, as any ironic sentence discloses ("That's a *bright* idea!?" or "That's a bright *idea!*"). But it should be of some practical consequence for the interpreter to know that he does have a precisely defined task, namely to discover the author's meaning. It is therefore not only sound but necessary for the interpreter to inquire, "What in all probability did the author mean? Is the pattern of emphases I construe the author's pattern?" But it is both incorrect and futile to inquire, "What does the language of the text say?" That question can have no determinate answer.

Verification

Since the meaning represented by a text is that of another, the interpreter can never be certain that his reading is correct. He knows furthermore that the norms of *langue* by themselves are far too broad to specify the particular meanings and emphases represented by the text, that these particular meanings were specified by particular kinds of subjective acts on the part of the author, and that these acts, as such, remain inaccessible. A less self-critical reader, on the other hand, approaches solipsism if he assumes that the text represents a perspicuous meaning simply because it represents an unalterable sequence of words. For if this "perspicuous" meaning is not verified in some way, it will simply be the interpreter's own meaning, exhibiting the connotations and emphases which he himself imposes. Of course, the reader must realize verbal meaning by his own subjective acts (no one can do that for him), but if he remembers that his job is to construe the author's meaning, he will attempt to exclude his own predispositions and to impose those of the author. But no one can establish another's meaning with certainty. The interpreter's goal is simply this: to show that a given reading is more probable than others. In hermeneutics, verification is a process of establishing relative probabilities.

To establish a reading as probable it is first necessary to show, with reference to the norms of language, that it is possible. This is the criterion of *legitimacy:* the reading must be permissible within the public norms of the *langue* in which the text was composed. The second criterion is that of *correspondence:* the reading must account for each linguistic component in the text. Whenever a reading arbitrarily ignores linguistic components or inadequately accounts for them, the reading may be presumed improbable. The third criterion is that of *generic appropriateness:* if the text follows the conventions of a scientific essay, for example, it is inappropriate to construe the kind of allusive meaning found in casual conversation.[11] But when these three preliminary criteria have been satisfied, there remains a fourth criterion which gives significance to all the rest, the criterion of plausibility or *coherence.* The three preliminary norms usually permit several readings, and this is by definition the case when a text is problematical. Faced with alternatives, the interpreter chooses the reading which best meets the criterion of coherence. Indeed, even when the text is not problematical, coherence remains the decisive criterion, since the meaning is "obvious" only because it "makes sense." I wish, therefore, to focus attention on the criterion of coherence, and shall take for granted the demands of legitimacy, correspondence, and generic appropriateness. I shall try to show that verification by the criterion of coherence, and ultimately, therefore, verification in general, implies a reconstruction of relevant aspects in the author's outlook. My point may be summarized in the paradox that objectivity in textual interpretation requires explicit reference to the speaker's subjectivity.

The paradox reflects the peculiar nature of coherence, which is not an absolute, but a dependent quality. The laws of coherence are variable; they depend upon the nature of the total meaning under consideration. Two meanings ("dark" and "bright," for example) which cohere in one context may not cohere in another.[12] "Dark with excessive bright" makes excellent sense in *Paradise Lost,* but if a reader found the phrase in a textbook on plant pathology, he would assume that he confronted a misprint for "Dark with excessive blight." Coherence depends on the context, and it is helpful to recall our definition of "context": it is a sense of the whole meaning, constituted of explicit partial meanings plus a horizon of expectations and probabilities. One meaning coheres with another because it is typical or probable with reference to the whole (coherence is thus the first cousin of implication). The criterion of coherence can be invoked only with reference to a particular context, and this context may be inferred only by positing the author's "horizon," his disposition toward a particular type of meaning. This conclusion requires elaboration.

The fact that coherence is a dependent quality leads to an unavoidable circularity in the process of interpretation. The interpreter posits meanings for the words and word-sequences he confronts, and, at the same time, he has to posit a whole meaning or context in reference to which the sub-meanings cohere with one another. The procedure is thoroughly circular; the context is derived from the sub-meanings and the sub-meanings are specified and rendered coherent with reference to the context. This circularity makes it very difficult to convince a reader to alter his construction, as every teacher knows. Many a self-willed student continues to insist that his reading is just as plausible as his instructor's, and, very often, the student is justified; his reading does make good sense. Often, the only thing at fault with the student's reading is that it is probably wrong, not that it is incoherent. The student persists in his opinion precisely because his construction *is* coherent and self-sustaining. In such a case he is wrong because he has misconstrued the context or sense of the whole. In this respect, the student's hardheadedness is not different from that of all self-convinced interpreters. Our readings are too plausible to be relinquished. If we have a distorted sense of the text's whole meaning, the harder we look at it the more certainly we shall find our distorted construction confirmed.

Since the quality of coherence depends upon the context inferred, there is no absolute standard of coherence by which we can adjudicate between different coherent readings. Verification by coherence implies therefore a verification of the *grounds* on which the reading is coherent. *It is necessary to establish that the context invoked is the most probable context.* Only then, in relation to an established context, can we judge that one reading is more coherent than another. Ultimately, therefore, we have to posit the most probable horizon for the text, and it is possible to do this only if we posit the author's typical outlook, the typical associations and expectations which form in part the context of his utterance. This is not only the single way we can test the relative coherence of a reading, but is also the only way to avoid pure circularity in making sense of the text.

An essential task in the process of verification is, therefore, a deliberate reconstruction of the author's subjective stance to the extent that this stance is relevant to the text at hand.[13] The importance of such psychological reconstruction may be exemplified in adjudicating between different readings of Wordsworth's "A Slumber Did My Spirit Seal." The interpretations of Brooks and Bateson, different as they are, remain equally coherent and self-sustaining. The implications which Brooks construes cohere beautifully with the explicit meanings of the poem within the context which Brooks adumbrates. The same may be said of Bateson's reading. The best way to show that one reading is more plausible and coherent than the other is to show that one context is more probable than the other. The problem of adjudicating between Bateson and Brooks is therefore, implicitly, the problem every interpreter must face when he tries to verify his reading. He must establish the most probable context.

Now when the *homme moyen sensuel* confronts bereavement such as that which Wordsworth's poem explicitly presents he adumbrates, typically, a horizon including sorrow and inconsolability. These are for him components in the very meaning of bereavement. Sorrow and inconsolability cannot fail to be associated with death when the loved one, formerly so active and alive, is imagined as lying in the earth, helpless, dumb, inert, insentient. And, since there is no hint of life in heaven but only of bodily death, the comforts of Christianity lie beyond the poem's horizon. Affirmations too deep for tears, like those Bateson insists on, simply do not cohere with the poem's explicit meanings; they do not belong to the context. Brooks's reading, therefore, with its emphasis on inconsolability and bitter irony, is clearly justified not only by the text but by reference to universal human attitudes and feelings.

But the trouble with such a reading is apparent to most Wordsworthians. The poet is not an *homme moyen sensuel;* his characteristic attitudes are somewhat pantheistic. Instead of regarding rocks and

stones and trees merely as inert objects, he probably regarded them in 1799 as deeply alive, as part of the immortal life of nature. Physical death he felt to be a return to the source of life, a new kind of participation in nature's "revolving immortality." From everything we know of Wordsworth's typical attitudes during the period in which he composed the poem, inconsolability and bitter irony do not belong in its horizon. I think, however, that Bateson overstates his case, and that he fails to emphasize properly the negative implications in the poem ("No motion has she now, no force"). He overlooks the poet's reticence, his distinct unwillingness to express any unqualified evaluation of his experience. Bateson, I would say, has not paid enough attention to the criterion of correspondence. Nevertheless, in spite of this, and in spite of the apparent implausibility of Bateson's reading, it remains, I think, somewhat more probable than that of Brooks. His procedure is also more objective. For even if he had botched his job thoroughly and had produced a less probable reading than that of Brooks, his method would remain fundamentally sound. Instead of projecting his own attitudes (Bateson is presumably not a pantheist) and instead of positing a "universal matrix" of human attitudes (there is none), he has tried to reconstruct the author's probable attitudes so far as these are relevant in specifying the poem's meaning. It is still possible, of course, that Brooks is right and Bateson wrong. A poet's typical attitudes do not always apply to a particular poem, although Wordsworth is, in a given period, more consistent than most poets. Be that as it may, we shall never be *certain* what any writer means, and since Bateson grounds his interpretation in a conscious construction of the poet's outlook, his reading must be deemed the more probable one until the uncovering of some presently unknown data makes a different construction of the poet's stance appear more valid.

Bateson's procedure is appropriate to all texts, including anonymous ones. On the surface, it would seem impossible to invoke the author's probable outlook when the author remains unknown, but in this limiting case the interpreter simply makes his psychological reconstruction on the basis of fewer data. For even with anonymous texts it is crucial to posit not simply some author or other, but a *particular* subjective stance in reference to which the construed context is rendered probable. That is why it is important to date anonymous texts. The interpreter needs all the clues he can muster with regard not only to the text's *langue* and genre, but also to the cultural and personal attitudes the author might be expected to bring to bear in specifying his verbal meanings. In this sense, all texts, including anonymous ones, are "attributed." The objective interpreter simply tries to make his attribution explicit, so that the grounds for his reading are frankly acknowledged. This opens the way to progressive accuracy in interpretation since it is possible, then, to test the assumptions behind a reading as well as the coherence of the reading itself.

The fact that anonymous texts may be successfully interpreted does not, however, lead to the conclusion that all texts should be treated as anonymous ones, that they should, so to say, speak for themselves. I have already argued that no text speaks for itself, and that every construed text is necessarily "attributed." These points suggest strongly that it is unsound to insist on deriving all inferences from the "text itself." When we date an anonymous text, for example, we apply knowledge gained from a wide variety of sources which we correlate with data derived from the text. This extrinsic data is not, however, read *into* the text. On the contrary, it is used to *verify* that which we read out of it. The extrinsic information has ultimately a purely verification function.

The same thing is true of information relating to the author's subjective stance. No matter what the source of this information may be, whether it be the text alone or the text in conjunction with other data, this information is *extrinsic* to verbal meaning as such. Strictly speaking, the author's subjective stance is not part of his verbal meaning even when he explicitly discusses his feelings and attitudes. This is Husserl's point again. The "intentional object" represented by a text is different from the "intentional acts" which realize it. When the interpreter posits the author's stance, he sympathetically re-enacts the author's "intentional acts," but although this imaginative act is necessary for realizing meaning, it must be distinguished from meaning as such. In no sense does the text *represent* the author's subjective stance: the interpreter simply adopts a stance in order to make sense of the text, and, if he is self-critical, he tries to verify his interpretation by showing his adopted stance to be, in all probability, the author's.

Of course, the text at hand is the safest source of clues to the author's outlook, since men do adopt different attitudes on different occasions. However, even though the text itself should be the primary source of clues and must always be the final authority, the interpreter should make an effort to go beyond his text wherever possible, since this is the only way he can avoid a vicious circularity. The harder one looks at a text from an incorrect stance, the more convincing the incorrect construction becomes. Inferences about the author's stance are sometimes difficult enough to make even when all relevant data are brought to bear, and it is self-defeating to make the inferential process more difficult than it need be. Since these inferences are ultimately extrinsic, there is no virtue in deriving them from the text alone. One must not confuse the result of a construction (the interpreter's understanding of the text's *Sinn*)* either with the *process* of construction or with a validation of that process. The *Sinn* must be represented by and limited by the text alone, but the process of construction and validation involve psychological reconstruction and should therefore be based on all the data available.

Not only the criterion of coherence but all the other criteria used in verifying interpretations must be applied with reference to a psychological reconstruction. The criterion of legitimacy, for example, must be related to a speaking subject, since it is the author's *langue*, as an internal possession, and not the interpreter's, which defines the range of meaning-possibilities a text can represent. The criterion of correspondence has force and significance only because we presume that the author meant something by each of the linguistic components he employed. And the criterion of generic appropriateness is relevant only so far as generic conventions are possessed and accepted by the author. The fact that these criteria all refer ultimately to a psychological construction is hardly surprising when we recall that to verify a text is simply to establish that the author probably meant what we construe his text to mean. The interpreter's primary task is to reproduce in himself the author's "logic," his attitudes, his cultural givens, in short his world. For even though the process of verification is highly complex and difficult, the ultimate verificative principle is very simple: the imaginative reconstruction of the speaking subject.[14]

Sinn: The work's unchanging "textual meaning," as opposed to the various types of "significance" that might be given to that meaning. —ED.

The speaking subject is not, however, identical with the subjectivity of the author as an actual historical person; it corresponds, rather, to a very limited and special aspect of the author's total subjectivity; it is, so to speak, that "part" of the author which specifies or determines verbal meaning.[15] This distinction is quite apparent in the case of a lie. When I wish to deceive, my secret awareness that I am lying is irrelevant to the verbal meaning of my utterance. The only correct interpretation of my lie is, paradoxically, to view it as being a true statement, since this is the only correct construction of my "verbal intention." Indeed it is only when my listener has *understood* my meaning (presented as true) that he can *judge* it to be a lie. Since I adopted a truth-telling stance, the verbal meaning of my utterance would be precisely the same, whether I was deliberately lying or suffering from the erroneous conviction that my statement was true. In other words, an author may adopt a stance which differs from his deepest attitudes in the same way that an interpreter must almost always adopt a stance different from his own.[16] But for the process of interpretation, the author's private experiences are irrelevant. The only relevant aspect of subjectivity is that which determines verbal meaning, or, in Husserl's terms, "content."

In a sense all poets are, of course, liars, and to some extent all speakers are, but the deliberate lie, spoken to deceive, is a borderline case. In most verbal utterances the speaker's public stance is not totally foreign to his private attitudes. Even in those cases where the speaker deliberately assumes a role, this mimetic stance is usually not the final determinant of his meaning. In a play, for example, the total meaning of an utterance is not the "intentional object" of the dramatic character; that meaning is simply a component in the more complex "intention" of the dramatist. The speaker himself is spoken. The best description of these receding levels of subjectivity was provided by the scholastic philosophers in their distinction between "first intention," "second intention," and so on. Irony, for example, always entails a comprehension of two contrasting stances ("intentional levels") by a third and final complex "intention." The "speaking subject" may be defined as the final and most comprehensive level of awareness determinative of verbal meaning. In the case of a lie the speaking subject assumes that he tells the truth, while the actual subject retains a private awareness of his deception. Similarly, many speakers retain in their isolated privacy a self-conscious awareness of their verbal meaning, an awareness which may agree or disagree, approve or disapprove, but which does not participate in determining their verbal meaning. To interpretation, this level of awareness is as irrelevant as it is inaccessible. In construing and verifying verbal meaning, only the speaking subject counts.

A separate exposition would be required to discuss the problems of psychological reconstruction. I have here simply tried to forestall the current objections to extrinsic biographical and historical information by pointing, on the one hand, to the exigencies of verification, and, on the other, to the distinction between a speaking subject and a "biographical" person. I shall be satisfied if this part of my discussion, incomplete as it must be, will help revive the half-forgotten truism that interpretation is the construction of *another's* meaning. A slight shift in the way we speak about texts would be highly salutary. It is natural to speak not of what a text says, but of what an author means, and this more natural locution is the more accurate one. Furthermore, to speak in this way implies a readiness (not notably apparent in recent criticism) to put forth a whole-hearted and self-critical effort at the primary level of criticism — the level of understanding.

Notes

1. The phrase, "piece of language," comes from the first paragraph of William Empson's *Seven Types of Ambiguity*, 3rd ed. (New York, 1955). It is typical of the critical school Empson founded.

2. *Vol. 1. Language*, trans. R. Manheim (New Haven, 1953). It is ironic that Cassirer's work should be used to support the notion that a text speaks for itself. The realm of language is autonomous for Cassirer only in the sense that it follows an independent development which is reciprocally determined by objective *and* subjective factors. See pp. 69, 178, 213, 249–250, et passim.

3. René Wellek and Austin Warren, *Theory of Literature*, 3rd ed. (New York, 1956), p. 144.

4. Every interpretation is necessarily incomplete in the sense that it fails to explicate all a text's implications. But this kind of incomplete interpretation may still carry an absolutely correct system of emphases and an accurate sense of the whole meaning. This kind of incompleteness is

radically different from that postulated by the inclusivists, for whom a sense of the whole means a grasp of the various possible meanings which a text can plausibly represent.

5. Cleanth Brooks, "Irony as a Principle of Structure," in M. D. Zabel, ed., *Literary Opinion in America*, 2nd ed. (New York, 1951), p. 736. F. W. Bateson, *English Poetry. A Critical Introduction* (London, 1950), p. 33 and pp. 80–81.

6. This is the "synchronic" as opposed to the "diachronic" sense of the term. See Ferdinand de Saussure, *Cours de linguistique générale* (Paris, 1931). Useful discussions may be found in Stephen Ullman, *The Principles of Semantics* (Glasgow, 1951), and W. v. Wartburg, *Einführung in die Problematik und Methodik der Sprachwissenchaft* (Halle, 1943).

7. See, for example, Cassirer, p. 304.

8. *Sewanee Review, 54,* 1946. Reprinted by W. K. Wimsatt, Jr., *The Verbal Icon* (Lexington, Ky., 1954).

9. T. S. Eliot, "From Poe to Valéry," *Hudson Review,* 2, 1949, p. 232.

10. The word is, in fact, quite effective. It conveys the sense of "memorable" by the component "memorial," and the sense of "never-to-be-forgotten" by the negative prefix. The difference between this and Jabberwocky words is that it appears to be a standard word occurring in a context of standard words. Perhaps Eliot is right to scold Poe, but he cannot properly insist that the word lacks a determinate verbal meaning.

11. This third criterion is, however, highly presumptive, since the interpreter may easily mistake the text's genre.

12. Exceptions to this are the syncategorematic meanings (color and extention, for example) which cohere by necessity regardless of the context.

13. The reader may feel that I have telescoped a number of steps here. The author's verbal meaning or "verbal intention" is the object of complex "intentional acts." To reproduce this meaning it is necessary for the interpreter to engage in "intentional acts" belonging to the same species as those of the author. (Two different "intentional acts" belong to the same species when they "intend" the same "intentional object.") That is why the issue of "stance" arises. The interpreter needs to adopt sympathetically the author's stance (his disposition to engage in particular kinds of "intentional acts") so that he can "intend" with some degree of probability the same "intentional objects" as the author. This is especially clear in the case of *implicit* verbal meaning, where the interpreter's realization of the author's stance determines the text's horizon.

14. Here I purposefully display my sympathies with Dilthey's concepts, *Sichhineinfühlen* and *Verstehen.* In fact, my whole argument may be regarded as an attempt to ground some of Dilthey's hermeneutic principles in Husserl's epistemology and Saussure's linguistics.

15. Spranger aptly calls this the "cultural subject." See Eduard Spranger, "Zur Theorie des Verstehens und zur geisteswissenschaftlichen Psychologie" in *Festschrift Johannes Volkelt zum 70. Geburtstag* (Munich, 1918), p. 369. It should be clear that I am here in essential agreement with the American anti-intentionalists (term used in the ordinary sense). I think they are right to exclude private associations from verbal meaning. But it is of some practical consequence to insist that verbal meaning is that aspect of an author's meaning which is interpersonally communicable. For this implies that his verbal meaning is that which, under linguistic norms, one *can* understand, even if one must sometimes work hard to do so.

16. Charles Bally calls this "dédoublement de la personalité." See his *Linguistique générale et linguistique française,* 2nd ed. (Bern, 1944), p. 37.

THEORY

*Supplying a vigorous affirmative answer to his question,
George Watson defends the practices of traditional literary history, practices which assume "a correspondence of
some kind between what the poet and his age might reasonably be thought to have in mind, on the one hand,
and the true meaning of the poem on the other." "The poet
and his age" is the key phrase here. Taking the author's
intention as the center of the poetic meaning, Watson
widens the argument to include the traditional concerns
of literary history as they bear on that center. So, in addition to strictly biographical information, we need to
consider, for example, genre (Hirsch's "generic appropriateness"), a subject with an important historical dimension. "When the literary historian identifies the lineage
of poems whose pedigrees have fallen into oblivion . . . he
is restoring to the consciousness of the reader knowledge
of an indispensable kind." At an even more fundamental
level, language itself is historically embedded. Those who
would substitute the "norms of language" for authorial
intention need to remember, says Watson, that the norms
of language are historically contingent. "To speak of the
norms of language is to concede, however unwittingly,
the case for an historical discipline." The practitioner of
this discipline, the literary historian, by reconstructing
the philosophical, political, and linguistic horizons of the
author's "age," constructs not only the author's probable
intentions but also the limits of the author's possible
meanings. Thus Watson's author-centered literary history, while a direct counterstatement to the formalists
we'll meet in the next chapter, is also a counter to the
very different historical approaches we'll meet in the
final chapter.*

Are Poems Historical Acts?

George Watson

Reprinted by permission of the author from George Watson,
The Study of Literature (London: Allen Lane, 1969), 70–77.

The nagging doubt about literary history in the present century does, after all, have more than a semblance of an objection of principle and is something more than a mere intellectual fashion. It is based upon a persuasive scepticism about the status of a poem as an historical act. The scepticism needs to be seen in perspective. Nobody has ever doubted that poems were written in the past. But it does not plainly follow that a poem is an historical document in the sense that it derives its chief interest and value from the personality and purpose of its author in the historical conditions under which he wrote. The debate surrounding the "intentional fallacy" has been concerned with this larger issue — an issue in which "the poet's intention" is only one of the problems involved. To speak of the intentional fallacy at all was to react against an historical view of literature which, by the 1940s, had been dominant in the West for over a hundred years. And to accept it as a fallacy was to offer a view deeply subversive to literary history, as it was meant to be, since the literary historian is bound to assume a correspondence of some kind between what the poet and his age might reasonably be thought to have in mind, on the one hand, and the true meaning of the poem on the other. When the historian investigates the question whether the figure of Shylock in *The Merchant of Venice* represents an anti-Semitic view, for instance, he regards the question as hardly distinguishable from a question about what Shakespeare and his first audience would have thought of Shylock. If the literary historian is to be told that the play now exists independently of its creator, and that the modern reader or actor is entitled to make what sense he can of it, then he had better gather up his writing materials and go elsewhere. Such an atmosphere is not for him.

In the following discussion, which is offered among other things as a refutation of the claim that intentionalism is a fallacy, I shall deliberately widen the scope of the argument to include issues beyond the intention of the poet himself. This procedure is justifiable to the extent that the issue involved in contemporary controversy is genuinely wider than the protagonists have always fully realized. What is involved here, at its widest extent, is the momentous issue whether literature is primarily to be studied as a purposive activity or not. It was among the greatest achievements of nineteenth-century historiography to emphasize, perhaps even to exaggerate, the sense of purpose out of which a great poem is born.

If this process is to be put into reverse, and if literature is now to be regarded as the first audiences for the Homeric poems perhaps regarded the *Iliad*, or as those who listen to pop-songs today regard what they hear — experiences involving curiosity about the performers, it may be supposed, rather than about the creators — then powerful reasons would be needed for supposing that such a reversal would represent a gain to civilized values. For most men who have valued the literary experience in the past century and more, literature is by contrast the supremely purposive activity: "an objective, a projected result," as Henry James once called it emphatically, adding sententiously: "it is life that is the unconscious, the agitated, the struggling, floundering cause."[1]

It was the Victorians themselves who raised the first protests against the prevailing obsession of their age with the pastness of the past. Robert Browning, who was perhaps the first Englishman to consider the issue in print, argued in a preface of 1852 on Shelley that, in the case of "objective" poets at least, biography may be dispensed with as "no more necessary to an understanding or enjoyment . . . than is a model or anatomy of some tropical tree to the right tasting of the fruit we are familiar with on the market-stall." Saintsbury sometimes claimed to believe — in his study of *Dryden* (1881), for example — that only the verbal analysis of poems can be defended in principle, though he practiced many other sorts himself. Matthew Arnold spent half a lifetime emphasizing the essential timelessness of great poetry. Oscar Wilde spoke of the work of art as having "an independent life of its own" which may "deliver a message far other than that which was put in its lips to say." Quiller-Couch, in his Cambridge lectures *On the Art of Writing* (1916), held that the greatest literature is always

seraphically free
From taint of personality.

E. M. Forster, in an essay of 1925 entitled "Anonymity," argued that "a poem is absolute," and that "all literature tends towards a condition of anonymity. . . . It wants not to be signed." Like so many campaigns against the Victorians, the campaign against literary history is itself Victorian in its origins. But the real reason for rehearsing these objections, which if placed beside the manifestoes of French *"l'art pour l'art"* and Proust's *Contre Sainte-*

Beuve would make a massive dossier, is to emphasize the scope and variety of the campaign rather than its antiquity. And many of these issues are rightly associated, various as they are. If in the following account I attempt to refute the case point by point, it is rather in the hope of marshalling a lucid argument in favour of a new tradition of literary history than out of any inclination to convict others of muddle or equivocation.

First, there is the issue of evaluation by intention. I mention this here only for the sake of completeness, since no one, it may be supposed, has ever seriously held that a poem is good because its author intended it to be so. To deny, against Wimsatt and Beardsley, that an author's intention is properly "a standard for judging ... success" is to consider a phrase that opens many issues: but so far as this one is concerned, it would be better to suppose that it had never existed.

The appeal to fulfilled intention, however, is a more serious matter, in the sense that it is a fallacy which is plausible enough to be believed. It is often suggested that a poet has done enough if he fully performs what he set out to do, and often objected that it is improper to demand of the author that he should have written a different book. But it is notable that good critics often demand of an author, and with good reason, that he should have written a different book. And it is not at all obvious that in principle they should not. When Dr. Johnson, in his Life of Dryden, complained of *Absalom and Achitophel* that

the original structure of the poem was defective; allegories drawn to great length will always break; Charles could not run continually parallel with David,

he is certainly regretting that Dryden had not written a radically different poem, and to object that he should accept the poem for what it is amounts to a demand that he should abdicate his function altogether. But then to fulfil an intention, in literature as in life, is not necessarily to behave as one should. If a man sets out to shoot his mother-in-law, and does so, one may applaud his marksmanship but not the deed itself.

If these were the only uses to which the determination of authorial intention were put by critics, it would be easy to agree that intentionalism is a fallacy. But they are not. After all, there is the wide and distinct issue of the distribution of literature: not just

in the way of mechanical improvements like the invention of printing, but in matters which affect the literary experience at its deepest roots. It is of much less than decisive importance that Chaucer did not intend his poems to be printed, for instance; though the fact that he probably intended his poems to be heard rather than silently perused is a fact of real interest. To print is to multiply copies, and the world is evidently right to assume that Chaucer's intentions in the matter are of little concern now. But a new form of distribution might represent a more radical change of emphasis than this. Milton is unlikely to have intended *Samson Agonistes* for the stage; Shakespeare designed his plays altogether for performance, and is unlikely to have taken much interest in their publication. Again, nobody supposes such intentions to be decisive upon posterity; but equally, the probability that *Samson* was written for the study rather than for the stage is a major fact about *Samson*. Anyone who supposed that Milton was attempting a theatrical rival to Dryden's *Conquest of Granada*, for example, would probably prove an unreceptive reader of Milton's play. It is said that Tibetan tea, which is partly composed of rancid butter, is revolting to Western tastes if considered as tea but acceptable if considered as soup. When we ask of a poem questions on the order of "What did the poet intend it for?" — whether stage or study, whether court audience or popular — the answer seems in principle likely to be useful to the extent that it is accurate. This is surely a good question to ask, and anybody who objects at this point that the search for the author's intention is necessarily a fallacy should be sent about his business.

It seems likely, too, that the purposive property of literature is under unnecessary attack at this point. To concede, for instance, that a good stage-play could be written by someone who is not trying to write a stage-play at all is not only to concede something vastly improbable in itself. It is also to humiliate the status of literature as a human act. As Wordsworth put it, a poet is a man speaking to men. On the whole, we listen to those who address us in order to discover what they mean. It is also true that, in rare and memorable instances, people say remarkable things without meaning them. But anybody who conducted his social life on the principle that conversation is worth listening to only or mainly for the sake of such instances would be guilty of continuous discourtesy and, still more important, would find himself much the worse for the bargain. Freaks in creation exist: Musset, for example, is said to have written his plays with no thought for the stage, though in fact they succeed there. But freaks are exactly what such cases are.

A further support for the doctrine of the poem as an historical act seems to arise from the study of the literary kinds. This is an extension of the preceding argument concerning the distribution of literature, and one to be distinguished from it only with difficulty. Nobody, in all probability, has ever denied that on the whole a novel is a novel, or an elegy an elegy, because its author intended it to be so. But in the anti-historical atmosphere of the early twentieth century it was possible to protest that, since works usually bear the evidence of the kind to which they belong on their faces, the historical critic had little to contribute by "going outside the poem." This view is certainly mistaken. When a reader recognizes a novel to be such, or chooses it because it is such, he is certainly using evidence from outside the work as well as evidence from within. He is recognizing features in the novel he holds in his hand which resemble those in other novels he has read. The uncertainty that overhangs early and unestablished literary forms, such as the novel in early eighteenth-century England, and the hesitating attempts to confer dignity and status upon such forms, as in Fielding's formula of the "comic epic in prose," are examples of the problems that ignorance or uncertainty concerning the literary kinds can raise. And when the literary historian identifies the lineage of poems whose pedigrees have fallen into oblivion—when he identifies one of *The Canterbury Tales* as a beast-fable, for instance, and another as a romance of courtly love—he is restoring to the consciousness of the reader knowledge of an indispensable kind. But then the achievements of genre-identification seem among the most massive and incontestable triumphs of historical criticism over the past two hundred years. To demonstrate the complex relation between Spenser's *Faerie Queen*, for instance, and the Italian epics which in the sixteenth century dominated the mode of romantic epic throughout Europe, is to restore to the English poem the status and interest of a masterpiece and rescue it from the imputation of a work that might otherwise barely survive as a loose collection of occasional beauties.

If the wider problem of language is considered in the same light, the historical status of literature grows steadily and inescapably clearer. It was sometimes objected of historical criticism that it encouraged a chaos of romantic individualism on the part of the poets in their use of language, whereas the fashionable demand in the earlier years of the century was for continuity, order and "the tradition." Words, it was emphasized by the New Critics and others, need to be disciplined to fit the norms of language, so that the poem itself might ideally exist in a void of space or time, a formal object or "well wrought urn." "The work after being produced must continue to exist independently of the author's intentions or thoughts about it. The idiosyncrasies of the author must not be repugnant to the norm."[2] But certain celebrated literary effects, after all, *are* repugnant to the norms of language as established in their age. The obscenities of Swift are repugnant to the norms of polite language in the Augustan age, as they were meant to be, and it is just their repugnancy—in this case, their power to shock—that makes them tell. Some English poets are well known to have used linguistic devices—Milton's syntax, Dylan Thomas's diction—which deviate from any known use of language in their age, and the reader is meant to sense that a deviation or perversion of usage is happening. It is admittedly tempting to suppose that there must be some limit to the degree of repugnancy that is admissible in literature; and certainly there is a point beyond which language can only turn into nonsense. But then nonsense can be literature too, and sometimes is—a warning that, if there is a limit to be placed, it may be worth insisting that it should be placed at some remote point.

In any case, to speak of norms of language is to concede, however unwittingly, the case for an historical discipline. The poem itself is not the norm, after all, and in itself it cannot reveal what the norm is. In order to demonstrate the idiosyncrasies of Milton's syntax in *Paradise Lost*, it is of no use to confine the discussion to the poem itself: one must look at other documents by Milton and by his contemporaries. The oddities of Thomas's diction exist only in relation to mid-twentieth-century usages outside his poems. If we are anxious to pretend that poems could ever "exist independently of the author's intentions," we had better banish all idea of the norm. And in banishing that, it is easy to see, a great deal of significance must go too. A reader content to suppose that Milton's language was the ordinary language of his age would certainly miss much of the significance of *Paradise Lost*. To evade in all circumstances the study of the author's intentions, in fact, is at times to evade the meaning of the poem itself.

What does it mean to speak usefully of an author's intentions in his poem? I emphasize "usefully," since it is right to concede at once that such discussions need not be useful at all; and doctrines like "the intentional fallacy" probably represent an exaggerated reaction to this realization, obvious as it is. But then the historian, whether of literature or of anything else, is in no way committed to the view that everything about the past is of equal interest: in fact it is precisely the historian who is expected to show the greatest skill and experience in sorting the important evidence from the insignificant. That is his trade. When we have shown that much skilful and informed speculation about the poet's intention does not help in reading his poems—a charge sometimes levelled against J. L. Lowes's study of Coleridge, *The Road to Xanadu*, for example—nothing decisive has been said or shown against the nature of such enquiries in general. If it sometimes helps, it does not follow that it always helps. Equally, the historical critic need not allow himself to be committed to the view that his enquiry is utterly limited to the question of what the poet intended. It is notorious that Shakespeare would not understand much modern Shakespearean criticism. But then that, in itself, is hardly an objection to what the critics are doing. Newton, equally, would presumably not understand modern physics. It seems likely that one or the other, if he could return to life, might be trained in understanding and would prove an unusually apt pupil; but to demand of the historical critic that he should in all circumstances limit himself to seeing in a Shakespeare play only as much as the dramatist himself might have seen and in something like the very terms in which he would have seen it is to ask, in large measure, that literary studies should be stopped.

On the other hand, the historical criticism of literature imposes a limit of another and more reasonable kind than this. If it does not forbid elucidation beyond the point where the poet himself might cease to follow the argument, it commonly forbids explanations that run counter to what the poet could have thought or felt. The enlargement of "intended" to "thought or felt" is a safety-device in this argument, but an allowable one if it is conceded how much wider than the conscious and articulate intention of the poet the scope of the modern argument about the poet's intention has proved. To set out to show that Shakespeare was something like a Marxist, or that he had a horror of autocracy and the police-state, is to attempt to prove something that runs counter not only to the texts of the plays but, short of the remotest freak of intellectual history, counter to anything an Elizabethan could have believed. When one exclaims "But Shakespeare *can't* have thought that," the curtain that drops upon the line of argument is a curtain that has good reason to be there.

Notes

1. "The Lesson of Balzac" (1905), reprinted in *The House of Fiction*, edited by Leon Edel (London, 1957), p. 64.
2. Wimsatt and Beardsley, in *Dictionary of World Literature*, edited by Joseph T. Shipley (New York, 1942), p. 327.

THEORY

Intention Floreat

Alastair Fowler

Alastair Fowler's "Intention Floreat" first appeared as the concluding essay to a book that gathered a number of pieces on both sides of the intentionalist controversy. We long to have done with the issue, says Fowler, but we can't because the problem of intentionality, "as ineluctable as meaning, as inseparable as human nature," haunts our understanding of interpretation. And rightly so, Fowler concludes, because finally authorial intention is the only solid basis for interpretation. He finds strong support for this view in the nearly universal belief that editors should deliver the author's exact words. Our instinct is right here, Fowler claims, and this belief entails consequences for the entire debate. But to see what these are, we need to investigate more fully the "phenomenology" of criticism. Fowler then offers a description of the reading process that might be profitably compared to those in the chapter on reader-response criticism. Like many critics in that context, Fowler is concerned to trace the steps by which readers "construct" the literary work. But much more than most reader-response critics, Fowler insists on the author's "realized intention" as the goal of our constructions. And much more than most formalist critics, he insists on historical limits to possible meanings. Even when biographical evidence is absent (as in the case of an anonymous poem), the question "Can the author have meant that?" may be answered in historical terms.

Like Hirsch, Fowler would in principle distinguish interpretation from evaluation (compare Hirsch's "meaning" and "significance"), but even more than Hirsch he finds the distinction very difficult in practice, acknowledging that we are so firmly situated in our own time that we cannot completely adopt the horizons of another

Reprinted by permission of the publisher and the author from David Newton-DeMolina, ed., *On Literary Intention* (Edinburgh: Edinburgh University Press, 1976), 242, 247–55. Copyright © 1976 by Edinburgh University Press. A portion of the essay has been omitted.

epoch. Sometimes we must remain "exiled from the original work by a feast of knowledge." This exile is also a freedom, allowing the critic to judge earlier or even contemporary works from wider or different horizons than those that bound the author. In this acknowledgment, Fowler leans toward the historical approaches we'll explore in the last chapter. But he immediately pulls back to remind us that, despite the difficulties, it is the fundamental task of interpretation to reconstruct the author's horizons and correctly understand the author's intentions. In so exhorting us to let intentionalism flourish, Fowler puts himself at odds with much of the critical theory of the last half-century; but he provides a rationale for much of its critical practice.

Our endless reasonings about authorial foreknowledge, about meaning and intention in literature, and about the relevance of discussion of intention in criticism and interpretation, begin to lose themselves in wandering mazes. But we are less apprehensive of scholasticism (for here terms are baggy-loose) than of the debate's losing momentum as it increases in volume, and turning vague. The meandering labyrinth may not only permit no progress but conceal no monster. How frustratingly the intentionalists and anti-intentionalists write at cross purposes: how seldom the lecturers wait behind to answer objections. We feel impelled to revolutionize the terms of a problem whose solution has become so intricate that it eludes our comprehension as easily as its own simplification. We want to move on, have done. Yet the classic problem of intentionality moves too, as ineluctable as meaning, as inseparable as human nature. Criticism at every turn challenges our policy towards intentionality.

•   •   •

The Sequence of Intentions

We may accept (with reservations that need not be entered into now) the idea of composition as an endless process in which editors, compositor and readers all participate creatively, so that continual reactualization or recreation of the work takes place. Let us grant that a compositor participates by deciphering manuscript; that an editor may impose house rules for orthography, and in old works (and some not so old) supply punctuation. Let us farther concede that substantive departures from the text originally intended can very occasionally produce a beauty which the author never thought of, or decided against. Given this situation, what characterizes the good compositor or scribe? In general he is agreed to be one who introduces no new words. Now examine his decision-making as he hesitates between two possible vocabulary-selections. Is not his criterion, rightly, whether the word was intended? There are no two ways about it: at this stage, at least, authorial intention rules. Editorial decisions are normally very little different in this respect. What we ask of an editor is that he transmit the author's vocabulary-selections as faithfully as possible. If he goes wrong and the error makes sense, this is a positive disadvantage. Exceptionally a Maxwell E. Perkins will rearrange or cut his author's text creatively; but then he is either literally a collaborator, or else he meets with approval just because he has rendered his confused author's main intention faithfully. The criterion of competent transmission remains conformity with the writer's vocabulary selections. A few qualifications of this either prove the rule or leave it materially unaltered. For example, oral literature (which has its own somewhat distinct model) may leave performers free to introduce local variations. And in very poorly transcribed texts even of written literature an editor will feel free to select, within limits and brackets, according to his general ideas of the work. Broadly speaking, however, unless one ignores the nature of literary transmission and communication links in general, one must acknowledge the privileged status of the particular set of words intended by the author.

This has never seriously been challenged. In fact, anti-intentionalists have conspicuously avoided the matter of transmission. Perhaps they have half-realized the difficulty of conceding the primacy of intention in this phase while rejecting it in all others. Transmission is indeed the thin end of an irresistible wedge, since vocabulary-choice carries almost every other authorial decision with it.

To see why, we need only think for a moment of the linguistic nature of the work (or, as Peckham prefers, of literary discourse). Choice of words by no means takes place in isolation from other features. It accords with a particular tone, for example; perhaps with a special diction and genre; certainly with many rhetorical structures. The lexical string expresses, in fact, the writer's grammatic and semantic intention; and in turn it binds the recipient to understand one specific communication, in contrast to countless others. There may be ambiguities. But in general the words entail a chain of discourse. If therefore the lexical string enjoys privileged status, so does the work's whole linguistic structure, and ultimately many of its literary features too. Because there is no bulkhead between the linguistic and literary components, there can be none between the privileged arrangement of words and the literary meaning originally implied by that arrangement. Respect for the text of an author seems to constitute *de facto* recognition of the privileged status of his intention.

But it is only the realized intention to which this status is conceded. Why trouble, then, to bring intention in at all? What difference can it make to speak of "the intended arrangement of words," "the author's meaning," etc., rather than simply "the work," "the meaning"? When the achieved meaning is in doubt, how can it help to invoke a far more shadowy intention? Surely Wimsatt and Beardsley were right to insist that the work's own form is best evidence for its meaning. If the author fulfilled his intention it remains "in" the work, available as impersonal form. If he did not, his intention is irrelevant. In "Genesis: A Fallacy Revisited" Wimsatt explains that his argument was never directed against the relevance of such intentions as can be inferred from the work itself. This eirenic clarification appears to satisfy any reasonable apprehension that he might have thrown a baby of value and integral personality out with the slops of wishy-washy biographical speculation. It seems that the anti-intentionalist position freely embraces intention, in the realized form that as we have seen counts for most. Has not Wimsatt conceded quite enough?

If it seems so, that is illusion; for he has really passed over the question of authorial privilege. In this he and Beardsley have unintentionally confused some of their readers. Alan Rodway suggests in *The Truths of Fiction* that most of the intentionalist controversy arises from misapprehension of what Wimsatt and Beardsley originally meant. They "omitted to use a separate term . . . to distinguish the apparent intention found within the work itself from that imported from outside (by scholarly deduction or the author's own statement). . . . And, of course, only the second sort of intention was declared to be fallacious as a measuring-rod." Now it is easy to interpret them (as also the Wimsatt *solus* of "Genesis") in this sense. But on closer consideration they appear never to have conceded that any sort of authorial intention could be acceptable as a *measuring-rod*, that is, a priv-

ileged criterion. To permit reference to realized intention is not to assign it any special status among other "versions" of the work. The authors of *The Verbal Icon* have never recanted the footnote, in which they roundly affirmed that "the history of words *after* a poem is written may contribute meanings which if relevant to the original pattern should not be ruled out by a scruple about intention." These are not the words of people who take realized intention as their measuring-rod.

The reason for insisting on intention is that without it the work disappears altogether. Abandon the search for authorial meaning, and there remains no common basis for criticism worth respecting. Intention may be hard, even impossible, to discover; it may have to be inferred and constructed; and it will certainly elude early attempts. But unless our efforts at least aim towards it, we have only Peckham's individualist "versions" to discuss: a dispersed horde of "works" competing for attention, each backed by more or less vociferous opinion. That is why it is vital that criticism concern itself with the intended work, and not merely with works.

This is not to say that the critic's sensibility should be repressed; that he should altruistically identify with the author, binding himself to what may after all be no more than a primitive or woolly conception of the work. Conceding authorial privilege means giving the author the first word, not the last. Unfortunately the relation between responsibility to intention and freedom of critical interpretation is obscure, and will perhaps remain so until we have a fuller phenomenology of criticism.

Phenomena of Interpretation

The need for a more adequate description of criticism is obvious enough. Above all we need to escape the limiting conception of its role as one of dealing with a given work. The common notion is that criticism starts from a text — "the words on the page" — which it proceeds to interpret and evaluate. But there is no such thing as words on pages, only ink marks. A reader has always to *construct* the words and the work, starting from marks on paper (or sound-waves in air). He does this by interpreting them, according to codes more or less fully shared with their encoder, as indications of the vocabulary choices intended. These choices, in turn, he interprets as signals of intended grammatical (or rhetorical, metrical, numerological, etc.) forms; and so on up the artifactual pyramid. At the top, as it were, above even the intended themes, the work's unity waits to be reconstructed. I have said that the levels are interpreted "in turn"; but it cannot be overemphasized how complex and organic the process is, whereby a reader's dawning apprehension of a work guides his construction of even its most subordinate elements. Feedback from his general view may fortunately supply the meaning of an unfamiliar usage; unfortunately, he may also misconstrue a constituent because of some ingenious misconception (already at this early stage) of what the work is all about.

We know by hard experience that critics may differ widely about what they have read. Commonly their opinions about the work are said then to differ. But it would often be truer to say that their opinions are about different things: they have constructed works so different, perhaps, that criticism of them must be at loggerheads or cross-purposes. This need not be an impasse. Though one almost hesitates to say it, so unorthodox has the idea become, variation of constructs is due to errors, which can be corrected. Errors in construction really are possible. I refer not to misinterpretation (though that can contribute, as we saw) but to invention of ghost constituents. At any level of the literary communication signals can be wrongly decoded, wrongly identified, or missed altogether. This may soon be obvious, as with the confusion of O. E. thorn and M. E. *p*, or ignorance of an obsolete grammatical rule. But often, as with the stylistic implications of rhetorical indicators, or with obsolete meanings of current words, it is far from clear when construction goes astray. Similarly with contemporary literature: codings may be unfamiliar because they are beyond the reader's emotional, social, or political experience; *avant-garde*; or too conservative to get an alert response. A profound work may be so demanding intellectually that it fails to establish coherent communication. And even with sentiments, though "a true feeler always brings half the entertainment along with him . . . 'Tis like reading *himself* and not the *book*," yet there is "little true feeling in the *herd* of the *world*" (Sterne, Letter to Dr. John Eustace, 9 Feb. 1768). In these ways, and many others, literary signals may meet with poor reception; so that the higher-level constituents they are meant to communicate are lost. Of course, the resulting errors are sometimes interesting—even worth consideration in their own right as Pater-like improvisations.

But every sensible reader will wish to get the signals right: to put together a construct that is neither random nor idiosyncratic, but that shares with other readers' constructs a common element corresponding to the original work. That original work may not be the whole subject for our different critical views. But it ought to be a component (and I think a main component) of that subject.

How, then, should the work be constructed? This large question has received little attention—not surprisingly, since in the absence of any phenomenology of criticism the constructive phase is confused with the interpretative. One of the few principles advanced to guide construction is Beardsley's "Principle of Plentitude": namely, "All the connotations that can be found to fit are to be attributed to the poem: it means all it *can* mean, so to speak" (*Aesthetics* (New York 1958) 144). For Robert Graves, in equally permissive mood, the meaning of a Shakespeare sonnet is the "one embracing as many meanings as possible, that is, the most difficult meaning." Indeed, one might call this affluent principle the primary constructive rule in our time. Richness is all.

Yet if it were possible to give general advice, it might well be against the tendency casually embraced by this rule. It is an unprincipled principle, which leads in the end to anything meaning anything. If Blake's Satanic mills can be industrial mills (as some have argued in pursuit of plenitude), why should not Spenser's false Una "framed of liquid air" be chastely cold? Any moderately fanciful reader can easily generate higher-level constituents that satisfy Beardsley's only restraining principle, Congruence. But far more constraints will be needed, to produce a valid construct. It is a common experience to have to change a construct that has proved faulty, yet in which the meanings once *seemed* to fit. And whenever we fault a former construct we acknowledge the artifactual structure to be closed to some congruent realizations. What limits its openness? Surely considerations of historical truth, for one thing. The field of criticism has a truth pole as well as an aesthetic interest pole: it matters to us which constituents are historically "in" the work. In saying "the work" I have in effect affirmed that the author's realized intention must exercise a farther constraint. What we try to construct is the original work, in the sense of the intention realized by the author. Scruples about intention will thus rule out many interesting meanings and other constituents.

Our criterial questions are Did the author intend this? and, minimally, Can he have meant that? These questions need not constitute appeals to biography. The case of anonymous literature shows that an imagined author can exert constraint on critical invention. And when we know the authorship it is still the accessible literary *persona* with whom we primarily deal as readers.

Interpretation and evaluation are distinct from construction and logically posterior to it. They are not, however, chronologically sequential phases. There would be far less confusion about intentionality if the critic could first construct the author's work and then criticize it. But the matter is less simple. Interpretation, like evaluation, necessarily deals for the most part with what interests the critic or his audience (preferably both). It speaks to their condition, even if the work does not. Consequently the focus and power of the reader's attention will vary with time and place in ways that no author can anticipate. Devices, levels of organization, even whole genres, may lose interest or delight (syntactic inversion; strict pentameter prosody; French Biblical epic). And to this Demogorgon of change the critic must, however reluctantly, pay some lip-service. An interpretation faithful to every proportion of the original, but lacking in relevance or interest, would be of very little use. The bearing of this truth on habits of construction is incalculable. How often do we unconsciously meet the choice between falsifying the construct or neglecting the work? It is repugnant to admit that we are temporarily or permanently incapable of receiving anything from what nevertheless was once a great work. But this may often be so. When the literary model alters, the parts of literature for which readers have competence must alter too. Nor are the changes only external or formal. The conception of meaning itself has undergone more than one profound development during the last millennium. In our own age allegoresis, for example, will simply not work as it worked for Dante or even for Shakespeare. And more inwardly still, the critic is exiled from the original work by a feast of knowledge. Inescapable hindsight shuts him out by making him incapable of a simple enough response. How could he ever feel the strangeness of the historically first exploration of an effect familiar to him from its subsequent exploitation and finesse?

The problem is not only a matter of historical stance: criticism's freedom legitimately extends to contemporary works. Living authors are subject to historical contingency too, in the deeper sense of human limitation. Consequently the reader is free to take a broader, deeper, or different view of the work from that of the limited author, if he can. He may well know more, or be more mature emotionally. And he feels perhaps that he can make a valuable contribution of his own in the selective assimilation of the values of the work.

The Responsibility of a Free Critic

This freedom, however, is not so unconditioned as some suppose. Northrop Frye scorns "the absurd quantum formula of criticism, the assertion that the critic should confine himself to 'getting out' of a poem exactly what the poet may vaguely be assumed to have been aware of 'putting in,'" that "it is simply his job to take a poem into which a poet has diligently stuffed a specific number of beauties or effects, and complacently extract them one by one, like his prototype Little Jack Horner" (*Anatomy of Criticism* (Princeton, N.J. 1957), 17–8). But, as we have seen, recognizing the privileged status of intention by no means entails a vague assumption of total consciousness. We are certainly free to talk about features that the author was unaware of, and to talk about any of the work's beauties in terms unavailable to him. In that sense we indeed discourse endlessly of beauties that the author did not "put in." But the critic's social contract, it seems to me, is to discuss beauties of existing features, not merely of notional ones. And features do not exist just because we "invent" or think them. Of course, not all theorists would accept this restriction. That in itself seems significant. Indeed, the intentionalist controversy almost seems as if it may now be starting to resolve itself into a more fundamental questioning of what criticism is about. Does criticism deal with actual literature only, or does it extend also to literature that exists potentially, or speculatively—without, as it were, having previous roots in history?

According to the view set out above, a critic's freedom is conditioned by responsibility to history. This responsibility has several components—not least the duty to avoid being oblivious to his own historical predicament. But from the present point of view the critic's responsibility is to include within his own broader vision the vision of the author. Ideally the original work will be incorporated in his construct, the original values (together perhaps with other critics' evaluations) encapsulated within his values, like the heart and growth rings of a tree. Only then, it seems, can he take his own historical place effectively, so that his interpretation, in turn, contributes to the healthy growth of the work.

This responsibility or "limitation" (as Frye would call it) is no more confining than thematic relevance to a poet or constancy to a lover. Far from restricting literature as an inexhaustible source of critical discoveries, it directs attention to the headwaters. True, it constrains the critic to distinguish discoveries from inventions. But by doing so, and therefore by obliging the critic to meet the challenges of different minds, it makes for a criticism that is more than just *interesting*.

Not all opponents of intentionalism are formalists or archetypists. Critics devoted mainly to instrumental values tend to dislike a critical exercise that goes farther back than interpretation. They prefer to believe in a work permanently available to the valuer. For them the work has a purely synchronic existence. It is always "there," in iconic immediacy and isolation, ready for the evaluative act. Even interpretation is a preliminary, to be despatched with a perfunctory word or two. Now, these critics need to be advised that such an attitude, despite its appearance of high seriousness, is really frivolous. The idea that the work continuously exists serves as a comforting defence; for what exists when the valuers come on the scene is a work that they have previously reconstructed themselves or taken over ready-made from other critics. Their wish to "take it as read" easily covers reluctance to look into the construct's specifications. From time to time an unsound construction collapses spectacularly. Criticism of a *White-Jacket* that contained the phrase "soiled fish of the sea" lost ground very quickly when the authenticity of the *White-Jacket* retaining Melville's "coiled fish of the sea" became obvious. But usually bad construction passes unnoticed. It takes a good deal of imagination to realize that not just vocabulary-selection but every component of a construct can be unsound, in ways less obvious but no less disastrous. Yet to a serious critic it makes all the difference whether a statement concerns Melville's work or another one like it.

Are all these counsels of perfection? It must be conceded that we cannot hope to construct an author's work without deficiency or superfluity. Our best attempts are blurred with probabilities and approximations. We cannot even look forward, in the general case, to some distant time when all uncertainties will have been resolved—as one might resolve a particular problem, such as the quality of a rhyme. Criticism's fundamental predicament is that it inescapably concerns itself with an intended work that it must inevitably fail to discover. A similar dilemma may be universally inherent in the nature of meaning. (However precisely a recipient's conception is formulated, it will at best specify a category which the intended meaning belongs to. He can never quite resolve the paradox of simultaneous identity and difference between the author's meaning and what E. D. Hirsch has called the "intrinsic genre.") But this dilemma of our contingency should not make us despair or turn to antinomian relativism. There is plenty to be done. Not to know as much as we can about the premises of our interpretations: not to accept every opportunity of learning the codes that form literary communication: not to pursue at least the true Florimel of the work itself: that would be to do less than the reasonable standard of criticism demands. It would be flinching, even, from the difficulties of historical engagement.

Serious critical enquiries are likely to be farthered by habitually orientating thought towards the *locus* of authorial intentions. Eventually, the critic's own unconscious volitions may then be schooled to cooperate in imaginative revivifying of actual literature.

APPLICATION

Shakespeare and the Idea of Obedience: Gonzalo in *The Tempest*

Paul Yachnin

If we want to understand The Tempest, *Paul Yachnin argues, we need to see it at "the historical moment of its production and reception." Although we know little about Shakespeare aside from his works, we can discover much about the audience for whom those works were intended, and this will be the surest guide to their meaning. In the case of* The Tempest, *a lack of this historical knowledge frequently causes modern readers to mistake both the genre of the play and its main theme. Genre, as Watson and Fowler remind us, has a historical dimension, and Yachnin locates the distinction between a "polemical" and a "literary" work in its specific historical context: "whether the work in question, at the historical moment of its production, seems more concerned with persuading readers with respect to an issue or more concerned with thinking about an issue." To see* The Tempest *as a literary work "does not necessarily foreclose the possibility of a particular political reading of the play: rather it simply requires that such a reading be grounded in a historically specific negotiation between the text and the* normal *political attitude of the theatre-audience."*

The "normal" attitude of the audience is the key. On this assumption, Yachnin takes issue with the numerous "new historical" and cultural materialist readings of The Tempest, *including those by Stephen Greenblatt and Paul Brown, on the grounds that these attempts to historicize our understanding are not historical enough; that is, they "do not adequately come to terms with the normative 1611 reception of* The Tempest's *politics." In short, the closer we get to the concerns of the intended audience, the closer we get to Shakespeare's meaning. Yachnin argues that in* The Tempest *these concerns were domestic and European rather than colonial and, on the central and conflicted issue of obedience to political*

Reprinted by permission from *Mosaic: A Journal for the Interdisciplinary Study of Literature*, 24.2 (Spring 1991): 1–18.

authority, weighted toward the conservative side. Modern readers, he concedes, have different concerns—hence, our tendency to mistake the play's original meaning.

The question of how far subjects were obliged to obey their princes was prominently contested in the Renaissance.[1] During the Reformation, struggles between Protestants on one side and the Catholic Church on the other threw into high relief the often opposing claims of conscience and political obedience, and moved the question of obedience near the center of the polemical wars ongoing from the time of Luther to the time of Milton. Of course, Catholic and Protestant positions on the duty of obedience were by no means consistent through the period; on the contrary, positions on both sides tended to shift depending upon which side was dominant in whatever nation was in question.

English Protestants, for example, who during the Marian exile had extended the Calvinist argument for the right of active resistance to include the common people as well as lesser magistrates retreated to a far more quiescent position once the Protestant Elizabeth acceded to the throne (Greaves 23). To the same effect, the Catholic Church, which in most matters espoused the necessity of submitting to authority, nonetheless was able to enjoin English Catholics to murder the Queen of England on the grounds that she was a tyrant responsible for endangering her subjects' souls: "there is no doubt," Gregory XIII's secretary wrote in 1580, "that whosoever sends her out of the world with the pious intention of doing God service, not only does not sin but gains merit" (qtd. in Greaves 33).

The clarity and assurance of the various positions adopted on both sides throughout the period depended upon suppressing the contradictions attendant upon the role played by power. The effective Elizabethan controversialist had *not* to know, had to forget that he had known, that English people had been enjoined to resist during Mary's reign, but were commanded to submit under Elizabeth; equally, he had to maneuver around the fact that Protestants under Catholic rule were said to be justified in following the dictates of conscience, but that Catholics in Elizabethan England were "justifiably" subject to severe punishments for obeying *their* consciences. Further, the Elizabethan doctrine of non-resistance in the face of wicked rulers depended upon suppressing the

fact that non-resistance—suffering rather than rebelling—was often difficult to distinguish from complicity. That is, if a subject did not actively resist a wicked ruler, was not s/he in fact complicit with the ruler's wickedness, even if s/he refused to carry out wicked orders? This point was brought out by John Ponet, one of the Marian exiles. Who, Ponet asked, was to be blamed for Nero's crimes: "He for doing them, or others for flattrying him, or the Senate and people of *Rome* in suffring him? Surely there is none to be excused, but all to be blamed, and chiefly those that might have bridled him, and did not" (16).

In spite of these contradictions, however, it seems clear that the majority of the English people throughout the Elizabethan and Jacobean periods both espoused a doctrine of political obedience and renounced any idea of active resistance. The Elizabethan doctrine of obedience, it should be noted, did not entail "blind" obedience, since both ruler and subject were seen to be under the ultimate authority of God. The ruler, however, was answerable only to God, and the subject, if conscience enjoined nonobedience, was merely to suffer but never to resist. Elizabethan and Jacobean arguments in favor of obedience built upon the earlier Henrician linking of political and religious obligations, according to which loyalty to civic authorities constituted a Christian duty. This linking of spheres of obligation constituted an attempt to obliterate the distincticn between the claims of conscience and the claims of obedience. The 1570 *Homily against Disobedience and Wilful Rebellion* undertook to inscribe the particular relations of power existing in Elizabethan England within the universal text of what—according to the Elizabethan authorities—had been ordained by God as natural, thus making rebellion a crime against the divine as well as against the political order:

> What shall subjectes do then? Shall they obey valiaunt, stoute, wyse and good princes, and contemne, disobey and rebell against chyldren beyng their princes, or against undiscrete and evyll governours? God forbid. For first what a perilous thing were it to commit unto the subjectes the judgement which prince is wyse and godly and his government good, and whiche is otherwise, as though the foote must judge of the head—an enterprise very heynous, and must needes breede rebellion. . . .
>
> How horrible a sinne against God and man rebellion is, can not possiblie be expressed according

unto the greatnesse therof. For he that nameth rebellion, nameth not a singular, or one only sinne . . .
but he nameth the whole poodle and sinke of all
sinnes against God and man. . . .

(*Certain Sermons* 213, 225)

Furthermore, Elizabethan and Jacobean arguments for obedience were absolutist in the sense
that they based the obligation of obedience to the
monarch on a metaphysical, as opposed to a merely
legal, legitimation of monarchical power (Sommerville 9–50). In this view, the monarch's power
was "absolute"—unconditional, independent, superior to all other civil authority—deriving from
God rather than from the people. In the Elizabethan
period, "absolutism" did not imply "arbitrary"
power, which is how it came to be conceived during the Civil War period (Daly 228–48). Nonetheless, the absolutism of monarchical power was
productive of a dilemma which vexed the question
of obedience in the culture at large. Whereas in
resistance theory, the claims of the state and of
conscience were distinct, since the power of the
monarch was normally seen to derive from the people rather than from God, in terms of Elizabethan/
Jacobean absolutism, the claims of the state and of
conscience were on an equal footing.

The Elizabethan/Jacobean idea of obedience also
derived support from what Jonathan Goldberg has
called "the absolutist trope of state secrets" (55–112,
230–39), a mystification of the commonsense idea
that the ruler has often to keep secret the reasons for
pursuing some course of action or for issuing some
command. This idea underlies Jonson's defense of
James's handling of the Spanish Marriage negotiations; Jonson's parliamentarian contemporary, Sir
Robert Phelips, conceded that members of Parliament "ought not to draw the veyles that princes are
pleased to sett between theyr secret ends and common eyes" (qtd. in Sharpe 16).

Shakespeare tends both to strengthen this defense
and also to put it in question by relating the argument for the necessity of secrecy to the wider issue of
epistemological uncertainty. Already broached, in a
truly dizzying fashion by Castiglione in *The Courtier*
(Strier 105–06), radical uncertainty in Shakespeare is
normally attendant on and supportive of positions
opposed to political resistance. John of Gaunt's refusal to punish Richard II for the murder of Thomas
of Gloucester is based on the conventional idea of the

king's absolute power, but also on his own uncertainty with respect to the moral status of the murder
itself:

God's is the quarrel, for God's substitute,
His deputy anointed in His sight,
Hath caus'd his death, *the which if wrongfully,*
Let heaven revenge, for I may never lift
An angry arm against His minister.

(*Richard II*, I.ii.37–41; emphasis mine)[2]

Finally, the Elizabethan/Jacobean doctrine of submission to divinely ordained civic authority derived
considerable urgency from Catholic arguments in favor of killing the English monarch. One example of
how Englishmen, especially during the Elizabethan
period and in the wake of the 1605 Gunpowder Plot,
came to identify the idea of active resistance with
"the Catholicke zeale to stab good Princes" is to be
found in James Cleland's 1607 courtesy-book, *The Institution of a Young Noble Man:* "What man is hee then
so rash and unadvised to saie or mainetaine that you
shoulde not obay your Soveraigne if hee be cruel or
rigorous? Where finde you that Gods commaunde-
ments will suffer Kings to bee throwne out of their
thrones? . . . This is the Papists doctrine: this is the
Romane Religion I wish you to beware of: this is the
Catholicke zeale to stab good Princes" (116).

In spite of this commonplace adherence to the
idea of political obedience, however, many English
people must have felt unsettled and disturbed by the
sheer "shiftiness" of official positions with regard to
the subject's duty of obedience. The political and religious instability of England itself throughout the
sixteenth century seems to have engendered in many
people an increasing degree of political and religious
free-thinking and even skepticism. The deep rifts in
the ideological system made visible by the instability
of the period spawned doubt in the minds of many.
A subject who thought about the issue of obedience
hard enough might begin to find the government's
position burdened by contradiction and special
pleading. Someone like Donne, intensely engaged in
the wars between Protestantism and Catholicism,
seems to have adopted a "self-centered" position
which ostensibly preserved both the integrity of
conscience and the duty of obedience, but only by
putting in question the connection between secular
rule and the divine authority which normally was
seen to constitute its legitimation. In "Satyre III"
(c. 1597; pub. 1633), Donne advised his reader,

Keepe the truth which thou hast found; men do not stand
In so ill case here, that God hath with his hand
Sign'd Kings blanck-charters to kill whom they hate,
Nor are they Vicars, but hangmen to Fate.   (139)

Donne's skeptical position remained unpublished during his lifetime. Others, often those working in more visible places, normally spoke in favor of the subject's duty to obey over the demands of conscience. In *Neptune's Triumph for the Return of Albion* (1624), written to whitewash the fiasco of the Spanish Marriage negotiations, Ben Jonson ruled out the issue of doubts about a prince's intelligence or integrity. In response to popular skepticism and resentment aroused by both King James's ineffectual management of the negotiations and by the negotiations themselves, Jonson suggested that James had in fact been testing his subjects' loyalty:

It was no envious stepdame's rage,
Or tyrant's malice of the age
     That did employ him [Prince Charles] forth
But such a wisdom that would prove,
By sending him, their hearts and love,
     That else might fear his worth.
                              (ll. 243–48)

It seems fair to say that the issue of political obedience was pursued in at least two distinct but permeable fields of discourse. The first is a "polemical" field marked by clearly defined and univocal positions founded on both the suppression of contradiction and a clear idea of the constituency and interpretive practices of the readership. The second is what I will call a "literary" field; here political quietism is coupled with a less constrained consideration of the problems attendant upon the opposing claims of obedience and conscience; here there is a willingness to allow the emergence of contradiction, a less settled sense of the make-up and politics of the readership, and far less authorial policing of the production of meaning.

The essential difference between the polemical and the literary might be defined, roughly, as the difference between a discourse of power (or persuasion) on the one hand, and a discourse of (powerless or non-persuasive) imaginative freedom on the other. Literary scholars are familiar with the modern version of this divided field, since the normal practice here is to inscribe one's own discourse within a "polemical" field and to locate the texts dis-

cussed within a "literary" field. The division of the universe of discourse in this way gives the critic power to speak persuasively *for* the literary texts which are thus constructed as unable to speak authoritatively for themselves. As Roger Seamon has suggested, modern criticism tends to assume that the text itself is "dumb," and that the business of criticism is to "speak" for it (296). One of my contentions is that many Renaissance texts constructed *themselves* as unable to speak authoritatively or powerfully about politics, and that by marking themselves as "dumb," such texts were freed from censorship and thus able to represent political issues in complex and candid ways ("Powerless Theater").

The polemical field includes works such as Jonson's *Neptune's Triumph* or the 1570 *Homily against Disobedience and Wilful Rebellion;* but it also includes works which argue for active resistance, such as Christopher Goodman's *How Superior Powers Oght to be Obeyd* (1558), and even openly subversive pamphlets such as Thomas Scot's *Vox Populi* (1624). The literary field includes works such as Thomas More's *Utopia* (1516), Donne's "Satyre III" or Thomas Browne's *Religio Medici* (1636; pub. 1642). Such categorization does not depend directly upon the formal features of the work itself; rather, it depends upon whether the work in question, at the historical moment of its production, seems more concerned with persuading readers with respect to an issue or more concerned with thinking about an issue. This distinction is often unstable, particularly with respect to "literary" writing. Indeed interpretive instability and changeability are two of the central features of the literary field. For this reason, works such as *Utopia* or Thomas Middleton's *A Game at Chess* (1624) or *Religio Medici* can be, and have been, inscribed within the polemical field and, consequently, have been interpreted as politically purposeful texts.

I want to suggest that *The Tempest*, at the historical moment of its production and reception, should be seen in terms of both the freedom to consider vexed political issues and the freedom from authorial policing of the production of meaning which are characteristic of texts inscribed in the literary field. Such a starting-place assumes that *The Tempest* was, largely, politically quiescent: free to "think" about political issues because constructed as powerless to speak authoritatively about such issues, powerless because of its openness to differing, even opposing, interpretations of its political meaning.

To locate *The Tempest* in the literary field does not necessarily foreclose the possibility of a particular political reading of the play; rather, it simply requires that such a reading be grounded in a historically-specific negotiation between the text and the *normal* political attitude of the theater-audience. Such a political reading recognizes the instability and change-ability of meaning, the fact that many Jacobean audience-members would have seen the play differently from how I will be suggesting it was normally seen; it also recognizes the fact that the meanings of *The Tempest* at the Globe in 1611 were not necessarily consonant with its meanings in London in 1674 (in Dryden's adaptation, *The Tempest,* or *The Enchanted Island*), or in Ernest Renan's 1878 adaptation (*Caliban: Suite de La Tempête*) in the wake of the Paris Commune, or at the 1988 meeting of the Shakespeare Association of America in Austin, Texas, where *The Tempest* was the focus of a special session on "Shakespeare and Colonialism." Furthermore, such a reading positions itself between left-wing and intentionalist interpretations of Shakespeare's politics (such as Curt Breight's recent interpretation of *The Tempest* as subversive or Richard Strier's similar study of *King Lear*) and Foucauldian readings of *The Tempest* as conservative and colonialist by scholars such as Stephen Greenblatt and Peter Hulme. These readings, while theoretically sophisticated, pay not enough attention to the centrality of the conscious activity both of writing on Shakespeare's part and of interpreting on the part of the Jacobean audience.

My reading of *The Tempest* as conservative, then, agrees with much new historicist and cultural materialist work on the play. I part company, however, from new historicist work by focusing on the European political scene in itself as central (as opposed to Europe in relation to the New World) and by insisting on the play's relative autonomy from determining discursive formations, whether discourses of colonialism, hierarchy or resistance. In particular, my emphasis on a conscious but never fully autonomous negotiation between author, players and audiences distinguishes my account of *The Tempest*'s meanings from Paul Brown's brilliant work on the play, since he sees the play's ideological complexity and instability as an effect of a conflicted discursive formation rather than as a product of the minds which had to respond to that discourse. Finally, my historicization of *The Tempest* differs from Kay Stockholder's recent psychoanalytic reading of what she sees as the play's conflicted figuration of power; she produces an effectively transhistorical authorial psyche by folding into the 1611 *Tempest* the conflicting readings which I want to see developing in history (197–232).

Accordingly, the supposed univocality of the political meaning of *The Tempest* must be seen to split along two separate axes—the first having to do with the heterogeneity of the political views of Shakespeare's contemporary audiences, the second having to do with the changing interpretations of *The Tempest* over time and in different cultural and political settings. My present discussion has to do only with the play as a conservative meditation, in 1611, on the necessity of political obedience over the demands of individual conscience in terms of the Reformation question of the subject's obligation to civil authority.

Such a focus disallows neither the view of *The Tempest* as subversive of domestic power relations (Breight) nor the "con-textualization" of the play in terms of its complicity with nascent colonialist discourse (Barker and Hulme; Brown; Erlich; Greenblatt; Hulme; Leininger). What I am suggesting, however, is that these views do not adequately come to terms with the normative 1611 reception of *The Tempest*'s politics—Breight's view because it is not sufficiently in tune with the play's affective structure (which invites identification with Prospero) and because it exaggerates popular disaffection with the monarchy; Barker and Hulme's view because it mistakes the particular range and contemporary import of the play's topical references. As Meredith Skura has argued recently, "colonialism" did not crystallize into a coherent discursive formation until after the first performances of *The Tempest* (52–57); consequently, one might argue that, in 1611, the play's allusions to the New World would have had reference primarily to Old World "domestic" concerns, rather than to the relationship between the Old and New Worlds. I would suggest, further, that such a domestic emphasis was equally in play in More's *Utopia* or in Montaigne's "Of the Caniballes," and even that European concerns in themselves constituted the determining emphasis for those works' early readers, a group which included Shakespeare. Equally, I would counter the new historicist view of the play as *automatically* supportive of colonialism's "euphemisation" of European exploitation of the New World, since such a view ignores both the constitutive function of the interpretation of "literary" texts and the differences of opinion which it is reasonable to assume existed between members of Shakespeare's original audiences.

• • •

The story of Gonzalo, the old counselor at the court of Alonso, lies at the center of the opposing claims of obedience and conscience in *The Tempest*. Although he is praised by Prospero, the play itself reveals—as Harry Berger pointed out in 1969—that Gonzalo was Antonio's accessory in the usurpation of Prospero. Gonzalo was in command of those who carried Prospero and Miranda from Milan and who abandoned them at sea; Gonzalo gave the castaways some necessities of life but abandoned them to death. According to Prospero, the agents of the usurpation carried him and Miranda out of Milan, bore them out to sea, and cast them adrift in "A rotten carcass of a butt, not rigg'd . . . the very rats/Instinctively have quit it" (I.ii. 146–48). In answer to a question from Miranda, Prospero reveals that the master of this heinous design was Gonzalo:

MIRANDA: How came we ashore?
PROSPERO: By Providence divine.
    Some food we had, and some fresh water, that
    A noble Neapolitan, Gonzalo,
    Out of his charity, who being then appointed
    Master of this design, did give us, with
    Rich garments, linens, stuffs, and necessaries,
    Which since have steaded much. . . .
                              (I.ii.159–65)

Unlike "polemical" works such as Jonson's *Neptune's Triumph* or King James's *Trew Law of Free Monarchies* (1598), *The Tempest* does not produce an incontestable conservative meaning; instead, the play "covers" its conservatism, so that only the interpretive efforts of a cooperative audience-member will "discover" the play's political meaning. We could say that *The Tempest* poses the case of Gonzalo as an interpretive problem whose solution produces a political argument. Gonzalo's participation in the overthrow of Prospero calls into question the validity of Prospero's praise of Gonzalo as his savior, and beyond that, calls into question Prospero's practical intelligence, acuity and authority. The play invites us to solve the problem of Gonzalo along lines that are predetermined by the requirement of recuperating Prospero as an authoritative and sympathetic figure. If Prospero is to remain the focus of our respect and sympathy, we will want to explain why he chooses to praise the very man who oversaw his ouster.

The reader or audience-member is entitled, of course, to decline the play's invitation to solve the problem of Gonzalo along the lines of the play's affective structure. It is possible to argue instead that Prospero's praise of Gonzalo reveals Prospero's inadequacy, lack of real authority, limited practical intelligence. This is Harry Berger's interpretation, one which suits both modern skepticism about authority and the current preference for irony as an interpretive technique. Moreover, Berger's ironic and skeptical reading would no doubt have been available to anti-absolutists or skeptics in Shakespeare's audience. Such a group might well have welcomed Berger's reading of Prospero as a ruler who refuses "to look too closely at the actual state of affairs, and more generally, at the world [he] live[s] in" (265); such a group might also have applauded Breight's (similar but different) historicized ironic reading of Prospero as a diabolically clever and successful politician who manufactures the threat of treason in order to legitimate and mystify his own claim to power.

I suggest, however, that neither of these ironic readings would have been normative in 1611, since the overall political climate at that juncture tended to be royalist rather than anti-royalist. Nor am I here simply invoking the fact that *The Tempest* was performed by the "King's Men," and performed by that company at court; that the court undoubtedly viewed the play as royalist does not necessarily mean that this was the way it was perceived by a large, public audience. Much more important is the massive positive reassessment of King James's ability, reputation and relations with his subjects which has been undertaken by scholars such as R. C. Munden and Jenny Wormald. In particular, in debunking the Whig interpretation of history by building a compelling refutation of the notion that Jacobean Parliaments constituted an "opposition" to the monarchy, Conrad Russell and Kevin Sharpe remove the ground underlying Breight's and Strier's arguments for seeing Shakespeare as a subversive playwright. Russell explains:

An opposition, as we know the term now, can hope to force changes of policy either by changing the government, or by appealing so eloquently to the public that the government is forced to change its ground. In this sense, opposition as we know the term now was impossible. It is also a characteristic of an "opposition" that it is united by some common body of beliefs, which it does not share with members of the government. This ideological gulf between "government" and "opposition" is impossible to find in Parliament before 1640. There were many disagreements on policy, often profound ones, but these were divisions which split the Council itself. On none of the great questions of the day did Parliamentary leaders hold any opinions not shared by members of the Council. Men who depend on persuasion to get their way, and who hold no beliefs incompatible with office, cannot be described as an "opposition" without grossly misleading modern readers. (18)

Thus, when Annabel Patterson attempts to strengthen her left-wing interpretation of *Coriolanus* by alluding to a contemporary parallel drawn between the Roman tribunes and what she calls "the opposition leaders in the Commons" (123), she is depending upon a no longer tenable view of Jacobean parliamentary relations with the crown. Breight refers to "oppositional discourse" rather than to an "opposition," and attempts to inscribe *The Tempest* within that discursive field. The exemplary oppositional texts he adduces, however, consist in the Marprelate tracts and, especially, in the dissident Catholic propaganda produced throughout the period on the Continent (3–4). As a consequence, Breight effectively aligns Shakespeare against the dominant views of his popular audience.

The prevailing royalism of Shakespeare's audience for which I am arguing need not be seen to preclude the possibility of satirical and skeptical theatrical representations of either James himself or the operations of power in general. Indeed, plays such as *Troilus and Cressida* (1601–02), *Eastward Ho!* (1605) and *A Game at Chess* (1624) demonstrate the persistence of satire and skepticism as elements in the theater's depiction of power throughout the Jacobean period. The point is, however, that the play in question must itself be satirical or, as is the case with *Game at Chess*, must encourage an ironic reception (Yachnin "*Game*"). *The Tempest*, like any literary text, can be interpreted ironically; however, because of its strong drive toward identification with Prospero, such an ironic interpretation would seem to require a powerful bias on the part of the interpretive community. Such a bias was perhaps characteristic of American Shakespeareans in the late 1960s and may be characteristic of modern left-wing Shakespeareans aligned against what they see as the conservative bias of New Historicism, but it was unlikely to be typical of Shakespeare's 1611 audience.

Also relevant is time of the play's performance. *The Tempest* was first performed before the death of the popular and militantly Protestant heir to the throne, Prince Henry, before the scandalous revelations surrounding the murder of Sir Thomas Overbury, and about seventeen months after the assassination of Henri IV, the Protestant ruler of France, an event which served to re-ignite English fears of Catholic subornation and treachery. Taken together with the revisionist account of the Jacobean political climate, these admittedly exemplary rather than decisive facts suggest that the first audiences of *The Tempest* would not have responded to the play against the bias of its affective structure.

In order to solve the problem of Gonzalo in a way which preserved Prospero's moral centrality and authority, Shakespeare's audience would have had to consider the contradictions and limitations attendant upon the idea of political obedience. The solution, that is, depends upon an endorsement of the idea of obedience *along with* an awareness of the moral and human costs that such obedience demands. Put another way, *The Tempest* invited the audience to formulate a critique of political obedience which demurred at the "obvious" next step of repudiation.

While the play's implicit support of obedience is uncongenial to modern readers, both because we value the rule of law and also because we have seen the heinous consequences of "following orders," it does not, of course, necessarily follow that Shakespeare's audience would have valued individual rights over the interests of the state, or would have associated political obedience with the abuses of fascism (as we do). Consequently, we have no reason to think either that *The Tempest* "fails" to repudiate the idea of obedience, or that the play does not repudiate obedience because Shakespeare lacked either courage or imagination. We can see, instead, that the subversion of and yet containment by the idea of political obedience is the effect of a negotiation between, on the one side, the powerless freedom itself of "literary" discourse and, on the other, a predominantly royalist audience, at a particular juncture in English history when resistance-theory tended to be identified with Catholic polemics against Protestantism and when actual opposition to authority tended to be identified with Catholic fifth-column activity.

The question of the opposing claims of obedience and conscience is also represented in *The Winter's Tale*. Written within a year of *The Tempest*, *The Win-*

ter's Tale provides two test cases which seek to emphasize the moral costs of political obedience and the value of obeying an absolute moral standard. That is, *The Winter's Tale* seeks to resolve the problem of obedience by pursuing a radical perspective and fails to do so because its nascent radicalism cannot be articulated in the absolutist terms dominant in the play. In the play, Camillo and Antigonus, two Sicilian lords in the Court of Leontes, respond in opposite ways to commands which each finds morally repugnant. Camillo, the first courtier, is commanded by Leontes to murder the innocent Polixenes. Camillo merely feigns compliance, and instead spirits Polixenes out of Sicilia. Antigonus, the second courtier, suppresses his moral repulsion in order to obey his prince. He obeys Leontes's wicked command to expose the baby, Perdita. Like Camillo, Antigonus carries an exile from Sicilia across the sea to Bohemia. Where Camillo's life-saving dereliction of duty is vindicated and rewarded, however, Antigonus's life-threatening obedience is punished by the aggregate forces of Nature, figured by the storm and by the bear which "mocks" him to death.

Gonzalo in *The Tempest* is closer to the bad example of Antigonus than he is to the good example of Camillo. Both Antigonus and Gonzalo are obedient to their princes; both are "throwers-out" of innocent victims; both are "masters of the design." Both are charitable in the commission of an evil act: Antigonus abandons Perdita with both a kind word and a small fortune in gold; Gonzalo abandons Prospero and Miranda with "some food," "some fresh water," "Rich garments, linens, stuffs, and necessaries," and Prospero's overprized books. Shakespeare arranges the details in order to make Gonzalo's act less clearly tantamount to murder; however, as Prospero suggests, their lives were saved by Providence, not by Gonzalo. In essence, therefore, the acts of Antigonus and Gonzalo are virtually identical.

If Prospero applied to his own situation the moral standard which serves to legitimate Antigonus's dismemberment in *The Winter's Tale,* he would not be able to praise Gonzalo. Moreover, if this moral standard were seen to obtain in general in *The Tempest,* we would have to conclude that Prospero is either a fool or a self-deceiver. As I want to argue, however, the moral standard of *The Winter's Tale* does not adequately cover events in *The Tempest.* Both plays adopt an absolutist paradigm, but *The Tempest'*s analysis of political acts and relations articulates the contradic-

tions which remain unarticulated in *The Winter's Tale.* Camillo's decision against murder is morally correct, Antigonus's decision in favor of the exposure of Perdita is immoral; but both courtiers' reasons for acting as they do are burdened by their inability to separate morality from political obedience. In contrast, Gonzalo's morally incorrect decision to obey Alonso's command to cast Prospero adrift is seen to have been undertaken in the knowledge that obedience requires culpable action.

When Camillo considers Leontes's regicidal command, the obvious moral objection to the murder of an innocent man is present in his mind, but his soliloquy swerves away from an articulation of the claims of morality as opposed to those of political hierarchy. As I have already suggested, Camillo turns away from the moral objection because the absolutist paradigm dominant in the play precludes the separation of political and religious spheres of obligation (just as in the 1570 *Homily against Disobedience*). Camillo is unable to say something like the following: "Poisoning Polixenes is morally wrong and therefore I will not do it." On the contrary, Camillo must think through his dilemma tortuously: "Poisoning Polixenes is morally wrong; my only reason to do it consists in my obedience to Leontes; but he is 'in rebellion with himself'; on the other hand, I might advance my career by doing it; but now that I think of it, I cannot recall hearing of anyone who has prospered by committing regicide; therefore I will not do it (and would not do it even if I were a villain [which I am not]; indeed, since I lose either way [does this entail moral or political loss?], I will do nothing—I will run away":

> What case stand I in? I must be the poisoner
> Of good Polixenes, and my ground to do't
> Is the obedience to a master; one
> Who, in rebellion with himself, will have
> All that are his so too. To do this deed,
> Promotion follows. If I could find example
> Of thousands that had struck anointed kings
> And flourish'd after, I'ld not do't; but since
> Nor brass nor stone nor parchment bears not one,
> Let villainy itself forswear't. I must
> Forsake the court. To do't, or no, is certain
> To me a break-neck.   (I.ii.351–62)

In a sense, *The Winter's Tale* achieves both its resolution of the problem of obedience and its preservation of hierarchy and morality by cheating. It must cheat, because to admit the full meaning of Camillo's disobedience would require not only a shift of the primary ground of authority from the divinely appointed monarch on the one side to the Law and the underlying principles of natural justice on the other; it would also require the virtual dissolution of the divine legitimation of the ruler's power over and against the state. Further, it would require Camillo to become his own master, to become — in a metaphysical sense — free. Yet although Camillo disobeys his master in Act I (for reasons he is unable fully to define), he remains personally and feudally bound to Leontes. The persistence of his fealty is token of the stability of the absolutist paradigm which his morally correct derogation has jeopardized. After fifteen years of serving Polixenes (whom he addresses as "sir," in contrast to his use of "my lord" for Leontes), he is called back home: "I desire to lay my bones there. Besides, *the penitent King, my master, hath sent for me,* to whose feeling sorrows I might be some allay (or I o'erween to think so), which is another spur to my departure" (IV.ii.6–9; emphasis mine).

The Tempest's account of the problem of obedience forces into the open the contradictions which vex absolutism's amalgamation of politics and religion. Further, the recollection of the repressed differences between political and religious spheres is made to take place as an aspect of the process of interpretation. Once we realize that Gonzalo is guilty of complicity in Prospero's overthrow, that he obeyed Alonso's command to cast Prospero and Miranda adrift, we will want to know why we should not view him as a mere time-server. From Prospero's viewpoint, Gonzalo's obedience to his master (even though it has entailed Prospero's suffering and near-death) is praiseworthy because political obedience guarantees the stability of government. Prospero's own experience with disobedient and treacherous subjects (Antonio and Caliban) underlies his praise of Gonzalo, whom he finds "good" both because Gonzalo tempered his immoral act by charitably providing food and other necessities and because Gonzalo did not allow his charity to violate the terms of his assignment:

O good Gonzalo,
My true preserver, and a loyal sir
To him thou follow'st!
(V.i.68–70)

This insight into the conditions of Prospero's praise of Gonzalo would have allowed Shakespeare's audience to see the politics of *The Tempest* as alto-

gether harsher and more reflective of the culpable nature of all public action than the politics of *The Winter's Tale.* For us as well, the idea that Gonzalo is guilty of an act tantamount to murder means that he is not what we have been used to thinking he was. He might be either a time-server (Berger's view) or a man who has subverted the integrity of conscience rather than the integrity of obedience (my view). What he cannot be is merely a doddering courtier — insignificant in terms of the play as a whole. That Prospero is aware of the guilt of the man he chooses to praise as "Holy Gonzalo, honorable man" (V.i.62) suggests the fullness of Prospero's acknowledgement of the moral cost of preserving political hierarchy.

Gonzalo's guilt valorizes his conduct and speech. His scorn of Antonio and Sebastian in II.i. has been noted (Orgel II.i.180–82n), but not the way his scorn shifts what would normally be the distribution of ridicule in this kind of scene. Conventionally, when two or more characters defame another character in asides, the third bears the full weight of ridicule (e.g., *Twelfth Night,* II.v; *Cymbeline,* I.ii; II.i). In *The Tempest,* II.i, in contrast, Gonzalo hears and understands Antonio's and Sebastian's "asides" (Shakespeare signals this variation of the convention at ll. 19, 166–70 [Orgel II.i.10–12n]). Therefore, instead of being the butt of their mockery, Gonzalo is shown as being tolerant and even contemptuous of their ineffectual cynicism:

ALONSO: Prithee no more; thou dost talk nothing to me.
GONZALO: I do well believe your Highness, and did it to minister occasion to these gentlemen, who are of such sensible and nimble lungs that they always use to laugh at nothing.   (II.i.171–75)

The "nothing" to which Gonzalo refers consists of a passage borrowed from Montaigne's essay "Of the Caniballes." His denigration of his own "golden age" speech, of course, reveals his awareness of its naiveté and so disarms Antonio's and Sebastian's ridicule. More important, Gonzalo's self-consciously edenic and egalitarian fantasy reflects the weight of the crime which was required by his station in a hierarchical political culture. Interestingly, Gonzalo's main additions to Montaigne consist in both an emphasis on boundaries or borders and a catalog of weapons, which together perhaps recall the "treacherous army" (I.ii.128) that invaded Milan. Florio's 1603 translation of Montaigne (qtd. in Kermode 146) has "partition"—division of property—where Shakespeare has "Bourn, bound of land":

> I' th' commonwealth I would, by contraries,
> Execute all things; for no kind of traffic
> Would I admit; no name of magistrate;
> Letters should not be known; riches, poverty,
> And use of service, none; contract, succession,
> *Bourn, bound of land,* tilth; vineyard, none;
> No use of metal, corn, or wine, or oil;
> No occupation; all men idle, all;
> And women too, but innocent and pure;
> No sovereignty—
> . . . . All things in common nature should produce
> Without sweat or endeavor: treason, felony,
> *Sword, pike, knife, gun, or need of any engine,*
> Would I not have. . . .
> (II.i.148–63; emphasis mine)

Gonzalo's encomium to Providence toward the end of the play also registers the burden of his crime, and his rejoicing signals his surprise at the sudden recuperation of the moral integrity he had chosen to subvert "when he was not his own." The last two lines span the ideological poles of absolutism. On one side is obedience: no man is "his own" since each man is determined by his station (Kermode V.i.213n); and on the other side is conscience: each man *is himself* because each values himself according to the integrity of his conscience:

> Was Milan thrust from Milan, that his issue
> Should become kings of Naples? O, rejoice
> Beyond a common joy, and set it down
> With gold on lasting pillars: in one voyage
> Did Claribel her husband find at Tunis,
> And Ferdinand, her brother, found a wife
> When he himself was lost; Prospero his dukedom
> In a poor isle; and all of us, ourselves,
> When no man was his own.   (V.i.205–13)

Gonzalo's commitment to political obedience is grounded as well on the problem of epistemological uncertainty. His skepticism with respect to the human capacity either to determine or to predict the consequences of actions is clear in his surprise at the happy ending of his own narrative, in his praise of the gods who "chalk'd forth the way / Which brought us hither" (V.i.203–04). Uncertainty about the ramifications of actions undermines evaluation of their moral status at a level above that of the motivation of the actor. For example, Henry's divorce from Katherine in *Henry VIII* is immoral at the motivational level because the king's desire for Anne Bullen

is at least as important as his wish to provide a male heir. In terms of consequences, however, the divorce is praiseworthy, since the offspring of Henry's marriage to Anne Bullen is the infant who will become Queen Elizabeth.

Both Gonzalo's suspension of judgment and his deference to higher powers indicate his acute sense of the limits placed upon action by uncertainty. He believes that the acts he performs cannot be meaningful in themselves (that is, that he cannot be certain of their meaning). He assumes that his acts have meaning only in terms of a larger hierarchical structure which includes the political, natural and cosmic worlds. The storm-scene (I.i.) provides a key instance of Gonzalo's hierarchical structuring of experience: in the face of imminent death which levels and demystifies conventional social categories (see the Boatswain's critique of hierarchy, ll. 16–27), Gonzalo preserves political order by enjoining the others to "assist" the king and prince at prayers. In contrast to the Boatswain's radically individualistic response to the threat of death—"None that I more love than myself"—Gonzalo draws a politically conservative lesson from the same threat—"The King and Prince at prayers, let's assist them, / For our case is as theirs" (ll. 54–55). Further, Gonzalo interprets the storm itself in terms of hierarchy, so that the wildness of nature which jeopardizes hierarchy (overturns it from the Boatswain's viewpoint) is seen to be merely an expression of hierarchy, an unwelcome but valorizing effect of divine agency whose import cannot be known but must be accepted nevertheless: "The wills above be done! but I would fain die a dry death" (ll. 67–68).

Political obedience is supported here by the conjoining of hierarchy with the uncertainty which undermines personal moral judgment. This does not mean that the moral implications of acts are of no consequence, but it does follow that the full moral import of any act cannot be known by the actor at the moment he or she performs it, and that the investiture of action with meaning must be projected into the future. To plot the movement of history along the lines of the "fortunate fall" (as Shakespeare does in *The Winter's Tale, The Tempest* and *Henry VIII*) arrests time's unending motion toward futurity, providing an authoritative moment of closure which crystallizes the meaning of individual acts. The "fortunate" ending of *The Tempest* reveals the mixed nature of Gonzalo's participation in the overthrow of Prospero. The fact that

Prospero has regained his dukedom, that Gonzalo's charity was conducive to Prospero's survival, and that Gonzalo maneuvered in order to preserve political hierarchy, suggests that although Gonzalo's act was tragically culpable, it has nevertheless been redeemed by the providential ordering of history.

It is true that the "fortunate" ending of the play barely manages to contain the subversive energies which threaten it: Caliban's credibility as a subversive, the obduracy of Antonio and Sebastian, Prospero's bitterness, Gonzalo's crime itself, the fact that the marriage accomplishes the very Neapolitan takeover of Milan which Prospero has decried. The point, however, is that these energies, while not erased, are contained for audience-members inclined to take sides with authority. In terms of my argument, the fact that an astute modern critic such as Anne Barton has judged the *felix culpa* ending to be deliberately flawed by uncontrolled subversive energies (37–39) should be seen, again, to indicate the lack of authorial policing of the production of meaning, and the changeability and historical specificity of the meaning of works in the literary field.

The particular historical context of *The Tempest*'s implied argument for obedience consists in the foreign threat to English sovereignty posed by European Catholic powers during the sixteenth and early seventeenth centuries. The 1570 *Homily against Disobedience* followed upon the rising of Catholic forces in the north of England (a rebellion fomented by expectations of Spanish military assistance) and upon the papal excommunication of Elizabeth (MacCaffrey 330–71).

The absolutist implications of the "problem of Gonzalo" do not, therefore, reflect primarily a general state of anxiety concerning lower-class rebellion (as Gary Schmidgall has argued [171–214]); nor do they suggest the Hobbesian idea that the political order is fundamentally artificial, the state of nature being a "war of all against all" which must be controlled by unquestioning submission to a ruler (as has been suggested by Jan Kott [272–73]). On the contrary, *The Tempest*'s endorsement of political obedience constitutes, in the broadest terms, a nationalist reaction to a threat which was seen to be primarily foreign rather than primarily domestic, in particular the danger of Spanish Catholic subornation of disaffected elements within the English Protestant commonwealth. The central threat to political order and national sovereignty, both in *The Tempest* and in Elizabethan and Jacobean England, was seen to consist in the intervention by foreign powers through the agency of dissident elements within the nation. This is the pattern in *The Tempest* where Prospero's throne is usurped by Antonio in collusion with the King of Naples (a betrayal that costs Milan both its *de jure* ruler and its sovereignty), and where, even in extremely reduced circumstances, Prospero's rule is threatened a second time by the domestic malcontent Caliban in league with the foreign invaders Stephano and Trinculo. In both cases, the internal menace to the political order is essentially powerless until it is abetted by a foreign master.

The patterning of sedition, invasion and usurpation in *The Tempest* is homologous with the popular conception of England's geopolitical situation throughout the Elizabethan and Jacobean period, according to which the English were the embattled representatives of apostolic Christianity, surrounded and vulnerable to subornation by the antichristian empire of Spain and Rome (Haller *passim*). Accordingly, I would argue that the conventional identification of Catholic fifth-column activity with resistance theory constituted the central determining factor in Shakespeare's audience's interpretation of the political meaning of *The Tempest*. To suggest this, of course, is not to preclude the possibility of subversive interpretations of the play in Shakespeare's time; however, it does mean that the normative meaning of *The Tempest* for Shakespeare's audience would have been conservative. Shakespeare's audience would have solved the "problem of Gonzalo" in a way productive of an argument in favor of political obedience; and the ending of the play, while allowing for the continuing operation of subversive forces within the body politic, would nonetheless have redeemed and valorized Gonzalo's choice of obedience over morality.

Ariel's last image of Gonzalo is evocative of the costs attendant upon Gonzalo's choice of obedience over conscience. The image suggests how structure itself can produce shelter even out of materials which are inherently unsound. Gonzalo's beard is figured as a shelter fashioned out of reeds, with reeds also being the metaphor used to symbolize Ferdinand's moral weakness in the face of death: "Ferdinand, / With hair up-staring (then like reeds, not hair), / Was the first man that leapt" (I.ii.212–14):

> but chiefly
> 'Him that you term'd, sir, "the good old Lord Gonzalo,"
> His tears run down his beard like winter's drops
> From eaves of reeds.   (V.i.14–17)

The contradictions of English Renaissance political culture are figured in Gonzalo's face. Absolutism's enhancement of political obedience *as loyalty* provides shelter from "winter's drops," but the drops do not represent a "natural" affliction. Instead they represent Gonzalo's ideologically-determined sorrow for culpable acts which were themselves determined by the idea of obedience. Finally, in terms of *The Tempest*'s interrogation and endorsement of political obedience in 1611, Gonzalo's weeping is earnest of his determination to persevere in the guilty business of government, and in this respect his attitude is like Prospero's bitter willingness to return into the world.[3]

Notes

1. For a brief overview of the issue of political obedience in the period, see Greaves; for a masterful survey of political theory in the period, see Skinner.
2. All Shakespeare quotations are from *The Riverside Shakespeare*.
3. An earlier version of this essay was presented at the CEMERS Renaissance Conference, 1987: I thank the members of that meeting for their instructive questions, and also my colleague Kay Stockholder for her valuable critique of a more recent version.

Works Cited

Barker, Francis, and Peter Hulme. "Nymphs and reapers heavily vanish: The Discursive Contexts of *The Tempest*." *Alternative Shakespeares*. Ed. John Drakakis. London: Methuen, 1985. 191–205.

Barton (Righter), Anne. "Introduction." *The Tempest*. Ed. Barton. Harmondsworth: Penguin, 1968.

Berger, Harry, Jr. "Miraculous Harp: A Reading of *The Tempest*." *Shakespeare Studies* 5 (1969): 253–83.

Breight, Curt. "'Treason doth never prosper': *The Tempest* and the Discourse of Treason." *Shakespeare Quarterly* 41.1 (1990): 1–28.

Brown, Paul. "'This thing of darkness I acknowledge mine': *The Tempest* and the Discourse of Colonialism." *Political Shakespeare: New Essays in Cultural Materialism*. Ed. Jonathan Dollimore and Alan Sinfield. Ithaca: Cornell UP, 1985. 48–71.

Certain Sermons or Homilies (1547) and A Homily against Disobedience and Wilful Rebellion (1570). Ed. Ronald B. Bond. Toronto: U of Toronto P, 1987.

Cleland, James. *The Institution of a Young Noble Man* (1607). Facsimile rpt. New York: Scholars, 1948.

Daly, James. "The Idea of Absolute Monarchy in Seventeenth-Century England." *Historical Journal* 21.2 (1970): 227–50.

Donne, John. *Poetical Works*. Ed. Herbert Grierson, 1912. Rpt. London: Oxford UP, 1966.

Erlich, Bruce. "Shakespeare's Colonial Metaphor: On the Social Function of Theatre in *The Tempest*." *Science & Society* 41.1 (1977): 43–65.

Goldberg, Jonathan. *James I and the Politics of Literature: Jonson, Donne, and Their Contemporaries*. Baltimore: Johns Hopkins UP, 1983.

Greaves, Richard L. "Concepts of Political Obedience in Late Tudor England: Conflicting Perspectives." *Journal of British Studies* 22.1 (1982): 23–34.

Greenblatt, Stephen. "Learning to Curse: Aspects of Linguistic Colonialism in the Sixteenth Century." *First Images of America: The Impact of the New World on the Old*. Ed. Fredi Chiappelli et al. 2 vols. Berkeley: U of California P, 1976. 2: 561–80.

Haller, William. *Foxe's Book of Martyrs and the Elect Nation*. London: Cape, 1963.

Hulme, Peter. *Colonial Encounters: Europe and the Native Caribbean, 1492–1797*. London: Methuen, 1986.

Jonson, Ben. *Neptune's Triumph for the Return of Albion. The Complete Masques*. Ed. Stephen Orgel. New Haven: Yale UP, 1969.

Kermode, Frank, ed. *The Tempest*. Arden Shakespeare. Cambridge: Harvard UP, 1958.

Kott, Jan. *Shakespeare Our Contemporary*. Trans. Boreslaw Taborski. New York: Anchor, 1966.

Leininger, Lorie Jerrell. "Cracking the Code of *The Tempest*." *Bucknell Review* 25 (1980): 121–31.

MacCaffrey, Wallace. *The Shaping of the Elizabethan Regime*. Princeton: Princeton UP, 1968.

Munden, R. C. "James I and 'the growth of mutual distrust': King, Commons, and Reform, 1603–1604." *Faction and Parliament: Essays on Early Stuart History*. Ed. Kevin Sharpe. Oxford: Clarendon, 1978. 43–72.

Orgel, Stephen, ed. *The Tempest*. The Oxford Shakespeare. Oxford: Clarendon, 1987.

Patterson, Annabel. *Shakespeare and the Popular Voice*. Oxford: Blackwell, 1989.

Ponet, John. *A short treatise of politike power, and of the true obedience which subjects owe to Kings and other civill Governours*, 1556. Rpt. [London] 1649.

Russell, Conrad. "Parliamentary History in Perspective 1604–1629." *History* 61 (1976): 1–27.

Schmidgall, Gary. *Shakespeare and the Courtly Aesthetic.* Berkeley: U of California P, 1981.

Seamon, Roger. "Poetics against Itself: On the Self-Destruction of Modern Scientific Criticism." *PMLA* 104.3 (1989): 294–305.

Shakespeare, William. *The Riverside Shakespeare.* Ed. G. Blakemore Evans. Boston: Houghton, 1974.

Sharpe, Kevin. "Parliamentary History 1603–1629: In or Out of Perspective?" *Faction and Parliament: Essays on Early Stuart History.* Ed. Sharpe. Oxford: Clarendon, 1978. 1–42.

Siegel, Paul N. "Historical Ironies in *The Tempest.*" *Shakespeare Jahrbuch* 119 (1983): 104–11.

Skinner, Quentin. *The Foundations of Modern Political Thought.* 2 vols. Cambridge: Cambridge UP, 1978.

Skura, Meredith Anne. "Discourse and the Individual: The Case of Colonialism in *The Tempest.*" *Shakespeare Quarterly* 40.1 (1989): 42–69.

Sommerville, J. P. *Politics and Ideology in England, 1603–1640.* London: Longman, 1986.

Stockholder, Kay. *Dream Works: Lovers and Families in Shakespeare's Plays.* Toronto: U of Toronto P, 1987.

Strier, Richard. "Faithful Servants: Shakespeare's Praise of Disobedience." *The Historical Renaissance: New Essays on Tudor and Stuart Literature and Culture.* Ed. Heather Dubrow and Richard Strier. Chicago: U of Chicago P, 1988, 104–33.

Wormald, Jenny. "James VI & I: Two Kings or One?" *History* 68.223 (1983): 187–209.

Yachnin, Paul. "*A Game of Chess:* Thomas Middleton's 'Praise of Folly.'" *Modern Language Quarterly* 48.1 (1987): 107–23.

———. "The Powerless Theater." *English Literary Renaissance,* forthcoming.

APPLICATION

Seeking a Way Home: The Uncanny in Wordsworth's Immortality Ode

Daniel W. Ross

Citing the readings by Trilling, Vendler, and McGann, among others, Daniel Ross notes that several critics have seen that the Immortality Ode is a highly conflicted poem, but few have seen that the poem achieves its power by dramatizing a deep conflict within the author's psyche. Using the concepts of Rank and Freud, Ross offers to illuminate that psyche and to demonstrate that "the power of the Ode is largely derived from the earliness of Wordsworth's feelings of separation and loss." To move from identifying a conflict in the poem to locating the source of that conflict in the author's unconscious is a maneuver typical of author-focused criticism. The explanation of the poem's power will lie not in its social circumstances nor in any conscious manipulation of poetic form; it will lie in the psyche of the author.

Aided by Wordsworth's preference for writing in the autobiographical mode, Ross ranges over the events of the author's life and cites several of his works and recorded comments to argue that the conflicts in the poem are reflections of serious and repressed conflicts in Wordsworth. These conflicts repeatedly surface in his writings, and they cannot be resolved by the rationalizations Wordsworth repeatedly offers; neither can they be resolved by the author's usual strategy of generalizing the conflicts, trying to make them "less personal." Whatever the manifest content of the poem, its latent content shows that these conflicts remain very personal and quite unresolved. "The Ode tries to describe deeply felt longings from Wordsworth's earliest memories; as psychoanalysis has since taught us, we can learn to live with those longings better by trying to work through them than by denying their power." And yet, in a further irony, the poem in this case may have served to protect the poet from the knowledge that would have destroyed him. Thus, "Wordsworth becomes the prototype of the modern artist-as-hero, struggling against the ultimate antagonist — the mind

Reprinted by permission from *SEL Studies in English Literature 1500–1900* 32.4 (1992): 625–43.

or, more specifically, the unconscious." In other words, the ultimate reality, like the ultimate antagonist, is psychological reality, and the greatest dramas take place within the individual psyche. This is where the critic must look for the poem's deepest meaning.

"I have always been regretting," said Henry David Thoreau, "that I was not as wise as the day I was born."[1] While Thoreau could express his regret with some detachment and humor, Wordsworth's desire for a return to childhood was the source of a deeper and more permanent longing. That longing is most evident in the Immortality Ode, where Wordsworth dramatized the power of childhood in his emotional life.

Yet in spite of much critical debate, there remains great uncertainty about Wordsworth's feelings for the child in the Ode. Much of the criticism of the Ode has focused on the question of whether or not we should accept Wordsworth's carefully rationalized conclusion that the "philosophic mind" is worth surrendering the powers of childhood for. I believe that we should not accept this resolution, but I also believe that the many arguments presented on this subject have not fully clarified *why* we should not.[2] What has been missing in criticism of the Ode is an understanding of the child's psychic power for Wordsworth, a power which generates his ambivalence. Douglas B. Wilson has taken us toward such an understanding by describing the significance of the uncanny throughout Wordsworth's work,[3] but the Ode itself still deserves further inquiry. In the Ode the child represents an uncanny link to an earlier self, a less conscious being unburdened by adult cares. And Wordsworth does not simply compare himself to or express envy for the child in this poem; rather, he confronts the child as a threat, a powerful psychic force.

My intention is, first, to review some problems in the argument of the Ode which signify the child's threat to the adult and then to describe the complex and mysterious encounter with the child by using Otto Rank's theory of the double and Freud's more general concept of the uncanny. To see the child as Wordsworth's double allows us to recognize a deeply embedded, infantile source of anxiety in the Ode which endangers the poet's self-unity. Freud's theory, meanwhile, helps us understand more clearly how and why the poet feels a sense of dislocation in the world he inhabits and how his efforts to defend himself against these feelings of dislocation break down in the Ode. These theories help us see that the power of the Ode is largely derived from the earliness of Wordsworth's feelings of separation and loss.

I

The Ode begins with an expression of the loss of light, of vision, of time, and of former connections to the natural and supernatural worlds. If Wordsworth cannot compensate for the loss of a higher destiny and his separation from the natural world, the rest of his life will consist only of pain and an increasing awareness of the "glory" he no longer has and never will have again. He thus argues for a compensation adequate to replace the lost glory, but the poem itself belies in many ways the sanguine conclusion of the final three stanzas.

The Ode also expresses a characteristic conflict in Wordsworth—the awareness of the loss of sensory power and the desire to thwart or avert that awareness. In his anxiety Wordsworth demonstrates what Thomas McFarland calls a "consciousness of self as a divided nature, a doubled and merely contradictory being."[4] Thoughts of the past, and of what has been lost, impinge on the poet's future happiness. Every action remembered from youth confirms the poet's awareness of loss; everything in nature reminds him "It is not now as it hath been of yore" (line 6).[5] Virtually every description of the child in the first 129 lines praises his advantages over the adult: he comes from "a glorious birth" (line 16), he is the "best Philosopher" (line 111), an "Eye among the blind" (line 112), a "Seer blest" (line 115), who can read "the eternal deep" (line 113). Wordsworth's overstatement of the child's powers has caused problems for many readers.[6] Because most of these descriptions come in stanza 8, the final stanza focused on the lost powers, I believe Wordsworth's overdetermination of childhood glory reflects his inability to accept his own passage out of childhood. Stanza 8 ends with a prediction of the child's final transition from the glory of youth to the diminished powers of adulthood:

> Full soon thy Soul shall have her earthly freight,
> And custom lie upon thee like a weight,
> Heavy as frost, and deep almost as life.
> (lines 127–29)

The images of weight and frost portend an adulthood of suffering and isolation which is abruptly denied in the rest of the poem.

Every reader of the Ode must ask how Wordsworth gets from these images of oppression, of the weary weight of the world, to the apostrophe ("O joy!") which opens the next stanza. How can memory compensate for the burden so convincingly described throughout the first 129 lines? Wordsworth never quite says; there is no transition from the burden to the joy. The change comes in an apparent leap of faith; we are to find joy in "the faith that looks through death." As Bostetter, McFarland, and others have argued, this type of affirmation tries to deny the reality of life and proves far less convincing than the poet's dramatization of his loss. The resolution provided in the last stanzas does not answer the specific questions posed in the poem; it merely answers Wordsworth's need for a resolution.

Other disturbing signs of inconsistent logic appear in the last three stanzas, including an increased use of first person plural rather than singular pronouns, as though Wordsworth can demystify his crisis of lost sensory powers by assuring us and himself that his feeling is universal.[7] This shift in pronoun focus, however, reflects a strategy which Clifford Siskin has found typical in Wordsworth's lyrics. Writing on "Tintern Abbey," Siskin notes that Wordsworth achieves closure by transferring the task of the poem to Dorothy, making the private issue public while eliminating himself from the poem.[8] Similarly, in the Ode Wordsworth directs his attention away from the personal loss of celestial light described in the opening stanza to the sight *"Our* souls" have in maturity ("Though inland far we be"), described in stanza 9. By making the conflict less personal, Wordsworth assuages much of his immediate pain, but only temporarily.

Throughout the latter part of the Ode Wordsworth tries to compensate for the loss of childhood powers, but much more striking than these bland accommodations is Wordsworth's sense in his earlier self of

> Blank misgivings of a Creature
> Moving about in worlds not realized,
> High instincts before which our mortal Nature
> Did tremble like a guilty Thing surprised.
> (lines 145–48)

Helen Vendler calls these lines (along with the three that precede them) "the heart of the poem." Having carefully traced Wordsworth's paired phrases throughout the poem, Vendler identifies this as the only "'unpaired' or 'nonce' passage in the poem" and warns that "commentary falters always before this passage and perhaps will always fail."[9]

Vendler, like many other readers, hears Miltonic echoes in such lines. But the more evident influence is Shakespearean. While this passage is not duplicated elsewhere in the Ode, it does allude to the Ghost's disappearance in the opening scene of *Hamlet:*

> And then it started like a guilty thing
> Upon a fearful summons.[10]

Jonathan Wordsworth, having recognized this allusion, associates Wordsworth's surprise with an intimation of the dead father.[11] But the scholar Horatio offers another reading:

> I have heard
> The cock, that is trumpet to the morn,
> Doth with his lofty and shrill-sounding throat
> Awake the god of day, and at his warning,
> Whether in sea or fire, in earth or air,
> The extravagant and erring spirit hies
> To his confine.   (I.i.149–55)

The summons, according to Horatio, calls one home, which is more readily associated with the mother than with the father. The Shakespearean analogy is but one reason why we should link the fear of "the guilty thing," and the rest of Wordsworth's anxiety in the Ode, with home and the mother.

The connection between home and the mother is also evident in Freud's essay on the uncanny and in the etymologies of that word and of "heimlich," its German equivalent. In his book on Dickens Robert Newsom has traced these etymological links. "Canny," of Scotch origin, has such traditionally feminine qualities as softness, snugness, and coziness. More specifically, "heimlich" is derived from "secret" and "private," suggesting the private parts of the female body and finding "its counterpart, if not a near equivalent, in the now obsolete Scotch 'canny-wife' and 'canny moment,' meaning 'midwife' and 'moment of birth,' respectively."[12] Using his experience as an analyst, Freud also linked home ("heimlich") with the mother:

> It often happens that male patients declare that they feel there is something uncanny about the female genital organs. This *unheimlich* place, however, is the entrance to the former *heim* [home] of all human beings, to the place where everyone dwelt once upon a time and in the beginning. There is a humorous saying: "Love is home-sickness," and whenever a man dreams of a place or a country

and says to himself, still in the dream, "this place is familiar to me, I have been there before," we may interpret the place as being his mother's genitals or her body. In this case, too, the *unheimlich* is what was once *heimish*, home-like, familiar; the prefix "un" is the token of repression.[13]

Hamlet, throughout his play, demonstrates his unease with the feminine; as we will see, Wordsworth evinces a similar unease throughout his work, but most particularly in the Ode.

Like Vendler, I find Wordsworth's "Blank misgivings" to be of central importance to the poem; the passage seems to bear the "trace" that André Green feels is in many texts. Even in joyful works, Green says, "We need only scratch the surface to discover, beneath the denial of anxiety, anxiety; beneath the negation of loss, the work of mourning."[14] And commentary does fail because criticism is a rational act, as is most of Wordsworth's poem, but in this "nonce" passage a special, irrational intuition disrupts the argument.[15] Thus, it would appear wise for us to detach ourselves from the argument and ask, "What is the source of these strange feelings?"

I suggest that Wordsworth's guilt is linked to his inability to explain, rationalize, or articulate his intimations. Though Wordsworth assures us he is grateful for such a creature, it seems clear that it provokes uncertainty, fear, and guilt in him. We must ask, "Who or what is that creature and why does he stir up such feelings?" I will argue that the passage represents an instance of the uncanny, more specifically, the double (Freud linked the two), aspects of which haunt Wordsworth throughout the Ode, and in other poems as well.

II

Freud begins his discussion of the uncanny (*das Unheimliche*) with questions of definition that bear directly on Wordsworth's poem. He concludes from this investigation that "heimlich" ultimately coincides with its opposite, "unheimlich" (uncanny). In other words, that which is most familiar can somehow become strange, dreadful, or mysterious. Thus, Freud writes, the uncanny feeling relates to one's feelings for his environment: "The better orientated in his environment a person is, the less readily will he get the impression of something uncanny in regard to objects and events in it" (p. 124).

Wordsworth's readers know the importance he attached to his environment and to the concept of "home": "Michael," "The Ruined Cottage," and *Home at Grasmere*, are just a few of the poems in which Wordsworth focuses on this subject.[16] The Ode is about a loss of home or orientation, its speaker describing his feeling that he no longer belongs in his environment.[17] He speaks of God as "our home" (line 65) which we have departed. The adult poet, stirred by intimations of that earlier connection to God, expresses some resentment toward "Earth" for helping us adapt to our new home and forget our old:

> And, even with something of a Mother's mind,
>   And no unworthy aim,
>   The homely nurse doth all she can
> To make her Foster-child, her inmate Man,
>   Forget the glories he hath known,
> And that imperial palace whence he came.
>   (lines 80–85)

While paying witness to Freud's claim that the "heimlich" can suddenly and strangely become "unheimlich," the lines express a powerful sense of separation anxiety, of being cut off from an aboriginal source of light and warmth. Nature, described in terms of a double negative, and having only "something of a Mother's mind," is portrayed here as a surrogate, an adoptive maternal force which seeks to confine the child and to obliterate from his memory any connections to his real mother. In short, these lines suggest that memory cannot be the solution to the problem of the poem; memory is part of the problem itself.

This shift from "heimlich" to "unheimlich" represents the more powerful of the two sources of the uncanny: the return of the repressed. Barbara Schapiro has previously noted that uncanny moments in Wordsworth's poetry signal "the sudden revelation of repressed unconscious emotions."[18] The questions we might now ask are what has been repressed and where is that former home from which the speaker feels displaced?[19] With the help of Freud and Rank, I can posit a hypothetical answer to each question: the thing repressed is another version of the self which was more unified and coherent than the one Wordsworth now feels he possesses. The former home is the womb, a place where the unity and coherence not only of self but of self with other can be re-experienced.

Throughout his poetry, especially in his confessional epic, *The Prelude*, Wordsworth describes emanations of another being existing within or alongside him. In one famous instance he speaks of an awareness that he seems

> Two consciousnesses, conscious of myself
> And of some other being.
> (Book II, lines 32–33)

As we will see, one of those consciousnesses invariably carries the trace of death, a trace that Wordsworth seeks to erase or forget. As Paul Jay has remarked, much of Wordsworth's poetry, especially that which emphasizes the restorative power of memory, "is actually rooted in a providential *forgetting* of what he experienced, and felt, in the past" (Jay's italics).[20] Writing, Jay argues, allows Wordsworth the means to remember imaginatively, to recreate his past in ways that he finds relatively unthreatening. Interactions between past and present selves in Wordsworth's poetry tend, as Jay notes,[21] to have restorative power, but lurking within the subtext of these interactions is the thing repressed, Wordsworth's ineffaceable secret sharer who refuses to be reconciled entirely to the past.

The double is one mode of the uncanny, and in this notion we can isolate several clues to the questions raised in the Immortality Ode. The theme of the double, as understood by Freud and Rank, is immortality, the titular subject of the Ode: "the 'double' was originally an insurance against the destruction of the ego, an 'energetic denial of the power of death,'. . . and probably the 'immortal' soul was the first 'double' of the body" ("The Uncanny," p. 141). Once the stage of primary narcissism has been passed, however, the double reverses itself and becomes a harbinger of death: "Originally conceived of as a guardian angel, assuring immortal survival to the self, the double eventually appears as precisely the opposite, a reminder of the individual's mortality, indeed, the announcer of death itself."[22] Once again, the "heimlich" has become "unheimlich." Wordsworth, by writing a poem on the soul's immortality, is certainly attempting to deny the power of death, but for him denial only confirms the supremacy and inevitability of death. His double, the child, the "Creature / Moving about in worlds not realized," becomes the harbinger of his own death, a reminder of his own "mortal Nature," but one who shows none of the signs of physical deterioration which spark the adult poet's feeling of alienation from the universe. In the Ode Wordsworth necessar-

ily confronts his harbinger of death; if he repressed it completely, he would run the risk of paralysis, suicide, or insanity — the fate of many of Wordsworth's eighteenth-century predecessors.

The double can be interpreted positively (as the prototype of personality) or negatively (as a symbol of death). In post-Enlightenment literature the double has most often been used negatively. This negative view began with German Romanticism: the German Romantics began "interpreting the theme of the Double as a Problem of the Self," a result of "their own split personality" (Rank, p. 68). The split personality, or double, looms as an "almost pathological loss of one's real self through a superimposed one" (Rank, p. 70). This is the threat the child as double poses for Wordsworth: the possibility of self-disintegration, of complete fragmentation and loss of being.

Rank notes that the use of the double as a representative of the soul has primitive roots (p. 73). Despite these primitive sources, however, Wordsworth's use of the double conforms to its modern evolution:

> Originally, the double was an identical self . . . promising personal survival in the *future;* later, the double retained together with the individual's life his personal *past.*   (Rank, pp. 81–82; his italics)

The later stage, involving the "personal past," best describes the double of the Ode and helps explain the insufficiency of Wordsworth's myth of memory. This myth fails for reasons Rank discusses: the double is an emanation from the unconscious, the irrational, and rationalizations such as Wordsworth's myth of memory do not dilute its extraordinary power. Indeed, rationalization is dangerous in such cases, as Wordsworth himself knew ("We murder to dissect"). The attempt in the last three stanzas of the Ode to dispel or repudiate the uncanny power of his double, the child, must not succeed because, if it does, the result will be self-annihilation: like it or not, the double is part of the self, one which the poet can only partially repress.

In this need to face his origins, the speaker's anxieties about his double and his loss of home meet, demonstrating his unresolved ambivalence about separation from the mother. It is Wordsworth's desire for reunion with the mother that most completely articulates what "home" meant to him. The Ode reveals a conflict between the poet's desire to merge or incorporate himself with the mother and the desire to be completely independent of her. The source of such an "oral-narcissistic" conflict is "a failure to negotiate successfully the transition from the infantile state of total narcissism and total dependence to one involving an awareness of the separate existence of others."[23] Wordsworth's child in the Ode represents the first state (total narcissism); the world he moves about in "not realized" represents the womb, the primary symbol of total union with and dependence on the mother. The return of this repressed "intimation" of unity with the mother traumatizes the speaker. At the end of the poem he moves, reluctantly, away from the womb, symbolized by the sea. This state of separation necessarily comes with maturity, but a narcissist does not give up the desire for union easily, as Philip Slater says: "But in direct proportion to his becoming less dependent, he becomes more aware of how overwhelming his dependency actually is, and looks back nostalgically to his previous oblivion."[24] Slater's paradox helps explain the speaker's frustration with his "homely Nurse" and his increased longing for infantile union and control over his environment. Wordsworth uses recollection in an effort to recapture this union, in fantasy if not in fact.

The uncanniness of Wordsworth's feelings for the child seems traceable to the extraordinary earliness of his intimations. Thus, while accepting Jerome C. Christensen's argument that Wordsworth is facing his origins in the Ode,[25] I see the primary conflict not, as he does, in Oedipal, but in preoedipal terms. Dyadic in nature and almost exclusively focused on the mother-child relationship, preoedipal conflicts are widely prevalent in Wordsworth's poetry. As Schapiro says, "The experience of loss connected with the mother-child relationship lies at the core of much of Wordsworth's poetry."[26] When Freud first identified the preoedipal phase in 1931, he assumed that it was much more important in the development of females than in males.[27] More recent research, however, suggests that the phase is similarly crucial in male development, especially in the separation/individuation process. Facing the stress of separation and loss, the child, in Freud's later observation, incorporates some portion of the external world into his/her ego, identifying with it as he/she internalizes it. This form of identification is a defensive response to separation and loss.[28] The Ode expresses Wordsworth's uneasiness with this coping mecha-

nism, his identification with nature as a mother imago no longer alleviating his separation anxiety. Certainly, as Ross Woodman has recently argued, the "homely nurse" of the Ode is a far cry from the nurse of the poet's moral being in "Tintern Abbey." This rhetorical shift mirrors the ideological shift that has occurred from one poem to the other. While the nurse in "Tintern Abbey" binds man to eternity, the later figure "binds day to day, imprisoning the poet for a crime he had not known he had committed until he was able to read the record of it in what he himself had written."[29] In Ned Lukacher's terms this is a case of memory being recognized only after it has been spoken—after the speaker overcomes the resistance that attempts to block the memory from consciousness.[30] In the Ode Wordsworth is searching deeper into the problems of origins and memory than he had in "Tintern Abbey." In this light it is hardly surprising that he rejects his homely nurse and yearns for the greater satisfaction of refusion with the mother.

We can see evidence of this desire to regain oneness throughout Wordsworth's life and work. Wordsworth's mother died when he was eight, before he would have reached the stage of independence that comes with adolescence. As any child would have, Wordsworth regarded her departure as a betrayal,[31] and his poetry is peopled by Bad Mothers who betray or even kill their children. The loss of the mother severely threatened Wordsworth's sense of self-unity. Throughout *The Prelude* he describes his feeling that he was cast early into a hostile world without the reassuring supports of motherhood. Wordsworth's desire for recapturing the union of infant and mother is most apparent in this famous passage:

> Blest the infant Babe,
> (For with my best conjecture I would trace
> Our being's earthly progress,) blest the babe,
> Nursed in his Mother's arms, who sinks to sleep
> Rocked on his Mother's breast; who, when his soul
> Claims manifest kindred with a human soul,
> Drinks in the feelings of his Mother's eye!
> (Book II, lines 232–38)

The images of oral incorporation are common in Wordsworth, expressing his response to an "unhomely" environment.[32] Just a few lines later Wordsworth refers to the alienation that followed his mother's death. The juxtaposition of these passages indicates that an extreme sense of rupture still haunts Wordsworth in adulthood. In fact, he idealizes the child in precisely the way Freud described in "On Narcissism": "That which he projects ahead of him as his ideal is merely his substitute for the lost narcissism of the childhood—the time when he was his own ideal."[33] Wordsworth's relationships with women reveal further ambivalence about separation and independence. Wordsworth depended on the praise he constantly received from Mary, Dorothy, Dora, and Sara Hutchinson, and he maintained a priestly manner in his household full of women. Other poems reflect ambivalence as well: e.g., the Lucy narrator's apparent desire to be reunited with Lucy in death,[34] and the boy's use of violence to avenge Nature's hold on him in "Nutting."

In contrast to such ghoulish or violent desires, Wordsworth also maintained a more satisfactory memory (or fantasy) of incorporation with Nature as a mother imago which he described in his remarks to Isabella Fenwick about the Ode:

[As a child] *I was often unable to think of external things as having external existence, and I communed with all that I saw as something not apart from, but inherent in, my own immaterial nature.* Many times while going to school have I grasped at a wall or tree to recall myself from this abyss of idealism to the reality. (*WP*, p. 978: my italics)

This passage most clearly demonstrates just how "heimlich" the world once was for Wordsworth and how integrated he felt with it. Once again, however, we must recall that this kind of incorporation is a defense against the anxiety of separation and loss. In addition, there are remarkable parallels between this passage and Freud's comparison in "The Uncanny" of the double to a "harking-back to particular phases in the evolution of the self-regarding feeling, a regression to *a time when the ego was not yet sharply differentiated from the external world and from other persons*" (p. 143; my italics).[35] The "time" Freud refers to here is the preoedipal phase when the mother represents the entirety of the child's world. The Ode shows the adult's longing to recapture that unity with the mother which his double (the child) enjoyed. But the poet faces the double ambivalently: while grateful for this link with nature, he is simultaneously frightened by it. He is frightened, it seems, that a maternal imago will again betray the heart that loves her.

III

Wordsworth's feelings about home and the return of the repressed are related to his obsession with immortality, evident in his recurring references to graves. No other English poet has written so much on epitaphs, monuments, and graves as Wordsworth. In writing and thinking about the Ode, he made three references to graves: to his brother Christopher, he said, "I could not believe that [I] should lie down quietly in the grave, and that my body would moulder into dust" (*WP*, p. 979). The other two references appear in stanza 8, which confronts most boldly the adult poet's sense of loss. The child is described there as one

On whom those truths do rest,
Which we are toiling all our lives to find,
In darkness lost, the darkness of the grave.
(lines 116–18)

This image, almost ghoulish, casts much doubt on the resolution that follows. If the darkness of adult life, deprived of the "celestial light" and "visionary gleam," is like the darkness of the grave, it becomes especially difficult to accept the compensations of memory and primal sympathy, offered in the next stanza, as adequate. But Wordsworth originally followed these lines with an astonishing suggestion of the way the child regards the grave, a way that contradicts what he said to Christopher. Though he deleted these lines in the 1815 edition of his poems, Wordsworth originally referred to the child in the first published versions of the Ode as one

To whom the grave
Is but a lonely bed without sense of sight
Of day or the warm light,
A place of thought where we in waiting lie.

This view of death parallels the primitive Christian doctrine of soul sleep, which sees death as an interim period, a time of "sleep" or "waiting" before Christ resurrects the body as well as the soul on Judgment Day.[36] But Coleridge, less comfortable with such a thought, protested against these lines and their "frightful notion of lying awake in the grave!"[37] For Wordsworth, the child, lacking a consciousness of death's possible finality, has no frightening thoughts of the grave, only thoughts suggesting the peace, warmth, security, and homeliness which are normally associated with the womb. This lack of fear is what the poet envies most in the child. In contrast to the child, Wordsworth, in his writing, shows great uneasiness about the soul's final destiny; a persistent consciousness of death, particularly of its "earthly" manifestations (graves, epitaphs, and the like) hardly bespeaks confidence in immortality.

But Wordsworth's monuments are palimpsests, concealing a primitive desire to confirm the soul's immortality, though not necessarily in a Christian way. According to Rank, "Prehistoric burial rites clearly indicate that the most primitive idea of a tomb for the dead was a housing for the soul—a replica of the maternal womb from which he was to be reborn" (p. 90). Freud also associated the feeling of being buried alive, the most uncanny feeling of all, with a fantasy of returning to the womb ("The Uncanny," p. 151). Thus, "tomb" and "womb" are examples of what Freud called the "antithetical sense of primal words": two words coming from the same root with apparently opposite meanings (a house for the dead soul, a house for the unborn soul), which originally expressed the same meaning. These etymological connections show that Wordsworth's lifelong fascination with graves and epitaphs is another sign of his deep, primordial desire not only to believe in some version of the soul's immortality, but to recapture his original sense of "home." In truth, the immortality he seeks, as my hypothesis suggested, is a permanent reunion with the mother.

The persistent recurrence in Wordsworth's great poetry of uncanny modes of being (such as the double) signify the importance of his repressed emotions.[38] The spots of time passages in *The Prelude* also signal terrifying and mysterious emanations from another world.[39] The Blind Beggar, for instance, makes the poet feel "As if admonished from another world" (Book 7, line 649), as does the paternal presence in nature which he senses after stealing the boat:

> but after I had seen
> That spectacle, for many days, my brain
> Worked with a dim and undetermined sense
> Of *unknown modes of being*
> (Book I, lines 390–93; my italics)

In this scene Wordsworth dramatizes another type of uncanny experience which Freud specifically cited: the delusion of being watched (p. 142). Still, the adult poet, no longer in close communion with external reality, longs to have such experiences again. Although the Ode is less known than *The Prelude* for "spots of

time," the uncanny sense of numinous presences, not the rational defense of the joy found in memory, provides the moving power of both works. Such presences are evident even in the conclusion of the Ode, where Wordsworth tries to erase them. Not only does the "guilty thing" suggest such a presence, but so too does Wordsworth's emphasis on a "primal sympathy." Sympathy does not exist within the self alone: De Quincey defined it as "the act of reproducing in our minds the feelings of another."[40]

The Ode, then, posits an awareness of man's dislocation, but its carefully rationalized conclusion finally evades the poem's darkest questions to insist that we should find joy in the rewards of adulthood. This conclusion evinces what McFarland calls "a blocking agent . . . an unconscious reluctance to allow the ultimate to happen."[41] This blocking out is a harbinger of Wordsworth's poetic decline, which occurred when Wordsworth stopped trying to answer those "obstinate questionings" that had obsessed him at the height of his career. The Ode tries to describe deeply felt longings from Wordsworth's earliest memories; as psychoanalysis has since taught us, we can learn to live with those longings better by trying to work through them than by denying their power.

In the Ode, Wordsworth becomes the prototype of the modern artist-as-hero, struggling against the ultimate antagonist—the mind or, more specifically, the unconscious. For modern readers the poem remains powerful because it dramatizes one of our earliest confrontations with the modern self. While trying to argue for the wholeness of selfhood and a linear growth from innocence to experience, the poem ironically portrays the contradictory, fragmented, and discontinuous structure of the self. But Wordsworth could confront the implications of his fragmented self and his desire for a return home only to a point before they overwhelmed him and drove him to despair; as Schapiro says, "the yearned-for fusion with the mother . . . must inevitably result in death."[42] Wordsworth stopped short of that point, occluding further contemplation of his intimations before they could drive him to the madness he so openly feared in "Resolution and Independence," a poem written contemporaneously with much of the Ode. Unable at last to resolve his conflict, Wordsworth wills a "Happy" conclusion in the last stanzas of the Ode. As a result, Wordsworth finally staves off his worst fears even while sensing the presence of a "Creature / Moving about in worlds not realized."[43]

However, he cannot tolerate for long the fear and guilt he unconsciously associates with this creature. For this reason the stated reconciliation between natural powers and the "philosophic mind" can hardly be accepted on faith. Wordsworth's conclusion is largely wishful thinking, which, says Rank, is found whenever the ego's destruction is feared (p. 203). Wordsworth's repressed anxieties remain in the unconscious from where they will surface again.

Ultimately, both memory and language fail Wordsworth. Nevertheless, the poem itself is a more effective compensation for his feeling of being lost in the world than is memory. Though Wordsworth cannot recapture his eidetic connections to the world, he does discover a new, if less perfect, version of the visionary gleam in his poetic vision. Artistic creation, Rank argues repeatedly (e.g., pp. 49–50), is man's one means of avoiding neurosis. By recreating life, art gains some measure of control over it (Rank, pp. 13–14).[44] The truest source of "joy" is not memory, which constantly reawakens the poet's sense of loss, but poetry, which provides a balm for his fear of encroaching mortality and for his loss of home. In the Ode Wordsworth engages himself in a self-healing project, and the poem is his best prescription to prevent the insanity or suicidal impulses he feared at the height of his poetic powers.

Notes

1. Henry David Thoreau, *Walden and Civil Disobedience,* ed. Sherman Paul (Boston: Houghton Mifflin, 1960), p. 68.
2. Of course, my dispute with the conclusion's affirmation is not universally accepted. Lionel Trilling's contention, in "The Immortality Ode," *The Liberal Imagination* (New York: Viking Press, 1942), pp. 129–53, that the Ode is "not only not a dirge sung over departing powers but actually a dedication to new powers" (p. 131), maintains much influence. In her "Lionel Trilling and 'Immortality Ode,'" *Salmagundi,* No. 41 (Spring 1978), 66–86, Helen Vendler takes issue with many of Trilling's claims, yet she agrees that Wordsworth succeeds in making the "philosophic mind" more attractive than the lost powers of youth (p. 69). In a similar vein Robert Langbaum sees the Ode, like many of Wordsworth's poems, as showing how the soul evolves. See his "The Evolution of Soul in Words-

worth's Poetry," in *The Prelude: A Casebook,* ed. W. J. Harvey and Richard Gravil (London: Macmillan, 1977): 218–36, 218. But the flaws of these more optimistic readings have been exposed by the criticism of Harold Bloom (beginning in *The Visionary Company*), Geoffrey Hartman, Edward E. Bostetter, and more recently, Thomas McFarland. Bostetter, in *The Romantic Ventriloquists* (Seattle: Univ. of Washington Press, 1975), perhaps best describes the unconvincing nature of the Ode's affirmation: "What seems at first glance triumphant affirmation is revealed on closer observation as a desperate struggle for affirmation against increasingly powerful obstacles." Bostetter further sees "affirmation hardening into an incantatory rhetoric sharply at odds with the perceptions and experiences it conveys" (p. 5). McFarland is equally explicit: "The great 'Immortality' Ode . . . generates its power by a logical argument that moves directly against that argument." See his "Wordsworth on Man, on Nature, and on Human Life," *SIR* 21, 4 (Winter 1982): 601–18, 601. And Jerome J. McGann, in *The Romantic Ideology: A Critical Investigation* (Chicago: Univ. of Chicago Press, 1983), describes the poem as "a very emblem of the tragedy of his epoch," because in the poem "Wordsworth imprisoned his true voice of feeling within the bastille of his consciousness" (p. 91).
3. See Wilson's "Wordsworth and the Uncanny: 'The Time Is Always Present,'" *TWC* 16, 2 (Spring 1985): 92–98.
4. Thomas McFarland, *Romanticism and the Forms of Ruin: Wordsworth, Coleridge, and the Modalities of Fragmentation* (Princeton: Princeton Univ. Press, 1981), p. 338. For a related argument, see Frederick Kirchhoff, "Reconstruction of the Self in Wordsworth's 'Ode: Intimations of Immortality from Recollections of Early Childhood,'" in *Narcissism and the Text: Studies in Literature and the Psychology of Self,* ed. Lynne Layton and Barbara Ann Schapiro (New York: New York Univ. Press, 1986), pp. 116–27. Reading the Ode from a Kohutian perspective, Kirchhoff also discusses the importance of fragmentation, showing that Wordsworth's depiction of nature as divided into "unrelated parts" (p. 120), such as the rainbow, the rose, the moon, represents the "fragmentation of the idealized selfobject" (p. 122). The Ode,

for Kirchhoff, dramatizes Wordsworth's attempt to restore the unity of both nature and self, but that restoration also brings Wordsworth to "the terminus of his creative life" (p. 127).

5. Quotations from the Ode and from passages of the prose are taken from the first volume of the Yale edition, *William Wordsworth: The Poems*, 2 vols., ed. John O. Hayden (New Haven: Yale Univ. Press, 1981). Where any ambiguity exists, I will use the abbreviation *WP* for this edition.

6. F. R. Leavis, for example, suggests that the "empty grandiosity" of these phrases is just one sign of a "general factitiousness" in the poem. See his *Revaluation* (London: Chatto and Windus, 1936), p. 184.

7. Wordsworth does use both singular and plural pronouns in the last three stanzas, but compared to the first eight stanzas the percentage of plural pronouns is greatly increased. In stanza 4, for example, all twelve pronouns are singular: in stanzas 9 and 10 plural pronouns outnumber singular ones.

8. Clifford Siskin, "Romantic Genre: Form and Revisionary Behavior in Wordsworth," *Genre* 16, 2 (Summer 1983): 137–55, 140–41.

9. Vendler, pp. 81–82.

10. I.i.148–49. Quotations from Shakespeare are from the edition by G. B. Harrison (New York: Harcourt, Brace, and World, 1968).

11. Jonathan Wordsworth, *William Wordsworth: The Borders of Vision* (Oxford: Clarendon Press, 1982), p. 64. I do not agree with all aspects of Jonathan Wordsworth's argument, but it is clear that both of us see "uncanny" manifestations here which are, for the poet, otherworldly. Wilson, for all his fine work on the uncanny, makes a crucial mistake in reference to the "guilty thing": "By uncanny analogy the boy's mortality trembles at a summons beyond death" (p. 96). But it is not the boy who trembles here—rather, it is the adult poet recalling his boyhood. As Wilson suggests elsewhere (p. 95), we have not an actual memory here, but a screen memory, a distortion of actual memory.

12. Robert Newsom, *Dickens on the Romantic Side of Familiar Things: "Bleak House" and the Novel Tradition* (New York: Columbia Univ. Press, 1977), p. 58.

13. Sigmund Freud, "The Uncanny," in *On Creativity and the Unconscious: Papers on the Psychology of Art, Literature, Love, Religion*, trans. Joan Riviere (New York: Harper and Row, 1958), pp. 122–61, 152–53. Italics in the original. All references will be taken from this edition and will be cited hereafter in the text.

14. André Green, "The Double and the Absent," in *Psychoanalysis, Creativity, and Literature: A French-American Inquiry*, trans. Ed Roland (New York: Columbia Univ. Press, 1978), pp. 271–92, 284.

15. Cf. Wilson's comment that the passage introduces "an irrational poetry that makes a strong claim upon our assent. The self here is liable to invasion by radical otherness" (p. 96).

16. The most extensive treatment of the leitmotif of the journey home in Wordsworth's poetry is M. H. Abrams, *Natural Supernaturalism: Tradition and Revolution in Romantic Literature* (New York: W. W. Norton, 1971), pp. 278–92.

17. Cf. David Ellis's argument in *Wordsworth, Freud, and the Spots of Time: Interpretation in "The Prelude"* (Cambridge: Cambridge Univ. Press, 1985), p. 19, that the "anxiety of hope" Wordsworth expresses in Book 11 of the 1805 *Prelude* "was probably no more than an eagerness to go home."

18. Barbara A. Schapiro, *The Romantic Mother: Narcissistic Patterns in Romantic Poetry* (Baltimore: Johns Hopkins Univ. Press, 1985), p. 100.

19. Wordsworth's references to God and even his Platonic imagery lead some readers to speculate that he longs for a reunion with the orthodox Christian God. Wordsworth himself disavowed any belief in the Platonic doctrine, calling it "far too shadowy a notion to be recommended to faith" (*WP*, p. 979). I can accept the idea that Wordsworth wanted the comforts that Christianity would offer, but it seems clear from the doubts and contradictions of the Ode that he could not, at least at this time in his life, readily adopt an orthodox perspective. Anya Taylor has recently offered a careful reading of the Ode in a Christian context. See her "Religious Readings of the Immortality Ode," *SEL* 26, 4 (Autumn 1986): 633–54. Under the rubric of an "argument from discontent" Taylor poses that Wordsworth, ultimately, is thankful "not for the recollections themselves, but for the dissatisfaction they arouse when recollections are contrasted with present realities" (p. 635). Wordsworth's poem does not seem to me to express thankfulness for dissatisfaction. Wordsworth's religious rhetoric is best approached with some caution. Though Abrams and others have

demonstrated Wordsworth's fondness for Christian apocalyptic metaphors, they also show that he put such language to secular use.

20. Paul Jay, *Being in the Text: Self-Representation from Wordsworth to Roland Barthes* (Ithaca: Cornell Univ. Press, 1984), p. 53.

21. Jay, p. 72.

22. Otto Rank, *Beyond Psychology* (1941; New York: Dover Books, 1958), p. 76. Rank discussed the double several times and even authored an early monograph on the subject (1914) which Freud knew. For consistency, I refer only to the discussion in chapter 2 of Rank's final book, *Beyond Psychology,* his most complete and integrated theory of the double. Future references to this work will be made in the text.

23. Philip E. Slater, *The Glory of Hera: Greek Mythology and the Greek Family* (Boston: Beacon Press, 1968), p. 88.

24. Slater, p. 149.

25. Jerome Christensen, "'Thoughts That Do Often Lie Too Deep for Tears': Toward a Romantic Concept of Lyrical Drama," *TWC* 12, 1 (Winter 1981): 52–64, 52–53.

26. Schapiro, *The Romantic Mother,* p. 101. Cf. the comment of the psychoanalyst David Beres: "There is evident in Wordsworth's life and work the precocious and unresolved oedipal development and the preoedipal impingements, the diminished boundaries between libidinal phases." See "Discussion" of Phyllis Greenacre's "The Family Romance of the Artist," *The Psychoanalytic Study of the Child* 13 (New York: International Universities Press, 1958): 40–42, 42.

27. Freud, "Female Sexuality," in *Sexuality and the Psychology of Love,* ed. Philip Rieff (New York: Macmillan, 1963), pp. 194–211, 199.

28. See Peter B. Neubauer, "Preoedipal Objects and Object Primacy," in *The Psychoanalytic Study of the Child* 40 (New Haven: Yale Univ. Press, 1985): 163–82, 177.

29. Ross Woodman, "Wordsworth's Crazed Bedouin: *The Prelude* and the Fate of Madness," *SIR* 27, 1 (Spring 1988): 3–30, 4.

30. Ned Lukacher, *Primal Scenes: Literature, Philosophy, Psychoanalysis* (Ithaca: Cornell Univ. Press, 1986), p. 12. For Lukacher such a moment represents a "primal scene." However, his use of that term is so radically different from Freud's original use that I do not find it helpful.

31. See Richard J. Onorato, *The Character of the Poet: Wordsworth in "The Prelude"* (Princeton: Princeton Univ. Press, 1971), p. 205.

32. For example, both Richard J. Onorato and David Ellis describe Wordsworth's desire in *The Prelude* to "drink in" as representing his "Oceanic" nature, evident in one who tries "to recapture the secure feeling of being 'at one' with the world which the baby at the breast supposedly experiences, either . . . because he feels he is absorbing his environment, or being absorbed by it" (Ellis, p. 33). Psychoanalysts have seen evidence of similar desires in patients. In a case study, P. J. Van der Leeuw describes a patient who visited bars to be near women. Always passive in his sexual relations, the patient invariably wanted to hear a woman's life story, especially the history of her relationships with men. The woman's narrative and everything about her, says Van der Leeuw, traced this desire to drink in to preoedipal conflicts similar to the ones I am ascribing to Wordsworth. See his "The Preoedipal Phase of the Male," in *The Psychoanalytic Study of the Child* 13 (New York: International Universities Press, 1958): 352–74, 365.

33. Freud, "On Narcissism: An Introduction," in *Collected Papers* 4, trans. Joan Riviere (New York: Basic Books, 1959): 30–59, 51.

34. Wilson, p. 93.

35. Even more remarkable is Wordsworth's interpretation of his childhood. Psychologists now agree that the process of differentiating the self from external reality begins at six months and is finished by age 3. For example, see Lynne Layton, "From Oedipus to Narcissus: Literature and Psychology of the Self," *Mosaic* 18, 1 (Winter 1985): 97–105, 98. Extraordinary a child as Wordsworth might have been, surely his development of separateness was not so protracted — to school age. That Wordsworth made this remark in his 70s makes its verity even more suspicious. However, if the recollections are even remotely accurate, it confirms my belief that Wordsworth was a narcissist who had extraordinary difficulty establishing his own independence.

36. Oscar Cullman, *Immortality of the Soul or Resurrection of the Dead?* (New York: Macmillan, 1958), pp. 49, 51, 56. I am grateful to Professor Jerome McGann, University of Virginia, for pointing out this connection to me.

37. Coleridge, *Biographia Literaria*, ed. George Watson (London: Dent, 1966), p. 262.
38. Schapiro, p. 100.
39. See, for example, Matthew C. Brennan's Jungian reading of the Discharged Soldier episode in " 'The ghastly figure moving at my side': The Discharged Soldier as Wordsworth's Shadow," *TWC* 18, 1 (Winter 1987): 19–23, for similarities to my reading of the Ode. Brennan reads the soldier as a shadow, a projection of the poet's self, representing an "encounter with his hellish side" (p. 21). Brennan also finds in the scene a longing for a return "home" to be reunited with the mother (p. 22).
40. Quoted in Adela Pinch, "Female Chatter: Meter, Masochism, and *The Lyrical Ballads*," *ELH* 55, 4 (Winter 1988): 835–52, 838.
41. Thomas McFarland, "Wordsworth's Best Philosopher," *TWC* 13, 2 (Spring 1982): 59–67, 59.
42. Schapiro, p. 110.
43. Francoise Meltzer persuasively argues that Freud does much the same thing in his essay on "The Uncanny." See her "The Uncanny Rendered Canny: Freud's Blind Spot in Reading Hoffmann's 'Sandman,' " in *Introducing Psychoanalytic Theory*, ed. Sander L. Gilman (New York: Brunner/Mazel, 1982), pp. 218–39. She says Freud "turns away from the abyss" in an effort to control the uncanny moment rather than to risk "exploring the uncertainty the uncanny embodies" (pp. 224–25, 228).
44. More specifically, many theorists of the creative process, such as Edith Jacobsen, see art as a means of sublimating desires that can be traced to infantile or preoedipal longings. See Van der Leeuw, p. 357.

APPLICATION

Feminist or Naturalist: The Social Context of Kate Chopin's *The Awakening*

Nancy Walker

Author-centered historical criticism makes its strongest claims when it offers not simply to deepen but drastically to revise our interpretations. Nancy Walker's analysis of the social context of The Awakening *is a case in point. While crediting feminist criticism for rediscovering and revaluing many important texts, Chopin's among them, Walker complains that critics have "hastened to find feminism where it did not exist and have ignored the cultural and literary milieu of the author." Walker's target here is not so much antihistorical formalism as it is a kind of radical historical relativism which assumes either that we cannot reconstruct an author's intentions or that we need not, since the work's relevance (compare Hirsch's "significance" as opposed to "meaning") is what we choose to make it. As Fowler notes, the distinction between what a work may have meant to its author and what it means to us, easy enough in theory, can be difficult in practice, and it becomes all the more difficult when the contested meanings are not matters of purely intellectual debate but are seen by the contestants as having consequences in the struggle to analyze and to alter current power relationships. In other words, Walker's real opponents, like Paul Yachnin's, are to be found in this book's concluding chapters. Against those who would see Chopin's work as a tract for our time, Walker asserts the creed of the author-centered literary historian: "The novel is best read with an eye to its [my emphasis] social and literary contexts." That social context is, for Walker, the Louisiana Creole community, and that literary context is the naturalistic conventions that Chopin knew and used. Developing her interpretation within these contexts, Walker offers a reading on what she claims are Chopin's terms, not ours. In subsequent chapters we will see some critics who will claim that Chopin's terms are closer to ours than Walker will allow; we'll also see some critics who will claim that Chopin's terms, whatever they may be, are not especially relevant. They are not genetic critics.*

The feminist movement has prompted rediscovery and/or reevaluation of a number of women writers and has thus been of great benefit to students of American culture who wish to have access to all points of view. Some critics of the "woman's novel," however, in their eagerness to establish a feminist tradition for such writers as Atwood, Lessing, and Rossner, have hastened to find feminism where it did not exist and have ignored the cultural and literary milieu of the author. A case in point is commentary concerning Kate Chopin's *The Awakening.*

Chopin has been regularly included in anthologies of women writers since the early 1960s. However, this anthologizing has led to the hasty assumption that all women writers have had the same concerns. For example, the editors of *American Voices, American Women* state that Chopin "chooses in . . . *The Awakening* to celebrate female sensuality at the same time as she shows the price for it exacted from women by external society and internalized social norms."[1] Louis D. Rubin speaks of Chopin's "urge to apply a French realism to the description of emancipated women."[2] And even her chief biographer refers to "her emancipationist writings" and "the female protest of *The Awakening,*" and speaks of the heroine's "open-eyed choice to defy illusions and to question the sacredness of morals."[3]

Indeed a mere summary of the plot would seem to support a feminist interpretation: Edna Pontellier becomes emotionally independent of her marriage after falling in love with another man, sends her children away to their grandmother, moves out of her husband's house, and has an affair which is based solely on physical attraction. Further, all of this takes place in the late nineteenth century South, in a culture assumed to be rigidly moralistic. The fact that Edna commits suicide at the end of the novel has been viewed as evidence that, in a "pre-liberation" era, this was the only option open to one who had dared to break society's rules in such a flagrant manner.

Much of the unfavorable comment the novel received when published concerned the sensual nature of the heroine; she expressed feelings of a sort not considered proper for the late nineteenth century. To-

day the sensual/sexual nature of woman is no longer a taboo subject, and Edna is ranked as an early liberationist by feminist critics. For example, Jacqueline Berke says that:

> . . . consciousness did not kill Edna; on the contrary, what killed Edna Pontellier was *a lack of consciousness* on the part of unawakened society, *a society which exerted so pervasively and persistently repressive an influence upon her* every effort to unfold as a total human being that she was forced finally to capitulate.[4] [latter italics mine]

But Chopin's rather flippant response to contemporary criticism is revealing:

> Having a group of people at my disposal, I thought it might be entertaining (to myself) to throw them together and see what would happen. I never dreamed of Mrs. Pontellier making such a mess of things and working out her own damnation as she did. If I had had the slightest intimation of such a thing I would have excluded her from the company.[5]

And Edmund Wilson was correct when he wrote:

> It is not . . . a "problem novel." No case for free love or women's rights or the injustice of marriage is argued. The heroine is simply a sensuous woman who follows her inclinations without thinking much about these issues or tormenting herself with her conscience.[6]

The novel is best read with an eye to its social and literary contexts. Whatever feminist beliefs Kate Chopin held, she makes it clear that Edna Pontellier is largely unaware of—and certainly unconcerned with—the reasons for her actions and that her awakening is a realization of her sensual nature, not of her equality or freedom as an individual. Cynthia Griffin Wolff, in a recent article, attempts to analyze the novel from a psychological standpoint in order to show that Chopin did not intend to write a feminist tract.[7] I propose that the proof is simpler and that much of Chopin's portrait of Edna depends upon the Louisiana Creole setting she chose and the naturalistic literary convention of her day.

Creole society was in some ways unlike any other in the United States. Occupying the southern half of Louisiana (and parts of Alabama and eastern Missouri), the Creoles were the descendants of French and Spanish colonists of the eighteenth century. Some of them became very wealthy as sugar cane planters; others were less successful economically, but all were bound by Catholicism, strong family ties, and a common language (French) into a cultural subgroup which had little in common with—indeed, was often in conflict with—Anglo-American society. The cultural patterns of the Creoles have been romanticized by local colorists, including Chopin, in her short stories, but some basic characteristics may be agreed upon.

Clement Eaton states that "the Creoles, to a greater degree than the Anglo-Americans, lived a life of sensation and careless enjoyment. They loved to dance, gamble, fish, attend feasts, play on the fiddle and to live without much thought of the morrow."[8] There are several reasons for this reputation for an easygoing attitude. One is Catholicism. The pre-Lenten celebrations known as Mardi Gras, and the Sunday after-Mass holiday spirit were shocking to visitors trained to the gloom of Calvinism. New Orleans was called a Southern Babylon because of the quadroon and octoroon mistresses supported openly by Creole men. Quadroons, having one-quarter Negro blood, were of course considered fully Negro by society (cf. the quadroon servants in *The Awakening*), and it is probable that the mother of a quadroon girl was pleased—and economically relieved—to have her daughter become the mistress of a wealthy white man.

Another reason for the reputed carpe diem philosophy no doubt is that the Creoles did not move westward in search of larger pieces of land, as did most colonists. They were content to remain in the vicinity of New Orleans, and made up about a third of its population in 1860. (About forty-five percent of the white population of the state then lived in New Orleans, which had until shortly before been the state capital.)[9] This lack of what the rest of the country would call "industry" did have its detrimental effects, for the same parcel of land had to be subdivided repeatedly among heirs, making it increasingly difficult for a single individual to benefit from the plantation system.

Since much of what we know of Creole culture comes from observers who were chiefly impressed with notable differences from their own environments, it is difficult to draw an accurate picture of these people. It is also difficult to ascertain how much change had taken place by the time Kate Chopin lived in southern Louisiana in the 1870s; but

since she had grown up in St. Louis, another area of Creole settlement, in the 1850s and 1860s, her description is probably a reliable one.

A close reading of the novel reveals that Chopin has not placed her heroine in a rigidly moralistic environment. Relatively unaffected by the puritanical mores of much of American society, the Creoles among whom Edna finds herself are openly sensual people. Ernest Earnest, referring to "The Storm," an unpublished story written after *The Awakening*, says, "The characters are all Creoles and therefore outside the Puritan tradition."[10] Warner Berthoff refers to "the languor, sensuality, frankness, and erotic sophistication of Creole manners."[11] And Larzer Ziff says of Chopin:

> The community about which she wrote was one in which respectable women took wine with their dinner and brandy after it, smoked cigarettes, played Chopin sonatas, and listened to the men tell risque stories. It was, in short, far more French than American, and Mrs. Chopin reproduced this little world with no specific intent to shock or make a point.... Rather, these were for Mrs. Chopin the conditions of civility.... People openly liked one another, enjoyed life, and savored its sensual riches.[12]

Hence, Edna is not behaving in a shocking, inexplicable manner in the novel; she is not flaunting the mores of the society she finds herself in. Rather, by succumbing to the sensuality of the Creoles, she is denying what she has been raised to believe, so that in some ways the novel deals with the clash of two cultures. She is a Kentucky Presbyterian by birth and has been thrown into a very different culture by virtue of her marriage to Leonce Pontellier.

Early in the novel Edna recalls a childhood day when she walked across a field in sensuous delight, drawn on despite herself:

> "Likely as not it was Sunday," she laughed; "and I was running away from prayers, from the Presbyterian service, read in a spirit of gloom by my father that chills me yet to think of."[13]

Edna's mother had died when the children were young, and Chopin implies that Edna's father was to some extent responsible for this when she writes, "The Colonel was perhaps unaware that he had coerced his own wife into her grave" (p. 186). The difference between two ways of life is also shown in the contrast between the Colonel and Leonce. If there is a domineering male in the book, it is Edna's father, not her husband. When both have become aware that Edna is behaving strangely upon the family's return to New Orleans, her father remarks to Leonce:

> You are too lenient, too lenient by far. . . . Authority, coercion are what is needed. Put your foot down good and hard; the only way to manage a wife. Take my word for it. (p. 186)

Soon after this the Colonel leaves New Orleans "With his padded shoulders, his Bible reading, his 'toddies' and ponderous oaths" (p. 185). Leonce, in contrast, is concerned and gentle, and asks the advice of Dr. Mandelet, who says, "Let your wife alone for a while. Don't bother her, and don't let her bother you" (p. 172). The Creole doctor embodies his culture's acceptance of human peculiarity, and Leonce agrees to follow his advice.

It is important to note that Edna Pontellier initially finds it difficult to participate in the easy intimacy of the Creoles.

> A characteristic which distinguished [the Creoles] and which impressed Mrs. Pontellier most forcibly was their entire absence of prudery. . . . Never would Edna Pontellier forget the shock with which she had heard Madame Ratignolle relating to old Monsieur Farival the harrowing story of one of her *accouchements,* withholding no intimate detail. . . . A book had gone the rounds of the *pension.* When it came her turn to read it, she did so with profound astonishment. She felt moved to read the book in secret and solitude, though none of the others had done so — to hide it from view at the sound of approaching footsteps. (pp. 23–24)

Even the simplest gestures of affection are foreign to her, and she becomes confused when Madame Ratignolle touches her hand during a conversation. "She was not accustomed to an outward and spoken expression of affection, either in herself or others" (p. 43). She describes herself as "self-contained," and remains largely so until the end of the novel, in the sense that she espouses no doctrine or set of principles outside herself. However, she does become a fully sexual being.

Edna's sexual awakening begins with the flirtations of Robert Lebrun, but it is apparent that this, too, is a part of the society in which Edna finds herself. No one is surprised that Robert is attentive to her — in fact, it is expected, even by Edna's husband. When Edna leaves Mass and goes to Madame An-

toine's with Robert, she says, upon awakening from her nap, "I wonder if Leonce will be uneasy!" And Robert replies, "Of course not; he knows you are with me" (p. 97). When Robert leaves for Mexico:

> Everyone seemed to take for granted that she missed him. Even her husband, when he came down the Saturday following Robert's departure, expressed regret that he had gone. "How do you get on without him, Edna?" he asked. "It's very dull without him," she admitted. (p. 120)

Before this point, Chopin has told us that "the Creole husband is never jealous; with him the gangrene passion is one which has been dwarfed by disuse" (p. 27). The relationship between Edna and Robert is, of course, expected to have limits. At one point, realizing that the situation could go beyond acceptable boundaries, Adele Ratignolle warns Robert: "She is not one of us; she is not like us. She might make the unfortunate blunder of taking you seriously" (pp. 50–51).

The warning is too late. Edna has realized by this point the feelings that she is capable of having for a man, and although Robert does the "gentlemanly" thing by going away, Edna translates her sexual feelings into love for him. And during the rest of the novel, she does not flee from her marriage, her children, and her social obligations; rather, she runs *toward* the promise of sexual fulfillment in the person of Robert. But *run* is the wrong word, for there is nothing frantic about Edna; in fact, she resembles a sleepwalker much of the time, not aware on an intellectual level of what she is doing.

It is on this point — Edna's lack of intellectual understanding of her actions — that setting, theme, and style converge. Chopin has caused Edna to be hypnotized by the sensuous Creoles, by the warmth and color of Grand Isle. In the process, Edna has experienced a sexual awakening, and because of its suddenness and power, she is not really in control of herself. To demonstrate this, Chopin uses the style of the naturalists in depicting a fated character. Echoing Crane's "None of them knew the color of the sky," in "The Open Boat," are numerous references to Edna which indicate a somnambulistic state: "she did not know why," "she was not aware," "she did not realize." It is significant, for example, that the first time she resists her husband's wishes, when he orders her to come inside in chapter eleven, Chopin writes, "She *could not at the moment have done other* than denied and resisted" (pp. 79–80; italics mine).

Evidence of this lack of command over her own feelings and actions continues to accumulate throughout the novel. Sailing to the Cheniere for Mass the day following the incident mentioned above, "Edna felt as if she were being borne away from some anchorage which had held her fast" (p. 87). This statement has been interpreted as meaning that she wants to be freed from her marriage. However, there are two reasons why this cannot be true. One is the passive nature of the statement: she is "being borne" by something other than her own will. More importantly, she has no thought of her husband or her marriage at this point in the novel; Chopin has merely provided words for an emotional state. The "anchorage" is emotional sterility; she feels free to respond to Robert's attentions. When she does "leave" Leonce, it is not so much a conscious action as a series of unplanned, unconnected moves. When she tells Mademoiselle Reisz, for example, that she is going to move into a house of her own, she has "only thought of it this morning," and when Mademoiselle asks for a reason,

> Neither was it quite clear to Edna herself; but it unfolded itself as she sat for a while in silence. Instinct had prompted her to put away her husband's bounty in casting off her allegiance. (p. 208)

In giving herself over to emotion, Edna has allowed her decisions to be made below the conscious level, so that they surprise even her, and she gives little thought to the consequences. When Edna writes what will be her last letter to her husband, Chopin remarks that "all sense of reality had gone out of her life; she had abandoned herself to Fate, and awaited the consequences with indifference" (p. 271). She has begun living for the day in the Creole manner. And, like that of a new convert, her devotion to this way of life is often extreme, causing Madame Ratignolle to remark, "In some way you seem to me like a child, Edna. You seem to act without a certain amount of reflection which is necessary in this life" (p. 250).

The last scene of the novel, that of Edna's suicide, reveals the same pattern of behavior. Significantly, the final chapter opens with Victor Lebrun's description to Mariequita of the dinner he had attended at Edna's, full of the sensual detail of flowers, golden goblets, and beautiful women. The young Creole, with his exaggerated account, thus sets the scene for Edna's final immersion into sensuality — the sea. She has not determined to commit suicide; in fact, on her way to the beach she talks with Victor about what will be served for dinner upon her return. And when she realizes that she hasn't the strength to swim back, the last images in the novel are serene, sensual ones; "the hum of bees, and the musky odor of pinks" (p. 303). In effect, Edna drifts into death because she does nothing to stop it; in this action, as in preceding ones, she has not controlled her own destiny.

Kate Chopin has written an important novel, and not the smallest factor in its importance is the author's open acceptance of the sensual nature of women, especially considering the era in which the novel was written. But the novel is also important as an examination of cultural patterns, and especially the collision of two cultures. Edna's awakening to sensuality — in which Chopin includes music, color, and food — occurs as a direct result of exposure to a society which valued these pleasures much more openly and unashamedly than did the one Edna had been reared in. Encouraged to develop her sense of freedom in enjoyment, Edna does so, with results that damage her marriage and eventually lead to her death. In addition, Chopin writes *The Awakening* from the perspective of a naturalist, giving Edna little control over her own destiny, and it is important to note that she is controlled by her own emotions, not by men or society. She has less "open-eyed choice" than Dreiser's Carrie. There is, in Chopin's novel, no stance about women's liberation or equality; indeed, the other married women in the novel are presented as happy in their condition. Perhaps those who read the novel as a feminist document are also affected by a clash of cultures: their own and that which the novelist inhabited.

Notes

1. Lee R. Edwards and Arlyn Diamond, eds., *American Voices, American Women* (New York: Avon, 1973), p. 16.
2. Louis D. Rubin, Jr., ed., *A Bibliographical Guide to the Study of Southern Literature* (Baton Rouge: Louisiana State Univ. Press, 1969), p. 174.
3. Per Seyersted, ed., *The Complete Works of Kate Chopin* (Baton Rouge: Louisiana State Univ. Press, 1969), I, 29, 33.
4. Jacqueline Berke, "Kate Chopin's Call to a Larger 'Awakening,'" *Kate Chopin Newsletter*, 1 (Winter 1975–76), 4.

5. Edmund Wilson, *Patriotic Gore: Studies in the Literature of the American Civil War* (New York: Oxford Univ. Press, 1962), p. 591.
6. Wilson, p. 591.
7. Cynthia Griffin Wolff, "Thanatos and Eros: Kate Chopin's *The Awakening*," *American Quarterly*, 25 (Oct. 1973), 449–71.
8. Clement Eaton, *The Civilization of the Old South*, ed. Albert D. Kirwan (Lexington: Univ. of Kentucky Press, 1968), p. 83.
9. Eaton, p. 99.
10. Ernest Earnest, *The American Eve in Fact and Fiction, 1775–1914* (Urbana: Univ. of Illinois Press, 1974), p. 262.
11. Warner Berthoff, *The Ferment of Realism: American Literature 1884–1919* (New York: The Free Press, 1965), p. 88.
12. Larzer Ziff, *The American 1890's: Life and Times of a Lost Generation* (New York: Viking Press, 1966), pp. 297–98.
13. Kate Chopin, *The Awakening* (New York: Capricorn, 1964), p. 42. (Subsequent references in the text are to this edition.)

CHAPTER TWO

Formal Criticism: Poem as Context

'Tis not a Lip, *or* Eye, *we Beauty call,*
But the joint Force and full Result *of all.*

—Pope, *An Essay on Criticism*

Historical critics argue that if we want to understand poems, we must look to their causes; reader-response critics insist we must look to their effects. Formal critics complain that both these views tend to overlook the poem itself, the central object that unites authors and readers and that offers a basis for an "objective" study of poetic art free from the difficulties and irrelevancies of author and reader psychology.

This argument tells us something about the way Anglo-American criticism has developed in our century. A simplified sketch of that development might well begin with the formalist challenge to the then-dominant historical criticism. It would trace the gradual progress of that challenge as the formalist argument found converts and the formalists themselves found prestigious academic positions. It might mark the 1950s as the apogee of the movement. This decade saw the formal approach established on nearly equal footing with historical studies in many graduate schools, and on more than equal footing in several critical journals. Even more telling, perhaps, the decade saw formal criticism also well established in hundreds of undergraduate classes in literature. If the sketch were then continued to the present day, it would show the last three decades dominated by attempts to challenge in turn the new formalist orthodoxy. Reader-response and historical approaches have found new defenders while other theorists have labored to revise formal methodology on formal principles and still others have argued that we must go "beyond" formalism in new directions.

In other words, the formal context holds a central position in modern Anglo-American criticism. To chart its development from the early writings of I. A. Richards and T. S. Eliot (though neither should be called simply a "formalist") through the important theoretical essays of such critics as John Crowe Ransom and Allen Tate to the widely influential critiques and textbooks by Cleanth Brooks and Robert Penn Warren and the inclusive and systematic theorizing of Austin Warren, René Wellek, and W. K. Wimsatt is to name a number of the important figures in mid-twentieth-century criticism. To recount the debates between these writers and others who were themselves essentially formalists, such as R. P. Blackmur, Kenneth Burke, Yvor Winters, and the "Chicago Critics" led by R. S. Crane, Richard McKeon, and Elder Olson, is to name still more.

At the same time, it would be misleading to suggest that formal criticism represents a new or peculiarly modern approach. This approach is at least as old as Aristotle, who asserted a basic formal axiom when he declared that skill in the use of metaphor was the true mark of poetic genius, and when Aristotle showed how his six tragic elements should relate to each other, how they must work together to achieve the ideal tragedy, he was performing a formal analysis. A more frequently cited father figure is Coleridge, who defined a poem as that species of composition that "proposes to itself such delight from the whole as is compatible with the distinct gratification from each component part," and who provided a very influential phrasing of formal principles when he declared that the poetic imagination revealed itself "in the balance or reconciliation of opposite or discordant qualities: of sameness, with difference; of the general, with the concrete; the idea, with the image; the individual, with the representative . . . a more than usual state of emotion, with more than usual order" (*Biographia Literaria*, 1817). Indeed, whenever the critic looks closely at the artistic design and devices of poems, whenever theory stresses the unity and coherence of the work of art, formal concepts are involved. In this sense, it is correct to say that the formal approach has been an important part of literary criticism from Aristotle's time to our own.

But only in our own century has the approach attained a well-developed theoretical base, and only in our own time has it achieved such popularity that it has become the central position against which other theories have had to define themselves. Since this popularity is sometimes obscured by the fact that not all analyses I here call "formal" are presented under that name, it will be useful to examine briefly some alternative labels, for each reveals something about the formalist's chief concerns.

The "New Criticism" is one of these labels, though one of the least helpful. The phrase was employed by John Crowe Ransom to refer to the work of Richards, Eliot, and others in the 1920s, but it was soon used to describe Ransom's own approach and that of his followers, and it has remained in the critical lexicon ever since to denote, and sometimes to dismiss, any formal analysis. The term was of doubtful value even when Ransom used it, and now that formal theories have been the center of critical discussion for several decades, the word "new" has taken on a distinctly ironic cast. But it does at least remind us that modern formalism developed first outside the established academic hierarchy and in opposition to the prevailing historical approaches. Since defenders of a position often define that position with reference to the most conspicuous opposition, this point is worth remembering.

A better descriptive term is "objective" criticism. The phrase is potentially misleading because it may call to mind a kind of scientific detachment or a dispassionate, methodical approach very far from the critic's actual purpose or practice. But the virtue of the term "objective" is that it stresses the "objectness" of the poem. The status of the poem as an "object," as something that exists independently of its creator and independently of any of its readers, is a key concept in formal theory. This concept implies, on the one hand, that we can have access to the poem quite apart from the mind of its creator or the circumstances of its creation and, on the other, that any reader's interpretation can be measured against and corrected by the "objective" standard of the poem itself, even if that reader should happen to be the author.

This view of the poem as independent "object," then, frees the formalist from the chief difficulties of the historical and affective contexts. When Ransom advertised for an "ontological" critic, he was asking for "objective" criticism in this sense. But the conception of the "objectness" of the poem has further implications. Poetry is a verbal art, which means that we must apprehend it first as a process while our eyes move down the page or the syllables fall on the ear. But the formal emphasis on the wholeness of the poem, on its "structure," on its "organic unity," on its "patterns" of images or motifs, inevitably suggests a spatial rather than a temporal mode of perception. This emphasis is apparent in the titles of such famous formalist works as Cleanth Brooks's *The Well Wrought Urn* or W. K. Wimsatt's *The Verbal Icon,* and it is implied in the formalist's belief that through many careful readings we can come to see the poetic object steadily and to see it *whole.*

This concern for the wholeness of the poetic object is an important characteristic of formalism, for the goal of formal analysis is to show how the various elements in the poem fit together, how the parts cohere to produce the whole, and how our understanding of the whole conditions our understanding of the parts. Such an analysis illustrates the central formal axiom that the primary context for the understanding of any part of the poem is the poem itself. Consider, as a brief example, the opening lines of William Blake's short poem "London": "I wander through each charter'd street / Near where the charter'd Thames does flow." (The complete poem appears in Jonathan Culler's essay in the Intertextual section.) Suppose we want to discover the meaning of the word "charter'd" in these lines. A large dictionary will give us several possible meanings for the word. A historical dictionary will give us the range of meanings generally known to Blake's contemporaries. A study of all of Blake's writings will tell us the various ways he used the word on other occasions. But none of these, says the formalist, will tell us exactly what the word means in the lines in question. Only a full understanding of their immediate context—that is, of the poem itself—will tell us that.

Thus, of the several recorded meanings of "charter'd," only some will fit the particular context that is this poem. But contextual pressures can create meanings as well as eliminate them. Whatever a "charter'd Thames" may mean in, say, nautical terms, when the phrase appears in juxtaposition with "charter'd streets" and with the thickly clustered imagery of bondage, restraint, and repression developed throughout the poem, it takes on a sinister resonance far beyond any recorded legal or cartographic senses. Such is the power of context to create connotations, overtones, implications, in brief, "meanings," beyond those cited in even the largest dictionaries. And the principle applies to all elements in the poem. What is the meaning of an image, a motif, a symbol, of a character or a pattern or a scene? In each case we must see how the element fits its context, how it functions in the poem. To investigate these relationships and the meanings they produce is the chief task of formal analysis.

"Formal criticism," then, is an accurate label for this context, as well as the most popular one. For when we consider the formalists' quarrel with the historical and reader-response approaches, their conception of the objective status of the poem, and their insistence that the context formed by the poem itself is the ultimate determiner of meaning, we see that their main concern is always with the unique verbal construct before them, with these particular words in this particular order. To put it another way, formalists refuse to separate form from content.

Other types of criticism fail, they argue, because they make that separation. Thus, the psychoanalytic critic or the myth critic, who may locate a poem's appeal in the latent content or underlying patterns it shares with other poems and with our dreams, is apt to overlook those specifically formal features that set poems apart from dreams and one poem apart from another. And biographical critics, in their concern with causes, are equally likely to ignore poetic form. Representatives of these other schools may regard this charge as minor as long as they can still claim to increase our understanding of the poem's meaning. But the formalists won't accept this separation. There is, they insist, no poetic meaning apart from poetic form.

This is the fundamental principle of formal criticism, and it leads directly to the formalist's famous distrust of the "paraphrase" on the grounds that too many readers are inclined to confuse the poem's paraphrasable content with its "meaning," an inclination encouraged, the formalist would argue, by other critical approaches. In reaction, formal critics are inclined to reverse the emphasis and locate poetic meaning in what can't be paraphrased. The goal of their analyses is to get us back to the poem itself, to show how it differs from the paraphrase, to point out those formal elements that make it a poem, and that particular poem, and not some other thing. By pointing to these formal elements, the formalist undertakes to show us not so much *what* the poem means, as "meaning" is usually understood in discursive contexts, but *how* it means. In large and complex structures like *Hamlet,* for instance, one critic may demonstrate a consistent image pattern, a second may remark the fitting of speech to character, a third may illuminate structural parallels, a fourth call attention to repeated motifs, and so on. In each case, the goal is to send the reader back to the play better equipped to see all the elements working together to create a verbal structure at once richly complex and highly coherent. Readers whose vision is thus armed will see that *how* a poem means is the same thing as *what* it means. They will understand that form is meaning.

Form is also value, the formalists argue. For we should value a thing for what it does essentially and always, not for what it does incidentally and occasionally. A poem may or may not heal or reveal its author's psychic wounds; it may or may not depict accurately the social or political conditions of its time; it may or may not do all or any of the many things that nonpoetic constructs do. But to be a poem at all, say the formalists, it must be a verbal structure possessing a high degree of complexity and coherence. Since it is the purpose of formal analysis to explicate these very qualities, we can understand the formalists' contention that such explication is in itself a demonstration of the poem's value as well as of its meaning. Explication *is* criticism.

This is a cogent argument, and it has persuaded many. The formalists claim to deal directly with poems and in poetic terms. They detach the poem from what they consider secondary contexts in order to concentrate on the poem itself, and they undertake to illuminate both poetic meaning and poetic value by the same kind of analysis. Even critics who remain skeptical are likely to concede that the formalist argument has had the salutary effect of forcing all types of critics to look more carefully at poems and to try to explain more fully the relevance of any information they offer about them. The formal approach also places interpreters in a somewhat different relationship to their audience. Whereas historical critics, for example, usually appear as experts who are supplying information obtained through months or years of research into an author's life or times, formal critics appear to be simply pointing to features or patterns in the poem that we might have overlooked. They seem to claim no special expertise beyond well-developed powers of observation and a sharpened sense of what to look for. And we can all play the game. We test their reading against the poem and accept, reject, or modify that reading as our own understanding of the text demands. Indeed, we *must* all play the game, for the analysis never substitutes for the poem. The critics can only tell us where to look and what to look for; we have to see for ourselves.

In a way, then, and despite the formalists' belief that we can and should approach a "best" reading, formal theory appears to democratize literary criticism. And this may in part account for the popularity of formal analysis as a classroom technique at many levels of instruction. At any rate, there seems to be no reason why the untrained reader equipped only with a sharp eye and a large dictionary should not explicate a given poem as well as the most experienced critic. That in practice the untrained reader can seldom do this is a phenomenon for which formal theory offers no clear explanation.

And here we touch on one of the perennial objections to the formal approach. Formal analysis, so this argument runs, is often better than formal theory because that analysis is actually based on knowledge imported from other contexts. In other words, the claim is that formalists do not in practice really isolate the poem. A more forceful form of this objection, as we have seen, insists that they dare not isolate it, and especially not from the historical context, because the idea of authorial meaning provides the only valid check against misinterpretation. Without it, the poem becomes either a truly closed system impervious to analysis, or an isolated verbal object open to any number of equally coherent readings but providing no valid way to choose among them. To this, formal critics reply that we can and should establish what the poem "means" apart from what the author might have "meant," and that the public nature of language and our knowledge of its norms and conventions guarantee the validity of this distinction. At this point the intertextual critics enter the debate, insisting that to talk of norms and conventions does indeed circumvent the genetic context, but only by placing the poem in the larger context of literature as a whole. This line of argument will be developed in another chapter. Here we should simply note that the concept of the poem as an object of determinate meaning existing apart from author or audience remains a central, and much contested, concept in formal criticism.

The formal theory of poetic value is also much contested. That formal analysis is designed to demonstrate the degree of complexity and coherence a poem possesses is clear; that such an analysis is therefore a demonstration of value can follow only if we are willing to accept complexity and coherence as the appropriate value terms. Some readers are reluctant to do so, and one frequent charge against formal criticism is that it ignores direct and simple literary works to concentrate instead on those special kinds of poems that allow considerable scope for critical ingenuity. Furthermore, even if it can be demonstrated that "tension," "irony," "paradox," and "ambiguity" are qualities of even apparently simple poems, it is still not clear why such forms of "complexity" as these should be considered valuable.

Now I. A. Richards, as we will see, had also been concerned to demonstrate the complexity and coherence of poems, and Richards was a strong influence on formal criticism. But Richards had grounded these terms in his affective theory of value. The complex poem is better than the simple poem because it appeals to a greater number of our desires and aversions. And a coherent poem is better than an incoherent poem because in organizing its diverse elements, it also organizes the reader's psyche. In this way, Richards furnished a cogent defense of complexity and coherence as value terms on strictly affective grounds. But most formal critics, though not necessarily denying that poems have the potential to do something like this for certain readers, rejected the entire reader-response approach as largely irrelevant. The poem, they argued, is not your experience or my experience; it is only a potential cause of experiences, and the adequacy of any subjective response must be tested against the "objective" poem itself. This argument eliminates some of the problems that trouble affective theories, but it also eliminates the affective defense of complexity and coherence as poetic values.

Indeed, as long as the poem is supposed to exist in isolation from other contexts, it is difficult to see how the formal critic can find a basis for any value scheme at all. But in practice most formalists do not really isolate the poem so completely. Part of the difficulty is simply a matter of rhetorical emphasis. Developing their views in opposition to the once more popular genetic and affective approaches, the formalists often insisted on the separateness of the poetic "object," but they chiefly meant its separateness from those particular contexts, from its possible causes or its possible effects. Some objectors, taking them literally, have charged that the formalists advocate "art for art's sake," that they wish to isolate the poem from "life," from "human significance." But this charge reveals a serious misunderstanding of the formalist position. Far from urging the poem's isolation from experience outside art, Anglo-American formal theory has usually insisted that the real function of poetry is to tell us the truth about that experience.

At the same time, the formalists, like many other modern critics, were unwilling to concede that the "scientific" model for truth is the only or the most adequate model. To be sure, the scientific picture of the world possesses a kind of truth. But the very nature of scientific inquiry dictates that this picture will be highly abstract and skeletal. The atomic physicist's conception of my desk, for example, which tells me that the desk is mainly space, or a time–space event, may well be true, but it doesn't appear to describe the knuckle-rapping, shin-barking solidity that is my experience of the desk. The world presented in literature seems to have more of this kind of concreteness. It describes more nearly the world as we experience it. It puts flesh on the scientist's skeletal picture and gives us, in Ransom's phrase, the "world's body."

And it does more. By presenting complex characters in complex situations, it offers us a world of actions with emotional and moral significance. For the poem, through the magic of the concrete symbol, mediates between the abstract world of the philosophic and moral precept and the solid but chaotic world of felt experience. It provides for the first a specific illustration, for the second, a significant form. If the poem is, as Aristotle said, a more philosophical thing than history, it is also, as he did not say, a more concrete thing than philosophy. Philosophy, like science, tends toward the abstract and the systematic. But these qualities are achieved only by simplification; life as we experience it remains multifaceted and contradictory. And poetry offers to deal with, to assimilate, all of it: Desdemona and Iago, Falstaff and Hotspur, Edgar and Edmund. This is why good poems must be "multivalent," "ambiguous," "paradoxical," and all the other things formal critics say they are, because these are the salient characteristics of the life poems seek to describe. These are all forms of complexity, and the good poem is complex because, more than any other kind of discourse, it deals faithfully with our complex experience of the world. It tells us the truth about that experience.

In other words, many formal critics ultimately ground their value theory in the mimetic or "imitative" context. And they do this so consistently that we might properly speak of the "formal-mimetic" critic. This phrase is rather awkward and hardly anyone uses it, but it has the virtue of being reasonably accurate, and its use would remind us that the formalists actually make very large claims for poetry. It might also remind us that very few critics are really "pure" formalists, perhaps for the simple reason that the poem "in itself" supplies no base for a theory of value. The mimetic context, on the contrary, offers the oldest and most popular value criterion, the appeal to truth. Of course, this criterion is not without its own difficulties, and it will be the business of another section to explore some of these. Here we should simply notice that if the formal critics are seldom "pure" formalists, neither are they "pure" mimeticists. Their concern for poetic form remains the defining feature of their criticism and the mainstay of their claim that their type of analysis is centrally relevant to poetry.

Now, since the term "form" seems to refer most directly to such elements as rhythm and repetition, to those patterns and structural devices that chiefly provide the poem's coherence, the formal critic is faced with a rather puzzling problem. Complexity, we saw, can be justified as a value on mimetic grounds. The complex poem is "congruent" with reality as we experience it and therefore "true." But it is not clear that "coherence" can be similarly explained. For many readers, in fact, reality as we experience it seems conspicuously to lack satisfactory design, to lack precisely that formal coherence we find in the poem. To be sure, in some philosophical systems — Plato's for one, and perhaps Aristotle's — there is no ultimate conflict between coherence or formal order and congruence or imitative accuracy, but the number of contemporary readers deeply committed to these or similar systems is small. For many of us, the claims of congruence are not easily reconciled with those of coherence. And while we may wish to assent to the argument that art, by selecting and arranging the material of ordinary experience, gives that material extraordinary intensity and significance, our empirical premises lead us to suspect that any selecting and arranging is necessarily a kind of falsification, a diminution of complexity, and that therefore coherence is a value different from and opposed to congruence.

It is this apparently polar opposition that causes our perplexity. As certain features of a prose narrative, for example, move toward the pole of congruence, as the characters and their actions take on the endless complication and apparent randomness of people and actions outside of art, our sense of shape and point diminishes. Only chaos truly mirrors chaos. But as we move toward the opposite pole, as the characters become simpler, the actions more directed, the plot more symmetrical, our sense of the incongruity of life and art increases. Perhaps the magic of great poetry lies in its ability to have it both ways, to reconcile the apparently rival claims of coherence and congruence in the same way it is said to combine the concrete and the universal. As W. K. Wimsatt, one of the most influential formal theorists, has put it, "poetry is that type of verbal structure where truth of reference or correspondence reaches a maximum degree of fusion with truth of coherence — or where external and internal relations are intimately mutual reflections" (*The Verbal Icon*, p. 149). Perhaps so. Yet it is difficult to avoid the feeling that formal criticism insists finally on two opposing principles of value — the mimetic principle of congruence and the formal principle of coherence — and that these are not easily reconcilable under one theory of value.

And this problem leads to a further difficulty, a difficulty inherent in the term "form" itself. We use this term in a number of senses, two of which are of particular interest here. When formal critics speak of "form," they mean nearly everything about the poem, these particular words in this particular order. In this sense, every poem is a unique form. But we also speak of form when we say this poem is a sonnet, a villanelle, a rondeau, or when, with less precision but more significance, we describe a work as a satire or a tragedy, an epic or a pastoral. That is, we also use the term "form" to suggest that this particular poem is a certain kind of poem.

These two senses of "form," then, are really quite different. One stresses the singularity or uniqueness of the poem, the other calls attention to features it shares with similar poems. "Formal" critics are very much concerned with form in the first sense, very little with form in the second. Indeed, they are often impatient with discussions of genre, feeling that the distinctions such discussions seek to draw are problematic, arbitrary, and generally irrelevant. Studies that attempt to show that *Hamlet* is or is not a "real" tragedy, that *Paradise Lost* is or is not a "true" epic, reveal more, the formalists think, about definitions than they do about poems. And like all "irrelevant" contexts, such studies distract our attention from the unique form that is the particular poem in question. So, for many formal critics, classifications such as "tragic novel" or "pastoral elegy" are similar to the historical categories "a Conrad novel" or "a seventeenth-century poem." Formalists may find it convenient to use the terms, but they have little use for the contexts these terms imply. Their task is to explicate the unique verbal object before them, and the poem, whether others call it tragic or comic, elegiac or satiric, will be good to the extent that it possesses a high degree of complexity and coherence. On these grounds, a good poem, regardless of its period or type, is simply a good poem, and the judgment needs no historic or generic qualification.

As we have seen, this "absolute" standard of value is ultimately grounded in the mimetic context. The more complex poem is better because it more adequately "imitates" complex reality. But can we account for poetic form on this ground? As long as we think primarily of the characters or plots of "realistic" plays or novels, we might be inclined to feel that these forms present imitations of human actions. And in a sense even a lyric poem is a small drama. The speaker is a character who undergoes emotional changes as the "plot" of the poem moves from mood to mood, from statement to counterstatement, from problem to solution. So even a Petrarchan sonnet may be said to possess character and plot and to imitate action. On the other hand, it also possesses an octave, a sestet, and five iambic feet per line, and in these respects it imitates nothing in the world at all—except other Petrarchan sonnets. Working back, then, from this point, we may be moved to argue that even the most "realistic" novel has a degree of conventionality and stylization, in short, a formal order that causes it to resemble more nearly a sonnet than it does the apparent formlessness of experience outside of art. It most resembles, of course, other "realistic" novels. In this way the opposition between congruence and coherence returns to haunt the key term "form" and makes it very difficult to account for literary form on mimetic grounds. Thus, to push the point to its paradoxical conclusion, to the extent that they have developed their evaluative principles on those grounds, "formal" critics can deal with nearly everything in the poem except its "form."

Here again formal practice has often been more flexible than its supporting theory, and admittedly I am highlighting only one of the several senses of the word "form." But it is an important sense, and the failure of formal theory to account for the formal principles of literature must be considered a deficiency. As we will see, intertextual critics offer to make good precisely this deficiency. But to do so, they must abandon some of the central tenets of the formalist position. So the debate between these two critical schools centers on their different conceptions of literary form. Meanwhile, many historical and reader-response critics remain unconvinced by the formalists' attempts to isolate the poem from its historical causes or its particular effects. And, to repeat, there is the central problem within formal theory of how to reconcile the conflicting claims of coherence and congruence, formal unity and imitative fidelity. So the formalists, holding their central position, find themselves open to challenges from all sides.

In part, these challenges are simply the price of success, and they remind us that in our own century the formal context is central historically as well as conceptually. And while formalists sometimes claim that other perspectives are often irrelevant to the main business of criticism, their own position is largely immune to that charge. Objectors may find formal theory limited, but they can't seriously claim that the formalists' concentration on the poem is irrelevant. In fact, even the most committed opponent will probably admit that the formalists' abiding concern with the poem—with these particular words and the specific pattern they make—has taught critics of all persuasions the value of close, careful reading. Furthermore, and despite the very real difficulties in formal theory, many "revisionists" have discovered that it is one thing to point out some problems with the formalists' key concepts, but quite another thing to try to do without them. The most basic of these concepts is the insistence that poetic form and poetic meaning are inseparable, are, in fact, one and the same thing, and that all relevant criticism must start from this principle. This concept will inevitably lead critics into some puzzling theoretical difficulties. But it also promises to lead them toward the central mysteries of the art of poetry. This promise is the strongest reason that formal criticism, under its various labels and adaptations, continues to thrive.

Suggestions for Further Reading

Formal criticism in its Anglo-American versions (still often called "New Criticism") is displayed in a group of central texts: William Empson, *Seven Types of Ambiguity* (rev. ed., 1947), John Crowe Ransom, *The World's Body* (1938), Cleanth Brooks, *The Well Wrought Urn* (1947), René Wellek and Austin Warren, *Theory of Literature* (3rd ed., 1956), and W. K. Wimsatt, Jr., *The Verbal Icon* (1954). Critics who share many of the formalists' basic assumptions include Kenneth Burke, *The Philosophy of Literary Form* (1941), R. P. Blackmur, *Language as Gesture* (1952), and the "Chicago" or "neo-Aristotelian" group represented by R. S. Crane, ed., *Critics and Criticism* (1952), and Wayne Booth, *The Rhetoric of Fiction* (rev. ed., 1982). Some attempts to restate and defend the formalist position are Monroe Beardsley, *The Possibility of Criticism* (1970), John Ellis, *The Theory of Literary Criticism* (1974), and Murray Krieger, *Theory of Criticism* (1976). Krieger's *The New Apologists for Poetry* (1956) is a sympathetic and insightful analysis of main-line Anglo-American formalism. Victor Erlich, *Russian Formalism* (2nd ed., 1965), describes the sometimes similar but largely unrelated Russian movement. Some of the key essays in that movement are translated in Lee Lemon and Marion Reis, *Russian Formalist Criticism* (1965). William J. Spurlin and Michael Fisher, eds., *The New Criticism and Contemporary Literary Theory* (1995) reprints some classic formalist essays and adds some recent evaluations of the movement.

THEORY

Cleanth Brooks has been one of the leading figures in Anglo-American formal criticism, and his essay "Irony as a Principle of Structure" illustrates several of the formalists' key ideas. One of these is the insistence that poetry is radically metaphorical—its meaning is bound to the particular, the concrete, and no paraphrase can carry the same meaning. Another key idea is that the parts of a good poem are "organically" related, so each part can have meaning only within the "context" of the work as a whole. As Brooks examines the contextual pressures exerted in a few short poems, he discovers that in each case these pressures produce a kind of "irony," and this is the mark of a mature or complex vision that takes in more than the simple or single vision. Good poetry, then, is congruent with experience (complex, ironic), but at the same time, unified and "coherent"; it is "a poetry which does not leave out what is apparently hostile to its dominant tone and which, because it is able to fuse the irrelevant and discordant, has come to terms with itself and is invulnerable to irony." To illustrate his points, Brooks explicates a few short poems, among them Wordsworth's "A slumber did my spirit seal." It is this explication that E. D. Hirsch found consistent with Wordsworth's text, but probably inconsistent with Wordsworth's meaning. Can the poem provide its own context? On this question the formal and the historical critics divide.

Irony as a Principle of Structure

Cleanth Brooks

One can sum up modern poetic technique by calling it the rediscovery of metaphor and the full commitment to metaphor. The poet can legitimately step out into the universal only by first going through the narrow door of the particular. The poet does not select an abstract theme and then embellish it with concrete details. On the contrary, he must establish the details, must abide by the details, and through his realization of the details attain to whatever general meaning he can attain. The meaning must issue from the particulars; it must not seem to be arbitrarily forced upon the particulars. Thus, our conventional habits of language have to be reversed when we come to deal with poetry. For here it is the tail that wags the dog. Better still, here it is the tail of the kite—the tail that makes the kite fly—the tail that renders the kite more than a frame of paper blown crazily down the wind.

The tail of the kite, it is true, seems to negate the kite's function: it weights down something made to rise; and in the same way, the concrete particulars with which the poet loads himself seem to deny the universal to which he aspires. The poet wants to "say" something. Why, then, doesn't he say it directly and forthrightly? Why is he willing to say it only through his metaphors? Through his metaphors, he risks saying it partially and obscurely, and risks not saying it at all. But the risk must be taken, for direct statement leads to abstraction and threatens to take us out of poetry altogether.

The commitment to metaphor thus implies, with respect to general theme, a principle of indirection. With respect to particular images and statements, it implies a principle of organic relationship. That is, the poem is not a collection of beautiful or "poetic" images. If there really existed objects which were somehow intrinsically "poetic," still the mere assemblage of these would not give us a poem. For in that case, one might arrange bouquets of these poetic images and thus create poems by formula. But the elements of a poem are related to each other, not as blossoms juxtaposed in a bouquet, but as the blossoms are related to the other parts of a growing plant. The beauty of the poem is the flowering of the whole plant, and needs the stalk, the leaf, and the hidden roots.

If this figure seems somewhat highflown, let us borrow an analogy from another art: the poem is like a little drama. The total effect proceeds from all elements in the drama, and in a good poem, as in a good drama, there is no waste motion and there are no superfluous parts.

In coming to see that the parts of a poem are related to each other organically, and related to the total theme indirectly, we have come to see the importance of *context*. The memorable verses in poetry—even those which seem somehow intrinsically "poetic"—show on inspection that they derive their poetic quality from their relation to a particular context. We may, it is true, be tempted to say that Shakespeare's "Ripeness is all" is poetic because it is a sublime thought, or because it possesses simple eloquence; but that is to forget the context in which the passage appears. The proof that this is so becomes obvious when we contemplate such unpoetic lines as "vitality is all," "serenity is all," "maturity is all,"—statements whose philosophical import in the abstract is about as defensible as that of "ripeness is all." Indeed, the commonplace word "never" repeated five times becomes one of the most poignant lines in *Lear*, but it becomes so because of the supporting context. Even the "meaning" of any particular item is modified by the context. For what is said is said in a particular situation and by a particular dramatic character.

The last instances adduced can be most properly regarded as instances of "loading" from the context. The context endows the particular word or image or statement with significance. Images so charged become symbols; statements so charged become dramatic utterances. But there is another way in which to look at the impact of the context upon the part. The part is modified by the pressure of the context.

Now the *obvious* warping of a statement by the context we characterize as "ironical." To take the simplest instance, we say "this is a fine state of affairs," and in certain contexts the statement means quite the opposite of what it purports to say literally. This is sarcasm, the most obvious kind of irony. Here a complete reversal of meaning is effected: effected by the context, and pointed, probably, by the tone of voice. But the modification can be most important even though it falls far short of sarcastic reversal, and it need not be underlined by the tone of voice at all. The tone of irony can be effected by the skillful disposition of the context. Gray's *Elegy* will furnish an obvious example.

> Can storied urn or animated bust
> Back to its mansion call the fleeting breath?
> Can Honour's voice provoke the silent dust,
> Or Flatt'ry soothe the dull cold ear of death?

In its context, the question is obviously rhetorical. The answer has been implied in the characterization of the breath as fleeting and of the ear of death as dull and cold. The form is that of a question, but the manner in which the question has been asked shows that it is no true question at all.

These are obvious instances of irony, and even on this level, much more poetry is ironical than the reader may be disposed to think. Many of Hardy's poems and nearly all of Houseman's, for example, reveal irony quite as definite and overt as this. Lest these examples, however, seem to specialize irony in the direction of the sardonic, the reader ought to be reminded that irony, even in its obvious and conventionally recognized forms, comprises a wide variety of modes: tragic irony, self-irony, playful, arch, mocking, or gentle irony, etc. The body of poetry which may be said to contain irony in the ordinary senses of the term stretches from *Lear,* on the one hand, to "Cupid and Campaspe Played," on the other.

What indeed would be a statement wholly devoid of an ironic potential—a statement that did not show any qualification of the context? One is forced to offer statements like "Two plus two equals four," or "The square of the hypotenuse of a right triangle is equal to the sum of the squares on the two sides." The meaning of these statements is unqualified by any context; if they are true, they are equally true in any possible context.[1] These statements are properly abstract, and their terms are pure denotations. (If "two" or "four" actually happened to have connotations for the fancifully minded, the connotations would be quite irrelevant: they do not participate in the meaningful structure of the statement.)

But connotations are important in poetry and do enter significantly into the structure of meaning which is the poem. Moreover, I should claim also—as a corollary of the foregoing proposition—that poems never contain abstract statements. That is, any "statement" made in the poem bears the pressure of the context and has its meaning modified by the context. In other words, the statements made—including those which appear to be philosophical generalizations—are to be read as if they were speeches in a drama. Their relevance, their propriety, their rhetorical force, even their meaning, cannot be divorced from the context in which they are imbedded.

The principle I state may seem a very obvious one, but I think that it is nonetheless very important. It may throw some light upon the importance of the term *irony* in modern criticism. As one who has certainly tended to overuse the term *irony* and perhaps, on occasion, has abused the term, I am closely concerned here. But I want to make quite clear what that concern is: it is not to justify the term *irony* as such, but rather to indicate why modern critics are so often tempted to use it. We have doubtless stretched the term too much, but it has been almost the only term available by which to point to a general and important aspect of poetry.

Consider this example: The speaker in Matthew Arnold's "Dover Beach" states that the world, "which seems to lie before us like a land of dreams . . . hath really neither joy nor love nor light. . . ." For some readers the statement will seem an obvious truism. (The hero of a typical Hemingway short story or novel, for example, will say this, though of course in a rather different idiom.) For other readers, however, the statement will seem false, or at least highly questionable. In any case, if we try to "prove" the proposition, we shall raise some very perplexing metaphysical questions, and in doing so, we shall certainly also move away from the problems of the poem and, finally, from a justification of the poem. For the lines are to be justified in the poem in terms of the context: the speaker is standing beside his loved one, looking out of the window on the calm sea, listening to the long withdrawing roar of the ebbing tide, and aware of the beautiful delusion of moonlight which "blanches" the whole scene. The "truth" of the statement, and of the poem itself, in which it is imbedded, will be validated, not by a majority report of the association of sociologists, or a committee of physical scientists, or of a congress of metaphysicians who are willing to stamp the statement as proved. How is the statement to be validated? We shall probably not be able to do better than to apply T. S. Eliot's test: does the statement seem to be that which the mind of the reader can accept as coherent, mature, and founded on the facts of experience? But when we raise such a question, we are driven to consider the poem as drama. We raise such further questions as these: Does the speaker seem carried away with his own emotions? Does he seem to oversimplify the situation? Or does he, on the other hand, seem to have won to a kind of detachment and objectivity? In other words, we are forced to raise the question as to whether the statement grows properly out of a context; whether it acknowledges the pressures of the context; whether it is "ironical"—or merely callow, glib, and sentimental.

I have suggested elsewhere that the poem which meets Eliot's test comes to the same thing as I. A. Richards' "poetry of synthesis"—that is, a poetry which does not leave out what is apparently hostile to its dominant tone, and which, because it is able to fuse the irrelevant and discordant, has come to terms with itself and is invulnerable to irony. Irony, then, in this further sense, is not only an acknowledgment of the pressures of a context. Invulnerability to irony is the stability of a context in which the internal pressures balance and mutually support each other. The stability is like that of the arch: the very forces which are calculated to drag the stones to the ground actually provide the principle of support—a principle in which thrust and counterthrust become the means of stability.

In many poems the pressures of the context emerge in obvious ironies. Marvell's "To His Coy Mistress" or Raleigh's "Nymph's Reply" or even Gray's "Elegy" reveal themselves as ironical, even to readers who use irony strictly in the conventional sense.

But can other poems be subsumed under this general principle, and do they show a comparable basic structure? The test case would seem to be presented by the lyric, and particularly the simple lyric. Consider, for example, one of Shakespeare's songs:

Who is Silvia: what is she
    That all our swains commend her?
Holy, fair, and wise is she;
    The heavens such grace did lend her,
That she might admired be.

Is she kind as she is fair?
    For beauty lives with kindness.
Love doth to her eyes repair,
    To help him of his blindness
And, being help'd, inhabits there.

Then to Silvia let us sing,
    That Silvia is excelling;
She excels each mortal thing
    Upon the dull earth dwelling:
To her let us garlands bring.

On one level the song attempts to answer the question "Who is Silvia?" and the answer given makes her something of an angel and something of a goddess. She excels each mortal thing "Upon the dull earth dwelling." Silvia herself, of course, dwells upon that dull earth, though it is presumably her own brightness which makes it dull by comparison. (The dull earth, for example, yields bright garlands, which the swains are bringing to her.) Why does she excel each mortal thing? Because of her virtues ("Holy, fair, and wise is she"), and these are a celes-

tial gift. She is heaven's darling ("The heavens such grace did lend her").

Grace, I suppose, refers to grace of movement, and some readers will insist that we leave it at that. But since Silvia's other virtues include holiness and wisdom, and since her grace has been lent from above, I do not think that we can quite shut out the theological overtones. Shakespeare's audience would have found it even more difficult to do so. At any rate, it is interesting to see what happens if we are aware of these overtones. We get a delightful richness, and we also get something very close to irony.

The motive for the bestowal of grace—that she might admired be—is oddly untheological. But what follows is odder still, for the love that "doth to her eyes repair" is not, as we might expect, Christian "charity" but the little pagan god Cupid ("Love doth to her eyes repair, / To help him of his blindnes"). But if Cupid lives in her eyes, then the second line of the stanza takes on another layer of meaning. "For beauty lives with kindness" becomes not merely a kind of charming platitude—actually often denied in human experience. (The Petrarchan lover, for example, as Shakespeare well knew, frequently found a beautiful and *cruel* mistress.) The second line, in this context, means also that the love god lives with the kind Silvia, and indeed has taken these eyes that sparkle with kindness for his own.

Is the mixture of pagan myth and Christian theology, then, an unthinking confusion into which the poet has blundered, or is it something wittily combined? It is certainly not a confusion, and if blundered into unconsciously, it is a happy mistake. But I do not mean to press the issue of the poet's self-consciousness (and with it, the implication of a kind of playful irony). Suffice it to say that the song is charming and delightful, and that the mingling of elements is proper to a poem which is a deft and light-fingered attempt to suggest the quality of divinity with which lovers perennially endow maidens who are finally mortal. The touch is light, there is a lyric grace, but the tone is complex, nonetheless.

I shall be prepared, however, to have this last example thrown out of court since Shakespeare, for all his universality, was a contemporary of the metaphysical poets, and may have incorporated more of their ironic complexity than is necessary or normal. One can draw more innocent and therefore more convincing examples from Wordsworth's Lucy poems.

She dwelt among the untrodden ways
   Beside the springs of Dove,
A maid whom there were none to praise
   And very few to love;

A violet by a mossy stone
   Half hidden from the eye!
Fair as a star, when only one
   Is shining in the sky.

She lived unknown, and few could know
   When Lucy ceased to be;
But she is in her grave, and, oh,
   The difference to me.

Which is Lucy really like—the violet or the star? The context in general seems to support the violet comparison. The violet, beautiful but almost unnoticed, already half hidden from the eye, is now, as the poem ends, completely hidden in its grave, with none but the poet to grieve for its loss. The star comparison may seem only vaguely relevant—a conventional and here a somewhat anomalous compliment. Actually, it is not difficult to justify the star comparison: to her lover's eyes, she is the solitary star. She has no rivals, nor would the idea of rivalry, in her unselfconscious simplicity, occur to her.

The violet and the star thus balance each other and between themselves define the situation: Lucy was, from the viewpoint of the great world, unnoticed, shy, modest, and half hidden from the eye, but from the standpoint of her lover, she is the single star, completely dominating that world, not arrogantly like the sun, but sweetly and modestly, like the star. The implicit contrast is that so often developed ironically by John Donne in his poems where the lovers, who amount to nothing in the eyes of the world, become, in their own eyes, each the other's world—as in "The Good-Morrow," where their love makes "one little room an everywhere," or as in "The Canonization," where the lovers drive into the mirrors of each other's eyes the "towns, countries, courts"—which make up the great world; and thus find that world in themselves. It is easy to imagine how Donne would have exploited the contrast between the violet and the star, accentuating it, developing the irony, showing how the violet was really like its antithesis, the star, etc.

Now one does not want to enter an Act of Uniformity against the poets. Wordsworth is entitled to his method of simple juxtaposition with no underscoring of the ironical contrast. But it is worth noting that the

contrast with its ironic potential is there in his poem. It is there in nearly all of Wordsworth's successful lyrics. It is certainly to be found in "A slumber did my spirit seal."

A slumber did my spirit seal;
   I had no human fears:
She seemed a thing that could not feel
   The touch of earthly years.

No motion has she now, no force;
   She neither hears nor sees,
Rolled round in earth's diurnal course,
   With rocks, and stones, and trees.

The lover's insensitivity to the claims of mortality is interpreted as a lethargy of spirit—a strange slumber. Thus the "human fears" that he lacked are apparently the fears normal to human beings. But the phrase has a certain pliability. It could mean fears *for* the loved one as a mortal human being; and the lines that follow tend to warp the phrase in this direction: it does not occur to the lover that he needs to fear for one who cannot be touched by "earthly years." We need not argue that Wordsworth is consciously using a witty device, a purposed ambiguity; nor need we conclude that he is confused. It is enough to see that Wordsworth has developed, quite "normally," let us say, a context calculated to pull "human fears" in opposed directions, and that the slightest pressure of attention on the part of the reader precipitates an ironical effect.

As we move into the second stanza, the potential irony almost becomes overt. If the slumber has sealed the lover's spirit, a slumber, immersed in which he thought it impossible that his loved one could perish, so too a slumber has now definitely sealed *her* spirit: "No motion has she now, no force; / She neither hears nor sees." It is evident that it is her unnatural slumber that has waked him out of his. It is curious to speculate on what Donne or Marvell would have made of this.

Wordsworth, however, still does not choose to exploit the contrast as such. Instead, he attempts to suggest something of the lover's agonized shock at the loved one's present lack of motion—of his response to her utter and horrible inertness. And how shall he suggest this? He chooses to suggest it, not by saying that she lies as quiet as marble or as a lump of clay; on the contrary, he attempts to suggest it by imagining her in violent motion—violent, but imposed motion, the same motion indeed which the very stones share, whirled about as they are in earth's diurnal course. Why does the image convey so powerfully the sense of something inert and helpless? Part of the effect, of course, resides in the fact that a dead life-lessness is suggested more sharply by an object's being whirled about by something else than by an image of the object in repose. But there are other matters which are at work here: the sense of the girl's falling back into the clutter of things, companioned by things chained like a tree to one particular spot, or by things completely inanimate, like rocks and stones. Here, of course, the concluding figure leans upon the suggestion made in the first stanza, that the girl once seemed something not subject to earthly limitations at all. But surely, the image of the whirl itself is important in its suggestion of something meaningless — motion that mechanically repeats itself. And there is one further element: the girl, who to her lover seemed a thing that could not feel the touch of earthly years, is caught up helplessly into the empty whirl of the earth which measures and makes time. She is touched by and held by earthly time in its most powerful and horrible image. The last figure thus seems to me to summarize the poem — to offer to almost every facet of meaning suggested in the earlier lines a concurring and resolving image which meets and accepts and reduces each item to its place in the total unity.

Wordsworth, as we have observed above, does not choose to point up specifically the ironical contrast between the speaker's formal slumber and the loved one's present slumber. But there is one ironical contrast which he does stress: this is the contrast between the two senses in which the girl becomes insulated against the "touch of earthly years." In the first stanza, she "could not feel / The touch of earthly years" because she seemed divine and immortal. But in the second stanza, now in her grave, she still does not "feel the touch of earthly years," for, like the rocks and stones, she feels nothing at all. It is true that Wordsworth does not repeat the verb "feels"; instead he writes "She neither *hears* nor *sees*." But the contrast, though not commented upon directly by any device of verbal wit, is there nonetheless, and is bound to make itself felt in any sensitive reading of the poem. The statement of the first stanza has been literally realized in the second, but its meaning has been ironically reversed.

Ought we, then, to apply the term *ironical* to Wordsworth's poem? Not necessarily. I am trying to account for my temptation to call such a poem ironical — not to justify my yielding to the temptation — least of all to insist that others so transgress. Moreover, Wordsworth's poem seems to me admirable, and I entertain no notion that it might have been more admirable still had John Donne written it rather than William Wordsworth. I shall be content if I can make a much more modest point: namely, that since both Wordsworth and Donne are poets, their work has at basis a similar structure, and that the dynamic structure — the pattern of thrust and counterthrust — which we associate with Donne has its counterpart in Wordsworth. In the work of both men, the relation between part and part is organic, which means that each part modifies and is modified by the whole.

Yet to intimate that there are potential ironies in Wordsworth's lyric may seem to distort it. After all, is it not simple and spontaneous? With these terms we encounter two of the critical catchwords of the nineteenth century, even as *ironical* is in danger of becoming a catchword of our own period. Are the terms *simple* and *ironical* mutually exclusive? What after all do we mean by *simple* or by *spontaneous?* We may mean that the poem came to the poet easily and even spontaneously: very complex poems may — indeed have — come just this way. Or the poem may seem in its effect on the reader a simple and spontaneous utterance: some poems of great complexity possess this quality. What is likely to cause trouble here is the intrusion of a special theory of composition. It is fairly represented as an intrusion since a theory as to how a poem is written is being allowed to dictate to us how the poem is to be read. There is no harm in thinking of Wordsworth's poem as simple and spontaneous unless these terms deny complexities that actually exist in the poem, and unless they justify us in reading the poem with only half our minds. A slumber ought not to seal the *reader's* spirit as he reads this poem, or any other poem.

I have argued that irony, taken as the acknowledgment of the pressures of context, is to be found in poetry of every period and even in simple lyrical poetry. But in the poetry of our own time, this pressure reveals itself strikingly. A great deal of modern poetry does use irony as its special and perhaps its characteristic strategy. For this there are reasons, and compelling reasons. To cite only a few of these reasons: there is the breakdown of a common symbolism; there is the general scepticism as to universals;

not least important, there is the depletion and corruption of the very language itself, by advertising and by the mass produced arts of radio, the moving picture, and pulp fiction. The modern poet has the task of rehabilitating a tired and drained language so that it can convey meanings once more with force and with exactitude. This task of qualifying and modifying language is perennial; but it is imposed on the modern poet as a burden. Those critics who attribute the use of ironic techniques to the poet's own bloodless sophistication and tired scepticism would be better advised to refer these vices to his potential readers, a public corrupted by Hollywood and the Book of the Month Club. For the modern poet is not addressing simple primitives but a public sophisticated by commercial art.

At any rate, to the honor of the modern poet be it said that he has frequently succeeded in using his ironic techniques to win through to clarity and passion. Randall Jarrell's "Eighth Air Force" represents a success of this sort.

> If, in an odd angle of the hutment,
> A puppy laps the water from a can
> Of flowers, and the drunk sergeant shaving
> Whistles *O Paradiso!*—shall I say that man
> Is not as men have said: a wolf to man?
>
> The other murderers troop in yawning;
> Three of them play Pitch, one sleeps, and one
> Lies counting missions, lies there sweating
> Till even his heart beats: One; One; One.
> *O murderers!* . . . Still, this is how it's done:
>
> This is a war. . . . But since these play, before they die,
> Like puppies with their puppy; since, a man,
> I did as these have done, but did not die—
> I will content the people as I can
> And give up these to them: Behold the man!
>
> I have suffered, in a dream, because of him
> Many things; for this last saviour, man,
> I have lied as I lie now. But what is lying?
> Men wash their hands, in blood, as best they can:
>   I find no fault in this just man.

There are no superfluous parts, no dead or empty details. The airmen in their hutment are casual enough and honest enough to be convincing. The raw building is domesticated: there are the flowers in water from which the mascot, a puppy, laps. There is the drunken sergeant, whistling an opera aria as he shaves. These "murderers," as the poet is casually to call the airmen in the next stanza, display a touching regard for the human values. How, then, can one say that man is a wolf to man, since these men "play before they die, like puppies with their puppy." But the casual presence of the puppy in the hutment allows us to take the stanza both ways, for the dog is a kind of tamed and domesticated wolf, and his presence may prove on the contrary that the hutment is the wolf den. After all, the timber wolf plays with its puppies.

The second stanza takes the theme to a perfectly explicit conclusion. If three of the men play pitch, and one is asleep, at least one man is awake and counts himself and his companions murderers. But his unvoiced cry "O murderers" is met, countered, and dismissed with the next two lines: ". . . Still this is how it's done: / This is a war. . . ."

The note of casuistry and cynical apology prepares for a brilliant and rich resolving image, the image of Pontius Pilate, which is announced specifically in the third stanza:

> I will content the people as I can
> And give up these to them: behold the man!

Yet if Pilate, as he is first presented, is a jesting Pilate, who asks "What is truth?" it is a bitter and grieving Pilate who concludes the poem. It is the integrity of Man himself that is at stake. Is man a cruel animal, a wolf, or is he the last savior, the Christ of our secular religion of humanity?

The Pontius Pilate metaphor, as the poet uses it, becomes a device for tremendous concentration. For the speaker (presumably the young airman who cried "O murderers") is himself the confessed murderer under judgment, and also the Pilate who judges, and, at least as a representative of man, the savior whom the mob would condemn. He is even Pilate's better nature, his wife, for the lines "I have suffered, in a dream, because of him, / Many things" is merely a rearrangement of Matthew 27:19, the speech of Pilate's wife to her husband. But this last item is more than a reminiscence of the scriptural scene. It reinforces the speaker's present dilemma. The modern has had high hopes for man; are the hopes merely a dream? Is man incorrigible, merely a cruel beast? The speaker's present torture springs from that hope and from his reluctance to dismiss it as an empty dream. This Pilate is even harder-pressed than was the Roman magistrate. For he must convince himself of this last savior's innocence. But he has lied for him before. He will lie for him now.

Men wash their hands, in blood, as best they can:
I find no fault in this just man.

What is the meaning of "Men wash their hands, in blood, as best they can?" It can mean: Since my own hands are bloody, I have no right to condemn the rest. It can mean: I know that man can love justice, even though his hands are bloody, for there is blood on mine. It can mean: Men are essentially decent: they try to keep their hands clean even if they have only blood in which to wash them.

None of these meanings cancels out the others. All are relevant, and each meaning contributes to the total meaning. Indeed, there is not a facet of significance which does not receive illumination from the figure.

Some of Jarrell's weaker poems seem weak to me because they lean too heavily upon this concept of the goodness of man. In some of them, his approach to the theme is too direct. But in this poem, the affirmation of man's essential justness by a Pilate who contents the people as he washes his hands in blood seems to me to supply every qualification that is required. The sense of self-guilt, the yearning to believe in man's justness, the knowledge of the difficulty of so believing—all work to render accurately and dramatically the total situation.

It is easy at this point to misapprehend the function of irony. We can say that Jarrell's irony pares his theme down to acceptable dimensions. The theme of man's goodness has here been so qualified that the poet himself does not really believe in it. But this is not what I am trying to say. We do not ask a poet to bring his poem into line with our personal beliefs—still less to flatter our personal beliefs. What we do ask is that the poem dramatize the situation so accurately, so honestly, with such fidelity to the total situation that it is no longer a question of our beliefs, but of our participation in the poetic experience. At his best, Jarrell manages to bring us, by an act of imagination, to the most penetrating insight. Partici-

pating in that insight, we doubtless become better citizens. (One of the "uses" of poetry, I should agree, is to make us better citizens.) But poetry is not the eloquent rendition of the citizen's creed. It is not even the accurate rendition of his creed. Poetry must carry us beyond the abstract creed into the very matrix out of which, and from which, our creeds are abstracted. That is what "The Eighth Air Force" does. That is what, I am convinced, all good poetry does.

For the theme in a genuine poem does not confront us as abstraction—that is, as one man's generalization from the relevant particulars. Finding its proper symbol, defined and refined by the participating metaphors, the theme becomes a part of the reality in which we live—an insight, rooted in and growing out of concrete experience, many-sided, three-dimensional. Even the resistance to generalization has its part in this process—even the drag of the particulars away from the universal—even the tension of opposing themes—play their parts. The kite properly loaded, tension maintained along the kite string, rises steadily *against* the thrust of the wind.

Note

1. This is not to say, of course, that such statements are not related to a particular "universe of discourse." They are indeed, as are all statements of whatever kind. But I distinguish here between "context" and "universe of discourse." "Two plus two equals four" is not dependent on a special dramatic context in the way in which a "statement" made in a poem is. Compare "two plus two equals four" and the same "statement" as contained in Housman's poem:

   —To think that two and two are four
     And neither five nor three
   The heart of man has long been sore
     And long 'tis like to be.

The Structure of the Concrete Universal

W. K. Wimsatt, Jr.

W. K. Wimsatt, one of the foremost theoreticians of formal criticism, here examines a question that has long interested philosophers of literature: "how a work of literature can be either more individual (unique) or more universal than other kinds of writing, or how it can combine the individual and the universal more than other kinds." A good formalist, Wimsatt finds the heart of the mystery in the idea of metaphor — "the structure most characteristic of concentrated poetry." And, like Cleanth Brooks, he concludes that the good poem will take in more of experience than the weak poem will: "The unity and maturity of good poems are two sides of the same thing. The kind of unity which we look for and find in poetry is attained only through a degree of complexity in design which itself involves maturity and richness." Having located the value of poetry in its form, Wimsatt argues that studies of authors, readers, and literary periods are simply off the point, for only an "objective" criticism carefully focused on the "form" of the verbal object can hope to tell us much about the meaning and value of poetry.

The central argument of this essay, concerning what I shall call the "concrete universal," proceeds from the observation that literary theorists have from early times to the present persisted in making statements which in their contexts seem to mean that a work of literary art is in some peculiar sense a very individual thing or a very universal thing or both. What that paradox can mean, or what important fact behind the paradox has been discerned by such various critics as Aristotle, Plotinus, Hegel, and Ransom, it will be the purpose of the essay to inquire, and by the inquiry to discuss not only a significant feature of metaphysical poetics from Aristotle to the present day but the relation between metaphysical poetics and more practical and specific rhetorical analysis. In the brief historical survey which forms one part of this essay it will not be my purpose to suggest that any of these writers meant exactly what I shall mean in later parts where I describe the structure of poetry. Yet throughout the essay I shall proceed on the theory not only that men have at different times used the same terms and have meant differently, but that they have sometimes used different terms and have meant the same or somewhat the same. In other words, I assume that there is continuity in the problems of criticism, and that a person who studies poetry today has a legitimate interest in what Plato said about poetry.

The view of common terms and their relations to classes of things from which I shall start is roughly that which one may read in the logic of J. S. Mill, a view which is not much different from the semantic view of today and for most purposes not much different from the Aristotelian and scholastic view. Mill speaks of the word and its denotion and connotation (the term, referent and reference, the sign, denotatum and designatum[1] of more recent terminologies). The denotation is the *it*, the individual thing or the aggregate of things to which the term may refer; the connotation is the *what*, the quality or classification inferred for the *it*, or implicitly predicated by the application of the term or the giving of the name.* One main difference between all modern positivistic, nominalistic, and semantic systems and the scholastic and classical systems is that the older ones stress the similarity of the individuals denoted by the common term and hence the real universality of meaning, while the modern systems stress the differences in the individuals, the constant flux even of each individual in time and space and its kinetic structure, and hence infer only an approximate or nominal universality of meaning and a convenience rather than a truth in the use of general terms. A further difference lies in the view of how the individual is related

to the various connotations of terms which may be applied to it. That is, to the question: What is it? the older writers seem to hold there is but one (essentially right) answer, while the moderns accept as many answers as there are classes to which the individual may be assigned (an indefinite number). The older writers speak of a proper essence or whatness of the individual, a quality which in some cases at least is that designated by the class name most commonly applied to the individual: a bench is a bench, essentially a bench, accidentally a heavy wooden object or something covered with green paint. "When we say *what* it is," observes Aristotle, "we do not say 'white,' or 'hot,' or 'three cubits long,' but 'a man' or 'a god.' "[2] And this view is also a habit scarcely avoidable in our own daily thinking, especially when we think of living things or of artifacts, things made by us or our fellows for a purpose. What is it? Bench, we think, is an adequate answer. An assemblage of sticks painted green, we consider freakish.

II

Whether or not one believes in universals, one may see the persistence in literary criticism of a theory that poetry presents the concrete and the universal, or the individual and the universal, or an object which in a mysterious and special way is both highly general and highly particular. The doctrine is implicit in Aristotle's two statements that poetry imitates action and that poetry tends to express the universal. It is implicit again at the end of the classic period in the mystic doctrine of Plotinus, who in his later writing on beauty reverses the Platonic objection that art does not know the ultimate reality of the forms. Plotinus arrives at the view that the artist by a kind of bypass of the inferior natural productions of the world soul reaches straight to the forms that lie behind in the divine intelligence.[3] Another version of the classic theory, with affinities for Plotinus, lies in the scholastic phrase *resplendentia formae*.

Cicero's account of how Zeuxis painted an ideal Helen from the five most beautiful virgins of Crotona is a typical development of Aristotelian theory, in effect the familiar neoclassic theory found in Du Fresnoy's *Art of Painting*, in the writings of Johnson, especially in the tulip passage in *Rasselas*, and in the *Discourses* and *Idlers* of Reynolds. The business of the poet is not to number the streaks of the tulip; it is to

---

*The terms "denotation" and "connotation" are commonly and loosely used by literary critics to distinguish the dictionary meaning of a term (denotation) from the vaguer aura of suggestion (connotation). Both these are parts of the connotation in the logical sense.

give us not the individual, but the species. The same thing is stated in a more complicated way by Kant in telling how the imagination constructs the "aesthetical normal Idea":

> It is the image for the whole race, which floats among all the variously different intuitions of individuals, which nature takes as archetype in her productions of the same species, but which seems not to be fully reached in any individual case.[4]

And Hegel's account is as follows:

> The work of art is not only for the sensuous apprehension as sensuous object, but its position is of such a kind that as sensuous it is at the same time essentially addressed to the *mind*.[5]

> In comparison with the show or semblance of immediate sensuous existence or of historical narrative, the artistic semblance has the advantage that in itself it points beyond self, and refers us away from itself to something spiritual which it is meant to bring before the mind's eye. . . . The hard rind of nature and the common world give the mind more trouble in breaking through to the idea than do the products of art.[6]

The excellence of Shakespeare, says Coleridge, consists in a "union and interpenetration of the universal and particular." In one terminology or another this idea of a concrete universal is found in most metaphysical aesthetic of the eighteenth and nineteenth centuries.

A modern literary critic, John Crowe Ransom, speaks of the argument of a poem (the universal) and a local texture or tissue of concrete irrelevance. Another literary critic, Allen Tate, manipulating the logical terms "extension" and "intension," has arrived at the concept of "tension" in poetry. "Extension," as logicians use the word, is the range of individuals denoted by a term (denotation); "intension" is the total of qualities connoted (connotation). In the ordinary or logical use of the terms, extension and intension are of inverse relationship—the wider the one, the shallower the other. A poem, says Tate, as I interpret him, is a verbal structure which in some peculiar way has both a wide extension and a deep intension.

Not all these theories of the concrete universal lay equal stress on the two sides of the paradox, and it seems indicative of the vitality of the theory and of the truth implicit in it that the two sides have been capable of exaggeration into antithetic schools and

theories of poetry. For Du Fresnoy, Johnson, and Reynolds poetry and painting give the universal; the less said about the particulars the better. This is the neoclassic theory, the illustrations of which we seek in Pope's *Essay on Man* or in Johnson's *Ramblers*, where the ideas are moral and general and concerned with "nature," "one clear, unchanged, and universal light." The opposite theory had notable expression in England, a few years before Johnson wrote *Rasselas*, in Joseph Warton's *Essay on Pope*:

> A minute and particular enumeration of circumstances judiciously selected, is what chiefly discriminates poetry from history, and renders the former, for that reason, a more close and faithful representation of nature than the latter.

And Blake's marginal criticism of Reynolds was: "THIS Man was Hired to Depress art." "To Generalize is to be an Idiot. To Particularize is the Alone Distinction of Merit. General Knowledges are those Knowledges that Idiots possess." "Sacrifice the Parts: What becomes of the whole?" The line from Warton's *Essay* to Croce's *Aesthetic* seems a straight and obvious one, from Thomson's specific descriptions of flowers to the individual act of intuition-expression which is art—its opposite and enemy being the concept or generality.[7] The two views of art (two that can be held by different theorists about the same works of art) may be startlingly contrasted in the following passages about fictitious character—one a well known statement by Johnson, the other by the philosopher of the *élan vital*.

> [Shakespeare's] characters are not modified by the customs of particular places, unpractised by the rest of the world; by the peculiarities of studies or professions, which can operate but upon small numbers; or by the accidents of transient fashions or temporary opinions: they are the genuine progeny of common humanity, such as the world will always supply, and observation will always find. His persons act and speak by the influence of those general passions and principles by which all minds are agitated, and the whole system of life is continued in motion. In the writings of other poets a character is too often an individual; in those of Shakespeare it is commonly a species.
>
> Hence it follows that art always aims at what is *individual*. What the artist fixes on his canvas is something he has seen at a certain spot, on a certain day, at a certain hour, with a colouring that

will never be seen again. What the poet sings of is a certain mood which was his, and his alone, and which will never return. . . . Nothing could be more unique than the character of Hamlet. Though he may resemble other men in some respects, it is clearly not on that account that he interests us most.[8]

Other critics, notably the most ancient and the most modern, have tried to hold the extremes together. Neither of the extremes gives a good account of art and each leads out of art. The theory of particularity leads to individuality and originality (Edward Young was another eighteenth century Crocean), then to the idiosyncratic and the unintelligible and to the psychology of the author, which is not in the work of art and is not a standard for judgment. The theory of universality as it appears in Johnson and Reynolds leads to platitude and to a standard of material objectivity, the average tulip, the average human form, some sort of average.[9]

III

"Just representations of general nature," said Johnson, and it ought to be noted, though it perhaps rarely is, that two kinds of generality are involved, as indeed they are in the whole neoclassic theory of generality. There is the generality of logic or classification, of the more general as opposed to the more specific, "essential" generality, one might say. And there is the generality of literal truth to nature, "existential" generality. The assumption of neoclassic theory seems to be that these two must coincide. As a matter of fact they may and often do, but need not. Thus: "purple cow" is a more general (less specific) term and concept than "tan cow with a broken horn," yet the latter is more general or true to nature. We have, in short, realism or fantasy, and in either there may be various degrees of the specific or the general. We have *A Journal of the Plague Year* and *The Rambler, Gulliver's Travels* and *Rasselas*. The fact that there are a greater number of "vicissitudes" and "miscarriages" (favorite *Rambler* events) in human experience than plagues at London, that there are more tan cows than tan cows with broken horns, makes it true in a sense that a greater degree of essential generality involves a greater degree of existential. But in this sense the most generally reliable concept is simply that of "being."

The question is how a work of literature can be either more individual (unique) or more universal than other kinds of writing, or how it can combine the individual and the universal more than other kinds. Every description in words, so far as it is a direct description ("The barn is red and square") is a generalization. That is the nature of words. There are no individuals conveyed in words but only more or less specific generalizations, so that Johnson is right, though we have to ask him what degree of verbal generality makes art, and whether "tulip" is a better or more important generality than "tulip with ten streaks," or whether "beauty" is not in fact a much more impressive generality than "tulip." On the other hand, one cannot deny that in some sense there are more tulips in poetry than pure abstracted beauty. So that Bergson is right too; only we shall have to ask him what degree of specificity in verbal description makes art. And he can never claim complete verbal specificity or individuality, even for Hamlet.

If he could, if a work of literary art could be looked on as an artifact or concrete physical work, the paradox for the student of universals would return from the opposite direction even more forcibly — as it does in fact for theorists of graphic art. If Reynolds' picture "The Age of Innocence" presents a species or universal, what species does it present? Not an Aristotelian essence — "a man," or "humanity," nor even a more specific kind of being such as "womanhood." For then the picture would present the same universal as Reynolds' portrait of Mrs. Siddons as "The Tragic Muse," and all differences between "The Age of Innocence" and "The Tragic Muse" would be aesthetically irrelevant. Does the picture then present girlhood, or barefoot girlhood, or barefoot girlhood in a white dress against a gloomy background? All three are equally valid universals (despite the fact that makeshift phrases are required to express two of them), and all three are presented by the picture. Or is it the title which tells us what universal is presented, "The Age of Innocence," and without the title should we not know the universal? The question will be: What in the individual work of art demands that we attribute to it one universal rather than another?

We may answer that for poetry it is the generalizing power of words already mentioned, and go on to decide that what distinguishes poetry from scientific or logical discourse is a degree of irrelevant concreteness in descriptive details. This is in effect what Ransom says in his doctrine of argument and local irrelevance, but it seems doubtful if the doctrine is not a version of the theory of ornamental metaphor. The argument, says Ransom, is the prose or scientific meaning, what the poem has in common with other kinds of writing. The irrelevance is a texture of concreteness which does not contribute anything to the argument but is somehow enjoyable or valuable for its own sake, the vehicle of a metaphor which one boards heedless of where it runs, whether crosstown or downtown—just for the ride. So Ransom nurses and refines the argument, and on one page he makes the remark that the poet searches for "suitability" in his particular phrases, and by suitability Ransom means "the propriety which consists in their denoting the particularity which really belongs to the logical object."[10] But the difference between "propriety" and relevance in such a context is not easy to see. And relevance is logic. The fact is that all concrete illustration has about it something of the irrelevant. An apple falling from a tree illustrates gravity, but apple and tree are irrelevant to the pure theory of gravity. It may be that what happens in a poem is that the apple and the tree are somehow made more than usually relevant.

Such a theory, not that of Johnson and Reynolds, not that of Warton and Bergson, not quite that of Ransom, is what I would suggest—yet less as a novelty than as something already widely implicit in recent poetical analyses and exegeses, in those of Empson, for instance, Tate, Blackmur, or Brooks. If a work of literature is not in a simple sense either more individual or more universal than other kinds of writing, it may yet be such an individual or such a complex of meaning that it has a special relation to the world of universals. Some acute remarks on this subject were made by Ruskin in a chapter of *Modern Painters* neglected today perhaps because of its distasteful ingredient of "noble emotion." Poetry, says Ruskin in criticizing Reynolds' *Idlers*, is not distinguished from history by the omission of details, nor for that matter by the mere addition of details. "There must be something either in the nature of the details themselves, or the method of using them, which invests them with poetical power." Their nature, one may add, as assumed through their relation to one another, a relation which may also be called the method of using them. The poetic character of details

consists not in what they say directly and explicitly (as if roses and moonlight were poetic) but in what by their arrangement they *show* implicitly.

IV

"One," observes Ben Jonson, thinking of literature, "is considerable two waies: either, as it is only separate, and by it self: or as being compos'd of many parts it beginnes to be one as those parts grow or are wrought together."[11] A literary work of art is a complex of detail (an artifact, if we may be allowed that metaphor for what is only a verbal object), a composition so complicated of human values that its interpretation is dictated by the understanding of it, and so complicated as to seem in the highest degree individual—a concrete universal. We are accustomed to being told, for example, that what makes a character in fiction or drama vital is a certain fullness or rotundity: that the character has many sides. Thus E. M. Forster:

> We may divide characters into flat and round. Flat characters were called "humours" in the seventeenth century, and are sometimes called types, and sometimes caricatures. In their purest form, they are constructed round a single idea or quality: when there is more than one factor in them, we get the beginning of the curve towards the round. The really flat character can be expressed in one sentence such as "I never will desert Mr. Micawber."

It remains to be said, however, that the many traits of the round character (if indeed it is one character and not a hodgepodge) are harmonized or unified, and that if this is so, then all the traits are chosen by a principle, just as are the traits of the flat character. Yet it cannot be that the difference between the round and flat character is simply numerical; the difference cannot be merely that the presiding principle is illustrated by more examples in the round character. Something further must be supposed—a special interrelation in the traits of the round character. Bobadil is an example of the *miles gloriosus,* a flat humour. He swears by "The foot of Pharaoh," takes tobacco, borrows money from his landlady, is found lying on a bench fully dressed with a hangover, brags about his feats at the siege of Strigonium, beats Cob, a poor water carrier, and so on. It is possible that he has numerically as many traits as Falstaff, one of the most vital of all characters. But one of the differences between Falstaff and Bobadil is that the things Falstaff says are funny; the things Bobadil says are not. Compared to Falstaff, Bobadil is unconscious, an opaque butt. There is the vitality of consciousness in Falstaff. And further there is the crowning complexity of self-consciousness. The fact that Morgann could devote a book to arguing that Falstaff is not a coward, that lately Professor Wilson has argued that at Gadshill Falstaff may exhibit, " 'all the common symptoms of the malady' of cowardice" and at the same time persuade the audience that he has " 'never once lost his self-possession,' " the fact that one can conceive that Falstaff in the Gadshill running-away scene really knows that his assailants are the Prince and Poins — all this shows that in Falstaff there is a kind of interrelation among his attributes, his cowardice, his wit, his debauchery, his presumption, that makes them in a special way an organic harmony. He is a rounded character not only in the sense that he is gross (a fact which may have tempted critics to speak of a rounded character) or in the sense that he is a bigger bundle of attributes, stuffed more full, than Bobadil or Ralph Roister Doister; but in the sense that his attributes make a circuit and connection. A kind of awareness of self (a high and human characteristic), with a pleasure in the fact, is perhaps the central principle which instead of simplifying the attributes gives each one a special function in the whole, a double or reflex value. Falstaff or such a character of self-conscious "infinite variety"* as Cleopatra are concrete universals because they have no class names, only their own proper ones, yet are structures of such precise variety and centrality that each demands a special interpretation in the realm of human values.

Character is one type of concrete universal; there are other types, as many perhaps as the central terms of criticism; but most can be learned I believe by examination of metaphor — the structure most characteristic of concentrated poetry. The language of poets, said Shelley, "is vitally metaphorical: that is, it marks the before unapprehended relations of things and perpetuates their apprehension." Wordsworth spoke of the abstracting and modifying powers of the imagination. Aristotle said that the greatest thing was the use of metaphor, because it meant an eye for

_____
*I do not mean that self-consciousness is the only principle of complexity in character, yet a considerable degree of it would appear to be a requisite for poetic interest.

resemblances. Even the simplest form of metaphor or simile ("My love is like a red, red rose") presents us with a special and creative, in fact a concrete, kind of abstraction different from that of science. For behind a metaphor lies a resemblance between two classes, and hence a more general third class. This class is unnamed and most likely remains unnamed and is apprehended only through the metaphor. It is a new conception for which there is no other expression. Keats discovering Homer is like a traveler in the realms of gold, like an astronomer who discovers a planet, like Cortez gazing at the Pacific. The title of the sonnet, "On First Looking into Chapman's Homer," seems to furnish not so much the subject of the poem as a fourth member of a central metaphor, the real subject of the poem being an abstraction, a certain kind of thrill in discovering, for which there is no name and no other description, only the four members of the metaphor pointing, as to the center of their pattern. The point of the poem seems to lie outside both vehicle and tenor.

To take a more complicated instance, Wordsworth's "Solitary Reaper" has the same basic metaphorical structure, the girl alone reaping and singing, and the two bird images, the nightingale in Arabian sands and the cuckoo among the Hebrides, the three figures serving the parallel or metaphorical function of bringing out the abstraction of loneliness, remoteness, mysterious charm in the singing. But there is also a kind of third-dimensional significance, in the fact that one bird is far out in the northern sea, the other far off in southern sands, a fact which is not part of the comparison between the birds and the girl. By an implication cutting across the plane of logic of the metaphor, the girl and the two birds suggest extension in space, universality, and world communication — an effect supported by other details of the poem such as the overflowing of the vale profound, the mystery of the Erse song, the bearing of the song away in the witness' heart, the past and future themes which the girl may be singing. Thus a central abstraction is created, of communication, telepathy in solitude, the prophetic soul of the wide world dreaming on things to come — an abstraction which is the effect not wholly of the metaphor elaborated logically (in a metaphysical way) but of a working on two axes, by association rather than by logic, by a three-dimensional complexity of structure.

To take yet a third instance, metaphoric structure may appear where we are less likely to realize it

explicitly—in poetic narratives, for example, ellipti-
cally concealed in the more obvious narrative outlines.
"I can bring you," writes Max Eastman, "examples of
diction that is metrical but not metaphoric—a great
part of the popular ballads, for example—and you
can hardly deny that they too are poetic." But the best
story poems may be analyzed, I believe, as metaphors
without expressed tenors, as symbols which speak for
themselves. "La Belle Dame Sans Merci," for example
(if a literary ballad may be taken), is about a knight,
by profession a man of action, but sensitive, like the
lily and the rose, and about a faery lady with wild,
wild eyes. At a more abstract level, it is about the loss
of self in the mysterious lure of beauty—whether
women, poetry, or poppy. It sings the irretrievable departure from practical normality (the squirrel's gra-
nary is full), the wan isolation after ecstasy. Each
reader will experience the poem at his own level of experience or at several. A good story poem is like a
stone thrown into a pond, into our minds, where ever
widening concentric circles of meaning go out—and
this because of the structure of the story.

"A poem should not mean but be." It is an epi-
gram worth quoting in every essay on poetry. And
the poet "nothing affirmeth, and therefore never li-
eth." "Sit quidvis," said Horace, "simplex dumtaxat
et unum." It seems almost the reverse of the truth.
"Complex dumtaxat et unum"* would be better.
Every real poem is a complex poem, and only in
virtue of its complexity does it have artistic unity. A
newspaper poem by Edgar Guest[†] does not have this

---

*First Latin phrase, "Let each thing be only simple and a
unit"; second Latin phrase, "Only complex and a unit."
—ED.

[†]A reader whose judgment I esteem tells me that such a
name appears in a serious discussion of poetics anom-
alously and in bad taste. I have allowed it to remain (in
preference to some more dignified name of mediocrity)
precisely because I wish to insist on the existence of bad-
ness in poetry and so to establish an antithetic point of
reference for the discussion of goodness. Relativistic argument often creates an illusion in its own favor by moving
steadily in a realm of great and nearly great art. See, for
example, George Boas, *A Primer for Critics* (Baltimore,
1937), where a cartoon by Daumier appears toward the
end as a startling approach to the vulgar. The purpose of
my essay is not judicial but theoretical, that is, not to exhibit original discoveries in taste, but to show the relationship between examples acknowledged to lie in the realms
of the good and the bad.

kind of unity, but only the unity of an abstractly
stated sentiment.

The principle is expressed by Aristotle when he
says that beauty is based on unity in variety, and by
Coleridge when he says that "The Beautiful, contemplated in its essentials, that is, in *kind* and not in *degree*,
is that in which the *many*, still seen as many become
one," and that a work of art is "rich in proportion to
the variety of parts which it holds in unity."

V

It is usually easier to show how poetry works than to
show why anyone should want it to work in a given
way. Rhetorical analysis of poetry has always tended
to separate from evaluation, technique from worth.
The structure of poems as concrete and universal is
the principle by which the critic can try to keep the
two together. If it be granted that the "subject matter"
of poetry is in a broad sense the moral realm, human
actions as good or bad, with all their associated feelings, all the thought and imagination that goes with
happiness and suffering (if poetry submits "the
shews of things to the desires of the Mind"), then the
rhetorical structure of the concrete universal, the
complexity and unity of the poem, is also its maturity
or sophistication of richness or depth, and hence its
value. Complexity of form is sophistication of content. The unity and maturity of good poems are two
sides of the same thing. The kind of unity which we
look for and find in poetry is attained only through a
degree of complexity in design which itself involves
maturity and richness. For a visual diagram of the
metaphysics of poetry one might write vertically the
word complexity, a column, and give it a head with
Janus faces, one looking in the rhetorical direction,
unity, and the other in the axiological, maturity.

A final point to be made is that a criticism of structure and of value is an objective criticism. It rests on
facts of human psychology (as that a man may love
a woman so well as to give up empires), facts, which
though psychological, yet are so well acknowledged
as to lie in the realm of what may be called public
psychology—a realm which one should distinguish
from the private realm of the author's psychology
and from the equally private realm of the individual
reader's psychology (the vivid pictures which poetry
or stories are supposed to create in the imagination,
or the venerable action of catharsis—all that poetry
is said to *do* rather than to *be*). Such a criticism, again,
is objective and absolute, as distinguished from the

relative criticism of idiom and period. I mean that this criticism will notice that Pope is different from Shakespeare, but will notice even more attentively that Shakespeare is different from Taylor the Water Poet and Pope different from Sir Richard Blackmore. Such a criticism will be interested to analyze the latter two differences and see what these differences have in common and what Shakespeare and Pope have in common, and it will not despair of describing that similarity (that formula or character of great poetry) even though the terms be abstract and difficult. Or, if we are told that there is no universal agreement about what is good — that Pope has not been steadily held in esteem, that Shakespeare has been considered a barbarian, the objective analyst of structures can at least say (and it seems much to say) that he is describing a class of poems, those which through a peculiar complexity possess unity and maturity and in a special way can be called both individual and universal. Among all recorded "poems," this class is of a relative rarity, and further this class will be found in an impressive way to coincide with those poems which have by some body of critics, some age of educated readers, been called great.

The function of the objective critic is by approximate descriptions of poems, or multiple restatements of their meaning, to aid other readers to come to an intuitive and full realization of poems themselves and hence to know good poems and distinguish them from bad ones. It is of course impossible to tell all about a poem in other words. Croce tells us, as we should expect him to, of the "impossibility of ever rendering in logical terms the full effect of any poetry or of other artistic work." "Criticism, nevertheless," he tells us, "performs its own office, which is to discern and to point out exactly where lies the poetical motive and to formulate the divisions which aid in distinguishing what is proper to every work."[12] The situation is something like this: In each poem there is something (an individual intuition — or a concept) which can never be expressed in other terms. It is like the square root of two or like pi, which cannot be expressed by rational numbers, but only as their *limit*. Criticism of poetry is like 1.414 . . . or 3.1416 . . . , not all it would be, yet all that can be had and very useful.

Notes

1. Charles W. Morris, "Esthetics and the Theory of Signs," in *Journal of Unified Science*, VIII (1939), 131–50.

2. *Metaphysics*, VII (Z), 1 (1028). Cp. Mortimer J. Adler, *The Problem of Species* (New York, 1940), 24–25.

3. "The arts are not to be slighted on the ground that they create by imitation of natural objects; for, to begin with, these natural objects are themselves imitations; then, we must recognize that they give no bare reproduction of the thing seen but go back to the ideas from which Nature itself derives." *Enneads*, V, viii, 1, *Plotinus — The Fifth Ennead*, Stephen MacKenna, tr. (London, 1926), 74.

4. *Kant's Critique of Judgment*, J. H. Bernard, tr. (London, 1931), 88–89.

5. *The Introduction to Hegel's Philosophy of Fine Art*, Bernard Bosanquet, tr. (London, 1886), 67. Cp. Walter T. Stace, *The Meaning of Beauty* (London, 1929), 41.

6. *The Introduction to Hegel's Philosophy of Fine Art*, 16. Cp. pp. 72–78, 133–37.

7. It is true that Croce has protested: "Ce qu'on démontre comme inconciliable avec le principe de la pure intuition, ce n'est pas l'universalité, mais la valeur intellectualiste et transcendante donnée dans l'art à l'universalité, sous la forme de l'allégorie ou du symbole." "Le Caractère de Totalité de l'Expression Artistique," in *Bréviaire d'Esthétique*, Georges Bourgin, tr. (Paris, 1923), 170. But the main drift of Croce's aesthetic, in being against conceptualization, is radically against the universal.

8. Henri Bergson, *Laughter, An Essay on the Meaning of the Comic* (New York, 1928), 161–62.

9. Roger Fry in his Introduction to Reynolds' *Third Discourse* argues that the species presented in painting are not those of the natural, but those of the social world, as king, knight, beggar. *Discourses*, Roger Fry, ed. (London, 1905), 46. And a modern critic of sculpture, R. H. Wilenski, offers what is perhaps the last retreat of the doctrine of universals in visual art: not man, flower, or animal but the forms of life analogous in (that is, common to) man, flower, and animal are abstracted and presented pure in sculptural art. R. H. Wilenski, *The Meaning of Modern Sculpture* (London, 1939), 159–60.

10. *The New Criticism* (Norfolk, 1941), 315. Maritain, coming from a different direction, arrives at somewhat the same poser. "If it pleases a futurist to paint a lady with only one eye, or a quarter of an eye, nobody denies him such a right: all

one is entitled to require—and here is the whole problem—is that the quarter eye is all the lady needs *in the given case.*" *Art and Scholasticism* (New York, 1937), 28. Here indeed is the whole problem. Aristotle said, "Not to know that a hind has no horns is a less serious matter than to paint it inartistically." *Poetics,* XXV, 5.

11. *Discoveries,* Maurice Castelain, ed. (Paris, 1906), 139. Jonson translates from Heinsius.
12. *Ariosto, Shakespeare and Corneille* (London, 1920), 146–47.

Technique as Discovery

Mark Schorer

Writing near mid century, Mark Schorer complains that although the arguments of formalists like Brooks and Wimsatt had largely carried the day for serious discussions of poetry, when it comes to prose fiction, the case for formal criticism had yet to be established. Readers of novels are still inclined to separate form from content and to locate value in a book's subject matter rather than in its art. But in fact, claims Schorer, the formalist argument holds for prose fiction just as surely as it holds for the carefully crafted lyric. Technique, strictly speaking, is "nearly everything" besides the raw experience that is the artist's starting point. It comprehends all those means by which that experience is converted to the achieved *content that is the finished work of art. Hence the formalist's claim that form and content are one and the same and that form* is *meaning. "Technique is the only means [the artist] has of discovering, exploring, developing his subject, of conveying its meaning, and, finally, of evaluating it." It follows, then, that "the writer capable of the most exacting technical scrutiny of his subject matter will produce works with the most satisfying content, works with thickness and resonance, works which reverberate, works with maximum meaning." But that "maximum meaning," we should remember, will be available only to those who read with careful attention to technique.*

To illustrate his case, Schorer focuses on two techniques: the artful use of language "to express the quality of the experience in question" and "the use of point of view not only as a mode of dramatic delimitation but, more particularly, of thematic definition." Applying these criteria first to two early novels, he finds Moll Flanders *a failure but* Wuthering Heights *a success, chiefly because Brontë had happened on a point of view that objectified her materials. "Technique alone objectifies the materials of art; hence technique alone evaluates those materials." Turning then to the twentieth century, Schorer argues that the fate of those writers who claimed to eschew technique in favor of some kind of direct mimesis of socially or psychologically compelling materials is instructive. Contrasting Wells with James and Lawrence with Joyce, he asserts that neither realism nor subjectivism can substitute for techniques adequate to discover the true meaning of experience. In a closing section that should be compared with the arguments of Alter and Paris in the mimetic chapter, Schorer is particularly scornful of those "realists" who see the mimetic impulse as an end in itself, a value that may override formal and thematic values. A thoroughgoing formalist, Schorer will not allow this separation. "In our committed realists, who deny the resources of art for the sake of life, whose technique forgives both innocence and slovenliness, there is a bush but it does not burn. . . . then, when we look again, we see that, really, the thing is dead."*

Modern criticism, through its exacting scrutiny of literary texts, has demonstrated with finality that in art beauty and truth are indivisible and one. The Keatsian overtones of these terms are mitigated and an old dilemma solved if for beauty we substitute form, and for truth, content. We may, without risk of loss, narrow them even more, and speak of technique and subject matter. Modern criticism has shown us that to speak of content as such is not to speak of art at all, but of experience; and that it is only when we speak of the *achieved* content, the form, the work of art as a work of art, that we speak as critics. The difference between content, or experience, and achieved content, or art, is technique.

When we speak of technique, then, we speak of nearly everything. For technique is the means by which the writer's experience, which is his subject matter, compels him to attend to it; technique is the only means he has of discovering, exploring, developing his subject, of conveying its meaning, and, finally, of evaluating it. And it follows that certain techniques are sharper tools than others, and will discover more; that the writer capable of the most exacting technical scrutiny of his subject matter will produce works with the most satisfying content, works with thickness and resonance, works which reverberate, works with maximum meaning.

We are no longer able to regard as seriously intended criticism of poetry which does not assume these generalizations; but the case for fiction has not yet been established. The novel is still read as though its content has some value in itself, as though the subject matter of fiction has greater or lesser value in itself, and as though technique were not a primary but a supplementary element, capable perhaps of not unattractive embellishments upon the surface of the subject, but hardly of its essence. Or technique is thought of in blunter terms than those that one associates with poetry, as such relatively obvious matters as the arrangement of events to create plot; or, within plot, of suspense and climax; or as the means of revealing character motivation, relationship, and development; or as the use of point of view, but point of view as some nearly arbitrary device for the heightening of dramatic interest through the narrowing or broadening of perspective upon the material, rather than as a means toward the positive definition of theme. As for the resources of language, these, somehow, we almost never think of as a part of the technique of fiction—language as used to create a certain texture and tone which in themselves state and define themes and meanings; or language, the counters of our ordinary speech, as forced, through conscious manipulation, into all those larger meanings that our ordinary speech almost never intends. Technique in fiction, all this is a way of saying, we somehow continue to regard as merely a means to organizing material which is "given" rather than as the means of exploring and defining the values in an area of experience which, for the first time *then*, are being given.

Is fiction still regarded in this odd, divided way because it is really less tractable before the critical suppositions which now seem inevitable to poetry? Let us look at some examples: two well-known novels of the past, both by writers who may be described as "primitive," although their relative innocence of technique is of a different sort—Defoe's *Moll Flanders* and Emily Brontë's *Wuthering Heights*; and three well-known novels of this century—*Tono Bungay*, by a writer who claimed to eschew technique; *Sons and Lovers*, by a novelist whose ideal of subject matter ("the poetry of the immediate present") led him in effect to eschew technique; and *A Portrait of the Artist as a Young Man*, by a novelist whose practice made claims for the supremacy of technique beyond those made by anyone in the past or by anyone else in this century.

Technique in fiction is, of course, all those obvious forms of it which are usually taken to be the whole of it, and many others; but for present purposes, let it be thought of in two respects particularly: the uses to which language, as language, is put to express the quality of the experience in question; and the uses of point of view not only as a mode of dramatic delimitation, but more particularly, of thematic definition. Technique is really what T. S. Eliot means by "convention": any selection, structure, or distortion, any form or rhythm imposed upon the world of action; by means of which, it should be added, our apprehension of the world of action is enriched or renewed. In this sense, everything is technique which is not the lump of experience itself, and one cannot properly say that a writer has no technique, or that he eschews technique, for, being a writer, he cannot do so. We can speak of good and bad technique, of adequate and inadequate, of technique which serves the novel's purpose, or disserves.

2

In the prefatory remarks to *Moll Flanders,* Defoe tells us that he is not writing fiction at all, but editing the journals of a woman of notorious character, and rather to instruct us in the necessities and the joys of virtue than to please us. We do not, of course, take these professions seriously, since nothing in the conduct of the narrative indicates that virtue is either more necessary or more enjoyable than vice. On the contrary, we discover that Moll turns virtuous only after a life of vice has enabled her to do so with security; yet it is precisely for this reason that Defoe's profession of didactic purpose has interest. For the actual morality which the novel enforces is the morality of any commercial culture, the belief that virtue pays—in worldly goods. It is a morality somewhat less than skin deep, having no relation to motives arising from a sense of good and evil, least of all, of evil-*in*-good, but exclusively from the presence or absence of food, drink, linen, damask, silver, and timepieces. It is the morality of measurement, and without in the least intending it, *Moll Flanders* is our classic revelation of the mercantile mind: the morality of measurement, which Defoe has completely neglected to measure. He fails not only to evaluate this material in his announced way, but to evaluate it at all. His announced purpose is, we admit, a pious humbug, and he meant us to read the book as a series of scandalous events; and thanks to his inexhaustible pleasure in excess and exagger-

ation, this element in the book continues to amuse us. Long before the book has been finished, however, this element has also become an absurdity; but not half the absurdity as that which Defoe did not intend at all—the notion that Moll could live a rich and full life of crime, and yet, repenting, emerge spotless in the end. The point is, of course, that she has no moral being, nor has the book any moral life. Everything is external. Everything can be weighed, measured, handled, paid for in gold, or expiated by a prison term. To this, the whole texture of the novel testifies—the bolts of goods, the inventories, the itemized accounts, the landlady's bills, the lists, the ledgers—all this, which taken together comprises what we call Defoe's method of circumstantial realism.

He did not come upon that method by any deliberation; it represents precisely his own world of value, the importance of external circumstance to Defoe. The point of view of Moll is indistinguishable from the point of view of her creator. We discover the meaning of the novel (at unnecessary length, without economy, without emphasis, with almost none of the distortions or the advantages of art) in spite of Defoe, not because of him. Thus the book is not the true chronicle of a disreputable female, but the true allegory of an impoverished soul, the author's; not an anatomy of the criminal class, but of the middle class. And we read it as an unintended comic revelation of self and of a social mode. Because he had no adequate resources of technique to separate himself from his material, thereby to discover and to define the meanings of his material, his contribution is not so much to fiction as to the history of fiction, and to social history.

The situation in *Wuthering Heights* is at once somewhat the same and yet very different. Here, too, the whole novel turns upon itself, but this time to its estimable advantage; here, too, is a revelation of what is perhaps the author's secret world of value, but this time, through what may be an accident of technique, the revelation is meaningfully accomplished. Emily Brontë may merely have stumbled upon the perspectives which define the form and the theme of her book. Whether she knew from the outset, or even at the end, what she was doing, we may doubt; but what she did and did superbly we can see.

We can assume, without at all becoming involved in the author's life but merely from the tone of somnambulistic excess which is generated by the writing itself, that this world of monstrous passion, of dark and gigantic emotional and nervous energy, is for the author, or was in the first place, a world of ideal value; and that the book sets out to persuade us of the moral magnificence of such unmoral passion. We are, I think, expected, in the first place, to take at their own valuation these demonic beings, Heathcliff and Cathy: as special creatures, set apart from the cloddish world about them by their heightened capacity for feeling, set apart, even, from the ordinary objects of human passion as, in their transcendent, sexless relationship, they identify themselves with an uncompromising landscape and cosmic force. Yet this is absurd, as much of the detail that surrounds it ("Other dogs lurked in other recesses") is absurd. The novelist Emily Brontë had to discover these absurdities to the girl Emily; her technique had to evaluate them for what they were, so that we are persuaded that it is not Emily who is mistaken in her estimate of her characters, but they who are mistaken in their estimate of themselves. The theme of the moral magnificence of unmoral passion is an impossible theme to sustain, and what interests us is that it was device—and, this time, mere mechanical device—which taught Emily Brontë—the needs of her temperament to the contrary, all personal longing and reverie to the contrary, perhaps—that this was indeed not at all what her material must mean as art. Technique objectifies.

To lay before us the full character of this passion, to show us how it first comes into being and then comes to dominate the world about it and the life that follows upon it, Emily Brontë gives her material a broad scope in time, lets it, in fact, cut across three generations. And to manage material which is so extensive, she must find a means of narration, points of view, which can encompass that material, and, in her somewhat crude concept of motive, justify its telling. So she chooses a foppish traveler who stumbles into this world of passionate violence, a traveler representing the thin and conventional emotional life of the far world of fashion, who wishes to hear the tale; and for her teller she chooses, almost inevitably, the old family retainer who knows everything, a character as conventional as the other, but this one representing not the conventions of fashion, but the conventions of the humblest moralism.

What has happened is, first, that she has chosen as her narrative perspective those very elements, conventional emotion and conventional morality, which her hero and heroine are meant to transcend

with such spectacular magnificence; and second, that she has permitted this perspective to operate throughout a long period of time. And these two elements compel the novelist to see what her unmoral passions come to. Moral magnificence? Not at all; rather, a devastating spectacle of human waste; ashes. For the time of the novel is carried on long enough to show Heathcliff at last an emptied man, burned out by his fever ragings, exhausted and willless, his passion meaningless at last. And it goes even a little further, to Lockwood, the fop, in the graveyard, sententiously contemplating headstones. Thus in the end the triumph is all on the side of the cloddish world, which survives.

Perhaps not all on that side. For, like Densher at the end of *The Wings of the Dove,* we say, and surely Hareton and the second Cathy say, "We shall never be again as we were!" But there is more point in observing that a certain body of materials, a girl's romantic daydreams, have, through the most conventional devices of fiction, been pushed beyond their inception in fancy to their meanings, their conception as a written book—that they, that is, are not at all as they were.

3

Technique alone objectifies the materials of art; hence technique alone evaluates those materials. This is the axiom which demonstrates itself so devastatingly whenever a writer declares under the urgent sense of the importance of his materials— whether these are autobiography, or social ideas, or personal passions—whenever such a writer declares that he cannot linger with technical refinements. That art will not tolerate such a writer H. G. Wells handsomely proves. His enormous literary energy included no respect for the techniques of his medium, and his medium takes its revenge upon his bumptiousness.

> I have never taken any very great pains about writing. I am outside the hierarchy of conscious and deliberate writers altogether. I am the absolute antithesis of Mr. James Joyce. . . . Long ago, living in close conversational proximity to Henry James, Joseph Conrad, and Mr. Ford Madox Hueffer, I escaped from under their immense artistic preoccupations by calling myself a journalist.

Precisely. And he escaped—he disappeared—from literature into the annals of an era.

Yet what confidence! "Literature," Wells said,

> is not jewelry, it has quite other aims than perfection, and the more one thinks of "how it is done" the less one gets it done. These critical indulgences lead along a fatal path, away from every natural interest towards a preposterous emptiness of technical effort, a monstrous egotism of artistry of which the later work of Henry James is the monumental warning. "It," the subject, the thing or the thought, has long since disappeared in these amazing works; nothing remains but the way it has been manipulated.

Seldom has a literary theorist been so totally wrong; for what we learn as James grows for us and Wells disappears is that without what he calls "manipulation," there *is* no "it," no "subject" in art. There is again only social history.

The virtue of the modern novelist—from James and Conrad down—is not only that he pays so much attention to his medium, but that, when he pays most, he discovers through it a new subject matter, and a greater one. Under the "immense artistic preoccupations" of James and Conrad and Joyce, the form of the novel changed, and with the technical change, analogous changes took place in substance, in point of view, in the whole conception of fiction. And the final lesson of the modern novel is that technique is not the secondary thing that it seemed to Wells, some external machination, a mechanical affair, but a deep and primary operation; not only that technique *contains* intellectual and moral implications, but that it *discovers* them. For a writer like Wells, who wished to give us the intellectual and the moral history of his times, the lesson is a hard one; it tells us that the order of intellect and the order of morality do not exist at all, in art, except as they are organized in the order of art.

Wells's ambitions were very large. "Before we have done, we will have all life within the scope of the novel." But that is where life already is, within the scope of the novel; where it needs to be brought is into novels. In Wells we have all the important topics in life, but no good novels. He was not asking too much of art, or asking that it include more than it happily can; he was not asking anything of it—as art, which is all that it can give, and that is everything.

A novel like *Tono Bungay,* generally thought to be Wells's best, is therefore instructive. "I want to tell— *myself,*" says George, the hero, "and my impressions of the thing as a whole"—the thing as a whole being the collapse of traditional British institutions in the twentieth century. George "tells himself" in terms of three stages in his life which have rough equivalents in modern British social history, and this is, to be sure, a plan, a framework; but it is the framework of Wells's abstract thinking, not of his craftsmanship, and the primary demand which one makes of such a book as this—that means be discovered whereby the dimensions of the hero contain the experiences he recounts—is never met. The novelist flounders through a series of literary imitations—from an early Dickensian episode, through a kind of Shavian interlude, through a Conradian episode, to a Jules Verne vision at the end. The significant failure is in that end, and in the way that it defeats not only the entire social analysis of the bulk of the novel, but Wells's own ends as a thinker. For at last George finds a purpose in science. "I decided that in power and knowledge lay the salvation of my life; the secret that would fill my need; that to these things I would give myself."

But science, power, and knowledge are summed up at last in a destroyer. As far as one can tell Wells intends no irony, although he may here have come upon the essence of the major irony in modern history. The novel ends in a kind of meditative rhapsody which denies every value that the book had been aiming toward. For of all the kinds of social waste which Wells has been describing, this is the most inclusive, the final waste. Thus he gives us in the end not a novel, but a hypothesis; not an individual destiny, but a theory of the future; and not his theory of the future, but a nihilistic vision quite opposite from everything that he meant to represent. With a minimum of attention to the virtues of technique, Wells might still not have written a great novel; but he would at any rate have established a point of view and a tone that would have told us what he meant.

To say what one means in art is never easy, and the more intimately one is implicated in one's material, the more difficult it is. If, besides, one commits fiction to a therapeutic function which is to be operative not on the audience but on the author, declaring, as D. H. Lawrence did, that "one sheds one's sicknesses in books—repeats and presents again one's emotions, to be master of them," the difficulty is vast. It is an acceptable theory only with the qualification that technique, which objectifies, is under no other circumstances so imperative. For merely to repeat one's emotions, merely to look into one's heart and write, is also merely to repeat the round of emotional bondage. If our books are to be exercises in self-analysis, then technique must—and alone can—take the place of the absent analyst.

Lawrence, in the introductory note to his *Collected Poems*, made a distinction between his "real" poems and what he seemed to think of as his "composed" poems, between the poems which expressed his demon directly and created their own form "willy-nilly," and the poems which, through the hocus-pocus of technique, he spuriously put together and could, if necessary, revise. His belief in a "poetry of . . . the immediate present," poetry in which nothing is fixed, static, or final, where all is shimmeriness and impermanence and vitalistic essence, arose from this notion of technique as a frustration of the demon, one's genius. And from this notion, an unsympathetic critic like D. S. Savage can construct a case which shows Lawrence driven "concurrently to the dissolution of personality and the dissolution of art." The argument suggests that Lawrence's early, crucial novel, *Sons and Lovers,* is another example of meanings confused by an impatience with technical resources.

The novel has two themes: the crippling effects of a mother's love on the emotional development of her son; and the "split" between kinds of love, physical and spiritual, which the son develops, the kinds represented by two young women, Clara and Miriam. The two themes should, of course, work together, the second being, actually, the result of the first: this "split" is the "crippling." So one would expect to see the novel developed, and so Lawrence, in his famous letter to Edward Garnett, where he says that Paul is left at the end "with the drift towards death," apparently thought he had developed it. Yet in the last few sentences of the novel, Paul rejects his desire for extinction and turns toward "the faintly humming, glowing town," to life—as nothing in his previous history persuades us that he could unfalteringly do.

The discrepancy suggests that the book may reveal certain confusions between intention and performance.

One of these is the contradiction between Lawrence's explicit characterization of the mother and father and his tonal evaluations of them. It is a problem not only of style (of the contradiction between expressed moral epithets and the more general texture of the prose which applies to them) but of point of view. Morel and Lawrence are never separated, which is a way of saying that Lawrence maintains for himself in this book the confused attitude of his character. The mother is a "proud, *honorable* soul," but the father has a "small, *mean* head." This is the sustained contrast; the epithets are characteristic of the whole, and they represent half of Lawrence's feelings. But what is the other half? Which of these characters is given his real sympathy—the hard, self-righteous, aggressive, demanding mother who comes through to us, or the simple, direct, gentle, downright, fumbling, ruined father? There are two attitudes here. Lawrence (and Morel) loves his mother, but he also hates her for compelling his love; and he hates his father with the true Freudian jealousy, but he also loves him for what he is in himself, and he sympathizes more deeply with him because his wholeness has been destroyed by the mother's domination, just as his, Lawrence-Morel's, has been.

This is a psychological tension which disrupts the form of the novel and obscures its meaning, because neither the contradiction in style nor the confusion in point of view is made to right itself. Lawrence is merely repeating his emotions, and he avoids an austerer technical scrutiny of his material because it would compel him to master them. He would not let the artist be stronger than the man.

The result is that, at the same time that the book condemns the mother, it justifies her; at the same time that it shows Paul's failure, it offers rationalizations which place the failure elsewhere. The handling of the girl, Miriam, if viewed closely, is pathetic in what it signifies for Lawrence, both as man and artist. For Miriam is made the mother's scapegoat, and in a different way from the way that she was in life. The central section of the novel is shot through with alternate statements as to the source of the difficulty: Paul is unable to love Miriam wholly, and Miriam can love only his spirit. These contradictions appear sometimes within single paragraphs, and the point of view is never adequately objectified and sustained to tell us which is true. The material is never seen as material; the writer is caught in it exactly as firmly as he was caught in his experience of it. "That's how women are with me," said Paul. "They want me like mad, but they don't want to belong to me." So he might have said, and believed it; but at the end of the novel, Lawrence is still saying that, and himself believing it.

For the full history of this technical failure, one must read *Sons and Lovers* carefully and then learn the history of the manuscript from the book called *D. H.*

Lawrence: A Personal Record, by one E. T., who was Miriam in life. The basic situation is clear enough. The first theme — the crippling effects of the mother's love — is developed right through to the end; and then suddenly, in the last few sentences, turns on itself, and Paul gives himself to life, not death. But all the way through, the insidious rationalizations of the second theme have crept in to destroy the artistic coherence of the work. A "split" would occur in Paul; but as the split is treated, it is superimposed upon rather than developed in support of the first theme. It is a rationalization made from it. If Miriam is made to insist on spiritual love, the meaning and the power of theme one are reduced; yet Paul's weakness is disguised. Lawrence could not separate the investigating analyst, who must be objective, from Lawrence, the subject of the book; and the sickness was not healed, the emotion not mastered, the novel not perfected. All this, and the character of a whole career, would have been altered if Lawrence had allowed his technique to discover the full meaning of his subject.

A Portrait of the Artist as a Young Man, like *Tono Bungay* and *Sons and Lovers,* is autobiographical, but unlike these it analyzes its material rigorously, and it defines the value and the quality of its experience not by appended comment or moral epithet, but by the texture of the style. The theme of *A Portrait,* a young artist's alienation from his environment, is explored and evaluated through three different styles and methods as Stephen Dedalus moves from childhood through boyhood into maturity. The opening pages are written in something like the Ulyssesean stream of consciousness, as the environment impinges directly on the consciousness of the infant and the child, a strange, opening world which the mind does not yet subject to questioning, selection, or judgment. But this style changes very soon, as the boy begins to explore his surroundings; and as his sensuous experience of the world is enlarged, it takes on heavier and heavier rhythms and a fuller and fuller body of sensuous detail, until it reaches a crescendo of romantic opulence in the emotional climaxes which mark Stephen's rejection of domestic and religious values. Then gradually the style subsides into the austere intellectuality of the final sections, as he defines to himself the outlines of the artistic task which is to usurp his maturity.

A highly self-conscious use of style and method defines the quality of experience in each of these sections, and, it is worth pointing out in connection with the third and concluding section, the style and method evaluate the experience. What has happened to Stephen is, of course, a progressive alienation from the life around him as he progressed in his initiation into it, and by the end of the novel, the alienation is complete. The final portion of the novel, fascinating as it may be for the developing esthetic creed of Stephen-Joyce, is peculiarly bare. The life experience was not bare, as we know from *Stephen Hero;* but Joyce is forcing technique to comment. In essence, Stephen's alienation is a denial of the human environment; it is a loss; and the austere discourse of the final section, abstract and almost wholly without sensuous detail or strong rhythm, tells us of that loss. It is a loss so great that the texture of the notation-like prose here suggests that the end is really all an illusion, that when Stephen tells us and himself that he is going forth to forge in the smithy of his soul the uncreated conscience of his race, we are to infer from the very quality of the icy, abstract void he now inhabits, the implausibility of his aim. For *Ulysses* does not create the conscience of the race; it creates our consciousness.

In the very last two or three paragraphs of the novel, the style changes once more, reverts from the bare, notative kind to the romantic prose of Stephen's adolescence. "Away! Away! The spell of arms and voices: the white arms of roads, their promise of close embraces and the black arms of tall ships that stand against the moon, their tale of distant nations. They are held out to say: We are alone — come." Might one not say that the austere ambition is founded on adolescent longing? That the excessive intellectual severity of one style is the counterpart of the excessive lyric relaxation of the other? And that the final passage of *A Portrait* punctuates the illusory nature of the whole ambition?

For *Ulysses* does not create a conscience. Stephen, in *Ulysses,* is a little older, and gripped now by guilt, but he is still the cold young man divorced from the human no less than the institutional environment. The environment of urban life finds a separate embodiment in the character of Bloom, and Bloom is as lost as Stephen, though touchingly groping for moorings. Each of the two is weakened by his inability to reach out, or to do more than reach out to the other. Here, then, is the theme again, more fully stated, as it were in counterpoint.

But if Stephen is not much older, Joyce is. He is older as an artist not only because he can create and lavish his godlike pity on a Leopold Bloom, but also because he knows now what both Stephen and Bloom mean, and *how much,* through the most brilliant technical operation ever made in fiction, they can be made to mean. Thus *Ulysses,* through the imaginative force which its techniques direct, is like a pattern of concentric circles, with the immediate human situation at its center, this passing on and out to the whole dilemma of modern life, this passing on and out beyond that to a vision of the cosmos, and this to the mythical limits of our experience. If we read *Ulysses* with more satisfaction than any other novel of this century, it is because its author held an attitude toward technique and the technical scrutiny of subject matter which enabled him to order, within a single work and with superb coherence, the greatest amount of our experience.

4

In the United States during the last twenty-five years, we have had many big novels but few good ones. A writer like James T. Farrell apparently assumes that by endless redundancy in the description of the surface of American life, he will somehow write a book with the scope of *Ulysses.* Thomas Wolfe apparently assumed that by the mere disgorging of the raw material of his experience he would give us at last our epic. But except in a physical sense, these men have hardly written novels at all.

The books of Thomas Wolfe were really journals, and the primary role of his editor in transforming these journals into the semblance of novels is well known. For the crucial act of the artist, the unique act which is composition, a sympathetic blue pencil and scissors were substituted. The result has excited many people, especially the young, and the ostensibly critical have observed the prodigal talent with the wish that it might have been controlled. Talent there was, if one means by talent inexhaustible verbal energy, excessive response to personal experience, and a great capacity for auditory imitativeness, yet all of this has nothing to do with the novelistic quality of the written result; for until the talent is controlled, the material organized, the content achieved, there is simply the man and his life. It remains to be demonstrated that Wolfe's conversations were any less interesting as novels than his books, which is to say that his books are without great interest as novels. Our response to the books is determined not so much by

their qualities as novels as by our response to him and his qualities as a temperament.

This is another way of saying that Thomas Wolfe never really knew what he was writing *about. Of Time and the River* is merely a euphemism for "Of a Man and His Ego." It is possible that had his conception of himself and of art included an adequate respect for technique and the capacity to pursue it, Wolfe would have written a great novel on his true subject — the dilemma of romantic genius; it was his true subject, but it remains his undiscovered subject, it is the subject which *we* must dig out for him, because he himself had neither the lamp nor the pick to find it in and mine it out of the labyrinths of his experience. Like Emily Brontë, Wolfe needed a point of view beyond his own which would separate his material and its effect.

With Farrell, the situation is opposite. He knows quite well what his subject is and what he wishes to tell us about it, but he hardly needs the novel to do so. It is significant that in sheer clumsiness of style no living writer exceeds him, for his prose is asked to perform no service beyond communication of the most rudimentary kind of fact. For his ambitions the style of the newspaper and the lens of the documentary camera would be quite adequate, yet consider the diminution which Leopold Bloom, for example, would suffer, if he were to be viewed from these technical perspectives. Under the eye of this technique, the material does not yield up enough; indeed, it shrinks.

More and more writers in this century have felt that naturalism as a method imposes on them strictures which prevent them from exploring through all the resources of technique the full amplifications of their subjects, and that thus it seriously limits the possible breadth of esthetic meaning and response. James Farrell is almost unique in the complacency with which he submits to the blunt techniques of naturalism; and his fiction is correspondingly repetitive and flat.

That naturalism had a sociological and disciplinary value in the nineteenth century is obvious; it enabled the novel to grasp materials and make analyses which had eluded it in the past, and to grasp them boldly; but even then it did not tell us enough of what, in Virginia Woolf's phrase, is "really real," nor did it provide the means to the maximum of reality coherently contained. Even the Flaubertian ideal of objectivity seems, today, an unnecessarily limited view of objectivity, for as almost every good writer of this century shows us, it is quite as possible to be objective about subjective states as it is to be objective about the circumstantial surfaces of life. Dublin, in *Ulysses,* is a moral setting: not only a city portrayed in the naturalistic fashion of Dickens's London, but also a map of the modern psyche with its oblique and baffled purposes. The second level of reality in no way invalidates the first, and a writer like Joyce shows us that, if the artist truly respects his medium, he can be objective about both at once. What we need in fiction is a devoted fidelity to every technique which will help us to discover and to evaluate our subject matter, and more than that, to discover the amplifications of meaning of which our subject matter is capable.

Most modern novelists have felt this demand upon them. André Gide allowed one of his artist-heroes to make an observation which considerably resembles an observation we have quoted from Wells.

> My novel hasn't got a subject . . . Let's say, if you prefer it, it hasn't got *one* subject . . . "A slice of life," the naturalist school said. The great defect of that school is that it always cuts its slice in the same direction; in time, lengthwise. Why not in breadth? Or in depth? As for me I should like not to cut at all. Please understand; I should like to put everything into my novel.

Wells, with his equally large blob of potential material, did not know how to cut it to the novel's taste; Gide cut, of course—in every possible direction. Gide and others. And those "cuts" are all the new techniques which modern fiction has given us. None, perhaps, is more important than that inheritance from French symbolism which Huxley, in the glittering wake of Gide, called "the musicalization of fiction." Conrad anticipated both when he wrote that the novel "must strenuously aspire to the plasticity of sculpture, to the colour of painting, and to the magic suggestiveness of music—which is the art of arts," and when he said of that early but wonderful piece of symbolist fiction, *Heart of Darkness,* "It was like another art altogether. That sombre theme had to be given a sinister resonance, a tonality of its own, a continued vibration that, I hoped, would hang in the air and dwell on the ear after the last note had been struck."

The analogy with music, except as a metaphor, is inexact, and except as it points to techniques which fiction can employ as fiction, not very useful to the sense of craftsmanship. It has had an approximate exactness in only one work, Joyce's final effort, an effort unique in literary history, *Finnegans Wake,* and here, of course, those readers willing to make the effort Joyce demands, discovering what appears to be an inexhaustible wealth and a scope beyond measure, are most forcibly reminded of the primary importance of technique to subject, and of their indivisibility.

The techniques of naturalism inevitably curtail subject and often leave it in its original area, that of undefined social experience. Those of our writers who, stemming from this tradition, yet, at their best, achieve a novelistic definition of social experience— writers like the occasional Sherwood Anderson, William Carlos Williams, the very early Erskine Caldwell, Nathanael West, and Ira Wolfert in *Tucker's People*—have done so by pressing naturalism far beyond itself, into positively Gothic distortions. The structural machinations of Dos Passos and the lyrical interruptions of Steinbeck are the maneuvers of men committed to a method of whose limitations they despair. They are our symbolists *manqué,* who end as allegorists.

Our most accomplished novels leave no such impressions of desperate and intentional struggle, yet their precise technique and their determination to make their prose work in the service of their subjects have been the measure of their accomplishment. Hemingway's *The Sun Also Rises* and Wescott's *The Pilgrim Hawk* are consummate works of art not because they may be measured by some external, neoclassic notion of form, but because their forms are so exactly equivalent with their subjects, and because the evaluation of their subjects exists in their styles.

Hemingway said that his contribution to younger writers lay in a certain necessary purification of the language; but the claim has doubtful value. The contribution of his prose was to his subject, and the terseness of style for which his early work is justly celebrated is no more valuable, as an end in itself, than the baroque involutedness of Faulkner's prose, or the cold elegance of Wescott's. Hemingway's early subject, the exhaustion of value, was perfectly investigated and invested by his bare style, and in story after story, no meaning at all is to be inferred from the fiction except as the style itself suggests that there is no meaning in life. This style, more than that, was the perfect technical substitute for the conventional commentator; it expresses and it measures that peculiar morality of the stiff lip which Hemingway borrowed from athletes. It is an instructive lesson, furthermore, to observe how the style breaks down when Hemingway moves into the less congenial subject matter of social affirmation: how the style breaks down, the effect of verbal economy as mute suffering, is lost, the personality of the writer, no longer protected by the objectification of an adequate technique, begins its offensive intrusion, and the entire structural integrity slackens. Inversely, in the stories and the early novels, the technique was the perfect embodiment of the subject and it gave that subject its astonishing largeness of effect and of meaning.

One should correct Buffon and say that style is the subject. In Wescott's *Pilgrim Hawk*—a novel which bewildered its many friendly critics by the apparent absence of subject—the subject, the story, is again in the style itself. This novel, which is a triumph of the sustained point of view, is only bewildering if we try to make a story out of the narrator's observations upon others; but if we read his observations as oblique and unrecognized observations upon himself the story emerges with perfect coherence, and it reverberates with meaning, is as suited to continuing reflection as the greatest lyrics.

The rewards of such respect for the medium as the early Hemingway and the occasional Wescott have shown may be observed in every good writer we have. The involutions of Faulkner's style are the perfect equivalent of his involved structures, and the two together are the perfect representation of the moral labyrinths through which he plunges and gropes, and of the ruined world which his novels repeatedly invoke and in which these labyrinths exist. The cultivated sensuosity of Katherine Anne Porter's style—as of Eudora Welty's and Carson McCullers's—has charm in itself, of course, but no more than with these others does it have esthetic value in itself; its values lie in the subtle means by which sensuous details become symbols, and in the way the symbols provide a network which is the story, and which at the same time provides the writer and us with a refined moral insight by means of which to test it. When we put such writers against a writer like William Saroyan, whose respect is reserved for his own temperament, we are appalled by the stylistic irresponsibility we find in him, and by the almost total absence of theme, or defined subject matter, and the abundance of unwarranted feeling. Such a writer inevitably becomes a sentimentalist be-

cause he has no means by which to measure his emotion. Technique, at last, is measure.

These writers, from Defoe to Porter, are of unequal and very different talent, and technique and talent are, of course, after a point, two different things. What Joyce gives us in one direction, Lawrence, for all his imperfections as a technician, gives us in another, even though it is not always the direction of art. In some of his stories and poems, where the demands of technique are less sustained and the subject matter is not autobiographical, Lawrence, who was less concerned with "perfection of the work" than of "the life," and in a quite different way from Joyce, comes to the same esthetic fulfillment. Emily Brontë, with what was perhaps her intuitive grasp of the need to establish a tension between her subject matter and her perspective upon it, achieves a similar fulfillment; and, curiously, in the same way and certainly by intuition alone, Hemingway's early work makes a moving splendor from nothingness.

And yet, whatever one must allow to talent and forgive in technique, one risks no generalization in saying that modern fiction at its best has been peculiarly conscious of itself and of its tools. The technique of modern fiction, at once greedy and fastidious, achieves as its subject matter not some singleness, some topic or thesis, but the whole of the modern consciousness. It discovers the complexity of the modern spirit, the difficulty of personal morality, and the fact of evil—all the untractable elements under the surface which a technique of the surface alone cannot approach. It shows us—in Conrad's words, from *Victory*—that we all live in an "age in which we are camped like bewildered travellers in a garish, unrestful hotel," and while it puts its hard light on our environment, it penetrates, with its sharp weapons, the depths of our bewilderment. These are not two things, but only an adequate technique can show them as one. In a realist like Farrell, we have the environment only, which we know from the newspapers; in a subjectivist like Wolfe, we have the bewilderment only, which we record in our own diaries and letters. But the true novelist gives them to us together, and thereby increases the effect of each, and reveals each in its full significance.

Elizabeth Bowen, writing of Lawrence, said of modern fiction, "We want the naturalistic surface, but with a kind of internal burning. In Lawrence every bush burns." But the bush burns brighter in some places than in others, and it burns brightest when a passionate private vision finds its objectification in exacting technical search. If the vision finds no such objectification, as in Wolfe and Saroyan, there is a burning without a bush. In our committed realists, who deny the resources of art for the sake of life, whose technique forgives both innocence and slovenliness, there is a bush but it does not burn. There, at first glance, the bush is only a bush; and then, when we look again, we see that, really, the thing is dead.

Reading
The Tempest

Russ McDonald

Like Paul Yachnin, Russ McDonald takes issue with
many of the recent new historical and cultural materialist interpretations of The Tempest, but while Yachnin
faults these for not paying enough attention to Shakespeare's time, McDonald faults them for not paying
enough attention to Shakespeare's text. Citing the essay
by Paul Brown in particular, McDonald notes that many
political readings do not simply ignore formal features
but are even "deliberately anti-aesthetic," fearful that
concentration on poetic features will distract our attention from the text's political implications. The result, according to McDonald, is interpretations as one-sided as
the earlier readings they claim to correct.

The true corrective in either case is close, careful
analysis with attention to "the most minute formal details." Such a reading discovers a more complex, ambiguous, and subtly nuanced text. "In The Tempest, as
in late Shakespeare generally, the effect of the poetry is to
promote uncertainty and to insist upon ambiguity, and
attention to the verse makes one increasingly dubious
about the bluntness of most political interpretation."
Some of the New Critics, McDonald acknowledges, may
have had their own ideological agendas, but formal
analysis is not itself an ideology. It is, rather, the surest
method to discover the true politics of a text. And despite
his reservations about the New Criticism, McDonald's
description of The Tempest sounds very much like
Cleanth Brooks's "Irony as a Principle of Structure":
"The play valorizes ambiguity and irony, ironizing its
own positions and insisting upon the inconclusiveness
of its own conclusions. The new orthodoxy, which exalts
the colonized, is as narrow as the old, which idealizes
and excuses the colonizer." In short, by failing to see
how the text means, we fail to see what it means.

Reprinted by permission of Cambridge University Press
and the author from *Shakespeare Survey* 43 (1991): 15–28.

My subject is *The Tempest* — how it has been read recently and how it might be read otherwise. My vehicle for approaching this subject is the poetic style, its most minute formal details. My immediate purpose is to read *The Tempest* in a way that offers an alternative to, and an implicit critique of, certain readings produced by American New Historicism and British Cultural Materialism. My larger aim is to discover uses for stylistic criticism that will reassert the value of textuality in a nontextual phase of criticism and that may contribute to the reconciliation of text and context, the aesthetic and the political.

I

It will come as no surprise to anyone who has followed developments in Renaissance studies that treatments of *The Tempest* seldom concern themselves with the verse. Recent criticism looks beyond textual details and formal properties to concentrate on cultural surroundings, addressing the play almost solely in terms of social and political contexts, particularly its relation to colonial discourse. The essay by Francis Barker and Peter Hulme in John Drakakis' *Alternative Shakespeares* is typical: 'The ensemble of fictional and lived practices, which for convenience we will simply refer to here as "English colonialism," provides *The Tempest*'s dominant discursive "contexts." We have chosen here to concentrate specifically on the figure of usurpation as the nodal point of the play's imbrication into this discourse of colonialism.'[1] If American New Historicists seem slightly less virulent than British Cultural Materialists, their concerns are scarcely less political and their methods similarly contextual.[2] The Virginia pamphlets, Shakespeare's personal association with contemporary colonial projects, Montaigne on cannibals, twentieth-century racism and political oppression and their relation to Caliban — these are the contexts that have dominated recent treatments of this text.[3]

Many of the readings that regard *The Tempest* primarily as what Paul Brown calls an "intervention" in European colonial history are tendentious in conception and narrow in scope. In disputing them, however, I do not wish to neglect their nuances nor to suppress the differences among them: Greenblatt's 1976 essay, "Learning to Curse: Aspects of Linguistic Colonialism in the Sixteenth Century," for example, contextualizes *The Tempest* in a way that is balanced and sensitive to ambiguity,[4] but recent readers have

become increasingly single-minded and reductive, often adopting a censorious and shrill tone in delineating the text's relation to the problems of cultural tyranny, political freedom, and exploitation. One of the most notable of these discussions, Paul Brown's "'This thing of darkness I acknowledge mine': *The Tempest* and the discourse of colonialism," printed in Dollimore and Sinfield's *Political Shakespeare*, states its purpose in a way that fairly represents the revisionist reading. "This chapter seeks to demonstrate that *The Tempest* is not simply a reflection of colonialist practices but an intervention in an ambivalent and even contradictory discourse. This intervention takes the form of a powerful and pleasurable narrative which seeks at once to harmonise disjunction, to transcend irreconcilable contradictions and to mystify the political conditions which demand colonialist discourse. Yet the narrative ultimately fails to deliver that containment and instead may be seen to foreground precisely those problems which it works to efface or overcome."[5] Something like this point of view is expressed more succinctly by Walter Cohen: "*The Tempest* uncovers, perhaps despite itself, the racist and imperialist bases of English nationalism."[6] And some critics decline to treat the work at all. Richard Strier, for example, considers *The Tempest* "more conservative than the plays, from *Hamlet* on, which precede it,"[7] and the adjective is not intended as a compliment.

As these remarks show, a basic argumentative move on the part of many poststructuralist critics has been to attack the play's sophistication. This gambit follows an earlier one, a critical usurpation of the dramatic sovereignty of Prospero and a concomitant attack on the idealist reading set forth in Frank Kermode's Introduction to the Arden edition.[8] Having cast the benevolent Prospero out to sea, New Historicists and Cultural Materialists have sought to exert their hegemony over the text (and interpretation of it) by urging the claims of discourse, usually asserting that *The Tempest* cannot be aware of its own participation in the language of oppression and colonial power.[9] Such readings are not simply uninterested in the contribution of poetic texture; in fact, much criticism of *The Tempest*, like much political reading in general, is deliberately anti-aesthetic. The verbal harmonics can too easily be considered a means of textual mystification, a tool in Prospero's magic trunk contributing to the "enchantment" that has made this play especially appealing and thus especially dangerous, made it "a powerful and plea-surable narrative." Some voices have been raised against the tendentious and monochromatic quality of much interpretation of *The Tempest:* Meredith Anne Skura, for example, in a persuasive psycholog-ical essay, argues that "recent criticism not only flat-tens the text into the mold of colonialist discourse and eliminates what is characteristically 'Shake-spearean' in order to foreground what is 'colonialist,' but it is also—paradoxically—in danger of taking the play further from the particular historical situa-tion in England in 1611 even as it brings it closer to what we mean by 'colonialism' today."[10] Despite this and a few other protests, the colonialist reading in the past decade has demonized Prospero, senti-mentalized Caliban, and tyrannized conferences and journals with a new orthodoxy as one-sided as that which it has sought to replace.

Sensitivity to the verse offers an alternative to both of these restrictive interpretations. In the first place, awareness of the poetic complexity of *The Tempest* suggests that the play is considerably more self-conscious than the recent demystifiers will al-low. Repetition—of vowels and consonants, words, phrases, syntactical forms, and other verbal effects—is a fundamental stylistic turn in *The Tempest;* these aurally reiterative patterns serve to tantalize the lis-tener, generating expectations of illumination and fixity but refusing to satisfy those desires. Such poetic echoes function in concert with the open-endedness of the romance form and with the reappearance of a host of familiar Shakespearian topoi: verbal and ideational patterns entice the audience by promising and withholding illumination, demonstrating the impossibility of significational certainty and creating an atmosphere of hermeneutic instability.

Moreover, the style and form of *The Tempest* en-gage the audience textually with the same issues of control and mastery—the problem of power—that are brought into sharp focus by considerations of his-torical context. The tendency of words and phrases to repeat themselves may be linked to the play's pro-found concern with reproduction, in various senses from the biological to the political. Versions of this very broad topic appear especially in those episodes that have appealed to recent critics: the story of the deceased Sycorax, the absent wife of Prospero, Anto-nio's usurpation, Prospero's taking the island from Caliban, the attempt of the "savage" to rape Miranda,

the enslavement of Ariel, the political ambitions of Stephano and Trinculo, the arranged marriages of Claribel and Miranda, the masque's concern with fer-tility and succession, the problem of dynasty, the ef-fort to reproduce the self through art. I shall argue that the stylistic implications of repetition offer a way of treating these political topics that is considerably more nuanced than most recent discussions of the play, more responsive to its balances and contradic-tions. The repetitions of the dramatic poetry help to expose the problems inherent in the art of cultural re-creation and to magnify their complexity, not to sup-ply answers. Virgil Thomson described "structural elements" in music as "expressive vocabularies, . . . repertories of devices for provoking feelings without defining them."[11] In *The Tempest,* as in late Shake-speare generally, the effect of the poetry is to promote *un*certainty and to insist upon ambiguity, and atten-tion to the verse makes one increasingly dubious about the bluntness of most political interpretation.

II

Repetition becomes a prominent figure in Shake-speare's late style generally, and *The Tempest* in partic-ular derives much of its poetic power from phonetic, lexical, and syntactical reiteration.[12] From the con-fused echoes of the first scene ("We split, we split!") through Prospero's re-creation of the past ("Twelve year since, Miranda, twelve year since") to the pleas-ing assonantal chiming of the Epilogue, aural patterns impart a distinctive texture to this text. And yet *The Tempest* is something of a stylistic paradox, being si-multaneously one of the most pleonastic and one of the briefest plays in the canon. The incantatory tone is in turn reinforced by the ellipses that represent a com-plementary and equally prominent feature of the late verse. But the repetition of sounds and words is only one type of larger and more frequently discussed modes of iteration, to which Jan Kott in particular has directed our notice: the replicated actions of usurpa-tion and assassination, the structural mirroring of the aristocratic and the servant plots, the allusion to and reproduction of major motifs from *The Aeneid,* the cre-ation of a masque within the play, and Shakespeare's representation of some of his own most familiar dra-matic actions and topics.[13] Likewise, omission makes itself felt narratively as well as stylistically. By this stage of his career Shakespeare has told the story of, say, regicide so many times that he now presents it in its most abbreviated and indicative fashion. Such a mimetic approach might be called abstract: the artist is sufficiently confident of his ability to tell a story and of his audience's capacity to receive it that he is able to signal an action rather than develop it in detail.[14] We are in the realm of the comedian performing at a convention of comedians: since everybody knows the jokes, he need only refer to a gag by number, and the house breaks into laughter.

Presence being easier to demonstrate than absence, I shall concentrate on figures of repetition, but a few words are in order about Shakespeare's impulse to omit. The gestural approach to storytelling corresponds to the poet's attempt at concentration and density throughout the last plays: Shakespeare strives for power of expression not only by contracting words and skipping over non-essential syllables, but also by discarding participles, pronouns (especially relative pronouns), conjunctions, and even nouns and verbs. Asyndeton appears about as frequently as in *King Lear* and *Antony and Cleopatra*, two plays of much greater length.[15] And the play is replete with verbless constructions: "Most sure the goddess / On whom these airs attend" (1.2.425–6); "No wonder, sir, / But certainly a maid" (1.2.431–2). Participles often do the work of longer noun/verb phrases, thus accelerating the tempo: "I, not rememb'ring how I cried out then, / Will cry it o'er again" (1.2.133–4). Anne Barton, in a brilliant discussion of this stripping away of nonessentials, points out that the vocabulary of *The Tempest* is spiked with spontaneous compounds ("sea-change," "cloud-capped," "hag-seed," "man-monster"), proposing that such phrases "seem to be driving towards some ultimate reduction of language, a mode of expression more meaningful in its very bareness than anything a more elaborate and conventional rhetoric could devise." She groups Shakespeare's urge towards linguistic compression with his disjunctive approach to characterization, observation of the unities, and reluctance to supply apparently pertinent details, all strategies by which *The Tempest* "continually gives the impression of being much bigger than it is."[16]

For all its compression and abbreviation, however, it is also pleonastic and reiterative—phonetically, rhythmically, lexically, syntactically, and architectonically. Although the structural and narrative replica-

tions are more likely to be the subject of critical interest than the aural, most listeners find themselves beguiled by the musical repetition of vowels and consonants, reduplication of words, echoing of metrical forms, and incantatory effect of this musical design. Even enthusiasts of prosody, however, are apt to weary of the repetitions of my close analysis, and so I beg the reader's indulgence as I lay the groundwork for the demonstration, in the second half of this essay, of how these effects function ideologically.

One of the play's most distinctive stylistic properties is the interlocking of aural effects in a way that recalls the etymology of *text* in weaving. Instances of consonance and assonance call attention to themselves in virtually every line: in a phrase such as "There's nothing ill can dwell in such a temple," "ill" is glanced at in "dwell," then both are altered with the repetition of the *e* and *l* in "temple," and these harmonies are augmented by the reiteration of the *th* and *n* sounds. Such interweavings are audible in lines that seem merely declarative ("For thou must now know farther") as well as in the obviously musical ("Wound the loud winds, or with bemocked-at stabs / Kill the still-closing waters"). They dominate Prospero's recitation of Ariel's history:

> within which rift
> Imprisoned thou didst painfully remain
> A dozen years, within which space she died
> And left thee there, where thou didst vent thy
> groans
> As fast as mill-wheels strike. Then was this
> island—
> Save for the son that she did litter here,
> A freckled whelp, hag-born—not honoured with
> A human shape. (1.2.279–86)

To begin with the smallest units, a series of vowel sounds spin themselves out to almost absurd lengths ("within which rift / Imprisoned thou didst painfully remain"); pairs of long vowels alternate with short ("she did litter here"): consonants can be repeated independently and then combined and split apart (in "put thyself / Upon this island as a spy," the *p*, *s*, and *i* sounds establish themselves separately and then coalesce in "spy"). This practice of joining and splitting phonemes creates what Stephen Booth has called "pulsating alliteration," a sensation of expansion and contraction that implies density and activity, making the text effectively "poetic" even when it may not sound conventionally so.[17]

Lexical repetition is largely responsible for the incantatory appeal of *The Tempest,* and thus for some of the most memorable passages in the play. Even in the prose of the opening shipwreck—"All lost! To prayers, to prayers! All lost!"; " 'We split, we split, we split!' "—the confused shouts of desperation take a reiterative form that functions poetically in the early speeches of Prospero and then throughout the work. Here, for instance, is a seven-line passage from the beginning of the play.

PROSPERO: . . .Tell your piteous heart
     There's no *harm done.*
MIRANDA: O woe the day!
PROSPERO: *No harm.*
     I have done nothing but in care *of thee,*
     Of thee, my dear one, *thee, my* daughter, who
     Art ignorant of what thou *art,* naught knowing
     Of whence *I am,* nor that *I am* more better
     Than Prospero, master of a full poor cell
     And thy no greater father.   (1.2.14–21)[18]

In addition to the italicized repetitions, the passage echoes with phonetic duplication: "heart . . . harm," "O, woe," "my dear . . . my daughter," "naught . . . daughter," "naught knowing," "full . . . cell," and "greater father." (Our uncertainty about Elizabethan pronunciation may limit but surely does not invalidate speculation about such phonetic echoes.) The regularity of certain metrical patterns and the isocolonic arrangement of clauses intensify the effect of the repeated words, notably "thee, my dear one, thee, my daughter" and "Of whence I am, nor that I am." And then there are all the negatives: "No," "no," "nothing," "naught," "knowing," "nor," "no."

To catch the repetitive flavour of Prospero's narrative to Miranda is to learn how to hear the language of the text as a whole; the following examples are taken from the first two hundred lines of the long second scene:

Which thou heard'st cry, which thou saw'st sink.
     Sit down,
For thou must now know farther.

If thou rememb'rest aught ere thou cam'st here,
How thou cam'st here thou mayst.

Twelve year since, Miranda, twelve year since

What foul play had we that we came from thence?
Or blessed was't we did?
                    Both, both, my girl.
By foul play, as thou sayst, were we heaved thence,
But blessedly holp hither.

                    how to grant suits,
How to deny them, *who t'*advance and *who*
To trash for over-topping, new *created*
The *creatures* that were mine, I say—*or* changed 'em
Or else new formed 'em; having both the key
Of *officer* and *office,* . . .

                    no screen between this part he
     played
And him he played it for

Which now's upon's, without the which this story

To cry to th'sea that roared to us, to sigh
To th'winds, whose pity, sighing back again

Sit still, and hear the last of our sea-sorrow.
Here in this island we arrived, and here
Have I, thy schoolmaster . . .

Since stylistic criticism often founders in an elaborate summation of what its examples have already disclosed, I leave it to the reader to note the poetic and rhetorical details, the instances of assonance, alliteration, epanalepsis, isocolon, several species of paronomasia (polyptoton, syllepsis, antanaclasis), not to mention the fundamental pleasures of the repeated sounds. The various kinds of verbal play impart energy and motion to what is dramatically a notoriously static scene.

That such echoing patterns are not confined to the protasis or to the protagonist but resound throughout the work is apparent by a glance at the episode in which Antonio seeks to inveigle Sebastian into fratricide, the temptation scene (2.1.204–311). The villain begins his scheme by priming his partner with anaphoric and rhythmic restatement: "They fell together all, as by consent; / They dropped as by a thunder-stroke" (2.1.208–9). He continues by arguing that Ferdinand's disappearance is Sebastian's good fortune, demonstrating the transformation linguistically:

SEBASTIAN: I have *no hope*
     That he's undrowned.
ANTONIO: O, out of that *"no hope"*
     What *great hope* have you! *No hope* that way is
     Another way *so high a hope* that even
     Ambition cannot pierce a wink beyond,
     But doubt discovery there.   (2.1.243–8)

Apart from the obvious echoes, the passage rings with assonance and consonance; in addition to the aural repetition, we also catch the relentless negatives characteristic of Shakespeare's villains; the glance at sleep imagery ("wink") to which the dra-

matic atmosphere of the scene and the island has ac-
climated us; and the self-conscious worrying of
words that extends the game begun earlier, when the
conspirators toy with the metaphor of "standing water" (226). As is often the case in *The Tempest*, language emerges as a subject itself, as speakers play
with it, take pleasure in it, test its capacities, and misuse it consciously and unconsciously, sometimes, as
here, at the same time.[19]

Antonio's principal trick is structural recapitulation, the stringing together of formally similar clauses.
Consider his appositional elaboration of Sebastian's
one-word speech, "Claribel":

> She that is Queen of Tunis; she that dwells
> Ten leagues beyond man's life; she that from Naples
> Can have no note—unless the sun were post—
> The man i'th'moon's too slow—till newborn chins
> Be rough and razorable; she that from whom
> We all were sea-swallowed, though some cast
>   again—
> And by that destiny, to perform an act
> Whereof what's past is prologue, what to come
> In yours and my discharge.   (2.1.251–9)

This string of clauses—the reader will have noticed
that it is not even a sentence—is calculated to inveigle the auditor into rhythmic sympathy with and, finally, assent to the speaker's claims. It depends for its
seductive power on the reiterative disposition of
phrases, specifically on the pattern known as *condu-
plicatio*, the repetition of words in succeeding clauses.
Antonio/Shakespeare strives for a kind of hypnosis
with simplicity of diction, at least in the first half,
where until "razorable" no word is longer than two
syllables and most are monosyllabic; with regular
disruption of the normal metrical structure, each of
the "she that" phrases being a trochee substituted for
an iamb;[20] and with syntactical recapitulation. Even
those qualifying clauses that violate the pattern of
"she that" develop their own rhythmic echo: "unless
the sun were post" and "The man i'th'moon's too
slow" are identical in length and regularity, similar in
the importance of consonance and assonance, and
completed with the repeated "o" sound. In these dramatic circumstances, Antonio's periphrastic style
amounts to verbal overkill, as even the dim Sebastian
seems to perceive in his response to the "Claribel"
speech: "What stuff is this?" But the local effect is less
important than the overriding dramatic goal: Antonio and Sebastian are merely the agents of a playwright seeking to seduce his audience with words.[21]

So it goes through other scenes and with other
speakers. Some of the richest passages in the text depend upon such lexical and sonic echo. One of the
play's axiological cruces, for example, the complex
relation between biology and culture, is set forth in
an aurally pleasing and complex frame:

> A devil, a born devil, on whose nature
> Nurture can never stick; on whom my pains,
> Humanely taken, all, all lost, quite lost.
>   (4.1.188–90)

"Full fathom five thy father lies," "Where the bee
sucks, there suck I"—the power of the play's songs
is at least partly attributable to various kinds of echo.
Finally, the notorious mystery surrounding Gonzalo's "Widow Dido" has been examined in almost
every conceivable context except, I think, that of aural identity, simple rhyme. Is it perhaps just another
case of internal rhyme that sounds as if it ought to
mean more than it does? Such density and concentration are essential to the sense of pregnancy upon
which *The Tempest* depends.

III

Verbal patterns are congruent with and supported by
larger networks of reiteration, most of them narrative and structural. Internal repetition of action has
been a staple of Shakespearian dramatic structure
since the early 1590s, the double wooing of Katherine and Bianca in *The Taming of the Shrew* being perhaps the most illustrative case. But rarely are the
symmetries and parodic constructions made so obvious—or so obviously the subject of comment—as
in *The Tempest*. The play is famous for the density
and congruity of its mirrored actions.[22] To mention
only those events associated with the celebrated example of usurpation, "the nodal point" of colonialist
readings: Antonio's prompting Sebastian to regicide
and fratricide seeks to repeat in Naples his own theft
of power in Milan and re-enacts Prospero's seizure of
the island and enslavement of Caliban, and all are
burlesqued in "that foul conspiracy / Of the beast
Caliban and his confederates / Against [Prospero's]
life" (4.1.139–41). This reticulum of stories contributes to a dramatic design that seems both familiar and wonderful.

But the pattern of narrative and thematic recapitulation goes far beyond this text. *The Tempest* is fla-
grantly intertextual, and the cluster of echoes is
especially audible, again, in the temptation scene. As

commentators since Coleridge have noticed, both in general structure and particular details — Antonio's hectoring Sebastian about "What thou shouldst be," the image of the crown, the sleep imagery implying failure to understand or to act, the suppression of conscience, even the image of the hungry cat (although it is used differently) — the episode restages the scene between the Macbeths before the killing of Duncan.[23] Everywhere in the scene Shakespeare is repeating himself, unashamedly gazing back over his entire *oeuvre* and summoning up scenes, persons, themes, metaphors, bits of vocabulary, and other minor theatrical strategies, so much so that the personal allegorists can hardly be blamed for the vigour with which they have approached this text. The recreated actions and speeches function as all allusions do, giving pleasure by exercising the mind and flattering veteran spectators on their perspicacity; and this audacious kind of authorial self-cannibalism contributes another layer of complexity, another apparently meaningful pattern of familiar and yet rearranged material. The duplication which constitutes the original source of meaning and pleasure, and which contains all the other patterns I have mentioned, is the troping by the play of the actual world: reality is (re)presented on the stage.[24] This act of repetition is the most general instance of the process I have been describing in little, in that the relationship of play to life would seem to amount to a meaningful pattern, and yet it is immensely difficult to articulate that meaning. As Stanley Wells puts it, "The enchanted island reverberates with sounds hinting at tunes that never appear fully formed."[25]

IV

The prominence of the figure of repetition in both the verbal style and dramatic structure of *The Tempest* leads perforce to the question of its importance — what does the figure import through the text to the audience? what is its function? how does it mean? Although for the most part I would decline to assign specific stylistic functions to particular sounds, certain aural configurations do undeniably accomplish certain small tasks of characterization and tone.[26] The hieratic style suggested by Prospero's repetitions is clearly appropriate to his vatic persona and elegiac frame of mind, it is a commonplace that some of his poetically knotted reiterations attest to his agitation at narratively recreating his deposition, and

Caliban's exultant "Freedom, high-day! High-day, freedom! Freedom, high-day, freedom!" ironically establishes his personal entrapment, his exchange of one master for another. But for the most part these and other such instances of functional echo constitute special cases. There is small profit in seeking "meaning" in Miranda's antanaclastic quibble on "your reason / For raising this sea-storm," in the vowels and consonants of Gonzalo's "If I should say I saw such islanders," or in most other lines.

I would argue that the operation of these acoustic and lexical echoes is musical, and that this music is only indirectly functional. The mutual effect of concentration and repetition creates a poetic counterpoint that challenges and exhilarates the auditor — Jan Kott describes *The Tempest* as a fugue[27] — and this contrapuntal effect induces aurally a sense of wonder corresponding to the aims and effects of the romantic or tragicomic mode. The operation of these verbal patterns is thus paradoxical, their greatest significance being precisely their ostensible significance combined with their refusal to signify. The effect is dream-like.[28] The verbal music is related to the oneiric and unreal atmosphere that attends and complicates the action of Shakespeare's late romantic forms; it promises much and delivers little, and I propose that it is just this dynamic that makes *The Tempest* uncommonly meaningful.

The insistent poetic reiterations interact with the elliptical verse style to mystify the audience about a function that never manifests itself. The play encourages its audience to scrutinize the linguistic and structural patterns for meaning, but it stoutly refuses to yield those meanings easily or fully. Eager to satisfy the desire for comprehension, we find ourselves both stimulated and frustrated. On the one hand, the repeated sounds or phrases in a brief and complicated text offer a kind of aural comfort: specifically, they create a richness of texture that seems to promise profundity. On the other, the text never fulfils the expectations of clarity which the discovery of such patterns engenders: in the rapid flow of the dialogue the repetitions themselves are succeeded by more repetitions which seem equally promising and equally unyielding. Such a strategy tantalizes the audience with the hope of clarification and fixity that art seems to promise, but it also demonstrates the difficulty and perhaps, finally, the impossibility of attaining them. Since order and comprehension seem always available but never thoroughly realized, the audience participates directly in the atmosphere of evanescence vital to this play.

The Tempest thus addresses itself directly to the problem of language and meaning, about which it registers extremely serious doubts. Denied or delayed communication becomes a minor but explicit motif as the action proceeds: numerous acts of communication (a speech, a song, a banquet, a masque) are broken off or delayed or redirected. Our position is something like that described by Caliban in his most memorable speech:

> Be not afeard. The isle is full of noises,
> Sounds, and sweet airs, that give delight and
>   hurt not.
> Sometimes a thousand twangling instruments
> Will hum about mine ears, and sometimes voices
> That if I then had waked after long sleep
> Will make me sleep again; and then in dreaming
> The clouds methought would open and show riches
> Ready to drop upon me, that when I waked
> I cried to dream again.   (3.2.138–46)

Often cited as evidence of natural sensitivity or of the magical atmosphere of the setting, these lines are most helpful as a statement of how the music of *The Tempest* impresses an audience. Robert Graves has shown that the confusion of tenses contributes to a feeling of arrested time;[29] lovely sounds "hum" about our ears; we seem to be about to receive the riches of meaning which remain forever elusive. The desired unity and gratification are contradicted by the brevity and compression of the text, and thus we find ourselves in what A. D. Nuttall has called an "atmosphere of ontological suspension" that pervades *The Tempest*, a region midway between promise and fulfilment.[30] And lest this seem too solemn let me add that this state of expectancy is also the source of immense pleasure. At this point one of my old teachers would have said, "You know. The Keats thing."

V

Tantalization is also one of the principal effects of the new mode of romance or tragicomedy that Shakespeare adopted in the late phase of his career, and the structure of the drama reinforces the fundamental erotic appeal of the verse by protracting but never seeming to supply the imminent resolution. Peter Brooks, commenting on an essay of Freud's, "Creative Writers and Day-Dreaming," writes about the aesthetic values of literary form, specifically what Freud calls "forepleasure."

> The equation of the effects of literary form with forepleasure in this well-known passage is perhaps less trivial than it at first appears. If *Lust* and *Unlust* don't take us very far in the analysis of literary texture, *Vorlust* — forepleasure — tropes on pleasure and thus seems more promising. Forepleasure is indeed a curious concept, suggesting a whole rhetoric of advance toward and retreat from the goal or the end, a formal zone of play (I take it that forepleasure somehow implicates foreplay) that is both harnessed to the end and yet autonomous, capable of deviations and recursive movements. When we begin to unpack the components of forepleasure, we may find a whole erotics of form, which is perhaps what we most need if we are to make formalism serve an understanding of the human functions of literature. Forepleasure would include the notion of both delay and advance in the textual dynamic, the creation of that "dilatory space" which Roland Barthes, in *S/Z*, claimed to be the essence of the textual middle. We seek to advance through this space toward the discharge of the end, yet all the while we are perversely delaying, returning backward in order to put off the promised end and perhaps to assure its greater significance.[31]

This suggestive paragraph is relevant to the way that Shakespeare's late style functions in, and in concert with, the voguish new dramatic mode. A more or less contemporary description of the process of narrative teasing is found in William Cartwright's prefatory verses in the 1647 Beaumont and Fletcher Folio:

> None can prevent the fancy, and see through
> At the first opening; all stand wondering how
> The thing will be, until it is; which hence
> With fresh delight still cheats, still takes the sense;
> The whole design, the shadow, the lights such
> That none can say he shews or hides too much.

The titillating diction of Cartwright's description is given special meaning in light of Brooks's plea for a textual erotics, for both capture the gamesome or sportive quality of romance or tragicomedy.[32]

Narrative progress towards the satisfactions of complete understanding, or closure, is indirect and irregular, and the chief pleasure rests in the delay and the circuitousness of the journey. Romance depends upon suspense, secrets, surprises, discoveries, peripeties, awakenings, revelations. Thus it automatically raises questions of epistemology but almost invariably leaves them open. It is a knowing form, a self-conscious mode reliant upon the audience's familiarity with conventions of tragic and comic storytelling and its willingness to be teased by the playwright's manipulation of generic signals. For similar reasons it is an ironic form in flattering the audience with privileged information; yet it deals in double ironies when it betrays this cosy relationship by a sudden reversal or surprise. Suspense and irony constitute only one pair of several antitheses inherent in tragicomic form (and implicit in its name); these have been described by Philip Edwards as "the pleasure of being kept out of the secret and the pleasure of being let into the secret."[33] Brooks's account of formal erotics is especially pertinent to the gestural narrative style of *The Tempest* and of the mode of romance generally.[34] Although the formal divagations are perhaps not as easy to discern in a compact work such as *The Tempest* as they are in *Cymbeline*, they are present none the less, and they recapitulate on a larger scale the sense of promise and profundity fostered by the texture of the verse.

VI

The sophisticated effects of form and style bespeak a degree of self-consciousness considerably greater than most recent political readings can admit, a self-awareness that comprehends the issues of politics and power central to the colonialist argument. The poetic and structural figures of repetition become directly pertinent to the critical debate over the European colonial impulse when that will to power is regarded as an effort to recreate the self in a new environment. Therefore the episodes and topics political critics have chosen to stress—the proprietary claims of the deceased Sycorax and her legacy to Caliban, Prospero's usurpation of the island from him, the enslavement of Ariel, the dynastic marriages of Claribel and Miranda—all these attest to the play's profound concern with reproduction, in various senses from the biological to the political to the aesthetic. Throughout its narrative *The Tempest* raises disturbing questions about the act of reproduction, not only the genetic possibilities ("Good wombs have borne bad sons") but also the difficulties of recreating society, beginning afresh, repairing in the new world the errors of the old, and it does so in a style that refuses to cease recreating itself.

The opening scene introduces the problem of sovereignty ("What cares these roarers for the name of king?"); Prospero's epilogue begs for remission and release ("let your indulgence set me free"): from beginning to end the playwright gives prominence to the problems of dominion, freedom, political failure, and the repetition of the past. Prospero's expository recital of how he lost control of himself and his dukedom is inflected with multiple variations on political failure and the repetition of past errors. He begins with a consideration of Miranda's memory, her ability to recreate the past imaginatively—"Of anything the image tell me that / Hath kept with thy remembrance" (1.2.43–4)—and the dimness of that memory prompts his rehearsal of the usurpation. Moreover, the daughter's piteous reaction to the tale reproduces emotionally the ordeal of banishment: she "will cry it o'er again" (1.2.134). His lecture reviews Antonio's seizure of power and renovation of the court, and, as Stephen Orgel points out, "this monologue is only the first of a series of repetitions."[35] Antonio encourages Sebastian to repeat the crime of deposing his brother; Prospero seeks to repair political division by arranging the dynastic marriage of Miranda and Ferdinand; Alonso is desperate at the loss of his son, which is the end of the biological line and the forfeiture of his future, Claribel being "lost" to him as well; Stephano, Trinculo, and Caliban seek to establish their own kingdom, taking power from Prospero who has himself seized the island from Caliban; Caliban has tried to reproduce himself by raping Miranda ("I had peopled else / This isle with Calibans"); the masque of Ceres dramatizes the importance of fertility, agriculture, and orderly succession; Prospero has sought by his magical art to remake his kingdom; and Shakespeare has sought by his theatrical art to reconstruct the material world. Looked at from one point of view, colonialism becomes a form of political and cultural reproduction congruent with the effort to transcend time through art, and both of these represent versions of the defence against death.

Considerations of political and artistic recreation lead us back to the poetry of *The Tempest*, for the stylistic and structural repetitions engage the audience textually with the same problems of authority and power that dominate political interpretation. The tendency of words and phrases to repeat themselves is a case of stylistic reproduction that creates, as I have shown, an atmosphere in which control of meaning remains necessarily elusive. The effect of the style throughout is to place the auditor in an intermediate state, and that region of indeterminacy is a version of the various other kinds of liminality associated with this text: the island is located midway between Africa and Europe; it apparently partakes of, or is hospitable to, the natural and supernatural realms; Miranda stands between childhood and maturity, Caliban between demon and human, Prospero between vengeance and mercy; even time seems arrested ("what's past is prologue"). The poetry seduces the audience into a state of stylistic suspension, an intuitive zone between sleep and wake, "a strange repose" like that felt by Sebastian (2.1.218) or that described in Caliban's lyric. It is a marginal condition between expectation and understanding, affirmation and scepticism, comedy and tragedy.

Poetic indeterminacy shows us how to evaluate the appropriation of the play by those who see it as a political act in the colonialist enterprise. It helps to complicate the ideology of *The Tempest*, indicating that the political ideas are more subtle and difficult than recent readings would suggest. Pleas for interpretative caution are often attacked as retrogressive politics, but the recognition that this is one of the most knowing, most self-conscious texts in the canon should warn us about pretensions to ideological certainty. On the very issues that have most deeply concerned materialist critics and their American cousins—power, social and political hierarchy, the theatre as a political instrument, freedom of action, education, and race—*The Tempest* is at its most elusive and complicated. The play valorizes ambiguity and irony, ironizing its own positions and insisting upon the inconclusiveness of its own conclusions. The new orthodoxy, which exalts the colonized, is as narrow as the old, which idealizes and excuses the colonizer.[36]

This stylistic interpretation is not, however, merely another version of New Criticism, a retreat, that is, into the restful shadows of irony and ambiguity. The difference is that this reading of *The Tempest* admits the importance of contextual study and historical location, just as it recognizes the inescapable affiliation of the political and the aesthetic. I acknowledge the capacity of new modes of criticism to identify and promote ideological issues and other points of departure that more traditional forms of criticism have neglected or deliberately suppressed. But I also seek to balance those virtues with a sensitivity to the claims of the text. It needs to be pointed out that as students and teachers of literature we are professionally concerned with political issues not just in themselves but as they are embodied in aesthetic forms. The dismissal of verse is dangerous, especially if the subject of inquiry is verse drama. In reaction to the excesses and orthodoxies of New Criticism, our own critical practice is moving farther and farther away from the text, and in reading this play stylistically I register a mild protest against the implicit cheapening of textuality. The poetry of *The Tempest* alerts us to the delicate relation between literature and ideology.

Which is what, according to Kenneth Burke, art ought to do. In an essay on the fictional uncertainties of Mann and Gide, he identifies the pleasures of the unfixed:

> so long as we feel the need of certitude, the state of doubt is discomforting, and by its very prolongation can make for our hysterical retreat into belief, as Hans Castorp descended from his mountain to the battlefield. But why could one not come to accept his social wilderness without anguish, utilizing for his self-respect either the irony and melancholy of Mann, or the curiosity of Gide? One need not suffer under insecurity any more than an animal suffers from being constantly on the alert for danger. In the unformed there are opportunities which can be invigorating to contemplate. This state of technical apprehension can be a norm, and certainly an athletic norm.[37]

The Tempest promotes in its audience a kind of moral and imaginative athleticism, an intellectual fitness that much recent interpretation, by relaxing— or stiffening—into a single mode of reading, has evaded. The play's epistemological sophistication is inconsistent with the baldness of a single-mindedly ideological interpretation. To listen to its language is to become deeply sceptical about the operation of all kinds of power—poetic, political, and critical too.

Notes

1. " 'Nymphs and reapers heavily vanish': the Discursive Con-texts of *The Tempest*," *Alternative Shakespeares*, ed. John Drakakis (London and New York: Methuen, 1985), pp. 191–205.

2. Recent British readers seem especially unsympathetic to the play, perhaps because, as Walter Cohen suggests, their response to its colonial associations undermines an otherwise unified vision of Shakespeare's political progressivism. See "Political Criticism of Shakespeare," in *Shakespeare Reproduced: The Text in History and Ideology,* ed. Jean E. Howard and Marion F. O'Connor (London: Methuen, 1987), p. 37.

3. Some of the essays that make the topic of colonialism their central theme are the following: Paul E. Brown, "'This thing of darkness I acknowledge mine': *The Tempest* and the Discourse of Colonialism," in *Political Shakespeare,* ed. Jonathan Dollimore and Alan Sinfield (Ithaca: Cornell University Press, 1985); Paul N. Siegel, "Historical Ironies in *The Tempest,*" *Shakespeare Jahrbuch,* 119 (1983), 104–11; Thomas Cartelli, "Prospero in Africa: *The Tempest* as Colonialist Text and Pretext," in Howard and O'Connor, *Shakespeare Reproduced,* pp. 99–115; Terence Hawkes, "Swisser-Swatter: Making a Man of English Letters," in Drakakis's *Alternative Shakespeares,* pp. 26–46; Stephen Orgel, "Prospero's Wife," *Representations,* 8 (1985), 1–13, and "Shakespeare and the Cannibals," in *Witches, Cannibals, Divorce: Estranging the Renaissance,* Selected Papers from the English Institute, NS II, ed. Marjorie Garber (Baltimore: Johns Hopkins University Press, 1986), pp. 40–66; Stephen Greenblatt, "Martial Law in the Land of Cockaigne," in *Shakespearean Negotiations: The Circulation of Social Energy in Renaissance England* (Berkeley: University of California Press, 1988), pp. 129–63.

4. The essay is printed in *First Images of America: The Impact of the New World on the Old,* ed. Fredi Chiappelli, 2 vols. (Berkeley: University of California Press, 1976), pp. 561–80.

5. (Ithaca: Cornell University Press, 1985), p. 48.

6. *Drama of a Nation: Public Theater in Renaissance England and Spain* (Ithaca: Cornell University Press, 1985), p. 401.

7. "Faithful Servants: Shakespeare's Praise of Disobedience," in *The Historical Renaissance: New Essays on Tudor and Stuart Literature and Culture,* ed. Heather Dubrow and Richard Strier (Chicago: University of Chicago Press, 1988), p. 133 n. 81.

8. *The Tempest,* ed. Frank Kermode (London: Methuen, 1954). Other studies now considered limited for their neglect of political issues would include those of G. Wilson Knight, *The Crown of Life* (Oxford: Clarendon Press, 1947), pp. 203–55; Reuben A. Brower, "The Mirror of Analogy: *The Tempest,*" in *The Fields of Light: An Experiment in Critical Reading* (New York: Oxford, 1951), pp. 95–122; Northrop Frye, Introduction to *The Tempest* in *The Complete Pelican Shakespeare,* gen. ed. Alfred Harbage (Baltimore: Penguin, 1969); D. G. James, *The Dream of Prospero* (Oxford: Clarendon Press, 1967); Harry Levin, "Two Magian Comedies: *The Alchemist* and *The Tempest,*" *Shakespeare Survey* 22 (1969), 47–58; Derek Traversi, *Shakespeare: The Last Phase* (London: Hollis and Carter, 1954); Harry Berger, "Miraculous Harp: A Reading of Shakespeare's *Tempest,*" *Shakespeare Studies,* 5 (1969), 253–83; Howard Felperin, *Shakespearean Romance* (Princeton: Princeton University Press, 1972); Joseph H. Summers, "The Anger of Prospero," in *Dreams of Love and Power: On Shakespeare's Plays* (Oxford: Clarendon, 1984).

9. For a fascinating commentary on this kind of critical power struggle, see Anthony B. Dawson, "*Tempest* in a Teapot: Critics, Evaluation, Ideology," in *Bad Shakespeare: Revaluations of the Shakespeare Canon,* ed. Maurice Charney (Rutherford, NJ: Fairleigh Dickinson University Press, 1988), pp. 61–73. Dawson is especially eloquent on "the way 'materialist' critics expose the hidden biases of traditional criticism . . . but fall into some of the same traps, particularly in the vexed area of evaluation and the ideological assumptions that the act of evaluating often makes plain" (71).

10. "Discourse and the Individual: The Case of Colonialism in *The Tempest,*" *Shakespeare Quarterly,* 40 (1989), 47. One of the earliest complaints about the excesses of recent political criticism was Edward Pechter's "The New Historicism and Its Discontents: Politicizing Renaissance Drama," *PMLA,* 102 (1987), 292–303. On the other hand, Carolyn Porter has attacked New Historicists for being insufficiently historical and insufficiently political: see "Are We Being Historical Yet?," *South Atlantic Quarterly,* 87 (1988), 743–86.

11. "Music Does Not Flow," *New York Review of Books,* 17 December 1981, p. 49.

12. Although everyone agrees that the poetry of the last plays is difficult and different from the earlier verse, surprisingly little has been written

about it. See F. E. Halliday, *The Poetry of Shakespeare's Plays* (London: Duckworth, 1954); J. M. Nosworthy's Introduction to the Arden edition of *Cymbeline* (London: Methuen, 1955), lxii–lxxiii; N. F. Blake, *Shakespeare's Language: An Introduction* (London: Methuen, 1983); John Porter Houston, *Shakespearean Sentences: A Study in Style and Syntax* (Baton Rouge: Louisiana State University Press, 1987); and George T. Wright, *Shakespeare's Metrical Art* (Berkeley: University of California Press, 1988). In preparing this essay I have also profited from Cyrus Hoy's "The Language of Fletcherian Tragicomedy," in *Mirror up to Shakespeare: Essays in Honour of G. R. Hibbard,* ed. J. C. Gray (Toronto: University of Toronto Press, 1984), pp. 99–113.

13. "*The Tempest,* or Repetition," in *The Bottom Translation: Marlowe and Shakespeare and the Carnival Tradition,* tr. Daniela Miedzyrzecka and Lillian Vallee (Evanston: Northwestern University Press, 1987).

14. For an intelligent discussion of the "abstract" qualities of Shakespeare's late work, see Marion Trousdale, "Style in *The Winter's Tale,*" *Critical Quarterly,* 18 (1976), 25–32.

15. On this and many points of stylistic criticism, I have been aided by the analysis of John Porter Houston in *Shakespearean Sentences.*

16. Introduction to *The Tempest* (Harmondsworth: Penguin, 1968), pp. 13–14.

17. *An Essay on Shakespeare's Sonnets* (New Haven: Yale University Press, 1969), pp. 87–8. Booth's comments on how poetic effects function in individual sonnets are extremely stimulating and applicable beyond their immediate subject. See also the essay by Kenneth Burke, "On Musicality in Verse," in which he demonstrates the complex effects of assonance and consonance in some poems of Coleridge: *The Philosophy of Literary Form* (Berkeley: University of California Press, rpt. 1973), pp. 369–79.

18. Here, as in a few other passages, I have added emphasis to illustrate certain poetic effects.

19. See Anne Barton, "Shakespeare and the Limits of Language," *Shakespeare Survey 24* (1971), 19–30.

20. On the expressive possibilities of this tactic, see Wright's *Shakespeare's Metrical Art,* especially chapter 13, "Trochees."

21. On the relative importance of specific and general effects in the last plays, see Anne Barton, "Leontes and the Spider: Language and Speaker in the Last Plays," *Shakespeare's Styles: Essays in honour of Kenneth Muir,* ed. Philip Edwards, G. K. Hunter, and Inga-Stina Ewbank (Cambridge: Cambridge University Press, 1980), pp. 131–50.

22. See, for example, Joan Hartwig, *Shakespeare's Analogical Scene: Parody as Structural Syntax* (Lincoln: University of Nebraska Press, 1983), chapter 8; Brower's *The Fields of Light;* and Knight's *The Crown of Life.*

23. For an excellent discussion of the densely allusive quality of this scene, see Paul A. Cantor, "Shakespeare's *The Tempest:* The Wise Man as Hero," *Shakespeare Quarterly,* 31 (1980), 64–75.

24. See Ruth Nevo's comments on this metatheatrical device: "The embedding of play within play dissolves representational boundaries so that the audience is required to suspend its attention, to negotiate a constant interchange between fictional reality and fictional illusion," *Shakespeare's Other Language* (London: Methuen, 1987), p. 136. This point of view is consistent with Shakespeare's late attitude toward a device that had served him well from the beginning, as Anne Barton points out: "On the whole, efforts to distinguish the fictional from the 'real,' art from life, tales from truth, come in the Romances to replace the older, moral concern with identifying hypocrisy and deceit." "Leontes and the Spider," p. 147.

25. "Shakespeare and Romance," in *Later Shakespeare,* ed. John Russell Brown and Bernard Harris, Stratford-upon-Avon Studies, 8 (London: Edward Arnold, 1966), p. 75.

26. From time to time aural echoes function as images do, pointing up crucial words and the ideas they raise. Consider the effect of "be" in the following exchange:

> ALONSO: Whe'er thou beest he or no,
> Or some enchanted trifle to abuse me,
> As late I have been, I not know: Thy pulse
> Beats, as of flesh and blood; and, since I saw thee
> Th'affliction of my mind amends, with which
> I fear a madness held me. This must crave—
> An if this be at all—a most strange story.
> Thy dukedom I resign, and do entreat
> Thou pardon me my wrongs. But how should Prospero
> Be living and be here?

PROSPERO (*to Gonzalo*): First, noble friend.
   Let me embrace thine age, whose honour cannot
   Be measured or confined.
   He embraces Gonzalo
GONZALO: Whether this be,
   Or be not, I'll not swear.   (5.1.113–24)

The hammering of the verb underscores the problem that Alonso and finally the audience must confront, the ontological status of what we are witnessing.

Stanley Fish has written brilliantly on the logical dangers of such interpretation, specifically on the circularity of thematic stylistics: "formal patterns are themselves the products of interpretation and . . . therefore there is no such thing as a formal pattern, at least in the sense necessary for the practice of stylistics: that is, no pattern that one can observe before interpretation is hazarded and which therefore can be used to prefer one interpretation to another." *Is There a Text in This Class?: The Authority of Textual Communities* (Cambridge, Mass.: Harvard University Press, 1980), p. 267. See also John Hollander, "The Metrical Frame," in *The Structure of Verse: Modern Essays on Prosody*, ed. Harvey Gross, rev. ed. (New York: Ecco Press, 1979), pp. 77–101.

27. *The Bottom Translation*, p. 97.
28. Of the many studies of the oneiric qualities of *The Tempest*, the most recent is found in Ruth Nevo's *Shakespeare's Other Language*, especially pp. 136–43.
29. *The White Goddess* (London: Farrar, 1948), p. 425.
30. *Two Concepts of Allegory: A Study of Shakespeare's "The Tempest" and the Logic of Allegorical Expression* (New York: Barnes and Noble, 1967), p. 158.
31. Peter Brooks, "The Idea of a Psychoanalytic Literary Criticism," *Critical Inquiry*, 13 (1987), 339.

32. Although I am sensitive to the various differences between the two kinds known as "romance" and "tragicomedy," it will be agreed that the forms share a number of fundamental features, and it is those similarities on which I am concentrating here.
33. "The Danger Not the Death: The Art of John Fletcher," in *Jacobean Theatre*, edited John Russell Brown and Bernard Harris (London: Edward Arnold, 1960), p. 164.
34. Patricia A. Parker brilliantly develops some of the same ideas as Brooks: "The suspensions which for Barthes become part of an erotics of the text recall not only the constant divagations of romance and its resistance to the demands of closure, but also the frustration in Ariosto of what Barthes calls the teleological form of vulgar readerly pleasure—the desire to penetrate the veil of meaning or to hasten the narrative's gradual striptease—by a continual postponement of revelation which leaves the reader suspended, or even erotically 'hung up.'" *Inescapable Romance: Studies in the Poetics of a Mode* (Princeton: Princeton University Press, 1979), pp. 220–1.
35. Introduction to his edition of *The Tempest*, p. 15.
36. See Skura, "The Case of Colonialism," in which she argues that new historicism "is now in danger of fostering blindness of its own. Granted that something was wrong with a commentary that focused on *The Tempest* as a self-contained project of a self-contained individual and that ignored the political situation in 1611. But something seems wrong now also, something more than the rhetorical excesses characteristic of any innovative critical movement" (pp. 46–7).
37. *Counter-statement* (rpt. Berkeley: University of California Press, 1968), p. 106.

Lionel Trilling and the Immortality Ode

Helen Vendler

In this essay, which first appeared in an issue of Salmagundi *devoted to the criticism of Lionel Trilling, Helen
Vendler takes up Trilling's very influential interpretation
of Wordsworth's Ode, in part, as she says, "to dispute its
conclusions, but also to ask to what degree its assumptions and methods are suited to the art of poetry."
Vendler's disagreements with Trilling point up some of
the tensions that might arise between the formal and
mimetic modes of criticism. Formal critics, as we have
seen, are also mimetic critics, and "complexity," that key
value term in the formal lexicon, is often grounded in the
mimetic context. Yet mimetic critics who treat a poem as
if it were a discursive statement and who fail to pay close
attention to the literary features that distinguish poems
from other kinds of discourse are apt to misinterpret.
This, according to Vendler, is where Trilling goes wrong.
"Adequacy to the complexity of experience is certainly
one—but only one—of the criteria by which we judge
great literature." Trilling's essential mistake is to detach
"the sentiments of the Ode from the only medium in
which they can live, the medium of their language." For
the formalist, that medium is the message. Only by exploring that medium carefully can we come to see how
the poem means. It "means," argues Vendler, by a number of specifically literary devices, and "most of all by its
ability to invent, mediating between the language of
childhood sense and its mirror-language of adult inwardness, a language of disorientation, which conveys the
difficulty inherent in the relation of consciousness to
sense-experience, that difficulty which the great poetry of
the Ode so triumphantly overcomes." Only a formal
reading can discover this meaning.*

Reprinted by permission of the publisher and the author
from *Salmagundi* 41 (1978): 66–86.

Lionel Trilling wrote more often about prose than about poetry, but he had a deeply-felt relation with at least two poets — Arnold and Wordsworth. What he loved in them was their moral insight: in one of the most autobiographical of his essays, he compares the writings of Wordsworth with the *Pirke Aboth,* a collection of Hebrew wisdom-writing that he read as a boy. It is not surprising, then, that when he wrote about Wordsworth's Immortality Ode (as he called it for convenience) his purpose was to defend the Ode from what he regarded as moral misrepresentation. He disliked the view that the Ode is "Wordsworth's conscious farewell to his art": "I believe the 'Ode' is not only not a dirge sung over departing powers, but actually a dedication to new powers." The "new powers" Trilling identifies as a "greater sensitivity and responsiveness" because "the 'philosophic mind' has not decreased but, on the contrary, increased the power to feel." The "new poetic subject matter" which Trilling finds implied in the Ode is tragedy — though he adds that Wordsworth was, in the event, incapable of writing the tragic verse announced in the Ode.

I take up Trilling's essay in part to dispute its conclusions, but also to ask to what degree its assumptions and methods are suited to the art of poetry. What, for Trilling, was poetry? It was — and this is the strangest of his assumptions — something other than, and less than, life. "Those critics," he says with considerable emphasis, "who . . . make the Ode relate only to poetical powers . . . conceive the Ode to be a lesser thing than it really is, for it is not about poetry, it is about life." A poet would scarcely assent to such a distinction; for poets, to make poetry is one of the modes of living, one of the ways in which life manifests itself. For Wordsworth especially, to create is to live, to become that "sensitive being" and "creative soul" for whom the essence of living is responding and creating.

Trilling's second assumption about a poem is that it is at heart a discursive statement, in which the author says what he means and means what he says, line by line: a poem is a statement "about something." The Ode is "about growing up," Trilling decides, and to judge by his description the Ode might be an essay or a homily:

> The first [of the two stanzas] *tells us* . . . the second movement . . . *tells us again* . . . the rainbow epigraph also *says* . . . Wordsworth *says* . . . he *says* . . . he *mentions* . . . Wordsworth *is speaking of a period* . . . Wordsworth *is talking about something* common to us all.

The phrases Trilling uses are proper to a notion of the poem as an utterance *à haute voix,* something close to moral instruction by example. The objections to such a view are familiar, but I must mention them briefly. Trilling's attitude fails to separate a poet's *intention* (which is often that of providing moral instruction, poets being only human) from his *accomplishment,* an accomplishment which separates the poet from common moral instructors — those who have not, as they uttered their instructions, composed a great poem. Secondly, such a view assumes that a poem is a discourse rather than an action; and thirdly, such a view takes no heed of Lawrence's famous warning — to trust not the teller but the tale. In his trust of his teller, in his use of a static discursive model, and in his failure to distinguish Wordsworth's mode from other modes of moral instruction, Trilling detaches the sentiments of the Ode from the only medium in which they can live, the medium of their language.

Assuming that Trilling is right, and that the Ode is not an elegy for youth but a poem about growing up, why, we may ask, should we prize it or listen to it? Its "message," as Trilling presents it, is by no means a new one, though it is suffused, in Trilling's presentation, by a then-fashionable Freudian aura. Wordsworth is, like all of us, says Trilling, ambivalent about the losses and gains of growing up:

> Inevitably we resist change and turn back with passionate nostalgia to the stage we are leaving. Still, we fulfill ourselves by choosing what is painful and difficult and necessary, and we develop by moving toward death. In short, organic development is a hard paradox which Wordsworth is stating in the discrepant answers of the second part of the Ode.

The "hard paradox" of "organic development" is not a new doctrine, but is rather one of the staples of both religious and secular literature. If any version of this "hard paradox" will do, of what particular value is Wordsworth's? Trilling imputes a virtue to Wordsworth's presentation of ambivalence, but when he adds that we find other examples of this ambivalence at leaving Eden (for instance in Milton and his creation Adam) he implies that Wordsworth is simply one of a long line of authors who present us with the pains and rewards of growth.

Adequacy to the complexity of experience is certainly one — but only one — of the criteria by which we judge great literature. It is disquieting how indistinguishable the Ode becomes, in Trilling's description, from an essay by Emerson, or a lecture by

Arnold. It is true that the moral conception of great art on which Trilling's writing is based is one found commonly among his American and English critical predecessors: "It is not by the mode of representing and saying, but by what is represented and said," says Ruskin, "that the respective greatness either of the painter or the writer is to be finally determined" (*Modern Painters* I, i, 2). And yet, for all his insistence on content, Ruskin rarely embarks on a set of remarks about an artist without making us feel the liveliest sense of the individual painter's manner as he perceives it. Here he is on Turner's representations of "the force of agitated water":

> He never loses himself and his subject in the splash of the fall, his presence of mind never fails as he goes down; he does not blind us with the spray, or veil the countenance of his fall with its own drapery . . . Thus, in the Upper Fall of the Tees, though the whole basin of the fall is blue and dim with the rising vapour, yet the attention of the spectator is chiefly directed to the concentric zones and delicate curves of the falling water itself; and it is impossible to express with what exquisite accuracy these are given. (*Modern Painters* II, v, 3)

In this description—which praises Turner's capacity to show airy smoke and foam without losing the structural concentric zones and curves behind the spray, and which admires Turner's combination of receptivity with presence of mind, of recording power with power of composition—Ruskin, without forgetting the sublimity of Turner's subject, remarks the finest details of Turner's conception and execution. Trilling does not seem to feel a comparable relish; he feels no impulse to delight in Wordsworth's invention or his manner. There is no mention in Trilling's essay of the large aesthetic problems—of scale, focus, perspective, structure, climax, and dénouement—solved by Wordsworth in the Ode, nor is there any admiring lingering on the smaller means—the registers of diction, the allusions, the internal cross-referencing, the sequence of events—by which local effects are given meaning. By addressing the import rather than the being of the poem, Trilling deprives us of any reason to believe in its assertions. Surely, even in poetry, perhaps especially in poetry, we do not believe assertions because they are asserted. If we are to assent to Wordsworth's "hard paradox"—that (in Trilling's version) "we develop by moving toward death"—it is because something *in the poem* compels our assent. It is not, as Trilling thinks, something in us that compels that assent.

Wordsworth, says Trilling, "is speaking of a period common to the development of everyone," and "critics who make the Ode refer to some particular and unique experience of Wordsworth's and who make it relate only to poetical powers have forgotten their own lives." This sort of remark imposes a false criterion of universality upon poetry. It is not necessary that the poet's experience should exactly resemble our own; it is enough if we find some analogy between the growth of the poet's mind and the growth of our own, non-poetic mind. But we should not be surprised if poetry about the growth of the poet's mind has special reference to the well-being of his creative powers.

If Trilling's method is insufficient to the Ode, what can be presented to supplement it? For I too believe with Trilling that the Ode "succeeds," that we "believe" Wordsworth's assertion that the possession of the "philosophic mind" is a greater good than the former possession of the lost "glory." I differ with Trilling, however, in the interpretation of the nature of the philosophic mind and of its powers. I do not believe that the philosophic mind can be said to have "increased the power to feel." Rather, the philosophic mind has enabled the composition of poetry, a quite different matter. The child who saw the visionary gleam was not a poet; he was not even a writer. He saw; he was; he existed in pure apprehension and pure feeling. I do not believe it to be true that "the knowledge of man's mortality . . . replaces the 'glory' as the agency which makes *things* significant and precious." Rather, the capacity to make natural things into metaphors of human life—the poet's gift, as Aristotle said—confers on those natural things an aura replacing the lost aura of celestial light. What the child cannot do, the poet can do—that is, he can see in every natural phenomenon an echo or mirror of the moral life of the human self:

> I love the Brooks which down their channels *fret*,
> Even more than *when I tripped lightly as they;*
> The *innocent* brightness of a *new-born* Day
> Is lovely yet;
> The Clouds that *gather round* the setting sun
> Do take a *sober* colouring from an eye
> That hath kept watch o'er man's mortality.

The eye that has seen the child "fretted" by its mother's kisses can perceive the brooks as "fretting"; the man remembering his own light tripping as a child can say of the brooks that they too "trip lightly"; the adult who has called a new-born child innocent can transfer the epithets "new-born" and "innocent" to a bright dawn; the eye that has kept a death-vigil can compare the clouds in a sunset to the watchers "gathering round" a deathbed, and can, *by the metaphor* of the deathwatch, confer a "sober colouring" on a sunset panorama which to the pure seeing of the visionary child would have represented simply a lively play of vivid sky-hues. The child, for all his possession of the visionary gleam, cannot say that the brooks "trip lightly" or "fret," or that the day is "new-born" and "innocent," or that the clouds which "gather round" the sun have a "sober" coloring. Not the knowledge of mortality alone, but the reflective knowledge of one's own life informs these metaphors. But the truly important thing about them is that they are metaphors. Everything in the world — *everything* — now reminds the adult Wordsworth of some aspect of human experience. He can no longer see a flower as the child in the Prelude (II) sees it. A fine passage in Trilling's essay describes the child's seeing:

> He does not perceive things merely as objects, he first sees them, because maternal love is a condition of his perception, as objects-and-judgments, as valued objects. He does not learn about a flower, but about the pretty-flower, the flower that I-want-and-that-mother-will-get-for-me . . . but the objects he sees are not in utter darkness.

This is probably as adequate a description of the psychological cause of the "glory" as one can give: but Trilling does not remark that the child's perception can as yet have no pathos of self-reference. The child cannot say, "the flower is innocent as I am innocent," or "the flower grows as I grow." Only with the advent of reflectiveness can metaphor arise. And it is the capacity for metaphor — for the drawing of analogies between natural emblems and human events — that is celebrated in the conclusion of the Ode. The child *feels* intensely — "the fullness of your bliss, I feel — I feel it all," says Wordsworth to the child, protesting too much. No-one can *feel* more strongly than the child. But one can *love* more strongly than the child does. "I love the brooks . . . *even more*," says Wordsworth. As a child he loved them, as he loved the sun, for their beauty; now, as an adult, he loves them more because they remind him, in their light and joyous motion, of his own careless steps as a child. The dawn was lovely to him when he was a child; it is "lovely yet" because it

seems the emblem of all new-born and innocent things. "A child, I loved the sun," but now the adult can confer things on nature, not merely receive impressions from it; the clouds take a coloring from his eye. What else is metaphor but a conferral of colors on the neutral world, an introduction of value where before there was only fact?

If every object in the adult poet's eye thus becomes weighty with possible meditation, he is no longer a stranger in the world, longing hopelessly for the "imperial palace whence he came." He has become, instead, naturalized in the world, as all its parts become colored by the feeling eye. This new analogizing habit of mind grows up imperceptibly, but eventually it becomes a habitual mode of vision. Wordsworth's aesthetic problem in the ode is to find languages appropriate to each of three stages described in the poem — the stage of "glory" and "obstinate questioning," the stage of loss, and the stage of metaphor. Ideally he must express — and we must be made to feel — the full reality of each stage. If he fails to do justice to any portion of his psychological journey, then readers, trusting not the teller but the tale, will be tempted to "believe" in one stage more than in another. Those critics whom Trilling wishes to refute — those who see the Ode as a dirge over departing powers — clearly "believe" in the rendition of the stages of glory and loss, but give less credence to the final repossession of the world by metaphor. Trilling's suggestion — that such critics could not read Wordsworth's plain declaration of compensatory value — does not seem credible. It is more plausible to say that those who read the Ode as a dirge have decided that Wordsworth's closing protestations ring false; and not all of Trilling's insistence on the "hard necessity" of "growing up" will convince them if Wordsworth's own words did not.

I should like to look at Wordsworth's "languages" for his three states in order to address this discrepancy of conviction between Trilling and the critics he attempts to refute. It is through religious language that Wordsworth at first describes his childhood: the light is "celestial," the gleam is "visionary," and "there hath past away a glory from the earth" — an ironic echo of Jesus' prophecy, "Heaven and earth shall pass away, but my words shall not pass away." The child comes from *God*, trailing clouds of *glory*; as a youth, he is still attended by the *vision* splendid, and is Nature's *priest*. The child lives with Immortality brooding over him like the Spirit who dove-like sat brooding o'er the vast abyss; his freedom is *heaven-born;* he is a *prophet* and a *seer,* a *Soul* in the "eternal Silence." Now this vocabulary comes from the most powerful cluster of poetic words, images, and concepts in English, the King James Bible (as transmitted, moreover, through Milton). All these lavish resources of language are spent on the initial rendition of the first stage, the stage of glory. It is no wonder that critics brought up—in home, school, and church—to believe this world of religious discourse superior to all others found this part of the poem irresistible. Wordsworth had dared to clothe the experience of his own human childhood in the most sublime of literary modes, the mode of revealed religion. If the earthly paradise has been transformed, in Wordsworth as in Milton, to "a paradise within," it only renders the archetypal loss of Eden more painful. Wordsworth has not been expelled; it is his sight which has been darkened: those things which he has seen he now can see no more. The paradox resides in the double use of "see": the things both are and are not still there. Wordsworth departs from tradition in showing the non-Edenic world not as "wild woods forlorn" but as wholly beautiful to *the neutrally aesthetic eye* which sees only natural forms; at best this eye, a non-creative one, uses personifications well-worn into cliché:

The Rainbow comes and goes
And *lovely* is the Rose,
The Moon doth *with delight*
Look round her when the heavens are bare;
Waters on a starry night
Are *beautiful and fair;*
The sunshine is a *glorious birth.*

The whole substance of the poem lies in Wordsworth's transition from this inherited language, springing solely from the eye, to the language of the concluding lines of the poem, which springs from the heart and is never without human reference. "The innocent brightness of a new-born Day is lovely yet," says the final voice, and we are meant to recognize the difference between the pathos of that statement and one which says that the rose is lovely and that the sunshine is a glorious birth.

In the midst of Wordsworth's religious language describing human childhood, two metaphors stand out in a discrepancy which will become useful in creating his passage to the stage of loss. The original radiant experience is called a "dream," and our place

of origin, elsewhere named "heaven," is represented as an "imperial palace." "Dream," invoking illusion rather than religious vision, hints at the inevitability of waking; the palace, in its haughtiness ("imperial," though suggested by "empyreal," remains a hierarchical word) foreshadows by contrast the humanizing process to come. These slight tremblings of diction away from the religious premise presage the imminent crumbling of Wordsworth's rapt first language of isolation and spectatorship.

A *frission* of another sort arises from the intrusion into the pastoral scenery of language like some overture to a later, as yet unannounced, drama of strength in the poem. After the relief brought by the "timely utterance" (which Trilling, for his own "growing up" thesis, decides, without much in the way of support, was not "My Heart Leaps Up" but "Resolution and Independence"), Wordsworth's vista enlarges beyond the lambs, the birds, and the accompanying rose, rainbow, and sunshine:

I again am strong:
The cataracts blow their trumpets from the steep;
No more shall grief of mine the season wrong;
I hear the echoes through the mountains throng,
The winds come to me from the fields of sleep.

The resolve—"No more shall grief of mine the season wrong"—is, as we know, premature: but Wordsworth's instinct toward strength, (later reappearing in the variant "We will *grieve* not, rather find / *Strength* in what remains behind") shows that the new emotion of resolve required a new scenery— the sublimity of cataracts and "the steep" and mountains and winds, the majestic orchestration of trumpets, over against the pipes and tabors of pastoral joy. The dream, the imperial palace, and this fugitive and mysterious early appearance of the sublime all prepare us for the great analysis of loss which follows the original grieving memory of celestial light.

The analysis of loss is carried on in the middle sections (7, 8, and 9) of the poem, in which Wordsworth uses language of exceptional variety and interest, and invents a series of structures that threaten to rupture lyric convention. The central structure of the poem is the remarkable diptych of the six-year-old "little Child." On the left, so to speak (st. 7), we see the Child wholly in exterior semblance, and the passage is consequently written in a satiric mode. On the right (st. 8) we see the Child in his immensity of soul, and the passage is written in the spiritual mode appropriate to pure substance wholly removed from accident. (Coleridge, who should have known better, called this passage an example of "mental bombast or thoughts and images too great for the subject" [*Biographia Literaria*, ch. xxii].) Both satire and the *via negativa* of theology are in essence disharmonious to lyric, because lyric requires sympathy *vis-à-vis* its subject, and needs the images of sense for its language. By severing the Child's exterior semblance from his soul's immensity, and by becoming in consequence educational satirist on the one hand and theologian of the inexpressible on the other, Wordsworth risks his whole poem. If the Child's exterior is soulless, his interior is lifeless (it is "deaf" and "silent"). Such a dissevering of one human presence into two aspects generates thematic and stylistic tension, and a compensatory will-toward-harmony presses us to reintegrate the separated human principles of the child, his appearance and his soul.

The satiric stanza on the child is rightly compared to the Prelude's mockery of the "model child": in each, Wordsworth's fine eye for human development is grimly accurate. In the Ode, we last saw the child on the lap of his homely nurse, his foster-mother the earth, but at six, the child fatally leaves the nursery behind, repudiates the female lap and maternal kisses, and eagerly prepares to join the masculine world of business, love, or strife. In Wordsworth's symbolic tableau, the child is already expected to be "a little man." He has outgrown his nursery skirts and is dressed in male clothing, which grotesquely makes him appear, to Wordsworth's eye, a dwarfish version of the adult male — "a six years' Darling of a pygmy size." He has discovered how to please his father — by imitating adult transactions. He is annoyed when his mother — who wishes he were still the baby on her lap — makes possessive forays on his attention. The father's approval is all he seeks:

> Behold the Child among his new-born blisses,
> A six-years' Darling of a pygmy size!
> See, where 'mid work of his own hand he lies,
> Fretted by sallies of his mother's kisses,
> With light upon him from his father's eyes!

"Behold, see, see," says our guide in developmental psychology. The scorn of the guide is interveined with the pathos of the sight. Children in their imitative play invariably betray their ignorance of what a wedding is, what funerals entail.

> See, at his feet, some little plan or chart,
> Some fragment from his dream of human life,
> Shaped by himself with newly-learned art;
>> A wedding or a festival,
>> A mourning or a funeral.

"His dream of human life" — the voice almost breaks in the judgment of experience on innocence. The little Actor, conning one part after another, plays all the persons "down to palsied Age" — but the voice knows, as the six-year-old child playing the palsied elder does not, what palsy is, what Age is. The voice cries out in protest: the child is socialized by male approval into all these rôles and dramas and dialogues, says the voice, "as if his whole vocation / Were endless imitation." We know that in Wordsworth's lexicon the opposite of imitation is creation, and the true human vocation is not to be imitative, but rather to be "a sensitive being, a *creative* soul."

The ironic vocabulary of the satiric tableau is hard to bear. The true new-born blisses of the visionary gleam are replaced by the "new-born blisses" of social imitation; the child's "celestial light" is replaced by the "light upon him from his father's eyes"; the "glory and the freshness of a dream" is replaced by the child's ignorant "dream of human life"; the joy of the babe who "leaps up on his Mother's arm" is replaced by the little Actor's "joy and pride" as he masters rôles under his approving father's glance. Heart, song, tongue, and art are enrolled in the service of "endless imitation." If there is a center of despair in the Ode, it comes in this oppressive tableau of socialization. And yet this too is "growing up." Trilling nowhere dwells on this stanza, but simply abstracts Wordsworth's remark about the weight of custom, and talks about "maturity, with its habits and its cares and its increase of distance from our celestial origin." This is to treat "maturity" as something imposed upon us, with "habits and cares" its inevitable concomitant. But Wordsworth keenly sees the child's own eagerness to "grow up," and emphasizes the paternal role in the socializing of the boy. The tone of this stanza was, I should guess, deeply offensive to Trilling, since it departs from the homiletic and the exalted; and the content, incriminating us in our own loss of the light, despairingly confronting our eagerness to please our parents, was threatening to the value Trilling placed on the "mature" acceptance of the adult rôle. Consequently, nobody reading Trilling's essay could ever guess that the Ode contains anything like this stanza of satiric externality.

The poetic voice, passing from satire into its own adult pain, the pain of those "in darkness lost, the darkness of the grave," grieves at the child's haste to attain adulthood. But before he expresses his anguished wish to halt the child's precipitous eagerness for adult status, the poet addresses the child in a second tableau, paired with the first. If it is true that all odes address a Divinity, then the Divinity of this Ode is Reciprocity—a mutual Divinity which consists of the child receptive to the Eternal Mind and Immortality brooding over the child. (The demonic or ironic version of this Romantic reciprocity can be seen in Coleridge's "Limbo," where, in the tableau of the blind man with uplifted head in moonlight, the man "seems to gaze at that which seems to gaze on him.") Wordsworth's ironic and satiric language gives way, in this moment of intensest penetration, to the language of inexpressibility. The child is all Eye, all Seer. While the "exterior" child listens to words, frames songs, and fits his tongue to dialogues, this "interior" child is deaf and silent. He "reads" a text at once illimitable and unfathomable, the eternal deep, voluminous in extent and profundity. The paradoxes of the passage are theological: the child is both slave to his Immortality and the possessor of heaven-born freedom; he actively reads eternity but is passively haunted by the eternal mind; he is fixed on the eternal deep but stands glorious on the height of being; he is a prophet but voiceless; he is a philosopher who does not enunciate truths, but on whom truths rest. The Seer *blest,* the Eye among the *blind,* is yet, in the activities of his own socialization, *"blindly* with [his] *blessedness* at strife." This last phrase "undoes" the former one, and dissolves the seer-child into one of us. The earthly freight of "custom" or social posture will bury the child, and in exchange for the eternal *deep,* the child will experience that weight *"deep* almost as life."

These two tableaux, which form the center of the Ode, are reactions by *one* mind to *one* object—the six-year-old child. If we consider this child as he strives toward male adulthood, in his misconceived external occupations and games, he is an object of scorn and pathos; but if we consider him in his soul, which is still, through no will of its own, an Eye haunted by an Eternal Mind, he is an object of stricken awe. In neither case is he humanly attractive. It is evident that

the pygmy Actor is a repellent, if innocent, form; but it needs to be said as well that the child who is deaf and silent and a slave is also, for all his "blessedness" and "freedom," a deprived form. That child will, in the course of the poem, achieve authentic hearing and speech (which may be contrasted to the false speech of the little Actor). We believe in the acquisition of that true hearing and speech because of our uneasiness at the double portrait of the child, falsely framing "adult" dramas and language on the one hand, deaf and silent on the other.

Trilling's remarks about this central portion of the poem are odd. In his view the Ode is divided into two large parts, of which the first (1–4) poses the question of the disappearance of the glory. "The second half of the Ode," says Trilling (ignoring the fact that what he calls "the second half" should more properly, in terms of length, be called "the last two-thirds") "is divided into two large movements, each of which gives an answer to the question with which the first part ends":

The two answers seem to contradict each other. The first (5–8) issues in despair, the second (9–11) in hope; the first uses a language strikingly supernatural, the second is entirely naturalistic. The two parts even differ in the statement of fact, for the first says that the gleam is gone, whereas the second says that it is not gone, but only transmuted. It is necessary to understand this contradiction, but it is not necessary to resolve it, for from the circuit between its two poles comes much of the power of the poem.

I believe that most of what Trilling says in this excerpt is false. In his view, the structure of the poem can be diagrammed:

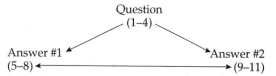

"Answer #1" and "Answer #2" remain opposed, Trilling has said, in a mutually energizing relation. "Answer #2" does not depend on "Answer #1" in this structure—they are autonomous parallel units. I would propose a counter-structure, wholly linear and sequential, divided into thirds, in which the closing stanzas (9–11) stand in a real and final relation to all that has preceded them. Because Trilling chooses not to mention the intensely "naturalistic" language of socialization in stanza 7 and in the close of stanza 8, he can represent the language of the first "answer" as "strikingly supernatural"; because he omits all mention of the race, the palms, the children on the shore of the immortal sea, and the faith that looks through death in stanzas 9–11, he can represent the language of the second "answer" as "entirely naturalistic." In following the fortunes of the gleam, he loses large portions of the poem, which retains its grasp on both ideality and reality throughout, and does not separate itself into "the supernatural" and "the naturalistic." Trilling even misrepresents the fate of the gleam: he says it is "transmuted" (a word not used by Wordsworth) and then, correcting himself, says it *"has not wholly fled, for it is remembered."* There is no contradiction between something which, itself, has wholly fled and something which is, though gone forever, remembered. Trilling confuses the remembered "truths that wake, to perish never" with the vanished "splendour in the grass, the glory in the flower." Wordsworth says, wholly explicitly, in the very "answer" where Trilling finds "transmutation," that "the radiance which was once so bright" is *"forever taken"* from his sight. That a "primal sympathy" remains is not to say that a gleam or a glory or a radiance remains. Trilling sees metaphor as a convenient way-station towards idea: but metaphor, for Wordsworth or any other poet, *is* idea. Had Wordsworth wished to say that the gleam was "transmuted" he would have said so.

In order to take issue with Trilling's troubling division of the ode into two autonomous "answers," it is necessary to establish the connections that Wordsworth draws between his despair at socialization and his final estimate of the value of the philosophic mind. As I see the Ode, Wordsworth implies, as much by the prior position of the one "answer" to the other as by any other means, that the acquisition of the philosophic mind depends on our participation, as we grow up, in a wedding or a festival, a mourning or a funeral; on those dialogues of "business, love, or strife"; on becoming, year by year, "all the Persons, down to palsied Age / That Life brings with her in her equipage." Wordsworth is saddened and irritated by the child's inordinate anticipation (in desire and act) of those stages: but the poem affirms (by its own schema of Child, Boy, Youth, and Man) that those stages are inescapable. They impose one terrible burden—the chill weight of custom—but they confer, at least on the "sensitive being, the *creative* soul," a benefit, wholly and amply described in the last two stanzas—a humanizing of the soul. Wordsworth's first mention of "the soothing thoughts that spring / Out of human suffering" is a cryptic one, but he subsequently gives convincing instances of those thoughts in his closing stanza.

It should also be mentioned, in contravention of Trilling, that Wordsworth is following, in his ode, the classic proportions of elegy. Every elegy descends to that point of death which is reached by Wordsworth in the weight of custom. The apotheosis or transfiguration which follows aims at the re-establishment of value, whether (in earlier poets) by the affirmation of a continuing life elsewhere or (since Milton, at least) the establishing of some domain corresponding to the paradise within. Trilling can of course choose to find Wordsworth's despair more convincing than Wordsworth's compensatory finale, and so represent them as two equally valid "answers": but the presence of the elegiac convention suggests that such was not Wordsworth's intent. Rather, he intended (as I believe his language shows) to "cure" the wounds of despair by his subsequent passages, not simply to offer two irreconcilable views of human life.

Wordsworth shows in the Ode a succession of wounds to the spirit. If we are to believe his closing assertions, and so see the poem as a cumulative experience, we must witness the healing of those wounds. Arnold was uncannily accurate in speaking of Wordsworth's "healing power": the Ode is in fact self-therapeutic, and in postulating his "two answers," irreconcilably if energetically co-existing, Trilling denies Wordsworth's therapeutic success. The success—which is a moral one achieved by literary means—rests on a powerfully plotted succession of what I have called "wounds" and "cures." The turn from the description of wounds to the performance of cures comes of course at the exclamation, "O joy!" *Embers* is cured by *remembers*; the cure for the loss of the light that has *died* away is something that doth *live*; the visionary gleam has *fled*, but nature yet remembers what was so *fugitive*; the child reading the *eternal* deep was a seer *blest*, but now memory breeds *perpetual benediction*; the *song* of the birds is replaced by the *song* of thanks and praise; the Immortality which was *master* to the child is, in the adult, the enduring *"master*-light" of recollection; its *cherishing* and *upholding* substitute for the *mother's* arm; its power to make "our noisy years seem moments in the being of the *eternal silence*" takes the place of the child's *silent* reading of the *eternal* mind. The truths that *wake* counteract the *sleep* of birth; the *sight* of the immortal sea and its children cures the *blindness* of adulthood; our ability to *travel* to that sea makes up for the fact that the Youth daily farther from the east must *travel*; the *hearing* of the mighty waters cures the *deafness* of the contemplative child. To join the youthful throng in *thought* becomes the appropriate response in lieu of the earlier strained wish to join in *feeling*; the initial thought of *grief* is refused in the resolve, "We will *grieve* not"; the premature "I again am *strong*" is renewed by the will to find "*strength* in what remains behind"; the "best *philosopher*" acquires the *philosophic* mind; and the faith that *looks through death* could only occur in a poem that had already looked back through birth (with a glance equally piercing a barrier) to "whence" the light flows, to "that imperial palace whence we came." In its great close, the Ode "cures" its own first lines: the meadows, groves, and streams have had added unto themselves fountains and hills; the *fountains* are a thematic and phonemic echo of the earlier *cataracts* in the *mountains*, while the *hills* are a memory of "the steep." In other words, the final landscape contains the sublimity missing in the first childhood pastoral scene, but subsequently incorporated in the first premature assertion of strength. The humanized brooks, day, clouds, and sunset replace the earlier exclusively visual items; the *setting* sun appears to recall "our life's star [which] hath had elsewhere its *setting*"; the *clouds* that gather round the setting sun replace the *clouds* of glory; the *sport* of the immortal children changes to the earnest *race* of the adult soul. We *live*, says Wordsworth, by the heart, by that something which doth *live* in our embers. Still, Wordsworth has not finished:

—But there's a Tree, of many, one,
A single Field which I have looked upon,
Both of them speak of something that is gone:
The Pansy at my feet
Doth the same tale repeat.

The admonitory Pansy *repeats* the *tale spoken* by the Tree and Field—a transfer of language from the poet to the elements in the landscape. The absence of which the landscape spoke must, above all, be "cured." The *apparel* of celestial light has been replaced by the *coloring* conferred on the clouds by the sobriety of the eye acquainted with the night; but what will, or can, the Pansy now say? Being a Pansy,

it will speak thoughts: but that alone is not enough. There is a deep fear in the poem that thought has replaced feeling: "we in *thought* will join your throng." And yet feeling, the heart, and love reappear intensely in the final stanza: "Yet in my *heart of hearts I feel* your might," "I *love* the Brooks . . . even *more*"; "thanks to the human *heart* by which we *live*." To end his poem, Wordsworth must place thought and feeling in some final and conclusive relation to each other; the landscape must be made to speak; and the new adjustment to "every *common* sight" must be established. Wordsworth generalizes his pansy, intensifies *common* into *mean*, translates *pensées* into *thoughts*, cures the weight of custom which "*lies deep* almost as life" with the thoughts which "*lie deep*" of the philosophic mind, and substitutes for the sublimity of cataracts which *blow* their trumpets and for the glory in the *flower*, the pathos of the *meanest flower that blows*:

To me the *meanest flower that blows* can give
Thoughts that do often *lie too deep* for tears.

It may be tedious so to anatomize Wordsworth's intense concentration of vocabulary (which I have by no means exhausted—see his plays on "forever" and "never," on "take" and "give," on "bring" and "bring back," on closing shades and gathering clouds, on guilt and innocence, etc.), but his moral import is convincing only because his homeopathic cure uses the vocabulary of the disease. By "solving" the answer of despair (deep-lying custom) with the answer of hope (deep-lying thoughts profounder than tears), Wordsworth intends to assert, as clearly as he can, that the feelings of despair are a waystation on the path to his ultimate powers of adulthood.

We return to the original question: to what extent is the Ode Wordsworth's dirge over departed powers? Wordsworth's original impulse—which everyone will agree was to lament those departed powers—still begins the Ode and sets an unforgettable tone. The long climb into compensatory complexity—painfully completed in thought during the two years in which Wordsworth left the Ode unfinished—was only completed in words during the composition of the last seven stanzas. Those readers who respond most strongly to the powerful adaptation of religious language at the opening of the ode will continue to feel that the dirge, having the "best" lines, is the "real" subject of the poem. Those who prefer the stoic and reparatory adult tone of the ending may agree with Trilling in rebuking the elegiac partisans. Those who, in conjunction with Trilling, see the weight of custom as an untranscended endpoint, will find an ineradicable pessimism in the Ode. But there is a passage which seems to escape the grasp of all these parties, and which is, nonetheless, the heart of the poem.

This passage, in the ninth stanza, embodies Wordsworth's *second* account of the psychological conditions he recalls from his childhood. Some extraordinary revaluation of his childhood experiences clearly occurred between the initial composition of the first four stanzas and the later completion of the poem. The first recollections had been ones purely of glory, dream, freshness, light, and gleam — the ravishments of sense. Wordsworth (in the Fenwich Notes) is perfectly explicit on the "dream-like vividness and splendour which invest objects of sight in childhood." There is, however, another, separate, and different recollection (italics mine):

> The poem rests entirely upon *two* recollections of childhood, *one* that of a splendour in the objects of sense which is passed away, and *the other* an indisposition to bend to the law of death as applying to our particular case. (W. to Mrs. Clarkson, Dec. 1814)

In the Fenwich Notes, Wordsworth speaks of the second recollection as an "abyss of idealism," says he wrote about it in the lines beginning "Obstinate questionings" etc., and adds that he was "often unable to think of external things as having external existence." De Selincourt cites a letter from Bonamy Price quoting Wordsworth: "There was a time in my life when I had to push against something that resisted, to be sure that there was anything outside me. I was sure of my own mind; everything else fell away, and vanished into thought" (*Works*, IV, pp. 463–467).

Trilling wrongly conflates these two separate recollections into one, saying, "We are told then, that light and glory consist, at least in part, of 'questionings,' 'fallings from us,' 'vanishings' and 'blank misgivings.'" Wordsworth nowhere says anything of the sort. What is most interesting about the poem is that Wordsworth chose first to recall only the ecstatic component in childhood, and to write a four-stanza lament for its disappearance. We can scarcely doubt that in the two years during which the unfinished Ode was troubling his mind, he thought more pro-

foundly about the nature of his childhood experience, and recognized that besides the ecstatic component clothing the world in light and glory, there was another component, dark, obscure, and subtractive. Nowhere in Wordsworth is there a stranger or more opaque description of human feeling than in the passage in which he declares that he is finally grateful not for childish delight or liberty or hope,

> But for those obstinate questionings
> Of sense and outward things,
> Fallings from us, vanishings;
> Blank misgivings of a Creature
> Moving about in worlds not realised,
> High instincts before which our mortal Nature
> Did tremble like a guilty Thing surprised.

This is, in language, virtually the only "unpaired" or "nonce" passage in the poem. In a work so consciously self-echoing, this characteristic alone marks the passage as one of special interest. In it, Wordsworth turns away entirely from the pictorial and imagistic language used to represent both the celestial light and the compensatory later vision of brooks, day, sunset, and flower. His vocabulary becomes abstract, unidiomatic ("fallings from us, vanishings"), and obsessive (question*ings*, th*ings*, fall*ings*, vanish*ings*, misgiv*ings*, Th*ing*). Commentary falters always before this passage, and perhaps will always fail. But a few observations may be risked. One myth behind the passage is that of our first parents apprehended by God in disobedience, or so I read the strong Miltonic echoes in "our mortal Nature . . . like a guilty Thing surprised." This hints at the difficulty of our attempt to liberate ourselves from "the spell / Of that strong frame of sense in which we dwell," as Wordsworth put it in one draft of the Ode. Our instinct for the high is in some sense a betrayal of our primary sense experience. The child's first creed has been that of sense; his "obstinate" questionings of sense are those of a heretic or a rebel. As outward things recede, the child feels literally robbed of his own corporeality: the loss of self expressed in "fallings *from us*, vanishings" is unnerving. One can only have "misgivings" where one has before had trust; just as one cannot be "obstinate" unless in the presence of a sovereign principle expecting submission. These are unpleasant experiences, inexplicable disorientations in a shadowy universe. Of course one would rather recall the "splendour in the objects of sense" than this mistrust of the "strong frame of sense," but

Wordsworth was able to complete the Ode only by at last recalling the first motions of *non*-sensuous instincts as the most valuable of his childhood experiences. The final human value affirmed by the Ode is that of thought arising from feeling. This value belongs rather to the realm of questioning and misgiving than to the splendor of transfigured sense. Had the Ode not contained this passage of awakened "high instinct" there could have been no continuity discovered between childhood and manhood: childhood would have been radiance and sense-experience, manhood the prison-house of waning responsiveness.

The epigraph to the Ode is often misread: it does not say, as an axiom, that the Child is Father of the Man. It says, in painful emotional relief, "The Child *is* Father of the Man; I had long doubted it; I wondered if any continuity of experience could be affirmed; but now I see that I am, in my adult state, descended from that child I once was; and if I should ever cease to feel this to be true, let me die!" Though the visionary gleam is *fled*, though the radiance is *forever* taken away, though *nothing* can bring back the hour of splendor and glory (and Wordsworth is explicit on the absolute disappearance of the *celestial* light), it is clear that the questionings and misgivings have not disappeared: on the contrary, they are the "truths that wake, / To perish never." Wordsworth does not say (as Trilling would have it) that "What was so intense a light in childhood becomes 'the fountain-light of all our day.'" He says rather that the misgivings and questionings of sense and outward things become that fountain-light. And they do so precisely because they are the foundation on which we construct our later trust in that inward affectional and intellectual reality "by which we live."

Trilling also maintains that in stanzas 9–11 Wordsworth "tells us of the everlasting connection of the *diminished person* with his own *ideal personality*. The child hands on to the *hampered adult* the imperial nature, the 'primal sympathy'" (italics mine). Nowhere, however, does Wordsworth suggest that the speaker had his *ideal personality* in childhood, or that he is now a *diminished person*, let alone a *hampered adult*. The deaf and silent Child-Seer is not describable as an ideal personality; he has in fact no personality at all. The adult capable of thoughts too deep for tears, who lives by the human heart, is not

diminished or hampered. In his inexplicable disregard for Wordsworth's own vocabulary and imagery, Trilling imposes on Wordsworth his own modernist sensibility. He was reading into Wordsworth the sort of thing he could find in Stevens:

> Now it is September and the web is woven. . . .
>
> It is all that you are, the final dwarf of you,
> That is woven and woven and waiting to be worn.

This is the sort of tone that Trilling's talk of the "diminished" and the "hampered" attributes to Wordsworth. And Trilling concludes his account of the Ode by saying that because Wordsworth was incapable of tragedy he could not write the poetry promised by his "bold declaration that he had acquired a new way of feeling."

If it is truer to say, as I believe it is, that the Ode represents the acquisition of the power of metaphor; that to rest in either the splendor of sense or in blank misgivings is not to be a poet; that to join the external world of sense-experience with the interior world of moral consciousness is to become an adult; that to express that juncture in metaphor is to become a poet — then all of Wordsworth's great poetry is the result of the process of the humanizing of sense and the symbolizing of interior experience described by the Ode. Affectional feeling (and not, as Trilling says, "the knowledge of man's mortality" alone) "replaces the 'glory' as the agency which makes things significant and precious." It is "thanks to the human *heart* . . . , its *tenderness*, its *joys* and *fears*," that a common flower can bear a new weight of meaning. In the epigraph to his poem "To the Daisy," Wordsworth quotes George Wither, who says his *Muse's divine skill* taught him

> That from everything I saw
> I could some instruction draw
> And raise pleasure to the height
> Through the *meanest object's* sight. (italics mine)

It is this capacity of the Muse — absolutely unattainable by the six-years' darling, however blessed his Soul's immensity — that is celebrated in the Ode.

In *The Meaning of a Literary Idea* Trilling proposed to examine "the relation which should properly obtain between what we call creative literature and what we call ideas," and he continues:

> When I consider the respective products of the poetic and of the philosophic mind, although I can see

that they are by no means the same and although I can conceive that different processes, even different mental faculties, were at work to make them and to make them different, I cannot resist the impulse to put stress on their similarity and on their easy assimilation to each other.

"We demand of our literature," Trilling asserts (appropriating the rest of us to his view by his grand "we"), "the authority, the cogency, the completeness, the brilliance, the *hardness* of systematic thought." And, he adds, "the aesthetic upon which the critic sets primary store is to the poet himself frequently of only secondary importance." These, among others, are the principles which led Trilling astray in his account of the Ode. Of course it was to Wordsworth wholly urgent to speak the truth about human life as he perceived it; but his utterance does not put "the aesthetic" secondary and "truth" primary. His truth lies in his way of speaking his truths. And if the critic is not to set primary store upon the aesthetic, how is he to explain his interest in this utterance at all? As for the cogency and authority and brilliance which Trilling seeks, they must be, in poetry, a cogency and authority and brilliance of expression and disposition of materials, not necessarily of "systematic thought." Trilling's "easy assimilation" of import to poem leads him, paradoxically, to a dispensing with genuine import, since he neglects import's imparting of itself. "My own interests," said Trilling writing *On the Teaching of Modern Literature*, "lead me to see literary situations as cultural situations, and cultural situations as great elaborate fights about moral issues." Perhaps he was uneasy with the lyric because it turns inward, away from polemic, away from any explicit concern with those "great elaborate fights" and away equally from the broad literary effects employed by epic, novel, and satire. Trilling recalled, in his essay on Isaac Babel, that what he had wanted in

his youth from the Russian Revolution was "an art that would have as little ambiguity as a proposition in logic." Though his adult self repudiated this boyish wish, something of it remains in his conviction that the Ode presents "statements" and "answers." Such a vocabulary is inadequate to an art devoted, in Wordsworth's view, to "the history and science of feeling." Our thoughts, to Wordsworth's mind, are not the repository of "systematic thought," but are rather "the representatives of all our past feelings." One feels that Trilling could never be quite happy with a work of literature that presents itself, as the Ode does, as a history and analysis of past and present feeling. A "great elaborate fight about a moral issue" was more to his taste; and his essay on the Ode did its best to see the Ode as a Freudian polemic, representing the diminution of the "oceanic feeling" into inevitable subjection to the superego, with a consequent literary commitment to tragedy, a subject unsuitable to its poet. He missed Wordsworth's complexity of presentation and the synthesis offered by *poesis* to the previous thesis and antithesis of childhood and custom. If Wordsworth's Ode means anything to us now, it is not as a convenient illustration of a pre-existent schema drawn from Freudian doctrine. It "means" by its hard-won setting of a later scene of consciousness against an earlier one; by virtue of the minutely-created antiphonal relation of the later to the earlier; by its refusal to affirm a unity of early and late selfhood without a unity of early and late language; and most of all by its ability to invent, mediating between the language of childhood sense and its mirror-language of adult inwardness, a language of disorientation, which conveys the difficulty inherent in the relation of consciousness to sense-experience, that difficulty which the great poetry of the Ode so triumphantly overcomes.

*While acknowledging the increasing sophistication of
Chopin criticism, John R. May complains that readers
are still inclined "to focus too exclusively on the heroine's 'awakening' to the demands of her sexuality." By
seizing on the most obvious or overt theme, we miss the
novel's wider significance. The remedy is closer reading.
Through careful analysis of the concrete details of setting
and structure we will come to see the work's more universal themes: the "human longing for freedom" and
the "agony of human limitations." By insisting that
the larger significance is in the smaller details, May reasserts Cleanth Brooks's point that "the poet can legitimately step out into the universal only by first going
through the narrow door of the particular" and W. K.
Wimsatt's argument that in the literary work of art the
universal inheres in the concrete particulars. In short, we
can discover the meaning of the whole only by a formal
analysis of the parts, and this is as true for prose fiction
as it is for a sonnet.*

*As May notes, there is an irony in his title, for "local
color" has long been used to denote and dismiss works
that seem to offer no more than local color—that is,
whose purpose appears to be only to trace the physical
and social characteristics of a region, to offer a travelogue
rather than insight into human experience. But in the
good novel, as the formalist reminds us, all details of
setting must be thematically relevant. Ideally, the novel
should achieve the same degree of unity and coherence we
expect from a lyric poem. As May sees it, Chopin's novel
meets this test. Analyzing the details of setting as these
function symbolically, May discovers a complex but coherent text that presents a universal statement about human freedom and limitations. But this "statement" is
available only to those readers who trouble to search for
the thematic implications of Chopin's "local color."*

Reprinted by permission of the author from *The Southern
Review* 6 (1970): 1031–40. Copyright © 1970 by John R.
May.

APPLICATION

Local Color in *The Awakening*

John R. May

The available criticism of Kate Chopin's *The Awak-ening*, although not impressive in quantity, reveals a remarkable and enthusiastic unanimity concerning the artistic value of the novel and the claim that it has to wider acceptance. Before the revival of interest in the novel in the early 1950s, the criticism was excessively moralistic in tone; yet even the recent critics — although past shock at its treatment of infidelity — seem still to focus too exclusively on the heroine's "awakening" to the demands of her sexuality. Typical of such interpretation is Larzer Ziff's statement that *"The Awakening* was the most important piece of fiction about the sexual life of a woman written to date in America."[1] Even Per Seyersted's recent critical biography of Kate Chopin leaves much to be desired on this score. Although he considers the existentialist theme of the "curse of Freedom," it is always within the consistent critical framework of his reading of the novel as "a eulogy on sex and a muted elegy on the female condition."[2] George Arms is the only commentator who has given lengthy treatment to another reading of the novel.[3]

Greater attention, it seems to me, has to be given to the integral relationship between local color in the novel and the development of its theme, as well as to Kate Chopin's use of related symbolism. There is no doubt a certain irony in suggesting a new reading of *The Awakening* in terms of its local color. It was precisely because of diminished interest in regional literature that many commentators feel it was so long ignored; there is the obvious implication that regional literature is somehow incompatible with universal appeal. In exploring both local color and related symbolism more fully though, it seems to me that critics will do greater justice to the profundity of Kate Chopin's theme. For the novel is not simply about a woman's awakening need for sexual satisfaction that her marriage cannot provide; sexuality in the novel represents a more universal human longing for freedom, and the frustration that Edna experiences is a poignant statement about the agony of human limitations.

Edna Pontellier is "an American woman."[4] Born of Presbyterian stock in the Kentucky bluegrass country, she marries into the Creole society of New Orleans — an environment of marked contrast to the severity of her own background. And the summer at Grand Isle, when the novel begins, puts her in closer contact with the Creoles than she had ever before experienced. She is profoundly impressed by "their en-tire absence of prudery" (p. 889), a freedom of expression that nonetheless seems to be quite reconcilable with the sense of chastity that is unmistakable in Creole women. She is shocked by the fact that the women openly relate the harrowing details of their *accouchements,* listen to droll stories told by the men, and trade and discuss publicly books that she is more inclined simply to read in secrecy. Nor is Edna at all accustomed to their "outward and spoken expression of affection" (p. 897); whatever friends she had had previously had been "all of one type — the self-contained" (p. 897). Moreover, the Creoles all seem to know each other well and at the Lebrun summer cottages live "like one large family" (p. 889). Owing primarily to the influence of Adèle Ratignolle, we are told, Edna begins "to loosen a little the mantle of reserve that had always enveloped her" (p. 893). These elements of local color — absence of prudery, familiarity, and open expression of affection — are all crucial to the atmosphere that causes Edna's "awakening," and they are qualities taken as a whole that seem quite unique — in America at least — to the French culture of the Creole society of Southern Louisiana.

There is a wealth of sensuous imagery in the novel, and this has been noted consistently by the critics; but what has not been noticed — apparently not even by Seyersted — is that sensuousness is a characteristic feature of the setting, a product of climate and the Creole temperament. And thus it must be considered primarily as constituting the new environment that Edna marries into, and not as directly supporting a preoccupation with sexual freedom. It is this environment that becomes the undoing of the American woman.

Kate Chopin appeals subtly to all of the reader's senses, and her descriptions are delicate impressionistic touches on her canvas of New Orleans and Grand Isle. In her use of color she is similar to Stephen Crane, yet somehow the strokes of her brush are less jarring. Léonce Pontellier watches his wife and Robert Lebrun approach the cottage: "He fixed his gaze upon a white sunshade that was advancing at a snail's pace from the beach. He could see it plainly between the gaunt trunks of the water-oaks and across the stretch of yellow camomile. The gulf looked far away, melting hazily into the blue of the horizon" (p. 882). When Edna goes with Arobin to the "pigeon-house" after her farewell party, she notices "the black line of his leg moving in and out so close to her against the yellow shimmer of her gown" (p. 975). The garden that Edna visits in the suburbs of New Orleans is "a small, leafy corner, with a few green tables under the orange trees" (p. 989).

The Gulf breeze that reaches the Lebrun cottages is "soft and languorous . . . , charged with the seductive odor of the sea" (p. 892). After the Lebrun party, as the guests leave for the beach, there are "strange, rare odors abroad—a tangle of the sea smell and of weeds and damp, new-plowed earth, mingled with the heavy perfume of a field of white blossoms somewhere near" (p. 907). "The everlasting voice of the sea" breaks "like a mournful lullaby upon the night" (p. 886).

As the story progresses there is an increasing emphasis on tactile imagery. When Victor ceremoniously apologizes for offending Edna, the touch of his lips is "like a pleasing sting to her hand" (p. 974). During her reunion with Robert, Edna notices the "same tender caress" (p. 982) of his eyes. Edna's "soft, cool delicate kiss" is a "voluptuous sting" (p. 991), penetrating Robert's whole being. When Edna leaves Adèle after the birth of her child, the air is "mild and caressing, but cool with the breath of spring and the night" (p. 995).

It is the personification of the sea, though, that dominates all the imagery. The sea is undoubtedly the central symbol of the novel; like all natural symbols it is basically ambiguous. Initially, though, it embodies for Edna all of the sensuousness of her new environment. The early passage describing the voice and touch of the sea becomes a poetic refrain when repeated at the close of the story. The sea presides over the dawn of Edna's awakening as it does over the night of her fate; but it is not just another sea, as Seyersted seems to imply.[5] The images attempt to capture the mystery and enchantment of the semi-tropical summer Gulf: "The voice of the sea is seductive; never ceasing, whispering, clamoring, murmuring, inviting the soul to wander for a spell in abysses of solitude; to lose itself in mazes of inward contemplation. The voice of the sea speaks to the soul. The touch of the sea is sensuous, enfolding the body in its soft, close embrace" (p. 893).

When the description appears again in the final chapter (pp. 999–1000), the words "for a spell" have been dropped and the first sentence ends with "solitude." The second sentence is not repeated. The effect of the repetition is to suggest that the end for Edna was indeed the beginning of her awakening. The omissions emphasize the finality of her solitude;

she gives herself to the sea only because she has already lost herself in a maze of self-contemplation.

The full symbolism of the novel is complex, yet Kate Chopin proves herself at all times to be the master of it. Supporting the rhythmic movement of the narrative from Grand Isle to the Creole quarter of New Orleans and back to Grand Isle are the basic symbols of sea and city. Even though the Lebrun cottages at Grand Isle the summer the novel begins are occupied exclusively by Creoles, there is a more relaxed atmosphere at the beach than in the winter of the city—because there one must "observe *les convenances*" (p. 932). The tension between freedom and restraint is evident in the use of the symbols.

Paralleling the significance of sea and city in the temporal sequence of the narrative is Edna's remembrance of the contrast between the Kentucky meadow and the Presbyterian household of her youth. She recalls the summer day when as a child she ran from the Sunday prayer service that her father always conducted "in a spirit of gloom" (p. 896). The meadow seemed like an ocean to her as she walked through it, "beating the tall grass as one strikes out in the water" (p. 896). "My sunbonnet obstructed the view," she tells Adèle; "I could see only the stretch of green before me, and I felt as if I must walk on forever, without coming to an end of it. . . . Sometimes I feel this summer as if I were walking through the green meadow again; idly, aimlessly, unthinking and unguided" (pp. 896–97).

The lady in black, the young lovers, and the mother-women represent the actual limits imposed by the Creole environment; as symbols they specify the restraint of the city. The lady in black is either "walking demurely up and down, telling her beads" (p. 882), or "reading her morning devotions" (p. 895). The young lovers lean upon each other like "water-oaks bent from the sea" (p. 901), "exchanging their vows and sighs" (p. 899) and showing an inclination "to linger and hold themselves apart" (p. 907). Yet it is the mother-women who seem to prevail: "It was easy to know them, fluttering about with extended, protecting wings when any harm, real or imaginary, threatened their precious brood. They were women who idolized their children, worshipped their husbands, and esteemed it a holy privilege to efface themselves as individuals and grow wings as ministering angels" (p. 888). By reason of her marriage and children, Edna rightfully belongs to this group; but she is not and cannot be a mother-woman.

In the criticism of the novel to date, no one has commented on the symbolic stages of Edna's rebellion against the restraints of Creole society—a withdrawal into solitude that poses as a quest for freedom. The sequence also adds irony to the final meaning of the sea. I refer here to the significance of the home on Esplanade Street, the "pigeonhouse" around the corner, the garden in the suburbs, and finally the sea. The Pontellier home on Esplanade is a perfect microcosm of the restraints of the Creole city. There Edna must be mistress of the household, receive callers on Tuesday afternoons, and be the perfect mother-woman. Yet, even while still there, Edna stops receiving callers, abandons the household to the erratic performance of the servants, and severs ties with her family. She refuses to attend her sister's wedding; and when her father terminates his shopping trip to New Orleans, which is also an abortive mission of persuasion, Edna is "glad to be rid of . . . his wedding garments and his bridal gifts, . . . his padded shoulders, his Bible reading, his 'toddies' and his ponderous oaths" (p. 954). At the farewell party, Edna's appearance suggests "the regal woman, the one who rules, who looks on, *who stands alone*" (p. 972, my emphasis). The "pigeonhouse," which Edna moves into in her husband's absence, the first stage of her actual physical withdrawal from Creole society, is just large enough to satisfy her needs. She knows that she will "like the feeling of freedom and independence" (p. 963). Seyersted's preoccupation with sexual freedom leads him at this point to ignore the obvious reference to the size of the place in relation to the home on Esplanade and to suggest that "it is to be a place of cooing love."[6]

After her disappointing reunion with Robert, Edna becomes the prey of alternating moods of hope and despondency. Robert does not return to see her during the days that follow. "Each morning she awoke with hope, and each night she was a prey to despondency" (p. 988). Then one night Arobin asks her to drive with him out to the lake. Her realization that it has become "more than a passing whim with Arobin to see her and be with her" (p. 988) leads to a second and more significant stage in her withdrawal. We are told that "there was no despondency when she fell asleep that night; nor was there hope when she awoke in the morning" (p. 989). Significantly, the very next scene takes place in a garden in the suburbs—a place "too modest to attract the attention of the people of fashion, and so quiet as to have escaped the notice of those in search of pleasure and dissipation" (p. 989).

The final stage of Edna's withdrawal is, of course, the return to Grand Isle and the sea. It is the day after Robert has left her the note which says: "I love you, Good-bye—because I love you" (p. 997). Despondency has returned to her and has not left. Now, at the beach, there is "no living thing in sight" (p. 999). "Absolutely alone," Edna removes her "unpleasant, pricking garments" (p. 1000) and swims out into the water. The sea which at first spoke sensuously to Edna of freedom has become finally the symbol of her liberation—but, also, ironically, of her complete withdrawal from society, her total isolation. It is curious that, as she swims on, Edna is drawn back in her memory to the days of her youth. She hears the voices of her father and sister, the barking of a chained dog, the clanging spur of the cavalry officer, and the hum of the bees. Seyersted, consistent as always with his critical motif, sees these final lines as "a parable on the female condition."[7] He ignores the voices and the barking dog to note the symbol of male dominance in the clanging spurs and the generative symbolism of the bees. The meaning of Edna's recollections is, at best, ambiguous. Although the sea and the meadow were associated earlier, she remembers now instead the sounds of her Presbyterian home. The gradual diminution of sound may indicate simply that her strength is gone, but it may also suggest ironically that Edna is returning home—defeated.

In what sense, then, has Edna been awakened by the alien Creole environment? I have already suggested that an explanation of her awakening simply in terms of a growing awareness of her sexual needs is too facile an interpretation of this rather complex novel. On a much deeper level Edna awakens to the reality of her own nature in relation to life. In seeking to possess Robert and be possessed by him, she has allowed herself to be duped by the sensuous freedom of the environment into thinking that she can satisfy her deepest human longings. Robert himself represents the unattainable, the possibilities that life offers, but never actualizes. During her farewell party on Esplanade Street, Edna experiences "the acute longing which always summoned into her spiritual vision the presence of the beloved one, overpowering her at once with a sense of the unattainable" (p. 972). It is longing which summons Robert as its symbol.

While still at Grand Isle, where her "awakening" begins, Edna is disturbed by dreams that leave "only an impression on her half-awakened senses of something unattainable" (p. 913). She pities Adèle Ratignolle because of the "colorless existence" that Adèle leads as a mother-woman, one "in which she would never have the taste of life's delirium" (p. 938), although Edna wonders at the time what she means by "life's delirium." The irony here, and Edna clearly awakens to this realization, is that life's delirium is never attainable. There are days when she feels as if life is passing her by, "leaving its promise broken and unfulfilled" (p. 956), yet others when she is "led on and *deceived* by fresh promises" (p. 956, my emphasis). Once when Edna is with Robert at Grand Isle and again when she returns from Adèle's at the end of the novel, she has the sensation of striving to overtake her thoughts (pp. 910, 995).

Life itself creates the longing within her, but it never fulfills its promise. Edna is not simply a dreamer, a romantic, because it was life that offered her the promise of the sad-eyed cavalry officer, the engaged young men, and the great tragedian. The fulfillment though was only the frustration of Léonce Pontellier, Alcée Arobin, and Robert Lebrun. Life among the Creoles promised familiarity, open expression of affection, and freedom from moral rigor, but then only as a mother-woman, a lady in black, or an innocent young lover.

It is nature and man that conspire to frustrate human longing. "As if a mist had been lifted from her eyes," Edna awakens to "the significance of life, that monster made up of beauty and brutality" (p. 967). Clearly, beauty and brutality correspond to vision and reality, promise and fulfillment. When, finally, Edna assists Adèle in childbirth, it is "with an inward agony, with a flaming, outspoken revolt against the ways of Nature" (p. 995). Doctor Mandelet, sensing the honest questions that Edna wants to ask, attempts an answer: "The trouble is . . . that youth is given up to illusions. It seems to be a provision of Nature; a decoy to secure mothers for the race. And Nature takes no account of moral consequences, of arbitrary conditions which we create, and which we feel obligated to maintain at any cost" (p. 996).

If Edna opens her eyes to the tyranny of life, she also becomes aware of her own nature. She is "a solitary soul," as Kate Chopin's original title for the novel indicated.[8] Nature has made her independent, willful, and selfish. When she moves from the home on Esplanade, she resolves "never again to belong to another than herself" (p. 963). She assures Robert, "I give myself where I choose" (p. 992). And when Doctor Mandelet asks if she is going abroad with her husband, Edna answers: "I'm not going to be forced into doing things. . . . I want to be let alone" (p. 995). Realizing that she is "wanting a good deal," she adds, "I don't want anything but my own way" (p. 996).

In reality, the Creole setting has simply provided a climate of psychological relaxation sufficient to allow Edna's true nature to reveal itself. Thus, because Edna is what she is, the longing for freedom has become the assertion of independence. The possibility of an open break with tradition has led simply to withdrawal from life. And the atmosphere of familiarity has revealed her radical incapacity to deal with anyone except on her own terms.

When Edna recalls that the friends of her youth had been of the self-contained type, the author notes: "She never realized that the reserve of her own character had much, perhaps everything, to do with this" (p. 897). Even Léonce Pontellier did not realize what was happening to his wife, "that she was becoming herself and daily casting aside that fictitious self which we assume like a garment with which to appear before the world" (p. 939). Only Mlle Reisz and Adèle Ratignolle seemed to sense, though vaguely, what was actually happening. Mlle Reisz had warned Edna, "The bird that would soar above the level plain of tradition and prejudice must have strong wings" (p. 966). Thus, expectedly, when Edna walks to the beach at Grand Isle for the last time, a bird with a broken wing hovers above her, "reeling, fluttering, circling disabled down, down to the water" (p. 999). And Adèle had pleaded with Robert, "Let Mrs. Pontellier alone. . . . She is not one of us" (p. 900).

Edna Pontellier's final revolt against nature, when she swims to her death in the sea, is certainly not an eventuality that the reader is unprepared for. Her innate sense of independence and her desire to assert her freedom, despite nature's refusal to satisfy her longing, have led her "step by inexorable step,"[9] in Stanley Kauffmann's phrase, to withdraw from life. The stages of her withdrawal into the solitude of complete isolation are symbolized, as we have seen, by the retreat from the home on Esplanade to the "pigeon-house," the garden, and the sea. The ultimate realization that she has awakened to is that the only way she can save herself is to give up her life (pp. 929, 999). She cannot accept the restrictions that nature and man have conspired to impose upon her, the perpetual frustration of desire that living entails. And so, paradoxically, she surrenders her life in order to save herself.

Although it is difficult—perhaps presumptuous—to write with assurance about the essence of local color, it seems safe to say that a local color novel is one in which the identity of the setting is integral to the very unfolding of the theme, rather than simply incidental to a theme that could as well be set anywhere. *The Awakening* is clearly of the former type. The greater freedom of the new environment—with all of its characteristic sensuousness—has tempted Edna to reach for the unattainable because, in contrast with the severity of her Kentucky background, the summer at Grand Isle actually deluded her into thinking that her deepest longings could be satisfied. By the time she awakens to the cruel illusion nurtured by life in her new environment, her independent and selfish temperament—which supported her vain efforts—has led her irrevocably into abysses of solitude.

Notes

1. Larzer Ziff, *The American 1890s* (New York, 1966), p. 304.
2. Per Seyersted, *Kate Chopin: A Critical Biography* (Baton Rouge: Louisiana State University Press, 1969), p. 160.
3. George Arms, "Kate Chopin's *The Awakening* in the Perspective of Her Literary Career," in *Essays on American Literature in Honor of Jay B. Hubbell*, ed. Clarence Gohdes (Durham, N. C., 1968), pp. 215–228.
4. *The Complete Works of Kate Chopin*, ed. Per Seyersted, Vol. II (Baton Rouge: Louisiana State University Press), p. 884. Page references hereafter incorporated in the text are to this recent edition, now the standard edition of Kate Chopin's works.
5. Seyersted, *Chopin: A Critical Biography*, p. 151.
6. *Ibid.*, p. 159.
7. *Ibid.*, p. 160.
8. Daniel S. Rankin, *Kate Chopin and Her Creole Stories* (Philadelphia, 1932), p. 171.
9. Stanley Kauffmann, "The Really Lost Generation," *New Republic*, CLV (December 3, 1966), 38.

CHAPTER THREE

Reader-Response Criticism: Audience as Context

'Tis with our Judgments *as our* Watches, *none*
Go just alike, *yet each believes his own.*

          —Pope, *An Essay on Criticism*

While genetic critics ground their approach on the firm fact that poems have authors, reader-response critics claim the equally solid ground that they also have audiences. By starting at this end of the communication line, they avoid most of the difficulties that trouble historical criticism. Certainly a poem is caused to exist at a particular time, but it continues to exist long after its causes have vanished. Authors grow old and die, and the circumstances of the poem's creation are soon lost in the irrevocable past. But the poem, a foster child of silence and slow time, remains for us in the perpetual present.

For reader-response, critics are most often concerned with the present audience. There are, it should be noted, audience-oriented critics with a historical bent who study the reception of poems over time. And there have long been studies focused on the poem's original audience. But these latter are really forms of historical criticism that assume if we could learn to think like the intended audience, we could recover the author's intended meaning. Most reader-response critics have little interest in authors or intended meanings. The poem exists now. It affects us now. These, they claim, are the crucial facts, and any relevant criticism must be built on them.

Not only do poems exist independently of their authors, they are almost always valued independently of their original contexts. Even historical criticism must start from this point. Milton's biography has received more attention than Cowley's because we have judged Milton's poems, not his life, to be more important than Cowley's. We may try to become Elizabethans to understand *The Tempest;* we do not read *The Tempest* to become Elizabethans. That is, we must first respond to the power of poems before we trouble to investigate their causes. What is that power, and what is the nature of our response to it? What happens when we read a novel, hear a poem, see a play? What is this interaction between audience and work without which that work would have no meaningful existence and certainly no value? The study of these questions, says the reader-response critic, is the chief business of literary criticism.

But before we consider what such study entails, we need to make some distinctions. Everyone agrees that we are affected by literature — delighted, disturbed, sometimes even instructed. Concern with the effects of poetry is as old as Aristophanes and as recent as the latest censorship case; and the long-playing debate about the moral and educative value of poetry has occasionally produced an attack, like Plato's, or a defense, like Shelley's, which are important documents in the history of literary criticism. But only very occasionally. Similarly, the sort of affectiveness found in numerous impressionistic essays that tell us how the critic felt while reading may seldom contribute directly to our general understanding of literature. In other words, while a good deal of the talk about literature has always been loosely affective, significant attempts to develop a consistent theory along these lines have been few, and most of these are quite modern.

There is, to be sure, the long and strong "rhetorical" tradition, which includes Aristotle, Horace, Cicero, Quintilian, and their legions of followers in Renaissance and post-Renaissance Europe. Certainly the language of this tradition is heavily "affective," stressing the ways authors can persuade or otherwise work upon their audiences. But in practice the rhetorical approach, especially when it was applied to poetry and drama, concentrated on the formal arrangement of elements within the work. It was assumed that these arrangements would produce certain effects, but little attempt was made to demonstrate this assumption or to study the responses of actual audiences. Consequently, the real heirs of this tradition have been the modern formalists who found they could use the well-developed terminology of the rhetoricians in their analyses while paying scant attention to the study of audience response.

But such study has become the focus of several other schools of modern criticism, and especially of those based on some form of psychology, for the very conception of the reader–poem context invites a psychological investigation. In fact, there are probably as many different approaches as there are different kinds of psychology. Experimental psychologists, for example, have wired readers to galvanometers, with sometimes hilarious results, and some other schools of psychology have appeared only slightly less clumsy when they have tried to deal with the subtleties of poetry. But two psychological theories, the Freudian and the Jungian, have seemed to hold a special promise to illuminate our reactions to literature. In the Freudian view, the poem, like the dream, has its manifest and latent content. Like the dream, it works for the reader's psyche. And like the dream, it yields its real meaning only to the critic trained in the proper psychoanalytic techniques. Until fairly recently, though, the reader-response applications of Freudian psychology have been less fully developed than the genetic or mimetic applications. The theories of Carl Jung, on the other hand, have been most frequently employed in the affective context to account for the power of poetry. Jung's model of the different facets of the human psyche, his idea of the "collective unconscious," and above all his conceptions of "symbol" and "archetype" have seemed to many critics directly applicable to our experience of literature.

Jungian ideas have strongly influenced a number of studies usually classed under the label "myth criticism." Such studies may show as well the influence of mythographers like G. S. Frazer, Gilbert Murray, and Joseph Campbell. As this diversity of influences suggests, "myth criticism" is not a single approach or a unified school, and in terms of the organization of this book "myth critics" can be found in most of our contexts. But they are found most often in the affective context for, whether they base their readings on Jung or on some other model of the human psyche, they agree that the power of literature chiefly resides in its presentation of special symbols, characters, and patterns of action to which we respond at the deepest levels of our being.

Great literature, in this view, is not great because it possesses complex verbal texture, realistic characters, fidelity to historical fact, or formal symmetry. A poem can have all these qualities and still be second-rate. Conversely, it can be marred by textual lacunae, as is the *Oresteia,* or by structural flaws, as is *Moby Dick,* and still succeed brilliantly. For in the imagery and characters of great works, in the green gardens and wintery wastelands, in the questing heroes and menacing villains, and in the archetypal patterns of their actions that form analogies to rites of spring and rites of passage, to cycles of death and rebirth, we recognize, usually at some subconscious level, the images and actions that haunt our dreams and that form the substance of our psychic lives. Here, too, as in the Freudian model, the poem is seen to have levels of meaning, a surface level available to formal or rhetorical analysis and a deeper level that can only be explained by those armed with the insights of psychological theory. Unarmed readers may believe they are responding to the surface level, but they are really being affected by the underlying patterns of archetypal symbolism.

But not all sophisticated forms of affective criticism depend on a type of depth psychology. In the third decade of this century, I. A. Richards, whose bent was empirical and behavioristic, developed an influential line of reader-response criticism, a line that included a fully argued theory of affective value. Since the strengths and the weaknesses of Richards's theory are in many respects representative, it will be worthwhile to examine his argument. Richards, an aesthetician, psychologist, and pioneering semanticist as well as a man well read in ancient and modern literature, differed from many twentieth-century critics in his willingness to concede that the scientific conception of truth is correct. Science provides accurate statements about the world; poems supply only "pseudo-statements." At the outset, then, Richards abandoned the traditional mimetic justifications for literature. With equal nonchalance, he abandoned the genetic researches so vigorously pursued by historical critics. The study of the circumstances of the poem's creation is simply not very relevant.

We are left, then, with some artfully constructed "pseudo-statements" and their readers. This may not look like a very promising basis for a defense of poetry. But people, Richards reminds us, do not live by scientific truth alone. Indeed, they live very little by it. Human beings are essentially bundles of desires and aversions, of "appetencies," to use Richards's term. Our lives consist of trying to satisfy as many of these appetencies as we can. And this task is not simple. The universe seldom seems designed to our purposes, other people's desires frequently contend with ours, and—perhaps most troublesome—our own appetencies are often in conflict.

Yet our psychic health depends entirely on our ability to harmonize and satisfy these appetencies. The desire for truth is only one appetency, and in awarding its satisfaction to science Richards was not awarding so much as it might seem. For people have many other needs, one of the most important being a need to construct a vision of the world in which we can feel at home. Religion used to supply this vision, but since we moderns have largely lost our religious beliefs without losing the wants they used to satisfy, it will fall to poetry to fill their place, just as Matthew Arnold had predicted. More accurately, we now see from this perspective that religion, myth, and poetry are functionally the same thing. They are all imaginative constructs. The mistake was to think of them as offering "truth" in the scientific sense. The real purpose of art is to answer the human need for an intelligible and satisfying vision of the universe and our place within it and to answer as well our many other psychic wants, few of which can be met by scientific truth or the brute facts of experience. And poetry, because it operates through language, the most potent and flexible artistic medium, can encompass the greatest part of our psychic life, can appeal to and harmonize the greatest number of our appetencies. Poetry is art *par excellence.*

One advantage of Richards's view is that it offers to account for all features of the literary work. As we noticed, the depth psychologists' attempts to explain the power of poems sometimes produce analyses that strip away the verbal texture and rhetorical structure of the work to reveal its underlying patterns, its embodiment of the dream or the myth that carries its true appeal. This focus on the latent content opens these methods to the charge that they are reductive, that they fail to deal with the art of poetry, and that, in their search for the mythic patterns or psychological mechanisms that inform many poems, such methods ignore the unique poem before them. If the oedipal conflict is the heart of *Hamlet,* in what ways does Shakespeare's play differ from an analyst's case history? If all tragedies embody the death–rebirth cycle, then why does *King Lear* affect us more strongly than *Alcestis* does, and why is a performance of *Oedipus Tyrannus* more powerful than a summary of its plot? These charges do not apply to Richards's approach. The orderly structure and rich verbal texture of literary works, their networks of images and motifs, their symmetrical designs, their tricks and tropes, their rhythms and rhymes are not decorative excrescences—they are in themselves important sources of our satisfaction. For art, to repeat, appeals to many of our appetencies. Poetry allows us the chance to experience, and to experience more fully, more of life's possibilities than our nonverbal existence ordinarily affords, and a great poem, like *Hamlet,* is great because it deals with a wider range of human experiences than does a lesser poem. This is why "complexity" is a value in art; the complex poem appeals to more appetencies than a simple poem does.

But complexity is only part of the effect. In ordinary existence, appetencies are often in conflict. In art, however, the formal unity of the artistic structure arranges and contains this complexity; it subdues even the painful and the ugly; it holds the disparate elements in a tensive balance; and it offers not the chaotic fragment but the harmonious whole. The more we look at *Hamlet,* the more we see that all its elements from the smallest to the largest, all its special and local effects, are working together. It takes in much more than a carefully wrought sonnet, but it is just as superbly organized, in fact, more superbly because there is more to organize. And when we read a great poem, as so many of our desires and aversions are brought skillfully into play, they are also brought—as they almost never are in experiences outside of art—into harmonious balance. The harmony in the poem becomes a harmony in the reader's psyche. This is why human beings need poetry. It is indispensable to our psychic health.

Thus, Richards constructs an ambitious and cogent defense of art on affective grounds, a defense that promises to deal with both the complexity and the coherence of poems and to account for each in terms of a fully articulated affective theory of value. Having explained his theory in *Principles of Literary Criticism* (1925), Richards went on to study the actual responses of readers in *Practical Criticism* (1929). He gave some Cambridge students several short poems that he felt varied widely in poetic quality. To eliminate any interference from preconditioned effects, he deleted all references to authors and dates, and he asked the students to read the poems as often as they wished and to record their reactions and evaluations. The widely disparate readings that resulted seemed to Richards to indicate that most people are poor readers of poetry. So Richards set about arranging, classifying, and analyzing the various ways his readers' responses had gone awry, and in the process he supplied his own analyses of the poems. Ironically, his analytical techniques were to be widely imitated in the next decades by many formalist critics who raised, at the same time, serious questions about his underlying affective theory.

The first and fundamental question is exactly whose response are we going to talk about? It is easy to speak in general terms about what "people" do, about the behavior of "audiences" or the reactions of "readers," but as Richards's research showed, and as a moment's reflection will confirm, different people react very differently to the "same" poem. Some see superficiality where others find profundity; some praise uplifting sentiments where others complain of clichés; some discover coherence where others see only chaos.

Is there any way to tell which of several responses is the best one? Richards thought there was, for he classified the various ways his respondents had deviated from the "right" or "more adequate" reading. And to illustrate that better reading, he appealed to "the poem itself." He pointed out what the words meant, how the sentiments expressed in the poem were or were not appropriate to the fictive speaker and situation, how the imagery developed consistently or inconsistently, how the parts fit or failed to fit together. In short, claims the formalist critic, Richards furnished a formal analysis, an analysis not of readers but of texts. Without this or some other standard, no way exists to decide if one response is better than another. In fact, without some standard there appears to be no alternative to complete relativism. For if, as many reader-response critics argue, the poem truly exists only when it is apprehended, then we seem to be driven toward the conclusion that there are as many *Hamlets* as there are readers of *Hamlet*. More accurately, there are as many *Hamlets* as there are readings, for our responses change from year to year, or even from day to day.

So this variability gives rise to one set of problems: How can reader-response critics avoid the conclusion, and the total relativism it entails, that a new poem is created with every reading? How can they establish a standard to measure the adequacy of any particular reading without assuming the stability of the text and importing that standard from some other context—in other words, without grounding meaning in the text, or the author, or the structure of language? And if reader-response critics do import a standard from some other context, how can they keep the discussion from shifting to that context, thus leaving behind as irrelevant the whole question of the responses of actual readers? In short, how can they talk *critically* about the poem–audience relationship?

These are problems, of course, only so long as the "better" interpretation is seen, as it usually has been seen, as the goal of literary criticism. For some reader-response critics, this goal is neither attainable nor even especially desirable. And they contend that our responses to literature are in themselves a subject of sufficient psychological interest as to require no further justification. Without disputing this contention, we should at least notice that the work of these critics differs in a fundamental way from that produced by critics working in other contexts. When historical critics, for example, offer us information about the author's life or intellectual background, they are claiming that this information will alter our understanding of poems, that it will confirm or eliminate certain interpretations. When formal critics point to a cluster of images or a pattern of motifs, they are claiming to show us something important that we may have overlooked, something that, now that we see it, will allow us to better understand and evaluate the poem. So they, too, are offering to confirm or eliminate readings. Reader-response critics who abandon this normative function (and certainly not all reader-response critics do abandon it) are simply not performing a parallel function. The claim to describe or even to explain the reactions of specific readers is a very different thing from the claim to supply insights that will alter or correct reactions. In each case, critics stand in quite a different relationship to the reader and the poem. Not until reader-response critics go beyond describing and analyzing responses and begin to tell us how and why we should respond do their statements really parallel those of critics in other contexts. And at exactly this point, of course, the critics encounter the first problem we discussed: how can they find, in the affective context, a normative standard for measuring the adequacy of any reading?

Some serious conceptual problems, then, face critics who work in this context. Even so, audience response seems to many critics so obviously central to the business of literature that the affective context has remained one of criticism's perennial interests. In recent decades, and partly in reaction to the dominance of formalist criticism, that interest has flourished. Practice in this context goes under a variety of names — "phenomenological" criticism, "speech-act" criticism, "transactive" criticism, "subjective" criticism, "rhetorical" criticism — but "reader-response" criticism continues to be the most popular label. And though all critics in this context are centrally concerned with the interaction between the audience and the literary work, they differ in the way they distribute their interest between these two poles, some keeping their focus near the text and only occasionally nodding toward actual readers, others concentrating on the responses of specific readers while paying scant attention to the text as a separable entity. Since this brief introduction can cite only a few representative examples of contemporary affective or reader-response criticism, it will be helpful to think of our exemplary critics as occupying a series of points along the imaginary line connecting the work and the reader.

Louise Rosenblatt, for instance, has a position near the textual terminus of that line. Although she has long argued that contemporary critical theory has given too little attention to the role of the reader, she is wary of "aggressively subjective" approaches that analyze responses but not texts, and she often remarks the need to distinguish "relevant" from "irrelevant" responses. Nevertheless, her "transactional" theory puts her well within the affective context. In her terminology, a "text" may exist independently of a reader, but a "poem" exists only when a reader "compenetrates" a text, that is, when he or she chooses to read it "aesthetically." Whether that choice is entirely free is not quite clear since Rosenblatt implies that some texts have features that invite an aesthetic reading and others — a newspaper article, for example — have features that do not. But this very ambiguity is consistent with her view that both the nature of the text and the nature of the reader determine the "poem as event," which is the "transaction" in her transactional theory.

A little further down the line, but still very much toward the textual end, we reach the position of Wolfgang Iser, a German critic whose work is well known in the United States. Iser shares with many other Continental critics a strong interest in phenomenology, a philosophy that stresses the perceiver's role in perception and that insists it is difficult to separate the thing known from the mind that knows it. Other European critics who share these assumptions include Roman Ingarden, Gaston Bachelard, and the "Geneva Critics" or "Critics of Consciousness," as they are sometimes called, of whom the best known to English readers is Georges Poulet. But whereas Bachelard, for example, is willing to follow at great length a train of personal associations set in motion by an image in the text, and whereas Poulet is often struggling to merge his "consciousness" with the "consciousness" of the author as that consciousness is revealed not only in a particular work but in everything the author has written, Iser's uses of phenomenology keep him much closer to the text. From another direction, although he has ties with the movement, he distances himself from the practitioners of "reception aesthetics," a line of inquiry that studies the history of a text's reception. Iser's concern is not with "actual readers"; he is interested, instead, in the "implied reader," a reader who "embodies all those predispositions necessary for a literary work to exercise its effect — predispositions laid down, not by an empirical outside reality, but by the text itself. Consequently, the implied reader as a concept has its roots firmly planted in the structure of the text; he is a construct and in no way to be identified with any real reader" (*The Act of Reading* 34).

Clearly, then, Iser wants to stay near the textual pole of our diagram. But he keeps a distance between himself and the formalist position as well. There can be no single best meaning that all readings must strive to approximate. The idea of a single meaning is not only at odds with Iser's phenomenological assumptions, but it is equally inconsistent with his view of our experience of literature and of the value of that experience. Much of that value lies exactly in the "indeterminacy" of the text. The text, for Iser, doesn't "contain" the meaning of the poem. Rather, we must "assemble" that meaning from the perspectives the text provides. In a complex novel such as Joyce's *Ulysses*, these perspectives are so many and varied that reconstructing the novel's meaning is like reconstructing reality itself. And our reconstructions always remain various because they always depend more on what the reader brings to the text than the formalist's model allows. It is true, and here Iser would agree with the intertextual critic, that readers must bring to the text a knowledge of the appropriate conventions or codes that will allow them to decode the poem. But here again Iser would insist on the poem's ability to transcend the code, to violate the conventions. It does so by presenting readers with "gaps" or "blanks" that they must bridge; in the process they have to construct, from the conventions they bring, new and unconventional meanings. So the text does offer a broad base of determinate meaning, as the formalist argues, and the "implied reader" brings to it a knowledge of the relevant conventions, as the intertextual critic claims, but the "poem itself" exists only in the interaction of the text and the reader, and the meaning that results is reducible neither to the conventions the reader has brought nor to the text.

Iser's position, then, allows for more "openness" in the text and more variability in our responses than critics operating in other contexts will usually admit. Equally to the point, Iser finds the value of literature largely in those indeterminacies that force readers to transcend the received codes as they construct, from their interaction with the text, new meanings. We should remember, though, that this value is most available to the "implied reader." Actual readers, who may lack the implied reader's mastery of the appropriate conventions and who may overlook important textual cues, will be more likely to misinterpret the text and to produce readings outside Iser's vaguely defined but certainly fairly narrow range of permissible "meanings."

A very different emphasis appears in the work of Norman Holland, who usually operates at a considerable distance from the textual end of our line. More accurately, he has operated at different distances over the years as his focus has moved ever closer to an exclusive concentration on the responses of actual readers. In his 1964 book *Psychoanalysis and Shakespeare,* Holland applied to Shakespeare's plays the terms and concepts of Freudian analysis. While he granted the usefulness of these concepts in the genetic and mimetic contexts, he thought their application in the reader-response context held the greatest potential for literary criticism, a potential that, aside from a few studies such as the pioneering work of S. O. Lesser, had remained largely unexplored. Holland continued to explore that potential with reference to a variety of texts in *The Dynamics of Literary Response* (1968). Here the text itself was seen as embodying various fantasies and their transformations. Readers "participate" in these to the extent that their own psychic imperatives allow, and to this extent the poem can "work" for them.

In his later writings, though, Holland has been more impressed by the reader's share in the transaction. In *Poems in Persons* (1973), in *5 Readers Reading* (1975), and in several later works, he has argued that an individual reader's psychic needs—more specifically, his or her "identity theme"—dictate that reader's perception of the text:

> By means of such adaptive structures as he has been able to match in the story, he will transform the fantasy content, which he has created from the materials of the story his defenses admitted, into some literary point or theme or interpretation. . . . He will, finally, render the fantasy he has synthesized as an intellectual content that is characteristic—and pleasing—for him.   (*5 Readers Reading* 121–22).

By now the reader's share in the transaction has become almost total, and we are very close to the view that a new poem is created with every reading. If two or more readers should happen to agree about an interpretation, this agreement could only arise because their "identity themes" were so similar to begin with that they created very similar poems as they read. All that remains, then, is to study readers reading.

Holland is not alarmed by this conclusion, but he is occasionally nagged by the difficulty of talking about a largely one-sided transaction. "The literary text may be only so many marks on a page—at most a matrix of psychological possibilities for its readers. Nevertheless only some possibilities truly fit the matrix" (12). This comment suggests that the text does set some boundaries to interpretation. But as soon as we try to measure these boundaries, the problem returns from the other direction. "A reader reads something, certainly, but if one cannot separate his 'subjective' response from its 'objective' basis, there seems no way to find out what that 'something' is in any impersonal sense. It is visible only in the psychological process the reader creates in himself by means of the literary work" (40). But neither is there any compelling need to find out what that "something" is, for the focus of study now is precisely this psychological process. As we study readers reading and see the various defenses and adaptations they adopt as they confront the text, we can hope to learn something about defenses and adaptations in general—our own and others'—in all kinds of situations.

Although we seem at this point to be very near the reader's end of the line, we are not quite near enough to suit David Bleich. While Bleich agrees in most respects with Holland's emphases (though not necessarily with his psychoanalytic terminology), he complains that Holland's refusal to distinguish between the "objective" and the "subjective" merely confuses the argument, and he suspects that Holland is really trying to find his way back to "objectivity." In Bleich's view, criticism has labored too long on the mistaken assumption that the poem can be profitably considered as an "object" independent of the perceiving "subject":

> The assumption derived from the objective paradigm that all observers have the same perceptual response to a symbolic object creates the illusion that the object is real and that its meaning must reside in it. The assumption of the subjective paradigm is that

collective similarity of response can be determined only by each individual's announcement of his response and subsequent communally motivated negotiative comparison. . . . The response must therefore be the starting point for the study of the
aesthetic experience (*Subjective Criticism* 98).

What the end point of such a study must be is not so clear. It could not be a progressively brighter illumination of the text, since this goal is ruled out from the start by
Bleich's epistemology. But presumably "communally motivated negotiative comparison" could throw light on our motives and strategies for reading. By honestly and
tolerantly exchanging information about our responses to literature, we might begin
to understand our own psyches, and this self-knowledge, for Bleich, is the larger
and more important goal, for "each person's most urgent motivations are to understand himself" (298).

Finally, then, though he endorses no particular school of psychology, Bleich
shares with Holland a psychological emphasis and a nearly exclusive focus on the
responses of actual readers. Assuming, as both critics do, that the poem as independent object is beyond our reach, they argue with some force that no other focus is
really available. Even so, the wary reader may wonder why their extreme skepticism about our ability to understand poetic objects should seem so relaxed when it
comes to our ability to understand perceiving subjects. For in such studies, readers
must become, in turn, perceived objects, and objects quite as complex as poems.

A last representative critic, and one who threatens to undermine my scheme of
placing affective critics at neat intervals on the line between text and reader, is Stanley Fish. When Fish first displayed his "affective stylistics," his position seemed to
be somewhere near Iser's. Like most recent reader-response critics, he was rebelling
against the formalist's doctrine that the poem "in itself" provided an objective standard of meaning, but he was rebelling more strongly against the formalists' view of
the poem as a static object, something to be grasped as a whole. Instead, he argued,
we really experience the poem as a sequence of effects. Analyzing *Paradise Lost* and
several other seventeenth-century poems on this premise, Fish sought to show how
the poem worked on the reader, setting up a pattern of responses or a set of expectations that it later violated or undercut. Our experience of the poem was sequential
and dynamic. The focus here was clearly on the reader, but Fish was careful to point
out that he had in mind a specially qualified reader, someone trained, as Fish himself was, in the conventions of seventeenth-century poetry. Such a figure is in some
ways like Iser's "implied reader," the reader the text seems to require.

But as Fish continued to explore the problems of interpretation, he came to feel
it was really inaccurate to speak of the text as directing the reader's response. It
would be more precise to say that the reader creates the poem in the very act of
perceiving it, and what we call "interpretation" is a more elaborate process of creation in which the formal features the reader claims to "find" in the text are "(illegit-
imately) assigned the responsibility for producing the interpretation which in fact
produced them" (*Is There a Text in This Class?* 163). Fish is willing to push this argument to its logical conclusion: each reading is a new creation, and the poem that results is the creature of whatever "interpretive strategies" the reader has employed.
The poem "in itself" has quite disappeared.

What, then, is the interpreter interpreting? "I cannot answer that question," Fish
admits, "but neither, I would claim, can anyone else." The illusion that we are reading the "same" poem seems to derive support from the fact that many readers can
agree about the text's meaning, and even more support from the fact that some readers will allow their readings of a poem to be "corrected." But this support is itself

illusory, argues Fish. Readers can agree when they are members of the same "interpretive community"; that is, when they share the same "interpretive strategies." And when readings are "corrected," they are simply brought into line with those agreed-upon strategies, not with the poem "itself." In Fish's later view, then, his own "affective stylistics," a way of reading that would place him nearer the textual end of our line than either Holland or Bleich, is simply one more arbitrarily chosen method, a method no more authorized by his theory than any other.

Fish's concept of interpretive communities has far-reaching implications, some of which we will consider in a later section. Most reader-response critics, though, continue to hold that they have very sound reasons for placing their focus where they do, and they are willing to argue that the nature of the poem, the nature of readers, or both combined dictate where the critics' emphasis should be if they are going to do justice to the literary experience. They differ, as we have seen, in their placement of that emphasis. Although no reader-response critic gives the text the autonomy that the formal critic would give it, some do see the text as considerably restricting the range of readings they will accept. So these critics must construct some hypothetical reader whose responses will be in conformity with the text's clues, and they show, consequently, little interest in the responses of actual readers. Other reader-response critics largely reverse this emphasis. We must start with the responses of actual readers, they argue, because that is all we can directly discover. So they complain that the first group is often practicing a type of disguised formalism and giving the text an illusory "objectivity." The first group, in turn, complains that the second, while showing us what some readers do, can never show us what they should do. So the various kinds of reader-response critics find much to argue about. But they agree on one main point: since the "poem" exists only when the reader (however defined) encounters the text, literary criticism must focus on that encounter.

Suggestions for Further Reading

The variety of contemporary reader-response criticism can be sampled in such collections as Susan Suleiman and Inge Crosman, eds., *The Reader in the Text* (1980), and Jane Tomkins, ed., *Reader-Response Criticism* (1980); both contain useful introductions and full bibliographies. The intersections of gender theory and reader-response criticism are explored in Elizabeth Flynn and P. P. Schweickart, eds., *Gender and Reading: Essays on Readers, Texts, and Contexts* (1986). See also Charles R. Cooper, ed., *Researching Responses to Literature and the Teaching of Literature: Points of Departure* (1985), Elizabeth Freund, *The Return of the Reader: Reader-Response Criticism* (1987), and Diane P. Freedman, Olivia Frey, and Frances Murphy Zauhor, eds., *The Intimate Critique: Autobiographical Literary Criticism* (1993). Since many "myth critics," and especially those influenced by Jung, are more concerned with literature's effect on the reader than with other contexts, they may be classed under this heading. John B. Vickery, ed., *Myth and Literature* (1966), provides the most convenient collection of essays on this large topic. Some representative books are Carl Jung, *Psyche and Symbol* (1958), Maud Bodkin, *Archetypal Patterns in Poetry* (1934), Joseph Campbell, *The Hero with a Thousand Faces* (1949), and Richard Chase, *Quest for Myth* (1949). I. A. Richards, in *Principles of Literary Criticism* (1925), makes a pioneering twentieth-century attempt to construct an affective poetics. Simon O. Lesser, in *Fiction and the Unconscious* (1957), offers one of the first books systematically to apply Freudian concepts to explain reader response. Norman Holland has continued work in that direction in *The Dynamics of Literary Response*

(1968) and, more radically, in *5 Readers Reading* (1975). Versions of continental phenomenological approaches are represented by Gaston Bachelard in *The Poetics of Reverie* (1960); by the Geneva Critics, handily described by Sarah Lawall in *Critics of Consciousness* (1968); and by Wolfgang Iser in *The Act of Reading* (1976). Reception aesthetics remains chiefly a German interest, and its historical emphasis might place it as logically in the last chapter of this book. The work of Hans Robert Jauss, represented by *Toward an Aesthetics of Reception* (1982), is central. The movement is described in Robert C. Holub, *Reception Theory: A Critical Introduction* (1984). Stanley Fish, *Self-Consuming Artifacts* (1972), and Louise Rosenblatt, *The Reader, The Text, The Poem* (1994), use reader-oriented approaches that see the text as largely controlling the reader's responses. Near the opposite pole is David Bleich, *Subjective Criticism* (1978), where the subject is the main object.

The Quest for "The Poem Itself"

Louise M. Rosenblatt

In her book The Reader, The Text, The Poem, *Louise Rosenblatt offers a "transactional" theory of the reading experience in which the reader and the text may exist separately but the "poem" comes into being only when the reader and the text "compenetrate." In the chapter reprinted here, Rosenblatt reviews the debates between the formal and genetic critics, debates that often found the formalists invoking "the poem itself" as the ultimate ground of meaning, and that usually found both sides ignoring the responses of the reader. Focusing on E. D. Hirsch's replay of the Brooks–Bateson argument over Wordsworth's "Slumber," she awards some points to both sides before providing her own reconciliation of opposites, one that promises to take into account the reader's share in the transaction and to explain in what ways different interpretations can still be valid interpretations. In the process, she furnishes a compact summary of the positions many contemporary reader-response critics are reacting against, as well as a succinct rationale for the renewed interest in the role of the reader.*

The dominant critical climate of the mid-century, it is usually pointed out, was largely shaped by reaction, on the one hand against the academic preoccupation with literary history, and on the other hand against romantic impressionism. A third influence often cited is the prestige of objective scientific modes of thought. All of these militated against recognition of the important role of the reader. A reaction, in turn, against the hegemony of the New Critics has now gained momentum. Yet resistance to emphasis on the reader's role still persists. In this chapter, I shall deal with two major current views of the nature of the literary work that rule out the transactional emphasis.

Reprinted with permission from *The Reader, The Text, The Poem: The Transactional Theory of the Literary Work* by Louise M. Rosenblatt. © 1994 by the Board of Trustees, Southern Illinois University. Parts of the chapter have been omitted, and the notes have been renumbered.

Excessive concern with the history of literature or with literature as an expression of biographical and social factors, the New Critics claimed, led to neglect of literature as an art. Building on one facet of I. A. Richards's work, they did much to rescue the poem as a work of art from earlier confusions with the poem either as a biographical document or as a document in intellectual and social history. A mark of twentieth-century criticism thus became depreciation of such approaches to literature and development of the technique of "close reading" of the work as an autonomous entity. The extraordinary success of some of the critical works and textbooks presenting this general approach established it as practically an unquestioned orthodoxy, if not for whole generations of readers emerging from our schools and colleges, certainly for those trained as specialists in literature.

The reaction against romantic impressionism fostered the ideal of an impersonal or objective criticism. Impressionist critics were charged with forgetting "the poem itself" as they pursued the adventures of their souls among masterpieces. Walter Pater, seeking to make of his own criticism a work of art, became (with only partial justice, I believe) the exemplar of the reader too preoccupied with his own emotions to remain faithful to the literary work. As so often happens, the reaction produced an equally extreme counter position—emphasis on something called "the work itself," treated as if it were an object whose parts could be analyzed without reference to the maker or the reader.

This trend in criticism undoubtedly paralleled, and was reinforced by, the ideal of the "impersonality" of the poet to which T. S. Eliot brought so much prestige. Spurning romantic self-expression, he declared poetry to be "not a turning loose of emotion, but an escape from emotion; it is not the expression of personality, but an escape from personality."[1] Thus, the literary work is seen as existing apart from the immediate circumstances in the poet's personal life that gave rise to it.

Eliot's famous phrase "the objective correlative"—despite the rather confused concepts associated with it, or perhaps because of its ambiguities*—also un-

doubtedly strengthened the view of the literary work as something existing in isolation. Eliot's definition of his key term does imply the presence of a reader, since the adequacy of the objective correlative depends on what it can evoke: "The only way of expressing emotion in the form of art is by finding an 'objective correlative'; in other words a set of objects, a situation, a chain of events which shall be the formula of that particular emotion; such that when the external facts, which must terminate in sensory experience, are given, the emotion is immediately evoked."[2] In this phrasing, however, the implied reader seems passively to wait for the signal or formula for a particular and already completely determined emotion. This is an oversimplification not only of the reader's response to a highly complex work like *Hamlet* but even to a simpler one—say, a lyric about life "under the greenwood tree." Even this, we have seen, requires the reader's active contribution. The danger of this formulation is the general assumption that the more uniform and automatic the response to an image or a scene, the better it is as an "objective correlative" and the better the work. This would reduce literature, at worst, to a series of automatic signals, like traffic lights, and, at best, to a collection of static symbols or emblems.

Eliot's basic contention is, rather, that, whatever the author's personal emotion, he must rely on the text to embody it. Reacting against the romantic emphasis on the poet's self-expression, Eliot is actually concerned with communication, and—a point in harmony with the transactional theory—he equates this with finding "a set of objects, a situation, a chain of events," that will enable *the reader* to produce the desired emotions. These were not the emphases generally drawn from the much-cited concept of the objective correlative, however. Freed from romantic identification with the biography and day-to-day personality of the author, the work, it seemed, existed objectively, impersonally, autonomously.

By analogy and example, evidently, rather than as the result of a clearly developed theory, the notion of the impersonality of the literary work of art was paralleled by the ideal of an impersonal, objective criticism. This tended to focus on explication, elaborate

---

*In "Hamlet and His Problems," Eliot uses the term in two ways. Part of the time he is discussing whether the situation and facts presented in the play justify Hamlet's emotions as expressed in the play. But Eliot primarily raises the question whether the total play is an adequate

"objective correlative" for the author's emotions. Eliot argues that the difficulty of interpreting the play demonstrates its inadequacy in relation to Shakespeare's confused generating emotions.

formal analysis, and discussion of the technique of the poem, viewed as an autonomous object. The author having been eliminated, the reader, too, was expected to approximate the impersonal transparency of the scientist.

Theory of Literature, by René Wellek and Austin Warren, published in 1949, contributed probably the clearest and most influential theoretical framework for concentration on "the poem itself," as against its study as a document in literary or social history. This work did much to provide a scholarly basis for consideration of major problems of critical theory. Yet, dominated by the notion of something nonpersonal, something apart from particular readers, which "is" the poem, their book has undoubtedly reinforced a narrow view of literary objectivity and a reluctance to recognize the contribution of the reader. Aware of the philosophical difficulties implicit in this problem, Wellek and Warren survey the various positions concerning the nature of the poem, and in their famous chapter 12 develop a sophisticated theory to support their view of "the mode of existence of the poem." Their arguments present in a more developed form what in the writings of their contemporaries is often merely arbitrary dictum or unquestioned assumption.

In the following statement, Wellek and Warren at first glance might seem to be attacking the position developed in the preceding chapters. But they set up as their target an extreme, even caricatured, version of the approach to the poem as embodied in unique evocations: "The view that the mental experience of a reader is the poem itself leads to the absurd conclusion that a poem is non-existent unless experienced and that it is recreated in every experience. There would thus not be one *Divine Comedy* but as many Divine Comedies as there are and were and will be readers. We end in complete scepticism and anarchy and arrive at the vicious maxim of *de gustibus non est disputandum.*"[3] One of the fallacies illustrated by this excerpt is the assumption that the title of a work or the term "the poem itself" must necessarily refer to an entity. Critical practice and literary pedagogy are frequently confused by this assumption. "The real poem," "the true poem," "the novel as it really is," "the genuine novel," "the poem itself," such phrases constantly invoked in *Theory of Literature* and other critical discussions, beg the question concerning whether there is indeed any single thing to which such a term might point. Thus, instead of the first sentence in the above excerpt, the

problem should be phrased: "Given the fact that a poem is re-created each time it is read, can we validly speak of anything as being 'the poem itself'?"

The statement by Wellek and Warren illustrates another current confusion—the assumption that recognition of the reader's activity in evoking the poem inevitably implies that any reading is as valid as any other. Any such view would of course lead to critical chaos. *But nothing in my insistence on the reader's activity necessitates such a conclusion.*

It is hard to liberate ourselves from the notion that the poem is something either entirely mental or entirely external to readers. "The poem" cannot be equated solely with *either* the text *or* the experience of a reader. Something encapsuled in a reader's mind without relevance to a text may be a wonderful fantasy, but the term "poem" or "literary work," in transactional terminology, would not be applicable to such a "mental experience" any more than to an entity apart from a reader. As soon as "poem" is understood to refer to the relationship between a reader and a text, the threatened critical anarchy does not follow; this and the following chapter will show that the basis exists for orderly and systematic criticism.

What each reader makes of the text is, indeed, *for him* the poem, in the sense that this is his only direct perception of it. No one else can read it for him. He may learn indirectly about others' experiences with the text; he may come to see that his own was confused or impoverished, and he may then be stimulated to attempt to call forth from the text a better poem. But this he must do himself, and only what he himself experiences in relation to the text is—again let us underline—*for him,* the work.

This point is frequently glossed over, evidently out of fear that it will lead to an assertion of brash literary egalitarianism. The solution is, rather, to face the uniquely personal character of literary experience, and then to discover how in this situation critical discrimination and sound criteria of interpretation can be achieved.

•   •   •

Wellek and Warren's effort to maintain the autonomy of "the work itself" apart from author and readers, does not succeed theoretically. Yet for at least a generation such arguments satisfied those who sought a rationalization for a formalistic criticism. In the recent reaction against the narrowness of the New Criticism, the historical and biographical approaches are being newly defended. Ironically, however, Wellek and Warren and the New Critics are being attacked for being too flexible in their view of the identity of the work, for conceding too much to the reader! For example, E. D. Hirsch, in his impressive *Validity in Interpretation,* not only insists on the identity of the work but condemns the New Critics for their "banishment of the author."[4] Since Hirsch is even more stringent than Wellek and Warren in his rejection of the reader, I shall briefly sketch some of his arguments and especially cite some of his applications. My main purpose is to make clear what the transactional view offers that is lost in concentration either on the hypostatized poem or on the author.

Hirsch also accepts the fact of the openness of the text, the fact that the same sequence of words can sponsor different meanings. But he rejects as leading only to critical confusion the idea that there can be more than one "correct" interpretation of the text. When the author wrote the text, he "meant" something by it; that must be the sole acceptable meaning. "For if the meaning of a text is not the author's then no interpretation can possibly correspond to *the* meaning of the text, since the text can have no determinate or determinable meaning" (p. 5). His purpose is to develop principles that will counteract skepticism concerning the "conception of absolutely valid interpretation" (p. viii).

Hirsch deplores the effects of the famous essay by W. K. Wimsatt and Monroe Beardsley, "the Intentional Fallacy," with its reminder of the distinction between an author's intention and his actual accomplishment in the text.[5] Agreeing that we "cannot get inside" the author's head and can never be certain of his intended meaning, Hirsch nevertheless argues that "common sense" tells us that author's meaning is the only universally acceptable norm. If genuine certainty in interpretation is impossible, the "aim of the discipline must be to reach a consensus, on the basis of what is known, that correct understanding of the author's meaning has *probably* been reached" (p. 17). This, of course, reflects a highly admirable scientific approach to knowledge in which valid conclusions are drawn on the basis of the available evidence and revised as new evidence emerges. If Hirsch settles on the question, what did the author mean to convey? as the *only* acceptable question, it is evidently because it lends itself to such a method. This search for correctness of the kind that, for example, we desire in interpreting a scientific formula or a logical state-

ment, is precisely what ultimately vitiates much that is insightful in Hirsch's discussion.

Of course, Hirsch cannot, we have seen, completely ignore the fact of the readers' experiential evocation of the work. His method is to relegate it to a theoretical limbo, a self-confirmatory imaginative guesswork,* which then must be scientifically tested against all the relevant knowledge available. The real work of arriving at the author's meaning is seen in the process of validation, which can be carried on "in the light of day" (p. 206). This sets up an arbitrary break between the process of shaping what I call an experienced meaning, and the process of critical validation.

In the course of scientific discovery, the scientist often proceeds by intuition and imagination to arrive at an idea or hypothesis which he then must test by evidence and logical principles.[6] The scientist retains and reports only the logical and evidential proof; the prior intuitive creative process is taken for granted. Hirsch seems to want to do the same thing for the literary work of art—and in stressing so much the logical processes of validation he has forgotten the essential difference between science and art. In dismissing the creative evocation of the poem as mere imaginative guesswork, Hirsch has thrown out the experienced work of art and retained only the scholarly apparatus.

• • •

Concentration on extrinsic evidence concerning the author's meaning unfortunately tends to lead to neglect of the poem or novel or play as primarily a work of art. (The New Critics were correct in this contention, although their solution, the fiction of a supposedly autonomous work, had its own unfortunate limitations.) In adjudicating between two contradictory interpretations of a text by Wordsworth, Hirsch exemplifies the way in which such disregard of the aesthetic event comes about (pp. 227 ff.).

---

*Northrop Frye, in *Anatomy of Criticism* (Princeton, N.J.: Princeton University Press, 1957), similarly dismisses the actual evocation of literary works to the limbo of "history of taste" (pp. 9–10). In his effort to develop a pseudoscientific taxonomy of literature, he sets up for his treatment of literature that model of the physicist analyzing nature. (Frye shows himself very much out of touch with contemporary philosophy of science, which would have shown him that the physicist's "nature" is no more completely "out there" than is our transactionally understood literary work.)

A slumber did my spirit seal;
  I had no human fears:
She seemed a thing that could not feel
  The touch of earthly years.

No motion has she now, no force;
  She neither hears nor sees;
Rolled round in earth's diurnal course,
  With rocks, and stones, and trees.

Hirsch presents excerpts from commentaries on the last two lines of this poem. The first is by Cleanth Brooks.

[The poet] attempts to suggest something of the lover's agonized shock at the loved one's present lack of motion—of his response to her utter and horrible inertness.... Part of the effect, of course, resides in the fact that a dead lifelessness is suggested more sharply by an object's being whirled about by something else than by an image of the object in repose. But there are other matters which are at work here: the sense of the girl's falling back into the clutter of things, companioned by things chained like a tree to one particular spot, or by things completely inanimate like rocks and stones.... [She] is caught up helplessly into the empty whirl of the earth which measures and makes time. She is touched by and held by earthly time in its mostly powerful and horrible image.

The second excerpt is from F. W. Bateson.

The final impression the poem leaves is not of two contrasting moods, but of a single mood mounting to a climax in the pantheistic magnificence of the last two lines.... The vague living-Lucy of this poem is opposed to the grander dead-Lucy who has become involved in the sublime processes of nature. We put the poem down satisfied, because its last two lines succeed in effecting a reconciliation between the two philosophies or social attitudes. Lucy is actually more alive now that she is dead, because she is now a part of the life of Nature, and not just a human "thing."

Somewhat too generously, in the light of his later comments on Bateson, Hirsch grants that "both the cited interpretations are permitted by the text." He proceeds to demonstrate that it is not possible validly to reconcile or fuse the two as somehow inherent in the ambiguity of the text. He then repeats his argument that the text can mean only what its author intended. Hence he argues from extratextual knowledge about the author: that is, that Wordsworth's "characteristic attitudes are somewhat pantheistic. Instead of regarding rocks and stones and trees as inert objects, he probably regarded them in 1799 as deeply alive." Hirsch is forced to concede, however, that "Bateson fails to emphasize the negative implications in the poem. He overlooks the poet's reticence, his distinct unwillingness to express any unqualified evaluation of his experience." Yet Hirsch concludes: "*Nevertheless, in spite of this, and in spite of the apparent implausibility of Bateson's reading*, it remains, I think, somewhat more probable than that of Brooks." (Italics added.)

Hirsch recognizes (rather belatedly) that "a poet's typical attitudes do not always apply to a particular poem." Why, then, can he not recognize that even a pantheist might undergo the initial shock of realizing the absence in death of the usual physical attributes of the live being? And why should Wordsworth not have recaptured that traumatic moment in a poem? Later, of course, he might find consolation in a pantheistic view of death, to be expressed in other poems. Nevertheless, Hirsch insists that Bateson's reading (despite its acknowledged failure to do justice to the negative aspect of the text) is more "probable" because he grounds it in external "data" concerning the poet's typical outlook. How far removed this is from any actual experienced meaning derived from the verbal stimuli! The impact of the exact words of the total text has been overshadowed, thrust aside, in the preoccupation with extrinsic information about the author. Arriving at an interpretation thus becomes an exercise in the logic of evidence. The essentiality of both reader and text is ignored.

Even if a letter were discovered tomorrow, in which Wordsworth stated his intention to express a consolatory pantheistic view of death in this poem, we should still have to ask: does the total text permit the evocation of such a poem? Would we not have to point out that the words of this text focus our attention on a mistaken lack of "human fears" of death and on death as an inert state, sans energy, motion, sight, or hearing? There is nothing *in the text* to arouse the feeling that rocks and stones and trees are "deeply alive, part of the immortal life of nature." On the contrary, their being "rolled round in earth's diurnal course" reinforces the link with the effect of inertness produced by the first lines of the stanza, so that even the trees are assimilated to the inert immobility of stones and rocks. If Wordsworth "meant" an optimistic, pantheistic poem, he did not provide a text that enables a reader not already a pantheist to evoke such a meaning. Other Wordsworthian texts, such as "Lines, Written above Tintern Abbey" or "The Prelude" do enable the reader to participate in pantheistic attitudes.

Brooks's interpretation, as Hirsch admits even while rejecting it, does greater justice to the negative emphasis of the text. Yet we must not forget that this, too, is Brooks's particular experience with the text. He infuses a quality, especially indicated through his repeated use of "horrible," that other readers may not elicit from the text. For example, I tend rather to feel, not horror, but an almost stunned realization of the brute fact of lifelessness. If we free ourselves from the obsession with a single correct reading, whether of the autonomous "poem itself" or of the author's meaning, we can recognize that such differences between what readers make of a text can validly exist. And extrinsic evidence can help us to differentiate the author's probably intended "meaning" from the meanings nevertheless validly derived from the text by contemporary or later readers.

•   •   •

Thus, I am ready to accept Hirsch's criteria of validity as *one* possible basis for evaluating a reading. As a student of comparative literature, I frequently read to discover the probable meaning of a text for the author and his contemporaries. My reading, then, should be judged in terms of the extent to which I have been able to limit myself to the horizon of the author and his age.

I am even ready to say that in most readings we seek the belief that a process of communication is going on, that one is participating in something that reflects the author's intention. And especially if our experience has been vivid or stirring, we may wish to ascertain what manner of temperament, life-situation, social or intellectual or philosophic environment, gave rise to this work. Especially if it is a text of the past, we may wish to discover to what degree our experience differs from that of the author's contemporaries. All of the approaches of the literary historian become potentially relevant—textual study, semantic history, literary, biographical, and other types of history. All of these may aid the reader to limit himself to the horizon of the author and his time.

Such acceptance of the traditional approach to the work as primarily the expression of a particular person, time and place, however, should first of all be qualified by an awareness of, and vigilant guarding against, the dangers of the absolutistic concern with the author's "meaning." We need to recognize the uncertainty of being able to duplicate the author's mentality or that of his contemporaries. Hence the danger of either unconsciously or, like Hirsch, consciously substituting knowledge *about* the author and his times in place of an actual aesthetic engagement with the text. The text thus becomes a document in the author's biography, a weak one at that, requiring support from more direct biographic and historical sources.

First and foremost, the priority of the lived-through relationship with the text should be maintained. Anything, any knowledge, that may help us to such participation is to be valued. With that clearly in mind, we can welcome any "background knowledge" that may enhance our ability to validly organize the experience generated by the text. Hence we can reject the nation of the intentional fallacy to the extent that knowledge of the author's intentions may alert us to textual clues that might have been overlooked.

To object to the monolithic views of Hirsch is not to reject the author but to recognize the complexity of the relationship between reader and author. Hirsch would lead us to make of the poem merely the starting point for a scholarly investigation. Rather, we need to keep our priorities clear. Whatever knowledge or insight we might gain by nonaesthetic means will be valued if it enhances the work-as-experienced. Anything else can be valued as biography, as literary history, as social documentation; but these will not be confused with or substituted for the literary experience.

Interest in the author's intention is not the only justification for reading a text. As in the cases of Blake's or Wordsworth's poems discussed above, other criteria of adequacy may be acceptable. A reader of the twentieth century may bring to these poems or to a Shakespeare play, be it *Hamlet* or *Coriolanus*, a "world" that enables him to evoke an experience whose intensity, complexity, subtlety, and human range can be judged to be an acceptable reading of the text, that is, to activate the actual words of the text and not to impose meanings for which the text offers no valid basis. Here, the criteria of adequacy are implicit in such words as intensity, complexity, subtlety, human range. Again, I am aware that such a reading may not meet the criterion limiting us to what we know of Elizabethan attitudes or beliefs, yet by the second yardstick the twentieth-century reading may rate higher. Often, but not necessarily always, the two sets of criteria may be satisfied by the same reading.

•   •   •

Those who bring a particular systematic ideology to the text especially need to weigh the effect of their criteria of validity. For example, early Christian exegetes read the Old Testament with the underlying assumption that the only acceptable interpretations were ones that made every part of the Old Testament a prefiguring of the New Testament. Only interpretations that, say, made Adam a foreshadowing of Jesus would be acceptable. A Jewish theologian who might argue that his interpretation did greater justice to the text would make little impression: the essential differences would reside in their standards of validity by which to evaluate the theologians' various interpretations, as well as their own. Those who apply a Freudian or a Marxist ideology to their readings are also usually introducing very special criteria of validity of interpretation.

It is sometimes maintained that readers tend to agree on the work and to differ only on matters of detail.* This impression—which is by no means generally supported by the evidence—is largely due to the fact that discussion of a text tends to be carried on among people sharing a common cultural climate. Within the setting of a particular time, culture, and social milieu, a group of readers or critics can bring a sufficiently similar experience to the text to be able to arrive at fairly homogeneous readings. And when they have in common a set of criteria of what constitutes a sound reading, they can then rank the various interpretations and agree on some "hierarchy of viewpoints." Despite the inevitable uniqueness of each life, readers under such circumstances may have acquired the language under similar conditions, had a similar literary training, read the same books, participated in the same social milieu, and acquired similar ethical and aesthetic values. Such a body of readers may thus be able to communicate easily with one another about their still, to some extent, diverse individual responses to a text. They may also be able

to come to a common judgment about which reading seems most satisfactory. But always this judgment will be in terms of particular linguistic, semantic, metaphysical factors appropriate to a particular time and place *and* a particular—more or less coherent— set of criteria for an adequate reading.

Actually, since the discussion of a reading of a particular work tends to be carried on among people within a particular cultural context, the text as "control" or "norm" usually seems to them to be paramount. The readers point toward the set of symbols as they seek to compare what the words called forth for them. The adequacy or inadequacy of a reading can be demonstrated by indicating the parts of the text which have been ignored, or which have not been woven into the rest of the semantic structure built on the text. The readers sharing a similar "background" take for granted their commonly held assumptions. Yet, as we have seen, even within the same general cultural situation, differences in what the reader brings to the text and differences in criteria of adequacy will make possible different though equally "acceptable" readings.

In the aesthetic orientation, the reader probably selects, out of many potential systems of limitations, an arc within which he seeks to synthesize all of the aspects of reference and feeling that the text evokes in him. He brings to this also a particular set of criteria for evaluating the soundness of his own performance. The more self-aware the reader, the more he will feel it necessary to critically scrutinize his own evocation of "the poem" as a transaction between himself and the text.

To speak of the text as a constraint rather than a norm or "system of norms" suggests a relationship rather than a fixed standard. Instead of functioning as a rigid mold, the signs serve as a pattern which the reader construes as verbal symbols—guides to the next step. The signs present limits or controls; the personality and culture brought by the reader constitute another type of limitation on the resultant synthesis, the lived-through work of art. The reader's attention constantly vibrates between the pole of the text and the pole of his own responses to it. The transactional view of the "mode of existence" of the literary work thus liberates us from absolutist rejection of the reader, preserves the importance of the text, and permits a dynamic view of the text as an opportunity for ever new individual readings, yet readings that can be responsibly self-aware and disciplined.

---

*See Wayne C. Booth, "Preserving the Exemplar," *Critical Inquiry* 3, 3 (1977), 412. Unanimous amusement at Mr. Collins's proposal to Elizabeth Bennet requires that Austen's readers share certain cultural assumptions, e.g., that marriage proposals should be couched in romantic terms.

Notes

1. T. S. Eliot, *Selected Essays*, new ed. (New York: Harcourt, Brace, 1950), p. 11.
2. Eliot, pp. 124–25.
3. René Wellek and Austin Warren, *Theory of Literature*, 3d ed. (New York: Harcourt, Brace and World, 1956), p. 146. All further references to this work appear in the text.
4. (New Haven, Conn.: Yale University Press, 1967), p. 1. All further references to this work appear in the text.
5. In W. K. Wimsatt, Jr., *The Verbal Icon* (New York: Noonday Press, 1958), pp. 5–18.
6. Banesh Hoffmann, *Albert Einstein* (New York: Viking, 1972); Marston Morse, "Mathematics, the Arts, and Freedom," *Thought*, 34 (Spring 1959); Norwood Russell Hanson, *Patterns of Discovery* (Cambridge University Press, 1958); Henri Poincaré, *The Foundations of Science*, tr. G. B. Halstead (New York: Science Press, 1913), chap. 9, "Science and Hypothesis"; Anthony Storr, *The Dynamics of Creation* (New York: Athenaeum, 1972), p. 67; Thomas S. Kuhn, *The Structure of Scientific Revolutions*, 2d ed. (University of Chicago Press, 1970); Stephen E. Toulmin, *Human Understanding* (Princeton University Press, 1972).

Readers and the Concept of the Implied Reader

Wolfgang Iser

In this chapter from The Act of Reading, *Wolfgang Iser explains his concept of the "implied reader." As Iser notes, reader-response critics can be divided into two groups: those who study the documented responses of "real" readers, and those who construct a "hypothetical" reader, "upon whom all possible actualizations of the text may be projected." One such hypothetical reader Iser calls the "ideal" reader. "It is difficult to pinpoint precisely where he is drawn from, though there is a good deal to be said for the claim that he tends to emerge from the brain of the philologist or critic himself." In fact, Iser argues, the ideal reader cannot exist because the concept denotes a reader who could "realize in full the meaning potential of the fictional text." The ideal reader, then, is a fiction, but often a useful fiction: "as a fiction he can close gaps that constantly appear in any analysis of literary effects and responses." Iser then proceeds to critique some of the ideal readers that other reader-response critics have constructed, among them Michael Riffaterre's "superreader," Stanley Fish's "informed reader," and Erwin Wolff's "intended reader." As a more adequate model of the reading process, Iser offers his own hypothetical reader, the "implied reader," a reader who "embodies all those predispositions necessary for a literary work to exercise its effect—predispositions laid down, not by an empirical outside reality, but by the text itself. Consequently, the implied reader as a concept has his roots firmly planted in the structure of the text; he is a construct and in no way to be identified with any real reader." But neither is the implied reader the same as the "fictitious reader," which is merely one of the perspectives offered by the fictional text. The convergence of all the textual perspectives—those of the narrator, the characters, the plot, and the fictitious reader—produce the "meaning" of the text, and this convergence must be visualized from a stand-*

Reprinted by permission of the publisher from Wolfgang Iser, *The Act of Reading: A Theory of Aesthetic Response*, pp. 27–38. Copyright © 1978 by The Johns Hopkins University Press. Notes have been renumbered.

*point outside the text. "Thus the reader's role is pre-
structured by three basic components: the different perspectives represented in the text, the vantage point from
which he joins them, and the meeting place where they
converge." Unlike the various forms of the "ideal
reader," Iser claims, the implied reader is not an abstraction from any real reader but a construction from the
text. The concept denotes "the role of the reader, which is
definable in terms of textual structure and structured
acts." As such, the concept of the implied reader "offers a
means of describing the process whereby textual structures are transmuted through ideational activities into
personal experiences."*

Northrop Frye once wrote: "It has been said of
Boehme that his books are like a picnic to which
the author brings the words and the reader the
meaning. The remark may have been intended as a
sneer at Boehme, but it is an exact description of all
works of literary art without exception."[1] Any attempt to understand the true nature of this cooperative enterprise will run into difficulties over the
question of which reader is being referred to. Many
different types of readers are invoked when the literary critic makes pronouncements on the effects of literature or responses to it. Generally, two categories
emerge, in accordance with whether the critic is concerned with the history of responses or the potential
effect of the literary text. In the first instance, we have
the "real" reader, known to us by his documented reactions; in the second, we have the "hypothetical"
reader, upon whom all possible actualizations of the
text may be projected. The latter category is frequently subdivided into the so-called ideal reader
and the contemporary reader. The first of these cannot be said to exist objectively, while the second,
though undoubtedly there, is difficult to mould to
the form of a generalization.

Nevertheless, no one would deny that there is
such a being as a contemporary reader, and perhaps
an ideal reader too, and it is the very plausibility of
their existence that seems to substantiate the claims
made on their behalf. The importance of this plausible basis as a means of verification can be gauged
from the fact that in recent years another type of
reader has sometimes been endowed with more than
merely heuristic qualities: namely, the reader whose
psychology has been opened up by the findings of
psychoanalysis. Examples of such studies are those
by Simon Lesser and Norman Holland, to which we

shall be referring again later. Recourse to psychology,
as a basis for a particular category of reader in whom
the responses to literature may be observed, has
come about not least because of the desire to escape
from the limitations of the other categories. The assumption of a psychologically describable reader has
increased the extent to which literary responses may
be ascertained, and a psychoanalytically based theory seems eminently plausible, because the reader it
refers to appears to have a real existence of his own.

Let us now take a closer look at the two main categories of readers and their place in literary criticism.
The real reader is invoked mainly in studies of the
history of responses, i.e., when attention is focused on
the way in which a literary work has been received
by a specific reading public. Now whatever judgments may have been passed on the work will also
reflect various attitudes and norms of that public, so
that literature can be said to mirror the cultural code
which conditions these judgments. This is also true
when the readers quoted belong to different historical ages, for, whatever period they may have belonged to, their judgment of the work in question will
still reveal their own norms, thereby offering a substantial clue as to the norms and tastes of their respective societies. Reconstruction of the real reader
naturally depends on the survival of contemporary
documents, but the further back in time we go, beyond the eighteenth century, the more sparse the documentation becomes. As a result, the reconstruction
often depends entirely on what can be gleaned from
the literary works themselves. The problem here is
whether such a reconstruction corresponds to the
real reader of the time or simply represents the role
which the author intended the reader to assume. In
this respect, there are three types of "contemporary"
reader—the one real and historical, drawn from existing documents, and the other two hypothetical: the
first constructed from social and historical knowledge of the time, and the second extrapolated from
the reader's role laid down in the text.

Almost diametrically opposite the contemporary
reader stands the oft quoted ideal reader. It is difficult to pinpoint precisely where he is drawn from,
though there is a good deal to be said for the claim
that he tends to emerge from the brain of the philologist or critic himself. Although the critic's judgment
may well have been honed and refined by the many
texts he has dealt with, he remains nothing more
than a cultured reader—if only because an ideal

reader is a structural impossibility as far as literary communication is concerned. An ideal reader would have to have an identical code to that of the author; authors, however, generally recodify prevailing codes in their texts, and so the ideal reader would also have to share the intentions underlying this process. And if this were possible, communication would then be quite superfluous, for one only communicates that which is *not* already shared by sender and receiver.

The idea that the author himself might be his own ideal reader is frequently undermined by the statements writers have made about their own works. Generally, as readers they hardly ever make any remarks on the impact their own texts have exercised upon them, but prefer to talk in referential language about their intentions, strategies, and constructions, conforming to conditions that will also be valid for the public they are trying to guide. Whenever this happens, i.e., whenever the author turns into a reader of his own work, he must therefore revert to the code, which he had already recoded in his work. In other words, the author, although theoretically the only possible ideal reader, as he has experienced what he has written, does not in fact *need* to duplicate himself into author and ideal reader, so that the postulate of an ideal reader is, in his case, superfluous.

A further question mark against the concept of the ideal reader lies in the fact that such a being would have to be able to realize in full the meaning potential of the fictional text. The history of literary responses, however, shows quite clearly that this potential has been fulfilled in many different ways, and if so, how can one person at one go encompass all the possible meanings? Different meanings of the same text have emerged at different times, and, indeed, the same text read a second time will have a different effect from that of its first reading. The ideal reader, then, must not only fulfill the potential meaning of the text independently of his own historical situation, but he must also do this exhaustively. The result would be total consumption of the text—which would itself be ruinous for literature. But there are texts which can be "consumed" in this way, as is obvious from the mounds of light literature that flow regularly into the pulping machines. The question then arises as to whether the reader of such works is really the one meant by the term "ideal reader," for the latter is usually called upon when the text is hard to grasp—it is hoped that he will help to unravel its

mysteries and, if there are no mysteries, his presence is not required anyway. Indeed, herein lies the true essence of this particular concept. The ideal reader, unlike the contemporary reader, is a purely fictional being; he has no basis in reality, and it is this very fact that makes him so useful: as a fictional being, he can close the gaps that constantly appear in any analysis of literary effects and responses. He can be endowed with a variety of qualities in accordance with whatever problem he is called upon to help solve.

This rather general account of the two concepts of ideal and contemporary readers reveals certain presuppositions, which frequently come into play when responses to fictional texts are to be assessed. The basic concern of these concepts is with the results produced rather than with the structure of effects, which causes and is responsible for these results. It is time now to change the vantage point, turning away from results produced and focusing on that potential in the text which triggers the recreative dialectics in the reader.

The desire to break free from these traditional and basically restrictive categories of readers can already be seen in the various attempts that have been made to develop new categories of readers as heuristic concepts. Present-day literary criticism offers specific categories for specific areas of discussion: there is the superreader (Riffaterre),[2] the informed reader (Fish),[3] and the intended reader (Wolff),[4] to name but a few, each type bringing with it a special terminology of its own. Although these readers are primarily conceived as heuristic constructs, they are nevertheless drawn from specific groups of real, existing readers.

Riffaterre's superreader stands for a "group of informants,"[5] who always come together at "nodal points in the text,"[6] thus establishing through their common reactions the existence of a "stylistic fact."[7] The superreader is like a sort of divining rod, used to discover a density of meaning potential encoded in the text. As a collective term for a variety of readers of different competence, it allows for an empirically verifiable account of both the semantic and pragmatic potential contained in the message of the text. By sheer weight of numbers, Riffaterre hopes to eliminate the degree of variation inevitably arising from the subjective disposition of the individual reader. He tries to objectify style, or the stylistic fact as a communicative element additional to the primary one of language.[8] He argues that the stylistic fact stands out from its context, thus pointing to a density within the encoded message, which is brought to light by intratextual contrasts that are spotted by the superreader. An approach like this bypasses the difficulties inherent in the stylistics of deviation, which always involves reference to linguistic norms that lie outside the text, in order to gauge the poetic qualities of a text by the degree it deviates from these presupposed extratextual norms. This argument, however, is not the core of Riffaterre's concept; the most vital point is that a stylistic fact can only be discerned by a perceiving subject. Consequently, the basic impossibility of formalizing the intratextual contrasts manifests itself as an effect that can only be experienced by a reader. And so Riffaterre's superreader is a means of ascertaining the stylistic fact, but owing to its nonreferentiality this concept shows how indispensable the reader is to the formulation of the stylistic fact.

Now even the superreader, as a collective term for a group of readers, is not proof against error. The very ascertaining of intratextual contrasts presupposes a differentiated competence and is dependent not least on the historical nearness or distance of the group in relation to the text under consideration. Nevertheless, Riffaterre's concept does show that stylistic qualities can no longer be exclusively pinpointed with the instruments of linguistics.

To a certain degree this also holds true of Fish's concept of the informed reader, which is not so much concerned with the statistical average of readers' reactions as with describing the processing of the text by the reader. For this purpose, certain conditions must be fulfilled:

> The informed reader is someone who 1.) is a competent speaker of the language out of which the text is built up. 2.) is in full possession of "semantic knowledge that a mature . . . listener brings to this task of comprehension." This includes the knowledge (that is, the experience, both as a producer and comprehender) of lexical sets, collocation probabilities, idioms, professional and other dialects, etc. 3.) has *literary* competence. . . . The reader, of whose responses I speak, then, is this informed reader, neither an abstraction, nor an actual living reader, but a hybrid—a real reader (me) who does everything within his power to make himself informed.[9]

This category of reader, then, must not only possess the necessary competence, but must also ob-serve his own reactions during the process of actualization[10] in order to control them. The need for this self-observation arises first from the fact that Fish developed his concept of the informed reader with close reference to generative-transformational grammar, and second from the fact that he could not take over some of the consequences inherent in this model. If the reader, by means of his competence, structures the text himself, this implies that his reactions will follow one another in time, during the course of his reading, and that it is in this sequence of reactions that the meaning of the text will be generated. To this extent Fish follows the model of transformational grammar. Where he diverges from this model is in his evaluation of surface structure: "It should be noted however that my category of response, and especially of meaningful response, includes more than the transformational grammarians, who believe that comprehension is a function of deep structure perception, would allow. There is a tendency, at least in the writings of some linguists, to downgrade surface structure—the form of actual sentences—to the status of a husk, or covering, or veil; a layer of excrescences that is to be peeled away or penetrated or discarded in favor of the kernel underlying it."[11]

The sequence of reactions aroused in the reader by the surface structure of a literary text is often characterized by the fact that the strategies of that text lead the reader astray—which is the prime reason why different readers will react differently. The surface structure sets off in the reader a process which in fact would grind to an almost immediate halt if the surface structure were meant only to unveil the deep structure. Thus, Fish abandons the transformational model at a point that is vital both for it and for his concept. The model in fact breaks down just when it reaches one of the most interesting tasks of all: clarifying the processing of literary texts—an act that would be grotesquely impoverished if reduced to terms of mere grammar. But it is also at this point that the concept of the informed reader loses its frame of reference and changes into a postulate that, for all the plausibility of its premises, is very difficult to consolidate. Fish himself is aware of the difficulty, and at the end of the essay he says of his concept: "In a peculiar and unsettling (to theorists) way, it is a method which processes its own user, who is also its only instrument. It is self-sharpening and what it sharpens is *you*. In short, it does not organize materials, but transforms minds."[12] The transformation, then, no longer relates to the text, but to the reader. Viewed from the standpoint of generative-transformational grammar, the transformation is just a metaphor, but it also shows clearly the limited range of the generative-transformational model, as there is no doubt that processing a text is bound to result in changes within the recipient, and these changes are not a matter of grammatical rules, but of experience. This is the problem with Fish's concept — it starts out from the grammatical model, justifiably abandons the model at a particular juncture, but can then only invoke an experience which, though indisputable, remains inaccessible to the theorist. However, we can see even more clearly from the concept of the informed reader than from that of the superreader that an analysis of text processing requires more than just a linguistic model.

While Fish concerns himself with the effects of the text on the reader, Wolff — with his intended reader — sets out to reconstruct the idea of the reader which the author had in mind.[13] This image of the intended reader can take on different forms, according to the text being dealt with: it may be the idealized reader,[14] or it may reveal itself through anticipation of the norms and values of contemporary readers, through individualization of the public, through apostrophes to the reader, through the assigning of attitudes, or didactic intentions, or the demand for the willing suspension of disbelief.[15] Thus the intended reader, as a sort of fictional inhabitant of the text,[16] can embody not only the concepts and conventions of the contemporary public but also the desire of the author both to link up with these concepts and to work on them — sometimes just portraying them, sometimes acting upon them. Wolff outlines the history of the democratization of the "reader idea," the definition of which, however, demands a relatively detailed knowledge of the contemporary reader and of the social history of the time, if the importance and function of this intended reader are to be properly evaluated. But, in any case, by characterizing this fictitious reader it is possible to reconstruct the public which the author wished to address.

There can be no doubting the usefulness, and indeed necessity, of ascertaining this figure, and equally certain is the fact that there is a reciprocity between the form of presentation and the type of reader intended,[17] but the question remains open as to why, generations later, a reader can still grasp the meaning (perhaps we should say *a* meaning) of the text, even though he cannot be the intended reader. Clearly, the historical qualities which influenced the author at the time of writing mould the image of the intended reader — and as such they may enable us to reconstruct the author's intentions, but they tell us nothing about the reader's actual response to the text. The intended reader, then, marks certain positions and attitudes in the text, but these are not yet identical to the reader's role, for many of these positions are conceived ironically (frequently the case in novels), so that the reader is not expected to accept the attitude offered him, but rather to react to it. We must, then, differentiate between the fictitious reader and the reader's role, for although the former is present in the text by way of a large variety of different signals, he is not independent of the other textual perspectives, such as narrator, characters, and plotline, as far as his function is concerned. The fictitious reader is, in fact, just one of several perspectives, all of which interlink and interact. The role of the reader emerges from this interplay of perspectives, for he finds himself called upon to mediate between them, and so it would be fair to say that the intended reader, as supplier of *one* perspective, can never represent more than one aspect of the reader's role.

The three concepts of reader that we have dealt with start out from different assumptions and aim at different solutions. The superreader represents a test concept which serves to ascertain the "stylistic fact," pointing to a density in the encoded message of the text. The informed reader represents a self-instructing concept that aims at increasing the reader's 'informedness,' and hence his competence, through self-observation with regard to the sequence of reactions set off by the text. The intended reader represents a concept of reconstruction, uncovering the historical dispositions of the reading public at which the author was aiming. But for all the diversity of their intentions, these three concepts have one common denominator: they all see themselves as a means of transcending the limitations of (1) structural linguistics, (2) generative-transformational grammar, or (3) literary sociology, by introducing the figure of the reader.

It is evident that no theory concerned with literary texts can make much headway without bringing in the reader, who now appears to have been promoted to the new frame of reference whenever the semantic and pragmatic potential of the text comes under scrutiny. The question is, what kind of reader? As we have seen, the different concepts, of real and of hypothetical readers, all entail restrictions that inevitably undermine the general applicability of the theories to which they are linked. If, then, we are to try and understand the effects caused and the responses elicited by literary works, we must allow for the reader's presence without in any way predetermining his character or his historical situation. We may call him, for want of a better term, the implied reader. He embodies all those predispositions necessary for a literary work to exercise its effect — predispositions laid down, not by an empirical outside reality, but by the text itself. Consequently, the implied reader as a concept has his roots firmly planted in the structure of the text; he is a construct and in no way to be identified with any real reader.

It is generally recognized that literary texts take on their reality by being read, and this in turn means that texts must already contain certain conditions of actualization that will allow their meaning to be assembled in the responsive mind of the recipient. The concept of the implied reader is therefore a textual structure anticipating the presence of a recipient without necessarily defining him: this concept prestructures the role to be assumed by each recipient, and this holds true even when texts deliberately appear to ignore their possible recipient or actively exclude him. Thus the concept of the implied reader designates a network of response-inviting structures, which impel the reader to grasp the text.

No matter who or what he may be, the real reader is always offered a particular role to play, and it is this role that constitutes the concept of the implied reader. There are two basic, interrelated aspects to this concept: the reader's role as a textual structure, and the reader's role as a structured act. Let us begin with the textual structure. We may assume that every literary text in one way or another represents a perspective view of the world put together by (though not necessarily typical of) the author. As such, the work is in no way a mere copy of the given world — it constructs a world of its own out of the material available to it. It is the way in which this world is constructed that brings about the perspective intended by the author. Since the world of the text is bound to have variable degrees of unfamiliarity for its possible readers (if the work is to have any "novelty" for them), they must be placed in a position which enables them to actualize the new view. This position, however, cannot be present in the text itself, as it is the vantage point for visualizing the world represented and so cannot be part of that world. The text must therefore *bring about* a standpoint from which the reader will be able to view things that would never have come into focus as long as his own habitual dispositions were determining his orientation, and what is more, this standpoint must be able to accommodate all kinds of different readers. How, then, can it evolve from the structure of the text?

It has been pointed out that the literary text offers a perspective view of the world (namely, the author's). It is also, in itself, composed of a variety of perspectives that outline the author's view and also provide access to what the reader is meant to visualize. This is best exemplified by the novel, which is a system of perspectives designed to transmit the individuality of the author's vision. As a rule there are four main perspectives: those of the narrator, the characters, the plot, and the fictitious reader. Although these may differ in order of importance, none of them on its own is identical to the meaning of the text. What they do is provide guidelines originating from different starting points (narrator, characters, etc.), continually shading into each other and devised in such a way that they all converge on a general meeting place. We call this meeting place the meaning of the text, which can only be brought into focus if it is visualized from a standpoint. Thus, standpoint and convergence of textual perspectives are closely interrelated, although neither of them is actually represented in the text, let alone set out in words. Rather they emerge during the reading process, in the course of which the reader's role is to occupy shifting vantage points that are geared to a prestructured activity and to fit the diverse perspectives into a gradually evolving pattern. This allows him to grasp both the different starting points of the textual perspectives and their ultimate coalescence, which is guided by the interplay between the changing perspectives and the gradually unfolding coalescence itself.[18]

Thus, the reader's role is prestructured by three basic components: the different perspectives represented in the text, the vantage point from which he joins them together, and the meeting place where they converge.

This pattern simultaneously reveals that the reader's role is not identical to the fictitious reader portrayed in the text. The latter is merely one component part of the reader's role, by which the author exposes the disposition of an assumed reader to interaction with the other perspectives, in order to bring about modifications.

So far we have outlined the reader's role as a textual structure, which, however, will be fully implemented only when it induces structured acts in the reader. The reason for this is that although the textual perspectives themselves are given, their gradual convergence and final meeting place are not linguistically formulated and so have to be imagined. This is the point where the textual structure of his role begins to affect the reader. The instructions provided stimulate mental images, which animate what is linguistically implied, though not said. A sequence of mental images is bound to arise during the reading process, as new instructions have continually to be accommodated, resulting not only in the replacement of images formed but also in a shifting position of the vantage point, which differentiates the attitudes to be adopted in the process of image-building. Thus the vantage point of the reader and the meeting place of perspectives become interrelated during the ideational activity and so draw the reader inescapably into the world of the text.

Textual structure and structured act are related in much the same way as intention and fulfillment, though in the concept of the implied reader they are joined together in the dynamic process we have described. In this respect, the concept departs from the latest postulate that the programmed reception of the text be designated as *"Rezeptionsvorgabe"* (structured prefigurement).[19] This term relates only to discernible textual structures and completely ignores the dynamic act which elicits the response to those structures.

The concept of the implied reader as an expression of the role offered by the text is in no way an abstraction derived from a real reader, but is rather the conditioning force behind a particular kind of tension produced by the real reader when he accepts the role. This tension results, in the first place, from the difference

> between myself as reader and the often very different self who goes about paying bills, repairing leaky faucets, and failing in generosity and wisdom. It is only as I read that I become the self whose beliefs must coincide with the author's. Regardless of my real beliefs and practices, I must subordinate my mind and heart to the book if I am to enjoy it to the full. The author creates, in short, an image of himself and another image of his reader; he makes his reader, as he makes his second self, and the most successful reading is one in which the created selves, author and reader, can find complete agreement.[20]

One wonders whether such an agreement can really work; even Coleridge's ever popular demand for a "willing suspension of disbelief" on the part of the audience remains an ideal whose desirability is questionable. Would the role offered by the text function properly if it were totally accepted? The sacrifice of the real reader's own beliefs would mean the loss of the whole repertoire of historical norms and values, and this in turn would entail the loss of the tension which is a precondition for the processing and for the comprehension that follows it. As M. H. Abrams has rightly stressed: "Given a truly impassive reader, all his beliefs suspended or anesthetized, (a poet) would be as helpless, in his attempt to endow his work with interest and power, as though he had to write for an audience from Mars."[21] However, the suggestion that there are two selves is certainly tenable, for these are the role offered by the text and the real reader's own disposition, and as the one can never be fully taken over by the other, there arises between the two the tension we have described. Generally, the role prescribed by the text will be the stronger, but the reader's own disposition will never disappear totally; it will tend instead to form the background to and a frame of reference for the act of grasping and comprehending. If it were to disappear totally, we should simply forget all the experiences that we are constantly bringing into play as we read—experiences which are responsible for the many different ways in which people fulfill the reader's role set out by the text. And even though we may lose awareness of these experiences while we read, we are still guided by them unconsciously, and by the end of our reading we are liable consciously to want to incorporate the new experience into our own store of knowledge.

The fact that the reader's role can be fulfilled in different ways, according to historical or individual circumstances, is an indication that the structure of the text *allows* for different ways of fulfillment. Clearly, then, the process of fulfillment is always a selective one, and any one actualization can be judged against the background of the others potentially present in the textual structure of the reader's role. Each actualization therefore represents a selective realization of the implied reader, whose own structure provides a frame of reference within which individual responses to a text can be communicated to others. This is a vital function of the whole concept of the implied reader: it provides a link between all the historical and individual actualizations of the text and makes them accessible to analysis.

To sum up, then, the concept of the implied reader is a transcendental model which makes it possible for the structured effects of literary texts to be described. It denotes the role of the reader, which is definable in terms of textual structure and structured acts. By bringing about a standpoint for the reader, the textual structure follows a basic rule of human perception, as our views of the world are always of a perspective nature. "The observing subject and the represented object have a particular relationship one to the other; the 'subject-object relationship' merges into the perspective way of representation. It also merges into the observer's way of seeing; for just as the artist organizes his representation according to the standpoint of an observer, the observer—because of this very technique of representation—finds himself directed toward a particular view which more or less obliges him to search for the one and only standpoint that will correspond to that view."[22]

By virtue of this standpoint, the reader is situated in such a position that he can assemble the meaning toward which the perspectives of the text have guided him. But since this meaning is neither a given external reality nor a copy of an intended reader's own world, it is something that has to be ideated by the mind of the reader. A reality that has no existence of its own can only come into being by way of ideation, and so the structure of the text sets off a sequence of mental images which lead to the text translating itself into the reader's consciousness. The actual content of these mental images will be colored by the reader's existing stock of experience, which acts as a referential background against which the unfamiliar can be conceived and processed. The concept of the implied reader offers a means of describing the process whereby textual structures are

transmuted through ideational activities into personal experiences.

Notes

1. Northrop Frye, *Fearful Symmetry. A Study of William Blake* (Boston, 1967), pp. 427f.
2. Michael Riffaterre, *Strukturale Stilistik,* transl. by Wilhelm Bolle (Munich, 1973), pp. 46ff.
3. Stanley Fish, "Literature in the Reader: Affective Stylistics," *New Literary History* 2 (1970): 123ff.
4. Erwin Wolff, "Der intendierte Leser," *Poetica* 4 (1971): 141ff.
5. Riffaterre, *Strukturale Stilistik,* p. 44.
6. Ibid., p. 48.
7. Ibid., p. 29, passim.
8. See also the critique by Rainer Warning, "Rezeptionsästhetik als literaturwissenschaftliche Pragmatik," in *Rezeptionsästhetik. Theorie und Praxis* (UTB 303), Rainer Warning, ed. (Munich, 1975), pp. 26ff.
9. Fish, "Literature in the Reader," p. 145.
10. Ibid., pp. 144–46.
11. Ibid., p. 143.
12. Ibid., p. 160f.
13. Wolff, "Der intendierte Leser," p. 166.
14. Ibid., p. 145.
15. Ibid., pp. 143, 151–54, 156, 158, 162.
16. Ibid., p. 160.
17. Ibid., pp. 159f.
18. For a more detailed discussion, see Part II, Chap. 4, pp. 96–99.
19. See Manfred Naumann et al., *Gesellschaft—Literatur—Lesen. Literaturrezeption in theoretischer Sicht* (Berlin and Weimar, 1973), p. 35, passim; see also my critique of this book, "Im Lichte der Kritik," in Warning's *Rezeptionsästhetik,* pp. 335–41, as well as that of H. R. Jauss, ibid., pp. 343ff.
20. Wayne C. Booth, *The Rhetoric of Fiction* (Chicago, 1963), pp. 137f.
21. M. H. Abrams, "Belief and Suspension of Disbelief," in *Literature and Belief* (English Institute Essays, 1957), M. H. Abrams, ed. (New York, 1958), p. 17.
22. Carl Friedrich Graumann, *Grundlagen einer Phänomenologie und Psychologie der Perspektivität* (Berlin, 1960), p. 14.

The Miller's Wife and the Professors: Questions about the Transactive Theory of Reading

Norman Holland

In contrast to Wolfgang Iser, who puts much of his emphasis on the ways the text controls the reader's responses, Norman Holland is more concerned with the ways actual readers control the text. Thus, while Iser offers a reader-response theory that explains why we should have similar reactions to the same text, Holland offers one that explains why we very often do not. Basing his literary theory on a psychoanalytic view of readers rather than on a phenomenological view of reading, Holland claims that each reader will impose his or her "identity theme" on the text, to a large extent recreating that text in the reader's image. And this process can be illustrated, Holland argues, even when the readers are professional literary analysts. This argument inevitably raises questions about the relative weight of "subjective" and "objective" data, about the possibility of "misreadings," and about the need to account for a reader's changing interpretations, questions that Holland undertakes to answer as he sets forth his own "transactive" theory of reading and defines his position with reference to several other reader-response critics.

The scene: spring at a large midwestern university, 10:15 A.M. A seminar room. Around the long table and in outer rows of seats are gathered a score or so of professorial-looking types from the English department, some senior, some junior. About a quarter are women, some of them, it turns out, faculty wives. They have assembled for a "Working Teachshop" by the Visiting Fireman.

It is the morning after the lecture and party the night before. People are gearing up for the day or, having taught 9:00s, gearing down. Those seated at the table are holding photocopies of a poem. As they banter, they seem to be approaching the morning's

Reprinted by permission of the publisher from *New Literary History* 17 (1986): pp. 423–47. Copyright © 1986 by The Johns Hopkins University Press.

exercise in a spirit of curiosity. Let's play the VF's game and see what happens.

The VF himself, neatly dressed if slightly hung over, sits in the middle of one long side. He speaks in a friendly but hesitant voice, feeling his way with this group, new to him. He begins by reading the poem aloud:

The Mill

The miller's wife had waited long,
    The tea was cold, the fire was dead;
And there might yet be nothing wrong
    In how he went and what he said;
"There are no millers any more,"
    Was all that she had heard him say;
And he had lingered at the door
    So long that it seemed yesterday.

Sick with fear that had no form
    She knew that she was there at last;
And in the mill there was a warm
    And mealy fragrance of the past.
What else there was would only seem
    To say again what he had meant;
And what was hanging from a beam
    Would not have heeded where she went.

And if she thought it followed her,
    She may have reasoned in the dark
That one way of the few there were
    Would hide her and would leave no mark:
Black water, smooth above the weir
    Like starry velvet in the night,
Though ruffled once, would soon appear
    The same as ever to the sight.

"The Mill" is by Edwin Arlington Robinson, 1920. This morning's consensus is: Not a great poem, but good. One senior man in American literature gravely opines that Robinson is "much underrated."

The VF remarks that he picked this particular poem because part of his lecture the night before dealt with Robert Frost's comments on it. He therefore thought the assembled company might find this poem a useful starting point. This morning, as advertised, he would like to consider how one might apply the theoretical ideas developed in the lecture (the transactive theory of reading, identity theory, feedback networks, cognitive psychology, the architecture of the brain) to something more practical, the teaching of literature. Would the professors be so kind as to fill in answers to the following five questions?

Actually, of course, the VF has a hidden agenda. As he goes to and fro on the earth, from campus to campus, explaining his devilish ideas about reading, he gets the same questions over and over. Last night's lecture was no exception. Three questions, in particular, always arise:

Doesn't this make every reading totally subjective, so that any one reading is as good as any other?

In teaching what do you do about misreadings?

Don't people change their readings? I know I read *Huckleberry Finn* differently now from the way I did when I was a child.

In answer, the VF has stated his views, his transactive theory of reading, many times. Although there are (obviously!) shared elements in the reading situation, we can represent someone's reading a poem or a story as a personal transaction — as an expression of character or identity. The VF is not abandoning the text or techniques of interpretation or the social situation within which interpretation takes place. He is not saying that a reading is not *also* a function of these things. Quite the contrary! he says. He is simply claiming that we *can* understand someone's reading as a function of personal identity.[1]

Sadly, however, the VF feels deep down inside him that no matter how clearly he says these, by now, to him, palpable truths, he will hear these same questions over and over again. To elicit them and discuss them and perhaps even lay to rest these recurring questions he has put together some materials for a workshop for professors of literature. If he coalesces several occasions on which he got groups of professors to work on his materials, he comes up with the scene with which this article began.

Meanwhile, back in that seminar room, the VF, ever hopeful, hands out questionnaires. He promises to hand out his own answers in exchange for their candor, but even so, the professors assembled around the seminar table are a little reluctant, a little shy, a little tested in their professional mettle.

1. To what does the clause "what was hanging from a beam" refer? _____
_____

2. To what does the clause "What else there was" refer? _____
_____

3. What is the most important single word in the poem? _____
Why? _____
_____

4. What does the miller's wife look like (features, build, clothing, etc.)? _____

_____

5. Whom does she remind you of, and why?

_____

_____

The questions artfully span a gamut from the most "objective" to the most "subjective." That is, question 1 asks a grammatical question which I think most professional readers would agree has one "right" and various "wrong" answers.

Question 2 looks like 1, but there probably is no definitely right answer. Still, some answers would be clearly wrong ("the wife," say) while a number of others would be acceptable and, in that sense, "right." I had in mind here Stanley Fish's concept of an "interpretive community." When we ask a grammatical question of a poem, we apply the procedures and conventions of the community of university readers, professors, and students to answer it. We use "interpretive strategies" that we learned from an "interpretive community." These, says Fish, "enable," "constitute," "make available" such ideas as a clause's referring to something.[2] Would the professors' answers demonstrate Fish's claim?

Question 3 asks for a more freely imaginative response. There are no "wrong" answers except (I suppose) words that do not occur in "The Mill." I took the question from David Bleich's book on "subjective" pedagogy in which the author says an answer to this question "begins in complete subjectivity and is then transformed into judgments that appear to be objective."[3]

Question 4 asks for even more projection, since the poem does not describe the wife at all. I wrote this question hoping to test Wolfgang Iser's model of response in which the text leaves gaps (here, the wife's appearance) which the reader feels impelled to fill.[4]

Question 5 admits a wholly personal response. That is, anyone would comprehend a description answering 4 (thin, gaunt, even "like an Eskimo"), but no one else in the room but the answerer could understand some of the answers possible for 5: my mother-in-law; a woman I saw once. Thus 5 calls for a "very subjective" and 1 for a "very objective" answer, and indeed the responses came out accordingly.

Most readers gave the "right" answer to question 1:

The miller

the miller's body

The miller's corpse

the miller

THE DEAD MILLER

refers to a new subj. serving as gr. subj. of verb "could not have heeded." serves as antecedent of "it"—applies to hanged miller.

Inevitably, there were a few who arrived at special results:

fear or the fear of what the future holds

I have no idea.

Seems something dead, fearful, underscoring her fright.

Question 2, allowing more leeway, elicited more varied answers and varied wording:

THE DEAD MILLER

Again it is referentially the hanged body of No. 1.

This also refers to the hanging body of the miller.

Various possibilities: Hanged miller—smell of hanged miller (bowels loosening, etc.—in contrast to pleasant "fragrance"), what was "there" beside the fear, finally given form—the scene & situation—

Maybe those who said in answer to 2 the miller's body (incorrect, in my reading) had some sort of carryover from question 1. They tended to use more language in answering question 2, possibly expressing uncertainty about their answers.

Some people wrote down what seems to me, at least, the "right" answer, namely, other things that embody the miller's outmoded craft:

The other reminders in the mill of the dead occupation.

Everything in the mill that reminds the wife of the Miller's life & that Millers are now unnecessary.

Still others suggested vague fears or futures or failures:

"what else there was" refers to "what he had meant" and "what was hanging from the beam." The referents are nonspecific and what floats around is the phantom of fear, or doubt or distrust—something that has no form.

It refers to that "something" that pervades the room, fills it with suspense. Not knowing what that something is is half the reason for its powerful effect.

It refers to the *non*-reassuring aspects of the mill — what speaks to her fears (of the future), not to her knowledge of the past. Fear directs itself toward the future.

Questions 1 and 2 should surely evoke the effects of Stanley Fish's interpretive communities. And they do. Clearly the professors were drawing on a common store of syntactic knowledge and shared principles of reading. On the other hand, there was no great unanimity. The idea of interpretive communities may be necessary, but it is not sufficient to explain these responses.

Question 3 elicited (as I had expected) a wide variety of answers:

dead. is right at beginning of poem & puts weight on everything that follows

"dead." It suggests what happens.

fear: Because of her first phrase "There are no millers anymore" which is, it appears, the point of her fear of economic downfall. Such things as yesterday, past, linger

Fear. It colors all responses to her encounters in the mill

hanging   Because he's hanging (the miller) in a society that no longer needs him.

hanging — everything in the poem seems to hang, be suspended, the wife waiting, the miller, no need, the dead miller, hope etc.

Some said there was *no* most important word, leaving the question blank or fussing with it:

There isn't one. To answer, though: dead so much death, everywhere — no more millers (other words seem to say again what it had meant).

I'm uncomfortable choosing — each word seems to be dependent on the others. "There" is used many times in different ways — as a place — as a nonplace — The poem draws attention to *place* (The Mill) as determining action.

Others showed remarkable ingenuity:

Same.   The irony that there are no millers anymore — and yet no change, no mark, everything still appears the same.

what   brings reader in

"No"   that which *is* disappears; connects to "nothing," "no millers," "no form," would not, "no mark."

MIL   The assonant found in "meal" & "miller" — it ties the entire poem together — especially in "mealy fragrance"

mealy?   pleasant, warm ground-down grain, devastated people, "mealy-mouthedness" of the probably — uncomplaining wife to the miller, & miller to anyone who might have heard or understood.

yet   she does not know — yet — and so the poem hangs in the moment before knowing, when she suspects, doesn't know, doesn't want to believe

And, of course, there was a joker. The most important word? " 'Hangs.' It jars you."

Surely one could say with Bleich that these answers begin in subjectivity and end in objectivity, but does that statement do more than describe what is taking place? Surely these answers are, finally, "subjective," yet they mark various "objective" appeals to the poem. There must be more helpful metaphors than "begins" and "ends" for developing the relation.

Asked in question 4 to project visually, some hesitated, agreed to make an image, but insisted they did not know for sure:

I remember nothing of her appearance. She seems an image — abstract — of domesticity.

She is not described at all, of course, and the poem seems to convey a sense of formlessness. There is a sense of evasion, of dimly making out the forms and outlines of things. Yet I see her as a heavy set woman, with a pale face, broad features, a woman who has worked hard all her life.

No clue in poem — probably small, plain, calico & gingham — anything but velvet

Others tried to reason an image into being:

? young?

She is *probably* short, as she must look up at the beam where he is hanging

Apron (tea). White face in fear, Hands red with hard work. Slightly overweight = the diet of poor people who eat a lot of starch.

Some simply went ahead and described her:

Older woman, motherly, has known hard time apron, thin, long hands & fingers, gaunt cheeks

Slightly over-weight, plain, middle-aged woman — wearing work clothes (housedress)

like a fat Russian peasant-woman in late middle-age

Others resorted to pictures and analogies:

not described—we are free to create our own image—I see a Brueghel.

Like a weaker version of the woman in Grant Wood's "American Gothic"

Several possibilities: the mother in the Katzenjammer Kids strip (older, obese/sturdy/hard-farm working immigrant with apron)—in this case suicide results of economy, *or* Nastasia Kinsky (grey peasant dress unbuttoned at the top showing inner breast & chest wall, hair seductively falling over left eye, pushed back, falls again)—then suicide due to jealousy, etc.

The variability in these pictures suggests to me a number of things about Iser's model. For one thing, Iser writes as though the bulk of the response were controlled by the poem and the reader simply fills in some inessential gaps. The poems these people describe, however, are *so* different (Grant Wood, Brueghel, thin, fat) that the balance seems rather the other way. Also, the answers to questions 1 and 2 suggest that, even in simple grammatical matters, readers are not constrained or limited. Third, it is not clear to me that readers are "impelled" to fill in gaps. Several of these professors simply refused.

To the last and most projective question of the five, there were the predictable blanks and responses like

no one

I can't think of anyone right now

—Can't think of a literary character just now

As in that last response, most of these professors of literature assumed, more or less automatically, that what was called for was a literary association, and most provided one. Some were predictable, others quite ingenious:

Chaucer—connotations of famous Miller?

The Wife in "Death of a Salesman"

Tristan, Romeo

Women in the Death of the Hired Man, Hedda Gabler

the old peasant woman whose shoes Heidegger writes about in "The Origin of Art"—because she seems to have been totally and unreflectively absorbed in her work (or her husband's) until the event which precipitates the poem occurs. Then, she is incapable of going on.

Others did what I had hoped for the purposes of my demonstration:

An old woman I saw once.

My grandmother—because she was old world & full of care & overworked

My Aunt Betty, who discovered her husband dead on his workshop floor

A former girlfriend, a timorous and dependent person, who gave meaning to her own life by identification with others—an identification with me I couldn't tolerate in the end.

They recalled figures entirely personal to themselves, people no one else in the room would know—except for

She does not remind me of anyone I know. In her fear that something may have happened to hurt a loved one, she reminds me of me.

Others turned to works of art or places, personal recollections but not entirely personal:

Woman figure in Dorothea Lange's depression photo. Sense of being lost, bereft, nowhere, empty.

Any Iowa farmer's wife, perhaps from a photo in the depression, black & white

I saw many working women in England who had that stoical air about them; they were worn by life, not very "well cared for" but still cheery and tough.

She's probably like that only without much fight left in her. Her ending seems so quiet and undramatic—just a bowing to the inevitable.

Finally others *imagined* a person to be reminded of:

She reminds me of someone who someone wants taking a less active role—content to let things happen "They also serve who stand & wait" She is unaffected by what's happening & partly paying no attention

And, of course, there was a joker. "Whom does she remind you of?" "The miller."

So far, we have been looking at answers by many different people to one question. Although these are skilled professional readers, although they are part of an interpretive community—American university teachers of literature—although most are drawing on an essentially similar "New Critical" training, their answers vary all over the place. Question 1 has "right" and "wrong" answers, but after that, responses go every which way.[5]

When we look at many answers to single questions, we can trace some rather vague patterns, but the whole picture is rather a jumble. We can get more coherence, however, if, instead of comparing everyone's answer to one question, we look at one person's answers to all five questions. For example:

1. body hanging there
2. the only thing that was left was his found body —
3. fear — gives feeling of dread
4. no idea — housewife — heavy set; placid air of waiting — doesn't pay much attention Keeps on with her
5. She reminds me of someone who someone wants taking a less active role — content to let things happen "They also serve who stand & wait" She is unaffected by what's happening & partly paying no attention

In these five answers by someone I'll call Professor One, I can read back from the last to the first and perceive a pattern. Answer 5 has a mistake: the repeated "someone," as if the final clause could stand alone, "Someone wants taking a less active role," as if the final clause could apply to Professor One herself as well as to the miller's wife. (Evidently she felt rushed — see 4.) To 5, the most projective of the questions, the one that allows most room, for individual feelings and associations, she speaks of someone "less active," who only stands and waits, who is partly paying no attention.

I see the same theme in her answer to question 4: placid, waiting, not paying attention. Again, as though what Professor One was saying applied equally to the miller's wife and to herself, she does not finish her last clause in 4. Perhaps she as well as the miller's wife is not paying attention. Perhaps she has identified herself with the wife.

In 3, she names "fear" as the most important word because it "gives feeling of dread." Again the phrasing is both passive and vague: the word *does something* to One, something vague. It "gives feeling." The verbs in 2 are exaggeratedly passive: "The only thing that was left was his found body." Finally, in 1, "body hanging there," we get a "correct" answer to this "objective" question, but stated so as to

emphasize the theme of passivity ("hanging") and vagueness ("there") that I find more obvious in her longer, more projective responses.

In tracing these themes, of course, I am primarily talking about her responses, only secondarily, inferentially about her. The distinction is essential, for two reasons. First, one cannot infer from One's writing alone what the relation is between her responses and her personality. The passivity I see in this specimen of her writing might be an overreaction by an intensely active person, or it might be a special frame of mind for reading, or it might simply be the result of the party the night before. Second, my reading of her response is as much a function of my identity as her reading of the poem is of hers. My conclusions, like hers, express me as well as what I am reading. Hence, what I am describing is a mutual interpretation. She reads the poem and the poem, so to speak, reads her. I read her response and her response, so to speak, reads me. My reading is my attempt to represent that systematically elusive process in words.

Possibly these interrelations will become clearer if we contrast One's reading with Professor Two's set of five responses:

1. refers to a new subj. serving as gr. subj. of verb "could not have heeded." serves as antecedent of "it" — applies to hanged miller.
2. 2d attribution of something in the mill — 1st thing being "fragrance"
3.
4. Unspecified — yet implied she follows, by drowning, her husband's departure by hanging.
5. Tristan, Romeo

Two is reluctant to project at all: he leaves 3 blank and insists in 4 that the wife's looks are "Unspecified." He makes up the lack by a process of inference which he attributes to the poem: the poem "implied" she drowned. Similarly, in 5, he pointed out by way of explanation, Tristan and Romeo fit in a sort of logical way. Each is a literary figure who dies in a double suicide or mutual love-death. His appeal to logic and observable behavior (as in 4) outweighed the woman's sex: very few respondents to 5 were reminded of men by the miller's *wife*.

The wife reminded him of literary figures, Tristan and Romeo, and he showed in 1 and 2 a similar focus on language (at the expense of the physical world). In 1 he spelled out a grammatical answer to a grammatical question exactly, almost fussily. In 2 he provided a grammatical answer — two grammatical answers — to a question that most people answered by an appeal to the events. In 4 he phrased the distressing facts of the poem in tangled euphemisms, "departure" for death or suicide, "follows" for the second death. From merely these brief responses, I can phrase a pair of themes that will unify Two's responses for me: displacement to logic, language, or demonstrable surface behavior; conversely, a reluctance to imagine what is not directly observable.

Young Professor Three was unusual in being witty:

1. The husband (miller) who has hanged himself. Poem draws attention to, depicts the transformation of person → object ("it" followed her); woman submerged beneath water, which then heals itself.
2. Various possibilities: Hanged miller — smell of hanged miller (bowels loosening, etc. — in contrast to pleasant "fragrance"), what was "there" beside the fear, finally given form — the scene & situation —
3. I'm uncomfortable choosing — each word seems to be dependent on the others. "There" is used many times in different ways — as a place — as a non-place — The poem draws attention to *place* (The Mill) as determining action.
4. We don't know; the poem doesn't tell us. Wet.
5. The miller.

She, too, is reluctant to project in 4 and 5. Her jokes in 4 and 5 serve as an evasion of the imagining the questionnaire asked her for. Her jokes take us, like Professor Two's focus on language, somewhat stubbornly back to what is demonstrable and obvious. Other themes: smells (2), body wastes (2) being "wet" (2,4), autonomy and dependency both for herself and for the words (3), persons as inanimate objects (1) and vice versa (1), delivering a precise and "professional" reading of the poem even if not called for (1). A psychoanalytic critic might well call this cluster of themes of self-rule and rule by others, obsessional, or, in a bodily terminology, "anal" themes. That is, to make a unity of this reading, I draw (from *my* interpretive community) psychoanalytic accounts of the kind of conflict parents and children have over who is autonomous and who is depen-

dent. Whose rules will be followed, particularly about delivering from one's body something that may or may not be a living part of oneself? Possibly that question applies to Professor Three's relation to this questionnaire as much as to the two-year-old on the potty.

I will call the next reader Professor Four, although I am not sure whether this woman was a professor or a graduate student.

1. fear or the fear of what the future holds
2. millers who are no more
3. fear: Because of her first phrase "There are no millers anymore" which is, it appears, the point of her fear of economic downfall. Such things as yesterday, past, linger
4. Older woman, motherly, has known hard times
5. poverty of a woman on the brink of it.

The themes that come across to me are fear — the word occurs four times — loss, and deprivation of poverty, specifically in an economic sense (2,3,4,5). In her metaphors, the future is a container that holds something to fear (1). Poverty is a pit one can fall into (5). She gives graphic versions to psychosocial deprivation from a "primary caretaker." I would call the container and pit symbols for what Four calls "motherly." The ultimate fear (in psychoanalytic theory) is annihilation at the hands of such a failing caretaker, and Four repeats that threat twice (2,3): one is no more, and she attributes the phrase to the wife. What defense Four expresses against this fear seems to be simply to face the danger, as the analysts might say, counterphobically: to fear the future, to know hard times, to be on the brink. If the choice is fight or flight, Four says fight: accept the fear and live with it.

The dominant motif in Professor Five's responses is also fear, but with a somewhat different tone:

1. The miller's wife's fears of her husband's suicide: she sees him *as if* hung
2. It refers to the *non*-reassuring aspects of the mill — what speaks of her fears (of the future), not to her knowledge of the past. Fear directs itself toward the future.
3. "Dead"
   The "dead" fire suggests the failures — and fears — which haunt the poem.

4. I remember nothing of her appearance. She seems an image—abstract—of domesticity.

5. She does not remind me of anyone I know. In her fear that something may have happened to hurt a loved one, she reminds me of me.

Five's last, candid answer suggests how his whole set of responses may reflect his own anxiety, leading to his error in the "objective" question, 1. The other answers suggest he may have a characteristic way of speaking about that fear: saying it applies to the unknown rather than the known, a kind of denial. The miller is only "as if" hung (1). Something "may have happened" (5). Fears apply to the necessarily unreadable future (2) and to abstractions, the "*non-reassuring aspects*" of a mill (2), or the "nothing" of an abstract image of domesticity (4). Five moves from relatively concrete images—"mill," "fire"—to abstractions—fear, failure, domesticity, future. The hanged man is only "as if" hung. He thus wards off literal fear: "She does not remind me of anyone I know." But he does make a mistake in 1.

Professor Six's responses somewhat resemble Five's:

1. The miller

2. His absence

3. "No" That which *is* disappears; connects to "nothing," "no millers," "no form," would not, "no mark."

4. apron, thin, long hands & fingers, gaunt cheeks

5. Woman figure in Dorothea Lange's depression photo. Sense of being lost, bereft, nowhere, empty.

If Five was defending against anxiety, Six was warding off a sense of absence, emptiness, or depression, as she (like Five) frankly says in her last response. She chooses "no" for the most important word, coupling it with phrasings of absence. In 2 she speaks of absence directly, and in 4 she imagines thinness and gauntness and, first of all, an apron obscuring the woman's body. In 1, perhaps one can find a significance in her speaking of "the miller" who is absent instead of "the miller's body" which is present.

In short, if I look at all the answers by one person, I can trace a theme or themes that permeate all five:

Professor One: being passive and vague

Professor Two: displacement to language

Professor Three: "anal" themes

Professor Four: loss from a mother

Professor Five: fear of loss, displacement to the unknown

Professor Six: depression at absence; painful acceptance.

If these themes permeate *all* of one person's answers, then they have entered into the answer to 1 just as much as the answer to 5. In other words, identical answers can be based on very different underlying concerns.[6] If we were to judge by the answers to questions 1 and 2 alone, we might very well say most of the professors were reading the same text in more or less the same way. We might conclude the text was constraining or limiting their responses. We might say they were applying the canons of an interpretive community. We might say they were constrained another way, by the workshop we were all engaged in.

Having the answers to questions 3–5 as well, though, we can see that they were reading the same text in very different ways. Some were concerned with realism, some with logic, some with language, some with literary form. Some were concerned with fear, others with loss, and others with deprivation.

Question 1 asked an "objective" question with "right" and "wrong" answers. The "right" answers all look more or less alike. Since question 5 asked each person to imagine or remember in a very personal way, people's answers to question 5 look very different. Behind the answers to both 1 and 5, however, is the same personal process, although it may be visible only in the answers to question 5 (or 4 or 3), and invisible in the answers to question 1 (or visible only as capitals or lower case or such slight differences in phrasing as "the miller," "the miller's body," "the miller's corpse," and so on). The "objective" and "subjective" answers draw on the same internal process in which themes of interest or concern to the answering professors shaped the way they worked with the text which was the same for all of them. *Both objective and subjective responses emerge from a process in which subjectivity shapes objectivity.*

The transactive theory of reading models this process as a person, with a certain identity, *using* (as an artist or a craftsman uses) the poem and the various codes, strategies, and settings to achieve a reading that *feels right*. For example, Professor Three was concerned with the relationship between person and thing. Her interest enabled her to *use* familiar interpretive techniques to read the poem as transforming persons to objects, for example, to understand the phrase "would soon appear / The same as ever to the sight" as "heals itself." Persons becoming objects also reflected some aspects of her personality or identity (as I read it). Her overall concern guided her use of shared techniques toward a particular reading that felt "right" to her. She was using the techniques many critics share with her, but using them to suit her unique identity. In the same way, Professor Six used them to suit her unique identity. In the same way, Professor Five used a critic's skill with ambiguity to manage his anxiety. Professor Two used a displacement to language that many critics would applaud, and he used it to serve his defensive needs as well as to interpret the poem. And so do we all.

I suggest that we all, as readers, use shared techniques to serve highly personal, even idiosyncratic, ends. We put hypotheses out from ourselves into the text. Indeed, the psychologists tell us this is the way we see and hear any chunk of the world.[7] Then we perceive *and feel* a return from the text. The poem seems delightful, pleasing, anxiety-arousing, incoherent, frustrating, satisfying, or whatever. Both emotionally and cognitively, then, both as a whole and part by part, we *feel* the poem responding to the hypotheses we bring to it.

For example, a VF hands us a questionnaire. It asks, "To what does the clause 'what was hanging from a beam' refer?" Those who have agreed to fill in the blanks approach the poem with hypotheses about grammar and antecedents. Within those hypotheses, the text enables us to arrive at some image of the miller's body which feels (emotionally and cognitively) like a satisfactory response to the VF's question. "To what does the clause 'What else there was' refer?" Here, the text does not give so clear a feedback to our hypotheses, and we respond differently. To some of us, flour bags and mice felt "right," to others the miller's body, and so on.

In other words, "The Mill," did not, on its own initiative, so to speak, cause what we saw. "The Mill" did not "constrain" a certain response among these professors. Rather, what the poem "did" depended on what we asked it to do. That in turn depended on what we brought to it: what questions, what expectation, what prejudices, what stock responses, what trust, what codes and rules. "The Mill" made a certain reading easy or difficult relative to the hypotheses *we* brought, hypotheses (in this instance) from the VF's questionnaire. If we had not been looking for antecedents for "what," we would not have seen the text the way we did.

That spring morning, the VF supplied the hypotheses. In the more usual situation, we supply our own. We may derive them from what we have been taught, from our culture (our "interpretive community"), or from the situation in which we find ourselves (a classroom, for example, or a theater). We may simply invent our own expectations for a poem. We always hypothesize, however, for that is the way we perceive not only poems and stories but everything. Hence, we perceive the text *only* as it responds to the hypotheses we bring to bear. The text can only affect our recreation reactively, the way the transparency of watercolors affects what a painter can do.

According to the transactive theory, then, reading is a creative process in which (one might say) subjectivity questions objectivity, thereby enabling objectivity to respond to and shape subjectivity. But that appealing paradox, obviously, does not provide a precise phrasing. We can imagine the reading of "The Mill" more rigorously, as a processing of information described by a feedback diagram (see Fig. 1).

While the appeal to a feedback model makes more precise various philosophical ways of stating the process (as dialectical, for example, or as deconstructive, perhaps), it has the further advantage of linking this account of reading to Piaget's idea of development, to theories of artificial intelligence, to brain physiology, to cognitive science, and to various psychological accounts of perception, symbolization, and memory.

In thinking through this picture (my students call it the "lima bean diagram") and the results of the questionnaire, however, it is essential to keep in mind a rather formal threefold definition of identity.[8] Identity is ARC—agency, representation, and consequence. That is, a person's identity is what initiates the feedback loops which are the way we sense and act on not only poems, but everything. In that sense, identity is an *agency:* it puts out hypotheses from our bodies into the world. The world (or a text) in turn gives back answers to those hypotheses, in a form which is ultimately sensory, and the way we feel about those answers determines the success or failure of the hypotheses. Identity is also therefore the cumulating *consequence* of those perceptions and ac-

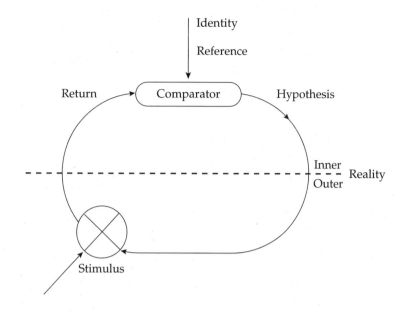

FIGURE 1 Perception

tions. We are the history of what we have experienced. Finally, however, and this is most important, identity is somebody's *representation* of that identity, just as a history is not just events but somebody's narrative of those events. In representing identity, I have urged the use of a theme and variations which I find most telling. Identity then becomes *the history of an identity theme and its variations.*

Evidently, if Professor Two's reading of "The Mill" is a function of his identity, my reading of Professor Two's identity and its recreation in his reading of the poem is a function of mine. In effect, the lima bean diagram is itself the loop in somebody else's lima bean diagram. If this is a schematic of Professor Two responding to "The Mill," one has to imagine another identity (mine) over to one side of this one hypothesizing this process of Two's and forming a narrative of it (see Fig. 2).

To use this concept of identity effectively, one has to keep all three components of this definition in mind at once, particularly the third. Omitting one or another leads to the common misunderstandings of the theory. In particular, if one neglects the idea of identity as representation, the concept becomes excessively deterministic. Unless one remembers identity is ARC, all three, the theory says that we have

identity themes imposed on us in early childhood and we can never ever change them.[9]

Thus, one finds people asking: "Don't people change their readings? I know I read *Huckleberry Finn* differently now from the way I did when I was a child." Yes, of course people change their readings, and it would be the task of a person phrasing an identity to represent those changes. That would involve showing *both* the sameness *and* the differences in someone's readings of *Huckleberry Finn*, since one recognizes difference against a pattern of sameness and sameness against a flow of differences. Putting these samenesses and differences into words neither causes nor limits them. It is not the phraser who can affect an AC-identity but the person with an AC-identity who can affect its phrasing (R).

For theories of reading, a feedback model is useful because it provides for *both* the reader's expression of self *and* the reader's use of semantic codes, taught techniques, interpretive communities, or, in general, the social, cultural, interpersonal, or transpersonal features of reading. One is not forced to such extreme claims as, "My language is not mine, just as my unconscious is not mine."[10]

Identity (loosely, "the subjective") enters the feedback loop in at least four different ways. First, identity

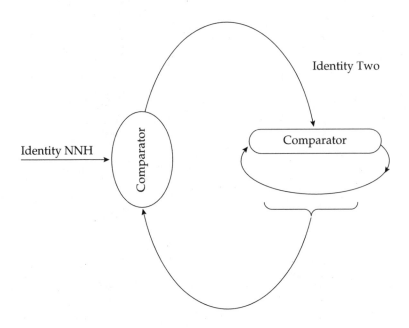

FIGURE 2 Perception of an Identity

was the agent. Each professor adapted from my questionnaire the hypotheses with which to approach the poem, doing so in as individual a style as they would later write their answers. Second, the poem did not simply "return" an answer. Each of us *heard* an answer, and we heard it with our own set of ears, our own linguistic usage, our own inner sentences, and all the rest. That is, we heard the questionnaire, and we heard "The Mill" answer the questions we asked of it—both in the idiom of our identities.

Third, what sounded "right" or satisfying or incoherent to each of us in the poem's answers to those hypotheses depended on the standards each of us applied. What seems coherent to you may not seem coherent to me. What pleases passive Professor One may not please fearful Professor Five. What suits Four as an answer to question 1 may not suit Two's more finely honed sense of grammar. All these criteria in turn are aspects of personality.

More precisely, they are the kinds of things we think about when we put someone's identity into words. When I say "fearful Professor Five," I am phrasing *my* reading of his standards for apprehending loss and anxiety, inferring them from the answers he wrote down and phrasing them in the light of my own standards and hypotheses. Hence we need to

imagine another identity in the lima bean diagram, one who is representing the identity of the reader under discussion.

Identity thus enters the feedback picture in at least four points. Identity frames the hypotheses, identity hears the return, and identity *feels* the discrepancy between that return and one's inner standards. Finally, *my* identity phrases the identity which does these things. Moreover, to avoid confusion, it is important to distinguish between different kinds of hypotheses an identity can put out into the text. Some are physiological. How fast can my eyes scan this novel? How fast can I absorb it? How much of the wording of this poem can I remember as I start the next page? How will the page division affect my reading? The answers to such questions would appear at the bottom of the feedback picture. They affect the answers the reader gets from his hypothesis in quite literal, physical ways.

Other hypotheses make use of cultural or semiotic codes. I intend "code" in the strict sense: a rule that makes a message possible.[11] I mean letters of the alphabet, numbers, grammar, dictionary meanings, and other things which have relatively fixed significations to all people in a given culture. For example, I see an *A* as an *A*. It would be very difficult for me to interpret it any other way. Indeed I learned this code so young and used it so often it would be well-nigh impossible for me to unlearn it. I could live for fifty years in Ulan Bator, reading nothing but Khalkha Mongol, and still, if I saw *A*, I would very likely think *A*.

Such codes are indispensable, enabling and constraining almost in the same sense as our bodies. We put them as hypotheses into the poem in order to read words, construe sentences, and arrive at meanings, and we do so automatically. The whole process is so fast and unconscious, we scarcely notice it unless we are dealing with a strange language. The only such code the questionnaire overtly used was syntax, in questions 1 and 2.

The other codes a professor uses to read a poem are of an entirely different order. We have seen our six readers seek unity in the poem ("each word . . . dependent on the others"). We have seen professors resist the idea of imagining either the look of the miller's wife or a private association to her. They are, I take it, tacitly following a rule: stick to the words on the page. I hear professors reaching for themes that go far beyond the immediate story of the poem, themes like irony, love–death, social determinism (Four), or negativity (Six).

Any one reader uses both kinds of rules, semiotic codes and interpretive canons, putting them out as hypotheses into the poem. The two kinds of rules are quite different, however. One can put aside a search for unity and start deconstructing as easily as one can drop the Odd Fellows and join the Elks.[12] One cannot so easily abandon seeing *A* as *A* or thinking in terms of subject–verb. One kind of rule, the interpretive canon, is chosen. The other, the cultural or semiotic code, is learned willy-nilly and can hardly be unlearned.

The "subjective" individual—an identity—puts forth these "objective" codes as hypotheses with which to read the text. The text in turn rewards some hypotheses and defeats others. As a result, the person senses both a cognitive and an emotional return from the text. The poem may feel delightful, moderately pleasing, anxiety-arousing, incoherent, frustrating—whatever. These sensations come about as we readers compare the return we get from the text with our inner standards for, perhaps, coherence, complexity, unity, or intensity. These inner standards are in turn functions of any one reader's personality or, better, identity. They may, of course, be learned. We

first apply them as the hypotheses we put forward (but those hypotheses may also be our use of convention, an interpretive community, a semiotic code, or even our physiology). We apply these standards to judge the return our hypotheses yield. These standards provide the language—the terms of the contract, so to speak—in which we hear the return from the text.

In short, a person—an identity—*uses* hypotheses with which to sense the poem. The poem responds to those hypotheses, and the individual *feels* whether it is a favorable or unfavorable response and so closes the loop, preparatory to sending another hypothesis out around it. This is the model that has been so closely questioned.[13]

"Doesn't all this make every reading totally subjective, so that any one reading is as good as any other?" That is the one question people most commonly ask me. What I can answer, on the basis of the identity-cum-feedback model, is that every reading inextricably combines subjective and objective aspects to the point where those words cease to be useful terms with which to address the problem. Merely to use those words is to assume that one could separate reading into subjective and objective parts, as though one could separate the process of painting into one part from the medium and another part from the artist, or a hammering into part from the carpenter and part from the hammer.

The metaphor hidden in "totally" raises the problem. It assumes that a reading can be "totally" or "more" or "less" subjective, as though it were addable parts. By my feedback picture, I am suggesting that we need to think of identity as *using, working with, building on, creating from* various hypotheses projected into the world. The world and the hypotheses are, in a manner of speaking, "objective." One cannot separate them from the hypothesizer and perceiver, however, any more than in a sculpture one can sort out the sculptor's subjectivity from the objectivity of the bronze.

One would quite lose sight of the process of sculpting by asserting this sculpture is less subjective than that. It is equally falsifying to assume that a reading could be totally subjective or more subjective than another reading, as the question does. Hence, there is no way to answer such a question. Properly, I am not saying all readings are equally or totally or even partially subjective. I am claiming that one cannot characterize readings as subjective or objective at all.[14]

The next most common question follows from the first. "In teaching, what do you do about misreadings?" Or sometimes, "If all readings are 'subjective,' what's the good of teaching reading?" One purpose of the identity-and-feedback model is precisely to enable us to sort out what we *are* doing when we teach people how to read. That was the reason I addressed a group of professors with it. That is, the model enables us to get beyond the old opposition of objective and subjective, and ask ourselves more tellingly what we are doing by any given classroom move. For example, some teaching consists simply of exposing the student to the world of letters: "Read Chapters 20–30 of *A Tale of Two Cities* by Wednesday." In terms of the model, that move simply places students in contact with what is labeled "Outer Reality." We expect the students to use the hypotheses they already have for addressing a text, the ability to put shapes together to form letters, letters to form words, words to form sentences, sentences to form plot, characters, setting — and so on. If one goes further, if one poses (in the manner of many textbooks) "Study Questions," one provides the student with ready-made hypotheses to try out on that (as did my questionnaire).

Just as a beginning reader learns how to use hypotheses to find the sound or meaning of an unknown word, so a more sophisticated reader learns how to use hypotheses to interpret a whole text. Higher level teaching tries to provide the student with hypotheses with which to address *any* text or, even better, the ability to hypothesize hypotheses which will give the best return from this particular text.

In general, then, the familiar modes of teaching literature address the *hypotheses* a student brings to a text, hypotheses like: You will be able to read the poem as referring to more than its ostensible subject (the obsolescence of millers). You will be able to shape the poem into a unity. Once you have done so, you will not be able to find an unnecessary word in this poem. Any changes you make in details will change the whole, probably for the worse. You will probably be able to find an irony crosscutting the poem, complicating it ("velvet," for example). You will probably be able to find a reference in the poem to its own creation; often such a reference will seem to deconstruct or cut across the ostensible sense of the poem.

At any given moment a teacher may be giving a student hypotheses or hypotheses for finding hypotheses or may be carrying a hypothesis through its testing to sense the return. All these are familiar strategies in teaching. All use the students' responses but seek a homogeneity of response. Typically this kind of teaching uses only those responses that can be generalized, shared, or otherwise made available to all the students. Like question 1 in the Visiting Fireman's questionnaire, they look objective because one is providing a pigment or a canvas for the picture of the poem the reader will paint. In fact, however, the identity of the artist will govern the use made of the hypothesis the teacher gives. Ultimately, whether the hypothesis is used at all or whether any given application feels right will depend on the response of the reader — his or her identity.

In recent years, another kind of response-centered teaching has grown up which addresses the nature of the reading process itself instead of some particular hypotheses associated with one or another school of criticism. Such teaching strives to make explicit the experience — the feelings — the student has in addition to or instead of the interpretive strategies. In terms of the model, the teacher does not talk about the hypotheses coming out of the right side of the student "comparator," so much as the "return" on the left. He asks students to be aware specifically of how a given return *feels* (as opposed to "fits"). The teacher may (but need not) go further and explore how a given hypothesis or return fits the identity of the reader in question so far as it has appeared in the classroom.[15] In terms of the model, this is a process quite distinct from examining the right and wrong applications of hypotheses.

In my experience, the two kinds of teaching are essentially independent (except that they cast one teacher in contrary roles, permissive and corrective). The familiar teaching of how-to-read-literature, by addressing the hypotheses by which one reads, directs attention away from the person applying the hypotheses. Reader-response teaching addresses the person as an applier of hypotheses, how that person feels, and what that person says when those hypotheses are applied. Hence reader-response teaching points away from a critique of the hypotheses themselves or the ways they are applied.

I cannot find any reason, however, why two teachers or even one could not apply both methods as they seemed appropriate. One could do the regular teaching only, as most teachers do. One could concentrate on responses only, as reader-response teachers do. Or one could consider the response as a function of both the person and the hypotheses chosen and applied. In that sense, a misreading would correspond to a wrong hypothesis or a wrong application of a right hypothesis. But it is not true that the transactive model of reading eliminates the idea of a misreading. It does ask, however, that the one who proclaims a misreading make the rule or context explicit that makes the reading a misreading. Too often teachers take it for granted — as part of a residual belief, I think, that modes of reading are self-evident, not to be questioned, eternal verities, linguistic competences, objective.

By contrast, the psychological theory of identity and the transactive model of reading let us tell a more coherent story of reading. I believe that, using these theories, we have obtained good evidence, both from these workshops on "The Mill" and earlier work with individual readers, for the proposition that each of us reads a poem or a story as a personal transaction. We, as individuals with individual styles, create literary experiences within those styles. In doing so, we *use* the text. We *use* the methods we have learned in school. We *use* the classroom or reading room or theater or learned conference in which we are responding. We *use* the canons of the interpretive community to which we have allied ourselves. And in reading, in using all these things, we recreate our personal identities (understood as the agency, consequence, and representation — ARC — of our own continuity in time).

It is too simple to say texts impose meanings or control responses. It is too simple to say there is a subjective part of reading and an objective part. Rather, we need to understand the text, the interpersonal situation, or the rules for reading, as all interacting with a self in a feedback (like painter's pigments) *in which the self is the active, creative element.* The interpretive community, the armchair or theater or classroom, even the text itself, affect our recreation only *reactively,* the way a chisel acts back on a carpenter's plans or as bronze both enables and limits a sculptor. The text, the rules, the codes are like musical instruments with which we play variations on our identity themes.[16]

In short, reading is an art like any other art. It has its medium, its techniques, its failures, and its successes. Above all, it has its mysteries. The three questions with which I began, however, are not among them.

Notes

1. I have expounded these theories through all too many years and stages of development. See *Poems in Persons: An Introduction to the Psychoanalysis of Literature* (New York, 1973); *5 Readers Reading* (New Haven, 1975); and *Laughing: A Psychology of Humor* (Ithaca, 1982).
2. Stanley Fish, *Is There a Text in This Class? The Authority of Interpretive Communities* (Cambridge, Mass., 1980), pp. 357, 338, 366, and passim.
3. David Bleich, *Readings and Feelings: An Introduction to Subjective Criticism* (Urbana, Ill., 1975), p. 49.
4. Wolfgang Iser, *The Act of Reading: A Theory of Aesthetic Response* (Baltimore, 1978).
5. In designing my questions, I now realize I had met some objections raised by Jonathan Culler to my work at an English Institute panel on reading. See his "Prolegomena to a Theory of Reading," in *The Reader in the Text: Essays on Audiences and Interpretation,* ed. Susan R. Suleiman and Inge Crosman (Princeton, 1980), pp. 46–66, esp. pp. 53–56. He objected to studying reading through the free associations of undergraduate readers on the grounds they were not competent, that the search for free associations will hide the agreement of "ninety-three out of a hundred" readers, and so on. Here, the readers are professors, committed to professional techniques in reading. The occasion was public, not a private interview. The questions pointed to the text rather than seeking associations "away" from the text. I believe this article shows that the conclusions of *5 Readers Reading* hold in this situation, *pace* Culler, as well as for undergraduate free associations.
6. Obviously, realizing this more complex process is important in basing psychological or literary research on questionnaires. The same answer may not express the same underlying process at all. If one is simply counting deodorant users or Democrats, that may not matter. If one is studying reading, it may matter very much. For example, I think my caveat is important for using such valuable survey work as the IEA (International Association for the Evaluation of Educational

Achievement) data bank or the 3rd National Assessment of Reading and Literature. See Alan C. Purves, "Using the IEA Data Bank for Research in Reading and Response to Literature," *Research in the Teaching of English,* 12 (1978), 289–96 and Anthony R. Petrosky, "The 3rd National Assessment of Reading and Literature Versus Norm- and Criterion-Referenced Testing," Paper presented at the Annual Meeting of the International Reading Association, May 1–5, Houston, 1978, ERIC Document No. 159599.

7. A brief, lucid, and authoritative introduction to modern perceptual theory is Edwin Land's "Our 'Polar Partnership' with the World Around Us," *Harvard Magazine,* 80 (1978), 23–26.

8. I have spelled out this concept of identity in detail most recently in my *Laughing: A Psychology of Humor,* chs. 9 and 11.

9. For instance, David Bleich can claim that with this theory "the idea of novelty loses its meaning altogether." See *Subjective Criticism* (Baltimore, 1978), p. 121. The theory, however, claims no more than that *one can trace* a consistent pattern in a person's behavior beginning in early childhood. Obviously, neither one's ability to trace nor a mere consistency implies that novelty drops out of human experience.

10. Culler, "Prolegomena," p. 56. One might ask with Freud, "Whose is it then?" "Unless the content of the dream . . . is inspired by alien spirits, it is a part of my own being." Sigmund Freud, "Moral Responsibility for the Content of Dreams," from "Some Additional Notes on Dream-Interpretation as a Whole" (1925), in *The Standard Edition of the Complete Psychological Works of Sigmund Freud,* tr. and ed. James Strachey et al. (London, 1961), XIX, 133.

11. I find conceptual difficulties in the loose sense of "code" some semioticians use. They announce what is no more than a personal interpretation as a code. In this sense, the famous Dorothea Lange photograph of the Depression farm wife to which several readers referred would be a "code" for poverty, obsolescence, or depression. Why not a code for the oppression of women? For aprons? For thinness? A code in this sense

simply decrees a single, universal meaning for what is patently variable.

12. Jonathan Culler, however, has called these interpretive rules, the conventional procedures of teachers of literature today, "literary competence," analogizing to Chomsky's idea of grammatical competence. His metaphor equates the deliberate, studied practice of a small group of people in universities with the syntactic rules an entire speech community is born into, acquires almost intuitively, without study, as children, and continues to live by. See Culler's "Literary Competence," in *Reader-Response Criticism: From Formalism to Post-Structuralism,* ed. Jane P. Tompkins (Baltimore, 1980), pp. 101–17, esp. 108–15.

13. The model, I find, bears some similarity to the "three worlds" hypothesis derived from studies of the brain by Sir Karl Popper and Sir John Eccles. Basically, World 2 (self-conscious mind), acting through World 3 (mental products such as language, arts, or theories), governs and is governed by World 1 (physical reality). See Karl Popper and John C. Eccles, *The Self and Its Brain* (Berlin and New York, 1977).

14. Working from a different point in the transactions, the interpretive community or cultural code, Stanley Fish comes to the same conclusion. See *Is There a Text in This Class?*, pp. 332, 336.

15. I have discussed this procedure as a Delphi ("know thyself") seminar. See Norman H. Holland (with Murray M. Schwartz), "The Delphi Seminar," *College English,* 36 (1975), 789–800; Norman H. Holland, "Transactive Teaching: Cordelia's Death," *College English,* 39 (1977), 276–85; and Norman N. Holland (with the members of English 692, Colloquium in Psychoanalytic Criticism), "Poem Opening: An Invitation to Transactive Criticism," *College English,* 40 (1978), 2–16.

16. You could, of course, in the manner of some deconstructionists, choose to read this feedback upside down. You could say *we* are the instruments on which the poem, the rules of interpretation, or the semiotic codes play out variations on *their* identities. That seems, however, a perversely difficult way of thinking about human perception.

APPLICATION

Anachronistic Themes and Literary Value: *The Tempest*

Ole Martin Skilleås

The responses of readers may vary not only from individual to individual, as Holland shows, but from group to group. Feminist critics, for example, and critics who focus on the dynamics of race and class have documented the differing reactions among these different "interpretive communities." Do readers of a particular era form a large interpretive community? Ole Skilleås argues that they do and illustrates his case with a "modern" reading of The Tempest *in which Prospero's powers are seen to represent the powers of the modern scientist to an audience familiar with the amazing benefits of scientific knowledge but also fearful of instant annihilation from nuclear war and slow death from ecological poisoning. This theme was, of course, unavailable to the original audience, or to the author. Conversely, the philosophical and ethical problems of white and black magic that concerned the Elizabethans are largely unavailable to modern readers, most of whom do not believe in magic of any kind.*

Skilleås concedes that these very different "topical" themes can be reconciled at a higher level of generality, but he maintains that "the change in the way the modern audience conceives of Prospero is profound." In fact, "it is arguable that The Tempest *is a play more relevant to the present audience than to Shakespeare's contemporary audience." This claim raises some large questions of interpretive theory. Does a literary work have a stable meaning through time, as Hirsch and others have argued? If so, will Hirsch's distinction between unchanging "meaning" and shifting "significance" dispose of the problems raised by Skilleås's "anachronistic" themes? Or is it rather the case, as many reader-response theorists assume, that different groups of readers will inevitably confer different meanings on a text? Or is there an intermediate possibility: are some texts, particularly those we call "classics," so constructed that they possess a special*

Reprinted by permission of Oxford University Press from the *British Journal of Aesthetics* 31:2 (April 1991): 122–33.

kind of "openness" to interpretation that makes them seem highly relevant to the different concerns of different eras?

In the second part of his essay, Skilleås explores these questions and, drawing on the work of Hans-Georg Gadamer, suggests a tentative reconciliation between "topical" and "perennial" themes. But he ends by posing an even larger question: is there an element of creativity or play in interpretation and are some literary works more valuable because they offer more scope for this play?

The primary concern of this paper is to explore how the concerns of the period in which a literary work is read and the concerns of the individual interpreter in that period influence interpretation. It would seem that if constructive activity beyond the level of determining sentence-meaning is involved in interpreting literature, then the assumptions and concerns of the interpreter, and consequently of the historical moment in which he or she lives, will play a part in determining which elements of the work are regarded as important, how they are related to each other by the interpreter and, more generally, how they are understood.

In order to provide an appropriate context for the discussion of this issue, part I of the paper provides a reading of *The Tempest*[1] which focuses on the role of Prospero as "prime mover," with particular reference to his "art" not only in steering the course of events, but also in the manipulation of the natural environment. This modern interpretation acknowledges that the concerns of today embrace an awareness of the power of modern science and technology to destroy the natural environment, and proposes that Prospero's position in the play with regard to his power on the island can be seen to be analogous to the power of the scientist to manipulate the environment in the present day.

It is plausible to suppose that the reader/spectator of today will approach Prospero's powers over the natural environment of the island through his "art" with an awareness of the powers of science over the natural environment of the earth. I shall argue that in the context of the play it is possible that a reflecting modern audience[2] will see Prospero's "art" as suggestive of the powers of today's science over the environment, be it through its most dramatic manifestation, nuclear weapons, or through other means devised by science to modify the nat-

ural environment. I shall further argue that the topicality of the connection between Prospero and modern science can lead to an identification of Prospero with humanity as a whole in a way that would not be plausible before, say, this century, because of the way our self-conception has changed with regard to our position in relation to nature. Only with the now almost boundless powers of knowledge, in the form of science, can this connection between Prospero and humanity be made. Thus, I argue, the topical theme of ecology leads easily into the perennial themes of "nature versus nurture," and/or "revenge and restraint." My discussion of *The Tempest* in the first part of this paper will therefore focus on the formation of such themes with close reference to the text of the play.[3] The theoretical soundness or otherwise of such moves, as well as the theoretical issues relating to theme formation, will be taken up in the latter part of the paper.

I

The central issue in any attempt to elicit *The Tempest*'s "ecological theme" is the nature of Prospero's command over the course of events in *The Tempest*. It seems that his powers do not go beyond the vicinity of the island:

> By accident most strange, bountiful
> Fortune . . . hath mine enemies
> Brought to this shore.[4]

As it is, his powers of manipulation on the island seem extensive. He creates the tempest, saves all the passengers from drowning, and has them stranded at different spots on the island's shore with their garments restored, and finally with the ship intact.

From the second scene of the first act the text emphasizes the importance of Prospero's powers, from the visual presence of his "magical garment"[5] to Miranda's plea that:

> If by your Art, my dearest Father, you have
> Put the wild waters in this roar, allay them.[6]

The scenes conjured up by Miranda's colourful imagination in the lines following this quotation bring home to the modern audience the fearful consequences the exercise of Prospero's powers could have. The world of the play, we are reminded, can be brought to the most terrible end by the powers of this man. The modern audience is unlikely to see or read this, and reflect,[7] without bringing knowledge of the present predicament to bear on the interpretation of the play. The development of physics, for example, has given us nuclear fission. With a power source of such immense force, anyone who possesses it holds a destructive potential over the real world of a magnitude at least matching that of Prospero's over his island.

Prospero, very modestly, calls himself "master of a full poor cell."[8] The discrepancy between this self-description and the power he has wielded to bring about the tempest borders on the self-deflatory as it is clear that the cell is where he keeps his books, which are the very source of his power. That it is a source is brought out by Prospero saying that:

> I'll to my book;
> For yet, ere supper-time, must I perform
> Much business appertaining.[9]

From this it is clear that the book (or books) is the source of his power, which in the fifth act is vindicated by his pledge to abjure his power[10] and consequently drown his book deep in the sea.[11] It is therefore less ironic when Prospero later refers to his "poor cell"[12] if he makes good his pledge.

The book, of course, should only strengthen the link the modern audience makes between Prospero and the notion of this character as a proto-scientist. A production might very well strengthen this link by showing the cell with book(s).

Much has been made of Prospero as magician, even "white magician" in contrast to Sycorax's black magic.[13] However, no matter what colour one attributes to his magic, it cannot be expected of the modern audience that it will interpret the character of Prospero in this way. The thought-world in which magic is a serious option is one which it takes great mental effort to enter. To relate to the powers of Prospero, and appropriate the themes of the play for present concerns, it seems more fruitful to see him as the proto-scientist suggested earlier.[14]

The modern audience may also note that the relation between Prospero and his powers is a role he can enter or leave at will, thus providing a further analogy to the modern scientist, who typically is a scientist by profession not vocation. The character of Prospero sanctions such an interpretation, since after Miranda had taken off his "magic garment" he addresses it: "Lie there, my Art." The modern popular conception of the scientist as a person in a white robe with a test tube in hand does nothing to undermine the plausibility of this connection.

An example of how the reception situation of *The Tempest* today gives us access via a topical to a perennial theme, that was not as readily available before, is the conflict of "revenge versus restraint."

With regard to the nature of Prospero's "art," it seems that his powers are significantly contrasted with the baser instincts of mankind, since his "art" does not stick on "the beast Caliban":

> A devil, a born devil, on whose nature
> Nurture can never stick; on whom my pains,
> Humanely taken, all, all lost, quite lost;
> And as with age his body uglier grows,
> So his mind cankers. I will plague them all,
> Even to roaring.[15]

It is evident here that Prospero's impotence in the face of unyielding nature torments him to distraction. He is quite clearly not omnipotent in the contest with stupid primitivity, represented by Caliban.[16] Prospero's inclination to take out his frustration on Caliban illustrates the conflict between the "Art" and the emotional immaturity of mankind, since the powerful Prospero does not automatically act virtuously despite all his knowledge and learning.

Knowing what we do about the probable effects of thermo-nuclear warfare, Prospero's battle with his own emotions is indeed a highly topical theme. It is natural to worry about what would happen if the power inherent in scientific knowledge was exercised by an over-heated brain. In *The Tempest* Prospero fights this battle within himself. The desire is for revenge over his brother, who usurped his political powers in Milan, and he battles with his rage against the obdurate ignorance of Caliban and the plot hatched by him and the drunkards. In the last act the "good" prevails[17] as he says:

> Yet with my nobler reason 'gainst my fury
> Do I take part: the rarer action is
> In virtue than in vengeance.[18]

Both in our world and in that of the play, power to command nature and power to command men are independent. In the play Prospero's powers to integrate them are at issue. He ends having shown his capacity to rule wisely. In our world, we hope against hope for a similar outcome.

A further, related, example of how the reception situation changes the theme of the interpretation is the new content the modern audience can give to the perennial theme of "nature versus nurture." "Nature," in this context, is understood in contrast to the socially conveyed virtues of "nurture." The fundamental change comes with the perception of Prospero as the scientist. The concept of "The Mage" implied a certain type of virtue, because the superior knowledge of "The Mage" made him wise. This connection is now missing, given the identification of Prospero with the scientist and the modern awareness that power and intelligence do not entail wisdom. The ability to react maturely to social and emotional conflicts and crises, we know, has not kept pace with the improvements in humanity's scientific knowledge. The awareness of the modern audience of this characteristic of the present situation highlights those aspects of the play that deal with similar situations. The failure of Prospero to improve the nature of Caliban is made all the more serious by the fact that Caliban is easily led by the drunkards Stephano and Trinculo.[19] Without the link between knowledge, power and virtue provided by the concept of "The Mage," the plot hatched by Caliban, Trinculo and Stephano[20] puts before us the possibility of a "Caliban mind" with "Prospero power."[21] In other words, the current situation makes it more likely that the modern audience will see these connections in the play. The concerns of the modern audience give a content to the theme of nature versus nurture that is different from any available to Shakespeare's contemporary audience.

So, if the modern audience looks for a fictional treatment of humanity's predicament of having the power to destroy the earth as we know it, yet still being immature in ability to resolve emotional conflicts, Prospero's dilemma with regard to revenge against his treacherous brother, his frustration with the unyielding nature of Caliban and the plot to oust him, offers scope for these themes. The conflicts fortunately also have happy endings. By the time Prospero is prepared to choose "virtue," he has more or less achieved his objectives and successfully fought the urge to take revenge—so graphically described in his rage against Caliban in the preceding act.[22]

Thus, for the modern audience Prospero resembles a symbol of modern science: frail in the face of evil and humanity's emotional immaturity, yet with a power that can, if injudiciously applied, be horrible in its consequences, and that on a scale far larger than Prospero's revenge. On the other hand, we also see that Prospero can use his "art" to please, not only manipulate for his own ends, as is shown in the masque he puts on for Miranda and Ferdinand:

> I must
> Bestow upon the eyes of this young couple
> Some vanity of mine Art; it is my promise,
> And they expect it from me.[23]

This contrast between the "revenge and reconciliation" aspects of his "art" is only resolved in the last act of the play in the soliloquy where he lists the various destructive and fiercely manipulative powers of his "so potent Art":

> But this rough magic
> I here abjure; and, when I have requir'd
> Some heavenly music,—which even now I do,—
> To work mine end upon their senses, that
> This airy charm is for, I'll break my staff,
> Bury it certain fadoms in the earth,
> And deeper than did ever plummet sound
> I'll drown my book.[24]

This is where Prospero relinquishes his powers. In his last act before breaking his staff and drowning his book he uses the power to give heavenly music to the senses of the people he manipulates.[25]

Having established the nature of Prospero's art and that it is confined to the island and its vicinity, the next step in an interpretation that tries to relate the play to the power of science over nature must be to inquire into the status of the island within such an interpretation.

In his *Shakespeare Our Contemporary* Jan Kott claimed that for the Elizabethans "the stage was the world, and the world was the stage."[26] Now, even if we do not accept this claim, or deem it irrelevant on the grounds that the modern audience will not bring Elizabethan assumptions to bear even on an interpretation of a play from that particular epoch, it still remains the case that for any audience the phenomenological character, in a certain sense of the term, of the spectator situation *makes* the world of the play to all intents and purposes appear to be the real world.

Both in our world and in that of the play, power to command nature and power to command men are independent. In the play Prospero's powers to integrate them are at issue. He ends having shown his capacity to rule wisely. In our world, we hope against hope for a similar outcome.

II

Given contemporary concern with the environment, and the quite recent realization that we might be in the process of destroying the basis of our way of life by the effects of the very same way of life, the "ecological theme" of *The Tempest* that I have outlined above is indeed topical.

It is maintained by most theorists who have discussed the nature and value of theme formation in literary criticism that topical themes are particularly fragile when put through the test of time.[27] They argue that it is the perennial themes which define great literature, and that the treatment of topical themes is the mark of ephemeral works. The interpretation of *The Tempest* proposed above can be seen to offer a new angle on this discussion.

For earlier critics Prospero has been "The Mage." With the modern, topical and anachronistic conception of Prospero as the scientist proposed in this essay, we can see that a new interpretation of the play is available to us that could not have been available to an earlier audience. This possibility arises from mankind's changing self-conception.

It is arguable that we live in "the age of science." The role of humanity has changed in important respects in a short period of time. The realm of the possible has expanded beyond the wildest dreams of earlier generations, and our daily lives have been radically transformed. If there is a single concept which represents the forces that have caused this momentous change it must be "science." It is thus plausible to claim that the present-day conception of humanity, our "self-conception," is that of "scientific man," and that this self-understanding has wide currency in present-day western societies. The next step, then, is to suggest that the topical interpretation of *The Tempest* in this paper implies that "Prospero the scientist" represents humanity as a whole. This transformation does not have to be at all abrupt in order for this relation to be productive in the understanding of the play. The transformation of Prospero the arch-scientist to Prospero as representing humanity happens just because of the change in self-conception which has occurred, in a historical perspective, quite recently.

Thus, the transformation of the role of Prospero from "Mage" to "Scientist" is brought about by the topicality of ecology and our manipulation of nature, and by our new self-conception. The further transformation of the character into a representative of humanity as a whole would appear to be virtually inevitable because of the present situation of the whole of humanity, posing a possible threat to ourselves by the power wielded by knowledge under the mantle of science. The upshot of these considerations is that the reception situation of today can change our interpretation of the play in a way previously impossible. At a higher level of generality the situation problematized by this interpretation is that of the perennial dilemmas of "revenge and restraint," and "nature versus nurture."[28] These are perennial themes which previous generations of interpreters may have arrived at through different topical themes, or not at all.

However, despite the possible identity of themes at a higher level of generality, the change in the way the modern audience conceives of Prospero is profound. As "Mage" Prospero is set apart from the modern audience by the mystical and esoteric nature of his knowledge. The "Mage" was further a marginal figure in the eyes of Elizabethan society as a whole. On the other hand, Prospero as "Scientist" brings him closer to the modern audience by the public nature of his "art," which also makes it much easier for the modern audience to identify with him. The powers of science are the powers of society. Despite the long initiation process, there is nothing inherently secret about the powers of science, and science is embraced by society. So much so, that I have argued that modern society may well be said to conceive of itself as "scientific society." Thus, it can be said that changes in society have brought Prospero from the elevated and esoteric level of the "Mage" down to the public in a way that was previously unthinkable. In terms of this background it is arguable that *The Tempest* is a play more relevant to the present audience than to Shakespeare's contemporary audience.

This raises the question how such a move can be justified in the face of interpretations more plausible from the point of view of readings rooted in the Elizabethan era.

Since the interpretation I have suggested here is based on assumptions about the concerns of the modern audience with topical questions, this is to enter upon a continuing debate about topical and perennial themes in literary works. The critic and theorist Frank Kermode seems to favour openness to topical themes:

> It seems that on a just view of the matter the books we call classics possess intrinsic qualities that endure, but possess also openness to accommodation which keeps them alive under endlessly varying dispositions.[29]

The more "austere" view is held by, among others, Stein Haugom Olsen.[30] He defines a topical theme as:

> a formulation of problems and issues of particular interest to a group of people (a society, a class, . . .) for a certain period. These problems and issues are related to specific situations in which that group of people sees itself or society/mankind as a whole as being, at that particular time.[31]

On this account the topical theme is transitory and cannot be used to explain how it is that the great works have survived over the ages to delight and enrich the lives of new generations. The austerity of his view is brought out by his strict definition of "literature" according to which, "it is necessary for a piece of discourse to invite construal in thematic terms if it is to merit the label 'literary work.'"[32] The only valuable themes are perennial ones: "Literary appreciation . . . always involves an attempt to apprehend the theme of a work using such thematic concepts as come closest to being perennial thematic concepts."[33] Olsen defines perennial themes in opposition to topical ones, such that, "a perennial theme differs from a topical theme in two respects: in the nature of the concepts which are used to define it, and in its lack of connection with a specific social/historical situation."[34] According to Olsen perennial concepts describe aspects of human nature and existence which have given rise to existential and metaphysical problems that we have not been able to solve, and which remain of continuing human interest.

However, it need not be the case that the views of Kermode and Olsen are irreconcilable. It can be argued that the great themes are the meta-level of more topical themes, and that the relation between them resembles that between type and token. Indeed, Olsen concedes that topical themes can constitute an element in the development of a perennial theme.[35] It is far from clear, however, whether this modification changes the general picture significantly. The most problematic element in Olsen's account lies in his assumption that thematic concepts and themes are *there* in the literary works.[36] It is an empirical fact that interpretations of literary works reach different results, and even if some of the interpretations are good and others bad, it does not follow that the demarcation criterion we employ is whether the interpreter has got *the* perennial theme right.

A common assumption underlying the various theories which assume that there is a single theme in a literary work is that the interpreter has no role to play other than eliciting whatever is there already. The assumption is, however, implausible, and Hans-Georg Gadamer's theory of understanding, his hermeneutics, helps us to see how it may be coherently rejected.

Gadamer offers a theoretical account of the relationship between text, reader and the situation of reception that takes account of the fact that in the process of understanding all three elements interact. One of the more provocative elements of his theory is that one's "prejudices" are the productive ground of understanding. "The overcoming of all prejudices, this global demand of the enlightenment, will prove itself to be a prejudice."[37] Gadamer is concerned to "rescue" the term from the enlightenment's discrediting account of it by pointing out that rather than impede understanding, the judgements one makes before encountering a phenomenon are preconditions for understanding the phenomenon. This is because "the prejudices of the individual, far more than his judgments, constitute the historical reality of his being."[38] This is because understanding takes place in a situation, and "the very idea of a situation means that we are not standing outside it and hence are unable to have any objective knowledge of it."[39] This rules out any purely "objective" conception of literary interpretation, since prejudices, in Gadamer's sense, will always be with the interpreter. In other words: prejudice is the very stuff understanding is made of.

Gadamer emphasizes "application" of the issues discussed to the situation of the interpreter as the very nature of hermeneutics, since the interpreter's situation and concerns are unavoidable elements in the process of understanding. Gadamer's model for the role of application in understanding is *legal* hermeneutics. The meaning of a law is not fixed by the original statement of the law, but is realized, expanded and modified, within limits, by its application to ever new situations which are seen to be governed by the law. The phenomenon of understanding a text works in a corresponding way: it is by applying the text to one's own situation that its meaning can be understood. This is part of the background for Gadamer's notorious claim that "we understand in a different way, if we understand at all."[40] However, to use Gadamer's term, the interpreter's relation to the text is one of "dialogue." As well as inviting discussion of a *Sache* (subject-matter), the text "speaks to you." This should be emphasized, since one can be misled by a relativist euphoria when encountering Gadamer for the first time. So, one's prejudices may well be confounded. However, the notion of *Sache* is problematic in literary interpretation. The reason may well be that Gadamer's hermeneutics is developed in response to questions that have arisen in the interpretation of philosophical, legal, theological and historical documents, but not specifically of literary works. One way to bring out this deficiency is to ask what the "sache" is in, for instance, Joseph Conrad's *Heart of Darkness*. Is it imperialism? Is it Conrad's own journey up the Congo? Can it be the nature of evil? The importance of moral restraint in the absence of social cohesion? The moral effects of culture shock? It is a good deal easier to answer questions about the *Sache* of different laws, Kant's *Kritik der reinen Vernunft* and Adam Smith's *Wealth of Nations;* the difference stems from the "openness" of literary works, their ability to address different issues and concerns. But there is one limiting factor at work in determining which issues or subject matters we take the literary works to address: the tradition which transmits preconceptions about the works through previous generations' encounters with them.[41] In Gadamer's terminology this is *wirkungsgeschichtliches Bewusstsein* (effective-historical consciousness).

The most important of these preconceptions or prejudices in the interpretative situation is that we deem the object for interpretation interesting. To do that we have to pre-judge the object to be worthy of our interest. The main class of objects which are judged worthy of interest for us by the culture in which we live are the classical works.

This is where we return to Kermode's claim about the intrinsic qualities of the text and its openness to accommodation. Gadamer's account allows for the possibility that the intrinsic qualities, the beautiful form, entertainment and the eternal truths[42] it contains are, along with its openness to accommodation,

the reasons why ever new generations return to the same texts. It can be argued that the spectacle and beauty, as well as the profundity of the soliloquies, are the main reasons for *The Tempest*'s standing. So we may not need to postulate treatment of perennial themes as the reason for the survival over the ages of the canonical, or great, works. This implies that we have an alternative conception to Olsen's, and that his view that: "a formulation of theme which does not go beyond the level of topical thematic concepts aborts the aesthetic significance of the work and is therefore unsatisfactory"[43] is itself unsatisfactory.

It is by reference to this broad theoretical background that I would claim theoretical validity and plausibility for the interpretation of *The Tempest* that I have presented above. The rationale for interpreting *The Tempest* in the way I have outlined is that it displays the play's relevance to the concerns of the modern audience, in a way that provides a fictional playing out through this great work of those concerns in a dialogue between the text/performance[44] and the concerns of the lives of the interpreters. I suggest that interpreters, in the constructive effort involved in interpretation, apply concepts and concerns from their own lives in a way that my interpretation illustrates. The question, then, is more specifically what *kind* of application this is.

In the interpretation of *The Tempest* provided above, for example, one can hold that on the one hand Prospero represents the scientist's power over the environment, enacting humanity's dilemma of the power we have and the frail character of the ecological status quo—the topical theme built around ecological concerns in the broad sense—and on the other hand that the play deals with the perennial themes of "revenge and restraint," and/or "nature versus nurture." The latter are only a more general description of the former and may not be available for the modern audience save through the topical theme and the topical thematic concepts which lead up to it. On this account, the relation between topical and perennial themes is such that the former provides access to the latter, and divining the perennial theme of one particular work is a creative and not a recreative activity. It also suggests that we can do without the added level of generality to explain why literary works survive over the ages.

However, it may also well be that one literary work can be interpreted as addressing different topical themes for different audiences, and that all of these can be seen at a higher level of generality to be perennial because the *types* of conflict, or comparable themes, are inherent in the human predicament. A consideration which supports Kermode's claim that "openness to accommodation" is a criterion for literary survival.

This leads us to a final question, which I shall only pose in this paper. It relates to the cognitive status of literary interpretation. Is there a rationale for reading and interpreting literature beyond entertainment and improving the performance of one's cerebral cortex?

My own emphasis in this paper has been on the creative activity of interpretation, an activity which can be seen as similar to children's play. It can be argued that children play, not in order to represent the world as it is, but to try out various ways it *could* be. Similarly, by interpreting literary works as addressing their own concerns, or those "of the age," the readers/spectators may add to the understanding of their world, and the various ways it could be. My suggestion is that the possibilities some literary works have for "application" to different concerns, and the "dialogue" with the audience that this feature invites are an important element in the value of literature. It is time that literary aesthetics took account of this quality.[45]

Notes

1. My references to *The Tempest*, given with act, scene and line number(s), are to the edition in The Arden Shakespeare, edited by Frank Kermode (London: Macmillan, 1954).
2. I shall use "the modern audience" in a more restricted sense than to mean just any contemporary audience or readership. I assume a higher degree of theatrical and literary knowledge and sophistication than one might expect from, say, picking a contemporary audience at random in London's West End.
3. Part I does not attempt to draw all the interrelated elements of the play together into a comprehensive interpretation. Rather, it is "a reading" in the sense that it presents a way of viewing a selection of aspects the modern audience may foreground when seeing or reading the play. This foregrounding does not entail blotting out other aspects of the play, such as the political themes, but is an expansion rather than an alternative.

Literary aesthetics has all too often taken for granted that the way critics present their papers is the way readers make sense of literary works. In my view this is a serious mistake.

4. I,ii,178–180.
5. I,ii,24.
6. I,ii,1–2.
7. The importance of reflection should be stressed, since interpretation is an activity which requires constructive activity. It is all too tempting for the theorist to assume that any audience will respond with a high degree of sophistication.
8. I,ii,20.
9. III,i,94–96.
10. V,i,50–51.
11. V,i,56–57.
12. In V,i,301.
13. See Frank Kermode's Editor's Introduction to the Arden Shakespeare, William Shakespeare, *The Tempest, The Arden Shakespeare* (London: Macmillan, 1954), for the distinction between Sycorax's and Prospero's magic, pp. xl–xli, and the nature of Prospero's magic, pp. xlvii–li.
14. "Magic sought power over nature; astrology proclaimed nature's power over man. Hence the magician is the ancestor of the modern practicing or 'applied' scientist, the inventor/ . . ." C. S. Lewis, *Studies in Medieval and Renaissance Literature*, Collected by Walter Hooper (Cambridge U.P., 1966), p. 56.
15. IV,i,188–193.
16. Note how the location of the island, between "primitive" Africa and Renaissance Italy, is also relevant in this conflict.
17. But they have suffered for their treason: IV,i,258–262.
18. V,i,26–28.
19. See the end of II,ii.
20. VI,i.
21. Cosmo Corfield, in "Why Does Prospero Abjure His 'Rough Magic'?" *Shakespeare Quarterly*, 36 (1985), pp. 31–48, argues that the opposition between Ariel and Caliban is an allegory of Prospero's mind. That would make "Prospero power with Caliban mind" a real alternative in the play.
22. VI,i,188–193.
23. IV,i,39–42.
24. V,i,50–57.
25. These now include the audience since they also will hear the music.

26. Jan Kott, *Shakespeare Our Contemporary*, translated by Boleslaw Taborski, second edition (London: Methuen, 1967), p. 250.

27. See in particular Anthony Savile, *The Test of Time: An Essay in Philosophical Aesthetics* (Oxford: Clarendon Press, 1982) and Stein Haugom Olsen, "Thematic Concepts: Where Philosophy Meets Literature," in *Philosophy and Literature*, edited by A. Phillips Griffiths (Cambridge U.P., 1984), pp. 75–93, and "Topical Themes and Literary Value," in *Forskningsprosjektet KRITIK och KONST*, edited by Goran Sorbom (Uppsala: Institutionen for Estetik, 1986), pp. 46–64.

28. At an even higher level of generality these two dilemmas can, I think, be unified in one theme. I shall not attempt to do so here, and it is in any case doubtful if such a move would serve any purpose.

29. Frank Kermode, *The Classic* (Cambridge, Massachusetts: Harvard U.P., 1983), p. 44.

30. Olsen is influenced by Savile.

31. Olsen in Sorbom, p. 54.

32. Stein Haugom Olsen, "Thematic Concepts: Where Philosophy Meets Literature," in *Philosophy and Literature*, edited by A. Phillips Griffiths, (Cambridge U.P., 1984), p. 81.

33. Olsen in Phillips Griffiths, p. 86.

34. Olsen in Sorbom, p. 58.

35. Olsen in Sorbom, p. 59.

36. Witness that he stresses that the correct description of the literary response to a literary work is "imaginative *reconstruction* of its literary aesthetic features" (my emphasis). Stein Haugom Olsen, *The End of Literary Theory* (Cambridge U.P., 1987), p. 16.

37. Hans-Georg Gadamer, *Truth and Method*, trans. by William Glen-Doepel, ed. by John Cumming and Garrett Barden from the second German ed. (1965) of *Wahrheit und Methode*, second English ed. (London: Sheed and Ward, 1979), p. 244.

38. Gadamer, p. 245.

39. Gadamer, p. 269.

40. Gadamer, p. 264.

41. Gadamer, p. 268.

42. What I mean by "eternal truths" is more like the statements of the text, such as "we are such stuff as dreams are made on"; and "our little life is rounded with a sleep," than the "perennial themes" Olsen argues for. The former may form part of the latter, but the "perennial themes" are at a higher level of generality and stand in relation to several elements of the work.

43. Olsen in Phillips Griffiths, p. 87.

44. I do not suggest that these modes of representation of *The Tempest* are similar, only that they in this respect play a corresponding role as the source for reflection and interpretation.

45. I am indebted to Dr Michael Bell, Helge Hoibraaten, Professor Stein Haugom Olsen and, in particular, Martin Warner for comments and discussions on drafts of this paper. Responsibility for remaining shortcomings is mine alone.

Wordsworth's Informed Reader

Susan Meisenhelder

In the introduction to her book, Wordsworth's Informed Reader, *Susan Meisenhelder claims that the tendency to see the biographical Wordsworth as a figure in his poetry has obscured the poet's own abiding concern with poetry's effect on its audience and has inhibited the study of the means by which he shapes his reader's responses. She seeks to redress the balance. Noting that Wordsworth saw his mission as that of transforming minds, Meisenhelder argues that he had developed a poetic theory "that strikingly resembles modern reader-response theories, particularly those of Wolfgang Iser. For Wordsworth, as for the modern response critics, the meaning of a text is not an extractable philosophical 'truth' but an interaction between text and reader" (2–3). It follows, then, that instead of focusing on the relationship between the author and the "I" of the poems, critics would do better to examine the means by which Wordsworth leads his readers through emotional and mental experiences, "even in those poems that seem most personal or traditionally descriptive" (27).*

In the selection that follows, Meisenhelder applies her approach to the Intimations Ode. Claiming that the 1815 edition of the poems was carefully designed to culminate with the experience of the Ode, she points up an intertextual dimension in reader-response criticism. Having read the earlier poems, the reader "initially joins the narrator in his sense of loss" and then, in a way reminiscent of Stanley Fish's affective stylistics, the informed reader comes to see the earlier reactions as necessary errors that can lead to the "growth of the mature mind."

By increasing the reader's distance from the mundane world and stripping objects gradually of sensory detail, Wordsworth moves his reader by the end of the 1815 edition to a "final eminence," a position above yet resting on the human "earthly, worm-like state." Although sensory forms are necessarily blurred from such a height, the result for the reader brought to this all-inclusive perspective and position of mental power is a recognition of the sense sublime.[1]

The movement toward the mind's sovereignty and recognition of the fruits reserved to such consciousness culminates in Wordsworth's Intimations Ode.[2] By the time of this poem, in all editions the final poem set off in a class by itself, the divestment of corporeality as a prop is almost complete. Having developed its power in earlier sections, the mind is able to work far removed from actual sensory experience, gleaning intimations from recollections. This characteristic influences the poetic texture of the entire poem, in important ways Wordsworth's richest yet most abstract. The palpable density of earlier poems is replaced by generality of both object and thought:

> The Rainbow comes and goes,
> And lovely is the Rose,
> The Moon doth with delight
> Look round her when the heavens are bare;
> Waters on a starry night
> Are beautiful and fair;
> The sunshine is a glorious birth.   (10–16)

By placing this poem last in his edition of the complete works, Wordsworth avoids, however, the emptiness of meaningless abstraction. Echoing earlier poems in nearly every line, he invests his generalities with a resonance enriching their apparent lack of specificity.

As Wordsworth's "Essay upon Epitaphs, II" indicates, he was aware of the power of apparently abstract language to echo a reader's concrete experience. Apologizing for the "monotonous" language of epitaphs, he illuminates how the language of the poems near the end of the 1815 edition, especially the Ode, works: "An experienced and well-regulated mind will not . . . be insensible to this monotonous language of sorrow and affectionate admiration; but will find under that veil a substance of individual truth" (*PrW* II: 66). He goes on to argue that a reader must have previously experienced the truths buried in generalizations for this resonance to be experienced. Commenting on epitaphs that "might be wholly uninteresting from the uniformity of the language which they exhibit" (*PrW* II: 68), he explains that "without previously participating in the truths upon which these general attestations are founded, it is impossible to arrive at that state or disposition of mind necessary to make those Epitaphs thoroughly felt" (*PrW* II: 68). The progression of poems leading up to the Ode in the 1815 edition allows Wordsworth to achieve this power for his poems. Because earlier concrete poems are buried beneath the abstractions of the Ode, Wordsworth ensures that the generalities are grounded in and derived from experience.[3]

In placing this poem last, Wordsworth also allows the reader to participate in the narrator's anguish. Because the poems have been ordered to parallel the course of human life, the experiences of childhood are as distant for the reader as they are for the narrator. With the memory of childhood that develops from having read the 1815 edition, the reader initially joins the narrator in his sense of loss. At this point, for reader as well as narrator,

> There was a time when meadow, grove, and stream,
> The earth, and every common sight,
>   To me did seem
>   Apparelled in celestial light,
> The glory and the freshness of a dream.
> It is not now as it hath been of yore;—
>   Turn wheresoe'er I may,
>   By night or day,
> The things which I have seen I now can see no more.
>   (1–9)

Out of the resonance of memory, the fact that earlier experiences of forms are preserved in the mind and that the soul does remember "how she felt" (*Prelude* II. 316), springs not only the narrator's but also the reader's despair.

Wordsworth's gradual development of the reader's powers also makes it possible to participate in the narrator's thoughts that transcend this anguish. The narrator's first solution is through an immersion in the animal delights of children, one that would invite the reader's immediate return to Wordsworth's earlier poems of "splendour in the grass" (182). As the progress of the narrator's thought makes clear, however, such a solution at this stage is not only insufficient but impossible. The empathetic union with the children ("I feel—I feel it all" [41]; "I hear, I hear, with joy I hear" [50]) only momentarily masks the gulf between childhood and maturity and the undeniable loss of "the visionary gleam."

An answer to the question, "Whither is fled the visionary gleam? / Where is it now, the glory and the dream?" (56–57), comes not from a simple immersion in childhood but from a search for its significance and value achieved because of temporal distance from it. What results from this investigation carried out through powers developed in the narrator and the reader but denied to the child is a recognition of essential and eternal form in the transitory experiences of this world.

Both the narrator and the reader ultimately see that the perception of glory and splendor is a limited response to specific objects rather than to form. The anguish expressed in the first part of the poem arises because the narrator looks at concrete objects in his search for glory and splendor. His opening lament makes this clear: "The *things* which I have seen I now can see no more" (9; emphasis added). Even as he experiences momentary joy with the particular birds, lambs, and children before him, this happiness evaporates when he remembers the splendid appearance of specific objects, a single tree, field, or pansy:

> —But there's a Tree, of many, one,
> A single Field which I have looked upon,
> Both of them speak of something that is gone:
> The Pansy at my feet
> Doth the same tale repeat:
> Whither is fled the visionary gleam?
> Where is it now, the glory and the dream?   (51–57)

An awareness of the distinction between form and thing is first revealed in the narrator's comments about childhood. While in reality the child is a "little Actor" (103) conning parts, the narrator is able to penetrate the "exterior semblance" (109), seeing the essential qualities of childhood:

> Thou best Philosopher, who yet dost keep
> Thy heritage, thou Eye among the blind,
> That, deaf and silent, read'st the eternal deep,
> Haunted for ever by the eternal mind,—
> Mighty Prophet! Seer blest!
> On whom those truths do rest,
> Which we are toiling all our lives to find.
> (111–17)

Although this would be an inflated, grandiose depiction of any specific child, the passage expresses a view of childhood similar to that of the Infant Babe passage (II. 232–65) of the *Prelude*. Underlying the

narrator's enthusiasm is not a deification of children but a recognition (achieved when childhood is looked on as form divested of its superfluous, worldly aspects) that qualities of childhood perception are the foundation on which rests all later, more mature grandeur of the human mind.

Thinking in this way about childhood, the narrator discovers that it is not the child's perception of splendor and glory in sensory objects that is most valuable, but his occasional transcendence of sensory reality, his questioning of things. The narrator thus praises childhood not for its "Delight" (137) in transient gleams of splendor,

> But for those obstinate questionings
> Of sense and outward things,
> Fallings from us, vanishings;
> Blank misgivings of a Creature
> Moving about in worlds not realised.   (142–46)

Though only an instinct (147) in the child, this mode of experience is the important seed from which grow higher minds. Since this perception comes to fruition in the narrator's ability to pierce "exterior semblance," the "truths" built on this initial childhood freedom from sensory objects are not transient ones. Rather, they are

> truths that wake,
> To perish never;
> Which neither listlessness, nor mad endeavour,
> Nor Man nor Boy,
> Nor all that is at enmity with joy,
> Can utterly abolish or destroy!   (156–61)

The narrator's investigation of the essential qualities of childhood—of childhood as a form of experience—from his distanced perspective thus results in an awareness that childhood is not an absolute value, the pinnacle of human experience, but the foundation on which rests later knowledge. As a foundation, however, childhood is an incomplete structure: the forms of childhood experience embody truths unrecognized by the child, who is immersed in the sensory delight of glory and splendor. Built atop the child's "primal sympathy" (182) are knowledge and reflective experience denied the child.[4] "The soothing thoughts that spring / Out of human suffering" (184–85) are not, as the Poems Referring to the Period of Childhood reveal, characteristics of childhood experience; for narrator and reader alike, they are acquired through a later, gradual process of development. Even though the child displays embryonically, in a poem such as "We Are Seven," the power of faith to overcome death, the faith that the narrator possesses and the reader has acquired through reading Epitaphs and Elegiac Pieces is a higher one—one not simply blind to death but, having faced it, able to look "through death" (186). Although the child is the "best Philosopher," unwittingly the possessor of truth, only gradually does the potentiality of this form become an actuality. Only in maturity are these truths recognized, valued, and acted on as truths; only "years . . . bring the philosophic mind" (187).

Anguish evaporates when the narrator accepts his distanced and abstracted position and the necessary loss of sensory delight in things that such a perspective entails. As the Wanderer's description of the mental power in old age indicated, the "finer passages of sense" (IX. 78) are exercised only when "the gross and visible frame of things / Relinquishes its hold upon the sense" (IX. 63–64) and becomes "unsubstantialized" (IX. 66). The final sections of the Ode reveal the perceptual power that results and the consolation allowed to a perceiver placed in such a position.[5] The narrator is able to join in the glee before him not through feeling elicited by sensory objects but by thought, a reflective power of mind more advanced than that of a child but built on a child's experiences:

> We in thought will join your throng,
>   Ye that pipe and ye that play,
>   Ye that through your hearts to-day
> Feel the gladness of the May! (172–75)

While to be one of the children is impossible, a recognition of the bond that links human days allows a different kind of connection, one achieved not with individual children but with childhood as a remembered form of experience:

>   Hence in a season of calm weather
>   Though inland far we be,
> Our Souls have sight of that immortal sea
>   Which brought us hither,
>   Can in a moment travel thither,
> And see the Children sport upon the shore,
> And hear the mighty waters rolling evermore.
>   (162–68)

The recognition of the continuity in human life—not a simple repetition of experiences but a repetition of *forms* of experience as "the ties / That bind the perishable hours of life / Each to the other" (*Prelude* VII. 461–63)—leads to Wordsworth's most mature re-

sponse to the dying taper in "Reply to Mathetes." When one recognizes these forms of experience as indestructible, one can respond to the dying taper of the soul not with sadness or "remonstrance" (*PrW* II: 18) but with positive joy:

> O joy! that in our embers
> Is something that doth live,
> That nature yet remembers
> What was so fugitive! (130–33)

Because forms of experience live in embers that are dying, the problem presented by transient immersion in childhood delight evaporates. The narrator's awareness of the distinction between sensory thing and eternal form is also clear in his final apostrophe to Nature. No longer bemoaning the loss of splendor in specific natural objects, a single tree or field, he attaches himself to their eternal forms:

> And O, ye Fountains, Meadows, Hills, and Groves,
> Forbode not any severing of our loves!
> Yet in my heart of hearts I feel your might;
> I only have relinquished one delight
> To live beneath your more habitual sway. (188–92)

This attachment to form represents a significant advance over the child's delight in sensory objects. In recognizing the eternal patterns of Nature, the narrator acknowledges their status as powers greater than objects, as laws for the human mind, and as informers of the soul.

The philosophic mind's awareness of the distinction between form and thing makes possible the final thought of the poem. Armed with a conscious ability to see through external semblance and thus to perceive form in objects, the mature philosophic mind, not demanding sensory glory in the flower as does the child, can return to the "meanest flower that blows" (203) and glean "Thoughts that do often lie too deep for tears" (204). Although splendor may be buried deep in the past, the narrator's metaphor of the depth of thought denies any loss of experience. For him as for the reader, it is possible to see in the flower and any sensory object a layered history of response, of which splendor is only one. Placing this poem as the culmination of the 1815 edition allows Wordsworth to recreate for his audience the depth experience of memory. After reading all of these poems, the reader can, in the lowest, "meanest" word or image, not only feel reverberations and hear echoes of other poems but respond with the maturity of thought characterizing the Wanderer.

In structuring the 1815 edition, Wordsworth incorporates a movement analogous to that seen in individual sections. Having raised his readers to this level of generality, Wordsworth invites them to make a similar review of experience.[6] While the river metaphor with which this chapter opened is an apt one for describing the progression of the 1815 edition toward the Intimations Ode, the journey on which Wordsworth leads his readers is actually even more complex, one he described in "Essay upon Epitaphs, I,"

> As, in sailing upon the orb of this planet, a voyage towards the regions where the sun sets, conducts gradually to the quarter where we have been accustomed to behold it come forth at its rising; and, in like manner, a voyage towards the east, the birthplace in our imagination of the morning, leads finally to the quarter where the sun is last seen when he departs from our eyes; so the contemplative Soul, travelling in the direction of mortality, advances to the country of everlasting life; and, in like manner, may she continue to explore those cheerful tracts, till she is brought back, for her advantage and benefit, to the land of transitory things—of sorrow and of tears. (*PrW* II: 53)

After leading readers in the "direction of mortality" through the 1815 edition and providing an experience of the "country of everlasting life" in the Intimations Ode, Wordsworth brings them ultimately back to the "land of transitory things." Because forms and poems are preserved in memory, it is possible to reread those early poems of the "meanest flower" and other sensory forms with a sophistication and complexity of consciousness beyond that at any earlier stage of reading. By thus building the function of memory into his edition, Wordsworth not only invests objects with layers of experience and multiple associations but also lays the foundation for the evocative power and rich complexity of his apparently simple poems. The reader can now look back on the experience of the 1815 edition and see its analogy to the river Wordsworth alluded to in "Reply to Mathetes." When earlier experiences of error are viewed from this perspective, the reader recognizes them as turnings of that river, necessary and important experiences in the growth of the mature mind.

Wordsworth strongly encourages such rereading by his addition in 1815 of the lines from "My Heart Leaps Up" as the epigraph of the Intimations Ode. The reader is thus invited to review the Poems Referring to the Period of Childhood from a distanced perspective that reveals the form within childhood experiences and the roots of the mind's power in those experiences. What is immediately clear is the limitation of the optimism expressed in "My Heart Leaps Up" and the early poems of that section. The immersion in childhood sensory delight, the heart forever leaping up at the rainbow, it is now clear, is not only impossible but undesirable. Only by virtue of the distance from such delights can the reader see the ultimate significance of childhood.

Notes

1. For Iser, this kind of strategy and the resulting transformation of the reader's consciousness characterizes all texts. Readers

   must be placed in a position which enables them to actualize the new view. This position, however, cannot be present in the text itself, as it is the vantage point for visualizing the world represented and so cannot be a part of that world. The text must therefore *bring about* a standpoint from which the reader will be able to view things that would never have come into focus as long as his own habitual dispositions were determining his orientation. (*The Act of Reading*, p. 35)

2. Ruoff, "Critical Implications of Wordsworth's 1815 Categorization," p. 81, has suggested that a reader-response interpretation of the Ode can resolve many of the problems critics have seen in it.

3. In other contexts, several critics have noticed the richness of Wordsworth's abstractions without any emphasis on how this quality is created for the reader. John Beer, "Wordsworth and the Face of Things," *The Wordsworth Circle* 10 (1979): 17, has pointed to the deceptive quality of Wordsworth's language that makes apparent truisms the embodiments of complex meaning. According to Donald Davie, *Articulate Energy: An Inquiry into the Syntax of English Poetry* (London: Routledge & Kegan Paul, 1955), p. 107, those words that look like abstractions acquire immense energy from their status as symbols. Josephine Miles, *Wordsworth and the Vocabulary of Emotion* (New York: Octagon, 1965), pp. 114–61, has commented on the resonance generally of Wordsworth's abstract language. She sees abstraction as Wordsworth's way of linking objects together. Ferguson, p. 94, has pointed to the Poems Proceeding from Sentiment and Reflection and the Poems Referring to the Pe-

riod of Old Age as Wordsworth's attempt to create an "after-life" for words.

4. In the extensive controversy surrounding the Intimations Ode, my reading agrees most closely with that of C. E. Pulos, "The Unity of Wordsworth's Immortality Ode," *Studies in Romanticism* 13 (1974): 179–88. He stresses that the "visionary gleam" is the child's limited recognition of natural light whose supernatural source is recognized only by the mature "philosophic mind."

5. My view of the narrator's ultimate recognition is similar to that of Sherry, p. 6, who stresses the child's lack of awareness and the adult's recognition, achieved only in recollection, of the value of childhood.

6. Briesmaster, p. 1, has suggested that Wordsworth encourages "reflective" readings of his poems without delineating his strategy for doing so.

Works Cited

Briesmaster, Allan. "Wordsworth as a Teacher of 'Thought.' " *The Wordsworth Circle* 11 (1980): 19–23.

Iser, Wolfgang. *The Act of Reading: A Theory of Aesthetic Response.* Baltimore: Johns Hopkins University Press, 1978.

Ruoff, Gene W. "Critical Implications of Wordsworth's 1815 Categorization, with Some Animadversions on Binaristic Commentary." *The Wordsworth Circle* 9 (1978): 75–82.

Sherry, Charles. *Wordsworth's Poetry of the Imagination.* Oxford: Clarendon Press, 1980.

Wordsworth, William. *The Prose Works of William Wordsworth.* Ed. W. J. B. Owen and Jane Worthington Smyser. 3 vols. Oxford: Clarendon Press, 1974. (abb. *PrW*)

Putting Audience in Its Place: Psychosexuality and Perspective Shifts in *The Awakening*

Pat Shaw

Pat Shaw sees the key to understanding The Awakening *in the novel's subtle shifts of perspective or point of view. As the story progresses, the reader is moved from "scientific" to "poetic" reality. We assume an increasingly intimate relationship with the main character and become not "external, dispassionate observers" but "direct participants in Edna's psychological (and physiological) trauma." Though Shaw's reader is not entirely passive (the reader must sometimes "put together" what the characters cannot), she or he is very much the generalized, "implied" reader described by Iser rather than the particular, "actual" reader studied by Holland, and Shaw's emphasis is on the way Chopin directs this reader's responses through her use of sophisticated narrative techniques, techniques that are more usually associated with modernist masters like Joyce and Faulkner. At times, though, Shaw wonders if we might better think of these techniques as directing both the reader and the author, speculating that they may be operating beyond the author's conscious control. Either way, she concludes, they work.*

Speaking generally of fictive heroines, Judith Fryer observes that unlike Henry James and other nineteenth-century male novelists who created women protagonists, Kate Chopin portrays Edna Pontellier of *The Awakening* "from the inside, in terms of her own consciousness."[1] Although Fryer's comment may separate Chopin's narrative technique from those of her male contemporaries, it is somewhat misleading in that Chopin does not *begin* her story from inside Edna's psyche. On the contrary, she carefully orchestrates events so that the audience is definitely "outside" Edna's thought processes for most of the novel, moving "inside" only when Edna is dying.[2] In Chopin's own words, the audience fol-

Reprinted by permission of the publisher from *American Literary Realism*, Volume 23, No. 1. Copyright © 1990 by McFarland & Company, Inc., Publishers, Jefferson NC 28640.

lows Edna from the "outward existence which conforms" to "the inward life which questions."[3] This unusual shift in audience perspective not only distinguishes an otherwise conventional story[4] but also acts as a key to the psychosexual dilemma underlying the narrative design.

Chopin's shift is predicated upon her management of two modes of reality. One is the substantive reality of actions and objects that are sensorily verifiable, while the other is the psychological reality defined by no quantifiable limits. In another context, Kenneth Burke employs the terms "scientific realism" for the former and "poetic realism" for the latter.[5] While Burke applies his terms to fiction generally and not specifically to Chopin, they are nonetheless apropos and we will borrow them in discussing Chopin's techniques. Chopin obviously cannot alter the extratextual "scientific" reality of the audience's world, but by shifting audience perspective relative to the fictive or "poetic" reality of her narrative she realizes what Burke refers to as a metonymic "strategy": "to convey some incorporeal or intangible state in terms of the corporeal or tangible."[6]

Chopin begins her narrative with a very tangible introduction to the scientific mode and thereafter grounds her various shifts upon it, or, more precisely, originates them from it. The initiatory "green and yellow parrot which hung in a cage outside the door"(p. 3) immediately orients the audience to perceiving a substantive reality within the fictive construct. The bird image ushers us into the narrative world as viewers of the garish parrot and coincidentally locates us exoterically, outside the "cage" surrounding the object of central concern. Insofar as the parrot-cage comes to symbolize Edna's incarcerated self, it is part of that scientific reality which transports us into the "poetic" or psychological mode. Functioning in this capacity, it transcends its corporeality and acts as a paradigm for the entire complex of external–internal shifting that ensues.[7]

The external–internal shifting motif commences immediately after the parrot has fixed the audience's vision. The motif permeates the entire text, but one typical passage will demonstrate how from the beginning Chopin uses literal narrative action to "convey some incorporeal or intangible state":

> Madame Lebrun was bustling in and out, giving orders in a high key to a yard-boy whenever she got inside the house, and directions in an equally high voice to a dining-room servant whenever she got outside. . . . Her starched skirts crinkled as she came and went. Farther down, before one of the cottages, a lady in black was walking demurely up and down, telling her beads. (p. 4)

Three times in this brief passage Chopin suggests external–internal transitions — first with the outside–inside "bustling," next with the "came and went" phrase, and finally with the "up and down" of the lady in black. What we literally "see" here is not sensational, but subliminally we are sensitized to an element that will soon attain conscious prominence: Edna's psychosexuality. The mundane in–out, enter–withdraw rhythm of Madame Lebrun's domestic activity not only introduces the many literal shifts that fill the novel (such as the travel between New Orleans and Grand Isle, the tides in and the tides out), but it also adumbrates the eroticism that dominates the figurative substructure of the narrative. As we will see, Chopin locates her audience in an increasingly intimate relationship with Edna so that the erotic boundaries between extratextual viewer and intratextual persona are progressively blurred.

With appropriate irony, Edna first comes into view as a secondary character in the background of narrative action. Léonce Pontellier, wearing eyeglasses which symbolize his myopia and personifying the male-dominated world that represses the feminine personae of the novel, directs our vision to "his wife, Mrs. Pontellier" (p. 4). Not until near the end of the first chapter does he walk away, leaving us to view Edna directly. However, Chopin continues to control our vision very carefully. In the opening lines of chapter II, we "see" explicit details of Edna's face and head: the hair color, the "horizontal" shape of her eyebrows, and the "yellowish brown" eyes (p. 5). The after four brief chapters that introduce additional characters, reiterate Edna's subservience to her husband, reveal her possible neglect of her children, and show her crying for no particular reason, Chopin subtly lowers our vision to see Edna "open her dress at the throat" (p. 16). We are unaware of it at the moment of occurrence, but this innocuous gesture inaugurates our participation in a kind of dramatic striptease. In the beginning we see a fully-clothed Edna through the eyes of an interposing character, but by the novel's end we are eyewitnesses to her nude descent into the Gulf waves. Thus, though such details as the facial description, the unbuttoning of the collar, and Chopin's control of audience vision seem trivial, they in fact initiate one of the essential motifs of the narrative: the uncovering of Edna's physical self that in turn reveals her psyche to us.[8]

A scene which exemplifies the link between loss of clothing and suppressed eroticism is in chapter XIII when Edna flees the "stifling atmosphere of the church" full of well-dressed worshipers (p. 36) to find sanctuary with Robert at Madame Antoine's cottage. Although the scene keeps the audience external to Edna's psyche, it makes an important alteration in our visual relationship with her. As we recall, Edna grows tired awaiting dinner and decides to rest.[9] In the bedroom, she removes "the greater part" of her clothes and stretches out "in the very center of the high, white bed." She loosens her long hair and caresses "the fine, firm quality and texture of her flesh" (p. 37). The powerful autoeroticism of the passage may momentarily distract us from noting that a kind of psychic translocation has occurred. Though Edna remains the center of audience awareness, she is now located *outside* her own body with the audience, "observing closely," as if her body "were something she saw for the first time" (p. 37). In prior narrative action she has been the object of perception, but now she is both perceived and perceiver.

However, the audience's response to the scene differs from Edna's. Having just observed her leave the church fully clothed and apparently safe from prying eyes, we suddenly stand beside her in bedroom privacy, watching as she caresses her nearly nude recumbent body. The shift from church to boudoir is startling enough that while we remain sympathetic to Edna's plight, and certainly enthralled by her physical presence, we tend unconsciously to evaluate from the same "caged" perspective implied by the worshipers inside the church. In short, we are at once erotically involved in Edna's performance and somewhat guilty for that vicarious eroticism—especially so because Edna seems to monitor our reactions. On the one hand Chopin locates us so that we join with the fictive Edna as co-observers of her autoeroticism, but on the other she requires that we remain "outside" that fictive world and judge Edna's narcissism. In light of this perspective ambiguity, the scene seems an authorial attempt to eradicate the barriers between the audience's scientific reality and the poetic reality of the text.

To further audience transference from this exterior, judgmental perspective to a sharing of Edna's inner life, Chopin depends on two strategically located art scenes. Previously explicated by other commentators in various contexts,[10] the vignettes are pertinent to our discussion because they demonstrate how Chopin uses surface reality to convey what F. K. Stanzel calls the "deep structure" of narrative design.[11] One scene is the sketching incident with Robert very early in the narrative and the other is the incident with Alcée Arobin's unfinished portrait shortly before Edna commits suicide. The two are intricately related. In the first episode, Edna is sketching on the beach at Grand Isle. Robert watches closely and praises her with "ejaculatory" expressions:

> During his oblivious attention [to her painting] he once quietly rested his head against Mrs. Pontellier's arm. As gently she repulsed him. Once again he repeated the offense. She could not but believe it to be thoughtlessness on his part; yet that was no reason she should submit to it. She did not remonstrate, except again to repulse him quietly but firmly. He offered no apology. (p. 13)

Superficially, the scene offers the external audience little reason for interpreting events as being anything other than a patient, motherly lady tolerating an interfering child—the same mundane domestic routine we witnessed in the Madame Lebrun set piece. Seen as part of Chopin's metonymic transference, however, the episode emblematizes Edna's psychosexual turmoil.

The subject of the sketch is Adèle Ratignolle, to whom Robert has recently "spoken words of love" and to whom Edna herself is aesthetically and perhaps homoerotically attracted. In rhetoric rich with sublimated eroticism, Chopin describes how Edna can no longer resist the urge "to try herself" on a woman with lips like "delicious crimson fruit" and "nothing subtle or hidden about her charms" (p. 10) and who sits "like some sensuous Madonna, with the gleam of the fading day enriching her splendid color" (p. 13). Until Robert interferes, Edna paints with "ease and freedom," happy in her vicarious intimacy with the stimulating Adèle. Even before commencing the sketch, Edna has entertained romantic thoughts about Robert and Adèle, for moments earlier she has coyly tried to convince herself how "unacceptable and annoying" it would be if Robert were to show the same love attention to her that he has shown to Adèle. Thus, after he rests his head upon her shoulder for the second time, she stops painting. Though she is satisfied with the technical artistry of the sketch, she suddenly defaces it with "a broad smudge of paint" and crumples "the paper between her hands" (p. 13).

At this early stage, the reader is hard put to understand Edna's petulant and symbolically self-destructive outburst. However, the second portrait episode, with her paramour Alcée Arobin as the subject, retrospectively clarifies her motivations for defacing Adèle's portrait. Though she is working from a photograph (itself emblematic of "scientific" reality as opposed to "poetic" or artistic reality), Edna is unable to complete the portrait of Alcée, just as she has been unable to complete the painting of Madame Ratignolle. In both instances she will not risk inadvertently creating a physical, perceivable record of her suppressed eroticism, not only as it relates to Robert specifically but to Adèle and others more generally. The two painting episodes—one coming early and one late in the narrative—offer tangible evidence that despite all her rebellion, Edna continues to allow societal mores to override her creative imagination and dictate her ethics. She dabbles in self awareness much as she dabbles in art, evincing a fatal dilettantism which explains why Mademoiselle Reisz's ridicule will later echo in her mind when she wades into the Gulf to drown: "And you call yourself an artist! . . . The artist must possess the courageous soul that dares and defies" (p. 114).

The painting episodes serve also to reveal how myopic Edna herself is in viewing Robert. Because Alcée's portrait is never finished, his photograph remains in her "pigeon-house" studio when Robert returns to her from Mexico. Demanding why Edna has the photograph, Robert jealously throws it aside (p. 99). This picture and Robert's immature reaction to it are in turn prefigured by an old photo of Robert as an "infant with a fist in his mouth" (p. 46) which Edna discovers. This and other pictures of Robert as an adolescent merely amuse Edna, who once again (as on the beach) seems more maternal than passionate in responding to her young admirer. We as audience, however, combine the photo scenes to "see" qualities about Robert that Edna does not clearly see and are thus reminded that the gerundive title of her narrative, like the unfinished portraits, implies an uncompleted process, not a completed one: she is *awakening*, but never *awakened*.[12] As the photograph album symbolizes by bringing the past graphically into the present, Robert has remained juvenile. He may deserve Edna's maternal patience, but he does not justify her sexual passion. And he is certainly unworthy of her immolation. Emanating too much from the cloying Genteel Tradition of nineteenth-century American fiction, he seems self-pitying and ineffective in context of a narrative which, as Per Seyersted points out, is in many respects even more modern in its naturalistic description of sex than Crane, Garland, Norris, and Dreiser.[13]

Indeed, our own angle of vision as dictated by our "reading room" or scientific reality will not long permit us to acquiesce to the relationship between the mature, passionate Edna and the callow Robert. Her desire for the scoundrel Arobin is convincing enough, but our willing suspension of disbelief can barely accommodate the Robert affair. Only if we see it as a tangible representation of the intangible authorial imagination can we appreciate that Robert functions metaphorically in the narrative design as a child-lover. As Hayden White points out, "a trope can be seen as the linguistic equivalent of a psychological mechanism of defense" for the author.[14] Viewing Robert in this tropic capacity, and given the mother–son implications of the Edna–Robert relationship, the aura of guilt surrounding Edna's dealings with her biological children, and the psychosexual implications of Edna's dying image of her domineering father, we can follow White's lead and plausibly speculate that Edna's desire for Robert (never consummated) may well have originated in Chopin's own incestuous impulses—impulses not as taboo as Freud taught but which were especially horrible to nineteenth-century mores.[15]

The hypothesis is supported by Chopin's destruction of her alter ego via suicide. Such resolution is compatible with both the literary and psychoanalytical elements of the Oedipal tradition. Kenneth Burke, for instance, discusses how the female in strongly patriarchal societies such as Sophoclean Greece or Creole Louisiana looks to suicide as an escape from "sexual ambivalent" impulses. This "killing of the old self" breaks the "total ancestral line."[16] Most often such self destruction is symbolic rather than literal, and it is obviously in the symbolic sense that Chopin uses the concept. In essence, by manifesting her psychosexual dilemma in a fictive other self and then killing that other self, Chopin hopes to recreate a psyche freed from the doubts and fears imparted by the patriarchal hegemony. Knowing that Chopin was widowed early in a society distrustful of female eroticism in any form and that she apparently sublimated her sexuality via children and a "proper" life, we should not be surprised (in fact might expect) that her fiction would serve as an objective epitome of her frustrated eroticism. Most actions in her narrative design may safely be viewed as objective correlatives of Chopin's need first to articulate and then to purge the guilts arising from her own psychosexuality.

Ironically, Edna's suicide therefore becomes positive, not only because it is the symbolic equivalent of rebirth but also because Chopin insists that the audience accompany Edna into death both as external, scientific observer and as psychic sharer. Just as Edna has previously crossed the invisible boundary between the poetic and scientific modes of reality to join us as viewer of her somatic self, so, too, do we ultimately cross to join her as psychic participant. In the suicide scene we complete the transposition from external, analytical viewer and move "inside" to become part of Edna's mind and—metonymically—part of Chopin's. Yet in the last narrative moments, when Edna's nude body in the gleaming water presents the most sensual image in the entire narrative and seems to demand "external" scrutiny, Chopin shifts her rhetorical emphasis from visual to auditory. Remembered sounds from her youth fill Edna's mind: the voice of her father; the barking of the dog; the jangle of the cavalry officer's spurs; the hum of bees. At last we "see" what Edna experiences, but our ears and not our eyes inform us. This sensory shift is literally necessary because the Gulf waves and the imminence of death shut off vision; but the intangible consequence is to define how much we as audience have changed—from external, dispassionate observers to direct participants in Edna's psychological (and physiological) trauma. Cut off suddenly from the sensuous intrusions that "vision" creates, we are privy to her most intimate memories. From removed, occasionally disinterested outsiders we suddenly find ourselves sharing mental space with one who is about to die. Beyond that, metonymy cannot carry us.

Wayne C. Booth warned some years ago that we risk drowning in confusion when we try to define or categorize "point of view," for all readers know from experience that a particular novel is more complex than any simple terminology can suggest.[17] That admonition holds true for The Awakening perhaps more so than for many novels because Chopin was on the leading edge of the late-nineteenth-century movement which carried the novel away from strict real-

ism and residual Romance and into psychology. Her narrative may therefore exhibit a lack of sophistication we should grant any pioneer. As we have already mentioned, for example, Robert's seemingly inappropriate character appears simplistic compared to the rich complexity of a character such as Edna, and we are never sure whether Chopin herself is conscious of the irony of such a paradoxical juxtaposition.[18] However, we are sure that Chopin's various transmutations and the external–internal shift clearly anticipated the modernists who subsequently made the technique into a standard mode of narrative management that would, as F. K. Stanzel establishes, shake the "theoretical foundations" of narrative criticism after World War II.[19] Stanzel correctly bases his conclusions on the writings of James Joyce, William Faulkner, and other modernists; but as we have seen Chopin was experimenting with the same sophisticated narrative modes a generation before the writers whom Stanzel cites. The true power of her narrative rests in that experimentation. As Mark Schorer noted about Emily Brontë and Wuthering Heights, "Whether she knew from the outset, or even at the end, what she was doing, we may doubt; but what she did and did superbly we can see."[20]

Notes

1. Judith Fryer, The Faces of Eve: Women in the Nineteenth-Century American Novel (New York: Oxford Univ. Press, 1976), p. 243.
2. Donald A. Ringe notices a double world in The Awakening, one within and one without, but Ringe's comment is incidental to his main focus on romantic imagery. See "Romantic Imagery in Kate Chopin's The Awakening," American Literature, 43 (Jan. 1972), 580–88.
3. Kate Chopin, The Awakening, ed. Margaret Culley (New York: W. W. Norton & Co., 1976), p. 15. Subsequent references to The Awakening are to this edition and will be cited in parentheses within the text.
4. Henry James and Stephen Crane—among others—had already accustomed readers to the plot Chopin develops: oppressions visited upon females by a ruling patriarchy. Thus, it was less the subject matter of The Awakening that caused Chopin to be so severely censured and more the authorial attitude.

5. Kenneth Burke, *A Grammar of Motives and a Rhetoric of Motives* (Cleveland: Meridian Books, 1962), p. 506.

6. Ibid., p. 507.

7. This shift in audience perspective correlates with Edna's difficulty in distinguishing reality from fantasy. Sam B. Girgus discusses this matter and recognizes parallels between R. D. Laing's theory of the schizoid personality and Edna's difficulty. Girgus, however, does not address the connections between Edna as objectifying persona and Chopin's own psychosexual impulses. See Sam B. Girgus, "R. D. Laing and Literature: Readings of Poe, Hawthorne and Kate Chopin," *Psychological Perspectives on Literature: Freudian Dissidents and Non-Freudians, A Casebook*, ed. Joseph Natoli (Hamden: The Shoe String Press, Inc., 1984), pp. 181–187. Also, for a more complete discussion of Chopin's use of bird imagery per se, see Judith Fryer, pp. 243–258.

8. Robert Collins offers another view of how Chopin uses clothing to characterize her protagonist. See "The Dismantling of Edna Pontellier: Garment Imagery in Kate Chopin's *The Awakening*," *Southern Studies* 23 (Summer 1984), 176–197.

9. This is but one of several hedonistic and sexually symbolic meals in the novel. Freud uses the term "totemic" for the entire complex of matriarchal, sexual impulses associated with women and food, and though his discussion is somewhat dated, it offers interesting observations applicable to Edna's conflicting guilts and desires. See especially *Totem and Taboo*, in *The Basic Writings of Sigmund Freud*, ed. and trans. A. A. Brill (New York: The Modern Library, 1966), pp. 909–914.

10. For example, Robert White correctly argues that Edna's art—perhaps more than any other single factor—emblematizes for the audience her attempt to increase her inner space. See "Inner and Outer Space in *The Awakening*," *Mosaic*, 17 (Winter 1984), 97–109.

11. F. K. Stanzel, *A Theory of Narrative*, trans. Charlotte Goedsche (London: Cambridge Univ. Press, 1984), p. 15.

12. In an early review, Percival Pollard offers a humorous debunking of Edna's "awakening." See *Their Day in Court* (New York: Neale Publishing, 1909), pp. 41–45; rpt. in *The Awakening*, ed. Margaret Culley (New York: W. W. Norton & Co., 1976), pp. 160–162.

13. Per Seyersted, *Kate Chopin: A Critical Biography* (Baton Rouge: Louisiana State Univ. Press, 1969), p. 190. One of the significant shortcomings of the narrative is the difficulty the audience has in accepting Robert as "man-enough" to justify Edna's passion for him. Especially for the modern audience, perhaps more so than for the audience of 1899, Edna's passion for him seems more ludicrous than convincing. Again, Percival Pollard noted this problem very early, pointing out the difficulty the audience has in believing that a mature, sexually active woman such as Edna would suddenly become "utterly unmanageable" after a "trifling encounter" with one such as Robert Lebrun (p. 160). Rosemary F. Franklin offers a significantly different explanation of Edna's relationship with Robert and Alcée. She likens Edna to the beautiful but mortal Psyche who must appease Aphrodite. Her affairs with Robert and Arobin parallel Psyche's affair with Eros. See "*The Awakening* and the Failure of Psyche," *American Literature* 56 (Dec. 1984), 510–526.

14. Hayden White, *Tropics of Discourse: Essays in Cultural Criticism* (Baltimore: Johns Hopkins Univ. Press, 1978), p. 2.

15. One of the best discussions of the post- or anti-Freudian complexities of the father–daughter, mother–son relationship as viewed by contemporary feminist theory is Jane Gallop, *The Daughter's Seduction: Feminism and Psychoanalysis* (Ithaca: Cornell Univ. Press, 1982).

16. Kenneth Burke, *The Philosophy of Literary Form* (Baton Rouge: Louisiana State Univ. Press, 1941), p. 274. The context of these observations is Burke's gentle disagreement with Freud's explanation of "totemism." Freud relates the concept to the patriarchal roots of society, but Burke (more logically it seems) sees it emanating from the matriarchal. Burke also discusses Freud's theories of "father-rejection" as a cause in "symbolic" suicides—and ultimately literal ones. Edna's relationship with her cold, domineering father is obviously pertinent in this context.

17. Wayne C. Booth, "Distance and Point-of-View: An Essay in Classification," *Essays in Criticism*, 11 (1961), 60–79; rpt. in *The Theory of the Novel*,

ed. Philip Stevick (New York: The Free Press, 1967), pp. 87–107.

18. For a discussion of another possible difficulty with the novel, see Suzanne Wolkenfeld, "Edna's Suicide: The Problem of the One and the Many," *The Awakening*, pp. 218–224.

19. Stanzel, p. 46.

20. Mark Schorer, "Technique as Discovery," *Hudson Review*, 1 (1948), 67–87; rpt. in *The Theory of the Novel*, ed. Philip Stevick (New York: The Free Press, 1967), pp. 65–84.

CHAPTER FOUR

Mimetic Criticism: Reality as Context

First follow NATURE, *and your Judgment frame*
By her just Standard, which is still the same

        —Pope, *An Essay on Criticism*

We saw in a previous section how formal critics often come to locate part of the poem's value in its ability to represent the world. Despite this mimetic drift, formalists deserve their name because their theory emphasizes that fitting of the parts to the whole that produces a coherent poem. A theory that emphasizes instead the correspondence of the poem to external reality is more properly called "mimetic." Critics who adopt such a theory join the great tradition in Western literary criticism. Among the ancients, the idea that literature was mimetic was not so much an argued conclusion as it was the unchallenged premise on which all arguments were built. And with few exceptions that premise continued to control discussions of literature well into the eighteenth century. Even when historical concerns began to dominate the academic study of literature, these concerns were not seen as opposing mimetic criticism. It was assumed that great literature revealed truth; this was what justified interest in its author and the circumstances of its creation. On this point, the academic critic and the common reader often agreed, and the mimetic value terms are at once the most venerable and the most popular. For many readers, words like "real," "true," and "lifelike" are assumed to name incontestable literary values.

This assumption is illustrated in censorship controversies and even court cases where the prosecution is likely to argue the affective line that the work in question, in its language or the actions it portrays, has a harmful effect on its audience, while the defense may respond with the mimetic argument that the work gives an accurate picture of reality. After all, people say and do such things, and the author is simply reporting the facts of life. Thus, one side appeals to goodness, the other to truth. (Very seldom do such cases admit an appeal to beauty.) For mimeticists, though, truth is a higher good. And sometimes their argument wins. The famous decision that allowed James Joyce's *Ulysses* to be sold in the United States, for example, justified the work in part as an honest and accurate portrait of middle-class

Dubliners at the turn of the century. Those who objected to the book's "too poignant preoccupation with sex" were reminded that Joyce's "locale was Celtic and his season Spring."

This commitment to "realism" is also reflected in our tendency to claim a mimetic justification for changes in literary fashions and conventions. As drama, for instance, dropped the use of meter and adopted "natural" speech and carefully detailed settings and costumes to portray contemporary bourgeois characters, each development was hailed as making drama more "realistic." Yet Chekhov, for one, looked on plays that employed all these devices as "unrealistic" in their presentation of well-made plots and of characters who could concentrate their attention on a single theme or follow the thread of a complex conversation. In the name of realism, he introduced the meandering dialogue, the "irrelevant" remark, and with these mimetic devices he anticipated some of the conventions of the "theater of the absurd," conventions that are in turn defended as "true to life." Similarly, techniques of modern prose fiction such as the stream of consciousness or the rigorously limited point of view have usually been explained as attempts to portray reality more accurately. That one generation's realistic device should so often be the next generation's "mere convention" might lead us to suspect the entire line of argument. But the prevalence of this line illustrates the potency of the mimetic appeal. We incline to believe that if we can claim for a device, a technique, or a whole work a "realistic" purpose, we have provided an ultimate justification.

It follows that a poem's failure on these grounds may be cause for condemnation. On such mimetic principles, Plato, in history's most famous attack on poetry, banished the poet from the ideal state. Actually, Plato said several and sometimes contradictory things about poets in his various writings, and he also objected to poetry on the affective grounds that it feeds and waters the passions. But his best-known remarks occur in *Republic X*, where he attacks poetry because it gives us a false view of the world. His argument is of interest chiefly for the answers it has inspired.

In Plato's philosophy, the world most of us call "real," the world apprehended by the senses, is an imperfect manifestation of the true reality, the world of immutable ideas or forms, the Parmenidean stasis that stands behind the Heraclitean flux of the sensuous world and that can be apprehended only by the mind. The idea of the perfect circle, for example, is prior to and apart from all circles we may draw or see, and that idea is the standard against which any physical circle can be measured. Obviously, only the mind can know the idea of a circle, and the mind must know that idea independently of any drawn circle. Likewise, when we see a pencil protruding from a glass of water, our sense of sight tells us that the pencil is bent, but the mind, which understands the truth, corrects the false report. And so for all knowledge. The business of humanity is to use our reason to pierce the veil of illusion, to transcend the false reports of the senses, to escape from the shadowy knowledge of the cave and to come to know the real world of the ideal forms. What furthers that knowledge is good; what inhibits it is harmful. Poetry inhibits it.

To explain his point, Plato resorts, as he often does, to visual metaphor. We start with the idea of a bed. A kind of practical artist, the carpenter, copies the idea of the bed to produce a physical bed. This bed, though a mere "imitation" and necessarily imperfect because a translation of an idea into a physical medium, has nonetheless a practical use. But when a painter paints a picture of that bed, he makes an imitation of an imitation that has no practical use. Worse, by copying the physical bed, which was itself a copy of the real bed, the painter produces a work twice removed from reality and so leads us not toward the realm of true knowledge but in the opposite direction.

By this argument, one of the world's greatest image makers and symbol wielders banished poets from his perfect state. The irony did not go long unnoticed, and at least as early as Plotinus we find art defended on the same Platonic grounds that Plato had used to condemn it. Philosophers who manage to escape the cave and enter the transcendent realm of pure forms can communicate what they have discovered only by means of metaphor and symbol. To talk at all about such a realm, the thinker must perforce become, like Plato, a poet. Thus Shelley, in one of the best-known Platonic defenses of poetry, can claim that

> poets, or those who imagine and express this indestructible order, are not only the authors of language and of music, of dance and architecture, and statuary, and painting; they are the institutors of laws, and the founders of civil society, and the inventors of the arts of life, and the teachers, who draw into a certain propinquity with the beautiful and the true, that partial apprehension of the agencies of the invisible world which is called religion.

In other words, the artist's bed need not be a copy of the carpenter's. The artist's vision can penetrate to the ideal realm, and the artist's skill can translate that vision into the artistic symbol that is, if not quite the idea itself, something that can lead us to conceive the idea. Like Keats's urn, the artist's symbol mediates between the physical world of flux and the immutable, transcendent realm. Through synesthesia and paradox it takes us past the mode of sensuous apprehension toward the unheard melodies beyond the sounded notes, the static pattern behind the frenzied action. It allows us to contemplate that realm beyond appearances where beauty and truth are indeed one and the same. This realm is the reality that art imitates and that *only* art can imitate. Thus, despite Plato's argument in the *Republic,* Platonic philosophy has most often been used to defend poetry, and specifically on mimetic grounds.

But the earliest reply to Plato had been argued on a different basis. At any rate, Aristotle's *Poetics* has generally been thought to have as one of its purposes the attempt to refute Plato's charge by redefining the sense in which poetry imitates reality. *Mimesis* is Aristotle's key word, and not all he says about it in this fragmentary document seems entirely clear and consistent. But his central concepts are plain enough. Like Plato, Aristotle builds his poetics on his metaphysics, but in solider Aristotle's scheme the reality that art imitates is quite literally a different matter. "Form" is no longer something beyond the physical world. The material world we apprehend with our senses is the real world, and everything in it consists of matter that is formed in some way. This concept is easy enough to conceive if we think of man-made things like a bed, or a poem, and in fact Aristotle's concepts provide the basis for "formal" criticism. But when we think of the forms of living things, the forms that poems imitate rather than the forms they possess, we are apt to misunderstand. The true "form" of a living thing is that which it most characteristically is. The form of a man, for example, is best represented by a vigorous adult who has reached that stage toward which childhood develops and from which old age declines. The form of an acorn is not a small and somewhat spherical object but a full-grown, majestic oak tree.

Now there is a sense in which this true form is never realized in nature. Warping winds, poor soil, impatient lumberjacks, and a hundred other "accidents" may prevent the acorn from achieving its true form. So Aristotle develops his own split between form and appearance, and this split has important implications for his concept of mimesis. For one thing, it explains how it is possible for a mimetic art to represent men as "better than they are" or things "as they ought to be," just as a sculptor may study several models in order to "imitate" a form possessed by none of the models. More importantly, it explains how the artist must look past the accidents, the individual peculiarities, to discover the essential or characteristic form that underlies them. The artist gives us the essence of a character, a situation, an action. The artist shows us not what that person or this person did, but what such people do. In perceiving this essential form and then imitating it in the medium of art so that we may perceive it, the poet achieves "a more philosophical and a higher thing than history: for poetry tends to express the universal, history the particular." Both the poet and the historian tell us truths, but the poet tells the more important truths.

Here is a mimetic defense of poetry as cogent as the Platonic and even more influential. Between them, these defenses provided the philosophic foundations for nearly every mimetic theory of literature until the eighteenth century, and their influence is still felt in many ways in contemporary criticism. Despite their considerable differences, the Platonic and Aristotelian views of mimesis have at least one important similarity: that is, whether art is thought to pierce the illusory veil of sense to enter the transcendent realm of the true forms, or whether it is thought to penetrate the accidents of local particularity to perceive the essential and universal character of persons and actions, each system offers a view that separates appearance and reality. Consequently, each avoids a serious problem that troubles many mimetic theories. Generally, the more heavily we stress the congruence of the poem to reality, the more difficult it becomes to explain the formal coherence of the poem. But if the poem is congruent not with the shifty and chaotic world of appearance but instead with some transcendent or underlying reality, the usual tension between coherence and congruence is considerably relaxed, perhaps even dissolved. In the Platonic scheme especially, the coherence of the work of art can be explained on mimetic grounds as an imitation of the coherence of the real world of ideal forms, that realm where coherence and congruence, beauty and truth, are one and the same. In the Aristotelian view, the gap between appearance and reality is not so wide. But it is wide enough to allow us to see artistic imitation as a process that strips away the peculiar, local, and temporary to reveal the characteristic, general, and permanent; and this view also exempts the poem from any need to conform closely to the appearance of things.

When we contemplate, for example, Aristotle's favorite play, *Oedipus Tyrannus,* we notice that by the standards of circumstantial realism it is a confabulation of implausible premises, improbable coincidences, and impossible circumstances. In fact, the famous economy and symmetry of its structure are salient among the things that set it apart from the world of ordinary experience. But, Aristotle implicitly argues, precisely those same things throw into sharp relief the essential action and, hence, the essential meaning of the play. The coherence of the poem, achieved by pruning away the distracting and confusing details of life as we usually experience it, is exactly what allows us to perceive the poem's universal relevance, its correspondence to the form beneath appearances. So the Aristotelian concept of mimesis, too, is able to lessen, if it cannot entirely eliminate, the troublesome opposition between coherence and congruence, between formal unity and imitative accuracy.

Increasingly, however, modern thought has been dominated by what may be called a pervasive "empirical" view of reality, which says that the world apprehended by the senses, the confusing flux of felt experience, is the real world. Such a view makes it much more difficult to separate the poet's truth from the historian's, or from the psychologist's, the sociologist's, or the physical scientist's. One solution is simply to give up poetry's claims to truth and to defend it on entirely different, usually affective, grounds. I. A. Richards, we noticed, attempted to do precisely that. But this radical solution has not appealed to most modern critics, and Richards's denial of the referential function of poetic language was in turn denied even by the formalist critics, who accepted his analytical techniques. These critics and others vigorously asserted the truth of poetry on empirical grounds and even against the claims of empirical science, and in the process they brought about a rather startling shift of perspective.

Aristotle, we saw, argued that poetry, because it was not confined as history was to the unique acts of specific persons at particular times and places, could reveal a higher and more universal truth. Certainly the poem presents particular characters and particular actions, but these are represented in their essentials, and the purpose of artistic shaping is to reveal their general truth. Samuel Johnson, who was often a staunch mimeticist, was very much in this tradition when he had his character Imlac declare that it is not the business of poetry to "number the streaks of the tulip"; its business is rather "to examine, not the individual, but the species; to remark general properties and large appearances." Sir Joshua Reynolds, Johnson's contemporary and a famous painter, took a similar view when he claimed that the "disposition to abstractions, to generalizing and classification, is the great glory of the human mind." It was this kind of remark that prompted William Blake to write in his *marginalia* on Reynolds, "To generalize is to be an idiot." Blake strikes the modern note. Many twentieth-century attempts to assert the claims of poetic truth against those of scientific truth have taken the tack we noticed in the discussion of formal criticism. Science obviously deals in "general" truths. Newton's apple and Humpty-Dumpty obey the same "laws," which can be stated in compact formulas to describe an infinite number of specific cases. But, replies the literary critic, such description is too general. It provides an even ghostlier paradigm than the Platonic forms. It is too abstract to describe the heft and feel, the smell and sound and sight, of the world as we actually experience it. For that we need a more concrete medium, something, if not more simple, at least more sensuous and passionate. We need poetry.

In this way modern critics come very often to stress the solidity and particularity of the poetic symbol, the complexity and tensions of the poetic structure. In doing so, we should remember, they are simply putting the emphasis on the other side of the same concrete–universal coin that is the poem. Aristotle and centuries of later critics, defining poetry with reference to the historian's particularity, stressed its universality. Many modern critics, defining poetry with reference to the universality of science, have emphasized its particularity. Each emphasis is understandable. Hamlet is interesting because he is in some sense every man, but Everyman is less interesting than Hamlet.

This is simply to note that the paradox of the concrete–universal becomes even more paradoxical as our view of reality becomes more empirical. But the empirical critic's vision gains clarity and force if it can be integrated within a larger system of thought. Psychological critics, for example, though they often focus their attention on the author, and sometimes on the audience, will also frequently operate in the mimetic context. Whether followers of Freud, Jung, Lacan, Maslow, or some other leading figure, such critics bring to their reading a fully developed theory about the way people really behave, and why; and this theory provides a standard by which they can measure the accuracy of the poet's representations. Such critics are often pleased, but not at all surprised, to find that the great poets' vision of human nature agrees with their own. Freud, for instance, noticed that creative writers had anticipated many of his own discoveries. He named his famous "Oedipus complex" after a play by Sophocles, and he suggested its application to one by Shakespeare. In doing so, we should notice, he was practicing mimetic criticism, for he was claiming that these playwrights were perceptive students of reality whose intuitive grasp of human nature was later confirmed by more methodical and scientific observation. "Not I, but the poets, have discovered the unconscious." And when we respond to these poets we do so because at some level of consciousness we recognize the truth of their representations. This approach is fundamentally different from that of the historical scholar who tells us, for example, that *Hamlet* must be understood in the light of some long-forgotten Renaissance theory of psychology that Shakespeare accepted or assumed his audience accepted. To the mimetic critic of a psychoanalytic persuasion, there is nothing anachronistic in reading classical or Elizabethan drama in Freudian terms. The psychologist and the poet study the same nature, and the truth of their findings, not at all limited by time and place, is always referable to this same standard, "at once the source, and end, and test of art." And of science.

So any psychology, indeed, any systematic view of human behavior, can provide the basis for a mimetic criticism of literature. In our own century, one of the most influential systems of thought has been the Marxist. To be sure, Marxist critics have often analyzed the social and economic forces acting on writers, and they have frequently been very much concerned with literature's effects. But these genetic and affective concerns are often based on a mimetic criterion: the work is good to the extent that it accurately depicts the clash of class interests, the forces of economic determinism, the dialectic process of history, in brief, the social reality as the critic's particular interpretation of Marxism may conceive it.

In other words, critics operating within a system of thought can account for the function of literature and measure its truth in terms of a larger framework of ideas. This is a potential strength, but only to the extent that we are willing to accept the whole system that supports the criticism. In practice, the great majority of readers has found the mimetic standards of most systems too partial, too limited, to deal adequately with the abundance and variety of literature that the world has generally called great. What system is capacious enough to comprehend Homer's cosmology and Milton's, Dante's ethics and de Sade's, Assisi's flowers and Baudelaire's? Or, take him all in all, what system can contain Shakespeare alone? Perhaps this is why the largest number of mimetic critics—and this number would include most of us at one time or another—feel no need to claim allegiance to a particular system of thought. Apparently unaffiliated and eclectic, they appeal to empiricism in its root meaning, to our common sense and our common experience of the world, to provide the mimetic standard, and what they may lose in philosophic rigor they gain in flexibility and wider assent.

But even the most eclectic and flexible forms of mimetic criticism must encounter some basic difficulties that seem to inhere in the problematic relationship between art and "reality," and the more firmly the criticism is based on empirical premises, the more troublesome these difficulties will be. One of these difficulties may be expressed in the form of two related questions: How does the poem, in conforming to a reality already known, give us knowledge? Or, if the reality is not already known, how can we be sure the poem does in fact conform to it? We may praise a work by remarking that it is congruent to life as we know it: this is the way things look; this is how people really behave. But it is not clear why we want to have such representations. Since we already possess the standard by which we judge them—that is, since we already know the reality imitated sufficiently well to judge the accuracy of the imitation—in what sense can we be said to learn anything from the poem?

This is not easy to answer. Aristotle's remarks that people learn by imitation and that they enjoy learning are not especially helpful, since he doesn't explain in what way people learn from artistic representations, and the example he gives muddies the waters further. Drawing on visual metaphor, he says that only those who know the original that the painter imitates can derive pleasure from the comparison; those who lack that knowledge derive what pleasure they have from some other, apparently nonmimetic, source. A better answer is offered by Fra Lippo Lippi, in Browning's poem of that name, when he explains, again using the "realistic" painting as his example, that we look at things every day but we don't really see them until the artist's picture calls our attention to them. Then we say, "That's the very man!" but in fact we hadn't been fully aware of the life around us until the artist taught us to see it.

This line is promising, and a critical theory could be developed at some length in this direction. But when we inquire how the artist has achieved this result, we seem to be faced with the paradox that it has been achieved by altering the very reality the artist claims to imitate. The alteration may take the form of simply selecting or rearranging details to heighten our awareness and focus our vision, but it is, nonetheless, alteration. And once we start to argue that even the most "realistic" plot, the most "lifelike" characters and actions, have some degree of distortion, then on the same principle we might argue that the most elaborate plots, the most outlandish caricatures, the most fantastic fictions can be similarly justified. For they too could be called heightenings and intensifications of reality. And by such arguments the so-called realistic devices and modes of literature lose their special standing. If forms such as "realistic" drama or "naturalistic" fiction achieve their ends by departing from direct imitation in at least some respects, then those same ends might be as well attained by forms such as epic, romance, pastoral, and others that depart from direct imitation in most respects. This line of argument does promise to account for the great variety of literature, but since it locates the special function and force of art in its power to select from, rearrange, and otherwise distort reality, it doesn't seem appropriate to call such a line mimetic.

So the question of just how an arrangement of words can be said to imitate reality remains a rather difficult question to answer, and so does the question of why we should want such imitations. And the answers are made all the more difficult when "reality" is defined in empirical terms. A related problem, how to reconcile the poem's formal coherence with its mimetic function, is also made more difficult. As we noticed, only idealistic philosophies like the Platonic can fully achieve this reconciliation. As the conception of reality becomes more empirical, the problem grows more troublesome, because any selection from the flux of felt experience and any imposition of formal pattern must to some extent lessen the poem's correspondence to empirical reality. As we should expect, formalists have often complained that many types of mimetic criticism ignore the very things that make poems, poems. Whatever ideology or philosophy is used to provide the standard of "truth," none can very well account for the art of poetry, and all are inclined to separate form and meaning, to extract the paraphrasable content of the poem and to judge that as if the poem were a philosophic treatise or a religious or economic tract. And even when the mimetic critic is willing to acknowledge the formal aspects of the poem, to grant its difference from discursive argument, the mimetic context cannot itself provide the concepts that will allow an explication or account of these formal aspects. Thus, the opposition between artistic design and imitative accuracy troubles virtually all mimetic theories, and it especially troubles those with an empirical basis.

This same opposition, we noticed, puzzled formal critics, though they approached the problem from the other direction. In fact, we could locate both formal and mimetic critics somewhere on that imaginary line that connects the work of art with reality as we experience it outside of art. The difference between them is often a matter of emphasis. Mimetic critics are primarily concerned to measure the poem's congruence with reality and to judge it on that basis, but they can neither entirely overlook nor, on mimetic grounds, adequately account for the formal features of the poem that set it apart from the world of experience and from other forms of discourse. Conversely, formal critics stress the uniqueness of poetic language and the inseparability of form and content, and their analyses are designed to explicate the poem's formal coherence. Yet they usually insist as well on the referential function of poetic language, and they often find the meaning and value of the poem's "complexity" in its correspondence to the complex reality of life as we experience it. So for both the formal and the mimetic critic, despite their different starting points, coherence and congruence are always necessary, but seldom easily reconcilable, principles.

A third problem confronting all mimetic approaches is brought into focus by a more radical objection. When formalists complain that mimetic critics cannot deal with the form of the poem, they mean by "form" these particular words in this particular order. When intertextual critics make the same complaint, they mean by "form" all the literary conventions that make up the poem. This objection is more radical because the intertextual perspective sees the poem not as an imitation of life but as an imitation of other poems. This perspective threatens, therefore, to undermine the mimetic premise entirely, to simply deny the referential function of art.

The development of this line of criticism is the subject of the next chapter. Here we shall simply note some implications of this objection. The mimetic perspective seems to bring naturally to mind narrative and dramatic structures, particularly those that offer "rounded" characters and "realistic" settings and actions and that seem to invite comparison with life outside of books. The novel, for example, is sometimes thought to be synonymous with the techniques of "circumstantial realism," and the tendency of much recent fiction to abandon these techniques has been seen by some to herald "the death of the novel." But the intertextual critics remind us that even so-called realistic techniques are simply conventions, and they call our attention to the myriad forms that make up the bulk of literature, the romances and pastorals, the farces and burlesques, the chameleon satire, that can infiltrate any form, and the encyclopedic work, like *Ulysses,* that can contain most. They remind us, further, that to defend *Ulysses* as a faithful picture of middle-class Dublin life at the turn of the century in the spring of the year may be judicially useful, but it is critically myopic. And they remind us, finally, that it is very difficult to account for the many generic conventions and their endless permutations on mimetic grounds. Yet these are the salient features of literary form, in a fundamental sense of the term, and a theory's inability to account for them must be considered a serious weakness.

Mimetic critics, then, encounter some difficult problems. On the one hand, they must face the charge of reductivism because they cannot easily cope with literary "form" in either the formal or the intertextual senses of the term. On the other hand, their own context is replete with philosophical puzzles about the relationship between verbal structures and the "reality" these structures are supposed to imitate. Although most of these problems are very old, they are made especially difficult by the prevailing modern tendency to define "reality" in empirical terms. Still, as the very hoariness of the problems indicates, their existence has never drastically diminished the popularity of the mimetic context. From Aristophanes' day to Samuel Johnson's, mimetic concerns dominated literary discussions, and these concerns have continued to play a major role in modern criticism.

Historical critics, of course, have always been centrally concerned with the representational aspects of literature. Anglo-American formalists, as we have seen, came to ground part of their theory of value in the poem's special ability to represent human experience. Freudians, Jungians, Marxists, Thomists, and other supporters of particular psychological or philosophical systems have perforce been interested in literature as a representation of human character and action, as have critics who focus on the issues of race, class, and gender as these are represented in literature. Indeed, as we will see, in the contexts of poststructural and cultural criticism, "representation" remains a central issue.

In other words, mimetic concerns, under a variety of names, continue to occupy much of our attention. There are good reasons that they should. The idea that literature in some way imitates life has been an axiom of Western thought from its earliest records, and while critics in some of our contexts have occasionally been willing to ignore that axiom, only certain kinds of structural and poststructural critics have been willing to deny it. Clearly, we are accustomed to thinking in mimetic terms. But more than habit may be involved. Almost any verbal representation, particularly one in narrative or dramatic form, seems to invite comparison with our nonliterary experience. Such comparison furnishes an obvious, an almost inevitable, point of reference for the viewer or reader, a standard automatically invoked whenever we remark the "consistency" of a character's behavior or the "plausibility" of an action. That is to say, our understanding of the characters and actions in literature seems to be at least partly, and almost by reflex, a matter of reference to the mimetic context.

Further, and perhaps most important, there is the large question of the value of literature. As we have seen, the attraction of mimetic theory has often been strongest here. To put it simply, if we can show that literature does, in some important ways, tell us the truth about experience, then the various forms of "scientific" thought can be met on their own ground and the vast enterprise connected with literature, and our own intense personal interest, can be given a widely accepted justification. Only the mimetic context promises to provide such justification.

Suggestions for Further Reading

Erich Auerbach, *Mimesis: The Representation of Reality in Western Literature* (1946), is a classic text; John D. Boyd, *The Function of Mimesis and Its Decline* (2nd ed., 1980), is a history of some of the key concepts. George Bisztray, *Marxist Models of Literary Realism* (1978), recounts the arguments among Marxist critics about this tricky term. Other explorations of "realism" include Ian Watt, *The Rise of the Novel* (1957); J. P. Sterne, *On Realism* (1973), Kathryn Hume, *Fantasy and Mimesis* (1984), Lilian R. Furst, *All Is True: The Claims and Strategies of Realist Fiction* (1995), and Arne Melberg, *Theories of Mimesis* (1996). Ernest Jones, *Hamlet and Oedipus* (1949), is a famous study asserting the psychological truth of Shakespeare's character on Freudian lines; Bernard Paris, *A Psychological Approach to Fiction* (1974), makes the case for mimetic criticism using a different psychological model. A. D. Nuttall, *A New Mimesis* (1983), Raymond Tallis, *In Defence of Realism* (1988), and Robert Alter, *The Pleasures of Reading in an Ideological Age* (1989), argue the viability of mimetic fiction in the face of structuralist and poststructuralist attacks.

Although feminist critics operate in most contexts, this diverse group may be cited here because their challenges to other forms of criticism, and to traditional ways of thinking about society, sex, and history, are often focused on questions of representation.

The variety of feminist criticism is best illustrated in collections of essays. Elaine Showalter, ed., *The New Feminist Criticism* (1985), reprints 18 of the most influential essays published in the previous decade. The same editor's *Speaking of Gender* (1989) marks the more recent shift from "woman-centered feminism" to concern with socially constructed gender differences. An even fuller picture is offered by Robyn Warhol and Diane Herndl, eds., *Feminism: An Anthology of Literary Theory and Criticism* (1991), which reprints 58 essays originally published between 1975 and 1991, and by Mary Eagleton, ed., *Feminist Literary Theory: A Reader* (2nd ed., 1996), which reprints excerpts from a great number of essays. Toril Moi, *Sexual/Textual Politics* (1985), and Janet Todd, *Feminist Literary History* (1988), are two helpful studies of the development of feminist criticism. Also useful is Jane Gallop, *Around 1981* (1992), which constructs a history of feminist criticism by analyzing several anthologies of feminist essays published since 1972. Also see Diana Fuss, *Essentially Speaking: Feminism, Nature, and Difference* (1989), Eve Kosofsky Sedgwick, *Epistemology of the Closet* (1990), Judith Butler, *Gender Trouble: Feminism and the Subversion of Identity* (1990), and Teresa L. Ebert, *Ludic Feminism and After: Postmodernism, Desire, and Labor in Late Capitalism* (1996).

THEORY

Noting the tendency of many recent theorists, especially those called structuralists and poststructuralists, to disparage the claims of mimetic criticism, Robert Alter undertakes a vigorous defense of these claims. As he sees it, the structuralists, with their elaborate linguistic analyses, and the poststructuralists, with their ideological objections to the idea of a unitary self, display a sophistication that is also a form of naïveté. They have achieved their insights by cultivating a kind of blindness, and they have lost sight of some old and important truths about literature. The most fundamental of these is that literature "is quintessentially a representational art," and what it represents is "the common stuff of our human existence."

Taking character as the "crucial test case for the link between literature and reality," Alter argues that while literary representation is, perforce, conventionalized, great writers have always known how to create characters who surpass the conventions, characters who impress us as "real" people. Confronted with such characters, "our recognition of the authority of the representation has to depend finally not on any internal mechanism of narrative but on a matching of experience and reading." Touching on an issue that Bernard Paris will develop more fully, Alter quotes with approval W. J. Harvey's remark that literary characters tend to exhibit "a surplus margin of gratuitous life." That "surplus" suggests that at times the mimetic impulse may override the formal and thematic impulses, and that readers may rightly be content that it should. "If the fascination of human types is an end in itself (and the novel generically reflects such an assumption), the deepened experiential knowing of the imagined individual is a process that justifies itself, and for which no formal limits or functions can be prescribed."

Character and the Connection with Reality

Robert Alter

Finally, then, Alter offers a defense of some of the oldest and strongest claims of mimetic criticism. Choosing examples ranging from Homer and the Bible to the twentieth century, he argues that humankind's problems and preoccupations tend to persist from time to time and from place to place, and that literature derives its power from its ability to represent these problems and preoccupations. Formal analysis, literary history, and other approaches may be useful and even necessary, but they all fail to account for "the powerful capacity of the literary work to refer its readers to a complex order of moral, emotional, and psychological realities. A criticism with no coherent vocabulary of discussing that power of reference will provide only a feeble guide to literature."

Literature is quintessentially a representational art, but the relation between the literary text and the world it represents has always been something of a puzzle, and recent trends in literary theory have compounded the puzzlement. The objects of literary representation belong to a wide range of heterogeneous categories, material, conceptual, emotional, relational, personal, and collective. They include states of feeling, moments of perception, memories (all characteristically treated in lyric poetry); buildings, neighborhoods, industrial processes, social institutions (as, for example, in the novels of Balzac); world-historical forces and theological ideas (as, respectively, in *War and Peace* and *The Brothers Karamazov*); imaginary personages and historical personages imaginatively reconstructed, which amounts to the same thing.

Fictional character is probably the crucial test case for the link between literature and reality. Very few people will take the trouble to read a novel or story unless they can somehow "identify" with the characters, live with them inwardly as though they were real at least for the duration of the reading. Modern avant-garde experiments in fiction that seek to block all possibility of such identification give signs of being not the wave of the future but no more than the exception that proves the rule. Literary theorists, among them critical promoters of such experiments, have frequently inveighed against the naïveté, or, indeed, the delusional habit, of reading fictional characters as though they were real people.

One objection that can be dismissed at the outset is that ordinary habits of reading betray a "metaphysics of presence," ignoring the ineluctable absence of all purported objects of representation in those columns of conventional signs of linguistic elements that constitute the printed page. The critic Denis Donoghue has pointed out with eminent good sense that such a reader is a straw man.[1] That is, unless a reader is delusional in a clinical sense, he or she never actually imagines that Emma Bovary or Isabel Archer or Huckleberry Finn is a real person. It is Don Quixote, in a fit of madness, who leaps onto the stage of Master Pedro's puppet theater, slashing at the evil Moors with his sword, but Cervantes' novel from the beginning is contrived to elicit from its readers a much saner and more complicated attitude toward the status of fictional personages.[2]

But if on some level we always know that characters in fiction are mere constructs, congeries of words, compounds of convention and invention, what is it about them that leads us to take them so seriously? Although there has been a great flowering of speculation on, and systematic description of, narrative in the past two decades, it offers little guidance, and in fact a good deal of misguidance, on this essential question. Let me describe briefly how this situation has come about before proposing an alternative way of thinking about character. As with the contemporary objections to the distinctiveness of literature, a move toward the marginalization of character has been undertaken on two fronts, one formal (and in part, linguistic), the other, in a much more intentional way, ideological.

The first great wave of contemporary narrative theory surfaced in France in the 1960s and, taking its models from Structuralist anthropology, sought to create a new discipline with a new name, narratology — that is, the systematic analysis of narrative as a set of formal relations and functions. Implicit in much of this discussion was a central metaphor of Structuralist thought, elsewhere applied to cultural systems and here to the literary text: the self-regulating machine. The systemic operations of narrative had largely been neglected by Anglo-American criticism, and by French criticism before the sixties, so there was definitely something to be learned from the new movement, but one may wonder whether the mechanizing conception of narrative as a system of functions offers an exhaustive account of it, as narratologists have tended to assume. What precisely is left out is the possibility of talking coherently about the nexus between text and what by consensus we are willing to call reality. It is symptomatic that narratology should be most conspicuously inadequate in its treatment of character because with its conception of narrative as a system of structural mechanisms, character can be little more than a function of plot. The narratologists have scarcely any critical vocabulary for encompassing the mimetic dimension of character.[3]

This inadequacy of Structuralist thinking about narrative is compounded by a fondness for seeing literary works in reductively linguistic terms. Because literary narrative is made up of words, it is imagined to be a language, or at the very least, a language-like system in which the purely internal differences among the components (tip from top or tap, villain from hero or helper) generate meanings. The elements of narrative, then, are conceived as analogous to or isomorphic with the elements of language, a notion that has led to some of the most embarrassing moments of the new narratology in which attempts have been made to identify in configurations of plot and character narrative adverbs, narrative adjectives, and so forth. In all this, there are scarcely grounds for helping us understand why the great fictional characters engage us so powerfully and even provide illumination for our lives.

Although the cluster of related intellectual trends called post-Structuralism withdraws from the Structuralist interest in system and rejects the project of a science of culture, it tacitly assumes as its point of departure in thinking about mimesis the supposed Structuralist demonstration that character is a mere function of narrative mechanisms. From the more ideological perspective of post-Structuralism, all the fuss and bother about a lowly function becomes suspect, if not actually ominous. Purportedly realistic character is now deemed a camouflage device or a mask (a notion already adumbrated in some of the Structuralists), or worse, a pernicious illusion working to sustain an oppressive ideology. Thus, the idealist, theological, and "logocentric" biases of Western culture are all encouraged by the illusion of character (an idea popular among the followers of Derrida and of Foucault); the notion of a coherent, unitary self embodied in realistic character is an evasion of all that is fissured and repressed in the self (an argument heard from Lacanians); the appealing consistency and meretricious intelligibility of character are merely instruments for enhancing the market value of literature (the objection of the neo-Marxists). All these lines of attack on character have been conveniently drawn together in a single article by the French critic Hélène Cixous, which is at once Derridean, Freudian, and Marxist.[4] She is so skeptical

about the reality of character that she uses the word in inverted commas only. Imparting an ideological impetus to the Stucturalist metaphor of the machine, she describes the literary work in which character occurs as a "machine of repression," and does not hesitate to conclude that "The marketable form of literature . . . is closely related to that familiar, decipherable human sign that 'character' claims to be."

What I would like to propose about all these attempts to undercut the mimetic validity of character is that they reflect the kind of sophistication that becomes its own egregious naïveté. Thus, Tzvetan Todorov, in an essay on verisimilitude that reflects French Structuralism in its heyday, proposes four different meanings for the term "verisimilitude" (correspondence to received opinion, correspondence to generic expectation, and so forth) after having announced flatly, "We shall discard only the first naive meaning, according to which a relation to reality is expressed."[5] This way of talking, which in various inflections has been in vogue since the sixties, is a means of exhibiting cleverness at the cost, as I have intimated, of a new sort of naïveté. To begin at the most rudimentary level, verisimilar fiction seeks to adhere to the laws of physical reality. If somebody throws an apple into the air in a story and it keeps going straight up, you know you are not reading verisimilar fiction, and this has nothing to do with received opinion. If someone in a novel runs a fever of 104° Fahrenheit, verisimilitude has been observed; if the fever is 114° Fahrenheit, verisimilitude has been violated. (Science fiction is an instructive mixed case because it tries to make fantasy seem verisimilar by extrapolating the physical laws of our own world to other worlds where somewhat different quantitative limits and relations may obtain.) Though there are not such easily measurable laws of human behavior, we nevertheless are able to make judgments when we read—and judgments not chiefly dependent on ideology, received opinion, genre, and so forth—about whether a bereaved father, a rejected mistress, a rebellious son is acting in a way that seems persuasively like reality. How such judgments are made will become clearer presently through illustration.

The very notion that literature is severed from reality because it is composed of conventions, both linguistic and literary, is an unexamined dogma of both Structuralist and post-Structuralist thought. The essential point of refutation, which ought to be self-evident but has been neglected in the general rage for sophistication, has been made with beautiful concision by A. D. Nuttall in his admirable book, *A New Mimesis:*

> Why should the presence of convention preclude reference to reality? The truth is almost exactly converse. All reference to reality (including pointing with the finger) is conventionally ordered. Language is an immensely rich system of conventions and is the best means we have of referring to the real.[6]

What this observation suggests is that discussion of the internal relations among elements of a literary work, however instructive, is never sufficient: ways have to be found to talk about how literature through its manifold conventions manages to address reality. To be sure, "reality" is a notoriously slippery term. I will use it here as an umbrella for the underlying aspects of our being in the world—the psychology of the individual; its matrices in biology and family; the complications of relating to others; social institutions; historical forces and events. About all of these we can talk with one another because to a large extent we share them as the common stuff of our human existence.

The simplifications of the ideological assault on mimetic character are as pronounced as those of the linguistic formalists, and attention to them will bring us closer to what occurs in literary mimesis. The whole idea of the realist work as a "machine of repression" is a piece of ideologically radical naïveté, for in the interests of displaying an impeccably liberated consciousness it entirely collapses the distinction between literature and propaganda. What is ignored is the polysemous, open-ended nature of literary texts; the evidence they abundantly offer for imaginative freedom variously exercised in the act of literary creation, often working against the grain of ruling ideologies; and hence the fundamental fact that ideology, like convention, is a context of literature but not its determinant, except when the writer slides into the propagandist. As for the idea of unitary character, comfortably familiar and decipherable, and as such both a market mechanism and an instrument of idealist deception, there may be some grounds for such a notion in modern popular literature from Western to romance, but in view of what serious writers have been doing with character since Homer and the Bible, it is as much of a straw man as the delusional reader naively addicted to a metaphysics of presence. In fact, many of the great fictional characters—King David, Othello, Captain Ahab, Anna Karenina, Leopold Bloom—are compelling precisely because there proves to be something ultimately indecipherable about them as they move through unforeseen twists and turns of self-revelation and self-concealment that put us in touch with what is uncanny, imponderable about our existence as human beings—and I begin my examples with one from the tenth or ninth century B.C.E. to stress that such purposefully troubling representation of character is hardly the invention of modernism.

The unity of character so often denounced as a sham by new wave critics is neither monolithic nor static, as they claim, but, on the contrary, is mobile, unstable, elusive even as it seems palpable in our reading experience—precisely like the complex unity of the literary artwork itself. Baruch Hochman astutely observes that the unity of character inheres in dynamic contradictions, which is also a basic fact of our psychological lives and as such helps explain the realistic persuasiveness of successfully achieved fictional character.[7] This is a perception shared in different terms by a good many writers but too often missed by contemporary theorists. The British novelist Elizabeth Bowen once proposed that character should seem unpredictable before any given act, inevitable after it. Vladimir Nabokov spoke in a chess metaphor of a "knight's move," in which the character hops over other pieces and then to one side, in ways that are unanticipated but prove after the fact to conform brilliantly to the rules (the rules in this case being the verisimilar dynamic unity of the character). And as long ago as 1927, E. M. Forster proposed that the test for what he called "round character" was that it was "capable of surprising in a convincing way" and in doing this possessed "the incalculability of life."[8]

How do we make such recognitions as we read, and what is the source in the writer's art for the mimetic power of such representations? The second question is probably unanswerable, though something may be gained by pondering it; the first question, at any rate, should come into clearer focus through some examples. Let us proceed from the unsurprising to the surprising, from pawn's march to knight's move.

A common mode of presenting character in the nineteenth-century novel, still occasionally used by novelists today, is a formal introductory portrait that defines the character's essential traits. As literary historians have noted, this practice derives from a minor nonnarrative genre popular in the seventeenth and eighteenth centuries, the Theophrastan character, which consists of a thumbnail sketch of a recognized social or vocational type (the country bumpkin, the pastor, the fop, and so forth). This is a convention that displays the familiar and the decipherable with a vengeance. Here, on the second page of Stendhal's *The Red and the Black* (1830), is the initial portrait of M. de Rênal, the pompous mayor of Verrières who will become Julien Sorel's employer and who will be cuckolded by Julien:

> At the sight of him all hats are quickly raised. His hair is graying and he is dressed in gray. He is a knight of several orders, he has a high forehead, an aquiline nose, and on the whole his face does not lack a certain regularity: one even finds, at first view, that it combines the dignity of a village mayor with that sort of appeal which can still be encountered in a man of forty-eight or fifty. But soon the visitor from Paris is shocked by a certain air of self-satisfaction and complacency mingled with a hint of limitation and unoriginality. One feels finally that this man's talent is limited to seeing that he is paid exactly what is owed him, and to paying on his part as late as possible when it is he that owes.
> Such is the mayor of Verrières, M. de Rênal.
> (I:l; my translation)

Everything about the mayor is related to social and characterological stereotypes. He has "that sort of appeal" we are all expected by experience to associate with certain men pushing fifty (and the indicative "that," reflecting an assumption of shared familiar knowledge, occurs frequently in these nineteenth-century thumbnail portraits). He has the smugness and provinciality of a small-town mayor, the narrowly calculating monetary habits of a perfect bourgeois, even a concert of gray hair and gray wardrobe to match the drab propriety of his life. Only the aquiline nose and the high forehead are a perfunctory effort to give him some individual physical traits. It is no wonder that the urbane narrator, who has assumed the stance of conducting a Parisian visitor on a tour of Verrières, can tightly tie up the whole package in an ostentatious ribbon: "Such is the mayor of Verrières, M. de Rênal."

The mayor is, I suppose, one variety of what E. M. Forster would call "flat character," a kind of character necessary to the artistic economy of the narrative;

Stendhal can afford to box him for public presentation in this fashion because no surprises will be required of him. Is such a procedure, with all its reliance on stereotype, antimimetic? At first thought, stereotypes may seem intrinsically unrealistic, but a little reflection will suggest that they are often approximations rather than misrepresentations of reality and that no one can get along without them. Baruch Hochman reminds us that relating individual character to general types is one of the principal mental operations we use in order to know people in real experience, and so the recourse to general types in fiction actually simulates a cognitive process repeatedly employed outside of reading.[9] Let us say we meet a bearded young man in a tie-dyed T-shirt, faded jeans, and sandals, with a little ponytail. A sixties type, we say to ourselves, a belated flower child. The stereotype calls to mind a whole cluster of associated traits, and we use it as an instrument of knowledge that enables us to "decipher" the individual by relating him to general categories. If all we see of the young man with the ponytail is what is caught by the passing eye in the street, there is an end to the matter; he remains a stereotype, like a flat character in a novel. Should we engage him in conversation, or actually enter into a continuing relationship with him, the stereotype might conceivably be confirmed (hence its initial function as an approximation); might require minor or major modifications; might need to be rejected altogether (if, for example, we discovered that the young man, despite appearances, was an investor in the stock market or a genetic engineer). A fiction with no dependable stereotypes would be radically disorienting, and that is indeed one way of describing the uncompromising iconoclasm of certain modernist writers like Kafka and Beckett. In the realist tradition, the approximation that is the stereotype serves as a foil of clear decipherability against which are played the more dynamic and more elusive major characters, for whom mere approximation will not do. What also sometimes happens is that the stereotypical character in the end manages to step outside the cage of stereotype. *The Red and the Black* offers the most instructive examples of the rendering of elusive unity in contrast to the stereotypical secondary character; for an instance of the self-transcendence of stereotype, we will have to look beyond the novels of Stendhal.

A few pages after the initial portrait of M. de Rênal, his wife is introduced—it should be noted, without the benefit of any thumbnail sketch. Instead, we see her in action, strolling with her husband and her three small sons, suddenly alarmed when her eleven-year-old threatens to climb up on a parapet. The narrator's sole initial comment is that she "appeared to be a woman of thirty, but still quite pretty." The age and the prettiness are needed narrative data because both will figure in her subsequent affair with Julien. Why doesn't the narrator simply tell us that she was thirty instead of saying that she looked thirty? If he knows that M. de Rênal is a knight of several orders, surely he could know Mme. De Rênal's exact age. It is a momentary renunciation of omniscience that goes hand in hand with his refusal to package Mme. de Rênal for us as he has just packaged her husband: we are kept on the outside, reminded that what we can know of this woman is a matter of inference from appearances, gestures, and speech. Her initial gestures show her as a solicitous mother calling her boy away from the parapet, and a loyal, indeed subservient, wife, patiently listening to her husband's tirade and praising him. He is incensed because a liberal Parisian journalist has arrived in town to investigate the local poorhouse and hospital for which he is overseer. The mayor expresses indignation to his wife over the scandalous articles such a fellow might place in the liberal newspapers. To which Mme. de Rênal, in what is only her second piece of dialogue in the novel, responds: "You don't read them, my dear" (I:2). The wonderful thing about these words is that we can't be sure how to take them. They may betray nothing more than naïveté, and that is surely how the husband construes them. They may conceal an ironic superiority of the demure wife to the fuming husband, her supposed naïveté perhaps exploited as a self-protective mask. Or they may reflect something we could call the incipience of ironic consciousness, in which the naïveté about politics and public opinion bears the seed of a cool shrewdness of perception that sets off the resourceful wife from her limited husband. In immediate context, the first of these three readings seems the most plausible—Mme. de Rênal has already been described as speaking "timidly" to her husband. But we read character developmentally, so that later discoveries compel a reconsideration of earlier views; and Mme. de Rênal's later behavior as Julien's passionate mistress exhibits a subtlety and a capacity for fine manipulation that make us suspect the presence of the ironist within the guise of the naive provincial wife.

These half-dozen words of dialogue, then, are a moment of formidably rich mimesis: the character's statement offers a revealing glimpse of those teasing ambiguities of motive and identity working in the frame of social institution about which we are obliged endlessly to infer in our lives outside of reading. Our recognition of the authority of the representation has to depend finally not on any internal mechanisms of the narrative but on a matching of experience and reading. Whatever we have gleaned from experience about men and women, marriage and politics, veiled irony as a weapon of the powerless, is instantaneously scanned as we imaginatively reconstruct the exchange between the spouses, and, if everything fits, this background of experiential knowledge confirms the rightness of the moment.

How did Stendhal manage to *know* this about Mme. de Rênal when he invented (writing, as a matter of fact, at breakneck speed) this line for her? Any explanation will remain highly conjectural, but it is important to note where no explanation is to be found. There is surely nothing in the structural necessities or formal requirements of the novel that could bring the writer to this moment of subtle comic illumination. And though as a novelist he must work with linguistic and literary convention, it is hard to imagine how convention, or even the swerving from convention, could in itself lead to such an insight. If we look beyond the formal configurations of the text to the man that produced them, we will find scant support for a mystique of the writer as a special repository of wisdom. Stendhal was in fact a shrewdly intelligent observer (something that could not be asserted of a good many great writers), but, particularly in his relations with women, he exhibited an astonishing capacity for repeated self-delusion that led to a long string of painful pratfalls and protracted frustrations. The case of Stendhal is exemplary. Between the unpredictable pattern of illumination in the work and the touching human foibles of the life, one is compelled to conclude that when fictional invention is going well, it is an activity that "privileges" the writer in some uncanny way: in the incandescence of the imagination that produces good fiction, elements of knowledge and bits of perception variously collected, many of them no doubt stored subliminally in the mind of the writer, coalesce, take on revelatory form in the speech and acts of imaginary personages. It is as if the very process of writing allowed the writer to tap unguessed levels of his own self, to achieve a kind of nonvolitional heightening of ordinary insight, as, analogously, the process of free association in psychoanalysis is supposed to do.

Fiction, then, involves above all an imaginative intercourse between the experience of the writer, beautifully focused as it would not be elsewhere, and the experience of the reader, which is both necessary to recognize adequately what the writer has produced and capable of being deepened by what the work of fiction offers. A. D. Nuttall nicely characterizes what has coalesced in the achieved fiction as a set of persuasive possibilities, probing hypotheses about human lives: "The fiction evokes from us, as we entertain the hypothesis, all the human energies and powers, the incipient commitments and defenses which occur in experiential knowing, but are absent from cool, conceptual knowing."[10] Such knowing, he goes on to say, is acquired through a gradual process of deepening and intensification, both in life and in the sequence of episodes that constitutes the work of fiction.

Mme. de Rênal, even though she is kept offstage for long stretches in The Red and the Black, provides an apt illustration of such a process of progressive revelation. Once she has fallen in love, the narrator observes that "her soul was entering unknown territory" (des pays inconnus), and Stendhal's characterization of her might be described as a continual, plausible destabilizing of any fixity of character we might at first have been tempted to attach to her. First she is compliant wife and devoted mother, then passionate mistress, then also cool actress in the interests of her love, then contrite penitent, and at the very end, passionate mistress again. But this instability is plausible because we sense certain common denominators, not easily specified, through all her changes. These would include: a spontaneity of feeling, a capacity for selfless devotion, a loyalty to her own emotions and to what she perceives as her values, a responsiveness or even malleability which sometimes has the look of passivity but is never quite that. There are, to be sure, other, less sympathetic ways of describing her character. Some critics, for example, have seen in her a morbid dependency exhibited first in her relationship with her husband and then with Julien. Different readings of this sort are possible both because we bring different predispositions and different backlogs of experience to the text and because the manifestations of character in fiction as in life leave a large margin of ambiguity.

What is important for our concern with the dynamic unity of character is that most readers intuit some set of common denominators, though they may debate over their precise nature.

It should be stressed that this dynamic complexity of character is relational and not just a matter of the individual self. A final example from The Red and the Black, one of the small, subtle knight's moves in the novel, will illustrate this relational dimension. After M. de Rênal has received an anonymous letter denouncing his wife and Julien, he confronts her, and in a conversation that goes on for two hours, she manages through the most ingenious histrionic contrivances to allay his suspicions, to make him feel guilty for having entertained them, and altogether to exhaust the poor man. In summarizing this interview, the narrator observes: "Once or twice, during this grand scene, Mme. De Rênal was on the verge of experiencing a certain sympathy for the emphatically real distress of this man, who for twelve years had been her friend [ami]. But true passion is selfish" (I:21). A momentary door is opened here on an unsuspected horizon: the possibility that such a man, now rendered helpless, might tempt such a woman to sympathy. This perception has that revelatory rightness of which I spoke earlier. M. de Rênal, mayor and man, is no doubt pompous, overbearing, conceited, obtuse, but all that does not preclude the possibility of a thread of companionship in the fabric of their marriage: he has been, after all, her ami. It seems equally right that the impulse of compassion is no more than a fleeting temptation: "But true passion is selfish." Note that the reversal is effected through the introduction of a moral maxim—of the sort, in fact, that Stendhal previously had put together in De l'Amour.

Although fictional character does not offer an abstract, conceptual kind of knowledge, the writer may draw on such knowledge to support his perception of character. Mme. de Rênal is splendidly individual, as her momentary turn of sympathy toward her obnoxious husband demonstrates, but the behavior of the individual can also be expected to conform in some ways to the laws of what Stendhal, with his roots in the eighteenth-century French philosophic tradition, conceived as a generally valid moral psychology. Most ages have their equivalents of such a body of knowledge. (Some version of Freudianism would probably serve for our own era.) To make character entirely contingent on general precepts would be to reduce fiction to didactic illustration, but as an ancillary device, the general principles enable writers to link the "incalculability of life" manifested in individual character with the elements of recurrence and typicality that allow us to decipher experience.

So far, I have stressed dynamic contradiction, subtlety, the capacity to surprise convincingly as measures of the mimetic force of character. We are all complicated creatures, but both introspection and observation of others suggest that we are not always or only complicated, and this is an understanding that is also registered in fictional mimesis. There are, that is to say, fictional characters that seem lifelike not in being complex but rather in being intensely, quite simply, themselves. The comic grotesque figures in Dickens and Smollett, those walking synecdoches, embodiments of a recurrent tic or metaphor, are not an abandonment of verisimilitude but bold stylizations that catch the terrible, absurd simplicity to which some people can reduce their lives—and so it may be a little misleading to call them "flat" characters. The realistic representation of simplicity of character is not, moreover, restricted to comic figures. There is a kind of serious character in which the sheer intensity of being consistently oneself becomes as compelling a hypothesis of human possibility as complexity in another kind of character. Let me offer an example which also illustrates the transcendence of stereotypes that is often produced by the momentum of fictional imagination in the realist novel.

Balzac is one of the most shameless traders in stereotype among the great nineteenth-century novelists. As a result, there are passages in his books that many of us today have to read in a spirit of camp as resounding expressions of the kitsch of his era. Nevertheless, he remains a major realist not only in his representation of places and processes and social institutions but also of character. His *Splendeurs et misères des courtisanes* (1847), a novel which in its most widely available English translation is called, with a certain music-hall jingle, *A Harlot High and Low*, provides a particularly instructive instance of a movement through stereotype to verisimilar characterization. The harlot in question is Esther Gobseck, the dazzling young woman who is Balzac's most memorable version of a nineteenth-century French stereotype of which he was particularly fond—*la belle Juive*, the beautiful Jewess. In one great set piece which is a kind of hymn to the pseudoscientific

racism of his age, he stresses the potency of genetically transmitted traits, even when the stock has been transported from one climate to another, and then associates Esther's beauty and her glowing sensuality with the brilliant azure of the Mediterranean skies, the smoldering sands of the desert, the rattle of Oriental tambourines, the sultriness of the seraglio (in all this rather extravagantly confusing the Hebrew Bible with *The Thousand and One Nights*). This cultural stereotype is crossbred with another one: the Whore with the Golden Heart, subspecies, True-Loving Courtesan. In a society of relentless self-seeking, Esther is the one person capable of total selfless devotion to the man she loves. This trait is an absolute given of her personality from the first pages of the novel; nothing she can undergo will induce her to swerve from it in the least degree.

The double stereotyping of Esther is reinforced by a characteristic Balzacian propensity to represent the character through a series of mythological images, sometimes actually arranging her as he describes her in iconographic poses. Thus, this "sublimist type of Asiatic beauty" is variously Mary Magdalen, the Madonna, and, with a switch of cultural spheres, Venus herself. These sundry stereotypes are much less defensible as approximations than, say, the social stereotypes Stendhal invokes in representing M. de Rênal because, deriving from literary and cultural conventions, they are fantasy projections of the mysterious Other (*la belle Juive*), sentimental simplifications (the Whore with the Golden Heart), and in sum, they seek less to understand than to heighten or monumentalize contemporary figures by assimilating them to mythic archetypes. In historical retrospect, all this may have a certain amusement value, but it is obviously not why we still read Balzac.

It might seem that Esther Gobseck as a plausible hypothesis of a real woman could not possibly extricate herself from the weight of stereotypical bric-a-brac with which the novelist has loaded her. In fact, she does, quite remarkably. Let us see how before speculating why. At first, she appears to be merely a pretty pawn manipulated by the sinister Vautrin, masquerading as a Spanish priest. Her absolute devotion to her lover Lucien—Vautrin's protégé—fits her nicely for this role of perfect passivity. From the moment Vautrin determines that she must give herself to the odious Baron de Nucingen in order to get the money needed for Lucien's social ascent, she begins to exhibit qualities of spunkiness, of self-protective shrewdness, at least in relation to the baron, that make her more believable as a precociously seasoned prostitute fanatically in love and utterly trapped by social circumstances.

Esther's great self-revelation, however, is posthumous. In the third of the four parts of the novel, after she has committed suicide and Lucien has been thrown into prison accused of complicity in her death, a letter written by Esther to Lucien on the morning of her death, delivered to his address after his arrest, falls into the hands of the police. Some quotation will be necessary to suggest the flavor of the letter—and it is eminently a text with a flavor—but since it goes on for five pages, a few excerpts will have to suffice. Balzac's punctuation here abounds in suspension points, presumably to indicate the broken, zigzag rhythm of Esther's last communication, so I will indicate my elisions by suspension points with brackets around them. Esther sits with a miniature of Lucien done on ivory, promising to send it with the letter. Then she thinks of Clothilde de Grandlieu, the flat-chested, unprepossessing young woman of good family whom Lucien seeks to marry in order to further his social ambitions.

> This portrait, my darling, hide it, don't give it to anyone . . . unless as a present it can win you the heart of that walking lath wearing dresses, that Clothilde de Grandlieu, who will make you black and blue when you sleep, her bones are so sharp. . . . Yes, I agree to that, I would still be good for something as when I was alive. Ah! to give you pleasure, or if it had just made you laugh, I'd have held myself close to a fire with an apple in my mouth to roast it for you! [. . .]
>
> Don't you see, I mean to make a beautiful corpse, I shall lie down, I shall stretch out in bed, I shall *pose* myself, eh! Then I shall press the berry against the soft palate, and I won't be disfigured either by convulsion, or by a ridiculous posture [. . .]
>
> You offered me a whole life the day before yesterday when you told me that if Clothilde still refused you, you would marry me. It would have been a calamity for both of us. I would have been all the more dead, so to speak; for deaths may be more or less bitter. Society would never have accepted us [. . .]
>
> Who will part your hair the way I did? Bah! I don't want to think about anything to do with life any longer, I have only five minutes left, I give them to God; don't be jealous of Him, my sweet angel, I want to talk to Him about you, ask Him

> to make you happy in return for my death and my punishment in the next world. It's such a nuisance to have to go to hell, I would have liked to see the angels and find out whether they are like you . . . [11]

Even in excerpt, one scarcely needs the context of the novel as a whole to see the effectiveness of the letter. Esther, scant minutes away from self-destruction, cannot suppress a jealous swipe at her skinny rival (she herself, needless to say, has a voluptuous figure), whose bones are so sharp they will bruise Lucien in bed. In one breath, her satiric language reveals the feisty young tart; in the next, the horrendous picture of roasting an apple in her mouth suggests her fanatic devotion, not without a strong tincture of masochism, to the feckless Lucien. (At this point, there is a strong resonance with what has preceded in the novel because in effect she *has* been roasting herself for Lucien's pleasure.) Then we encounter the exquisitely feminine narcissism of Esther's contemplation of suicide. (Her lover exhibits his own style of narcissism which is a good deal less engaging.) Through all her brief life, she has had only her beauty to trade on, and so it seems powerfully right that even in suicide she should be concerned to pose herself for a perfect death, with no disfigurement, anticipating the touch against the palate of the rare, painless poison as a sensual fulfillment.

Alternately spunky, self-sacrificing, and theatrical, Esther is also capable of shrewd perception, as in her comment that no happy ending was possible for them because society would never have accepted Lucien's marriage to a kept woman. It is Lucien, not she, who, as she understands, desperately needs society. The last paragraph about God and the angels, which occurs just before she signs the letter, is a wonderful climax of self-revelation. Before the moment of death, she recalls an intimate gesture of amorous solicitude: "Who will part your hair the way I did?" Then she must excuse herself for devoting her last minutes to prayer by begging her lover not to be jealous of God: even confronting eternity, she can, after all, imagine things only with the reflexes of someone whose life has been defined by passion, jealousy, the threat of sexual rivalry. Heaven and hell themselves are conceived in the image of her unflagging devotion to her "angelic" Lucien, though the reader is sharply aware that her lover is in fact a will-less instrument of the satanic Vautrin.

What is this posthumous letter doing in the penultimate section of Balzac's novel? It plays no real role

in the plot; thematically, it does no more than reinforce an obvious irony: the life of its intended recipient has been shattered, and he, too, will commit
suicide, not out of the pride of passion like Esther
but out of the weakness of despair. Any claim, then,
that this revelation of character primarily serves a
function in the internal mechanisms of the narrative is implausible. But the functionally superfluous
passage is really what fictional character is all about.
W. J. Harvey, in a happy phrase, has observed that
character tends to exhibit "a surplus margin of gratuitous life,"[12] and this encore performance by a
dead and buried Esther illustrates the aptness of that
formula in the most literal way. From the viewpoint
of the novelist, what is involved is a kind of zest in
the sheer "doing" of Esther that has no strong relation to the structural necessities of the novel. One
easily imagines Balzac entering into the pleasure, the
powerful imaginative momentum, of embodying (it
would be nice to be able to say ensouling) this individual woman, here made more splendidly individual in her last moments than she was at any point
earlier in the novel. The stereotypes to which he had
frequent recourse before are set aside like a discarded scaffolding as he invents these last individual
gestures of an arresting human possibility, Esther
Gobseck.

The answering pleasure we experience as readers
stems from the perception of a distinctive presence,
and subtlety or complexity does not play much of a
role in this perception. Granted, the character of Esther is not monolithic, as the rapid, psychologically
plausible leaps in the letter from attitude to attitude
indicate. But what engages the imagination, I think,
is not the element of surprise that one encounters
in novelists like Stendhal, Tolstoy, James, Proust,
Nabokov, but rather the fact that Esther is so intensely herself: the traits, the motives, might all have
been predicted from her previous representations in
the novel; the pleasure of discovery is in the verisimilar details of speech and gesture which manifest
those traits and motives so vividly. If one wants to
use a spatial metaphor for Esther and the whole
class of fictional characters who resemble her, one
should say they are neither round nor flat, but deep.
If the fascination of human types is an end in itself
(and the novel generically reflects such an assumption), the deepened experiential knowing of the
imagined individual is a process that justifies itself,

and for which no formal limits or functions can be
prescribed.

The sense of illuminating connection we feel as
readers between fictional character and real human
possibility does not depend on a particular narrative
technique. Ultimately, I suppose, it flows from the
kind of leap of intuition by the writer that I tried to
describe earlier. Some writers realize such intuition
through a purely external presentation of character.
Balzac generally restricts himself to outside views of
Esther (as he does with most of his characters), and
then uses the final letter as a kind of soliloquy. Stendhal, on the other hand, renders Mme. de Rênal (and
his other major characters) through mixed means
of presentation: we are offered summaries of her
thoughts and feelings, the third-person miming of
inward speech that is called *style indirect libre*, the
narrator's analysis of her motives and acts, and the
report of her speech and actions. These shifting techniques of presentation may help suggest a quality of
dynamic fluidity in the character, but that is by no
means the only way to achieve such an effect.

As a matter of literary history, the novel devotes
much more attention than do earlier narrative genres
to the minute emotional and cognitive fluctuations
of inner states, and in a later chapter we will consider
in detail the technical operations of this attention. Beginning in the eighteenth century with the epistolary
novels of Richardson, Sterne's fantastically associative narrative, the emotional perspectivism of novels
like Prévost's *Manon Lescaut* and Diderot's *The Nun*,
the novel perfects subtle new techniques for representing the movements of consciousness—new,
though not without certain remarkable anticipations
in biblical and classical literature. The most supple of
these is the *style indirect libre*, though by the first
decades of our own century some writers would step
beyond it to interior monologue when immediacy,
difficulty, and the sheer sense of process became central mimetic values. I would guess that many readers of the great realist novels carry around in their
heads little anthologies of perfectly realized moments of experiential realism, novelistic equivalents
of the hand-held camera: Kitty ascending the great
stairs to the ball early in *Anna Karenina* with eyes
open to the wondrous glitter of the scene; Emma Bovary at the end of all her resources, running through
the woods with the trees spinning around her night-
marishly; the child Pip on the second page of *Great*

Expectations confronted by the looming figure of a fierce man dressed in gray, his body lacerated, one leg in a great iron. It should be recognized, however, that these are only one set of possibilities for the realism of character; elsewhere — for example, in the novels of Fielding, Scott, Mark Twain, Trollope — such realism is achieved with little or no representation of the kinesis of consciousness.

It is important to keep this variety in mind because it will help us to see the continuities between the mimesis of character in the novel and in earlier and other genres. In fact, the supposedly pure conventionality of novelistic realism has been argued on historical grounds in the following terms: What we call the individual is a product of emergent capitalism, Protestantism, the breakdown of village society, the dissolution of the extended family, and so forth. It would have made no sense to a medieval person or to someone living in classical antiquity. The novel, then, does not represent men and women as they "really" are but rather gives us a historically conditioned, ideologically slanted conception of individual identity that may always have been partly illusory. In any event, its time is now passed and it will be replaced by some new notion of the serial self, the collective self, or whatever answers the requirements of a new era. The argument is by no means a foolish one. There were significant forces in intellectual and cultural history only recently in evidence around the year 1600 that put new value on the individual and that in the course of time would lead to a concept of the originality of the self which would have been unintelligible to earlier eras. Without such a concept, the novel would scarcely have been what it proved to be. And yet, it strains credibility to imagine that the individual is solely a product of transient historic conditioning. There are, perhaps, human societies in which a person feels himself to be no more than a component of some corporate identity, but the evidence of the Western literary tradition beginning with the Greeks and the Hebrews suggests that at least in this tradition there have been no close approximations of this sort of human beehive. The individual has certainly been modified through the ages but not rebuilt from the ground up.

What enables us to become imaginatively engaged with characters in works of fiction produced in the early nineteenth century, the turn of the seventeenth century, or even the eighth century B.C.E.?

Obviously, even a moderately sophisticated reader has to be capable of a certain amount of historical reconstruction. Jane Austen's heroines live long before feminism, the sexual revolution, the electronic environment, the drug culture, and their quandaries will seem nonsense to a late twentieth-century reader unless he or she is able to imagine the different moral coordinates that defined the life of a young woman in rural England during the time of the Regency. Nevertheless, many people still read Jane Austen, quite avidly, not as an exercise of archaeological reconstruction because, for all the drastic historical changes, there remain strong and meaningful continuities between the human possibilities so finely represented in her novels and the human possibilities with which we still contend in our lives.

Let me illustrate the point with two episodes involving fathers and sons that are historically removed from us by nearly three millennia. The first is from the sixth book of the *Iliad*. Hektor, in full battle gear, has been taking leave of his wife, Andromache, before going out to fight the Achaians.

> So speaking glorious Hektor held out his arms to his baby,
> who shrank to his fair-girdled nurse's bosom
> screaming, and frightened at the aspect of his father,
> terrified as he saw the bronze and the crest with its horse-hair,
> nodding dreadfully, as he thought, from the peak of the helmet.
> Then his beloved father laughed out, and his honoured mother,
> and at once glorious Hektor lifted from his head the helmet
> and laid it in all its shining upon the ground. Then taking
> up his dear son he tossed him about in his arms, and kissed him. . . .
>
> (VI:466–474; Lattimore translation)

The heroes and heroines of the Homeric epics are not yet the highly particularized individuals of the realist novel. It is not only that individuating details of personal history are usually much sparser but, more crucially, that these figures belong to a much more stable world of fixed roles and values. The heroic epithet, however much it served the technical needs of oral-formulaic composition, is a key expression of this stability. Like an eternal force of nature, Hektor is repeatedly "glorious Hektor," and the family relations are preassigned and universalized, "beloved father," "honoured mother." These elements of distance from our own cultural situation need to be registered, even in a passage which, out of context, looks as though it could serve the disarmament movement of the 1980s. (Homer's poem, of course, actually celebrates martial virtues, though with a pained consciousness of the cost they exact.)

Yet with all that has changed, some things have not changed, and that is precisely what enables us to be moved by these lines 2,700 years after their composition in a world alien to ours. The terror of the startled, uncomprehending child; the affection of the laughing father; the throat-catching contrast between human father revealing himself to his son and terrible man of war, features hidden beneath horsehair and bronze—none of this needs explaining to us because we still are conscious of many of the same things about fathers and children, about the terrible tension between familial love and the savagery of war. It need not be claimed that human nature is fixed and unchanging, but after three millennia, sufficiently powerful continuities persist in the literary representation of human realities to make us feel when we read that writers then and now are engaged with many of the same fundamental objects of representation.

My other illustration is an equally memorable moment from ancient literature, in a narrative written perhaps 150 years or more before the *Iliad* (the dating remains quite uncertain), several hundred miles to the east. King David's throne has been usurped by his son Absalom, and David has fled to Transjordan with fighting men still loyal to him. When the rebels and the loyalists are about to meet in battle, the aging king, who will not himself now enter the fray, gives explicit instructions that no harm be done to "the lad Absalom." However, David's hard-bitten commander-in-chief Joab concludes that paternal sentiment should not be allowed to interfere with the need to be rid of this dangerous adversary, and when Absalom is caught in the oak tree, Joab himself stabs him to death. In a spectacular scene, David sits waiting between the two gates of the city while a watchman overhead makes out first one runner, then another hurrying toward them. When the second of these responds to David's anxious question by at last conveying the news of Absalom's death, the king mounts to the chamber over the gate,

weeping as he climbs and crying out these words: "O my son Absalom! my son Absalom! Would that I had died in thy place, O Absalom, my son, my son!" (2 Samuel 19:33).[13]

Although biblical narrative often uses distinctive techniques that involve subtleties of perception which may easily be lost on later readers, David's words here readily move us without any guide. Altogether, David is more of an individualized character, full of dynamic psychological contradictions, than any of the Homeric heroes. Elsewhere a master of poised, politic speech, and of poetic eloquence, bereavement here reduces him to a stammer of anguish. We may no longer live in a society where lines of relation, as in the David story, are defined by polygamy, vendetta, anointed monarchy, exercise of cultic functions, and public sexual possession of a rival's concubines; but the bond between father and son is a biological given of our shared human condition that continues to dictate essentially the same spectrum of emotional and moral possibilities. In the first part of his story David is chiefly a public—and hidden—person; we begin to see the private David only after the catastrophe of his adultery with Bathsheba and his vicarious murder of Uriah in 2 Samuel 11. Absalom's rebellion forces an absolute conflict between David's public and private roles. When he learns of his son's death, the public man collapses, leaving only the helpless old father with his unbearable loss. David's long gasp of pain rendered in these few repeated words addressed to a dead son seems as immediate as though it were written yesterday.

The claim I am making is a fairly modest one, which it seems to me is variously and abundantly confirmed by the evidence of five millennia or more of cultural artifacts: not that there is an immutable human nature but that there are certain lines of persistence that cross over from one era and one culture to another. Much about the way we perceive ourselves and the world manifestly changes as society, language, ideology, and technology change; but we also continue to share much as creatures born of woman, begotten by man, raised with siblings, endowed with certain appetites, conscious of our own mortality, confronting nature from our various locations in culture. To say that humanity continues to hold some things in common across the ages is not to imply that what is held in common is confidently known. On the contrary, the most arresting writers, even in the ancient period, often treat the human awareness of being in the world, in the family, in society, in history, as something to puzzle over endlessly. The characters and life situations of the narratives of different eras speak to us not because they reflect a knowledge which never changes but rather because they express a set of enigmas with which we continue to wrestle.

My examples from antiquity highlight the aspect of continuity in the mimetic enterprise of literary tradition. The complementary, and necessary, perspective of literary history concentrates on evolution and transformation. Formal analysis of literature in turn focuses on conventions and technical devices, in which quite often the shifting of aesthetic values and cultural codes is most perceptible. But what needs emphasis at this late point in the course of criticism is that literature cannot be adequately accounted for merely as a set of changing and arbitrary codes. What is left out in such a view is the powerful capacity of the literary work to refer its readers to a complex order of moral, emotional, and psychological realities. A criticism with no coherent vocabulary for discussing that power of reference will provide only a feeble guide to literature.

Literary fashions, generic constraints, cultural assumptions, manifestly change from era to era, but literary tradition constitutes itself as a trans-historical human community. In fact, a good many of the cultural codes invoked in literature may not be arbitrary but rather may be stylizations of certain perdurable aspects of human existence perpetuated from one era to another—perpetuated precisely because they answer so well to what we share as people. It is not only that later writers, by allusion and imitation, converse with the writers of earlier ages, but that through this polyphonous conversation all of them point toward shared objects of representation, turning and turning the sundry artifices of language to reveal the incalculability of life.

Notes

1. Denis Donoghue, "The Limits of Language," *The New Republic*, July 7, 1986, pp. 40–45.
2. I have discussed this issue in *Don Quixote* at length in *Partial Magic: The Novel as a Self-Conscious Genre* (Berkeley and Los Angeles, 1975), Chapter 1.
3. For an incisive critique of this general trend, see Hugh Bredin, "The Displacement of Character in Narrative Theory," *British Journal of Aesthetics*, Autumn 1982.
4. Hélène Cixous, "The Character of 'Character,'" *New Literary History* 5 (1974).
5. Tzvetan Todorov, *The Poetics of Prose*, trans. Richard Howard (Ithaca, 1977), p. 82. In fairness to Todorov, it should be said that by the 1980s he renounced many of these early extremist views.
6. A. D. Nuttall, *A New Mimesis: Shakespeare and the Representation of Reality* (London, 1983), p. 53.
7. Baruch Hochman, *Character in Literature* (Ithaca, 1985), p. 50.
8. E. M. Forster, *Aspects of the Novel* (New York, 1927), p. 78.
9. Hochman, p. 46.
10. Nuttall, p. 75.
11. Balzac, *Splendeurs et misères des courtisanes*, ed. Pierre Barberis (Paris, 1973), pp. 431–436 (my translation).
12. W. J. Harvey, *Character in the Novel* (Ithaca, 1968), p. 187.
13. I have introduced small emendations into the King James Version for the sake of accuracy.

The Uses of Psychology

Bernard Paris

Critics have often applied psychological theories in the genetic context to get at the author's psyche, and in the affective context to get at the reader's. Bernard Paris argues that these theories can also be applied in the mimetic context to help us understand fictional characters, including "implied authors." Like Robert Alter, Paris is fully aware of the objections to treating fictional characters as if they were real people, but he finds the arguments on the other side more persuasive, especially in the case of "realistic" novels where "representation" is the dominant mode. As his later work on Shakespeare indicates, Paris would include certain kinds of drama here as well. Citing such proponents of realism as Erich Auerbach, Georg Lukács, and Ian Watt, Paris claims that with the great novels of psychological realism "thematic and formal analysis can't begin to do justice to the psychological portraiture which is often the greatest achievement of these works." We need, instead, a mimetic criticism deploying the insights of modern psychology. Although he later argues specifically for the uses of "third force" psychology associated with such figures as Karen Horney and Abraham Maslow, Paris presents in his opening chapter a general defense of mimetic criticism and a rationale for applying psychological theories to fictional characters "as though they were real people."

Norman Holland finds it "hard to see how a psychology [can] deal with a work of art *qua* work of art," and observes that in practice psychoanalytic critics "do not."[1] Psychology cannot consider works of art in themselves, he argues, because psychology as such is concerned "not with literature, but with minds" (p. 293). "Any psychological system," there-

---

Reprinted by permission of the author from Bernard Paris, *A Psychological Approach to Fiction*, pp. 1–13, 23–27. Copyright © 1974 by Indiana University Press. A part of the chapter has been omitted, and the notes have been renumbered.

fore, "must deal, not with works of art in isolation, but with works of art in relation to man's mind" (p. 151). The "three possible minds to which the psychological critic customarily refers" are the author's mind, a character's mind, and the audience's mind. It is only the study of the audience's mind, Holland feels, that can lead "to a bonafide method; the other two tend to confusion" (p. 294). I believe that there are two kinds of minds within realistic novels that can be studied in psychological terms: they are the minds of the implied authors and the minds of the leading characters.

Holland argues that "we should use psychology on our own real and lively reactions" to the work "rather than on the characters' fictitious minds" (p. 308). He feels that character study is useful and legitimate only when it is incorporated into our analysis of the audience's mind. Then it is seen to "identify 'latent impulses' of the characters which may be considered as stimuli to or projections of latent impulses of the audience" (p. 283). Character study is not legitimate when, as in most psychological criticism, it talks "about literary characters as though they were real people" (p. 296). Holland's strongest argument in support of this position is that "Homo Fictus and Homo Dramaticus do not so much what Homo Sapiens would do in similar circumstances, but what it is necessary for them to do in the logical and meaningful realities of the works of art in which they live" (pp. 305–306). The artist "hovers between *mimesis*, making like, and *harmonia*, the almost musical ordering of the events he depicts. . . . The psychoanalytic critic of character neglects the element of *harmonia*, the symbolic conceptions that must modify the mimetic" (p. 306). Other critics of literature have learned to avoid this mistake: ". . . as a plain matter of fact, most literary critics do not—any more—treat literary characters as real people" (p. 296).[2]

Holland is participating in what W. J. Harvey calls "the retreat from character" in modern criticism, a retreat which Harvey's book, *Character and the Novel*, is intended to halt. "What has been said about character" in the past forty years, Harvey observes, "has been mainly a stock of critical commonplaces used largely to dismiss the subject in order that the critic may turn his attention to other allegedly more important and central subjects—symbolism, narrative techniques, moral vision and the like."[3] In the criticism of realistic fiction this has been especially unfortunate, for "most great novels exist to reveal and

explore character" (p. 23). There are many reasons for this retreat, Harvey continues, the most important of which is the rise of the New Criticism:

> The New Criticism was centrally concerned to apply close and rigorous analytical methods to lyric poetry; it is noticeable how ill at ease its practitioners have been when they have approached the bulky, diffuse and variegated world of the novel. What we might expect is in fact the case; the new critic, when dealing with fiction, is thrown back upon an interest in imagery, symbolism or structural features which have little to do with characterization. (p. 200)

The danger that the critic of novels must now be warned against is not the neglect of *harmonia*, but the neglect of *mimesis*; for *harmonia* has had its due of late, and "a mimetic intention" was, after all, "the central concern of the novel until the end of the nineteenth century" (p. 205).

No study of character should ignore the fact that characters in fiction participate in the dramatic and thematic structures of the works in which they appear and that the meaning of their behavior is often to be understood in terms of its function within these structures. The less mimetic the fiction, the more completely will the characters be intelligible in terms of their dramatic and thematic functions; and even in highly realistic fiction, the minor characters are to be understood more functionally than psychologically. But, as Harvey points out, the authors of the great realistic novels "display an appetite and passion for life which threatens to overwhelm the formal nature of their art" (pp. 187–188). There is in such novels "a surplus margin of gratuitous life, a sheer excess of material, a fecundity of detail and invention, a delighted submergence in experience for its own sake" (p. 188). The result is "that characterization often overflows the strict necessities of form" (p. 188). This is especially true in the characterization of the protagonists, of "those characters whose motivation and history are most fully established, who conflict and change as the story progresses . . ." (p. 56). What we attend to in the protagonist's story "is the individual, the unique and particular case. . . . We quickly feel uneasy if the protagonist is made to stand for something general and diffused; the more he *stands for* the less he *is*" (p. 67). Though such characters have their dramatic and thematic functions, they are "in a sense . . . end-products"; we often feel that "they are what the novel exists for; it exists to reveal them" (p. 56).

The retreat from character of which Harvey complains has been in part a reaction against reading plays, stories, impressionistic novels, and other tightly structured or basically symbolic works as though they were realistic fiction. This has frequently resulted, ironically, in the study of realistic novels as though they were tightly structured or basically symbolic forms. In our avoidance of what Northrop Frye would call a low-mimetic provincialism, we have often failed to do justice to the low-mimetic forms themselves.

Fortunately, the most recent trend in literary criticism has been to emphasize the qualities that distinguish the literary modes and kinds from each other. In the study of narrative art, we are learning to appreciate a variety of forms and effects; and this, in turn, is enabling us to grasp the distinctive characteristics of each form with greater precision.[4] We are coming to see, among other things, that character is central in many realistic novels and that much of the characterization in such fiction escapes dramatic and thematic analysis and can be understood only in terms of its mimetic function. A careful examination of the nature of realistic fiction as modern criticism is coming to conceive it will show that in certain cases it *is* proper to treat literary characters as real people and that only by doing so can we fully appreciate the distinctive achievement of the genre.

The diversity of aesthetic theories and of critical approaches is in part a reflection of the multiplicity of values to be found in literature and in part a product of the varying interests and temperaments with which different critics come to literature. Not all approaches are equally valid: the most satisfying kind of criticism is that which is somehow congruent with the work and which is faithful to the distribution of interests in the work itself. The approach employed here attempts to stress values which are inherently important in realistic fiction and to make these values more accessible to us than they hitherto have been.

The primary values of fiction can be described in a variety of terms; I shall classify them as mimetic, thematic, and formal. Fiction is mainly concerned with the representation, the interpretation, and the aesthetic patterning of experience.[5] In different works and in different fictional modes the distribution of emphasis varies; and in some works one of these interests may be far more important than the others. When a work concerns itself seriously with more than one of

these interests, it must bring its various impulses into harmony if it is to be organically unified.

From the middle of the eighteenth to the beginning of the twentieth century, the novel attempted, by and large, to realize all of these values; but its primary impulse seems to have been the mimetic one. Henry James is reflecting not only his own taste, but the essential nature of the genre when he characterizes the novel as "a picture" and proclaims that "the only reason for the existence of a novel is that it does attempt to represent life."[6] It is not its interpretation of life or its formal perfection but its "air of reality (solidity of specification)" that James identifies as "the supreme virtue of a novel" (p. 14). Arnold Kettle distinguishes between the moral fable, which is dominated by "pattern" or "significance" and the novel, in which "pattern" is subordinate to "life." Despite a frequently strong commitment to thematic interests, the great realists, says Kettle, "are less consciously concerned with the moral significance of life than with its surface texture. Their talent is devoted first and foremost to getting life on to the page, to conveying across to their readers the sense of what life as their characters live it really feels like."[7]

The view of realistic fiction that we are developing is confirmed by such classic works on the subject as Ian Watt's *The Rise of the Novel* and Ereich Auerbach's *Mimesis*. Formal interests cannot be paramount in a genre that, as Watt describes it, "works by exhaustive presentation rather than by elegant concentration."[8] Like E. M. Forster, Watt sees "the portrayal of 'life by time' as the distinctive role which the novel has added to literature's more ancient preoccupation with portraying 'life by values'" (p. 22). The domain of the novel is the individual and his social relationships, and it tends to present its subject less in terms of ethical categories than in terms of chronological and causal sequences. The distinctive characteristics of the novel are, for Watt, its emphasis upon the particular, its circumstantial view of life, and its full and authentic reporting of experience (pp. 31–32).

To our statement that the novel's primary impulse is a mimetic one, we must add the qualification that the reality imitated is not general nature or the world of Ideas, but the concrete and temporal reality of modern empirical thought. The novel came into being in a world dominated by secularism and individualism, a world in which men were losing their belief in the supernatural and institutional bases of life. "Both the philosophical and the literary innovations," says Watt, "must be seen as parallel manifestations of a larger change—that vast transformation of Western civilization since the Renaissance which has replaced the unified world picture of the Middle Ages with another very different one—one which presents us, essentially, with a developing but unplanned aggregate of particular individuals having particular experiences at particular times and at particular places" (p. 31).

For Erich Auerbach the foundations of modern realism are first, "the serious treatment of everyday reality, the rise of more extensive and socially inferior human groups to the position of subject matter for problematic-existential representation"; and, second, "the embedding of random persons and events in the general course of contemporary history, the fluid historical background."[9] Throughout *Mimesis* Auerbach is concerned with the contrast between the classical moralistic and the problematic existential ways of presenting reality. The distinction is basically between the representation of life in terms of fixed canons of style and of ethical categories which are a priori and static, and a stylistically mixed, ethically ambiguous portrayal which probes "the social forces underlying the facts and conditions" that it presents (p. 27). The problematic existential perception of reality, which *Mimesis* exists to celebrate, is one that is informed by the insights of Historicism. It is characterized by an awareness that "epochs and societies are not to be judged in terms of a pattern concept of what is desirable absolutely speaking but rather in every case in terms of their own premises"; by "a sense of historical dynamics, of the incomparability of historical phenomena and of their constant inner mobility"; and by a "conviction that the meaning of events cannot be grasped in abstract and general forms of cognition" (p. 391).

It is evident that in fiction employing the classical moralistic perspective, interpretation will outweigh and, indeed, govern representation, whereas in fiction written from a problematic existential point of view the mimetic impulse will be predominant. In many realistic novels, however, the classical moralistic perspective continues to exist alongside of, and often in disharmony with, the concrete, "serio-problematic" representation of life. Auerbach observes that Balzac, for example, "aspires to be a classical moralist" but that "this suits neither his style nor his temperament" (pp. 422–423). In his novels "the clas-

sically moralistic element very often gives the impression of being a foreign body." It expresses itself in the narrator's "generalized apophthegms of a moral cast," which are "sometimes witty as individual observations," but which are often "far too generalized" and are sometimes "plain 'tripe'" (p. 422).

Realism for Auerbach means essentially social realism—the presentation of events in terms of the network of historical relations in which they exist and a concern for all of the forces at work, not simply for a limited, class-determined set of causes. His distinction between the categorical and the historistic views of experience applies just as readily to the presentation of character as it does to the rendering of society, though Auerbach himself has little to say about psychological realism. Representation is the primary interest of realistic fiction, and the two chief objects of representation are character and social milieu. Some novels are profoundly concerned with both character and society; others focus primarily on social or on psychological reality. Novels in which psychological realism predominates tend to present society from the point of view of the individual; novels of social realism often take a sociological rather than a psychological view of character.

Though realistic fiction is more concerned with mimesis than it is with theme and form the latter are, nonetheless, very important elements in the majority of novels. Indeed, one of the basic problems of the novel as a genre is that it attempts to integrate impulses which are disparate and often in conflict. The problematic existential portrayal of reality defies, by its very nature, authorial attempts at analysis and judgment. The great realists see and represent far more than they can understand. And, as Northrop Frye observes, "the realistic writer soon finds that the requirements of literary form and plausible content always fight against each other."[10] Form derives from generic conventions, and ultimately from mythic patterns, which are inherently unrealistic; realistic content obeys the laws of probability, of cause and effect, and belongs to a different universe of discourse. The integration of theme, form, and mimesis is an extremely difficult task.

Critics of realistic fiction, even some of those who best understand its nature, come to it demanding formal and thematic perfections which very few novels can achieve. The novel "may have a distinctive representational technique," says Ian Watt, "but if it is to be considered a valuable literary form it must also have, like any other literary form, a structure which is a coherent expression of all its parts" (p. 104). The novel, Watt feels, must "supplement its realism of presentation with a realism of assessment." If the interpretive element is weak "we shall be wholly immersed in the reality of the characters and their actions, but whether we shall be any wiser as a result is open to question" (p. 288). Arnold Kettle recognizes that "there are writers, and great ones, whose books have more vividness than wisdom, more vitality than significance"; but he feels that "the central core of any novel is what it has to say about life." Novels with more life than pattern, or in which life and pattern are not integrated, are wanting in the quality of their perception (pp. 14–16).

It is my impression that if we come to novels expecting moral wisdom and coherent teleological structures we are usually going to be disappointed. Such expectations are frequently aroused by the works themselves, and it is natural for the reader to want them fulfilled; but the mimetic impulse that dominates most novels often works against total integration and thematic adequacy. Even so, the novel is a valuable literary form. As Watt himself says, "In the novel, more perhaps than in any other literary genre, the qualities of life can atone for the defects of art . . ." (p. 301). The novel's weaknesses are in many cases the defects of its virtues, and its virtues are very great indeed. Some novels, of course, are integrated: they are usually those in which the interpretive element either is almost nonexistent or is incorporated into the mimesis. Such novels have coherent teleological structures, but they do not provide the kind of wisdom that Kettle, Watt, and many other critics seem to be looking for.

It is because they contain highly individualized characters or extremely detailed pictures of society that many novels lack total artistic integration. In novels of psychological realism (on which we shall focus here) there is a character-creating impulse which has its own inner logic and which tends to go its own way, whatever the implied author's formal and thematic intentions may be. As critics we demand, indeed, that the central characters of realistic fiction be like real people, that they have a life of their own beyond the control of their author. The novelist, says Harvey, "must accept his characters as asserting their human individuality and uniqueness in the face of all ideology (including his own limited point of view)" (p. 25). In realistic fiction, proclaims

Georg Lukács, "what matters is the picture conveyed by the work; the question to what extent this picture conforms to the views of the authors is a secondary consideration."[11] "A great realist," Lukács continues,

> . . . if the intrinsic artistic development of situations and characters he has created comes into conflict with his most cherished prejudices or even his most sacred convictions, will, without an instant's hesitation, set aside these his own prejudices and convictions and describe what he really sees, not what he would prefer to see. This ruthlessness towards their own subjective world-picture is the hall-mark of all great realists, in sharp contrast to the second-raters, who nearly always succeed in bringing their own *Weltanschauung* into "harmony" with reality. . . .
> (p. 11)

Lukács is chiefly concerned with the portrayal of social reality, but his observations apply also to the presentation of character:

> The characters created by the great realists, once conceived in the vision of their creator, live an independent life of their own; their comings and goings, their development, their destiny is dictated by the inner dialectic of their social and individual existence. No writer is a true realist—or even a truly good writer, if he can direct the evolution of his own characters at will.
> (p. 11)

The point I am trying to make has been most brilliantly developed by E. M. Forster, in his discussion of flat and round characters. "The novelist," he observes, "has a very mixed lot of ingredients to handle." He is telling a story ("life in time") which has a meaning ("life by values"). His story is "about human beings":

> The characters arrive when evoked, but full of the spirit of mutiny. For they have these numerous parallels with people like ourselves, they try to live their own lives and are consequently often engaged in treason against the main scheme of the book. They "run away," they "get out of hand": they are creations inside a creation, and often inharmonious towards it; if they are given complete freedom they kick the book to pieces, and if they are kept too sternly in check, they revenge themselves by dying, and destroy it by intestinal decay.[12]

What Forster has described here is the dilemma of the realistic novelist. If his characters are truly alive they will have a motivational life of their own and will tend to subvert the main scheme of the book. If he keeps his characters subordinated to their aesthetic and thematic functions, however, they will be lifeless puppets and his book will be flawless in a different and more serious way.

In their excellent book on narrative literature, Robert Scholes and Robert Kellogg recapitulate and refine many of our most recent insights into the nature of realistic fiction. Their division of characters into three types—aesthetic, illustrative, and mimetic—provides the best taxonomy that we have to date and offers a convenient way of formulating the thesis which I have been developing.

Characters should be understood in terms of the kind of function that they perform. Aesthetic types— "villains, ingénues, *ficelles*, choral characters, *nuntii*, and so on"—serve mainly to create formal patterns and dramatic impact. They have little inner depth or moral significance. Illustrative characters are most important in works governed by the classical moralistic perspective:

Illustration differs from representation in narrative art in that it does not seek to reproduce actuality but to present selected aspects of the actual, essences referable for their meaning not to historical, psychological, or sociological truth but to ethical and metaphysical truth.

Illustrative characters

. . . are concepts in anthropoid shape or fragments of the human psyche masquerading as whole human beings. Thus we are not called upon to understand their motivation as if they were whole human beings but to understand the principles they illustrate through their actions in a narrative framework. (p. 88)

Behind realistic fiction there is a strong "psychological impulse" that "tends toward the presentation of highly individualized figures who resist abstraction and generalization, and whose motivation is not susceptible to rigid ethical interpretation" (p. 101). When we encounter a fully drawn mimetic character "we are justified in asking questions about his motivation based on our knowledge of the ways in which real people are motivated" (p. 87).

There are aesthetic and illustrative types in realistic novels, of course, and in the central characters there is often a mixing of and a tension between illustrative, mimetic, and aesthetic functions. But in novels of psychological realism the main characters exist primarily as mimetic portraits whose intricacies escape the moral and symbolic meanings assigned to them. Many aspects of their characterization which are of little formal or thematic interest become very significant when we see them as manifestations of the characters' inner being, as part of the author's unfolding of character for its own sake.

The great gift of the psychological realists, then, even of the most intellectually proficient and ethically sensitive of them, is not in the interpretation but in the representation of the experience of their characters. Their characters may have important functions in the thematic and formal structures of the works in which they exist, but thematic and formal analysis cannot begin to do justice to the psychological portraiture which is often the greatest achievement of these works, and it frequently blinds us to the fact that the experience represented does not always sustain the dramatic and thematic effects for which the work is striving.

Ortega y Gasset contends that all of the

. . . psychological knowledge accumulated in the contemporary mind . . . is to no small degree responsible for the present failure of the novel. Authors that yesterday seemed excellent appear naive today because the present reader is a much better psychologist than the old author.[13]

This is true only if we judge the old authors primarily in terms of their analyses and assessments of their characters' behavior. Given the fact that the old authors were not necessarily gifted as analysts and moralists, that their value judgments were bound to be influenced by their own neuroses, and that the psychological theories available to them were inadequate to their insights, it was inevitable that their interpretations would be inferior to their representations of experience and that the beneficiaries of a more advanced psychological science would feel superior to them. If we do justice to their representations of character, however, we will see that they were excellent psychologists indeed, and that we need all of the resources of modern knowledge to understand and appreciate their achievement.

•　　•　　•

The question of what kind of illumination art—or, in our case, realistic fiction—*does* supply is too large to be dealt with completely here; but it is central to our concerns, and I shall attempt to offer a partial answer. If we have realism of presentation without realism of assessment, says Ian Watt, "we shall be wholly immersed in the reality of the characters and their actions, but whether we shall be any wiser as a result is open to question" (p. 288). Immersion in the inner reality of characters provides a kind of knowledge which is not wisdom, though it may be the basis of wisdom, and which realistic fiction is especially fitted to supply. If we understand by phenomenology the formulation of "an experience of the world, a contact with the world which precedes all" judgment and explanation,[14] we can say that highly mimetic fiction gives us a phenomenological knowledge of reality. It gives us an immediate knowledge of how the world is experienced by the individual consciousness and an understanding of the inner life in its own terms. It enables us to grasp from within the phenomena which psychology and ethics treat from without.

As Wayne Booth has observed, when we read novels in which there are deep inside views "that . . . give the reader an effect of living thought and sensation" (p. 324), we tend to abandon judgment and analysis. When we are immersed in the "indomitable mental reality" (p. 323) of a character, we adopt his perspective and experience his feelings as though they were our own. This kind of experience, which is one of the great gifts of fiction, is acceptable to Booth only when the character's perspective is, in his view, an ethically acceptable one. It is very dangerous, he feels, if the character's values are destructive, for then the reader is liable to be corrupted by his identification with unhealthy attitudes. I feel that Booth has overestimated both the danger which the reader is in and the effectiveness of rhetoric as a corrective, and that he has underestimated the value of deep inside views, though he admits that they "can be of immeasurable value in forcing us to see the human worth of a character whose actions, objectively considered, we would deplore" (p. 378). Robbe-Grillet's *The Voyeur* "does, indeed, lead us to experience intensely the sensations and emotions of a homicidal maniac. But is this," Booth asks, "really what we go to literature for?" (p. 384). My answer is, Yes.

We go to literature for many things, and not the least of them is the immediate knowledge that it gives to variously constituted human psyches. The novel makes its revelations not only through mimetic portraits of characters, but also, in many cases, through the picture that it creates of the implied author. As both Wayne Booth and Sheldon Sacks point out, when the implied author functions as interpreter, he often makes a multitude of particular judgments as his characters display their temperaments and confront their choices. This gives rise to "a much more detailed ordering of values" than we ever encounter in systematic philosophy. Even if we cannot accept the implied author's values as adequate either to his fictional world or to life outside, we have a marvellously rich portrayal of a particular kind of consciousness making ethical responses to a variety of human situations. Through the novel's rhetoric we become aware of the meaning which the characters' experience has for a mind like that of the implied author, and we enter thus into his subjective world.

What I am suggesting, then, is that if we view him as a fictional persona, as another dramatized consciousness, rather than as an authoritative source of values, the implied author, too, enlarges our knowledge of experience. What we have, in effect, is a deep inside view of *his* mind, a view which makes us phenomenologically aware of *his* experience of the world. When we see him as another consciousness, sometimes the most fascinating one in the book, it becomes more difficult to regret the technical devices by which he is revealed, even when they produce aesthetic flaws. To see him in this way we must set aside the fictional conventions which encourage us to invest him with the authority which Wayne Booth would like him to have; but it is essential to do so if we are to appreciate many great narrators whose wisdom we must question and whose obtrusiveness we must otherwise regret.

As long as we regard the implied author as a kind of God whose will we must understand but never question, it seems quite inappropriate to analyze him psychologically. His contradictions are manifestations of a higher harmony which we have not yet grasped; and his judgments, being right, require no explanation. When we see him as a dramatized consciousness whose values can be as subjective and as confused as those of an ordinary man, psychological analysis becomes a necessity.

I have tried to show by an analysis of the genre that it is often appropriate to study the characters and implied authors of realistic novels by a psychological method. In the interpretations of individual novels that will follow our discussion of Third Force psychology, I hope to demonstrate that the approach employed here helps us to appreciate some of fiction's most important values and to resolve some difficult critical problems.

I am aware, however, that the very arguments by which I have attempted to justify a psychological approach may seem to preclude it. I have argued that one of the chief interests of realistic fiction is a mimetic characterization which gives us a phenomenological grasp of experience in its immediacy and ambiguity and that the value of such characterization lies precisely in its continual resistance to the patterns by which the author has tried to shape and interpret it. It may be objected that the values of such characterization are incommensurate with any kind of analysis and that to intellectualize them is to destroy them. My reply must be that any criticism, whether it be psychological or not, is bound to operate with categories and abstractions which, if they are allowed to replace the values of literature, will destroy them. Criticism can make literature more accessible to us, but we must use it as a means to rather than as a substitute for the aesthetic encounter.

A common complaint about the psychological analysis of character is that it does violence to the literary values of fiction by reducing the novel to a case history, the character to his neurosis. We must recognize that literature and criticism belong to different universes of discourse. As Northrop Frye says, "the axiom of criticism must be, not that the poet does not know what he is talking about, but that he cannot talk about what he knows."[15] The function of criticism is to talk about what the artist knows, and to do that it must speak in the language of science and philosophy rather than in the language of art. But if we are aware of what we are doing this does not convert art into science or philosophy. Criticism points to a reality which is far more complex and of a different nature than itself; the values of which it speaks can be experienced only in the aesthetic encounter. All criticism is reductive. Psychological analysis is our best tool for talking about the intricacies of mimetic characterization. If properly conducted, it is less reductive than any other critical approach.

It is extremely valuable to bring literature and psychology together. The psychologist and the artist often know about the same areas of experience, but they comprehend them and present their knowledge in different ways. Each enlarges our awareness and satisfies our need to master reality in a way that the other cannot. The psychologist enables us to grasp certain configurations of experience analytically, categorically, and (if we accept his conceptions of health and neurosis) normatively. The novelist enables us to grasp these phenomena in other ways. Fiction lets us know what it is like to be a certain kind of person with a certain kind of destiny. Through mimetic portraits of character, novels provide us with artistic formulations of experience that are permanent, irreplaceable, and of an order quite different from the discursive formulations of systematic psychology. And, if we view him as a fictional persona, as a dramatized consciousness, the implied author, too, enlarges our knowledge of the human psyche.

Taken together, psychology and fiction give us a far more complete possession of experience than either can give us by itself. Psychology helps us to talk about what the novelist knows; fiction helps us to know what the psychologist is talking about.

Notes

1. *Psychoanalysis and Shakespeare* (New York, 1966), p. 151. Whenever the source is clear, page numbers will be given parenthetically in the text.
2. There is a slight modification of Holland's position in *The Dynamics of Literary Response* (New York, 1968), Chapter 10 ("Character and Identification"): Psychoanalytic critics regularly apply psychological concepts from the world of everyday reality to characters who exist in a wholly different kind of world — it should not work but it does" (p. 267). My contention is that it should work, and it does.
3. (Ithaca, 1965), p. 192.
4. See especially, Robert Scholes and Robert Kellogg, *The Nature of Narrative* (New York, 1966); Northrop Frye, *The Anatomy of Criticism* (Princeton, 1957); Wayne C. Booth, *The Rhetoric of Fiction* (Chicago, 1961); and Sheldon Sacks, *Fiction and the Shape of Belief* (Berkeley and Los Angeles, 1964).
5. There is an element of interpretation in all representation, of course, in that representation is not mere copying but involves artistic selection for the purpose of creating a more effective mimetic portrait. When I distinguish between representation and interpretation, I am using "interpretation" to mean analysis and judgment."
6. "The Art of Fiction," in *Myth and Method, Modern Theories of Fiction*, ed. James E. Miller, Jr. (Lincoln, 1960), pp. 24–25.
7. Arnold Kettle, *An Introduction to the English Novel* (Harper Torchbook ed.: New York, 1960), Vol. 1, p. 21.

8. (Berkeley and Los Angeles, 1965), p. 30.
9. *Mimesis, The Representation of Reality in Western Literature,* trans. by Willard Trask (Anchor Book ed.: New York, 1957), pp. 433–434.
10. "Myth, Fiction, and Displacement," in *Fables of Identity* (New York, 1963), p. 36.
11. *Studies in European Realism* (New York, 1964), p. 10.
12. *Aspects of the Novel* (London, 1927), Chapter 4.
13. *The Dehumanization of Art* (Anchor Book ed.: Garden City, 1956), p. 92.
14. Merleau-Ponty, quoted by Herbert Spiegelberg, *The Phenomenological Movement: A Historical Introduction* (The Hague, 1960), Vol. 2, p. 416.
15. *Anatomy of Criticism,* p. 5.

Beyond the Net: Feminist Criticism as a Moral Criticism

Josephine Donovan

Noting that much contemporary feminist criticism has passed beyond the "images of women" focus that was the movement's starting point, Josephine Donovan here returns to that focus to argue that the representation of women remains a key issue in feminist criticism. "Feminist criticism is rooted in the fundamental a priori intuition that women are seats of consciousness; are selves, not others." But in much literature, Donovan complains, and in much that is called the greatest, women are represented not as complex human beings and free moral agents but as stereotypes of good or evil, creatures whose function is simply to help or hinder the male hero's progress. In short, women are represented as others, not selves. This misrepresentation reflects the pervasive sexist bias of society; even worse, it serves to perpetuate that bias. In this context, misrepresentation is an intellectual error with serious moral consequences, and it must be combated by a serious moral criticism. On the one hand, then, the feminist critic must become a "negative" critic, a resisting reader who refuses to deny her own experience in order to identify with the fictional male hero and who refuses to accept the stereotype for the reality. On the other hand, the feminist critic must champion those works that do portray their characters, male and female, realistically, that is, as authentic, autonomous, and fully human beings. "Most literature that we call great expresses . . . universal, fundamental human experience." Looking back to the beginning of Western criticism in the mimetic theories of Plato and Aristotle, and glancing toward the work of Iris Murdoch, a modern student of Plato, Donovan puts the case for a feminist criticism that, by resisting false representations and praising true ones, will achieve a reconciliation of the Good and the True and become, thereby, a truly moral criticism.

Reprinted by permission of the author from *Denver Quarterly* 17, 4 (1983): 40–57.

The death of a beautiful woman is the most poetical topic in the world.

—Edgar Allan Poe, "The Philosophy of Composition"

While feminist literary criticism has diversified considerably in the past few years, I wish in this article to return to the "images of women" approach that dominated feminist literary studies of the early 1970s and is still central to the pedagogy of Women's Studies in literature. Through the "images of women" approach the critic determines how women characters are presented in literature. Usually the critic discovers that the images are *Other,* and therefore that the literature is alien. The task may be labeled "negative criticism" if one wishes to adapt the dialectical terms of the Frankfurt school of Marxist criticism.[1] It is "negative" because the critic is in effect saying "no" to reified perceptions, structures, and models that have historically denied full humanity to women. This means looking "negatively" at much of Western literature. Here I wish to set down a theoretical moral basis for this critique.

Feminist criticism is rooted in the fundamental *a priori* intuition that women are seats of consciousness; are selves, not others. As Dorin Schumacher has pointed out, the dominant criticism of the past, which she labels "masculinist," has gone on the opposite assumption: "Man [is] self, or normative, and woman [is] other, or deviant."[2] Schumacher's analysis derives, of course (as any "images of women" criticism must, I believe), from Simone de Beauvoir's brilliant application of Existentialist phenomenology to women.

In her introduction to *The Second Sex,* Beauvoir, echoing Heidegger and Sartre, asserted that "Otherness is a fundamental category of human thought."[3] The fundamental duality between the Self and the Other "is as primordial as consciousness itself" (p. xvi). By the time Beauvoir was writing *The Second Sex,* Claude Lévi-Strauss had in fact identified (in *Les Structures élémentaires de la parenté*) the transition from "nature" to "culture" as one which required the development of a binary consciousness. Beauvoir seems to have been influenced by this thesis, so fundamental to structuralism.

Beauvoir perceived, moreover, that the Self-Other dichotomy quickly becomes expressed in political terms: it is the socially dominant group which establishes itself as Self, as the norm, the essential; while subordinate groups are Other, which means they are perceived as deviant, inessential, objects (p. xvii). In our society the masculine is the norm; the feminine, the aberrant.

Women in literature written by men are for the most part seen as Other, as objects, of interest only insofar as they serve or detract from the goals of the male protagonist. Such literature is alien from a female point of view because it denies her essential selfhood. Beauvoir cemented her point by citing a seventeenth-century critic, Poulain de la Barre: "All that has been written about women by men should be suspect, for the men are at once judge and party to the lawsuit" (p. xxii).

The primary assumption a critic in the "images of women" school must make is an evaluation of the *authenticity* of the female characters.[4] Authenticity is another concept borrowed from the Existentialists, in particular Heidegger, who meant by it whether an individual has a self-defined critical consciousness, as opposed to a mass-produced or stereotypical identity.[5] Sartre defined the latter as the *en-soi,* the *in-itself* or the object-self, as opposed to the authentic *pour-soi* or *for-itself,* which is the critical or reflective consciousness capable of forming projects.[6]

The concept of authenticity in feminist criticism is therefore not a free-floating, "impressionistic" notion, as has been suggested.[7] Judgments which evaluate a character's authenticity are rooted in the extensive body of Existentialist theory on the subject. Such judgments are made according to whether the character has a reflective, critical consciousness, whether s/he is a moral agent, capable of self-determined action, whether, in short, s/he is a Self, not an Other. Such judgments enable the feminist critic to determine the degree to which sexist ideology controls the text.[8] Sexist ideology necessarily promotes the concept of woman-as-object or woman-as-other. Sometimes the critic may note an interplay between the ideology and a critique of it expressed in the text (this is usually only in works written by women). Sometimes the critic has to supply the critique herself. Thus, one discovers that the "cult of true womanhood," a particular nineteenth-century American version of sexist ideology which essentially consigned women to true "otherhood," is embedded in scores of sentimentalist texts of the period. But one may also note ways in which the female authors somewhat subverted the ideology through plot and character.[9] Again one must stress that the feminist *a priori* is that women have in all historical periods been seats of consciousness and moral agents (i.e., selves), no matter how circumscribed their spheres or range of actions may have been. Any text which does not recognize the fundamental moral reality of women is sexist.

In order to illustrate how an author may create and exploit inauthentic female characters, thereby promulgating sexist ideology, I am first going to look at several contemporary films. In many of these we find visual examples of exploitation for aesthetic purposes, as in Poe's aesthetic excitement over the death of a beautiful woman. (I am not even addressing here the whole realm of pornographic treatment of women except to note that pornography is the ultimate objectification of women and represents the far end of the continuum of alien literature.)

Molly Haskell noted in her study of film images of women: "The conception of woman as idol, art object, icon and visual entity is . . . the first principle of the aesthetic of film as a visual medium."[10] Or, as Laura Mulvey, a Freudian feminist critic, pointed out:

> [In film] the determining male gaze projects its fantasy onto the female figure, which is styled accordingly. In their traditional exhibitionist role women are simultaneously looked at and displayed, with their appearance coded for strong visual and erotic impact so that they can be said to connote *to-be-looked-at-ness*.[11]

In other words, women characters in film are usually presented as objects or as *Other* to the male protagonist and for the pleasure of the male viewer. Such objectification is mitigated only when strong women film personalities take over the role, making of it something not intended by writer or director.

Some films of Ingmar Bergman provide excellent if subtle examples of the phenomenon of aesthetic exploitation of women characters. *Cries and Whispers* (1972) is a film which one might, on first viewing, hail as a sensitive portrayal of the lives of four women. The extraordinary visual beauty of the film is seductive enough to promote this judgment. However, on reflection one comes to realize that the women are used aesthetically as if they were on the same level of moral importance as the red decor of their surroundings. Like Poe, Bergman finds women's agonies aesthetically interesting because he sees them from without and not from within. He can visually appreciate the screams and agonized wriggling of Agnes.

But, as Constance Penley wrote in an important feminist critique of the film, the women's suffering is morally gratuitous. "Since the film is not about women coming to realizations of self-knowledge through their struggles, then their suffering must serve some other function."[12] That function is aesthetic.

I am using *aesthetic* here in the sense given it at least since Kant, that of a disinterested appreciation of a phenomenon that exists as a discrete entity in space and time, which is pleasing within these or because of these spatio-temporal coordinates. As we shall see, I believe that the imputed divorce between aesthetics and morals which this view entails is specious, masking as it does ideological exploitation of female figures. Nevertheless, aesthetics since the Renaissance has relied upon this divorce; spatio-temporal perspectives are the governing principle.[13] Consequently an artist like Bergman can treat his female figures as objects within a spatio-temporal continuum that are of use only insofar as they fit into the total aesthetic vision he has fashioned. In *Cries and Whispers* there is no moral resolution for the women characters because they are not conceived as moral creatures, as possessing authenticity. These women gain no wisdom. Their lot does not get any better. It gets worse. Theirs is a universe deprived of hope, a world that is irredeemably fallen; suffering is to no redemptive purpose. In *Cries and Whispers* that world, largely female, is damned to total alienation and meaningless suffering, saved only by the camera eye, an aesthetic redemption. One may argue that male protagonists in a modern world are also subjected to alienation and non-redemptive suffering; but female characters tend to be used more for aesthetic effects which divert attention from their moral existence.

Despite the fact that *Scenes from a Marriage* (1973) was touted as a "liberated" break-through in which male and female characters hold equal power, the woman character remains submissive to the end. She is unable to function autonomously, because Bergman does not allow her to. When tension between the couple escalates, it is the male character who is physically abusive. After a brutal scene in which the woman is kicked at length by her husband, she comes crawling back for more, and we, the audience, are expected to feel pity for her abuser because he lost his self-control and presumably his self-respect. The female character is used as a vehicle for the male's growth in self-awareness.

In *Face to Face* (1976) the female protagonist is even more limited. In this film Liv Ullmann plays a career/professional woman who is separated from her husband. As in most misogynist literature the unmated female is gratuitously abused because she has dared to attempt autonomy; she has rejected a male and refused to play the role of traditional wife-and-mother—which is the only acceptable female role in this misogynist vision because it is utterly passive and non-disruptive of predestined male triumph.[14]

The movie opens with the rape of the female protagonist. The experience precipitates her complete unravelment and breakdown. While the role is a tour de force for Liv Ullmann, the film provides no moral resolution to the great suffering that has been displayed. In no way is the enormity of the suffering justified. The sheer imbalance in the movie is the clue that Bergman relished aesthetically every nuance of the breakdown; that was sufficient cause for her suffering. Once again the suffering is viewed from without; it serves superficial aesthetic purposes. Ultimately such exploitation of suffering is an example of artistic bad faith, an author's immoral use of his characters. Unlike the great works of Western literature where suffering for the male protagonist leads to wisdom, to knowledge, to growth, or to positive social change, here the suffering is without meaning. Nor is there any catharsis for the female viewer (or the male viewer who may care for the protagonist). The only point of the movie is to show the marvelous acting *technique* of Liv Ullmann and filming *technique* of Bergman. But this is not art in its profoundest sense, for all great art is sustained by the integrity of a moral vision. It cannot depend on gratuitous suffering which is tantamount to torture. Later I will discuss what a feminist/humanist moral vision in art entails.

Another contemporary film which helps to illustrate my thesis is Woody Allen's *Interiors* (1978). Once again we have a visually seductive film, aesthetically very beautiful. All the frames are in aesthetic balance, and the colors of the interiors are aesthetically pleasing. But in the end the "interiors" of the characters are of no more moral substance than the house and apartment interiors they live in. This film, modeled whether consciously or not on Chekhov's masterwork *The Three Sisters*, attempts to portray and in some sense justify aesthetically the suffering of the female characters, primarily that of the mother-wife played by Geraldine Page. Once

again the role is a tour de force for a supremely talented actress; but the overall resolution of the film is not satisfactory for the viewer who identifies with, or empathizes with, or simply cares for the central female character. Why is this the case? To answer this I must discuss the nature of aesthetic satisfaction.

The aesthetic dimension of literature and of film cannot be divorced from the moral dimension, as we have facilely come to assume under the influence of technique-oriented critical methodologies (New Criticism, for example). Since Aristotle, the aesthetic experience has in fact been understood as one which provides release, relief, catharsis, and the pleasure of wholeness. The events within this aesthetic frame may be horrible or violent but they are ultimately redeemed by the fact that they take their place within an order. This order cannot be a superficial order, i.e., it is not sufficient to simply frame a scene of grotesque suffering. It has to be placed within a moral order of great consequence. All the "great works" of Western literature intend and depend upon a moral order. The events of the work take their place within an order that satisfies one's sense of justice or one's sense of irony, which itself requires a belief in an order beyond the events of the work.

When one identifies too closely with a character's suffering in a work of art, or when that suffering is exploited to the point where it breaks the boundaries of appropriateness within the moral context of the work, the aesthetic continuity is dislocated; the suffering cannot be justified, morally or aesthetically.[15] So that when *Interiors* comes to its aesthetic ending (the three women are artistically arranged like beautiful motionless statues staring at the ocean), the resolution is not sufficient to justify the enormous suffering of the mother-wife character. No knowledge, no wisdom, no growth, no change has resulted. Passive reduction to beautiful objects is the resolution for those female characters who are still alive at the end of the film. This is not a sufficient moral resolution for the engaged spectator.

By contrast, Chekhov's play *The Three Sisters* exists on a plane far above the exploitation of female suffering seen in these contemporary films. The great themes of Chekhov's drama point to the vanity of human purposes and the corrosion of the human fabric through time. The male and the female characters equally suffer disillusionments and defeats inherent in the human condition. The strongest and most noble figure in the work, indeed, is a woman,

Olga. Chekhov clearly has full compassion and empathy for his female characters.

The great tragedies of Western literature intend the existence of a moral order that transcends and in some way justifies the evil and suffering that is occasioned in the text. As examples, consider *King Lear* and *Oedipus at Colonus*. The protagonist in each play experiences excruciating suffering. But the suffering is not morally meaningless. It is justified by the fact that wisdom and positive social change result (or have resulted in the case of Oedipus).

A powerful passage in Aeschylus's *Agammemnon* states this principle succinctly:

Zeus, who guided men to think,
who has laid it down that wisdom
comes alone through suffering.

. . .

From the gods who sit in grandeur
grace comes somehow violent.
Trans. Richmond Lattimore

The tragic cycle of suffering, death, growth, rebirth fits into a universal human expectation of the death of vegetation in winter and its rebirth in the spring (the ancient ritual of the dying year god). Such mythic expectations are not sex-linked; they are universal. Most literature that we call great expresses such universal, fundamental human experiences.

In the case of *King Lear* and *Oedipus at Colonus*, suffering and evil are not hypostasized and projected onto a female Other, as they are in misogynist literature. It is true that Goneril and Regan, Lear's treacherous daughters, are irretrievably evil, but so is Edmund, the bastard son of Gloucester. Cordelia's honesty and loyalty are paralleled by Kent's faithful service to the mad Lear. Feminists (indeed, most viewers/readers) may regret that Shakespeare did not allow Cordelia to survive, along with Edgar, Gloucester's good son, and Kent; nevertheless, the dénoument goes beyond sexist scapegoating. Within the context of the play the deaths are morally and aesthetically necessary; they signify the expulsion of evil and error from the social body; they are necessary to the establishment of a viable moral order.[16] Similarly in *Oedipus at Colonus*, another work that concerns filial piety, Oedipus is assisted by his daughters Antigone and, to a lesser extent, Ismene in his final days. The charitable acts of the women are not the mechanical gestures of an Other, but are the acts of great compassion. That Shakespeare and Sophocles chose women—Cordelia and Antigone—

to exemplify the compelling power of love is not to be construed as sexist stereotyping. Rather, these women are simply humans moved to help a fallen figure in distress. Unfortunately, much of our literature does not reach this stage of grace.[17]

Much of our literature in fact depends upon a series of fixed images of women, stereotypes. These reified forms, surprisingly few in number, are repeated over and over again through much of Western literature. The objectified images have one thing in common, however: they define the woman insofar as she relates to, serves, or thwarts the interests of men.

In the Western tradition these stereotypes tend to fall into two categories, reflecting the endemic Manicheistic dualism in the Western world-view. Female stereotypes symbolize either the spiritual or the material, good or evil. Mary, the mother of Jesus, came through time to exemplify the ultimate in spiritual goodness, and Eve, the partner of Adam, the most sinister of evil physicality. The following diagram shows how this dualism is conceived:

spiritual	material
spirit/soul	body
virginal ideal	sex object
Mary	Eve
inspiration	seductress
good	evil

Under the category of the good-woman stereotypes, that is, those who serve the interests of the hero, are the patient wife, the mother/martyr, and the lady. In the bad or evil category are deviants who reject or do not properly serve men or his interests: the old maid/career woman, the witch/lesbian, the shrew or domineering mother/wife. Several works, considered archetypal masterpieces of the Western tradition, rely upon these simplistic stereotypes of women.

The *Odyssey* is not only the first masterwork of the Western tradition, it provides its archetypal sexist plot, depending as it does on a series of female stereotypes. The *Odyssey* relates the far-flung life adventures of a male hero on his return home to love and security. Tending the home during his twenty-year absence, faithful wife Penelope does little but fend off potential suitors and weave. It has been argued that Penelope matches her "wily" husband in character because she outwits the suitors, as he has outwitted various enemies (most of them women) on his journey. However, her role is so slight and her character so thinly developed that she remains little more than the stereotype of the patient wife.

On his travels, which have the ostensible goal of returning home, he is delayed by a series of female figures. As they present obstacles to his true course, they are seen as evil and fall into the category of "bad" woman. They are all sexual beings, as opposed to Penelope, and they successfully seduce Odysseus, thus delaying his proper progress.

His first encounter is with Calypso, an enchantress-seductress with whom he spends seven years, although he claimed he never gave consent in his heart (*Od.* IX). Next came Circe, a witch, whose brew turned Odysseus's men into pigs. Odysseus has a potion that renders him immune to her liquor, and so he can sleep with her for a year before moving on. Next come the sirens whose seductive songs threaten to delay him once again. Finally, there are Scylla and Charybdis, female monsters, who eat six crewmen.

There are other women in the *Odyssey,* but the central figures are these. They are defined solely in terms of whether they help or hinder the hero on his course. They are presented as wholly evil or wholly good, depending upon that role. Odysseus himself seems to bear no guilt or responsibility for his dallying. The fault, in this original statement of the double standard, is theirs.

Dante's *Commedia,* completed in 1321, is usually interpreted as an allegory of the soul's descent through hell and ascent through purgatory and into paradise. On his journey Dante is guided by various figures. In the *Inferno* and *Purgatorio* his guide is Virgil, who is usually interpreted as representing human reason. Female figures become especially evident in the *Paradiso.* Dante's primary guide in this section is Beatrice, an idealized version of an early romantic involvement he had supposedly had in real life (and which is described in an early work of the courtly love tradition, *La Vita Nuova*). Beatrice is the ultimate expression of the salvific woman, the muse, she who inspires the despairing artist. For this role she is promoted to the levels of highest significance in Dante's personal cosmos, which is extrapolated in the *Commedia* to be the moral cosmos of the Christian myth.

Also in the ultimate reaches of the *Paradiso* is a beatified Virgin Mary, the ultimate symbol in the work of love and grace. The *Commedia* presents, therefore, among other things, one of the greatest elaborations of the ideal spiritual woman, who is nevertheless defined (and in this case elevated to the ranks of ultimate goodness) in terms of her service to the male protagonist.[18]

Faust, completed in 1832 by Goethe, considered one of the greatest of the Western masterworks, also relies on a conception of woman as the inspiration for the man of genius. The final line of this massive dramatic poem is "das Ewig-Weibliche zieht uns hinan," translated: "The eternal feminine draws us upward." In this work the salvific female has been hypostasized as the ultimate inspirational and energizing force of the universe. A summary of the plot of this work will show that this force has been extrapolated from the sacrifice of a rather pathetic female figure, Margaret (or Gretchen).

Faust describes the reinspiration and therefore salvation of a scientist-scholar who has grown despondent and bored with the world. As the work opens, he is looking for something to recharge him. He turns to various means, one of which is a flirtation with a country maid named Gretchen whom he abandons pregnant. Eventually she kills her child, is imprisoned, and dies.

The unappealing philosophy underlying this work is that lesser people like Gretchen and most women are fuel for the great dynamic energy of the great male geniuses of history like Faust. Therefore the destruction of such "little people" is justified as a sacrifice to the greater good that a person like Faust represents in Goethe's dynamic universe. Faust is finally saved in Goethe's romantic version of the legend because he never gave up striving; his energy never ceased. And the reason he continued in a state of "becoming" or growth was due to the inspiration effected by various incarnations of womanhood, who are hypostasized finally as "das Ewig-Weibliche."

These works, central to the Western tradition—the *Odyssey,* the *Commedia,* and *Faust*—do not present the "inside" of women's experience. We learn little, if anything, of the women's own personal responses to events. They are simply vehicles for the growth and salvation of the male protagonist. The women are Other in Beauvoir's sense of the term, and therefore this literature must remain alien to the female reader who reads as a woman.

One can argue, of course, that a woman reader can suspend her femaleness and appreciate great works which have male protagonists (and objectified women) when the protagonists are wrestling with universal human problems. In other words, one can argue that one can transcend one's sex in appreciating a literary work.[19] To some extent I believe that this is indeed possible. One is certainly impelled when viewing or reading *Hamlet* to identify with, or simply to care for, the central character simply because he represents the active consciousness in the work. In *Hamlet* it would take a supreme act of the will to be more concerned about Ophelia, who is minor and whose appeal is largely aesthetic. The same is true for Penelope, Beatrice, and Gretchen.

The real question is not whether a woman *can* identify with the subjective consciousness or the self if it is male, but whether she *should*, given her own political and social environment. In other words, isn't it morally misleading to encourage a person who is barred from action to identify with an individual whose dilemma (in the case of Hamlet) is simply whether to act? Action, taking charge, is a choice that historically has been denied women and still is unavailable to them in many areas. Until, however, ideological socialization ceases, we as female readers cannot authentically transcend our sex. Such literature as treated in this article must remain alien. This does not mean that we should throw out or refuse to read these works, but that they should be read with a perspective that recognizes the sexism inherent in their moral vision.

All moral criticism of literature is based on the assumption that literature affects us, that it changes our attitudes and our behavior; in other words it assumes that literature can precipitate action, harmful or otherwise, in the "real" world. One of the oldest critical observations is Horace's comment that the purpose of art is to teach or to delight (*aut prodesse aut delectare*). Going back further, even Aristotle, often presented as the first technique-oriented critic (as opposed to Plato), couched his theory of mimesis in moral terms:

> Since the objects of imitation are men in action, and these men must be either of a higher or lower type (for moral character [ethos] mainly answers to these divisions, goodness and badness being the distinguishing marks of moral differences), it follows that we must represent men either as better than in real life, or as worse, or as they are (*Poetics* ii, 1; trans. S. H. Butcher).

It is clear in the rest of the *Poetics* that Aristotle prefers the form that imitates the actions of good men (tragedy). In his discussion of character (*ethos*) he

stipulates that the most important trait is "goodness." But Aristotle specifies further that "even a woman may be good, and also a slave; though the woman may be said to be an inferior being, and the slave quite worthless" (*Poetics* xv, 1). Thus, while moral criticism is quite old, the morality expressed has been for the most part sexist. Feminist criticism is a moral criticism which attempts to redress the balance.

John Gardner in *On Moral Fiction* has recently returned to the great moral tradition in criticism. An artistic medium is "good," he says,

> only when it has a clear positive moral effect, presenting valid models for imitation, eternal verities worth keeping in mind, and a benevolent vision of the possible which can inspire human beings toward virtue, toward life affirmation as opposed to destruction or indifference.[20]

Gardner is not talking about a facile didacticism. Instead, and rather courageously, given the epistemological quandary of contemporary ethics, he is trying to talk in everyday terms about values and literature.

Feminist criticism is moral because it sees that one of the central problems of Western literature is that in much of it women are not human beings, seats of consciousness. They are objects, who are used to facilitate, explain away, or redeem the projects of men. Western projects of redemption almost always depend upon a salvific woman. On the other hand, in some Western literature women are the objects, the scapegoats, of much cruelty and evil. Much Western thought and literature has failed to come to grips with the problem of evil because it facilely projects evil upon woman or other hypostasized "Others," such as the Jew, the Negro, thereby denying the reality of the contingent order.[21]

Feminist criticism becomes political when it asserts that literature, academic curricula, and the standards of critical judgment should be changed, so that literature will no longer function as propaganda furthering sexist ideology. The feminist critic recognizes that literature is an important contributing element to a moral atmosphere in which women are derrogated. Moreover, the feminist critic joins other critics of Western thinking in decrying the endemic Manicheism that projects evil upon the Other. Following is a discussion of some literary and ethical values which suggest a way beyond this cultural impasse.

"Moral action is action which affirms life," claims Gardner (p. 23). For a feminist, moral literature is one which affirms the life of women, as well as all other creatures. As Gardner points out, one of the most important criteria that a moral critic can use is to determine whether an author cares for his or her characters, or whether, as we have seen in our analysis of the films, s/he is simply using them for other purposes (pp. 84–85). A great writer must never "sink" to stereotype for even the most minor characters" (p. 109). "Beauty . . . should not be conceived only as a matter of the technique . . . but as the effect of emotional honesty as well . . ." (p. 145). These are fundamental criteria for the feminist critic.

Linguistic analysis and semiological studies can tell us much about how cultural ideologies are expressed in literary form. But only when style is studied in the context of the author's or the culture's moral view of women can it be of feminist significance. Unfortunately much formalist analysis in the past has relied on the convenient divorce between values and aesthetics described above. For this reason it has been able to evade the central evaluative issue that criticism must face: that of the moral stature of the work.

Criticism, by ignoring central questions of content, has become dehumanized in the same way as modern art did when it gave way to exclusively formal concerns. As Gardner notes,

> In all the arts, our criticism is for the most part inhumane. We are rich in schools which speak of how art "works" and avoid the whole subject of what work it ought to do. . . . Structuralists, formalists, linguistic philosophers who tell us that works of art are . . . simply objects for perception—all avoid on principle the humanistic question: who will the work of art help? (pp. 16–17)

Literature on its most profound level is a form of learning. We learn, we grow from the knowledge of life, of psychology, of human behavior and relationships that we discover in worthwhile works of art. The notion that art teaches is as old as criticism. But how it teaches is an equally old and perhaps unanswerable question.

Conversely, bad or immoral art can and does promote evil behavior, just as evil films promote evil acts. Again, as Iris Murdoch has noted, *how* art promotes behavior is a difficult question.[22] Gardner sees fiction as a kind of laboratory wherein moral ideas can be tested both by the author and the reader. The net effect of good literature on the reader should be moral growth, a learning of the effects of good and evil behavior. Much of Western literature does not provide women with such models of behavior and only provides the moral learning experience described above if she engages in inauthentic suspension of her female identity.

Tolstoy's *What Is Art?* is one of the best-known pieces of moral criticism. For all its faults it presents a view of art that is central to a moral critique. Art for Tolstoy is one of the highest forms of communication among humans:

> To evoke in oneself a feeling one has once experienced, and having evoked it in oneself, then, by means of movements, lines, colors, sounds, or forms expressed in words, so to transmit that feeling that others may experience the same feeling— that is the activity of art. Art is a human activity in this, that one . . . hands on to others feelings he has lived through, and that other people are infected by these feelings and also experience them.[23]

"It is a means of union" among peoples, "joining them together in the same feelings, and indispensable for the life and progress toward well-being of individuals and of humanity" (p. 52). Ultimately it is a religious idea of the good that art strives to communicate, according to Tolstoy. That art should be accessible to all, not just an elite, is one of his cardinal principles (p. 96).

Tolstoy argues that one may determine whether a work of art is worthwhile if it evokes "that feeling . . . of joy and of spiritual union with another (the author) and with others (those who are also infected by it)" (p. 139). Again, such spiritual union is hardly possible for a woman when the work involves the derogation of women. (Tolstoy himself was, of course, guilty of considerable misogyny.)

Like Gardner, Tolstoy specifies as one of the hallmarks of great literature a quality of emotional honesty, or what we might call integrity. Tolstoy's preference is for rural pre-industrial literature, the Greek epics, certain Biblical stories. Today, he would have probably loved a film like *Tree of Wooden Clogs* (1978) or, earlier, the short stories of Sarah Orne Jewett.

But it is British novelist Iris Murdoch who, in a series of essays, has developed the most appealing discussions of the moral purpose of art. Murdoch's view of art is that it is a form of education, that it promotes moral growth by helping us to *see* beyond the usual illusions and facile stereotypes by which we habitually organize the chaos of "reality." Following

Simone Weil, Murdoch argues that our most serious moral weakness is our tendency to see by means of "fantasy mechanisms."

This concept derives from Simone Weil's notion of gravity, as discussed in *La Pesanteur et la grâce* (1948). In human relations, Weil argues, there are phenomena similar to "gravity" that function as if mechanically. These mechanisms describe the way the psyche orients itself in the world. For example, if one is abused, one has a tendency to retaliate in kind rather than absorb the injury. This injury-retaliation cycle tends to take the shape of a continuing mechanism; it functions almost as predictably as a physical phenomenon like gravity.

Similarly, Weil maintains, we tend to "fill the void" with an endless stream of fabrications, imaginings, myths, etc., which give us a feeling of significance. Sexist mythology promotes males' feelings of significance. These fantasies are stories which magically redeem one from the contingent order by denying its reality; they are false, or inauthentic, attempts at transcendence. The logic of this kind of thinking is deductive. The premises are assumed, and reality is pressed into a kind of unstated, defective syllogism: Women are unimportant; I am not a woman; Therefore I am important.

In "Diving into the Wreck," an early poem, Adrienne Rich wrote,

the thing I came for:
the wreck itself and not the story of the wreck
the thing itself and not the myth.[24]

Such an approach points to the moral alternative described by Iris Murdoch. In wanting to get back to the "thing itself" Rich is attempting to get beyond (or under) the network of mythic confabulations we are enshrouded in. Getting back to the thing itself means not cramming it into a received syllogism; it means functioning by means of a kind of inductive logic (always considered women's strong point). It means starting not from mythic premises, but rather proceeding inductively from concrete, experiential realities, building and gathering knowledge from the events themselves. Women have been criticized in the past for their so-called inability to see the forest for the trees. But perhaps this "inability" is simply a resistance on the part of women to imposing mythic conceptions upon empirical events, knowing, as we do, how easily one's own reality, one's self, can be falsified by public myths.

Unlike Ludwig Wittgenstein, Murdoch does not despair of getting under this reified net of myths. She does not see us as irretrievably imprisoned behind linguistic and semiological barriers which keep us from the thing itself. Such entrapment is not a part of the human condition, Murdoch maintains; it is rather a condition we fall into out of moral weakness. In other words, while Wittgenstein (in the *Tractatus*) argues that the world is only that which we construct theoretically or mythically—and therefore a web of lies—Murdoch insists that we fall into the habit of mythic construction out of fear, weakness, or inertia. Murdoch proposes that we can get out of this epistemological trap by means of moral effort—by a redirection of the will and attention. Such a redirection can lead us to a moral knowledge of the real and of the good.

Murdoch's first novel illustrates concerns similar to Rich's of getting "under the net" (the novel's title), back to reality itself. Jake, the protagonist, is a good example of a person who has fallen into the habit of mythicizing; he continually fantasizes upon reality. His relationship with Anna is particularly illustrative: he constantly tries to see her in terms of various mythic paradigms (e.g., a fairy princess).

Anna herself (following in this regard Wittgenstein himself) has, by contrast, developed a philosophy of silence. Her position seems to be that at this stage of our moral development it is only through silence—only by "knowing the void" (Weil's concept)—that we can begin to see one another as we actually are. Only in this way can we overcome the psychic mechanisms that tend to make us construe people in terms of received myth. While the ending of the novel is somewhat irresolute, it is clear that Jake has moved away from the automatic mythicizing of the early sections toward the beginnings of an acceptance of the reality of the contingent world, of the reality of creatures other than himself and of their diversity. "It seemed," he reflects, "as if, for the first time, Anna really existed now as a separate being, and not as part of myself."[25]

Murdoch sees art and literature, in particular the novel, as an important vehicle for the liberation of people from "fantasy mechanisms." It can foster the growth of moral attention to contingent realities beyond the self and beyond self-promoting fantasies. An essay entitled "On 'God' and 'Good'" presents Murdoch's position most cogently. In this essay she argues that finally it is love that enables us to get under the mythic net, for love demands an awareness of realities beyond the self. The love Murdoch speaks of is, of course, not romantic love, which is itself a mythic mechanism, but rather an orientation toward the world that involves reverential attention. This kind of orientation can be developed and encouraged. It is not necessarily "natural"; at the same time it does not depend on supranatural intervention. It can be developed by a strengthening of our powers of attention, and we can decide to work at such strengthening. That is, we can choose to discipline our awareness; it is an act of will. Great artists exhibit such discipline and compel our awareness similarly. The discipline involves a focusing of the attention without:

> The direction of attention is, contrary to nature, outward, away from self which reduces all to a false unity, toward the great surprising variety of the world, and the ability to so direct attention is love.[26]

Murdoch borrowed the concept of attention from Simone Weil, as she acknowledges. Weil used the term to mean "the idea of a just and loving gaze directed upon an individual reality."[27] Such attention, Murdoch notes, is "the characteristic and proper mark of the active moral agent" (p. 34). Such attention counteracts such "states of illusion" as are fostered by stereotypic or mythic expectations (p. 37).

Seeing clearly through proper attentiveness brings one to proper conduct. It effects moral growth: "True vision occasions right conduct."

> The more the separateness and differentness of other people is realized, and the fact seen that another . . . has needs and wishes as demanding as one's own, the harder it becomes to treat a person as a thing (p. 66).

True liberation therefore lies in the capacity to apprehend realities beyond the self and its promotion:

> It is in the capacity to love, that is to *see*, that the liberation of the soul from fantasy consists. The freedom which is a proper human goal is the freedom from fantasy, that is the realism of compassion (p. 66).

Ideally, the work of great artists helps us to *see* reality in all its conflicting diversity and therefore to make choices that are truly responsible to the real contexts in which they are made.

In "The Sublime and the Good," Murdoch argues further that art and morals are rooted in the same impulse:

> The essence of both of them is love. Love is the perception of individuals. Love is the extremely diffi-

cult realization that something other than oneself is real. Love, and so art and morals, is the discovery of reality.[28]

Both intend the "non-violent apprehension of difference" (p. 54). Great novelists, she argues elsewhere, are not "afraid of the contingent." They display "a real apprehension of persons other than the author as having a right to exist and to have a separate mode of being which is important and interesting to themselves."[29]

Much of the literature of our Western tradition has not risen to such heights. Its male authors do not reach that "extremely difficult realization" that women, "something other than" themselves, exist, are real. Their works are morally insufficient, for they do not attend to the independent reality of women. This is a fundamental critique offered by an "images of women" approach to literature.

Notes

1. This article follows from the assumptions about feminist criticism as a negative criticism laid down in my "Afterword: Critical Re-Vision," *Feminist Literary Criticism. Explorations in Theory.* ed. Josephine Donovan (Lexington: University Press of Kentucky, 1975), p. 75.
2. "Subjectivities," *Feminist Literary Criticism,* p. 34.
3. *The Second Sex* (New York: Knopf, 1953); p. xviii. Other references will follow in the text.
4. As Marcia Holly pointed out in "Consciousness and Authenticity: Toward a Feminist Aesthetic," *Feminist Literary Criticism,* pp. 38–47.
5. See Martin Heidegger, *Being and Time,* trans. John MacQuarrie and Edward Robinson (New York: Harper, 1962), pp. 164–243.
6. Jean-Paul Sartre, *Being and Nothingness: An Essay in Phenomenological Ontology,* trans. Hazel E. Barnes (New York: The Citadel Press, 1966), pp. lxvi, 54, 535.
7. See Stuart Cunningham, "Some Problems of Feminist Literary Criticism," *Journal of Women's Studies in Literature,* 1, No. 2 (Spring, 1979), 159–78. Cunningham's thesis that more attention must be paid by American feminist critics to the role ideology plays in shaping stereotypes is, however, a useful suggestion.
8. Terry Eagleton explains Marxist and Freudian methodology in similar terms in *Criticism and Ideology* (London: Verso, 1978), pp. 91–101.

9. See Barbara Welter, "The Cult of True Womanhood: 1820–1860," *American Quarterly,* 18, No. 2, Pt. 1 (Summer, 1966), 151–74; Helen Papashvily, *All the Happy Endings* (New York: Harper, 1956); and Nina Baym, *Woman's Fiction* (Ithaca: Cornell University Press, 1978).

10. *From Reverence to Rape: The Treatment of Women in the Movies* (New York: Penguin, 1974), p. 7.

11. "Visual Pleasure and Narrative Cinema," *Women and the Cinema: A Critical Anthology,* ed. Karyn Kay and Gerald Peary (New York: E. P. Dutton, 1977), p. 418.

12. "Cries and Whispers," *Movies and Methods: An Anthology,* ed. Bill Nichols (Berkeley: University of California Press, 1976), p. 207.

13. Erwin Panofsky's "Die Perspektive als 'symbolische Form,'" *Vorträge der Bibliothek Warburg 1924–1925* (Berlin: B. G. Tuebner, 1927), presents a brilliant discussion of the emergence of the mathematical paradigm as the governing aesthetic notion in the Renaissance.

14. See Katharine Rogers, *The Troublesome Helpmate: A History of Misogyny in Literature* (Seattle: University of Washington Press, 1966), pp. 201–57, for a brief history of attacks on the single woman.

15. Elsewhere I have argued that such is the case in Faulkner's *Light in August.* In that work the suffering and destruction of the spinster woman Joanna Burden, as well as her demoniacal evil, lead one to consider her existence improbable and beyond the pale of aesthetic and moral appropriateness (using once again Aristotelian criteria). When one character is so out of bounds, the whole moral and therefore the aesthetic universe of the work collapses. I noted that "it is impossible for a feminist to accept the aesthetic imperative of Faulkner's novel which requires that the author create an inauthentic woman and use her immorally for aesthetic ends" ("Feminism and Aesthetics," *Critical Inquiry,* 3, No. 3 [Spring, 1977], 608).

16. Even Cordelia exhibited the kind of moral intransigence that we associate with tragic hybris. One may argue whether she deserved her fate, but one cannot see her as doomed *because* she is a woman. I am relying here in part on A. C. Bradley's classic study, *Shakespearean Tragedy* (1904). Bradley does not see Cordelia as contributing to her fate, however, but rather as an innocent victim accidentally destroyed in the process of the expulsion of evil. For recent feminist analyses of Shakespeare see Carolyn Ruth Swift Lenz, Gayle Green, and Carol Thomas Neely (eds.), *The Woman's Part: Feminist Criticism of Shakespeare* (Urbana: University of Illinois Press, 1980).

17. The question of the extent to which tragedy as a *form* is inherently sexist would take us beyond the confines of this article. On the subject see Carol Gelderman, "The Male Nature of Tragedy," *Prairie Schooner,* 49, No. 3 (Autumn, 1975), 220–27.

18. Joan M. Ferrante presents a fully detailed analysis in *Woman as Image in Medieval Literature* (New York: Columbia University Press, 1975), Chap. 5.

19. I presented some of the ideas in the following two paragraphs in "Comment," *College English,* 38, No. 3 (November, 1976), 301–02.

20. *On Moral Fiction* (New York: Basic Books, 1978), p. 18. Further references will follow in the text.

21. See Jean-Paul Sartre's *Anti-Semite and Jew* (1956) and *Saint Genet* (1952), as well as Thomas Szasz, *The Manufacturer of Madness* (New York: Dell, 1970) for an exploration of this thesis. Szasz applies the concept of Otherness to witches, the insane, and homosexuals.

22. Iris Murdoch, *The Fire and the Sun: Why Plato Banished the Artists* (Oxford: Clarendon Press, 1977), p. 77.

23. Leo Tolstoy, *What Is Art?* trans. Aylmer Maude (Indianapolis: Bobbs-Merrill, 1960), p. 51. Further references will follow in the text.

24. *Diving into the Wreck—Poems 1971–72* (New York: W. W. Norton & Co., 1973), p. 23.

25. *Under the Net* (New York: Viking Press, 1954), p. 261.

26. "On 'God' and 'Good,'" in *The Sovereignty of Good* (New York: Schocken, 1971), p. 66.

27. Murdoch, "The Idea of Perfection," *The Sovereignty of Good,* p. 34. Further references follow in the text.

28. "The Sublime and the Good," *Chicago Review,* 13 (Autumn, 1959), p. 51. Further references follow in the text.

29. "The Sublime and the Beautiful Revisited," *Yale Review,* 69 (December, 1959), p. 257.

The Tempest

Bernard Paris

*In Bargains with Fate: Psychological Crises and Con-
flicts in Shakespeare and His Plays, Bernard Paris continues his project of applying psychological theories to
fictional characters and to implied authors. In the selection
that follows, Paris concentrates on the character of Prospero, producing a reading of that character considerably at
odds with Prospero's own estimate and with much traditional criticism. In the selection from Paris in the Theory
section of this chapter, he had raised the possibility that in
some literary works the mimetic impulse may be in conflict with the thematic impulse. Paris finds just such a
conflict in* The Tempest. *There is a discrepancy, he argues, between the play's thematic thrust and its representation of character. "When we understand Prospero's
psychological development, he seems different from the
figure celebrated by so many critics. Those who interpret*
The Tempest *as a story of magnanimity, forgiveness, and
reconciliation are responding correctly, I believe, to Shakespeare's thematic intentions, whereas those who take a
more "hard-nosed" view of the play are responding to the
psychological portrait of Prospero." As Paris sees it, those
who concentrate on the psychological portrait are going to
get closer to the play's real meaning.*

*T*he Tempest is one of only two Shakespearean plays
whose plot, as far as we know, is entirely the author's invention. More than any other play, it is
Shakespeare's fantasy. What, we must ask, is it a fantasy of? What psychological needs are being met?
What wishes are being fulfilled? One way of approaching these questions is to look at the unrealistic
elements in the play, particularly Prospero's magic.
The function of magic is to do the impossible, to grant

Reprinted by permission of the author from *Bargains with
Fate: Psychological Crises and Conflicts in Shakespeare and His
Plays.* New York: Insight Books, 1991: 263–76. This selec-
tion is a retitled excerpt from chapter 9, *"The Tempest:*
Shakespeare's Ideal Solution."

wishes that are denied to us in reality. What is his magic doing for Prospero? And for Shakespeare? What impossible dream does it allow to come true?

These questions can be approached from a variety of psychological perspectives. In Freudian theory, for instance, magic is associated with a belief in the omnipotence of thought, and it is employed in an effort to restore the delusions of grandeur that accompanied infantile megalomania. By giving him magical powers, Shakespeare grants Prospero the mastery of time, space, and matter that we once thought we enjoyed and that we still desire. In *Totem and Taboo*, Freud argued that man's conception of the universe has passed through three stages, the animistic, the religious, and the scientific:

> we have no difficulty in following the fortunes of the "omnipotence of thought" through all these phases. In the animistic stage man ascribes omnipotence to himself; in the religious he has ceded it to the gods, but without seriously giving it up, for he reserves to himself the right to control the gods by influencing them in some way or other in the interest of his wishes. In the scientific attitude toward life there is no longer any room for man's omnipotence; he has acknowledged his smallness and has submitted to death as to all other natural necessities in a spirit of resignation. (n.d., 115)

Most of Shakespeare's comedies and romances are written from a religious perspective; wishes are fulfilled through the cooperation or even the direct intervention of providential forces. Perhaps Northrop Frye, for whom domination by the pleasure principle is the glory of literature, calls *The Tempest* the "bedrock of drama" (1969, 67) because it is written from an animistic perspective. Prospero is indebted to "providence divine" for guiding him to the island and for placing his enemies within his reach, but to a large extent the powers given to the gods and to providence in the other romances are conferred here upon a human being. No doubt, the appeal of *The Tempest* lies, in part, in the directness and immediacy of its wish-fulfillment, in its regression to one of the earliest stages of primary-process thinking. One question we must ask, of course, is why Prospero gives up his magic. Is it a sign of movement to a religious or a scientific perspective?

This approach sheds a good deal of light upon the play, especially upon the ending, but it does not relate Prospero's magic to his personality and show us how it helps him to satisfy his specific psychological needs. Before he is overthrown, Prospero is a predominantly detached person. The detached person craves serenity, dislikes responsibility, and is averse to the struggle for power. His "two outstanding neurotic claims are that life should be . . . effortless and that he should not be bothered" (Horney 1950, 264). Prospero turns his responsibilities as duke over to his brother, rejects the pursuit of "worldly ends," and retires into his library, which is "dukedom large enough!" (II, ii). He immerses himself in a world of books, seeking glory not through the exercise of his office, which involves him in troublesome relations with other people, but through the pursuit of knowledge. As a result of his studies, he becomes "the prime duke, being so reputed / In dignity, and for the liberal arts / Without a parallel" (II, ii). He is not without ambition and a hunger for power, but he satisfies these needs in a detached way.

Prospero's study of magic is highly congruent with his personality. The detached person has an aversion to effort and places the greatest value upon freedom from constraint. Magic is a means of achieving one's ends without effort and of transcending the limitations of the human condition. It is a way of enforcing the claim that mind is the supreme reality, that the material world is subject to its dictates. Indeed, it symbolizes that claim. Through his withdrawal into the study of magic, Prospero is pursuing a dream of glory that is far more grandiose than any available to him as Duke of Milan. It is no wonder that he "prize[s]" his "volumes . . . above [his] dukedom." He becomes "transported / And rapt in secret studies" and grows a "stranger" to his state (I, ii).

Reality intrudes upon Prospero in the form of Antonio's plot, which leads to his expulsion from the dukedom. Although many critics have blamed Prospero for his neglect of his duties, Prospero does not seem to blame himself or to see himself as being responsible in any way for his fate. He interprets his withdrawal as a commendable unworldliness and presents his behavior toward his brother in a way that is flattering to himself:

> and my trust,
> Like a good parent, did beget of him
> A falsehood in its contrary as great
> As my trust was, which had indeed no limit,
> A confidence sans bound. (I, ii)

There are strong self-effacing tendencies in Prospero that lead him to think too well of his fellows and to bestow upon them a trust they do not deserve. Overtrustingness has disastrous consequences in the history plays and in the tragedies, but it has no permanent ill-effects in the comedies and romances. Prospero glorifies his excessive confidence in his brother and places the blame for what happens entirely upon Antonio's "evil nature." He seems to have no sense of how his own foolish behavior has contributed to his fate.

Antonio's betrayal marks the failure of Prospero's self-effacing bargain; his goodness to his brother, which he had expected to be repaid with gratitude and devotion, is used by Antonio to usurp the dukedom. This trauma is similar to those that precipitate psychological crises in the protagonists of the tragedies, crises from which none of them recover. Prospero's case is different because of his magic. Like the protagonists of the tragedies, Prospero is furious with those by whom he has been injured and craves a revenge that will assuage his anger and repair his idealized image. Unlike the characters in the realistic plays, however, he has a means of restoring his pride without being destructive to himself and others. He spends the next twelve years dreaming of his revenge and perfecting his magic in preparation for his vindictive triumph. *The Tempest* is the story of his day of reckoning.

Prospero has numerous objectives on this day, all of which he achieves through his magic. He wants to punish his enemies, to make a good match for his daughter, to get back what he has lost, to prove through his display of power that he was right to have immersed himself in his studies, and to demonstrate that he is the great man that he has felt himself to be, far superior to those who have humiliated him. The most important function of his magic, however, is that it enables him to resolve his psychological conflicts. Once he has been wronged, Prospero is caught between contradictory impulses. He is full of rage that he has a powerful need to express, but he feels that revenge is ignoble and that he will be as bad as his enemies if he allows himself to descend to their level. What Prospero needs is what Hamlet could not find and what Shakespeare is trying to imagine: a way of taking revenge and remaining innocent. This is a problem that only his magic can solve. *The Tempest* is above all a fantasy of innocent revenge. The revenge is Prospero's, but the fantasy is Shakespeare's, whose conflicting needs are similar to those of his protagonist.

The storm with which the play opens is an expression of Prospero's rage. It instills terror in his enemies and satisfies his need to make them suffer for what they have done to him. If the vindictive side of Prospero is embodied in the storm, his compassionate side is embodied in Miranda, who is full of pity for the suffering of the "poor souls" who seem to have "perish'd" (I, ii). Since Miranda is the product of Prospero's tutelage, she represents his ideal values, at least for a woman; and it is important to recognize that she is extremely self-effacing. When Prospero begins to tell the story of their past, her "heart bleeds / To think o' th' teen that I have turn'd you to"; and when he describes their expulsion, she exclaims, "Alack, what trouble / Was I then to you!" (I, ii). She wants to carry Ferdinand's logs for him, feels unworthy of his love, and swears to be his servant if he will not marry her (III, i). Like her father before his fall, she has an idealistic view of human nature. The "brave vessel" that has sunk "had no doubt some noble creature in her" (I, ii), and when she first sees the assembled company, she exclaims, "How beauteous mankind is! O brave new world / That has such people in't!" (V, i). Prospero is no longer so idealistic, but he has retained many of his self-effacing values and has instilled them in Miranda. He approves of her response to "the wrack, which touch'd / The very virtue of compassion in thee" (I, ii) and assures her that "There's no harm done." Through his "art" he has "So safely ordered" the storm that there is "not so much perdition as an hair / Betid to any creature in the vessel / Which thou heard'st cry." Miranda says that if she had "been any god of power" she would never have permitted the wreck to happen, and neither does Prospero. Through his magic, the wreck happens and does not happen. His magic permits him to satisfy his vindictive needs without violating the side of himself that is expressed by Miranda.[1] To further alleviate his discomfort with his sadistic behavior and Miranda's implied reproaches, Prospero claims that he has "done nothing but in care" of her and justifies his actions by telling the story of Antonio's perfidy.

Prospero's delight in the discomfiture of his enemies is revealed most vividly in his response to Ariel's account of his frightening behavior during the tempest. He asks Ariel if he has "Perform'd to point the tempest" he had commanded; and when Ariel replies that he has, Prospero's sadistic pleasure is evident: "My brave spirit! / Who was so firm, so

constant, that this coil / Would not infect his reason?"
His enthusiastic response inspires Ariel to elaborate:

> Not a soul
> But felt a fever of the mad and play'd
> Some tricks of desperation. All but mariners
> Plung'd in the foaming brine and quit the vessel,
> Then all afire with me. The King's son Ferdinand,
> With hair up-staring (then like reeds, not hair),
> Was the first man that leapt; cried "Hell is empty,
> And all the devils are here!"   (I, ii)

Once again Prospero expresses his approval: "Why, that's my spirit!" Since Ariel has carried out his orders "To every article," we must assume that the madness and desperation Ariel describes are precisely what Prospero intended. He is pleased not only by the terror of his enemies, but also by that of Ferdinand, his future son-in-law. He is rather indiscriminate in his punishments, as he is later in his forgiveness.

Prospero can enjoy the terror of his victims because he has not injured them physically: "But are they, Ariel, safe?" Not only are they safe, but their garments are "fresher than before" (I, ii). In the history plays and the tragedies, revengers incur guilt and bring destruction upon themselves by doing physical violence to their enemies. Prospero is a cunning and sadistic revenger who employs his magic to inflict psychological violence upon his enemies while he shields them from physical injury and thereby preserves his innocence. In his mind, as long as no one is physically injured, "There's no harm done" (I, ii). Having everyone fear imminent destruction, including the good Gonzalo, having them run mad with terror at Ariel's apparitions, having Ferdinand and Alonso believe each other dead, such things, for Prospero, do not constitute harm.

Prospero's cruelty toward his enemies may not appear to say much about his character because it seems justified by their outrageous treatment of him. He is prone to react with aggression, however, whenever he can find a justification, however slight, for doing so.[2] He says he will put Ferdinand in chains and force him to drink sea water and to eat mussels, withered roots, and acorn husks, and he makes him remove thousands of logs, "lest too light winning" of Miranda "Make the prize light" (I, ii). This seems a weak excuse for his sadistic behavior. His pleasure with Ariel for his management of the tempest is followed by a scene in which he threatens to "rend an oak / And peg [him] in his knotty entrails till / [He]

has howl'd away twelve winters" (I, ii). He even threatens Miranda when she beseeches him to have pity upon Ferdinand: "Silence! One word more / Shall make me chide thee, if not hate thee" (I, ii).

Prospero is usually benevolent until he feels that his kindness has been betrayed or unappreciated, and then he becomes vindictive. He feels betrayed by Antonio, of course, and unappreciated by Ariel when that spirit presses for liberty. He justifies his enslavement of Ariel by reminding him that it was his "art" that freed him from Sycorax's spell, and he threatens him with torments similar to those Sycorax had inflicted if he continues to complain. Prospero's threats seem to me an overreaction. He will peg Ariel in the entrails of an oak merely for murmuring. Prospero makes enormous claims on the basis of his kindness, and if others do not honor these claims he becomes enraged. If he is ready to punish Ariel and to hate Miranda for very slight offenses, think of the vindictiveness that he must be feeling toward Antonio. Ariel is self-effacing and knows how to make peace with Prospero. He thanks him for having freed him and promises to "be correspondent to command / And do [his] spriting gently" (I, ii). This allows Prospero to become benevolent once again, and he promises to discharge Ariel in two days. Ariel then says what Prospero wants to hear: "That's my noble master!" This is the way Prospero insists upon being perceived. Indeed, his anger with Ariel when he murmurs derives partly from the fact that Ariel has threatened his idealized image by making him seem unkind.

Ariel plays Prospero's game, but Caliban does not. Prospero is initially very kind to Caliban; he strokes him, gives him treats, educates him, and lodges him in his cell. And Caliban initially reciprocates; he loves Prospero and shows him "all the qualities o' the isle" (I, ii). Prospero turns against Caliban, however, when he seeks to violate Miranda's honor, and from this point on he treats Caliban with great brutality. Here, too, Prospero overreacts. He is so enraged, I propose, because Caliban has repeated Antonio's crime, accepting Prospero's favors and repaying them with treachery. Prospero discharges onto him all the anger that he feels toward the enemies back home who, before the day of reckoning, are beyond his power. Even after he enslaves Caliban, Prospero expects him to behave submissively. He complains to Miranda that Caliban "never / Yields us kind answer," but then he summons Caliban in a way that reveals the unreasonableness of his expectation: "What, ho!

slave! Caliban / Thou earth, thou! Speak!" (II, ii). When Caliban responds to being treated like dirt by being bitterly resentful, Prospero takes this as a sign of his irreclaimable nature.

There is a major contradiction in Prospero's attitude toward Caliban. He feels that Caliban is subhuman, but he holds him morally responsible for his acts and he punishes him severely. If Caliban is subhuman, then he is not morally responsible and should simply be kept away from Miranda, a precaution Prospero could easily effect. If he is a moral agent, then he needs to be shown the error of his ways; but Prospero's punishments are merely designed to torture him and to break his spirit. The contradiction in Prospero's attitude results from conflicting psychological needs. He needs to hold Caliban responsible because doing so allows him to act out his sadistic impulses, but he also needs to regard Caliban as subhuman because this allows him to avoid feeling guilt. If Caliban is subhuman, he is not part of Prospero's moral community, and Prospero's behavior toward him is not subject to the shoulds and taboos that are operative in his relations with his fellow human beings. Caliban provides Prospero with a splendid opportunity for justified aggression, for being vindictive without losing his nobility.

Prospero's rationalization of his treatment of Caliban works so well that the majority of critics have accepted his point of view and have felt that Caliban deserves what he gets, though some have been sympathetic toward Caliban's suffering and uneasy about Prospero's behavior (Auden 1962, 129). Prospero is constantly punishing Caliban, not just for the attempted rape, but also for the much lesser crimes of surliness, resentment, and insubordination. When Caliban is slow in responding to Prospero's summons ("Slave! Caliban! / Thou earth, thou!"), Prospero calls him again in an even nastier way: "Thou poisonous slave, got by the devil himself / Upon thy wicked dam, come forth!" (I, ii). Caliban does not yield a "kind answer" but enters with curses: "As wicked dew as e'er my mother brush'd / With raven's feather from unwholesome fen / Drop on you both!" Prospero responds by promising horrible punishments:

> For this, be sure, to-night thou shalt have cramps,
> Side-stitches that shall pen thy breath up; urchins
> Shall, for that vast of night that they may work,
> All exercise on thee; thou shalt be pinch'd
> As thick as honeycomb, each pinch more stinging
> Than bees that made 'em. (I, ii)

This is a very unequal contest, since Caliban's curses are merely words, an expression of ill-will, while Prospero has the power to inflict the torments he describes. Despite his "crime" in attempting Miranda (a natural act for an uncivilized being), Caliban seems to have reason for his resentment. He feels that the island is his (he was his "own king" before Prospero arrived), he has been turned into a drudge, and he is subject to vicious abuse. Prospero looks for penitence, submissiveness, and gracious service from Caliban and punishes him severely for his spirit of defiance. He seems to be trying to torture him into being a willing slave, like Ariel, and he is embittered by his lack of success.

Prospero and Caliban are caught in a vicious circle from which there seems to be no escape. The more Caliban resists what he perceives as Prospero's tyranny, the more Prospero punishes him; and the more Prospero punishes him, the more Caliban resists. He curses Prospero even though he knows that his spirits hear him and that he may be subject to retaliation—"yet I needs must curse" (II, ii). The need for this emotional relief must be powerful indeed in view of what may be in store for him:

> For every trifle are they set upon me;
> Sometimes like apes that mow and chatter at me,
> And after bite me; then like hedgehogs which
> Lie tumbling in my barefoot way and mount
> Their pricks at my footfall; sometime am I
> All wound with adders, who with cloven tongues
> Do hiss me into madness. (II, ii)

It is remarkable that Caliban's spirit has not been broken as a result of such torments. And it is no wonder that Caliban seizes the opportunity he thinks is presented by Stephano and Trinculo to revolt against Prospero. "I am subject," he tells them, "to a tyrant, / A sorcerer, that by his cunning hath / Cheated me of the island" (III, ii). Is this far from the truth? He claims that Prospero's spirits "all do hate him / As rootedly as I." It is impossible to say whether or not this is true, but it might be. Even Ariel must be threatened with terrible punishments and reminded once a month of what Prospero has done for him.

Prospero does not need to use his magic to resolve inner conflicts in his relationship with Caliban because regarding Caliban as subhuman allows him to act out his vindictive impulses without guilt or restraint. The combination of his sadistic imagination and his magic makes him an ingenious torturer. He could have used his magic more benignly if he had regarded Caliban as part of his moral community, but this would have generated conflicts and deprived him of his scapegoat. (See Berger 1970, 261, on Caliban as scapegoat.) He insists, therefore, that Caliban is uneducable: "A devil, a born devil, on whose nature / Nurture can never stick! on whom my pains, / Humanely taken, all, all lost, quite lost!" (IV, i). His judgment is reinforced by Miranda, who abhors Caliban, in part, because his vindictiveness violates her self-effacing values, and by Caliban's plot, which seems to demonstrate his innate depravity. Since there is no point in being humane to a born devil, Prospero is free to "plague" him "to roaring."[3]

Many critics agree that Caliban is a hopeless case, but some are impressed by his sensitivity in "The isle is full of noises" speech (III, ii) and by his declaration that he will "seek for grace" (V, i) (see also Berger 1970, 255). His plot can be seen as a reaction to Prospero's abuse rather than as a sign that he is an "abhorred slave / Which any print of goodness wilt not take" (I, ii). Prospero must hold onto his image of Caliban as a devil in order to hold onto his idealized image of himself. If Caliban is redeemable, then Prospero has been a monster. The exchange of curses between Prospero and Caliban indicates that they have much in common. What Prospero hates and punishes in Caliban is the forbidden part of himself. His denial of moral status to Caliban is in part a rationale for his vindictive behavior and in part a way of denying the similarities that clearly exist between them. Prospero is doing to Caliban what Caliban would do to Prospero if he had the power.

Prospero is much more careful in his treatment of his fellow humans, some of whom strike us as being considerably more depraved than Caliban. Indeed, Prospero calls Caliban a devil but feels that Antonio and Sebastian "are worse than devils" (III, iii). Nonetheless, he regards them as fellow human beings and his shoulds and taboos are fully operative in relation to them. Not only does he conceal his vindictiveness from himself (and from many of the critics) by employing his magic to punish them without doing any "harm," but he justifies his treatment of them by seeing it as conducive to their moral growth. His object is not revenge but regeneration and reconciliation. Ariel articulates Prospero's perspective in the banquet scene. He accuses the "three men of sin" of their crimes against "good Prospero," threatens them with "ling'ring perdition," and indicates that they can escape Prospero's wrath only by "heart's sorrow / And

a clear life ensuing" (III, iii). Even as Prospero is knitting them up in "fits" and exulting in the fact that "they are now in [his] pow'r," he is being presented in a very noble light. He manages to take revenge in such a way that he emerges as the benefactor of his victims.

After he has tormented them so much that "the good old Lord Gonzalo" is in tears at the sight and even Ariel has "a feeling / Of their afflictions," Prospero relents, as he had intended to do all along:

Though with their high wrongs I am struck to th'
  quick,
Yet with my nobler reason 'gainst my fury
Do I take part. The rarer action is
In virtue than in vengeance. They being penitent,
The sole drift of my purpose doth extend
Not a frown further.   (V, i)

Although Prospero is still furious with the evil three, his perfectionistic and self-effacing shoulds are stronger than his vindictive impulses. He releases them from his spell, in part, because his cruelty is making him uneasy and, in part, because his need for revenge has been assuaged by their suffering. He proclaims that "the rarer action is / In virtue than in vengeance," but he says this only after he has gotten a goodly measure of vengeance. He makes it seem that his only purpose has been to bring the men of sin to penitence, but that is hardly the case. This is a play not only about renouncing revenge but also about getting it.

There has been much debate over whether Prospero's enemies are indeed repentant. Prospero's forgiveness is made contingent upon penitence and a clear life after, but only Alonso seems to merit his pardon. Alonso displays his remorse again and again, but Sebastian and Antonio show no sign of repentance or promise of reformation. They have plotted against Prospero in the past; they try to kill Alonso during the course of the play; and they seem at the play's end still to be dangerous fellows. Many critics have speculated upon the likelihood of their continued criminality upon the return to Italy. In 1797, F. G. Waldron wrote a sequel to *The Tempest* in which Antonio and Sebastian betray Prospero during the voyage home and force him to retrieve his magic.

Why, then, does Prospero forgive them? It may be that he thinks they have repented, but I do not think he does. While Antonio is still under his spell, Prospero says, "I forgive thee, / Unnatural though thou art" (V, i); and when he has returned to full consciousness, Prospero forgives him again, in an even more contemptuous way:

> For you, most wicked sir, whom to call brother
> Would even infect my mouth, I do forgive
> Thy rankest fault—all of them . . .   (V, i)

As Bonamy Dobrée (1952) suggested, there is a nasty quality about Prospero's forgiveness. More like revenge than a movement toward reconciliation, it is a vindictive forgiveness that satisfies his need to express his scorn and bitterness while appearing to be noble. Antonio's undeservingness contributes to Prospero's sense of moral grandeur; the worse Antonio is, the more charitable is Prospero to forgive him. This is Prospero's perspective and that of the play's rhetoric; but from a psychological point of view, Prospero's forgiveness seems compulsive, indiscriminate, and dangerous. It is inappropriate to the practical and moral realities of the situation but necessary if Prospero is to maintain his idealized image.

For most of the play, Prospero's idealized image contains a combination of arrogant-vindictive and self-effacing traits that are reconciled by means of his magic. He needs to see himself as a humane, benevolent, forgiving man, and also as a powerful, masterful, dangerous man who cannot be taken advantage of with impunity and who will strike back when he has been injured. The first four acts of the play show Prospero satisfying his needs for mastery and revenge, but in ways that do not violate his perfectionistic and self-effacing dictates. By the end of act 4, he has achieved his objectives. He has knit up Antonio, Sebastian, and Alonso in his spell and has thwarted the plot of Caliban, Stephano, and Trinculo, with a final display of innocent delight in the torture of the conspirators. Prospero sets his dogs (two of whom are aptly named Fury and Tyrant) upon them, and tells Ariel to charge his "goblins that they grind their joints / With dry convulsions, shorten up their sinews / With aged cramps, and more pinch-spotted make them / Than pard or cat o' mountain" (IV, i). "At this hour," Prospero proclaims, "Lie at my mercy all mine enemies." From this point on, he becomes increasingly self-effacing. At the beginning of the next act, he gives up his vengeance and determines to renounce his magic. Once he gives up his magic, he has no choice but to repress his vindictive trends, for it was only through his magic that he was able to act them out innocently.

Prospero represses his vindictive side for a number of reasons. He has shown his power. Now, in order to satisfy his self-effacing shoulds, he must show his mercy. He cannot stop behaving vindictively until his anger has been partially assuaged, but he cannot continue once his enemies are in his power. That he is still angry is clear from the manner of his forgiveness, but the imperative to forgive is now more powerful than the need for revenge. Given his inner conflicts, Prospero is bound to feel uncomfortable about his aggressive behavior; and now that he has had his day of reckoning, his negative feelings about it become dominant. He regards revenge as ignoble and "abjures" his "rough magic" (V, i). His choice of words here is significant. He seems to feel ashamed of his magic (even as he celebrates its powers) and guilty for having employed it. Why else would he use the word "abjure," which means to disavow, recant, or repudiate? Whereas earlier he was able to enjoy his power, he now has a self-effacing response to it. He gives up his magic because he needs to place himself in an humble position and to show that he has not used his power for personal aggrandizement, but only to set things right, to bring about moral growth and reconciliation.

Although *Henry VIII* was yet to come, *The Tempest* is often read as Shakespeare's farewell to the theater, and Prospero is seen as his supreme embodiment of the artist figure. Though it is impossible to tell to what extent Prospero is Shakespeare's alter ego, there are some striking parallels. Prospero uses his magic and Shakespeare uses his art to attain mastery and to achieve disguised or innocent revenge. Shakespeare condemns or even kills off in his plays the kinds of people who have hurt him or of whom he is most afraid, but, like Prospero, he maintains a posture of benevolence and wisdom.[4] Again like Prospero, he seems after a certain point (*Timon*) to become more and more self-effacing; and he prematurely relinquishes his magic, perhaps because he, too, feels guilty about his exercise of power and needs to embrace "the blessedness of being little" (*Henry VIII*, IV, ii).

In the Epilogue, with his "charms . . . o'erthrown," Prospero adopts an extremely self-effacing posture. Since he can no longer "enchant," he can "be reliev'd" only by prayer,

> Which pierces so that it assaults
> Mercy itself and frees all faults.
> As you from crimes would pardon'd be,
> Let your indulgence set me free.

Prospero sees himself here not as the avenger, but as the guilty party, perhaps because of his revenge; and he tries to make a self-effacing bargain in which he judges not so that he will not be judged. We can now understand more fully his motives for forgiving the men of sin. Beneath his self-righteousness, Prospero has hidden feelings of guilt and fears of retribution. By refusing to take a more severe form of revenge, to which he certainly seems entitled, he protects himself against punishment. By forgiving others, he ensures his own pardon. Giving up his magic serves a similar purpose. It counteracts his feelings of pride and places him in a dependent, submissive position. Although Prospero's remarks in the Epilogue are partly a conventional appeal to the audience, he remains in character and expresses sentiments that are in keeping with his psychological development.

When we understand Prospero's psychological development, he seems different from the figure celebrated by so many critics. Those who interpret *The Tempest* as a story of magnanimity, forgiveness, and reconciliation are responding correctly, I believe, to Shakespeare's thematic intentions, whereas those who take a more "hard-nosed" view of the play are responding to the psychological portrait of Prospero. There is in this play, as in some others, a disparity between rhetoric and mimesis that generates conflicting critical responses and reflects the inner divisions of the author (see Paris 1991).

In his presentation of Prospero, Shakespeare employs a powerful rhetoric both of justification and of glorification. He employs numerous devices that justify Prospero's behavior toward Antonio, Sebastian, Alonso, Caliban, Ariel, Ferdinand, Stephano, and Trinculo—toward all the characters, in effect, whom Prospero treats harshly. Early in the play, there is some rhetoric of glorification and some rhetoric of justification toward the end, but by and large the justification occurs when Prospero is being punitive and the glorification occurs after he gives up his vengeance. We learn early in the play of Prospero's betrayal by his brother, of the dangers to which he was exposed, of Ariel's impatience, of Caliban's treachery, of the need to test Ferdinand, and of the continued perfidy of Antonio and Sebastian. All these things justify Prospero's harshness, as does Miranda's condemnation of Caliban and Ariel's acceptance of Prospero's reproaches. As the play progresses, Prospero is increasingly surrounded by a rhetoric of glorification. He is praised by Ariel ("my

noble master") and Ferdinand ("so rare a wonder'd father"), and he receives a tribute even from Caliban, who is impressed by his fineness and determines to "seek for grace." (Though Prospero cannot afford to recognize it, Caliban reforms when Prospero stops torturing him and holds out the prospect of pardon.)

The rhetoric of the play justifies the vindictive Prospero and glorifies the self-effacing one. It confirms Prospero's idealized image of himself as a kindly, charitable man who punishes others much less than they deserve and only for their own good. Meanwhile, the action of the play shows us a Prospero who is bitter, sadistic, and hungry for revenge. The disparity between rhetoric and mimesis is a reflection of Prospero's inner conflicts and of Shakespeare's. The rhetoric rationalizes and disguises Prospero's vindictiveness and celebrates his moral nobility.[5] Its function is similar to that of Prospero's magic. The magic enables Prospero to have his revenge and to remain innocent in his own eyes and in the eyes of the other characters. The magic and the rhetoric together enable Shakespeare to deceive himself and the audience as to Prospero's true nature.

Notes

1. Kahn observed that Prospero achieves "a brilliant compromise between revenge and charity, which allows him to have his cake and eat it too." The trials to which he subjects Antonio, Sebastian, and Alonso "would add up to a tidy revenge were they not sheer illusion . . . and were they not perpetrated for the sake of arousing 'heart-sorrow and a clear life ensuing.' They are and are not revenge" (1981, 223).

2. I am one of the relatively small number of critics who subscribe to what Harry Berger, Jr., calls "the hard-nosed" as opposed to the "sentimental" view of Prospero (1970, 279). See also Leech (1961), Abenheimer (1946), Auden (1962, 128–34), and Dobrée (1952).

3. In his response to my interpretation of *The Tempest* at the 1985 Florida Conference on Shakespeare's Personality, J. Dennis Huston pointed out that Prospero may have yet another motive for classifying Caliban as subhuman: "he does not have to recognize that he, like Antonio, has used raw power to usurp a kingdom belonging to another: if Caliban is really subhuman, he can hardly have valid claims to the island."

4. As A. D. Nuttall observed in his response to this chapter, "You can kill people in plays without hurting anyone."
5. David Sundelson observed that "much in the play that might pass for dissent only adds to Prospero's stature—the brief quarrel with Ariel, for example." He speaks of the "sanctioned narcissism of Prospero" (1980, 38, 39).

Works Cited

Abenheimer, K. M. 1946. "Shakespeare's *Tempest*: A Psychological Analysis." *Psychoanalytic Review* 33:339–415.

Auden, W. H. 1962. *The Dyer's Hand.* New York: Random House.

Berger, Harry, Jr. 1970. "The Miraculous Harp: A Reading of Shakespeare's *Tempest.*" *Shakespeare Studies* 5:254–83.

Dobrée, Bonamy. 1952. "The Tempest." *New Series of Essays and Studies* 5:13–25.

Freud, Sigmund. [n.d.]. *Totem and Taboo.* New York: Vintage Books.

Frye, Northrop. 1969. Introduction to *The Tempest.* In *Twentieth Century Interpretations of the Tempest.* Edited by Hallet Smith. Englewood Cliffs, NJ: Prentice-Hall.

Horney, Karen. 1950. *Neurosis and Human Growth: The Struggle Toward Self-Realization.* New York: Norton.

Kahn, Coppélia. 1981. *Man's Estate: Masculine Identity in Shakespeare.* Berkeley and Los Angeles: University of California Press.

Leech, Clifford. 1961. *Shakespeare's Tragedies.* London: Chatto & Windus.

Paris, Bernard J. 1991. *Character as a Subversive Force in Shakespeare: The History and the Roman Plays.* Rutherford, NJ: Fairleigh Dickinson University Press.

Sundelson, David. 1980. "So Rare a Wonder'd Father: Prospero's *Tempest.*" In *Representing Shakespeare: New Psychoanalytic Essays.* Edited by Murray M. Schwartz and Coppélia Kahn. Baltimore: Johns Hopkins University Press.

The Immortality Ode

Lionel Trilling

Lionel Trilling's essay is perhaps the most widely known commentary of Wordsworth's Ode, and it is frequently taken as a point of reference by later critics, as the selections in this book attest. But while critics like Vendler, for example, object that Trilling is not sufficiently formalist in his reading, Trilling's own quarrel was with the then-dominant historical and biographical interpretations that saw the poem as Wordsworth's "conscious farewell to his art, a dirge sung over his departing powers." Against this biographical reading, Trilling opposes a mimetic reading: this is not a poem about Wordsworth growing old; it is a poem about a human being growing up. "If we understand that Wordsworth is speaking of a period common to the development of everyone, we are helped to see that we cannot identify the vision of that period with his peculiar poetic power . . . for what we must now see is that Wordsworth is talking about something common to us all, the development of the sense of reality."

The speaker of the poem, in short, is not Wordsworth but Everyman. In drawing on Freud and the insights of psychoanalysis to illuminate the poem, Trilling is not offering to analyze the psyche of the author (cf. the essay by Ross in chapter 1) but instead to use Freud's insights into general human nature to analyze the psyche of the speaker as representative human figure. Wordsworth here is not the analysand but the analyst, an equally perceptive student of human nature whose insights are confirmed by science. "Wordsworth, like Freud, was preoccupied by the idea of reality, and, again like Freud, he knew that the child's way of apprehension was but a stage which, in the course of nature, would give way to another." Finally, then, Trilling takes the oldest and strongest mimetic line: human nature does not change

Reprinted from *The Liberal Imagination*. New York: The Viking Press, 1950: 129–34, 141–47. Copyright © 1950 by Lionel Trilling. Reprinted by permission of The Wylie Agency, Inc. Parts of the essay have been omitted, and the notes have been renumbered.

much from time to time nor from place to place, and
great literature achieves its power by representing this
nature. Historical and biographical readings, by making
the general personal and the universal local, diminish
this power. "It seems to me that those critics who made
the Ode refer to some particular and unique experience
of Wordsworth's and who make it relate only to poetical
powers have forgotten their own lives and in conse-
quence conceive the Ode to be a lesser thing than it
really is, for it is not about poetry, it is about life."

Criticism, we know, must always be concerned
with the poem itself. But a poem does not always exist only in itself: sometimes it has a very
lively existence in its false or partial appearances.
These simulacra of the actual poem must be taken
into account by criticism; and sometimes, in its effort
to come at the poem as it really is, criticism does well
to allow the simulacra to dictate at least its opening
moves. In speaking about Wordsworth's "Ode: Intimations of Immortality from Recollections of Early
Childhood," I should like to begin by considering an
interpretation of the poem which is commonly
made. According to this interpretation—I choose for
its brevity Dean Sperry's statement of a view which
is held by many other admirable critics—the Ode is
"Wordsworth's conscious farewell to his art, a dirge
sung over his departing powers."

How did this interpretation—erroneous, as I believe—come into being? The Ode may indeed be
quoted to substantiate it, but I do not think it has
been drawn directly from the poem itself. To be sure,
the Ode is not wholly perspicuous. Wordsworth
himself seems to have thought it difficult, for in the
Fenwick notes he speaks of the need for competence
and attention in the reader. The difficulty does not lie
in the diction, which is simple, or even in the syntax,
which is sometimes obscure, but rather in certain
contradictory statements which the poem makes,
and in the ambiguity of some of its crucial words. Yet
the erroneous interpretation I am dealing with does
not arise from any intrinsic difficulty of the poem itself but rather from certain extraneous and unexpressed assumptions which some of its readers make
about the nature of the mind.

Nowadays it is not difficult for us to understand
that such tacit assumptions about the mental processes are likely to lie hidden beneath what we say
about poetry. Usually, despite our general awareness
of their existence, it requires great effort to bring

these assumptions explicitly into consciousness. But
in speaking of Wordsworth one of the commonest of
our unexpressed ideas comes so close to the surface
of our thought that it needs only to be grasped and
named. I refer to the belief that poetry is made by
means of a particular poetic faculty, a faculty which
may be isolated and defined.

It is this belief, based wholly upon assumption,
which underlies all the speculations of the critics
who attempt to provide us with explanations of
Wordsworth's poetic decline by attributing it to one
or another of the events of his life. In effect any such
explanation is a way of *defining* Wordsworth's poetic
faculty: what the biographical critics are telling us is
that Wordsworth wrote great poetry by means of a
faculty which depended upon his relations with Annette Vallon, or by means of a faculty which operated
only so long as he admired the French Revolution, or
by means of a faculty which flourished by virtue of
a particular pitch of youthful sense-perception or by
virtue of a certain attitude toward Jeffrey's criticism
or by virtue of a certain relation with Coleridge.

Now no one can reasonably object to the idea of
mental determination in general, and I certainly do
not intend to make out that poetry is an unconditioned activity. Still, this particular notion of mental
determination which implies that Wordsworth's genius failed when it was deprived of some single
emotional circumstance is so much too simple and so
much too mechanical that I think we must inevitably
reject it. Certainly what we know of poetry does not
allow us to refer the making of it to any single faculty. Nothing less than the whole mind, the whole
man, will suffice for its origin. And such was Wordsworth's own view of the matter.

There is another unsubstantiated assumption at
work in the common biographical interpretation of
the Ode. This is the belief that a natural and inevitable warfare exists between the poetic faculty
and the faculty by which we conceive or comprehend general ideas. Wordsworth himself did not believe in this antagonism—indeed, he held an almost
contrary view—but Coleridge thought that philosophy had encroached upon and destroyed his own
powers, and the critics who speculate on Wordsworth's artistic fate seem to prefer Coleridge's psychology to Wordsworth's own. Observing in the Ode
a contrast drawn between something called "the visionary gleam" and something called "the philosophic mind," they leap to the conclusion that the

Ode is Wordsworth's conscious farewell to his art, a dirge sung over departing powers.

I am so far from agreeing with this conclusion that I believe the Ode is not only not a dirge sung over departing powers but actually a dedication to new powers. Wordsworth did not, to be sure, realize his hopes for these new powers, but that is quite another matter.

As with many poems, it is hard to understand any part of the Ode until we first understand the whole of it. I will therefore say at once what I think the poem is chiefly about. It is a poem about growing; some say it is a poem about growing old, but I believe it is about growing up. It is incidentally a poem about optics and then, inevitably, about epistemology; it is concerned with ways of seeing and then with ways of knowing. Ultimately it is concerned with ways of acting, for, as usual with Wordsworth, knowledge implies liberty and power. In only a limited sense is the Ode a poem about immortality.

Both formally and in the history of its composition the poem is divided into two main parts. The first part, consisting of four stanzas, states an optical phenomenon and asks a question about it. The second part, consisting of seven stanzas, answers that question and is itself divided into two parts, of which the first is despairing, the second hopeful. Some time separates the composition of the question from that of the answer; the evidence most recently adduced by Professor de Selincourt seems to indicate that the interval was two years.

The question which the first part asks is this:

Whither is fled the visionary gleam?
Where is it now, the glory and the dream?

All the first part leads to this question, but although it moves in only one direction it takes its way through more than one mood. There are at least three moods before the climax of the question is reached.

The first stanza makes a relatively simple statement. "There was a time" when all common things seemed clothed in "celestial light," when they had "the glory and the freshness of a dream." In a poem ostensibly about immortality we ought perhaps to pause over the word "celestial," but the present elaborate title was not given to the poem until much later, and conceivably at the time of the writing of the first part the idea of immortality was not in Wordsworth's mind at all. Celestial light probably means

only something different from ordinary, earthly, scientific light; it is a light of the mind, shining even in darkness — "by night or day" — and it is perhaps similar to the light which is praised in the invocation to the third book of *Paradise Lost*.

The second stanza goes on to develop this first mood, speaking of the ordinary, physical kind of vision and suggesting further the meaning of "celestial." We must remark that in this stanza Wordsworth is so far from observing a diminution of his physical senses that he explicitly affirms their strength. He is at pains to tell us how vividly he sees the rainbow, the rose, the moon, the stars, the water and the sunshine. I emphasize this because some of those who find the Ode a dirge over the poetic power maintain that the poetic power failed with the failure of Wordsworth's senses. It is true that Wordsworth, who lived to be eighty, was said in middle life to look much older than his years. Still, thirty-two, his age at the time of writing the first part of the Ode, is an extravagantly early age for a dramatic failure of the senses. We might observe here, as others have observed elsewhere, that Wordsworth never did have the special and perhaps modern sensibility of his sister or of Coleridge, who were so aware of exquisite particularities. His finest passages are moral, emotional, subjective; whatever visual intensity they have comes from his response to the object, not from his close observation of it.

And in the second stanza Wordsworth not only confirms his senses but he also confirms his ability to perceive beauty. He tells us how he responds to the loveliness of the rose and of the stars reflected in the water. He can deal, in the way of Fancy, with the delight of the moon when there are no competing stars in the sky. He can see in Nature certain moral propensities. He speaks of the sunshine as a "glorious birth." But here he pauses to draw distinctions from that fascinating word "glory": despite his perception of the sunshine as a glorious birth, he knows "That there hath past away a glory from the earth."

Now, with the third stanza, the poem begins to complicate itself. It is *while* Wordsworth is aware of the "optical" change in himself, the loss of the "glory," that there comes to him "a thought of grief." I emphasize the word "while" to suggest that we must understand that for some time he had been conscious of the "optical" change *without* feeling grief. The grief, then, would seem to be coincidental with but not necessarily caused by the change.

And the grief is not of long duration, for we learn that

A timely utterance gave that thought relief,
    And I again am strong.

It would be not only interesting but also useful to know what that "timely utterance" was, and I shall hazard a guess; but first I should like to follow the development of the Ode a little further, pausing only to remark that the reference to the timely utterance seems to imply that, although the grief is not of long duration, still we are not dealing with the internal experiences of a moment, or of a morning's walk, but of a time sufficient to allow for development and change of mood; that is, the dramatic time of the poem is not exactly equivalent to the emotional time.

Stanza IV goes on to tell us that the poet, after gaining relief from the timely utterance, whatever that was, felt himself quite in harmony with the joy of Nature in spring. The tone of this stanza is ecstatic, and in a way that some readers find strained and unpleasant and even of doubtful sincerity. Twice there is a halting repetition of words to express a kind of painful intensity of response: "I feel—I feel it all," and "I hear, I hear, with joy I hear!" Wordsworth sees, hears, feels—and with that "joy" which both he and Coleridge felt to be so necessary to the poet. But despite the response, despite the joy, the ecstasy changes to sadness in a wonderful modulation which quite justifies the antecedent shrillness of affirmation:

    —But there's a Tree, of many, one,
    A single Field which I have looked upon,
    Both of them speak of something that is gone:
    The Pansy at my feet
    Doth the same tale repeat.

And what they utter is the terrible question:

    Whiter is fled the visionary gleam?
    Where is it now, the glory and the dream?

•   •   •

The second half of the Ode is divided into two large movements, each of which gives an answer to the question with which the first part ends. The two answers seem to contradict each other. The first issues in despair, the second in hope; the first uses a language strikingly supernatural, the second is entirely naturalistic. The two parts even differ in the statement of fact, for the first says that the gleam is gone, whereas the second says that it is not gone, but only transmuted. It is necessary to understand this contradiction, but it is not necessary to resolve it, for from the circuit between its two poles comes much of the power of the poem.

The first of the two answers (stanzas V–VIII) tells us where the visionary gleam has gone by telling us where it came from. It is a remnant of a pre-existence in which we enjoyed a way of seeing and knowing now almost wholly gone from us. We come into the world, not with minds that are merely *tabulae rasae*, but with a kind of attendant light, the vestige of an existence otherwise obliterated from our memories. In infancy and childhood the recollection is relatively strong, but it fades as we move forward into earthly life. Maturity, with its habits and its cares and its increase of distance from our celestial origin, wears away the light of recollection. Nothing could be more poignantly sad than the conclusion of this part with the heavy sonority of its last line as Wordsworth addresses the child in whom the glory still lives:

    Full soon thy Soul shall have her earthly freight,
    And custom lie upon thee with a weight,
    Heavy as frost, and deep almost as life!

Between this movement of despair and the following movement of hope there is no clear connection save that of contradiction. But between the question itself and the movement of hope there is an explicit verbal link, for the question is: "Whither has *fled* the visionary gleam?" and the movement of hope answers that "nature yet remembers / What was so *fugitive*."

The second movement of the second part of the Ode tells us again what has happened to the visionary gleam: it has not wholly fled, for it is remembered. This possession of childhood has been passed on as a legacy to the child's heir, the adult man; for the mind, as the rainbow epigraph also says, is one and continuous, and what was so intense a light in childhood becomes "the fountain-light of all our day" and a "master-light of all our seeing," that is, of our adult day and our mature seeing. The child's recollection of his heavenly home exists in the recollection of the adult.

But what exactly is this fountain-light, this master-light? I am sure that when we understand what it is we shall see that the glory that Wordsworth means is very different from Coleridge's glory, which is Joy. Wordsworth says that what he holds in memory as the guiding heritage of childhood is exactly not the Joy of childhood. It is not "delight," not "liberty," not even "hope"—not for these, he says, "I raise / The song of thanks and praise." For what then does he raise the song? For this particular experience of childhood:

> . . . those obstinate questionings
> Of sense and outward things,
> Fallings from us, vanishings;
> Blank misgivings of a Creature
> Moving about in worlds not realised.

He mentions other reasons for gratitude, but here for the moment I should like to halt the enumeration.

We are told, then, that light and glory consist, at least in part, of "questionings," "fallings from us," "vanishings," and "blank misgivings" in a world not yet *made real*, for surely Wordsworth uses the word "realised" in its most literal sense. In his note on the poem he has this to say of the experience he refers to:

> . . . I was often unable to think of external things as having external existence, but I communed with all that I saw as something not apart from, but inherent in, my own material nature. Many times while going to school have I grasped at a wall or tree to recall myself from this abyss of idealism to the reality. At this time I was afraid of such processes.

He remarks that the experience is not peculiar to himself, which is of course true, and he says that it was connected in his thoughts with a potency of spirit which made him believe that he could never die.

The precise and naturalistic way in which Wordsworth talks of this experience of his childhood must cast doubt on Professor Garrod's statement that Wordsworth believed quite literally in the notion of pre-existence, with which the "vanishings" experience is connected. Wordsworth is very careful to delimit the extent of his belief; he says that it is "too shadowy a notion to be recommended to faith" as an evidence of immortality. He says that he is using the idea to illuminate another idea—using it, as he says, "for my purpose" and "as a poet." It has as much validity for him as any "popular" religious idea might have, that is to say, a kind of suggestive validity. We may regard pre-existence as being for Wordsworth a very serious conceit, vested with relative belief, intended to give a high value to the natural experience of the "vanishings."[1]

The naturalistic tone of Wordsworth's note suggests that we shall be doing no violence to the experience of the "vanishings" if we consider it sci-entifically. In a well-known essay, "Stages in the Development of the Sense of Reality," the distinguished psychoanalyst Ferenczi speaks of the child's reluctance to distinguish between himself and the world and of the slow growth of objectivity which differentiates the self from external things. And Freud himself, dealing with the "oceanic" sensation of "being at one with the universe," which a literary friend had supposed to be the source of all religious emotions, conjectures that it is a vestige of the infant's state of feeling before he has learned to distinguish between the stimuli of his own sensations and those of the world outside. In *Civilization and Its Discontents* he writes:

> Originally the ego includes everything, later it detaches from itself the outside world. The ego-feeling we are aware of now is thus only a shrunken vestige of a more extensive feeling—a feeling which embraced the universe and expressed an inseparable connection of the ego with the external world. If we may suppose that this primary ego-feeling has been preserved in the minds of many people—to a greater or lesser extent—it would co-exist like a sort of counterpart with the narrower and more sharply outlined ego-feeling of maturity, and the ideational content belonging to it would be precisely the notion of limitless extension and one-ness with the universe—the same feeling as that described by my friend as "oceanic."

This has its clear relation to Wordsworth's "worlds not realised." Wordsworth, like Freud, was preoccupied by the idea of reality, and, again like Freud, he knew that the child's way of apprehension was but a stage which, in the course of nature, would give way to another. If we understand that Wordsworth is speaking of a period common to the development of everyone, we are helped to see that we cannot identify the vision of that period with his peculiar poetic power.

But in addition to the experience of the "vanishings" there is another experience for which Wordsworth is grateful to his childhood and which, I believe, goes with the "vanishings" to make up the "master-light," the "fountain-light." I am not referring to the

> High instincts before which our mortal Nature
> Did tremble like a guilty Thing surprised,

but rather to what Wordsworth calls "those first affections."

I am inclined to think that with this phrase Wordsworth refers to a later stage in the child's development which, like the earlier stage in which the external world is included within the ego, leaves vestiges in the developing mind. This is the period described in a well-known passage in Book II of *The Prelude,* in which the child learns about the world in his mother's arms:

> Blest the infant Babe,
> (For with my best conjecture I would trace
> Our Being's earthly progress), blest the Babe,
> Nursed in his Mother's arms, who sinks to sleep,
> Rocked on his Mother's breast; who with his soul
> Drinks in the feelings of his Mother's eye!
> For him, in one dear Presence, there exists
> A virtue which irradiates and exalts
> Objects through widest intercourse of sense.
> No outcast he, bewildered and depressed:
> Along his infant veins are interfused
> The gravitation and the filial bond
> Of nature that connect him with the world.
> Is there a flower, to which he points with hand
> Too weak to gather it, already love
> Drawn from love's purest earthly fount for him
> Hath beautified that flower; already shades
> Of pity cast from inward tenderness
> Do fall around him upon aught that bears
> Unsightly marks of violence or harm.
> Emphatically such a Being lives,
> Frail creature as he is, helpless as frail,
> An inmate of this active universe:
> For feeling has to him imparted power
> That through the growing faculties of sense,
> Doth like an agent of the one great Mind
> Create, creator and receiver both,
> Working but in alliance with the works
> Which it beholds. — Such, verily, is the first
> Poetic[2] spirit of our human life,
> By uniform control of after years,
> In most, abated or suppressed; in some,
> Through every change of growth and of decay
> Pre-eminent till death.

The child, this passage says, does not perceive things merely as objects; he first sees them, because maternal love is a condition of his perception, as objects-and-judgments, as valued objects. He does not learn about a flower, but about the pretty-flower, the flower that-I-want-and-that-mother-will-get-for-me; he does not learn about the bird and a broken wing but about the poor-bird-whose-wing-was-broken. The safety, warmth, and good feeling of his mother's conscious benevolence is a circumstance of

his first learning. He sees, in short, with "glory"; not only is he himself not in "utter nakedness" as the Ode puts it, but the objects he sees are not in utter nakedness. The passage from *The Prelude* says in naturalistic language what stanza v of the Ode expresses by a theistical metaphor. Both the *Prelude* passage and the Ode distinguish a state of exile from a state of security and comfort, of at-homeness; there is (as the *Prelude* passage puts it) a "filial bond," or (as in stanza x of the Ode) a "primal sympathy," which keeps man from being an "outcast . . . bewildered and depressed."

The Ode and *The Prelude* differ about the source of this primal sympathy or filial bond. The Ode makes heavenly pre-existence the source, *The Prelude* finds the source in maternal affection. But the psychologists tell us that notions of heavenly pre-existence figure commonly as representations of physical pre-natality — the womb is the environment which is perfectly adapted to its inmate and compared to it all other conditions of life may well seem like "exile" to the (very literal) "outcast."[3] Even the security of the mother's arms, although it is an effort to re-create for the child the old environment, is but a diminished comfort. And if we think of the experience of which Wordsworth is speaking, the "vanishings," as the child's recollection of a condition in which it was very nearly true that he and his environment were one, it will not seem surprising that Wordsworth should compound the two experiences and figure them in the single metaphor of the glorious heavenly pre-existence.[4]

I have tried to be as naturalistic as possible in speaking of Wordsworth's childhood experiences and the more-or-less Platonic notion they suggested to him. I believe that naturalism is in order here, for what we must now see is that Wordsworth is talking about something common to us all, the development of the sense of reality. To have once had the visionary gleam of the perfect union of the self and the universe is essential to and definitive of our human nature, and it is in that sense connected with the making of poetry. But the visionary gleam is not in itself the poetry-making power, and its diminution is right and inevitable.

That there should be ambivalence in Wordsworth's response to this diminution is quite natural, and the two answers, that of stanzas V–VIII and that of stanzas IX–XI, comprise both the resistance to and the acceptance of growth. Inevitably we resist change and turn back with passionate nostalgia to the stage we are leaving. Still, we fulfill ourselves by choosing what is painful and difficult and necessary, and we develop by moving toward death. In short, organic development is a hard paradox which Wordsworth is stating in the discrepant answers of the second part of the Ode. And it seems to me that those critics who made the Ode refer to some particular and unique experience of Wordsworth's and who make it relate only to poetical powers have forgotten their own lives and in consequence conceive the Ode to be a lesser thing than it really is, for it is not about poetry, it is about life. And having made this error, they are inevitably led to misinterpret the meaning of the "philosophic mind" and also to deny that Wordsworth's ambivalence is sincere. No doubt it would not be a sincere ambivalence if Wordsworth were really saying farewell to poetry, it would merely be an attempt at self-consolation. But he is not saying farewell to poetry, he is saying farewell to Eden, and his ambivalence is much what Adam's was, and Milton's, and for the same reasons.[5]

To speak naturalistically of the quasi-mystical experiences of his childhood does not in the least bring into question the value which Wordsworth attached to them, for, despite its dominating theistical metaphor, the Ode is largely naturalistic in its intention. We can begin to see what that intention is by understanding the force of the word "imperial" in stanza VI. This stanza is the second of the four stanzas in which Wordsworth states and develops the theme of the reminiscence of the light of heaven and its gradual evanescence through the maturing years. In stanza V we are told that the infant inhabits it; the Boy beholds it, seeing it "in his joy"; the Youth is still attended by it; "the Man perceives it die away, / And fade into the light of common day." Stanza VI speaks briefly of the efforts made by earthly life to bring about the natural and inevitable amnesia:

Earth fills her lap with pleasures of her own;
Yearnings she hath in her own natural kind,
And even with something of a Mother's mind,
    And no unworthy aim,
    The homely Nurse doth all she can
To make her Foster-child, her Inmate Man,
    Forget the glories he hath known,
And that imperial palace whence he came.

"Imperial" suggests grandeur, dignity, and splendor, everything that stands in opposition to what, in *The Excursion*, Wordsworth was to call "littleness." And "littleness" is the result of having wrong notions about the nature of man and his connection with the universe; its outcome is "deadness." The melancholy and despair of the Solitary in *The Excursion* are the signs of the deadness which resulted from his having conceived of man as something less than imperial. Wordsworth's idea of splendid power is his protest against all views of the mind that would limit and debase it. By conceiving, as he does, an intimate connection between mind and universe, by seeing the universe fitted to the mind and the mind to the universe, he bestows upon man a dignity which cannot be derived from looking at him in the actualities of common life, from seeing him engaged in business, in morality and politics.

Yet here we must credit Wordsworth with the double vision. Man must be conceived of as "imperial," but he must also be seen as he actually is in the field of life. The earth is not an environment in which the celestial or imperial qualities can easily exist. Wordsworth, who spoke of the notion of imperial pre-existence as being adumbrated by Adam's fall, uses the words "earth" and "earthly" in the common quasi-religious sense to refer to the things of this world. He does not make Earth synonymous with Nature, for although Man may be the true child of Nature, he is the "Foster-child" of Earth. But it is to be observed that the foster mother is a kindly one, that her disposition is at least quasi-maternal, that her aims are at least not unworthy; she is, in short, the foster mother who figures so often in the legend of the Hero, whose real and unknown parents are noble or divine.[6]

Wordsworth, in short, is looking at man in a double way, seeing man both in his ideal nature and in his earthly activity. The two views do not so much contradict as supplement each other. If in stanzas V–VIII Wordsworth tells us that we live by decrease, in stanzas IX–XI he tells us of the everlasting connection of the diminished person with his own ideal personality. The child hands on to the hampered adult the imperial nature, the "primal sympathy / Which having been must ever be," the mind fitted to the universe, the universe to the mind. The sympathy is not so pure and intense in maturity as in childhood, but only because another relation grows up beside the relation of man to Nature — the relation of man to his fellows in the moral world of difficulty and pain. Given Wordsworth's epistemology the new relation is bound to change the very aspect of Nature itself:

the clouds will take a sober coloring from an eye that hath kept watch o'er man's mortality, but a sober color is a color still.

There is sorrow in the Ode, the inevitable sorrow of giving up an old habit of vision for a new one. In shifting the center of his interest from Nature to man in the field of morality Wordsworth is fulfilling his own conception of the three ages of man which Professor Beatty has expounded so well. The shift in interest he called the coming of "the philosophic mind," but the word "philosophic" does not have here either of two of its meanings in common usage — it does not mean abstract and it does not mean apathetic. Wordsworth is not saying, and it is sentimental and unimaginative of us to say, that he has become less a feeling man and less a poet. He is only saying that he has become less a youth. Indeed, the Ode is so little a farewell to art, so little a dirge sung over departing powers, that it is actually the very opposite — it is a welcome of new powers and a dedication to a new poetic subject. For if sensitivity and responsiveness be among the poetic powers, what else is Wordsworth saying at the end of the poem except that he has a greater sensitivity and responsiveness than ever before? The "philosophic mind" has not decreased but, on the contrary, increased the power to feel.

> The clouds that gather round the setting sun
> Do take a sober colouring from an eye
> That hath kept watch o'er man's mortality;
> Another race hath been and other palms are won.
> Thanks to the human heart by which we live,
> Thanks to its tenderness, its joys, and fears,
> To me the meanest flower that blows can give
> Thoughts that do often lie too deep for tears.

The meanest flower is significant now not only because, like the small celandine, it speaks of age, suffering, and death, but because to a man who is aware of man's mortality the world becomes significant and precious. The knowledge of man's mortality — this must be carefully noted in a poem presumably about immortality — now replaces the "glory" as the agency which makes things significant and precious. We are back again at optics, which we have never really left, and the Ode in a very honest fashion has come full circle.

Notes

1. In his *Studies in the Poetry of Henry Vaughan*, a Cambridge University dissertation, Andrew Chiappe makes a similar judgment of the quality and degree of belief in the idea of pre-existence in the poetry of Vaughan and Traherne.

2. The use here of the word "poetic" is either metaphorical and general, or it is entirely literal, that is, it refers to the root-meaning of the word, which is "to make" — Wordsworth has in mind the creative nature of right human perception and not merely poetry.

3. "Before born babe bliss had. Within womb won he worship. Whatever in that one case done commodiously done was." — James Joyce, *Ulysses*. The myth of Eden is also interpreted as figuring either childhood or the womb — see below Wordsworth's statement of the connection of the notion of pre-existence with Adam's fall.

4. Readers of Ferenczi's remarkable study, *Thalassa*, a discussion, admittedly speculative but wonderfully fascinating, of unconscious racial memories of the ocean as the ultimate source of life, will not be able to resist giving an added meaning to Wordsworth's lines about the "immortal sea / Which brought us hither" and of the unborn children who "Sport upon the shore." The recollection of Samuel Butler's delightful fantasy of the Unborn and his theory of unconscious memory will also serve to enrich our reading of the Ode by suggesting the continuing force of the Platonic myth.

5. Milton provides a possible gloss to several difficult points in the poem. In stanza VIII, the Child is addressed as "thou Eye among the blind," and to the Eye are applied the epithets "deaf and silent"; Coleridge objected to these epithets as irrational, but his objection may be met by citing the brilliant precedent of "blind mouths" of "Lycidas." Again, Coleridge's question of the propriety of making a master *brood* over a slave is in part answered by the sonnet "On His Being Arrived at the Age of Twenty-three," in which Milton expresses his security in his development as it shall take place in his "great Task-master's eye." Between this sonnet and the Ode there are other significant correspondences of thought and of phrase, as there also are in the sonnet "On His Blindness."

6. Carlyle makes elaborate play with this idea in his account of Teufelsdröckh, and see the essay on *The Princess Casamassima* in this volume, page 62. The fantasy that their parents are really foster parents is a common one with children, and it is to be associated with the various forms of the belief that the world is not real.

APPLICATION

*Like Nancy Walker, Cynthia Griffin Wolff disagrees with
those critics who find the chief interest and power of
Chopin's novel in its "anticipation of the woman question." But Wolff's objection, unlike Walker's, is not that
these readings are anachronistic, too much concerned
with our time and too little with the author's, but too
chronistic, too much concerned with changing social circumstances and too little with the timeless truths of human nature. Echoing Josephine Donovan's mimetic credo
that most literature we call great depicts not sex-linked
experiences but "universal, fundamental human experiences," Wolff claims that Edna Pontellier interests us
"not because she is a 'woman'" but "because she is
human — because she fails in ways which beckon seductively to all of us." Wolff then provides a detailed
psychological analysis of Chopin's main character, drawing on the insights of Freud, R. D. Laing, and Helene
Deutsch. Chopin, of course, had never read these analysts. But, the mimetic argument runs, she was a keen
observer of human nature, which varies little over time
and space, and her work embodies fundamental truths
about human behavior, truths which, as Paris argues,
art can help us discover and psychology can help us
talk about. But is there such a thing as "universal, fundamental" human experience? In the final chapter we'll
meet some radically historical critics who will question
this foundational assumption of much mimetic criticism.*

Thanatos and Eros: Kate Chopin's *The Awakening*

Cynthia Griffin Wolff

After its initially dramatic reception, *The Awakening* slipped into an undeserved state of neglect;
now, partly as a result of the new feminist criticism,
the pendulum has swung in quite the other direction, and Chopin has been hailed as an early advocate of women's rights. Edmund Wilson sees *The
Awakening* as an anticipation of D. H. Lawrence in its
treatment of infidelity.[1] Kenneth Eble maintains that

Reprinted by permission from *American Quarterly*, Volume
25, no. 4. Copyright © 1973 by the American Studies
Association.

"the novel is an American *Madame Bovary*, though such a designation is not precisely accurate. Its central character is similar: the married woman who seeks love outside a stuffy, middle-class marriage."[2] Jules Chametzky is even more explicit: "What does surprise one is the modernity . . . of Mrs. Chopin's insights into 'the woman question.' It is not so much that she advocates woman's libidinal freedom or celebrates the force of the body's prerogatives. . . . What Kate Chopin shows so beautifully are the pressures working against woman's true awakening to her condition, and what that condition is."[3]

There are differences, of course, among these evaluations, but the underlying similarity is unmistakable: all see the power of the novel as growing out of an existential confrontation between the heroine and some external, repressive force. Thus, one might say that it is the woman against stifling sexual standards or that it is the woman against the tedium of a provincial marriage. Chametzky offers, perhaps, the most detailed explanation: "The struggle is for the woman to free herself from being an object or possession defined in her functions, or owned, by others."[4] Certainly elements of the novel serve to confirm these interpretations, especially if one takes seriously some of the accusations leveled by the heroine in moments of anger or distress. Edna is disillusioned by marriage; to her "a wedding is one of the most lamentable spectacles on earth" (p. 172).[5] Even so, the contemporary readings of the novel which stress Edna's position as a victim of society's standards do not capture its power; for although it is not a great novel—perhaps it is even a greatly flawed novel because of the elusiveness of its focus—reading it can be a devastating and unforgettable experience. And such an experience can simply not grow out of a work whose importance lies in the fact that it anticipates Lawrence or that it is a sort of American *Madame Bovary*. Such evaluations are diminishing. The importance of Chopin's work does not lie in its anticipation of "the woman question" or of any other question; it derives from its ruthless fidelity to the disintegration of Edna's character. Edna, in turn, interests us not because she is "a woman," the implication being that her experience is principally important because it might stand for that of any other woman. Quite the contrary; she interests us because she is human—because she fails in ways which beckon seductively to all of us. Conrad might say that, woman *or* man, she is "one of us."

It is difficult to define Edna's character as it might have existed before we meet her in the novel, for even at its opening such stability as she may have had has already been disrupted. We do learn something of her background. She is the middle child of an ambiguously religious family. "She comes of sound old Presbyterian Kentucky stock. The old gentleman, her father, I have heard, used to atone for his week-day sins with his Sunday devotions. I know for a fact, that his race horses literally ran away with the prettiest bit of Kentucky farming land I ever laid eyes upon" (pp. 171–72). The family has two faces, then: it "sins" (during the week) with its racing and land-grabbing; and it "atones" (on Sundays) with pious condemnations. The character of each of the daughters reflects this contradiction. So Margaret, the oldest "has all the Presbyterian undiluted" (p. 172); she is "matronly and dignified, probably from having assumed matronly and house-wifely responsibilities too early in life, their mother having died when they were quite young. Margaret was not effusive; she was practical" (pp. 43–44). She was also, quite possibly, in her remote and disapproving way, the principal mother-figure for Edna. Janet, on the other hand, "the youngest is sometime of a vixen" (p. 172). Edna, caught between the two extremes, can live comfortably with neither portion of the family's double standard; instead she tries to evolve a habit or manner which will accommodate both.

The attempt to internalize this contradiction combines with other of Edna's psychic needs to produce an "identity" which is predicated on the conscious process of concealment. In some sense there are two Ednas: "At a very early period she had apprehended instinctively the dual life—that outward existence which conforms, the inward life which questions" (p. 35). Therefore she is very little open to sustained emotional relationships because those elements of character which she might want to call her "real" self must remain hidden, revealed only to herself. "Edna had had an occasional girl friend, but whether accidentally or not, they seemed to have been all of one type—the self-contained. She never realized that the reserve of her own character had much, perhaps everything, to do with this" (p. 44). Not that Edna *wants* to be so entirely alone. On the contrary, the cool distancing tone of her "visible" character conceals an ardent yearning for intensity, for passion. So Edna provides the passion she needs in the only manner which seems safely available to her—through daydreaming.

Edna often wondered at one propensity which sometimes had inwardly disturbed her without causing any outward show or manifestation on her part. At a very early age—perhaps it was when she traversed the ocean of waving grass—she remembered that she had been passionately enamored of a dignified and sad-eyed cavalry officer who visited her father in Kentucky. She could not leave his presence when he was there, nor remove her eyes from his face, which was something like Napoleon's, with a lock of black hair falling across the forehead. But the cavalry officer melted imperceptibly out of her existence.

At another time her affections were deeply engaged by a young gentleman who visited a lady on a neighborhood plantation. It was after they went to Mississippi to live. The young man was engaged to be married to the young lady, and they sometimes called upon Margaret, driving over of afternoons in a buggy. Edna was a little miss, just merging into her teens; and the realization that she herself was nothing, nothing, nothing to the engaged young man was a bitter affliction to her. But he too, went the way of dreams.

She was a grown young woman when she was overtaken by what she supposed to be the climax of her fate. It was when the face and figure of a great tragedian began to haunt her imagination and stir her senses. *The persistence of the infatuation lent it an aspect of genuineness. The hopelessness of it colored it with the lofty tones of a great passion.*

The picture of the tragedian stood enframed upon her desk. Any one may possess the portrait of a tragedian without exciting suspicion or comment.

(pp. 45–46, italics added)

The emotional change here must be described as the development of an increasingly resistant barrier between the "real" external world and that world which was most authentic in Edna's experience — the inner world of her fantasies. Thus her libidinal energies are focused first on a real man who is in some ways genuinely available to her; he is apparently unmarried, unattached and a frequent visitor to the family home. Still, he is a good deal older than she, and his chief attraction seems to be his resemblance to Napoleon (and perhaps the romantic aura attached to his having been a cavalry officer—one calls to mind the clanging spurs which echo in Edna's memory as she is drowning). The next object of Edna's affection is manifestly unavailable since he is engaged to her sister's friend, and although the realization that she was "nothing, nothing, nothing to the engaged man" may have made Edna consciously miserable, there is a form of safety, too, in nothingness. The passion is never expressed, always controlled, with only the substantial threat of "dreams," which melt away. Characteristically, she reserves her greatest passion for a figure of pure fantasy, the tragedian whose picture one can possess "without exciting suspicion or comment."

Given the apparent terror which genuine emotional involvement inspires in Edna, her marriage to a man like Léonce Pontellier is no accident. No one would call him remarkable; most readers might think him dull, insensitive, unperceptive, even callous. Certainly he is an essentially prosaic man. If one assumed that marriage was to be an intimate affair of deep understanding, all of these qualities would condemn Léonce. Yet for Edna they are the very qualities which recommend him. "The acme of bliss, which would have been a marriage with the tragedian, was not for her in this world" (p. 47); such bliss, indeed, is not for anyone *in this world*. It is a romantic illusion, a dream—defined by its very inability to be consummated. What is more, the intensity of dreams such as these may have become disturbing to Edna. So she chooses to marry Léonce; after all "as the devoted wife of a man who worshiped her, she felt she would take her place with a certain dignity in the world of reality, closing the portals forever behind her upon the realm of romance and dreams" (p. 47). The marriage to such a man as Léonce was, then, a defensive maneuver designed to maintain the integrity of the two "selves" that formed her character and to reinforce the distance between them. Her outer self was confirmed by the entirely conventional marriage while her inner self was safe—known only to Edna. An intuitive man, a sensitive husband, might threaten it; a husband who evoked passion from her might lure the hidden self into the open, tempting Edna to attach her emotions to flesh and blood rather than phantoms. Léonce is neither, and their union ensures the secret safety of Edna's "real" self. "It was not long before the tragedian had gone to join the cavalry officer and the engaged young man and a few others; and Edna found herself face to face with the realities. She grew fond of her husband, realizing with some unaccountable satisfaction that no trace of passion or excessive and fictitious warmth colored her affection, *thereby threatening its dissolution*" (p. 47, italics added).

If we try to assess the configuration of Edna's personality when she comes to Grand Isle at the novel's beginning, we might best do so by using R. D. Laing's description of the "schizoid" personality. As Laing would describe it, the schizoid personality consists of a set of defenses which have been established as an attempt to preserve some semblance of coherent identity. "The self, in order to develop and sustain its identity and autonomy, and in order to be safe from the persistent threat and danger from the world, has cut itself off from direct relatedness with others, and has endeavoured to become its own object: to become, in fact, related directly only to itself. Its cardinal functions become phantasy and observation. Now, in so far as this is successful, one necessary consequence is that the self has difficulty sustaining any *sentiment du réel* for the very reason that it is not 'in touch' with reality, it never actually 'meets' reality."[6]

Laing's insights provide at least a partial explanation for elements of the novel which might otherwise be unclear. For example, Edna's fragility or susceptibility to the atmosphere at Grand Isle (as compared, for example, with her robust friend Madame Ratignolle, or the grand aloofness of Madame Reisz) can be traced to the circular ineffectiveness of the schizoid mechanism for maintaining identity. To be specific, such a person must be simultaneously alert to and protected from any invitation to interact with the real world since all genuine interactions leave the hidden "real" self exposed to potential danger. Vigilance begets threat which in turn precipitates withdrawal and renewed vigilance.[7]

More important, interpersonal relationships can be conceived of only in cataclysmic terms; "there is a constant dread and resentment at being turned into someone else's thing, of being penetrated by him, and a sense of being in someone else's power and control. Freedom then consists in being inaccessible."[8] Such habits of mind comport with Edna's outbursts concerning her own relationships. Certainly her rather dull husband seems not to notice her except as a part of the general inventory of his worldly goods: thus early in the novel he is described as "looking at his wife as one looks at a valuable piece of personal property which has suffered some damage" (p. 4). Yet his attentions, such as they are, are rather more indicative of indifference than otherwise. Indeed, at every point within the narrative when he might, were he so inclined, assert his "rights," he declines to do so. After the evening swimming party, for example, when he clearly desires sexual intercourse and his wife does not wish to comply, he utters but a few sharp words and then, surprising for a man so supposedly interested in the proprietary relationship, slips on a robe and comes out to keep her company during her fitful vigil (see pp. 78–81). After their return to New Orleans, he reacts to Edna's disruption of her "wifely functions" with but momentary impatience; he does not attempt coercion, and he goes to the lengths of consulting a physician out of concern for her well-being. Even when Edna has taken up residence in her diminutive "pigeon house" Léonce decides to leave her to her own ways. His only concern — a small-minded one, to be sure — is to save appearances.

It is hard to cast such an ultimately insignificant man in the role of villain — compared with a man like Soames Forsyte or with some of the more brutal husbands in Chopin's short stories, Léonce is a slender vehicle to carry the weight of society's repression of women. Yet Edna sees herself as his possession, even as she sees herself the prisoner of her children's demands. Her dying thoughts confirm this fixation: "She thought of Léonce and the children. They were a part of her life. But they need not have thought that they could possess her, body and soul" (p. 302). Now if Léonce is not able to rise to the occasion of possessing her body and soul, the children as they are portrayed in the novel, seem to exercise even less continuous claim upon her. They are always accompanied by a nurse whose presence frees Edna to pursue whatever interests she can sustain; what is more, they spend much of their time with their paternal grandmother, who seems to welcome them whenever Edna wishes to send them. Her emotional relationship with them is tenuous at best, certainly not demanding and by no stretch of the imagination stifling. "She was fond of her children in an uneven, impulsive way. She would sometimes gather them passionately to her heart; she would sometimes forget them" (p. 47). Given the extraordinary latitude that Edna did in fact have, we might better interpret her feelings of imprisonment as projections of her own attitudes and fears. The end of the novel offers an ironic affirmation of such a view, for when she returns home from Madame Ratignolle's accouchement, even her apparently positive expectations with regard to Robert follow the same familiar definition: "She could picture at that moment no greater bliss on earth than possession of the beloved one" (p. 291). The wording is somewhat ambiguous—she might possess him, he might possess her, the "possession" might be understood as a synonym for sexual union—still the key word here is *possession*, and it is Edna's word.

Possession, as descriptive of any intense emotional involvement, is both tempting and terrifying. To yield to possession is to become engulfed, to be nothing. The antiphonal emblematic figures that appear like phantoms while Edna is staying at Grand Isle reflect the dilemma. On the one hand there are the lovers, intimate, always together, seemingly happy, a beckoning vision of replenishment which carries always with it the fear of annihilation. And then there is the woman in black, the emblem of the self-destroyed in a bizarre act of self-preservation, withdrawn from all personal interaction—"safe" and "free."

One solution for the problem Edna faces would be to formulate a way to have her relationship with Robert without ever *really* having it. Temporarily she does effect such a solution, and she does so in two ways. First, while she is at Grand Isle, she systematically denies the possibility of an adult relationship with him; this denial takes the form of her engulfing him ("possessing" him, perhaps) by a kind of incorporation of his personality into her own. She accepts his attentions, his services, his affection; and in so far as these are important to her, she comes to regard them as extensions of her own will or desire. Robert is not conceived of as a separate, individuated being, and thus she repeatedly is surprised and dismayed when his actions unaccountably (to her) deviate from her wishes. We can see this aspect of their relationship very early in a trivial incident when Robert leaves her one evening and fails to return. "She wondered why Robert had gone away and left her. It did not occur to her to think he might have grown tired of being with her the livelong day. She was not tired, and she felt that he was not. She regretted that he had gone. It was so much more natural to have him stay, when he was not absolutely required to leave her" (p. 103). This scene and Edna's reaction is a foreshadowing of the much more distressing separation when Robert leaves for Mexico. "But can't you understand? I've grown used to seeing you, to having you with me all the time, and your action seems unfriendly, even unkind. You don't even offer an excuse for it. Why, I was planning to be together, thinking of how pleasant it would be to see you in the city next

winter" (p. 114). She finds it difficult, if not impossible, to separate his will or his wishes from her own, to acknowledge his existence independent of hers. Only after he has left can she safely *feel* the intensity of passion that later comes to be associated with him; and she can do so because once physically absent, he can be made magically present as a phantom, an object in her own imagination, a figure which is now truly a part of herself. She has reawakened the cavalry officer, the young engaged man, the tragedian; "for the first time she recognized anew the symptoms of infatuation which she had felt incipiently as a child, as a girl in her earliest teens, and later as a young woman" (p. 116). As a woman, however, Edna wants more.

Thus she evolves a second solution by which she can have a relationship with Robert without being forced to fuse the outer and the inner "selves" that comprise her identity. This stratagem is the affair with Arobin. She can respond sensually to the kiss which initiates their relationship precisely because she has no feeling for him. Her feelings are fixed safely on the *image* of Robert; "there was Robert's reproach making itself felt by a quicker, fiercer, more overpowering love, which had awakened within her toward him" (p. 219). And this arrangement frees her from anxiety, leaving only a "dull pang of regret."[9] When Robert does, in fact, return, the problem of fusing the outer world with the "real" world within returns with him; and, as before, the fantasy is easier to deal with. "A hundred times Edna had pictured Robert's return, and imagined their first meeting. It was usually at her home, whither he had sought her out at once. She always fancied him expressing or betraying in some way his love for her. And here, the reality was that they sat ten feet apart, she at the window, crushing geranium leaves in her hand and smelling them, he twirling around on the piano stool" (pp. 256–57).

Robert's return and his sensuous awakening to her kiss (pp. 282–84) precipitates the final crisis from which she must flee. She cannot, in the end, yield her "self" to the insistence of his passionate plea to stay; and his own subsequent flight destroys the fantasy lover as well. Both of Edna's selves are truly betrayed and barren, and she retrenches in the only manner familiar to her, that of a final and ultimate withdrawal. As Laing says: "If the whole of the individual's being cannot be defended, the individual retracts his lines of defence until he withdraws within a central citadel. He is prepared to write off everything he is, except his 'self.' But the tragic paradox is that the more the self is defended in this way, the more it is destroyed. The apparent eventual destruction and dissolution of these in schizophrenic conditions is accomplished not be external attacks from the enemy (actual or supposed), from without, but by the devastation caused by the inner defensive manoeuvres themselves."[10]

This description of Edna's defensive patterns is an invaluable aid in understanding the novel; however, taken alone it does not lead to a complete explanation. We can understand, perhaps, why Edna's act of self-destruction seems the logical culmination of other apparently nondestructive behavior, but we cannot yet comprehend the manner of her dissolution, nor the significance to Edna (which must have been central) of Madame Ratignolle's accouchement or of Edna's own children, who seem to haunt her even though their *physical* presence scarcely enters the novel. More important, the tone of the novel — perhaps its most artistically compelling element — cannot yet be described or explained in any but the most general terms as a reflection of Edna's schizoid affinity for fantasy. Even the title of the work, *The Awakening*, suggests a positive quality with which Edna's systematic annihilation of self (albeit from the most "self-preserving" motives) seems oddly at variance. Thus though we might accept the psychic anatomy defined by Laing as schizoid, we must go beyond simple categorizing to understand the novel as a whole.

We might begin with the title itself. Surely one unavoidable meaning of the title has to do with Edna's secret "real" self. She had married a Creole and yet she "was not thoroughly at home in the society of Creoles. . . . A characteristic which distinguished them and which impressed Mrs. Pontellier most forcibly was their entire absence of prudery. Their freedom of expression was at first incomprehensible to her, though she had no difficulty in reconciling it with a lofty chastity which in the Creole woman seems to be inborn and unmistakable" (pp. 22–23). The unfamiliar mode of conduct which seems most puzzling to Edna is the ability to have affect — to show feeling, even passion — without going beyond certain socially approved limits; that is, it is not just the "freedom" of the Creole society but the coupling of that freedom with a confident sense of decorum, "lofty chastity," which confounds her. "A book had

gone the rounds of the *pension.* When it came her turn to read it, she did so with profound astonishment. She felt moved to read the book in secret and solitude, though none of the others had done so — to hide it from view at the sound of approaching footsteps. It was openly criticised and freely discussed at table. Mrs. Pontellier gave over being astonished, and concluded that wonders would never cease" (pp. 23–24). As we have seen, "freedom" for Edna has always meant isolation and concealment, an increasingly sterile and barren existence; now suddenly she finds herself among people who have a different kind of freedom, the freedom to express feelings openly and without fear. What a temptation to the insistent inner being whose authenticity Edna so feverishly guards from attack! For this is a self which is starving — and Grand Isle offers nourishment in bounteous abundance.

However, danger lies in the possibility that this hidden self will emerge as voracious, omnivorous and insatiable. Such a fear is probably always present in the schizoid personality; for these defense mechanisms "can be understood as an attempt to preserve a being that is precariously structured. . . . The initial structuralization of being into its basic elements occurs in early infancy. In normal circumstances, this occurs in such a way as to be so conclusively stable in its basic elements (for instance, the continuity of time, the distinction between the self and not-self, phantasy and reality), that it can henceforth be taken for granted: on this stable base, a considerable amount of plasticity can exist in what we call a person's 'character,' "[11] (It is precisely this plasticity which Edna observes among the Creoles and which she finds not shocking but deeply puzzling because it is absent in her own personality.) It is at this most elementary level that Edna's hidden self subsists. "The orientation of the schizoid personality is a primitive oral one, concerned with the dilemma of sustaining its aliveness, while being terrified to 'take in' anything. It becomes parched with thirst, and desolate."[12] And out of this desolation Edna's "self" ventures forward to seek resuscitation and confirmation.

The awakening is a sensuous one. It is important, however, not to accept this term as an exclusively or even primarily sexual one. To be sure, Edna's awakening involves a liaison with Arobin, and the novel leaves little doubt that this attachment includes sexual activity. Yet it would be naïve and limiting to suppose that Edna's principal complaint ought to be described in terms of sexual repression (though she might find it reassuring to do so). Gratifying sexual experience cannot be isolated from sensuous experience in general, and entering into a sexual relationship is an act which necessarily "awakens" memories—echoes, if you will—of earlier sensuous needs and experiences. As Freud has observed, the mind is unique in its development, for "only in the mind is such a preservation of all the earlier stages alongside of the final form possible."[13] Now a reader of Chopin's novel might find himself more absorbed by the apparently genital aspects of Edna's sensuous life, the love affair with Robert and the attachment to Arobin; after all, this is in some sense the "appropriate" level for the expression of passion in an adult woman. The narrator, however, directs our attention in a different direction. "That summer at Grand Isle she began to loosen a little the mantle of reserve that had always enveloped her. There may have been— there must have been—influences, both subtle and apparent, working in their several ways to induce her to do this; but the most obvious was the influence of Adèle Ratignolle. The excessive physical charm of the Creole had first attracted her, for Edna had a sensuous susceptibility to beauty" (p. 35).

Why is Adèle and not Robert singled out as the primary force that rouses Edna from her slumber? Our introduction to Adèle gives some hints. "There are no words to describe her save the old ones that have served so often to picture the by-gone heroine of romance and the fair lady of our dreams" (p. 19). If some portion of Edna's self has been arrested in dreams, perhaps Adèle is the embodiment of those dreams. And yet, despite the "spun-gold hair" and blue eyes, she is scarcely a conventional heroine. Her beauty derives its power from a sense of fullness, ripeness and abundance. Her very essence might be described as a kind of plump succulence, and the narrator reverts to terms of nourishment as the only appropriate means of rendering her nature. She had "two lips that pouted, that were so red one could only think of cherries or some other delicious crimson fruit in looking at them. She was growing a little stout, but it did not seem to detract an iota from the grace of every step, pose, gesture" (p. 20). Her hours are spent delightfully (to her) in mending and sorting children's clothes, and she is pregnant—a fact which pleases her and becomes her principal topic of conversation—when Edna meets her. She might

have been painted by Renoir. She is, in Edna's terms, the quintessential "mother-woman."

Though Edna's own instincts for mothering are fitful, she is clearly attracted to the bounty of Adèle's nature, allowing herself to slip into caressing intimacy like a grateful child. "Madame Ratignolle laid her hand over that of Mrs. Pontellier, which was near her. Seeing that the hand was not withdrawn, she clasped it firmly and warmly. She even stroked it a little, fondly, with the other hand, murmuring in an undertone, 'Pauvre cherie.' The action was at first a little confusing to Edna, but she soon lent herself readily to the Creole's gentle caress" (p. 43). So far as one can tell, this is the first sensuous contact that Edna has had with anyone—perhaps in her conscious memory, certainly since adolescence. "During one period of my life," she confides to Adèle, "religion took a firm hold upon me; after I was twelve and until—until—why, I suppose until now, though I never thought much about it—just driven along by habit" (pp. 42–43). This sensuous awakening loosens Edna's memory, and her mind drifts back through childhood, recalling the enveloping sea of grass, the succession of phantom lovers. "Edna did not reveal so much as all this to Madame Ratignolle that summer day when they sat with faces turned to the sea. But a good part of it escaped her. She had put her head down on Madame Ratignolle's shoulder. She was flushed and felt intoxicated with the sound of her own voice and the unaccustomed taste of candor. It muddled her like wine, or like a first breath of freedom" (p. 48).

The almost blinding intensity of this episode between Edna and Adèle contrasts vividly with the emotional paleness of Edna's real-world interactions with Robert (which must not be confused with her fantasies about him, especially after he leaves, nor with her increasingly narcissistic appreciation of her own body). Thus Edna's coming to rest upon Adèle's shoulder with trusting openness is preceded by an episode between Edna and Robert which is similar in action and yet altogether different in tone. "During his oblivious attention he once quietly rested his head against Mrs. Pontellier's arm. As gently she repulsed him. Once again he repeated the offense. She could not but believe it to be thoughtlessness on his part; yet that was no reason she should submit to it. She did not remonstrate, except again to repulse him quietly but firmly" (p. 29). Several things must be noted here: Edna views Robert's action not as sensuously stimulating but as an imposition, even an affront; her resistance betrays no conflict (that is, the narrator does not suggest that she was tempted by the possible sexual content of his gesture or that she felt threatened or guilty), quite the contrary; her attitude is coolly distant. But then Robert is a man whose quasi-sexual flirtations are not to be taken seriously.

In many ways his patterns of behavior are similar to Edna's, and to some extent, this similarity makes him non-threatening. He does not seek genuine emotional or sexual involvements, preferring to attach his affections to those women who are "safely" unattainable. "Since the age of fifteen, which was eleven years before, Robert each summer at Grand Isle had constituted himself the devoted attendant of some fair dame or damsel. Sometimes it was a young girl, again a widow; but as often as not it was some interesting married woman" (p. 25). His psychic life is more firmly rooted in the world than Edna's; he does not pursue figures of pure fantasy. Still, his propensity for playing the role of hopeless, love-sick youth is so well known as to be able to be anticipated by those who know him. Thus "many had predicted that Robert would devote himself to Mrs. Pontellier when he arrived" (p. 25). His attentions, gratefully received by a number of the ladies, more often than not take the form of ministering to their creature comforts: he fetches bouillon for Adèle, blankets and shawls for Edna.

Indeed, an astonishing proportion of that part of the novel which deals with Edna's sojourn at Grand Isle is paced by the rhythm of her basic needs, especially the most primitive ones of eating and sleeping. If one were to plot the course of Edna's life during this period, the most reliable indices to the passage of time would be her meals and her periods of sleep. The importance of these in Edna's more general "awakening" can be suggested if we examine the day-long boat trip which she makes with Robert.

There is an almost fairy-tale quality to the whole experience; the rules of time seem suspended, and the mélange of brilliant sensory experiences—the sun, the water, the soft breeze, the old church with its lizards and whispered tales of pirate gold—melts into a dreamlike pattern. It is almost as if Edna's fantasy world had come into being. Indeed, there is even some suggestion that after the event, she incorporates the memory of it into her fantasy world in such a way that the reality and the illusion do, in fact, become confused. Later on in the novel when Edna is invited to tell a true anecdote at a dinner party, she speaks "of a woman who paddled away with her lover one night in a pirogue and never came back. They were lost amid the Baratarian Islands, and no one ever heard of them or found trace of them from that day to this. It was pure invention. She said that Madame Antoine had related it to her. That, also, was an invention. Perhaps it was a dream she had had. But every glowing word seemed real to those who listened" (pp. 182–83).

Yet even this jewel-like adventure with Robert is dominated by the insistence of the infantile life-pattern—sleep and eat, sleep and eat. Edna's rest had been feverish the night prior to the expedition; "She slept but a few hours" (p. 82), and their expedition begins with a hurried breakfast (p. 84). Her taste for sight-seeing, even her willingness to remain with Robert, is so overwhelmed by her lassitude that she must find a place to rest and to be alone. Strikingly, however, once she is by herself, left to seek restful sleep, Edna seems somewhat to revive, and the tone shifts from one of exhaustion to one of sensuous, leisurely enjoyment of her own body. "Left alone in the little side room, [she] loosened her clothes, removing the greater part of them. . . . How luxurious it felt to rest thus in a strange, quaint bed, with its sweet country odor of laurel lingering about the sheets and mattress! She stretched her strong limbs that ached a little. She ran her fingers through her loosened hair for a while. She looked at her round arms as she held them straight up and rubbed them one after the other, observing closely, as if it were something she saw for the first time, the fine, firm quality and texture of her flesh" (p. 93). Powerfully sensuous as this scene is, we would be hard put to find genital significance here. Reduced to its simplest form, the description is of a being discovering the limits and qualities of its own body—discovering, and taking joy in the process of discovery. And having engaged in this exploratory "play" for a while, Edna falls asleep.

The manner of her waking makes explicit reference to the myth of the sleeping beauty. "'How many years have I slept?' she inquired. 'The whole island seems changed. A new race of beings must have sprung up, leaving only you and me as past relics'" (p. 96). Robert jokingly falls in with the fantasy: "'You have slept precisely one hundred years. I was left here to guard your slumbers; and for one hundred years I have been out under the shed reading a book'" (p. 96). In the fairy tale, of course, the princess awakens with a kiss, conscious of love; but Edna's libidinal energies have been arrested at a pregenital level—so she awakens "very hungry" (p. 95)—and her lover prepares her a meal! "He was childishly gratified to discover her appetite, and to see the relish with which she ate the food which he had procured for her" (p. 97). Indeed, though the title of the novel suggests a re-enactment of the traditional romantic myth, it never does offer a complete representation of it. The next invocation is Arobin's kiss, "the first kiss of her life to which her nature had really responded" (p. 218); but as we have seen earlier, this response is facilitated, perhaps even made possible, by the fact that her emotional attachment is not to Arobin but to the Robert of her fantasy world. The final allusion to an awakening kiss is Edna's rousing of Robert (p. 280); and yet this is a potentially genital awakening from which both flee.

Edna's central problem, once the hidden "self" begins to exert its inexorable power, is that her libidinal appetite has been fixated at the oral level. Edna herself has an insistent preoccupation with nourishment; on the simplest level, she is concerned with food. Her favorite adjective is "delicious": she sees many mother-women as "delicious" in their role (p. 19); she carries echoes of her children's voices "like the memory of a delicious song" (p. 248); when she imagines Robert she thinks "how delicious it would be to have him there with her" (p. 270). And the notion of something's being good because it might be good to "eat" (or internalize in some way) is echoed in all of her relationships with other people. Those who care about her typically feed her; and the sleep-and-eat pattern which is most strikingly established at the beginning of the novel continues even to the very end. Not surprisingly, in the "grown-up world" she is a poor housekeeper, and though Léonce's responses are clearly petty and self-centered, Edna's behavior does betray incompetence, especially when we compare it (as the novel so often invites us to) with the nurturing capacities of Adèle. It is not surprising that the most dramatic gesture toward freedom that Edna makes is to move out of her husband's house; yet even this gesture toward "independence" can be comprehended as part of an equally powerful wish to regress. It is, after all, a "tiny house" that she moves to; she called it her "pigeon house," and if she were still a little girl, we might call it a playhouse.

The decision to move from Léonce's house is virtually coincidental with the beginning of her affair with Arobin; yet even the initial stages of that affair are described in oral terms—Edna feels regret because "it was not love which had held this cup of life to her lips" (p. 219). And though the relationship develops as she makes preparations for the move, it absorbs astonishingly little of Edna's libido. She is deliberately distant, treating Arobin with "affected carelessness" (p. 221). As a narrator observes, "If he had expected to find her languishing, reproachful, or indulging in sentimental tears, he must have been greatly surprised" (p. 221). She is "true" to the fantasy image of Robert. And in the real world her emotional energy has been committed in another direction. She is busy with elaborate plans—for a dinner party! And it is on this extravagant sumptuous oral repast that she lavishes her time and care (see pp. 225–37). Here Edna as purveyor of food becomes not primarily a nourisher (as Adèle is) but a sensualist in the only terms that she can truly comprehend. One might argue that in this elaborate feast Edna's sensuous self comes closest to some form of expression which might be compatible with the real world. The dinner party itself is one of the longest sustained episodes in the novel; we are told in loving detail about the appearance of the table, the commodious chairs, the flowers, the candles, the food and wines, Edna's attire—no sensory pleasure is left unattended. Yet even this indulgence fails to satisfy. "As she sat there amid her guests, she felt the old ennui overtaking her; the hopelessness which so often assailed her, which came upon her like an obsession, like something extraneous, independent of volition. It was something which announced itself; a chill breath that seemed to issue from some vast cavern wherein discords wailed" (p. 232). Edna, perhaps, connects this despair to the absence of Robert. "There came over her the acute longing which always summoned into her spiritual vision the presence of the beloved one, overpowering her at once with a sense of the unattainable" (p. 232). However, the narrator's language here is interestingly ambiguous. It is not specifically *Robert* that Edna longs for; it is "the presence of the beloved one"—an indefinite perpetual image, existing "always" in "her spiritual vision." The longing, so described, is an immortal one and, as she acknowledges, "unattainable"; the vision might be of Robert, but it might equally be of the cavalry officer, the engaged young man, the tragedian—even of Adèle, whose mothering attentions first elicited a sensuous response from Edna and whose own imminent motherhood has kept her from the grand party. The indefinite quality of Edna's longing thus described has an ominous tone, a tone made even more ominous by the rising specter of those "vast caverns" waiting vainly to be filled.

Perhaps Edna's preoccupation with the incorporation of food is but one aspect of a more general concern with incorporating what which is external to her. Freud's hypotheses about the persistence in some people of essentially oral concerns makes Edna's particular problem even clearer.

> Originally the ego includes everything, later it separates off an external world from itself. Our present ego-feeling is, therefore, only a shrunken residue of a much more inclusive—indeed, an all-embracing—feeling which corresponded to a more intimate bond between the ego and the world about it. If we may assume that there are many people in whose mental life this primary ego-feeling has persisted to a greater or less degree, it would exist in them side by side with the narrower and more sharply demarcated ego-feeling of maturity, like a kind of counterpart to it. In that case, the ideational contents appropriate to it would be precisely those of limitlessness and a bond with the universe . . . the 'oceanic' feeling.[14]

A psychologically mature individual has to some extent satisfied these oral desires for limitless fusion with the external world; presumably his sense of oneness with a nurturing figure has given him sustenance sufficient to move onward to more complex satisfactions. Yet growth inevitably involves some loss. "The feeling of happiness derived from the satisfaction of a wild instinctual impulse untamed by the ego is incomparably more intense than that derived from sating an instinct that has been tamed."[15] To some extent all of us share Edna's fantasy of complete fulfillment through a bond with the infinite; that is what gives the novel its power. However for those few people in whom this primary ego-feeling has persisted with uncompromising force the temptation to seek total fulfillment may be both irresistible and annihilating.

Everywhere and always in the novel, Edna's fundamental longing is postulated in precisely these terms. And strangely enough, the narrator seems intuitively to understand the connection between this longing for suffusion, fulfillment, incorporation, and the very earliest attempts to define identity.

> But the beginning of things, of a world especially, is necessarily vague, tangled, chaotic, and exceedingly disturbing. How few of us ever emerge from such a beginning! How many souls perish in its tumult!
>
> The voice of the sea is seductive; never ceasing, whispering, clamoring, murmuring, inviting the soul to wander for a spell in abysses of solitude; to lose itself in mazes of inward contemplation. The voice of the sea speaks to the soul. The touch of the sea is sensuous, enfolding the body in its soft, close embrace. (p. 34)

Ultimately, the problem facing Edna has a nightmarish circularity. She has achieved some measure of personal identity only by hiding her "true self" within—repressing all desire for instinctual gratification. Yet she can see others in her environment—the Creoles generally and Adèle in particular—who seem comfortably able to indulge their various sensory appetites and to do so with easy moderation. Edna's hidden self longs for resuscitation and nourishment; and in the supportive presence of Grand Isle Edna begins to acknowledge and express the needs of that "self."

Yet once released, the inner being cannot be satisfied. It is an orally destructive self, a limitless void whose needs can be filled, finally, only by total fusion with the outside world, a totality of sensuous enfolding. And this totality means annihilation of the ego.

Thus all aspects of Edna's relationship with the outside world are unevenly defined. She is remarkably vulnerable to feelings of being invaded and overwhelmed; we have already seen that she views emotional intimacy as potentially shattering. She is equally unable to handle the phenomenal world with any degree of consistency or efficiency. She is very much at the mercy of her environment: the atmosphere of Mademoiselle Reisz' room is said to "invade" her with repose (p. 252); Mademoiselle Reisz' music has the consistent effect of penetrating Edna's outer self and playing upon the responsive chords of her inner yearning; even her way of looking at objects in the world about her becomes an act of incorporation; "she had a way of turning [her eyes] swiftly upon an object and holding them there as if lost in some inward maze of contemplation or thought" (p. 7). Once she has given up the pattern of repression that served to control dangerous impulses, she becomes engaged in trying to maintain a precarious balance in each of her relationships. On the one hand she must resist invasion, for with invasion comes possession and total destruction. On the other hand she must resist the equally powerful impulse to destroy whatever separates her from the external world so that she can seek union, fusion and (so her fantasies suggest) ecstatic fulfillment.

In seeking to deal with this apparently hopeless problem, Edna encounters several people whose behavior might serve as a pattern for her. Mademoiselle Reisz is one. Mademoiselle Reisz is an artist, and as such she has created that direct avenue between inner and outer worlds which Edna seeks in her own life. Surely Edna's own attempts at artistic enterprise grow out of her more general desire for sustained ecstasy. "While Edna worked she sometimes sang low the little air, 'Ah, si tu savais!'" (p. 149). Her work is insensibly linked with her memories of Robert, and these in turn melt into more generalized memories and desires. The little song she is humming "moved her with recollections. She could hear again the ripple of the water, the flapping sail. She could see the glint of the moon upon the bay, and could feel the soft, gusty beating of the hot south wind. A subtle current of desire passed through her body, weakening her hold upon the brushes and making her eyes burn" (p. 149). In some ways, Edna's painting might offer her an excellent and viable mode for coming to terms with the insistent demands of cosmic yearning. For one thing, it utilizes in an effective way her habit of transforming the act of observing the external world into an act of incorporation: to some extent the artist must use the world in this way, incorporating it and transforming it in the act of artistic creation. Thus the period during which Edna is experimenting with her art offers her some of the most satisfying experiences she is capable of having. "There were days when she was very happy without knowing why. She was happy to be alive and breathing when her whole being seemed to be one with the sunlight, the color, the odors, the luxuriant warmth of some perfect Southern day. . . . And she found it good to dream and to be alone and unmolested" (p. 149).

Yet when Edna tells Mademoiselle Reisz about her efforts, she is greeted with skepticism: "You have

pretensions," Mademoiselle Reisz responds. "'To be an artist includes much; one must possess many gifts—absolute gifts—which have not been acquired by one's own effort. And moreover, to succeed, the artist must possess the courageous soul. . . . The brave soul. The soul that dares and defies'" (p. 165). One implication of Mademoiselle Reisz' half-contemptuous comment may well be the traditional view that the artist must dare to be unconventional; and it is this interpretation which Edna reports later to Arobin, saying as she does, however, "'I only half comprehend her'" (p. 217). The part of Mademoiselle Reisz' injunction that eludes Edna's understanding concerns the sense of purposiveness which is implied by the image of a courageous soul. Mademoiselle Reisz has her art, but she has sacrificed for it—perhaps too much. In any case, however, she has acknowledged limitations, accepted some and grappled with others; she is an active agent who has defined her relationship to the world. Edna, by contrast, is passive.

The words which recur most frequently to describe her are words like melting, drifting, misty, dreaming, shadowy. She is not willing (perhaps not able) to define her position in the world because to do so would involve relinquishing the dream of total fulfillment. Thus while Mademoiselle Reisz can control and create, Edna is most comfortable as the receptive vessel—both for Mademoiselle Reisz' music and for the sense impressions which form the basis for her own artistic endeavor. Mademoiselle Reisz commands her work; Edna is at the mercy of hers. Thus just as there are moments of exhilaration, so "there were days when she was unhappy, she did not know why, —when it did not seem worthwhile to be glad or sorry, to be alive or dead; when life appeared to her like a grotesque pandemonium and humanity like worms struggling blindly toward inevitable annihilation. She could not work on such a day, nor weave fantasies to stir her pulses and warm her blood" (pp. 149–50). Art, for Edna, ultimately becomes not a defense against inner turmoil, merely a reflection of it.

Another possible defense for Edna might be the establishment and sustaining of a genuine genital relationship. Her adolescent fantasies, her mechanical marriage, her liaison with Arobin and her passionate attachment to the fantasy image of Robert all suggest imperfect efforts to do just that. A genital relationship, like ego-relationships, necessarily involves limitation; to put the matter in Edna's terms, a significant attachment with a real man would involve relinquishing the fantasy of total fulfillment with some fantasy lover. In turn, it would offer genuine emotional nourishment—though perhaps never enough to satisfy the voracious clamoring of Edna's hidden self.

Ironically, Adèle, who seems such a fount of sustenance, gives indications of having some of the same oral needs that Edna does. Like Edna she is preoccupied with eating, she pays extravagant care to the arrangement of her own physical comforts, and she uses her pregnancy as an excuse to demand a kind of mothering attention for herself. The difference between Edna and Adèle is that Adèle can deal with her nurturing needs by displacing them onto her children and becoming a "mother-woman." Having thus segregated and limited these desires, Adèle can find diverse ways of satisfying them; and having satisfied her own infantile oral needs, she can go on to have a rewarding adult relationship with her husband. Between Adèle and M. Ratignolle there is mutual joining together: "The Ratignolles understood each other perfectly. If ever the fusion of two human beings into one has been accomplished on this sphere it was surely in their union" (p. 144). The clearest outward sign of this happy union is that the Ratignolles converse eagerly and clearly with each other. M. Ratignolle reports his experiences and thoughts to his wife, and she in turn "was keenly interested in everything he said, laying down her fork the better to listen, chiming in, taking the words out of his mouth" (p. 145). Yet this picture of social and domestic accord is indescribably dismaying to Edna. She "felt depressed rather than soothed after leaving them. The little glimpse of domestic harmony which had been offered her, gave her no regret, no longing" (p. 145).

Again, what has capitulated is the fantasy of complete and total suffusion; the Ratignolles have only a union which is as perfect as one can expect *on this sphere* (italics added). Yet the acme of bliss which Edna has always sought "was not for her in this world" (p. 47). Edna wishes a kind of pre-verbal union, an understanding which consistently surpasses words. Léonce is scarcely a sensitive man (that is, as we have seen, why she chose to marry him). Yet Edna never exerts herself to even such efforts at communication with him as might encourage a supportive emotional response. She responds to his unperceptive clumsiness by turning inward, falling into silence. Over and over again their disagreements follow the pattern of a misunderstanding which Edna refuses to clarify. At the very beginning of the novel when Léonce selfishly strolls off for an evening of gambling, Edna's rage and sense of loneliness are resolutely hidden, even when she seeks to discover the cause of her unhappiness. "She said nothing, and refused to answer her husband when he questioned her" (p. 13). Perhaps Léonce could not have understood the needs which Edna feels so achingly unfulfilled. And he is very clumsy. But he does make attempts at communication while she does not, and his interview with the family doctor (pp. 168–74) shows greater concern about Edna's problems than she manages to feel for his.

The attachment to Robert, which takes on significance only after he has left Grand Isle, monopolizes Edna's emotions because it does temporarily offer an illusion of fusion, of complete union. However, this love affair, such as it is, is a genuinely narcissistic one; the sense of fusion exists because Edna's lover is really a part of herself—a figment of her imagination, an image of Robert which she has incorporated into her consciousness. Not only is her meeting with Robert after his return a disappointment (as we have seen earlier); it moves the static, imaginary "love affair" into a new and crucial stage; it tests, once and for all, Edna's capacity to transform her world of dreams into viable reality. Not surprisingly, "some way he had seemed nearer to her off there in Mexico" (p. 268).

Still she does try. She awakens him with a kiss even as Arobin has awakened her. Robert, too, is resistant to genuine involvement, and his initial reaction is to speak of the hopelessness of their relationship. Edna, however, is insistent (despite the interruption telling her of Adèle's accouchement). "'We shall be everything to each other. Nothing else in the world is of any consequence. I must go to my friend; but you will wait for me? No matter how late; you will wait for me, Robert?'" (p. 283). And at this point, Edna seems finally to have won her victory. "'Don't go; don't go! Oh! Edna, stay with me,' he pleaded. . . . Her seductive voice, together with his great love for her, had enthralled his senses, had deprived him of every impulse but the longing to hold her and keep her" (p. 284). And at this moment, so long and eagerly anticipated, Edna leaves Robert!

Robert's own resolve weakens during the interval, and it would be all too easy to blame Edna's failure on him. Certainly he is implicated. Yet his act does not explain *Edna's* behavior. "Nothing else in the world is of any consequence," she has said. If this is so, why then does she leave? No real duty calls her. Her presence at Adèle's delivery is of virtually no help. The doctor, sorry for the pain that the scene has caused Edna even remonstrates with her mildly for having come. "'You shouldn't have been there, Mrs. Pontellier. . . . There were a dozen women she might have had with her, unimpressionable women'" (pp. 290–91). To have stayed with Robert would have meant consummation, finally, the joining of her dream-like passion to a flesh and blood lover; to leave was to risk losing that opportunity. Edna must realize the terms of this dilemma, and still she chooses to leave. We can only conclude that she is unconsciously ambivalent about achieving the goal which has sustained her fantasies for so long. The flesh and blood Robert may prove an imperfect, unsatisfactory substitute for the "beloved" of her dreams; what is more, a relationship with the real Robert would necessarily disenfranchise the more desirable phantom lover, whose presence is linked with her more general yearning for suffusion and indefinable ecstasy.

The totality of loss which follows Edna's decision forces a grim recognition upon her, the recognition that all her lovers have really been of but fleeting significance. "To-day it is Arobin; to-morrow it will be some one else. . . . It makes no difference to me. . . . There was no one thing in the world that she desired. There was no human being whom she wanted near her except Robert; and she even realized that the day would come when he, too, and the thought of him would melt out of her existence, leaving her alone" (pp. 299–300). Her devastation, thus described, is removed from the realm of romantic disappointment; and we must see Edna's final suicide as originating in a sense of inner emptiness, not in some finite failure of love. Her decision to go to Adèle is in part a reflection of Edna's unwillingness to compromise her dream of Robert (and in this sense it might be interpreted as a flight from reality). On the other hand, it might also be seen as a last desperate attempt to come to terms with the anguish created by her unfulfilled "Oceanic" longing. And for this last effort she must turn to Adèle, the human who first caused her to loosen the bonds of repression.

The pre-eminence of Adèle over Robert in Edna's emotional life, affirmed by Edna's crucial choice, is undeniably linked to her image as a nurturing figure and, especially here, as a mother-to-be. In this capacity she is also linked to Edna's own children—insistent specters in Edna's consciousness; and this link is made explicit by Adèle's repetition of the cryptic injunction to "think of the children" (p. 298).

Now in every human's life there is a period of rhapsodic union or fusion with another, and this is the period of early infancy, before the time when a baby begins to differentiate himself from his mother. It is the haunting memory of this evanescent state which Freud defines as "Oceanic feeling," the longing to recapture that sense of oneness and suffused sensuous pleasure—even, perhaps, the desire to be reincorporated into the safety of pre-existence. Men can never recreate this state of total union. Adult women can—when they are pregnant. Most pregnant women identify intensely with their unborn children, and through that identification in some measure re-experience a state of complete and harmonious union. "The biologic process has created a unity of mother and child, in which the bodily substance of one flows into the other, and thus one larger unit is formed out of two units. The same thing takes place on the psychic level. By tender identification, by perceiving the fruit of her body as part of herself, the pregnant woman is able to transform the 'parasite' into a beloved being. Thus, mankind's eternal yearning for identity between the ego and the nonego, that deeply buried original desire to reachieve the condition once experienced, to repeat the human dream that was once realized in the mother's womb, is fulfilled."[16] Adèle is a dear friend, yes; she is a nurturing figure. But above all, she is the living embodiment of that state which Edna's deepest being longs to recapture. Trapped in the conflict between her desire for "freedom," as seen in her compulsive need to protect her precarious sense of self, and her equally insistent yearning for complete fulfillment through total suffusion, Edna is intensely involved with Adèle's pregnancy.

Edna's compulsion to be with Adèle at the moment of delivery is, in the sense which would have most significance for her, a need to view individuation at its origin. For if pregnancy offers a state of total union, then birth is the initial separation: for the child it is the archetypal separation trauma; for the mother, too, it is a significant psychic trauma. It is the ritual reenactment of her own birth and a brutal reawakening to the world of isolated ego. "To make it the being that is outside her, the pregnant mother must deliver the child from the depths of herself. . . . She loses not only it, but herself with it. This, I think, is at the bottom of the fear and foreboding of death that every pregnant woman has, and this turns the giving of life into the losing of life."[17] Edna cannot refuse to partake of this ceremony, for here, if anywhere, she will find the solution to her problem.

Yet the experience is horrendous; it gives no comfort, no reassuring answer to Edna's predicament. It offers only stark, uncompromising truth. Adèle's ordeal reminds Edna of her own accouchements. "Edna began to feel uneasy. She was seized with a vague dread. Her own like experiences seemed far away, unreal, and only half remembered. She recalled faintly an ecstasy of pain, the heavy odor of chloroform, a stupor which had deadened sensation, and an awakening to find a little new life to which she had given being" (p. 288). This is Nature's cruel message. The fundamental significance to Edna of an awakening is an awakening to separation, to individual existence, to the hopelessness of ever satisfying the dream of total fusion. The rousing of her sensuous being had led Edna on a quest for ecstasy; but the ecstasy which beckoned has become in the end merely an "ecstasy of pain," first in her protracted struggle to retain identity and finally here in that relentless recognition of inevitable separation which has been affirmed in the delivery, "an awakening to find a little new life." Edna is urged to leave, but she refuses. "With an inward agony, with a flaming, outspoken revolt against the ways of Nature, she witnessed the scene of torture" (p. 288).

In this world, in life, there can be no perfect union, and the children whom Adèle urges Edna to remember stand as living proof of the inevitability of separation. Edna's longing can never be satisfied. This is her final discovery, the inescapable disillusionment; and the narrator calls it to our attention again, lest its significance escape us. "'The years that are gone seem like dreams,'" Edna muses, "'if one might go on sleeping and dreaming—but to wake up and find—'" (p. 292). Here she pauses, but the reader can complete her thought—"a little new life." "'Oh! well! Perhaps it is better to wake up after all, even to suffer rather than to remain a dupe to illusions all one's life'" (p. 292).

One wonders to what extent Edna's fate might have been different if Robert had remained. Momentarily, at least, he might have roused her from her de-

spondency by offering not ecstasy but at least partial satisfaction. The fundamental problem would have remained, however. Life offers only partial pleasures, and individuated experience.

Thus Edna's final act of destruction has a quality of uncompromising sensuous fulfillment as well. It is her answer to the inadequacies of life, a literal denial and reversal of the birth trauma she has just witnessed, a stripping away of adulthood, of limitation, of consciousness itself. If life cannot offer fulfillment of her dream of fusion, then the ecstasy of death is preferable to the relinquishing of that dream. So Edna goes to the sea "and for the first time in her life she stood naked in the open air, at the mercy of the sun, the breeze that beat upon her, and the waves that invited her" (p. 301). She is a child, an infant again. "How strange and awful it seemed to stand naked under the sky! how delicious! She felt like some new-born creature, opening its eyes in a familiar world that it had never known" (p. 301). And with her final act Edna completes the regression, back beyond childhood, back into time eternal. "The touch of the sea is sensuous, enfolding the body in its soft, close embrace" (p. 301).

Notes

1. *Patriotic Gore* (New York: Oxford Univ. Press, 1966), p. 590.
2. *The Awakening*, with introduction by Kenneth Eble (New York: Capricorn, 1964), pp. vii–viii.
3. "Our Decentralized Literature: A Consideration of Regional, Ethnic, Racial, and Sexual Factors," from a paper delivered before the German American Studies Association in Heidelberg, June 5, 1971.
4. Ibid.
5. The quotation and all other quotations from *The Awakening* have been taken from the Capricorn edition (cited above) and will be identified in the text by page number. The hard cover edition—Kate Chopin, *The Awakening*, Vol. 2 in *The Complete Works of Kate Chopin*, edited and with an introduction by Per Seyersted, foreword by Edmund Wilson (Baton Rouge: Louisiana State Univ. Press, [1969]), may be found in libraries but is not readily available to the general public.
6. Ronald D. Laing, *The Divided Self* (London: Penguin Books, 1965), p. 137.
7. See Laing, pp. 138–39.

8. Ibid., p. 113.

9. Laing cites a maneuver which is remarkably similar. "A patient, for instance, who conducted his life along relatively 'normal' lines outwardly but operated this inner split, presented as his original complaint the fact that he could never have intercourse with his wife but only with his own image of her. That is, his body had physical relations with her body, but his mental self, while this was going on, could only look on at what his body was doing and/or *imagine* himself having intercourse with his wife as an object of his imagination. . . . This is an example of what I mean by saying that phantasy and reality are kept apart. The self avoids being related directly to real persons but relates itself to itself and to the objects which it itself posits. *The self can relate itself with immediacy to an object which is an object of its own imagination or memory but not to a real person*" (p. 86).

10. Ibid., p. 77.

11. Ibid.

12. Ibid., p. 161.

13. Sigmund Freud, "Civilization and Its Discontents," in *The Standard Edition of the Complete Psychological Works*, ed. James Strachey (London: Hogarth Press, 1971), 21:71.

14. Ibid., p. 68.

15. Ibid., p. 79.

16. Helene Deutsch, *The Psychology of Women* (New York: Grune and Stratton, 1971), 2:139.

17. Ibid., p. 160.

CHAPTER FIVE

Intertextual Criticism: Literature as Context

Be Homer's *Works your* Study, *and* Delight,
Read them by Day, *and meditate by* Night
 —Pope, *An Essay on Criticism*

Poems do not imitate life; they imitate other poems. This is the central idea of the perspective I have labeled "intertextual criticism," a perspective that says the poem can best be understood by seeing it in the larger contexts of the linguistic and literary conventions it employs. Unless we know these, says the intertextualist, we can't know the poem at all.

Not all of the many critics who have adopted this perspective consider themselves members of the same critical school, and perhaps only a few would answer to the name I have given to their approach. I can only plead that no other term would meet with greater recognition. And this is odd, because the approach itself has a history as old and as rich as any other. But this approach has never had a widely accepted label, and often it has had no label at all. Northrop Frye states the case, and the problem, in an essay on *Lycidas:*

> In the writing of *Lycidas* there are four creative principles of particular importance. . . . One is convention, the reshaping of the poetic material which is appropriate to this subject. Another is genre, the choosing of the appropriate form. A third is archetype, the use of appropriate, and therefore recurrently employed, images and symbols. The fourth, for which there is no name, is the fact that the forms of literature are autonomous: that is, they do not exist outside of literature. Milton is not writing an obituary: he does not start with Edward King and his life and times, but with the conventions and archetypes that poetry requires for such a theme.

This fourth principle, "for which there is no name," includes the other three; to name it is to name the entire context. But critics have failed to agree on an appropriate label.

To supply this lack, some have tried to promote one of the other words to the status of cover term, and each label tells us something about the interests of this perspective. So we hear, for example, of "genre criticism," and clearly any conception of genre does fall within this context. But as a cover term, "genre criticism" has two drawbacks. First, it suggests to many minds a rigid and even hierarchic conception of discrete forms and a concern with arid distinctions parodied in Polonius's pedantic taxonomy: "tragedy, comedy, history, pastoral, pastoral-comical, historical-pastoral, tragical-historical, tragical-comical-historical-pastoral." This reaction may be prejudice, but it is strong enough to erode the usefulness of the term. More importantly, the concept "genre" is itself reducible to an indefinite number of conventions by which we recognize the various "kinds" of literature. Consequently, many critics can operate in this context without being directly concerned with "genre" in the usual sense of the word.

The word "archetype" offers another possibility, and Frye himself is often called an "archetypal" or a "myth" critic. Some justification exists for these terms if they are understood to have the special meanings Frye sometimes gives them. Unfortunately, Frye uses the term "myth" in several different senses and, even more confusing, it has long been used to label critical approaches very different from his own. "Archetype" presents similar problems. Frye's sense of "recurrently employed images and symbols" clearly fits the context I am describing here, though, like "genre," it too seems reducible to "convention." But the chief difficulty is that "archetype" inevitably suggests to many readers the very different Jungian sense of the word. The fact that Frye is still often classed with "myth" critics or with "archetypal" critics of a Jungian persuasion shows that these labels are likely to cause confusion.

There remains, then, the basic term "convention." Archetype, in Frye's sense, and "genre" as well, are simply elaborations of this more fundamental concept. And a concern with the conventional aspects of art is indeed the characteristic feature of the criticism we are here describing. All art, in this view, is conventional, and any work of art can be understood only by those who know the conventions it employs. So it would be both accurate and appropriate to call this approach "conventional" criticism. I can think of only one disadvantage to this name: the obvious and fatal one that "conventional" criticism, like "conventional" wisdom, will be taken to mean the dull, the ordinary, the uninspired, and that would be neither accurate nor appropriate. Convention, nevertheless, remains the key concept. Our understanding of a particular work is an analogical process by which we measure its conformity to the linguistic and literary conventions we know. The conformity is never absolute; in this sense each work is "unique." Yet, if the work were truly unique, if it used no conventions we knew, it would be simply unintelligible. This is the primary reason I have labeled the approach to literature by way of its conventional elements an "intertextual" approach.

The term has achieved some currency, particularly in connection with the related terms "semiotics" and "structuralism," which we'll need to glance at again later in this introduction. Here I simply note that "semiotics" and "structuralism" are used to describe movements in several intellectual fields besides literary criticism. That is, they are both more and less than approaches to literature. But when structuralists or semioticians do concentrate on literature, they are primarily concerned with the conventional and self-referential aspects of the art, with literature as a system of signs. So "intertextual" is an appropriate cover term for most semiotic and structural, and even for much "poststructural," criticism.

But I use "intertextual" here in an even wider yet fairly obvious sense. While interest in structuralism and semiotics is a relatively recent phenomenon, especially among English-speaking critics, interest in "intertextual" relations, under a variety of cover terms, is very old and very widespread. In this broad sense of the term, whenever critics focus on the conventional elements of literature and relate the poem not to "reality" but, by analogy, to other poems, they are practicing "intertextual" criticism.

The term understood in this sense helps to clarify the crucial distinction between the genetic and the generic perspectives. Studies that attempt to trace the literary influences on a particular poem have long been a staple of genetic or historical criticism. As the words "genetic" and "influence" imply, such studies seek the causes of poems and necessarily operate in chronological sequence. With a tradition as diffuse as that of the pastoral and with an author as learned as Milton, tracing the sources of a poem like *Lycidas* becomes difficult and frustrating. The difficulty results from the vast number of parallels that exist for many features of the poem. The frustration follows from our inability to know precisely which of these parallels Milton had in mind when he wrote. But when we shift from the genetic to the intertextual perspective, the difficulty evaporates. We need to know pastoral conventions to understand *Lycidas,* and therefore we need to know other pastoral poems, but it makes little difference on this view whether we know only those pastoral poems that Milton knew. For that matter, our knowledge of later poems in the genre may be quite as helpful as our knowledge of earlier ones. Yet clearly no one would argue that Arnold's "Thyrsis," say, or Shelley's "Adonais" in any way "influenced" Milton's poem.

Similarly, our comprehension of the *Aeneid* is improved when we read it with *Paradise Lost* in mind, and our understanding of the *Iliad* is conditioned by our reading of Virgil's epic, even though the "lines of influence" in each case run in the opposite direction. And the process operates when there are no clear lines of influence at all. The question of how much Shakespeare could have known about Sophocles' drama is, on this view, less important than the reciprocal illumination that results when their plays are compared. The relationships in all these instances are not genetic but generic, not diachronic but synchronic, not causal but analogical. Robert Frost, though he probably never used the term, has furnished a succinct description of intertextual reading: "A poem is best read in the light of all the other poems ever written. We read A the better to read B (we have to start somewhere; we may get very little out of A). We read B the better to read C, C the better to read D, D the better to go back and get something out of A. Progress is not the aim, but circulation. The thing is to get among the poems where they hold each other apart in their places as the stars do" (*Selected Prose*, New York, 1966, pp. 96–97).

"Intertextual" criticism, then, is something neither new nor strange, and the idea that our understanding of literature depends on a knowledge of its conventions may often go unremarked because it goes, as we say, without saying. But quite as often, one suspects, it goes unsaid because it is *unseen.* A curious thing about conventions is that the more firmly established they are, the less likely we are to notice them. Scarcely any visitor to a museum remarks the absence of octagonal paintings, and few concertgoers in the West notice departures from five-tone or quarter-tone scales. Literary critics have often displayed a similar inattention to literary convention.

Perhaps for this reason much of the history of intertextual criticism is to be found in the observations and, above all, in the practice of the poets themselves. It now seems clear, for example, that the *Iliad* and the *Odyssey,* those songs of "Homer" that for us stand at the beginning of Western literature, achieved their final form only at the end of several centuries of oral heroic poetry. During these illiterate centuries, the characters, the actions, the meter, and the hundreds of formulaic phrases that make up these poems were gradually developed, refined, and transmitted from poet to poet. How much of either poem can be attributed to an individual genius is quite impossible to determine and, for the intertextualist, quite unnecessary to determine. But the image of the self-effacing lyre-smiter, the Phemios or the blind Demodokos, who must quite sincerely invoke the aid of Memory's daughters, is very much to the point. For what these bards must remember are all the other poems on the same themes and all the formulae with which they will build their own at each performance. They tell the old stories in the old way, and their success consists in doing well what many others have done before.

Traditional poets may be self-effacing, but their art is very important. That art is sometimes called the "collective memory" of the tribe, but it is really more like the tribe's collective imagination. The epic poem, under the guise of recreating the distant past, actually creates a world of more heroic characters and more significant actions than those its hearers know from life. So the worlds of Achilles and Odysseus, far from mirroring the lives of their listeners, provide an image of greatness, an imagined standard, against which those lives can be measured. The mirror may tell us what we are; memory may tell us what we were; but only the imagination can tell us what we might be. It is the function of art to provide these imagined worlds, and to the extent that artists work with the materials of this world, they must not copy but transform those materials. "All the world," said Mallarmé, "exists in order to make a book," a bit of "decadent aestheticism" anticipated many centuries earlier by Homer's Phaiakian king, who gives the poet's game away when he reminds the weeping Odysseus that the whole tragic action of Troy had been fashioned by the gods "so that it might become a song for future generations."

Most often, however, what the poets transform is not the raw material of life but the conventions of their medium. And this is why, says the intertextualist, only an absurdly small proportion of the world's literature can be accounted for on "mimetic" principles. It is not the mimetic but the conventional elements in art that enable us to understand it, and the great poets from Homer to the present have always known this. Pope pictures Virgil as closing up the barren leaves of art to turn directly to nature as the model for his Roman epic, only to discover that Homer had already produced the faithful copy. In actuality, it is very unlikely that Virgil ever contemplated any such thing; and neither did Pope. Virgil follows Homer at every turn because he wants his readers to know that the *Aeneid* is a heroic poem, and that meant for him, as it means for us, a poem that looks like the *Iliad* and the *Odyssey*. He also follows Homer at every turn because he wants his readers to know how profoundly his vision differs from Homer's. In other words, Virgil carefully copies the Homeric poems because much of the meaning of his work depends on our marking these comparisons. And there is reason to believe that "Homer" relates to his predecessors in the same way. For the same reasons, Milton takes pains to copy Homer and Virgil in *Paradise Lost*, and Pope, in turn, draws on all these in *The Rape of the Lock*.

The last is, of course, a mock heroic. But from the intertextual perspective, all poems are to some degree "mock" forms. That is, it may be readily admitted that Pope's *Rape of the Lock* will not be very meaningful to anyone who doesn't understand the conventions of heroic poetry and that the reader who comes to the poem with a knowledge of the epics of Homer and Virgil and Milton is better equipped than one who brings only a knowledge of Pope's life, or of Arabella Fermor's. But a knowledge of the conventions of heroic poetry is equally indispensable, says the intertextual critic, to our understanding of the "primary" works. And this knowledge can be gained only by studying heroic poems.

And so with every other form or "genre." It can be said that Pope, like Milton, never sat down to write a poem; he always wrote some "kind" of poem. All poets must do this, the intertextualist claims, but not all poets have been equally conscious of the fact. One of the few things that makes Wordsworth's 1800 "Preface" to the *Lyrical Ballads* a truly revolutionary critical document is his inclination to talk about poetry with no reference to generic type and with little reference to convention, except for those conventions he wishes to extirpate. Somehow the term "decorum" has become attached to those conventions, and the poor reputation of the word dates from about this time. This represents a clear and symptomatic decline from the term's earlier meaning of "suitability," specifically that suiting of image, diction, style, and tone to theme and subject that Milton had in mind when he pronounced "decorum" to be "the grand masterpiece to observe," a pronouncement that makes sense only in the context of some conception of genre and convention.

The intertextual critic will point out, of course, that Wordsworth's poems, despite his critical theory, are quite as conventional as any others. But the tendency to overlook this fact is by no means limited to Wordsworth. Perhaps, as some have argued, the modern emphasis on individualism and "originality" has served to further obscure the conventional and communal elements in literature. At any rate, it is the case that until fairly recently modern critical theory has tended to play down the role of convention. Yet most readers remain at least dimly aware that many of the masterpieces of Western literature, including the works of Virgil, Dante, Chaucer, Shakespeare, and Milton, are profoundly "conventional" poems, though we may prefer to call them "highly allusive" instead; and few works require a greater knowledge of literary conventions than do such modernist masterpieces as *The Waste Land* and *Ulysses.* This interdependence is not really surprising, argues the intertextual critic, for poetry, being an art, must go on rediscovering, recreating, and recombining the conventions of that art if it is to exist at all. And poetry must continue to do so even when critical theory takes little notice of the fact and even when its readers come less and less to share similar assumptions and similar training.

This last is a serious difficulty, and for the past two hundred years, as the number of readers has increased several times over but the number trained as Pope and Milton were trained has steadily declined, poets have lamented their plight. Yeats, like Blake before him, tried to solve the problem by making of his own poems an interlocking set of images and symbols, a sounding box in which the individual poem may resonate. Eliot complained that the modern poet and his readers lacked anything like the extensive system of attitudes and symbols that Dante shared with his audience, but then proceeded to write poetry nearly as allusive as Dante's. Each solution illustrates the intertextualist's point: the poet can speak only through the conventions of poetry.

In his famous essay "Tradition and the Individual Talent" (1917), Eliot asserted that "honest criticism and sensitive appreciation are directed not upon the poet but upon the poetry," and the essay has been often cited as an opening shot in the formalists' battle against genetic criticism. But the formalists largely ignored, and their theory cannot easily deal with, the chief thesis of that essay in which Eliot explained that "no poet, no artist of any art, has his complete meaning alone." He urged both the poet and the critic to develop what he called a "historical sense," which "involves a perception, not only of the pastness of the past, but of its presence; the historical sense compels a man to write not merely with his own generation in his bones, but with a feeling that the whole of the literature of Europe from Homer and within it the whole of the literature of his own country has a simultaneous existence and composes a simultaneous order." While we may hesitate to call this synchronic view a "historical" sense, Eliot's vision of all the works of Western literature, not strung out in fixed sequence but arranged in some kind of conceptual space to form a context for the understanding of each poem, is precisely the vision of intertextual criticism.

From this perspective, the intertextual critic offers to explain a central fact that nearly everyone recognizes but that no other theory can adequately account for: people who have read a lot of poetry can generally interpret a given poem better than people who have not. We noticed in particular that critics operating in the formal and mimetic contexts find this phenomenon difficult to explain, and for the simple reason that these contexts have no way of dealing with literary convention. The problem goes much deeper than "allusion." In discussing formalism, I remarked that formalists sometimes appear to confront the poem armed only with their wits and a dictionary. But this immensely oversimplifies the case. In the first place, if the poem is in English, any reader has already more or less—and it is always more or less—mastered several systems of conventions that make up "written English." That certain marks should stand for certain sounds and that these sounds should stand for things, actions, and relationships are matters quite arbitrary and peculiar to each language. In English, for example, we depend almost exclusively on word order to signal meaning, and we are required to describe a certain spatial relationship by saying, "the cat is on the mat" rather than "the mat is on the cat." These devices are not the result of our perception of the world; they are purely conventional elements. But unless one has mastered these conventions, one cannot understand even the simplest English sentence.

Now poems, says the analogist, present analogous cases. But to explain literary conventions by analogy to linguistic conventions somewhat clouds the issue, for a poem is in the first place a system of linguistic conventions, the "system" itself being one of the conventional elements. It differs from other utterances in the same language, the intertextual critic would argue, by also employing a number of supralinguistic conventions peculiar to or characteristic of literature. This fact explains, incidentally, why poems are and are not translatable. Linguistic conventions and the literary conventions most closely bound to them, such as meter, rhythm, and rhyme, are notoriously difficult to reproduce in another language. But devices of structure and plot, techniques of character representation, and a vast reservoir of images and symbols are conventions that most of the Western literatures, at least, have in common, and these easily cross linguistic boundaries. But, like the conventions of language, they have meaning only to those who have learned them. As Eliot says in the same essay, the literary tradition "cannot be inherited, and if you want it you must obtain it by great labour."

This idea that literary conventions must be learned is a crucial point that sets intertextual critics apart from most "myth" critics. The latter, whatever their psychological or anthropological affiliation, are generally affectivists who locate the power of poems in special patterns or symbols that have the ability to appeal directly and forcefully to our subconscious minds. They may, like the Jungians, account for this power on the basis of some theory of inherited racial memory, or like the Freudians, they may feel that the essential similarity of human experience offers sufficient explanation. In either case they are concerned only with certain special poetic "conventions" (though they would surely find that word too slight) and, as we noticed in the discussion of reader-response criticism, while their view offers an apparently plausible explanation of why some of us respond intensely to certain works, it offers no explanation at all of why many of us do not. Intertextual critics, by contrast, though not necessarily denying that certain symbols may have special potency, feel no need to locate the power of myths or symbols in the unconscious or in the extraliterary. Like the conventions of language, literary conventions are arbitrary, and they must, therefore, be learned. From this perspective, readers who fail to respond to *King Lear,* say, or to *Moby Dick,* are not psychologically defective; they simply don't know how to read well enough.

It is the fundamental task of literary criticism to teach them, first by explaining what they need to know and then by showing how they may most efficiently acquire that knowledge. What they need to know, of course, are the conventions of literature, and here the only singing school is studying the monuments themselves. That is, in the intertextual view, the study of literature cannot be based on psychology, anthropology, sociology, or biography, nor can it be grounded in religious, economic, or political history. None of these contexts can directly tell us much about how literary conventions carry meaning. For similar reasons, the traditional genetic categories of author, period, and nation often prove less than ideal organizing forms for the study of literature. From the intertextual perspective, the best context for the understanding of any poem is all the other poems that employ similar conventions. These may or may not include poems by the same author or from the same historical period, but they are almost never limited to these, and they are seldom limited to the writings of a single nation or a single language.

This range suggests that in practice the intertextual study of literature may best be organized along generic lines, lines that keep our attention on conventional elements and that cut across national, temporal, and linguistic boundaries. The problem, again, is how to arrange this vast body of simultaneously existing works so that it may be most efficiently studied. Or, in terms of our definition of criticism, the problem is how to assure that the relevant information can be brought to bear on whatever work we have placed at the center of our attention. Generic concepts are helpful here, but generic distinctions are not. The critical task is not to define tragedy, or pastoral, or epic, but to assemble for our understanding the most useful comparisons. With large works, like *The Faerie Queen* or *Paradise Lost,* this purpose very quickly takes us beyond "generic" concerns to a contemplation of the vast networks of conventional images, symbols, and patterns of action that give such poems their multileveled meanings and their astonishing richness. In this view, the reader of *Ulysses* may need to know very little about Dublin at the turn of the century in the springtime, but a great deal about Western literature since Homer's time.

To be sure, nothing short of a total knowledge of all literature will guarantee that one will come to a given poem with all the relevant conventions in mind. But it's not difficult to imagine a course of study by which readers could acquire much of what the intertextual critics claim they must know to understand most works in the Western tradition. Such a study would concentrate early and long on the classical languages and literatures. It would emphasize the *Iliad* and the *Odyssey:* the plays of Aeschylus, Sophocles, Euripides, and Aristophanes; the dialogues of Plato. It would include some Greek lyrics, Plautus and Terence, Virgil and Ovid and Horace. It would very likely include Dante's *Commedia,* and it would certainly include intensive study of the Bible. Above all, it would conceive of Western literature as a unit, and it would largely ignore national boundaries. Obviously, this course of study resembles, in content if not in methodology, the curriculum of "liberal" education as that phrase was generally understood in the centuries before our own. And this resemblance is not surprising, for readers who follow this curriculum would be learning the conventions of literature in much the same way that the poets they want to read had learned them. As the intertextual critic sees it, these works, quite aside from their intrinsic merit, form the "grammar" and the basic "vocabulary" of European literary language, and consequently a knowledge of them is as indispensable to readers of Barth and Borges, Pynchon and Joyce, Eliot and Stevens as it is to readers of Spenser or Milton or Pope. For all art, says the intertextualist, is conventional.

This is the fundamental tenet. And the intertextualist can demonstrate it with even the briefest example. Consider, as a case in point, another Blake lyric, "The Sick Rose":

> O Rose, thou art sick.
> The invisible worm
> That flies in the night
> In the howling storm
>
> Has found out thy bed
> Of crimson joy,
> And his dark secret love
> Does thy life destroy.

To the intertextual critic, it seems pointless to look to Blake's life for the meaning of these words, and equally pointless to examine the responses of readers, until we know which readers have the best responses. Furthermore, although the poem, short as it is, exhibits a complex structure and a high degree of formal coherence, these in themselves do not account for the referential sense of the words. Now, ordinarily referential meaning implies correspondence to the world of nonverbal experience. Yet as a botanical description, Blake's poem is, like most poems, negligible if not downright ridiculous. But the intertextual critic argues that the real frame of reference for poetic language is not the world of nonverbal experience but the world of poetry, the world that literature creates and is.

If, ignoring considerations of rhythm and rhyme, we substitute "tulip" for "rose," "insect" for "invisible worm," "dawn" for "night," and so forth, we can construct a poem that would not only be equally coherent, but that would present at least as accurate a picture of the nonverbal world. As a poem, though, it would be a very poor thing, for it would lack the extensive range of conventional associations that Blake's words have. The rose, for example, has been long established in the Western tradition as a symbol of beauty. This is not a matter of perception or "aesthetics" in the basic sense. Under the aspect of eternity, we may suppose, all plants are equally beautiful, and many people may prefer tulips to roses in their gardens or vases. But not in their verses. The convention is too strong. One thinks of the *Romance of the Rose,* of Dante's Rose of Heaven, of Eliot's rose garden, of Waller's lovely rose and Housman's withered rose and Thomas's crooked rose, and on and on through a hundred other poems great and small. The only limit is our reading and our memory. And "worm," whatever its relation to real roses, has a similarly extensive literary pedigree. It calls to mind those snakes and serpents that slither through countless other poems and that have, whatever their possible psychological sources, a necessarily sinister resonance because of the pervasive influence of the Bible, a resonance reinforced here by the conventional associations of "invisible," "night," "howling storm," "dark," and "secret." Most of us do not need a Freudian analyst to tell us that "bed of joy" has sexual associations, nor that "crimson" in this context is "multivalent."

Indeed, the whole poem is wonderfully multivalent, or "plurisignificant." We can construct upon it a coherent "religious" reading, an equally coherent "sexual" reading, and any number of other readings within or around these. Short as it is, the poem can support pages of relevant commentary and not be exhausted because it is

a coherent arrangement of elements that were already highly charged with poetic —
that is, with "conventional" — significance. Blake didn't invent these associations
any more than he invented the dictionary definitions of his words. His business as
a poet was to be unusually sensitive to the conventional associations of words and
to have the genius to combine deftly these already charged particles to create that
supercharged verbal structure that is his poem. But that poem, the intertextualist reminds us, is fully available only to readers who have mastered the relevant conventions of literature. "The Sick Rose" has eight lines; *Paradise Lost* has 10,565. We begin
to see what Eliot meant by "great labour." Happily, most of this labor consists of
reading poems.

This, then, is a sketch of the intertextual critic's argument, and even skeptical
readers might grant that it has much to recommend it. But they might also feel that
the perspective raises some difficult questions. Consider, for example, the question
of the poem's relationship to the world. We have noticed that the mimetic critic, by
definition, and the formal critic, often more hesitantly, locate the value of poetry in
its correspondence to reality, however subtly such correspondence is defined and
qualified. And this "reality" is usually the empiricist's reality, the world of experience. This mimetic grounding causes difficulties, but since correspondence to reality
is the definition of "truth" in most commonsense views, poetry's claim to mimetic
accuracy, to "truth-revealing" powers, seems to many critics to offer the only stable
ground for poetic value. Yet the intertextual critic, by arguing that poems imitate
other poems and not the world of experience, appears to surrender that claim at the
outset. Literature becomes, as I. A. Richards had said it was, a system of purely hypothetical or "pseudo" statements.

But in defense of this position, the intertextualist can urge two arguments that
were not so readily available in Richards's affective context. The first argument, interestingly, simply accepts the empirical view of "truth." The poem does provide
cognitive knowledge, but knowledge of imagined worlds. By showing us not what
life is but in what ways it could be better or worse, poetry becomes, in Matthew
Arnold's phrase, a "criticism of life." For the only standard by which we can measure actuality must be an imagined standard. The characters and actions we find
in literature are, in this view, less imitations of things than things to be imitated, or
shunned, images of desire or aversion. This, I assume, is what Northrop Frye means
when he says that one of the functions of art is to provide the "goals of work" for
civilization. Looked at this way, what we call civilization is our collective attempt to
create, from the world of nature we find, something approximating the world we
imagine. And in this sense, life does indeed imitate art. As that arch-antimimeticist,
Oscar Wilde, reminds us, nature has good intentions, but she can't carry them out.

This argument meets the empiricists on their own ground because it assumes that
the correspondence definition of truth holds and that the world experienced outside
of art is the "real" world. Only now, paradoxically, the value of literature seems to inhere not in its correspondence to that world but in its difference from it. This reversal, admittedly, offers as many evaluative difficulties as does the correspondence
standard. But such a view is at least better able to account for the many forms of literature, and it would serve to counter the modern, mimetic prejudice against forms
such as epic, romance, and pastoral that flaunt their "unrealistic" conventions.

And yet, the more we contemplate the conventional aspects of poems, the more
it appears that all verbal constructs are to a high degree conventional. Carried to its
logical conclusion, such a view undercuts empiricism itself. It does so not by denying the existence of "reality" but by denying that it can be known apart from the

structure of the mind that knows it. Perception, as Kant perceived, is itself creation, and to the extent that art organizes our perceptions, we can understand the more profound implications of Wilde's remark that "life imitates are far more than art imitates life." This begins to sound like Kant's structuralist answer to the empiricism that Hume had pushed to its logical and paradoxical limits, and while the intertextual perspective in criticism does not require any particular philosophical orientation, it is not surprising that many intertextual critics should feel comfortable with what we might call, broadly speaking, a "structuralist" outlook. At any rate, it is typical of neo-Kantian philosophers, such as Ernst Cassirer, and of structuralist thinkers, such as Ferdinand de Saussure and Claude Lévi-Strauss and their many followers in literary criticism, to emphasize the conventional, symbolic, and self-referential elements in all systems of thought. In such philosophies the empiricist's truth of correspondence tends to disappear. There is instead only truth of coherence.

In other words, the truth of any statement must be judged not by its correspondence to empirical reality, for this correspondence cannot be directly known, but by its coherence, its ability to fit into the system of other statements that we have already accepted as "true." And there is not only one system; there are several. Mathematics, for instance, appears to some thinkers to be a clear example of such a system of complex and totally coherent relationships that, as a system, is congruent with, or corresponds to, nothing at all outside mathematics. By analogy, what we call "history" and "sociology" and "physics" are also self-contained systems. For in this view even the physicists, the hardest of the "hard" scientists, cannot tell us if a statement corresponds to reality. They can only tell us, in the first place, if the terms of that statement have any meaning within the universe of discourse we call physics and, in the second, if the statement is consistent with other statements that constitute that universe of discourse.

And so with all systems of thought. Clearly it is beyond the scope of this book to explore such large philosophic questions as whether truth is a matter of coherence or of correspondence. But we can at least note briefly a few of the consequences for literary criticism that are implied in a "structuralist" view of the mind's relationship to the world. Such a view suggests, in the first place, that no system of thought has a firm empirical base and that all are imaginative constructs. It follows that the critic who adopts this view is in a very different position than Richards was, for Richards denied truth of correspondence to poetry but granted it to science; the "coherence" theory denies truth of correspondence to everybody. Further, whereas mimetic critics operating with the empirical or correspondence model have difficulty separating poems from other kinds of discourse because they assume that all verbal constructs are "imitations" of reality, critics operating on the coherence model have the same difficulty for the opposite reason. If all verbal structures are imaginative structures, then what we call poems can again differ from other types of discourse only in degree, not in kind.

But though defining poetry from this perspective may be difficult, it is also unnecessary. We need instead to define criticism, that system of discourse that is centrally concerned with the conventional elements of symbolic or metaphorical structures. This shift of perspective eliminates two problems that sometimes trouble critics. On the one hand, if all verbal structures are metaphorical or symbolic, literary critics need not worry about getting "out of their field" if they comment on, say, the writings of Xenophon or Thucydides, Gibbon or Hume, Mill or Marx, nor need they worry too much whether biography or autobiography is within their ken. Their business is metaphor wherever they find it, and they find it everywhere. On the other hand, the literary critic, understood in this sense, has no reason to object to the historian, the psychologist, the economist, or anyone else making statements about poems. For the statements they make would not be literary criticism simply because they were about poems; their statements would continue to be history, psychology, economics, or whatever the discipline being applied was named.

To put the matter differently, it is not a question of what we study but of *how* we study. In this view, literary criticism has often appeared confused because critics have tried to define their subject of study by their object of study. They have tried to set poems apart from other verbal structures, and then they have tried to borrow their methodology — their way of seeing the object — from some other discipline. By this route we get such terms as "sociological criticism," "psychological criticism," and "historical criticism." From the perspective we are exploring here, this attempt is nonsense. One cannot borrow an approach or a methodology from another discipline because the approach or methodology *is* the discipline. Disciplines are ways of seeing, not things to be seen; subjects, not objects. And what literary critics must master is not a definition of their object, but the discipline of criticism, which involves a systematic knowledge of the conventions from which metaphoric or symbolic forms are created and through which they can be understood.

These, I believe, are a few of the consequences that follow from accepting what I have called a "structuralist" view of criticism, but one doesn't need to get to this view by way of that label, nor is the critic who wishes to adopt an intertextual perspective compelled also to adopt this view of the mind and all that it seems to entail. As we have seen, even an empiricist can operate comfortably in the intertextual context.

But whatever their philosophic orientation may be, critics who employ the intertextual approach to literature will face some conceptual difficulties. One of these is the problem of circularity. We saw one version of this circularity in formalist theory, which holds that any part of the work can be understood and evaluated only in terms of the whole work, although (necessarily) that whole can be known only through its parts. In intertextual criticism, a similar difficulty returns on a larger scale. A particular poem can be understood only by someone who understands its conventions, but these conventions must be learned by studying similar poems, and a reading of each of these requires in turn a knowledge of conventions. But this problem, like the formalist's circularity, is less serious in practice than in theory, and again the parallel to language is instructive. We can understand, and even produce, new utterances in English because, through a complex, little understood, and never quite completed process, we have learned the conventions of our language, and this learning was gained by attending to other utterances in English. Thus the continuous interplay between convention and particular construct presents little practical difficulty at this level, however mysterious it may be to logic.

But this interplay points to a more serious problem, and that is the tendency of intertextual criticism to lose its focus on the individual work in question. Granted, this loss of focus is a problem mainly when criticism is defined, as in this book, as having as its primary goal the interpretation of particular poems. But if we hold to this conception — and most critics do — then the inclination of intertextual criticism to dissolve the particular work into an aggregate of conventions opens the approach to the charge of reductivism. If all poems are conventional, what makes some poems more effective than others? Does *Paradise Lost* have more, or better, conventions than Blackmore's *Prince Arthur*? Does *Lycidas* employ a greater number of conventional elements than lesser pastorals? Or does the better poem simply employ its conventions more effectively? Surely the latter is the case, the formalists would answer. And, while they must grant the reader's need to know the conventions used in any poem, formalists will persist in regarding such knowledge as no different in kind from a knowledge of dictionary definitions. A dictionary and *Hamlet,* they might argue, consist of conventional meanings just as a marble quarry and the Parthenon consist of stone: the particular arrangement makes all the difference.

This analogy, as the intertextualists will remind us, is greatly complicated by the fact that in literature, as in architecture, the arrangement itself is largely a matter of convention. Nevertheless, formalists, the *intra*textualists, will continue to insist on the importance of "form" in their sense of the term, the special meaning that results from these particular words in this particular order, and so they will try to pull the reader's attention along the horizontal axis to the center of our diagram while the intertextual critics pull the reader's attention toward the larger context of literary and linguistic conventions. As long as the understanding of the particular poem remains the primary, if not the ultimate, goal of criticism, this tension is difficult to relax. But it is also relatively easy to live with, and the formal and intertextual perspectives are probably more compatible than other combinations that might be formed among our contexts. Still, in spite of this compatibility, or perhaps because of it, the formalist's complaint that intertextual criticism has difficulty keeping a clear and useful focus on the individual poem is one of the most troublesome objections to the intertextual approach.

It is not, of course, the only objection. Mimetic critics, for example, will point out that if it is hard to see why we should value a poem simply because of its fidelity to empirical reality, it is also hard to see why we should value some departures from that standard more than others. Reader-response critics will want to know why some conventions, or some uses of conventions, will produce greater or lesser emotional impact, and genetic critics, even if they grant the importance of the conventional and communal elements in literature, will continue to maintain that some conception of "authorial" meaning is necessary to provide a standard for valid interpretation. Only this, they insist, will allow us to separate what the poem does mean from what it could mean.

The intertextual perspective, in short, has not resolved all the issues. It has, however, gained many adherents. In the English-speaking world, Northrop Frye's influence alone has been considerable; it has helped to create, as it has profited from, a climate of opinion that finds many literary theorists interested in philosophers like Ernst Cassirer or art critics like E. H. Gombrich, who emphasize the role of convention in all art and thought. And on the continent, and increasingly in Britain and the United States, the concepts of structuralism and semiotics, long applied in the fields of linguistics and anthropology, have been employed to elucidate the conventional elements in literary structures. This climate may also account in part for the enthusiastic reception given the work of Mikhail Bakhtin. Though much of that work was done in the first half of the century, its impact was slight before the 1970s; since then, though, Bakhtin's influence has been strong, and several of his key terms, like "dialogic," "heteroglossia," "polyglossia," "chronotope," and "carnival" have been frequently adopted. For Bakhtin, carnival reflected the "lived life" of medieval and early modern peoples. In carnival, official authority and high culture were jostled "from below" by elements of satire, parody, irony, mimicry, bodily humor, and grotesque display. This jostling from below served to keep society open, to liberate it from deadening, because univocal, authority. In "carnivalesque" literature, epitomized by the writings of Rabelais, these same elements jostle the univocal and elevated language of "high" art and high society, and to the same effect. The result is a many-voiced, multileveled, polymodal "novel" whose inclusiveness is similarly liberating.

As early as 1929, in his study of Dostoevsky, Bakhtin had seen the "novel" as the heteroglossic form *par excellence*, an antigeneric genre that undercut the authority of the single voice traditionally found in the lyric or epic. For Bakhtin, the "novel" was a kind of literary equivalent to carnival. As such, it could be traced back not only to Rabelais and Cervantes but, as he shows in "From the Pre-History of Novelistic Discourse," all the way to Hellenistic literature where "monoglossia," the myth of one language, had to give way to the reality of "polyglossia," the clash and mixture of many languages. Bakhtin, then, is interested in the historical development of literary forms, and in their interaction with social forces. His concept of the "chronotope" assumes that each era has its own way of perceiving and representing time and space, and his concepts like "carnival" and "heteroglossia" assume close connections between language, literature, and ideology. An apostle of heterogeneity, Bakhtin argues that all periods are characterized by competing ideologies, competing social forces, and, intimately bound to these, competing voices. For these reasons he could be placed as well in my final context, where his influence has also been strong.

But this may serve to remind us that the intertextual context doesn't represent a single school of thought. Like the other contexts, it includes various schools and movements as well as unaffiliated individuals, some of whom may feel uncomfortable in the company I have assigned them, and many of whom may want to argue with parts of the position I have sketched. Our concern, however, is with basic orientations to the literary work, and on this principle I have classed together those critics who, despite their many differences, share a central interest in the conventional aspects of literature. This interest defines the perspective and sets it apart from the others we have considered. And, while the objections to this perspective are not negligible, the critics who adopt it enjoy some real advantages. They, like the formal and the mimetic critics, find it possible to discuss the meaning of poems without appealing to the psyches of particular authors or particular readers, and so they avoid most of the difficulties that trouble genetic and reader-response approaches. By orienting the poem toward the world of poetic convention rather than toward the world of empirical reality, they eliminate the problems that haunt mimetic attempts to explain how verbal constructs can "imitate" this reality, or why we should want them to. And by arguing that poems imitate other poems and take their meaning from these literary relationships, they can account for literary form in the sense that the "formal" critics cannot. Finally, and this is by no means the least of their strengths, the intertextual critics' theory will explain, as no other theory will, why a study of poetry should help one understand poems.

Suggestions for Further Reading

In the English-speaking world, Northrop Frye, though he was an intertextualist *avant la lettre*, has been the most influential figure in this context, and *Anatomy of Criticism* (1957) is the fullest expression of his views. Among his later books, *The Educated Imagination* (1964) is a brief introduction to his main ideas. Studies more self-consciously "structural" or "semiotic" include Roland Barthes, *Elements of Semiology* (1967); Edward Said, *Beginnings* (1975); Umberto Eco, *A Theory of Semiotics* (1975); Seymour

Chatman, *Story and Discourse* (1978); Tzvetan Todorov, *Introduction to Poetics* (1981); Gerard Genette, *Figures of Literary Discourse* (1982); A. J. Greimas, *On Meaning: Selected Writings in Semiotic Theory* (1987); and Michael Riffaterre, *Fictional Truths* (1990). Adena Rosmarin, *The Power of Genre* (1985), analyzes several influential concepts of genre.

E. H. Gombrich, *Art and Illusion* (1961), is a study of perception and convention in the visual arts that has influenced literary theory. The fictional structuring of "historical" narrative is treated in Hayden White, *Metahistory* (1973); Paul Fussell, *The Great War and Modern Memory* (1975); and Frank Kermode, *The Genesis of Secrecy* (1979). Mikhail Bakhtin's work may be represented by *The Dialogic Imagination: Four Essays* (1981); Bakhtin's complex career and ideas are given a book-length exposition in Gary Saul Morson and Caryl Emerson, *Bakhtin: Creation of a Prosaics* (1990).

For the entire context, three interpretive works in recommended order of reading: Terence Hawkes, *Structuralism and Semiotics* (1977); Jonathan Culler, *Structuralist Poetics* (1975); and Robert Scholes, *Semiotics and Interpretation* (1982). Michael Worton and Judith Still, eds., *Intertextuality: Theories and Practices* (1990), and Jay Clayton and Eric Rothstein, eds., *Influence and Intertextuality in Literary History* (1991), are useful collections of essays. Udo J. Hebel, *Intertextuality, Allusion, and Quotation: An International Bibliography* (1989), is a well-indexed, multilingual, 2,033-entry bibliography.

THEORY

The Critical Path

Northrop Frye

Northrop Frye's influential writings provided a rationale for intertextual criticism well before structuralist and semiotic critics came to be widely known in the English-speaking world. In the retrospective opening chapter to The Critical Path, *Frye describes the critical scene when he began to write, and he explains why the genetic, formal, and reader-response contexts seemed to him not quite the right bases for the study of literature, each being too limited and extraliterary: "I felt that no critic had given his full attention to what seemed to me the first operation of criticism: trying to see what meaning could be discovered in works of literature from their context in literature." Frye's exploration of this context led to his concentration on "conventions, genres, and recurring image groups," which he called "archetypal" criticism. It also led to the charge that such intertextual criticism lacks social relevance. Frye goes on to suggest that since literature provides the "models" or "goals of work" for civilization, literary study has a great deal of social relevance, and this relevance is most clearly understood by the kind of criticism that can see literature as a whole in its social context.*

The phrase "The Critical Path" is, I understand, a term in business administration, and was one that I began hearing extensively used during the preparations for the Montreal Expo of 1967. It associated itself in my mind with the closing sentences of Kant's *Critique of Pure Reason*, where he says that dogmatism and skepticism have both had it as tenable philosophical positions, and that "the critical path is alone open." It also associated itself with a turning point in my own development. About twenty-five years ago, when still in middle life, I lost my way in the dark wood of Blake's prophecies, and looked around for some path that would get me out of there. There were many paths, some well trodden and equipped with signposts, but all pointing in what for me were the wrong directions. They directed me to the social conditions of Blake's time, to the history of the occult tradition, to psychological factors in Blake's mind, and other subjects quite valid in themselves. But my task was the specific one of trying to crack Blake's symbolic code, and I had a feeling that the way to that led directly through literature itself. The critical path I wanted was a theory of criticism which would, first, account for the major phenomena of literary experience, and, second, would lead to some view of the place of literature in civilization as a whole.

Following the bent that Blake had given me, I became particularly interested in two questions. One was: What is the total subject of study of which criticism forms part? I rejected the answer: "Criticism is a subdivision of literature," because it was such obvious nonsense. Criticism is the theory of literature, not a minor and non-essential element in its practice. This latter notion of it is not surprising in outsiders, or in poets, but how a critic himself can be so confused about his function as to take the same view I could not (and cannot yet) understand. Of course criticism has a peculiar disability in the number of people who have drifted into it without any vocation for it, and who may therefore have, however unconsciously, some interest in keeping it theoretically incoherent.

Literary criticism in its turn seemed to be a part of two larger but undeveloped subjects. One was the unified criticism of all the arts; the other was some area of verbal expression which had not yet been defined, and which in the present book is called mythology. The latter seemed more immediately promising: the former I felt was the ultimate destiny of the subject called aesthetics, in which (at least at that time) relatively few technically competent literary critics appeared to be much interested. I noticed also the strong centrifugal drift from criticism toward social, philosophical and religious interests, which had set in at least as early as Coleridge. Some of this seemed to me badly motivated. A critic devoting himself to literature, but without any sense of his distinctive function, is often tempted to feel that he can never be anything more than a second-class writer or thinker, because his work is derived from the work of what by his postulates are greater men. I felt, then, that a

conception of criticism was needed which would set the critic's activity in its proper light, and that once we had that, a critic's other interests would represent a natural expansion of criticism rather than an escape from it.

The other question was: How do we arrive at poetic meaning? It is a generally accepted principle that meaning is derived from context. But there are two contexts for verbal meaning: the imaginative context of literature, and the context of ordinary intentional discourse. I felt that no critic had given his full attention to what seemed to me to be the first operation of criticism: trying to see what meaning could be discovered in works of literature from their context in literature. All meaning in literature seemed to be referred first of all to the context of intentional meaning, always a secondary and sometimes the wrong context. That is, the primary meaning of a literary work was assumed to be the kind of meaning that a prose paraphrase could represent. This primary meaning was called the "literal" meaning, a phrase with a luxuriant growth of semantic tangles around it which I have discussed elsewhere and return to more briefly here.

When I first began to write on critical theory, I was startled to realize how general was the agreement that criticism had no presuppositions of its own, but had to be "grounded" on some other subject. The disagreements were not over that, but over the question of what the proper subjects were that criticism ought to depend on. The older European philological basis, a very sound one, at least in the form in which it was expounded by August Boeckh and others in the nineteenth century, had largely disappeared in English-speaking countries. In some places, notably Oxford, where I studied in the thirties, it had declined into a much narrower conception of philology. This was partly because the shifting of the centre of literary study from the Classical to the modern languages had developed a prejudice, derived from one of the more bizarre perversions of the work ethic, that English literature at least was a merely entertaining subject, and should not be admitted to universities unless the main emphasis fell on something more beneficial to the moral fibre, like learning the classes of Old English strong verbs. In most North American universities the critical establishment rested on a mixture of history and philosophy, evidently on the assumption that every work of literature is what Sir Walter Raleigh said *Paradise Lost* was, a monument to dead ideas. I myself was soon identified as one of the critics who took their assumptions from anthropology and psychology, then still widely regarded as the wrong subjects. I have always insisted that criticism cannot take presuppositions from elsewhere, which always means wrenching them out of their real context, and must work out its own. But mental habits are hard to break, especially bad habits, and because I found the term "archetype" an essential one, I am still often called a Jungian critic, and classified with Miss Maud Bodkin, whose book I have read with interest, but whom, on the evidence of that book, I resemble about as closely as I resemble the late Sarah Bernhardt.

The reason for this rather silly situation was obvious enough. As long as the meaning of a poem, let us say for short, is sought primarily within the context of intentional discourse, it becomes a document, to be related to some verbal area of study outside literature. Hence criticism, like Los Angeles, becomes an aggregate of suburbs, with no central area in literature itself. One of these suburbs is the biographical one, where the literary work is taken to be a document illustrating something in the writer's life. The most fashionable time for this approach was the nineteenth century, and its strongest proponent Carlyle, for whom great poetry could only be the personal rhetoric of a great man. The theory demands that Shakespeare, for instance, should be an obviously and overwhelmingly great man, which is why so much nineteenth-century critical energy was expended in trying to invent a sufficiently interesting biography for Shakespeare out of fancied allusions in the poetry. This misguided industry has now largely been restricted to the sonnets, where, as Mutt says in *Finnegans Wake,* "he who runes may rede it on all fours." Carlyle's essay on Shakespeare, in *Heroes and Hero-Worship,* comes as close to pure verbiage, to rhetoric without content, as prose sentences can in the nature of things get. Something seems to be wrong with the theory, at least in this form. One is better off with Goethe, but even there the sense of personal greatness may be connected less with the quality of the poetry than with the number of things Goethe had been able to do besides writing poetry.

I am not talking here about real biography, but about the assumption that the poet's life is the essential key to the deeper understanding of the poetry. It often happens that interesting literature is produced by an uninteresting man, in the sense of one who disappoints us if we are looking for some kind of culture-hero. In fact it happens so often that there is clearly no correlation between the ability to write poetry and any other ability, or, at least, it is clearly absurd to assume that every real poet must be a certain kind of person. Hence the formula "this poem is particularly notable for the way in which it throws light on," etc., soon ceases to carry much conviction for all but a selected group of poets. Something else, more deeply founded in a wider literary experience, is needed for critical understanding.

In these days, a biographical approach is likely to move from the manifest to the latent personal content of the poem, and from a biographical approach properly speaking to a psychological one. At the present time and place this means very largely a Freudian, or what I think of as a Luther-on-the-privy, approach. A considerable amount of determinism enters at this stage. All documentary conceptions of literature are allegorical conceptions of it, and this fact becomes even more obvious when poems are taken to be allegories of Freudian repressions, unresolved conflicts, or tensions between ego and id, or, for another school, of the Jungian process of individuation. But what is true of allegorical poetry is equally true of allegorical criticism: that allegory is a technique calling for tact. Tact is violated when the whiteness of Moby Dick is explained as a Lockian *tabula rasa,* or when Alice in Wonderland is discussed in terms of her hypothetical toilet training, or when Matthew Arnold's line in *Dover Beach,* "Where ignorant armies clash by night," is taken as a covert reference to the copulation of his parents. One is reminded of the exempla from natural history made by medieval preachers. According to Richard Rolle in the fourteenth century, the bee carries earth in its feet to ballast itself when it flies, and thereby reminds us of the Incarnation, when God took up an earthly form. The example is ingenious and entertaining, and only unsatisfying if one happens to be interested in bees.

If we tire of the shadow-play of explaining real poems by assumed mental states, we may be driven to realize that the ultimate source of a poem is not so much the individual poet as the social situation from which he springs, and of which he is the spokesman and the medium. This takes us into the area of historical criticism. Here again no one can or should deny the relevance of literature to history, but only rarely in historical criticism is there any real sense of the fact that literature is itself an active part of the historical process. Poets are assumed to have a sensitive litmus-paper response to social trends, hence literature as a whole is taken to be something that the historical process acts on, and we have still not escaped from a documentary and allegorical procedure.

Once more, some historical critics, like the biographical ones, will want to go from manifest to latent social content, from the historical context of the poem to its context in some unified overview of history. Here again determinism, the impulse to find the ultimate meaning of literature in something that is not literature, is unmistakable. At the time of which I am speaking, a generation ago, a conservative Catholic determinism was fashionable, strongly influenced by Eliot, which adopted Thomism, or at least made references to it, as the summit of Western cultural values, and looked down benignantly on everything that followed it as a kind of toboggan slide, rushing through nominalism, Protestantism, liberalism, subjective idealism, and so on to the solipsism in which the critic's non-Thomist contemporaries were assumed to be enclosed. Marxism is another enlarged historical perspective, widely adopted, and perhaps inherently the most serious one of them all. Literature is a part of a social process; hence that process as a whole forms the genuine context of literature. Theoretically, Marxism takes a social view of literature which is comprehensive enough to see it within this genuine context. In practice, however, Marxism operates as merely one more determinism, which avoids every aspect of literature except one allegorical interpretation of its content.

All these documentary and external approaches, even when correctly handled, are subject to at least three limitations which every experienced scholar has to reckon with. In the first place, they do not account for the literary form of what they are discussing. Identifying Edward King and documenting Milton's attitude to the Church of England will throw no light on *Lycidas* as a pastoral elegy with specific Classical and Italian lines of ancestry. Secondly, they do not account for the poetic and metaphorical language of the literary work, but assume its primary meaning to be a non-poetic meaning. Thirdly, they do not account for the fact that the genuine quality of a poet is often in a negative relation to the chosen context. To understand Blake's *Milton* and *Jerusalem* it is useful to know something of his quarrel with Hayley and his sedition trial. But one also needs to be aware of the vast disproportion between these minor events in a quiet life and their apocalyptic transformation in the poems. One should also know enough of criticism, as well as of Blake, not to ascribe the disproportion to paranoia on Blake's part. Similarly, a scholar may write a whole shelf of books about the life of Milton studied in connexion with the history of this time, and still fail to notice that Milton's greatness as a poet has a good deal to do with his profound and perverse misunderstanding of the history of his time.

By the time I began writing criticism, the so-called "new criticism" had established itself as a technique of explication. This was a rhetorical form of criticism, and from the beginning rhetoric has meant two things: the figuration of language and the persuasive powers of an orator. New criticism dealt with rhetoric in the former sense, and established a counterweight to the biographical approach which treated poetry as a personal rhetoric. The great merit of explicatory criticism was that it accepted poetic language and form as the basis for poetic meaning. On that basis it built up a resistance to all "background" criticism that explained the literary in terms of the non-literary. At the same time, it deprived itself of the great strength of documentary criticism: the sense of context. It simply explicated one work after another, paying little attention to genre or to any larger structural principles connecting the different works explicated.

The limitations of this approach soon became obvious, and most of the new critics sooner or later fell back on one of the established documentary contexts, generally the historical one, although they were regarded at first as anti-historical. One or two have even been Marxists, but in general the movement, at least in America, was anti-Marxist. Marxists had previously condemned the somewhat similar tendency in Russian criticism called "formalism," because they realized that if they began by conceding literary form as the basis for literary significance, the assumptions on which Marxist bureaucracies rationalized their censorship of the arts would be greatly weakened. They would logically have to end, in fact, in giving poets and novelists the same kind of freedom that they had reluctantly been compelled to grant to the physical scientists.

More recently, Marshall McLuhan has placed a formalist theory, expressed in the phrase "the medium is the message," within the context of a neo-Marxist determinism in which communication media play the same role that instruments of production do in more orthodox Marxism. Professor McLuhan drafted his new mosaic code under a strong influence from the conservative wing of the new critical movement, and many traces of an earlier Thomist determinism can be found in *The Gutenberg Galaxy*. An example is the curiously exaggerated distinction he draws between the manuscript culture of the Middle Ages and the book culture of the printed page that followed it.

It seemed to me obvious that, after accepting the poetic form of a poem as its primary basis of meaning, the next step was to look for its context within literature itself. And of course the most obvious literary context for a poem is the entire output of its author. Just as explication, by stressing the more objective aspect of rhetoric, had formed a corrective to the excesses of biographical criticism, so a study of a poet's whole work might form the basis of a kind of "psychological" criticism that would operate within literature, and so provide some balance for the kind that ends in the bosom of Freud. Poetry is, after all, a technique of communication: it engages the conscious part of the mind as well as the murkier areas, and what a poet succeeds in communicating to others is at least as important as what he fails to resolve for himself.

We soon become aware that every poet has his own distinctive structure of imagery, which usually emerges even in his earliest work, and which does not and cannot essentially change. This larger context of the poem within its author's entire "mental landscape" is assumed in all the best explication — Spitzer's, for example. I became aware of its importance myself, when working on Blake, as soon as I realized that Blake's special symbolic names and the like did form a genuine structure of poetic imagery and not, despite his use of the word, a "system" to which he was bound like an administrator to a computer. The structure of imagery, however, as I continued to study it, began to show an increasing number of similarities to the structures of other poets. Blake had always been regarded as a poet with a "private symbolism" locked up in his own mind, but this conception of him was so fantastically untrue that overcoming it carried me much further than merely correcting a mistaken notion of Blake.

I was led to three conclusions in particular. First, there is no private symbolism: the phrase makes no sense. There may be private allusions or associations that need footnotes, but they cannot form a poetic structure, even if the poet himself is a psychotic. The structure of the poem remains an effort at communication, however utterly it may fail to communicate. Second, as just said, every poet has his own structure of imagery, every detail of which has its analogue in that of all other poets. Third, when we follow out this pattern of analogous structures, we find that it leads, not to similarity, but to identity. Similarity implies uniformity and monotony, and any conclusion that all poets are much alike, in whatever respect, is too false to our literary experience to be tenable. It is identity that makes individuality possible: poems are made out of the *same* images, just as poems in English are all made out of the same language. This contrast of similarity and identity is one of the most difficult problems in critical theory, and we shall have to return to it several times in this book.

I was still not satisfied: I wanted a historical approach to literature, but an approach that would be or include a genuine history of literature, and not simply the assimilating of literature to some other kind of history. It was at this point that the immense importance of certain structural elements in the literary tradition, such as conventions, genres, and the recurring use of certain images or image-clusters, which I came to call archetypes, forced itself on me. T. S. Eliot had already spoken of tradition as a creative and informing power operating on the poet specifically as a craftsman, and not vaguely as a merely cultivated person. But neither he nor anyone else seemed to get to the point of identifying the factors of that tradition, of what it is that makes possible the creation of new works of literature out of earlier ones. The new critics had resisted the background approach to criticism, but they had not destroyed the oratorical conception of poetry as a personal rhetoric.

And yet convention, within literature, seemed to be a force even stronger than history. The difference between the conventions of medieval poets writing in the London of Richard II and those of Cavalier poets writing in the London of Charles II is far less than the difference in social conditions between the two ages. I began to suspect that a poet's relation to poetry was much more like a scholar's relation to his scholarship than was generally thought. Whatever one is producing, the psychological processes involved seem much the same. The scholar cannot be a scholar until he immerses himself in his subject, until he attaches his own thinking to the body of what is thought in his day about that subject. A scholar, *qua* scholar, cannot think for himself or think at random: he can only expand an organic body of thought, add something logically related to what he or someone else has already thought. But this is precisely the way that poets have always talked about their relation to poetry. From Homer onward, poets have continually insisted that they were simply places where something new in literature was able to take its own shape.

From here it is clear that one has to take a step. Criticism must develop a sense of history within literature to complement the historical criticism that relates literature to its non-literary historical background. Similarly, it must develop its own form of historical overview, on the basis of what is inside literature rather than outside it. Instead of fitting literature into a prefabricated scheme of history, the critic should see literature as a coherent structure, historically conditioned but shaping its own history, responding to but not determined in its form by an external historical process. This total body of literature can be studied through its larger structural principles, which I have just described as conventions, genres and recurring image-groups or archetypes. These structural principles are largely ignored by most social critics. Their treatment of literature, in consequence, is usually superficial, a matter of picking things out of literary works that seem interesting for non-literary reasons.

When criticism develops a proper sense of the history of literature, the history beyond literature does not cease to exist or to be relevant to the critic. Similarly, seeing literature as a unity in itself does not withdraw it from a social context: on the contrary, it becomes far easier to see what its place in civilization is. Criticism will always have two aspects, one turned toward the structure of literature and one turned toward the other cultural phenomena that form the social environment of literature. Together, they balance each other: when one is worked on to the exclusion of the other, the critical perspective goes out of focus. If criticism is in proper balance, the tendency of critics to move from critical to larger social issues becomes more intelligible. Such a movement need not, and should not, be due to a dissatisfaction with the narrowness of criticism as a discipline, but should be simply the result of a sense of social context, a sense

present in all critics from whom one is in the least likely to learn anything.

There was another difficulty with new criticism which was only a technical one, but still pointed to the necessity for a sense of context. Whenever we read anything there are two mental operations we perform, which succeed one another in time. First we follow the narrative movement in the act of reading, turning over the pages and pursuing the trail from top left to bottom right. Afterwards, we can look at the work as a simultaneous unity and study its structure. This latter act is the critical response properly speaking: the ordinary reader seldom needs to bother with it. The chief material of rhetorical analysis consists of a study of the poetic "texture," and such a study plunges one into a complicated labyrinth of ambiguities, multiple meanings, recurring images, and echoes of both sound and sense. A full explication of a long and complex work which was based on the reading process could well become much longer, and more difficult to read, than the work itself. Such linear explications have some advantages as a teaching technique, but for publishing purposes it is more practical to start with the second stage. This involves attaching the rhetorical analysis to a deductive framework derived from a study of the structure, and the context of that structure is what shows us where we should begin to look for our central images and ambiguities.

The difficulty in transferring explication from the reading process to the study of structure has left some curious traces in new critical theory. One of them is in Ransom, with his arbitrary assumption that texture is somehow more important for the critic than structure; another is again in McLuhan, who has expanded the two unresolved factors of explication into a portentous historical contrast between the "linear" demands of old printed media and the "simultaneous" impact of the new electronic ones. The real distinction however is not between different kinds of media, but between the two operations of the mind which are employed in every contact with every medium. There is a "simultaneous" response to print; there is a "linear" response to a painting, for there is a preliminary dance of the eye before we take in the whole picture; music, at the opposite end of experience, has its score, the spatial presentation symbolizing a simultaneous understanding of it. In reading a newspaper there are two preliminary linear operations, the glance over the headlines and the following down of a story.

This point is crucial for critical theory, because the whole prose-paraphrase conception of "literal" meaning is based on an understanding which is really pre-critical. It is while we are striving to take in what is being presented to us that we are reducing the poetic to the intentional meaning, attending to what the work explicitly says rather than to what it is. The pre-critical experience of literature is wordless, and all criticism which attempts to ground itself on such experience tends to assume that the primary critical act is a wordless reaction, to be described in some metaphor of immediate and nonverbal contact, such as "taste." Verbal criticism, in this view, is a secondary operation of trying to find words to describe the taste. Students who have been encouraged to think along these lines often ask me why I pay so little attention to the "uniqueness" of a work of literature. It may be absurd that "unique" should become a value-term, the world's worst poem being obviously as unique as any other, but the word brings out the underlying confusion of thought very clearly. Criticism is a structure of knowledge, and the unique as such is unknowable; uniqueness is a quality of experience, not of knowledge, and of precisely the aspect of experience which cannot form part of a structure of knowledge.

A better word, such as "individuality," would raise deeper problems. The basis of critical knowledge is the direct experience of literature, certainly, but experience as such is never adequate. We are always reading *Paradise Lost* with a hangover or seeing *King Lear* with an incompetent Cordelia or disliking a novel because some scene in it connects with something suppressed in our memories, and our most deeply satisfying responses are often made in childhood, to be seen later as immature overreacting. The right occasion, the right mood, the right state of development to meet the occasion, can hardly coincide more than once or twice in a lifetime. Nevertheless, the conception of a definitive experience in time seems to be the *hypothesis* on which criticism is based. Criticism, surely, is designed to reconstruct the kind of experience that we could and should have had, and thereby to bring us into line with that experience, even if the "shadow" of Eliot's *The Hollow Men* has forever darkened it. As a structure of knowledge, then, criticism, like other structures of knowledge, is in one sense a monument to a failure of experience, a tower of Babel or one of the "ruins of time" which, in Blake's phrase, "build mansions in eternity." Hence the popularity of the evaluative or taste-criticism which seems to point backwards to a greater intensity of response than the criticism itself can convey. It corresponds to a popular view of poetry itself, that whatever the poet writes down is merely salvaged from an original "inspiration" of a much more numinous kind. There is a real truth here, though it needs to be differently stated.

There are two categories of response to literature, which could be well described by Schiller's terms naive and sentimental, if used in his sense but transferred from qualities inherent in literature to qualities in the experience of it. The "naive" experience is the one we are now discussing, the linear, participating, pre-critical response which is thrown forward to the conclusion of the work as the reader turns pages or the theatre audience expectantly listens. The conclusion is not simply the last page or spoken line, but the "recognition" which, in a work of fiction particularly, brings the end into line with the beginning and pulls the straight line of response around into a parabola. A pure, self-contained pleasure of participating response is the end at which all writers aim who think of themselves as primarily entertainers, and some of them ignore, resist, or resent the critical operation that follows it.

Such pleasure is however a state of innocence rarely attained in adult life. Many of us have "favorite" authors who set up for us a kind of enclosed garden in which we can wander in a state of completely satisfied receptivity. But for each reader there are very few of these, and they are usually discovered and read fairly early. The sense of guilt about reading "escape" literature is a moral anxiety mainly derived from a feeling that it is a substitute for an unattained experience, and that if escape literature really did what it professes to do it would not be escape literature. As a rule our pleasure in direct response is of a more muted and disseminated kind. It arises from a *habit* of reading or theatre-going, and much of this pleasure comes from a greatly enlarged kind of expectation, extending over many works and many years. Instead of trying to operate the gambling machine of an ideal experience, which may never pay off, we are building something up, accumulating a total fund of experience, each individual response being an investment in it.

It is a central function of criticism to explain what is going on in the habit of reading, using "reading" as a general term for all literary experience. If reading formed simply an unconnected series of experiences, one novel or poem or play after another, it would have the sense of distraction or idle time-filling about it which so many of those who are afraid of leisure believe it to have. The real reader knows better: he knows that he is entering into a coherent structure of experience, and the criticism which studies literature through its organizing patterns of convention, genre and archetype enables him to see what that structure is. Such criticism can hardly injure the "uniqueness" of each experience: on the contrary, it rejects the evaluating hierarchy that limits us to the evaluator's reading list, and encourages each reader to accept no substitutes in his search for infinite variety. It is simply not true that the "great" writers supply all the varieties of experience offered by the merely "good" ones: if Massinger is not a substitute for Shakespeare, neither is Shakespeare a substitute for Massinger.

Still less does the study of the recurring structural patterns of literature lead the reader to the conviction that literature is everywhere much alike. For such study, as just said, does not keep bringing the student back to similar points, but to the same point, to the sense of an identity in literary experience which is the objective counterpart to his own identity. That variety and novelty can be found only at the place of identity is the theme of much of the most influential writing in our century, of the Eliot Quartets with their garlic and sapphires clotting a bedded axletree, of the Pound Cantos which insist on "making it new" but remain at the center of the "unwobbling pivot," of that tremendous hymn to the eternal newness of the same which is *Finnegans Wake*. Twentieth-century criticism which does not understand a central theme of the literature of its own time can hardly be expected to make much sense of the literature of the past.

This brings us to the "sentimental" type of response, which starts where criticism starts, with the unity of the work being read. In modern literature there has been a strong emphasis on demanding a response from the reader which minimizes everything "naive," everything connected with suspense or expectation. This emphasis begins in English literature with the Blake Prophecies, *Milton* and *Jerusalem* particularly, which avoid the sense of linear narration

and keep repeating the central theme in an expanding series of contexts. Fiction tends increasingly to abolish the teleological plot which keeps the reader wondering "how it turns out"; poetry drops its connective tissue of narrative in favor of discontinuous episodes; in Mallarmé and elsewhere it even avoids the centrifugal movement of naming or pointing to objects thought of as external to the poem. The emphasis, though it starts with unity, is not on unity for its own sake, but on intensity, a word which brings us back to the conception of an ideal experience. Hopkins with his "inscape" and "instress," Proust with his instants of remembrance and recognition, Eliot with his timeless moments at the world's axis, and a host of more recent writers with their mystiques of orgasm, drugs, and quasi-Buddhist moments of enlightenment, are all talking about a form of ideal experience, which in one way or another seems to be the real goal of life. The ideal experience itself, for the shrewder of these writers at least, never occurs, but with intense practice and concentration a deeply satisfying approximation may occur very rarely. The curious link with religion—for even writers who are not religious still often employ religious terminology or symbolism in this connexion, as Joyce and Proust do—indicates that this direct analogy of ideal experience is typically the way of the mystic or saint rather than the artist—"an occupation for the saint," as Eliot calls it, though he immediately adds that it cannot be in any sense an occupation.

Traditional Christian thought had an explanation for the dilemma of experience which at least made sense within its own postulates. According to it, Adam was capable of a preternatural power of experience before his fall, and we have lost this capacity. Our structures of reason and imagination are therefore analogical constructs designed to recapture, within the mental processes that belong to our present state, something of a lost directness of apprehension. Thus Milton can define education as "an attempt to repair the ruin of our first parents by regaining to know God aright." Similar language continues in our day. Proust concludes his colossal analysis of experience by saying that the only paradises are lost paradises; Yeats, in a much more light-hearted way, tells us in "Solomon and the Witch," anticipating the more recent orgasm cults, that a single act of perfect intercourse would restore the unfallen world. In this view, literature, philosophy and religion at least are all articulate analogies of an experience that goes not only beyond articulateness, but beyond human capacity as well.

The Christian fallen world is only one form of a conception which has run through human imagination and thought from earliest times to the present, according to which the existing world is, so to speak, the lower level of being or reality. Above it is a world which may not exist (we do not actually know that it exists even if we seem to have an experience of it), but is not nothing or non-existence; is not a merely ideal world, because it can act as an informing principle of existence, and yet cannot convincingly be assigned to any intermediate category of existence, such as the potential. This world, related by analogy to the intelligible world of the philosopher and scientist, the imaginable world of the poet, and the revealed world of religion, is increasingly referred to in our day by the term "model." In religion, as noted, this model world is usually projected as an actually existing world created by God, though at present out of human reach. In philosophy it appears in such concepts as Aristotle's final cause, and in the more uninhibited structures of the poets it is the idealized world of romance, pastoral, or apocalyptic vision. As such it suggests a world with which we should wish to identify ourselves, or something in ourselves, and so it becomes the world indicated by the analogy of ideal experience just mentioned.

A direct experience or apprehension of such a world would be a microcosmic experience, an intelligence or imagination finding itself at the centre of an intelligible or imaginable totality, and so experiencing, for however brief an instant, without any residue of alienation. It would thus also be an experience of finally attained or recovered identity. Most of us, at least, never reach it directly in experience if it is attainable in experience at all, but only through one of the articulated analogies, of which literature is a central one. Whatever it is, it represents the end of our critical path, though we have not as yet traversed the path.

As we proceed to do this, we must keep to a middle way between two uncritical extremes. One is the centrifugal fallacy of determinism, the feeling that literature lacks a social reference unless its structure is ignored and its content associated with something non-literary. No theory is any good unless it explains facts, but theory and facts have to be in the same plane. Psychological and political theories can explain only psychological and political facts; no literary facts can be explained by anything except a literary theory. I remember a student, interested in the Victorian period, who dismissed several standard critical works in that area as "totally lacking in any sense of social awareness." I eventually learned that social awareness, for him, meant the amount of space given in the book, whatever the announced subject, to the Chartist movement. Chartism and similar social movements have their relevance to literature, certainly; but literature is all about something else, even when social protest is its explicit theme.

The other extreme is the centripetal fallacy, where we fail to separate criticism from the pre-critical direct experience of literature. This leads to an evaluating criticism which imposes the critic's own values, derived from the prejudices and anxieties of his own time, on the whole literature of the past. Criticism, like religion, is one of the sub-academic areas in which a large number of people are still free to indulge their anxieties instead of studying their subject. Any mention of this fact is apt to provoke the response: "Of course you don't understand how important our anxieties are." I understand it sufficiently to have devoted a good deal of this essay to the subject of social anxiety and its relation to genuine criticism. We note that the two fallacies mentioned above turn out to be essentially the same fallacy, as opposed extremes so often do.

Structuralism
and Literature

Jonathan Culler

*Like Northrop Frye, Jonathan Culler believes we must
see the individual poem within the context of literature if
we are to understand it fully, and especially if we are to
know how we understand it. Structuralism, as Culler
views it, offers in the first place "not a new way of interpreting literary works, but an attempt to understand
how it is that works do have meaning for us." So structuralist critics speak of genres and conventions and of
the "system" or "institution" of literature. And they frequently take our understanding of language as the base
and analogy for our understanding of literature. They
may also show, as Culler does, considerable sympathy for
some forms of reader-response criticism, for they will be
much concerned with what the reader needs to know to
attain "literary competence." At the same time, since
structuralists define the competent reader as one who has
mastered the relevant conventions, the number of readings they accept as competent must be considerably restricted. But this definition of competence is also the
structuralists' great strength, for their theory offers a rationale for literary study as a discipline through which
one can progressively come to know the conventions of
literature. Structuralism, then, presents the intertextual
context as the fundamental context, the one that ultimately grounds our understanding. Yet although Culler
initially stresses the distinction between this generalized
understanding and the interpretation of particular poems, he suggests at the end of his essay how the structuralist view may also facilitate specific interpretations.*

Reprinted by permission from Hilda Schiff, ed., *Contemporary Approaches to English Studies*, pp. 59–76. Copyright ©
1977 by Barnes & Noble Books, Totowa, N.J.

My main purpose here is to show that despite its more extreme manifestations structuralism is not an abstruse or recondite theory but that, on the contrary, a structuralist approach to literature is directly relevant to the practical study and teaching of literature. Further, I am going to assume from the first that the teaching of literature involves a concern with the fact that the objects of study are literary works rather than simply documents about interpersonal relations, and that students are supposed to learn about literature and how to read it, rather than about life and how to live.

There are, of course, good reasons for using literary works as ways of finding out about the possibilities of human experience: the images they offer are both more complex and less embarrassing to discuss than, say, another individual's account of relationships with parents or friends. And I think there would be much to be said from a structuralist or semiological point of view about the way in which attention of this kind tries to organize our world; but that is not what I am concerned with here. I shall assume that studying literature and teaching literature involve the development and mastery of special operations and procedures which are required for the reading of literature, as opposed to the reading of other kinds of texts.

First I shall try to explain what structuralism is and why it is especially relevant to the study of literature. Then I shall outline a structuralist approach to literature, both in general and with respect to several examples. But I should like to emphasize from the outset that I am not proposing a structuralist "method" of interpretation: structuralism is not a new way of interpreting literary works, but an attempt to understand how it is that works do have meaning for us.

First, then, what is structuralism? Roland Barthes once defined it, in its "most specialized and consequently most relevant version," as a method for the study of cultural artefacts derived from the methods of contemporary linguistics.[1] Now there are two possible ways of using linguistic methods in the study of literature. The first would be to describe in linguistic terms the language of literary texts. Many critics speak eloquently of the benefits of this approach, but it is not, I think, what Barthes meant by his definition nor is it the kind of structuralism with which I am concerned here. The second approach would be to take linguistics as a model which indi- cates how one might go about constructing a poetics which stands to literature as linguistics stands to lan- guage. In other words, one takes linguistics as an analogy which indicates how other cultural artefacts should be studied. For this kind of structuralism only a few fundamental principles of linguistics are di- rectly relevant, of which the most important is Ferdi- nand Saussure's distinction between *langue* and *parole*.

La langue, the linguistic system, is what one knows when one knows English. *La parole*, specific utter- ances or speech arts, are instances of language, *la langue*. Saussure argued that *la langue*, the linguistic system, was the proper object of linguistics, and he went on to say that "dans la langue il n'y a que des différences, sans termes positifs." In the linguistic system there are only differences, with no positive terms. Study of *la langue* is an attempt to determine the nature of a system of relations, oppositions, and differences which makes possible *la parole*. In learn- ing a language we master a linguistic system which makes actual communication possible, and the lin- guist's task is to describe and to make explicit what it is we have mastered.[2]

Taking this as a point of departure we can say that structuralism and its close relation semiology are based on two fundamental insights: first, that social and cultural phenomena do not have essences but are defined by a network of relations, both internal and external; and, secondly, that in so far as social and cultural phenomena, including literature, have meaning they are signs.

If one wished to distinguish between structural- ism and semiology (and the reasons for the distinc- tion are historical rather than logical), one could do so in these terms: structuralism studies the structures or systems of relations by which cultural objects are defined and distinguished from one another; semiol- ogy studies cultural objects as signs that carry mean- ings. But I think that it is extremely important *not* to make the distinction, not to try to separate the two enterprises, since one entails the other where a prof- itable study of literature is concerned. If the two are separated one risks either discovering patterns of re- lations and oppositions which are irrelevant in that they have no sign function (this is the danger of the kind of linguistic analysis best represented by Ro- man Jakobson[3]), or else investigating signs on a one- to-one basis without due regard to the systems of convention which produce them (this is the danger of a limited semiological approach).

The task of structural analysis, we may then say, is to formulate the underlying systems of convention which enable cultural objects to have meaning for us. In this sense structuralism is not hermeneutic: it is not a method for producing new and startling interpretations of literary works (although in another sense which I shall mention below it *is* hermeneutic). It asks, rather, how the meanings of literary works are possible.

I should perhaps digress for a moment at this point to correct a frequent misapprehension about the relative status of literary theory and critical interpretation. It is common to speak of interpretations of particular works as though they were the central activity of literary criticism and to think of literary theory as something peripheral and altogether secondary, but of course the truth is quite the reverse. Interpretations of authors and works are wholly parasitic on the activity of reading literature: the critic who writes about an author is simply producing a more thorough and perhaps more perceptive version of what readers of literature do for themselves. But to enquire about the *nature* of literature, a theoretical task, is to ask what is involved in reading something *as* literature, and this is to tackle questions which are fundamental to anyone engaged in critical interpretation in that implicit answers are necessarily presupposed both by the activity of reading literature, and by the development of a discipline concerned with the study of literature as an institution.

The best way to ease oneself into this structuralist perspective is to take linguistics as a model and to think of the relationship between an utterance and the speaker/hearer. A sentence which I utter comes to you as a series of physical events, a sequence of sounds which we might represent by a phonetic transcription. You hear this sequence of sounds and give it a meaning. The question linguistics asks is how is this possible, and the answer, of course, is that you bring to the act of communication an immense amount of implicit, subconscious knowledge. You have assimilated the phonological system of English which enables you to relate these physical sounds to the abstract and relational phonemes of English; you have assimilated a grammatical system, so complex that we are only beginning to understand it, which enables you to assign a structural description to the sentence, to ascertain the relations among its parts, and to recognize it as grammatically well-formed, even though you have never heard it before; and fi-

nally, your knowledge of the semantic component of the language enables you to assign an interpretation to this string of sounds. Now we may say, if we wish, that the phonological and syntactic structure and the meaning are *properties* of the utterance, so long as we remember that they are properties of the utterance only with respect to the complex grammar which speakers of English have assimilated. Without the complex knowledge brought to the communicative act, they have none of these properties.

Moving from language to literature, we find an analogous situation. Imagine someone who knows English but has no knowledge of literature and indeed no acquaintance with the concept of literature. If presented with a poem he would be quite baffled. He would understand words and sentences, certainly, but he would not know what this strange thing was; he would not, quite literally, know what to do with this curious linguistic construction. What he lacks is a complex system of knowledge that experienced readers have acquired, a system of conventions and norms which we might call "literary competence." And we can say that just as the task of linguistics is to make explicit the system of a language which makes linguistic communication possible, so in the case of literature a structuralist poetics must enquire what knowledge must be postulated to account for our ability to read and understand literary works.

Lest you be sceptical about the importance of this implicit knowledge that we bring to the act of reading poetry, let me offer a simple and crude example. Take a perfectly ordinary sentence, such as "Yesterday I went into town and bought a lamp," and set it down on a page as a poem:

> Yesterday I
> Went into town and bought
> A lamp.

The words remain the same, and if meanings change it is because we approach the poem with different expectations and interpretative operations. What sort of things happens? First of all, "Yesterday" takes on a different force: it no longer refers to a particular day but to the set of possible yesterdays and serves primarily to set up a temporal opposition within the poem (between present and recent past). This is due to our conventions about the relationship of poems to the moment of utterance. Secondly, we expect the lyric to capture a moment of some significance, to be thematically viable; and we thus apply to "lamp" and "bought" conventions of symbolic extrapolation. The traditional associations of *lamp* are obvious; *buying* we can take as one mode of acquisition as opposed to others; and we thus acquire potential thematic material. Thirdly, we expect a poem to be a unified whole and thus we must attempt to interpret the fact that this poem ends so swiftly and inconclusively. The silence at the end can be read as a kind of ironic comment, a blank, and we can set up an opposition between the action of buying a lamp, the attempt to acquire light, and the failure to tell of any positive benefits which result from yesterday's action. This general structure can, of course, support a variety of paraphrases, but any interpretation of the poem is likely to make use of these three elementary operations enshrined in any institution of poetry. The conventions of the lyric create the possibility of new and supplementary meanings.

Note also, and this is important, that though in one sense these meanings are in the poem — they are public, can be argued about, and do not depend upon individual subjective associations — in another sense, which is more important given the current critical climate, they are not *in* the poem. They depend on operations performed by readers (and assumed by poets).

Though this may seem obvious, there are good reasons for insisting on it. What we still call the New Criticism, in its desire to free the text from a controlling authorial intention, wanted to convince us that meanings could be there in the language of the text. The poem was to be thought of as complete in itself, a harmonious totality, not unlike an autonomous self-sufficient natural organism. Despite the salutary effects of this Coleridgean line of criticism, which I should not in the least want to deny, it was perhaps inevitable that it should lead to the notion that the critic or reader, like a good empiricist, approaches the poem without preconceptions and attempts to appreciate fully what is there. Such a notion leads to a theoretical impasse, to a hopeless attempt to show how the language of poetry itself differs from the language of prose or everyday speech.

Structuralism leads us to think of the poem not as a self-contained organism but as a sequence which has meaning only in relation to a literary system, or rather, to the "institution" of literature which guides the reader. The sense of a poem's completeness is a function of the totality of the interpretive process, the result of the way we have been taught to read poems. And to avoid misunderstanding I should perhaps emphasize that, though it is preferable to talk about reading rather than writing, we are dealing with conventions which are assumed by the writer. He is not just setting words down on paper but writing a poem. Even when he is in revolt against the tradition, he still knows what is involved in reading and writing poems; and when he chooses among alternative words or phrases, he does so as a master of reading.

Although this notion of a literary system or of literary competence may be anathema to many, the reasons which lead one to postulate it are quite convincing. First of all, the claims of schools and universities to offer literary training cannot be lightly dismissed: it is, alas, only too clear that knowledge of English and a certain experience of the world do not suffice to make someone a perceptive reader of literature. Something else is required, something which literary training is designed to provide. And a poetics ought to be able to go some way towards specifying what is supposed to be learned. We presume, after all, to judge a student's progress towards literary competence: our examinations are not designed merely to check whether he or she has read and remembered certain books but to test his or her progress as a reader of literature. And that presumption suggests that there is something to be learnt here.

Secondly, it seems obvious that the study of one work facilitates the study of the next. We gain not only points of comparison but a sense of how to read — general formal principles and distinctions that have proved useful, questions which one addresses to certain kinds of texts, a sense of what one is looking for. We can speak if we like of extrapolating from one work to another, so long as we do not thereby obscure the fact that it is precisely this extrapolation which requires explanation. If we are to make any sense of the process of literary education we must assume, as Northrop Frye says, the possibility of "a coherent and comprehensive theory of literature . . . some of which the student unconsciously learns as he goes along, but the main principles of which are as yet unknown to us."[4]

What are the obstacles to this kind of enterprise? First, critics are accustomed to think of their task as that of producing new and subtler interpretations of literary works, and to ask them to attend to what must be taken for granted by experienced readers of literature cannot but seem an impoverishment of the critical enterprise. Just as most people are more interested in using their language than in trying to determine the nature of their linguistic competence, so most critics are more interested in exercising their understanding of literature than in investigating what it involves. But of course in the first case we do not deceive ourselves that those engaged in using their linguistic competence are thereby participating in the study of language, whereas in the second case critics have succeeded in making us believe that their discussion of individual works constitutes the study of literature. This notion is a significant obstacle; but if we are at all concerned with the nature of literature itself, and if we recognize the desirability of understanding what it is that we expect our students to learn, we would do well to grant poetics its proper status at the centre of literary studies.

The second obstacle seems more serious: the difficulty of determining what will count as evidence for literary competence, evidence about the assumptions and operations of reading. It might seem that critics differ so widely in their interpretations as to undermine any notion of a general literary competence. But I should stress first of all that this is not, in fact, an obstacle which must be overcome initially, but a matter which will resolve itself in practice. Since what one is trying to do is to determine the conventions and operations which will account for certain effects, one begins by specifying what effects in fact one is attempting to explain, and then constructs models to account for them. As it is obvious that there is a range of acceptable readings for any poem, what one attempts to discover are the operations which account for this range of readings. In the case of the brief poem which I discussed above, I assumed that the sentence had different possible meanings when set down as a poem rather than as a prose statement, and offered some crude hypotheses to explain why this should be so. If you think that it is not so, if the meanings do not strike you as acceptable in terms of your own literary competence, you will reject the hypotheses and the explanation as false. The only danger, in other words, is that you will find what I have to say irrelevant because I am trying to account for facts which you do not accept. However, even if one were to succeed only in describing in an explicit fashion one's own literary competence, that would be a significant achievement. And because literary competence is the result of an interpersonal experience of reading and dis-

cussion, any account of it will doubtless cover much common ground.

Moreover it cannot be emphasized too strongly that some kind of literary competence is presupposed by everyone who discusses or writes about literature. Any critic who claims to offer more than a purely personal and idiosyncratic response to a text is claiming that his interpretation derives from operations of reading that are generally accepted, that it is possible to convince readers of its validity because there are shared points of departure and common notions of how to read, and that both critic and audience know what counts as evidence for a reading, what can be taken for granted, and what must be explicitly argued for. What I am asking is that we try to grasp more clearly this common basis of reading and thus to make explicit the conventions which make literature possible.

A structuralist approach starts by stressing the artificiality of literature, the fact that though literature may be written in the language of information it is not used in the "language-game" of giving information. It is obvious, for example, that by convention the relationship of speaker to utterance is different when we are dealing with a poem and with another speech act. The poet does not stand in the same relation to a lyric as to a letter he has written, even if the poem be Ben Jonson's "Inviting a Friend to Supper." This initial strangeness, this artifice, is the primary fact with which we have to deal, and we can say that the techniques of reading are ways of simultaneously cherishing and overcoming this strangeness — ways of "naturalizing" the text and making it something of a communication. To naturalize a text — I use this word in preference to what some of the French theorists call *vraisemblablisation*—is to transform it so that it can be assimilated to an order of *vraisemblance*. This is absolutely basic to the reading of literature, and a simple example would be the interpretation of metaphor. When Shelley writes "my soul is an enchanted boat" we must, in order to "understand" this, naturalize the figure; we must perform a semantic transformation on "enchanted boat" so as to bring it under a particular order of *vraisemblance*, which here we might call "possible characteristics of the soul." Of course, the fact that understanding involves more than translation of this kind must be stressed: we must preserve the distance traversed in the act of translation as a sign in its own right. Here, for example, we have a sign of a particular lyric posture, of the poetical character, of the inadequacy of ordinary discourse, and so on.

Now there are various levels at which we can naturalize, various sets of conventions which can be brought into play. And of course these change with the institution of literature itself, so that once a style or mode of discourse becomes established it is possible to naturalize a poem as a comment upon this literary mode. When we read Lewis Carroll's "A-Sitting on a Gate" as a parody of Wordsworth's "Resolution and Independence" we naturalize the former and make its strange features intelligible as commentary upon the latter.

The conventions of literature guide the process of naturalization and provide alternatives to what might be called "premature naturalization." This is a direct move from poem to utterance which ignores the former's specifically literary characteristics, as if we were to naturalize Donne's "The Good Morrow" by saying: the poet was in bed with his mistress one morning when the sun rose and, being still befuddled with drink, he uttered this statement in the hope that the sun would go away and shine elsewhere. If one had no knowledge of the institution of literature this is what one might be tempted to do, but even the least advanced student knows that this is an inappropriate step, that he must naturalize at another level which takes into account some of the conventions of literature. The protest to the sun is itself a figure; the situation of the utterance of a poem is a fiction which must be incorporated in our interpretation. We are likely to naturalize "The Good Morrow" as a love poem which uses this situation as an image of energy and annoyance, and hence as a figure for a strong, self-sufficient passion.

This ought at least to indicate what I mean by naturalization: it is the process of making something intelligible by relating it to what is already known and accepted as *vraisemblable*. We are guided in this process by various codes of expectations which we ought to try to make explicit. In discussing prose fiction Roland Barthes identifies five different codes, but I shall mention just two by way of example.[5]

What Barthes calls the semic code is an especially good case of literary conventions which produce intelligibility. As we go through a novel we pick out items which refer to the behaviour of characters and use them, as we say, to create character. Generally this involves considerable semantic transformation. Cultural stereotypes enable us to move from de-

scriptions of dress or behaviour to qualities of persons, and we admit in fiction moves which we would not accept in ordinary circumstances. We do not believe that there is a real correlation between perfect or blemished complexions and perfect or blemished moral character, but certain *genres* permit inferences of this kind. We do not believe that blonde women as a class have different qualities from brunettes as a class, but the conventions of literature provide us with a set of opposed qualities with which the opposition between a blonde and a dark heroine may be correlated. Indeed, in order to see literature as an agent of moral education, as Christopher Butler has urged, we have to assume that literature will provide us with models of personality and ways of relating action to motive which are not the fruit of our ordinary experience; one of the things a reader of literature learns, that is to say, is how to construct personalities out of the notations that the text offers. He acquires mastery of the semic code.

The symbolic code is one of the oddest and most difficult to discuss. It is also the code with which students have the greatest difficulty, and both students and teachers ought to attempt to gain clearer notions of what it involves than we have at present. What governs the perception and interpretation of symbols? There are obviously a few symbols, consecrated by tradition, which seem to bear an intrinsic meaning, but most potential symbols are defined by complex relations with a context. The rose, for example, can lead in a variety of directions, and within each of these semantic fields (religion, love, nature) its significance will depend on its place in an oppositional structure. Sun and moon can signify almost anything, provided the opposition between them is preserved. Although, as I say, this code is poorly understood, it seems clear that symbolic extrapolation is a teleological process with a set of goals which limit the range of plausible interpretations and specify what kind of meanings serve as adequate *terminii ad quem* [ends or boundaries]. For example, there is a rule of generalization: to be told that in a phrase like "shine on my bowed head, O moon" the moon symbolizes "the quarterly production quota set by the district manager" is bathetic. We quickly learn that there is a set of semantic oppositions, such as life and death, simplicity and complexity, harmony and strife, reality and appearance, body and soul, certainty and doubt, imagination and intellect, which are culturally marked as in some way "ultimate" and hence as goals in the process of symbolic extrapolation. But we ought to be able to say a good deal more about this process which we expect students to master.

After these sketchy indications of the problems involved, I should like to turn by way of example to the kind of fundamental expectations concerning poetry which govern the operation of codes and the process of naturalization. We might start with a short poem by William Carlos Williams:

> This Is Just to Say
>
> I have eaten
> the plums
> that were in
> the icebox
>
> and which
> you were probably
> saving
> for breakfast
>
> Forgive me
> they were delicious
> so sweet
> so cold

The fact that this is printed on a page as a poem brings into play our expectations concerning poetry (as sentences in a novel it would, of course, be read differently), the first of which we might call the convention of distance and impersonality. Although at one level the sentences are presented as a note asking forgiveness for eating plums, since poetry is by convention detached from immediate circumstances of utterance we deprive it of this pragmatic function, retaining simply the reference to a context as an implicit statement that this kind of experience is important, worthy of poetry. By doing this we avoid the premature naturalization which says, "the poet ate the plums and left this note on the table for his wife, writing it as verse because he was a poet."

Starting then with the assumption that this is not a pragmatic utterance but a lyric in which a fictional "I" speaks of eating plums, we are faced with the question of what to do with this object, how to structure it. We expect poems to be organic wholes and we possess a variety of models of wholeness: the simplest is the binary opposition which is given a temporal dimension (not X but Y); another is the unresolved opposition (neither X nor Y but both simultaneously); next there is the dialectical resolution of a binary opposition; and finally, remaining with simple models of wholeness, the four-term homology (X is to Y as A is to B) or the series closed and summed up by a transcendent final term. In studying this poem we need to apply a model of completeness so as to secure an opening up of the poem and to establish a thematic structure into which we can fit its elements, which thus become sets of features subject to thematic expansion. Our elementary model of the opposition can here take the thematic form of rule and transgression: the plums were to be saved for breakfast but they have been eaten. We can then group various features on one side or the other: on the side of "eating" we have "delicious," "sweet" and "cold," stressed by their final position (this is a conventional rule) and implying that eating plums was indeed worth it; on the other side we have the assumed priority of domestic rules about eating (one recognizes them and asks for forgiveness), the reference to "breakfast," the orderly life represented by the hypostatization of meal-times. The process of thematic interpretation requires us to move from facts towards values, so we can develop each thematic complex, retaining the opposition between them. Thus we have the valuing of immediate sensuous experience, as against an economy of order and saving, which is also valued, though transgressed.

Then, presumably, the question we must ask ourselves is whether this structure is complete: whether the opposition is a simple one, a move from X to Y, or whether the attitude of the poem is in fact more complex and requires us to call upon other models. And here we can take account of what we earlier set aside — the fact that the poem masquerades as a note asking forgiveness. We can say that the poem itself acts as a mediating force, recognizing the priority of conventions (by the act of writing a note) but also seeking absolution. We can also give a function at this level to the deictics, the "I" and "you" which we had set aside, taking the relationship as a figure of intimacy, and say that the note tries to bring this realm of immediate sensuous experience into the realm of interpersonal relations, where there will be tension, certainly, but where (as the abrupt ending of the poem implies) there is hope that intimacy and understanding will resolve the tension.

Although I have been naming and paraphrasing, what I am producing is, of course, a thematic structure which could be stated in various ways. The claim is simply that in interpreting a poem like this we are implicitly relying on assumptions about poetry and structural models without which we could not proceed: that our readings of the poem (which will, of course, differ) depend upon some common interpretive operations.

Interpretation might generally stop here, but if we think about the fact that these sentences are presented as a poem we can go a step further by asking "why?" Why should this sort of banal statement be a poem? And here, by an elementary reversal which is crucial to the reading of modern poetry, we can take banality of statement as a statement about banality and say that the world of notes and breakfast is also the world of language, which must try to make a place for this kind of immediate experience which sounds banal and whose value can only be hinted at. This, we could go on to say, is why the poem must be so sparse and apparently incomplete. It must produce, as it were, a felt absence, a sense of missing intensity and profundity, so that in our desire to read the poem and to make it complete we will supply what the poem itself dare not claim: the sense of significance.

Let me turn now to a poem of a rather different kind, one which is usually read as a political statement and act of engagement, Blake's "London."

> I wander through each chartered street,
> Near where the chartered Thames does flow,
> And mark in every face I meet
> Marks of weakness, marks of woe.
>
> In every cry of every Man,
> In every Infant's cry of fear,
> In every voice, in every ban,
> The mind-forged manacles I hear.
>
> How the Chimney-sweeper's cry
> Every black'ning Church appalls;
> And the hapless Soldier's sigh
> Runs in blood down Palace walls.
>
> But most thro' midnight streets I hear
> How the youthful Harlot's curse
> Blasts the new-born Infant's tear,
> And blights with plagues the Marriage hearse.

I don't want to suggest that this isn't a political poem, but I would like to impress upon you how much work we must do in order to make it a political statement and what a variety of extremely artificial conventions we must call upon in order to read it in this way.

The poem is organized as a list of things seen and heard: I mark marks; I hear manacles; I hear how. . . . And it is obvious from the outset that the things

heard or seen are bad (marks of weakness, marks of woe, manacles, blasts and blights). This gives us our initial opposition between the perceiving subject and the objects of perception and provides a thematic centre which helps us to organize details. We may start with the assumption, based on the convention of unity, that we have a series which will cohere at some level (the second stanza with its repetitions of "every" is ample warrant for that). But it is quite difficult to produce this coherence. In the third stanza we can try to collate the two propositions in order to discover their common subject: I hear how the cry of the sweep and the sigh of the soldier act upon the church or palace. This gives us a sound (which fits into the series of "marks" which the "I" perceives), an actor (who, our cultural model tells us, counts among the oppressed), and an institution which they affect. The opposition between institution and oppressed is one whose parameter we know: the possibilities are those of protest and submission, the results the indifference or guilt of the institution. And in fact the structure which Blake has established is ambiguous enough to preclude our really knowing which to choose here. One critic, citing historical evidence, argues that the sigh of the soldier is the murmur of possible rebellion and that the visionary can already see the blood on palace walls in a native version of the French Revolution. But we can also say, in an alternative naturalization, that the palace is bloody because it is responsible for the blood of soldiers whom it commands. Both readings, of course, are at some distance from the "sigh running in blood," but we are sufficiently accustomed to such interpretive operations for this not to worry us.

What, though, of the chimney-sweep? One might assume that the Church is horrified ("appalled") at the conditions of child labour, but the convention of coherence invariably leads critics to reject this reading and to emphasize that "appall" means to make pale or (since by convention puns are permitted when relevant) to cast a pall over and to weaken the Church's moral authority. The "black'ning" church either becomes black, with guilt as well as soot, or makes things black by its indifference and hypocrisy; and the cry of the sweep changes its colour either by making it pale or by casting a pall of metaphorical soot over it. Our ability to perform these acts of semantic transference, moving "black" and "soot" around from sweep to church to its moral character, works as a kind of proof of the poem, a demonstration that there is a rich logical coherence and semantic solidarity here. The point, however, is that the lines do not carry an obvious meaning; they cannot be naturalized as an intimation of oppression without the help of a considerable amount of condensation and displacement.

The last stanza too has an initial strangeness which is difficult to naturalize. The speaker hears how a harlot's curse blasts a tear. We could, of course, read this as a harlot cursing at the fact that her own baby is crying, but since this is to be the climax of the poem we are constrained to reject this interpretation as premature naturalization. Indeed, such is the force of conventional expectations that no commentary I have read cites this reading, though it is the most obvious. To produce unity we must discover mind-forged manacles, and the best candidate for manacling is the infant. If we are to allow his tear to be blasted we must perform semantic operations on it: the tear can be an expression of protest and feeling, of innocence also perhaps, which is cursed and manacled not so much by the curse of the harlot (and again we become involved in semantic transfers) as by her existence. Her curse becomes her sign or mark and thus fits into the series of sounds which the narrator hears. By another transfer we can say that the infant himself is cursed, as he becomes an inhabitant of this world of harlots and charters. Similarly, in the last line we can transfer epithets to say that it is marriage itself which is blighted, so that the wedding carriage becomes a hearse, through the existence of the harlot. We could, of course, work out a casual relationship here (marriage is weakened if husbands visit harlots), but the level of generality at which the poem operates suggests that this will make coherence difficult. "London " is not after all a description of specific social evils, and that, if we read the poem as a protest, is a fact with which we must now contend.

We must ask, in other words, what we are to say about the fact that the poem goes some way towards defeating our expectations: the cries are not cries of misery only but every cry of every man, even the shouts of street vendors. What are we to make, shall we say, of this odd semiotic procedure and of the interpretive requirements which the poem imposes upon us? There is a great distance which the reader must traverse in order to get from the language of the text to political protest. What does this signify? And the answer is, I think, that here, in the kind of

reading which the poem requires, we have a representation of the problems of the visionary state. The distance between every cry and mind-forged manacles is great, so great that there is a possible ambiguity about whose mind is manacled. The speaker "marks marks"; is it because he is "marking" that he sees marks? He perceives, after all, the same thing in every street cry, in every face. In order to make sense of this we must construct an identity for the "I" of the poem; we must postulate the figure of a visionary who sees what no one else sees, who can traverse these distances and read signs whose meaning is obscure to other observers. The city is not itself aware of its problems, its grief. The gap between appearance and awareness is presented, we can say, as the greatest terror of London. The true misery of manacles forged in the mind lies in the fact that they restrict the perception of misery and that no one else, not even the reader until the poem has forced him to exercise his symbolic imagination, can see the blood run down palace walls.

This has been a laboured account of what seems required if we are to read the poem as we do. It is not a structuralist interpretation for it agrees, except for the last paragraph, with customary readings of the poem. If it seems different, that is because it tries to make explicit some of the operations which we are accustomed to taking for granted. Some of these operations are highly conventional; they involve a special logic of literary interpretation, and it is not at all strange that critics prefer to take them for granted. But I think that if we are concerned with the nature of literature itself, or with dispelling the popular notion of the interpretation of literary texts as involving a complex guessing game, it is important to think more explicitly about the operations which our interpretations presuppose.

I think also, and my final remarks on "London" were designed to provide some hint of this, that the last stage in our interpretation of a poem ought to be one which returns dialectically to its source, which takes into consideration the kind of naturalization and the interpretive conventions which the poem has compelled us to use, and which asks what these demands signify. For finally the meaning of a poem will lie in the kinds of operations which it forces us to perform, in the extent to which it resists or complies with our expectations about literary signs. It is in this sense that the structuralist poetics can be hermeneutic. If we become accustomed to thinking of literature as a set of interpretive norms and operations, we will be better equipped to see (and this is crucial in the case of the most modern and difficult texts) how and where the work resists us, and how it leads to that questioning of the self and of received modes of ordering the world which has always been the result of the greatest literature.

My readers, says the narrator at the end of *A la recherche du temps perdu*, will become "les propres lecteurs d'eux-mêmes." In my book, he says, they will read themselves and their own limits. How better to facilitate a reading of the self than by gaining a sense of the conventions of intelligibility that define the self, than by trying to make explicit one's sense of order and disorder, of the significant and the insignificant, of the naturalized and the bizarre? In its resolute artificiality, literature challenges the limits we set to the self as an agent of order and allows us to accede, painfully or joyfully, to an expansion of self. But that requires, if it is to be fully accomplished,

a measure of awareness of the modes of ordering which are the components of one's culture, and it is for that reason that I think a structuralist poetics has a crucial role to play, not only in advancing an understanding of literature as an institution but also in promoting the richest experience of reading.

Notes

1. "Science versus Literature," *Times Literary Supplement*, 28 September 1967, p. 897.
2. See F. de Saussure, *Course in General Linguistics*, London, Fontana, 1974.
3. See Roman Jakobson, *Questions de poétique*, Paris, Seuil, 1973. For discussion see Culler, *Structuralist Poetics*, chapter III.
4. *Anatomy of Criticism*, New York, Atheneum, 1965, p. 11.
5. Roland Barthes, *S/Z*, Paris, Sevil, 1970.

THEORY

Defining a Theory
of Genre

Adena Rosmarin

In The Power of Genre, *Adena Rosmarin develops a
"pragmatic" definition of genre and tests the concept
with particular reference to the dramatic monologue.
The first chapter of her book, which is reprinted here, is
a wide-ranging discussion of "genre," its various definitions, and the problems these raise, which prove to be
many and complex. At their most fundamental, these are
versions of old and large philosophical problems: the one
versus the many, deduction versus induction, idealism
versus empiricism. And these problems, in one form or
another, haunt all discussions of intertextual criticism.
Examining a number of influential theories of genre,
including those of E. D. Hirsch, E. H. Gombrich, and
Northrop Frye, Rosmarin notes a pervasive bias against
the deductive and in favor of the inductive and "representative." Against this bias, she argues the case for a
deductive and pragmatic theory that would see genre as
"the critic's heuristic tool, his chosen or defined way of
persuading his audience to see the literary text in all its
previously inexplicable and 'literary' fullness and then
to relate this text to those that are similar or, more precisely, to those that may be similarly explained."*

*In the process of making her case, Rosmarin gives a
summary of several competing theories of genre and a
probing analysis of the philosophical issues involved. The
result is a challenging essay in a number of senses. And
while the issues may be difficult, Rosmarin is convinced
they are of fundamental importance. "Genre is the most
powerful explanatory tool available to the literary critic.
It is our most reasoned way of talking about and valuing
the literary text. When both genre and its definitional
nature are made explicit rather than denied, our explanations acquire the defensive strengths of self-awareness
and internal consistency. . . . But a knowing use of genre
generates a constructive strength as well: it is the way of*

Reprinted by permission from *The Power of Genre*. Minneapolis: University of Minnesota Press, 1985: 23–51.

talking that, despite our traditional opinion to the contrary, most fully unfolds the characteristics that make the text seem valuable to us as a literary text."

Metaphysical systems . . . are intrinsically metaphorical systems.

—M. H. Abrams

We reason about them with a late reason.

—Wallace Stevens

Similitude and Difference

Our word "genre" comes from the Greek *genus,* meaning "kind" or "sort." To argue, as do Richards and Gombrich, that "all thinking is sorting" is to argue that thought habitually begins with the generic or general: it defines similarity; it repeats in spite of difference.[1] The argument, which is characteristically modern, is also ancient: Aristotle in his *Poetics* argues that "the greatest thing by far is to have a command of metaphor. This alone cannot be imparted by another; it is the mark of genius, for to make good metaphors implies an eye for resemblances."[2] It implies, that is, the power to see similarity in difference, to define the general in a multitude of particulars. And this power is no less primary for the critic or theorist than for the poet. Aristotle thus begins his own treatise generically and, what we shall find to be much the same, deductively: "I propose to treat of poetry in itself and of its various kinds, noting the essential quality of each."[3]

But it is mainly under the name of "repetition" that "resemblance" or what Shelley called "similitude" enters modern poetics.[4] In his brilliantly suggestive "Lexicon Rhetoricae" Kenneth Burke argues that "repetitive form, the restatement of a theme by new details, is basic to any work of art, or to any other kind of orientation, for that matter. It is our only method of 'talking on the subject.' "[5] Barbara Herrnstein Smith argues similarly in *Poetic Closure,* dramatizing at length the explanatory power of her primary premise: "Repetition is the fundamental phenomenon of poetic form."[6] But even such straightforward affirmations of the general are twisted into paradox by the presence of the particular: "repetitive form" is "the restatement of a theme *by new details.*" We name something a "repetition" when it reminds us of something else so strongly that it seems to be that some-

thing else, to be not itself but a repetition of a prior self. Yet what makes us attend to that reminder and, indeed, perceive it *as* a reminder is precisely if paradoxically these "new details," the ways in which its restatement or present self seems to differ from the prior statement that these details paradoxically enable us to infer. Thus in *Wuthering Heights* Hareton reminds Heathcliff of Catherine because he simultaneously repeats and fails to repeat Catherine, because his face at once resembles and differs from the face that is primary among that novel's multiple and unrecoverable origins.

The previous chapter stated the paradoxical dynamics of repetition in terms of visual representation: the illusion is always striving to convince its audience that it is what it seems. Cubism has critiqued visual representation by forcing the members of this paradox apart: it deconstructs or "unbuilds" this seeming by issuing conspicuously representational invitations that it no less conspicuously refuses to make good. These refusals, what Gombrich calls "reversals," force the beholder's "attention to the plane" (p. 284), making him see not only a guitar but also a painting of a guitar. Cubism thus builds its contradiction of its topic *into* its topic, accomplishing what Gombrich says is "strictly" or representationally speaking impossible: it makes our illusion conscious. It simultaneously gives the painting a substance and stature of its own. A mere copy no longer, it becomes a creation.

The procedures and consequences of deconstructing writing have proven closely analogous. The representational seemings of literary and critical texts alike have also been undone, their constitutive metaphors unbuilt, brought to light, unearthed, or, to use the textual metaphor itself, unraveled. The critical text has been shown to repeat the literary text and, as well, to display the "new details" that inhabit that repetition. As in painting, this display makes the criticism self-conscious or theoretical. It is what gives the critical text substance and stature, making it "visible" in its own right or, what is the same, in its own terms. Any convincing attempt to paint illusionistically or explain representationally in the wake of such undoings must somehow contain those undoings within itself, must somehow, as the Israeli painter Avigdor Arikha has said, perform "both the transgression and the inclusion of doubt."[7]

We shall find that an expressly deductive genre criticism is just such a performance. It would make its reader aware of its premises and, simultaneously, convince him of their explanatory power. It achieves both ends by interweaving two quite different repetitions: by repeating in its own text particulars of the text explained; by repeating the "new details" of that repetition when explaining a different literary text.[8] This second or terminological repetition, the aforementioned "display," is the traditional self-validating procedure of genre criticism and, unlike the first repetition, which is the traditional self-validating procedure of "literary" or covertly generic criticism, is itself infinitely repeatable. An expressly deductive genre criticism, however, refuses the choice between these two traditional routes and instead proposes a way around. This way is marked out or constrained by the critic's suasive purpose and constructed by his simultaneous and overt use of both repetitions. It is, in other words, fully pragmatic and rhetorical, deliberately argued from purpose to premise to particular text. It is also explicitly critical: it places constitutive or constructive power in the genre, and defines the genre neither "historically" nor "theoretically" but in terms of its use in critical explanation. The genre is the critic's heuristic tool, his chosen or defined way of persuading his audience to see the literary text in all its previously inexplicable and "literary" fullness and then to relate this text to those that are similar or, more precisely, to those that may be similarly explained.

Because it seeks to convince its reader of the explanatory power of genre, an expressly deductive genre criticism can readily acknowledge what more traditionally conceived genre criticism, whether "historical" or "theoretical," must conceal or deny. That an eye for resemblance is always also an eye for difference. That not only is perfect repetition impossible—to repeat is always also to differ—but that similarity or the general becomes convincing only when embedded in difference or the particular. That explanatory power, like affective power, tends to be greatest when the affinities are surprising, when the yokings unite seemingly incongruous matter across seemingly unbridgeable gaps. That likening evening to "a patient etherized upon a table" surprises more than likening it to a "nun breathless with adoration" precisely because Eliot's repetition is more crossed by contrast than Wordsworth's, because we have had to work harder to "find" the similarity. That this interpretive work, what Gombrich calls "the beholder's share," commits us to our finding, engendering our belief or conviction. That if "trace" is the presence of difference in similarity, it is also and simultaneously the presence of similarity in difference.[9] That reason may respect difference and imagination similitude (as Shelley said) or vice versa (as Plato might have said), but this respect is always relational, the degree of difference always being just that: a matter of degree. That once genre is defined as pragmatic rather than natural, as defined rather than found, and as used rather than described, then there are precisely as many genres as we need, genres whose conceptual shape is precisely determined by that need. They are designed to serve the explanatory purpose of critical thought, not the other way around.

A Dissonance of Theories: Genre and Representation

Genre theory, however, has traditionally chosen just this other way around. With few exceptions criticism has treated genre not as the critic's explanatory tool but as a hypothesis, a probable stab at the truth, something whose inherence in a particular literary text or whose independent existence as a schema is potentially verifiable or, at least, refutable. The characteristic treatment, in other words, has been either to naturalize or historicize the genre by retrospectively "finding" it in the literary text or to hypostatize it, making it "theoretical." But this treatment, which is in either case representational, is neither necessary nor ultimately persuasive, for both historicized and hypostatized genres similarly lose credibility as their unacknowledged definitional nature becomes increasingly obvious with increasing use. Whereas in either case the critic presents himself as describing or representing what antecedes his text—the historical genre being derived from observation of preexisting literary facts, the theoretical genre being deduced from a preexisting theory of literature—in both cases the genre is actually conceptualized, textualized, and justified by the critic's present-tense act, by his writing of the genre's definition.[10]

Although it is commonly assumed that making the critic's act explicit weakens criticism, undoing its transparence or "validity," in actuality the attempt to conceal this act is what ultimately proves weakening. This is particularly so when, as in genre criticism, the schemata or premises are conspicuous.

Genres, in other words, are always and obviously open to question, and this questioning inevitably discovers the inconsistency between the critic's descriptive claim and his constitutively powerful premises. This vulnerability, however, is a consequence not of genre per se but of trying to write genre criticism while simultaneously making representational claims. It is a consequence of denying not only genre criticism's deductiveness but also its pragmatism, of denying not only the premises and procedures of its reasoning but also their origin in the critic's explanatory purpose and their present-tense existence in his explaining text.

The weakening consequences of this denial are most easily seen in E. D. Hirsch's *Validity in Interpretation*.[11] In his earlier study, "Objective Interpretation," Hirsch had constrained the potential indeterminacy of literary meaning by defining it as the author's, but in *Validity* he refines this definition, arguing that the author's most determining act is his choice of type or genre, that this genre constitutes or determines the text's meaning, and that reconstructing or inferring this genre makes possible the representation of that meaning.[12] The argument is a typical post-Kantian blend of induction and deduction, of media used as if they were powerless or "descriptive" on one level (here meaning "theory") and powerful or constitutive on another (here meaning "criticism").[13]

"All understanding of verbal meaning," Hirsch begins, "is necessarily genre-bound" (p. 76). This does not mean that we never change our minds about which genre is "right"—we obviously can and do replace old genres with new—but "ultimately everything we understand will have been constituted . . . by the new generic conception" (p. 76). He goes on to explain that "this description of the genre-bound character of understanding is, of course, a version of the hermeneutic circle, which in its classical formulation has been described as the interdependence of part and whole: the whole can be understood only through its parts, but the parts can be understood only through the whole" (p. 76). Like Karl Viëtor, René Wellek, and others, Hirsch here treats one of genre study's most frequently asked questions as a special case of the hermeneutic circle.[14] It is a question that has been most clearly posed by Wellek: "How can we arrive at a genre description from history without knowing beforehand what the genre

is like, and how can we know a genre without its history, without a knowledge of its particular instances?"[15] Wellek's answer necessarily begs the question—"It can be solved in the concrete dialectics of past and present, fact and idea, history and aesthetics"—because the question is, as Wellek himself points out, paradoxical or unanswerable.[16] Indeed, as Gustavo Pérez Firmat observes, the question is not even properly asked of genre: "a work does not belong to a genre as a part belongs to a whole . . . since not every feature of a work is genre-bound. . . . Unlike the whole, it is less than the sum of its parts; and what is equally important, it is not simply less, it is also *different* from its parts."[17]

But the hermeneutic circle, despite its increasingly recognized difficulties, has continued to be used, primarily because it gives us a way of articulating the problem of "grounding" or "validating" interpretation. Increasingly many of those who use it, however, recognize that it also perpetuates that problem. Hirsch's next words accordingly come as no surprise:

> This traditional formulation, however, clouds some of the processes of understanding in unnecessary paradox. It is true that an idea of the whole controls, connects, and unifies our understanding of parts. It is also true that the idea of the whole must arise from an encounter with parts. But this encounter could not occur if the parts did not have an autonomy capable of suggesting a certain kind of whole in the first place. A part—a word, a title, a syntactical pattern—is frequently autonomous in the sense that some aspect of it is the same no matter what whole it belongs to. (Pp. 76–77)

Hirsch here reduces the paradox of the hermeneutic circle by defining the independence and priority of the part: it has the "*autonomy* capable of suggesting a certain kind of whole *in the first place*." But if Hirsch has just asserted the constitutive power of genre, how can he now assert that the text has the power to "suggest" or constitute the genre? He can do so because he defines the genre as "intrinsic," as a concealed given or ground that is contained *within* the text and that will accordingly remain "the same no matter what whole it belongs to." This conclusion phrases in generic terms Hirsch's more sweeping claims in *Aims of Interpretation*: that stylistics is the enemy of synonymity, that "an absolutely identical meaning" can survive its translation into different linguistic and conventional forms, and that upon this synonymity "genuine knowledge" and our discipline depend.[18]

As his argument proceeds, Hirsch sharpens both his claim and the paradoxical dilemma of traditionally conceived genre criticism. Interpretation begins, he tells us, with the interpreter's "guess about the kind of meaning he confronts" (p. 78). (This dilemma is prefigured in Hirsch's phrasing: he yokes the interpreter's guess, which is a conjectural or propositional act, with a confrontational metaphor, which denies that very action.) This guess or genre has "a necessary heuristic function in interpretation, and it is well known that heuristic instruments are to be thrown away as soon as they have served their purpose" (p. 76). So far Hirsch reads like Vaihinger, for whom the conceptual fiction has a purely pragmatic existence, its proper use being to be "used up." But because Hirsch has committed himself to the premise that "understanding is itself genre-bound," he also argues that "a generic conception is not simply a tool that can be discarded once understanding is attained" (p. 78). He thus concludes that "the generic conception serves both a heuristic and a constitutive function" (p. 78).

This contradiction, however, could be transformed from a logical weakness to an argumentative strength by adapting Vaihinger's thesis: by arguing that genre is heuristic when we explicitly use it pragmatically and suppositionally, *as if* it constituted the text. Indeed, if read carefully, most criticism, even that which professes its disinterest in the generic and the suppositional alike, reveals that it is already both. Let us, for example, recall the exact words of Blanchot's disclaimer: "A book no longer belongs to a genre; every book arises from literature alone, *as if* the latter possessed in advance, in its *generality*, the secrets and the formulas that alone allow book reality to be given to that which is written. Everything would happen *as if*, genres having dissipated, literature alone was affirmed, alone shined in the mysterious light that it spreads and that every literary creation sends back to it while multiplying it—*as if* there were an '*essence*' of literature" (emphasis added.)[19] Nor need *we* always add the emphasis. Kenneth Burke, for example, has argued "that one can, at times, most clearly indicate the structure of a work by treating it *as if* it were designed to point a moral."[20]

But Hirsch refuses the pragmatic and suppositional in hope of finding the certain or, at least, the probable: "To know the intrinsic genre is to know almost everything" (p. 88). This refusal initiates the traditional and endless search for the "natural" stopping place, the ground that will interpret without itself needing interpretation: "An extrinsic genre is a wrong guess, an intrinsic genre a correct one. One of the main tasks of interpretation can be summarized as the critical rejection of extrinsic genres in the search for the intrinsic genre of a text" (pp. 88–89).[21] This concern with the right or wrong of a genre, with whether it is the one the author intended (intrinsic) or the one the critic intends (extrinsic), is a purely representational worry. It equates the genre's "rightness," its correspondence to the author's intention, with its power to explain the text. But this equation, perhaps the most basic assumption of genre theory, is both unwarranted and, in actual critical practice, tacitly ignored. Thus even the rare genre of whose authoritative rightness we are assured can fall before a genre of superior pragmatic virtue. Henry Fielding, to take but one example, defined the genre of *Joseph Andrews* in his preface, but critics have nevertheless felt free to replace the "comic epic poem in prose" with genres of their own devising.[22] It is the *theorist* who typically insists on the critical genre's authoritative rightness, even when, as is most often the case, that authority is impossible either to confirm or refute. It is the *critic* who in any case insists on the genre's pragmatic power.

R. S. Crane seems to argue an even more purely inductive or *a posteriori* line than Hirsch, but when he moves from "practical" genre theory to critical theory, from proposing a critical language to discussing critical languages *as* languages, the deductiveness of his argument or, to be precise, of one of his arguments becomes obvious. This inductive-deductive ambivalence typifies neo-Aristotelian or "Chicago" criticism, the theory and practice of which has most thoroughly explored the explanatory power of deductive genre and, simultaneously, has most firmly "grounded" that power in the text. Throughout "Towards a More Adequate Criticism of Poetic Structure," Crane explicitly argues that an inductive poetics is not only desirable but possible, that a transparent or constitutively powerless medium for criticism exists, and that this medium is the proper "language of criticism."[23] He accordingly attacks critics for their deductiveness, for unwittingly letting their languages or genres determine their reading:

It is fatal therefore to think that we can know the shaping principle of any poem in advance or, what amounts to the same thing in practice, that we can get at it in terms of any predetermined conception or model of what structure in poetry or in this or that special branch of poetry in general either is or ought to be. Yet this is exactly what most of the critics who have concerned themselves with questions of structure in practical criticism have attempted to do. They have come to poems equipped, so to speak, with paradigms of poetry, or of epic, tragedy, lyric, and so on, and hence with more or less definite specifications concerning the nature of the structural patterns they ought to look for; and they have as a consequence been unable to see any structural principles in poems except those already contained in their preferred definitions and models.

(P. 146)

Crane uses Robert Heilman's formalist reading of *Othello* to exemplify this attack on the powerful paradigm: whereas "the question of the structure of *Othello* could surely be approached inductively," Heilman's argument is "a simple application of this paradigm to the facts of the text which it enables him to select as significant data" (p. 147). This exposé of deductive criticism is meant to convince us both that Heilman's paradigm has indeed powerfully constituted his explanation and that it shouldn't have, that that power wrongs the text. And these convictions are meant to engender another: that we need "a language in which we can envisage our questions as questions of fact rather than of relations of ideas" (p. 149). What we need, in short, is a transparent language.

Crane proposes that Aristotle's *Poetics* offers just such a language. It perfectly reflects what he defines as the essence of the literary text: "the most important thing about any poetic production is the characteristic power it has to affect us in this definite way rather than that" (p. 179). And its procedures are self-effacing: it allows us to conduct "inquiries of an *a posteriori* type which move inductively . . . from particulars to the universals they embody" (p. 155). We need criticize neither Crane's choice of language nor his superlative use of that language, as in "The Concept of Plot and the Plot of *Tom Jones*,"[24] in order to note, first, that his language seems transparent to its object because his definitions of the literary text and of his language share a common origin in the *Poetics* and, second, that his attitude toward this transparency depends upon whether he speaks as a theorist or as a metatheorist. When speaking as a theorist, as one concerned with ways of explaining literature, he values transparency or powerlessness in critical languages: "if we are to allow the facts to speak for themselves, we must in some fashion supply them with a language in which to talk" (p. 174). But when in "The Multiplicity of Critical Languages" he moves one "level" up and speaks as a metatheorist, as one concerned with ways of explaining criticism, he values those same languages for their opacity or power:

> Literary criticism is not, and never has been, a single discipline, to which successive writers have made partial and never wholly satisfactory contributions, but rather a collection of distinct and more or less incommensurable "frameworks" or "languages," within any one of which a question like that of poetic structure necessarily takes on a different meaning and receives a different kind of answer from the meaning it has and the kind of answer it is properly given in any of the rival critical languages in which it is discussed.[25]

Crane, then, mounts two distinct and contradictory arguments, one from the theorist's point of view, the other from the metatheorist's. When the critical language is the interpretive medium, he argues that it, like all perfect representational media, should be transparent, fully deferential to the object or text described. But when it is the interpretive ground, itself the object of description, he argues that it, like all perfect grounds, should be powerful or opaque, something to be looked at, not through. Representational theory desires only commensurable languages, those whose overlappings "imply" or make visible the literary ground they represent in common. Incommensurable languages are undesirable because they defeat synonymity of meaning or, rephrased in pluralist terms, the argument that there are many different and "valid" ways of representing the same text. Incommensurable languages leave their traces or "new details" in the text explained. They make their power "visible." In Gombrich's terms, they force our attention to the critical plane, making us "see" not only *Othello* but the paradigm that selects the "significant data" of *Othello*.

Of course, it is precisely the inscribing power of Heilman's paradigm that enables him to write his reading. This power is also what makes the reading "visible" to Crane, what gives it sufficient substance and stature to make it a fit topic for metacritical analysis. In other words, to inscribe the "significant data" of *Othello* is to explain the significance of *Othello,* and to reinscribe that inscription is to explain the significance of Heilman's reading. The importance of Crane's work for contemporary genre studies is that it lets us see this common ground, the way in which the practical critic's use of the powerful medium is linked to the metatheorist's recognition of that power. But Crane's work is also important because it simultaneously displays the stance of the traditional theorist: his built-in antagonism to both critical practice and its explanation, his preference for a medium distinguished by neither its usefulness nor its visibility but, rather, by its disinterestedness and invisibility. Crane as theorist, in sum, denies the very power that, when writing as a practical critic, he uses and, when writing as a metatheorist, he describes.

Even the most conspicuously schematic of genre theorists, one whose openly deductive premises and procedures lead us to expect a similarly open acknowledgment of those premises and procedures, makes a point of their denial. Northrop Frye opens his *Anatomy of Criticism* by arguing that "the first thing the literary critic has to do is . . . to make an inductive survey of his own field and let his critical principles shape themselves solely out of his knowledge of that field."[26] Moreover, this critic should in good inductive fashion keep his values from contaminating that knowledge: "Value-judgments are founded on the study of literature; the study of literature can never be founded on value-judgments" (p. 20). Such professions of inductiveness not surprisingly prove short-lived, the force and visibility with which Frye wields his schemata quickly forcing him to concede their existence: he has, he tells us, "proceeded deductively" (p. 29). But he also tells us that he has done so in order "to keep the book within the bounds that would make it possible to write and publish it" and that "the deductiveness does not extend further than tactical method" (p. 29). In other words, Frye admits his deductiveness but insists on its superficiality, an admission that, given his conspicuous schemata, must be more feint than finesse. But his opening gestures to induction are nevertheless important—not because they argue the inductiveness and thus the "validity" of his theory but because they instance the institutional sway of inductive pretense, its power to turn even a conspicuously deductive theory of genre against itself,

making it vulnerable to the charges of inconsistency and self-ignorance.

Not surprisingly, Frye's inductive gestures have done little to deflect his critics, who, while routinely remarking Frye's "brilliance" and "scintillating erudition," no less routinely find his overt schematism to be too much of an already dangerous thing. Correcting Frye has accordingly become a creative first step for subsequent theories of genre, a theoretical practice that works according to the theoretical "rhythm" defined in the preceding chapter: that of correction and schema.[27] We thus find Tzvetan Todorov, in the opening chapter of *The Fantastic,* strongly faulting Frye's deductiveness.[28] But the strength of Todorov's faultfinding is less interesting than its obliquity, than the way representational pressure once again skews toward induction even those arguments that announce their deductiveness. For Todorov begins as a champion of deduction—or so it seems:

> One of the first characteristics of scientific method is that it does not require us to observe every instance of a phenomenon in order to describe it; scientific method proceeds rather by deduction. We actually deal with a relatively limited number of cases, from them we deduce a general hypothesis, and we verify this hypothesis by other cases, correcting (or rejecting) as need be.   (P. 4; p. 8)

The inductive-deductive ambiguity of this passage depends upon semantic slippage in the word "deduce": Todorov uses it not in its logical or rigorous sense, meaning to argue from a premise, from general statement to particular instances, but in its colloquial or Sherlock Holmesian sense, meaning to move inferentially from particulars to generality. The former sense lingers, giving the semblance of neo-Kantian self-awareness and explanatory power to an otherwise traditional argument for representational validity. Todorov's inductiveness, however, is all but explicit by the essay's end: "The genres we deduce from the theory must be verified by reference to the texts: if our deductions fail to correspond to any work we are on a false trail" (p. 21; p. 26). His concern with falsity, verification, and correspondence is purely representational, as is his censure of Frye's categories.

But it is, of course, precisely these censured characteristics that distinguish Fyre's genres. Todorov shows that these genres are purposefully defined by Frye rather than "discovered" in the text, that they contradict the text's literariness, that they usurp its autonomy and constitutive power. Any traditional theorist would fault Frye in just this way, if not this astutely. But Todorov's argument, because of the semantic slippage on which it is built, has paradoxically purchased the power to reflect on itself and discover its own impossibility:

> No observation of works can strictly confirm or invalidate a theory of genres. If I am told: a certain work does not fit any of your categories, hence your categories are wrong, I could object: your "hence" has no reason to exist; works need not coincide with categories, which have merely a constructed existence; a work can, for example, manifest more than one category, more than one genre. We are thus led to an exemplary methodological impasse: how to prove the descriptive failure of any theory of genres whatever? The reproach we made to Frye appears to apply to any work, ours included. (P. 22; p. 26)

As indeed it does. But the reproach becomes necessary only within a purely representational theory of interpretation. Because the procedures of genre criticism are ineluctably deductive—always in however concealed a fashion, moving from general to particular—and because representation only tolerates the reverse movement, genre criticism and representational theory are inherently at odds, their attempted union an inevitable embarrassment. Hence Todorov's reproach and self-reproach. Only when using a rhetorical and pragmatic language, whose grammar and vocabulary allow us to explain the constitutive power of genre as instrumental to critical thought, do such reproaches become themselves unnecessary.

Todorov's "impasse" is remarkable not only for its self-awareness but for its clear outline. In his second chapter, entitled "Definition of the Fantastic," Todorov states the premise from which he will deduce specific instances of the genre, thereby explaining them: "The fantastic is that hesitation experienced by a person who knows only the laws of nature, confronting an apparently supernatural event" (p. 25; p. 29). The explanations that follow are powerful and, as such, fully justify his definition or chosen premise. But they cannot, as critical practice more generally cannot, validate this or any definition. Theory's desire for the explaining text's complete and traceless grasp of the explained must remain unfulfilled, as must practical criticism's inductive desire for consti-

tutively powerful textual particulars, those capable of announcing their "correct" or "intrinsic" genre. Taken together, the practical strength and conceptual candor of *The Fantastic* enact our most open staging of representation's linked dilemmas: the theoretical and practical impossibilities of its self-defined fulfillment. But a complex and concealed staging would prove yet more instructive, and for this we turn to Hans Robert Jauss's "Theories of Genres and Medieval Literature."[29] Jauss's theory, like Todorov's, is justified by a powerful practice, but, once again, this justification wears a mask of validation, a mask whose conspicuous and unavoidable slippage sets the theory's articulation at odds with its premises.

The complexity of Jauss's theory of genre is in part due to his use of not one but many schemata, in part to their location on different "levels," in part to his repeated gesturing toward a real-world context, in part to his alternating display and denial of his own interpretive act. Jauss's theory, in other words, stages the three-way conflict analyzed in the previous chapter: constitutive or explanatory power is in rapid and alternating succession located in genres, in the particulars of the historical text and context, in the theorist's "envisioning" of those genres and particulars. But Jauss, despite his proclaimed interest in the world from which literature arises and in which it is "received," is far less interested in the particulars of that world than in its literary genres and the theoretical schemata that will best "illuminate" or explain them for his present-day audience.

Jauss's argument, in other words, is fully if not quite admittedly pragmatic, carefully argued from purpose to premise to particular text. Indeed, Jauss begins by explicitly stating his purpose: "it seems worthwhile to develop a theory of literary genres within a field of inquiry that lies between the opposites of singularity and collectivity, of the artistic character of literature and its merely purposive or social character" (p. 76). Also in beginning, he defines the present-day context of genre study, thereby opening a conceptual space for his own theory: "The theory of literary genres is at the point of seeking a path between the Scylla of nominalist skepticism that allows for only *a posteriori* classifications, and the Charybdis of regression into timeless typologies, a path along which the historicization of genre poetics and of the concept of form are upheld" (p. 78). Jauss then proposes as a first step in his theory's justification the correction of a previous theory: "To initiate a justification of this path with a critique of Croce recommends itself not merely on the grounds of an interdisciplinary discussion. For Croce pushed to an extreme the critique of the universal validity of the canon of genres, a critique that had been growing since the eighteenth century, so that the necessity of founding a historical systematics of literary genres once again becomes apparent" (p. 78).

Jauss defines the "relationship between the individual text and the series of texts formative of a genre . . . as a process of the continual founding and altering of horizons. The new text evokes for the reader (listener) the horizon of expectations and 'rules of the game' familiar to him from earlier texts, which as such can then be varied, extended, corrected, but also transformed, crossed out, or simply reproduced" (p. 88). This "rhythm" is essentially that of Gombrich's "schema and correction," and, like Gombrich's, is both an aesthetic model and a critical model. Its explanatory power, that is, operates on more than one level, its ambidexterity enabling the critic to explain a text in terms of its historical reading and that reading in terms of the text. Quoting J. G. Drosen on literary genres, Jauss says as much: "they transform themselves to the extent that they have history, and they have history to the extent that they transform themselves'" (p. 89).

In one of the distinguishing leaps of his theory, Jauss now defines aesthetic value in terms of this transformation: "the more stereotypically a text repeats the generic, the more inferior is its artistic character and its degree of historicity" (p. 89). But this definition, given more fully in his earlier "Literary History as a Challenge to Literary Theory," is not an altogether happy one.[30] Although texts that challenge the norm are frequently, even usually, the ones esteemed, they are not necessarily esteemed, either at the time of their writing or later, nor are texts that do not challenge the norm necessarily not esteemed, either at the time of their writing or later. Jauss emphasizes both this "later" and these "necessities," implying that even within the ranks of genius a Stravinsky necessarily outranks a Mozart and that the subsequent reception of a text is more self-evident, stable, and unambivalent than its original reception.[31] But "conventional" texts are not infrequently valued over "challenging" texts, a valuation that is itself always open to reevaluation and in need of interpretation. Moreover, at any point in its interpretive history a text can be simultaneously valued and not valued. Most importantly, however, that point is always itself interpreted from within what Jauss himself calls the "perspective" of the present interpreter. In other words, the correlation between aesthetic value and "challenge" is always in practice a matter of the present interpreter's purpose, as in his own essay it is for Jauss. But despite its problems, Jauss's reciprocal definition of genre and aesthetic value is important, for assignation of genre, as I shall argue, is invariably a valuative act on the part of the interpreter. This act, however, involves deciding not whether genre is connected to aesthetic value but how.

Jauss in part "solves" his three-way conflict by positing a "ground" that constitutes both the text's genre and its reception:

A theory of genres grounded in an aesthetics of reception necessarily will add to the study of the structural relations between literature and society, work and audience, where the historical system of norms of a "literary public" lies hidden in a distant past; there it can most readily still be reconstructed through the horizon of expectations of a genre system that pre-constituted the intention of the works as well as the understanding of the audience.

(P. 108)

But placing his "ground" on the "horizon," where it is definitively and forever just out of sight, defers rather than solves the problem of defining the site of constitutive authority. This deferral, of course, is precisely what enables Jauss to claim both social significance and generic rigor for the ground and to present it as not defined but "discovered" or, more precisely, discoverable. But the deliberate vagueness of this ground is too obvious for its authority to be convincing, and the conflict of its presentation with Jauss's repeated acts of terminological definition further weakens the argument.

Its most serious weakness, however, lies in Jauss's repeated denial of this conflict: "the modern theory of genres can proceed only descriptively, and not by definition" (p. 95); genres "cannot be deduced or defined, but only historically determined, delimited, and described" (p. 80). Whether or not we agree with these claims, Jauss's own practice could not be in fuller or more explicit disagreement, whether he is, as in his "Literary History" essay, announcing the "premises" from which he will "develop the principle of representation of a literary history" (p. 38), or whether he is, as in the following, unfolding his generic premises and the act of their definition:

> If one follows the fundamental rule of the historicization of the concept of form, and sees the history of literary genres as a temporal process of the continual founding and altering of horizons, then the metaphorics of the courses of development, function, and decay can be replaced by the nonteleological concept of the playing out of a limited number of possibilities. In this concept a masterwork is definable in terms of an alteration of the horizon of the genre that is as unexpected as it is enriching; the genre's prehistory is definable in terms of a trying and testing of possibilities; and its arrival at a historical end is definable in terms of formal ossification, automatization, or a giving-up or misunderstanding of the "rules of the game," as is often found in the last epigones. But the history of genres in this perspective also presupposes reflection on that which can become visible only to the retrospective observer: the beginning character of the beginnings and the definite character of an end; the norm-founding or norm-breaking role of particular examples; and finally, the historical as well as the aesthetic significance of masterworks, which itself may change with the history of their effects and works, and thereby may also differently illuminate the coherence of the history of their genre that is to be narrated. (P. 94)

The act of terminological definition could hardly be made more explicit, nor could its metaphoricity, nor could the emplotting or constitutive power of the "retrospective" observer's vision, nor could the narrative nature of that "vision." But it is important to recognize that Jauss's difficulty in consistently conceptualizing the emplotment or writing of literary history is less a particular difficulty than one built into the genre of "history" itself, at least as it is traditionally defined. As Hayden White has shown, the very beginning-middle-endness that gives histories their plot and thereby their appeal and significance is precisely what endangers that appeal and significance.[32] The problem, which looks philosophical but is actually rhetorical, results from the contradictory demands made by the audience of a history, whether it be literary or otherwise: we desire it to have both the feel of reality and the finish of the ideal. When Jauss insists that he is not defining but describing, he is attempting to fulfill the former desire. When he insists, as here, on the coherence of his "narrated" history, he is attempting to fulfill the latter. The two fulfillments are logically incompatible, but the appearance of their compatibility is at least provisionally achieved by the historian's strategic use of either or both of representation's traditional metaphors, preferably in "dead" form. He can present himself as "seeing" the history's coherence, as Jauss does here, or he can, as White explains, present it as "found," as a product of archaeological search and discovery:

> The historical narrative, as against the chronicle, reveals to us a world that is putatively "finished," done with, over, and yet not dissolved, not falling apart. In this world, reality wears the mask of a meaning, the completeness and fullness of which we can only *imagine*, never experience. Insofar as historical stories can be completed, can be given narrative closure, can be shown to have had a *plot* all along, they give to reality the odor of the *ideal*. This is why the plot of a historical narrative is always an embarrassment and has to be presented as "found" in the events rather than put there by narrative techniques.[33]

It is not necessary to deny—nor am I doing so—that the poet or novelist knew his genre in order to accept that our narrations of his generic manipulation are nevertheless informed by our present-tense explanatory purpose. Nor should the occasional coincidence of a critical genre with a genre similarly named in history confuse the issue by leading us either to naturalize or to hypostatize that genre, concealing thereby its definitional nature and the deductively unfolded knowledge that it enables. Even less should we be tempted to hypostatize a posited generic model or to claim its "intrinsicality" when, as is the case with the dramatic monologue, it did not as currently named exist for the writers who used it. Whether "theoretical" as in the passage above—"the genre's prehistory is definable in terms of a trying and testing of possibilities"—or "historical"—"there were in the Middle Ages basically four schemata of division at one's disposal that could, in varying degrees, serve the explanation of genres" (p. 95)—the genres that Jauss chooses or defines are similarly "grounded" in explanatory purpose. That they succeed pragmatically, that they fulfill this purpose by proving useful in making explanations, is their only possible justification. It is also the only "proof" that we, in this or in any other case, should demand.

Ralph Rader's work is a rare instance of explicitly purposeful and deductive genre criticism. Consider this passage, which follows Rader's definition of the "realism-plot-judgment form," as exemplified by *Pamela*:

> I will call this conception and others to be developed later *models*, in order to emphasize their hypothetical character and their function as artificial similitudes of independently cognitive form. The model is a revision of the R. S. Crane-Sheldon Sacks concept of represented action designed to make it meet clearly the condition just mentioned, namely to define the principle of the realism-plot-judgment class and to exclude *Moll Flanders*. I should say that the models are deductive models; that is, they are meant to define the most general differentiating principle of a work's form in such a way that its more particular aspects can be rigorously deduced from it.[34]

Rader is proceeding in explicitly deductive fashion. He is defining, not discovering, and he is defining with an explicit purpose: to exclude *Moll Flanders* from the set of literary texts called "novels" and thereby to purchase greater explanatory power and precision. He emphasizes the model's pragmatism, its definitional and purposeful nature, and openly deduces particulars from this model — not the other way around.

The strength of Rader's criticism is a function of the strength of his premise or model and of the rigor or consistency of its unfolding. The suasive force of this consistency, however, depends upon its explicitness, upon his premise and procedures being explicitly acknowledged and justified. Hence the theoretical justification that opens "Fact, Theory, and Literary Explanation":

> Hypothesis — interpretive assumption — does not follow from the observation of fact but necessarily precedes and structures it, so that agreement between hypothesis and fact is to some degree foreordained. The implications of this relationship have been powerfully developed in the philosophy of Sir Karl Popper, who argues that all our knowledge is inherently and permanently hypothetical, that knowledge can never begin with "the facts" but only with a conjecture about the facts, and that the test of a conjecture (read hypothesis or theory) is not the degree to which it finds confirmation in facts — the significance of which it effectively constructs — but the degree to which it risks refutation by independent facts which it does not have immediately in view. In this conception knowledge is not built up inductively from local fact to gradually justified generalization, but deductively, by extending a strong generalization over the widest possible range of fact toward potential refutation.[35]

A rhetorical and pragmatic theory of explanation welcomes this powerful argument for the deductive nature of critical thought. But Rader, like Gombrich, is arguing according to the "rhythm of schema and correction," and, like Gombrich, he therefore needs a "correcting" tool. Hence the "independent facts" to which he grants a special constitutive power, that of "refutation." But if hypothesis "necessarily precedes and structures" facts, how can these facts have the power to refute the hypothesis? Rader answers this version of the hermeneutic-circle question by stipulating that these particular facts be not "immediately in view," by placing them on the hermeneutic "horizon." But by the logic of his own theory this answer will not do. It defers rather than solves the problem, leaving the theory vulnerable to further questioning: What is the hypothesis or model that will let us "see" these correcting facts? What are the facts that will in turn provide *its* correction? The questions are infinitely regressive or, what is the same, ultimately unanswerable.

But this inconsistency, the inevitable and potentially devastating by-product of attempting to unite the theories of genre and representation, is, once again, unnecessary. One solution to Rader's problem would be to retain the "independent fact" but emphasize its definitional and pragmatic nature. Kant himself remarks the heuristic function of the *ding an sich* — for that is what Rader's "fact" actually is — and Vaihinger insists on its fictionality, arguing simultaneously that the fictional is useful only insofar as it is explicitly presented as such.[36] A related solution would be to follow through on the reversed "rhythm," that of "correction and schema," which Rader himself articulates in the first quotation. There he explicitly "grounds" his model in explanatory purpose — "to define the most general differentiating principle of a work's form in such a way that its more particular aspects can be readily deduced from it" — and locates its origin in his revision, "correction," or, more precisely, rewriting of the Crane-Sacks model. Rader could, that is, consistently treat his models or genres as the pragmatic and deductive beginnings he posits them to be, as chosen or defined to serve the purposes of our critical thought and, particularly, to begin the processes of that thought. Such a correction would make possible the fully pragmatic theory of genre to whose statement we now turn.

Syllogism, Metaphor, and the Logic of Criticism

Genre is the most powerful explanatory tool available to the literary critic. It is our most reasoned way of talking about and valuing the literary text. When both genre and its definitional nature are made explicit rather than denied, our explanations acquire the defensive strengths of self-awareness and internal consistency. They thereby reduce their vulnerability to ironic discounting or extra-mural deconstruction, although they, not inconsistently, welcome revision or rewriting by explanations yet to be written. But a knowing use of genre generates a constructive strength as well: it is the way of talking that, despite our traditional opinion to the contrary, most fully unfolds the characteristics that make the text seem valuable to us *as a literary text*. We value the explanation that appropriates both these defensive and constructive strengths, that can make sense both in the explanation's own terms, meaning that it is closely and consistently reasoned, and in terms of its topic, meaning that it unfolds the literary text's value as a literary text. And we value most highly the genre that helps us to make such explanations.

These valued or "literary" characteristics are, of course, themselves definitional rather than natural. Most obviously in modern poetics, they are defined aesthetically: in terms of the text's "feel" of uniqueness, particularity, and richness; in terms of an indwelling order, which is itself variously defined, being at times an "organic" unity, at times a syllogistic logic, at times an "uncanny" illogic. But these characteristics have also been defined ethically, although less in the traditional mimetic sense, in terms of the real-world value of a represented content, than in the Romantic or Shelleyan sense, in terms of the text's heuristic power, which is primarily a power to make the reader better than he was when he began to read.[37] He becomes expert in recognizing and negotiating the difficulties of reading and writing texts, particularly the textualized selves manifest in those texts. And he learns the prodigious significance of rewriting those texts, an act commonly termed "judgment" but more usefully termed "correction" and "completion." The good literary text, that is, has been most successfully defined as a text that is well made *and* as a text

that makes well. And the good critical text, I am suggesting, is in this manner also well defined, particularly in terms of genre.[38]

The primary act of the generic critic is suppositional and metaphoric: let us explain this literary text by reading it in terms of that genre. Just as the painter manipulates his schema until he thinks that his audience will "recognize" a particular face, so this critic proceeds to manipulate his genre, to deduce particulars from it until he thinks that his audience will "recognize" a particular text. The "stopping place" of his schematic correction will vary from text to text, depending on its interpretive history and his audience. For some texts he will need to correct or specify at length, for some very little. But in each case his purpose or goal is to convince his audience that the posited genre is more "like" the text than the genres used to carry on previous critical discussions of the same text, that this genre, in other words, is the vehicle that most fully and precisely captures the tenor or text.[39]

When defined thus—pragmatically and rhetorically rather than "naturally" or representationally—this conviction happens without the critic's concealing the fact that the genre can no more be perfectly like that which is not-itself than can any medium. He acknowledges and builds upon the fact that it will always leave its trace in the text and always be blind to many particulars. But how, then, can the reading convince? It convinces because it takes place in an intertextual world, in which readings are expressly conscious not only of themselves as readings but also of previous readings, all of which have been generic but not all of which have used the same genre. A text's interpretive history, which is a textualized pastiche of the many genres that have "read" the text, is recalled by the critic to his audience. It thus becomes itself a suasive instrument, its various successes and failures becoming available for the critic's present suasive use. When recalled and themselves "read," they give the critic a way of substantiating and, finally, justifying his procedures of correction and construction, procedures which, when sufficiently substantial and justified, write an explanation that we call convincing or true.

I have been talking of "deducing" a text from a genre, but what exactly does this mean? Most generally, it means asserting particular instances of the traits stated or implied by the posited genre. This assertion, however, proceeds not randomly but rigorously, indeed syllogistically:

All men are mortal.
Socrates is a man.
Socrates is mortal.

The first or major premise of the classical syllogism asserts that all members of one class belong to a second class. (The classes may be the same size and in generic syllogisms typically are.) The minor premise asserts that an entity belongs to the first class, and the conclusion states that it therefore belongs to the second class as well.

Let us exemplify this reasoning with a particular genre:

Dramatic monologues invite their readers to distinguish the characterized speaker's meaning from the poem's.

"Andrea del Sarto" is a dramatic monologue.

"Andrea del Sarto" invites its reader to distinguish its speaker's meaning from the poem's.

The major premise asserts that all members of the genre "dramatic monologue" belong to the class of poems that invite their readers to distinguish the characterized speaker's meaning from the poem's. The syllogism then concludes that if a particular poem belongs to the first class it therefore belongs to the second class as well. All generic criticism proceeds thus, although the syllogistic pattern not only varies greatly in its explicitness but is usually abbreviated as an enthymeme ("'Andrea del Sarto' invites its readers to distinguish its speaker's meaning from the poem's because it is a dramatic monologue") or as an "if-then" assertion ("If 'Andrea del Sarto' is a dramatic monologue, then it invites its readers to distinguish its speaker's meaning from the poem's").

The syllogistic pattern, however, does not merely begin the critic's argument. It is repeated throughout the explanation, the conclusion of the opening syllogism becoming the major premise of the next, whose conclusion in turn is always potentially and perhaps actually yet another major premise. Thus the above conclusion will in the next chapter be followed by a minor premise ("The reader makes this distinction when the speaker seems to understand his discourse less well than the reader does"), which leads to another and more specific conclusion ("Andrea seems not to 'see' his discourse, in particular his tropes, as clearly as he might"). This sorites or series of syllo-

gisms forms the conceptual skeleton of all well-reasoned critical explanation. And it often, as it does throughout this study, takes the shape of a question-answer series, which is a version of the "correction-schema" series, the revised "rhythm" proposed in the last chapter. We accordingly ask: How do we learn that Andrea's "seeing" is faulty, that his insight is clouded by blindness? Because, we answer, he himself repeatedly corrects his vision, thereby displaying the fact that he uses tropes much as he uses his painter's "faultless" brush: to close rather than to open meaning, to achieve limited perfection rather than limitless imperfection. But if Andrea's correction of his vision is what teaches us to see its faults, how, then, does our vision come to surpass his? Because our repeated views of his tropological misuse tutor us in its recognition, so that when he seems suddenly to go blind to the damning implications of his "faultlessness," that blindness becomes itself visible to the reader. The reader thus achieves an insight denied the speaker, although the process of its achievement warns that that insight contains within itself a yet-to-be-discovered blindness.

I would emphasize, therefore, not any particular phrasing but rather a pattern of reasoning that explicitly moves from definition of genre to defining specific instances of that genre and then to the unfolding of that specificity, an unfolding structured by the sorites and fleshed out by citations from the poem itself. These citations fuse the poet's text and the critic's text, a conflation that brings the sorites to a close and, simultaneously, convinces the reader of the genre's power to "reveal" the text. This reasoning pattern, moreover, is just that: a conceptual model for the way critical argument effectively moves. It is not an attempt to imitate a "horizonal" historical reality, an "intrinsic" textual reality, a "theoretical" genre, or the process by which the critic actually "discovered" his argument. The priority of the premise is purely logical, as Kenneth Burke in the opening paragraph of his essay, "Definition of Man," points out:

First, a few words on definition in general. . . .
when used in an essay, as with Aristotle's definition of tragedy in his *Poetics*, a definition so sums things up that all the properties attributed to the thing defined can be as though "derived" from the definition. In actual development, the definition may be the last thing a writer hits upon. Or it may be formulated somewhere along the line. But logically it

is prior to the observations that it summarizes. Thus, insofar as all the attributes of the thing defined fit the definition, the definition should be viewed as "prior" in this purely nontemporal sense of priority. (P. 3)

The reason for this reasoning, moreover, is purely pragmatic: it is justified wholly insofar as it helps us make better or more convincing critical arguments, those that acknowledge their premises and whose reasoning is consistent with those premises. And this pragmatic reason or purpose is what decides both the sorites' beginning point or premise and its stopping point or conclusion. It will be instructive here to consider Paul de Man's observation on the sorites or its various phrasings: "The question-and-answer structure, like the foreground-background or the conscious-preconscious structures, are abyssal frames that engender each other without end or *telos*. In the process, however, they create a sequence of apparent syntheses that convey an impression of methodological mastery."[40] While agreeing that there is no "natural" end to these procedures and that their display does indeed create an impression of methodological mastery, we should also recognize that the sorites does in fact always have a beginning and an end, as is shown, for example, in the above analysis of Jauss, whose practice de Man is here discussing. The notion that the "frames" are "abyssal" and self-engendering is a belated representational notion, one developed from our increasing awareness that the representational search for the "natural" beginning and end, traditionally termed either "bedrock" or the "horizon," is always infinitely regressive. A rhetorical and pragmatic theory of explanation has no need to place beginnings and ends "out of sight" because it locates them in the interpreter's suasive purpose, which in large part is the creation of that very "impression of methodological mastery" remarked by de Man, an end that in a representational theory must remain an incidental by-product of the interpreter's philosophic questing.

The overtness of its premises and the consistency of its reasoning endow an explanation with defensive strength, the power of prolepsis. By acknowledging rather than concealing its constitutive metaphors, it anticipates and thus defends against their extramural deconstruction or "unbuilding." But an explicitly generic criticism generates constructive strengths as well. Perhaps the most straightforward benefit of making our use of genre explicit is the greater con-

versational range and economy of the resulting criticism. Recall that traditional formalist criticism, fascinated with the unique and multifarious verbal surface, tends to move from particular text to particular text. This restricted and local movement, which characterizes even the best formalist criticism, even, for example, Cleanth Brooks's *The Well Wrought Urn*, both requires and is required by the denial of genre. Speaking generically, however, enables us to exemplify many texts in a single discussion. Thus Rader's reading of *Pamela*, explicitly and consistently deduced from his model of the novel, not only explains *Pamela* but by extension enables him to explain all novels like *Pamela*. Thus the generic explicitness of the following readings makes it possible to explain deduced texts in varying detail and length, the extension of the early readings enabling later abbreviation. But such synecdochic explanation is not only more economical, it is also more suggestive and, thereby, more powerfully convincing. Because we normally assume, as Gombrich has noted, "that to see a few members of a series is to see them all," because we expect to contribute our "beholder's share," critics, like painters, can invoke the "etc. principle" to suggest completion from very little indeed (p. 220). And it is the interpretive work necessary to complete this suggestion that works to make the conviction ours.

Genre, in other words, is a finite schema capable of potentially infinite suggestion. It is a special case of what Douglas Hofstadter calls a "strange loop": "what else is a loop but a way of representing an endless process in a finite way?"[41] But how does a "strange loop" differ from "normal" representation, which also seeks to capture the infinite in the finite? By making its beholder or reader aware of the "gaps" that he must fill or bridge in order to make sense. A strange loop calls attention to itself or, more precisely, to its finitude, and by so doing makes us attend to the dynamics of our attention itself, to the ways in which we accomplish the interpretive work of making sense. This redoubled attention is what makes it "strange." Put otherwise, normal and strange loops differ in the same way that illusionism differs from cubism: the one tries to conceal its difference from what is represented, the other uses, even flaunts its difference in order to convince us of the value of the representing text.

A strange loop, then, is not simply a suggestively incomplete series but one that explicitly turns back on itself, remarking its own incompletion. This turning, which is a kind of tropological maneuver, is what closes the infinite regress of representation, making the series seem complete. In the special case of genre, this illusion of completion is created when the literary text is incompletely represented (which always happens) and when attention is explicitly drawn to that incompletion (which happens only when genre is used rhetorically and pragmatically). This theoretical paradox, in other words, proves a powerful practical logic, for it is precisely the explicit incompletion of the explaining text that creates the seeming completion or fullness of the text explained. It makes the literary text seem to elude us, to contain more than we can know. And if we examine the notion of genre in terms of its other and no less inevitable representational failing—the trace or error it injects into the literary text—we end with a similar and similarly useful paradox. For no genre can represent its texts without reordering, reemphasizing, or in some way leaving its schematic imprint. There is *always* a difference between the universal and the particular, and this difference is a consequence not only of leaving something out but of putting something in. Once foregrounded, the latter proves no less useful in explanation than the former, for just as incompletion leads us to complete, difference (or, as we more usually and less precisely say, "error") leads us to "correct," to define similitude. And the activity of this "correction," no less than the activity of completion, commits us to its product, to the literary text that we have "made."

If, as Vaihinger observes, "what we generally call truth, namely a conceptual world coinciding with the external world, *is merely the most expedient error*,"[42] then what the critic seeks is not a "fit" but the most suggestive "misfit," the most expedient "error" or, as we have been saying, difference. And what is most expedient in literary criticism? We have already discussed the benefits of economy and range in explicitly generic explanation. But what about "literariness"? Genre criticism, of course, is the traditional enemy of the literary text as it has been most frequently defined and valued since the Romantics: as aesthetically rich and heuristically potent. However, if "fit" is acknowledged to be philosophically impossible but pragmatically possible, if our purpose is not finding accurate comparisons but, in Gombrich's words, "inventing comparisons which work," then we are free to define "work" as we will (p. 301). We can define it as the suggestion of just these characteristics.

One way to make this suggestion, to accomplish this simultaneously critical and "literary" purpose, is

to refine our genres: "Whenever the difference between species matters, the schema is modified to meet the distinction" (Gombrich, p. 121). The distinction made in the following chapters between dramatic monologues and mask lyrics is just such a refinement, one that allows us to justify more fully the aesthetic and ethical value of such poems as "Prufrock." But a total refinement is neither possible nor desirable. Genres can never be perfectly coincident with texts unless we posit as many genres as texts—at which point we fall back into a Crocean world, into treating each text in isolation. Nor is sensitivity an absolute good. For certain conversational purposes we may want to *de*sensitize a given genre, making it less aware of differences, more emphatic of similarity. But whether we move toward greater or lesser sensitivity is, once again, not a philosophic but a pragmatic question. Just as Wordsworth's likening of the evening to a nun's breathless adoration was more apt for his meditative purpose, despite its being less surprising than Eliot's contrast-crossed metaphor, so it happens that likeness will work better than difference for certain explanatory purposes and not for others. Structuralism's search for the ever more basic underlying structures, the elemental likenesses that explain the greatest set of differences and, thereby, "define the conditions of meaning," is our boldest enactment of such a critical purpose.[43] It is also and not incidentally the least "literary" of contemporary critical languages, the least interested in saying how any particular text is just that: particular, inexplicable in general terms alone.

I have been discussing generic argument as syllogistic, as a reasoned way of discovering or, more precisely, defining the particular in the general, but the preceding remarks remind us that speaking generically is also metaphoric, a way of defining likeness in difference.[44] This kinship of syllogistic and metaphoric reasoning can be made explicit by revising our model thus:

> Let us define dramatic monologues as poems that invite their readers to distinguish the characterized speaker's meaning from the poem's.
>
> Let us discuss "Andrea del Sarto" as a dramatic monologue.
>
> Let us discuss "Andrea del Sarto" as inviting its readers to distinguish the speaker's meaning from the poem's.

The movement remains the same—from general to particular—but the asserted relationship between the two has become explicitly definitional rather than implicitly intrinsic or "natural." No longer claiming that "Andrea del Sarto" *is* a dramatic monologue, that there is some intrinsic or natural connection between the two, we now propose a pragmatic thought-experiment: let us explore what "Andrea del Sarto" is like when we read it in terms of the genre here defined as "dramatic monologue." The syllogistic process of deducing the poem from the genre is now refined—and redefined—as the unpacking of metaphoric equivalences.

But because metaphors are as crossed by contrast as they are confirmed by similarity, the process is ultimately an unpacking of difference as well, and it is here that the gap between literature and our thought about literature is finally closed. For genre, like metaphor, is powerfully persuasive not only because it leads us to perceive similarity but because it leads us to perceive that similarity in the midst of and in spite of difference. Like all metaphor, it is a way of talking "about things in terms of what they are not."[45] Like all metaphor, it perpetrates a contradiction in terms or, more precisely, in texts. For genre is not, as is commonly thought, a class but, rather, a classifying statement. It is therefore itself a text. It is writing about writing, distinguished by its topic and its way of handling that topic, the way it takes a set of literary texts and defines their relationship. This definition yokes it to its topic, the text it writes about, but it also sets it apart from that topic, articulating their difference, what Hofstadter would call the strangeness of the "loop." The text called "genre" is always different from the text it writes about.

Yet our perception of the genre's difference from the literary text leads not to suasive failure—the explicitly deductive critic defends against this failure by foregrounding the constitutive power of his genre—but to an impression of that text's value, of its particularity and power. For when the genre's trace and incompletion are acknowledged, their discovery "in" the text does not so much impugn the genre as create an impression of a distinctly *literary* text, one that seems infinitely particular and heuristically powerful precisely because it eludes our generalizing grasp. But the use of explicitly deductive genre reconciles the poem to its poetics in another way as well: by starting with the general we can deduce the most minute and numerous particulars, whereas when we purportedly start with those particulars we commit ourselves to moving away from

them, to reducing them to the general. Thus does the very direction of explicitly deductive argument encourage "discovery" of an *ir*reducible text, one capable of being indefinitely because never conclusively unfolded.

But certain combinations of similarity and difference are more persuasive of this literariness than others, and those that create affinities at once surprising and profound are most persuasive of all. We shall find, for example, that it is neither surprising nor useful to connect two recognized dramatic monologues because they possess in common the use of a characterized speaker. This trait is too obvious: the similarity it remarks has, with repetition, come to seem superficial, powerless before increasingly noticed difference. It is an explanatory metaphor that has died. But to connect two monologues, as Robert Langbaum did, because they generate a common effect, is to construct a similarity that surprises us with its capacity to subsume those increasingly noticed and hitherto inexplicable differences.[46]

When the critic asserts that a particular genre is like a particular literary text, he makes a conceptual promise to his reader. He fulfills this promise by displaying both the *extensiveness* of his metaphor's power, showing how it subsumes surprisingly many poems, and its *intensiveness*, showing how it unfolds a given poem in surprising detail. Using the sorites, he reasons his way from generic premise to actual citation—in poem after poem, novel after novel. But the critic also and effectively displays how the texts of a given genre are *unlike* each other. This display, which bears a paradoxical relationship to the first, creates both the impression of each individual poem's literariness, thereby confirming its power to resist generalization, and the impression of an irresistible genre, thereby confirming its power to define difference in the midst of similarity. Taken together, these displays suggest that the "best" or most explanatorily potent genre to use for any particular discussion is the one that will extend what seems a profound similarity over a wide range of difference and that is capable of dramatizing this extension by "discovering" that difference intensively.

This extension, however, is not limitless, nor is it desirable that it should seem so. To explain everything by something is a purely representational ideal, a performance whose practical and theoretical impossibilities have been repeatedly dramatized in modern poetics. But were the performance possible, would it be desirable? Would it enable us to make better explanations of literary texts? In his analysis of poetic form Burke notes that "the peril of power is monotony,"[47] and, we might answer, so it is in critical explanation as well. The attempt to explain all or even many poems in terms of a single similarity or genre is a false economy: it would purchase extensive power by sacrificing the explanatory powers that are of particular importance in literary studies, those of subtlety and intensity.

Moreover, such an attempt would be inconsistent with a knowing use of genre. Once we define genre as constitutively powerful, we commit ourselves to the logical consequences of that definition, one of which is the recognition that a genre can no more be perfectly coincident with the literary text than it can be perfectly transparent or constitutively powerless. There are always, in other words, two "as if" or suppositional decisions made in generic criticism. One is obvious: we will discuss a group of poems as if they are *like* each other and their genre. The other is not: we will discuss a group of poems as if they are *unlike* each other and their genre. Moreover, we will discuss them as if they were *unlike* poems not included in the group. This display of difference is no less necessary to critical explanation than the display of similitude. Each implies the other, and each uses the other to do its interpretive work. The terms of difference are precisely what create the possibility of talk about similitude — and vice versa.

All of which means that a generic explanation best persuades not only by displaying its power to explain a great many poems in great detail but also by pushing itself to its explanatory limits. This last act both sharpens the explanation's metaphoric program — by showing us how *Moll Flanders* is not like *Pamela*, Rader shows us more clearly what *Pamela* is like — and constructs the credibility or defensive strength of that program. But it is also a creative strength, the process of completion and correction being the most suggestive of all knowledge-making processes. As our rigorous use of the genre pushes it to its explanatory limits and quite literally uses it up, its disintegration yields a hermeneutic detritus that has the "feel" of interpretive fact: what remains when the genre has been exhausted seems nothing other than the poem itself.[48] The following discussion of dramatic monologues, here defined as poems that are like "Andrea del Sarto," gradually gives way to discussion of Frost's "A Servant to Servants" and Browning's "Fra Lippo Lippi," which are less like

dramatic monologues, and finally to discussion of Tennyson's "Ulysses," Browning's "Childe Roland," and Eliot's "Prufrock," which are defined to be unlike dramatic monologues in a distinctive way. The distinctiveness of this way defines a new similarity or genre, the "mask lyric," which "corrects" previous readings of these poems by making these newly defined poems seem more like each other and less like those with which they were previously said to be congeneric. But this genre also has its distinctive and acknowledged limits and, like all explanatory definitions, fully anticipates and welcomes its own future redefinition.

What, then, is a genre? The preceding pages have answered this and the other opening questions by arguing that genre is most usefully defined as a tool of critical explanation, as our most powerful and reasoned way of justifying the value we place or would place on a literary text. But to argue thus is not to claim that one of the most repeated questions of contemporary genre studies — Are genres "historical" or "theoretical"? — can only have wrong answers but, rather, is to suggest that the question is not very useful to ask. It leads us to treat as "real" a conflict that is itself invented, a terminological definition made to serve philosophical purposes that have largely passed into history. And its either-or terms effectively keep us from answering the question that compels the attention of contemporary literary studies: How can we make explanations of the literary text that are at once reasoned and yet distinctly "literary"? The answer here proposed is that we make such explanations by explicitly choosing our premises and deducing our texts. The argumentative energy of these explanations goes not into concealment but into reasoning, not into denials of the premise and the critic's act but into justifying his chosen premise by the consistency and richness of the reasoning that follows.

The critic, of course, may and often does argue the value of his genre in "historical" terms. He may, for example, argue that Browning intended us to read "Andrea del Sarto" as a dramatic monologue as here defined. But the value of such argument nevertheless remains a pragmatic rather than a "realistic" question: How well does this genre explain the poem? More precisely: How valuable is this poem when explained in terms of this genre? What makes a genre "good," in other words, is its power to make the literary text "good" — however that "good" be presently defined by our audience. Similarly, the critic may and often does argue the value of his genre in "theoretical" terms. But however laudable the internal rigor and scope of his theoretical system, any genre within the system nevertheless needs to justify itself pragmatically, by justifying the literary value of the text explained. Even Frye's strongest advocates accordingly fault him for not "practicing" the genres he preaches.

Several theorists of genre have recently observed that the historical-theoretical distinction is another way of making the inductive-deductive distinction and that the "historical" genre is a masked "theoretical" genre. The "historical" critic has simply—or not so simply—concealed his first or a priori step.[49] I agree with these observations but would take them one step further by noting that the "theoretical" genre is itself a mask. Like the "historical" genre, it is a way of "grounding" critical discourse in the not-itself, of displacing constitutive power from the critic's explanatory purpose and textualized act. Criticism, however, does not derive power from what it is not—whether a text or schema. Rather, it engenders power by what it does. Therefore, it is by explicitly returning constitutive power to the place where it in practice always resides—in the purpose and act of criticism—that we fully realize the power of genre. The questions of origin and change are answered by this "return." As exemplified by my use of the mask lyric, a genre is chosen or defined to fit neither a historical nor a theoretical reality but to serve a pragmatic end. It is meant to solve a critical problem, a problem that typically involves justifying the literary text's acknowledged but seemingly inexplicable value. The critic accordingly "finds" his genre by correcting a previous genre, in this case the dramatic monologue, a genre that is erroneous not because it is inherently wrong but because for certain poems it explains insufficiently well.[50] And the new genre is correct not inherently but pragmatically: because it explains sufficiently well, the power to explain being identical with the power to correct the old genre, to remedy its deficiencies, to make it workable. Like the "theoretical" genre, this chosen or defined genre constitutes the poem, causing us to "see" it in the genre's terms. It can and does constrain interpretation. But unlike the "theoretical" genre, its choice or definition is not itself constrained by a "deeper" ground, whether it be an entity or a category. It is always constrained prag-

matically and rhetorically, by the critic's suasive purpose and audience.

This last point raises the "descriptive or prescriptive" question. As any reader of genre theory quickly learns, "descriptive" and "prescriptive" are themselves prescriptive terms, not neutral or descriptive but judgmental: a "good" genre describes, a "bad" genre prescribes. The judgment is Crocean. It is the way genre theory has played out the role of theory per se: to "look at" practice, not to affect it. Hence René Wellek and Austin Warren: "Modern genre theory is, clearly, descriptive. It doesn't limit the number of possible kinds and doesn't prescribe rules to authors."[51] Hence Paul Hernadi: "It seems to me that the better part of modern genre criticism has been more philosophical than historical or prescriptive: it has attempted to describe a few basic types of literature that *can* be written, not numerous kinds of works that *have* or, in the critic's view, *should have* been written."[52] Wellek and Warren are claiming descriptive validity for their definition of genre, but Hernadi is claiming both this validity and prescriptive power: his ideal genre *describes* the types of literature that *can* be written. This descriptive-prescriptive contradiction is yet another phrasing of the contradiction that always occurs when genre theory is yoked to a traditional or representational theory of knowledge. As in Crane and Jauss in particular, the descriptive claim is meant to mask and launder the prescriptive, but, again as in Crane and Jauss, it can't. For even as Hernadi is claiming the prescriptive powerlessness of his ideal genre, its inability to map literary practice, he is claiming that it has the power to do just that. The dilemma, however, drops away once we construe this mapping as not literary but critical.

In other words, the rhetorical and pragmatic answer to the "descriptive or prescriptive" question is that the critical genre is prescriptive, but what it prescribes is not literary but critical practice. The critic who explicitly uses his genre as an explanatory tool neither claims nor needs to claim that literary texts should be or will be written in its terms but that, at the present moment and for his implied audience, criticism can best justify the value of a particular literary text by using these terms. As shown above, this end is in part accomplished by the critic's manipulating the genre to the point at which it is used up or deductively exhausted. He thus justifies the value of his explanation by justifying the value of the poem. But he also justifies his explanation by showing it to be knowing, to be both self-aware and closely reasoned. Both justifications are finally one, similarly made possible by the explicitness of his premise and procedures, similarly concluding in the citations that conflate his text with the poet's. But his explanation's awareness of its provisional and pragmatic nature also leads to a further and paradoxical claim: that it is powerful because it has not only the power to correct previous readings but also the power to inspire the future readings that constitute its own correction.

Notes

1. E. H. Gombrich, *Art and Illusion: A Study in the Psychology of Pictorial Representation* (Princeton: Princeton University Press, 1960), p. 301; I. A. Richards, *The Philosophy of Rhetoric* (New York: Oxford University Press, 136), p. 30. Further citations will be included in the text. See also Hayden White, *Tropics of Discourse: Essays in Cultural Criticism* (Baltimore: Johns Hopkins University Press, 1978): "the beginning of all understanding is classification" (p. 22).

2. Aristotle, *Poetics*, in *Critical Theory Since Plato*, ed. Hazard Adams (New York: Harcourt, Brace and Jovanovich, 1971), p. 62. The connection between the biologist's attempts at classification and the critic's may be said to originate with Aristotle, who was a naturalist and who begins his *Poetics* by announcing just such an attempt: "I propose to treat of poetry in itself and of its various kinds, noting the essential quality of each . . ." (p. 48). In post-Linnaean times, the genus has become the biologist's way of organizing its member species and the species his way of organizing its member individuals. The analogy with literary genres and their member texts is, strictly speaking, with the latter pairing, and, indeed, such eighteenth-century writers as Samuel Johnson and Hugh Blair referred to "genres" as "species," the term "genre" not coming into use until the nineteenth century. This change, however, did not affect the analogy since the general-particular relationship repeats on all levels of bionomial nomenclature.

    The field of literary studies characteristically distinguishes its use of classification from that of the natural sciences. The distinction, however, typically depends upon a misunderstanding

of the status and function of classification in both disciplines, a misunderstanding exemplified by Tzvetan Todorov's analysis in the opening chapter of *The Fantastic*, trans. Richard Howard (Cleveland: Press of Case Western University, 1973): "the birth of a new tiger does not modify the species in its definition. The impact of individual organisms on the evolution of the species is so slow that we can discount it in practice" (p. 6). Although it is true that evolutionary changes are reflected in the bionomial nomenclature, they account for only a small percentage of biology's ongoing and multitudinous reclassifications. In avian nomenclature, for example, 84 percent (674 of 798) of North American species have, on some taxonomic level, been reclassified between the fifth (1957) and sixth (1983) editions of the *Checklist of North American Birds*. Purely nomenclatural changes—corrections made to conform to the grammar of the classical languages, those made to accord with the principle of historical priority of names, those made to eliminate the inadvertent duplication of names—account for twenty changes. The rest, which involve either "lumping" groups previously classed as separate or "splitting" groups previously classed as one, reflect new opinion on the actual or potential breeding behavior of the groups involved, opinion that is variously based on morphological, ethological, or biochemical data. Moreover, individual populations not infrequently undergo multiple reclassifications. The Thayer's Gull, for example, was not distinguished from the Herring Gull till 1915, when it was granted full species status. In 1925 it was demoted to a subspecies of the Herring Gull, then in 1973 once again was granted full species status. And at present, "there exists some feeling that Thayer's Gull should, again, be lumped—this time with Iceland" (Paul Lehman, "The Identification of Thayer's Gull in the Field," *Birding* 12 [1980]: 198). My point is that biological classification is itself an explanatory system, which has been devised primarily to make sense of an otherwise disparate group of individuals and which is changed primarily in order to improve that sense. While robins and poems are obviously different, the attempt to make a reasoned sense similarly dominates their study.

3. Aristotle, *Poetics*, p. 48.

4. Percy Bysshe Shelley, *A Defense of Poetry*, in Adams, *Critical Theory Since Plato*, p. 499.

5. Kenneth Burke, *Counter-Statement* (Berkeley: University of California Press, 1968), p. 125.

6. Barbara Herrnstein Smith, *Poetic Closure: A Study of How Poems End* (Chicago: University of Chicago Press, 1968), p. 38.

7. Avigdor Arikha, *Time*, 30 July 1979, 71. A recent attempt to perform "both the transgression and the inclusion of doubt" is David Carroll's *The Subject in Question: The Languages of Theory and the Strategies of Fiction* (Chicago: The University of Chicago Press, 1982). Carroll opens by stating his premise and purpose: "Rather than place theory and literature (in this case theory and fiction) against each other in sterile opposition, in this book I use fiction strategically to indicate the limitations of theory and theory to indicate the limitations of fiction—each revealing the premises, interests, and implications of the other. Each is not so much opposed to the other as always implicated in the other" (p. 2).

8. My distinction between the two repetitions, which an expressly deductive genre theory and practice interweaves, has its most immediate theoretical antecedents in Jacques Derrida, "Différance," *Bulletin de la Société française de philosophie* 62 (1968); rpt. in *Speech and Phenomena: And Other Essays on Husserl's Theory of Signs* (Evanston: Northwestern University Press, 1973), pp. 129–60, and Gilles Deleuze, *Logique du Sens* (Paris: Les Editions de Minuit, 1969). Derrida phrases the two repetitions in terms of difference and delay—"In the one case 'to differ' signifies nonidentity; in the other case it signifies the order of the *same*' (p. 129)—and then joins them in the term *différance*. Deleuze phrases the two repetitions thus: "Let us consider two formulations: 'only that which resembles itself differs,' 'only differences resemble one another.' It is a question of two readings of the world in that one asks us to think of difference on the basis of preestablished similitude or identity, while the other invites us on the contrary to think of similitude and even identity as the product of a fundamental disparity" (p. 302). My most immediate practical antecedent is J. Hillis Miller's use of these two repetitions in *Fiction and Repetition: Seven English Novels* (Cambridge, Mass.: Harvard University Press, 1982). Miller opens with their theoretical definition (he invokes Deleuze's definition, among others, and I accordingly cite his translation) and proceeds to use that definition to perform critical practice. This usage transfers in the present study to the practices of both genre theory and genre criticism. See also Derrida's "The Law of Genre," trans. Avital Ronell, *Critical Inquiry* 7 (1980): 55–81, one of the theses of which is that "every text participates in one or several genres, there is no genreless text; there is always a genre and genres, yet such participation never amounts to belonging" (p. 65).

9. Barbara Johnson observes that in deconstructionist criticism "truth is preserved in the notion of error" ("Nothing Fails Like Success," *SCE Reports* 8 [1980]: 14). Richard Rorty makes a similar point (about Derrida's notion of "trace") in "Philosophy as a Kind of Writing: An Essay on Derrida," *New Literary History* 10 (1978–79); rpt. in Rorty, *Consequences of Pragmatism (Essays: 1972–1980)* (Minneapolis: University of Minnesota Press, 1982), pp. 90–109.

10. Gustavo Pérez Firmat argues similarly: that "the genre achieves textual existence in the present-day critic's own discourse" ("The Novel as Genres," *Genre* 12 [1979]: 276). I find Firmat's study, although on several points it differs from my own, to be the most insightful recent inquiry into genre. Especially valuable is his analysis of Todorov and the inductive-deductive problem (pp. 277–84). See also Stanley Fish's argument that "the claims of independence and priority are the same" in "Interpreting the *Variorum*," *Critical Inquiry* 2 (1976); rpt. in *Is There a Text in This Class? The Authority of Interpretive Communities* (Cambridge, Mass.: Harvard University Press, 1980), p. 162. In other words, to claim that the genre preexists the critic's description is to claim that it is independent of that description.

11. E. D. Hirsch, Jr., *Validity in Interpretation* (New Haven: Yale University Press, 1967). Further citations will be included in the text.

12. E. D. Hirsch, Jr., "Objective Interpretation," *PMLA* 75 (1960); rpt. in ibid., pp. 209–44. Hirsch argues the stated points in chap. 3 of *Validity*.

13. The best contemporary example of this blend is Stanley Fish's theory of interpretive strategies (see chaps. 13 through 16 of *Is There a Text in This Class?*). Like Kant, Fish takes a category or, as he

says, "interpretive strategy" as his object of description. He emphasizes the constitutive power of this "strategy," its power to make meaning, but he also assumes the power of his metatheory to describe that "strategy" accurately, without contamination from its own strategies. This latter power is paradoxical, being a power of powerlessness: it is that of the perfectly polished mirror, the perfectly transparent lens. Conceived thus, the theoretical medium neither causes nor constitutes meaning but, rather, reflects critical meaning, enabling the theorist to *describe* how our critical strategies cause or constitute the literary meaning that they, in like fashion, present themselves as describing. Kant's categories differ from Fish's primarily in that Kant's are essentially unchanging whereas Fish's are never not changing—except at the precise moment of their description. But the similarity of their categories is more important than this difference: just as Fish conceives of the formal features of a text as a product of interpretation, not its cause, so Kant conceives of it as a datum of sense experience to be itself categorized. Kant argues this point in the *Critique of Pure Reason* (1781), trans. Norman Kemp Smith (London: Macmillan, 1929), sec. I ("Transcendental Doctrine of Elements"), bk. I, chap. 2, "The Deduction of the Pure Concepts of Understanding." The point is further emphasized in the much revised second edition (1787). Like Fish and Hirsch, Kant never explains how we know the categories (or "strategies," or "wholes") themselves, nor how we know which category is in force. The question of how to make philosophical assertions or, in terms of our discipline, how to begin critical argument is raised in the *Critique*, but left unanswered.

14. Karl Viëtor, "Die Geschichte literarischer Gattungen," in *Geist und Form* (Bern: A. Franke, 1952), pp. 292–309. See following note for Wellek. The "hermeneutic circle" problem is discussed at length by Claudio Guillén, *Literature as System: Essays toward the Theory of Literary History* (Princeton: Princeton University Press, 1971), essay 4, "On the Uses of Literary Genre," pp. 107–34, and by Gustavo Pérez Firmat (see below in text), whose discussion exposes the faulty analogy that engenders the problem. See also Allan Rodway, "Generic Criticism: The Approach through Type, Mode and Kind," in *Contemporary Criticism*, Stratford-upon-Avon Studies 12 (New York: St. Martin's Press, 1970). Rodway similarly sees the genre question as a phrasing of the "hermeneutic circle" problem and, like Hirsch, posits an inductive solution: "We escape, so to speak, by edging out, tacking from evidence to hypothesis to further evidence to renewed hypothesis" (p. 94).

15. René Wellek, *Discriminations: Further Concepts of Criticism* (New Haven: Yale University Press, 1970), p. 252.

16. Ibid., p. 252.

17. Firmat, "The Novel as Genres," p. 278.

18. E. D. Hirsch, Jr., "Stylistics and Synonymity," *Critical Inquiry* 1 (1975); rpt. in *Aims of Interpretation* (Chicago: University of Chicago Press, 1976), pp. 50–73.

19. Maurice Blanchot, *Le livre à venir* (Paris: Gallimard, 1959), p. 293. See my theoretical introduction (no. 22 above) for further information.

20. Kenneth Burke, "Formalist Criticism: Its Principles and Limits," *Texas Quarterly* 9 (1966); rpt. in *Language as Symbolic Action: Essays on Life, Literature, and Method* (Berkeley: University of California Press, 1966), p. 489.

21. For a lucid and suggestive exposition of the infinitely regressive ground problem as it troubles literary studies, in particular literary history, see Michael McCanles, "The Authentic Discourse of the Renaissance," *Diacritics* 10 (1980): 77–87, discussed in my introduction.

22. Perhaps the strongest and most explicitly critical redefinition of *Joseph Andrews* is that of Sheldon Sacks, *Fiction and the Shape of Belief: A Study of Henry Fielding with Glances at Swift, Johnson and Richardson* (Chicago: University of Chicago Press, 1964), pp. 70–102. The genre is defined along Aristotelian lines, as an "action": "Actions . . . are works in which characters about whose fates we are made to care are introduced in unstable relationships which are then further complicated until the complication is finally resolved by the complete removal of the represented instability" (p. 24). Sacks is explicit about formulating a "Grammar of the Types of Fiction" (chap. 1) and about the purposefulness of that grammar: "The primary justification for establishing three classes—obviously others equally 'correct' are possible—is to formulate a meaningful general question, or possibly ques-

tions, about the relation between a novelist's be-liefs and the forms of his novels" (p. 27). Sacks argues thus even as he quotes Howard Mum-ford Jones's observation: that *Joseph Andrews* is "the first English novel consciously fulfilling an aesthetic theory" ("Introduction" to *Joseph An-drews* [New York: Random House, Modern Li-brary College Editions, 1950], p. vii; quoted by Sacks on p. 236). Only occasionally will a critic make explicit the typically determining criterion of the critical premise or model, namely, its worth in explanation. For an example from the interpretive history of the monologue, see Linda K. Hughes, "Dramatis and Private Personae: 'Ulysses' Revisited," *Victorian Poetry* 17 (1979): 192–203. In conclusion Hughes argues thus: "If this reading of the poem does not coincide ex-actly with Tennyson's own conception of scene and audience, it at least accords well with the movement of the poem. More important, this reading can perhaps answer to what is at best a minor criticism of 'Ulysses'—its apparent con-tradictions in setting, movement, and audience" (p. 203).

23. R. S. Crane, "Towards a More Adequate Criti-cism of Poetic Structure," in *The Languages of Criticism and the Structure of Poetry* (Toronto: Uni-versity of Toronto Press, 1953), pp. 140–94. Fur-ther citations will be included in the text. For a searching critique of Crane's inductivism see Kenneth Burke, "The Problem of the Intrinsic," in *A Grammar of Motives* (Berkeley: University of California Press, 1969), pp. 465–84. See also W. K. Wimsatt, Jr.'s analysis of the inductive-deductive wavering of Richard McKeon's liter-ary theory in Wimsatt, "The Chicago Critics: The Fallacy of the Neoclassic Species," *Comparative Literature* 5 (1953); rpt. in Wimsatt, *The Verbal Icon: Studies in the Meaning of Poetry* (Lexington: University of Kentucky Press, 1954), p. 43. For a recent "Chicago" statement on genre, see David H. Richter, "Pandora's Box Revisited: A Review Article," *Critical Inquiry* 1 (1974): 453–78.

24. R. S. Crane, "The Concept of Plot and the Plot of *Tom Jones*," in *Critics and Criticism: Ancient and Modern*, ed. R. S. Crane (Chicago: University of Chicago Press, 1952), pp. 616–47. The novel, like the dramatic monologue, has particularly at-tracted the attention of theorists of genre. The two genres are conceptually challenging for

many of the same reasons: their deft interweav-ing of the spoken and written word, the de-signed blurring of borders between text and world, their tendency toward various kinds of calculated incompletion and polyvocality, what Bakhtin has called "heteroglossia." See M. M. Bakhtin, *The Dialogic Imagination: Four Essays*, ed. Michael Holquist, trans. Caryl Emerson and Michael Holquist (Austin: University of Texas Press, 1981). The first essay, "Epic and the Novel: Toward a Methodology for the Study of the Novel," exemplifies Bakhtin's never fully sys-tematized notion of genre as both textually determining and itself determined by its socio-historical context.

25. R. S. Crane, "The Multiplicity of Critical Lan-guages," in *The Languages of Criticism*, p. 13.

26. Northrop Frye, *Anatomy of Criticism: Four Essays* (Princeton: Princeton University Press, 1957), pp. 6–7. Further citations will be included in the text. Criticizing or "correcting" Frye is one of the three most frequent starting points for contem-porary genre theories (the other two being Croce and Todorov). Among such corrections, that of Hazard Adams comes closest to mine: "My own objection to Frye's argument is that . . . I do not believe he can hold to the philosophical neutral-ity of his method" (*The Interests of Criticism: An Introduction to Literary Theory* [New York: Har-court, Brace & World, 1969], p. 130). Frye's the-ory, Adams decides, is "neo-Kantian," and I agree. See also Murray Krieger, ed., *Northrop Frye in Modern Criticism: Selected Papers from the English Institute* (New York: Columbia Univer-sity Press, 1966), particularly Krieger's introduc-tory essay, "Northrop Frye and Contemporary Criticism: Ariel and the Spirit of Gravity." Else-where Krieger acknowledges "the practical im-possibility of keeping criticism inductive . . . once we first concede—in post-Kantian man-ner—the constitutive role of our categories" ("Literary Analysis and Evaluation—and the Ambidextrous Critic," *Contemporary Literature* 9 [1968]; rpt. in Krieger, *Poetic Presence and Illusion: Essays in Critical History and Theory* [Baltimore: Johns Hopkins University Press, 1979], p. 307). And in his essay on Frye's *Anatomy* we find this footnoted but telling comment: "Originally I thought of using *systematics* instead of *schematics* here. But, as Frye points out . . . , his categories

and modes might better be thought of as schematic rather than systematic creations" (p. 5).

27. For an elegant, historical, and schematic critique of the overly schematic theory from Plato and Aristotle onward, see Gérard Genette, *Introduction à l'architexte* (Paris: Éditions du Seuil, 1979). Discussing Frye's *Anatomy*, Genette comments that "on peut sans doute contester la procédure, mais non l'intérêt du résultat (p. 50). Hence Frye's power as a starting place.

28. Tzvetan Todorov, *The Fantastic: A Structural Approach to a Literary Genre*, trans. Richard Howard (Cleveland: Press of Case Western Reserve University, 1973). Further citations will be included in the text, the first page number referring to the English text, the second to the French (*Introduction à la littérature fantastique* [Paris: Seuil, 1970]). Howard's translation closely follows the original, so I will not give the French text here. I have, however, replaced the confusing punctuation of the passage beginning "no observation" with Todorov's own. Todorov's opening chapter is rapidly replacing Frye's *Anatomy* as *the* theory to "correct." See Firmat, "The Novel as Genres"; Richter, "Pandora's Box Revisited"; and Christine Brooke-Rose, *A Rhetoric of the Unreal: Studies in Narrative and Structure, Especially of the Fantastic* (Cambridge: Cambridge University Press, 1981), chap. 3, "Historic Genres/Theoretical Genres: Todorov on the Fantastic," pp. 55–71.

29. Hans Robert Jauss, "Theory of Genres and Medieval Literature," in *Toward an Aesthetic of Reception*, trans. Timothy Bahti (Minneapolis: University of Minnesota Press, 1982), pp. 76–109. Further citations will be included in the text.

30. Hans Robert Jauss, "Literary History as a Challenge to Literary Theory," in *Toward an Aesthetics of Reception*, particularly pp. 25–28. Further citations will be included in the text. The core of Jauss's definition is as follows: "The way in which a literary work, at the historical moment of its appearance, satisfies, surpasses, disappoints, or refutes the expectations of its first audience obviously provides a criterion for the determination of its aesthetic value. The distance between the horizon of expectations and the work, between the familiarity of previous aesthetic experience and the 'horizonal change' demanded by the reception of the new work, determines the artistic character of a literary work, according to an aesthetics of reception: to the degree that this distance decreases, and no turn toward the horizon of yet-unknown experience is demanded of the receiving consciousness, the closer the work comes to the sphere of 'culinary' or entertainment art [*Unterhaltungskunst*]" (p. 25).

31. Jauss's notion of "originality" is thoroughly Romantic and insufficiently complex. His aesthetics could not, for example, make the following discrimination concerning Mozart: "[He is] original in a different sense from Haydn, who astonished, amused, and charmed the people of his time by the freshness, wit, and insouciance of his ideas. Mozart seems never to want to exceed the bounds of convention. He wanted to *fulfill* the laws, not to violate them. Yet he constantly violates the spirit of the music of the eighteenth century—by his seriousness, his amiability (which was no longer the amiability of the *rococo* period), his artistry of combination" (Alfred Einstein, *Greatness in Music* [London: Oxford University Press, 1945], p. 153). Mozart's "conventional" greatness is perhaps best explained by Leonard B. Meyer, who, in his "Grammatical Simplicity and Relational Richness: The Trio of Mozart's G Minor Symphony," *Critical Inquiry* 2 (1976): 693–761, shows how the "unassuming, conventional means" of the Trio nevertheless can yield "rich" results. Not incidentally, Meyer's essay exemplifies many of the points I am making in this chapter and those following. He concentrates, as does Gombrich, on "relational results" rather than "material means," and emphasizes that when explaining these relationships "what seems crucial is that premises be made explicit and arguments from them consistent" (pp. 693, 759).

32. Hayden White, "The Value of Narrativity in the Representation of Reality," *Critical Inquiry* 7 (1980): 5–27.

33. Ibid., p. 24.

34. Ralph W. Rader, "Defoe, Richardson, Joyce, and the Concept of Form in the Novel," in *Autobiography, Biography and the Novel* (Los Angeles: University of California Press, 1973), p. 33.

35. Ralph W. Rader, "Fact, Theory, and Literary Explanation," *Critical Inquiry* 1 (1974): 245–46.

36. See Hans Vaihinger, *The Philosophy of "As If": A System of the Theoretical, Practical and Religious*

Fictions of Mankind, trans. C. K. Ogden (London: Routledge & Kegan Paul, 1924), pp. 74–76, 313–18.

37. See Shelley, *A Defense of Poetry,* p. 503.

38. The aesthetic valuative criteria used in this study are most obviously manifest in formalist and de-constructionist criticism, the ethical criteria in reader-response criticism, particularly that of Stanley Fish. See Fish's *Self-Consuming Artifacts: The Experience of Seventeenth-Century Literature* (Berkeley: University of California Press, 1972), particularly chaps. 1 and 7. See Albert Camus, *La Chute* (Paris: Gallimard, 1956), for a "literary" inquiry into the powers and perfidies of judgment. By repeatedly manipulating its reader into judgments or readings that are repeatedly shown to be misjudgments or misreadings, the "récit" dramatizes even as it thematizes both the inevitability of judgment and its danger.

39. All generic explanations happen within the ongoing conversation that I am here calling the text's interpretive history. John Reichert initially seems to agree with this point: "the placing of a work in one genre can never rule out the interpretive questions raised by some other genre to which it may also belong" ("More than Kin and Less than Kind: The Limits of Genre Theory," in *Theories of Literary Genre,* ed. Joseph P. Strelka [University Park: Pennsylvania State University Press, 1978], p. 65). Reichert, however, argues on the assumption that a text may or may not *intrinsically* belong to a given genre or genres. My point is that a generic argument is convincing in part because it comprehends a text's previous generic definitions, whether by rebuttal, assimilation, or revision.

40. Paul de Man, "Introduction" to Jauss, *Toward an Aesthetic of Reception,* p. xiii.

41. Douglas Hofstadter, *Gödel, Escher, Bach: An Eternal Golden Braid* (New York: Random House, 1980), p. 15. Hofstadter's formulation of self-reflexivity, the "strange loop," is indebted to Gödel's Incompleteness Theorem, which states that in any sufficiently complex or powerful system there are true statements whose proof is beyond the resources of that system. These statements (which, for Gödel, were statements of number theory) can be understood on two different levels: as statements of number theory and as statements about those statements. This latter "level" analogizes with critical theory, the former with critical practice, and the formulation itself thereby offers an extremely suggestive if dizzying analogy for the fusion of theory and practice in our own discipline.

42. Vaihinger, *The Philosophy of "As If,"* p. 108.

43. See Jonathan Culler, *Structuralist Poetics: Structuralism, Linguistics and the Study of Literature* (Ithaca: Cornell University Press, 1975), particularly pp. 207–13.

44. See Paul Ricoeur, "The Metaphorical Process as Cognition, Imagination, and Feeling," *Critical Inquiry* 5 (1978): 143–59, for a challenging attempt to define in terms of metaphor the unity of cognitive, imaginative, and emotional processes. Ricoeur's notion of "predicative assimilation," defined as a "*making* similar, that is, semantically proximate, the terms that the metaphorical utterance brings together" (p. 148), is related to the notion of deductive genre as here defined. See also Hayden White's argument in *Tropics of Discourse* that "the model of the syllogism itself displays clear evidence of troping": "The move from the major premise (all men are mortal) to the *choice* of the datum to serve as the minor (Socrates is a man) is itself a tropological move, a 'swerve' from the universal to the particular which logic cannot preside over, since it is logic itself that is being served by this move. Every *applied* syllogism contains an enthymemic element, this element consisting of nothing but the *decision* to move from the plane of universal propositions (themselves extended synecdoches) to that of singular existential statements (these being extended metonymies)" (p. 3). See also Georg Wilhelm Friedrich Hegel, *The Logic of Hegel,* 2d rev. ed., trans. William Wallace (London: Oxford University Press, 1892), pp. 314–29.

45. Kenneth Burke, "Definition of Man," *Hudson Review* 17 (1963–64); rpt. in *Language as Symbolic Action,* p. 5.

46. Robert Langbaum, *The Poetry of Experience: The Dramatic Monologue in Modern Literary Tradition* (New York: W. W. Norton, 1957).

47. Burke, *Counter-Statement,* p. 160.

48. Chaim Perelman has observed that "everything that promotes perception of a device—the mechanical, farfetched, abstract, codified, and for-

mal aspects of a speech—will prompt the search for a reality that is dissociated from it" (Chaim Perelman and L. Olbrechts-Tyteca, *The New Rhetoric: A Treatise on Argumentation,* trans. John Wilkinson and Purcell Weaver [Notre Dame: University of Notre Dame Press, 1969], p. 453). Perelman is speaking of argumentation generally, but we can usefully transfer his insight to genre criticism, wherein genre equals the "device" which, when foregrounded, prompts us to go beneath and behind in search of the textual reality it necessarily reduces and distorts. It is when the device is thoroughly exposed or used up through the sorites that we come face to face with citations from the poem itself, citations that I am here calling "hermeneutic detritus." Thus does the working of genre, by a paradoxical logic and by its yoking with the unique demands made of a *literary* explanation, finally depend upon the genre's *not* working in the more usual sense. For an explicit example of this process, see Avrom Fleishman, "*Wuthering Heights:* The Love of a Sylph and a Gnome," in *Fiction and the Ways of Knowing: Essays on British Novels* (Austin: University of Texas Press, 1978), pp. 37–51. Fleishman begins thus: "The premise stated in the title of this essay will require provisional justification, although its credibility can only gradually be gained" (p. 37). Fleishman then proceeds to this justification, reading the novel in terms of alchemical doctrines. When he has used up their explanatory power, he concludes by juxtaposing citations from both *Wuthering Heights* and alchemical texts, then remarking that "these doctrines may be related to *Wuthering Heights* in a sequence of declining specificity" and that "at this point, the theories of the alchemists begin to distinguish themselves sharply from the wider Gnostic tradition, and by the same token their application to the novel becomes increasingly problematic" (p. 50).

49. The most lucid and forceful statement of this point is Firmat's (in "The Novel as Genres"), which is phrased as a critique of Todorov's distinction, which, in turn, typifies that made by most theorists of genre:

If one reviews Todorov's remarks, it becomes clear, first of all, that these two categories do not in fact designate two kinds of genres, but rather two ostensibly different ways of arriving at generic concepts. When he states that historical genres are "le fruit d'une observation des faits littéraires," while theoretical genres "sont deduits d'une théorie de la littérature," Todorov is in effect discriminating between inductive and deductive concept formation. The fact that he regards historical genres as subsets of complex theoretical genres bears out their essential likeness. Were the two categories qualitatively different, that is, were Todorov really defining two *kinds* of genres, this subordination would be impossible. . . . The two seem to be dissimilar only insofar as they were reached by different avenues. . . . What separates historical and theoretical genealogy is simply an illusion, the illusion that one can form theories in a rigorously inductive manner." (pp. 275–76)

Firmat refers us to Karl Popper's *The Logic of Scientific Discovery* (New York: Basic Books, 1959), as does Rader ("Fact, Theory, and Literary Explanation"). Popper's deductivism, his argument that induction necessarily leads to an infinite regress (p. 29), his definition of a theory's power in terms of its explanatory range—all make his theory seem readily transferable to literary studies. As in part it surely is. But we should keep in mind that Popper is explaining theories that would explain the world rather than texts, theories that, unlike literary theories or genres, can be falsified.

50. As I am arguing throughout, "insufficiently" and "sufficiently" are pragmatic and rhetorical criteria. They measure an explanation's success in terms of its function, purpose, and audience—terms that are open to change in time and, even at any given time, may be particularized in more than one way.

51. René Wellek and Austin Warren, *Theory of Literature* (New York: Harcourt, Brace & World, 1956), pp. 234–35.

52. Paul Hernadi, *Beyond Genre: New Directions in Literary Classification* (Ithaca: Cornell University Press, 1972), p. 184. For a "historical genre" study, which also proposes to be a theory of genre, see Alastair Fowler, *Kinds of Literature: An Introduction to the Theory of Genres and Modes* (Cambridge, Mass.: Harvard University Press, 1982). Fowler is primarily a historian of genre, interested in how genres evolve, die, and revive. He defines his theory against systematizing theories such as Frye's or Hernadi's. Finally, see Fredric Jameson, *The Political Unconscious: Narrative as a Socially Symbolic Act* (Ithaca: Cornell University Press, 1981),

particularly chap. 2, "Magical Narratives: On the Dialectical Use of Genre Criticism." For the purposes of the present study, Jameson's most interesting point comes at the end of his lengthy and rigorous Marxist inquiry, where he notes that the "final moment of the generic operation, in which the working categories of genre are themselves historically deconstructed and abandoned, suggests a final axiom, according to which *all* generic categories, even the most time-hallowed and traditional, are ultimately to be understood (or "estranged") as mere ad hoc, experimental constructs, devised for a specific textual occasion and abandoned like so much scaffolding when the analysis has done its work" (p. 145). This "final axiom" is, in effect, my beginning premise.

APPLICATION

In the course of his long career, Northrop Frye frequently wrote about The Tempest. *The late essay that follows is his most extensive commentary on the play. He begins, typically, by addressing questions of genre, claiming that Shakespeare's final romances are the "genuine culmination" of his career, the plays wherein he "reaches the bedrock of drama, the musical, poetic, and spectacular panorama of magic and fantasy in which there is no longer tragedy or comedy, but an action passing through tragic and comic moods to a conclusion of serenity and peace." Appropriately, from Frye's point of view, these transcendent dramatic structures are built from the crudest and most primitive materials, and* The Tempest, *particularly, has aspects of mystery, magic, and fairy tale. All such terms, of course, imply a contrasting "reality" as a point of reference, but it is precisely that sense of reality that is put in question by the action of the play.*

Although Frye touches in passing on issues like the magus as modern scientist or Caliban as oppressed colonial, for him the center of the play is this conflict between illusion and reality. In our earlier selection from The Critical Path, *Frye remarks on the importance of the conception of an "unfallen" world, a world most of us can experience only through the "articulated analogies" of literature, especially in the "idealized world of romance, pastoral, or apocalyptic vision." Such a vision, the end or goal of our literary experience, is fittingly supplied in Shakespeare's last great work. Yet the play's movement from illusion to reality is paradoxical, and "it seems highly significant that this vision of the reality of nature from which we have fallen away can be attained only through some kind of theatrical illusion." That is to say, only through some kind of "articulated analogy" that art, and only art, can supply. At this level, only the imagination can deliver the real world.*

Shakespeare's *The Tempest*

Northrop Frye

Reprinted by permission of the estate of Northrop Frye from *The Northrop Frye Newsletter* 2 (Summer 1990): 19–27.

In Shakespeare's day, if a cultivated person had been asked what a comedy was, he would probably have said that it was a play which depicted people in the middle and lower ranks of society, observed their foibles and follies, and was careful not to diverge too far from what would be recognized as credible, if not necessarily plausible, action. This was Ben Jonson's conception of comedy, supported by many prefaces and manifestos, and is illustrated by the general practice of English comic writers down to our own day. But the earlier Elizabethan dramatists — Peele, Greene, Lyly — wrote in a very different idiom of comedy, one which introduced themes of romance and fantasy, as well as characters from higher social ranks. The first fact about Shakespeare, considered as a writer of comedy, is that he followed the older practice and ignored the Jonsonian type of comedy, even in plays which are later than Jonson's early ones.

One reason for this is not hard to see. Observing men and manners on a certain level of credibility demands a degree of sophistication, whereas the fairy tale plots of Peele's *Old Wives' Tale* and Lyly's *Endymion* appeal to a more childlike desire to see a show and be told a story, without having to think about whether the story is "true to life" or not. The child wants primarily to know what comes next; he may not care so much about the logic of its relation to what it follows. If the adult completely loses this childlike response, he loses something very central to the dramatic experience, and Shakespeare was careful never to lose it as a playwright. Jonson tends to scold his audiences for not being mature enough to appreciate him: Shakespeare says (in the epilogue to *Twelfth Night*), "We'll strive to please you every day," and never fails to include some feature or incident that is incredible, that belongs to magic, fairyland, folktale, or farce rather than to the observation of men and manners. In Jonsonian comedy the play is intended to be a transparent medium for such observation: we learn about life through the comedy. In Shakespearean comedy the play is opaque: it surrounds us and wraps us up, with nothing to do but to see and hear what is passing. This does not mean that an unusual or unfamiliar type of story is wanted: again, the simple and childlike response is to the familiar and conventional, new variants of well-loved stories that have been told many times before. Shakespeare's comedies are all very different from one another, but he understands this response well enough to keep repeating his comic devices.

Further, not only does Shakespeare adhere to the pre-Jonsonian type of comedy, but he moves closer to it as he goes on. The plays are classified by the First Folio as comedies, histories, and tragedies, but criticism has isolated a fourth genre, that of romance, to which Shakespeare devoted his main attention in his last years. We have also come to realize that the romances are not a relaxation or letdown after the strenuous efforts of *King Lear* or *Macbeth*, as often used to be said, but are the genuine culmination of Shakespeare's dramatic achievement. These are the plays in which Shakespeare reaches the bedrock of drama, the musical, poetic, and spectacular panorama of magic and fantasy in which there is no longer tragedy or comedy, but an action passing through tragic and comic moods to a conclusion of serenity and peace.

We notice that the plays that seem most to have influenced Shakespeare in writing the romances were much cruder than those of Peele or Lyly. One of them was *Mucedorus*, a play of the 1590s revived around 1609, which clearly held the affections of the reading public as well as playgoers, as it went through seventeen editions in about eighty years. It is a very simple-minded play about a prince who goes in disguise to another country to woo a princess, and who gains her after baffling a cowardly villain and rescuing her and himself from a wild man in a forest. There is a prologue in which two figures named "Comedy" and "Envy" engage in a sharp dispute about the shape of the forthcoming action, the former promising a happy ending and the latter many pitfalls along the way. In another early play, *The Rare Triumphs of Love and Fortune*, which features a magician and his daughter, like *The Tempest*, we begin with an assembly of gods and a debate between Fortuna and Venus, again over the character of the story that is to follow.

From such unlikely (as it seems to us) sources, Shakespeare drew hints for an expanding stage action that can include not only all social levels from royalty to clowns, but gods and magicians with superhuman powers as well. The romances end happily, or at any rate quietly, but they do not avoid the tragic: *The Winter's Tale* in particular passes through and contains a complete tragic action on its way to a more festive conclusion, and *Cymbeline*, which has at least a token historical theme (Cymbeline was a real king of Britain, and his coins are in the British Museum), is actually classified as a tragedy in the Folio.

Such plays are "tragicomedies," a genre that not only Shakespeare but Beaumont and Fletcher were popularizing from about 1607 onward. In the preface to Fletcher's *Faithful Shepherdess* (ca. 1609), it is said that in a tragicomedy a god is "lawful," i.e., superhuman agents can be introduced with decorum.

But to expand into a divine world means reducing the scale of the human one. The jealousy of Leontes and Posthumus is quite as unreasonable as that of Othello, but it is not on the gigantic human scale of Othello's: we see it from a perspective in which it seems petty and ridiculous as well. The form of the romance thus moves closer to the puppet show, which again, as Goethe's *Wilhelm Meister* reminds us, is a form of popular drama with a strong appeal to children, precisely because they can see that the action is being manipulated. The debates of Comedy and Envy in *Mucedorus,* and of Venus and Fortuna in *The Rare Triumphs* introduce us to another approach to the manipulating of action. Here we are told that the play to follow is connected with certain genres, and that characters who personify these genres are taking a hand in the action. The notion of Comedy as a character in the action of a comedy may seem strange at first, but is deeply involved in the structure of Shakespearean comedy. Let us look at a comedy of Shakespeare that many people have found very puzzling, *Measure for Measure,* from this point of view.

In *Measure for Measure,* Vincentio, the Duke of Vienna (which Shakespeare seems to have thought of as an Italian town), announces his departure, leaving his deputy Angelo in charge to tighten up laws against sexual irregularity. Everything goes wrong, and Angelo, who sincerely wants to be an honest and conscientious official, is not only impossibly rigorous, condemning to death young Claudio for a very trifling breach of the law, but is thrown headlong by his first temptation, which is to seduce Claudio's sister Isabella when she comes to plead for his life. The action leads up to the dialogue of the condemned Claudio and his sister in prison. Claudio's nerve breaks down under the horror of approaching death, and he urges Isabella to yield to Angelo. Isabella, totally demoralized by her first glimpse of human evil, and, perhaps, by finding herself more attracted to Angelo and his proposal than she would ever have thought possible, explodes in a termagant fury. She says: "I'll pray a thousand prayers for thy death" — hardly a possible procedure for any Christian, though

Isabella wants to be a cloistered nun. Everything is drifting toward a miserable and total impasse, when the disguised Duke steps forward. The rhythm abruptly changes from blank verse to prose, and the Duke proceeds to outline a complicated and very unplausible comic plot, complete with the naive device known as the "bed trick," substituting one woman for another in the dark. It is clear that this point is the "peripety" or reversal of the action, and that the play falls into the form of a diptych, the first half tragic in direction and the second half comic. Vincentio has the longest speaking part of any character in Shakespearean comedy: a sure sign that he has the role of a subdramatist, a deputy producer of the stage action. *Measure for Measure,* then, is not a play about the philosophy of government or sexual morality or the folly of trying to legislate people into virtue. It is a play about the relation of the structure of comedy to these things. The Duke's actions make no kind of realistic sense, but they make structural dramatic sense, and only the structure of comedy, intervening in human life, can bring genuine repentance out of Angelo and genuine forgiveness out of Isabella.

In *The Winter's Tale* the action also forms a diptych, and again we have first a tragic movement proceeding toward chaos and general muddle. This action comprises Leontes' jealousy, the disappearance of his wife Hermione, the death of his son Mamillius, the exposing of the infant Perdita, and the devouring of Antigonus, who exposes her, by a bear. Then a shepherd and his son enter the action: as in *Measure for Measure,* the rhythm immediately changes from blank verse to prose. The shepherd finds the infant and the son sees the death of Antigonus, and the shepherd's remark, "Thou mettest with things dying, I with things new born," emphasizes the separating into two parts of the total action. This separating of the action is referred to later on in a recognition scene, not presented but reported in the conversation of some gentlemen: "all the instruments that aided to expose the child were even then lost when it was found." Such phrases indicate that the real dividing point in the action is the finding of Perdita at the end of the third act, not the sixteen years that are said to elapse before the fourth act begins. In the final scene of the play Paulina, the widow of Antigonus, says to Hermione, who is pretending to be a statue: "our Perdita is found." This is the formula that first draws speech from Hermione.

Paulina, though an agent of the comic structure of the second half of the play, is not its generator: that appears to be some power connected with the Delphic oracle, which had previously announced that Leontes would live without an heir "if that which is lost be not found."

In *The Tempest* there is no clearly marked peripety or reversal of action. The reason is that the entire play is a reversal of an action which has taken place before the play begins. This concentration on the second half of a total dramatic action accounts for many features of *The Tempest*. It is quite a short play, which is why Prospero's role has fewer lines than Vincentio's, though he dominates the action even more completely. Again, we are constantly aware of the passing of a brief interval of time, an interval of a few hours, very close to the period of time we spend in watching the play. The dramatic action is generated by Prospero and carried out by Ariel, whose role is parallel to that of Pauline in *The Winter's Tale*. But because only the second or rearranging half of the action is presented, the characters have no chance to mess up their lives in the way that Angelo and Leontes do. The theme of frustrated aggressive action recurs several times: when Ferdinand tries to draw his sword on Prospero, when Antonio and Sebastian attempt to murder Alonso and Gonzalo, and later to attack Ariel, and when Stephano's conspiracy is baffled. Prospero's magic controls everything, and the effect is of an audience being taken inside a play, so that they not only watch the play but, so to speak, see it being put on.

Ordinarily, in our dramatic experience, this sense of a play being created before our eyes is one that we can only get when we are watching an action that seems to be partly improvised on the spot, where we know the general outline of the story but not its particulars. Various devices such as Brecht's "alienating" techniques and the Stanislavski method of acting attempt to create such a feeling in modern audiences. In Shakespeare's day this type of improvising action appeared in the *commedia dell' arte*, which was well known in England, and influenced Shakespeare in all periods of his production. Some of the sketchy plot outlines (*scenari*) of this type of play have been preserved, and we note that they feature magicians, enchanted islands, reunions of families, clown scenes (*lazzi*), and the like. Such *scenari* are probably as close as we shall ever get to finding a general source for *The Tempest*.

Not only does Prospero arrange the action, but we are seldom allowed to forget that it is specifically a dramatic action that is going on. Prospero orders Ariel to disguise himself as a nymph of the sea, while remaining invisible to everyone else. In reading the play, we might wonder what point there is in dressing up so elaborately if he is to remain invisible, but in the theater we realize at once that he will not be invisible to us. Again, an illusory banquet is presented to and snatched away from the Court Party, and Ariel, as a harpy, makes a somber speech condemning the "three men of sin." It is an impressive and oracular speech, but we hardly notice this because Prospero immediately undercuts it, coming forward to commend Ariel on doing a good actor's job. The opposite emphasis comes in the epilogue, when Prospero says:

As you from crimes would pardon'd be,
Let your indulgence set me free.

The epilogue represents only the convention of asking the audience to applaud the play, so we hardly notice how grave the tone is. Yet it is clear that the restructuring of the lives of the characters in the play is being said to be a deeply serious operation, with an application in it for ourselves. We have not merely been watching a fairy tale, we feel, but participating in some kind of mystery. What kind of mystery?

The Tempest is almost a comic parody of a revenge tragedy, in which there is repentance, forgiveness, and reconciliation instead of revenge. The characters are divided into three groups and each is put through ordeals, illusions, and a final awakening to some kind of self-knowledge. There is hardly a character in the play who is not believed by other characters to be dead, and in the final recognition scene there is something very like a sense that everyone is being raised from the dead, as there is with Hermione in the last scene of *The Winter's Tale*. Prospero actually claims the power of raising the dead in his renunciation speech, and he also pretends that Miranda was drowned in the storm he raised.

The Court Party goes through a labyrinth of "forthrights and meanders" with strange shapes appearing and disappearing around them, but nevertheless they finally arrive at a state of self-recognition where Gonzalo is able to say that each has found himself "when [formerly] no man was his own." Gonzalo himself is on the highest moral level of the

Court Party: in contrast to Antonio and Sebastian, he finds the island a pleasant place and his garments fresh, and he is excluded from Ariel's condemnation of the "three men of sin." Alonso comes next: his repentance and his gaining of self-awareness seem equally genuine, and he is clearly the focus of Prospero's regenerative efforts. Next is Sebastian, a weak and ineffectual person who does what the stronger characters around him suggest that he do. In the final scene he seems quite cheerful, and we feel that, while nothing very profound has happened to him, he will be as easily persuaded to virtue as to vice. Antonio, who speaks only once in the last scene, in reply to a direct question, is a more doubtful quantity. Stephano, Trinculo, and Caliban go through a kind of parody of the Court Party ordeals and illusions, yet they too reach some level of self-awareness. Stephano is reconciled to losing his imaginary kingdom, and Caliban, who has emerged as much the most intelligent of the three, is apparently ready to be weaned from idolatry, and so to take the first step in self-knowledge himself.

To the extent that people are acquiring self-knowledge, then, they seem to be taking their places in a moral hierarchy. Yet as we look further into it, it seems to be less a moral hierarchy than an imaginative one. They move from illusion to reality as the play presents these categories. What is illusion? Primarily, it is what such people as Antonio consider reality. As soon as Alonso falls asleep, Antonio starts a plot to murder him: this is *Realpolitik*, the way things are done in the real world. Similarly, he takes a very "realistic" view of the island, in contrast to Gonzalo's. But the play itself moves toward a reversal of this view of reality. Antonio's one remark in the last scene is that Caliban is a "plain fish"—one of several indications that living on his level is symbolically living under water. The illusions in the mazy wanderings of the Court Party are more real than Antonio's life without conscience.

What, then, is reality, as the play presents it? That is more difficult, and Prospero seems to agree with T. S. Eliot that whatever reality is, humankind cannot bear very much of it. But just as "reality" for Antonio turns out to be illusion, so perhaps what is illusion on the much higher level of Ferdinand and Miranda might turn out to be closer to reality. The masque put on for their benefit by Prospero is a vision of the highest form of "reality" in our cultural tradition: the vision of what in Christianity is called

"unfallen" nature, the original world before the fall, the model divine creation that God observed and saw to be good. The dance of nymphs and August reapers seems to suggest the "perpetual spring" which is a traditional attribute of Paradise, and the three goddesses of earth, sky, and rainbow suggest the newly washed world after Noah's flood, when the curse was lifted from the ground and a regularity of seasons was promised. The vision, however, is one of a renewed power and energy of nature rather than simply a return to a lost Paradise: a sense of a "brave new world" appropriate as a wedding offering to a young and attractive couple. And it seems highly significant that this vision of the reality of nature from which we have fallen away can be attained only through some kind of theatrical illusion.

The action of the play, then, moves from illusion to reality in a paradoxical way. What we think of as reality is illusion: not all of us are realistic in the criminal way that Antonio is, but, as Prospero's great speech at the end of the masque says, in our world everything that we call real is merely an illusion that lasts a little longer than some other illusions. At the other end, what we think of as real can come to us only as a temporary illusion, specifically a dramatic illusion. This is what the wedding masque symbolizes in the play: the masque is presented to Ferdinand and Miranda, but the whole play is being presented to us, and we must be sure that we omit no aspect of it.

The play keeps entirely within the order of nature: there are no gods or oracles, though Alonso expects them, and Prospero's magic operates entirely within the four elements below the moon. Sycorax, like other witches, could draw down the moon, i.e., bring "lunatic" influences to bear on human life, but this is not Prospero's interest, though it may be within his power. In the action that took place before the play began, when Prospero was Duke of Milan, his brother Antonio had become the *persona* or dramatic mask of the absentminded Prospero, and gradually expanded until he became "absolute Milan," the entire Duke, until Prospero and the infant Miranda vanished into another world in an open boat (for Milan, like Bohemia in *The Winter's Tale*, appears to have a seacoast). On the enchanted island this dramatic action goes into reverse, Prospero expanding into the real Duke of Milan and Antonio shrinking to a kind of discarded shell. Prospero's life in Milan is what passes for real life in our ordinary experience:

the action of *The Tempest* presents us with the aspect of nature which is real but, like the dark side of the moon, constantly hidden from us. We note in passing the folktale theme of the struggle of brothers, the rightful heir exiled only to return later in triumph.

The feeling that the play is some kind of mystery or initiation, then, is a quite normal and central response to it. The connection between drama and rites of initiation probably goes back to the Old Stone Age. In classical times there were several mystery religions with dramatic forms of initiation, the most celebrated being those of Eleusis, near Athens, which were held in honor of the earth goddess Demeter, the Roman Ceres who is the central figure in Prospero's masque. In the eighteenth century Bishop Warburton suggested that the sixth book of the *Aeneid*, depicting Aeneas's journey to the lower world, was a disguised form of Eleusinian initiation, and in 1921 Colin Still, in *Shakespeare's Mystery Play*, applied a similar theory to *The Tempest*. He noted that the route of the Court Party, from Tunis in Africa to the coast of Italy, paralleled the route of Aeneas from Carthage, and the otherwise pointless identification of Tunis with Carthage made by Gonzalo in Act II, along with the equally pointless amusement of Antonio and Sebastian, seems to be emphasizing the parallel. I suspect that Colin Still's book was an influence on T. S. Eliot's *Waste Land*, published the next year, though Eliot does not mention Still before his preface to Wilson Knight's *Wheel of Fire* in 1930.

Colin Still, recognizing that Shakespeare could have had no direct knowledge of classical mystery rites, ascribed the symbolic coincidences he found with *The Tempest* to an inner "necessity," to the fact that the imagination must always talk in some such terms when it gets to a sufficient pitch of intensity. I should add only that the "necessity" is specifically a necessity of dramatic structure. We can see this more clearly if we turn to a dramatic form which not only did not influence Shakespeare but was nowhere in his cultural tradition, the No play of Japan. In a No play what usually happens is that two travelers encounter a ghost who was a famous hero in his former life, and who recreates the story of his exploits in this ghostly world, which is also presented as a world of reconciliation and mutual understanding. This type of drama is linked to Buddhist beliefs in a world intervening between death and rebirth, but we do not need such beliefs to make imaginative sense of No plays. We do recognize in them, however, a very

powerful and integral dramatic structure. When we enter the world of *The Tempest*, with its curious feeling of being a world withdrawn from both death and birth, we recognize again that that world is being specifically identified with the world of the drama.

As often in Shakespeare, the characters in *The Tempest* are invited to a meeting to be held after the play in which the puzzling features of their experiences will be explained to them. This seems a curious and unnecessary convention, but it is true to the situation of drama, where the audience always knows more about what is going on than the characters do, besides being in a greater state of freedom, because they are able to walk out of the theater. Each character in *The Tempest*, at the beginning of the play, is lost in a private drama of his own. This is true even of Prospero, in the long dialogues he holds with Miranda, Ariel, and Caliban in Act I, mainly for the benefit of the audience. Through the action of the play, a communal dramatic sense gradually consolidates, in which all the characters identify themselves within the same drama, a drama which the audience is finally invited to enter.

The Tempest, like its predecessor *The Winter's Tale*, is both comedy and romance. In the tradition of comedy that Shakespeare inherited from Plautus and Terence, what typically happens is that a young man and a young woman wish to get married, that there is parental opposition, and that this opposition is eventually evaded and the marriage takes place. Comedy thus moves toward the triumph of youth over age, and toward the vision of the renewal and rebirth of nature which such a triumph symbolizes, however little of nature there may be in a Roman comedy. In *The Tempest*, the conventionally comic aspect of the play is represented by the marriage of Ferdinand and Miranda. Prospero puts up a token opposition to this marriage, apparently because it is customary for fathers to do so, and he forces Ferdinand into the role of servant, as part of the token tests and ordeals which traditionally make the suitor worthy of his mistress.

The corresponding comic element in *The Winter's Tale* centered on the successful marriage of Florizel and Perdita in the teeth of strenuous parental opposition. Florizel temporarily renounces his princely heritage and exchanges garments with the thief Autolycus, just as Ferdinand takes over Caliban's role as a bearer of logs. Here again the renewal of nature is a part of the theme, more explicitly because of the romance element in the play. The great sheep-shearing festival in the fourth act of *The Winter's Tale* is a vision of the power of nature extending through four seasons, that being probably what the dance of the twelve satyrs symbolizes. Nature has it all her own way throughout this scene, and Perdita, the child of nature, announces that she will have nothing to do with "bastard" flowers adulterated by art. Nor will she listen to Polixenes' sophisticated idealism about art as being really nature's way of improving nature. The traditional symbol of the domination of art over nature, Orpheus, whose music could command animals and plants, appears only in parody, in connection with the ballads of Autolycus.

But this triumph of nature and its powers of renewal and rebirth, with its center of gravity in the future, is only the lesser recognition in the play. The main emphasis comes not on the successful wooing of the younger pair, but, as usual in Shakespearean romance, on the reintegrating of the world of their elders. The greater recognition scene takes place in a world of art, Paulina's chapel, where we are told that we are being presented with a work of sculpture and painting, where music is heard, where references to the art of magic are made. In the vision of the triumph of art, the emphasis is not on renewal and rebirth but on resurrection, the transformation from death to life. And just as the vision of nature's renewal and rebirth relates primarily to the future, so the triumph of art and resurrection relates primarily to the past, where the words of the oracle, spoken sixteen years earlier, are brought to life in the present, and where old sins and blunders are healed up. In his essay *The Decay of Lying*, Oscar Wilde says of music that it "creates for one a past of which one has been ignorant, and fills one with a sense of sorrows that have been hidden from one's tears." Perhaps it is the function of all art to "create a past" in this sense of revealing to us the range of experience that our timid senses and reasonings largely screen out. The power of nature gives us a hope that helps us to face the future: the power of art gives us a faith that helps us to face the past.

The Tempest is concerned even more than *The Winter's Tale* with the triumph of art, and much less with the triumph of nature. This is mainly because Prospero is a magus figure: in Elizabethan English "art" meant mostly magic, as it does here. Prospero renounces his magic at the end of the play: this was conventional, for while magic was a great attraction as dramatic entertainment, it was a highly suspicious operation in real life; hence all dramatic magicians were well advised to renounce their powers when the play drew to a close. But there is more to Prospero's renunciation of magic than this. We recall the deep melancholy of his "our revels now are ended" speech at the end of the masque, and his somber comment on Miranda's enthusiasm for her brave new world: "'tis new to thee." In the world of reality that we can reach only through dramatic illusion, the past is the source of faith and the future the source of hope. In the world of illusion that we take for reality, the past is only the no longer and the future only the not yet: one vanishes into nothingness and the other, after proving itself to be much the same, vanishes after it.

As a magus, Prospero is fulfilling the past, reliving and restructuring his former life as Duke of Milan. To do so, he must take an obsessive interest in time: "the very minute bids thee ope thine ear," he says to Miranda, referring to astrology, and he later tells her that the fortunes of all the rest of his life depend on his seizing the present moment. Antonio's urging the same plea on Sebastian later is a direct parody of this. Prospero's anxiety about time interpenetrates very curiously with his anxieties as a theatrical producer, making sure that Ariel comes in on cue and that his audience is properly attentive and impressed. Such strain and such anxiety cannot go on for long, and all through the play Prospero, no less than Ariel, is longing for the end of it.

Prospero's magic summons up the romantic enthusiasm for magic with which the sixteenth century had begun, in Agrippa and Paracelsus and Pico della Mirandola and the legendary Faust. It continued for most of the next century, and among contemporary scholars Frances Yates in particular has speculated about its curious relation to Shakespeare's romances. But this vision of a power and wisdom beyond human scope seems to be passing away when Ariel is released and melts into the thin air from whence he came. Whether magic was a reality or a dream, in either case it could only end as dreams do. In Shakespeare's day magic and science were very imperfectly separated, and today, in a postscientific age when they seem to be coming together again, the magus figure has revived in contemporary fiction, with much the same dreams attached to it. Such a return may make *The Tempest* more "relevant" to us today, but if so, the weariness and disillusionment of Prospero are equally "relevant."

Just as the mere past, the vanishing age, seems to be summed up in the figure of Ariel, so the mere future, the yet-to-vanish new age, seems to be summed up in the figure of Caliban. Caliban's name seems to echo the "cannibals" of Montaigne's famous essay, a passage from which forms the basis for Gonzalo's reverie about an ideal commonwealth in Act II. Around the figure of Caliban, again, there are many phrases indicating Shakespeare's reading in contemporary pamphlets dealing with the first English efforts to settle on the American coast. Every editor of *The Tempest* has to record this fact, while pointing out that Prospero's island is in the Mediterranean, not the Atlantic, and has nothing to do with the New World. Still, the historical situation of *The Tempest*, coming at the end of an age of speculative magic and at the beginning of an age of colonization in the New World, seems to give Caliban a peculiar and poignant resonance. Caliban is the shape of things to come in the future "real" world, not a brave new world of hope, but, for the most part, a mean and cruel world, full of slavery and greed, of which many Calibans will be the victims.

Of course, we had rather have the past of faith and the future of hope than the past of dream and the future of nightmare, but what choice have we? This is perhaps another way of asking what *The Tempest*, as dramatic illusion, has to give us in the way of reality. When Shakespeare touches on such subjects he is apt to bury what he says in unlikely places, passages of dialogue that the eye and ear could easily pass over as mere "filler." We find such a passage in the inane babble of Antonio and Sebastian at the beginning of the second act. Sebastian's response to a narrow escape from drowning is a kind of giggling hysteria, and Antonio falls in with this mood and encourages it, because he knows what he wants to do with Sebastian later on. In the course of the dialogue Gonzalo, who is speaking with a wisdom and insight not his own, assures the others that "Tunis was Carthage." We pick up the implication that *The Tempest*, as explained, is repeating the experience of Aeneas voyaging from Carthage to Italy to build a new Troy, and presenting an imaginative moment, at once retrospective and prospective, in the history of the third Troy, as England was conventionally supposed to be. The dialogue goes on:

> ANT. What impossible matter will he make easy next?
> SEB. I think he will carry this island home in his pocket, and give it his son for an apple.
> ANT. And, sowing the kernels of it in the sea, bring forth more islands.

Gonzalo never claims to make impossible matters easy, but Prospero can do so, and by implication Shakespeare himself can. And it is Shakespeare who gives us, as members of his audience, his island, as one would give a child an apple, but with the further hope that we will not stop with eating the apple, but will use its seeds to create for ourselves new seas and even more enchanted islands.

APPLICATION

Anne Williams argues that although many sensitive and sympathetic critics have complained of elements of incoherence in Wordsworth's Ode, the poem's order and unity become clear when we see the Ode in its proper literary context: "All its divergent strains are subservient to one plot or mythos . . . a pattern of death and rebirth, specifically that of the myth of the fortunate fall, as told by Milton." A genetic critic, like Ross, will read the poem as autobiography; a mimetic critic, like Trilling, will read it as a representation of the general human development toward a sadder but wiser maturity; both kinds of readers may be inclined to see the conclusion as less triumphant than the speaker claims. But, Williams argues, both kinds of readers have chosen the wrong contexts. "Once it is recognized, the Ode's pervasive undertone of Miltonic allusion transforms our sense of the Ode's coherence and suggests a persuasive explication of its concluding stanza." Readers attuned to the Miltonic echoes will see that Wordsworth has, characteristically, replayed Milton's epic in lyric form and restaged the great Christian theme of the fortunate fall in the mind of the speaker. And readers attuned to generic conventions will see that as the Ode develops, it modulates from the muted voice of the pastoral elegy to the bardic voice of the great ode. Thus, to see the poem in its literary context is to see

that the apparent disunity is really a calculated shift of generic models that appropriately signals the speaker's new level of understanding. "To recognize that Wordsworth's ode embodies, consciously and pointedly, a structural pattern common to Paradise Lost *and made manifest at the psychological, stylistic, and generic levels of the poem, is to see its often alleged disunity in quite a new context." Specifically, it is to see it in an intertextual context, the context which, Williams claims, yields the fullest understanding of the poem.*

The *Intimations Ode:* Wordsworth's Fortunate Fall

Anne Williams

Reprinted by permission from *Romanticism Past and Present* 5:1 (1981): 1–13.

Most readers profess to admire the *Intimations Ode*; yet for many it exemplifies that paradox of literature, the imperfect masterpiece. A surprising number of sensitive and sympathetic critics have noted disturbing intimations of incoherence in the poem.[1] Certainly the *Ode* embraces a bewildering association of the personal and the universal, of thought and feeling, of sorrow and celebration. I propose, however, that the *Ode*'s order and unity are more than merely adequate. All its divergent strains are subservient to one plot or *mythos*: the plot, "soul of the work" (Aristotle's phrase), is a pattern of death and rebirth, specifically that of the myth of the fortunate fall, as told by Milton. The *Ode* is full of buried (and seldom noted) allusions to *Paradise Lost* which indicate a consistent analogy of situation and a consistent pattern of psychological response, that response being to a loss which touches the speaker of the poem both as man and as poet.

This unfamiliar thesis rests on several familiar assumptions about the nature of Miltonic influence and about the *Ode*. First, Harold Bloom has specified Milton's influential role as that of a "precursor" (though Bloom is thinking primarily of "Lycidas"). Second, Brooks, Hirsch, and others have assumed, as I do, that the *Ode* concerns the development of imagination. Third, the autobiographical dimension of the poem—the fact that the *Ode* is about the poet and his poetry—has long been recognized.[2] And my reading is also fundamentally indebted to M. H. Abrams' thesis, stated in *Natural Supernaturalism*, that the Romantics "undertook . . . to save traditional concepts, schemes, and values which had been based on the relation of the Creator to his creature and creation, but to reformulate them within the prevailing two-term system of subject and object, ego and nonego."[3] Once it is recognized, the *Ode*'s pervasive undertone of Miltonic allusion transforms our sense of the *Ode*'s coherence and suggests a persuasive explication of its concluding stanzas. The *Ode* is no antechapel but the apse of Wordsworth's poetic cathedral; or, if we prefer, it is an epithalamion for the marriage of mind and nature.

I

A primary theme of the *Intimations Ode* is the transition from innocence to experience—the process of growing up, as Trilling observes.[4] The *Ode* is ostensibly a natural history. But its structure specifically echoes Milton's epic retelling of the Christian myth—a tragedy ultimately less tragic when seen as a step toward a higher theodicy. The foremost indication of this parallel is Wordsworth's paradoxical thanksgiving for loss and suffering, for "fallings . . . vanishings" (1. 147), which he declares after the shift in mood between stanzas 8 and 9.[5] His gratitude is even less equivocal than Adam's, who states that, "full of doubt I stand / Whether I should repent me now of sin / . . . or rejoice / Much more, that much more good thereof shall spring" (*P.L.*, XII, 473–76).[6]

Once heard, this echo suggests the possibility of further parallels between the situation of Adam and that of Wordsworth's speaker. And indeed there are several, though in a characteristic Wordsworthian compression of psychological insight and religious metaphor, the whole experience is transposed into the microcosm of mind and nature. In the *Ode*, the mind's "High instincts" (1. 150) assume the role of God the Father; Wordsworth's "mortal Nature" (1. 150) behaves like Milton's Adam and Eve after the Fall. Conscious of sin, they tremble before God as guilty things surprised. When Eve falls, "Earth felt the wound" of sin (*P.L.*, IX, 782); in the experience of Wordsworth's speaker, the change is felt as a decay of his own faculties, not of nature. The sign of Adam's innocence is a garden, which, once damaged, all his tilling can never restore. Wordsworthian innocence is manifested in spontaneous imaginative vision, which, once lost, "we are toiling all our lives to find" (1. 116).

According to the *Ode*, the child dwells in an Edenic state ("Heaven lies about us . . ." [1. 66]) of supreme imagination. But this state, though blissful, is as limited as Eden was. "Blest" (1. 114) in his "heaven-born freedom" (1. 26), the child is also, paradoxically, a prisoner: over him "Immortality / Broods like the day, a Master o'er a Slave, / A presence which is not to be put by" (11. 119–121). A slave is still bound, even though his master be divine. And it is one aspect of this particular slave's servitude that he is unaware of his bondage, blinded by his vision. Eden was a walled garden, a symbol of the insight—more explicit in Wordsworth—that ignorance *is* bliss.

In contrast to Adam's fall, the child's is not consciously chosen, nor is it an isolated event. Each story, however, includes an element of seduction. Nature, the kindly nurse and foster mother of the *Ode*, innocently offers fruit which, far from being forbidden, is necessary food. Yet this fruit is as dangerous as the serpent's, for it also comes from the tree of knowledge, the fatal apple of worldly experience. But this "naturalization" of the soul is the result of collaboration. Some of the child's own best spiritual qualities, his yearning to know and to be, lead him forward along the inevitable path as he imitates the fallen (adult) state of his parents. Thus he takes what nature offers and gradually leaves Eden; the celestial light fades "into the light of common day" (1. 76).

Adam had an angel to instruct him in the significance of his fall; Wordsworth has a child who is in part an externalized, objectified version of his remembered earlier self, and at the same time a figure of mythic overtones, recalling the holy, archetypal child who is the son of a sky father and an earth mother, and thus a symbol of creative union between spirit and matter. In *Paradise Lost*, the Archangel Michael permits Adam a vision of human history which is the last stage of his preparation to depart from Eden. After observing this world to come, Adam exclaims:

How soon hath thy prediction, Seer blest,
Measur'd this transient World, the Race of time,
Till time stand fixt: beyond is all abyss,
Eternity, whose end no eye can reach.
Greatly instructed I shall hence depart,
Greatly in peace of thought. . . .   (XII, 554–58)

In the *Ode* it is the speaker's *own* eye "That hath kept watch o'er man's mortality" (1. 202). But his encounter with his childhood self, the "Mighty Prophet, Seer blest" (1. 114), is as crucial as was Michael's revelation to Adam. The deepest sorrow springs from the knowledge that this child, every child, must lose his original brightness; yet the subsequent, climactic, and paradoxical joy springs from the same revelation.

Like all profoundly religious insights, this one is a recognition of order, of unity, of community. All is One: the child's "celestial light" (1. 4) and the man's memory of "What was so fugitive" (1. 136). Thus the man may now, through memory, travel back to the edge of that "immortal sea" (1. 167). The child is a prophet in Wordsworth's eyes because he looks forward to the man's supreme moment of recognition. And this attribution of prophecy before the nadir of despair in the poem is a silent preparation for the final "access of joy."

Like the Divine Goodness which makes a fortunate fall of Adam's sin, the enduring and restorative capacities of the mind preside over Wordsworth's recognition of gain through loss. The history recounted in the *Ode* therefore summarizes and recapitulates an idea familiar elsewhere in Wordsworth, particularly in *The Prelude*, where he describes the "spots of time." These remembered experiences reassert the dominion of mind and have a "fructifying," "vivifying," "renovating" virtue. Through such memories, writes Wordsworth, the mind is "nourished and invisibly repaired":

A virtue, by which pleasure is enhanced,
That penetrates, enables us to mount,
When high, more high, and lifts us up when fallen.
(*The Prelude*, XII, 215–18)[7]

The *Ode* presents the archetype (in a precise sense) of such experiences, for the history it records is treated as personal and universal, at once individual and shared by all. The phrase from *The Prelude*, "lifts us up when fallen," so relevant to my reading of the *Ode*, hints that the Wordsworthian and universally human fall is, unlike Adam's, a recurrent failure of spirit from which one may repeatedly recover.

The speaker describes sources of strength new to him in maturity; all of them indicate new power and boundaries overcome. All demonstrate the two most essential Wordsworthian values: the dominance of mind over "outward sense" and the ability to hear the still, sad music of humanity. All are born of the marriage of mind and nature. "The soothing thoughts that spring / Out of human suffering" (11. 187–88) evoke the notion of tragic catharsis, which may be seen as an aesthetic counterpart of the fortunate fall—and in the *Ode*, as Wordsworth's translation of Adam's observation that evil may be turned into good (*P.L.*, XII, 471). The philosophic mind, the supreme Wordsworthian reward, has, unlike the child's mind, the capacity to grow and to change, to accommodate external realities. It does not imitate, but instead shapes. Implicit in the *Ode*, then, is *The Prelude*'s declared theme, the growth of the poet's mind.

II

I have refrained until now from discussing the most obvious Miltonic allusion in the *Ode*: from the beginning, the speaker describes his loss as the disappearance of a "celestial light." This is Milton's phrase, appearing in the Invocation to Book III, where the poet mourns his blindness:

. . . cloud . . . and ever-during dark
Surrounds me, from the cheerful ways of men
Cut off, and for the Book of knowledge fair
Presented with a Universal blanc.   (11. 45–48)

From Milton, too, a visionary gleam was fled, but his solution is clear and immediate: "So much the rather thou Celestial Light / Shine inward, and the mind through all her powers / Irradiate...." (11. 51–53). Wordsworth's appropriation of the Miltonic words is characteristic, and invites the reader to explore the analogy so unobtrusively proposed.[8]

The spiritual loss of vision sustained by Wordsworth's speaker, figuratively expressed, echoes Milton's references to his own physical loss. Each knows that nature continues in her course, that the change is a personal deficiency. Each turns inward in an attempt to find a new illumination which will enable him to "see and tell / Of things invisible to mortal sight" (P.L., III, 54–55). The "Celestial Light" to which Milton turns is the heavenly muse; Wordsworth's light is childhood's imaginative experience which he comes to recognize as yet alive, though transformed, "fallen," into another mode of being.

The "Celestial Light" in its new Wordsworthian context becomes broader in meaning, and a way of wedding particular with universal experience in the Ode. In its various manifestations as star, ember, and sunset light, it is a metaphor for all human spiritual experience and development. But its prior, Miltonic sense of divine poetic inspiration remains relevant to Wordsworth the poet, since the allusion reminds us that Wordsworth's loss of the gleam had the same poetic implications that troubled Milton. Thus we recognize a final way in which Milton's theme of the fortunate fall illuminates the Ode.[9]

Milton appropriated the epic tradition to convey his myth of the loss of Eden. It is fitting that Wordsworth's psychological version of the same plot is presented in a lyric form. If we wished to describe the poem's generic affinities precisely, we should say that an elegy is resolved by—and into—an ode. This generic transformation subtly dramatizes the notion of the fortunate fall in a guise especially reassuring to the poet who mourns the loss of "Celestial Light."

Any traditional genre, by virtue of the fact that it is traditional, implies its own context. Reading an elegy, for instance, one not only remembers elegiac conventions and earlier examples; one also expects a certain range of themes, attitudes, strategies, styles. The choice of genre is one means of controlling a reader's expectations. In terms of genre, however, something rather curious happens in the Ode which critics have not fully acknowledged: the substitution of a major for a minor lyric kind. If one is justified in seeing genres as a significant dimension of the work's meaning, then this shift may itself reflect, at a literary level, the emotional and phenomenological change it describes.[10]

If we attend to the conventional signals, the Intimations Ode begins as a pastoral elegy. Bloom is quite correct in noting Wordsworth's debt to "Lycidas" in the first four stanzas, in which a first-person-singular voice speaks of "something that is gone" (1. 53). In a springtime pastoral world of lambs and shepherds, this voice stresses isolation and loss. In an ironic compression of the elegiac convention in which the speaker typically observes nature herself mourning, Wordsworth's speaker acknowledges that nature's reflection of this loss springs from within: the rainbow, rose, and moonlight are still lovely—only their glory is departed. Yet this elegiac strain abruptly ceases after the speaker poses his overwhelming question: "Whither is fled the visionary gleam? / Where is it now, the glory and the dream?" (11. 56–57).

The first-person singular is then replaced by a first-person plural, a more public voice which speaks of "our birth" (1. 57), "our life's Star" (1. 59). The "I" does not return until after another, even more abrupt change—the modulation from sorrow to joy between stanzas 8 and 9. This middle portion we may call the "ode" proper, for it follows the eighteenth-century convention that the ode should express themes of high import and public character. Odes, declared Plato, should sing the praises of gods and heroes. In their enthusiasm for "Pindarics," many eighteenth-century critics echoed this exalted sense of the genre's proper sphere; typical among them was John Dennis, who in 1704 wrote that the "greater lyrick," or ode, was the form most suited to the expression of religious truth.[11] The ode was generally ranked near the top of the generic hierarchy and as near epic and tragedy as any lyric could be. Elegy remained near the bottom of the scale. The elegiac voice, therefore, is implicitly the voice of a bereaved shepherd, mourning the loss of his beloved, while the speaker of the ode is ideally a bard, the quintessentially reliable narrator, who "present, past, and future sees."

Assuming that this modulation of a lesser into a greater lyric form is artistically significant, what are its implications? First, one recognizes that Wordsworth has not merely treated Milton's epic theme in lyric form, but also that this form has imposed upon him the necessity of treating the theme from exactly the opposite perspective. Milton's treatment of the universal human experience of loss ("the root of all our woe") begins with a symbol, the prototypical man, Adam. Milton's strategy is to "humanize" the actors of this drama—his various abstract representatives of man, woman, good, evil. His challenge is to make them into credible human characters with the power to evoke empathy from readers. When, less than two centuries later, Wordsworth attempts the same theme, however, it is apparently impossible to write an epic based on mythical material, as he reveals in describing his search for a theme in Book I of *The Prelude*. The epistemological revolution, the rise of empiricism manifest in the Romantic ethos, now finds most convincing a truth that is grounded in human experience rather than being the testimony of divine revelation.

Thus for Wordsworth (as for most of the Romantics) the lyric has a special appropriateness and a special validity, being the mode which most readily supports the portrayal of unique and private experience. This subjective angle of vision, however, always threatens to imply solipsism: how can the poet be sure that what seems true from his perspective is true from that of others? Wordsworth's solution is evident in the *Ode:* instead of beginning with revealed truth, as Milton did, he is constrained to begin with his own lived truth. Wordsworth does so in the knowledge that he must still bridge the gulf between himself and other men.

He does so by means of a generic shift; the conventional associations of elegy and ode offer him the possibility of being coherent while yet remaining faithful to the inherently paradoxical nature of his theme. The traditional pastoral elegy speaks of a personal loss which is ultimately resolved by reference to some principle of order which places the loss in a universal perspective. In the *Ode*, Wordsworth's loss of the visionary gleam, proposed in a context of pastoral elegy, is resolved in the intervening "ode" by recognition of just such a universal spiritual truth—that nature yet remembers what was so fugitive. Having stated the problem and asked its meaning, his speaker assumes a bardic voice and tells a story, a myth in fact, of the soul's journey, fall, and survival. This remains, however, a myth still grounded in individual experience, even as the poet's rhetoric implies revealed truth in the myth, an authority by which one traditionally expected the bard to speak.

There is a second, and possibly more speculative, significance in this generic modulation. The shift from "elegy" to "ode" coincides with the point at which Wordsworth suspended composition for two years—after stanza 4. Whatever biographical data

may be relevant to this pause—or impasse—his choosing to resume the poem in a new voice is at least congruent with the thematic development signalled by the generic shift, for it suggests that the initial question was unanswerable in the terms in which it had been asked. The new "prophetic voice" was not only desirable, therefore, but became a psychological and poetic necessity. Accordingly, Wordsworth chose, upon publication of the first edition of the *Ode*, an epigraph from Virgil's fourth eclogue, *Paulo majora canamus:* "Let us sing of somewhat greater things." Eclogue, which combines elements of pastoral and prophecy alike, is the perfect choice of intermediate genre to signal Wordsworth's generic modulation.

The final stanzas of the *Intimations Ode* show the re-emergence of the "I," but without deserting the earlier "we": "The thought of *our* past years in *me* doth breed / Perpetual benediction" (11. 137–38—italics mine). And so Wordsworth proceeds to celebrate that truth now known because it has been learned through pain. It is a truth concerning the poet's allegiance to the supreme human imagination and its triumphant marriage to the natural world. Nature, he sees, is a necessary participant in this consummation. Before the turning point, the *Ode* describes two states of human development: a first in which mind is dominant, and a second in which nature is dominant. The third and last state, however, entails a balancing of the first two, or as Wordsworth elsewhere calls it, a marriage. Earth as the dominant force appears earlier as a female principle, showing figurative aspects that Wordsworth attributes to it elsewhere: nurse and foster mother. The unobtrusive personification immediately after the elegiac turn in the phrase, "nature yet remembers" (1. 135), subtly continues this metaphorical strategy. It is Wordsworth who remembers, of course, but nature provides the motive and impetus to remember; mind and nature are involved in a relationship almost impossible to disentangle: a union.

Hence the implicit third metaphor of nature as bride. Reexamination of the poem shows that this figure has been carefully anticipated. In the first section (stanzas 1–4), the natural world prepares for a festival, which may well be a wedding. It is a springtime holiday; "all the earth is gay" (1. 29)

While Earth herself is adorning,
This sweet May-morning. (11. 43–44)

Children are gathering flowers "In a thousand valleys far and wide" (1. 47). But the speaker, though he concedes that "My head hath its coronal" (1. 40), does not perceive the significance of this wreath. He feels, one infers, like the ungracious wedding guest in the Biblical parable who was bidden to the wedding feast, but refused to go. He has the grace to feel ashamed of his inadequacy ("Oh evil day! if I were sullen" [1. 42]), but he is unable to join in the celebration, not knowing that *he* is the anointed bridegroom.

Later, in stanza 7, as Wordsworth describes the child's education in the ways of the world, the image of the wedding recurs; the child "shapes" indiscriminately, some "fragment from his dream of human life" (11. 91–92),

> A wedding or a festival,
> A mourning or a funeral. (11. 93–94)

At this point one recalls that the poem's opening was all of these. The child toys with each activity thoughtlessly, heartlessly; these "dialogues of business, love, or strife" are not the true and fructifying exchange between mind and nature which is creative, and which also preserves freedom from nature's prison.

But stanzas 10 and 11 significantly return to the opening scene. The speaker has now joined the festival in spirit and in truth, by means of "thought" (1. 175) and imagination which have restored the original dominance of mind over nature, temporarily lost. His final apostrophe to nature is a love song which is also, fittingly, an epithalamion:

> And O, ye Fountains, Meadows, Hills, and Groves,
> Forebode not any severing of our loves! (11. 191–92)

In a tone far more assured than in *Tintern Abbey,* Wordsworth expresses hope for a future that threatens no divorce, no widowhood. He anticipates a quiet marriage to nature, lived "beneath [its] more habitual sway" (1. 195).

Most important to the resolution of the poem is Wordsworth's demonstration that this marriage is a *creative* relationship: "The Clouds that gather round the setting sun / Do take a sober colouring from an eye / That hath kept watch o'er man's mortality" (11. 200–202), he says, and adds, "To me the meanest flower that blows can give / Thoughts that do often lie too deep for tears" (11. 206–207). The equality between partners is emphatic: both mind and nature give, both receive. The earlier broodings upon mortality, the fosterings of nature, have finally led to this consummation, to this paradise regained (Wordsworth's version of the Miltonic "paradise within"). The *Ode*'s conclusion describes that paradise which

the mind "when wedded to this goodly universe / In love and holy passion" shall find "A simple produce of the common day."[12] The apparently doomed youth who saw the visionary gleam fade was left with this "light of common day"; he has gradually become the redeemed man, who finds in that very loss a new Heaven and a new Earth.

I repeat, then, a note sounded at the beginning of this essay: to recognize that Wordsworth's ode embodies, consciously and pointedly, a structural pattern common to *Paradise Lost* and made manifest at the psychological, stylistic, and generic levels of the poem, is to see its often alleged disunity in quite a new context. Disunified it may be in one sense — as a piece of music might be termed "disunified" if it began in soft minor strains and ended in triumphant major harmonies of another key. But the shift or modulation, however surprising, however far it might place the ending — at first listening — from the beginning, is nevertheless deliberate, even necessary. For the great Biblical and Miltonic myth which seemed to Wordsworth congruent with the history of his own and every man's spiritual development, contained as the essence of its shape this transformation from one mode to another — from E minor to C major, from the loss of the visionary gleam to the birth of "the philosophic mind." This transformation is one instance in which, as Coleridge put it when speaking of organic form, the substance of a work could only grow by its own principles, "shaping itself from within." If the resolution of the *Ode* has puzzled some readers, it must be at least in part because they have failed to recognize the poem's shape and the region "whence it came."

III

Milton, in word and deed, provides a supreme model for the poet who matures from the merely personal lyric, through experience, into "something like prophetic strain," as he wrote at the end of the early "Il Penseroso." (Of the three allusions to Milton in Dorothy's journals, two mention Wordsworth's reading of this poem.) As we have seen, this is the pattern of growth which Wordsworth has so pointedly enacted in the *Ode.*

Unfallen Adam in the garden might be seen as the prototype, not only of man, but also of the Wordsworthian lyric pastoral poet whose perceptions overflow into expression. According to legend, speech was simple and uncomplicated in Eden, perception and expression virtually the same. As the animals were led before Adam for the first time, he named them, "as it were from a fountaine of prophesie."[13] But when innocence is gone, the gleam fled, Eden lost, Adam and the Wordsworthian poet must then perceive and speak in a different mode, one which reflects that experience of loss, and yet bespeaks a wider world, a higher reality. Michael speaks to fallen Adam shortly before his departure into the fallen world:

> . . . only add
> Deeds to thy knowledge answerable, add Faith,
> Add Virtue, Patience, Temperance, add Love,
> By name to come called Charity, the soul
> Of all the rest: then wilt thou not be loath
> To leave this Paradise, but shall possess
> A paradise within thee, happier far.   (XII, 581–87)

Virtue, patience, temperance, love—these are moral qualities, and in Michael's list all the words but Faith concern man's relation with his fellow man. Eden was isolated compared with the world to come, as the elegy is private compared with the epic—or the ode. The paradise the angel describes to Adam is clearly akin to Wordsworth's "humanized" imagination, which must concern itself with greater things—man, nature, and human life.

The characteristic quality of the unfallen state for Wordsworth is joy, akin to Adam's paradisal bliss; in the fallen state it is "strength," which is associated, like the fallen Adam's fortitude, with power, knowledge, and new freedom. The poet of such powers, writes Wordsworth,

> . . . oft
> Must turn elsewhere—to travel near the tribes
> And fellowships of men, and see ill sights
> Of madding passions mutually inflamed;
> Must hear humanity in fields and groves
> Pipe solitary anguish. . . .[14]

Wordsworth, in his later poetry, did turn more and more to "greater things," to broader canvasses of human life and suffering which he sought to render in the voice of the bard. *The Excursion* shows his adherence to the vow, "*Paulo majora canamus.*" But the voice finally faltered into silence and *The Recluse* was never completed. Thus the *Ode* is tragic in the same sense that *Paradise Lost* is tragic: nothing can bring back the hour of splendour in the grass. But within the bounds of the poem, for the moment recorded there, the precarious transformation from personal to prophetic seems complete, and the loss itself another Fortunate Fall.

Notes

1. John Jones sees the poem as a "preparation for the defeat of imaginative monism" in *The Egotistical Sublime* (London: Chatto and Windus, 1954), p. 167; Florence G. Marsh calls it "fractured" in "Wordsworth's *Ode*: Obstinate Questionings," *SiR* VI (1965), 226; Cleanth Brooks writes that the conclusion is not as fully realized poetically as the earlier expression of loss, that it is "asserted rather than dramatized," in *The Well-Wrought Urn* (New York: Harcourt, Brace and World, 1947), p. 148; David Perkins questions the success of the work's ethical conclusion in *The Quest for Permanence* (Cambridge, MA: Harvard Univ. Press, 1959), p. 80; Alan Grob finds the poem set apart from the body of Wordsworth's work: "The *Ode* remains alone *sui generis* set apart in magnificent isolation," *The Philosophic Mind* (Columbus, OH: Ohio State Univ. Press, 1973), pp. 261–62. The edition of the *Intimations Ode* used throughout and cued by line in the text of the essay appears in *The Poetical Works of William Wordsworth,* ed. Ernest de Selincourt, rev. Helen Darbishire, 5 vols. (1940–49; rpt. Oxford: Clarendon, 1952–54), IV, 279–85.
2. Harold Bloom, *A Map of Misreading* (New York: Oxford Univ. Press, 1975), p. 145; Brooks, pp. 124–150; E. D. Hirsch, *Wordsworth and Schelling: A Typological Study of Romanticism* (New Haven: Yale Univ. Press, 1960), pp. 177–78.
3. M. H. Abrams, *Natural Supernaturalism* (New York: W. W. Norton, 1971), p. 13.
4. Lionel Trilling, "The Immortality Ode," in *The Liberal Imagination* (1940; rpt. New York: Charles Scribner's Sons, 1953), pp. 129–159.
5. The grammar as well as the substance of stanza 9 is notoriously puzzling of course, and the Fenwick note, written decades after the *Ode*, has done little to clarify it. *Without* the note, I suggest, the passage would be less perplexing because the reader might more readily see the universal paradox of the fortunate fall in Wordsworth's language. The note, however, specifies and particularizes the reference so as to make it idiosyncratic—just what Wordsworth was apparently trying to avoid in the poem itself. In fact,

Brooks was the *first* to emphasize the crucial paradoxes in the *Ode.* A careful reading of the note, however, does not contradict my thesis. The memory of the "fallings, vanishings" is gratifying because the experience of loss remembered is his best evidence of the previous state when he "communed with all that I saw as something not apart from but inherent in, my own immaterial nature." Like Eden, this state can only be known by contrast. The "fallings . . . etc." are not identical with the power also called the gleam, but the moments at which its true power could be most intensely felt and hence known.

6. John Milton, *Complete Poems and Major Prose,* ed. Merritt Y. Hughes (New York: The Odyssey Press, 1957). All quotations from Milton are taken from this edition.

7. Ernest de Selincourt and Helen Darbishire, eds. *The Prelude* (Oxford: Clarendon Press, 1959). Quotations are from the 1850 text.

8. Trilling notes that this "celestial light" is perhaps similar to the light which is praised in the invocation to the third book of *Paradise Lost*" (p. 132).

9. Helen Vendler also alludes to the poetic development spurred by the loss of the gleam as a "fortunate fall," but does not pursue the Miltonic context of allusion, in her essay, "Lionel Trilling and the *Immortality Ode,*" *Salmagundi,* 41 (1978), 664–86.

10. My conception of the poetic uses of genre is indebted to Rosalie Colie, *The Resources of Kind* (Berkeley, Los Angeles, and London: Univ. of California Press, 1973), and to Ralph Rader, "The Concept of Genre and Eighteenth-Century Studies," in *New Approaches to Eighteenth-Century Literature: Selected Papers from the English Institute,* ed. Phillip Harth (New York and London: Columbia Univ. Press, 1974), 79–116.

11. " . . . as great Passion only is the adequate Language of the greater poetry [epic, tragedy, the ode], so the greater poetry is the only adequate language of Religion." John Dennis, "The Grounds of Criticism in Poetry," *Critical Works of John Dennis,* ed. E. N. Hooker (Baltimore: The Johns Hopkins Univ. Press, 1929), I, 340. Norman MacLean emphasizes this public tradition of the eighteenth-century ode in his essay "From Action to Image: Theories of the Lyric in the Eighteenth Century," in *Critics and Criticism,* ed. R. S. Crane (Chicago: Univ. of Chicago Press, 1952), pp. 408–462.

12. "The Prospectus," 11. 53–55.

13. Edward Topsell, *A History of Four-Footed Beasts,* facsimile reprint (New York: Da Capo Press, 1967), A3.

14. "The Prospectus," 11. 72–77.

The Second Coming of Aphrodite: Kate Chopin's Fantasy of Desire

Sandra Gilbert

While not denying the significance of those readings that see The Awakening *as a "realistic" novel whose immediate context seems to be its late-nineteenth-century social setting, Sandra Gilbert proposes here to read the novel in mythic and archetypal terms. The novel initially presents a realistic surface, but "realism," Gilbert reminds us, is itself a set of literary conventions. Furthermore, as the story progresses, the novel's generic form becomes more equivocal. Taking Edna Pontellier's "baptismal" swim in chapter 10 as the turning point, Gilbert claims that Edna "swims not only toward a female paradise but out of one kind of novel—the work of Eliotian or Flaubertian 'realism' she had previously inhabited— and into a new kind of work, a mythic/metaphysical romance that elaborates her distinctively female fantasy of paradisiacal fulfillment and therefore adumbrates much of the feminist modernism that was to come within a few decades." Focusing, as Frye says the critic should, on "convention, genres, and recurring image groups or archetypes," Gilbert locates the heroine with reference to mythic figures like Aphrodite, Eve, Phaedra, and Isolde, and she locates the novel with reference to the work of, among others, Flaubert, Whitman, Swinburne, Dickinson, Wagner, Baudelaire, the Brontë sisters, George Eliot, Wilde, Yeats, Cather, H. D., Sexton, and Stevens. In this admittedly "hyperbolic" reading, a* tour de force *of intertextual criticism, Gilbert performs what Frye calls "the first operation of criticism: trying to see what meaning could be discovered in works of literature from their context in literature."*

First published in *The Kenyon Review*—New Series, Summer 1983, Vol. V, No. 3. Copyright by Kenyon College. Reprinted with permission of the author and *The Kenyon Review*.

The radiant ancient Venus, the Aphrodite born from the white foam of the sea, has not traversed the horrifying darkness of the Middle Ages with impunity. . . . She has retired into the depths of a cave . . . lighted up by fires which are not those of the benign Phoebus.

—Charles Baudelaire, "R. Wagner & Tannhäuser in Paris," 1861

Then to me so lying awake a vision
Came without sleep over the seas and touched me,
Softly touched mine eyelids and lips; and I too,
  Full of vision,

Saw the white implacable Aphrodite,
Saw the hair unbound and the feet unsandalled
Shine as fire of sunset on western waters . . .

—A. C. Swinburne, "Sapphics," 1865

I was born under the star of Aphrodite, Aphrodite who was also born on the sea, and when her star is in the ascendant, events are always propitious to me.

—Isadora Duncan, *My Life*, 1927

Swiftly re-light the flame,
Aphrodite, holy name . . .

return, O holiest one,
Venus whose name is kin

to venerate,
venerator.

—H. D., *Tribute to the Angels*, 1945

Toward the end of Kate Chopin's *The Awakening* there is a dinner party scene which has been ignored by many critics though it has fascinated and puzzled a few. On the verge of leaving her husband's house for a nearby cottage that she hopes will become both a spiritual and material room of her own, Edna Pontellier has invited a "select" group of friends to join her at a birthday dinner which will also be a ceremonial celebration of her departure from one household and her entrance into another. Splendid in gold satin and lace "the color of her skin," she presides over an equally splendid table, which is similarly decked in "pale yellow satin," lit by "wax candles in massive brass candelabra," and heaped with "full, fragrant roses." More strikingly still, "the

ordinary stiff dining chairs" have been "discarded for the occasion and replaced by the most commodious and luxurious which could be collected throughout the house" while "before each guest [stands] a tiny glass that [sparkles] like a garnet gem," containing a special, magical-looking cocktail. Enthroned at the head of the table, Edna herself appears equally magical, for there is "something in her attitude, in her whole appearance, which [suggests] the regal woman, the one who rules, who looks on, who stands alone." At the same time, however—even in the midst of gold champagne, crimson cocktails, and general merrymaking which climaxes in one of the women guests weaving a pagan garland of roses to crown the dark curls of the handsome young man beside her—we are told that Edna feels an "old ennui overtaking her . . . a chill breath that seemed to issue from some vast cavern wherein discords wailed" (chapter 30). Ranging as it does from sumptuous feasting to secret, inexplicable sadness, from gorgeousness to gloom, the dinner party chapter represents, as Cynthia Griffin Wolff observes, "one of the longest sustained episodes in the novel."[1]

Perhaps it is because so many contemporary critics would agree with Lawrence Thornton's recent description of *The Awakening* as a "political romance"[2] that so few have paid close attention to this scene. Though in the last decade *The Awakening* has become one of the most frequently taught and persistently analyzed American novels, commentators on the book commonly describe Edna's party, if they discuss it at all, as just one more occasion when Chopin's half-mad housewife experiences and expresses "unfocused yearning" for romantic transfiguration or social liberation.[3] Besides occupying an exceptionally elaborate chapter in a novel of economical, obliquely rendered episodes, however, Edna's dinner party constitutes an extraordinarily complex literary structure, a scene whose images and allusions as well as its dramatic plot suggest surprisingly rich veins of symbolic significance. What does it mean, after all, when the narrator of this apparently "realistic" work suddenly calls her heroine "the regal woman, the one who rules, who looks on, who stands alone"? The vocabulary of such a description seems more appropriate to a fantasy, a romance, or a fairytale, and yet this mysterious definition seems also to evoke the narrator's next perception of the "chill breath" her queenly heroine feels, together with Edna's corollary, equally mystical and mysterious sense of "acute longing which always summoned into her spiritual vision the presence of the beloved one." Who or what, indeed, is the oddly vague "beloved one"? And why, finally, does the enigmatically wise Mlle. Reisz take her leave of Edna with a French sentence— *"Bonne nuit, ma reine, soyez sage"*—that seems to confirm our feeling that this magical hostess is clothed in a paradoxical veil of power and vulnerability?

As a speculative explanation of these puzzles I want to argue that *The Awakening* is a female fiction that both draws upon and revises *fin de siècle* hedonism to propose a feminist and matriarchal myth of Aphrodite/Venus as an alternative to the masculinist and patriarchal myth of Jesus. In the novel's unfolding of this implicit myth, the dinner party scene is of crucial importance, for here, as she presides over a Swinburnian Last Supper, Edna Pontellier definitively (if only for a moment) "becomes" the powerful goddess of love and art into whose shape she was first "born" in the Gulf near Grand Isle and in whose image she will be suicidally borne back into the sea at the novel's end. Thus when Victor, the dark-haired young man who was ritually draped and garlanded at the climax of the feast, tells his friend Mariequita that "Venus rising from the foam could have presented no more entrancing a spectacle than Mrs. Pontellier, blazing with beauty and diamonds at the head of the board," he is speaking what is in some deep sense the truth about Kate Chopin's heroine.

To see *The Awakening* in these terms is not, of course, to deny that it is also the work most critics and readers have thought it is: a "Creole Bovary," a feminist "critique of the identity of 'mother-women,'" a New Orleans version of "the familiar transcendentalist fable of the soul's emergence, or 'lapse' into life," "a eulogy on sex and a muted elegy on the female condition," a turn-of-the-century "existentialist" epiphany, and "a tough-minded critique of the Victorian myths of love."[4] Taken together, all of these definitions of the novel articulate the range of political, moral, and philosophical concerns on which Chopin meditates throughout this brief but sophisticated work. What unifies and dramatizes these often divergent matters, however, is the way in which, for all its surface realism, *The Awakening* is allusively organized by Kate Chopin's half-secret (and perhaps only half-conscious) but distinctly feminist fantasy of the second coming of Aphrodite.

To be sure, Chopin's "Creole Bovary" has always been understood to be, like its French precursor, a novel that both uses fantasy and comments upon fantasy in order to establish the character of its heroine and the nature of her character. From the severest early reviewers to the most enthusiastic recent writers, however, most critics see such fantasies as, like Emma Bovary's, symptoms of inadequacy, of an "over-idealization of love" and a "susceptibility to romantic codes." People like Edna Pontellier and Emma Bovary, wrote Willa Cather in 1899, "are the spoil of the poets, the Iphigenias of sentiment." Edna's commitment to fantasy, concludes Cynthia Griffin Wolff in a somewhat extreme summary of this position, is the ultimate mark of the "schizoid" personality which causes her "disintegration."[5] I will argue, however, that the details of desire which the text of *The Awakening* records ultimately shape themselves into a tale of romantic transfiguration that not only uses and comments upon fantasy but actually becomes a fantasy, albeit a shadowy one. Both seriously and ironically this fantasy of Kate Chopin's shows, from a female point of view, just what would "really" happen to a mortal, turn-of-the-century woman who tried to claim for herself the erotic freedom and power owned by the classical queen of love.

I will argue, moreover, that to see this novel as such a shadowy fantasy or fantasy *manqué* is to begin to explain a number of qualities that have puzzled its severe critics as well as its enthusiastic admirers: its odd short chapters, its ambiguous lyricism (what Willa Cather called its "flexible iridescent style"), its editorial restraint, its use of recurrent images and refrains, its implicit or explicit allusions to writers like Whitman, Swinburne, Flaubert, and its air of moral indeterminacy. In addition, I will suggest more specifically that to see *The Awakening* as such a fantasy is to begin to grasp the purpose of some of the scenes in the book that have always appeared problematical—the often ignored or misrepresented episode of the dinner party, for example, and the even more controversial scene of Edna's suicide. Finally, I will show that in creating this realistically surfaced, generically equivocal fantasy, Kate Chopin was working in a mode of mingled naturalism and symbolism exactly analogous to the one explored by her near contemporary George Moore and his younger countryman James Joyce. Learned from such varied continental precursors as Turgenev and Balzac, Maupassant and Chekhov, this artful combination of surface and symbol evolved through Moore's *The Untilled Field* and Joyce's *Dubliners* to a famous culmination in *Ulysses*. But Kate Chopin in America, inheriting the same tradition and similar techniques, also began to give emphasis to the fantastic or mythic radiance that might at any moment flash through ordinary reality. Because she was female, however, she saw such epiphanies from a feminine point of view and in what we would now call feminist terms. Indeed, the next literary woman to employ the same mode and the same techniques would be Virginia Woolf, and she too would use them to valorize and mythologize femaleness.

Appropriately enough, Kate Chopin's portrait of Aphrodite as a Creole Bovary begins and ends at a seaside resort, on the margin between nature and culture, where a leisured or, anyway, a lucky few may be given (as only a few have always been given) the chance to witness the birth of erotic power in the foam. To start with, however, despite the nearness of the sea and the incessant sound of its "seductive" voice, Chopin offers scenes that seem determinedly realistic, low-key, landbound. In addition, as if briefly but formally acknowledging Flaubert's influence, she opens her novel about a woman's fateful transformation by examining her heroine from a solid and stolid male perspective. *Madame Bovary*, of course, begins with a brief summary of Charles Bovary's history, including a description of the way Emma Rouault looks to the bovine but passionate young physician whom she will soon marry. Similarly, *The Awakening*'s author-omniscient first chapter emphasizes the point of view of Edna Pontellier's conventional husband, Léonce.

Like Madame Bovary's husband-to-be, who at one point gazes at Emma as she stands beneath a parasol that colors "the white skin of her face with shifting reflections,"[6] Mr. Pontellier watches from a porch on the main building of Madame Le Brun's Grand Isle summer colony as "a white sunshade [advances] at a snail's pace from the beach" with his wife Edna and her friend Robert Le Brun strolling "beneath its pink-lined shelter" (chapter 1). In both cases, the woman appears first as an object, and Edna in particular, whether she "is" herself or the walking sunshade that contains her, is presented as she seems to Léonce: valuable, even treasured, but nevertheless, a *thing* to be possessed and guarded rather than a person to be heard or heeded. Even this early in her novel, however, and even while acknowledging her debt to Flaubert, Chopin swerves

from him by emphasizing this last point. For where the French novelist creates sympathy for Charles with his devastating portrait of the first Madame Bovary, a skinny pimpled Jocasta who is not only old enough to be the young doctor's mother but has actually been chosen for him by his mother, Chopin immediately characterizes Léonce as an impatient businessman who scrutinizes his wife for sunburn "as one looks at a valuable piece of personal property which has suffered some damage" (chapter 1).

Most of *The Awakening* is told from Edna's perspective, with occasional editorial interpolations from the narrator, but despite (or perhaps because of) its unrepresentative point of view and its air of almost impressionistic improvisation, this opening chapter constitutes a surprisingly complete introduction to the problems and personae of the novel. As an overture, in fact, it includes many of the major leitmotifs of the work to follow: symbolic objects (houses, clothing, jewelry, food); symbolic activities (piano playing, swimming, housecleaning, gambling); symbolic figures, both human and inhuman (the birds, the lady in black, the twins, Edna and Robert, Mr. Pontellier, Madame Le Brun); symbolic places (the Gulf, the beach, the city, the summer colony on Grand Isle), and crucial relationships (husbands and wives, mothers and children). First encountered here, most of these ultimately extraordinary elements seem ordinary enough, or rather they seem as vividly literal as objects in a painting by Renoir or Seurat. It is only as one scene dissolves into another, as the narrative point of view gradually enters Edna's strengthening consciousness, and as objects and activities insistently recur, like elements of a protracted dream, that they begin to gain what eventually becomes an almost uncanny power. Porches and pianos, mothers and children, skirts and sunshades—all these are the props and properties of domesticity, the key elements of what in the nineteenth century was called "woman's sphere," and it is in this sphere, on the edge of a blue gulf, that Edna Pontellier is securely caged when she first appears in the novel that will tell her story. In a larger sense, however, she is confined in what is not only literally a "woman's sphere" but, symbolically speaking, the Woman's House—the place to which in civilized as in primitive cultures women are ritually assigned at crucial times in their lives. Here, therefore, every object and figure has not only a literal domestic function and a dreamlike symbolic radiance but a distinctively female symbolic significance.

The self-abnegating "mother-women" who seem "to prevail that summer at Grand Isle," the mutually absorbed young lovers who always appear in the neighborhood of the sepulchrally religious lady in black, Edna's own children trailed by their omnipresent quadroon nurse with her "faraway, meditative air," awkward and imperious Mademoiselle Reisz in her "rusty black lace" and artificial violets, the Farival twins "always clad in the virgin's colors," the skirt-dancing little girl in black tulle, even Edna herself sharing out her husband's gift of *friandises*— all seem like faintly grotesque variations on the figures from "La Vie d'une Femme" who appear in Charlotte Brontë's *Villette:* the young girl, the bride, the mother, the widow. That the *pension* in which all these women have gathered is ruled by the pretty but powerful widow Madame Le Brun, who sews and oversees in a light airy room with a view at the top of the house, seems quite appropriate. At the same time, however, it seems quite appropriate that the novel begins with the comical curse of the caged parrot—"*Allez vous-en! Allez vous-en! Sapristi!*"— and with the information that this same bird also speaks "a language which nobody understood, unless it was the mocking bird that hung on the other side of the door. . . ." For, as we shall see, these birds together prefigure both Edna's restlessness and her irony, her awakening desire for freedom and her sardonic sense that freedom may ultimately be meaningless, her yearning for solitude and her skeptical worries about loneliness.

Before these desires and fears become fully conscious, however, and even while it is slowly becoming clear that the domesticity of these early chapters is symbolically as well as literally important, Chopin begins to dramatize her heroine's summer of discontent through a series of traditionally "realistic" interactions between Edna and her husband. Indeed, though the technique and structure of these exchanges may be derived in part from French writers like Flaubert and Maupassant, they are most thematically indebted to the female literary tradition in English, of which Kate Chopin was surely an heir. Thus, depicting Léonce's casual self-absorption and Edna's mild rebelliousness, the narrator of *The Awakening* at first seems primarily concerned to represent with Austenian delicacy a marriage on the edge of Eliotian fissures. Pontellier is not, of course, either a Casaubon or a Grandcourt, but that seems in fact to be Chopin's revisionary point. For as she depicts

both his power and his imperiousness in swift, understated domestic episodes—the scene in chapter three when he wakes Edna and the children, for instance, or his offhand gifts of money and *friandises*— she shows that he too is possessed by the possessive male will which speaks differently but equally in the tyrannical husbands of *Daniel Deronda* and *Middlemarch*. To begin with, therefore, Edna's "awakening" is both domestic and prosaic. Like Dorothea Brooke and Gwendolyn Harleth, she awakens from the romantic dreams of girlhood first to find herself a married woman and then to find that the meaning of marriage is very different from what she had supposed. Like another nineteenth-century heroine— Emily Brontë's Catherine Earnshaw Linton—she experiences what Chopin calls "an indescribable oppression" which seems to come at least in part from her sense of herself as, in Brontë's words, "the wife of a stranger; an exile, and outcast . . . from what had been [her] world."[7] For when, like the subject of one of Emily Dickinson's poems, she rises to "His Requirements" and takes on "the honorable work of Woman and of Wife," she seems to have accepted a spiritual confinement that excludes all visions of "Amplitude and Awe."[8]

For George Eliot's comparatively docile Dorothea and her chastened Gwendolyn, even for Emily Brontë's more satanically ambitious Catherine, such a recognition of domestic entrapment along with its corollary spiritual diminution is the climax of a long process of social reconciliation that must ultimately end in these heroines accepting their own comparative powerlessness. For Edna, on the other hand, this maritally-induced recognition of "her position in the universe as a human being, and . . . her relations as an individual to the world within and about her" (chapter 6) is only the beginning of a more metaphysical awakening to all the visionary intimations and implications of her own femaleness. To be sure, once she has left her husband's bed to sit on the porch and listen to "the everlasting voice of the sea," she has already, like Eliot's and Brontë's heroines, acquired what her author ironically calls "more wisdom than the Holy Ghost is usually pleased to vouchsafe to any woman." But, like Emily Dickinson, Chopin wants to record not only the body's rebellion at confinement but the soul's "moments of Escape" (Johnson 512), along with the visions that empower such escapes. In addition, because she is a fiction writer, she wants to create a narrative that will enact and record those visions. After her first, realistically rendered discoveries of spiritual uneasiness, therefore, Edna's "awakenings" become increasingly fantastic and poetic, stirrings of the imagination's desire for amplitude and awe rather than protests of the reason against unreasonable constraint.

Paradoxically, however, it is just Edna's realistic awakenings to domestic confinement and her domestic confinement itself that make possible these later, more visionary awakenings. Specifically, I would argue, Edna awakens to the possibilities as well as the problems of "her position in the universe" not only because she finds herself enclosed in woman's literal sphere and inhabiting a figurative House of Women but also because she has come to spend the summer in what is both literally and figuratively a female colony, a sort of parodic Lesbos. In fact, though not many critics have noticed this, Madame Le Brun's *pension* on Grand Isle is very much a woman's land, not only because it is owned and run by a single woman and dominated by "mother-women" but also because (as in so many summer colonies today) its principal inhabitants are actually women and children whose husbands and fathers visit only on weekends. No wonder, then, that, as Chopin observes, "that summer at Grand Isle [Edna] had begun to loosen a little the mantle of reserve that had always enveloped her" (chapter 7) and had begun to do so under "the influence" first of beautiful and sensual Adèle Ratignolle and, later, of more severe and spiritual Mlle. Reisz.

From the eighteenth century on, after all, middle-class women's culture has often been fragmented by the relegation of each wife to a separate household, by the scattering of such households to genteel suburbs, and by the rituals of politeness that codified visiting behavior and other interchanges between the ladies of these separate households. While husbands joined to work and play in a public community of men, women were isolated in private parlors or used, in brief stylized public appearances, as conspicuous consumers to signify their husbands' wealth. Only a few situations, most notably the girls' school and the summer hotel, offered the isolated lady any real chance to participate in an ongoing community of women, one based on extended experiences of intimacy with others of their own sex. And, as *The Awakening* shows, for married adult women of Edna Pontellier's age and class the quasi-utopian communal household of the vacation hotel

must have offered a unique opportunity to live closely with other women and to learn from them. My use here of the word "colony" is, therefore, deliberately ambiguous. For if a summer colony like Madame Le Brun's *pension* is, on the one hand, a place where women have been colonized—that is, dominated and confined by men who have conquered them—in another sense this female-occupied *pension* is a place where women have established a colony or encampment of their own, an outpost of the lively dream queendom that Charlotte Perkins Gilman called "Herland."[9]

Finally, then, the punning phrase "the Bonds of Womanhood" that Nancy Cott wisely uses as the title of her historical study of American women is also useful here.[10] For in this close-knit summer colony locks become links: bonds in the negative sense of "fetters" gradually give way to bonds in the positive sense of "ties." Given this transformation of bondage into bonding, moreover, it is inevitable that both Adèle Ratignolle, the antithetical "mother-woman," and Mlle. Reisz, the equally antithetical spinster/artist, facilitate Edna's passage into the metaphorically divine sexuality that is *her* fated and unique identity. Responding to Adèle's interrogations in chapter seven, for instance, Edna begins to formulate her sense of the desirous quest for significant desire that has shaped her life. Similarly, responding in chapter nine to the implicit challenge posed by Mlle. Reisz's music, she becomes conscious that "the very passions themselves were aroused within her soul, swaying it, lashing it, as the waves daily beat upon her . . . body."

The oceanic imagery embedded in Chopin's description of Edna's response to Mlle. Reisz's music is neither casual nor coincidental; rather it suggests yet another agency through which Mme. Le Brun's predominantly female summer colony on Grand Isle awakens and empowers this Creole Bovary. For Chopin's Aphrodite, like Hesiod's is born from the sea, and born specifically because the colony where she comes to consciousness is situated, like so many places that are significant for women, outside patriarchal culture, beyond the limits of the city where men make history, on one of those magical shores that mark the margin where nature intersects with culture. Here power can flow from outside, from the timelessness or from, in Mircea Eliade's phrase, the "Great Time" that is free of historical constraints; and here, therefore, the sea can speak in a seductive voice, "never ceasing, whispering, clamoring, murmuring, inviting the soul to wander for a spell in abysses of solitude; to lose itself in mazes of inward contemplation" (chapter 6).

It is significant, then, that not only Edna's silent dialogue with Mlle. Reisz but also her confessional conversation with Adèle Ratignolle incorporates sea imagery. Reconstructing her first childhood sense of self for her friend, Edna remembers "a meadow that seemed as big as the ocean" in which as a little girl she "threw out her arms as if swimming when she walked, beating the tall grass as one strikes out in the water" (chapter 7). Just as significantly she speculates that, as she journeyed through this seemingly endless grass, she was most likely "running away from prayers, from the Presbyterian service, read in a spirit of gloom by my father that chills me yet to think of." She was running away, that is, from the dictations and interdictions of patriarchal culture, especially of patriarchal theology, and running into the wild openness of nature. Even so early, the story implies, her quest for an alternative theology, or at least for an alternative mythology, had begun. In the summer of her awakening on Grand Isle, that quest is extended into the more formalized process of learning not to run but to swim.

Edna's education in swimming is, of course, obviously symbolic, representing as it does both a positive political lesson in staying afloat and an ambiguously valuable sentimental education in the consequences of getting in over one's head. More important, however, is the fact that swimming immerses Edna in an *other* element—an element, indeed, of otherness—in whose baptismal embrace she is mystically and mythically revitalized, renewed, reborn. That Chopin wants specifically to emphasize this aspect of Edna's education in swimming, moreover, is made clear by the magical occasion on which her heroine's first independent swim takes place. Following Mlle. Reisz's evocative concert, "someone, perhaps it was Robert [Edna's lover-to-be], thought of a bath at that mystic hour and under that mystic moon." Appropriately, then, on this night that sits "lightly upon the sea and land," this night when "the white light of the moon [has] fallen upon the world like the mystery and softness of sleep," the previously timid Edna begins for the first time to swim, feeling "as if some power of significant import had been given her" and aspiring "to swim far out, where no woman had swum before" (chapter 10). Her new strength and her new

ambition are symbolically fostered by the traditionally female mythic associations of moonlight and water, as well as by the romantic attendance of Robert Le Brun and the seemingly erotic "heavy perfume of a field of white blossoms somewhere near." At the same time, however, Chopin's description of the waves breaking on the beach "in little foamy crests . . . like slow white serpents" suggests that Edna is swimming not only with new powers but into a kind of alternative paradise, one that depends upon deliberate inversions and conversions of conventional theological images, while her frequent reminders that this sea is a *gulf* reinforce our sense that its waters are at least as metaphysical as those of, say, the Golfo Placido in Conrad's *Nostromo*. Thus, even more important than Edna's swim are both its narrative and its aesthetic consequences, twin textual transformations that influence and energize the rest of Chopin's novel. For in swimming away from the beach where her prosaic husband watches and waits, Edna swims away from the shore of her old life, where she had lingered for twenty-eight years, hesitant and ambivalent. As she swims, moreover, she swims not only toward a female paradise but out of one kind of novel—the work of Eliotian or Flaubertian "realism" she had previously inhabited—and into a new kind of work, a mythic/metaphysical romance that elaborates her distinctively female fantasy of paradisiacal fulfillment and therefore adumbrates much of the feminist modernism that was to come within a few decades.

In a literal sense, of course, these crucial textual transformations can be seen as merely playful fantasies expressed by Robert and Edna as part of a "realistically" rendered courtship. I am arguing, though, that they have a metaphorical intensity and a mythic power far weightier than what would appear to be their mimetic function, and that through this intensity they create a ghostly subtextual narrative that persists with metaphysical insistence from Edna's baptismal swimming scene in chapter ten through her last, suicidal swim in chapter thirty-nine. For when Edna says "I wonder if any night on earth will ever again be like this one," she is beginning to place herself in a tale that comes poetically "true." Her dialogue with Robert, as the two return from their moonlit midnight swim in the Gulf, outlines the first premises of this story. "It is like a night in a dream," she says. "The people about me are like some uncanny, half-human beings. There must be spirits abroad tonight" (chapter 10). Robert's reply picks up this idea and elaborates upon it. It is "the twenty-eighth of August," he observes, and then explains, fancifully, that

> on the twenty-eighth of August, at the hour of midnight, and if the moon is shining—the moon must be shining—a spirit that has haunted these shores for ages rises up from the Gulf. With its own penetrating vision the spirit seeks some one mortal worthy to hold him company, worthy of being exalted for a few hours into realms of the semicelestials. His search has always hitherto been fruitless, and he has sunk back, disheartened, into the sea. But tonight he found Mrs. Pontellier. Perhaps, he will never wholly release her from the spell. Perhaps she will never again suffer a poor, unworthy earthling to walk in the shadow of her divine presence.
> (chapter 10)

Fanciful as it seems, however, this mutual fantasy of Edna's and Robert's is associated, first, with a real change in their relationship, and then, with a real change in Edna. Sitting on the porch in the moonlight, the two fall into an erotic silence that seems to be a consequence of the fiction they have jointly created: "No multitude of words could have been more significant than those moments of silence, or more pregnant with the first-felt throbbings of desire" (chapter 10). And the next day, when Edna awakens from her night of transformative dreaming, she finds herself "blindly following whatever impulse moved her, as if she had placed herself in alien hands for direction, and freed her soul of responsibility" (chapter 12).

The scenes that follow—Edna's waking of Robert in chapter twelve, their voyage in the same chapter to the Chenière Caminada, their attendance at church in chapter thirteen, Edna's nap at Madame Antoine's cottage again in chapter thirteen, and their return to Grand Isle in chapter fourteen—constitute a wistful adult fairytale that lies at the heart of this desirous but ultimately sardonic fantasy. Journeying across the Gulf to Mass on the nearby island of Chenière Caminada—the island of live oaks—Edna and Robert find themselves in the Felliniesque company of the lovers, the lady in black, and a barefooted Spanish girl (apparently Robert's sometime girlfriend) with the allegorical name of Mariequita. Yet despite all this company Edna feels "as if she were being borne away from some anchorage which had held her fast, whose chains had been loosening," and together with Robert she dreams of "pirate gold" and of yet another voyage, this one to the legendary-sounding island of "Grande Terre," where they will "climb up the hill to the old fort and look at the little wriggling gold snakes and watch the lizards sun themselves" (chapter 12). When she finally arrives at the "quaint little Gothic church of Our Lady of Lourdes," therefore, she is not surprisingly overcome by "a feeling of oppression and drowsiness." Like Mariequita, the Church of Our Lady of Lourdes is named for the wrong goddess, and Edna inevitably struggles—as she did when "running away from prayers" through the Kentucky meadow—to escape its "stifling atmosphere . . . and reach the open air."

Everything that happens after she leaves the church further implies that she has abandoned the suffocation of traditional Christian (that is, traditional patriarchal) theology for the rituals of an alternative, possibly matriarchal but certainly female religion. Attended by the ever-solicitous Robert, she strolls across the "low, drowsy island," stopping once—almost ceremonially—to drink water that a "mild-faced Acadian" is drawing from a well. At "Madame Antoine's cot," she undresses, bathes, and lies down "in the very center of [a] high, white bed," where like a revisionary Sleeping Beauty, she sleeps for almost a whole day. When she awakens, for the fifth or sixth but most crucial time in this novel of perpetual "awakening," she wonders, "How many years have I slept? . . . The whole island seems changed. A new race of beings must have sprung up . . . and when did our people from Grand Isle disappear from the earth?" (chapter 13). Again she bathes, almost ceremonially, and then she eats what appear to be two ritual meals. First she enters a room where she finds that though "no one was there . . . there was a cloth spread upon the table that stood against the wall, and a cover was laid for one, with a crusty brown loaf and a bottle of wine beside the plate." She bites "a piece from the brown loaf, tearing it with strong, white teeth" and drinks some of the wine. Then, after this solitary communion, she dines à deux with Robert, who serves her "no mean repast." Finally, as the sun sets, she and Robert sit—again ceremonially—at the feet of fat, matriarchal Madame Antoine, who tells them "legends of the Baratarians and the sea," so that as the moon rises Edna imagines she can hear "the whispering voices of dead men and the click of muffled gold" (chapter 13).

Having bathed, slept, feasted, communed, and received quasireligious instruction in an alternate theology, she seems definitely to have entered a fictive world, a realm of gold where extraordinary myths are real and ordinary reality is merely mythical. Yet of course the pagan fictive world Edna has entered is absolutely incompatible with the fictions of gentility and Christianity by which her "real" world lives. Metaphorically speaking, Edna has become Aphrodite, or at least an ephebe of that goddess. But what can be — must be — her fate? Shadowing her earlier "realism" with the subtextual romance she has developed in these chapters of swimming and boating, sleeping and eating, Chopin devotes the rest of her novel to examining with alternate sadness and sardonic verve the sequence of struggles for autonomy, understandings and misunderstandings, oppressions and exaltations, that she imagines would have befallen any nineteenth-century woman who experienced such a fantastic transformation. If Aphrodite — or at least Phaedra — were reborn as a *fin-de-siècle* New Orleans housewife, says Chopin, Edna Pontellier's fate would be her fate.

Because it is primarily a logical elaboration of the consequences of Edna's mythic metamorphosis, the rest of *The Awakening* can be summarized and analyzed quite briefly. Having awakened to her "true" self — that is, to a different and seemingly more authentic way of formulating her identity — Edna begins "daily casting aside that fictitious self which we assume like a garment with which to appear before the world." Yet as the self-consciously fictive episode on the Chenière Caminada reveals, neither she nor her author are eschewing fictions and fantasies altogether. Rather, Chopin has allowed the moon, the sea, the female summer colony, and Madame Antoine to recreate Edna Pontellier as a quasilegendary character in search of a story that can contain her and her power. That such a tale will be both hard to find and hard to tell, however, is revealed almost at once by Robert Le Brun's abrupt departure from Grand Isle. As the would-be lover of a newborn goddess, the Hippolytus to Edna's Phaedra, the Tristan to her Isolde, even the Leon to her Emma, he consciously struggles to do what is both morally and fictionally "right," accurately perceiving that because he is a "good" man and not a seducer, the traditional plot in which he imagines himself enmeshed now calls for renunciation. By the end of the novel, Edna will have created a different story, one in which Robert plays Adonis to her Venus, and, "no longer one of Mr. Pontellier's possessions to dispose of or not," she can declare that, like the Queen of Love, "I give myself where I choose" (chapter 36). But in chapter fifteen, as she struggles toward such an ambitious self-definition, she finds herself incapable of proposing any serious plot alternatives. Significantly, however, she does notice that Robert has announced his plans "in a high voice and with a lofty air [like] some gentlemen on the stage." Just as significantly, she retires to her cottage to tell her children a story that she does not, perhaps cannot, end, so that "instead of soothing, it excited them ... [and] she left them in heated argument, speculating about the conclusion of the tale" (chapter 15).

The tale of her own life moves just as haltingly to its strange conclusion. As Edna becomes increasingly aware that she is "seeking herself and finding herself," she struggles with growing ferocity to discard and even destroy the conventions by which she has lived — her wedding ring, her "reception day," even her "charming home" that has been so well stocked with Mr. Pontellier's "household goods." Yet though she stamps on her ring, "striving to crush it ... her small boot heel [does] not make an indenture, not a mark upon the little glittering circlet" (chapter 14). And though she plots to move out of her big house on Esplanade Street into a smaller cottage nearby, a home of her own she fictionalizes as the "Pigeon House," her husband counters with a fiction of his own "concerning the remodeling of his home, changes which he had long contemplated, and which he desired carried forward during his temporary absence" (chapter 32).

Edna's painting, her gambling, and her visits to the races as well as her relationships with Mlle. Reisz and Adèle Ratignolle, with the Flaubertian Alcée Arobin (clearly a sort of Rodolphe) and his friends Mr. and Mrs. Highcamp, constitute similar attempts at revisionary self-definition. Painting, for instance, allows her to recreate both her present and her past in more satisfactory forms. Mlle. Reisz brings her closer to Robert and to the oceanic passions and poetic ideals that had inspired her feelings for him from the first. Adèle Ratignolle reinforces her sense of the "blind contentment" implicit in the sequestered domesticity she has rejected (chapter 18). Her trips to the racetrack remind her of the freedom of her Kentucky childhood, when the "racehorse was a friend and intimate associate"—a spirit like herself, let loose in illimitable fields. And her rapidly developing sexual relationship with Arobin acts "like a narcotic upon her," offering her a "cup of life" that drugs and drains her awakening egotism even while her choice to drink it down manifests the new freedom she is attempting to define.

Yet none of these relationships succeed in yielding what we might call an open space in the plot that encloses Edna. In fact, precisely because these entanglements participate in a mutually agreed-upon social reality that gives them "realistic" plausibility as therapeutic possibilities, none is equal to the intensity of what is by now quite clearly Edna's metaphysical desire, the desire that has torn her away from her ordinary life into an extraordinary state where she has become, as Chopin's original title put it, "a solitary soul." Stranded in this state, having been visited by the Holy Ghost of the allegorical-sounding "Gulf," who rarely vouchsafes so much "ponderous" wisdom "to any woman," she can only struggle to make her own persuasive fictions, such as the story she tells at one point about "a woman who paddled away with her lover one night in a pirogue and never came back. They were lost amid the Baratarian Islands, and no one ever heard of them or found trace of them from that day to this" (chapter 23).

As Edna eventually realizes, however, even such a fiction defines desire through the banalities of second-rate romance, so that ultimately her dinner party in chapter thirty is the most authentic story she can tell and the one that is most radically revisionary. Here, as I began by noting, Edna Pontellier actually enacts the part of the person she has metaphorically become: "the regal woman, the one who rules, who looks on, who stands alone." Yet of course, in terms of the alternative theology that haunts Kate Chopin's story of this "solitary" heroine's mythologized life, the story of Edna's dinner party is the tale of a Last Supper, a final transformation of will and desire into bread and wine, flesh and blood, before the painful crucifixion of the "regal woman's" inevitable betrayal by a fictional scheme in which a regenerated Aphrodite has no viable role. More specifically, it is a Last Supper that precedes Edna's betrayal by a plot that sets both Adèle Ratignolle, the "mother-woman," and Robert Le Brun, the conventional lover, against her. In one way or another, each of these characters will remind her of her instrumentality—Adèle, exhausted by childbirth, whispering that she

must "think of the children," and Robert passionately envisioning a transaction in which Mr. Pontellier might "set" her "free" to belong to *him*.

Finally, therefore, Edna can think of only one way "to elude them," to assert her autonomy, and to become absolutely herself, and that is through her much-debated suicidal last swim. Once again, however, our interpretation of this dénouement depends on our understanding of the mythic subtextual narrative that enriches it. Certainly if we see Edna's decision to swim into the sea's "abysses of solitude" as simply a "realistic" action, we are likely to disapprove of it, to consider it—as a number of critics have—"a defeat and a regression, rooted in a self-annihilating instinct, in a romantic incapacity to accommodate . . . to the limitations of reality."[11] But though this may appear almost perversely metaphorical, I think it is possible to argue that Edna's last swim is not a suicide—that is, a death—at all, or, if it is a death, it is a death associated with a resurrection, a pagan, female Good Friday that promises a Venusian Easter. Certainly, at any rate, because of the way it is presented to us, Edna's supposed suicide enacts not a refusal to accommodate the limitations of reality but a subversive questioning of the limitations of both reality and "realism." For, swimming away from the white beach of Grand Isle, from the empty summer colony and the equally empty fictions of marriage and maternity, Edna swims, as the novel's last sentences tell us, not into death but back into her own life, back into her own vision, back into the imaginative openness of her childhood.

It is significant, after all, that in depicting Edna's last swim Chopin seems quite consciously to have swerved from precursors like Flaubert and Pierre Louÿs as well as from such a descendant as Edith Wharton, all of whom not only show the beautiful and desirous Aphroditean woman dead but actually linger over the details of her mortification. Flaubert, for instance, follows his sardonic Extreme Unction with horrifying visions of Emma's dead mouth "like a black hole at the bottom of her face," pouring forth "black liquid . . . as if she were vomiting." Similarly, in *Aphrodite* Pierre Louÿs undercuts his Chrysis's triumphant epiphany as Aphrodite with a ghastly picture of her dead body, a "thread of blood" flowing from one "diaphanous nostril" and "some emerald-colored spots . . . softly [tinting] the relaxed belly." Even Wharton, in *The House of Mirth*, though she depicts the dead "semblance of Lily Bart" more gently, imagines her heroine's "estranged and tranquil face" definitely motionless and thereby, through that motionlessness, offering her watching lover "the word which made all clear."[12] By contrast, Kate Chopin never allows Edna Pontellier to become fixed, immobilized. Neither perfected nor corrupted, she is still swimming when we last see her, nor does she ever in Dickinson's phrase, "Stop for Death." To be sure, we are told that "her arms and legs were growing tired," that "exhaustion was pressing upon and overpowering her" (chapter 39). It is clear enough that both reality and realism will contain her by fatiguing her, drowning her, killing her. Yet Chopin seems determined to regenerate Edna through a regeneration of romance, of fantasy.

No wonder, then, that as she enters the water for her last swim, this transformed heroine finally divests herself of "the unpleasant, pricking garments" of her old life as a "real" woman—a wife, mother, and mistress—and stands "naked under the sky . . . like some new-born creature, opening its eyes in a familiar world that it had never known." Together, her ceremonial nakedness, the paradoxically unknown familiarity of the world she is entering, and the "foamy wavelets [that curl and coil] like serpents about her ankles" (chapter 39) tell us that she is journeying not just toward rebirth but toward a regenerative and revisionary genre, a genre that intends to propose new realities for women by providing new mythic paradigms through which women's lives can be understood. Even in the last sentences of Chopin's novel, then, Edna Pontellier is still swimming. *And how, after all, do we know that she ever dies?* What critics have called her "suicide" is simply our interpretation of her motion, our realistic idea about the direction in which she is swimming. Yet as Chopin's last words tell us, that direction is toward the mythic, the pagan, the aphrodisiac. "There was the hum of bees, and the musky odor of pinks filled the air." Defeated, even crucified, by the "reality" of nineteenth-century New Orleans, Chopin's resurrected Venus is returning to Cyprus or Cythera.

This reading of *The Awakening* is of course hyperbolic, so that it is certainly not meant to displace those readings which honor the text's more obvious intentions. Rather, it is meant to suggest the argument between realistic and mythic aesthetic strategies that complicates and illuminates Chopin's brilliant novel. More, it is meant to make a few points about the literary history as well as the poetical significance of the goddess Aphrodite in the nineteenth and twentieth centuries. Finally, it is intended to clarify the dialectical relationship into which Chopin, as a pioneering feminist mythmaker, entered with such crucial precursors as Flaubert, Whitman, and Swinburne.

To take the last point first, I want to emphasize how important it is for us to remember that Chopin was a woman of the nineties, a writer of the *fin de siècle*. What did it mean, though, to be a *woman*, a female artist, of the *fin de siècle*, with all that such a faintly exotic, voluptuously apocalyptic French phrase implied? Superficially, at least, the *fin de siècle* meant, for literary women as for literary men, a kind of drawingroom sophistication—smoking Turkish cigarettes, subscribing to *The Yellow Book*, reading (and translating) French fiction, all of which Kate Chopin did, especially in the St. Louis years of her widowhood, which were the years of her major literary activity. More centrally, the *fin de siècle* was associated, for women as for men, with artistic and intellectual revolutionaries like Beardsley and Wilde, together with their most significant precursors— Swinburne, Pater, Whitman, Wagner, Baudelaire. For women, however, the nineties also meant the comparatively new idea of "free love" as well as the even newer persona of "The New Woman." In addition, to be a woman of the nineties meant to have come of age in a new kind of literary era, one whose spirit was, if not dominated by literary women, at least shared and shaped by female imaginations. For it was only in the nineteenth century, after all, that women entered the profession of literature in significant numbers.

Such a sharing of the literary terrain had, however, double and mutually contradictory consequences. On the one hand, a number of male writers consciously or unconsciously perceived this commercial as well as aesthetic strengthening of the female imagination as a threatening cultural event. Belated heirs of a long patrilineage, they feared that with the entrance of women into high culture, history's originatory male center might no longer hold; lawless and unsponsored, the female imagination might fragment or even ruin civilization. On the other hand, women writers for the first time experienced the validation of a literary matrilineage. The earliest heiresses of a brief but notably enlivened cultural past, they now felt empowered to imagine a powerful future. At the same time, though, they had to contend against the male anxieties that saw them a the ruinous daughters of Herodias, rousing terrible winds of change and presaging apocalypse.[13]

Given these cultural developments, it became inevitable that a work like *The Awakening* would enter into a complicated dialectic with contextual works by both male and female artists. If we once again compare Chopin's novel to its most obvious precursor, for instance—Flaubert's *Madame Bovary*—we can see that where the French writer dramatizes what he considers the destructive power of the female imagination, Chopin struggles to articulate what is positive in that power, never copying Flaubert (the way Cather and others thought she did) but always responding to him. Thus, for Flaubert, water is, as D. L. Demorest noted in 1931, "the symbol of Venus the delectable" (as it is for Chopin) but what this means in Flaubert's case is that throughout *Madame Bovary* "images of fluidity" dissolve and resolve to "evoke all that is disastrous in love." Emma's girlish sentimentality, for instance, is represented in what the writer himself called "milky oceans of books about castles and troubadours" while the final destructive horror of her imagination pours as black liquid, a sort of morbid ink, from her dead mouth, as if she were vomiting the essential fluid which had inscribed the romantic fictions that killed her and would eventually destroy her uxorious husband. Such Flaubertian images slowly filter the very idea of the fluid female imagination—the idea, that is, of female fluency—through what Sartre called "a realism more spiteful than detached" (and it is possible to speculate that they are general defensive strategies against the developing cultural power of women as well as specific defenses by which Flaubert armored himself against Louise Colet, a woman of letters on whom he felt helplessly dependent, defenses—to quote Sartre again—"in the diplomacy of Flaubert with regard to this pertinacious poetess"[14]). Whatever the source of Flaubert's anxieties, however, Chopin vigorously defends herself and other literary women against such Flaubertian defenses, for she consistently revises his negative images of female "fluency" to present not a spitefully realistic but a metaphysically lyric version of the seductive mazes of the sea from which her Venus is born, substituting the valorizations of myth for the devaluations of realism.

But of course Chopin was aided in this revisionary struggle by aesthetic strategies learned from other precursors, both male and female. Surely, for example, she learned from Whitman and Swinburne, both of whom she much admired, to see the sea the way she did—as, implicitly, "a great sweet mother" uttering "the low and delicious word 'death'" even while rocking her heroine in life-giving "billowy drowse." In a sense, in fact, her Edna Pontellier is as much a cousin of the twenty-eight-year-old "twenty-ninth bather" in Whitman's "Song of Myself" as she is a niece of Flaubert's Emma Bovary. "Handsome and richly dressed," Edna, like Whitman's woman, has had "twenty-eight years of womanly life, and all so lonesome," hiding "aft the blinds of the window," and now, "dancing and laughing," she comes along the beach to bathe in the waters of life. Yet again, much as she had learned from Whitman, Chopin swerves from him, less radically than, but almost as significantly as, she had from Flaubert, to create a woman who does not enter the sea to "seize fast" to twenty-eight young men but rather to seize and hold fast to herself. Similarly, she swerves from Swinburne to create an ocean that is not simply an other—a "fair, green-girdled mother"—but also a version of *self*, intricately veined with "mazes of inward contemplation" and sacramental precisely because emblematic of such subjectivity.[15]

In this last respect, indeed, the sea of Chopin's *Awakening* has much in common with the mystically voluptuous ocean Emily Dickinson imagines in a love poem like "Wild Nights—Wild Nights!" For when Dickinson exclaims "Rowing in Eden— / Ah, the Sea! / Might I but moor—Tonight— / In Thee!" (Johnson 249), she is imagining an ocean of erotic energy that will transform and transport her, an ocean that exists *for* her and in some sense *is* her. More, in identifying this sea with Eden, she is revising the vocabulary of traditional Christian theology so as to force it to reflect the autonomy and urgency of female desire. Such a revision is of course exactly the one that Chopin performed throughout *The Awakening*. Thus where the Extreme Unction that Flaubert intones over the corpse of Emma Bovary (stroking the oil of reductive metaphor over her no longer impassioned eyes, nostrils, lips, hands, and feet) functions as a final, misogynistic exorcism of the ferocity of the imagining and desirous woman, Kate Chopin's redefined sacraments of bread and wine or crimson cocktails function, like Dickinson's, to vindicate female desire in yet another way. For in creating a heroine as free and golden as Aphrodite, a "regal woman" who "stands alone" and gives herself where she "pleases," Chopin was exploring a vein of revisionary mythology allied not only to the revisionary erotics of free love advocates like Victoria Woodhull and Emma Goldmann but also to the feminist theology of women like Florence Nightingale, who believed that the next Christ might be a "female Christ," and Mary Baker Eddy, who argued that because "the ideal woman corresponds to life and to Love . . . we have not as much authority for considering God masculine as we have for considering Him feminine, for Love imparts the clearest idea of Deity."[16] Finally, therefore, Chopin's allusive subtextual narrative of the second coming of Aphrodite becomes an important step in the historical female struggle to imagine a deity who would rule and represent a strong female community, a woman's colony transformed into a woman's country.

To be sure, men from Wagner (in *Tannhäuser*) to Baudelaire (writing on Wagner), Swinburne (in "Lais Veneris," "Sapphics," and, by implication, his version of "Phaedra"), Beardsley (in "Under the Hill"), and Pierre Louÿs (in *Aphrodite* and *Songs of Bilitis*) had begun to examine the characteristics of the goddess of love, who had in the past, as Paul Friedrich points out in his useful study of *The Meaning of Aphrodite*, often been "avoided" by poets and scholars because they found her female erotic autonomy both "alarming" and "alluring."[17] But for the most part even these revolutionary nineteenth-century artists used Aphrodite the way Flaubert used Emma Bovary—to enact a new anxiety about female power. For Chopin, however, as for such feminist descendants as Isadora Duncan and H. D., Aphrodite/Venus becomes a radiant symbol of the erotic liberation that turn-of-the-century women had begun to allow themselves to desire.

The source of Aphrodite's significance for this revisionary company of women is not hard to discern. Neither primarily wife (like Hera), mother (like Demeter), nor daughter (like Athena), Aphrodite is, and has her sexual energy, for herself, her own grandeur, her own pleasure. As Friedrich observes, moreover, all her essential characteristics—her connections with birds and water, her affinity for young mortal men, her nakedness, her goldenness, and even her liminality, as well as her erotic sophistication—empower her in one way or another.[18] Her dove- or swan-drawn chariot enables her to travel between earth and sky, while her sea-birth places her

between earth and sea. Naked yet immortal, she moves with ease and grace between the natural and the super-natural, the human and the inhuman, nature and culture. Golden and decked in gold, she is associated with sunset and sunrise, the liminal hours of transformative consciousness—the entranced hours of awakening or drowsing—that mediate between night and day, dream and reality. Almost inevitably, then, she is the patron goddess of Sappho, whom that paradigmatic literary feminist Virginia Woolf called "the supreme head of song"[19] and whose lyric imagination famously fostered and was fostered by unique erotic freedom. Inevitably, too, she became a crucial image of female divinity in the increasingly feminist years of the *fin de siècle*, and almost as inevitably Kate Chopin (perhaps half-consciously, perhaps consciously) made her a model for a "regal" sea-borne, gold-clad, bird-haunted woman whose autonomous desire for freedom, and for a younger man, edged her first out of a large patriarchal mansion into a small female cottage and then across the shadowline that separates the clothing of culture from the nakedness of nature.

It is no coincidence, after all, that Kate Chopin imagined her Venus rising from the foam of a ceremonial dinner party in 1899, the same year that another American artist, Isadora Duncan, was beginning to dance the dances of Aphrodite in London salons while the feminist classicist, Jane Ellen Harrison, who would soon recover the matriarchal origins of ancient Greek religion, chanted Greek lyrics in the background. Within a few years, Duncan, haunted by her own birth "under the star of Aphrodite," was to sit "for days before the *Primavera*, the famous painting of Botticelli" and create a dance "in which I endeavoured to realise the soft and marvelous movements emanating from it; the circle of nymphs and the flight of the Zephyrs, all assembling about the central figure, half Aphrodite, half Madonna, who indicates the procreation of spring in one significant gesture."[20] Musing on the "sweet, half-seen pagan life, where Aphrodite gleamed through the form of the gracious but more tender Mother of Christ," this prophetess of the beauty of female nakedness was struggling, as Chopin had, to see the power of the pagan through the constraints of the Christian and the triumph of the female through the power of the pagan. She was striving, as H. D. would, to "relight the flame" of "Aphrodite, holy name," and of "Venus, whose name is kin / to venerate, / venerator." And she was laboring, as Chopin had, to define the indefinable mythic essence of "a familiar world that [she] had never known."

Like Chopin's and H. D.'s, too, Duncan's revisionary program marked an apex of feminist confidence in the female erotic autonomy of Aphrodite. But even as these artists struggled to reimagine and reappropriate the ancient powers of the Queen of Love, a few literary women who were their contemporaries or descendants had begun to formulate darker counterimaginings, visions of Venus in which the old feminine mistrust of female sensuality surfaced once again. Most notable among these visions is Willa Cather's sardonically brilliant "Coming, Aphrodite!" a retelling of Louÿs's *Aphrodite* which seems also to revise and subvert the allusive terms of *The Awakening,* and to do this so dramatically that it might almost be considered an extension of Cather's earlier censorious review of Chopin's book.[21] Specifically, Cather's story presents us with an ambitious Illinois farm girl named *Edna* Bowers who, along with devouring "Sapho" [sic] and "Mademoiselle de Maupin," has resolved to become a great actress-singer named "Eden Bower." Just as important, she has easily and casually stepped outside of ordinary social confinement and made herself erotically autonomous. When the story begins, she is being kept (entirely for her own convenience and in the furtherance of her career) by a handily absent Chicago millionaire in a New York flat next door to a studio occupied by Don Hedger, a struggling artist. Tracing the stages of their romance, Cather splits Chopin's erotic and artistic Edna into two characters: the metaphysically awakened painter, who falls in love with Eden by peering at her through a hole in the wall of his closet, and the physically awakened Eden, whom he watches as, like a latterday Isadora, she exercises naked before a mirror until, like both Edna and Isadora, she takes on a mythic radiance. Thus, at the tale's most intense, Hedger thinks of her body "as never having been clad, or as having worn the stuffs and dyes of all the centuries but his own. And for him [Eden has] no geographical associations; unless with Crete, or Alexandria, or Veronese's Venice. She [is] the immortal conception, the perennial theme" (page 22).

Throughout the tale, however, Cather hints that when this naked Aphrodite ceases to be paradigmatic and becomes personal, or to put it differently, when she refuses to be merely an artwork—a "conception"

or a "theme"—and asserts herself as an autonomous being, she becomes not an embodiment of Edna but a troublesome and anti-Edenic Eve. Early on, for instance, she threatens Hedger's masculinity by scorning his phallic bulldog, Caesar (who does, in fact, "seize her" and is in return seized and silenced by his master, who has himself been seized and stupefied by desire). Later, when Hedger tells an extravagant story about a sexually voracious Aztec princess who gelds and enslaves a captive prince, we understand the fable to be a monitory one: the power of female desire may be castrating, even murderous. Finally, therefore, Cather separates the lovers with the suggestion that Eden's sensual desirousness also implies a material greed that would ruin the aesthetic career of Hedger, the "true" artist. And indeed, by the end of the tale this anti-Edenic Eve's autonomy and ambition have led to a death of the soul even more terrible than the dissolution Cather associated with Edna Pontellier's erotic dreams. Now a major international star, scheduled to sing in an operatic version of Louÿs's *Aphrodite,* Eden has learned that Hedger, whom she hasn't seen in twenty years, has become an originary figure, "decidedly an influence in art," and it is plain that he has become this by freeing himself from her influence. As she drives off in her luxurious car her face becomes "hard and settled, like a plaster cast; so a sail, that has been filled by a strong breeze, behaves when the wind suddenly dies. Tomorrow night the wind would blow again, and this mask would be the golden face of Aphrodite. But a 'big' career takes its toll, even with the best of luck" (page 63). Cather's point seems clear: as in Louÿs's novel and as in Hedger's fable of "The Forty Lovers of the Queen," female erotic autonomy, imaged in the golden nakedness of Aphrodite, is inexorably doomed to rigidify and reify, killing not only any lover unlucky enough to remain captive but also the shining queen of love herself.

There is no doubt, of course, that Willa Cather had a number of personal motives for writing a story like "Coming, Aphrodite!" which reimagines Aphrodite so bitterly. These motives probably included both a deep anxiety about heterosexual desire and a deep identification with the closeted artist who admires and desires the naked girl next door.[22] When we look at the tale as a revisionary critique of *The Awakening,* however, we can see that the creator of Edna/Eden Bower(s) is withdrawing unsympathetically from Chopin's Edna precisely because the earlier

Aphrodite had to swim away from the solid ground of patriarchal reality and dive into what was no more than a myth of erotic power. As Mlle. Reisz tells Edna, the artist "must possess the courageous soul. . . . The brave soul. The soul that dares and defies" (chapter 21), but Edna, naked and defeated on the beach, is haunted by a bird with a broken wing, "reeling, fluttering, circling disabled down, down to the water" (chapter 38). Given her own anxieties, Cather must have needed to clarify this problem for herself; and after all, her anxieties about female eroticism were representatively female even while they had personal origins; more, they were anxieties that accurately (if paradoxically) summarized Chopin's own wounded reaction to the hostile reviews *The Awakening* received from, among others, Willa Cather. Thus, Cather implicitly decides in "Coming, Aphrodite!" that Edna Pontellier cannot be an artist because she is desirous; art, which requires courage and demands survival, must be left to the (male) Hedgers of this world, who hedge their bets by renouncing desire and protecting themselves against women with a snarling canine Caesar. Yet as Chopin keenly understood, it is precisely because she is desirous that Edna becomes an artist in the first place, and her art, as at her dinner party, is as much an art of eroticism as it is a "pure" aesthetic activity.

What is the way out of this vicious circle? Even so recent a descendent of Chopin, Cather, Duncan, and H. D. as Anne Sexton could see none. In a posthumous volume, *Words for Dr. Y.*, her daughter Linda Gray Sexton prints a piece called "To Like, To Love" in which the poet addresses "Aphrodite, / my Cape Town lady, / my mother, my daughter" and admits that though "I dream you Nordic and six foot tall, / I dream you masked and blood-mouthed," in the end "you start to cry, / you fall down into a huddle, / you are sick . . . because you are no one." It is as if for women, struggling to recapture the autonomy of desire, there was one moment of Aphroditean rebirth—the neo-Swinburnian moment, say, when Edna enthroned herself in gold satin at the head of a fictive dinner table and Isadora Duncan theatrically brooded before Botticelli's *Primavera*—and then, as Virginia Woolf wrote of the erotic in a slightly different context, "the close withdrew; the hard softened. It was over—the moment."[23] "Realism," declares Cather, may be more than a fictional mode; it may in fact reflect a social reality in which the golden Aphrodite is no more than a metal mask.

Perhaps it is not insignificant, then, that among recent poets it is a male artist, Wallace Stevens, who would have responded most sympathetically to the desire implicit in the allusive structure of the tale Kate Chopin's *The Awakening* tells, for he would have been free from the anxieties that serious identification with a mythic figure necessarily entails, free as Swinburne, for instance, was, and as neither Chopin nor Cather could ever be. Certainly when Stevens's "paltry nude" starts, like Edna Pontellier, on her early voyage, he too imagines a second coming, not of a rough beast like the slouching nightmare creature of Yeats's visionary apocalypse, but of a "goldener nude," a more triumphantly secular goddess, "of a later day."[24] Still, because Chopin was a woman writer, her imagining was at least as different from his as his was from Yeats's. She, after all, painfully dreamed a surrogate self into that visionary nakedness. Imagining (even if failing to achieve) transformation, she was haunted by her longing for a redeemed and redemptive Aphrodite, who would go "like the center of sea-green pomp" into a future of different myths and mythic difference.

Notes

1. Since there are so many different editions of this novel, all references will be to chapter numbers and will be given in the text; Cynthia Griffin Wolff, "Thanatos and Eros: Kate Chopin's *The Awakening*," *American Quarterly*, 25 (October 1973): 463.

2. Lawrence Thornton, "*The Awakening*: A Political Romance," *American Literature*, 52, no. 1 (March 1980): 51.

3. Thornton, "Political Romance," p. 64. Even those writers who analyze the feast more sympathetically tend to be perfunctory, bewildered, or both in their treatment of the event. Bernard J. Koloski, for instance, the first critic to identify the lines from Swinburne quoted by one of the dinner guests, finally reads the scene entirely in terms of those lines as Edna's Swinburnian "Song before Death." (See Koloski, "The Swinburne Lines in *The Awakening*," *American Literature*, 45 [1974]: 608–10.) Only Per Seyersted, still Chopin's most perceptive critic, defines the party as "a sensuous feast with subtle overtones of a ritual for Eros." (See Seyersted, *Kate Chopin* [Oslo: Universitetsforlaget, and Baton Rouge: Louisiana State University Press, 1969], p. 157.)

4. Willa Cather, review of *The Awakening* by Kate Chopin, *Pittsburgh Leader,* 8 July 1899, p. 6; reprinted in Margaret Culley, ed., *The Awakening: A Norton Critical Edition* (New York: W. W. Norton, 1976), pp. 153–55; Helen Taylor, introduction to *The Awakening* (London: The Women's Press, 1978), p. xviii; Warner Berthoff, *The Ferment of Realism: American Literature, 1884–1919* (New York: Free Press, 1965), p. 89; Seyersted, *Kate Chopin,* p. 161; Stanley Kauffman, "The Really Lost Generation," *The New Republic,* 3 December 1966, pp. 37–38; Otis B. Wheeler, "The Five Awakenings of Edna Pontellier," *The Southern Review,* 11 (1975), 118–28.

5. Culley, *Norton Critical,* p. 154; Thornton, "Political Romance," p. 51; Wolff, "Thanatos and Eros," pp. 453, 450.

6. Gustave Flaubert, *Madame Bovary,* edited and with a substantially new translation by Paul de Man (New York: Norton Critical Edition, 1965), p. 13. All references hereafter will be to this edition and will be included in the text.

7. Emily Brontë, *Wuthering Heights,* rev. ed., ed. William M. Sale, Jr. (New York: Norton Critical Edition, 1972), p. 107.

8. J. 732, in *The Poems of Emily Dickinson,* ed. Thomas Johnson, 3 vols. (Cambridge, Mass.: Belknap Press, 1955). All references hereafter will be to Johnson's numbers and will be included in the text.

9. See Charlotte Perkins Gilman, *Herland,* with an introduction by Ann J. Lane (New York: Pantheon, 1979).

10. Nancy Cott, *The Bonds of Womanhood: "Woman's Sphere" in New England, 1780–1835* (New Haven: Yale University Press, 1977). For an essay that also explores the paradoxically positive aspects of the privatized world of nineteenth-century women, see Carroll Smith-Rosenberg, "The Female World of Love and Ritual: Relations Between Women in Nineteenth-Century America," *Signs* 1 (Autumn 1975): 1–29.

11. Suzanne Wolkenfeld, "Edna's Suicide: The Problem of the One and the Many," in Culley, *Norton Critical,* p. 220.

12. *Collected Works of Pierre Louÿs* (New York: Shakespeare House, 1951), p. 178; Edith Wharton, *The House of Mirth* (New York: New American Library, 1964), pp. 338, 342.

13. Oscar Wilde's *Salome* (1894) and W. B. Yeats's "Nineteen Hundred and Nineteen" are only two of many works that focus on a desirous female as a sign of imminent apocalypse. For further discussions of this figure, see Mario Praz, *The Romantic Agony* (London & New York: Oxford University Press, 1970).

14. D. L. Demorest, ["Structures of Imagery in *Madame Bovary*"], in Norton Critical *Madame Bovary,* p. 280; Flaubert, letter to Louise Colet, 3 March 1852, *ibid.,* p. 311; Jean-Paul Sartre, ["Flaubert and *Madame Bovary:* Outline of a New Method"], *ibid.,* p. 303, fn 3.

15. See Swinburne, "The Triumph of Time," line 257; Whitman, "Out of the Cradle Endlessly Rocking," line 168, and "Song of Myself," line 452, ll. 199–224; and "The Triumph of Time," line 265. Portions of this last poem do, however, foreshadow the dénouement of *The Awakening:* disappointed in love, the speaker dreams of a suicide by drowning, and imagines himself first casting off his clothes and then being reborn in the sea:

> This woven raiment of nights and days,
>   Were it once cast off and unwound from me,
> Naked and glad would I walk in thy ways,
>   Alive and aware of thy ways and thee;
> Clear of the whole world, hidden at home,
> Clothed with the green and crowned with the foam,
> A pulse of the life of thy straits and bays,
>   A vein in the heart of the streams of the sea.
>   (lines 281–88)

16. Florence Nightingale, *Cassandra* (Old Westbury, N.Y.: The Feminist Press, 1979), p. 53. Mary Baker Eddy, *Science and Health with Key to the Scriptures* (Boston: First Church of Christ Scientist, 1875), p. 517.

17. Paul Friedrich, *The Meaning of Aphrodite* (Chicago: University of Chicago Press, 1978), p. 1.

18. Friedrich, *Aphrodite, passim,* but esp. pp. 33–35, 132–148.

19. Virginia Woolf, *A Room of One's Own* (New York: Harcourt Brace, 1929), p. 69.

20. See Jill Silverman, "Introduction to 'André Levinson on Isadora Duncan,'" *Ballet Review* 6, no. 4 (1977–78): 4. Silverman notes that Harrison also "guided the young dancer through the Greek collections at the British Museum," and adds that "Harrison's . . . glorification of matriarchal structures in archaic Greece . . . undoubtedly influenced the early development of Duncan's art"

(*loc. cit.*); see also Isadora Duncan, *My Life* (New York: Liveright, 1927), p. 114. Another connection between Duncan and Chopin is suggested by Elizabeth Kendall, who points out that the dancer's mother, Mary Dora Grey Duncan, was a "bold-minded St. Louis Irish girl about the same age as . . . Kate Chopin" ("Before the World Began," *Ballet Review* 6, no. 4 [1977–78]: 24).

21. Willa Cather, "Coming, Aphrodite!" in *Youth and the Bright Medusa* (New York: Vintage, 1975). All references hereafter will be to the Vintage edition and will be included in the text. It is important to note, however, that this story also exists in a somewhat bowdlerized version which was published as "Coming, Eden Bower!" in the *Smart Set* (August 1920). For a detailed study of variants between these two texts, see the appendix to *Uncle Valentine and Other Short Stories: Willa Cather's Uncollected Short Fiction, 1915–1929,* ed. Bernice Slote (Lincoln: University of Nebraska Press, 1973). Perhaps the two most significant changes are the title change and the change in the opera that Eden Bower stars in: in the *Smart Set* version, she sings Clytemnestra in Straus's *Elektra,* while in the book version she sings Aphrodite in Erlanger's *Aphrodite,* based on Louÿs's novel. Both changes suggest Cather's consciousness of the erotic centrality of Aphrodite in the story she really wanted to write. (For further background information, see Slote's introduction to *Uncle Valentine,* pp. xxi–xxii.)

22. On Cather's sexual ambivalence, see James Woodress, *Willa Cather* (New York: Pegasus, 1970), pp. 86–87, 91–94.

23. Anne Sexton, *Words for Dr. Y.,* ed. Linda Gray Sexton (Boston: Houghton Mifflin, 1978), pp. 38–39; Virginia Woolf, *Mrs. Dalloway* (New York: Harcourt Brace, 1953), p. 47.

24. See W. B. Yeats, "The Second Coming"; see also "The Paltry Nude Starts on a Spring Voyage," in *The Collected Poems of Wallace Stevens* (New York: Knopf, 1955), pp. 5–6.

CHAPTER SIX

Poststructural Criticism: Language as Context

Others for Language *all their Care express*
　　　—Pope, *An Essay on Criticism*

In the earlier chapters of this book I have defined and illustrated five contexts for criticism, five ways of looking at the literary work to decide what it means. And I have claimed that these contexts are the fundamental grounds for interpretation because questions of meaning must first be decided within one of these contexts before the significance of that meaning can be gauged. Perhaps the wary reader was inclined to accept this distinction, and the contexts themselves, only provisionally. This same reader may have noticed that occasionally the symmetrical diagram mapped some asymmetrical concepts. The mimetic context, for example, does not go exactly on all fours with the others, since it seems to offer a standard for evaluating rather than determining meanings. Not surprisingly, then, the discussion of mimeticism opened easily to the larger concerns of significance.

All similes limp, as the proverb has it, and if the inclusion of the mimetic context has hobbled my metaphor, it has allowed us to at least touch upon some ideas that have been central to thinking about art from the time of ancient Greece. It has also allowed us to touch upon some difficult conceptual problems. For not only will explorers in this context soon encounter such large questions as what is "truth" and what is "reality"; they will also quickly meet the related question of how truth or reality, however it may be defined, can be presented, or represented, in language. And even to state the case this way may beg the question since it assumes that there is a truth or reality independent of language that is to be represented by means of language.

But this is merely to say that the problems of the mimetic context appear sooner rather than later. Explorers on the vertical axis of our diagram will eventually encounter their own puzzles. The author, that solid center of genetic meaning who is the object as well as the subject of biography, gradually diminishes to the vanishing point as one pursues the day, the hour, the instant when the "real" poem was fully present to the author's consciousness. And that same apparently solid center expands, diffuses, and quite evaporates again as one pursues in the opposite direction the forces, the ideas, the "spirit of the age" that made the author that made the work. In either case the center and origin of meaning in genetic criticism, the meaner, disappears, and only language remains. Attempts to center meaning in the reader, we have noticed, will encounter parallel problems. Critics who report the behavior of actual readers offer us an embarrassing variety of different meanings; those who try to ground interpretation in some version of an ideal reader tend to shift the argument to one of the other contexts. And neither those critics who claim to interpret poems, nor those who claim merely to interpret readers, are ever free from the web of words.

Whatever line we follow then, it seems that thought finally reaches an impasse and begins to turn back on itself. Obviously these problems do not stop us from interpreting, since we cannot read at all without interpreting. But if we pause to face the problems, we may be moved to wonder how far our practice of interpreting, and our confidence in that practice, depends on our ability to suppress these problems, to become blind to the impasses. We have discovered often enough, as we moved from context to context, from argument to argument, that critics who were very clear-sighted in spotting the difficulties of other approaches appeared to be rather less perceptive about their own perceptions. Since metaphors in such discussions turn frequently to the visual, we may say we have here several variations on an old problem: it is very difficult to examine the lens you see with, to look *at* the instrument you are looking *through.*

But the visual metaphor, like all metaphors, may obscure as well as enlighten. For one constant in all these paradoxes and impasses is that they appear to arise from the nature of language itself. If language is our instrument of thought, as it is certainly our instrument of expression, then we are always in the position of trying to think about language in language. And if, as some philosophers maintain, we can escape this predicament (though the etymology of "predicament" offers little encouragement here), we must then fall into another, for we must at any rate talk about language in language, and even at this level the potential for confusion is high.

The problems of language, then, haunt all our contexts. But the formal and intertextual critics have often seemed to be most fully aware of these problems, and to have wrestled most strenuously with them. We recall that the formalist usually begins by separating the language of poetry from other kinds of language. The words of a poem may be quite ordinary—as, for example, in "London" or "The Sick Rose"—but the contextual pressures within the poem itself create tensions, ambiguities, paradoxes, ironies, in short, special meanings that arise from this unique and supercharged arrangement of words. Furthermore, elements that would be irrelevant and distracting in conversation or in a laboratory report—such as rhythm, rhyme, meter, image, metaphor, and symbol—all combine in the poem to *form* meaning. As a consequence of these synergistic pressures, quite ordinary words become extraordinary language as their extensive and intensive meanings fuse in tensive balance. The result, the formalist argues, is an indissoluble unity of form and content that can express important truths, truths that cannot be stated, or rather, imaged, in any other pattern of words.

We have already examined many aspects of this argument; here we should note three points in particular. First, by asserting the truth-telling or referential function of the poem, the formalists purchase a powerful argument for poetic value, but at a price. For now they must deal with all the difficulties of the mimetic context, most centrally the (re)presentational problems noted earlier. And the formalists' claim that the poem is a special kind of verbal structure that is in some mysterious way pecu-

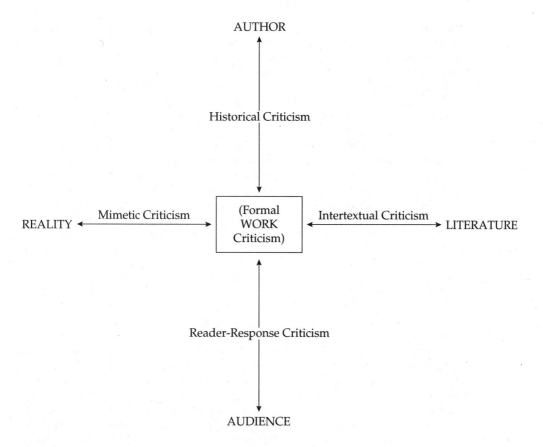

AUTHOR

Historical Criticism

REALITY ← Mimetic Criticism → (Formal WORK Criticism) ← Intertextual Criticism → LITERATURE

Reader-Response Criticism

AUDIENCE

liarly suited to capture the complexities of nonverbal reality is a claim that has not been accepted by all students of language.

Second, as we saw earlier, the formalists threaten to undercut their own mimetic ground when they emphasize the poem's apparently nonreferential qualities of unity and coherence. But are unity and coherence really features of the poem, or are they simply functions of the critics' own rage for order? And can the formalists escape the relativism of reader-response criticism by appealing to the "text" as a stable origin and center of meaning? Or does the radically metaphorical nature of poetic language, the same metaphorical nature that the formalists have always taken as a starting point, undercut this claim? For one could argue that precisely because poetic language is radically metaphorical, it is radically indeterminate. This is, poetic language will always elude readings that seek to impose upon it a complete unity or to determine exactly its range of meanings. Other equally coherent readings will always be possible, and instead of a stable center for determinate meaning, the text becomes, from this perspective, a network for the free play of an indefinite number of meanings.

And this argument leads to the third point. For if these are the consequences of taking very seriously the metaphorical or "rhetorical" nature of poetic language, what follows if we examine closely, with a formalist's trained eye for implied image and submerged metaphor, the "nonpoetic" language used in other forms of discourse, and we discover that this language too—in fact, all language—is radically metaphorical or rhetorical? One thing that will follow is that the formalists' enabling distinction between "poetic" and "nonpoetic" language will begin to get fuzzy. If the language explaining a poem is itself poetic, then the poet and the critic, the poem and the commentary, will begin to blur and meld in an unsettling way, all the more unsettling because here, too, the conclusion that shakes the formalist's premises appears to follow directly from those premises.

Now the intertextual critics, and particularly those most committed to a structuralist perspective, have recognized some of these difficulties. By taking the system of language as their base and model, they acknowledge more fully than do critics in any other context the central place of language in all matters of interpretation. Furthermore, by stressing the self-referential nature of the system, they are able to defer (indefinitely, some would argue) the problems of mimesis or correspondence. "Meanings" are generated and deciphered within the self-contained system of signs. In this view we humans are essentially structuring or signifying animals, and our entire culture—the foods we eat, the clothes we wear, the sounds we utter—is a system of sign systems, a layering of codes. Hence the broad claim that all the world, at least as it can be known to *homo significans,* is "text," and all understanding, all deciphering, is "intertextual."

This is, of course, a radical structuralist's view of the world. Not all intertextual critics feel compelled to extend the notion of "text" this far. Yet even if we confine ourselves to more traditional literary problems, the intertextual emphasis on system or code seems to have wide explanatory power. Perhaps most importantly it offers to explain how readers may come to know literature in the same way that they progressively come to know their own language. At least by analogy, then, we can talk of the "language" of poetry, or of painting, of architecture, of music, and so forth. In each medium the competent "readers"—and, perforce, the competent artists—would be those who had mastered the conventions, the "language," of their art. From this perspective, the study of poetry could become the coherent, progressive discipline that Frye and others have called for, and "literary criticism" would be the name of that discipline.

Thus, intertextual critics offer their perspective as the interpretive context *par excellence,* for they undertake to show not simply what a particular poem means but how it is possible for a poem to carry meaning at all and how it is possible for the competent reader to understand that meaning. Consequently, they would argue that my diagram is misleading. In place of a number of perspectives set at equal distance from the work and from each other, with the formalist perspective apparently closer or more central than the rest, the intertextual critics would image a pyramid with the intertextual perspective at the base, since to understand anything in language at all, they would claim, is to understand "intertextually," that is, within a system of conventional signs. In other words, the textual meaning that formalists claim as their ground is in turn grounded on intertextual meaning. And so is every other kind of meaning.

But how solid is that ground? One suggestion of sponginess appears when we try to separate the "literary" elements in a work from the "nonliterary" elements. "The Sick Rose" is a poem in English. It would mean little to a highly competent reader of French poetry who knew no English. But it would also mean little to a native speaker of English who knew nothing about poetry and who happened to be in search of gardening instruction. And if we set about learning the language of poetry—that system of conventions somehow independent of particular linguistic systems, although always expressed within one of them—is there any principle of limitation we could apply? Or will the right side of our diagram expand indefinitely until we are driven once more to the position of the radical structuralist and must see the strands of any text interwoven with the strands of all texts? If so, then again the world becomes "text," no clear line can be drawn between one kind of text and another kind, or between one text and another text, and the meaning of any individual text becomes radically indeterminate because potentially limitless. In this view, intertextual meaning seems not merely a rather spongy ground for textual meaning but a quicksand that threatens to submerge the individual poem in a slough of signs.

This threat may not be as serious as it sounds as long as the individual reader can supply the focus. But it is not easy to see how readers are going to keep their feet on this ground either. We may be, as the structuralists claim, structuring animals. But it is at least as true to say that we are structured animals, as much products as producers of systems, as much creatures as creators of our structures. Language once again supplies the paradigm. Any language is a system of systems—phonological, morphological, syntactical, lexical. Those who know the phonemes of English, for example, can immediately structure the speech sounds they hear into clusters of sounds, grouping together as one "sound" all variations that never contrast meanings in English (paying no attention, say, to the change from aspirated to unaspirated "p" in the word *pip*) but sharply distinguishing differences in sound that are significant in the system (such as the voicing of the initial consonant that changes *pip* to *bip*). We say that English listeners "structure" the sounds they hear, but only to the extent that those sounds conform to the independent and impersonal structure of English. And if the English phonemic system is the only one they know, listeners will quite automatically "hear" any language the same way, which means that they will miss some significant sounds when listening to a different language. So it would be as accurate to say that English has structured their hearing, has formed their perceptions. In this respect, surely, we are much less creators than we are creatures of "our" language.

And language, to repeat, is the paradigm case, the simple instance of structured humanity. If our analogy holds, the idea of what qualifies one as a competent hearer of English could be expanded to explain what makes one a competent reader of *Hamlet* by showing how much of the system of English and how much of the system of "literature" such a reader would need to master—or be mastered by. Such an explanation would be immensely complex, yet at any point within these multilayered and interlocking systems the paradigm case would apply: readers could read only according to the way they had been structured. Thus the idea of the sturdy, autonomous "ego" controlling meaning as it reads begins to sink into the same slough of signs.

Another troublesome feature of structures emerges when we try to think of their origin and development. For if the "system" must be already in place before any element in that system can have meaning, it is difficult to conceive of an origin or starting point. The problem here is not the infinite regress of the diachronic vision where each cause must have its prior cause, *ad infinitum*, but the impossibility of regressing at all. For try as we might to image in its pristine isolation the first meaningful utterance, the first systemless "sign" around which the system could form, imagination fails us. There can be no meaning, no sign, except within the system that confers meaning. So the system must be already there at the beginning; it must be always already there. In short, from this perspective we can't very well account for the phenomenon of change at all, and this thoroughly synchronic vision seems to throw up new versions of the ancient paradoxes propounded by Zeno the Eleatic that appeared to show that change itself was but an illusion.

So the intertextual line, too, ends in paradox and puzzle. We start with the plausible view that meaning takes place within a conventional system, with "ordinary language" serving as the paradigm, and we construct on this ground a vision of literary criticism as a progressive and coherent discipline that might explain the system of literature as linguistics explains the system of language. Yet these premises, which promise to explain much, seem to lead logically to larger and more radical claims and to some puzzling problems. The very notion of "intertextuality," while showing how texts can have meaning, seems to undercut any way of delimiting meaning. For while it is easy to see that meaning must be limited by context, it is hard to see how context can be limited. Furthermore, the idea of structure begins to double-back on itself in odd ways if one pushes the structuralist premises far enough. At the end of the line, the coder and decoder of the message come to appear not as autonomous creators and masters of structures they employ but, at least in part, as creatures structured by the codes, employees of the system, with the notion of the autonomous ego itself being merely a device of language. The difficulty we have in thinking of the origin of the system, of imaging that first, lonely, "sign," may be a symptom of this condition. This is, perhaps, a strange conclusion to structuralist thought, but it is one that appears to follow logically from structuralist assumptions.

We may say, then, that even those critics who have wrestled most strenuously with the problems of language have come off with nothing better than a draw. Their own premises seem to carry implications that, when fully unfolded, serve to undercut those premises. To demonstrate that this is always the case is the main task or project of the "deconstructive" critics. The chief figure here, and the man who has provided the name and many of the key terms for the movement, is the French philosopher Jacques Derrida. Derrida's way of working—he will not call it a method—is to concentrate his considerable analytical powers on a particular text, usually a piece of discursive or "philosophical" prose, and to deconstruct or "unbuild" that text to show how it was constructed, to reveal its underlying metaphorical base. In this description, Derrida appears to practice some combination of formal and structural analysis, and that appearance is not entirely misleading, for Derrida could be called a superformalist or a superstructuralist, a reader who is willing to push the assumptions of the formal and structural perspectives to their logical, and paradoxical, conclusions. Above all else, he is a philosopher who takes the problems of language seriously and who argues that Western "metaphysics" from Plato to the present has contrived to ignore or suppress those problems. As Derrida sees it, metaphysicians have typically thought of truth or ultimate reality as something above or beyond language. They have then sought, or simply assumed, an "unproblematic" language, a transparent medium that would contain or express this truth, a "philosophical discourse" that would rise above the ambiguities of ordinary language and the obscuring rhetoricity of poetry. By subjecting "philosophical" texts to careful, formal analysis, Derrida seeks to show that there is no such language. All philosophical texts, all texts of any kind, he argues, are radically metaphorical or "poetic," and thus the very nature of language undoes the metaphysicians' attempts to get through or beyond language, to convey their thoughts directly without imposing an intervening screen of rhetoric.

Some philosophers who have been acutely aware of these problems have tried to circumvent this screening effect by claiming to concentrate on those moments when the objects of thought were most fully "present" to the thinker, and the speaker of those thoughts most fully "present" to his or her hearers. Socrates' famous distrust of writing is a case in point. These attempts, according to Derrida, have led to the widespread and mistaken "privileging" of speech over writing, which has led in turn to Derrida's already notorious reversal of that priority, his counter-privileging of writing and the science of "grammatology." By such reversals and transpositions, Derrida wants to decenter our thought so we can see how it was centered in the first place. In the case of speech and writing, for example, the paradoxical position that writing is prior to speech becomes more understandable when we notice that by "writing" Derrida means something like the system of language, and in this he shows himself a thoroughgoing structuralist as well as a thoroughgoing formalist. For, as we have noted, the necessary condition for any meaningful utterance is that it be structured according to a system that is, in Derrida's phrase, "always already" in place and quite independent of the speaker—already "written," one might say.

As a formalist, then, Derrida deconstructs the text to reveal its metaphorical basis, its inherent rhetoricity, conditions necessarily at odds with the idea of philosophical prose as a transparent, undistorting medium for present-ing nonverbal reality. As a structuralist, he deconstructs the text to show how it is structured by the system of language, a condition that once again limits the control of the speaker or author. Furthermore, as a radical structuralist, he subjects the concept of "structure" to the same deconstructive analysis. This maneuver is illustrated in his reading of the structural anthropologist Claude Lévi-Strauss in the essay "Structure, Sign, and Play," which follows in this section. Here Derrida reveals at the "center" of structuralist thought an insoluble paradox: structuralists argue that they can critique empiricism because any knowledge empirically derived can be recognized as knowledge only within a system already in place; yet structuralists simultaneously argue that their own understanding of the system was empirically derived and can, therefore, be altered by new empirical discoveries. In other words, the structuralists claim to operate outside structure while claiming that such operation is impossible. And both claims are necessary to their enterprise.

This paradox haunts our attempts to think about structure at any and all levels. It is surely lurking in the tension we noted between the formalist's "empirical" view of form as the unique possession of the individual poem and the intertextualist's "structural" view of form as what the poem shares with other poems. For to make critical statements at all, each must accommodate the other's viewpoint. At a higher level of abstraction, the paradox is central to the long-playing debate between those who claim that truth is a matter of empirically discovered correspondence to "the way things are" and those who claim that truth is a matter of coherence, of conformity to a system of beliefs already in place. For empiricists must finally defend their view on the ground that it is consistent with our other beliefs, while their opponents must finally argue that the coherence theory does indeed correspond to "the way things are."

Closer to hand, the reader can discover a convenient example of the problem in the design of this book, since it should now be apparent that our program—to examine three target texts from different perspectives, and to measure the usefulness of these perspectives by what they revealed about the texts—could be pursued only by ignoring this empiricist–structuralist paradox. If we assume we can apply, say, a formal approach to *The Tempest*, and then a historical approach, an intertextual approach, and so forth, and see which approach works best, or see to what extent each "works," we implicitly claim that we possess already a standard of critical adequacy independent of any approach. We will know what "works" when we see it. This is the empiricist view, and our willingness to accept this as the commonsense view shows our empirical bias. Yet if we must always read some way, within some context, then the structuralist view reasserts itself, for if we can never know the poem apart from some approach, then we can never use the "poem" to test the adequacy of an approach. We may prefer one context to another, but we could never point to the poem to ground that preference, could never claim one perspective was more "illuminating" than another, for the idea of what counted as illumination would itself be determined within the context we were defending. By such reasoning we simultaneously undercut our structures while revealing our inability to do without them.

These, then, are some of the consequences of deconstructive thought. As the sample essay illustrates, Derrida is difficult to paraphrase or summarize. Since he claims to approach each text on its own terms, even if only to show that these terms are not what the author thought they were, he claims to be something of an empiricist himself. Yet he knows full well that he cannot escape the dilemma he reveals in Lévi-Strauss's thought. Furthermore, because he is acutely aware of the metaphorical nature of language and of our tendency to overlook that nature, he has adopted a strategy of changing his key terms, his key metaphors, from book to book, or even from essay to essay, to prevent them hardening into unexamined starting points. By such shifts and dodges he hopes to keep his readers alive to the rhetorical basis of his own language and to remind us that he doesn't offer a method or a system. Rather, he offers a way of reading that focuses our attention on the problematic nature of language and that deconstructs the methods and systems of others.

Yet despite his claim to offer no method, or perhaps because of it, Derrida's way of reading has attracted a number of followers, especially in the field of literary criticism. On this side of the Atlantic, three of the most prominent figures associated with deconstruction are Paul de Man, Geoffrey Hartman, and J. Hillis Miller. Each of these men was an established critic before adopting the name and some of the aims of deconstruction, and each has a different emphasis and practices a different kind of deconstructive analysis. Hartman, for example, has been most concerned with the theoretical implications of the movement for the entire enterprise of criticism, often celebrating the ludic and "liberating" elements in deconstruction. Miller shares some of these interests but tends to downplay theory and to focus, like a good formalist, on specific texts. For him, deconstruction is yet one more critical perspective that may help him in his attempt to get at what he calls "the oddity of literary language." This focus on individual texts is even more intense in the work of Paul de Man, whose patient, probing, careful analyses are in some ways ideal formalist readings.

As even these few examples show, deconstruction is hardly a unified school of criticism, and given Derrida's starting point, that is scarcely surprising. Nonetheless, the work of Derrida and his followers has been much discussed and often imitated in the past two decades, so much so that we may soon have in print a deconstructive reading of most major literary texts. And this seems, in some ways, a rather strange prospect. After all, it might be exciting and liberating to argue, as Derrida does, that "philosophical" texts are radically metaphorical or tropical, that they have not achieved a truth-bearing medium free from the distortions of rhetoric or poetry, but it can hardly be news that poems are radically metaphorical or rhetorical. The formal and intertextual critics have asserted that all along. And up to a certain point, the deconstructive critic always performs some version of formal or intertextual analysis.

But it is the mark of the deconstructive critics not to stop at any certain point. As formalists—and the rigorous analyses of Paul de Man may be taken as exemplary here—they will be concerned with the rhetorical or tropical nature of the text's language, but they will not start with the formalist assumption of unity or coherence. Instead, given their view of language, they will work from the opposite assumption and will seek to show how the rhetoricity of the text will undo or undercut any single or unified meaning. Thus the language of the poem, sharing with all language a radically rhetorical nature, shares too the condition of being radically undecidable or indeterminate. Ironically, de Man, starting from this assumption, occasionally comes to re-distinguish and re-privilege specifically "poetic" language as the only language aware of its own condition. The poem, by frankly announcing itself as a rhetorical or metaphorical structure, rather than trying to conceal this condition as "nonpoetic" language does, becomes the only truly honest language. This seems to be the deconstructivists' version of the old idea that poets never lie because they never affirm. In this version, the poet's language affirms only that it lies—which at least puts it one up on everybody else's language.

As formalists, then, the deconstructive critics keep all the formalist assumptions, except the central one that coherence and unity are the defining features of poetry. Likewise, as intertextualists, they accept most of the structuralist assumptions: the poem is an utterance encoded in a system of signs, a *parole* in the *langue* of literature; the text is a dense fabric of threads stretching out to other texts. The exemplary figure here might be Roland Barthes as he carries his structuralist enterprise to its elaborate and playful conclusion in *S/Z*, a book-length reading of a Balzac short story in terms of several layered codes. Looked at one way, the book is the apogee of structuralism. Yet one gets the impression that these codes lack the firmness that the typical structuralist would want. It seems they could easily be more or fewer or other than they are, and rather than revealing a "competent" reader who has mastered a system of literary codes firmly controlling large but determinate meanings, the book displays instead a subtle and playful intelligence exulting in the creation of signs, "codes," and alternative versions of the story he is "reading." As intertextualists, then, deconstructive critics accept the main structuralist assumptions, but refuse to accept the limits that the concepts of structure or system are generally thought to impose.

In other words, the relationship between structuralism and "poststructuralism" is complex. Poststructuralism is sometimes simply another name for deconstruction, but even in this restricted sense it is potentially confusing. As Derrida's critique of Lévi-Strauss illustrates, in important ways deconstruction is not so much a break from structuralism as an extension of it. Structuralist thinkers had already applied the linguistic model to all cultural phenomena, had already "textualized" the world. And in the process they had gone some way toward decentering the "individuals" who were supposed to control these all-encompassing semiological systems. Yet structuralist thought is characterized, as the term "structure" implies, by an emphasis on order, form, and limit. Authors and readers may be less in control than they imagine, but the system, the structure, remains always in place to stabilize meaning. It is exactly this stability that the deconstructive critique of structure destabilizes, revealing a system that guarantees only free play, a ceaseless slide of signifiers, an endless deferral of meaning with all possible points of fixity—origin, telos, center, circumference—now deconstructed. And this critique, we should remember, takes place at the level of language itself, the foundation and paradigm of structuralist thought.

Deconstructive criticism, then, is poststructural in at least three senses: it comes after structuralism; it deconstructs the central concept of "structure"; yet at the same time it continues many of the key ideas of structuralism, among them the ideas that humans are signifying creatures, that human culture is a system of sign systems, and that the source and pattern for these systems is language.

While Derrida and other deconstructive critics have concentrated their analyses on literary and philosophical texts, other writers have applied these ideas and these analytical strategies to different layers of cultural coding. If, as the structuralists claim, all culture is a language, then the deconstructive critique of language will similarly destabilize all cultural codes. With that realization, language, as Derrida has put it, "invaded the universal problematic." Poststructuralism, then, may be more broadly defined as the application of a deconstructive language model to all aspects of culture and thought.

While poststructuralism in this expanded sense has received considerable play in recent Anglo-American criticism, French thinkers have clearly been the leaders in this context, and three of the most influential have been Jacques Lacan, Jean-François Lyotard, and Jean Baudrillard. None of these writers is primarily a "literary" critic in the usual sense of the term; each developed his views independently of Derridean deconstruction; and they disagree among themselves about much. Yet their areas of agreement are more important, and their influences have been very much in the same direction. They agree, for example, that most modern philosophy from Descartes to the present has been built on the false premise that philosophy could provide a foundation for knowledge solid enough to support totalizing or universal claims. Instead, they are inclined to accept the views of skeptical thinkers like Nietzsche and Heidegger who argue that all perspectives are partial and all representation inevitably mediated and distorted by language. They agree, too, that the autonomous, rational, unified "individual" posited by most philosophical systems is a fiction, and they are inclined to speak instead of the decentered, fragmented, and linguistically constructed "subject." Above all, they agree that language in its problematicized form is the key to understanding subjects, objects, history, and culture.

For Jacques Lacan, language is not only the base and model for all cultural formations, it is the element that literally creates and structures our psychic life. A psychoanalyst, Lacan rewrites Freud in terms of language. As the child enters the "Symbolic Order," the "pure desire" of prelinguistic existence is dominated, channeled, and repressed. "The law of man has been the law of language" (*Ecrits* 61). The result is the linguistically created "subject," including both conscious and unconscious levels. Further, the unconscious thus created is structured by language on the pattern of language. Conflating Freud's "displacement" and "condensation" with "metaphor" and "metonymy," Lacan reads the unconscious as one reads a literary language. But then, for the poststructuralist, all language is literary language.

Lyotard comes at the problematic of language from a philosophical background. Adopting aspects of Nietzsche's critique, he rejects all foundationalist and essentialist modes of thought and he parallels, on a political level, Derrida's concept of "dissemination," the insight that signification always eludes and exceeds structural constraints. For Lyotard, political struggle is very much a matter of language and depends on our using deconstructive strategies to decenter and undermine the "dominant" discourses. The goal, however, cannot be to replace one dominant discourse with another, but rather to maintain a multiplicity of discourses.

If Lyotard's extension of the poststructuralist critique of language to political discourses ends in a vision of a pluralist utopia, Baudrillard's further extension of that critique takes on a distinctly dystopian cast. While Lacan saw the unconscious as structured like a language and Lyotard subsumed politics to discourse theory, the early Baudrillard explained economics on the model of language. Deconstructing the Marxist distinctions between base and superstructure, use value and exchange value, he pictured the economy as an endless circulation of signs with no values that could be grounded outside the system. In effect, exchange value was the only value. Here again we replace foundational systems of thought, like those of Freud or Marx, which claim to get beneath superficial appearances to reveal the real meaning, the real forces, underneath, with something resembling the deconstructivist language model. In the later work of Baudrillard this model, now extended to the entire textualized world, to all aspects of culture, yields the vision of "hyperreality." We live, says Baudrillard, in a postmodern age of "radical semiurgy," an era of proliferated signs where the boundaries between sign and signified have "imploded" and the very basis of the "real" has simply disappeared. "Life" imitates "art," Disneyland becomes the exemplar, and the entire world is simulacra, signs without referents. "Whoever lives by meaning dies by meaning."

An extreme view, certainly, though one that was perhaps implicit all along in the poststructural critique of language and representation. Once the deconstructive view of language was combined with the structuralist idea that language is the model for all cultural formations, the road was open to Baudrillard's hyperreality. To be sure, not all poststructuralists have been willing to go as far as Baudrillard, but most have worked to extend the critique of language and representation to various aspects of culture. In the process, they have profoundly influenced the way we think about language, literature, philosophy, politics, and the psyche. Their terminology, their analytical strategies, and their key ideas have been adopted and adapted by writers in all these fields, often by writers who in important ways disagree with them.

We will see some of these influences and disagreements in the next chapter. If we focus now on the more limited area of "literary" study as it is usually defined, we can say that on one level poststructural criticism offers a way of reading texts that combines and extends formal and intertextual analysis, but with the crucial differences noted above. On another level, and perhaps more importantly, it offers a metacritical and skeptical critique of all contexts and systems and theories of reading. By subjecting language to deconstructive analysis, poststructuralists remind us that our constructs are, after all, constructs and that the metaphors we think with are, after all, metaphors. By following the premises of our interpretative systems to their paradoxical conclusions, they remind us that we often achieve our insights by turning a blind eye to those impasses where our line of thought turns back upon itself. We will, of course, go on thinking and speaking in metaphors, for we have no other way to think or speak. And we will go on interpreting in one context or another, for we have no other ways to interpret. But if we have absorbed the lessons of poststructural thought, we will suspect that our practices rest on very shaky theoretical foundations. Language has indeed "invaded the universal problematic."

Suggestions for Further Reading

For deconstruction, the work of Jacques Derrida is central; Peggy Kamuf, ed., *A Derrida Reader* (1991), offers a convenient selection. Roland Barthes, *S/Z* (1970), shows this protean writer in one of his poststructuralist phases. Some representative texts by American critics associated with deconstruction are Paul de Man, *Blindness and Insight* (1983); Geoffrey Hartman, *Criticism in the Wilderness* (1980); J. Hillis Miller, *The Linguistic*

Moment from Wordsworth to Stevens (1985); and Barbara Johnson, *The Critical Difference* (1980). Three explanatory works on deconstruction, in recommended order of reading: Christopher Norris, *Deconstruction: Theory and Practice* (rev. ed. 1991); Jonathan Culler, *On Deconstruction* (1982); and Vincent Leitch, *Deconstruction: An Advanced Introduction* (1983). Lacan's work can be sampled in *Ecrits: A Selection* (1977), Lyotard's in Andrew Benjamin, ed., *The Lyotard Reader* (1989), and Baudrillard's in Mark Poster, ed., *Jean Baudrillard: Selected Writings* (1988). The variety of poststructuralist practice is illustrated in collections like Josue V. Harari, ed., *Textual Strategies: Perspectives in Post-Structuralist Criticism* (1979), and Richard Machin and Christopher Norris, eds., *Post-Structuralist Readings of English Poetry* (1987). Anthony Easthope, *British Post-Structuralism* (1988), and Art Berman, *From the New Criticism to Deconstruction* (1988), examine the impact of poststructuralist thought on British and American criticism.

THEORY

When Jacques Derrida presented his "Structure, Sign, and Play" at a conference on the "Sciences of Man" at Johns Hopkins University in 1966, it marked the entrance of deconstruction onto the Anglo-American literary scene. While no single essay can fully represent Derrida's thought, or capture his shifting terminology, this influential paper shows some aspects of that thought in operation and introduces a number of terms—supplementarity, presence, différance—which have become part of the lexicon of poststructural criticism. It also displays Derrida's characteristic way of going to work. Examining the thought of Claude Lévi-Strauss, probably the world's best-known structural anthropologist, Derrida deconstructs structuralism itself. Since deconstructivists are often called "poststructuralists," it is worth noticing that this name is potentially misleading. For although Derrida's critique proceeds by uncovering an irreducible contradiction built into structuralist thought, he does not claim to pass beyond structuralism nor to replace it with another, contradiction-free system of thought. Rather, the critique of structuralism presented here is exemplary. All systems of thought are subject to a similar deconstruction, since we cannot very well think of a centerless system, one that does not claim to be grounded finally on some presence, foundation, origin (archè), or end (telos) beyond freeplay. Each of the "contexts" of this book, for example, proposes a locus or ground for meaning (author, text, audience, reality, literature), and all are open to the same critique. As long as we continue to interpret interpretation, structure, sign, and freeplay in the hope of finding an end where interpretation itself can come to rest, we are, Derrida concludes, deluded by our habits of mind and language.

Structure, Sign, and Play in the Discourse of the Human Sciences[1]

Jacques Derrida

Perhaps something has occurred in the history of the concept of structure that could be called an "event" if this loaded word did not entail a meaning which it is precisely the function of structural—or structuralist—thought to reduce or to suspect. But let me use the term "event" anyway, employing it with caution and as if in quotation marks. In this sense, this event will have the exterior form of a *rupture* and a *redoubling*.

It would be easy enough to show that the concept of structure and even the word "structure" itself are as old as the *epistèmè*—that is to say, as old as western science and western philosophy—and that their roots thrust deep into the soil of ordinary language, into whose deepest recesses the *epistèmè* plunges to gather them together once more, making them part of itself in a metaphorical displacement. Nevertheless, up until the event which I wish to mark out and define, structure—or rather the structurality of structure—although it has always been involved, has always been neutralized or reduced, and this by a process of giving it a center or referring it to a point of presence, a fixed origin. The function of this center was not only to orient, balance, and organize the structure—one cannot in fact conceive of an unorganized structure—but above all to make sure that the organizing principle of the structure would limit what we might call the *freeplay* of the structure. No doubt that by orienting and organizing the coherence of the system, the center of a structure permits the freeplay of its elements inside the total form. And even today the notion of a structure lacking any center represents the unthinkable itself.

Nevertheless, the center also closes off the freeplay it opens up and makes possible. *Qua* center, it is the point at which the substitution of contents, elements, or terms is no longer possible. At the center, the permutation or the transformation of elements (which may of course be structures enclosed within a structure) is forbidden. At least this permutation has always remained *interdicted*[2] (I use this word deliberately). Thus it has always been thought that the center, which is by definition unique, constituted that very thing within a structure which governs the structure, while escaping structurality. This is why classical thought concerning structure could say that the center is, paradoxically, *within* the structure and *outside* it. The center is at the center of the totality, and yet, since the center does not belong to the totality (is not part of the totality), the totality *has its cen-*

ter elsewhere. The center is not the center. The concept of centered structure—although it represents coherence itself, the condition of the *epistèmè* as philosophy or science—is contradictorily coherent. And, as always, coherence in contradiction expresses the force of a desire. The concept of centered structure is in fact the concept of a freeplay based on a fundamental ground, a freeplay which is constituted upon a fundamental immobility and a reassuring certitude, which is itself beyond the reach of the freeplay. With this certitude anxiety can be mastered, for anxiety is invariably the result of a certain mode of being implicated in the game, of being caught by the game, of being as it were from the very beginning at stake in the game.[3] From the basis of what we therefore call the center (and which, because it can be either inside or outside, is as readily called the origin as the end, as readily *archè* as *telos*), the repetitions, the substitutions, the transformations, and the permutations are always *taken* from a history of meaning [*sens*]—that is, a history, period—whose origin may always be revealed or whose end may always be anticipated in the form of presence. This is why one could perhaps say that the movement of any archeology, like that of any eschatology, is an accomplice of this reduction of the structurality of structure and always attempts to conceive of structure from the basis of a full presence which is out of play.

If this is so, the whole history of the concept of structure, before the rupture I spoke of, must be thought of as a series of substitutions of center for center, as a linked chain of determinations of the center. Successively, and in a regulated fashion, the center receives different forms or names. The history of metaphysics, like the history of the West, is the history of these metaphors and metonymies. Its matrix—if you will pardon me for demonstrating so little and for being so elliptical in order to bring me more quickly to my principal theme—is the determination of being as *presence* in all the senses of this word. It would be possible to show that all the names related to fundamentals, to principles, or to the center have always designated the constant of a presence—*eidos, archè, telos, energeia, ousia* (essence, existence, substance, subject), *aletheia*, transcendentality, consciousness, or conscience, God, man, and so forth.

The event I called a rupture, the disruption I alluded to at the beginning of this paper, would presumably have come about when the structurality of structure had to begin to be thought, that is to say, repeated, and this is why I said that this disruption was repetition in all of the senses of this word. From then on it became necessary to think the law which governed, as it were, the desire for the center in the constitution of structure and the process of signification prescribing its displacements and its substitutions for this law of the central presence—but a central presence which was never itself, which has always already been transported outside itself in its surrogate. The surrogate does not substitute itself for anything which has somehow pre-existed it. From then on it was probably necessary to begin to think that there was no center, that the center could not be thought in the form of a being-present, that the center had no natural locus, that it was not a fixed locus but a function, a sort of nonlocus in which an infinite number of sign-substitutions came into play. This moment was that in which language invaded the universal problematic; that in which, in the absence of a center or origin, everything became discourse— provided we can agree on this word—that is to say, when everything became a system where the central signified, the original or transcendental signified, is never absolutely present outside a system of differences. The absence of the transcendental signified extends the domain and the interplay of signification *ad infinitum*.

Where and how does this decentering, this notion of the structurality of structure, occur? If would be somewhat naïve to refer to an event, a doctrine, or an author in order to designate this occurrence. It is no doubt part of the totality of an era, our own, but still it has already begun to proclaim itself and begun to *work*. Nevertheless, if I wished to give some sort of indication by choosing one or two "names," and by recalling those authors in whose discourses this occurrence has most nearly maintained its most radical formulation, I would probably cite the Nietzschean critique of metaphysics, the critique of the concepts of being and truth, for which were substituted the concepts of play, interpretation, and sign (sign without truth present); the Freudian critique of self-presence, that is, the critique of consciousness, of the subject, of self-identity and of self-proximity or self-possession; and, more radically, the Heideggerean destruction of metaphysics, of onto-theology, of the determination of being as presence. But all these destructive discourses and all their analogues are trapped in a sort of circle. This circle is unique. It describes the form of the relationship between the his-

tory of metaphysics and the destruction of the history of metaphysics. *There is no sense* in doing without the concepts of metaphysics in order to attack metaphysics. We have no language—no syntax and no lexicon—which is alien to this history; we cannot utter a single destructive proposition which has not already slipped into the form, the logic, and the implicit postulations of precisely what it seeks to contest. To pick out one example from many: the metaphysics of presence is attacked with the help of the concept of the *sign*. But from the moment anyone wishes this to show, as I suggested a moment ago, that there is no transcendental or privileged signified and that the domain or the interplay of signification has, henceforth, no limit, he ought to extend his refusal to the concept and to the word sign itself—which is precisely what cannot be done. For the signification "sign" has always been comprehended and determined, in its sense, as sign-of, signifier referring to a signified, signifier different from its signified. If one erases the radical difference between signifier and signified, it is the word signifier itself which ought to be abandoned as a metaphysical concept. When Lévi-Strauss says in the preface to *The Raw and the Cooked*[4] that he has "sought to transcend the opposition between the sensible and the intelligible by placing [himself] from the very beginning at the level of signs," the necessity, the force, and the legitimacy of his act cannot make us forget that the concept of the sign cannot in itself surpass or bypass this opposition between the sensible and the intelligible. The concept of the sign is determined by this opposition: through and throughout the totality of its history and by its system. But we cannot do without the concept of the sign, we cannot give up this metaphysical complicity without also giving up the critique we are directing against this complicity, without the risk of erasing difference [altogether] in the self-identity of a signified reducing into itself its signifier, or, what amounts to the same thing, simply expelling it outside itself. For there are two heterogenous ways of erasing the difference between the signifier and the signified: one, the classic way, consists in reducing or deriving the signifier, that is to say, ultimately in *submitting* the sign to thought; the other, the one we are using here against the first one, consists in putting into question the system in which the preceding reduction functioned: first and foremost, the opposition between the sensible and the intelligible. The *paradox* is that the metaphysical reduction of the sign needed the opposition it was reducing. The

opposition is part of the system, along with the reduction. And what I am saying here about the sign
can be extended to all the concepts and all the sentences of metaphysics, in particular to the discourse
on "structure." But there are many ways of being
caught in this circle. They are all more or less naïve,
more or less empirical, more or less systematic, more
or less close to the formulation or even to the for-
malization of this circle. It is these differences which
explain the multiplicity of destructive discourses and
the disagreement between those who make them. It
was within concepts inherited from metaphysics that
Nietzsche, Freud, and Heidegger worked, for example. Since these concepts are not elements or atoms
and since they are taken from a syntax and a system,
every particular borrowing drags along with it the
whole of metaphysics. This is what allows these de-
stroyers to destroy each other reciprocally—for example, Heidegger considering Nietzsche, with as
much lucidity and rigor as bad faith and miscon-
struction, as the last metaphysician, the last "Platon-
ist." One could do the same for Heidegger himself,
for Freud, or for a number of others. And today no
exercise is more widespread.

What is the relevance of this formal schéma when
we turn to what are called the "human sciences"?
One of them perhaps occupies a privileged place—
ethnology. One can in fact assume that ethnology
could have been born as a science only at the moment when a de-centering had come about: at the
moment when European culture—and, in consequence, the history of metaphysics and of its concepts—had been *dislocated,* driven from its locus,
and forced to stop considering itself as the culture of
reference. This moment is not first and foremost a
moment of philosophical or scientific discourse, it is
also a moment which is political, economic, technical, and so forth. One can say in total assurance that
there is nothing fortuitous about the fact that the critique of ethnocentrism—the very condition of ethnology—should be systematically and historically
contemporaneous with the destruction of the history
of metaphysics. Both belong to a single and same era.

Ethnology—like any science—comes about
within the element of discourse. And it is primarily
a European science employing traditional concepts,
however much it may struggle against them. Consequently, whether he wants to or not—and this does
not depend on a decision on his part—the ethnolo-
gist accepts into his discourse the premises of ethnocentrism at the very moment when he is employed in
denouncing them. This necessity is irreducible; it is
not a historical contingency. We ought to consider
very carefully all its implications. But if nobody can
escape this necessity, and if no one is therefore responsible for giving in to it, however little, this does
not mean that all the ways of giving in to it are of an
equal pertinence. The quality and the fecundity of a
discourse are perhaps measured by the critical rigor
with which this relationship to the history of metaphysics and to inherited concepts is thought. Here it
is a question of a critical relationship to the language
of the human sciences and a question of a critical responsibility of the discourse. It is a question of putting
expressly and systematically the problem of the status
of a discourse which borrows from a heritage the resources necessary for the deconstruction of that heritage itself. A problem of *economy* and *strategy.*

If I now go on to employ an examination of the
texts of Lévi-Strauss as an example, it is not only because of the privilege accorded to ethnology among
the human sciences, nor yet because the thought of
Lévi-Strauss weighs heavily on the contemporary
theoretical situation. It is above all because a certain
choice has made itself evident in the work of Lévi-
Strauss and because a certain doctrine has been elaborated there, and precisely in a *more or less explicit
manner,* in relation to this critique of language and to
this critical language in the human sciences.

In order to follow this movement in the text of
Lévi-Strauss, let me choose as one guiding thread
among others the opposition between nature and culture. In spite of all its rejuvenations and its disguises,
this opposition is congenital to philosophy. It is even
older than Plato. It is at least as old as the Sophists.
Since the statement of the opposition—*physis/nomos,
physis/techné*—it has been passed on to us by a whole
historical chain which opposes "nature" to the law, to
education, to art, to technics—and also to liberty, to
the arbitrary, to history, to society, to the mind, and so
on. From the beginnings of his quest and from his
first book, *The Elementary Structures of Kinship,*[5] Lévi-
Strauss has felt at one and the same time the necessity of utilizing this opposition and the impossibility
of making it acceptable. In the *Elementary Structures,*
he begins from this axiom or definition: that belongs
to nature which is *universal* and spontaneous, not depending on any particular culture or on any determi-

nate norm. That belongs to culture, on the other hand, which depends on a system of *norms* regulating society and is therefore capable of *varying* from one social structure to another. These two definitions are of the traditional type. But, in the very first pages of the *Elementary Structures,* Lévi-Strauss, who has begun to give these concepts an acceptable standing, encounters what he calls a *scandal,* that is to say, something which no longer tolerates the nature/culture opposition he has accepted and which seems to require *at one and the same time* the predicates of nature and those of culture. This scandal is the *incest-prohibition.* The incest-prohibition is universal; in this sense one could call it natural. But it is also a prohibition, a system of norms and interdicts; in this sense one could call it cultural.

> Let us assume therefore that everything universal in man derives from the order of nature and is characterized by spontaneity, that everything which is subject to a norm belongs to culture and presents the attributes of the relative and the particular. We then find ourselves confronted by a fact, or rather an ensemble of facts, which, in the light of the preceding definitions, is not far from appearing as a scandal: the prohibition of incest presents without the least equivocation, and indissolubly linked together, the two characteristics in which we recognized the contradictory attributes of two exclusive orders. The prohibition of incest constitutes a rule, but a rule, alone of all the social rules, which possesses at the same time a universal character (p. 9).

Obviously there is no scandal except in the *interior* of a system of concepts sanctioning the difference between nature and culture. In beginning his work with the *factum* of the incest-prohibition, Lévi-Strauss thus puts himself in a position entailing that this difference, which has always been assumed to be self-evident, becomes obliterated or disputed. For, from the moment that the incest-prohibition can no longer be conceived within the nature/culture opposition, it can no longer be said that it is a scandalous fact, a nucleus of opacity within a network of transparent significations. The incest-prohibition is no longer a scandal one meets with or comes up against in the domain of traditional concepts; it is something which escapes these concepts and certainly precedes them — probably as the condition of their possibility. It could perhaps be said that the whole of philosophical conceptualization, systematically relating itself to the nature/culture opposition, is designed to leave in the domain of the unthinkable the very thing that makes this conceptualization possible: the origin of the prohibition of incest.

I have dealt too cursorily with this example, only one among so many others, but the example nevertheless reveals that language bears within itself the necessity of its own critique. This critique may be undertaken along two tracks, in two "manners." Once the limit of nature/culture opposition makes itself felt, one might want to question systematically and rigorously the history of these concepts. This is a first action. Such a systematic and historic questioning would be neither a philological nor a philosophical action in the classic sense of these words. Concerning oneself with the founding concepts of the whole history of philosophy, deconstituting them, is not to undertake the task of the philologist or of the classic historian of philosophy. In spite of appearances, it is probably the most daring way of making the beginnings of a step outside of philosophy. The step "outside philosophy" is much more difficult to conceive than is generally imagined by those who think they made it long ago with cavalier ease, and who are in general swallowed up in metaphysics by the whole body of the discourse that they claim to have disengaged from it.

In order to avoid the possibly sterilizing effect of the first way, the other choice — which I feel corresponds more nearly to the way chosen by Lévi-Strauss — consists in conserving in the field of empirical discovery all these old concepts, while at the same time exposing here and there their limits, treating them as tools which can still be of use. No longer is any truth-value attributed to them; there is a readiness to abandon them if necessary if other instruments should appear more useful. In the meantime, their relative efficacy is exploited, and they are employed to destroy the old machinery to which they belong and of which they themselves are pieces. Thus it is that the language of the human sciences criticizes *itself.* Lévi-Strauss thinks that in this way he can separate *method* from *truth,* the instruments of the method and the objective significations aimed at by it. One could almost say that this is the primary affirmation of Lévi-Strauss; in any event, the first words of the *Elementary Structures* are: "One begins to understand that the distinction between state of nature and state of society (we would be more apt to say today: state of nature and state of culture), while lacking any acceptable historical signification, presents a value which fully justifies its use by modern sociology: its value as a methodological instrument."

Lévi-Strauss will always remain faithful to this double intention: to preserve as an instrument that whose truth-value he criticizes.

On the one hand, he will continue in effect to contest the value of the nature/culture opposition. More than thirteen years after the *Elementary Structures*, *The Savage Mind*[6] faithfully echoes the text I have just quoted: "The opposition between nature and culture which I have previously insisted on seems today to offer a value which is above all methodological." And this methodological value is not affected by its "ontological" non-value (as could be said, if this notion were not suspect here): "It would not be enough to have absorbed particular humanities into a general humanity; this first enterprise prepares the way for others . . . which belong to the natural and exact sciences: to reintegrate culture into nature, and finally, to reintegrate life into the totality of its physiochemical conditions" (p. 327).

On the other hand, still in *The Savage Mind*, he presents as what he calls *bricolage*[7] what might be called the discourse of this method. The *bricoleur*, says Lévi-Strauss, is someone who uses "the means at hand," that is, the instruments he finds at his disposition around him, those which are already there, which had not been especially conceived with an eye to the operation for which they are to be used and to which one tries by trial and error to adapt them, not hesitating to change them whenever it appears necessary, or to try several of them at once, even if their form and their origin are heterogeneous—and so forth. There is therefore a critique of language in the form of *bricolage*, and it has even been possible to say that *bricolage* is the critical language itself. I am thinking in particular of the article by G. Genette, "Structuralisme et Critique littéraire," published in homage to Lévi-Strauss in a special issue *L'Arc* (no. 26, 1965), where it is stated that the analysis of *bricolage* could "be applied almost word for word" to criticism, and especially to "literary criticism."[8]

If one calls *bricolage* the necessity of borrowing one's concepts from the text of a heritage which is more or less coherent or ruined, it must be said that every discourse is *bricoleur*. The engineer, whom Lévi-Strauss opposed to the *bricoleur*, should be the one to construct the totality of his language, syntax, and lexicon. In this sense the engineer is a myth. A subject who would supposedly be the absolute origin of his own discourse and would supposedly construct it "out of nothing," "out of whole cloth," would be the creator of the *verbe*, the *verbe* itself. The notion of the engineer who had supposedly broken with all forms of *bricolage* is therefore a theological idea; and since Lévi-Strauss tells us elsewhere that *bricolage* is mythopoetic, the odds are that the engineer is a myth produced by the *bricoleur*. From the moment that we cease to believe in such an engineer and in a discourse breaking with the received historical discourse, as soon as it is admitted that every finite discourse is bound by a certain *bricolage*, and that the engineer and the scientist are also species of *bricoleurs* then the very idea of *bricolage* is menaced and the difference in which it took on its meaning decomposes.

This brings out the second thread which might guide us in what is being unraveled here.

Lévi-Strauss describes *bricolage* not only as an intellectual activity but also as a mythopoetical activity. One reads in *The Savage Mind*, "Like *bricolage* on the technical level, mythical reflection can attain brilliant and unforeseen results on the intellectual level. Reciprocally, the mythopoetical character of *bricolage* has often been noted" (p. 26).

But the remarkable endeavor of Lévi-Srauss is not simply to put forward, notably in the most recent of his investigations, a structural science of knowledge of myths and of mythological activity. His endeavor also appears—I would say almost from the first—in the status which he accords to his own discourse on myths, to what he calls his "mythologicals." It is here that his discourse on the myth reflects on itself and criticizes itself. And this moment, this critical period, is evidently of concern to all the languages which share the field of the human sciences. What does Lévi-Strauss say of his "mythologicals"? It is here that we rediscover the mythopoetical virtue (power) of *bricolage*. In effect, what appears most fascinating in this critical search for a new status of the discourse is the stated abandonment of all reference to a *center*, to a *subject*, to a privileged *reference*, to an origin, or to an absolute *archè*. The theme of this decentering could be followed throughout the "overture" to his last book, *The Raw and the Cooked*. I shall simply remark on a few key points.

1. From the very start, Lévi-Strauss recognizes that the Bororo myth which he employs in the book as the "reference-myth" does not merit this name and this treatment. The name is specious and the use of the myth improper. This myth deserves no more than any other its referential privilege:

> In fact the Bororo myth which will from now on be designated by the name *reference-myth* is, as I shall try to show, nothing other than a more or less forced transformation of other myths originating either in the same society or in societies more or less far removed. It would therefore have been legitimate to choose as my point of departure any representative of the group whatsoever. From this point of view, the interest of the reference-myth does not depend on its typical character, but rather on its irregular position in the midst of a group (p. 10).

2. There is no unity or absolute source of the myth. The focus or the source of the myth are always shadows and virtualities which are elusive, unactualizable, and nonexistent in the first place. Everything begins with the structure, the configuration, the relationship. The discourse on this acentric structure, the myth, that is, cannot itself have an absolute subject or an absolute center. In order not to short change the form and the movement of the myth, that violence which consists in centering a language which is describing an acentric structure must be avoided. In this context, therefore it is necessary to forgo scientific or philosophical discourse, to renounce the *epistème* which absolutely requires, which is the absolute requirement that we go back to the source, to the center, to the founding basis, to the principle, and so on. In opposition to *epis-tèmic* discourse, structural discourse on myths — *mythological* discourse — must itself be *mythomorphic*. It must have the form of that of which it speaks. This is what Lévi-Strauss says in *The Raw and the Cooked*, from which I would now like to quote a long and remarkable passage:

> In effect the study of myths poses a methodological problem by the fact that it cannot conform to the Cartesian principle of dividing the difficulty into as many parts as are necessary to resolve it. There exists no veritable end or term to mythical analysis, no secret unity which could be grasped at the end of the work of decomposition. The themes dupli-

cate themselves to infinity. When we think we have disentangled them from each other and can hold them separate, it is only to realize that they are joining together again, in response to the attraction of unforeseen affinities. In consequence, the unity of the myth is only tendential and projective; it never reflects a state or a moment of the myth. An imaginary phenomenon implied by the endeavor to interpret, its role is to give a synthetic form to the myth and to impede its dissolution into the confusion of contraries. It could therefore be said that the science or knowledge of myths is an *anaclastic*, taking this ancient term in the widest sense authorized by its etymology, a science which admits into its definition the study of the reflected rays along with that of the broken ones. But, unlike philosophical reflection, which claims to go all the way back to its source, the reflections in question here concern rays without any other than a virtual focus. . . . In wanting to imitate the spontaneous movement of mythical thought, my enterprise, itself too brief and too long, has had to yield to its demands and respect its rhythm. Thus is this book, on myths itself and in its own way, a myth.

This statement is repeated a little farther on (p. 20): "Since myths themselves rest on second-order codes (the first-order codes being those in which language consists), this book thus offers the rough draft of a third-order code, destined to insure the reciprocal possibility of translation of several myths. This is why it would not be wrong to consider it a myth: the myth of mythology, as it were." It is by this absence of any real and fixed center of the mythical or mythological discourse that the musical model chosen by Lévi-Strauss for the composition of his book is apparently justified. The absence of a center is here the absence of a subject and the absence of an author: "The myth and the musical work thus appear as orchestra conductors whose listeners are the silent performers. If it be asked where the real focus of the work is to be found, it must be replied that its determination is impossible. Music and mythology bring man face to face with virtual objects whose shadow alone is actual. . . . Myths have no authors" (p. 25).

Thus it is at this point that ethnographic *bricolage* deliberately assumes its mythopoetic function. But by the same token, this function makes the philosophical or epistemological requirement of a center appear as mythological, that is to say, as a historical illusion.

Nevertheless, even if one yields to the necessity of what Lévi-Strauss has done, one cannot ignore its risks. If the mythological is mythomorphic, are all discourses on myths equivalent? Shall we have to abandon any epistemological requirement which permits us to distinguish between several qualities of discourse on the myth? A classic question, but inevitable. We cannot reply—and I do not believe Lévi-Strauss replies to it—as long as the problem of the relationships between the philosopheme or the theorem, on the one hand, and the mytheme or the mythopoem(e), on the other, has not been expressly posed. This is no small problem. For lack of expressly posing this problem, we condemn ourselves to transforming the claimed transgression of philosophy into an unperceived fault in the interior of the philosophical field. Empiricism would be the genus of which these faults would always be the species. Trans-philosophical concepts would be transformed into philosophical naïvetés. One could give many examples to demonstrate this risk: the concepts of sign, history, truth, and so forth. What I want to emphasize is simply that the passage beyond philosophy does not consist in turning the page of philosophy (which usually comes down to philosophizing badly), but in continuing to read philosophers *in a certain way*. The risk I am speaking of is always assumed by Lévi-Strauss and it is the very price of his endeavor. I have said that empiricism is the matrix of all the faults menacing a discourse which continues, as with Lévi-Strauss in particular, to elect to be scientific. If we wanted to pose the problem of empiricism and *bricolage* in depth, we would probably end up very quickly with a number of propositions absolutely contradictory in relation to the status of discourse in structural ethnography. On the one hand, structuralism justly claims to be the critique of empiricism. But at the same time there is not a single book or study by Lévi-Strauss which does not offer itself as an empirical essay which can always be completed or invalidated by new information. The structural schemata are always proposed as hypotheses resulting from a finite quantity of information and which are subjected to the proof of experience. Numerous texts could be used to demonstrate this double postulation. Let us turn once again to the "Overture" of *The Raw and the Cooked*, where it seems clear that if this postulation is double, it is because it is a question here of a language on language:

Critics who might take me to task for not having begun by making an exhaustive inventory of South American myths before analyzing them would be making a serious mistake about the nature and the role of these documents. The totality of the myths of a people is of the order of the discourse. Provided that this people does not become physically or morally extinct, this totality is never closed. Such a criticism would therefore be equivalent to reproaching a linguist with writing the grammar of a language without having recorded the totality of the words which have been uttered since that language came into existence and without knowing the verbal exchanges which will take place as long as the language continues to exist. Experience proves that an absurdly small number of sentences . . . allows the linguist to elaborate a grammar of the language he is studying. And even a partial grammar or an outline of a grammar represents a valuable acquisition in the case of unknown languages. Syntax does not wait until it has been possible to enumerate a theoretically unlimited series of events before becoming manifest, because syntax consists in the body of rules which presides over the generation of these events. And it is precisely a syntax of South American mythology that I wanted to outline. Should new texts appear to enrich the mythical discourse, then this will provide an opportunity to check or modify the way in which certain grammatical laws have been formulated, an opportunity to discard certain of them and an opportunity to discover new ones. But in no instance can the requirement of a total mythical discourse be raised as an objection. For we have just seen that such a requirement has no meaning (pp. 15–16).

Totalization is therefore defined at one time as *useless*, at another as *impossible*. This is no doubt the result of the fact that there are two ways of conceiving the limit of totalization. And I assert once again that these two determinations coexist implicitly in the discourses of Lévi-Strauss. Totalization can be judged impossible in the classical style: one then refers to the empirical endeavor of a subject or of a finite discourse in a vain and breathless quest of an infinite richness which it can never master. There is too much, more than one can say. But nontotalization can also be determined in another way: not from the standpoint of the concept of finitude as assigning us to an empirical view, but from the standpoint of the concept of *freeplay*. If totalization no longer has any meaning, it is not because the infinity of a field cannot be covered by a finite glance or a finite discourse, but because the nature of the field—that is, language and a finite language—excludes totalization. This field is in fact that of *freeplay,* that is to say, a field of infinite substitutions in the closure of a finite ensemble. This field permits these infinite substitutions only because it is finite, that is to say, because instead of being an inexhaustible field, as in the classical hypothesis, instead of being too large, there is something missing from it: a center which arrests and founds the freeplay of substitutions. One could say—rigorously using that word whose scandalous signification is always obliterated in French—that this movement of the freeplay, permitted by the lack, the absence of a center or origin, is the movement of *supplementarity.* One cannot determine the center, the sign which *supplements*[9] it, which takes its place in its absence—because this sign adds itself, occurs in addition, over and above, comes as a *supplement.*[10] The movement of signification adds something, which results in the fact that there is always more, but this addition is a floating one because it comes to perform a vicarious function, to supplement a lack on the part of the signified. Although Lévi-Strauss in his use of the word supplementary never emphasizes as I am doing here the two directions of meaning which are so strangely compounded within it, it is not by chance that he uses this word twice in his "Introduction to the Work of Marcel Mauss,"[11] at the point where he is speaking of the "superabundance of signifier, in relation to the signifieds to which this superabundance can refer":

> In his endeavor to understand the world, man therefore always has at his disposition a surplus of signification (which he portions out amongst things according to the laws of symbolic thought—which it is the task of ethnologists and linguists to study). This distribution of a *supplementary* allowance [ration *supplémentaire*]—if it is permissible to put it that way—is absolutely necessary in order that on the whole the available signifier and the signified it aims at may remain in the relationship of complementarity which is the very condition of the use of symbolic thought (p. xlix).

(It could no doubt be demonstrated that this *ration supplémentaire* of signification is the origin of the *ratio* itself.) The word reappears a little farther on, after Lévi-Strauss has mentioned "this floating signifier, which is the servitude of all finite thought":

In other words—and taking as our guide Mauss's precept that all social phenomena can be assimilated to language—we see in *mana, Wakau, oranda* and other notions of the same type, the conscious expression of a semantic function, whose role it is to permit symbolic thought to operate in spite of the contradiction which is proper to it. In this way are explained the apparently insoluble antinomies attached to this notion. . . . At one and the same time force and action, quality and state, substantive and verb, abstract and concrete, omnipresent and localized—*mana* is in effect all these things. But is it not precisely because it is none of these things that *mana* is a simple form, or more exactly, a symbol in the pure state, and therefore capable of becoming charged with any sort of symbolic content whatever? In the system of symbols constituted by all cosmologies, *mana* would simply be a *valeur symbolique zéro,* that is to say, a sign marking the necessity of a symbolic content *supplementary* [my italics] to that with which the signified is already loaded, but which can take on any value required, provided only that this value still remains part of the available reserve and is not, as phonologists put it, a group-term.

Lévi-Strauss adds the note:

> Linguists have already been led to formulate hypotheses of this type. For example: "A zero phoneme is opposed to all the other phonemes in French in that it entails no differential characters and no constant phonetic value. On the contrary, the proper function of the zero phoneme is to be opposed to phoneme absence." (R. Jakobson and J. Lutz, "Notes on the French Phonemic Pattern," *Word,* vol. 5, no. 2 [August, 1949], p. 155). Similarly, if we schematize the conception I am proposing here, it could almost be said that the function of notions like *mana* is to be opposed to the absence of signification, without entailing by itself any particular signification (p. 1 and note).

The *superabundance* of the signifier, its *supplementary* character, is thus the result of a finitude, that is to say, the result of a lack which must be *supplemented.*

It can now be understood why the concept of freeplay is important in Lévi-Strauss. His references to all sorts of games, notably to roulette, are very frequent, especially in his *Conversations,*[12] in *Race and History,*[13] and in *The Savage Mind.* This reference to the game or freeplay is always caught up in a tension.

It is in tension with history, first of all. This is a classical problem, objections to which are now well worn or used up. I shall simply indicate what seems to me the formality of the problem: by reducing history, Lévi-Srauss has treated as it deserves a concept which has always been in complicity with a teleological and eschatological metaphysics, in other words, paradoxically, in complicity with that philosophy of presence to which it was believed history could be opposed. The thematic of historicity, although it seems to be a somewhat late arrival in philosophy, has always been required by the determination of being as presence. With or without etymology, and in spite of the classic antagonism which opposes these significations throughout all of classical thought, it could be shown the concept of *epistèmè* has always called forth that of *historia,* if history is always the unity of a becoming, as tradition of truth or development of science or knowledge oriented toward the appropriation of truth in presence and self-presence, toward knowledge in consciousness-of-self.[14] History has always been conceived as the movement of a resumption of history, a diversion between two presences. But if it is legitimate to suspect this concept of history, there is a risk, if it is reduced without an express statement of the problem I am indicating here, of falling back into an anhistoricism of a classical type, that is to say, in a determinate moment of the history of metaphysics. Such is the algebraic formality of the problem as I see it. More concretely, in the work of Lévi-Strauss it must be recognized that the respect for structurality, for the internal originality of the structure, compels a neutralization of time and history. For example, the appearance of a new structure, of an original system, always comes about—and this is the very condition of its structural specificity—by a rupture with its past, its origin, and its cause. One can therefore describe what is peculiar to the structural organization only by not taking into account, in the very moment of this description, its past conditions: by failing to pose the problem of the passage from one structure to another, by putting history into parentheses. In this "structuralist" moment, the concepts of chance and discontinuity are indispensable. And Lévi-Strauss does in fact often appeal to them as he does, for instance, for that structure of structures, language, of which he says in the "Introduction to the Work of Marcel Mauss" that it "could only have been born in one fell swoop":

> Whatever may have been the moment and the circumstances of its appearance in the scale of animal life, language could only have been born in one fell swoop. Things could not have set about signifying progressively. Following a transformation the study of which is not the concern of the social sciences, but rather of biology and psychology, a crossing over came about from a stage where nothing had a meaning to another where everything possessed it (p. xlvi).

This standpoint does not prevent Lévi-Strauss from recognizing the slowness, the process of maturing, the continuous toil of factual transformations, history (for example, in *Race and History*). But, in accordance with an act which was also Rousseau's and Husserl's, he must "brush aside all the facts" at the moment when he wishes to recapture the specificity of a structure. Like Rousseau, he must always conceive of the origin of a new structure on the model of catastrophe—an overturning of nature in nature, a natural interruption of the natural sequence, a brushing aside *of* nature.

Besides the tension of freeplay with history, there is also the tension of freeplay with presence. Freeplay is the disruption of presence. The presence of an element is always a signifying and substitutive reference inscribed in a system of differences and the movement of a chain. Freeplay is always an interplay of absence and presence, but if it is to be radically conceived, freeplay must be conceived of before the alternative of presence and absence; being must be conceived of as presence or absence beginning with the possibility of freeplay and not the other way around. If Lévi-Strauss, better than any other, has brought to light the freeplay of repetition and the repetition of freeplay, one no less perceives in his work a sort of ethic of presence, an ethic of nostalgia for origins, an ethic of archaic and natural innocence, of a purity of presence and self-presence in speech[15]—an ethic, nostalgia, and even remorse which he often presents as the motivation of the ethnological project when he moves toward archaic societies—exemplary societies in his eyes. These texts are well known.

As a turning toward the presence, lost or impossible, of the absent origin, this structuralist thematic of broken immediateness is thus the sad, *negative*, nostalgic, guilty, Rousseauist facet of the thinking of freeplay of which the Nietzschean *affirmation*—the joyous affirmation of the freeplay of the world and without truth, without origin, offered to an active interpretation—would be the other side. *This affirmation then determines the non-center otherwise than as loss of the center.* And it plays the game without security. For there is a *sure* freeplay: that which is limited to the *substitution of given and existing, present,* pieces. In absolute chance, affirmation also surrenders itself to *genetic in*determination, to the *seminal* adventure of the trace.[16]

There are thus two interpretations of interpretation, of structure, of sign, of freeplay. The one seeks to decipher, dreams of deciphering, a truth or an origin which is free from freeplay and from the order of the sign, and lives like an exile with the necessity of interpretation. The other, which is no longer turned toward the origin, affirms freeplay and tries to pass beyond man and humanism, the name man being the name of that being who, throughout the history of metaphysics or of ontotheology — in other words, through the history of all of his history — has dreamed of full presence, the reassuring foundation, the origin and the end of the game. The second interpretation of interpretation, to which Nietzsche showed us the way, does not seek in ethnography, as Lévi-Strauss wished, the "inspiration of a new humanism" (again from the "Introduction to the Work of Marcel Mauss").

There are more than enough indications today to suggest we might perceive that these two interpretations of interpretation — which are absolutely irreconcilable even if we live them simultaneously and reconcile them in an obscure economy — together shared the field which we call, in such a problematic fashion, the human sciences.

For my part, although these two interpretations must acknowledge and accentuate their difference and define their irreducibility, I do not believe that today there is any question of *choosing*—in the first place because here we are in a region (let's say, provisionally, a region of historicity) where the category of choice seems particularly trivial; and in the second, because we must first try to conceive of the common ground, and the *différance* of this irreducible difference.[17] Here there is a sort of question, call it historical, of which we are only glimpsing today the *conception, the formation, the gestation, the labor.* I employ these words, I admit, with a glance toward the business of childbearing — but also with a glance toward those who, in a company from which I do not exclude myself, turn their eyes away in the face of the as yet unnameable which is proclaiming itself and which can do so, as is necessary whenever a

birth is in the offing, only under the species of the non-species, in the formless, mute, infant, and terrifying form of monstrosity.

Notes

1. "La Structure, le signe et le jeu dans le discours des sciences humaines." The text which follows is a translation of the revised version of M. Derrida's communication. The word "jeu" is variously translated here as "play," "interplay," "game," and "stake," besides the normative translation "freeplay." All footnotes to this article are additions by the translator.
2. *Interdite:* "forbidden," "disconcerted," "confounded," "speechless."
3. ". . . qui naît toujours d'une certaine manière d'être impliqué dans le jeu, d'être pris au jeu, d'être comme être d'entrée de jeu dans le jeu."
4. *Le cru et le cuit* (Paris: Plon, 1964).
5. *Les structures élémentaires de la parenté* (Paris: Presses Universitaires de France, 1949).
6. *La pensée sauvage* (Paris: Plon, 1962).
7. A *bricoleur* is a jack-of-all trades, someone who potters about with odds-and-ends, who puts things together out of bits and pieces.
8. Reprinted in: G. Genette, *Figures* (Paris: Editions du Seuil, 1966), p. 145.
9. The point being that the word, both in English and French, means "to supply a deficiency," on the one hand, and "to supply something additional," on the other.
10. ". . . ce signe s'ajoute, vient en sus, en *supplément.*"
11. "Introduction à l'oeuvre de Marcel Mauss," in: Marcel Mauss, *Sociologie et anthropologie* (Paris: Presses Universitaires de France, 1950).
12. Presumably: G. Charbonnier, *Entretiens avec Claude Lévi-Srauss* (Paris: Plon-Julliard, 1961).
13. *Race and History* (Paris: UNESCO Publications, 1958).
14. ". . . l'unité d'un devenir, comme tradition de la vérité dans la présence et la présence à soi, vers le savoir dans la conscience de soi."
15. ". . . de la présence à soi dans la parole."
16. "Tournée vers la présence, perdue ou impossible, de l'origine absente, cette thématique structuraliste de l'immédiateté rompue est donc la face triste, *négative,* nostalgique, coupable, rousseauiste, de la pensée du jeu dont *l'affirmation*

nietzschéenne, l'affirmation joyeuse du jeu du monde et de l'innocence du devenir, l'affirmation d'un monde de signes sans faute, sans vérité, sans origine, offert à une interprétation active, serait l'autre face. *Cette affirmation détermine alors le* non-centre *autrement que comme perte du centre. Et elle joue sans sécurité. Car il y a un jeu sûr:* celui qui se limite à la *substitution* de piéces *données et existantes, présentes.* Dans le hasard absolu, l'affirmation se livre aussi à l'indétermination *génétique,* à l'aventure *séminale* de la trace."

17. From *différer,* in the sense of "to postpone," "put off," "defer." Elsewhere Derrida uses the word as a synonym for the German *Aufschub:* "postponement," and relates it to the central Freudian concepts of *Verspätung, Nachträglichkeit,* and to the *"détours* to death" of *Beyond the Pleasure Principle* by Sigmund Freud (Standard Edition, ed. James Strachey, vol. XIX, London, 1961), Chap. V.

THEORY

Semiology and Rhetoric

Paul de Man

After reviewing some recent forms of criticism that as-
sume a continuity between grammar and rhetoric or
figurative language, Paul de Man proceeds to challenge
that assumption. Citing Kenneth Burke, Charles Sanders
Peirce, and Jacques Derrida as others who have ques-
tioned that continuity, he begins with the playful exam-
ple of a "rhetorical" question as it might be viewed by an
"archie Debunker," moves on to a deconstructive reading
of four lines by Yeats, and ends with an extended analy-
sis of a passage from Proust. In each case, his reading
argues that rhetoric undoes grammar, and vice versa.
Having sketched an immense deconstructive project for
criticism along the lines suggested by his analyses, de
Man cautions us that the superior status this project
seems to confer on the philosopher-critic is an illusion.
The poet has always been there first and the task of the
deconstructive critic is to follow closely, like a good for-
malist, the text the poet has given him. "Poetic writing
is the most advanced and refined mode of deconstruction,"
de Man insists and, as he demonstrates, it demands the
closest of close readers. But such readers will discover
not the formalist's unity and coherence but the text's
propensity to deconstruct itself. "Literature," he con-
cludes, "as well as criticism—the difference between
them being delusive—are condemned (or privileged) to
be forever the most rigorous and, consequently, the most
unreliable language in terms of which man names and
modifies himself."

To judge from various recent publications, the spirit of the times is not blowing in the direction of formalist and intrinsic criticism. We may no longer be hearing too much about relevance but we keep hearing a great deal about reference, about the non-verbal "outside" to which language refers, by which

Reprinted by permission from *Diacritics* 3 (Fall 1973): 27–33. Copyright © 1973 by The Johns Hopkins University Press.

it is conditioned and upon which it acts. The stress falls not so much on the fictional status of literature — a property now perhaps somewhat too easily taken for granted — but on the interplay between these fictions and categories that are said to partake of reality, such as the self, man, society, "the artist, his culture and the human community," as one critic puts it. Hence the emphasis on hybrid texts considered to be partly literary and partly referential, on popular fictions deliberately aimed towards social and psychological gratification, on literary autobiography as a key to the understanding of the self, and so on. We speak as if, with the problems of literary form resolved once and forever, and with the techniques of structural analysis refined to near-perfection, we could now move "beyond formalism" towards the questions that really interest us and reap, at last, the fruits of the ascetic concentration on techniques that prepared us for this decisive step. With the internal law and order of literature well policed, we can now confidently devote ourselves to the foreign affairs, the external politics of literature. Not only do we feel able to do so, but we owe it to ourselves to take this step: our moral conscience would not allow us to do otherwise. Behind the assurance that valid interpretation is possible, behind the recent interest in writing and reading as potentially effective public speech acts, stands a highly respectable moral imperative that strives to reconcile the internal, formal, private structures of literary language with their external, referential and public effects.

I want, for the moment, to consider briefly this tendency in itself, as an undeniable and recurrent historical fact, without regard for its truth or falseness or for its value as desirable or pernicious. It is a fact that this sort of thing happens, again and again, in literary studies. On the one hand, literature cannot merely be received as a definite unit of referential meaning that can be decoded without leaving a residue. The code is unusually conspicuous, complex and enigmatic; it attracts an inordinate amount of attention to itself and this attention has to acquire the rigor of a method. The structural moment of concentration on the code for its own sake cannot be avoided and literature necessarily breeds its own formalism. Technical innovations in the methodical study of literature only occur when this kind of attention predominates. It can legitimately be said, for example, that, from a technical point of view, very little has happened in American criticism since the in-

novative works of New Criticism. There certainly have been numerous excellent books of criticism since, but in none of them have the techniques of description and interpretation evolved beyond the techniques of close reading established in the thirties and the forties. Formalism, it seems, is an all-absorbing and tyrannical muse; the hope that one can be at the same time technically original and discursively eloquent is not borne out by the history of literary criticism.

On the other hand — and this is the real mystery — no literary formalism, no matter how accurate and enriching in its analytic powers, is ever allowed to come into being without seeming reductive. When form is considered to be the external trappings of literary meaning or content, it seems superficial and expendable. The development of intrinsic, formalist criticism in the twentieth century has changed this model: form is now a solipsistic category of self-reflection and the referential meaning is said to be extrinsic. The polarities of inside and outside have been reversed, but they are still the same polarities that are at play: internal meaning has become outside reference and the outer form has become the intrinsic structure. A new version of reductiveness at once follows this reversal: formalism nowadays is mostly described in an imagery of imprisonment and claustrophobia: the "prison house of language," "the impasse of formalist criticism," etc. Like the grandmother in Proust's novel ceaselessly driving the young Marcel out into the garden, away from the unhealthy inwardness of his closeted reading, critics cry out for the fresh air of referential meaning. Thus, with the structure of the code so opaque, but the meaning so anxious to blot out the obstacle of form, no wonder that the reconciliation of form and meaning would be so attractive. The attraction of reconciliation is the elective breeding-ground of false models and metaphors; it accounts for the metaphorical model, of literature as a kind of box that separates an inside from an outside, and the reader or critic as the person who opens the lid in order to release in the open what was secreted but inaccessible inside. It matters little whether we call the inside of the box the content or the form, the outside the meaning or the appearance. The recurrent debate opposing intrinsic to extrinsic criticism stands under the aegis of an inside/outside metaphor that is never being seriously questioned.

Metaphors are much more tenacious than facts and I certainly don't expect to dislodge this age-old model in one short expository talk. I merely wish to speculate on a different set of terms, perhaps less simple in their differential relationship than the strictly polar, binary opposition between inside and outside and therefore less likely to enter into the easy play of chiasmic reversals. I derive these terms (which are as old as the hills) pragmatically from the observation of developments and debates in recent critical methodology.

One of the most controversial among these developments coincides with a new approach to poetics or, as it is called in Germany, poetology, as a branch of general semiotics. In France, a semiology of literature comes about as the outcome of the long-deferred but all the more explosive encounter of the nimble French literary mind with the category of form. Semiology, as opposed to semantics, is the science or study of signs as signifiers; it does not ask what words mean but how they mean. Unlike American New Criticism, which derived the internalization of form from the practice of highly self-conscious modern writers, French semiology turned to linguistics for its model and adopted Saussure and Jakobson rather than Valéry or Proust for its masters. By an awareness of the arbitrariness of the sign (Saussure) and of literature as an autotelic statement "focused on the way it is expressed" (Jakobson) the entire question of meaning can be bracketed, thus freeing the critical discourse from the debilitating burden of paraphrase. The demystifying power of semiology, within the context of French historical and thematic criticism, has been considerable. It demonstrated that the perception of the literary dimensions of language is largely obscured if one submits uncritically to the authority of reference. It also revealed how tenaciously this authority continues to assert itself in a variety of disguises, ranging from the crudest ideology to the most refined forms of aesthetic and ethical judgment. It especially explodes the myth of semantic correspondence between sign and referent, the wishful hope of having it both ways, of being, to paraphrase Marx in the German Ideology, a formalist critic in the morning and a communal moralist in the afternoon, of serving both the technique of form and the substance of meaning. The results, in the practice of French criticism, have been as fruitful as they are irreversible. Perhaps for the first time since the late eighteenth century, French critics can come at least somewhat closer to the kind of linguistic awareness that never ceased to be operative in its poets and novelists and that forced all of them including Sainte Beuve to write their main works "contre Sainte Beuve." The distance was never so considerable in England and the United States, which does not mean, however, that we may be able, in this country, to dispense with a preventative semiological hygiene altogether.

One of the most striking characteristics of literary semiology, as it is practiced today, in France and elsewhere, is the use of grammatical (especially syntactical) structures conjointly with rhetorical structures without apparent awareness of a possible discrepancy between them. In their literary analyses, Barthes, Genette, Todorov, Greimas and their disciples all simplify and regress from Jakobson in letting grammar and rhetoric function in perfect continuity, and in passing from grammatical to rhetorical structures without difficulty of interruption. Indeed, as the study of grammatical structures is refined in contemporary theories of generative, transformational and distributive grammar, the study of tropes and of figures (which is how the term rhetoric is used throughout this paper, and not in the derived sense of comment or of eloquence or persuasion) becomes a mere extension of grammatical models, a particular subset of syntactical relations. In the recent *Dictionnaire encyclopédique des sciences du language*, Ducrot and Todorov write that rhetoric has always been satisfied with a paradigmatic view over words (words substituting for each other), without questioning their syntagmatic relationship (the contiguity of words to each other). There ought to be another perspective, complementary to the first, in which metaphor, for example, would not be defined as a substitution but as a particular type of combination. Research inspired by linguistics or, more narrowly, by syntactical studies, has begun to reveal this possibility—but it remains to be explored. Todorov, who calls one of his books a *Grammar of the Decameron*, rightly thinks of his own work and that of his associates as first explorations in the elaboration of a systematic grammar of literary modes, genres and also of literary figures. Perhaps the most perceptive work to come out of this school, Genette's studies of figural modes, can be shown to be assimilations of rhetorical transformations or combinations to syntactical, grammatical patterns. Thus a recent study, now printed in *Figures III* and entitled *Metaphor and Metonymy in Proust*, shows the combined presence, in a wide and astute selection of passages, of paradigmatic, metaphorical figures with syntagmatic, metonymic structures. The combination of both is treated descriptively and nondialectically without suffering the possibility of logical tensions.

One can ask whether this reduction of figure to grammar is legitimate. The existence of grammatical structures, within and beyond the unit of the sentence in literary texts is undeniable, and their description and classification are indispensable. The question remains if and how figures of rhetoric can be included in such a taxonomy. This question is at the core of the debate going on, in a wide variety of apparently unrelated forms, in contemporary poetics, but I do not plan to make clear the connection between this "real" problem and the countless pseudo-problems that agitate literary studies. The historical picture of contemporary criticism is too confused to make the mapping out of such a topography a useful exercise. Not only are these questions mixed in and mixed up within particular groups or local trends, but they are often co-present, without apparent contradiction, within the work of a single author.

Neither is the theory of the question suitable for quick expository treatment. To distinguish the epistemology of grammar from the epistemology of rhetoric is a redoubtable task. On an entirely naïve level, we tend to conceive of grammatical systems as tending towards universality and as simply generative, i.e. as capable of deriving an infinity of versions from a single model (that may govern transformations as well as derivations) without the intervention of another model that would upset the first. We therefore think of the relationship between grammar and logic, the passage from grammar to propositions, as being relatively un-problematic: no true propositions are conceivable in the absence of grammatical consistency or of controlled deviation from a system of consistency no matter how complex. Grammar and logic stand to each other in a dyadic relationship of unsubverted support. In a logic of acts rather than of statements, as in Austin's theory of speech acts, that has had such strong influence on recent American work in literary semiology, it is also possible to move between speech acts and grammar without difficulty. The performance of what is called illocutionary acts such as ordering, questioning, denying, assuming etc. within the language is congruent with the grammatical structures of syntax in the corresponding imperative, interrogative, negative, optative sentences. "The rules for illocutionary acts," writes Richard Ohman in a recent paper, "determine whether performance of a given act is well-executed, in just the same way as *grammatical* rules determine whether the product of a locutionary act—a sentence—is well formed [...]. But whereas the rules of grammar concern the relationships among sound, syntax, and meaning, the rules of illocutionary acts concern relationships among people" ("Speech, Literature, and the Space in between," *New Literary History* IV, No. 1 [Autumn 1972]; p. 50). And since rhetoric is then conceived exclusively as persuasion, as actual action upon others (and not as an intralinguistic figure or trope), the continuity between the illocutionary realm of grammar and the perlocutionary realm of rhetoric is self-evident. It becomes the basis for a new rhetoric that, exactly as is the case for Todorov and Genette, would also be a new grammar.

Without engaging the substance of the question, it can be pointed out, without having to go beyond recent and American examples, and without calling upon the strength of an age-old tradition, that the continuity here assumed between grammar and rhetoric is not borne out by theoretical and philosophical speculation. Kenneth Burke mentions *Deflection* (which he compares structurally to Freudian displacement), defined as "any slight bias or even unintended error," as the rhetorical basis of language, and deflection is then conceived as a dialectical subversion of the consistent link between sign and meaning that operates within grammatical patterns; hence Burke's well-known insistence on the distinction between grammar and rhetoric. Charles Sanders Peirce who, with Nietzsche and Saussure, laid the philosophical foundation for modern semiology, stressed the distinction between grammar and rhetoric in his celebrated and so suggestively unfathomable definition of the sign. He insists, as is well known, on the necessary presence of a third element, called the interpretant, within any relationship that the sign entertains with its object. The sign is to be interpreted if we are to understand the idea it is to convey, and this is so because the sign is not the thing but a meaning derived from the thing by a process here called representation that is not simply generative, i.e. dependent on a univocal origin. The interpretation of the sign is not, for Peirce, a meaning but another sign; it is a reading, not a decodage, and this reading has, in its turn, to be interpreted into another sign, and so on *ad infinitum*. Peirce calls this process by means of which "one sign gives birth to another" pure rhetoric, as distinguished from pure grammar, which postulates the possibility of unproblematic, dyadic meaning and pure logic, which postulates the possibility of the universal truth of meanings. Only if the sign engendered meaning in the same way that the object engenders the sign, that is, by representation, would there be no need to distinguish between grammar and rhetoric.

These remarks should indicate at least the existence and the difficulty of the question, a difficulty which puts its concise theoretical exposition beyond my powers. I must retreat therefore into a pragmatic discourse and try to illustrate the tension between grammar and rhetoric in a few specific textual examples. Let me begin by considering what is perhaps the most commonly known instance of an apparent symbiosis between a grammatical and a rhetorical structure, the so-called rhetorical question, in which the figure is conveyed directly by means of a syntactical device. I take the first example from the subliterature of the mass media: asked by his wife whether he wants to have his bowling shoes laced over or laced under, Archie Bunker answers with a question: "What's the difference?" Being a reader of sublime simplicity, his wife replies by patiently explaining the difference between lacing over and lacing under, whatever this may be, but provokes only ire. "What's the difference" did not ask for difference but means instead "I don't give a damn what the difference is." The same grammatical pattern engenders two meanings that are mutually exclusive: the literal meaning asks for a concept (difference) whose existence is denied by the figurative meaning. As long as we are talking about bowling shoes, the consequences are relatively trivial; Archie Bunker, who is a great believer in the authority of origins (as long, of course, as they are the right origins) muddles along in a world where literal and figurative meanings get in each other's way, though not without discomforts. But suppose that it is a *de*-bunker rather than a "Bunker," and a de-bunker of the arche (or origin), an archie Debunker such as Nietzsche or Jacques Derrida for instance, who asks the question "What is the Difference"—and we cannot even tell from his grammar whether he "really" wants to know "what" the difference is or is just telling us that we shouldn't even try to find it. Confronted with the question of the difference between grammar and rhetoric, grammar allows us to ask the question, but

the sentence by means of which we ask it may deny the very possibility of asking. For what is the use of asking, I ask, when we cannot even authoritatively decide whether a question asks or doesn't ask?

The point is as follows. A perfectly clear syntactical paradigm (the question) engenders a sentence that has at least two meanings of which the one asserts and the other denies its own illocutionary mode. It is not so that there are simply two meanings, one literal and the other figural, and that we have to decide which one of these meanings is the right one in this particular situation. The confusion can only be cleared up by the intervention of an extra-textual intention, such as Archie Bunker putting his wife straight; but the very anger he displays is indicative of more than impatience; it reveals his despair when confronted with a structure of linguistic meaning that he cannot control and that holds the discouraging prospect of an infinity of similar future confusions, all of them potentially catastrophic in their consequences. Nor is this intervention really a part of the mini-text constituted by the figure which holds our attention only as long as it remains suspended and unresolved. I follow the usage of common speech in calling this semiological enigma "rhetorical." The grammatical model of the question becomes rhetorical not when we have, on the one hand, a literal meaning and on the other hand a figural meaning, but when it is impossible to decide by grammatical or other linguistic devices which of the two meanings (that can be entirely contradictory) prevails. Rhetoric radically suspends logic and opens up vertiginous possibilities of referential aberration. And although it would perhaps be somewhat more remote from common usage, I would not hesitate to equate the rhetorical, figural potentiality of language with literature itself. I could point to a great number of antecedents to this equation of literature with figure; the most recent reference would be to Monroe Beardsley's insistence in his contribution to the *Essays* to honor William Wimsatt, that literary language is characterized by being "distinctly above the norm in ratio of implicit (or, I would say rhetorical) to explicit meaning" (p. 37).

Let me pursue the question of rhetorical question through one more example. Yeats' poem "Among School Children," ends with the famous line: "How can we know the dancer from the dance?" Although there are some revealing inconsistencies within the commentaries, the line is usually interpreted as stating, with the increased emphasis of a rhetorical device, the potential unity between form and experience, between creator and creation. It could be said that it denies the discrepancy between the sign and the referent from which we started out. Many elements in the imagery and the dramatic development of the poem strengthen this traditional reading; without having to look any further than the immediately preceding lines, one finds powerful and consecrated images of the continuity from part to whole that makes synecdoche into the most seductive of metaphors: the organic beauty of the tree, stated in the parallel syntax of a similar rhetorical question, or the convergence, in the dance, of erotic desire with musical form:

> O chestnut tree, great rooted blossomer
> Are you the leaf, the blossom or the bole?
> O body swayed to music, O brightening glance
> How can we know the dancer from the dance?

A more extended reading, always assuming that the final line is to be read as a rhetorical question, reveals that the thematic and rhetorical grammar of the poem yields a consistent reading that extends from the first line to the last and that can account for all details in the text. It is equally possible, however, to read the last line literally rather than figuratively, as asking with some urgency the question we asked at the beginning of this talk within the context of contemporary criticism: *not* that sign and referent are so exquisitely fitted to each other that all difference between them is at times blotted out but, rather, since the two essentially different elements, sign and meaning, are so intricately intertwined in the imagined "presence" that the poem addresses, how can we possibly make the distinctions that would shelter us from the error of identifying what cannot be identified? The clumsiness of the paraphrase reveals that it is not necessarily the literal reading which is simpler than the figurative one, as was the case in our first example; here, the figural reading, which assumes the question to be rhetorical is perhaps naïve, whereas the literal reading leads to greater complications of theme and statement. For it turns out that the entire scheme set up by the first reading can be undermined or deconstructed, in the terms of the second, in which the final line is read literally as meaning that, since the dancer and the dance are not the same, it might be useful, perhaps even desperately necessary—for the question can be given a ring of urgency, "Please tell me, how *can* I know the dancer from the dance"—to tell them apart. But this will replace the reading of each symbolic detail by a divergent interpretation. The oneness of trunk, leaf and blossom, for example, that would have appealed to Goethe, would find itself replaced by the much less reassuring Tree of Life from the Mabinogion that appears in the poem "Vacillation," in which the fiery blossom and the earthly leaf are held together, as well as apart, by the crucified and castrated God Attis, of whose body it can hardly be said that it is "not bruised to pleasure soul." This hint should suffice to suggest that two entirely coherent but entirely incompatible readings can be made to hinge on one line, whose grammatical structure is devoid of ambiguity, but whose rhetorical mode turns the mood as well as the mode of the entire poem upside down. Neither can we say, as was already the case in the first example, that the poem simply has two meanings that exist side by side. The two readings have to engage each other in direct confrontation, for the one reading is precisely the error denounced by the other and has to be undone by it. Nor can we in any way make a valid decision as to which of the readings can be given priority over the other; none can exist in the other's absence. There can be no dance without a dancer, no sign without a referent. On the other hand, the authority of the meaning engendered by the grammatical structure is fully obscured by the duplicity of a figure that cries out for the differentiation that it conceals.

Yeats' poem is not explicitly "about" rhetorical questions but about images or metaphors, and about the possibility of convergence between experiences of consciousness such as memory or emotions—what the poem calls passion, piety and affection—and entities accessible to the senses such as bodies, persons or icons. We return to the inside/outside model from which we started out and which the poem puts into question by means of a syntactical device (the question) made to operate on a grammatical as well as on a rhetorical level. The couple grammar/rhetoric, certainly not a binary opposition since they in no way exclude each other, disrupts and confuses the neat antithesis of the inside/outside pattern. We can transfer this scheme to the act of reading and interpretation. By reading we get, as we say, inside a text that was first something alien to us and which we now make our own by an act of understanding. But this understanding becomes at once the representation of an extra-textual meaning; in Austin's terms, the illocutionary speech act becomes a perlocutionary actual act—in Frege's terms, *Bedeutung* becomes *Sinn*. Our recurrent question is whether this transformation is semantically controlled along grammatical or along rhetorical lines. Does the metaphor of reading really unite outer meaning with inner understanding, action with reflection, into one single totality? The assertion is powerfully and suggestively made in a passage from Proust that describes the experience of reading as such a union. It describes the young Marcel, near the beginning of Combray, hiding in the closed space of his room in order to read. The example differs from the earlier ones in that we are not dealing with a grammatical structure that also functions rhetorically but have instead the representation, the dramatization, in terms of the experience of a subject, of a rhetorical structure—just as in many other passages, Proust dramatizes tropes by means of landscapes or descriptions of objects. The figure here dramatized is that of metaphor, an inside/outside correspondence as represented by the act of reading. The reading scene is the culmination of a series of actions taking place in enclosed spaces and leading up to the "dark coolness" of Marcel's room.

> I had stretched out on my bed, with a book, in my room which sheltered, trembling, its transparent and fragile coolness against the afternoon sun, behind the almost closed blinds through which a glimmer of daylight had nevertheless managed to push its yellow wings, remaining motionless between the wood and the glass, in a corner, poised like a butterfly. It was hardly light enough to read and the sensation of the light's splendor was given me only by the noise of Camus [. . .] hammering dusty crates; resounding in the sonorous atmosphere that is peculiar to hot weather, they seemed to spark off scarlet stars; and also by the flies executing their little concert, the chamber music of summer: evocative not in the manner of a human tune that, heard perchance during the summer, afterwards reminds you of it; it is connected to summer by a more necessary link: born from beautiful days, resurrecting only when they return, containing some of their essence, it does not only awaken their image in our memory; it guarantees their return, their actual, persistent, unmediated presence.
>
> The dark coolness of my room related to the full sunlight of the street as the shadow relates to the ray of light, that is to say it was just as luminous and it gave my imagination the total spectacle of

the summer, whereas my senses, if I had been on a walk, could only have enjoyed it by fragments; it matched my repose which (thanks to the adventures told by my book and stirring my tranquility) supported, like the quiet of a motionless hand in the middle of a running brook the shock and the motion of a torrent of activity. (*Swann's Way*. Paris: Pléiade, 1954; p. 83. Author's translation.)

From the beginning of the passage, inwardness is valorized positively as something desirable that has to protect itself against the intrusion of outside forces, but that nevertheless has to borrow, as it were, some of its constitutive properties from the outside. A chain of binary properties is set up and antithetically differentiated in terms of the inside/outside polarity: properties of coolness, darkness, repose, silence, imagination and totality, associated with inwardness, contrast with the heat, the light, the activity, the sounds, the senses and the fragmentation that govern the outside. By the act of reading, these static oppositions are put in motion, thus allowing for the play of substitutions by means of which the claim for totalization can be made. Thus, in a beautifully seductive effect of chiaroscuro, mediated by the metaphor of light as a poised butterfly, the inner room is convincingly said to acquire the amount of light necessary to reading. In the wake of this light, warmth can also enter the room, incarnate in the auditive synaesthesia of the various sounds. According to the narrator, these metaphorical substitutions and reversals render the presence of Summer in the room more complete than the actual experience of Summer in the outside world could have done. The text achieves this synthesis and comments on it in normative terms, comparable to the manner in which treatises of practical rhetorics recommend the use of one figure in preference to another in a given situation: here it is the substitutive totalization by metaphor which is said to be more effective than the mere contiguity of metonymic association. As opposed to the random contingency of metonymy ("par hasard"), the metaphor is linked to its proper meaning by, says Proust, the "necessary link" that leads to perfect synthesis. In the wake of this synthesis, the entire conceptual vocabulary of metaphysics enters the text: a terminology of generation, of transcendental necessity, of totality, of essence, of permanence, and of unmediated presence. The passage acts out and asserts the priority of metaphor over metonymy in terms of the categories of metaphysics and with reference to the act of reading.

The actual test of the truth of the assertion comes in the second paragraph when the absurd mathematical ratio set up at the beginning has to be verified by a further substitution. This time, what has to be exchanged are not only the properties of light and dark, warm and cool, fragment and totality (part and whole), but the properties of action and repose. The full seduction of the text can only come into being when the formal totalization of light and dark is completed by the transfer from rest to action that represents the extratextual, referential moment. The text asserts the transfer in the concluding sentence: "The dark coolness of my room [. . .] supported, like the quiet of a motionless hand in the middle of a running brook, the shock and the motion of a torrent of activity." The verb "to support" here carries the full weight of uniting rest and action ("repos et activité"), fiction and reality, as firmly as the base supports the column. The transfer, as is so often the case in Proust, is carried out by the liquid element of the running brook. The natural, representational connotation of the passage is with coolness, so particularly attractive within the predominant summer-mood of the entire *Recherche*. But coolness, it will be remembered, is one of the characteristic properties of the "inside" world. It cannot therefore by itself transfer us into the opposite world of activity. The movement of the water evokes a freshness which in the binary logic of the passage is associated with the inward, imaginary world of reading and fiction. In order to accede to action, it would be necessary to capture one of the properties belonging to the opposite chain such as, for example, warmth. The mere "cool" action of fiction cannot suffice: it is necessary to reconcile the cool immobility of the hand with the heat of action if the claim made by the sentence is to stand up as true. The transfer is carried out, always within the same sentence, when it is said that repose supports "a torrent of activity." The expression "*torrent d'activité*" is not, or no longer, a metaphor in French: it is a cliché, a dead, or sleeping metaphor that has lost the suggestive, connotative values contained in the word "torrent." It simply means "a great deal of activity," the amount of activity that is likely to agitate one to the point of getting hot. Heat is thus surreptitiously smuggled into the passage from a cold source, closing the ring of antithetical properties and allowing for their exchange and substitution: from the moment tranquility can be active and warm without losing its cool and its distinctive quality of repose, the fragmented experience of real-

ity can become whole without losing its quality of being real.

The transfer is made to seem convincing and seductive by the double play on the cliché "torrent of activity." The proximate, contiguous image of the brook awakens, as it were, the sleeping beauty of the dozing metaphor which, in its common use, had become the metonymic association of two words united by sheer habit and no longer by the inner necessity, the necessary link of a transcendental signification. "Torrent" functions in a double semantic register: in its reawakened literal meaning it relays the attribute of coolness that is actually part of the running water, whereas in its figural non-meaning it designates the quantity of activity connotative of the contrary property of warmth.

The rhetorical structure of this sentence is therefore not simply metaphorical. It is at least doubly metonymic, first because the coupling of words, in a cliché, is not governed by the necessary link that reveals their potential identity but by the contingent habit of proximity; second, because the reawakening of the metaphorical term "torrent" is carried out by a statement that happens to be in the vicinity, but without there being any necessity for the proximity on the level of the referential meaning. The most striking thing is that this doubly metonymic structure is found in a text that also contains highly seductive and successful metaphors (as in the chiaroscuro effect of the beginning, or in the condensation of light in the butterfly image) and that explicitly asserts the superiority of metaphor over metonymy in terms of metaphysical categories.

That these metaphysical categories do not remain unaffected by such a reading would become clear from an inclusive reading of Proust's novel or would become even more explicit in a language-conscious philosopher, such as Nietzsche who, as a philosopher, has to be concerned with the epistemological consequences of the kind of rhetorical seductions exemplified by the Proust passage. It can be shown that the systematic critique of the main categories of metaphysics undertaken by Nietzsche in his late work, the critique of the concepts of causality, of the subject, of identity, of referential and revealed truth, etc. occurs along the same pattern of deconstruction that was operative in Proust's text; and it can also be shown that this pattern exactly corresponds to Nietzsche's description, in texts that precede *The Will to Power* by more than fifteen years, of the structure of the main rhetorical tropes. The key to this critique of metaphysics, which is itself a recurrent gesture throughout the history of thought, is the rhetorical model of the trope or, if one prefers to call it that, literature. It turns out that, in these innocent-looking didactic exercises we are in fact playing for very sizable stakes.

It is therefore all the more necessary to know what is linguistically involved in a rhetorically conscious reading of the type here undertaken on a brief fragment from a novel and extended by Nietzsche to the entire text of post-Hellenic thought. Our first examples dealing with the rhetorical questions were rhetorizations of grammar, figures generated by syntactical paradigms, whereas the Proust example could be better described as a grammatization of rhetoric. By passing from a paradigmatic structure based on substitution, such as metaphor, to a syntagmatic structure based on contingent association such as metonymy, the mechanical, repetitive aspect of grammatical forms is shown to be operative in a passage that seemed at first sight to celebrate the self-willed and autonomous inventiveness of a subject. Figures are assumed to be inventions, the products of a highly particularized individual talent, whereas no one can claim credit or the programmed pattern of grammar. Yet, our reading of the Proust passage shows that precisely when the highest claims are being made for the unifying power of metaphor, these very images rely in fact on the deceptive use of semi-automatic grammatical patterns. The deconstruction of metaphor and of all rhetorical patterns such as mimesis, paranomasis or personification that use resemblance as a way to disguise differences, takes us back to the impersonal precision of grammar and of a semiology derived from grammatical patterns. Such a deconstruction puts into question a whole series of concepts that underlie the value judgments of our critical discourse: the metaphor of primacy, of genetic history and, most notably, of the autonomous power to will of the self.

There seems to be a difference, then, between what I called the rhetorization of grammar (as in the rhetorical question) and the grammatization of rhetoric, as in the de-constructive readings of the type sketched out in the passage from Proust. The former end up in indetermination, in a suspended uncertainty that was unable to choose between two modes of reading, whereas the latter seems to reach a truth, albeit by the negative road of exposing an error, a false pretense. After the de-constructive reading of the Proust passage, we can no longer believe the assertion made in

this passage about the intrinsic, metaphysical superiority of metaphor over metonymy. We seem to end up in a mood of negative assurance that is highly productive of critical discourse. The further text of Proust's novel, for example, responds perfectly to an extended application of this de-constructive pattern: not only can similar gestures be repeated throughout the novel, at all the crucial articulations or all passages where large aesthetic and metaphysical claims are being made—the scenes of involuntary memory, the workshop of Elstir, the septette of Vinteuil, the convergence of author and narrator at the end of the novel—but a vast thematic and semiotic network is revealed that structures the entire narrative and that remained invisible to a reader caught in naïve metaphorical mystification. The whole of literature would respond in similar fashion, although the techniques and the patterns would have to vary considerably, of course, from author to author. But there is absolutely no reason why analyses of the kind here suggested for Proust would not be applicable, with proper modifications of technique, to Milton or to Dante or to Hölderlin. This will in fact be the task of literary criticism in the coming years.

It would seem that we are saying that criticism is the deconstruction of literature, the reduction to the rigors of grammar of rhetorical mystifications. And if we hold up Nietzsche as the philosopher of such a critical deconstruction, then the literary critic would become the philosopher's ally in his struggle with the poets. Criticism and literature would separate around the epistemological axis that distinguishes grammar from rhetoric. It is easy enough to see that this apparent glorification of the critic-philosopher in the name of truth is in fact a glorification of the poet as the primary source of this truth; if truth is the recognition of the systematic character of a certain kind of error, then it would be fully dependent on the prior existence of this error. Philosophers of science like Bachelard or Wittgenstein are notoriously dependent on the aberrations of the poets. We are back at our unanswered question: does the grammatization of rhetoric end up in negative certainty or does it, like the rhetorization of grammar, remain suspended in the ignorance of its own truth or falsehood?

Two concluding remarks should suffice to answer the question. First of all, it is not true that Proust's text can simply be reduced to the mystified assertion (the superiority of metaphor over metonymy) that our reading deconstructs. The reading is not "our" reading, since it uses only the linguistic elements provided by the text itself; the distinction between author and reader is one of the false distinctions that the deconstruction makes evident. The deconstruction is not something we have added to the text but it constituted the text in the first place. A literary text simultaneously asserts and denies the authority of its own rhetorical mode and by reading the text as we did, we were only trying to come closer to being as rigorous a reader as the author had to be in order to write the sentence in the first place. Poetic writing is the most advanced and refined mode of deconstruction; it may differ from critical or discursive writing in the economy of its articulation, but not in kind.

But if we recognize the existence of the deconstructive moment as constitutive of all literary language we have surreptitiously reintroduced the categories that this deconstruction was supposed to eliminate and that have merely been displaced. We have, for example, displaced the question of the self from the referent into the figure of the narrator, who then becomes the *signifié* of the passage. It becomes again possible to ask such naïve questions as what Proust, or Marcel's, motives may have been in thus manipulating language: was he fooling himself, or was he represented as fooling himself and fooling us into believing that fiction and action are as easy to unite, by reading, as the passage asserts? The pathos of the entire section, which would have been more noticeable if the quotation had been a little more extended, the constant vacillation of the narrator between guilt and well-being, invites such questions. They are absurd questions, of course, since the reconciliation of fact and fiction occurs itself as a mere assertion made in the text, and is thus productive of more text at the moment when it asserts its decision to escape from textual confinement. But even if we free ourselves of all false questions of intent and rightfully reduce the narrator to the status of a mere grammatical pronoun, without which the deconstructive narrative could not come into being, this subject remains endowed with a function that is not grammatical but rhetorical, in that it gives voice, so to speak, to a grammatical syntagm. The term voice, even when used in a grammatical terminology as when we speak, of the passive or interrogative voice is, of course, a metaphor inferring by analogy the intent of the subject from the structure of the predicate. In the case of the deconstructive discourse that we call literary, or rhetorical, or poetic, this creates a dis-

tinctive complication illustrated by the Proust passage. The deconstructive reading revealed a first paradox: the passage valorizes metaphor as being the "right" literary figure, but then proceeds to constitute itself by means of the epistemologically incompatible figure of metonymy. The deconstructive critical discourse reveals the presence of this delusion and affirms it as the irreversible mode of its truth. It cannot pause there however. For if we then ask the obvious and simple next question, whether the rhetorical mode of the text in question is that of metaphor or metonymy, it is impossible to give an answer. Individual metaphors, such as the chiaroscuro effect or the butterfly, are shown to be subordinate figures in a general clause whose syntax is metonymic; from this point of view, it seems that the rhetoric is superseded by a grammar that deconstructs it. But this metonymic clause has as its subject a voice whose relationship to this clause is again metaphorical. The narrator who tells us about the impossibility of metaphor is himself, or itself, a metaphor, the metaphor of a grammatical syntagm whose meaning is the denial of metaphor stated, by antiphrasis, as its priority. And this subject-metaphor is, in its turn, open to the kind of deconstruction to the second degree, the rhetorical deconstruction of psycholinguistics, in which the more advanced investigations of literature are presently engaged, against considerable resistance.

We end up therefore, in the case of the rhetorical grammatization of semiology, just as in the grammatical rhetorization of illocutionary phrases, in the same state of suspended ignorance. Any question about the rhetorical mode of a literary text is always a rhetorical question which does not even know whether it is really questioning. The resulting pathos is an anxiety (or bliss, depending on one's momentary mood or individual temperament) of ignorance, not an anxiety of reference—as becomes thematically clear in Proust's novel when reading is dramatized, in the relationship between Marcel and Albertine, not as an emotive reaction to what language does, but as an emotive reaction to the impossibility of knowing what it might be up to. Literature as well as criticism—the difference between them being delusive—are condemned (or privileged) to be forever the most rigorous and, consequently, the most unreliable language in terms of which man names and modifies himself.

THEORY

*Stanley Fish's concept of "interpretive communities" fits
well within the poststructural context, for it is premised
on the "antifoundational" and "antiessentialist" arguments that are characteristic of this context. But it gives
these arguments an interesting twist. Language may
indeed be inherently indeterminate, but "meaning" is
always determinate, Fish argues, because interpreters,
who make meaning, make it so. On this score his position seems to resemble Norman Holland's. But while
Holland sees the reader imposing his or her individual
identity on the text, producing thereby a highly individualized interpretation, Fish argues that we always read
as members of an interpretive community who share an
accepted interpretive strategy. Thus, Fish offers to explain both why our interpretations can agree, and why
they often do not. Members of the same interpretive community may produce similar readings and may even allow their interpretations to be "corrected" according to
the rules of that community's strategy. Within such a
community, interpretation can be the progressive discipline several critics have called for, and almost any literature class will furnish a microcosmic example of the
process. On a larger scale, each of this book's contexts is
an interpretive community, or a collection of such communities, sharing fundamental assumptions about where
literary meaning is located and how we can get at it.
But the strategies and assumptions of one context are
not those of another, hence the large amount of radical
disagreement in critical discussions and the apparent
futility of trying to talk across the boundaries of these
contexts or to offer a strategy they can all agree upon.
Since "meaning" is itself the product of interpretation,*

What Makes an Interpretation Acceptable?

Stanley Fish

in Fish's view, all attempts to circumvent interpretive strategies are doomed to fail. "Interpretation is the only game in town." And since the acceptability of an interpretation can be decided only within an interpretive community, we are reminded that the argument all along has been about what critical context one should choose. But on this crucial point, Fish, as an antifoundationalist and antiessentialist, has no advice to offer.

Last time I ended by suggesting that the fact of agreement, rather than being a proof of the stability of objects, is a testimony to the power of an interpretive community to constitute the objects upon which its members (also and simultaneously constituted) can then agree. This account of agreement has the additional advantage of providing what the objectivist argument cannot supply, a coherent account of *dis*agreement. To someone who believes in determinate meaning, disagreement can only be a theological error. The truth lies plainly in view, available to anyone who has the eyes to see; but some readers choose not to see it and perversely substitute their own meanings for the meanings that texts obviously bear. Nowhere is there an explanation of this waywardness (original sin would seem to be the only relevant model), or of the origin of these idiosyncratic meanings (I have been arguing that there could be none), or of the reason why some readers seem to be exempt from the general infirmity. There is simply the conviction that the facts exist in their own self-evident shape and that disagreements are to be resolved by referring the respective parties to the facts as they really are. In the view that I have been urging, however, disagreements cannot be resolved by reference to the facts, because the facts emerge only in the context of some point of view. It follows, then, that disagreements must occur between those who hold (or are held by) different points of view, and what is at stake in a disagreement is the right to specify what the facts can hereafter be said to be. Disagreements are not settled by the facts, but are the means by which the facts are settled. Of course, no such settling is final, and in the (almost certain) event that the dispute is opened again, the category of the facts "as they really are" will be reconstituted in still another shape.

Nowhere is this process more conveniently on display than in literary criticism, where everyone's claim is that his interpretation more perfectly accords with the facts, but where everyone's purpose is to persuade the rest of us to the version of the facts he espouses by persuading us to the interpretive principles in the light of which those facts will seem indisputable. The recent critical fortunes of William Blake's "The Tyger" provide a nice example. In 1954 Kathleen Raine published an influential essay entitled "Who Made the Tyger" in which she argued that because the tiger is for Blake "the beast that sustains its own life at the expense of its fellow-creatures" it is a "symbol of . . . predacious selfhood," and that therefore the answer to the poem's final question — "Did he who made the Lamb make thee" — "is, beyond all possible doubt, No."[1] In short, the tiger is unambiguously and obviously evil. Raine supports her reading by pointing to two bodies of evidence, certain cabbalistic writings which, she avers, "beyond doubt . . . inspired *The Tyger*," and evidence from the poem itself. She pays particular attention to the word "forests" as it appears in line 2, "In the forests of the night:" "Never . . . is the word 'forest' used by Blake in any context in which it does not refer to the natural, 'fallen' world" (p. 48).

The direction of argument here is from the word "forests" to the support it is said to provide or a particular interpretation. Ten years later, however, that same word is being cited in support of a quite different interpretation. While Raine assumes that the lamb is for Blake a symbol of Christ-like self-sacrifice, E. D. Hirsch believes that Blake's intention was "to satirize the singlemindedness of the Lamb": "There can be no doubt," he declares, "that *The Tyger* is a poem that celebrates the holiness of tigerness."[2] In his reading the "ferocity and destructiveness" of the tiger are transfigured and one of the things they are transfigured by is the word "forests": " 'Forests' . . . suggest tall straight forms, a world that for all its terror has the orderliness of the tiger's stripes or Blake's perfectly balanced verses" (p. 247).

What we have here then are two critics with opposing interpretations, each of whom claims the same word as internal and confirming evidence. Clearly they cannot both be right, but just as clearly there is no basis for deciding between them. One cannot appeal to the text, because the text has become an extension of the interpretive disagreement that divides them; and, in fact, the text as it is variously characterized is a *consequence* of the interpretation for which it is supposedly evidence. It is not that the meaning of the word "forests" points in the direction of one interpretation or the other; rather, in the light on an already assumed interpretation, the word will be seen to *obviously* have one meaning or another. Nor can the question be settled by turning to the context—say the cabbalistic writings cited by Raine—for that too will only be a context for an already assumed interpretation. If Raine had not already decided that the answer to the poem's final question is "beyond all possible doubt, No," the cabbalistic texts, with their distinction between supreme and inferior deities, would never have suggested themselves to her as Blake's source. The rhetoric of critical argument, as it is usually conducted in our journals, depends upon a distinction between interpretations on the one hand and the textual and contextual facts that will either support or disconfirm them on the other; but as the example of Blake's "Tyger" shows, text, context, and interpretation all emerge together, as a consequence of a gesture (the declaration of belief) that is irreducibly interpretive. It follows, then, that when one interpretation wins out over another, it is not because the first has been shown to be in accordance with the facts but because it is from the perspective of its assumptions that the facts are now being specified. It is these assumptions, and not the facts they make possible, that are at stake in any critical dispute.

Hirsch and Raine seem to be aware of this, at least subliminally; for whenever their respective assumptions surface they are asserted with a vehemence that is finally defensive: "The answer to the question . . . is beyond all possible doubt, No." "There can be no doubt that *The Tyger* is . . . a poem that celebrates the holiness of tigerness." If there were a doubt, if the interpretation with which each critic begins were not firmly in place, the account of the poem that follows from that interpretation could not get under way. One could not cite as an "obvious" fact that "forests" is a fallen word or, alternatively, that it "suggests tall and straight forms." Whenever a critic prefaces an assertion with a phrase like "without doubt" or "there can be no doubt," you can be sure that you are within hailing distance of the interpretive principles which produce the facts that he presents as obvious.

In the years since 1964 other interpretations of the poem have been put forward, and they follow a predictable course. Some echo either Raine or Hirsch by arguing that the tiger is either good or evil; others assert that the tiger is *both* good and evil, or beyond good and evil; still others protest that the questions posed in the poem are rhetorical and are therefore

not meant to be answered ("it is quite evident that the critics are not trying to understand the poem at all. If they were, they would not attempt to answer its questions").[3] It is only a matter of time before the focus turns from the questions to their asker and to the possibility that the speaker of the poem is not Blake but a limited persona ("Surely the point . . . is that Blake sees further or deeper than his *persona*").[4] It then becomes possible to assert that "we don't know who the speaker of 'The Tyger' is" and that therefore the poem "is a maze of questions in which the reader is forced to wander confusedly."[5] In this reading the poem itself becomes rather "tigerish" and one is not at all surprised when the original question—"Who made the Tiger?"—is given its quintessentially new-critical answer: the tiger is the poem itself and Blake, the consummate artist who smiles "his work to see," is its creator.[6] As one obvious and indisputable interpretation supplants another, it brings with it a new set of obvious and indisputable facts. Of course each new reading is elaborated in the name of the poem itself, but the poem itself is always a function of the interpretive perspective from which the critic "discovers" it.

A committed pluralist might find in the previous paragraph a confirmation of his own position. After all, while "The Tyger" is obviously open to more than one interpretation, it is not open to an infinite number of interpretations. There may be disagreements as to whether the tiger is good or evil, or whether the speaker is Blake or a persona, and so on, but no one is suggesting that the poem is an allegory of the digestive processes or that it predicts the Second World War, and its limited plurality is simply a testimony to the capacity of a great work of art to generate multiple readings. The point is one that Wayne Booth makes when he asks, "Are we *right* to rule out at least some readings?"[7] and then answers his own question with a resounding yes. It would be my answer too; but the real question is what gives us the right so to be right. A pluralist is committed to saying that there is something in the text which rules out some readings and allows others (even though no *one* reading can ever capture the text's "inexhaustible richness and complexity"). His best evidence is that in practice "we all in fact" do reject unacceptable readings and that more often than not we agree on the readings that are to be rejected. Booth tells us, for example, that he has never found a reader of *Pride and Prejudice* "who sees no jokes against Mr. Collins" when he gives his reasons for wanting to marry Elizabeth Bennet and only belatedly, in fifth position, cites the "violence" of his affection.[8] From this and other examples, Booth concludes that there are justified limits to what we can legitimately do with a text, for "surely we could not go on disputing at all if a core of agreement did not exist." Again, I agree, but if, as I have argued, the text is always a function of interpretation, then the text cannot be the location of the core of agreement by means of which we reject interpretations. We seem to be at an impasse: on the one hand there would seem to be no basis for labeling an interpretation unacceptable, but on the other we do it all the time.

This, however, is an impasse only if one assumes that the activity of interpretation is itself unconstrained; but in fact the shape of that activity is determined by the literary institution which at any one time will authorize only a finite number of interpretive strategies. Thus, while there is no core of agreement *in* the text, there is a core of agreement (although one subject to change) concerning the ways of *producing* the text. Nowhere is this set of acceptable ways written down, but it is a part of everyone's knowledge of what it means to be operating within the literary institution as it is now constituted. A student of mine recently demonstrated this knowledge when, with an air of giving away a trade secret, she confided that she could go into any classroom, no matter what the subject of the course, and win approval for running one of a number of well-defined interpretive routines: she could view the assigned text as an instance of the tension between nature and culture; she could look at the text for evidence of large mythological oppositions; she could argue that the true subject of the text was its own composition, or that in the guise of fashioning a narrative the speaker was fragmenting and displacing his own anxieties and fears. She could not, however, at least at Johns Hopkins University today, argue that the text was a prophetic message inspired by the ghost of her Aunt Tilly.

My student's understanding of what she could and could not get away with, of the unwritten rules of the literary game, is shared by everyone who plays that game, by those who write and judge articles for publication in learned journals, by those who read and listen to papers at professional meetings, by those who seek and award tenure in innumerable departments of English and comparative literature, by the armies of graduate students for whom knowledge of the rules is the real mark of professional initiation. This does not mean that these rules and the practices they authorize are either monolithic or stable. Within the literary community there are subcommunities (what will excite the editors of *Diacritics* is likely to distress the editors of *Studies in Philology*), and within any community the boundaries of the acceptable are continually being redrawn. In a classroom whose authority figures include David Bleich and Norman Holland, a student might very well relate a text to her memories of a favorite aunt, while in other classrooms, dominated by the spirit of Brooks and Warren, any such activity would immediately be dismissed as nonliterary, as something that isn't done.

The point is that while there is always a category of things that are not done (it is simply the reverse or flip side of the category of things that *are* done), the membership in that category is continually changing. It changes laterally as one moves from subcommunity to subcommunity, and it changes through time when once interdicted interpretive strategies are admitted into the ranks of the acceptable. Twenty years ago one of the things that literary critics didn't do was talk about the reader, at least in a way that made his experience the focus of the critical act. The prohibition on such talk was largely the result of Wimsatt's and Beardsley's famous essay "The Affective Fallacy," which argued that the variability of readers renders any investigation of their responses ad-hoc and relativistic: "The poem itself," the authors complained, "as an object of specifically critical judgment, tends to disappear."[9] So influential was this essay that it was possible for a reviewer to dismiss a book merely by finding in it evidence that the affective fallacy had been committed. The use of a juridical terminology is not accidental; this was in a very real sense a *legal* finding of activity in violation of understood and institutionalized decorums. Today, however, the affective fallacy, no longer a fallacy but a methodology, is committed all the time, and its practitioners have behind them the full and authorizing weight of a fully articulated institutional apparatus. The "reader in literature" is regularly the subject of forums and workshops at the convention of the Modern Language Association; there is a reader newsletter, which reports on the multitudinous labors of a reader industry; any list of currently active schools of literary criticism includes the school of "reader response," and two major university presses have published collections of essays designed both to display the variety of reader-centered criticism (the emergence of factions within a once interdicted activity is a sure sign of its having achieved the status of an orthodoxy) and to detail its history. None of this of course means that a reader-centered criticism is now invulnerable to challenge or attack, merely that it is now recognized as a competing literary strategy that cannot be dismissed simply by being named. It is acceptable not because everyone accepts it but because those who do not are now obliged to argue against it.

The promotion of reader-response criticism to the category of things that are done (even if it is not being done by everyone) brings with it a whole new set of facts to which its practitioners can now refer. These include patterns of expectation and disappointment, reversals of direction, traps, invitations to premature conclusions, textual gaps, delayed revelations, temptations, all of which are related to a corresponding set of authors' intentions, of strategies designed to educate the reader or humiliate him or confound him or, in the more sophisticated versions of the mode, to make him enact in his responses the very subject matter of the poem. These facts and intentions emerge when the text is interrogated by a series of related questions — What is the reader doing? What is being done to him? For what purpose? — questions that follow necessarily from the assumption that the text is not a spatial object but the occasion for a temporal experience. It is in the course of answering such questions that a reader response critic elaborates "the structure of the reading experience," a structure which is not so much discovered by the interrogation but demanded by it. (If you begin by assuming that readers do something and the something they do has meaning, you will never fail to discover a pattern of reader activities that appears obviously to be meaningful.) As that structure emerges (under the pressure of interrogation) it takes the form of a "reading," and insofar as the procedures which produced it are recognized by the literary community as something that some of its members do, that reading will have the status of a competing interpretation. Of course it is still the case, as Booth insists, that we are "right to rule out at least some readings," but there is now one less reading or kind of reading that can be ruled out, because there is now one more interpretive procedure that has been accorded a place in the literary institution.

The fact that it remains easy to think of a reading that most of us would dismiss out of hand does not mean that the text excludes it but that there is as yet no elaborated interpretive procedure for producing that text. That is why the examples of critics like Wayne Booth seem to have so much force; rather than looking back, as I have, to now familiar strategies that were once alien and strange sounding, they look forward to strategies that have not yet emerged. Norman Holland's analysis of Faulkner's "A Rose for Emily" is a case in point. Holland is arguing for a kind of psychoanalytic pluralism. The text, he declares, is "at most a matrix of psychological possibilities for its readers," but, he insists, "only some possibilities . . . truly fit the matrix": "One would not say, for example, that a reader of . . . 'A Rose for Emily' who thought the 'tableau' [of Emily and her father in the doorway] described an Eskimo was really responding to the story at all — only pursuing some mysterious inner exploration."[10]

Holland is making two arguments: first, that anyone who proposes an Eskimo reading of "A Rose for Emily" will not find a hearing in the literary community. And that, I think, is right. ("We are right to rule out at least some readings.") His second argument is that the unacceptability of the Eskimo reading is a function of the text, of what he calls its "sharable promptuary" (p. 287), the public "store of structured language" (p. 287) that sets limits to the interpretations the words can accommodate. And that, I think, is wrong. The Eskimo reading is unacceptable because there is at present no interpretive strategy for producing it, no way of "looking" or reading (and remember, all acts of looking or reading are "ways") that would result in the emergence of obviously Eskimo meanings. This does not mean, however, that no such strategy could ever come into play, and it is not difficult to imagine the circumstances under which it would establish itself. One such circumstance would be the discovery of a letter in which Faulkner confides that he has always believed himself to be an Eskimo changeling. (The example is absurd only if one forgets Yeats' *Vision* or Blake's Swedenborgianism or James Miller's recent elaboration of a homosexual reading of *The Waste Land*.) Immediately the workers in the Faulkner industry would begin to reinterpret the canon in the light of this newly revealed "belief" and the work of reinterpretation would involve the elaboration of a symbolic or allusive system (not unlike mythological or typological criticism) whose application would immediately transform the text into one informed everywhere by Eskimo meanings. It might seem that I am admitting that there is a text to be transformed, but the object of transformation would be the text (or texts) given by whatever interpretive strategies the Eskimo strategy was in the process of dislodging or expanding. The result would be that whereas we now have a Freudian "A Rose for Emily," a mythological "A Rose for Emily," a Christological "A Rose for Emily," a regional "A Rose for Emily," a sociological "A Rose for Emily," a linguistic "A Rose for Emily," we would in addition have an Eskimo "A Rose for Emily," existing in some relation of compatibility or incompatibility with the others.

Again the point is that while there are always mechanisms for ruling out readings, their source is not the text but the presently recognized interpretive strategies for producing the text. It follows, then, that no reading, however outlandish it might appear, is inherently an impossible one. Consider, for another example, Booth's report that he had never found a reader who sees no jokes against Mr. Collins, and his conclusion that the text of *Pride and Prejudice* enforces or signals an ironic reading. First of all, the fact that he hasn't yet found such a reader does not mean that one does not exist, and we can even construct his profile; he would be someone for whom the reasons in Mr. Collins's list correspond to a deeply held set of values, exactly the opposite of the set of values that must be assumed if the passage is to be seen as obviously ironic. Presumably no one who has sat in Professor Booth's classes holds that set of values or is allowed to hold them (students always know what they are expected to believe) and it is unlikely that anyone who is now working in the Austen industry begins with an assumption other than the assumption that the novelist is a master ironist. It is precisely for this reason that the time is ripe for the "discovery" by an enterprising scholar of a nonironic Austen, and one can even predict the course such a discovery would take. It would begin with the uncovering of new evidence (a letter, a lost manuscript, a contemporary response) and proceed to the conclusion that Austen's intentions have been misconstrued by generations of literary critics. She was not in fact satirizing the narrow and circumscribed life of a country gentry; rather, she was celebrating that life and its tireless elaboration of a social fabric, complete with values, rituals, and self-perpetuating goals (marriage, the preservation of great houses, and so on). This view, or something very much like it, is already implicit in much of the criticism, and it would only be a matter of extending it to local matters of interpretation, and specifically to Mr. Collins's list of reasons which might now be seen as reflecting a proper ranking of the values and obligations necessary to the maintenance of a way of life.

Of course any such reading would meet resistance; its opponents could point for example to the narrator's unequivocal condemnation of Mr. Collins; but there are always ways in the literary institution of handling this or any other objection. One need only introduce (if it has not already been introduced) the notion of the fallible narrator in any of its various forms (the dupe, the moral prig, the naif in need of education), and the "unequivocal condemnation" would take its place in a structure designed to glorify Mr. Collins and everything he stands for. Still, no matter how many objections were met and explained away, the basic resistance on the part of many scholars to this revisionist reading would remain, and for a time at least *Pride and Prejudice* would have acquired the status of the fourth book of *Gulliver's Travels*, a work whose very shape changes in the light of two radically opposed interpretive assumptions.

Again, I am aware that this argument is a tour-de-force and will continue to seem so as long as the revolution it projects has not occurred. The reading of *Pride and Prejudice*, however, is not meant to be persuasive. I only wanted to describe the conditions under which it might *become* persuasive and to point out that those conditions are not unimaginable given the procedures within the literary institution by which interpretations are proposed and established. Any interpretation could be elaborated by someone in command of those procedures (someone who knows what "will do" as a literary argument), even my own "absurd" reading of "The Tyger" as an allegory of the digestive processes. Here the task is easy because according to the critical consensus there is no belief so bizarre that Blake could not have been committed to it and it would be no trick at all to find some elaborate system of alimentary significances (Pythagorean? Swedenborgian? Cabbalistic?) which he could be presumed to have known. One might then decide that the poem was the first-person lament of someone who had violated a dietary prohibition against eating tiger meat, and finds that forbidden food burning brightly in his stomach, making its fiery way through the forest of the intestinal tract, beating and hammering like some devil-wielded anvil. In his distress he can do nothing but rail at the tiger and at the mischance that led him to mistake its meat for the meat of some purified animal: "Did he who made the Lamb make thee?" The poem ends as it began, with the speaker still paying the price of his sin and wondering at the inscrutable purposes of a deity who would lead his creatures into digestive temptation. Anyone who thinks that this time I have gone too far might do very well to consult some recent numbers of *Blake Studies*.

In fact, my examples are very serious, and they are serious in part because they are so ridiculous. The fact that they *are* ridiculous, or are at least perceived to be so, is evidence that we are never without canons of acceptability; we are always "right to rule out at least some readings." But the fact that we can imagine conditions under which they would *not* seem ridiculous, and that readings once considered ridiculous are now respectable and even orthodox, is evidence that the canons of acceptability can change. Moreover, the change is not random but orderly and, to some extent, predictable. A new interpretive strategy always makes its way in some relationship of opposition to the old, which has often marked out a negative space (of things that aren't done) from which it can emerge into respectability. Thus, when Wimsatt and Beardsley declare that "the Affective Fallacy is a confusion between the poem and its *results*, what it *is* and what it *does*," the way is open for an affective critic to argue, as I did, that a poem *is* what it does. And when the possibility of a reader-centered criticism seems threatened by the variability of readers, that threat will be countered either by denying the variability (Stephen Booth, Michael Riffaterre) or by controlling it (Wolfgang Iser, Louise Rosenblatt) or by embracing it and making it into a principle of value (David Bleich, Walter Slatoff).

Rhetorically the new position announces itself as a break from the old, but in fact it is radically dependent on the old, because it is only in the context of some differential relationship that it can be perceived as new or, for that matter, perceived at all. No one would bother to assert that Mr. Collins is the hero of *Pride and Prejudice* (even as an example intended to be absurd) were that position not already occupied in the criticism by Elizabeth and Darcy; for then the assertion would have no force; there would be nothing in relation to which it could be surprising. Nei-

ther would there be any point in arguing that Blake's tiger is both good and evil if there were not already readings in which he was declared to be one or the other. And if anyone is ever to argue that he is both old and young, someone will first have to argue that he is *either* old or young, for only when his age has become a question will there be any value in a refusal to answer it. Nor is it the case that the moral status of the tiger (as opposed to its age, or nationality, or intelligence) is an issue raised by the poem itself; it becomes an issue because a question is put to the poem (is the tiger good or evil?) and once that question (it could have been another) is answered, the way is open to answering it differently, or declining to answer it, or to declaring that the absence of an answer is the poem's "real point."

The discovery of the "real point" is always what is claimed whenever a new interpretation is advanced, but the claim makes sense only in relation to a point (or points) that had previously been considered the real one. This means that the space in which a critic works has been marked out for him by his predecessors, even though he is obliged by the conventions of the institution to dislodge them. It is only by their prevenience or prepossession that there is something for him to say; that is, it is only because something has already been said that he can now say something different. This dependency, the reverse of the anxiety of influence, is reflected in the unwritten requirement that an interpretation present itself as remedying a deficiency in the interpretations that have come before it. (If it did not do this, what claim would it have on our attention?) Nor can this be just any old deficiency; it will not do, for example, to fault your predecessors for failing to notice that a poem is free of split infinitives or dangling participles. The lack an interpretation supplies must be related to the criteria by which the literary community recognizes and evaluates the objects of its professional attention. As things stand now, textbook grammaticality is not one of those criteria, and therefore the demonstration of its presence in a poem will not reflect credit either on the poem or on the critic who offers it.

Credit *will* accrue to the critic when he bestows the *proper* credit on the poem, when he demonstrates that it possesses one or more of the qualities that are understood to distinguish poems from other verbal productions. In the context of the "new" criticism, under many of whose assumptions we still labor, those qualities include unity, complexity, and universality, and it is the perceived failure of previous commentators to celebrate their presence in a poem that gives a critic the right (or so he will claim) to advance a new interpretation. The unfolding of the interpretation will thus proceed under two constraints: not only must what one says about a work be related to what has already been said (even if the relation is one of reversal) but as a consequence of saying it the work must be shown to possess in a greater degree than had hitherto been recognized the qualities that properly belong to literary productions, whether they are unity and complexity, or unparaphrasability, or metaphoric richness, or indeterminacy and undecidability. In short, the new interpretation must not only claim to tell the truth about the work (in a dependent opposition to the falsehood or partial truths told by its predecessors) but it must claim to make the work better. (The usual phrase is "enhance our appreciation of.") Indeed, these claims are finally inseparable since it is assumed that the truth about a work will be what penetrates to the essence of its literary value.

This assumption, along with several others, is conveniently on display in the opening paragraph of the preface to Stephen Booth's *An Essay on Shakespeare's Sonnets.*[11]

> The history of criticism opens so many possibilities for an essay on Shakespeare's sonnets that I must warn a prospective reader about what this work does and doesn't do. To begin with the negative, I have not solved or tried to solve any of the puzzles of Shakespeare's sonnets. I do not attempt to identify Mr. W. H. or the dark lady. I do not speculate on the occasions that may have evoked particular sonnets. I do not attempt to date them. I offer neither a reorganization of the sequence, nor a defense of the quarto order. What I have tried to do is find out what about the sonnets has made them so highly valued by the vast majority of critics and general readers.

This brief paragraph can serve as an illustration of almost everything I have been saying. First of all, Booth self-consciously locates and defines his position in a differential opposition to the positions he would dislodge. He will not, he tells us, do what any of his predecessors have done; he will do something else, and indeed if it were not something else there would be no reason for him to be doing it. The reason he gives for doing it is that what his predecessors

have done is misleading or beside the point. The point is the location of the source of the sonnets' value ("what about the sonnets has made them so highly valued") and his contention (not stated but strongly implied) is that those who have come before him have been looking in the wrong places, in the historical identity of the sequence's characters, in the possibility of recovering the biographical conditions of composition, and in the determination of an authoritative ordering and organization. He, however, will look in the right place and thereby produce an account of the sonnets that does them the justice they so richly deserve.

Thus, in only a few sentences Booth manages to claim for his interpretation everything that certifies it as acceptable within the conventions of literary criticism: he locates a deficiency in previous interpretations and proposes to remedy it; the remedy will take the form of producing a more satisfactory account of the work; and as a result the literary credentials of the work—what makes it of enduring value—will be more securely established, as they are when Booth is able to point in the closing paragraph of his book to Shakespeare's "remarkable achievement." By thus validating Shakespeare's achievement, Booth also validates his own credentials as a literary critic, as someone who knows what claims and demonstrations mark him as a competent member of the institution.

What makes Stephen Booth so interesting (although not at all atypical) is that one of his claims is to have freed himself and the sonnets from the very institution and its practices. "I do not," he declares, "intentionally give any interpretations of the sonnets I discuss. I mean to describe them, not to explain them." The irony is that even as Booth is declaring himself out of the game, he is performing one of its most familiar moves. The move has several versions, and Booth is here availing himself of two: (1) the "external-internal," performed when a critic dismisses his predecessors for being insufficiently literary ("but that has nothing to do with its qualities *as a poem*"); and (2) the "back-to-the-text," performed when the critical history of a work is deplored as so much dross, as an obscuring encrustation ("we are in danger of substituting the criticism for the poem"). The latter is the more powerful version of the move because it trades on the assumption, still basic to the profession's sense of its activities, that the function of literary criticism is to let the text speak for itself. It is thus a move drenched in humility, although it is often performed with righteousness: those other fellows may be interested in displaying their ingenuity, but *I* am simply a servant of the text and wish only to make it more available to its readers (who happen also to be my readers).

The basic gesture, then, is to disavow interpretation in favor of simply presenting the text; but it is actually a gesture in which one set of interpretive principles is replaced by another that happens to claim for itself the virtue of not being an interpretation at all. The claim, however, is an impossible one since in order "simply to present" the text, one must at the very least describe it ("I mean to describe them") and description can occur only within a stipulative understanding of what there is to be described, an understanding that will produce the object of its attention. Thus, when Booth rejects the assumptions of those who have tried to solve the puzzles of the sonnets in favor of "the assumption that the source of our pleasure in them must be in the line by line experience of reading them," he is not avoiding interpretation but proposing a change in the terms within which it will occur. Specifically, he proposes that the focus of attention, and therefore of description, shift from the poem conceived as a spatial object which *contains* meanings to the poem conceived as a temporal experience in the course of which meanings become momentarily available, before disappearing under the pressure of other meanings, which are in their turn superseded, contradicted, qualified, or simply forgotten. It is only if a reader agrees to this change, that is, agrees to accept Booth's revisionary stipulation as to where the value and the significance of a poem are to be located, that the facts to which his subsequent analyses point will be seen to be facts at all. The description which Booth offers in place of an interpretation turns out to be as much of an interpretive construct as the interpretations he rejects.

Nor could it be otherwise. Strictly speaking, getting "back-to-the-text" is not a move one can perform, because the text one gets back to will be the text demanded by some other interpretation and that interpretation will be presiding over its production. This is not to say, however, that the "back-to-the-text" move is ineffectual. The fact that it is not something one can do in no way diminishes the effectiveness of claiming to do it. As a rhetorical ploy, the announcement that one is returning to the text will be powerful so long as the assumption that criticism is

secondary to the text and must not be allowed to overwhelm it remains unchallenged. Certainly, Booth does not challenge it; indeed, he relies on it and invokes it even as he relies on and invokes many other assumptions that someone else might want to dispute: the assumption that what distinguishes literary from ordinary language is its invulnerability to paraphrase; the assumption that a poem should not mean, but be; the assumption that the more complex a work is, the more propositions it holds in tension and equilibrium, the better it is. It would not be at all unfair to label these assumptions "conservative" and to point out that in holding to them Booth undermines his radical credentials. But it would also be beside the point, which is not that Booth isn't truly radical but that he *couldn't* be. Nor could anyone else. The challenge he mounts to some of the conventions of literary study (the convention of the poem as artifact, the convention of meaningfulness) would not even be *recognized* as a challenge if others of these conventions were not firmly in place and, for the time being at least, unquestioned. A wholesale challenge would be impossible because there would be no terms in which it could be made; that is, in order to be wholesale, it would have to be made in terms wholly outside the institution; but if that were the case, it would be unintelligible because it is only within the institution that the facts of literary study—texts, authors, periods, genres—become available. In short, the price intelligibility exacts (a price Booth pays here) is implication in the very structure of assumptions and goals from which one desires to be free.

So it would seem, finally, that there are no moves that are not moves in the game, and this includes even the move by which one claims no longer to be a player. Indeed, by a logic peculiar to the institution, one of the standard ways of practicing literary criticism is to announce that you are avoiding it. This is so because at the heart of the institution is the wish to deny that its activities have any consequences. The critic is taught to think of himself as a transmitter of the best that had been thought and said by others, and his greatest fear is that he will stand charged of having substituted his own meanings for the meanings of which he is supposedly the guardian; his greatest fear is that he be found guilty of having interpreted. That is why we have the spectacle of commentators who, like Stephen Booth, adopt a stance of aggressive humility and, in the manner of someone who rises to speak at a temperance meeting, declare that they will never interpret again but will instead do something else ("I mean to describe them"). What I have been saying is that whatever they do, it will only be interpretation in another guise because, like it or not, interpretation is the only game in town.

Notes

1. *Encounter,* June 1954, p. 50.
2. *Innocence and Experience* (New Haven: Yale University Press, 1964), pp. 245, 248.
3. Philip Hosbaum, "A Rhetorical Question Answered: Blake's *Tyger* and Its Critics," *Neophilologus,* 48, no. 2 (1964), 154.
4. Warren Stevenson, "The 'Tyger' as Artefact," *Blake Studies,* 2, no. 1 (1969–70), 9.
5. L. J. Swingle, "Answers to Blake's 'Tyger': A Matter of Reason or of Choice," *Concerning Poetry,* 2 (1970), 67.
6. Stevenson, " 'Tyger' as Artefact," p. 15.
7. "Preserving the Exemplar," *Critical Inquiry,* 3, no. 3 (Spring 1977), 413.
8. Ibid., 412.
9. *The Verbal Icon* (Lexington: University of Kentucky Press, 1954), p. 21.
10. *5 Readers Reading* (New Haven: Yale University Press, 1975), p. 12.
11. New Haven: Yale University Press, 1969.

Tempest

Stephen J. Miko

The many and various interpretations of The Tempest, *several of which are noted in Stephen J. Miko's first footnote, could furnish a striking illustration of Stanley Fish's "interpretive communities" in action. But Miko's reading of the play is poststructural in another sense, for while each of these interpretations shows a strategy for determining meaning, this text, as Miko sees it, remains radically indeterminate. Thus the various interpretations point not to "some hinted idea to which the variety can be subordinated," but instead to "the multiplicity and possibly deliberate inconclusiveness of Shakespeare's last plays." A text's unity and coherence, the poststructuralists argue, is largely a function of the critic's will to order, his or her willingness to turn a blind eye to elements that won't fit the critic's reading. As Miko puts it, "the neatness of this (and possibly any) work of art depends on how strongly one insists on details that seem to violate a defined, usually conventional pattern." Miko's own reading insists strongly on precisely those details. The play's inconclusiveness may "possibly" be deliberate; what's true of this play may "possibly" be true of any. Miko is appropriately tentative about large claims, beyond the claim that this play is appropriately tentative. By tugging firmly at the play's "loose ends," he produces a reading which, by a deManian paradox, finds the text's meaning in its very inconclusiveness. "All the mirrors are chipped and cracked," and "the main point, to which Shakespeare consistently returns, is that attempts to match words and things, wishes and realities, inevitably leave disjunctions."*

How beauteous mankind is! O brave new world,
That has such people in't!

V,i,183–4

Many ironies sit here. Except for the most obvious one, residing in the gap between Miranda's innocence and our knowledge that some of these beauties are attempted homicides, there is little agreement either about what they are or how far they go. Miranda speaks from a tableau, just revealed by a magician to those who astonish her, and who have just been released by the same magician from a charmed circle. They are astonished too. The language of miracle and wonder is appropriate on both sides; a father is reunited with his son, gains a daughter, reconciles himself with conscience. Yet the magician who managed all this says almost nothing about the "strange maze" which he has led these wanderers through. He calls their miracles "accidents," which he promises to make "seem probable," along with the story of his life. Later, after the play is over. To clear the way for thinking ("every third thought") of his grave. The ironies I speak of multiply as these elements are heightened into contrasts.

To harp on ironies is to harp on (possible) problems. The range of disagreement as to how to take this play is itself astonishing.[1] If Miranda's world is, demonstrably, neither brave nor new, what degree of mockery may be lurking here? To complicate matters further, this last scene, especially by virtue of being a last scene, has given rise to talk about mystery. That has in turn led to talk of symbol, allegory, and mysticism. Something cryptic appears to most critics to be going on, and the usual (but certainly not universal) response has been to fill in Shakespeare's meaning with religious and moral hierarchies. Yet anything thought cryptic may also be an invitation to ask questions about explanations, to wonder, finally, whether explanation itself may be mocked in Prospero's promises to tell all some other time some other place.

What we have just noticed is at least an obvious manipulation of most of the characters into a position where they must be astonished, and, further, must behave themselves. Moral correction is another matter. So is forgiveness. The new world is most obviously new in being rearranged; rearrangement took place in careful isolation, on an island, with the help of a lot of magic and tricks. Yet the trickster is willingly giving up his magic powers to return, without notable enthusiasm, to rule Milan by conventional methods. He takes with him two unredeemed villains, one redeemed villain, a loyal retainer, two humiliated buffoons, and a wholly conventional romantic couple. He leaves behind both his magic emissary and his enslaved monster, probably, after Prospero himself, the two most intriguing characters of the play. There is not much agreement about what these final groupings mean, and very little sense that Prospero has *solved* anything. Both his future and Caliban's seem open questions — it is not even clear that Caliban will remain. What is clear is that Prospero has succeeded in his manipulations of bodies (if not destinies) and that he is packing up his tricks. Perhaps the playwright is also packing up his tricks, completing his play by completing its island actions, rounding them out but not (because of their very nature) fully resolving them. Once one looks at what finally happens to the various characters and the themes they embody, it is difficult to accept either Prospero's or Shakespeare's manipulations as a series of exalted gestures, part of a symbolic package that points toward (even if it doesn't actually show) a grand, coherent, or transcendent completion of Shakespeare's highest art. Neither is it possible to read the play as "just a play," without meanings of various symbolic kinds, in fact many kinds. I propose, then, to look at the play as if it is, in a stronger sense than is usually conceded, experimental. Shakespeare may be experimenting with the very assumptions that lead us to expect poetic justice, symbolic neatness, and "resolved" endings for plays. I think, in fact, that he is demonstrating the limits of all three sets of expectation.

II Loose Ends

Does this play have loose ends or not? Those who lean toward heavily symbolic readings tend to think not; those who favor character analysis and even moral analysis tend to think it does. I belong to the second group, though my reasons perhaps differ from those most often given or implied. The neatness of this (and possibly any) work of art largely depends on how strongly one insists on details that seem to violate a defined, usually conventional pattern. For example, isn't Antonio an embarrassment to the dominant moral pattern of the play? Unlike

Alonzo he shows no repentance whatever, and some question the sincerity of Prospero's forgiving him.[2] In the same vein, does Caliban's intention to "seek for grace" represent a lurch upward toward moral stature? Both show stubborn resistance to redemption, or even to claims that the *tone* of the ending is grandly affirmative. Yet one can always insist that exceptions prove the rule: Antonio and Caliban only show us that moral ideals exist in an imperfect world — all the more are just, forgiving, philosopher-magician-kings required. And from a certain comfortable distance this may do; why should we want to find a loose end in what can be seen as a reflection (though inverted) of the need for grace, or help, or even a civilized culture to keep evil (both natural and unnatural) in check?[3] One ready answer is that these reflections just as easily suggest something very different, though not exactly contradictory. In these stubborn characters we may also see limits: to Prospero's power and all that it may represent, including Shakespeare's power in art, or *the* power of art.

Probably more than any of Shakespeare's other plays, *The Tempest* leaves "reflection" a live metaphor. It has even been read as a kind of cypher to contemporary biographical, political, or religious events, quite beside the theories of more general symbolic construction alluded to already.[4] I do not propose another attempt to sort these theories out, but to note that this variety must mean something — not, I think, some hinted idea to which the variety can be subordinated, but something about the multiplicity and possibly the deliberate inconclusiveness of Shakespeare's last plays. However we evaluate these many interpretations, we can consistently infer that the play which occasions such riches must itself be rich and strange. Both the richness and strangeness are functions, it seems to me, of Shakespeare's testing, or at least playing with, the limits of his — and maybe anyone's — playmaking, including powerful gestures of affirmation while affirming, in Sidney's sense, nothing. In short, there are loose ends indeed, of the most fundamental sort: the art and magic of playmaking questions both its matter (the themes) and its own power, affirming only in understood, limited ways.

What, then, are these affirmations? Beside the usual "romance" themes of forgiveness, reconciliation, and regeneration I would put a list that has a negative cast, because it derives from ironic perspectives: men and their desires need checking and or-

dering, a process which makes (limited) fulfillment of desire possible, and may even transform coarse emotion into something higher (or at least more interesting); "natural" is a profoundly ambiguous term, but all good (and, less clearly, most evil) is an art that nature makes; true love requires civilizing (another kind of limiting); plays and the art of making them are special, deliberately artificial distortions of the "real" world, meant less to teach than to present interesting, sometimes heartening, analogies; art is no avenue to higher realms but a modest (yet at best very impressive) image of man's desires reflected back through his intelligence, which shapes and approves selectively; and even spectacular magic art has very little consequence in the world "outside." I think all these points are made by the play — are, in fact, its central affirmations. I don't see how such things could be asserted in a play without, at least in the most conventional senses, loose ends. The failure to carry out fully the pattern of moral correction may be seen, then, as just the most obvious refusal to make this play neat. If my list is accurate, the cast of mind dominating the play is neither tragic, nor, in the celebratory sense, comic; it is skeptical, yet genial.

III Prospero: Theurgist, Mage, Goetist, Trickster, Stage Manager

This is Prospero's play, with no very close parallel in Shakespeare. Whatever symbolic freight we make visible, Prospero is either carrying it or managing the carrying. It is no doubt obvious already that my emphasis will drift from left to right on the scale listed above: although we are surely impressed by Prospero's ability to disintegrate and reassemble ships, quick-dry (and even freshen) costumes, cast spells, put on spirit-masques, and pinch out punishments, there are hints throughout the play that invite us — quite inconclusively — to subordinate this power, this Art, to something approaching hypnosis, the creation of dream states for moral psychotherapy. The magic lore that creeps into the play is capable of causing embarrassment both to those who prefer the notion that they all just dreamt the tempest and the transportations and those who say magic is magic, usually invoking John Dee and insisting that at least it's white.[5] To be very short on this issue, transportations are not likely dreamt if you actually end up in other places, alive when you thought you had drowned, and we can hardly doubt that Ariel and company exist. On the other hand all this power results in only one indisputable conversion (Alonzo), the tempest is also obviously *inside* most of the characters, the magic shows are dispensable and vanish without trace or consequence, the selves everyone finds when released from trance are much the same as they were earlier, and we can't be sure that Prospero isn't embroidering a little—the Ovidian list including raising the dead (V,i,41–50) embarrasses almost everyone. We seem to be put repeatedly in the position of trying to decide what the magic means before we can say what it is. And that meaning, or those meanings, are all extensions of Prospero.

It may be helpful to descend for a while into the unambiguous. Although I think that Prospero's magic tricks shift in emphasis from magic to tricks, and that this shift is emblematic of much else in the play's movement, some solid "facts" about Prospero are given us, mostly in the usual first act history, and much also follows from them.

Besides an enormously powerful magician—the play begins, of course, with the ship disintegrating in Prospero's tempest—Prospero is an overprotective father and an uneasy, apparently disillusioned idealist. His exile is a consequence both of the natural evil in his brother and his own retreat from ducal responsibility into studies—magic and the liberal arts. He takes blame for his condition, claiming to have brought out the evil in Antonio and to have lived too much in his mind (his dream?). Once the initial hardship of the journey was overcome, his magic books and powers made him a god of his island, displacing Caliban. So for a dozen years Prospero has been running everything, even, it would appear, the local weather. He has not seen fit to tell his daughter her own early history or his, and he has failed only in redeeming—making human, more-or-less—his "devil-whelp." His child at fifteen is the very type of virginal virtue, full of sympathy for fellow creatures she has never seen but has apparently learned of from books and paternal instruction. The preservation of her innocence—of evil, especially sexual evil—has been a central concern, nearly foiled by Caliban's attempted rape. Now that the outside world must again be confronted (Prospero cannot neglect this providential opportunity to master his enemies), Miranda gets her history in careful doses, with considerable solicitousness for the shock to her delicate system and to her credulity.

A few obvious inferences follow easily from this list: first, we can expect no real trouble in any plans Prospero has to control the movements of his enemies; if he can do tempests, he can do most anything. Second, the single but striking failure with Caliban gives basis for a more fundamental sort of anxiety: Prospero's power does not extend to minds or souls, so we may wonder how much external manipulation can touch natural evil, which we soon discover also continues in Antonio and Sebastian. What effect, then, can Prospero's external powers have on internal (moral, spiritual) states? The whole plot seems to hinge on this question, yet it is begged early on. What in fact transpires is a series of scenes illustrating Prospero's control, especially of two kinds: the testing of goodness and the interruption—not the correction or extinction—of evil. In short, a series of magic shows allowing the characters to *show themselves*. The metaphor of "finding" a self is, I believe, ironic well before the end of the play.

How we take these shows inevitably depends on how much we take them, either in themselves or by various allusive procedures, to have symbolic or allegorical meanings—and, in turn, whether these meanings arrange themselves into consistent pictures, or lessons, or larger "wholes." Even more fundamentally, what we construct as interpretation depends directly on how serious we think Shakespeare was in presenting *his* shows, or, more narrowly, what sort of seriousness is appropriate to them.

What follows will reveal at least two assumptions about this seriousness: first, that the easiest way to encompass the divergent earnestness of so many critics is to assume that their earnestness led to their divergence; second, the play's failure to achieve an unambiguous resolution, its resistance to any available version of a neat, closed form, suggests that games with closed form may be going on, and the mode of these may be playful (yet not *without* seriousness). *The Tempest* is more like a comedy than a tragedy, neat in very abstract ways only (the much-noticed unities at last observed), yet lacking in mysteries that resonate, either ethical, religious, or aesthetic.

By this thinking, then, a central point (or meaning) of Prospero's magic is that it defines moral limits by illustrating (mostly) psychological obduracy, including Prospero's own. If we do read his behavior as stubborn and reluctant to leave his island kingdom, we may also without strain read it as a preference for art (and dream) over "reality." But that cannot in turn be assumed to be *Shakespeare's* prefer-ence.[6] If Prospero's art is a type (in any sense) of Art, the most obvious inference is not that Shakespeare yearns for a dream world, but that Art comes from one, or constitutes one, and that any effects Art has on the world "outside" must include recognizing this. Perhaps drowning the book and breaking the staff enact not the rejection of Art but of ideas that Art can, even in its own realm, control the desires it reflects. Even as *model* Art rejects Absolutes. Prospero is not, apparently, very happy about this; Shake-speare may or may not have been, but he certainly accepted limits gracefully elsewhere, although he tested them constantly. In this play and also, strik-ingly, in *The Winter's Tale* they become part of the subject matter.

In so far as this play is "about" art it requires a broad acceptance of artificiality. The sequence of Prospero's magic shows illustrates an increased will-fulness and arbitrariness, moving from the impres-sive tempest to a nuptial masque introduced as a "vanity" and petulantly interrupted (although es-sentially over) and then to a tableau imitating an em-blem book (the chess game).[7] The villains and their burlesque counterparts, once their homicidal intents are recognized and foiled on stage, receive magical punishments mostly out of sight, all repetitive of the early demonstrations of power over bodies (freeze them and pinch them), descending into mud and horsepiss—although it has been noted that the is-land reveals no other sign of horses. I doubt that any audience can worry, once Ariel saves Alonzo and Gonzalo, that evil may triumph after all, especially with Ariel's constant reassurances and effortless ubiquity. Yet the point does not seem to be to mock evil or reduce it by parody, but to show us, as many have noticed, that it's *always there,* fully preventable only in a magical world, where it may become the occasion for jokes.[8] What is most directly mocked is stupidity and narrow egotism, the traditional targets of comedy, yet unlike what happens in most comedy the mockery does not convincingly triumph; the magical garden continues to harbor real snakes.

So Prospero's magic is limited in several ways: it does not touch man's inner nature; its use descends into stage shows and trickery; it must be put aside fully to confront the "real" world (outside island and play). We can read it, then, as emblematic of good in-tentions, whose goodness is compromised by self-indulgence, but more fundamentally compromised by the necessary element of illusion in equating art with magic—not only Prospero's illusion, but ours.[9] Shakespeare's art both uses and criticizes such equa-tions, as I hope will be made clearer by some closer looks.

IV Art, Magic, and Illusion

I have suggested that Prospero is a manager of shows. He runs versions of a living theatre, both pro-ducing and directing—although the latter function is often Ariel's—to test, to punish, and to convert. Those tested, however, don't need it: Ferdinand car-ries logs absurdly to prove he respects virginity; no real temptation is allowed him. Miranda (we must strain to include her) has her sympathy and new love tested through the same log-carrying; she offers to help, properly anguished over "her" Ferdinand's suffering. Both pass, foregone conclusions. Ferdi-nand, in fact, is so without passion some critics don't like him; his protestations that his honor won't melt appear comic. All those whose conversions are sought resist but one, and we easily doubt Alonzo's need for all the browbeating and lying he gets, especially the repeated "news," cheerfully delivered by the play's only teacher of sympathy, that his son is dead.[10] Both the tests and conversions, then, degenerate into pun-ishments. So the putative intent of most of Prospero's shows fails to coincide with their results. Prospero is apparently caught in moral justifications that fail to fit his shows because they were not really, or mainly, or purely, moral shows.

What are they then? Obviously enough, they are entertainments. But for whom, and to what point? That is not easy to answer. Or there are several, per-haps not fully consistent, answers.

First, they are for Prospero. A vanity of his art, a demonstration of control, and perhaps a demonstra-tion of longing to stay on the island. Like Leontes in *The Winter's Tale* Prospero enjoys making the world over to fit his dreams. The log-carrying and the harpied banquet seem obvious instances of a father punishing bad children by whatever dramatic expe-dient may occur to him. Only in the former the chil-dren are not bad at all, so that Prospero has to apologize for these activities, and in the latter the bad children are too bad to be affected. We can under-stand and even approve, however, Prospero's tours de force: to freeze swords in the air, taunt villains (and credulous Gonzalo) with disappearing acts, and mock the folly of airslicing. The victims are also, of course, an audience, forced to appreciate Prospero's power, only the point, even for this audience, seems to be more showmanship than power. Everyone's dreams have to be subordinate to Prospero's dreams, however arbitrary. Behavior is controlled largely by controlling perception, emphasizing that the world is as it is seen.

For the next audiences, Prospero and then us, the shows flirt, even through their allusions, with the idea that art itself is to some important degree arbitrary.[11] We are also made conscious that, if we are not to take log-carrying with the seriousness of a "real" test, nor dismiss it as a wholly arbitrary entertainment, it may be part of a literary or dramatic game Shakespeare is playing with us, this time with Prospero as the "forced" actor. The curious combination of Prospero's real power and real impotence, both functions of his involvement in his own magical (here read "imaginative") world, seems an excellent—and once one notices this pattern, inevitable—metaphor for the powers and limits of Shakespeare's own imaginative world, and by not too forced an extension, art in general. Art affirms nothing largely in the sense that Prospero's magic "comes to" nothing: As Alonzos we may want, inspired by renewed consciousness of guilt, or reawakened goodness, or any other *already resident* characteristic, to act, "led" to this action by art. But if this is causation, it is indirect, crucially dependent on our being largely "there" already. Meanwhile, shows go on, and we must learn not to expect too much of them, or, if we do, suffer Prospero's moodiness and unresolved state, or possibly even Alonzo's wish for suicide. In art or in magic shows black may be white, emblems may appear as realities, wishes may become harpies, but they are all spirits that vanish into thin air, and we forget this at the cost (at least) of being bemired in our folly.

Prospero's (and the play's) most famous speech (IV,i,147–158) takes these ideas a step further. As the spirit masque, so the world, meaning our world, or any world known to men. This burst of eloquence, variously noticed as a curious intrusion or a striking change of tone seems, depending on how we read it, to ally this play with tragedy, to provide a metaphysical dimension hardly hinted at before, to undercut all of Prospero's efforts before or after, to change our perspective on *The Tempest* by enforcing a new degree of detachment. My general argument

has been that all these things are already there in the various forms of inconclusiveness we have been noting—although I would play down tragic undertones. This speech is indeed central, but it need not be taken with the sadness and weariness that Prospero apparently feels during its delivery.

It is tempting to read it at a discount. Prospero is obviously in a funk, which is not adequately justified by the reason he gives for introducing the "strange, hollow, and confused noise" that cuts off the show. If the "minute of their plot" is almost come, the drama of their entry is curiously attenuated, leaving room for Ariel to be amusing in his description of the helpless plotters, left dancing up to their chins in a filthy mantled pool. And Prospero's subsequent mutterings about the "born devil" hardly sound a grave note either, less even than Caliban's threat of driving a nail into his head did earlier. Yet Prospero seems genuinely upset, as his daughter notices, and if it is not about threats of evildoing, it is most likely about the content of that eloquent speech. The masque, a creation of Prospero's imagination, is interrupted by another creation of his imagination—in short, by the thought that the whole world is no more stable or meaningful than the imagination which "creates" it.

This is indeed metaphysics, but our consciousness that a troubled brain is here expressing itself warns us not to leap at once into Tragic Apprehension; it is just this reminder that Prospero needs to prepare to detach himself from a world where his dreams are everything, yet "amount" to nothing. And there is a positive side to this gloomy view of the ephemerality of things: if we are such stuff as dreams are made on, we make ourselves by dreaming, and much of "the world" too. Our lovers are an obvious case in point; Ferdinand really would do anything for his Miranda, and he very likely really believes, as he says just before the interruption, that "So rare a wonder'd father and a wise / Makes this place paradise." What the naive Ferdinand doesn't yet know (and let him take his time finding out) is that the wisdom and the paradise are both also dreams, already infected beyond repair.

We, on the other hand, are expected to know these things by now, and to be reminded pointedly, here, by Prospero. If this speech undercuts both the moral gravity and magical powers of the play—and even, I would argue, undercuts itself—it is not a violent change or misplaced comment on what has been going on all along. Both here and in *The Winter's Tale* Shakespeare has been setting up his audience for reflections of this kind, which include consciousness of deliberate artifice, especially as it reveals the gap, sometimes trivial but always present, between desire and act, dream and the real world.

The last act collects these matters for us. For instance, Prospero's famous lesson in sympathy, noted by the Arden editor as a "gnomic and vital idea":

Yet with my nobler reason 'gainst my fury
Do I take part: the rarer action is
In virtue than in vengeance: they being penitent,
The sole drift of my purpose doth extend
Not a frown further.   (V,i,27–31)

This is in response to Ariel's vivid description of the three villains distracted, wept over by Gonzalo. How can we ignore that two of the three are *not* (even in the slightest degree) penitent? They merely have temporarily boiled brains, a result of Prospero's art. Yet the rarer action *is* in virtue, even if helped along by a delusion grown out of a wish. As art is. The irony points both back into the play and at us, who are also wishers for powers like Prospero's, and perhaps too ready to give them to Shakespeare.

Or, even more strikingly, this speech a little further on, after the major speech abjuring magic. It has often been read with great solemnity.

                              Most cruelly
Didst thou, Alonzo, use me and my daughter:
Thy brother was a furtherer in the act.
Thou art pinch'd for't now, Sebastian. Flesh and
     blood,
You, brother mine, that entertain'd ambition,
Expell'd remorse and nature; whom, with
     Sebastian,—
Whose inward pinches therefore are most strong,—
Would here have kill'd your king; I do forgive thee,
Unnatural though thou art.   (V,i,71–79)

Not, "unnatural hast thou been." The gesture of forgiveness, which we have no reason to think phony, rebounds off Sebastian's consistent (unnatural) malice, although Prospero wants in the same breath to insist that the pinching was "inward"—which must mean, pinching of conscience, the agenbite of inwit. But it wasn't, and Prospero knows it, hence the ambivalence in the speech, shortly followed up by further admission that remorse and nature remain expelled.[12] So we have another show, with some of the actors playing the parts Prospero has "written,"

others just walking through them, deliberately distracted. They want to write their own parts, and do. Prospero doesn't like to admit this, but surely *we* should. Nor do we need to deny that there is a serious moral lesson here, only the emphasis of the play seems as much on illfitting yet necessary illusions as on either the fallen world or, especially, on grand regenerations and moral uplift.

We are further reminded that this isle is full of subtleties that distort the taste and encumber belief (perhaps fatally). Gonzalo, with his usual blindness to subtleties of any kind, unwittingly blurts out a few lines that summarize much of what has been going on:

All torment, trouble, wonder and amazement
Inhabits here: some heavenly power guide us
Out of this fearful country!   (V,i,104–6)

Heavenly power is indeed needed, since the fearful country is, variously, the magical illusions, the imagination, and the mind and soul. Nothing is there that they didn't bring, nor will they leave these things there when they go—except Ariel, and perhaps Caliban. Gonzalos will find wonder and amazement at home too, Antonios will replace them with wisecracks and plots, and Prosperos will retire, along with Alonzos, chastened by overreaching.

Prospero, despite his inability not to frown at the recalcitrants, appears to be having a good time, as he promised himself earlier, gloating that they were all at his mercy. If he can't properly be a heavenly power, he can at least run the show his way, even teasing lugubrious Alonzo:

ALONZO: When did you lose your daughter?
PROSPERO: In this last tempest.   (V,i,152–3)

Their trances and boiled brains, not very effectual morally, are just the thing to reduce them to an ideal audience for a chess game. And the chess game, suggestive as you please of elegant aristocracy, suggests also isolation, especially the sort necessary to maintain the protestations of romantic love. Miranda's wondering expletives are echoed, as Kermode especially notices, by Caliban, both of them much taken by elegant attire:

O Setebos, these be brave spirits indeed!
How fine my master is!   (V,i,261–2)

Prospero's mild retort to his enthusiastic daughter fits as well here.

'Tis new to thee.

V Art, Nature, and Caliban

O ho, O ho! would't had been done!
Thou didst prevent me; I had peopled else
This isle with Calibans.

Perhaps Shakespeare has. As many critics emphasize, Caliban is an appealing demi-devil, whose
shape, though deformed in some unspecified way, is
human. E. E. Stoll has with particular relish laid out
the psychology of the "brute," who loves his sensual
pleasures and is more amoral than immoral, and
who may be allowed an imagination—*must* be allowed one, if we refuse to dismiss his lyrical speech
on dream-inducing music (III,ii,133–40) as out of
character.[13] Few besides Stoll are willing to stop
here, however, including me.

With many others I think Caliban should be promoted from a natural man, or a brute man, to Natural Man, and maybe even Us. I don't of course
mean we all secretly yearn to rape virgins or murder
our bosses, but that Caliban's attempts to understand enough to control his own life have obvious
similarities to the rest of the cast, to Prospero, to any
playmaker, and to us. In short I would play down
the contrasts—which are certainly there in the
play—to the idealized romantic and moral paradigms which Miranda and Ferdinand keep assuring
us they live by, and which Prospero pays rather ambivalent service to, and emphasize instead that our
sympathy with and pleasure in this brute qualifies,
if not refutes, Prospero's rants about him and makes
any strict belief that nurture will never stick false. At
least Caliban has learned that gods don't reside in
bottles and that his admiration—and even, he says
once, love—for his master isn't all inverted into resentment and hatred, nails or no nails. If not redeemed into goodness, Caliban is very likely to
know much better what to do when the next batch
of civilized creatures visit him. And the gift of language is far from stagnant in him, either for cursing
or celebrating.

Like everyone else in the play, Caliban lives, or
tries to live, in illusions that the play shows inadequate. In this context he specially emphasizes that illusions, even fond dreams of evildoing, are *natural,*
opening wide the door to a popular paradox (or
would-be paradox) of Shakespeare's time as well as
to modern philosophizing on the mysteries of "natural" man—in both cases fallen and hoping to rise.
Polixenes' argument with Perdita in *The Winter's Tale*

(IV,iv,85–100) is sufficient footnote here to contemporary debate on the natural and the artificial, and
applications to notions of the noble savage may be
pursued extensively in D. G. James' *Dream of Prospero.* The basic point, as I take it anyhow, is that good
and evil are built into most of us (perhaps all—I'm
holding out Miranda), and most of us are capable of
being better—especially of being taught to be better.
This may finally mean better at moral action or better at imagining—two activities ideally connected,
but in practice sometimes opposed, since desire inevitably remains in the picture. Moral art as well as
the art of illusion are natural, so the common split in
the word's use—unnatural acts being either magical
or immoral—are not contradictions but isolations in
a hierarchy under the rubric of Polixenes, "the art
that nature makes." That brothers can kill each other
is unnatural only from the point of view of someone
who insists that natural always means moral—an
unusually rigid or didactic playwright, for example.
Even the innocent Miranda knows better, when she
comforts her father over Antonio's evildoing in Act
One. And the other use of "unnatural" in this play,
the unnatural events that Prospero has brought about,
remain unnatural only as we remain ignorant of
what's in those magic books, or, if larger mysteries
are preferred, what providential forces brought the
boat into range of the tempest. Yet is seems odd to call
providence unnatural. God must be allowed His own
magic tricks, and so must Shakespeare. We have
room to choose how earnestly we receive either.[14]

The main point, to which I think Shakespeare consistently returns, is that attempts to match words and
things, wishes and realities, inevitably leave disjunctions, especially for those who insist on neatness and
univocality. Shakespeare most certainly did not, and
Caliban's "puzzling" bursts of poetry point this up.
Perhaps his uncertain future does too. In trying to be
a junior Prospero he got minor tortures and a large
wallow—and a little more common sense. Prospero
proper got everyone at his mercy, a son-in-law, and
his city back—all three rather qualified victories,
and basic, fundamental evil is just untouched.

Neither Caliban nor his master could typecast;
nature wouldn't have it. That nature wouldn't is one
of the play's main messages, one of its "truths about
life," one of its loose ends. Art, like life, orders by acts
of wishing and willing and above all imagining; the
results are bound to be a little messy. They can be
neat only if will dominates all.

I hope this makes it clearer why I think of *The Tempest* as experimental, tentative among its wonderful reconciliations. It is tempting, but I think too neat, to identify Caliban with some sort of reality principle, evil itself, or perhaps original sin. Auden seems closer to the truth in making Caliban both the interrogating audience and a voice which becomes, finally, Shakespeare's own—after a kind of reverse metamorphosis from Ariel, the soaring spirit collapsed into the undeniable body.[15] If as I believe Shakespeare will not allow either unequivocal idealization or consistent, "realistic" parody, all the characters are mirrors of us, especially as we are all artist-dreamers, and all the mirrors are chipped and cracked.

Notes

1. The extremes in the range of interpretation may be represented by Colin Still's *The Timeless Theme* (London, 1936) and E. E. Stoll's "The Tempest," *PMLA* 47 (1932). The former finds the whole play an allegory, the latter denies any secondary meanings whatever. Between them there is considerable variety, but the central division seems to be between those who take the play as a serious and coherent moral or religious statement and those who find it problematic, ironic, or otherwise resistant to allegorical interpretations. The majority still favor what I call the earnest view—that Shakespeare is in this play culminating (or even summarizing) his career, probably saying farewell to the stage, making a symbolic statement of unusual economy, resonance, and power. The minority offer various more skeptical readings, tend to be critical of Prospero, find ambiguities or loose ends, and generally find the play not fully explained by symbolic patterns. Representative of the majority are Derek Traversi, *Shakespeare: The Last Phase* (Stanford, 1955), R. G. Hunter, *Shakespeare's Comedy of Forgiveness* (New York, 1955), D. G. James, *The Dream of Prospero* (Oxford, 1967); Frank Kermode, Arden Edition to *The Tempest* (London, 1954); G. Wilson Knight, *The Shakespearean Tempest* (Oxford 1932). Representatives of the minority are Bonamy Dobree in *Twentieth Century Interpretations of The Tempest*, ed. Hallet Smith (Englewood Cliffs, 1969); Harry Berger's "Miraculous Harp: A Reading of Shakespeare's *Tempest*," *Shakespeare Studies V* 1970; and Clifford Leech, *Shakespeare's Tragedies* (London, 1950). Berger's essay overlaps most with my own, although it focuses more intensely on Prospero's psychology.

   Norman Rabkin's comments on Shakespeare's consciousness of art and artifice in *Shakespeare and the Common Understanding* (New York, 1967) also resemble mine, but he differs strikingly in the seriousness with which he responds to symbolic patterns and to tone generally. My own emphasis here is on a much more relaxed view of the play, with special interest in the way Shakespeare's last plays remind us of limits: of dreams, desires, acts, and particularly the ordering action of art. All subsequent references to these authors will be to the works already cited, unless otherwise noted.

2. Dobree and Berger, for example.

3. These last few sentences crudely summarize the views of D. G. James. I found this a fascinating and helpful book, although James' elegiac view of the play is almost a polar opposite to mine.

4. See especially Robert Graves, *Poetic Unreason* (New York, 1968).

5. D. G. James (Chapter II) insists that there are "two tempests," the first an illusion, but no one I have read is quite willing to claim all the play's action is somehow just "dreamt." If there is a prevalent view about the "actual" force of Prospero's powers, it seems to be that they do indeed exceed what we now mean by magician's tricks, yet most critics proceed without much troubling over this to discussing what the magic may mean in the play. James sees Prospero's rejection of it as the rejection by the seventeenth century of magical explanations in favor of the new science. See C. J. Sisson, "The Magic of Prospero," *Shakespeare Survey* II (1958), for a neat summary of Elizabethan notions, legal and philosophical, concerning black and white magic.

6. Harry Berger argues these points strongly.

7. In "New Uses of Adversity: Tragic Experience in *The Tempest*," Stephen Orgel has the reading most plausibly claiming that the masque is functional. For him it represents, as masques traditionally do, a world outside time and also, as a masque of Ceres omitting winter, a natural order shaped by man's idealization (the imagination). In short, it is a version of Prospero's imagined

wishes, so that "Prospero's interruption is full of a consciousness of the dangers not only of the conspiracy he has forgotten but also of the imaginative world that has tempted him to forget it." This reading appears to me to reinforce my own, even though Orgel takes the idea of suffering more seriously than I do throughout. Orgel notes at the play's ending some of the loose ends I do, but for him they represent tragic implications. His essay appeared in *In Defense of Reading*, Richard Poirier and Reuben Brower, eds. (New York, 1962).

8. See R. G. Hunter, who thinks the evil *is* reduced, against Harry Berger.

9. All the more extreme symbolic readings, especially Still's, appear to want to assert metamorphic powers (acting on us) in *The Tempest*. In my view the play mocks them.

10. Although we feel much less cruelty here, Alonzo's punishments resemble Isabel's in *Measure for Measure*, where the Duke requires her to forgive her brother's executioner before he tells her there was no execution.

11. For the banquet scene, for example, R. G. Hunter favors an interrupted communion, finding this a more precise analogy than a symbol of deceitful desire (such as Northrop Frye, in his introduction to the *Pelican Shakespeare*) or allusion to Christ's temptation (such as Kermode in his introduction to the Arden Shakespeare). I prefer the more general sort of suggestion (Frye's), since to insist on close Christian parallels would require precisely the narrowness of didactic focus which I would argue against. My point is simply that the scene invites various interpretations without requiring one "right" reading.

12. Sebastian does make one pious remark — "O most high miracle" — but this hardly constitutes an obvious change of heart. He also says Prospero is possessed by the devil, and Prospero's remarks to Antonio don't seem to suppose a conversion. If we are to believe, as Gonzalo appears to, that everyone has found himself and become virtuous too, Shakespeare has strikingly left out reassurances we might reasonably expect, especially if we bear in mind his usual attention to such loose ends in his comedies.

13. See also John Wain, who sees in Caliban under-privileged people everywhere. Wain's essay appears in Hallett Smith's anthology, *Twentieth Century Interpretations of The Tempest*.

14. Again, this whole argument can be conceived as a game exploring limits, as I try to elaborate in a companion essay on *The Winter's Tale*. I don't think J. M. Murry got it quite right when he argued that Polixenes — and Shakespeare — were saying that "Where man's art improves nature, it is nature's art in man; where it makes nature worse, it is man's art alone." The problem is in calling "man's art alone" unnatural, as usage both in Shakespeare's time and ours amply illustrates. Are elaborately synthetic poisons unnatural? Man makes them by natural wit from natural elements. Is evil unnatural? It is the profoundest urge of some human creatures, as Shakespeare's tragedies fully show. To shift the terms in the way I favor is merely to call attention, as I think Shakespeare does often, to man's tendency to use the label unnatural for things he doesn't like, want, or understand. Here he meets his own limits — of, naturally enough, taste, desire, and knowledge, and finally, if he acts, in what he produces — like plays.

15. *The Sea and The Mirror*. I am not sure I understand all that Caliban is meant to be here, and I think Shakespeare stops short of Auden's apparently religious solution, but I find most of Caliban's musings close to mine. Especially this, where he speaks as audience:

> You yourself, we seem to remember, have spoken of the conjured spectacle as 'a mirror held up to nature,' a phrase misleading in its aphoristic sweep but indicative at least of one aspect of the relationship between the real and the imagined, their mutual reversal of value, for isn't the essential artistic strangeness to which your citation of the sinisterly biased image would point just this: that on the far side of the mirror the general will to compose, to form at all costs a felicitous pattern becomes the *necessary cause* of any particular effort to live or act or love or triumph or vary, instead of being as, in so far as it emerges at all, it is on this side their *accidental effect*?

> It seems to me that Shakespeare has in this play also included the second perspective, that of accidental effect.

"Timely Utterance" Once More

Geoffrey H. Hartman

Geoffrey Hartman begins by citing a number of cruxes or puzzles in Wordsworth's Ode, but unlike critics in other contexts, he does not cite these in order to resolve them: "I multiply questions because I suspect that a simple solution, or stabilizing specificity, cannot be found." In fact, many of Wordsworth's strongest phrases, he claims, are simply not—or not simply—referential in the ordinary ways of reference, and Hartman's style of reading "refuses to substitute ideas for words." As he puts it in a characteristic reversal, "ideas may be simple, but words are always complex." Formalists, of course, have always known that words are complex, but as the poststructuralist sees it, formalists have often been unwilling to explore the full range of that complexity.

To illustrate his case, Hartman provides a playful, punning, free-ranging analysis of the implications and ambiguities of "timely." His reading is intertextual as well as formal, but intertextual with a poststructural turn: "the construction of an intertextual field is disconcerting as well as enriching because intertextual concordance produces a reality-discord, an overlay or distancing of the referential function of speech, of the word-thing, word-experience relation." By the time Hartman's "intertextual leaping" comes to rest, the reader has been led a lively intellectual dance and treated to much that is disconcerting as well as enriching. If this essay is, as the author says, only "mildly deconstructive," it is nonetheless thoroughly poststructural in its treatment of language and representative, as well, of the ludic strain in poststructural criticism.

Reprinted by permission from Robert Con Davis and Ronald Schleifer, eds., *Rhetoric and Form: Deconstruction at Yale.* © University of Oklahoma Press, 1985: 37–49.

et sonitus me sacer intus agit

—Milton

"It would be not only interesting but also useful to know what the 'timely utterance' was," Lionel Trilling wrote in 1941 concerning Wordsworth's Intimations Ode. He eventually does "hazard a guess."[1] Time has not diminished our fascination with the phrase: the guessing continues, while Trilling's interpretation has become part of the poem's aura and has entered the consciousness of many readers. Just as we find a ring of cosmic junk around planets, so it is with interpretive solutions stabilized by the gravitational field of a well-known poem. Moreover, Trilling's critical style is itself of interest. To "hazard a guess" indicates a modest attitude (he does not speak as a specialist, rather as an educated, reflective reader) but also, perhaps, a subdued sense of venture. For Wordsworth's diction is a riddle as well as a puzzle, and we answer it at the risk of appearing foolish, of exposing our superficial views on language and life.[2]

"Timely utterance," of course, is not the only crux in Wordsworth's Ode, nor the only mystery-phrase singled out by readers. There is the bombast (Coleridge's term) of stanza 8, addressed to the Child as Prophet and Philosopher; there is the delicate vatic vagueness of "fields of sleep"; there is, at the end, "thoughts that do often lie too deep for tears."

These cruxes—and there are others—all share a problem of reference: we do not know what the "timely utterance" was; "fields of sleep" is a periphrasis that should yield a proper name, perhaps of a place as mythic as the Elysian fields ("fields of light," cf. *Aeneid* 6.640); the sublime words that describe the infant seem really to describe some other, more fitting, subject; and who knows what the deep thoughts are about.

Let me clarify, in a preliminary way, this problem of reference. Those deep thoughts: their occasion is clear (the simplest thing, the meanest flower), and their emotional impact also is clear. But where precisely do they lie, where is "too deep for tears"? Is it, to quote a moving sonnet in which Wordsworth mourns the loss of his daughter Catherine, that "spot which no vicissitude can find"?[3] Or is the obverse suggested, that they are *not* thoughts of loss, mortality, or the grave, but arise from a still deeper level, from under or beyond the grave? Or is Wordsworth adjuring himself not to cry, not to give in to a pathos permitted even to Aeneas ("Sunt lacrymae rerum . . . ," *Aeneid* 1.468), as he forbids mourning despite nature's valedictory intimations:

> And O, ye Fountains, Meadows, Hills, and Groves,
> Forebode not any severing of our loves!

I multiply questions because I suspect that a simple solution, or stabilizing specificity, cannot be found. Yet the nonspecific quality of such verses does not harm them. It acts somewhat like formal perspective, in which an abstract reference-point allows the imaginative construction of naturalistic space. For, with the partial exception of stanza 8 on the sublime Child, we remain very much in a familiar world. Wordsworth extends, it is true, the boundary of natural events, yet never crosses it decisively into another region. Plato's doctrine of anamnesis or pre-existence is made to support ordinary feelings, to give them a memorable frame, not to justify fantastic speculation. The Ode's closing sentiment even limits the kind of thoughtful brooding (the "philosophic mind") that is its very concern: there is neither analytic nor visionary excess.

The more we press toward precision of reference, the more a Wordsworthian thought-limit appears. One is tempted to ask: are the thoughts secretly apocalyptic? Or so sentimental that they border on a crazy sort of concreteness, as mind passes from the "meanest" sign to the sublimest natural laws via an elided corpse? (For one could imagine the poet thinking: This flower at my feet may be nourished by the putrefaction of the dead, who are remembered unto life in this way.)[4]

Matthew Arnold's eulogy of the poet is to the point.

> The cloud of mortal destiny,
> Others will front it fearlessly—
> But who, like him, will put it by?

Wordsworth's poetry has the strength to absorb thoughts that potentially unbalance the mind. "Dim sadness—and blind thoughts," he calls them in "Resolution and Independence," "I knew not, nor could name." The "burthen of the mystery" is acknowledged—and lightened. Alas, the "burthen of the mystery" is another of those strange phrases, strong yet vague. I turn now to what occasioned these preliminary reflections: "timely utterance."

I

The context is not as much help as it might be.

> To me alone there came a thought of grief:
> A timely utterance gave that thought relief....
> (22–23)

The thought is almost as unspecific as what gives it relief. Perhaps it does not have to be specific, since the stanza's first verses suggest that what mattered was the contrast of thought and season. To me alone, among all beings, there came this untoward thought, like an untimely echo. Hence, after it is dispelled, Wordsworth vows: "No more shall grief of mine the season wrong." Only "seasonable sweets" (Keats) from now on. One possibility for interpretation, therefore, is that he was interested in expressing a relation, or a broken and then restored relation, rather than the precise detail of a single experience. The broken relation between his heart and the "heart of May" is always to be repaired. There may even be a repetition of that relational structure in the very next lines:

> The cataracts blow their trumpets from the steep;
> No more shall grief of mine the season wrong;
> I hear the Echoes through the mountains throng,
> The Winds come to me from the fields of sleep....
> (25–28)

Two types of utterance are presented here in asyndetic sequence: one comes from nature (the cataracts) and seems to heighten, like a punctuation from above, the timely utterance (indeed, there is a possibility that it was the timely utterance); and one comes from within the poet ("No more shall grief..."), as if to answer or echo nature (relation having been restored) and so to confirm that the disturbing fancy has passed. This echo-structure is made literal by "I hear the Echoes through the mountains throng." Together with "The Winds come to me from the fields of sleep," it suggests an extension of sensibility, some inner horizon opening up, as the poet hears into the distance. What is heard is not just waterfall or winds (whatever their message), but the principle of echo itself. Hence the echoes "throng"; they are suddenly everywhere; as thick as sheep at folding time. The stanza as a whole evokes a *correspondence* of breezes, sounds, feelings, one that has absorbed discordant elements (cf. 1850 *Prelude* 1.85, 96 ff., 340–50). Its culmination is the hallooing of "Shout round me, let me hear thy shouts, thou happy Shepherd boy!" (Ode, 35).

In this verse, which concludes the stanza, the movement of empathy is so strong that we almost feel its apostrophe as a self-address, representing the poet as that "Child of Joy" (34). His flock, as in Shelley's "Adonais," is composed of "quick Dreams, / The passion-winged Ministers of thought." And though we are moving toward the opposite of a pastoral elegy, the double or echo aspect of this provisional climax ("Shout ... shout") may be modifying as well as intensifying. Is not the cry optative rather than indicative in mood, an utterance that *projects* an ideal utterance, so that it is hard to tell the spontaneous from the anticipated joy? The "let me hear" repeats as a variant "Shout round me" and points it inward: it seems to appeal for a sound so strong that the poet cannot but hear. Yet "I hear, I hear, with joy I hear" is delayed to the next stanza, and then immediately counterpointed: " —But there's a Tree, of many, one ..." An inward and meeting echo, a reciprocal response, is not assured even now.

II

Broken column, broken tower, broken ... response. The theme of lost Hellenic grace or harmony is not relevant except as it is also more than Hellenic and recalls the "echo" formula of a poetry at once pastoral and elegiac:

> All as the sheepe, such was the shepeheards looke,

Spenser writes in "January," the first eclogue of the *Shepheardes Calender.* And

> Thou barrein ground, whome winters wrath hath wasted,
> Art made a myrrhour, to behold my plight....

This correspondence of season with mood, or of nature with human feelings, is the simplest form of the echo-principle in pastoral verse. Echo is something more than a figure of speech:

> Now lay those sorrowfull complaints aside,
> And hauing all your heads with girland crownd,
> Helpe me mine owne loues prayses to resound,
> Ne let the same of any be enuide:
> So Orpheus did for his owne bride,
> So I vnto my selfe alone will sing,
> The woods shall to me answer and my Eccho ring.

Spenser gives himself away in an *Epithalamion* of his own making: his poetry participates in the marriage, it weds the world, the word, to his desire, or more exactly to the *timing* which builds his rhyme, and which can call for silence ("And cease till then our tymely joyes to sing, / The woods no more vs answer, nor our eccho ring") as well as for responsive sound. In this sense, poetry is itself the "timely utterance"—not Spenser's *Epithalamion* as such, nor "Resolution and Independence" (or a part of it, as Trilling and Barzun suggest[5]), or any other identifiable set of verses.

Yet what is meant by *poetry* cannot be formalized, as I have seemed to suggest, in terms of generic features. I might like to claim that "timely utterance" opens every poetic form to the incursion of pastoral;[6] and Wordsworth himself gives some purchase on such a view:

—The Poets, in their elegies and songs
Lamenting the departed, call the groves,
They call upon the hills and streams to mourn,
And senseless rocks; nor idly; for they speak,
In these their invocations, with a voice
Obedient to the strong creative power
Of human passion.　　(*The Excursion* 1.475–81)

Yet what matters is neither the pastoral setting nor the overt, figurative expression of sympathy ("Sympathies there are," Wordsworth continues, "More tranquil, yet perhaps of kindred birth, / That steal upon the meditative mind, and grow with thought.") What matters is the sense of a *bond* between man and nature, of a *responsiveness* that overcomes the difference of human speech and creaturely muteness, or articulate and inarticulate utterance.

　　. . . Far and wide the clouds were touched,
And in their silent faces could be read
Unutterable love.
. . . in the mountains did he *feel* his faith.
All things, responsive to the writing, there
Breathed immortality, revolving life,
And greatness still revolving; infinite. . . .
　　　　(*The Excursion* 1.203–05; 206–29)

The capacity for "timely utterance" in this timeless, mute, or unutterable situation maintains the bond, and justifies the poetry. "The strong creative power / Of human passion" is equivalent to poetry in this respect. "Passion" often has, for Wordsworth, the sense of passionate speech that identifies with "mute, insensate things." "My heart leaps up"—an "extempore" lyric whose final lines come to serve as an epigraph to the Intimations Ode, and which has been nominated by some scholars as the "timely ut-

terance"—is about this bond. The lyric is remarkable as an utterance, as a speech act that falls somewhere between vow and passionate wish:

My heart leaps up when I behold
　　A rainbow in the sky:
So was it when my life began;
So is it now I am a man;
So be it when I shall grow old,
　　Or let me die!

That "Or let me die!" is a true "fit of passion," one of those Wordsworthian moments where feeling seems to overflow and be in excess of its occasion. It is, one might say, *untimely*.

Yet we intuit its emotional truth, and it becomes timely again once we recall another utterance, that of the creator when he makes the rainbow a sign of *His* bond:

I have set My bow in the cloud, and it shall be a token of a covenant between Me and the earth. And it shall come to pass, when I bring clouds over the earth, and the bow is seen in the cloud, that I will remember My covenant, which is between Me and you and every living creature of all flesh; and the waters shall no more become a flood to destroy all flesh.　　(Genesis 9:13–16)

If Wordsworth's vow recalls that primal vow, it is a response that says: This is *my* bond, *my* way of binding each day to each and continuing in time. Cut the link of nature to human feelings and the bond is broken. Once dead to nature, I might as well die. Poetry is a marriage-covenant with nature, a "spousal verse" even more demanding of "dew" response than Spenser's *Epithalamion*.

III

To utter things in a timely way is the ideal situation, of course; and Wordsworth usually represents the ideal in its wishful or miscarried form. So the hyperbolic "Or let me die!" is followed by a second hyperbole that expresses more patently a disturbed sense of temporal continuity. "The Child is father of the Man" reverses the way we think about fathers and children; yet it quickly naturalizes itself as a sort of proverb. We assimilate its unexpectedness, as with "Or let me die!"; and since the words themselves are simple enough (however complex the thought), we do not have to, indeed we cannot, keep unfolding them. The very opening of *The Prelude*, similarly, is a "passion" that makes us aware, as it generates itself, of an ideal of harmony or correspondence that proves fallible. As an utterance it comes closer to "tempest" than "tempus." The "correspondent breeze" turns into "A tempest, a redundant energy / Vexing its own creation" (*Prelude* 1.37–8). There is a disproportion or discord between the "gentle breeze" of the poem's first verse and this tempestuous, self-forcing power. The *untimely* is never far away (cf. 1.94–105).

But our own solution may have been untimely, that is, premature. Even should "timely utterance" be an inspired periphrasis for "poetry," and exclude the promoting of a particular poem or passage, we continue to think of poetry as a *manifold* of utterances that is *one* only if the idea of vocation is adduced: if poetry is also "poesy." Poetic utterances are not only characterized by being timely (either vis-a-vis others or oneself); they are unified by being timely. That should be their essential quality, or the predicate pointing to a predicament. A reader alerted by the Vergilian motto of the Ode ("paulo majora canamus") would recognize the question of poetic growth and maturation: of the *career* of the poet. Is there a future for Wordsworth as poet, or for poetry itself? Has the time for poetry, as "timely utterance," passed?

Moreover, the Ode's vacillating strain, its blend of humble and prophetic tones, recalls Milton's stylized hesitation in *Lycidas*: poetry is conceived by Milton as a precarious venture that may be prematurely launched, untimely tried by "forc'd fingers rude." It is Milton who linked poetry's timeliness explicitly to a vocation that was imperious, prophetic, hazardous. If not now, when?

The "Now" that begins stanza 3 of Wordsworth's Ode may therefore be more than a pivoting or idling word. Its place in time, as well as its syntactical position, is not easily fixed. It is like the anchor of hope. Its prepositional and propositional components fuse into an absolute construction. The word stands outside the events it qualifies: like a symbol in mathematics it could refer to every phrase that follows. The sequence of tenses in stanza 3 shifts, moreover, from present to past to present, as everything tends toward that "Now." Coming to it, after two reflective and chiefly elegiac stanzas, it is as if a person were to draw a deep breath, then to exhale it, signaling a new start. The present, or this very utterance, cancels what has been. "Now" is, in its virtuality, the temporal word *par excellence*.

To make so ordinary a word extraordinary may be self-defeating in terms of the diction of poetry.

Yet poetic language, it could be argued, is ordinary language in its always residual or always future promise. What a difference between this "now" and its two prefigurative echoes in lines 6 and 9 of the first stanza! That common word may also remarkably index "A Presence which is not to be put by" (Ode, 120). It intimates the possibility—not the fact—of a decisive turning point, something about to be, or about to be . . . uttered. Within the flow of language it is an open-vowelled *nunc stans*, a fleeting epiphanic sound. And the transition from "thought of grief" to "relief," which it introduces, and then, in the next stanza, to "blessing," comes through drinking in a surround of sounds: the utterance itself, the cataracts, echoes, winds, and the first clear vocative of the poem, "Shout round me. . . ." It is as if Wordsworth had been released into voice as well as blessing, into a voice that is a blessing.

> Ye blessed Creatures, I have heard the call
>   Ye to each other make. . . .   (36–7)

It is a moment similar to the removal of the curse from the Ancient Mariner in Coleridge's poem. There is the same feeling of relief, the creatures (*res creatae*) are acknowledged and blessed. Coleridge, however, separates blessing and utterance, as if timely utterance were not, or not yet, possible.

> O happy living things! no tongue
> Their beauty might declare:
> A spring of love gushed from my heart,
> And I blessed them unaware.

Yet in Wordsworth too a hesitation of the tongue is felt, or some impediment to the coincidence of voice and blessing. It emerges when we ask whether the action of stanza 4 takes place in real or wishful time. "Ye blessed Creatures, I have heard the call / Ye to each other make; I see / The heavens laugh with you . . ." need not be a descriptive statement about what is happening then and there. It could be an anticipatory and envisioning response to "Shout round me, let me hear thy shouts . . ." A wish-fulfillment, then, a proleptic extension of the poet's own vocative, his pausal "Now." The "I have heard" may refer to the past ("There was a time") or it may come so close to the moment of speaking that it is a confirmatory "Roger." Wordsworth does not actually say that *he* is laughing with the creatures; but as he looks round once more, repeating the "turning" described in the opening stanzas, he sees and hears the things he said he could no more.

The reader, of course, no less wishful than the poet, would like to assume that the thought of grief has passed and that the birds and beasts did in fact sing and bound, and that only the discordant heart of the poet had to be tuned. But the "Now" remains slightly apart, hyper-referential, or just plain *hyper*. It is a wishing-word. The music of Wordsworth's Ode is so elaborate that it untunes the timely-happy connection between heaven and nature, as between heart and nature, a connection the poet is always re-establishing. His poem is the most complex Music Ode in English, conveying and absorbing the difference between voice and blessing, words and wishes, being and being-in-time.

IV

All things, responsive to the writing
— Wordsworth

I have offered a mildly deconstructive reading: one that discloses in words "a 'spirit' peculiar to their nature as words" (Kenneth Burke). Such a reading refuses to substitute ideas for words, especially since in the empiricist tradition after Locke ideas are taken to be a faint replica of images, which are themselves directly referable to sense-experience. One way of bringing out the spirit peculiar to words, and so, paradoxically, making them material—emphasizing the letter in the spirit—is to evoke their intertextual echoes. Ideas may be simple, but words always are complex. Yet the construction of an intertextual field is disconcerting as well as enriching because intertextual concordance produces a reality-discord, an overlay or distancing of the referential function of speech, of the word-thing, word-experience relation. Even though the *fact* of correspondence between language and experience is not in question (there is a complex answerability of the one to the other), the *theory* of correspondence remains a problem. I want to conclude my remarks by suggesting that intertextual awareness follows from the character of words, and that it does not divorce us from dearly-beloved experience, or Wordsworth's "the world, which is the world of all of us."

"There was a time" (line 1) immediately introduces the motif of time in a colloquial and inconspicuous way. Yet as the poem proceeds, the expression begins to border on myth. It becomes reminiscent of the *illo tempore,* the "in those days," of mythical thought. Wordsworth locates that mythical epoch at the barely scrutable edge of everyone's memory of childhood. During this numinous time, a "celestial light" invests natural objects, although later we learn also about darker moments, "Blank misgivings of a Creature / Moving about in worlds not realized" (Ode, 144–45). The darkness and the light are intervolved, as in a Grasmere storm. But the metaphor of light predominates, and the poet's loss is described in terms of it.

The third stanza deepens as well as qualifies that sense of loss. The "to me alone" of line 22 points to an event closer to augury than subjective feeling; it singles the poet out. He haruspicates himself. His inability to respond fully to nature, what does it mean? Was the vanished natural light perhaps an inner and now failing light, not *given* from outside but rather *bestowed* from within by imagination?

That gleam, moreover, whatever its source, seems preternatural. It suggests that the bond between nature and imagination is precarious from the outset, with imagination seeking to wed itself to nature, in order to become poetry rather than prophecy. That is certainly how it seemed to Blake when he read the Ode. He was deeply moved by it, but denounced the "natural man" in Wordsworth always rising up, as he put it, against the imaginative man.

Those acquainted with Wordsworth know that a simple turn of thought can trigger a radical turning about of his mind, and release a near-apocalyptic sense of isolation. Blake is right in the sense that even when the final mood-swing or *"envoi"* of the Ode ends ominously,

> And O, ye Fountains, Meadows, Hills, and Groves,
> Forebode not any severing of our loves! (187–88),

Wordsworth pretends that the portent comes from nature rather than from himself. He will not acknowledge that the bond with nature—more psychic than epistemic—is broken. "I could wish my days to be / Bound each to each by natural piety."

"I *could* wish"? How strangely tentative that sounds! The wish hesitates, I suspect, because its very success, its potential fulfillment, might go against nature by confirming the omnipotence of wishful thought. A similar scruple may hover over stanza 3 and the "timely utterance" that allows the

Ode to turn upward instead of spiraling downward or breaking off. The very discretion of the phrase protects it from being construed as a wish, or any sort of direct — imperative — speech-act.

"Timely utterance," then, does not pose only a problem of reference. The indirect phrasing involves signifier as well as signified: the poet's attitude toward a higher mode of speech, whether wishful or prophetic. Wordsworth's expression is guarded: he does not actually wish; rather, he "could wish" that the bond with nature should continue, and that the mutability suggested by "There was a time" should not bode an end to time itself, a discontinuity between *illo tempore* and his present or future state. The "timely utterance" meets that anxiety about time; and as "utterance" it suggests that someone else has made a wish for the poet and so relieved him of the responsibility. It is as if a thought had been taken out of his heart and uttered. The structure is similar to that of the famous dedication scene in *The Prelude*, which makes him aware of his calling as poet. "I made no vows, but vows / Were then made for me; bond unknown to me / Was given . . ." (5.534–6).[7] In the Ode too we do not know who utters what. Even if the utterance took place within the poet, it was not his but some other voice. A "discours de l'Autre" (Jacques Lacan) takes away the burden of wishful or visionary speech. There exists, in fact, one such Discourse of the Other that is *timely* and *bonding* and even joins the theme of speaking to that of giving light:

> And God said, Let there be light: and there was light. And God saw the light, that it was good: and God divided the light from the darkness. And God called the light Day, and the darkness he called Night. And there was evening and there was morning, one day.

These are "timely" words indeed: they create time, they establish it beyond all misgiving. What is founded, moreover, bonds a responsive nature (or what is to be nature) to an utterance, and God to his own work, for he acknowledges by direct acts of naming and blessing what has been called into being.

I am tempted, at last, to make an assertion and identify the "timely utterance." "Let there be light: and there was light" utters itself in the poet's mind as a proof-text, that is, not only as a deeply subjective wish for the return of the light whose loss was lamented in the first two stanzas, but also as that wish in the form of God's first words, His "Let there be."

I have taken one phrase as my starting point, and made many angels dance on it. These revels would be in vain if Wordsworth's Ode were not involved in the question of voice as well as light: in what connection there still might be between poetry and prophecy. "A Voice to Light gave Being," Wordsworth writes in a later Great Ode, alluding to fiat or logos. Yet there is a fear lest poetic voice, in its very power, may call on darkness, and become decreative rather than creative and so a "counter-spirit" or parody of the "divine I AM." Then the prophetic or poetic voice would serve, however involuntarily, the cause of cursing, not of blessing, and wish for an end, a dissolution of word and world. The utterance that surprised Wordsworth is, from one perspective, an archetypal instance of wish-fulfillment or omnipotence of thoughts. Yet from another perspective it is an exemplary instance of poetry as a creative speech-act that leads to natural piety rather than to apocalyptic solipsism or transcendence.

Wordsworth's most felicitous poetry merges wishing, responding, and blessing: merges, in fact, a first timely utterance, the fiat, and a second timely utterance, the convenant. If, in stanza 3 of his Ode, the sounding cataracts and the "timely utterance" are echo-aspects of each other, it is because what was founded must be founded a second time, on the flood; just as the light that was has to be lit again, now. The Covenant is a second creation confirming the first; while the rainbow as a timely sign recalls an utterance that could make the poet's heart leap up. The Intimations Ode is the third of this series. It is the poet's response, his covenant-sign, his own "timely utterance," incorporating mutely — as silent light — the divine *davar*, that is, the text on which my own intertextual leaping comes to rest.

Notes

1. "The Immortality Ode," reprinted in *The Liberal Imagination* (New York: Viking, 1950).
2. That we are reluctant to develop the resonances of a critic's prose, even a critic as deliberate as Trilling, does not mean they are not felt. Ironically, Trilling's answer, when it does come (in the fourth section of his essay) is one that leads to a displacement from one phrase or word-complex to

another, and so enlightens without disburdening the poem. It does not give a final relief to thought.

3. "Surprised by joy—impatient as the Wind" (1815).

4. Compare, in the second stanza of "A slumber did my spirit seal," the verse: "Wheeled round in earth's diurnal course." An image of *gravitational* elides or displaces that of the *grave;* and the tacit verbal pun is reenforced by the fact that "di*ur*nal" is followed by "course," a word that sounds like the archaic-poetic pronunciation of "corpse." (I owe this insight to Jay Farness.) Could one show, in Wordsworth, a convergence of nature's eliding (subliming) of the corpse, and poetry's eliding (subliming) of the referent?

5. See Trilling, *The Liberal Imagination,* p. 139.

6. I agree with Paul de Man ("The Dead-End of Formalist Criticism," *Blindness and Insight,* 2d ed., 1983) in his understanding of pastoral as much more than convention or genre. "There is no doubt that the pastoral theme is, in fact, the only poetic theme, that it is poetry itself." De Man's insight comes by way of a critique of Empson and the doctrine of "reconciliation," a critique that limits the rigorous and principled criticism initiated by Richards.

7. The placement of "unknown" causes an ambiguity. It could refer to the bond or to its character vis-a-vis the receiver. "An unknown bond was given—to me, who was unaware (unknowing) of it at the time." The "unknown" points to what is knowable yet difficult to locate as conscious knowledge at a single spot in time. Its place in the verse-line is self-displacing.

APPLICATION

Patricia S. Yaeger claims that when we read The Awakening *as a novel about sexual liberation, "we read it with
our patriarchal biases intact" and, further, that novels
of female adultery, Chopin's included, are usually only
"mildly transgressive," for they depict behavior easily
accommodated within the bourgeois code. She also takes
exception to Sandra Gilbert's mythopoeic reading, though
she feels this approach has promise, and to Cynthia Griffin Wolff's psychoanalytic reading, for whereas Wolff
sees Edna Pontellier's problems as psychological, Yaeger
sees them as "linguistic and social." "If* The Awakening
*can be defined as an emancipatory text, if it voices a con-
flict between men's speech and the speaking of women,
this is a conflict articulated as a struggle between men's
normative language and something unvoiced and enigmatic." On this premise, Yaeger offers a feminist, poststructural reading that could as easily fit in the next
chapter of this book. It isn't always clear, for example, if
Yaeger is arguing that her way of reading discovers the
novel's true transgressive force, or confers it. But this
kind of intentionalist or genetic distinction is of little
concern to most poststructural critics. And if Yaeger is
a cultural critic in her interest in the kind of cultural
work the novel can be made to do, in the opportunity it
offers us "to construct a new, utopian image of the emergence of women's antithetical desires," she is very much
a poststructural critic in her insistence that the novel's
conception of language is the key to its meaning. Drawing on the work of Michel Foucault, Julia Kristeva, Jean
François Lyotard, and Jacques Lacan, she furnishes a
poststructural analysis of the novel centering on a language whose very inadequacy makes it the only adequate
vehicle.*

"A Language Which Nobody Understood": Emancipatory Strategies in *The Awakening*

Patricia S. Yaeger

Despite the academy's growing commitment to producing and publishing feminist interpretations of literary texts, insofar as feminist critics read Kate Chopin's *The Awakening* as a novel about sexual liberation, we read it with our patriarchal biases intact. Of course *The Awakening*'s final scene is breathtaking; Edna Pontellier transcends her circumscribed status as sensual entity—as the object of others' desires—and stands before us as her own subject, as a blissfully embodied being: ". . . she cast the unpleasant, pricking garments from her, and for the first time in her life she stood naked in the open air, at the mercy of the sun, the breeze that beat upon her, and the waves that invited her."[1] It is because of this new dignity and visibility Chopin gives to women's desires that *The Awakening* has been celebrated as one of the great subversive novels—a novel belonging to the tradition of transgressive narratives Tony Tanner describes in *Adultery in the Novel*. But in this essay I will suggest that Tanner's ideas are inadequate to account for the real transgressive force of Chopin's novel. Instead, I want to locate this force in Chopin's representation of a language Edna Pontellier seeks but does not possess, in her representation of "a language which nobody understood."[2]

In *Adultery in the Novel* Tanner explains that eighteenth- and nineteenth-century novels derive a "narrative urgency" from their power to interrupt the status quo by representing characters or ideas which impinge on society's stability. While most bourgeois novels affirm marriage, the nuclear family, or genealogical continuity as the source of social stability, these same novels gather momentum by representing "an energy that threatens to contravene that stability of the family on which society depends": an energy frequently embodied in the adulterous woman.[3] While prostitutes, orphans, adventurers, and other marginal characters dominate the early phases of the novel and disrupt its representations of family stability with a raw transgressive force, Tanner suggests that in the novel's later incarnations this same energy is embodied in the motive or act of adultery. "Marriage, to put it at its simplest . . . is a means by which society attempts to bring into harmonious alignment patterns of passion and patterns of property" (15).

According to Tanner, marriage and adultery are central to the bourgeois novel because marriage mediates between the opposed demands of private desire and public law. "If society depends for its existence on certain rules governing what may be combined and what should be kept separate, then adultery, by bringing the wrong things together in the wrong places (or the wrong people in the wrong beds), offers an attack on those rules, revealing them to be arbitrary rather than absolute" (13). This is a fine observation, and resembles the critique Edna Pontellier applies to her husband and children while contemplating suicide. But Edna's critique of her position within the nuclear family, her sense of herself as someone who should not be regarded as her husband's or children's property, is only a part of her story: her realization does not begin to explain the forces in her society that resist critique. While the adulterous impulses of the novelistic heroine challenge one form of patriarchy, I want to suggest that they enhance another: the power of woman's "extramarital" desire does not have the revolutionary power Tanner predicates.

Obsessed with the other, murdered, ostracized, or killed by her own hand, the adulterous woman is caught in an elaborate code that has already been negotiated by her society. Her actions may be defined as abnormal, but they are only mildly transgressive; adultery remains well within the arena of permissible social trespass. Edna Pontellier falls in love with Robert Lebrun precisely *because* this possibility is inscribed within her, because adulterous desire is covertly regarded in her society as a path for woman's misconduct: such desire continues to involve an obsessional valorization of the masculine.

> Edna often wondered at one propensity which sometimes had inwardly disturbed her. . . . At a very early age . . . she remembered that she had been passionately enamored of a dignified and sad-eyed cavalry officer who visited her father in Kentucky. She could not leave his presence when he was there, nor remove her eyes from his face, which was something like Napoleon's. (18–19)

Participating in the bourgeois family is one expression of the romantic obsession that shapes and destroys the bourgeois heroine. Participating in licentious desire for a man other than her husband is simply another. At the Pontelliers' dinner party early in the novel we can see how this desire remains within the schema of approved social narratives:

> The Colonel, with little sense of humor and of the fitness of things, related a somber episode of those

dark and bitter days, in which he had acted a conspicuous part and always formed a central figure. Nor was the Doctor happier in his selection, when he told the old, ever new and curious story of the waning of a woman's love, seeking strange, new channels, only to return to its legitimate source after days of fierce unrest. It was one of the many little human documents which had been unfolded to him during his long career as a physician. The story did not seem especially to impress Edna.   (70)

With this generous construction of what is and is not "legitimate," the doctor has told a story in Tanner's "New Testament tradition." According to Tanner, Christ is the ideal narrator, the narrator who, when "confronted with the woman taken in adultery," tries to make the "would-be lawgivers aware of her problematical reality, calling into question both the impersonal application of the law and the justification and rights of the would-be legislators. Effectively this implies the disintegration of society-as-constituted" (14). But what else might it imply? Christ, despite his distinct "femininity," and Mandelet, despite his generosity, still claim jural power by virtue of their gender; their acts and judgments do not imply "the disintegration of society as constituted," but rather its "fatherly" reformation, since these paternal figures define—if not society's center—then its gentlemanly margins. In their "generous" revisions of law we find the same plot transferred to another patriarchal economy. Neither Christ nor Dr. Mandelet suggests a revision of the traditional heterosexual plot which, while it may or may not involve marriage, always involves a hierarchical reading of woman's relation to man.

Tanner has more to say; he argues that even "without anything or anyone necessarily having changed place or roles (in social terms), the action of adultery portends the possible breakdown of all the mediations on which society itself depends, and demonstrates the latent impossibility of participating in the interrelated patterns that comprise its structure" (17). This apocalyptic view of transgression is appealing, but wrong. For Edna, the thought or practice of adultery seems revolutionary but is actually a conservative gesture within the larger scheme of things, another mode of social acquiescence.[4] The most radical act of trespass Chopin's novel describes is not Edna's propensity to fall in love, or even the way she acts after falling, but the fact that she is disturbed by her own obsessions.

Before her romance with Lebrun intervenes, Chopin's novel holds Edna's awakening open for us as an extraordinary event that Chopin refuses to attach—except peripherally—to Lebrun until we have witnessed Edna's preliminary attempts at self-dialogue and self-knowledge. We should therefore take exception to Tanner's paradigm, his notion that adultery

> introduces an agonizing and irresolvable category— confusion—into the individual and thence into society itself. . . . If society depends for its existence on certain rules governing what may be combined and what should be kept separate, then adultery, by bringing the wrong things together in the wrong places (or the wrong people in the wrong beds), offers an attack on those rules, revealing them to be arbitrary rather than absolute. In this way, the adulterous woman becomes the "gap" in society that gradually extends through it. In attempting to ostracize her, society moves toward ostracizing itself.
> (12–13)

Society may read itself through the absence of the adulterous woman, but she, being absent, cannot read herself. It is the absence of such critique and not the absence of adultery that allows the maintenance of a sex/gender system that remains repressive and hierarchical and victimizes women by making them not only wives, but objects of romantic or domestic narratives. *The Awakening*'s most radical awareness is that Edna inhabits a world of limited linguistic possibilities, of limited possibilities for interpreting and reorganizing her feelings, and therefore of limited possibilities for action. In Edna's world what sorts of things are open to question and what things are not? Although Edna initially attempts to move into an arena in which she can begin to explore feelings which lie outside the prescribed social code, finally she can only think about herself within that code, can only act within some permutation of the subject-object relations her society has ordained for her.

If this is so, can we still define *The Awakening* as one of the grand subversive novels, as a novel belonging to a great tradition of emancipatory fiction? We can make such claims for *The Awakening* only if Chopin has been successful in inventing a novelistic structure in which the heroine's very absence of speech works productively, in which Edna's silence offers a new dialogic ground from which we can measure the systematic distortions of her old ground of being and begin to construct a new, utopian image of the emergence of women's antithetical desires. Does Chopin's novel offer such utopian structures?

"She had put her head down on Madame Ratignolle's shoulder. She was flushed and felt intoxicated with the sound of her own voice and the unaccustomed taste of candor. It muddled her like wine, or like a first breath of freedom" (20). What are the conditions that permit Edna to feel intoxicated with the sound of her own voice, to experience this "unaccustomed taste of candor" in conversation with a friend? These feelings are customary, this rapture quite ordinary, in fictions by men. "The earth is all before me," Wordsworth insists in *The Prelude*. "With a heart / Joyous, nor scared at its own liberty, / I look about; and should my chosen guide/ Be nothing better than a wandering cloud, / I cannot miss my way. I breathe again!"[5] We know, of course, that Wordsworth has it wrong, that he has miles to go before he discovers anything remotely resembling liberty. Intoxicated by his own voice, thrilled at the prospect of articulate freedom, Wordsworth still claims prophetic powers; he permits his mind to wander and releases his voice to those "trances of thought and mountings of the mind" which hurry toward him. This makes gorgeous poetry, but for whom does it speak? Such moments are rarely recorded by women writers either on their own behalf or on behalf of their fictional heroines. In the scene in *The Awakening* where Edna returns to the beach from her unearthly swim, it is Robert Lebrun who speaks for her, who frames and articulates the meaning of her adventure, and the plot he invents involves a mystical, masculine sea-spirit responsible for Edna's sense of election, as if romance were the only form of elation a heroine might feel. Edna repudiates Robert's story: " 'Don't banter me,' she said, wounded at what appeared to be his flippancy" (30). And yet Robert's metaphors quickly become Edna's own:

> Sailing across the bay to the *Chênière Caminada*, Edna felt as if she were being borne away from some anchorage which had held her fast, whose chains had been loosening—had snapped the night before when the mystic spirit was abroad, leaving her free to drift whithersoever she chose to set her sails. Robert spoke to her incessantly ...   (35)

The tension between Edna's imagined freedom and Robert's incessant speech is palpable, but unlike the speech of Edna's husband, Robert's words invite dialogue: "I'll take you some night in the pirogue when the moon shines. Maybe your Gulf spirit will whisper to you in which of these islands the treasures are hidden—direct you to the very spot, perhaps.' 'And in a day we should be rich!' she laughed. 'I'd give it all to you, the pirate gold and every bit of treasure we could dig up'" (35). Not only is Robert's vision one that Edna can participate in and help to create, but it is also like a fairy-tale: romantic, enticing, utopian. As a "utopia" Robert's vision is not at all emancipatory; it offers only the flip side, the half-fulfilled wishes of an everyday ideology.

> "How many years have I slept?" she inquired. "The whole island seems changed. A new race of beings must have sprung up, leaving only you and me as past relics. . . ."
>   He familiarly adjusted a ruffle upon her shoulder.
>   "You have slept precisely one hundred years. I was left here to guard your slumbers; and for one hundred years I have been out under the shed reading a book. The only evil I couldn't prevent was to keep a broiled fowl from drying up."   (38)

This comic repartee is charming: as Foucault explains in *The Order of Things*, utopias afford us special consolation. "Although they have no real locality there is nevertheless a fantastic, untroubled region in which they are able to unfold; they open up . . . countries where life is easy, even though the road to them is chimerical. . . . This is why utopias permit fables and discourse: they run with the very grain of language and are part of the fundamental dimension of the *fabula*."[6] What Robert Lebrun offers Edna is a continuing story, a mode of discourse which may be chimerical, but unlike Edna's talk with her husband is also potentially communal. This discursive mode cannot, however, invite its speakers to test the limits of their language; instead, it creates a pleasurable nexus of fancy through which Edna may dream. Freed from the repressive talk of her husband, Edna chooses another mode of oppression, a speech-world that offers space for flirtation that Edna finds liberating. But this liberation is also limiting, a form of stultification, and in exchanging the intoxicating sound of her own voice as she speaks on the beach for Robert's romantic voice, Edna Pontellier's growing sense of self is stabilized, frozen into a mode of feeling and consciousness which, for all its promise of sexual fulfillment, leaves her essentially without resources, without an opportunity for other internal dialogues.[7] We may see *The Awakening* as a novel praising sexual discovery and critiquing the asymmetries of the marriage plot, but we must also recognize that this is a novel in which the heroine's capacities for thought are shut down, a novel in which Edna's temptations *to think* are repressed by the moody discourse of romance. In fact, the novel's explicitly utopian constructs partake of this romance framework; they do not function transgressively. Does Chopin offer her heroine — or her reader — any emancipatory alternative?

Let us begin to answer this question by considering a moment from Lacan's essay "From Love to the Libido" — a moment in which Lacan turns upon his audience and denies that we can ever define ourselves through another's language.

> What I, Lacan . . . am telling you is that the subject as such is uncertain because he is divided by the effects of language. Through the effects of speech, the subject always realizes himself more in the Other, but he is already pursuing there more than half of himself. He will simply find his desire ever more divided, pulverized, in the circumscribable metonymy of speech.[8]

The hearing of a lecture, the writing of a psychoanalytic text, the reading of a novel: these are moments of self-divisiveness, of seeking what we are in that which we are not. It is this drive toward self-realization in the speech of the other that we have begun to discover in *The Awakening*. Chopin's novel focuses from its beginning on the difficulties we have maneuvering within the precincts of language. It opens with an exotic and showy image: "A green and yellow parrot, which hung in a cage outside the door, kept repeating over and over: *Allez vous-en! Allez vous-en! Sapristi! That's all right!*" (3). The parrot's speech is nonsensical and yet it illuminates its world in an intriguing way. An amalgam of English and Creole, this exotic speech alerts us to the fact that the parrot inhabits a multilingual culture and suggests the babble and lyricism bred by mixing world views. But in addition to giving us a glimpse of the worlds we will encounter within the larger novel, these opening paragraphs make enigmatic statements about our relation to language itself; they open up an intriguing linguistic matrix.

> Mr. Pontellier, unable to read his newspaper with any degree of comfort, arose with an expression and an exclamation of disgust. He walked down the gallery across the narrow "bridges" which connected the Lebrun cottages one with the other. . . .

> He stopped before the door of his own cottage, which was the fourth one from the main building and next to the last. Seating himself in a wicker rocker which was there, he once more applied himself to the task of reading the newspaper. The day was Sunday; the paper was a day old. (3)

In contrast to the giddy plurality of the parrot's speech, Mr. Pontellier's meditations are redundant and single-minded. Chopin asks us to associate his propriety with the backward tug of words which are "a day old" and already emptied of meaning.[9] The parrot, on the other hand, speaks a language emptied of meaning but full of something else. "He could speak a little Spanish, and also a language which nobody understood, unless it was the mocking-bird that hung on the other side of the door, whistling his fluty notes out upon the breeze with maddening persistence" (3). Repetitive, discontinuous, incomprehensible: the speech of this parrot points to an immediate contrast between everyday speech and a more extraordinary speech world. The parrot mixes modes of speech at random; its polyvocal discourse directs our attention to a potential lack of meaning in words themselves — to a register of meaning beyond the reach of its language which is paradoxically articulated in *The Awakening* as "a language which nobody understood."

In reading the parrot's speech we are in the vicinity of what Lacan calls "metonymy":

> A lack is encountered by the subject in the Other, in the very intimation that the Other makes to him by his discourse. In the intervals of the discourse of the Other, there emerges in the experience of the child something that is radically mappable, namely, *He is saying this to me, but what does he want?*
>
> In this interval intersecting the signifiers . . . is the locus of what, in other registers of my exposition, I have called metonymy. It is there that what we call desire crawls, slips, escapes, like the ferret. The desire of the Other is apprehended by the subject in that which does not work, in the lacks of the discourse of the Other, and all the child's *whys* reveal not so much an avidity for the reason of things, as a testing of the adult, a *Why are you telling me this?* ever-resuscitated from its base, which is the enigma of the adult's desire. (214)

Reading Chopin's text we find ourselves, from our first overhearing of the parrot's empty speech, in the position of the child who asks "Why?" but unlike the child we can begin to formulate an answer. The register of desire — of something not described within language but premised and promised there—is provided for us in the "empty" referents of the parrot's speech and its highly charged iterations of the mockingbird's song. It is this enigmatic "language" Mr. Pontellier attempts to shun as he navigates his newspaper and the "bridges" connecting the coherent and well-mapped spaces between the cottages. But it is in the unmapped spaces, the spaces between words, the unspoken sites of desire that Edna Pontellier initially resides, and in order to understand how this transgressive impulse is structured into Chopin's novel we need to see that Chopin herself has divided the linguistic topography of *The Awakening* into an extra-linguistic zone of meaning imaged for us at the beginning of the novel in the speech of the parrot, a "language which nobody understood," and a countervailing region of linguistic constraints imaged for us in Mr. Pontellier's speech.

Although Lacan's reading of "metonymy" helps us to identify this linguistic topography, the novel's missing register of language should not be confused with the irrecoverable "lack" that Lacan defines at the heart of discourse, or the psychic dyslexia in which Kristeva says "Woman" resides. Although "the feminine," in Kristeva's early essays, is said to be synonymous with the a-linguistic ("What I mean by 'woman' is that which is not represented, that which is unspoken, that which is left out of namings and ideologies"[10]), I want to suggest that Edna's absent language is not a manifestation of women's permanent expulsion from "masculine speech" but of what Jean-François Lyotard calls *"le différend."*

Lyotard explains that "in the *différend* something 'asks' to be put into sentences, and suffers the wrong of not being able to be at the moment. . . . It is the concern of a literature, of a philosophy, perhaps of a politics, to testify to these *différends* by finding an idiom for them."[11] Chopin testifies to these *"différends"* by using the metaphor of an absent or displaced vocality ("the voice of the sea," the multivoiced babble of the parrot) to emphasize Edna's need for a more passionate and intersubjective speech that would allow Edna to revise or rearticulate her relations to her own desire and to the social reality that thwarts this desire. This is to argue that *The Awakening* is a text that asks for another idiom to fill in the unspoken voices in Edna's story: an idiom that contemporary women writers and feminist critics have begun to provide.[12] Thus Edna Pontellier speaks an unfinished discourse that reaches out to be completed by other speaking human beings: her "lost" speech—

represented by her own speech fragments, by the sibilant voice of the sea and the chatter of the trilingual parrot—is not unfinished on an a-historical, metaphysical plane. Instead, Chopin's displaced metaphors of vocality help us to envision for her heroine a more radical speech situation, a linguistic practice that would reach out to the *"différend,"* to a politics that is not yet a politics, to a language that should be phrased but cannot yet (or could not then) be phrased.[13] In this reading of Chopin's text the emancipatory moments in *The Awakening* do not consist of those instances of adulterous desire that drive Edna toward the transgressive side of the marriage plot. Instead, such emancipatory moments are contained in those unstable instances of self-questioning and dialogue with herself and with other women that the novel's romance plot helps to elide.

Before looking more closely at the way the *"différend"* operates in Chopin's novel, let us consider the moment of Edna's awakening in more detail. On the evening when Edna first begins, consciously, to recognize her powers and wants "to swim far out, where no woman had swum before" (28), her experience is one of multiple moods, of emotions which seem confused and inarticulate: "A thousand emotions have swept through me to-night. I don't comprehend half of them. . . . I wonder if any night on earth will ever again be like this one. It is like a night in a dream. The people about me are like some uncanny, half-human beings. There must be spirits abroad to-night" (30). Sensing the extraordinary reach of her feelings, Lebrun answers in kind:

> "There are," whispered Robert. "Didn't you know this was the twenty-eighth of August?"
> "The twenty-eighth of August?"
> "Yes. On the twenty-eighth of August, at the hour of midnight, and if the moon is shining—the moon must be shining—a spirit that has haunted these shores for ages rises up from the Gulf. With its own penetrating vision the spirit seeks some one mortal worthy to hold him company, worthy of being exalted for a few hours into realms of the semi-celestials. His search has always hitherto been fruitless, and he has sunk back, disheartened, into the sea. But tonight he found Mrs. Pontellier. Perhaps he will never wholly release her from the spell. Perhaps she will never again suffer a poor, unworthy earthling to walk in the shadow of her divine presence." (30)

While Robert Lebrun may have "penetrated her mood," he has also begun to alter its meaning.

Edna's experience has been solitary and essentially mysterious; her swim has been a surpassing of limits, a mythic encounter with death—an experience suffused with metaphor, beyond comprehension. Robert's words do not begin to encompass its meaning, but he does attempt to communicate with her, to understand her mood. And since Edna lacks an alternative register of language to describe her tumultuous feelings, Robert's conceit soon becomes her own; his language comes to stand for the nameless feelings she has just begun to experience. Just as Edna's initial awakening, her continuing journey toward self-articulation and self-awareness is initially eccentric and complex, so this journey is finally diminished and divided, reduced in the romantic stories that she is told and the romantic stories she comes to tell herself, to a simplistic narrative that falsifies the diversity of her awakening consciousness. From this perspective, the pivotal event of Chopin's novel is not Edna's suicide, nor her break with her husband, but her openness to Robert Lebrun's stories, her vulnerability to the romantic speech of the other which has, by the end of the novel, become her speech as well:

> "I love you," she whispered, "only you; no one but you. It was you who awoke me last summer out of a life-long, stupid dream. Oh! you have made me so unhappy with your indifference. Oh! I have suffered, suffered! Now you are here we shall love each other, my Robert. We shall be everything to each other. Nothing else in the world is of any consequence. I must go to my friend; but you will wait for me? No matter how late; you will wait for me, Robert?" (107)

Edna's final retelling of her story is not an accurate self-portrait, but a radical betrayal of the "awakening" that emerges at the novel's beginning. This initial "awakening" does not involve the violent triangulation of adultery, romance, and erotic storytelling, but the exploration of a discontinuous series of images that are promisingly feminocentric. In fact, what is disturbing about Edna's last speech to Robert is its falsification of her story, its naming of Lebrun as author of her growth, as source of her awakening. For what this last speech denies is the essential strangeness of Edna's initial self-consciousness, the tantalizing world of unvoiced dreams and ideas that Edna encounters at the novel's inception. By the end of the novel Edna has drifted into a system of self-explanation that—while it seems to account for her experience—also falsifies that experience by giving

it the gloss of coherence, of a continuous narrative line. Edna's thoughts at the beginning of the novel are much more confused—but they are also more heterogeneous and promising.

In the opening scenes of *The Awakening* this struggle among different social possibilities, among diverse points of view, fails to take place as explicitly realized dialogue. Even Edna's husband does not have the power to challenge the voices which annoy him, but only "the privilege of quitting their society when they ceased to be entertaining." "The parrot and the mocking-bird were the property of Madame Lebrun," Chopin tells us, "and they had the right to make all the noise they wished" (3). The detail seems trivial, but it is worth noting that just as Mr. Pontellier's reaction to the parrot's nonsensical speech is defined in terms of his relation to the parrot as someone else's possession, so his wife is defined in terms of property relations as well. " 'What folly to bathe at such an hour and in such heat! . . . You are burnt beyond recognition,' he added, looking at his wife as one looks at a valuable piece of personal property which has suffered some damage" (4). In Pontellier's linguistic world, the roles of speaker and listener are clearly defined in terms of social and material hierarchies. Edna Pontellier is someone her husband feels free to command and free to define, but she is not someone to whom Mr. Pontellier listens:

> "What is it?" asked Pontellier, looking lazily and amused from one to the other. It was some utter nonsense; some adventure out there in the water, and they both tried to relate it at once. It did not seem half so amusing when told. They realized this, and so did Mr. Pontellier. He yawned and stretched himself. Then he got up, saying he had half a mind to go over to Klein's hotel and play a game of billiards. (5)

When Pontellier—feeling "very talkative"—returns from Klein's hotel late at night, he blithely awakens his wife to converse.

> He talked to her while he undressed, telling her anecdotes and bits of news and gossip that he had gathered during the day. From his trousers pockets he took a fistful of crumpled bank notes and a good deal of silver coin, which he piled on the bureau indiscriminately with keys, knife, handkerchief, and whatever else happened to be in his pockets. (7)

Pontellier expects his words to have the same weight as his silver; the only difference is that he dispenses his language with greater abandon. But Edna Pontellier inhabits a speech-world very different from her husband's, a world oddly bereft of his cultural symbols. "Overcome with sleep," she continues dreaming as he speaks and answers him "with little half utterances." For her husband, Edna's separateness is maddening. Her words, like the words of the parrot Pontellier cannot abide, seem nonsensical; her "little half utterances" suggest a replay of the early morning scene on the beach. But this time the hierarchies are played out in earnest, and Pontellier reacts to his wife's inattention with a burgher-like furor. Nominally concerned for his children, he stalks to their rooms, only to find them inhabiting their own bizarre speech-worlds: "He turned and shifted the youngsters about in bed. One of them began to kick and talk about a basket full of crabs" (7).

While *The Awakening* traces the closure of its own intervals of desire and self-questioning, Chopin is also engaged in the radical mapping of those moments of speech in which our desires begin to address us. If the socio-symbolic world we inhabit encourages us to displace unspoken polyphanies with repetition, with customary stories, with narrative lines, the force of *The Awakening*'s subversive nocturnes, its metonymic intervals, belies the permanence of Pontellier's social forms and suggests a linguistic counterplot which glitters through the text with dis-articulate meaning. The child's response throws his father's patriarchal assumptions into even higher relief when Pontellier responds to his son's "utter nonsense" by chiding his wife: "Mr. Pontellier returned to his wife with the information that Raoul had a high fever and needed looking after. . . . He reproached his wife with her inattention, her habitual neglect of the children. If it was not a mother's place to look after children, whose on earth was it?" (7). When Pontellier uses his power of speech to awaken his wife and to define her, Edna answers with deliberate silence. But when Pontellier drifts off to sleep, this silence loses its power. "Turning, she thrust her face, steaming and wet, into the bend of her arm, and she went on crying there, not caring any longer to dry her face, her eyes, her arms. She could not have told why she was crying." What is remarkable about this episode is Chopin's emphasis on the unspoken, the unsayable:

> An indescribable oppression, which seemed to generate in some unfamiliar part of her consciousness, filled her whole being with a vague anguish. It was like a shadow, like a mist passing across her soul's summer day. It was strange and unfamiliar;

it was a mood. She did not sit there inwardly upbraiding her husband, lamenting at Fate, which had directed her footsteps to the path which they had taken. She was just having a good cry all to herself. The mosquitoes made merry over her, biting her firm, round arms and nipping at her bare insteps. (8)

The oppression Edna feels is not merely "indescribable" and "vague," it also comes from an "unfamiliar" region of consciousness and can only be described through analogy. Edna's mood closes as swiftly as it has opened: "The little stinging, buzzing imps succeeded in dispelling a mood which might have held her there in the darkness half a night longer" (8). The biting mosquitoes add an ominous note and operate upon Edna like her husband's alien language; it is as if their determined orality forecloses on Edna's own right to speak.

In the morning the talk between wife and husband is amicably re-established through an economic transaction: "Mr. Pontellier gave his wife half the money which he had brought away from Klein's hotel the evening before" (9). When Mr. Pontellier responds with the appropriate cultural symbols, Edna is as trapped as she was in her conversations with Robert; she can only voice gratitude. " 'It will buy a handsome wedding present for Sister Janet!' she exclaimed, smoothing out the bills as she counted them one by one. 'Oh! we'll treat Sister Janet better than that, my dear,' he laughed, as he prepared to kiss her good-by" (9). This happiness continues when Mr. Pontellier returns to New Orleans. The medium of this continued harmony is something oral or edible, something, like language, that Edna can put in her mouth:

> A few days later a box arrived for Mrs. Pontellier from New Orleans. It was from her husband. It was filled with *friandises*, with luscious and toothsome bits—the finest of fruits, *patés*, a rare bottle or two, delicious syrups, and bonbons in abundance.
>
> Mrs. Pontellier was always very generous with the contents of such a box; she was quite used to receiving them when away from home. The *patés* and fruit were brought to the dining-room; the bonbons were passed around. And the ladies, selecting with dainty and discriminating fingers and a little greedily, all declared that Mr. Pontellier was the best husband in the world. Mrs. Pontellier was forced to admit that she knew of none better. (9)

Chopin's description of Edna's acquiescence, her praise of her husband, is edged with an undeclared violence; Edna is "forced to admit" what she does not feel. But what else could she say? "Mr. Pontellier was a great favorite, and ladies, men, children, even nurses, were always on hand to say good-by to him. His wife stood smiling and waving, the boys shouting, as he disappeared in the old rockaway down the sandy road" (9). Edna has no words for describing her intricate feelings, and if she did, who would listen? She could only speak in a private "language which nobody understood, unless it was the mocking-bird that hung on the other side of the door, whistling his fluty notes out upon the breeze . . ."

In her essay on *The Awakening* Cynthia Griffin Wolff argues that Edna's central problem is psychological, that once her "hidden self" has begun "to exert its inexorable power" we can see that Edna's "libidinal appetite has been fixated at the oral level."[14] I have begun, in contrast, to suggest that Edna's problem is linguistic and social, that her "orality" is frustrated, exacerbated by her social milieu. Wolff insists on the correspondence between Edna's "preoccupation with nourishment" and an infantile, "orally destructive self, a limitless void whose needs can be filled, finally, only by total fusion with the outside world, a totality of sensuous enfolding" (208, 211). She explains that this totality "means annihilation of the ego." But we have seen that Edna's need for fusion, her preoccupation with nourishment or oral surfeiting, does not arise from Edna's own infantility but from social prescription. Married to a Creole, Edna does not feel at home in his society, and she feels especially ill at ease with the Creole manner of speech. If the gap between Creole and Anglo-American cultures gives Edna a glimpse of the inadequacies of each, Edna's inability to deal fluently in the language her husband and lovers speak remains a sign of her disempowerment. As she sails across the bay with Robert to the *Chênière Caminada*, he flirts with a "young barefooted Spanish girl" named Mariequita. Mariequita is coy and flirtatious: she teases Lebrun and asks him sweet, ribald questions:

> Edna liked it all. She looked Mariequita up and down, from her ugly brown toes to her pretty black eyes, and back again.
> "Why does she look at me like that?" inquired the girl of Robert.
> "Maybe she thinks you are pretty. Shall I ask her?"
> "No. Is she your sweetheart?"

> "She's a married lady, and has two children."
> "Oh! well! Francisco ran away with Sylvano's wife, who had four children. They took all his money and one of the children and stole his boat."
> "Shut up!"
> "Does she understand?"
> "Oh, hush!"   (34)

The scene is gay, but Mariequita's questions are filled with foreboding. Robert's knowledge of several languages, his power to control what others hear and speak, is a sign of his "right" to preside in a context where "no one present understood what they said" (34).

In a conversation with Alcée Arobin later in the novel we see how the paths for women's self-expression are continually limited. As Edna begins to explore her own deviance from social codes, Alcée Arobin usurps her role as story-teller; he begins to define her himself:

> "One of these days," she said, "I'm going to pull myself together for a while and think—try to determine what character of a woman I am; for, candidly, I don't know. By all the codes which I am acquainted with, I am a devilishly wicked specimen of the sex. But some way I can't convince myself that I am. I must think about it."
> "Don't. What's the use? Why should you bother thinking about it when I can tell you what manner of woman you are." His fingers strayed occasionally down to her warm, smooth cheeks and firm chin, which was growing a little full and double.   (82)

The text moves from an emphasis on Edna's power of thought and speech to an emphasis on her erotic power, her flesh, as Arobin reasserts the old codes and "feeds" her with stories. Earlier in the novel Adèle Ratignolle is similarly primed. Counselling Robert Lebrun to leave Mrs. Pontellier alone, Madame Ratignolle is rebuked for her efforts to speak: " 'It isn't pleasant to have a woman tell you—' " Robert Lebrun interrupts, "unheedingly, but breaking off suddenly: 'Now if I were like Arobin—you remember Alcée Arobin and that story of the consul's wife at Biloxi?' " Lebrun's speech operates not only as a form of entertainment, but as a form of repression. "And he related the story of Alcée Arobin and the consul's wife; and another about the tenor of the French Opera, who received letters which should never have been written; and still other stories, grave and gay, till Mrs. Pontellier and her possible propensity for taking young men seriously was apparently forgotten" (21). Lebrun dismisses Madame Ratignolle's concern for Edna and reminds us that the women in Chopin's novel taste little if any verbal freedom. Visiting the Ratignolles Edna observes that

> The Ratignolles understood each other perfectly. If ever the fusion of two human beings into one has been accomplished on this sphere it was surely in their union.
>
> . . . .
>
> Monsieur Ratignolle . . . spoke with an animation and earnestness that gave an exaggerated importance to every syllable he uttered. His wife was keenly interested in everything he said, laying down her fork the better to listen, chiming in, taking the words out of his mouth. (56)

If Edna "is remarkably vulnerable to feelings of being invaded and overwhelmed," if, as Wolff insists, "she is very much at the mercy of her environment," this is because her environment *is* invasive and overwhelming, not only limiting her self-expression to acts of eating, but also rewarding women who, like Madame Ratignolle, are dutifully "delicious" in their roles, who put men's words in their mouths, who have "eaten" their husbands' language.

We have established that *The Awakening* revolves around the heroine's limiting life in the courts of romance and describes, as well, a frightening antagonism between a feminine subject and the objectifying world of discourse she inhabits. "The letter was on the bookshelf. It possessed the greatest interest and attraction for Edna; the envelope, its size and shape, the postmark, the handwriting. She examined every detail of the outside before opening it" (47). What men say, what they write grows more and more portentous, and the cumulative weight of their saying is often the same: "There was no special message to Edna except a postscript saying that if Mrs. Pontellier desired to finish the book which he had been reading to her, his mother would find it in his room, among other books there on the table" (47). The world of alien discourse seems omnipresent in the novel, and when Edna tries to make her own mark, her efforts are fruitless. "Once she stopped, and taking off her wedding ring, flung it upon the carpet. When she saw it lying there, she stamped her heel upon it, striving to crush it. But her small boot heel did not make an indenture, not a mark upon the little glittering circlet" (53). In frustration Edna seizes a glass vase and flings it to the hearth. "She wanted to destroy something. The crash and clatter were what

she wanted to hear" (53). If *The Awakening* can be defined as an emancipatory text, if it voices a conflict between men's speech and the speaking of women, this is a conflict articulated as a struggle between men's normative language and something unvoiced and enigmatic—a clatter, a "language which nobody understood." Edna's anger is speechless; her gesture all but impotent, for when a maid sidles into the room to clean up the glass she rediscovers her mistress's cast-off ring: "Edna held out her hand, and taking the ring, slipped it upon her finger" (53).

It is, in fact, only women of property like Madame Lebrun, the owner of the summer resort where the Pontelliers are staying, or artists like Mademoiselle Reisz who have the power of public expression. But Mademoiselle Reisz (who would seem, initially, to offer Edna another model for female self-hood) is surprisingly complicitous in limiting Edna's options. We find the strongest image of her complicity midway through the novel when she hands Edna the letter from Robert and asks Edna to read it while Mademoiselle Reisz plays heart-rending music. "Edna did not know when the Impromptu began or ended. She sat on the sofa corner reading Robert's letter by the fading light." As Edna reads Mademoiselle plays like a manic cupid, gliding "from the Chopin into the quivering lovenotes of Isolde's song, and back again to the Impromptu with its soulful and poignant longing" (64). The music grows fantastic; it fills the room, and Edna begins to sob "as she had wept one midnight at Grand Isle when strange, new voices awoke her." Now she hears one voice only and this voice has an oppressive material weight. "Mademoiselle reentered and lit a candle. Robert's letter was on the floor. She stopped and picked it up. It was crumpled and damp with tears. Mademoiselle smoothed the letter out, restored it to the envelope, and replaced it in the table drawer" (64). Like Mr. Pontellier's crumpled bank notes and small change, the letter has come to possess its own objectivity, its own material power. But if this is a letter that Mademoiselle Reisz can exchange for the pleasure of Edna's visit, it also represses her particular sonority. Mademoiselle Reisz's music is replaced by Robert's tune: "Robert's voice was not pretentious. It was musical and true. The voice, the notes, the whole refrain haunted her memory."

The speech of the masculine "other" becomes, for Edna Pontellier and the women in her society, an arena of self-loss and inner divisiveness. Madame

Lebrun's expressions, like Edna's, remain vestigial, enigmatic. Her sewing machine echoes the "clatter" of Edna's broken vase.

> "I have a letter somewhere," looking in the machine drawer and finding the letter in the bottom of the work-basket. "He says to tell you he will be in Vera Cruz the beginning of next month"—clatter, clatter!—"and if you still have the intention of joining him"—bang! clatter, clatter, bang!
> "Why didn't you tell me so before, mother? You know I wanted—" Clatter, clatter, clatter! (23)

If Madame Lebrun does not possess Alcée Arobin's power of definition, she does possess his power of interruption, and the noise of her sewing machine half-prepares us for her jibe at her younger son: "Really, this table is getting to be more and more like Bedlam every day, with everybody talking at once. Sometimes—I hope God will forgive me—but positively, sometimes I wish Victor would lose the power of speech" (42).

Translated into the language of the other, Edna's own story fails to materialize. But what might it have looked like? What is the rhythm and content of Edna's speech when she is neither speaking like her father or lover nor to him? First, we have seen that Chopin plays with the hiatus between the stories Edna inherits and what, in Edna, is heterogeneous to these stories, but is not bound by them. In *The Awakening* a story or framing device is frequently set against a "remainder" or supplement of meaning not encompassed within that frame. This remainder, this "excess" of meaning represents a *"différend"* which challenges the framing story's totalizing power, its explanatory validity. (Adorno puts this another way in his *Negative Dialectics:* "A matter of urgency to the concept would be what it fails to cover, what its abstractionist mechanism eliminates, what is not already a case of the concept.")[15] It is never a question of Edna's transcendence of local mythology, but rather of a negative and dialectical play between myth and that which resists mythic closure:

> "Of whom—of what are you thinking?" asked Adèle of her companion. . . .
> "Nothing," returned Mrs. Pontellier, with a start, adding at once: "How stupid! But it seems to me it is the reply we make instinctively to such a question. Let me see . . . I was really not conscious of thinking of anything; but perhaps I can retrace my thoughts."

> "Oh! never mind!" laughed Madame Ratignolle. "I am not quite so exacting. . . . It is really too hot to think, especially to think about thinking."

Clearly Adèle Ratignolle's dislike of "thinking" is normative in Edna's society and acts as near-absolute rule. But Edna ventures into areas of the mind that are not well mapped, into memories excluded from Adèle Ratignolle's cultural typology. And in thinking of "Nothing," something old and familiar emerges:

> "But for the fun of it," persisted Edna. "First of all, the sight of the water stretching so far away, those motionless sails against the blue sky, made a delicious picture that I just wanted to sit and look at. The hot wind beating in my face made me think—without any connection that I can trace—of a summer day in Kentucky, of a meadow that seemed as big as the ocean to the very little girl walking through the grass . . . She threw out her arms as if swimming when she walked, beating the tall grass as one strikes out in the water, Oh, I see the connection now!"
> "Where were you going that day in Kentucky, walking through the grass?"
> . . . .
> "Likely as not it was Sunday," she laughed, "and I was running away from prayers, from the Presbyterian service, read in a spirit of gloom by my father that chills me yet to think of." (17–18)

As practitioners of free association and students of Freud we may see little that is remarkable in Edna's response. But this is to underestimate the radical quality of her awareness, to dismiss its acrobatic integrity. It is as if Chopin is aware, as Edna is only naively, that the mind wants to go beyond itself, to go toward extremes, to test the accuracy of its own boundaries. Even as the social order demands a closing of ranks—a synthesis or yoking together of disparate ideas in such a way that their disparity grows invisible—the individual has the capacity to challenge her own syntactic boundaries. Edna's talks with Madame Ratignolle present us with a radical example of thought as disconnection, of Edna's capacity to separate ideas from one context to pursue them in another. This is the precondition for dialectic, the capacity for critique that Hegel defines in his *Phenomenology:*

> The activity of dissolution is the power and work of the *Understanding,* the most astonishing and mightiest of powers, or rather the absolute power.

The circle that remains self-enclosed and, like substance, holds its moments together, is an immediate relationship, one therefore which has nothing astonishing about it. But that an accident as such, detached from what circumscribes it, what is bound and is actual only in its context with others, should attain an existence of its own and a separate freedom—this is the tremendous power of the negative; it is the energy of thought, of the pure "I." [16]

What does this "power of the negative" mean for Edna, and what does it do for her? The images she conjures up seem aimless and accidental, beyond further synthesis, beyond dialectic. But this is precisely their virtue.

In escaping her father's old sermons, Edna strikes out into new physical space; she veers toward an arena of free feeling not designated by the paterfamilias. Similarly, in walking to the beach, Adèle Ratignolle and Edna have slipped momentarily outside the zone of paternal definition. "In some unaccountable way they had escaped from Robert," Chopin explains (15). The problem, of course, is that their escape is *literally* unaccountable, that outside the other's language they enter the arena of "Nothing," of a language which nobody speaks. And yet in talking with Adèle Ratignolle Edna begins to see connections she has not seen before; her thoughts become unsystematic—they go forward before going astray. "Thought," as Maire Jaanus Kurrik suggests, "must admit that it is not only cogency but play, that it is random and can go astray, and can only go forward because it can go astray. Thought has an unshielded and open aspect, which is unsystematic, and which traditional philosophy has repressed for fear of chaos." [17] She adds that thought must "abdicate its idea of hegemony and autarky, and practice a disenchantment of the concept, its transcendence," if it is to challenge its own preconceptions (221). Edna is not so self-conscious about the nature of her thinking, but as her mind plays over the past in a random and heterodox fashion, we can recognize in her thoughts the potential disenchantment of the concept that most binds her, the concept of an obsessive attachment to men, of a romantic and excessive bondage to father-like figures. The image of the beloved cavalry officer that Edna remembers is followed by a series of images or memories of men who have "haunted" Edna's imagination and "stirred" her senses. These broken images come to her not as images of love, but as sources of puzzlement, disaf-

fection, and wonder. Edna is open to thinking about the mystery of her affections; she notes in past amours an obsessive quality that demands perusal.

But something prevents Edna from thinking further, from becoming fully aware of the conditions which bind her. In this instance the conversation between Edna and Adèle is interrupted; as they converse on the beach their voices are blurred by "the sound of approaching voices. It was Robert, surrounded by a troop of children, searching for them" (20). Unable to continue their conversation, interrupted in the very moment when Edna had begun to feel "intoxicated with the sound of her own voice . . . the women at once rose and began to shake out their draperies and relax their muscles," and Madame Ratignolle begins to lean "draggingly" on Robert's arm as they walk home (20).

Thought should, perhaps, be "unshielded" and "open"; if thinking is to occur at all the mind must open itself to what is playful, random and unsystematic. But thought can only go so far afield before it ceases to be thought at all; as Hegel suggests, mind or spirit possesses its power only "by looking the negative in the face, and tarrying with it. This tarrying with the negative is the magical power that converts it into being" (19). And this "tarrying with" is something that occurs over time and in a community of speakers; it is not the product of an instant. What prevents Edna's "tarrying with" the negative is not her own inadequacy or some incapacity inherent in speech as such, but Edna's lack of a speech community that will encourage these new speculations, her lack of a group of fellow speakers who will encourage the growth of her thought and its translation into praxis. Though Madame Ratignolle is sympathetic and offers Edna both physical solace and a sympathetic ear, open conversation between them is rare; they speak different languages. "Edna had once told Madame Ratignolle that she would never sacrifice herself for her children, or for any one. Then had followed a rather heated argument." Edna finds herself speaking a language as impenetrable to others as the parrot's babble: "The two women did not appear to understand each other or to be talking the same language" (48). The pull of the libidinal speech-world Edna shares with Robert, then, is immense. (Robert, Chopin explains, "talked a good deal about himself. He was very young, and did not know any better. Mrs. Pontellier talked a little about herself for the same reason. Each was interested in what the other said" [6].) What emerges from their conversation is not a critique of society, however, but gay, utopian play, a pattern of speech in which Edna is once again caught within the semiotic, the bodily residues of her social code, and is not permitted the range of meaning or the control over culturally established symbols that Robert Lebrun is able to command.

Given the power that Robert (and the romance plot itself) exerts over Edna's ordinary patterns of associative thinking, it is worth noting that Chopin's novel ends in a more heterogeneous zone, with Edna's attention turned neither toward Robert nor her husband and children, but toward her own past:

> She looked into the distance, and the old terror flamed up for an instant, then sank again. Edna heard her father's voice and her sister Margaret's. She heard the barking of an old dog that was chained to the sycamore tree. The spurs of the cavalry officer clanged as he walked across the porch. There was the hum of bees, and the musky odor of pinks filled the air. (114)

This lyrical ending is as enigmatic as the novel's beginning; it might be read as a regression toward oral passivity: toward an infantile repudiation of the validity claims, the social responsibilities adult speech requires. But I would suggest this extralinguistic memory comes to Edna at the end of her life because it is in such a sequence of images, and not the language of Robert Lebrun, that Edna can find the most accessible path to her story—that even in death Edna is seeking (as she sought on the beach) a path of emancipation; she is seeking a register of language more her own.

At the end of the novel as Edna swims out to sea and tries to address Robert once more, she fails again; she finds herself trying to speak a language no one understands. " 'Good-by—because, I love you.' He did not know; he did not understand. He would never understand" (114). The story that Edna has told herself about her affection for Robert is inadequate. Close to death, she turns her mind toward the blurred edge of her womanhood, and the novel ends as it has begun, with a medley of distinct and disconnected voices. Here they represent a point of possible origin; they trace that moment in time when, still experiencing the world as a multitude of sounds, Edna's attention begins to shift from the plural voices of childhood toward the socially anticipated fulfillment of her sexual rhythms, toward the obsessive "clang" of the cavalryman's spurs. Just as the novel begins with the parrot's strange speech, with an order of speaking that satirizes and escapes from the epistemological confines of the heroine's world, so Edna's own awakening begins with and returns at her death to the rich and painful lure of desires that are still outside speech and beyond the social order. We must look again at this excluded order of meaning.

In *The Order of Things* Michel Foucault describes the discontinuity and disjunction he feels in perusing a list of incommensurable words or objects encountered in a story by Borges. Foucault experiences the variable terms of this list as "monstrous" and unnerving—Borges' reader is presented with an "order of things" which refuses orderly synthesis. This mode of disorder Foucault defines as a "heteroclite," a state in which "things are 'laid,' 'placed,' 'arranged' in sites so very different from one another that it is impossible . . . to define a *common locus* beneath them all" (xvii–xviii). In the opening sentences of *The Awakening* the parrot's speech presents us with a similar confusion. Here different syntactic and semantic units from different language systems mingle but refuse to cohere, and we find ourselves contemplating a potential "heterotopia," a discontinuous linguistic space in which the communicative function of language itself is called into question. These discontinuous linguistic spaces, these "heterotopias," are disturbing "because they secretly undermine language . . . because they shatter or tangle common names, because they destroy 'syntax' in advance, and not only the syntax with which we construct sentences but also that less apparent syntax which causes words and things . . . to 'hold together'" (xviii). The opening sentences of Chopin's text have a similar effect upon their reader.[18] In the discrepancies between different languages and the fractioned idioms these languages produce, we are presented with several categories of words and of things that cannot be held, simultaneously, in consciousness. The novel begins by challenging orthodoxy; it posits a world of saying in which ordinary ways of looking at things are called into question.

Chopin's novel pushes us from its beginning toward an arena of speech which asks us to become aware of disjunctions between the disorder of words and the social order, between our usual perceptions and the world these perceptions are designed to organize. The potent, possible syntheses between the self and its world — the syntheses the symbolic order insists we believe in — are challenged and in their place we discover a universe that is anomalous, asynchronic, confusing: a world not so much out of joint as out of its inhabitants' thought, a world outrageously unthinkable. Chopin insists that Mr. Pontellier's manner of organizing himself within this world is to ignore its arch nonsense, to cling to its objects for fetishistic support. He reads his newspaper, fingers his vest pocket: "There was a ten-dollar bill there. He did not know: perhaps he would return for the early dinner and perhaps he would not" (5). Within the novel an extraordinary register of speech is always opening up and then quietly shutting down — a closure which returns us, inevitably, to the circumscribed world of other people's objects and other people's speech, to a linear world in which the intervals of desire are stabilized by cultural symbols that determine the perimeters of self-knowledge.

Chopin makes us aware that the world her novel is designed to represent is itself a heteroclite; her text points to a discrepancy between one kind of social order and its possible others. "It is here," as Foucault says in *The Order of Things*, in the region where the heteroclite becomes visible,

> that a culture, imperceptibly deviating from the empirical orders prescribed for it by its primary codes, instituting an initial separation from them, causes them to lose their original transparency, relinquishes its immediate and invisible powers, frees itself sufficiently to discover that these orders are perhaps not the only possible ones or the best ones; this culture then finds itself faced with the stark fact that there exists, below the level of its spontaneous orders, things that are in themselves capable of being ordered, that belong to a certain unspoken order . . .   (xx)

To argue that Edna Pontellier commits suicide because she lacks a language, because of this "unspoken order," seems a cruel oversimplification of her character and of her material situation. And yet at the end of *The Awakening* we are, like Edna, subjected to a multiplication of points of view and can see no way to contain this multiplicity within the novel's heterosexist milieu. To argue that Edna lacks a language, then, is not only to say that culture has invaded her consciousness, has mortgaged her right to original speech, but that Edna's language is inadequate to her vital needs, that it is singular when it should be plural, masculine when it should be feminine, phantasmic when it should be open and dialectical. And what becomes clear by the novel's end is that Robert Lebrun has served as an iconic replacement for that which Edna cannot say; his name functions as a hieroglyph condensing Edna's complex desires — both those she has named and those which remain unnameable.

In *Powers of Horror* Julia Kristeva suggests that "phobia bears the marks of the frailty of the subject's signifying system," and Edna's love for Robert — although it is not phobic as such, reproduces this frailty as symptom; when Edna seeks nothing but the speech of her beloved, it makes her "signifying system" frail.[19] Edna Pontellier has no language to help her integrate and interrogate the diversity of her feelings; she experiences neither world nor signifying system capacious enough to accommodate her desires. But by the end of the novel these contradictory desires become noisy, impossible to repress. As Edna helps Adèle Ratignolle through a difficult childbirth the romantic interlude that Edna has shared with Robert becomes faint; it seems "unreal, and only half-remembered" (108), and once again language fails her. When Dr. Mandelet asks if she will go abroad to relax, Edna finds herself stumbling for words: " 'Perhaps — no, I am not going. I'm not going to be forced into doing things. I don't want to go abroad. I want to be let alone. Nobody has any right — except children, perhaps — and even then, it seems to me — or it did seem —' She felt that her speech was voicing the incoherency of her thoughts, and stopped abruptly" (109). After watching Adèle give birth and listening to her painful repetitions ("Think of the children, think of them"), Edna begins to re-experience the bodily sensations and feelings for her children that she has repressed; her extra-marital desires grow more tumultuous. Once more her sentences split with the weight of this conflict, and as Mandelet tries to put them together, as he offers to "talk of things you never have dreamt of talking about before," Edna refuses his kind and magian powers, just as, in childhood, she refused her father's chill summons to prayer. She gives herself, instead, to the "voice" of the sea, to that sibilance in which every name drowns. And her mind returns to what she can claim of her childhood, to the story she told Adèle Ratignolle on the hot summer beach.

Kristeva has suggested that we consider "the phobic person as a subject in want of metaphorical-ness" (37), and I have suggested that the same becomes true of a woman in love, a woman who becomes the subject of her culture's romantic fantasies. "Incapable of producing metaphors by means of signs alone," Kristeva argues,

> [this subject] produces them in the very material of drives—and it turns out that the only rhetoric of which he is capable is that of affect, and it is projected, as often as not, by means of *images*. It will then fall upon analysis to give back a memory, hence a language, to the unnamable and namable states of fear, while emphasizing the former, which make up what is more unapproachable in the unconscious. (37)

I am not suggesting that Edna is in need of a Freudian or even a Kristevan analysis. I am suggesting instead that we can locate the power of the novel's final images in Edna's desire "to give back a memory, hence a language," to that within her which remains nameless.

> There is a fact which our experience of speech does not permit us to deny, the fact that every discourse is cast in the direction of something which it seeks to seize hold of, that it is incomplete and open, somewhat as the visual field is partial, limited and extended by an horizon. How can we explain this almost visual property of speaking on the basis of this object closed in principle, shut up on itself in a self-sufficient totality, which is the system of *langue*?[20]

The "voice" of the sea Edna tries to embrace is more than a harbinger of death, more than a sign of dark and unfulfilled sexuality; the novel's final images frame and articulate Edna's incessant need for some other register of language, for a mode of speech that will express her unspoken, but not unspeakable needs.

Notes

1. Kate Chopin, *The Awakening,* ed. Margaret Culley (New York: Norton, 1976), p. 113. All further references will be cited in the text.
2. For readings of Edna that celebrate her sexual awakening, see, for example, Per Seyersted's emphasis on "Edna's slow birth as a sexual and authentic being" (153) in *Kate Chopin: A Critical Biography* (New York: Octagon, 1980), pp. 134–63, and Sandra M. Gilbert's excellent "The Second Coming of Aphrodite: Kate Chopin's Fan-

tasy of Desire" in *Kenyon Review* (Summer 1983), pp. 42–66. Gilbert's enthusiastic description of Edna as a "resurrected Venus . . . returning to Cyprus . . . a radiant symbol of the erotic liberation that turn-of-the-century women had begun to allow themselves to desire" (58, 62), endows Edna with an archetypal complicity in erotic myth that Chopin herself takes pains to critique. For a reading that is less passionate than Gilbert's but truer to the novel's sexual ambiguities, see Paula Treichler's "The Construction of Ambiguity in *The Awakening*: A Linguistic Analysis," in *Women and Language in Literature and Society,* ed. Sally McConnell-Ginet et al. (New York: Praeger, 1980), pp. 239–57.
3. Tony Tanner, *Adultery in the Novel: Contract and Transgression* (Baltimore: Johns Hopkins University Press, 1979), p. 4. All further references will be cited in the text.
4. For a similar view of Tanner's work and an extended critique of the ways in which critics have refused to see the difference between "transgression" and real social change, see Allon White's "Pigs and Pierrots: The Politics of Transgression in Modern Fiction" in *Raritan* (Summer 1982), pp. 51–70.
5. William Wordsworth, *The Prelude* in *Selected Poems and Prefaces: William Wordsworth,* ed. Jack Stillinger (Boston: Riverside, 1965), p. 193.
6. Michel Foucault, *The Order of Things: An Archaeology of the Human Sciences* (New York: Vintage, 1973), p. xviii. All further references will be cited in the text.
7. Gilbert argues that Robert's telling of these "wistful adult fairy tale[s]" (53) aids in reproducing a modern Aphrodite's birth from the foam—a birth in which Edna is "mystically and mythically revitalized." Gilbert imagines that Robert's words are without distorting power because she envisions Grand Isle as a woman's world, a colony situated "outside patriarchal culture, beyond the limits of the city where men make history. . . . Here power can flow from outside . . . from the timelessness . . . that is free of historical constraints" (51). The point of my essay is that these "historical constraints" invade Edna's fantasies of "timelessness" as insistently as they invade Mr. Pontellier's city life.
8. Jacques Lacan, *The Four Fundamental Concepts of Psycho-Analysis,* ed. Jacques-Alain Miller, trans.

Alan Sheridan (New York: Norton, 1978), p. 188. All further references will be cited in the text.

9. Edna is also associated with old print. Early in the novel Adèle Ratignolle "brought the pattern of drawers for Mrs. Pontellier to cut out, a marvel of construction, fashioned to enclose a baby's body so effectually that only two small eyes might look out from the garment, like an Eskimo's." This is a world where characters are cut to fit the language they speak, where Edna's manufacture of a pattern for her children's garments can be read as a parable for her condition within language: "Mrs. Pontellier's mind was quite at rest concerning the present material needs of her children . . . but she did not want to appear unamiable and uninterested, so she had brought forth newspapers which she spread upon the floor of the gallery, and under Madame Ratignolle's directions she had cut a pattern of the impervious garment" (10).

10. Julia Kristeva, "Interview-1974," trans. Claire Pajaczkowska, *m/f* (5/6 1981), p. 166.

11. Jean-François Lyotard, *Le différend* (Paris: Minuit, 1983), p. 30. All further references will be cited in the text. This translation is from Peter Dews' "The Letter and the Line: Discourse and Its Other in Lyotard," in *Diacritics* (Fall 1984), p. 49. See also in the same issue "Interview," trans. Georges Van Den Abbeele, pp. 16–21, and David Carroll's "Rephrasing the Political with Kant and Lyotard: From Aesthetic to Political Judgments," pp. 74–87.

12. See, for example, Margaret Culley's "Edna Pontellier: 'A Solitary Soul'" in her edition of *The Awakening*; Susan J. Rosowski's "The Novel of Awakening" in *The Voyage In: Fictions of Female Development*, ed. Elizabeth Abel, Marianne Hirsch, and Elizabeth Langland (Hanover: University Press of New England, 1983); Paula Treichler's "The Construction of Ambiguity in *The Awakening*: A Linguistic Analysis" in *Women and Language in Literature and Society*, ed. Sally McConnell-Ginet, Ruth Borker, and Nelly Furman (New York: Praeger, 1980); Anne Goodwyn Jones' "Kate Chopin: The Life Behind the Mask" in *Tomorrow Is Another Day: The Woman Writer in the South, 1859–1936* (Baton Rouge: Louisiana State University Press, 1981); and Sandra M. Gilbert's "The Second Coming of Aphrodite:

Kate Chopin's Fantasy of Desire," in *Kenyon Review* (Summer 1983), pp. 42–66.

13. Gilbert wants to discover a more definite, definable symbolic matrix than Chopin's novel provides. Still, her essay itself is a beautiful testimonial to the *"différend"* in Chopin's novel. Gilbert finds *The Awakening* prophetic, and argues that Chopin's novel calls out toward new paradigms: Edna "is journeying not just toward rebirth but toward a regenerative and revisionary genre, a genre that intends to propose new realities for women by providing new mythic paradigms through which women's lives can be understood" (59). But Gilbert argues that this transformation actually occurs as Edna swims "out of one kind of novel—the work of Eliotian or Flaubertian 'realism' she had previously inhabited—and into a new kind of work, a mythic/metaphysical romance that elaborates her distinctively female fantasy of paradisiacal fulfillment and therefore adumbrates much of the feminist modernism that was to come within a few decades" (52). In other words, Gilbert experiences the novel primarily through its *différend*, through the future discourse it calls toward. This may distort Gilbert's reading of Chopin, but it transforms her essay into a form of feminist myth-making that uplifts and inspires.

14. Cynthia Griffin Wolff, "Thanatos and Eros" in *The Awakening*, ed. Margaret Culley (New York: Norton, 1976), p. 208. All further references will be cited in the text.

15. Theodor W. Adorno, *Negative Dialectics*, trans. E. B. Ashton (New York: Continuum, 1983), p. 8.

16. G. W. F. Hegel, *Phenomenology of Spirit*, trans. A. V. Miller (London: Oxford University Press, 1977), pp. 18–19.

17. Maire Jaanus Kurrik, *Literature and Negation* (New York: Columbia University Press, 1979), p. 221. Kurrik's ideas have been useful throughout in helping me come to terms with Edna Pontellier's way of thinking. See also Adorno's *Negative Dialectics*, pp. 3–57.

18. I have focused on the opening sentences, but this sense of the "heteroclite" pervades Chopin's text. The most bizarre and recurrent instance of a set of characters who simultaneously inhabit Mr. Pontellier's world and live in some other, in-

commensurable realm is the pair of lovers and their surreal duenna:

> The lovers were just entering the grounds of the *pension*. They were leaning toward each other as the water-oaks bent from the sea. There was not a particle of earth beneath their feet. Their heads might have been turned upside-down, so absolutely did they tread upon blue ether. The lady in black, creeping behind them, looked a trifle paler and more jaded than usual. (22)

19. Julia Kristeva, *Powers of Horror: An Essay in Abjection*, trans. Leon S. Roudiez (New York: Columbia, 1982), p. 35. All further references will be cited in the text.
20. Lyotard, *Le différend*, p. 32. This translation is from Peter Dews' "The Letter and the Line: Discourse and Its Other in Lyotard," in *Diacritics* (Fall 1984), p. 41.

CHAPTER SEVEN

Historical Criticism II: Culture as Context

The Face of Nature we no more Survey
— Pope, *An Essay on Criticism*

The most notable trend in recent literary theory has been a turn to historical criticism. I stress the term "theory," for much critical practice, we should remember, has continued to be historical in the senses used in the first chapter of this book. Genetic studies that investigate an author's life and times to determine what that author might have meant in a given work continue to be produced in large numbers. But the recent turn toward history is not quite a return to genetic criticism. The newer historians, though reacting against the ahistorical thrust of much contemporary theory, are new precisely because they have absorbed many ideas from these ahistorical approaches.

The reaction was probably predictable. Ever since formalism challenged the then-dominant genetic criticism, the chief theoretical debates have been among competing forms of ahistorical, or even antihistorical, theories. Reader-response critics, for example, have usually been content to study the responses of contemporary readers. Mimetic critics — and often formalists are mimetic critics in this respect — have usually argued that literature imitates universal human nature and conveys timeless truths. Intertextual critics, especially those most influenced by structuralist thought, have generally pictured literature as a synchronic system of simultaneously present works. To be sure, none of these contexts, except perhaps formalism in its Anglo-American versions, is inherently ahistorical. Reception aesthetics, for example, traces reader responses over different historical periods. Mimesis can accommodate imitation of historically contingent as well as timeless conditions. And intertextual studies — Bakhtin's work comes to mind — can have a diachronic as well as a synchronic basis. Even so, the emphasis in all these contexts has been heavily ahistorical.

This is also true of poststructuralist criticism, which has occasionally been antihistorical as well. Deconstructive critics have often pushed formalist and structuralist arguments to their logical, or illogical, conclusions, pointing up irreducible tensions in the work or tracing the strands by which that work is woven into the larger text that is the only world man-the-signifier can know. In the process, they have strongly emphasized the ahistorical bent of these approaches. But deconstruction has also offered a more direct challenge to historical criticism. By calling into question the very concepts of origin, telos, and cause, deconstruction has threatened to deconstruct the historian's as well as the metaphysician's enterprise.

In sum, historical criticism has been decidedly on the margins of most theoretical debates in the last half-century, so much so that some historical critics have claimed that virtually all the critical controversies since the New Criticism are merely in-house squabbles among competing formalisms. Against this background, the call for a "return to history" is sometimes taken as a vindication of genetic criticism in its various forms. But the kinds of historical criticism that have moved to the center in recent theoretical discussions are not those that have simply rejected the ahistorical approaches. Among these newer historical criticisms one can identify a few loosely formed groups or "interpretive communities." Somewhat confusingly, the New Historicism is the name for one of these groups. Others call their own work "sociological poetics" or "cultural studies" or "cultural criticism." Much of this work has been influenced by Marxist thought, and Marxist critics who have in turn been influenced by structuralism, deconstruction, and postmodernism might also be included here among the poststructuralist historians. In addition, the turn to history can be seen in the work of many feminist critics and in the growing number of studies that focus on the issues of race, ethnicity, and postcolonialism.

This turn to history, then, includes a large and diverse group of critics. But they share several concerns, and often the things that unite them are the things they have taken over from formalism, structuralism, and poststructuralism. One of these is an emphasis on "textuality" and the problems of "representation." They agree that no text can offer a transparent window to historical fact. On the contrary, all texts must be scrutinized with formalist rigor and with a formalist's eye to the implications of even the smallest textual features. Further, many of the newer historians have accepted the poststructuralist deconstruction of the "self," the "individual," the "autonomous ego," which they associate with "liberal humanism," and they speak instead of the "subject," a social or linguistic construct. Most also accept the deconstruction of such long-standing oppositions as that between the literary and the non-literary, or that between high and popular culture, and they are inclined to collapse the disciplinary walls that are built on such oppositions. They agree with the genetic critics that we need to look at the historical causes of literary productions, but they would add that we need also to look at their historical consequences. And we need to look, too, they would say, at the "situatedness" of the historian; we need to be aware of how much of our present we carry into our investigations of the past. Most generally, and most importantly, the newer historians have absorbed the poststructuralists' skepticism toward any universalizing or totalizing claims, and they are adept at using the techniques of deconstruction to argue that nearly everything we may have thought was "natural" — from the superiority of Shakespeare's poetry to one's sexual or racial identity — is actually a social and historically contingent construction.

The New Historicism is a case in point. It's not clear how many people apply this label to themselves. Stephen Greenblatt, who is often cited as the leading New Historicist, prefers to call his work "cultural poetics," and a recent anthology of *The New Historicism* (Veeser) reveals several points of disagreement or differing emphases among figures like Greenblatt, Louis Montrose, Joel Feinman, and Catherine Gallagher, all critics associated with the movement. But the assumptions they share are numerous and important. Some of these can be traced to the influence of the French historian/philosopher/sociologist/"archeologist," Michel Foucault. Foucault's work is hard to classify because one of his goals was to erase or blur such classifications. His project was to examine the intricately structured power relations that obtain in a society at a given time, to show how that society constructs, defines, and thus controls its members. Most often, Foucault argues, society maintains control by making its constructed categories, say, of "crime" or "madness" or "sexuality," appear to be natural, things given rather than made, and so beyond question or change. Yet such constructs do change over time, as historical study can show us, thus leading us to suspect the "naturalness" of our own constructs. Nevertheless, in tracing the changes in power relations, Foucault is not claiming to offer a history that moves from origin to end, or from worse to better. Neither does he see power as a necessarily oppressive force from which we must be liberated or even from which we could be liberated, for Foucault is impressed by society's ability to absorb opposition and to maneuver those who would challenge existing power relations into actually supporting the status quo. In other words, Foucault often shows considerable respect — too much respect, his critics say — for the totalizing power of society. He is also keenly aware of the difficulties of seeing the past except through the lenses, the constructs, of the present. Yet these difficulties make the historian's task not less but more necessary, not an impossibility but the only possibility. If we can find no transcendent standpoint and no "natural," nonhistorical anchors for our key ideas ("madness" really means . . . "sexuality" truly is . . .), all we can do is conduct archeological expeditions, patiently constructing the genealogies of these ideas from the sedimented layers of the past. Our key ideas, in other words, have no essence; they have only a history.

Several of Foucault's interests can be seen in the work of Greenblatt and other New Historicists. Like Foucault, they think of history in terms of power relations and they are fascinated by the "circulation" of power within society. They also traverse traditional disciplinary boundaries, collapsing distinctions between the literary and the nonliterary, between the foreground and the background. And they are deeply suspicious of any appeals to "universal" truths or "natural" behavior. Greenblatt, who has worked chiefly with the English Renaissance, positions his "cultural poetics" between the two extremes of earlier kinds of literary history: on the one hand, studies that paint with a broad brush the main ideas of an "age" and then find those ideas directly reflected in the period's chief literary works and, on the other, highly specialized studies that turn every work into a political allegory. Instead, Greenblatt produces what anthropologists like Clifford Geertz have called "thick descriptions," linking literary works with contemporary cultural phenomena in sometimes startling ways — *King Lear* with a now-obscure attack on exorcism, for example. Like Foucault, Greenblatt has been chided by more politically committed critics for describing power relations as a mysterious and agentless totality. Other critics have complained that his work represents an abandonment of "literary" criticism, though it could equally be argued that it represents the extension of literary criticism to all aspects of culture. Either way, the question depends on a distinction of little concern to Greenblatt, for whom "literature" is simply a "part of the system of signs that constitutes a given culture."

Jerome McGann is another writer who has tried to steer criticism toward a more historical course. In several books and essays dealing mainly with the English Romantic poets, McGann has argued the need for a "sociological poetics" that will go beyond the formalist's ahistorical focus on the text but also beyond the genetic critic's focus on the author and even beyond the wider but still "literary" focus of traditional literary history. Only a social history, he asserts, can fully elucidate the poem's "network of social relations." Acknowledging a debt to Marxism, Russian Formalism, and the work of Bakhtin, McGann calls for a criticism that will explicate all the stages of a poem's "socializations," starting with the material conditions of its place and mode of publication and going on to trace not only its original reception but also the history of its reception over time. For our present responses "are clearly tied to this entire historical development, whether we are aware of it or not" (*Inflections* 54).

While both McGann's "sociological poetics" and Greenblatt's "cultural poetics" would considerably broaden the scope of literary study, neither includes all the diverse practices that cluster under the labels "Cultural Studies" or "Cultural Criticism." Here again one of the chief goals of those who accept these labels is to traverse disciplinary and departmental boundaries, so it's not surprising that they resist attempts to define and thus rebound them. Indeed, "traversing" and "resisting" are terms that figure prominently in the lexicon of Cultural Studies. If we try to shackle this Proteus by applying the traditional schema of sources, techniques, and ends, we can say that British Cultural Criticism begins with the work of Raymond Williams, Richard Hoggart, and E. P. Thompson in the 1950s and 1960s. This work, strongly influenced by Marxism, questioned the distinctions between "high" and popular culture and argued that working-class culture, generally misunderstood and undervalued, was a proper subject for serious study. While never abandoning this class-conscious and egalitarian origin, Cultural Studies in their British, American, and Continental forms have subsequently been heavily influenced by the same structuralist and poststructuralist ideas that have changed the intellectual landscape in many fields. They have also been heavily influenced by the competing voices that have put issues of gender, race, and ethnic identity on the agenda alongside or ahead of social class. So today the cultural critic will apply the techniques of poststructural criticism to any and all cultural phenomena from opera to sporting events, from classical drama to television shows, from museum exhibits to graffiti. Clearly "culture" in this context is defined expansively.

But while there is no limit to the objects of cultural study, cultural critics, despite their antidisciplinary stance, usually share similar goals. Above all, the end of their inquiry is to show what kind of "cultural work" the object under scrutiny has done, or is doing, or could be made to do. Like Foucault, the cultural critic is concerned with relations of power within society. But even more than the New Historicists, cultural critics are likely to stress the present implications of their studies and to see their own work, even when it's focused on the past, as an intervention into current political arrangements. Almost always that intervention is in opposition to existing power structures and designed to empower groups historically disadvantaged. Along these lines, the thrust of many recent studies of popular culture has been to point up the element of political "resistance" to be found not only in such phenomena as "skinhead" or "punk" groups but also in the ways the apparently passive audiences of mass-appeal entertainments convert these to their own purposes. Such studies often show the influence of the Italian Marxist Antonio Gramsci, who described the "hegemonic" power of the prevailing ideology, but who also stressed the possibilities of local or "micropolitical" opposition to this power, and of Bakhtin, whose idea of the "carnivalesque" emphasizes the oppositional role of popular culture.

This activist agenda figures in other distinguishing features of cultural criticism. For example, the urge to collapse distinctions between high and popular culture, between canonical and noncanonical literature, between one field of study and another, is motivated not only by skepticism about the ontological status of these distinctions but perhaps more by the belief that such distinctions serve to maintain the existing power relations in society. Similarly, cultural critics' objections to terms like "humanism" and "universal truth" rest not so much on epistemological grounds as on the fact that these terms have historically been used to privilege the views of one small group—white males of European descent, who have had the power to impress their own image on the "human" and the "universal." Hence the worry among cultural critics that they are themselves in danger of becoming a recognized discipline, or even an academic department, or that they may inadvertently establish a canonical countercanon. An institutionalized opposition is always something of an oxymoron.

Quite consistently, therefore, cultural critics have joined other poststructuralist historians in stressing the inquirer's need for self-awareness. As we attempt to investigate cultural phenomena across geographical, temporal, and class boundaries, we need to know what cultural baggage we carry with us and how we acquired it. One result of this emphasis has been a number of investigations into literary study itself as a cultural practice. What gets defined as "literature," what texts get assigned in schools and colleges, what kinds of topics get discussed in classes and in standard exams? And who decides the answers to these questions? In short, what social forces influence reading practices and what are the social consequences of these practices? Not surprisingly, feminist cultural critics have led the way in raising these questions, but they have been joined by many others who have been concerned to point out the economic and social class implications of literary study, especially as it has been organized in the schools.

In these and other ways, the Marxist influence in cultural criticism has remained strong, as it has in most of the newer historicisms. Although relatively few in these groups may call themselves simply "Marxist" ("cultural materialist" is a favored name among some British cultural critics), many acknowledge that Marxist ideas have shaped their thinking. But influences run in both directions, and Marxist critics have also had to confront the powerful challenges of formalism, structuralism, and poststructuralism. So we should include in this latest turn to history the work of writers like Terry Eagleton and Fredric Jameson, two leading Marxist critics who have appropriated many poststructuralist concepts. Both eschew simple dichotomies like base versus superstructure or form versus content, both use formalist and poststructuralist techniques to investigate the ideological implications of literary forms, and both find the relations between literary texts and their social contexts multidirectional and highly complex. Of the two, Jameson is the more difficult theorist. Indeed, some readers have complained that his absorption of other critical approaches has been so comprehensive and his account of social and literary relations so refined that his Marxism has been obscured. Nevertheless, Jameson has continued to insist that the Marxist view of history remains the unboundable "horizon" that bounds all other critical approaches.

In addition to these loosely defined groups and practices, the latest turn to history includes the work of a large number of unaffiliated or multiaffiliated critics who may disagree about much but who agree that literary studies must become more historical and more engaged with "real-world" problems. I include here the growing number of writers who have made issues of gender, race, and postcolonialism the focus of their work. This focus almost demands some kind of historical approach, and in recent years these approaches, too, have been strongly influenced by poststructuralist thought. Feminist critics, for example, have been quick to see the uses of poststructuralist analysis for deconstructing oppressive stereotypes and undermining patriarchal power. But feminist perspectives have in turn been subjected to the same kind of analysis by those who find some feminist work complicit in maintaining the dominant heterosexual ideology and by those who would assert the importance of race or class over gender as the crucial social determinant. And just as feminist criticism has questioned the "representation" of women in literary works, these other voices have critiqued the representation of homosexuals, African Americans, native Americans, and other colonized peoples, questioning not only the images that purport to represent these groups but also the authority of those who claim to speak as their representatives.

Such studies have often asked as well in what language these representatives should speak. In the context of theories that stress the decisive influence of language upon thought, this issue becomes central for colonized voices. Again following the pattern of feminists who questioned the adequacy of "patriarchal" language to represent them, minority and Third-World critics have examined both the problems and the subversive potentials entailed in adopting the colonizer's language. Most often, of course, that language has been English, which has been imposed not only on millions within the British Isles but on hundreds of millions around the globe. Given the intimate connections between language and culture, a merging of the poststructuralist emphasis on language with the historicist emphasis on culture has seemed inevitable.

The New Historicism, "sociological poetics," cultural criticism, revisionist Marxism, studies of race, gender, ethnicity, and postcolonialism, the social history of literary study—a mixed bag, and a shapeless one. Yet as different as these practices are, they all represent a turn to history, and the history they turn to is markedly different in many ways from the kinds of history explored in the opening chapter. What sets these newer practices apart, as we have seen, is the extent to which they reflect the assumptions and techniques of formal and poststructural criticism. In fact, we might use "poststructuralist history" as a convenient cover term for this entire context.

The complaint, then, that there is little new in the newer histories is easily answered. But the charge that what's new isn't historical may have more substance. This charge has been leveled both by undeconstructed Marxists and by unreconstructed geneticists. The latter, for example, have continued to object to the extreme historical relativism that would see readers as largely limited to their own cultural horizons. The virtues of self-awareness and self-reflexivity, they argue, can become vices if the recognition of one's supposedly "inescapable" biases becomes an excuse not to try to escape them. More seriously, if we are really in thrall to our own perspective, we can't really "do" history at all. Finding this position epistemologically dubious as well as self-defeating, genetic critics continue to claim that with care and effort we can reconstruct with reasonable accuracy the perspectives of people who lived in other times and places. Yet the model these critics invoke of an independent subject observing an independent, but knowable, object is a model that has been under heavy attack in virtually all critical contexts from reader-response criticism to deconstruction.

From another direction, some Marxists have objected to New Historical practice on the grounds that its "thick descriptions" can be historically disabling in two ways. On the one hand, disclosure of surprising links between the most disparate elements in a society (e.g., between witchcraft and "high" art) may imply power relationships at once so intricate and so agentless as to render futile any attempts to change them. On the other hand, these "thick descriptions" are like snapshots or stills that present a detailed picture of a society at a point in time but that offer no way to move from one time frame to another. In short, the method is synchronic rather than diachronic. Having no way to explain changes from one period to another, it is not really "historical" at all, certainly not in any Marxist sense of the term. In both cases the problem is an inability to establish a cause-and-effect relationship. Yet while it is difficult to think of doing history without some sense of causality, it is also difficult to think of any causal links that poststructural analysis couldn't dissolve.

These and similar objections point to a basic problem—the very assumptions and techniques that define poststructuralist history also make it difficult to do poststructuralist history. This raises the suspicion that poststructuralist history may be not a new element but a highly unstable compound in which historicist and sometimes interventionist elements mix incompletely with formal and deconstructive elements. To change the metaphor, many of the practices in this context appear to involve a two-stage operation in which deconstructive analysis is brought in for the ground-clearing demolition work, then moved safely off-site when the reconstruction work begins.

If, for example, you want to open the "canon" to previously marginalized works, you will find it useful to deconstruct the binary opposition of center and margin and to subject the process of canon formation to a demystifying analysis that will show all claims for literary value to be historically contingent. But these procedures will make it equally difficult to justify any alternative reading lists. If you want to dissolve the limiting stereotypes of, say, the "feminine," or the "African American," deconstruction and historical genealogy will be effective solvents. But if you then want to reconstruct the "feminine" or the "African American" as a characteristic form of writing or as a site for exposing and opposing oppression, it's not clear how your reconstruction will be able to resist these same solvents. If your task is to decenter the bourgeois "individual" of capitalism, or the autonomous "ego" of ego psychology, or the independent "self" of liberal humanism, here again deconstruction and Foucauldian archeology will be useful tools. But in a society populated entirely by socially constructed "subject formations in transit," it's not apparent where you will be able to fix the responsibility for anyone's actions. In the same way, the need of subaltern groups to form strong bonds of self-recognition and group identity finds ambiguous aid from poststructuralist analysis. Though such analysis will delegitimize the claims of any group currently holding power, it also threatens to delegitimize any proposed substitutions, undercut any "essentialist" definitions around which oppositional groups might unite, and fracture any basis for solidarity. Where in such a world will socially (de)constructed subjects find the "justice" that is their goal?

Many of the internal stresses in this amalgam I have labeled poststructuralist history center on the embattled term "representation." The fact that "representation" is a key word both for poststructuralists and for most of the newer historians obscures the point that it means something rather different in each context. For poststructuralists, as we have seen, "representation" is primarily a linguistic and epistemological problem. Working from the model of structural linguistics, they argue that signifiers inevitably slide, meaning is always deferred, and true "representation" ever eludes us. For poststructuralist historians, who focus on power relations in society and on issues of class, gender, and race, "representation" is also the central issue. More exactly, subaltern groups of all types have echoed the feminists' complaint that the main problem is "misrepresentation." As Edward Said has put it, the task of the "oppositional" critic is to understand and ultimately to change the "ideological power of misrepresentation." Such a critic must expose those works that misrepresent women or gays or people of color and laud those works that tell it like it is, or was. "Oppositional" critics, then, have a considerable stake in the possibility of accurate representation, and, indeed, they will often value highly works of "social realism" that purport to offer a direct mimesis of social conditions. In short, for the oppositional critic, misrepresentation is largely a result, as well as a cause, of maldistributed power in society. For the poststructuralist, it is an inherent condition of human language. Any group whose goal is the undistorted self-representation of all groups will find an uncomfortable ally in a theory that rules out the possibility of undistorted representation. And since all critics who claim to be "historical," whether oppositional or not, have a similar stake in the possibility of accurate representation, "poststructuralist" history is necessarily a highly problematic concept.

Once again, then, we find that our context consists of a cluster of critical practices marked by apparently inherent and irreducible tensions. This will come as no surprise to those who have absorbed the lessons of deconstruction, and despite much talk about the blindness that enables insight, many poststructuralist historians are keenly aware of the tensions within their own work. At the same time, they are unwilling to abandon either the "worldly" thrust of their history or the textual thrust of poststructural analysis. Whether or not they think of themselves as "oppositional" critics, they agree on the two chief points that are the source of these tensions: literary study must become more historical, and historical study must become more poststructural.

Certainly they agree that the sociohistorical connections between the text and the world, the sense of a text as the product of social causes as well as the producer of social effects, has been too much neglected in literary study. For these critics, the formal concentration on the isolated text, the intertextual focus on literary relations, and the poststructural emphasis on the linguistically constructed universe are merely progressively larger cells in the prisonhouse of language. Yet given the right twist, each of these contexts offers useful insights for those who would see the literary work in its cultural contexts. Such critics will remind us that Derrida's famous remark, "there is nothing outside the text," though often seen as isolating the text from the world, could also be seen as an invitation to read the whole world as text and so open all aspects of culture to poststructuralist "literary" analysis.

Therein lies the promise, and the problem. As we have seen, the analytical strategies of poststructural criticism can indeed open up cultural issues in exciting and disturbing ways. They are especially effective for dismantling foundationalist and essentialist arguments, for demolishing totalizing claims, for deconstructing ideologies, for delegitimizing power, and generally for demonstrating that nearly everything called universal, timeless, and natural is really local, historically contingent, and socially constructed. So poststructuralist history, perhaps more than most kinds of historical study, offers to free us from the past. But as we have also seen, poststructuralist analysis constantly threatens to subvert any historical project, to deconstruct any political agenda, and to reenclose any inquiry in the endless loop of sliding signifiers. The challenge, then, as in our other contexts, is to harness the energy in these tensions and to channel it to productive uses. The burgeoning number of studies in this context indicates that, at the moment, this energy is considerable.

Suggestions for Further Reading

For the New Historicism, Michel Foucault's work, represented by Paul Rabinow, ed., *The Foucault Reader* (1984), is an important influence. Stephen Greenblatt, *Shakespearean Negotiations: The Circulation of Social Energy in Renaissance England* (1988), and Catherine Gallager, *The Industrial Reformation of English Fiction: Social Discourse and Narrative Form, 1832–1867* (1988), are two examples of New Historical practice. H. Aram Veeser, ed., *The New Historicism* (1989) contains a few essays by these and other writers illustrating the New Historicism along with several essays critiquing it. Another useful collection is Jeffrey N. Cox and Larry J. Reynolds, eds., *New Historical Literary Study* (1993). Brook Thomas, *The New Historicism and Other Old-Fashioned Topics* (1991), is a series of essays probing the movement's key concepts. Jerome J. McGann's work is represented by *The Beauty of Inflections: Literary Investigations in Historical Method and Theory* (1985).

Three founding texts of British cultural studies are Richard Hoggart, *The Uses of Literacy: Changing Patterns in English Mass Culture* (1958); Raymond Williams, *The Long Revolution* (1961); and E. P. Thompson, *The Making of the English Working Class* (1963). Contemporary "cultural materialism" is illustrated in Alan Sinfield, *Literature, Politics, and Culture in Postwar Britain* (1989), and Jonathan Dollimore and Alan Sinfield, eds., *Political Shakespeare: New Essays in Cultural Materialism* (1985). The diverse practices of contemporary cultural studies are displayed in Lawrence Grossberg, et al., eds., *Cultural Studies* (1992), which prints 40 essays by cultural critics from most parts of the English-speaking world. John Story, ed., *What Is Cultural Studies? A Reader* (1996), reprints 22 essays that offer to define, rather than to illustrate, the aims of cultural studies. Patrick Brantlinger, *Crusoe's Footprints: Cultural Studies in Britain and America* (1990), is a sympathetic but probing analysis of the various movements within cultural studies. See also Michael Berube, *Public Access: Literary Theory and American Cultural Politics* (1994).

Terry Eagleton, *Criticism and Ideology: A Study in Marxist Literary Theory* (1978), and Fredric Jameson, *The Political Unconscious: Narrative as a Socially Symbolic Act* (1981), are representative of the work of these two prolific authors. Jameson's ideas receive a helpful exposition in William C. Dowling, *Jameson, Althusser, Marx: An Introduction to "The Political Unconscious"* (1984). More general studies of Marxist thought and its relation to contemporary literary theory are Michael Ryan, *Marxism and Deconstruction* (1982); Martin Jay, *Marxism and Totality* (1984); and John Frow, *Marxism and Literary History* (1986). Eagleton's *Ideology* (1991) is a book-length examination of this key concept. Chris Bullock and David Peck, eds., *A Guide to Marxist Literary Criticism* (1980), is a useful bibliography. Terry Eagleton and Drew Milne, eds., *Marxist Literary Theory: A Reader* (1996) is a collection of representative essays from Marx to the present.

The subversive possibilities of taking over or "deterritorializing" the colonizer's language are explored in studies like Gilles Deleuze and Felix Guattari, *Kafka: Toward a Minor Literature* (1975), and Henry Louis Gates, Jr., *The Signifying Monkey: A Theory of Afro-American Literary Criticism* (1988). The concerns of feminist, Third-World, and poststructuralist criticism intersect in the work of Gayatri Spivak, *In Other Worlds: Essays in Cultural Politics* (1987). Edward Said, *The World, the Text, and the Critic* (1983), calls for a "worldly" criticism that will emphasize the text's, and the critic's, interaction with history and society. Issues of postcolonial literature and criticism are treated in Bill Ashcroft, Gareth Griffiths, and Helen Tiffin, *The Empire Writes Back* (1989), and in Padmini Mongia, ed., *Contemporary Postcolonial Theory: A Reader* (1996).

Jane Tomkins, *Sensational Designs* (1985), Russell Reising, *The Unusable Past* (1986), and John Guillory, *Cultural Capital* (1993), discuss questions of canon formation. Literary study as an institutional practice is viewed from an American perspective in Gerald Graff, *Professing Literature* (1987), and from a British perspective in Chris Baldick, *The Social Mission of English Criticism, 1848–1932* (1983); Ian Hunter, *Culture and Government* (1988); and Brian Doyle, *English and Englishness* (1989).

THEORY

Literature and History

Terry Eagleton

In the first chapter of his Marxism and Literary Criticism, *Terry Eagleton asserts that critical explanation should mean grasping literary forms, styles, and meaning "as products of a particular history." In opposition, then, to those critics who claim that great literature transcends the circumstances of its creation, the Marxist critic will stress its ties to those circumstances. The result will be a historical criticism, but one very different from the author-centered, intentionalist criticism we saw in the first chapter. From the Marxist perspective, authors are likely to be profoundly unaware of the true significance of their work, for they generally lack the "revolutionary understanding of history" that permits the Marxist critic to explain the literary work's relationship to the "ideology" of its age. Eagleton defines ideology here as "the way men live out their roles in class-society, the values, ideas and images which tie them to their social functions and so prevent them from having a true knowledge of society as a whole." Ideology, in this sense (see Eagleton's* Ideology *[1991] for a fuller discussion of this key term), is something like "false consciousness," and Eagleton stresses his point that the literary work's relation to the ideology of its age is likely to be much more complicated than the "vulgar Marxist" will generally allow, neither simply supporting that ideology nor directly challenging it. A truly "scientific" criticism, Eagleton claims, will "seek to explain the literary work in terms of the ideological structure of which it is a part, yet which it transforms in its art."*

Marx, Engels and Criticism

If Karl Marx and Frederick Engels are better known for their political and economic rather than literary writings, this is not in the least because they regarded literature as insignificant. It is true, as Leon Trotsky remarked in *Literature and Revolution* (1924), that "there are many people in this world who think as revolutionists and feel as philistines"; but Marx and Engels were not of this number. The writings of Karl Marx, himself the youthful author of lyric poetry, a fragment of verse-drama and an unfinished comic novel much influenced by Laurence Sterne, are laced with literary concepts and allusions; he wrote a sizeable unpublished manuscript on art and religion, and planned a journal of dramatic criticism, a full-length study of Balzac and a treatise on aesthetics. Art and literature were part of the very air Marx breathed, as a formidably cultured German intellectual in the great classical tradition of his society. His acquaintance with literature, from Sophocles to the Spanish novel, Lucretius to potboiling English fiction, was staggering in its scope; the German workers' circle he founded in Brussels devoted an evening a week to discussing the arts, and Marx himself was an inveterate theatre-goer, declaimer of poetry, devourer of every species of literary art from Augustan prose to industrial ballads. He described his own works in a letter to Engels as forming an "artistic whole," and was scrupulously sensitive to questions of literary style, not least his own; his very first pieces of journalism argued for freedom of artistic expression. Moreover, the pressure of aesthetic concepts can be detected behind some of the most crucial categories of economic thought he employs in his mature work.[1]

Even so, Marx and Engels had rather more important tasks on their hands than the formation of a complete aesthetic theory. Their comments on art and literature are scattered and fragmentary, glancing allusions rather than developed positions.[2] This is one reason why Marxist criticism involves more than merely restating cases set out by the "sociology of literature." The sociology of literature concerns itself chiefly with what might be called the means of literary production, distribution and exchange in a particular society—how books are published, the social composition of their authors and audiences, levels of literacy, the social determinants of "taste." It

also examines literary texts for their "sociological" relevance, raiding literary works to abstract from them themes of interest to the social historian. There has been some excellent work in this field,[3] and it forms one aspect of Marxist criticism as a whole; but taken by itself it is neither particularly Marxist nor particularly critical. It is, indeed, for the most part a suitably tamed, degutted version of Marxist criticism, appropriate for Western consumption.

Marxist criticism is not merely a "sociology of literature," concerned with how novels get published and whether they mention the working class. Its aim is to *explain* the literary work more fully; and this means a sensitive attention to its forms, styles and meanings.[4] But it also means grasping those forms, styles and meanings as the products of a particular history. The painter Henri Matisse once remarked that all art bears the imprint of its historical epoch, but that great art is that in which this imprint is most deeply marked. Most students of literature are taught otherwise: the greatest art is that which timelessly transcends its historical conditions. Marxist criticism has much to say on this issue, but the "historical" analysis of literature did not of course begin with Marxism. Many thinkers before Marx had tried to account for literary works in terms of the history which produced them;[5] and one of these, the German idealist philosopher G. W. F. Hegel, had a profound influence on Marx's own aesthetic thought. The originality of Marxist criticism, then, lies not in its historical approach to literature, but in its revolutionary understanding of history itself.

Base and Superstructure

The seeds of that revolutionary understanding are planted in a famous passage in Marx and Engels's *The German Ideology* (1845–6):

> The production of ideas, concepts and consciousness is first of all directly interwoven with the material intercourse of man, the language of real life. Conceiving, thinking, the spiritual intercourse of men, appear here as the direct efflux of men's material behaviour . . . we do not proceed from what men say, imagine, conceive, nor from men as described, thought of, imagined, conceived, in order to arrive at corporeal man; rather we proceed from the really active man . . . Consciousness does not determine life: life determines consciousness.

A fuller statement of what this means can be found in the Preface to *A Contribution to the Critique of Political Economy* (1859):

> In the social production of their life, men enter into definite relations that are indispensable and independent of their will, *relations of production* which correspond to a definite stage of development of their material productive *forces.* The sum total of these relations of production constitutes the economic structure of society, the real foundation, on which rises a legal and political superstructure and to which correspond definite forms of social consciousness. The mode of production of material life conditions the social, political and intellectual life process in general. It is not the consciousness of men that determines their being, but on the contrary, their social being that determines their consciousness.

The social relations between men, in other words, are bound up with the way they produce their material life. Certain "productive forces"—say, the organisation of labour in the middle ages—involve the social relations of villein to lord we know as feudalism. At a later stage, the development of new modes of productive organisation is based on a changed set of social relations—this time between the capitalist class who owns those means of production, and the proletarian class whose labour-power the capitalist buys for profit. Taken together, these "forces" and "relations" of production form what Marx calls "the economic structure of society," or what is more commonly known by Marxism as the economic "base" or "infrastructure." From this economic base, in every period, emerges a "superstructure"—certain forms of law and politics, a certain kind of state, whose essential function is to legitimate the power of the social class which owns the means of economic production. But the superstructure contains more than this: it also consists of certain "definite forms of social consciousness" (political, religious, ethical, aesthetic and so on), which is what Marxism designates as *ideology.* The function of ideology, also, is to legitimate the power of the ruling class in society; in the last analysis, the dominant ideas of a society are the ideas of its ruling class.[6]

Art, then, is for Marxism part of the "superstructure" of society. It is (with qualifications we shall make later) part of a society's ideology—an element in that complex structure of social perception which ensures that the situation in which one social class has power over the others is either seen by most members of the society as "natural," or not seen at all. To understand literature, then, means understanding the total social process of which it is part. As the Russian Marxist critic George Plekhanov put it: "The social mentality of an age is conditioned by that age's social relations. This is nowhere quite as evident as in the history of art and literature."[7] Literary works are not mysteriously inspired, or explicable simply in terms of their author's psychology. They are forms of perception, particular ways of seeing the world; and as such they have a relation to that dominant way of seeing the world which is the "social mentality" or ideology of an age. That ideology, in turn, is the product of the concrete social relations into which men enter at a particular time and place; it is the way those class-relations are experienced, legitimized and perpetuated. Moreover, men are not free to choose their social relations; they are constrained into them by material necessity—by the nature and stage of development of their mode of economic production.

To understand *King Lear, The Dunciad* or *Ulysses* is therefore to do more than interpret their symbolism, study their literary history and add footnotes about sociological facts which enter into them. It is first of all to understand the complex, indirect relations between those works and the ideological worlds they inhabit—relations which emerge not just in "themes" and "preoccupations," but in style, rhythm, image, quality and (as we shall see later) *form.* But we do not understand ideology either unless we grasp the part it plays in the society as a whole—how it consists of a definite, historically relative structure of perception which underpins the power of a particular social class. This is not an easy task, since an ideology is never a simple reflection of a ruling class's ideas; on the contrary, it is always a complex phenomenon, which may incorporate conflicting, even contradictory, views of the world. To understand an ideology, we must analyze the precise relations between different classes in a society; and to do that means grasping where those classes stand in relation to the mode of production.

All this may seem a tall order to the student of literature who thought he was merely required to discuss plot and characterization. It may seem a confusion of literary criticism with disciplines like politics and economics which ought to be kept separate. But it is, nonetheless, essential for the fullest explanation of any work of literature. Take, for example, the great Placido Gulf scene in Conrad's *Nostromo*. To evaluate the fine artistic force of this episode, as Decoud and Nostromo are isolated in utter darkness on the slowly sinking lighter, involves us in subtly placing the scene within the imaginative vision of the novel as a whole. The radical pessimism of that vision (and to grasp it fully we must, of course, relate *Nostromo* to the rest of Conrad's fiction) cannot simply be accounted for in terms of "psychological" factors in Conrad himself; for individual psychology is also a *social* product. The pessimism of Conrad's world view is rather a unique transformation into art of an ideological pessimism rife in his period—a sense of history as futile and cyclical, of individuals as impenetrable and solitary, of human values as relativistic and irrational, which marks a drastic crisis in the ideology of the Western bourgeois class to which Conrad allied himself. There were good reasons for that ideological crisis, in the history of imperialist capitalism throughout this period. Conrad did not, of course, merely anonymously reflect that history in his fiction; every writer is individually placed in society, responding to a general history from his own particular standpoint, making sense of it in his own concrete terms. But it is not difficult to see how Conrad's personal standing, as an "aristocratic" Polish exile deeply committed to English conservatism, intensified for him the crisis of English bourgeois ideology.[8]

It is also possible to see in these terms why that scene in the Placido Gulf should be artistically fine. To write well is more than a matter of "style"; it also means having at one's disposal an ideological perspective which can penetrate to the realities of men's experience in a certain situation. This is certainly what the Placido Gulf scene does; and it can do it, not just because its author happens to have an excellent prose-style, but because his historical situation allows him access to such insights. Whether those insights are in political terms "progressive" or "reactionary" (Conrad's are certainly the latter) is not the point—anymore than it is to the point that most of the agreed major writers of the twentieth century—Yeats, Eliot, Pound, Lawrence—are political conservatives who each had truck with fascism. Marxist criticism, rather than apologising for the fact, explains it—sees that, in the absence of genuinely revolutionary art, only a radical conservatism, hostile like Marxism to the withered values of liberal

bourgeois society, could produce the most significant literature.

Literature and Superstructure

It would be a mistake to imply that Marxist criticism moves mechanically from "text" to "ideology" to "social relations" to "productive forces." It is concerned, rather, with the *unity* of these "levels" of society. Literature may be part of the superstructure, but it is not merely the passive reflection of the economic base. Engels makes this clear, in a letter to Joseph Bloch in 1890:

> According to the materialist conception of history, the determining element in history is *ultimately* the production and reproduction in real life. More than this neither Marx nor I have ever asserted. If therefore somebody twists this into the statement that the economic element is the *only* determining one, he transforms it into a meaningless, abstract and absurd phrase. The economic situation is the basis, but the various elements of the superstructure—political forms of the class struggle and its consequences, constitutions established by the victorious class after a successful battle, etc.—forms of law—and then even the reflexes of all these actual struggles in the brains of the combatants: political, legal, and philosophical theories, religious ideas and their further development into systems of dogma—also exercise their influence upon the course of the historical struggles and in many cases preponderate in determining their *form*.

Engels wants to deny that there is any mechanical, one-to-one correspondence between base and superstructure; elements of the superstructure constantly react back upon and influence the economic base. The materialist theory of history denies that art can *in itself* change the course of history; but it insists that art can be an active element in such change. Indeed, when Marx came to consider the relation between base and superstructure, it was art which he selected as an instance of the complexity and indirectness of that relationship:

> In the case of the arts, it is well known that certain periods of their flowering are out of all proportion to the general development of society, hence also to the material foundation, the skeletal structure, as it were, of its organisation. For example, the Greeks compared to the moderns or also Shakespeare. It is even recognised that certain forms of art, e.g. the epic, can no longer be produced in their world

epoch-making, classical stature as soon as the production of art, as such, begins; that is, that certain significant forms within the realm of the arts are possible only at an undeveloped stage of artistic development. If this is the case with the relation between different kinds of art within the realm of art, it is already less puzzling that it is the case in the relation of the entire realm to the general development of society. The difficulty consists only in the general formulation of these contradictions. As soon as they have been specified, they are already clarified.[9]

Marx is considering here what he calls "the unequal relationship of the development of material production . . . to artistic production." It does not follow that the greatest artistic achievements depend upon the highest development of the productive forces, as the example of the Greeks, who produced major art in an economically undeveloped society, clearly evidences. Certain major artistic forms like the epic are only *possible* in an undeveloped society. Why then, Marx goes on to ask, do we still respond to such forms, given our historical distance from them?

> But the difficulty lies not in understanding that the Greek arts and epic are bound up with certain forms of social development. The difficulty is that they still afford us artistic pleasure and that in a certain respect they count as a norm and as an unattainable model.

Why does Greek art still give us aesthetic pleasure? The answer which Marx goes on to provide has been universally lambasted by unsympathetic commentators as lamely inept:

> A man cannot become a child again, or he becomes childish. But does he not find joy in the child's naiveté, and must he himself not strive to reproduce its truth at a higher stage? Does not the true character of each epoch come alive in the nature of its children? Why should not the historic childhood of humanity, its most beautiful unfolding, as a stage never to return, exercise an eternal charm? There are unruly children and precocious children. Many of the old peoples belong in this category. The Greeks were normal children. The charm of their art for us is not in contradiction to the undeveloped stage of society on which it grew. [It] is its result, rather, and is inextricably bound up, rather, with the fact that the unripe social conditions under which it arose, and could alone rise, can never return.

So our liking for Greek art is a nostalgic lapse back into childhood—a piece of unmaterialistic sentimentalism which hostile critics have gladly pounced on. But the passage can only be treated thus if it is rudely ripped from the context to which it belongs—the draft manuscripts of 1857, known today as the *Grundrisse*. Once returned to that context, the meaning becomes instantly apparent. The Greeks, Marx is arguing, were able to produce major art not *in spite of* but *because of* the undeveloped state of their society. In ancient societies, which have not yet undergone the fragmenting "division of labour" known to capitalism, the overwhelming of "quality" by "quantity" which results from commodity-production and the restless, continual development of the productive forces, a certain "measure" or harmony can be achieved between man and Nature—a harmony precisely dependent upon the *limited* nature of Greek society. The "childlike" world of the Greeks is attractive because it thrives within certain measured limits—measures and limits which are brutally overridden by bourgeois society in its limitless demand to produce and consume. Historically, it is essential that this constricted society should be broken up as the productive forces expand beyond its frontiers; but when Marx speaks of "striv[ing] to reproduce its truth at a higher stage," he is clearly speaking of the communist society of the future, where unlimited resources will serve an unlimitedly developing man.[10]

Two questions, then, emerge from Marx's formulations in the *Grundrisse*. The first concerns the relation between "base" and "superstructure"; the second concerns our own relation in the present with past art. To take the second question first: how can it be that we moderns still find aesthetic appeal in the cultural products of past, vastly different societies? In a sense, the answer Marx gives is no different from the answer to the question: How is it that we moderns still respond to the exploits of, say, Spartacus? We respond to Spartacus or Greek sculpture because our own history links us to those ancient societies; we find in them an undeveloped phase of the forces which condition us. Moreover, we find in those ancient societies a primitive image of "measure" between man and Nature which capitalist society necessarily destroys, and which socialist society can reproduce at an incomparably higher level. We ought, in other words, to think of "history" in wider terms than our own contemporary history. To ask how Dickens relates to history is not just to ask how he relates to Victorian England, for that society was itself the product of a long history which includes men like Shakespeare and Milton. It is a curiously narrowed view of history which defines it merely as the "contemporary moment" and relegates all else to the "universal." One answer to the problem of past and present is suggested by Bertolt Brecht, who argues that "we need to develop the historical sense . . . into a real sensual delight. When our theatres perform plays of other periods they like to annihilate distance, fill in the gap, gloss over the differences. But what comes then of our delight in comparisons, in distance, in dissimilarity—which is at the same time a delight in what is close and proper to ourselves?"11

The other problem posed by the *Grundrisse* is the relation between base and superstructure. Marx is clear that these two aspects of society do not form a *symmetrical* relationship, dancing a harmonious minuet hand-in-hand throughout history. Each element of a society's superstructure—art, law, politics, religion—has its own tempo of development, its own internal evolution, which is not reducible to a mere expression of the class struggle or the state of the economy. Art, as Trotsky comments, has "a very high degree of autonomy"; it is not tied in any simple one-to-one way to the mode of production. And yet Marxism claims too that, in the last analysis, art is determined by that mode of production. How are we to explain this apparent discrepancy?

Let us take a concrete literary example. A "vulgar Marxist" case about T. S. Eliot's *The Waste Land* might be that the poem is directly determined by ideological and economic factors—by the spiritual emptiness and exhaustion of bourgeois ideology which springs from that crisis of imperialist capitalism known as the First World War. This is to explain the poem as an immediate "reflection" of those conditions; but it clearly fails to take into account a whole series of "levels" which "mediate" between the text itself and capitalist economy. It says nothing, for instance, about the social situation of Eliot himself—a writer living an ambiguous relationship with English society, as an "aristocratic" American expatriate who became a glorified City clerk and yet identified deeply with the conservative-traditionalist, rather than bourgeois-commercialist, elements of English ideology. It says nothing about that ideology's more general forms—nothing of its structure, content, in-

ternal complexity, and how all these are produced by the extremely complex class-relations of English society at the time. It is silent about the form and language of *The Waste Land*—about why Eliot, despite his extreme political conservatism, was an *avant-garde* poet who selected certain "progressive" experimental techniques from the history of literary forms available to him, and on what ideological basis he did this. We learn nothing from this approach about the social conditions which gave rise at the time to certain forms of "spirituality," part-Christian, part-Buddhist, which the poem draws on; or of what role a certain kind of bourgeois anthropology (Fraser) and bourgeois philosophy (F. H. Bradley's idealism) used by the poem fulfilled in the ideological formation of the period. We are unilluminated about Eliot's social position as an artist, part of a self-consciously erudite, experimental élite with particular modes of publication (the small press, the little magazine) at their disposal; or about the kind of audience which that implied, and its effect on the poem's style and devices. We remain ignorant about the relation between the poem and the aesthetic theories associated with it—of what role that aesthetic plays in the ideology of the time, and how it shapes the construction of the poem itself.

Any complete understanding of *The Waste Land* would need to take these (and other) factors into account. It is not a matter of *reducing* the poem to the state of contemporary capitalism; but neither is it a matter of introducing so many judicious complications that anything as crude as capitalism may to all intents and purposes be forgotten. On the contrary: all of the elements I have enumerated (the author's class-position, ideological forms and their relation to literary forms, "spirituality" and philosophy, techniques of literary production, aesthetic theory) are directly relevant to the base/superstructure model. What Marxist criticism looks for is the unique *conjuncture* of these elements which we know as *The Waste Land*.12 No one of these elements can be conflated with another: each has its own relative independence. *The Waste Land* can indeed be explained as a poem which springs from a crisis of bourgeois ideology, but it has no simple correspondence with that crisis or with the political and economic conditions which produced it. (As a poem, it does not of course *know itself* as a product of a particular ideological crisis, for if it did it would cease to exist. It needs to translate that crisis into "universal" terms—to grasp it as part of an unchanging human condition, shared alike by ancient Egyptians and modern man.) *The Waste Land's* relation to the real history of its time, then, is highly *mediated;* and in this it is like all works of art.

Literature and Ideology

Frederick Engels remarks in *Ludwig Feuerbach and the End of Classical German Philosophy* (1888) that art is far richer and more "opaque" than political and economic theory because it is less purely ideological. It is important here to grasp the precise meaning for Marxism of "ideology." Ideology is not in the first place a set of doctrines; it signifies the way men live out their roles in class-society, the values, ideas and images which tie them to their social functions and so prevent them from a true knowledge of society as a whole. In this sense *The Waste Land* is ideological: it shows a man making sense of his experience in ways that prohibit a true understanding of his society, ways that are consequently false. All art springs from an ideological conception of the world; there is no such thing, Plekhanov comments, as a work of art entirely devoid of ideological content. But Engels's remark suggests that art has a more complex relationship to ideology than law and political theory, which rather more transparently embody the interests of a ruling class. The question, then, is what relationship art has to ideology.

This is not an easy question to answer. Two extreme, opposite positions are possible here. One is that literature is *nothing but* ideology in a certain artistic form—that works of literature are just expressions of the ideologies of their time. They are prisoners of "false consciousness," unable to reach beyond it to arrive at the truth. It is a position characteristic of much "vulgar Marxist" criticism, which tends to see literary works merely as reflections of dominant ideologies. As such, it is unable to explain, for one thing, why so much literature actually *challenges* the ideological assumptions of its time. The opposite case seizes on the fact that so much literature challenges the ideology it confronts, and makes this part of the definition of literary art itself. Authentic art, as Ernst Fischer argues in his significantly entitled *Art Against Ideology* (1969), always transcends the ideological limits of its time, yielding us insight into the realities which ideology hides from view.

Both of these cases seem to me too simple. A more subtle (although still incomplete) account of the relationship between literature and ideology is provided by the French Marxist theorist Louis Althusser.[13] Althusser argues that art cannot be reduced to ideology: it has, rather, a particular *relationship* to it. Ideology signifies the imaginary ways in which men experience the real world, which is, of course, the kind of experience literature gives us too—what it feels like to live in particular conditions, rather than a conceptual analysis of those conditions. However, art does more than just passively reflect that experience. It is held within ideology, but also manages to distance itself from it, to the point where it permits us to "feel" and "perceive" the ideology from which it springs. In doing this, art does not enable us to *know* the truth which ideology conceals, since for Althusser "knowledge" in the strict sense means *scientific* knowledge—the kind of knowledge of, say, capitalism which Marx's *Capital* rather than Dickens's *Hard Times* allows us. The difference between science and art is not that they deal with different objects, but that they deal with the same objects in different ways. Science gives us conceptual knowledge of a situation; art gives us the experience of that situation, which is equivalent to ideology. But by doing this, it allows us to "see" the nature of that ideology, and thus begins to move us towards that full understanding of ideology which is scientific knowledge.

How literature can do this is more fully developed by one of Althusser's colleagues, Pierre Macherey. In his *Pour une Théorie de la Production Littéraire* (1966), Macherey distinguishes between what he terms "illusion" (meaning, essentially, ideology), and "fiction." Illusion—the ordinary ideological experience of men—is the material on which the writer goes to work; but in working on it he transforms it into something different, lends it a shape and structure. It is by giving ideology a determinate form, fixing it within certain fictional limits, that art is able to distance itself from it, thus revealing to us the limits of that ideology. In doing this, Macherey claims, art contributes to our deliverance from the ideological illusion.

I find the comments of both Althusser and Macherey at crucial points ambiguous and obscure; but the relation they propose between literature and ideology is nonetheless deeply suggestive. Ideology, for both critics, is more than an amorphous body of free-floating images and ideas; in any society it has a certain structural coherence. Because it possesses such relative coherence, it can be the object of scientific analysis; and since literary texts "belong" to ideology, they too can be the object of such scientific analysis. A scientific criticism would seek to explain the literary work in terms of the ideological structure of which it is part, yet which it transforms in its art: it would search out the principle which both ties the work to ideology and distances it from it.

Notes

1. See M. Lifshitz, *The Philosophy of Art of Karl Marx* (London, 1973). For a naively prejudiced but reasonably informative account of Marx and Engels's literary interests, see P. Demetz, *Marx, Engels and the Poets* (Chicago, 1967).

2. See Karl Marx and Frederick Engels, *On Literature and Art* (New York, 1973), for a compendium of these comments.

3. See especially L. Schücking, *The Sociology of Literary Taste* (London, 1944); R. Escarpit, *The Sociology of Literature* (London, 1971); R. D. Atlick, *The English Common Reader* (Chicago, 1957); and R. Williams, *The Long Revolution* (London, 1961). Representative recent works have been D. Laurenson and A. Swingewood, *The Sociology of Literature* (London, 1972), and M. Bradbury, *The Social Context of English Literature* (Oxford, 1971). For an account of Raymond Williams's important work, see my article in *New Left Review* 95 (January–February, 1976).

4. Much non-Marxist criticism would reject a term like "explanation," feeling that it violates the "mystery" of literature. I use it here because I agree with Pierre Macherey, in his *Pour une Théorie de la Production Littéraire* (Paris, 1966), that the task of the critic is not to "interpret" but to "explain." For Macherey, "interpretation" of a text means revising or correcting it in accordance

with some ideal norm of what it should be; it consists, that is to say, in refusing the text *as it is*. Interpretative criticism merely "redoubles" the text, modifying and elaborating it for easier consumption. In saying *more* about the work, it succeeds in saying *less*.

5. See especially Vico's *The New Science* (1725); Madame de Staël, *Of Literature and Social Institutions* (1800); H. Taine, *History of English Literature* (1863).

6. This, inevitably, is a considerably over-simplified account. For a full analysis, see N. Poulantzas, *Political Power and Social Classes* (London, 1973).

7. Quoted in the Preface to Henri Arvon's *Marxist Aesthetics* (Ithaca, 1970).

8. On the question of how a writer's personal history interlocks with the history of his time, see J. P. Sartre, *The Search for a Method* (London, 1963).

9. Introduction to the *Grundrisse* (Harmondsworth, 1973).

10. See Stanley Mitchell's essay on Max in Hall and Walton (eds.), *Situating Marx* (London, 1972).

11. Appendices to the "Short Organum on the Theatre," in J. Willett (ed.), *Brecht on Theatre: The Development of an Aesthetic* (London, 1964).

12. To put the issue in more complex theoretical terms: the influence of the economic "base" on *The Waste Land* is evident not in a direct way, but in the fact that it is the economic base which in the last instance determines the state of development of each element of the superstructure (religious, philosophical and so on) which went into its making, and moreover determines the structural interrelations between those elements, of which the poem is a particular conjuncture.

13. In his "Letter on Art in reply to André Daspre," in *Lenin and Philosophy* (London, 1971). See also the following essay on the abstract painter Cremonini.

THEORY

*Catherine Belsey's "Literature, History, Politics" touches
on a number of this context's chief concerns: literature
versus Literature, classical versus revisionary Marxism,
the constructed "subject" versus the autonomous "ego,"
criticism as an institution, the fluidity of disciplinary
boundaries, the study of the past as an intervention in
current power relations. The institution of literary criticism, Belsey complains, is still dominated by the formal-
mimetic belief that literature represents universal truths.
The dominance of this belief is clearly demonstrated, she
feels, by standard examination questions, just as the
power of the institution is demonstrated by the existence
of such examinations. But when we claim to read trans-
historically, we may reveal only that we are totally bound
by our own horizons. The antidote is "history," but not
traditional literary history. "When the institution of literary criticism in Britain invokes history, whether as
world picture or as long-lost organic community, it is
ultimately in order to suppress it, by showing that in
essence things are as they have always been." Structuralism, though it seemed to challenge the critical establishment, has turned out to be little help in this regard,
for it largely continued the dominance of the synchronic
view and so served to further suppress history and politics. And American deconstruction, Belsey claims, for all
its supposed radicalism, has had much the same effect.
But in the work of other poststructuralists—and especially in the work of Foucault—Belsey sees the promise
of a new history, a "poststructuralist history" that will
be "explicitly partial, from a position and on behalf of a
position" and whose effect will be "to locate the present
in history and in process."*

*One of the first steps toward truly historicizing liter-
ary study is to take a historical view of literary study
itself, and Belsey notes that in recent years this kind*

Literature,
History, Politics[1]

Catherine Belsey

Reprinted by permission of the author and publisher from
Literature and History 9 (Spring 1983): 17–27.

of analysis has done much to expose the ideological assumptions of the institution of literary criticism, and to "relativize its claims to universality." But, says Belsey, as we strive to unite literature, history, and politics, to undermine literary study "as currently constituted," and to "challenge the category of Literature"—all worthy goals, she agrees—we do not need to ignore "literary" texts entirely. The study of even canonical texts can further these goals if we go about it in the right ways. We can, for example, extend the concept of "intertextuality" to include the "nonliterary" and thereby encounter "the discourses themselves in their uncertainty, their instability, their relativity." Further, while admitting that we can read any text any way, Belsey feels that "fictional" texts "offer a space for the problematisation of the knowledge they invoke" in ways that other kinds of texts do not. She hastens to add that she is not trying to "privilege literature (and certainly not Literature) but only to allow it a certain specificity which identifies its use-value in the construction of the history of the present." "The construction of the history of the present" might stand as a brief description of the goals of most poststructural historians. If we can see how power relations that offer themselves as natural and timeless have in fact been historically constructed, we may feel empowered to change them. This kind of poststructural history, this way of uniting literature, history, and politics, is "a stake through the heart of Eternal Man, and the world of practice as well as theory is consequently laid open to effective political action."

To bring these three terms together is hardly to do anything new. *Literature and History* has been doing it since its inception; the Essex Conference volumes do it; Raymond Williams has spent his life doing it; historians like E. P. Thompson and Christopher Hill, glancing sideways at literature, have frequently done it; a venerable tradition of Marxist criticism all over Europe does it. Less marginally, as far as the institution of literary criticism in Britain is concerned, T. S. Eliot, F. R. Leavis and E. M. W. Tillyard did it when they constructed between them a lost Elizabethan utopia where thought and feeling were one, where the native rhythms of speech expressed in poetry the intuitive consciousness of an organic community, and everyone recognised in the principle of order the necessity of submission to the proper authorities, social and divine.

And yet paradoxically to bring these three terms together *explicitly* is still to scandalise the institution

of literary criticism, because it is to propose a relationship between the transcendent (literature), the contingent (history) and the merely strategic (politics). The institution is dedicated to the infinite repetition of the best that has been thought and said in the world, and this luminous heritage, however shaded by the Discarded Image of medieval ideas, or the Victorian Frame of Mind, stands ready to be released from history by the apparatus criticus which the academic profession supplies, and to reappear resplendent before every new generation of student-critics. The model for the institution's conception of history as a kind of perpetual present, and its conviction of the vulgarity of politics, is Arnold's essay, "The Study of Poetry," where it is clear from the "touchstones" Arnold invokes that great poetry from Homer to Milton, despite minor differences of language and setting, has always taught the same elegiac truth, that this world is inevitably a place of sorrow and that the only heroism is a solitary resignation of the spirit.

The sole inhabitant of the universe of literature is Eternal Man (and the masculine form is appropriate), whose brooding, feeling presence precedes, determines and transcends history as it precedes and determines the truths inscribed in the English syllabus, the truths examination candidates are required to reproduce. "'When we read Chaucer's early poems we feel the author's awareness of how complex and involved the events and circumstances of life are, of how they defy any single interpretation.' Discuss." (Oxford Honour School of English Language and Literature, "Chaucer and Langland," 1980.) Miraculously, Chaucer's awareness of the complexity of it all precisely resembles mine, ours, everyone's. Every liberal's, that is, in the twentieth century: a modern "recognition" is rendered eternal by literary criticism. Examination questions, the ultimate location of institutional power, identify the boundaries of the discipline, and define what it is permissible to "discuss," as they so invitingly and misleadingly put it (Davies, 1982, p. 39). "'The sense of a peculiarly heightened personal dignity is at the centre of Donne's work.' (Alvarez) *Either* discuss with reference to Donne *or* describe the sense of personal dignity in any other writer of the period." (Oxford Honour School.... "English Literature from 1600 to 1740," 1980.) Or any other writer of any other period, perhaps, because it is a reading from the present, from a position of liberal humanism, which finds the sense of personal dignity at issue wherever it looks.

Historians have been quite clear, at least since Eric Hobsbawm's seminal articles were published in *Past and Present* in 1954, that the seventeenth century was a period of general crisis. That general crisis has apparently no repercussions whatever for the literature of the period as it is defined in the broad run of examinations at O Level, at A Level and in the universities. Where the crisis is glimpsed, it is instantly depoliticised: " 'Courtly poetry without a court.' What do the Cavalier poets gain or lose by the decline and final absence of a Court? Discuss one or more poets." (Cambridge English Tripos, Part II, "Special Period, 1616–60," 1981.) Had the question asked what was gained or lost from the collapse of the Court by agricultural labourers, by an emerging feminism or by radical politics, the answer might have mattered. But that would be history. What matters in English is the implications of the Revolution of the 1640s for the Cavalier poets. Alternatively, the crisis is personalised as the idiosyncratic interest of an individual: " 'Throughout *Paradise Lost* Milton's concern is to present and investigate a crisis of authority.' Discuss." (Oxford Honour School . . . "Spenser and Milton," 1980.) What it is not possible to say in answer to that question is how a crisis of authority is at the heart of *Paradise Lost*, not as a matter for the author's investigation, but as a source of fragmentation within the poem and the writing of the poem. It is precisely the location of authority—in God and in the human will, in the subjectivity of the narrator and in a signification which is outside the narrator and appeals to all human cultures—or rather, it is these contradictory locations of authority which insist on the inadequacy of any reading of the poem that looks for "Milton's concern" as a guide to its possible meanings. And among these possible meanings is the limits of what can be said about authority in a period when authority is in crisis.

When the institution of literary criticism in Britain invokes history, whether as world picture or as long-lost organic community, it is ultimately in order to suppress it, by showing that *in essence* things are as they have always been. The function of scholarship, as of conventional criticism, is finally to reinstate the continuity of felt life which the ignorance of a trivialising society obscures. No history: no politics. Because if there has never been change at a fundamental level, there are no rational grounds for commitment to change. No politics—or rather, no overt politics, since there is, of course, no political neutrality in the assertion of an unchanging essential human nature.

The radical theoretical work of the last twenty years has not always confronted the suppression of history and politics in literary criticism. Structuralism, widely regarded, when it began to appear in Britain in the sixties and early seventies, as the beginning of the end of civilization as we know it, quite failed to challenge the institution on this central issue. Saussure's *Course in General Linguistics* is a remarkably plural text. Insofar as its readers confined themselves to its discovery of an opposition which precisely replicated the classic liberal opposition between the individual and society, structuralism offered no threat to the equilibrium of the free West. Fired by the concept of the difference between *langue* and *parole*, which permitted utterance within the permutations already authorized by the language-system, the structuralists set off in quest of similar timeless enabling systems in other spheres, the form of all societies, the pattern of all narrative, the key to all mythologies. It was the signifying system itself which was held to lay down, long before the drama of history was inscribed in it, the elementary structures of culture and of subjectivity (Lacan, 1977, p. 148). Structuralism thus proclaimed Eternal Man and the suppression of history with a new and resounding authority. Ironically, Saussure's analysis of language as a system of differences was invoked to initiate the elimination of all difference.

But it was also Saussure's work, in conjunction with the Marxist analysis of ideology, which permitted Roland Barthes on behalf of anarchism to identify Eternal Man as the product and pivot of bourgeois mythology (Barthes, 1972, p. 140), and subsequently to repudiate the structuralist equalization of all narrative "under the scrutiny of an indifferent science" (Barthes, 1975, p. 3). This was possible because one of the effects of the *Course in General Linguistics* was to relativise meaning by detaching it from the world outside language. Insofar as the value of a specific sign differs from one language to another, and insofar as language is the condition of meaning and thought, meaning and thought differ from one language to another, one culture to another. As linguistic habits alter, cultures are transformed. Difference, history, change reappear.

They disappear again, however, in American deconstructionism, which nails its colours to the free play of the eternal signifier. Here all writing and all speech is fiction in a timeless present without presence, and the subject celebrates its own non-being in an infinite space where there is no room for politics. Deconstructionism has nothing to say about the relationship between literature and history, or the political implications of either. Nothing explicit, that is.

What is at stake here is the elision of the signified. Saussure distinguished three terms of orders—the signifier (the sound or written image), the signified (the meaning) and the referent (the thing in the world). A certain elusiveness in Saussure's theory concerning the relationship between meaning and *intention* prompted Derrida's deconstruction of Saussure's phono-centrism, and in the interests of contesting the notion of a pure, conceptual intelligibility, a "truth in the soul" which precedes the signifier (Derrida, 1976, p. 15), Derrida in that context treats as suspect, as he puts it, the difference between signifier and signified (p. 14). The order of the signified is subsumed under "presence," which is understood indiscriminately as concept, intention or referent, so that meaning, being and truth are collapsed together. Elsewhere Derrida's notion of *différence* does not eliminate the possibility of signification. Meaning exists, neither as being nor as truth, but as linguistic difference, textually produced, contextually deferred (Derrida, 1973, pp. 129–60). But the opening pages of *Grammatology* invite vulgar deconstructionists to take it that there is no such thing as meaning, and in consequence, since meaningless language is literally unthinkable, that words mean whatever you want them to mean. This *Looking-Glass* reasoning leads at best to an anarchic scepticism, the celebration of undecidability as an end in itself, and at worst to the reinstatement of the mirror phase, where the critic-subject at play rejoices in its own linguistic plenitude. In the constant and repeated assertion of the evaporation of meaning there is no place to analyse the contest for meaning, and therefore no politics, and there is no possibility of tracing changes of meaning, the sliding of the signified, in history.

It was at this point in the debate that political post-structuralism began to turn more insistently to the work of Foucault. (It was also, perhaps, at this point in the debate that Foucault's own work became more explicitly political.) Foucault goes beyond Derridean scepticism to the extent that he identifies the relationship between meaning (or discourse-as-knowledge) and power. Conceding that language does not map the world, but distinguishing signified from referent and intention, knowledge from what is true (because guaranteed by being or by things), Foucault reinstates politics in a post-structuralist world which, despite the heroic efforts of Althusser, could not support the concept of science. *I, Pierre Rivière . . .* documents Pierre Rivière's murder in 1835 of his mother, his sister and his brother. It is made clear that the meaning of Pierre's memoir exceeds any single reading of it, since reading always takes place from a position and on behalf of a position. The question is not, "what is the *truth* of Pierre Rivière's behaviour?," "was he *really* mad?" but "from what positions, inscribed in what knowledge, did the contest between the legal and the medical professions for control of Pierre Rivière take place?" And in addition, "what possibilities of a reading of these documents are available now which were not available in the 1830s?" From the perspective of the present, the records of Pierre Rivière's act of unauthorized resistance can be read as a part of the history of the present, because they demonstrate the social and discursive construction of a deviant and at the same time permit him to speak. The "humanitarian" practice which confines the criminally insane for life silences them even more effectively than execution, since whatever they say is rendered inaudible, "mad."

Foucault's work politicizes the polyphony of the signified. The plurality of meaning is not exclusively a matter of infinite play, as recent history demonstrates. Meanings produce practices and generate behaviour. It was explicitly in a contest for the meaning of "aggression"—as colonialism, as theft, or as violence—that British and Argentine soldiers killed and mutilated each other in the South Atlantic, both sides using might to establish that might is not right. In this as in all other just wars it was evident that the letter kills. While the American deconstructionists play, Reagan is preparing to reduce us all to radioactive rubble to preserve our freedom. The control of meanings—of freedom, democracy, the American way of life—the control of these meanings is political power, but it is a mistake to suppose that the abolition of the signified is the abolition of power. On the contrary, deconstructionalism collaborates with the operations of meaning-as-power precisely insofar as it protests that there is no such thing.

Foucault's work brings together two of my three terms, history and politics, in its analysis of the ways in which power produces new knowledges. It is a history of ideas in which ideas are understood as generating practices, a history of discourses in which discourses define and are reproduced in institutions. It offers a challenge to classical Marxist politics to the extent that it refuses to find a central and determining locus of power in the mode of production, and a challenge to empiricist history in its refusal to treat documents as transparent. In a sense we needed both challenges. Whatever the inadequacies of Althusserian Marxism, it was impossible for a post-structuralist politics subsequently to retreat from the decentring concept of overdetermination. To attribute a relative autonomy to ideology was to open up the possibility of a history of the forms in which people become conscious of their differences and begin to fight them out. These forms are precisely the classical superstructural forms of law, metaphysics, aesthetics, and so on, but with the addition of those areas where struggle has become increasingly pressing in the twentieth century — sexuality, the family, subjectivity. The theory of relative autonomy, however vulnerable in itself, permitted attention within Marxism to these areas as sites of struggle.

But if post-structural politics implied the dispersal of history into new areas, it also implied a historiography which was both more and less than the transcription of lost experience. To take a single example of the problem, Lawrence Stone's book, *The Family, Sex and Marriage in England, 1500–1800,* published in 1977, is extremely welcome insofar as it tackles precisely one of those areas which politics (specifically, in this instance, feminist politics) had brought to prominence. But Stone's vocabulary of "evidence," "sources," "documents" and "sampling" define the historian's quarry, however elusive, as something anterior to textuality, revealed through its expression in the mass of diaries, memoirs, autobiographies and letters cited. History is seen as the recovered presence of pure, extra-discursive, representative experience, "how it (usually) felt." What Stone produces in consequence is a smooth, homogeneous evolution, with overlapping strata for enhanced verisimilitude, from the open lineage family of the late middle ages to the affective nuclear family in the seventeenth and eighteenth centuries. But the affective nuclear family begins to be glimpsed in discourse in the mid-sixteenth century, and there is evidence (if evidence is what is at stake) that this concept of a private realm, in which power is exercised invisibly for the public good, defines itself in this period in opposition to a control of marriage exercised directly but precariously by the sovereign as head of the church. What Stone's quest for the representative experience behind the documents eliminates is the *politics* of the history of the family, precisely the issue which put it on the feminist map, the contest for power, which is also a contest for meaning in its materiality, the struggle about the meaning and practice of family life.

Representative experience is understood to be whatever a lot of people said they felt, and it is held to be the origin of, and to issue in, representative behaviour. This notion of the "fit" between documented feelings and recorded behaviour relegates to the margins of history any feelings or behaviour which were not dominant. Struggle thus becomes marginal, always the province, except in periods of general struggle, of the idiosyncratic few. But more important, modes of resistance to what was dominant are ignored if they could not be formulated in so many words, were not allowed a voice, were not experienced as resistance or can be defined as deviant. Stone makes no space, for instance, for a consideration of witchcraft as a practice of offering women a form of power which was forbidden precisely by orthodox concepts of the family.

The point is worth dwelling on because Stone is by no means an isolated case. Even among those radical historians for whom struggle is heroic, if still idiosyncratic, the quest for experience and the belief that documents are ultimately transparent remain common. But documents do not merely transcribe experience: to the extent that they inevitably come from a context where power is at stake, they are worth analysis not as access to something beyond them, not as evidence of how it felt, but as themselves locations of power and resistance to power.

A post-structuralist history needs to re-examine Stone's mass of documents (and perhaps others), and to address to them a different series of questions. These include the following (borrowed, in modified form, from Foucault):

> What are the modes and conditions of these texts?
>
> Where do they come from; who controls them; on behalf of whom?
>
> What possible subject positions are inscribed in them?
>
> What meanings and what contests for meaning do they display?
>
> (cf. Foucault, 1977, p. 138)

The answers to these questions give us a different history of the family, sex and marriage. This is the history not of an irrecoverable experience, but of meanings, of the signified in its plurality, not the referent in its singular but imaginary presence. It is, therefore, a history of struggle and, in consequence, a political history.

Such a history is not offered as objective, authoritative, neutral or true. It is not outside history itself, or outside the present. On the contrary, it is part of history, part of the present. It is irreducibly textual, offering no place outside discourse from which to interpret or judge. It is explicitly partial, from a position and on behalf of a position. It is not culturally relative in so far as relativism is determinist and therefore a-political: "I think like this because my society thinks like this." But its effect is to relativise the present, to locate the present in history and in process.

Foucault's work gives us a methodology for producing our own history and politics, a history which is simultaneously a politics, but it has little to say about my third term, literature. Literature is not a knowledge. Literary criticism is a knowledge, produced in and reproducing an institution. Some of the most important and radical work of the last decade has been devoted to analysis of the institution of literary criticism, challenging its assumptions, exposing its ideological implications and relativising its claims to universality and timelessness.[2] One of the central concerns of this work has been the interrogation of the idea of literature itself as "the central co-ordinating concept of the discourse of literary criticism, supplying the point of reference to which relationships of difference and similarity within the field of writing are articulated" (Bennett, 1981, p. 139). Tony Bennett's point here is an important one. "Literature" signifies as an element in a system of differences. It is that which is *not* minor, popular, ephemeral or trivial, as well as that which is not medicine, economics, history or, of course, politics. "Literature" designates a value and a category.

That conjunction—of value and category—issues in English departments as we know them, and generates, I have argued, the continuous production and reproduction of hierarchies of subjectivity (Belsey, 1982). We need, therefore, as Tony Bennett argues, to call into question both the category—the autonomy of literary studies—and the value—Literature as distinct from its residue, popular fiction. We need to replace the quest for value by an "analysis of the social contestation of value" (Bennett, 1981, p. 143).

Work on the institution of literary criticism is centrally concerned with the reception of literary texts, with the text as site of the range of possible meanings that may be produced during the course of its history, and with the knowledges inscribed in both dominant and radical discourses. Its importance seems to me to be established beyond question. Here is a field of operations which brings together literature, history and politics in crucial ways, undermining the power of the institution and challenging the category of Literature.

The effect of this project, in other words, is to de-centre literary criticism, to displace "the text," the "primary material," from its authoritative position at the heart of the syllabus, to dislodge the belief in the close reading of the text as the critic's essential and indispensable skill. Quite whether we can afford to dispose of the literary text altogether is not usually made clear, but it seems implicit in the project that we can do without it for most of the time. What is to be read closely is criticism, official reports on the teaching of English, examination papers, and all the other discursive displays of institutional power.

But before we throw out the Arden Shakespeares and the Penguin English Library (in order to make a space for the Critical Heritage and the Newbolt Report), I want to propose a way of recycling the texts, on the grounds that work on the institution is not the only way of bringing together literature, history and politics, of undermining literary studies as currently constituted, or of challenging the category of Literature. I want to argue in favour of at least one additional way of doing all those things (in the hope of forestalling one of those fierce bouts of either-orism which periodically dissipate the energies of the left).

Literature (or fiction: the fields defined by the two words are not necessarily co-extensive: what about Bacon's *Essays*, Donne's sermons, the "Epistle to Dr. Arbuthnot," *The Prelude*? But perhaps we read these texts as fiction now, so the term will perhaps serve to modify the ideological implications of Literature)—literature or fiction is not a knowledge, but it is not only a site where knowledge is produced. It is also the location of a range of knowledges. In this sense the text always exceeds the history of its reception. While on the one hand meaning is never single, eternally inscribed in the words on the page, on the other hand readings do not spring unilaterally out of the subjectivities (or the ideologies) of readers. The text is not an empty space, filled with meaning from outside itself, any more than it is the transcription of an authorial intention, filled with meaning from outside language. As a signifying practice, writing always offers raw material for the production of meanings, the signified in its plurality, on the understanding, of course, that the signified is distinct from the intention of the author (pure concept) or the referent (a world already constituted and re-presented).

The intertextual relations of the text are never purely literary. Fiction draws not only on other fiction but on the knowledges of its period, discourses in circulation which are themselves sites of power and the contest for power. In the case of *Macbeth,* for instance, the Victorian fable of vaulting ambition and its attendant remorse and punishment is also a repository of Reformation Christianity, morbid, demonic, apocalyptic; of the Jacobean law of sovereignty and succession; of Renaissance medicine; and of Stuart history. Equally, since narrative fiction depends on impediments (where there are no obstacles to be overcome there's no story), *Macbeth* depends on resistance to those knowledges, on what refuses or escapes them: on witchcraft seen as a knowledge which repudiates Christian knowledge, on regicide, madness, suicide, as evasions of a control which is thereby shown to be precarious. A political and historical reading of *Macbeth* might analyze these discourses, not in the manner of Tillyard, as a means of a deeper understanding of the text, and at the same time a lost golden world where nature itself rose up to punish resistance to the existing order, but on the contrary, as a way of encountering the discourses themselves in their uncertainty, their instability, their relativity.

Narrative necessarily depends on the establishment within the story of fictional forms of control and resistance to control, norms and the repudiation of norms. And in the period to which English departments are centrally committed, from the Renaissance to the present, the criterion of verisimilitude, towards or against which fiction has consistently pressed, has necessitated that these concepts of control and normality be intelligible outside fiction itself. Thus, sovereignty, the family, subjectivity are defined and redefined in narrative fiction, problematised and reproblematised. *Macbeth* (again) offers, in the scene with Lady Macduff, an early instance of the emerging concept of the affective nuclear family — a

private realm of domestic harmony shown as vulnerable to crisis in a public and political world which is beginning to be perceived as distinct from it. It presents, on the other hand, the fragmentation of the subject, Macbeth, under the pressure of a crisis in which the personal and the political are still perceived as continuous.

In *Critical Practice* I tried to distinguish between three kinds of texts, which I identified as declarative, imperative and interrogative. The declarative text imparts "knowledge" (fictional or not) to the reader, the imperative text (propaganda) exhorts, instructs or orders the reader, and the interrogative text poses questions by enlisting the reader in contradiction (Belsey, 1980, pp. 90 ff.). It now seems to me that this classification may have been excessively formalistic, implying that texts can unilaterally determine their reception by the reader. As we know, a reading practice which actively seeks out contradiction can *produce* as interrogative a text which has conventionally been read as declarative. Nonetheless, the categories may be useful if they enable us to attribute a certain kind of specificity to literary/fictional texts. The danger of formalism is to be set against the structuralist danger of collapsing all difference. That there is a formal indeterminacy does not mean that we can never speak of form, any more than the polyphony of "freedom" prevents us from condemning police states. In the period of *Macbeth* many of the available written texts are imperative — sermons, tracts, pamphlets, marked as referring to a given external reality, and offering the reader a position of alignment with one set of values and practices and opposition to others (divorce, for instance, or patriarchal sovereignty). Fictional (declarative or interrogative) texts, by contrast, marked as alluding only indirectly to "reality," informing without directly exhorting, offer a space for the problematisation of the knowledges they invoke in ways which imperative texts cannot risk.[3] Radically contradictory definitions of marriage in a divorce pamphlet inevitably reduce its propaganda-value: plays, on the contrary, can problematise marriage without affecting the coherence of the story.

To say this is not, I hope, to privilege literature (and certainly not Literature) but only to allow it a certain specificity which identifies its use-value in the construction of the history of the present. A vest is not a sock, but it is not in consequence obvious that one is better than the other. On the basis of this specificity which is neither privilege nor autonomy, I want to urge that lyric poetry, read as fiction, is also worth recycling. Sexuality and subjectivity are the twin themes of the lyric, and since any text longer than, say, an imagist poem, moves towards argument or narrative, and therefore toward crisis, similar definitions and problematisations of these areas of our history offer themselves for analysis here. Sexuality, gender, the subject are not fixed but slide in history, and this sliding is available to an analysis which repudiates both the quarry of an empiricist history (experience, the world) and the quarry of conventional criticism (consciousness, the author).

The quest is for, say, the subject in its meanings. The word, "I," the fixed centre of liberal humanism, may always *designate* the speaker, but it *means* something new in the late sixteenth century, and something new again in the early nineteenth century. Equally, sexuality is not given but socially produced. We don't have access to the eighteenth-century experience of sexuality, but we can analyse the contest in that period for its meaning. It may be the case that the size of household in Britain has not changed much since the middle ages (Laslett, 1977), but the meaning of the family, institutionally and in practice, has changed fundamentally—and can therefore change again. This kind of analysis is a stake through the heart of Eternal Man, and the world of practice as well as theory is consequently laid open to effective radical political action.

The reading practice implied by this enterprise—the production of a political history from the raw material of literary texts—is a result of all that poststructuralism has urged about meaning: its often marginal location, its disunity and discontinuity, as well as its plurality. In this way the text reappears, but not as it "really is," or "really was." On the contrary, this is the text as it never was, though it was never anything else—dispersed, fragmented, produced, politicized. The text is no longer the centre of a self-contained exercise called literary criticism. It is one of the places to begin to assemble the political history of the present.

I say "to begin" because it is immediately apparent that such a history is not bounded by the boundaries of Literature or literature. Literary value becomes irrelevant: political assassination is problematised in Pickering's play, *Horestes* (1567) as well as in *Hamlet*. Equally, the subject is a legal and a psychoanalytic category just as much as a literary one;

the family is defined by medical and religious discourses as well as by classic realist texts. And so the autonomy of literature begins to dissolve, its boundaries to waver as the enterprise unfolds. The text does not disappear, though the canon does; and fiction is put to work for substantial political ends which replace the mysterious objectives of aesthetic satisfaction and moral enrichment.

Two projects, related but distinct, immediately present themselves. The first is the synchronic analysis of a historical moment, starting possibly but not inevitably from literary texts. This has perhaps been the project of the Essex conferences, focussed on a series of crises (1848, 1936, 1642, 1789), and subtitled, "the Sociology of Literature." The Essex volumes have made available some excellent work, but if the projected archaeology did not materialise in its entirety, there are reasons for this which have little to do with the value or the practicality of the project itself. I suspect that one of these reasons was that the project was not shared by all participants. (There is no reason why it should have been: it makes no exclusive claims.) Ideally the project is a collective one, but it's not easy to work collectively if you meet only once a year. It's also a long-term project involving deliberate and patient analysis, and it may be that the conference paper is not an ideal place for its presentation and discussion.

But if the Essex conferences have not achieved everything that was hoped for, they have produced work which in various ways suggests important directions for the future.[4] And in addition, there is a second and analogous project—what Foucault sporadically calls a genealogy because it traces change without invoking a single point of origin (Foucault, 1977, pp. 139–64, etc.). This is a diachronic analysis of specific discontinuities—in sovereignty, gender, the subject, for instance. And where else should we begin this analysis but by looking at fiction, poetry, autobiography? If we start with the texts on the syllabus—because they are available and for no other very specific reason—we shall not end with them, because the enquiry inevitably transgresses the boundaries of the existing discipline.

The proposal is to reverse the Leavisian enterprise of constructing (inventing) a lost organic world of unfallen orality, undissociated sensibility and uncontested order. In fact, in so far as it concerns the sixteenth and seventeenth centuries, the kind of archaeology I have in mind uncovers a world of violence, disorder and fragmentation. The history of the present is not a history of a fall from grace but of the transformations of power and resistances to power. The claim is not that such a history, or such a reading of literary texts, is more accurate, but only that it is more radical. No less partial, it produces the past not in order to present an ideal of hierarchy, but to relativise the present, to demonstrate that since change has occurred in those areas which seem most intimate and most inevitable, change in those areas is possible for us.

According to Foucault, who invents the verb "to fiction" in order to undermine his own use of the word "truth," "one 'fictions' a history starting from a political reality that renders it true, one 'fictions' a politics that doesn't as yet exist starting from a historical truth" (Foucault, 1979, pp. 74–5). I want to add this: the literary institution has "fictioned" a criticism which uncritically protests its own truth; we must instead "fiction" a literature which renders up our true history in the interests of a politics of change.

Notes

1. I am grateful for the comments of Francis Barker and Chris Weedon on an earlier draft of this essay.
2. See for example the work of Renée Balibar; Francis Mulhern, *The Moment of Scrutiny* (London: NLB, 1979); Tony Bennett, *Formalism and Marxism* (London: Methuen, 1979); Peter Widdowson ed., *Re-Reading English* (London: Methuen, 1982); the LTP (Literature Teaching Politics) conferences and journal.
3. I am indebted for this idea to Simon Barker.
4. See particularly in the *1642* volume (ed. Francis Barker *et al.*) essays by Francis Barker, Peter Hulme, Christine Berg and Philippa Berry.

Bibliography

Barker, Francis *et al.*, (1981) *1642: Literature and Power in the Seventeenth Century,* University of Essex.

Barthes, Roland, (1972) *Mythologies,* trs. Annette Lavers, London, Cape.

Barthes, Roland, (1975) *S/Z,* trs. Richard Miller, London, Cape.

Belsey, Catherine, (1980) *Critical Practice,* London, Methuen.

Belsey, Catherine, (1982) "Re-Reading the Great Tradition." *Re-Reading English,* ed. Peter Widdowson, London, Methuen, pp. 121–135.

Bennett, Tony, (1981) "Marxism and Popular Fiction," *Literature and History,* VII, pp. 138–165.

Davies, Tony, (1982) "Common Sense and Critical Practice: Teaching Literature," *Re-Reading English,* ed. Peter Widdowson, London, Methuen, pp. 32–43.

Derrida, Jacques, (1973) *Speech and Phenomena,* trs. David B. Allison, Evanston, Ill. Northwestern U.P.

Derrida, Jacques, (1976) *Of Grammatology,* trs. Gayatri Chakravorty Spivak, Baltimore and London, Johns Hopkins U.P.

Foucault, Michel, (1977) *Language, Counter-Memory, Practice,* ed. Donald Bouchard, Oxford, Blackwell.

Foucault, Michel, ed., (1978) *I, Pierre Rivière . . . ,* Harmondsworth, Penguin.

Foucault, Michel, (1979) *Power, Truth, Strategy,* ed. Meaghan Morris and Paul Patton, Sydney, Feral Publications.

Lacan, Jacques, (1977) *Ecrits,* trs. Alan Sheridan, London, Tavistock.

Laslett, Peter, (1977) *Family Life and Illicit Love in Earlier Generations,* Cambridge, CUP.

Stone, Lawrence, (1977) *The Family, Sex and Marriage in England, 1500–1800,* London, Weidenfeld and Nicolson.

Culture

Stephen Greenblatt

*Stephen Greenblatt is a leading figure in the "New His-
toricism." But he prefers to call his own work "cultural
poetics," and we have seen others in this context who call
themselves cultural historians, cultural materialists, and
cultural critics. Why, asks Greenblatt, should the term
"culture" be useful to students of literature? Characteristically, he immediately transforms the question: "how can
we get the concept of culture to do more work for us?"
Reading culture in Foucault's terms as a system of constraints and freedoms, Greenblatt proposes a set of "cultural questions" we could ask about a literary work. The
answers will be "historical," but they will require a poststructural history quite different from the author-centered
history explored in the first chapter. Greenblatt's questions
will certainly lead us to investigate what Eagleton calls
the "ideology" of an age, though not necessarily with all
of Eagleton's Marxist assumptions. And they will also
get us into some of the territory that Catherine Belsey
maps out. At first glance, though, Greenblatt's program
looks less radical than Belsey's. Greenblatt stresses the
importance of formal analysis, talks unabashedly about
"great literature," and seems to argue that we should
take the past on its, rather than on our, terms. But he
also points out that cultural poetics will quickly dissolve
the formalist's distinction between what's "within" and
what's "outside" the text and will just as quickly dissolve the distinction between "high" and "popular" culture. Further, though he admits his own writings may
have given the impression that art simply reinforces the
boundaries of its culture, he recognizes that art sometimes
challenges these boundaries, becoming thereby a "transgressive force" that may open the way to intervention in
our own cultural scene. "If it is the task of cultural criticism to decipher the power of Prospero, it is equally its*

Reprinted by permission from Frank Lentricchia and
Thomas McLaughlin, eds. *Critical Terms for Literary Study*.
Chicago: University of Chicago Press, 1995: 225–232.
Copyright © 1995 by the University of Chicago Press.

task to hear the accents of Caliban." Having explained how a concept of culture can be useful to students of literature, Greenblatt reminds us that the initial question was backward noting that "in a liberal education broadly conceived, it is literary study that is the servant of cultural education."

The term "culture" has not always been used in literary studies, and indeed the very concept denoted by the term is fairly recent. "Culture or Civilization," wrote the influential anthropologist Edward B. Tylor in 1871, "taken in its wide ethnographic sense, is that complex whole which includes knowledge, belief, art, morals, law, custom, and any other capabilities and habits acquired by man as a member of society." Why should such a concept be useful to students of literature?

The answer may be that it is not. After all, the term as Tylor uses it is almost impossibly vague and encompassing, and the few things that seem excluded from it are almost immediately reincorporated in the actual use of the word. Hence we may think with a certain relief that at least "culture" does not refer to material objects—tables, or gold, or grain, or spinning wheels—but of course those objects, as used by men and women, are close to the center of any particular society, and we may accordingly speak of such a society's "material culture." Like "ideology" (to which, as a concept, it is closely allied), "culture" is a term that is repeatedly used without meaning much of anything at all, a vague gesture toward a dimly perceived ethos: aristocratic culture, youth culture, human culture. There is nothing especially wrong with such gestures—without them we wouldn't ordinarily be able to get through three consecutive sentences—but they are scarcely the backbone of an innovative critical practice.

How can we get the concept of culture to do more work for us? We might begin by reflecting on the fact that the concept gestures toward what appear to be opposite things: *constraint* and *mobility*. The ensemble of beliefs and practices that form a given culture function as a pervasive technology of control, a set of limits within which social behavior must be contained, a repertoire of models to which individuals must conform. The limits need not be narrow—in certain societies, such as that of the United States, they can seem quite vast—but they are not infinite, and the consequences for straying beyond them can

be severe. The most effective disciplinary techniques practiced against those who stray beyond the limits of a given culture are probably not the spectacular punishments reserved for serious offenders—exile, imprisonment in an insane asylum, penal servitude, or execution—but seemingly innocuous responses: a condescending smile, laughter poised between the genial and the sarcastic, a small dose of indulgent pity laced with contempt, cool silence. And we should add that a culture's boundaries are enforced more positively as well: through the system of rewards that range again from the spectacular (grand public honors, glittering prizes) to the apparently modest (a gaze of admiration, a respectful nod, a few words of gratitude).

Here we can make our first tentative move toward the use of culture for the study of literature, for Western literature over a very long period of time has been one of the great institutions for the enforcement of cultural boundaries through praise and blame. This is most obvious in the kinds of literature that are explicitly engaged in attack and celebration: satire and panegyric. Works in these genres often seem immensely important when they first appear, but their power begins quickly to fade when the individuals to whom the works refer begin to fade, and the evaporation of literary power continues when the models and limits that the works articulated and enforced have themselves substantially changed. The footnotes in modern editions of these works can give us the names and dates that have been lost, but they cannot in themselves enable us to recover a sense of the stakes that once gave readers pleasure and pain. An awareness of culture as a complex whole can help us to recover that sense by leading us to reconstruct the boundaries upon whose existence the works were predicated.

We can begin to do so simply by a heightened attention to the beliefs and practices implicitly enforced by particular literary acts of praising or blaming. That is, we can ask ourselves a set of cultural questions about the work before us:

> What kinds of behavior, what models of practice, does this work seem to enforce?

> Why might readers at a particular time and place find this work compelling?

> Are there differences between my values and the values implicit in the work I am reading?

Upon what social understandings does the work depend?

Whose freedom of thought or movement might be constrained implicitly or explicitly by this work?

What are the larger social structures with which these particular acts of praise or blame might be connected?

Such questions heighten our attention to features of the literary work that we might not have noticed, and, above all, to connections among elements within the work. Eventually, a full cultural analysis will need to push beyond the boundaries of the text, to establish links between the text and values, institutions, and practices elsewhere in the culture. But these links cannot be a substitute for close reading. Cultural analysis has much to learn from scrupulous formal analysis of literary texts because those texts are not merely cultural by virtue of reference to the world beyond themselves; they are cultural by virtue of social values and contexts that they have themselves successfully absorbed. The world is full of texts, most of which are virtually incomprehensible when they are removed from their immediate surroundings. To recover the meaning of such texts, to make any sense of them at all, we need to reconstruct the situation in which they were produced. Works of art by contrast contain directly or by implication much of this situation within themselves, and it is this sustained absorption that enables many literary works to survive the collapse of the conditions that led to their production.

Cultural analysis then is not by definition an extrinsic analysis, as opposed to an internal formal analysis of works of art. At the same time, cultural analysis must be opposed on principle to the rigid distinction between that which is within a text and that which lies outside. It is necessary to use whatever is available to construct a vision of the "complex whole" to which Tylor referred. And if an exploration of a particular culture will lead to a heightened understanding of a work of literature produced within that culture, so too a careful reading of a work of literature will lead to a heightened understanding of the culture within which it was produced. The organization of this volume makes it appear that the analysis of culture is the servant of literary study, but in a liberal education broadly conceived it is literary study that is the servant of cultural understanding.

I will return to the question of extrinsic as opposed to intrinsic analysis, but first we must continue to pursue the idea of culture as a system of constraints. The functioning of such a system is obvious in poems like Pope's "Epistle to Doctor Arbuthnot" or Marvell's "Horatian Ode" on Cromwell, works that undertake to excoriate dullness as embodied in certain hated individuals and celebrate civic or military virtue as embodied in certain admired individuals. Indeed culture here is close to its earlier sense of "cultivation"—the internalization and practice of a code of manners. And this sense extends well beyond the limits of satire and panegyric, particularly for those periods in which manners were a crucial sign of status difference.

Consider, for example, Shakespeare's *As You Like It*, where Orlando's bitter complaint is not that he has been excluded from his patrimony—Orlando accepts the custom of primogeniture by which his brother, as the eldest son, inherits virtually all the family property—but rather that he is being prevented from learning the manners of his class: "My father charged you in his will to give me a good education: you have train'd me like a peasant, obscuring and hiding from me all gentleman-like qualities." Shakespeare characteristically suggests that Orlando has within him an innate gentility that enables him to rise naturally above his boorish upbringing, but he equally characteristically suggests that Orlando's gentility needs to be shaped and brought to fruition through a series of difficult trials. When in the Forest of Arden the young man roughly demands food for his aged servant Adam, he receives a lesson in courtesy: "Your gentleness shall force / More than your force moves us to gentleness." The lesson has a special authority conferred upon it by the fact that it is delivered by the exiled Duke, the figure at the pinnacle of the play's social order. But the entire world of *As You Like It* is engaged in articulating cultural codes of behavior, from the elaborate, ironic training in courtship presided over by Rosalind to the humble but dignified social order by which the shepherds live. Even the simple country wench Audrey receives a lesson in manners from the sophisticated clown Touchstone: "bear your body more seeming, Audrey." This instruction in the management of the body, played no doubt for comic effect, is an enactment in miniature of a process of acculturation occurring everywhere in the play, and occurring most powerfully perhaps on an almost subliminal level, such as the distance we automatically keep from others or the way we position our legs when we sit down. Shakespeare wittily parodies this process—for example, in Touchstone's elaborate rule-book for insults—but he also participates in it, for even as his plays represent characters engaged in negotiating the boundaries of their culture, the plays also help to establish and maintain those boundaries for their audiences.

Art is an important agent then in the transmission of culture. It is one of the ways in which the roles by which men and women are expected to pattern their lives are communicated and passed from generation to generation. Certain artists have been highly self-conscious about this function. The purpose of his vast romance epic, *The Faerie Queene*, writes the Renaissance poet Edmund Spenser, is "to fashion a gentleman or noble person in virtuous and gentle discipline." The depth of our understanding of such a project, extended over a complex plot involving hundreds of allegorical figures, depends upon the extent of our grasp of Spenser's entire culture, from its nuanced Aristotelian conception of moral hierarchies to its apocalyptic fantasies, from exquisite refinement at court to colonial violence in Ireland. Most precisely, we need to grasp the way in which this culture of mixed motives and conflicting desires seemed to Spenser to generate an interlocking series of models, a moral order, a set of ethical constraints ranged against the threat of anarchy, rebellion, and chaos.

To speak of *The Faerie Queene* only in terms of the constraints imposed by culture is obviously inadequate, since the poem itself, with its knights and ladies endlessly roaming an imaginary landscape, is so insistent upon mobility. We return to the paradox with which we started: if culture functions as a structure of limits, it also functions as the regulator and guarantor of movement. Indeed the limits are virtually meaningless without movement; it is only through improvisation, experiment, and exchange that cultural boundaries can be established. Obviously, among different cultures there will be a great diversity in the ratio between mobility and constraint. Some cultures dream of imposing an absolute order, a perfect stasis, but even these, if they are to reproduce themselves from one generation to the next, will have to commit themselves, however tentatively or unwillingly, to some minimal measure of movement; conversely, some cultures dream of an absolute mobility, a perfect freedom, but these too have always been compelled, in the interest of survival, to accept some limits.

What is set up, under wildly varying circumstances and with radically divergent consequences, is a structure of improvisation, a set of patterns that have enough elasticity, enough scope of variation, to accommodate most of the participants in a given culture. A life that fails to conform at all, that violates absolutely all the available patterns, will have to be dealt with as an emergency—hence exiled, or killed, or declared a god. But most individuals are content to improvise, and, in the West at least, a great many works of art are centrally concerned with these improvisations. The novel has been particularly sensitive to the diverse ways in which individuals come to terms with the governing patterns of culture; works like Dickens' *Great Expectations* and Eliot's *Middlemarch* brilliantly explore the ironies and pain, as well as the inventiveness, of particular adjustments.

In representing this adjustment as a social, emotional, and intellectual education, these novels in effect thematize their own place in culture, for works of art are themselves educational tools. They do not merely passively reflect the prevailing ratio of mobility and constraint; they help to shape, articulate, and reproduce it through their own improvisatory intelligence. This means that, despite our romantic cult of originality, most artists are themselves gifted creators of variations upon received themes. Even those great writers whom we regard with special awe, and whom we celebrate for their refusal to parrot the clichés of their culture, tend to be particularly brilliant improvisers rather than absolute violaters or pure inventors. Thus Dickens crafted cunning adaptations of the melodramatic potboilers of his times; Shakespeare borrowed most of his plots, and many of his characters, from familiar tales or well-rehearsed historical narratives; and Spenser revised for his own culture stories first told, and told wonderfully, by the Italian poets Ariosto and Tasso.

Such borrowing is not evidence of imaginative parsimony, still less a symptom of creative exhaustion—I am using Dickens, Shakespeare, and Spenser precisely because they are among the most exuberant, generous, and creative literary imaginations in our language. It signals rather a further aspect of the cultural mobility to which I have already pointed. This mobility is not the expression of random motion but of *exchange*. A culture is a particular network of negotiations for the exchange of material goods, ideas, and—through institutions like enslavement, adoption, or marriage—people. Anthropologists are centrally concerned with a culture's kinship system—its conception of family relationships, its prohibitions of certain couplings, its marriage rules—and with its narratives—its myths, folktales, and sacred stories. The two concerns are linked, for a culture's narratives, like its kinship arrangements, are crucial indices of the prevailing codes governing human mobility and constraint. Great writers are precisely masters of these codes, specialists in cultural exchange. The works they create are structures for the accumulation, transformation, representation, and communication of social energies and practices.

In any culture there is a general symbolic economy made up of the myriad signs that excite human desire, fear, and aggression. Through their ability to construct resonant stories, their command of effective imagery, and above all their sensitivity to the greatest collective creation of culture—language—literary artists are skilled at manipulating this economy. They take symbolic materials from one zone of the culture and move them to another, augmenting their emotional force, altering their significance, linking them with other materials taken from a different zone, changing their place in a larger social design. Take, for example, Shakespeare's *King Lear:* the dramatist borrows an often-told pseudo-historical account of an ancient British king, associates with it his society's most severe anxieties about kinship relations on the one hand and civil strife on the other, infuses a measure of apocalyptic religious expectation mingled paradoxically with an acute skepticism, and returns these materials to his audience, transformed into what is perhaps the most intense experience of tragic pleasure ever created. A nuanced cultural analysis will be concerned with the various matrices from which Shakespeare derives his materials, and hence will be drawn outside the formal boundary of the play—toward the legal arrangements, for example, the elderly parents in the Renaissance made with their children, or toward child-rearing practices in the period, or toward political debates about when, if ever, disobeying a legitimate ruler was justified, or toward predictions of the imminent end of the world.

The current structure of liberal arts education often places obstacles in the way of such an analysis by separating the study of history from the study of literature, as if the two were entirely distinct enterprises, but historians have become increasingly sensitive to the symbolic dimensions of social practice, while literary critics have in recent years turned with growing interest to the social and historical dimensions of symbolic practice. Hence it is more possible, both in terms of individual courses and of overall programs of study, for students to reach toward a sense of the complex whole of a particular culture. But there is much to be done in the way of cultural analysis even without an integrated structure of courses, much that depends primarily on asking fresh questions about the possible social functions of works of art. Indeed even if one begins to achieve a sophisticated historical sense of the cultural materials out of which a literary text is constructed, it remains essential to study the ways in which these materials are formally put together and articulated in order to understand the cultural work that the text accomplishes.

For great works of art are not neutral relay stations in the circulation of cultural materials. Something happens to objects, beliefs, and practices when they are represented, reimagined, and performed in literary texts, something often unpredictable and disturbing. That "something" is the sign both of the power of art and of the embeddedness of culture in the contingencies of history. I have written at moments as if art always reinforces the dominant beliefs and social structures of its culture, as if culture is always harmonious rather than shifting and conflict-ridden, and as if there necessarily is a mutually affirmative relation between artistic production and the other modes of production and reproduction that make up a society. At times there is precisely such an easy and comfortable conjunction, but it is by no means necessary. The ability of artists to assemble and shape the forces of their culture in novel ways so that elements powerfully interact that rarely have commerce with one another in the general economy has the potential to unsettle this affirmative relation. Indeed in our own time most students of literature reserve their highest admiration for those works that situate themselves on the very edges of what can be said at a particular place and time, that batter against the boundaries of their own culture.

Near the end of his career Shakespeare decided to take advantage of his contemporaries' lively interest in New World exploration. His play *The Tempest* contains many details drawn from the writings of adventurers and colonists, details that are skillfully displaced onto a mysterious Mediterranean island and interwoven with echoes from Virgil's *Aeneid*, from other art forms such as the court masque and pastoral tragicomedy, and from the lore of white magic. The play reiterates the arguments that Europeans made about the legitimacy and civilizing force of their presence in the newly discovered lands; indeed it intensifies those arguments by conferring upon Prospero the power not only of a great prince who has the right to command the forces of this world but of a wizard who has the ability—the "Art" as the play terms it—to command supernatural forces as well. But the intensification has an oddly discordant effect: the magical power is clearly impressive but its legitimacy is less clear.

As magician Prospero resembles no one in the play so much as Sycorax, the hated witch who had preceded him as the island's ruler. The play, to be sure, does not endorse a challenge to Prospero's rule, any more than Shakespeare's culture ever encouraged challenges to legitimate monarchs. And yet out of the uneasy matrix formed by the skillful interweaving of cultural materials comes an odd, discordant voice, the voice of the "savage and deformed slave" Caliban:

> This island's mine, by Sycorax my mother,
> Which thou tak'st from me. When thou cam'st first
> Thou strok'st me, and made much of me; wouldst give me
> Water with berries in't; and teach me how

> To name the bigger light, and how the less,
> That burn by day and night: and then I lov'd thee,
> And show'd thee all the qualities o'th'isle,
> The fresh springs, brine-pits, barren place and fertile:
> Curs'd be I that did so! All the charms
> Of Sycorax, toads, beetles, bats, light on you!
> For I am all the subjects that you have,
> Which first was mine own King: and here you sty me
> In this hard rock, whiles you do keep from me
> The rest o'th'island.

Caliban, of course, does not triumph: it would take different artists from different cultures—the postcolonial Caribbean and African cultures of our own times—to rewrite Shakespeare's play and make good on Caliban's claim. But even within the powerful constraints of Shakespeare's Jacobean culture, the artist's imaginative mobility enables him to display cracks in the glacial front of princely power and to record a voice, the voice of the displaced and oppressed, that is heard scarcely anywhere else in his own time. If it is the task of cultural criticism to decipher the power of Prospero, it is equally its task to hear the accents of Caliban.

Suggested Readings

Bakhtin, Mikhail. 1968. *Rabelais and His World.*
Benjamin, Walter. 1968. *Illuminations.*
Elias, Norbert. 1978. *The Civilizing Process.*
Geertz, Clifford. 1973. *The Interpretation of Cultures.*
Williams, Raymond. 1958. *Culture and Society, 1780-1950.*

APPLICATION

"If it is the task of cultural criticism to decipher the power of Prospero," writes Stephen Greenblatt, "it is equally its task to hear the accents of Caliban." Paul Brown is one of the many cultural critics who have taken up these tasks, and his essay answers as well as Catherine Belsey's call for a "poststructuralist" history and Terry Eagleton's call for criticism to "explain the literary work in terms of the ideological structure of which it is a part, yet which it transforms in its art." Alive to the complex relations between art and ideology, Brown offers to demonstrate that "The Tempest is not simply a reflection of colonialist practices but an intervention in an ambivalent and even contradictory discourse." His use of words like "intervention" and "discourse" is characteristic of cultural criticism, and his definition of the latter term encompasses the chief interests of critics in this context: "By 'discourse' I refer to a domain or field of linguistic strategies operating within particular areas of social practice to effect knowledge and pleasure, being produced by and re-producing or reworking power relations between classes, genders and cultures." And near the end of his essay, Brown offers an explicit and detailed account of the workings of what Fredric Jameson calls "the political unconscious."

In a number of ways, then, Brown's essay is thoroughly representative of cultural criticism, and in its reading of The Tempest in terms of "the discourse of colonialism," it is also thoroughly representative of much contemporary criticism of this play. So markedly has this become the dominant strain in Tempest criticism that, as we have seen, critics in other contexts have begun to counterattack, frequently citing Brown's essay as the exemplary cultural critique.

"This Thing of Darkness I Acknowledge Mine": *The Tempest* and the Discourse of Colonialism

Paul Brown

Reprinted from *Political Shakespeare: Essays in Cultural Materialism*, 2nd ed., edited by Jonathan Dollimore and Alan Sinfield. Copyright © Manchester University Press, 1985, 1994. Used by permission of the American publisher, Cornell University Press.

It has long been recognised that *The Tempest* bears traces of the contemporary British investment in colonial expansion. Attention has been drawn to Shakespeare's patronal relations with prominent members of the Virginia Company and to the circumstances of the play's initial production at the expansionist Jacobean court in 1611 and 1612–13. Borrowings from a traditional and classical stock of exotic stereotypes, ranging from the wild man, the savage and the masterless man to the tropology of the pastoral *locus amoenus* and the wilderness, have been noted. Semi-quotations from contemporary propagandist pamphlets and Montaigne's essay on cannibals have been painstakingly logged.[1] However, a sustained historical and theoretical analysis of the play's involvement in the colonialist project has yet to be undertaken.[2] This chapter seeks to demonstrate that *The Tempest* is not simply a reflection of colonialist practices but an intervention in an ambivalent and even contradictory discourse.[3] This intervention takes the form of a powerful and pleasurable narrative which seeks at once to harmonise disjunction, to transcend irreconcilable contradictions and to mystify the political conditions which demand colonialist discourse. Yet the narrative ultimately fails to deliver that containment and instead may be seen to foreground precisely those problems which it works to efface or overcome. The result is a radically ambivalent text which exemplifies not some *timeless* contradiction internal to the discourse by which it inexorably undermines or deconstructs its "official" pronouncements, but a moment of *historical* crisis. This crisis is the struggle to produce a coherent discourse adequate to the complex requirements of British colonialism in its initial phase. Since accounts of the miraculous survival of members of the company of the Sea Adventure, wrecked off Bermuda in 1609, are said to have provided Shakespeare with an immediate source for his production, let an incident in the later life of one of those survivors serve as a ground for this analysis.

In 1614 John Rolfe, a Virginia planter, wrote a letter seeking the Governor's blessing for his proposed marriage with Pocahontas, abducted daughter of Powhatan, chief-of-chiefs. This remarkable document announces a victory for the colonialist project, confirming Rolfe in the position of coloniser and Pocahontas in the position of a savage other. The letter is an exposure of Rolfe's inner motives to public scrutiny, a production of his civilised "self" as a text to be read by his superiors, that is, his Governor and his God. What lurks in Rolfe's "secret bosome" is a desire for a savage female. He has had "to strive with all my power of body and minde, in the undertaking of so mightie a matter, no way led (so farre forth as mans weaknesse may permit) with the unbridled desire of carnall affection: but for the good of this plantation, for the honour of our countrie, for the glory of God, for my own salvation, and for the converting to the true knowledge of God and Jesus Christ, an unbeleeving creature, namely Pokahuntas."[4] As the syntax of the sentence indicates, the whole struggle, fought on the grounds of psychic order, social cohesion, national destiny, theological mission, redemption of the sinner and the conversion of the pagan, is conducted in relation to the female body. "Carnall affection" would appear, despite Rolfe's disavowal, to have been a force which might disrupt commitments to conscience, Governor and God.

Pocahontas had posed a problem that was "so intricate a laborinth, that I was even awearied to unwinde my selfe thereout." Yet whether good or evil, Pocahontas cannot fail to operate as a sign of Rolfe's election, since if reformable, she is the space to be filled with the saintly seed of civility, if obdurately irreformable, she assures the godliness of him who is called to trial (the whole ethos of the godly community in the wilderness depended upon such proximity and exposure to evil). Rolfe's supposedly problematic letter may therefore be said to *produce* Pocahontas as an other in such a way that she will always affirm Rolfe's sense of godly duty and thus confirm him as a truly civil subject.

Inexorably, the text moves from the possible beleaguerments of carnality — variously constituted as the threat of the tempting wilderness, the charge that Rolfe's own interests in this matter are purely sexual, and the possible detraction of "depravers and turbulent spirits" within the colony — towards a more positive presentation. Now the carnal affection which might fracture Rolfe's sense of duty becomes re-encoded as a vital part of God's commandments: "why was I created? If not for transitory pleasures and worldly vanities, but to labour in the Lord's vineyard, there to sow and plant, to nourish and increase the fruites thereof, daily adding with the good husbandman in the Gospell, somewhat to the tallent, that in the end the fruites may be reaped, to the comfort of the laborer in this life, and his salvation in the world to come?" Given this imperative, mutual sexual desire, including the female's "own inticements," can be admitted. Now it would be unmasterly not to desire her, as husbandman. The other incites the godly project: the godly project is embodied in the other. With the word thus made flesh and with Rolfe's self-acquittal in the court of conscience, all that remains to be achieved is the reorientation of those potential detractors into public witnesses of Rolfe's heroism, that "all the world may truly say: this is the work of God, and it is marvelous in our eies."

The threats of disruption to Rolfe's servitude to conscience, Governor and God have thus become the site of the affirmation of psychic, social and cosmic order. The encounter with the savage other serves to confirm the civil subject in that self-knowledge which ensures self-mastery. Of his thoughts and desires he can say: "I know them all, and have not rashly overslipped any." The letter, then, rehearses the power of the civil subject to maintain self-control and to bring the other into his service, even as it refers to a desire which might undermine that mastery.

After his initial calls for Rolfe to be denounced as a traitor, James I allowed the "princess," newly christened "Lady Rebecca," into court as visible evidence of the power of civility to transform the other. Pocahontas was to die in England a nine day's wonder; Rolfe returned to his tobacco plantation, to be killed in the great uprising of the Indians in 1622. The Pocahontas myth was only beginning, however.[5]

Even this partial analysis of one aspect of such myth-making serves to demonstrate the characteristic operations of the discourse of colonialism. This complex discourse can be seen to have operated in two main areas: they may be called "masterlessness" and "savagism." Masterlessness analyses wandering or unfixed and unsupervised elements located in the internal margins of civil society (in the above example, Rolfe's subjective desire and potential detractors within the colony). Savagism probes and categorises alien cultures on the external margins of expanding civil power (in the same example, the Amerindian cultures of Virginia). At the same time as they serve to define the other, such discursive practices refer back to those conditions which constitute civility itself. Masterlessness reveals the mastered (submissive, observed, supervised, deferential) and masterful (powerful, observing, supervising, teleological) nature of civil society. Savagism (a-sociality and untrammelled libidinality) reveals the necessity of psy-

chic and institutional order and direction in the civil regime. In practice these two concepts are intertwined and mutually reinforcing. Together they constitute a powerful discourse in which the non-civil is represented to the civil subject to produce for Rolfe a "laborinth" out of which, like Theseus escaping from the Minotaur's lair, he is to "unwinde" his "selfe."

That such an encounter of the civil and non-civil should be couched in terms of the promulgation/resistance of fulfilling/destructive sexual desire, as it is in Rolfe's case, deserves careful attention, as this strategy is common in colonialist discourse. Such tropes as that of the coloniser as husbandman making the land fruitful, or of the wilderness offering a dangerous libidinal attraction to the struggling saint, are ubiquitous. The discourse of sexuality in fact offers the crucial nexus for the various domains of colonialist discourse which I have schematised above. Rolfe's letter reorients potentially truant sexual desire within the confines of a duly ordered and supervised civil relationship. *The Tempest* represents a politicisation of what for Rolfe is experienced as primarily a crisis of his individual subjectivity. For example, the proof of Prospero's power to order and supervise his little colony is manifested in his capacity to control not *his,* but his *subjects'* sexuality, particularly that of his slave and his daughter. Rolfe's personal triumph of reason over passion or soul over body is repeated publicly as Prospero's triumphant ordering of potentially truant or subversive desires in his body politic. Similarly, Prospero's reintegration into the political world of Milan and Naples is represented, in Prospero's narrative, as an elaborate courtship, a series of strategic manoeuvres with political as well as "loving" intentions and effects. This will be examined further in due course. For the moment I am simply seeking to show connection between a class discourse (masterlessness), a race discourse (savagism) and a courtly and politicised discourse on sexuality. This characteristically produces an encounter with the other involving the coloniser's attempts to dominate, restrict, and exploit the other even as that other offers allurements which might erode the order obtaining within the civil subject or the body politic. This encounter is truly a labyrinthine situation, offering the affirmation or *ravelling up* of the civil subject even as it raises the possibility of its undoing, its erosion, its *unravelling.*[6] A brief survey of British colonial operations will help us to establish a network of relations or discursive matrix *within and against which* an analysis of *The Tempest* becomes possible.

Geographically, the discourse operated upon the various domains of British world influence, which may be discerned roughly, in the terms of Immanuel Wallerstein, as the "core," "semiperiphery" and "periphery."[7] Colonialism therefore comprises the expansion of royal hegemony in the English-Welsh mainland (the internal colonialism of the core), the extension of British influence in the semiperiphery of Ireland, and the diffuse range of British interests in the extreme periphery of the New World. Each expansive thrust extended British power beyond existing spheres of influence into new margins. In the core, these areas included the North, Wales and other "dark corners" such as woods, wastes and suburbs. In the semiperiphery, the Pale around Dublin was extended and other areas subdued and settled. In America, official and unofficial excursions were made into "virgin" territory. I have given one example of the production of an American other; the production of core and Irish others will exemplify the enormous scope of contemporary colonialist discourse.

In his "archaeology" of the wild man type, Hayden White discusses the threat to civil society posed by the very proximity of anti-social man: "he is just out of sight, over the horizon, in the nearby forest, desert, mountains, or hills. He sleeps in crevices, under great trees, or in the caves of wild animals."[8] Many of these characteristics are shared by the more socially specific production of the "masterless man,"[9] the ungoverned and unsupervised man without the restraining resources of social organisation, an embodiment of directionless and indiscriminate desire. Masterless types were discerned in royal proclamations to exist in the very suburbs of the capital.[10] These and other texts produce a counter-culture within the margins of civility, living in disorder, requiring surveillance, classification, expulsion, and punishment. A typical example is Richard Johnson's *Look Upon Me London* (1613) in which warnings against the city's many "alectives to unthriftinesse" are given. To counter such traps for the ingenuous sons of the gentry, Johnson produces a taxonomy of bad houses, hierarchically arranged according to the social standing of their clientele, of which the worst are "out of the common walkes of the magistrates."[11] These are "privy houses," privy in that they are hidden and secret and also in that they attract the dirt or excremental elements of the body politic. Such dirt is continually viewed as a dire threat to civil order in this literature. Johnson specifically warns that "if the shifters in, and within the level of London, were truly mustered, I dare boldly say they would amaze a good army" (p. 20). The masterless are, here, produced as an other, that "many-headed multitude" common in such writing.[12]

This other is a threat around which the governing classes might mobilise, that is, around which they might recognise their common class position, as governors, over and against the otherwise ungoverned and dangerous multitudes. In *The Tempest* Stephano the "drunken butler" and the "jester" Trinculo obviously represent such masterless men, whose alliance with the savage Caliban provides an antitype of order, issuing in a revolt requiring chastisement and ridicule. The assembled aristocrats in the play, and perhaps in the original courtly audiences, come to recognise in these figures their own common identity — and the necessity for a solidarity among the ruling class in face of such a threat. This solidarity must take priority over any internecine struggles; the masterless therefore function to bind the rulers together in hegemony. They were produced as a counter-order, sometimes classified according to rigid hierarchies of villainy in some demonic parody of good order,[13] sometimes viewed as a reserve army of potential recruits for rebellion, sometimes offered as a mere negative principle, the simple absence of the requirements of civility, attracting the sons of the gentry through its very spaciousness, irresponsibility and dirtiness.

Johnson's text produces a complex pleasure beyond the simple production of an instrumental knowledge of the masterless other. This knowledge is certainly offered for the services of magistracy and no doubt produces the antitype by which good order might be defined. Yet this moral and serviceable discourse displays in its descriptive richness precisely the intense and voyeuristic fascination for the other which it warns the gentry against. The text ostensibly avoids the taint of voyeurism by declaring that since this probing and exposing of dirt is required for the sober gaze of magistracy, a certain specular pleasure may be allowed. Again, at least officially, a potentially disruptive desire provoked by the "alective" other of masterlessness is channelled into positive civil service. This encoding of pleasure within the production of useful knowledge for the advantage of civil power is specifically described by Francis Bacon in his essay "Of Truth" as an erotic and courtly activity: the pursuit of knowledge is a "love-making or wooing."[14] Bacon implicitly offers an ideal of Renaissance sovereignty which can unite what Foucault terms "power-knowledge-pleasure."[15] Here pleasure is not simply disruptive, something produced by the other to deform or disturb the civil subject; it is a vital adjunct to power, a utilisation of the potentially disruptive to further the workings of power. In courtly fictions we can see this movement in operation: the other is incorporated into the service of sovereignty by reorienting *its* desires.

Such fictions include celebrations which centre upon the figure of the good sovereign. In these, the mere presence of the royal personage and the power of the royal gaze are able to transmute hitherto recalcitrant elements of the body politic, engendering in the place of disorderly passion a desire for service that is akin to an erotic courtship. In progresses, processions and masques such powers were continually complimented. In 1575, for example, at Kenilworth, Elizabeth I was confronted by an "Hombre Salvagio." In dangerous marginal space, beyond the confines of the great house, at the edge of the wild woods, at a most dangerous hour (nine o'clock in the evening), the Virgin Queen encountered the very emblem of marginality. But at this moment of maximum threat the wild man is metamorphosed into her eloquent and loving subject. He says:

> O queen, I must confesse it is not without cause
> These civile people so rejoice, that you should give them lawes.
> Since I, which live at large, a wilde and savage man,
> And have ronne out a wilfull race, since first my life began,
> Do here submit my selfe, beseeching yow to serve.[16]

The Hombre's entry into a loving relationship with Elizabeth is also his entry into interpersonal language (he has hitherto only spoken to his echo) and into subjection to a lawful sovereign: his very capacity to represent himself as "I" is in the gift of the sovereign. She confers on him the status of a linguistic and a legal subject, he now operates in a courtly idiom and in the "sentence" of the sovereign law.[17] Such taming of the wild man by a courtly virgin is a ubiquitous trope in medieval and Renaissance literature, as Richard Bernheimer has shown.[18] It serves as an emblem of courtly power, of the capacity to reorient masterlessness and savagism into service without recourse to the naked exercise of coercive power. This tropology is of great importance in the delineation of the Miranda–Caliban relationship, as I shall show later.

The discourse of masterlessness was embodied also in proclamations and statutes requiring that the bodies of vagrant classes, for example, should be modified.[19] Those condemned as persistent vagrants could literally be marked (whipped, bored, branded) with public signs announcing their adulteration, the hallmark of vice. Alternatively they could suffer the discipline of the work-house or the Bridewell. Yet no apparatus seemed sufficient to keep their numbers down. The constant vilification and punishment of those designated masterless by the ruling classes was not simply a strategy designed to legitimate civil rule: it also evidences a genuine anxiety. This took several forms: a real fear of the power of the governed classes should they mobilise against their betters; a complex displacement of the fear of aristocratic revolt on to the already vilified; a realisation that the increasing numbers of mobile classes evidenced a fundamental social change and a great threat to traditional modes of deference; and, finally, perhaps, a recognition of the restrictive nature of that deference society registered precisely in the continuous fascination for the disorderly other.

The thrust into Ireland from the 1530s sought to consolidate and expand British political control and economic exploitation of a strategic marginal area previously only partially under British authority.[20] D. B. Quinn has shown that the major policies of this expansion included plantation of British settlements in key areas, the establishment of a docile landed elite, the fossilisation of the social order in areas under British control, the conversion of Gaelic customs into their "civil" counterparts and the introduction of English as the sole official language.[21] These policies were exercised partly through a vast discursive production of Ireland and the Irish. The virtuous and vicious potentialities that were attributed to Pocahontas predominate in such discourse. Ireland was therefore a savage land that might yet be made to flow with milk and honey like a new Canaan. Similarly the Irish were seen as both savage Gaels and lapsed civil subjects. This arose out of historic claims that the land was *both* a feudal fief under British lordship (then, under the Tudors, under direct British sovereignty), whose truant subjects needed reordering and pacification *and* also a colony, where the savage other needed to be civilised, conquered, dispossessed.[22] The discourse afforded a flexible ensemble to be mobilised in the service of the varying fortune of the British in their semiperiphery.

In this highly complex discourse an "elementary ethnology" was formulated in which the various cultures of Ireland might be examined, and evidence gathered to show their inferiority to civility even as their potential for exploitation was assessed (Quinn, p. 20). As with the Negro or Amerindian, the Irish might be constituted as bestial or only marginally human and, as such, totally irreformable. For example, in 1594 Dawtrey drew upon a whole stock of commonplaces to give his opinion of the possibility of change in the Irish: "an ape will be an ape though he were clad in cloth of gold" (quoted in Quinn, pp. 36–7). It should be noted that Stephano's and Trinculo's masterless aping of the aristocrats in IV.i, where they steal rich clothes off a line, bears the weight of this stereotypicality—and their subsequent punishment, being hunted with dogs, draws full attention to their bestiality.

Even if granted human status, Gaelic modes of social behaviour were viewed as the antithesis of civil codes. In Spenser's account of booleying (the seasonal migration of livestock and owners to summer pasture), this wandering and unsupervised operation enables its practioners to "grow thereby the more barbarous and live more licentiously than they could in towns, . . . for there they think themselves half exempted from law and obedience, and having once tasted freedom do, like a steer that hath long been out of his yoke, grudge and repine ever after to come under rule again."[23] Barbarity is opposed to the life of the town or *polis,* and the booleyers evade the law, conferring upon themselves the status of truants or outlaws—masterless men. Each social relegation marks the Irish off again as beast-like, requiring the management of the British husbandman.

Within this general delineation of masterless barbarity, particular classes of footloose Irish were specifically targeted, especially jesters (again notice how Trinculo is related to such exemplary antitypes), "carrows" (or gamblers), wolvine "kernes" (or foot soldiers) and bards. Such figures literally embodied the masterless/savage threat and their suppression became a symbolic statement of British intent for the whole of uncivil Ireland.

More positive versions of Ireland were also produced, particularly in those texts which advocated plantation of the English beyond the Pale. Such versions produce Irish culture, generally, along the lines of a "negative formula," in which the alien is afforded no positive terms but merely displays the absence of those qualities that connote civility, for example, no law, no government, no marriage, no social hierarchy, no visible mode of production, no permanent settlement.[24] Again *The Tempest* is implicated in such a strategy. Gonzalo's description of his imagined island kingdom in II.i, culled from Montaigne, rehearses the standard formula by which the colonised is denigrated even as it appears to be simply the idle thoughts of a stranded courtier.

At its most optimistic the negative formula represents the other as a natural simplicity against which a jaded civility might be criticised, yet even here the other is produced for the use of civility, to gauge *its* present crisis. Nevertheless, the other's critical function must not be overlooked, as I hope to demonstrate with *The Tempest.* The more typical orientation of the other around the negative formula, however, is the production of a *tabula rasa.* Eden's translation of Peter Martyr's *Decades* (1555) provides a central statement of such a strategy. The Amerindians are "Gentiles" who "may well be likened to a smooth, bare table unpainted, or a white paper unwritten, upon the which you may at the first paint or write what you list, as you cannot upon tables already painted, unless you raze or blot out the first forms."[25] Here the other is an empty space to be inscribed at will by the desire of the coloniser. In some accounts of Ireland the land and the bulk of its peasantry were this unpainted table. Yet contradictorily, for instance in the version of Sir John Davies, before it could be painted at will certain obdurate forms, tyrannical lords and customs had to be razed.[26]

So vacuous or vicious, docile or destructive, such stereotypical production announced the triumph of civility or declared the other's usefulness for its purposes. But a dark countertruth needed to be acknowledged. The inferior culture of the Gaels had absorbed the Old English invaders, as Davies noted with horror: "The English, who hoped to make a perfect conquest of the Irish, were by them perfectly and absolutely conquered" (p. 290). The possibility of "going native" was constantly evidenced in this example, which Davies likened to the vicious transformation of Nebuchadnezzar or the Circean swine (p. 297). The supposed *binary* division of civil and other into virtue/vice, positive/negative, etc., was shown to be erodable as the forces of the subordinate term of the opposition seeped back into the privileged term. The blank spaces of Ireland provided not only an opportunity for the expansion of civility; they were also sites for the possible undoing of civil man, offering a "freedom" (Spenser's term for the avoidance of civility in the quotation above) in which he might lapse into masterlessness and savagism. The same discourse which allows for the transformation of the savage into the civil also raises the possibility of a reverse transformation. As Davies could announce a hope for the homogenisation of the Irish into civility "so that we may conceive an hope that the next generation will in tongue and heart and every way else become English" (Davies, p. 335), so Spenser could remark of civil man: "Lord, how quickly doth that country alter men's natures" (p. 51).

Given the importance of the colonisation of Ireland for British expansionism, together with its complex discursive formation which I have outlined briefly, it is surprising that such scant attention has been paid to such material in relation to *The Tempest*. I am not suggesting that Irish colonial discourse should be ransacked to find possible sources for some of the play's phraseology. Rather (as Hulme and Barker suggest) we should note a general analogy between text and context; specifically, between Ireland and Prospero's island. They are both marginally situated in semiperipheral areas (Ireland is geographically semiperipheral, its subjects both truant civilians and savages, as Prospero's island is ambiguously placed between American and European discourse). Both places are described as "uninhabited" (that is, connoting the absence of civility) and yet are peopled with a strange admixture of the savage and masterless other, powerfully controlling and malcontentedly lapsed civil subjects. Both locations are subject to powerful organising narratives which recount the beleaguerments, loss and recovery—the ravelling and unravelling—of colonising subjects. Such discourse provides the richest and the most fraught discussion of colonialism at the moment of the play's inception.

Much of my analysis above has been theoretically informed by Edward Said's account of orientalist discourse.[27] Orientalism is not simply a discourse which produces a certain knowledge of the East, rather it is a "western style for dominating, restructuring and having authority over the Orient" (p. 3). Although it cannot be simply correlated with the process of *material* exploitation of the East, the discourse produces a form of knowledge which is of great utility in aiding this process—serving to define the West as its origin, serving to relegate alien cultures, serving even the voyeuristic and libidinal desire of the western man who is denied such expression elsewhere.

Homi K. Bhabha's recent account of the colonialist stereotype effects a critique of Said, suggesting that even in the stereotype there is something which prevents it from being *totally* useful for the coloniser.[28] Bhabha says the stereotype "connotes rigidity and an unchanging order as well as disorder, degeneracy and demonic repetition" (p. 18). This is to say that at the heart of the stereotype, a discursive strategy designed to locate or "fix" a colonial other in a position of inferiority to the coloniser, the potentiality of a disruptive threat must be admitted. For example, if a stereotype declares the black to be rapacious, then even as it marks him as inferior to the self-controlled white, it announces his power to violate, and thus requires the imposition of restraint if such power is to be curtailed: so the stereotype cannot rest, it is always impelled to *further* action.

To summarise, I have begun to suggest that colonialist discourse voices a demand both for order and disorder, producing a disruptive other in order to assert the superiority of the coloniser. Yet that production is itself evidence of a struggle to restrict the other's disruptiveness to that role. Colonialist discourse does not simply announce a triumph for civility, it must continually *produce* it, and this work involves struggle and risk. It is this complex relation between the intention to produce colonialist stereotypicality, its beleaguerments and even its possible erosion in the face of the other that I now wish to trace through *The Tempest*.

The play begins in an apparent disruption of that social deference and elemental harmony which characterise the representation of courtly authority in Renaissance dramaturgy. Yet this initial "tempest" becomes retroactively a kind of antimasque or disorderly prelude to the assertion of that courtly authority which was supposedly in jeopardy. From Prospero's initial appearance it becomes clear that disruption was produced to create a series of problems precisely in order to effect their resolution. The dramatic conflict of the opening of the play is to be reordered to declare the mastery of Prospero in being able to initiate and control such dislocation and dispersal. This narrative intention is a correlate of the courtly masque proper, in which, conflict having been eradicated, elaborate and declarative compliment might be made to the supervising sovereign (as in the Hombre Salvagio episode, above). Prospero's problems concerning the maintenance of his power on the island are therefore also problems of representation, of his capacity to "forge" the island in his own image. The production of narrative, in this play, is always related to questions of power.

In his powerful narrative, Prospero interpellates the various listeners—calls to them, as it were, and invites them to recognise themselves as subjects of his discourse, as beneficiaries of his civil largesse. Thus for Miranda he is a strong father who educates and protects her; for Ariel he is a rescuer and taskmaster; for Caliban he is a coloniser whose refused offer of civilisation forces him to strict discipline; for the shipwrecked he is a surrogate providence who corrects errant aristocrats and punishes plebeian revolt. Each of these subject positions confirms Prospero as master.

The second scene of the play is an extended demonstration of Prospero's powerful narration as it interpellates Miranda, Ariel and Caliban. It is recounted as something importantly rescued out of the "dark backward and abysm of time" (I.ii.50), a remembrance of things past soon revealed as a mnemonic of power. This is to say, Prospero's narrative demands of its subjects that they should accede to *his* version of the past. For Miranda, Prospero's account of her origins is a tale of the neglect of office, leading to a fraternal usurpation and a banishment, followed by a miraculous landfall on the island. Prospero first tells of his loss of civil power and then of its renewal, in magic, upon the marginal space of the island. This reinvestiture in civil power through the medium of the non-civil is an essentially colonialist discourse. However, the narrative is fraught because it reveals internal contradictions which strain its ostensible project and because it produces the possibility of sites of resistance in the other precisely at the moment when it seeks to impose its captivating power.

In the recitation to Miranda, for example, Prospero is forced to remember his own past *forgetfulness*, since it was his devotion to private study that al-

lowed his unsupervised brother, masterlessly, to seize power. He is forced to recall a division between liberal and stately arts which are ideally united in the princely magus of masquing fiction. However as the recitation continues, this essentially political disjunction becomes simply the pretext or initial disruption that is replaced by a mysterious account of the recovery of civil power, the reunification of the liberal artist and the politic sovereign. It is re-presented as a *felix culpa*, a fortunate fall, in which court intrigue becomes reinscribed in the terms of romance, via a shift from the language of courtiership to that of courtship, to a rhetoric of love and charity.

This is marked by a series of tropes deriving from courtly love conventions, as Kermode notes (p. 18). The deposed duke becomes a helpless exile who cries into the sea, which charitably responds, as does the wind, with pity (148–50). The deposition becomes a "loving wrong" (151)—again the very form of oxymoron is typical of Petrarchan love sonnetry. These romance tropes effect a transition from a discourse of power to one of powerlessness. This mystifies the origin of what is after all a colonialist regime on the island by producing it as the result of charitable acts (by the sea, the wind and the honest courtier, Gonzalo, alike) made out of pity for powerless exiles. Recent important work on pastoral and amatory sonnet sequences has shown how such a rhetoric of love, charity and romance is always already involved in the mediation of power relations.[29] Prospero's mystifying narrative here has precisely these effects. Further, his scheme for the resumption of his dukedom and his reintegration with the larger political world is also inscribed in such terms, as a courtship of "bountiful Fortune," his "dear lady," or of an auspicious star which "If now I court her not, but omit, my fortunes / Will ever after droop" (see 179–84). And, of course, a major strategy of this scheme is to engineer another courtship, between Miranda and the son of his old enemy—his daughter having been duly educated for such a role in the enclosed and enchanted space of the island. The entire production of the island here, ostensibly an escape or exile from the world of statism, is thoroughly instrumental, even if predicated upon an initial loss of power.

In the same scene Prospero reminds Ariel of his indebtedness to the master, an act of memory which it is necessary to repeat monthly (261–3). This constant reminding operates as a mode of "symbolic violence":[30] What is really at issue is the underlining of a power relation. Ariel is, paradoxically, *bound* in service by this constant reminder of Prospero's gift of *freedom* to him, in releasing him from imprisonment in a tree. That bondage is reinforced by both a promise to repeat the act of release when a period of servitude has expired and a promise to repeat the act of incarceration should service not be forthcoming. In order to do this, Prospero utilises the previous regime of Sycorax as an evil other. Her black, female magic ostensibly contrasts with that of Prospero in that it is remembered as viciously coercive, yet beneath the apparent voluntarism of the white, male regime lies the threat of precisely this coercion. This tends to produce an identification between the regimes, which is underscored by biographical similarities such as that both rulers are magicians, both have been exiled because of their practices, both have nurtured children on the isle. The most apparent distinction between black and white regimes[31] would seem to be that the latter is simply more powerful and more flexible. Part of its flexibility is its capacity to produce and utilise an other in order to obtain the consent of Ariel to his continued subjugation.

Caliban, on the other hand, is nakedly enslaved to the master. The narrative of I.ii legitimises this exercise of power by representing Caliban's resistance to colonisation as the obdurate and irresponsible refusal of a simple educative project. This other, the offspring of a witch and a devil, the wild man and savage, the emblem of morphological ambivalence (see Hulme, "Hurricans in the Caribees," p. 67ff), was even without language before the arrival of the exiles. It was Miranda, the civil virgin, who, out of pity, taught Caliban to "know thine own meaning" (358). Yet, as with the Hombre Salvagio above, the "gift" of language also inscribes a power relation as the other is hailed and recognises himself as a linguistic subject of the master language. Caliban's refusal marks him as obdurate yet he must voice this in a curse in the language of civility, representing himself as a subject of what he so accurately describes as *"your* language" (367, my stress). Whatever Caliban does with this gift announces his capture by it.

Yet within the parameters of this capture Caliban is able to create a resistance. Ostensibly *produced* as an other to provide the pretext for the exercise of naked power, he is also a *producer*, provoking reaction in the master. He does not come when called, which makes Prospero angry (315–22). Then he greets the colonisers with a curse, provoking the master to curse in reply, reducing the eloquent master of civil language to the raucous registers of the other (323–32). Third, he ignores the civil curse and proceeds with his own narrative, in which Prospero himself is designated as usurping other to Caliban's initial monarchy and hospitality (333–46). Such discursive strategies show that Caliban has indeed mastered enough of the lessons of civility to ensure that its interpellation of him as simply savage, "a born devil, on whose nature / Nurture can never stick" (IV.i.188–9), is inadequate. Paradoxically, it is the eloquent power of civility which allows him to know his *own* meaning, offering him a site of resistance even as civility's coercive capacities finally reduce him to silence (373–5).

The island itself is an "uninhabited" spot, a *tabula rasa* peopled fortuitously by the shipwrecked. Two children, Miranda and Caliban, have been nurtured upon it. Prospero's narrative operates to produce in them the binary division of the other, into the malleable and the irreformable, that I have shown to be a major strategy of colonialist discourse. There is Miranda, miraculous courtly lady, virgin prospect (cf. Virginia itself) and there is Caliban, scrambled "cannibal," savage incarnate. Presiding over them is the cabalist Prospero, whose function it is to divide and demarcate these potentialities, arrogating to the male all that is debased and rapacious, to the female all that is cultured and needs protection.

Such a division of the "children" is validated in Prospero's narrative by the memory of Caliban's attempted rape of Miranda (I.ii.347–53), which immediately follows Caliban's own account of his boundless hospitality to the exiles on their arrival (333–46). The issue here is not whether Caliban is actually a rapist or not, since Caliban accepts the charge. I am rather concerned with the political effects of this charge at this moment in the play. The first effect is to circumvent Caliban's version of events by reencoding his boundlessness as rapacity: his inability to discern a concept of private, bounded property concerning his own dominions is reinterpreted as a desire to violate the chaste virgin, who epitomises courtly property. Second, the capacity to divide and order is shown to be the prerogative of the courtly ruler alone. Third, the memory legitimises Prospero's takeover of power.

Such a sexual division of the other into rapist and virgin is common in colonialist discourse. In *The*

Faerie Queene, for example, Ireland is presented as both Irene, a courtly virgin, and Grantorto, a rapacious woodkerne from whom the virgin requires protection, thus validating the intervention of the British knight, Artegall, and his killing machine, Talus.[32] Similarly, in Purchas's *Virginia's Verger* of 1625 the uprising of 1622 is shown to be an act of incestuous rape by native sons upon a virgin land, and this declares the rightfulness of the betrothal of that land to duly respectful civil husbandmen, engaged in "presenting her as a chaste virgin to Christ" (see Porter, *The Inconstant Savage,* p. 480). Miranda is represented as just such a virgin, to be protected from the rapist native and presented to a civil lover, Ferdinand. The "fatherly" power of the coloniser, and his capacity to regulate and utilise the sexuality of his subject "children," is therefore a potent trope as activated in *The Tempest* and again demonstrates the crucial nexus of civil power and sexuality in colonial discourse. The other is here presented to legitimate the seizure of power by civility and to define by antithesis (rape) the proper course of civil courtship—a channelling of desire into a series of formal tasks and manoeuvres and, finally, into courtly marriage. Such a virtuous consummation is predicated upon the disruptive potential of carnality, embodied in the rapist other and in the potentially truant desires of the courtly lovers themselves, which Prospero constantly warns them against (as at IV.i.15–23 and 51–4). With little evidence of such truancy, Prospero's repeated warnings reassert his power to regulate sexuality just at the point when such regulatory power is being transferred from father to husband. Yet his continued insistence on the power of desire to disrupt courtly form surely also evidences an unease, an anxiety, about the power of civility to deliver control over a force which it locates both in the other and in the civil subject.

A capacity to divide and demarcate groups of subjects along class lines is also demonstrated. The shipwrecked courtiers are dispersed on the island into two groups, aristocrats and plebeians. The usurping "men of sin" in the courtly group are first maddened, then recuperated; the drunken servants, unmastered, are simply punished and held up to ridicule. This division of masterless behaviour serves a complex hegemonic function: the unselfmastered aristocrats are reabsorbed, after correction, into the governing class, their new solidarity underscored by their collective laughter at the chastened revolting plebeians. The class joke acts as a recuperative and defusive strategy which celebrates the renewal of courtly hegemony and displaces its breakdown on to the ludicrous revolt of the masterless.

Such binarism is also apparent in productions such as Ben Jonson's *Irish Masque at Court* (first put on in December, 1613).[33] Here indecorous stage-Irish plebeians are banished from the royal presence, to be replaced with the courtly exemplars of newly-converted Anglo-Irish civility. In this James I's coercive power is celebrated as music. Now Ireland has stooped to "the music of his peace, / She need not with the spheres change harmony." This harmonics of power causes the Irish aristocrats to slough off their former dress and customs to emerge as English court butterflies; the ant-like rabble are precluded from such a metamorphosis.

This last example demonstrates another strategy by which sovereign power might at once be praised and effaced *as power* in colonialist discourse. In this masque, power is represented as an *aesthetic* ordering. This correlates with Prospero's investment in the power of narrative to maintain social control and with *The Tempest's* production of the origins of colonialism through the rhetoric of romance, its representation of colonial power as a gift of freedom or of education, its demonstration of colonialist organisation as a "family romance" involving the management and reordering of disruptive desire. The play's observation of the classical unities (of space, time and action), its use of harmonious music to lead, enchant, relax, restore, its constant reference to the leisured space of pastoral[34] and the dream, all underline this aesthetic and disinterested, harmonious and non-exploitative representation of power. In a sermon of Richard Crashaw (1610), the latent mechanisms of power which actually promote the metamorphosis of jaded civil subjects is acknowledged: the transplanted, if "subject to some pinching miseries and to a strict form of government and severe discipline, do often become new men, even as it were cast in a new mould" (quoted in Porter, pp. 369–70). *The Tempest* is, therefore, fully implicated in the process of "euphemisation," the effacement of power—yet, as I have begun to demonstrate, the play also reveals precisely "the strict form of government" which actually underpins the miraculous narrative of "sea change." The play oscillates uneasily between mystification and revelation and this is crucially demonstrated in the presentation of the plebeian revolt.

The process of euphemisation depends upon the rebellious misalliance of Caliban and Stephano and Trinculo being recognised as a kind of antimasque, yet there are features of this representation which disrupt such a recognition. Ostensibly the "low" scenes of the play ape courtly actions and demonstrate the latter's superiority. The initial encounter of the masterless and the savage, for example, is analogous to the encounter between the civil and the savage narrated by Prospero, and to the encounter of the New World virgin and the gallant courtier enacted before the audience. Caliban's hospitality to Prospero is repeated as an act of voluntary subjection to the actually powerless exile, Stephano. This act is a bathetic version of the idealised meeting of civil and savage epitomised in the Hombre Salvagio episode—Caliban misrecognises *true* sovereignty and gives his fealty rather to a drunken servant. Unlike the immediate recognition of a common courtly bond which Miranda and Ferdinand experience, the savage and the masterless reveal a spontaneous *non-civil* affinity. More locally, as the courtly exiles brought Caliban the gift of language, so the masterless donate "that which will give language to you, cat"—a bottle (II.ii.84–5); the former imposes linguistic capture and restraint, the latter offers release.

Yet the issue is more complex, for what this misalliance mediates, in "low" terms, is precisely a colonising situation. Only here can the colonising process be viewed as nakedly avaricious, profiteering, perhaps even pointless (the expense of effort to no end rather than a proper teleological civil investment). Stephano, for example, contemplates taming and exhibiting Caliban for gain (II.ii.78–80). Also, the masterless do not lead but are led around by the savage, who must constantly remind them of their rebellious plans (see IV.i.231–2). This low version of colonialism serves to displace possibly damaging charges which might be levied against properly-constituted civil authority on to the already excremental products of civility, the masterless. This allows those charges to be announced and defused, transforming a possible anxiety into pleasure at the ludicrous antics of the low who will, after all, be punished in due course.

This analysis still produces the other as being in the (complex) service of civility, even if the last paragraph suggests that a possible anxiety is being displaced. Yet there is a manifest contradiction in the representation of the misalliance which I have not considered so far: in denigrating the masterless, such scenes foreground more positive qualities in the savage. The banter of the drunkards serves to counterpoint moments of great eloquence in the obdurate slave. Amid all the comic business, Caliban describes the effects of the island music:

> the isle is full of noises,
> Sounds and sweet airs, that give delight, and hurt not.
> Sometimes a thousand twangling instruments
> Will hum about mine ears; and sometimes voices,
> That, if I then had wak'd after long sleep,
> Will make me sleep again: and then, in dreaming,
> The clouds methought would open, and show riches
> Ready to drop upon me: that, when I wak'd,
> I cried to dream again   (III.ii.133–41)

Here the island is seen to operate not for the coloniser but for the colonised. Prospero utilises music to charm, punish and restore his various subjects, employing it like James I in a harmonics of power. For Caliban, music provokes a dream wish for the riches which in reality are denied him by colonising power. There seems to be a quality in the island beyond the requirements of the coloniser's powerful harmonics, a quality existing for itself, which the other may use to resist, if only in dream, the repressive reality which hails him as villain—both a feudalised bonded workhorse and evil incarnate.

This production of a site beyond colonial appropriation can only be represented through colonialist discourse, however, since Caliban's eloquence is after all "your language," the language of the coloniser. Obviously the play itself, heavily invested in colonialist discourse, can only represent this moment of excess through that very discourse: and so the discourse itself may be said to produce this site of resistance. Yet what precisely is at stake here?

The answer I believe is scandalously simple. Caliban's dream is not the *antithesis* but the *apotheosis* of colonialist discourse. If this discourse seeks to efface its own power, then here at last is an eloquent spokesman who is powerless; here such eloquence represents not a desire to control and rule but a fervent wish for release, a desire to escape reality and return to dream. Caliban's production of the island as a pastoral space, separated from the world of power, takes *literally* what the discourse in the hands of a Prospero can only mean *metaphorically*. This is to say, the colonialist project's investment in the processes of euphemisation of what are really powerful relations here has produced a utopian moment where powerlessness represents *a desire for powerlessness*. This is the danger that any metaphorical system faces, that vehicle may be taken for tenor and used against the ostensible meanings intended. The play registers, if only momentarily, a radical ambivalence at the heart of colonialist discourse, revealing that it is a site of *struggle* over meaning.

Prospero's narrative can be seen, then, to operate as a reality principle, ordering and correcting the inhabitants of the island, subordinating their discourse to his own. A more potent metaphor, however, might be the concept of dreamwork[35]—that labour undertaken to represent seamlessly and palatably what in reality is a contest between a censorship and a latent drive. The masterful operations of censorship are apparent everywhere in *The Tempest*. In the terminology of the analysis of dreamwork developed by Freud, these political operations may be discerned as displacement (for example, the displacement of the fear of noble insurrection on to the easily defeated misalliance), condensation (the condensation of the whole colonial project into the terms of a patriarchal demarcation of sexuality), symbolisation (the emblems of the vanishing banquet, the marriage masque, the discovery of the lovers at chess) and secondary revision (the ravelling up of the narrative dispersal of the storm scene, the imposition of Prospero's memory over that of his subjects, etc.). As I have attempted to show above with specific examples, such operations encode struggle and contradiction even as they, or *because* they, strive to insist on the legitimacy of colonialist narrative.

Further, as this narrative progresses, its master appears more and more to divest himself of the very power he has so relentlessly sought. As Fiedler brilliantly notes, in the courtship game in which Miranda is a pawn, even as Prospero's gameplan succeeds he himself is played out, left without a move as power over his daughter slips away (Fiedler, *The Stranger in Shakespeare*, p. 206). So the magus abjures his magic, his major source of coercive power (V.i.33–57). This is ostensibly replaced by civil power as Prospero resorts to his "hat and rapier," twin markers of the governor (the undoffed hat signifying a high status in a deference society, as the rapier signifies the aristocratic right to carry such weaponry). Yet this resumption of power entails the relinquishing of revenge upon the usurpers, an end to the exploitation and punishment of the masterless and the savage,

even an exile from the island. Further, he goes home not to resume public duty but to retire and think of death (see V.i.310–11). The completion of the colonialist project signals the banishment of its supreme exponent even as his triumph is declared.

Is this final distancing of the master from his narrative an unravelling of his project? Or is this displacement merely the final example of that courtly euphemisation of power outlined above? One last example must serve to demonstrate that the "ending" of the play is in fact a struggle between the apotheosis and the aporia of colonialist discourse. The marriage masque of IV.i demonstrates Prospero's capacity to order native spirits to perform a courtly narrative of his own design. In addition, this production is consented to by the audience of two courtly lovers, whose pleasure itself shows that they are bound by the narrative. As such, the masque is a model of ideological interpellation, securing chastity, a state which the master continually *demands* of the lovers, through active consent rather than coercive power. Further, Prospero's instructions to his audience before the masque begins implicitly rehearse his ideal subject-audience: "No tongue! All eyes! be silent" (IV.i.59). Yet the masque is disrupted, as Prospero is drawn back from this moment of the declaration of his triumph into the realm of struggle, for Caliban's plot must be dealt with. Although the plot is allowed for in his timetable (see IV.i.141–2) and is demonstrably ineffectual, this irruption of the antimasque into the masque proper has a totally disproportionate effect to its actual capacity to seize power. The masque is dispelled and Prospero utters a monologue upon the illusory nature of all representation, even of the world itself (IV.i.153–8). Hitherto he has insisted that his narrative be taken as real and powerful—now it is collapsed, along with everything else, into the "stuff" of dreams. The forging of colonialist narrative is, momentarily, revealed as a forgery. Yet, Prospero goes on to meet the threat and triumph over it, thus completing his narrative. What is profoundly ambivalent here is the relation between narrative declaration and dramatic struggle. Prospero requires a struggle with the forces of the other in order to show his power: struggle is therefore the precondition for the announcement of his victory. Yet here the moment of declaration is disrupted as a further contest arises: Prospero must repeat the process of struggle. It is *he* who largely produces the ineffectual challenge as a dire threat.

This is to say, the colonialist narrative requires and produces the other—an other which continually destabilises and disperses the narrative's moment of conviction. The threat must be present to validate colonialist discourse; yet if present it cannot but impel the narrative to further action. The process is interminable. Yet the play has to end.

Given this central ambivalence in the narrative, and given Prospero's problematic relationship to the restitution of civil power, it falls upon the honest old courtier, Gonzalo, actually to announce the closure of the narrative. He confirms that all is restored, including "all of us ourselves / When no man was his own" (see V.i.206–13). True civil subjectivity is declared: the encounter with the forces of otherness on the island produces a signal victory. Yet the architect of that victory is to retire and die, his narrative a mere entertainment to while away the last night on the isle, his actor reduced in the epilogue to beg for the release of applause. When apportioning the plebeians to the masters, he assigns Caliban to himself, saying "this thing of darkness I / Acknowledge mine" (V.i.275–6). Even as this powerfully designates the monster as his property, an object for his own utility, a darkness from which he may rescue self-knowledge, there is surely an ironic identification *with* the other here as both become interstitial. Only a displacement of the narrating function from the master to a simpler, declarative civilian courtier can hope to terminate the endless struggle to relate self and other so as to serve the colonialist project. At the "close" of the play, Prospero is in danger of becoming the other to the narrative declaration of his own project, which is precisely the ambivalent position Caliban occupies.

The Tempest, then, declares no all-embracing triumph for colonialism. Rather it serves as a limit text in which the characteristic operations of colonialist discourse may be discerned—as an instrument of exploitation, a register of beleaguerment and a site of radical ambivalence. These operations produce strategies and stereotypes which seek to impose and efface colonialist power; in this text they are also driven into contradiction and disruption. The play's "ending" in renunciation and restoration is only the final ambivalence, being at once the apotheosis, mystification and potential erosion of the colonialist discourse. If this powerful discourse, thus mediated, is finally reduced to the stuff of dreams, then it is still dreamwork, the site of a struggle for meaning. My project has been to attempt a repunctuation of the play so that it may reveal its involvement in colonial practices, speak something of the ideological contradictions of its *political* unconscious.[36]

Notes

1. Such scholarship is summarised in Frank Kermode's Introduction to his edition of William Shakespeare, *The Tempest* (London: Methuen, 6th ed., corrected, 1964), *passim*. All quotations of the play are taken from this edition.
2. Some of the major incursions into this field are to be found in the notes below. At a late stage in the production of this paper I learnt of Peter Hulme's and Francis Barker's collaboration on an analysis of *The Tempest* in the forthcoming *Alternative Shakespeares*, ed. John Drakakis (London: Methuen, 1985). I was very pleased to see a draft of this important intervention which, unfortunately, I have not space to comment fully upon here. However, I hope I have begun to answer their call for a historical "con-textual" analysis of the play.
3. By "discourse" I refer to a domain or field of linguistic strategies operating within particular areas of social practice to effect knowledge and pleasure, being produced by and reproducing or reworking power relations between classes, genders and cultures.
4. The text is reproduced in Warren M. Billings, ed., *The Old Dominion in the Seventeenth Century: a Documentary History of Virginia* (Chapel Hill: University of North Carolina Press, 1975), pp. 216–19.
5. See Grace Steele Woodward, *Pocahontas* (Norman: University of Oklahoma Press, 1969), especially pp. 153–89.
6. Actually "ravelling" is a radically ambivalent term, meaning both to entangle and disentangle. It has peculiar descriptive relevance for my analysis of *The Tempest*.
7. See Immanuel Wallerstein, *The Modern World System: vol. I* (New York: Academic Press, 1974), ch. 2, *passim*.
8. Hayden White, "The Forms of Wildness: Archaeology of an Idea," in Edward Dudley and Maximillian Novak, eds., *The Wild Man Within: an Image in Western Thought from the Renaissance to Romanticism* (Pittsburgh University Press, 1972), pp. 20–1.

9. On the masterless classes see particularly Christopher Hill, *The World Turned Upside Down* (1972; rpt. Harmondsworth: Penguin, 1975), ch. 3, *passim.*

10. See Paul L. Hughes and James F. Larkin, ed., *Tudor Royal Proclamations* (New Haven: Yale University Press, 1969), vol. II, no. 622 and vol. III, nos. 762 and 809, for examples.

11. Richard Johnson, "Look Upon Me London . . ." in J. Payne Collier, ed., *Illustrations of Early English Popular Literature* (1863; rpt. New York: Benjamin Blom, 1966), part 7, p. 19. Jonathan Dollimore, above p. 76, quotes a remarkably similar phrase in George Whetstone's *Mirror for Magistrates,* which is undoubtedly the most important immediate source for Johnson's plagiarism and serves to underline the chronic ubiquity of such a trope.

12. See Christopher Hill, "The Many-Headed Monster in Late Tudor and Early Stuart Political Thinking," in Charles H. Carter, ed., *From the Renaissance to the Counter-Reformation* (New York: Random House, 1965), pp. 296–324.

13. See for example the collection of A. V. Judges, ed., *The Elizabethan Underworld* (1930; rpt. London: Routledge, 1965).

14. In Francis Bacon, *Essays (1625),* ed. Michael Hawkins (London: Dent, 1973), p. 4.

15. See the theorisation of power–knowledge–pleasure in Michel Foucault, *The History of Sexuality: vol. I: An Introduction,* trans. Robert Hurley (Harmondsworth: Penguin, 1981), *passim.*

16. In John Nichols, ed., *The Progresses and Public Processions of Queen Elizabeth* (1823; rpt. New York: Burt Franklin, 1966), vol. I, pp. 436–8.

17. On the assimilation of the language of the other for the service of colonialism see Stephen J. Greenblatt, "Learning to Curse: Aspects of Linguistic Colonialism in the Sixteenth Century," in Fredi Chiapelli, ed., *First Images of America: The Impact of the New World on the Old* (Berkeley and Los Angeles: University of California Press, 1970), 561–80. This article and that of Peter Hulme, "Hurricans in the Caribbees: the Constitution of the Discourse of English Colonialism," in Francis Barker *et al.*, eds., *Literature and Power in the Seventeenth Century: Proceedings of the Essex Conference on the Sociology of Literature, July 1980* (Colchester: University of Essex, 1981), pp. 55–

83, offer important commentary on Caliban and civil language.

18. Richard Bernheimer, *Wild Men in the Middle Ages: a Study in Art, Sentiment and Demonology* (1952; rpt. New York: Octagon Press, 1970), pp. 136–55.

19. For a listing of the acts relating to vagrancy see Ken Powell and Chris Cook, *English Historical Facts: 1485–1603* (London: Macmillan, 1977), pp. 56–8.

20. For a short account of this bloody history see Grenfell Morton, *Elizabethan Ireland* (London: Longmans, 1971), *passim.*

21. See David Beers Quinn, *The Elizabethans and the Irish* (Ithaca: Cornell University Press, 1966), especially ch. 10; and Michael Hechter, *Internal Colonialism: the Celtic Fringe in British Colonial Development 1536–1966* (London: Routledge and Kegan Paul, 1975), especially part 2.

22. Hence the discourses regarding the Irish and the Amerindians were mutually reinforcing. See on this issue Nicholas P. Canny, "The Ideology of English Colonization," *William and Mary Quarterly,* 30 (1973), 575–98. Throughout this section I am indebted to the work of Bernard W. Sheehan, *Savagism and Civility: Indians and Englishmen in Colonial Virginia* (Cambridge University Press, 1980), *passim.*

23. Edmund Spenser, *A View of the Present State of Ireland* (1596), ed. W. L. Renwick (Oxford: Clarendon Press, 1970), p. 50.

24. See Sheehan, ch. 1, *passim* and Margaret T. Hogden, *Early Anthropology in the Sixteenth and Seventeenth Centuries* (Philadelphia: University of Pennsylvania Press, 1964), *passim.*

25. Quoted in H. C. Porter, *The Inconstant Savage: Englishmen and the North American Indian* (Duckworth, 1979), p. 28.

26. Sir John Davies, "A Discovery of the True Causes Why Ireland Was Never Subdued . . . Until the Beginning of His Majesty's Happy Reign," in Henry Morley, ed., *Ireland Under Elizabeth and James I* (London: George Routledge, 1890), p. 341.

27. Edward W. Said, *Orientalism* (London: Routledge, 1978), p. 2.

28. Homi K. Bhabha, "The Other Question," *Screen* 24 (1983), no. 6, pp. 18–36.

29. On the relation of courtship and courtiership see Peter Stallybrass and Ann Rosalind Jones, "The

Politics of *Astrophil and Stella*," *Studies in English Literature*, 24 (1984), 53–68. On the mediation and effacement of power relations in courtly discourse see Louis A. Montrose, " 'Eliza, Queene of Shepheardes,' and the Pastoral of Power," *English Literary Renaissance*, 10 (1980), 153–82. For a short account of courtly theatre see Stephen Orgel, *The Illusion of Power: Political Theatre in the English Renaissance* (Berkeley and Los Angeles: University of California Press, 1975), *passim*.

30. On this concept see Pierre Bourdieu, *Outline of a Theory of Practice*, trans. Richard Nice (Cambridge University Press, 1977), pp. 190–7.

31. As noted in Leslie A. Fiedler, *The Stranger in Shakespeare* (St. Albans: Paladin, 1974), p. 64.

32. Edmund Spenser, *The Faerie Queene*, ed. T. P. Roche and C. P. O'Donnell (Harmondsworth: Penguin, 1978), book V, cantos xi–xii, *passim*.

33. Ben Jonson, *The Complete Masques*, ed. Stephen Orgel (New Haven: Yale University Press, 1968), pp. 206–12.

34. For the use of pastoral in colonialist discourse see Howard Mumford Jones, *O Strange New World: American Culture: the Formative Years* (New York: Viking Press, 1964), pp. 185–93.

35. On dreamwork see Sigmund Freud, *Introductory Lectures in Psychoanalysis: the Pelican Freud Library Vol. I*, trans. James Strachey, ed. James Strachey and Angela Richards (Harmondsworth: Penguin, 1973), especially chs. 9–11. Stephen Greenblatt notes in his *Renaissance Self-Fashioning: from More to Shakespeare* (University of Chicago Press, 1980), p. 173, that it was Freud who first drew the analogy between the political operations of colonialism and the modes of psychic repression. My use of Freudian terms does not mean that I endorse its ahistorical, Europocentric and sexist models of psychical development. However, a materialist criticism deprived of such concepts as displacement and condensation would be seriously impoverished in its analysis of the complex operations of colonialist discourse and its addressing of subjects of its power. This paper attempts to utilise psychoanalytic concepts for a strictly historical analysis of a particular text, foregrounding the representation of the embattled subjectivity of the (white, governing, patriarchal) coloniser.

36. The term is that of Fredric Jameson in his *The Political Unconscious: Narrative as a Socially Symbolic Act* (London: Methuen, 1983), *passim*. This represents the most profound attempt to assimilate psychoanalytic concepts into a materialist account of narrative production.

I would like to record my deepest thanks to the editors and to Peter Stallybrass, Ann Jones, Andrew Crozier, Alan Fair, Eric Woods and especially Barry Taylor for their enormous help in the preparation of this paper. My main debt, as ever, is to Lesly Brown.

APPLICATION

*Like other critics in this context, Jerome McGann wants
to free criticism from "the prison-house of language"
where, he feels, formal and structural theories have largely
confined it. And again like other critics in this context,
he believes that "culture," "history," and "ideology" are
the key terms that will unlock the gate. "To take up the
subject of poetry's conceptual and ideological elements is
to allow criticism once again to intersect with those other
traditional fields of inquiry so long alienated from the
center of our discipline: textual criticism, bibliography,
book production and distribution, reception history." This
intersection, however, will produce something rather different from traditional author-centered literary history
and something much closer to a revelation of the text's
"political unconscious." When critics undertake the
socio-historical investigation of Romantic poems, they
discover that "the works tend to develop different sorts
of artistic means with which to occlude and disguise
their own involvement in a certain nexus of historical
relations." This is the "ideology" of Romantic poetry,
and critics who would expose it must read against the
grain of the author's conscious intentions and beneath
the manifest content of the poem's surface. For frequently
a poem will be most deeply involved in its "historical relations" when it seems to say least about them.*

*Taking Wordsworth as the exemplary case, McGann-
offers readings of "The Ruined Cottage" and "Tintern
Abbey" before focusing on the Intimations Ode where
"the processes of elision which I have been describing
reach their notorious and brilliant apogee." Although
Wordsworth's consciousness turns out to be false, his
poem is nevertheless great—precisely because it is "a
rare, original, and comprehensive record of the birth and
character of a particular ideology." But to see that, the*

Wordsworth and the Ideology of Romantic Poems

Jerome J. McGann

Reprinted by permission from *The Romantic Ideology: A
Critical Investigation,* Chicago: University of Chicago Press,
81–92. Copyright © 1983 by the University of Chicago.

critic has to put the poem in the right context. The irony is that Wordsworth, by so artfully displacing the social to the psychological and the historically specific to the "universal," has fooled not only himself but most of his critics as well. When we read him on his own terms, we misread him. Only an explicitly "ideological" reading will serve as a corrective "not merely because ideology is a central . . . factor in Romantic works, but also because it is a central factor in the criticism of Romantic works." A thorough socio-historical criticism, then, will elucidate our own ideology as well as the author's.

At this point we can return to consider in greater detail the problem of ideology in Romantic poems. In my reconsideration of Swingle's arguments I tried to put the subject matter of poetry back into the general aesthetic field of a poem's operation. The advantage of such a move, from the point of view of critical method, is that it supplies the critic with more ways for defining the special character of poetic works. The critic need not feel obliged to work within the narrow limits of a poem's purely linguistic elements. To take up the subject of poetry's conceptual and ideological elements is to allow criticism once again to intersect with those other traditional fields of inquiry so long alienated from the center of our discipline: textual criticism, bibliography, book production and distribution, reception history. On all fronts the critic will move to enlarge the concept of the poetical work beyond that of a special kind of linguistic system, beyond even a certain type of semiological structure. The critic will be asked to expand the concept of the poem-as-text to the poem as a more broadly based cultural product: in short, to the poem as poetical work. This hardly means that we cease being interested in the linguistic and semiological aspects of poems; rather, it simply entails that those matters will be taken up in a cultural context which is at once more comprehensive (theoretically) and more particular (socially and historically).[1]

These general considerations lead us to conclude, then, that the "Isms" of Romantic poetry should not be set aside when we come to study Romantic poems. On the contrary, certain features which are peculiar to poems from the Romantic Period make it crucial to pay attention to those "Isms." I want now to consider two of the most important of these features. The patterns I shall be marking out are widespread in the works of the period. I shall concentrate here on Wordsworth, however, because his works—

like his position in the Romantic Movement—are normative and, in every sense, exemplary.

We begin by forcing the critical act to attend to the specific referential patterns which appear in specific poems. These references may be factual or cognitive, but in all cases they will be historically and socially specific. In the case of Romantic poems, we shall find that the works tend to develop different sorts of artistic means with which to occlude and disguise their own involvement in a certain nexus of historical relations. This act of evasion, as it were, operates most powerfully whenever the poem is most deeply immersed in its cognitive (i.e., its ideological) materials and commitments. For this reason the critic of Romantic poetry must make a determined effort to elucidate the subject matter of such poems *historically:* to define the specific ways in which certain stylistic forms intersect and join with certain factual and cognitive points of reference.

Rather than speak of the method in such general terms any longer, however, let me commence with "The Ruined Cottage,"[2] partly because it is a great poem, and partly because its structural methods for dealing with substantive issues are so clear. In his Fenwick note Wordsworth says that the work was based upon incidents and conditions which he had himself observed in 1793 in the southwest of England. The information is to an extent supererogatory since no one reading the story when it was first published in 1814, still less if it had been read earlier in a manuscript version, would have been unaware of the context in which the tragic events are embedded.

Margaret's husband Robert is a weaver and the poem focuses upon the precarious state in which this cottage industry found itself in the late eighteenth and early nineteenth century. Two bad harvests coupled with "that worse affliction . . . the plague of war" (136) bring Robert's family to the point of ruin, as he becomes one among those "shoals of artizans" who

> Were from their daily labor turned away
> To hang for bread on parish charity.
> They and their wives and children.   (154–7)

Eventually Robert joins the army in a pathetically incompetent and misplaced effort to free his family from their economic plight. Robert disappears in the gulf of war while his wife and child are left to the beautiful slow-motion narrative of their painfully slow-motion demise.

I have myself re-narrated these well-known details because the strategy of Wordsworth's poem is to elide their distinctiveness from our memories, to drive the particulars of this tragedy to a region that is too deep either for tears or for what Wordsworth here calls "restless thoughts" (198). Margaret's cottage is gradually overgrown and "ruined" when "Nature" invades its neglected precincts. This — the poem's dominant and most memorable process — finally comes to stand as an emblem of the endurance of Nature's care and ceaseless governance, just as it glances obliquely at the pathetic incompetence of individual, cultural, and institutional efforts to give stability to human affairs. Not England, not Robert's social and economic institutions, not even Robert by himself can afford protection against "A time of trouble." Margaret's cottage will collapse under their "neglect," which Wordsworth sees as inevitable, indeed, as a function of the social *rerum natura*.

This gradual collapse of the cottage into what Wordsworth calls, in his characteristic form of Romantic wit, Nature's "silent overgrowings" (506), has yet another analogue, however, in the poem's narrative method itself. To read Wordsworth's retelling of this pitiful story is to be led further and further from a clear sense of the historical origins and circumstantial causes of Margaret's tragedy. The place of such thoughts and such concerns is usurped, overgrown. Armytage, poet, and reader all fix their attention on a gathering mass of sensory, and chiefly vegetable, details. Hypnotized at this sensational surface, the light of sense goes out and "The secret spirit of humanity" emerges.

> I stood, and leaning o'er the garden gate
> Reviewed that Woman's suff'rings; and it seemed
> To comfort me while with a brother's love
> I blessed her in the impotence of grief.
> At length towards the cottage I returned
> Fondly, and traced with milder interest,
> That secret spirit of humanity
> Which, 'mid the calm oblivious tendencies
> Of nature, 'mid her plants, her weeds and flowers,
> And silent overgrowings, still survived.
> The old man seeing this resumed, and said,
> "My Friend, enough to sorrow have you given,
> The purposes of wisdom ask no more:
> Be wise and chearful, and no longer read
> The forms of things with an unworthy eye.
> She sleeps in the calm earth, and peace is here.
> (497–512)

Margaret's devotion, love, and fidelity to her house speak to Wordsworth's "restless" narrator from beyond the grave and transfer his allegiance from "The Party of Humanity" to its secret spiritual replacement. "The Ruined Cottage" aims to effect a similar translation of attention and commitments in the reader:

> I well remember that those very plumes,
> Those weeds, and the high spear-grass on that wall,
> By mist and silent rain-drops silvered o'er,
> As once I passed, did to my mind convey
> So still an image of tranquility,
> So calm and still, and looked so beautiful
> Amid the uneasy thoughts which filled my mind,
> That what we feel of sorrow and despair
> From ruin and from change, and all the grief
> The passing shews of being leave behind,
> Appeared an idle dream that could not live
> Where meditation was. I turned away,
> And walked along my road in happiness." (513–24)

"The Ruined Cottage" is an exemplary case of what commentators mean when they speak of the "displacement" that occurs in a Romantic poem. An Enlightenment mind like Diderot's or Godwin's or Crabbe's would study this poem's events in social and economic terms, but Wordsworth is precisely interested in preventing — in actively countering — such a focus of concentration. The displacement is reproduced in the poem's subtle transformation of Wordsworth's 1793–4 world — including the social and political discontents which dominated his life at that time — into the changed world of 1797–8, when he began to write the poem in the exuberant atmosphere of Racedown and Alfoxden. Wordsworth himself becomes a poetic narrator, and the focus of his original feelings of dislocation are displaced from France and the Bishop of Llandaff to the more homely and immediate discomforts of the walking tourist (lines 18–26). In such circumstances, the story of Margaret produces in the narrator a sense of shame and humility before a great suffering, and an overflow of sympathy and love for the sufferer rather than, as in 1793–4, a sense of outrage, and an overflow of angry judgment upon those whom Wordsworth at the time held accountable for helping to maintain the social conditions which generated a surplus of social evil.

I shall have more to say about the poetic significance of these erasures and displacements in a later part of this essay. Here I am interested in the fact of the displacement, and in the extent to which — including the manner in which — it is brought about. In works like "The Ruined Cottage" and the Salisbury Plain poems we are kept in a direct contact with the particular social circumstances with which these works are concerned. Nevertheless, James Butler is right to say that "*The Ruined Cottage* is not a work of social protest,"[3] a fact about the poem which appears in the process of attenuation which I have been remarking upon. Yet the character and extent of the displacement in "The Ruined Cottage" is quite different — is far less extreme — from what we may observe in "Tintern Abbey."

Here the temporal displacement is at once more exact and yet less clear, more specific and yet not so easy to understand. The "Five Years" of which the poem speaks delimit on the one hand Wordsworth's trip to Salisbury Plain and North Wales in the summer of 1793, and on the other his return visit, particularly to the abbey, on July 13, 1798. In the course of the poem not a word is said about the French Revolution, or about the impoverished and dislocated country poor, or — least of all — that this event and these conditions might be structurally related to each other. All these are matters which had been touched upon, however briefly, in "The Ruined Cottage," but in "Tintern Abbey" they are further displaced out of the narrative.

But not entirely displaced. As in "The Ruined Cottage," these subjects are present in the early parts of the poem, only to be completely erased after line 23. But their presence is maintained in such an oblique way that readers — especially later scholars and interpreters — have passed them by almost without notice. Recently Marjorie Levinson, in a brilliantly researched and highly controversial polemic, has redrawn our attention to the importance of the date in the subtitle, and to the special significance which Tintern Abbey and its environs had for an informed English audience of the period.[4] Her argument is complex and detailed and neither can nor need be rehearsed here. Suffice it to say — and to see — that Wordsworth situates his poem (and his original experience) on the eve of Bastille Day. Secondly, the force of lines 15–23 depends upon our knowing that the ruined abbey had been in the 1790s a favorite haunt of transients and displaced persons — of beggars and vagrants of various sorts, including (presumably) "female vagrants." Wordsworth ob-

serves the tranquil orderliness of the nearby "pastoral farms" and draws these views into a relation with the "vagrant dwellers in the houseless woods" of the abbey. This relation contains a startling, even a shocking, contrast of social conditions. Even more, it suggests an ominous social and economic fact of the period: that in 1793 no great distance separated the houseless vagrant from the happy cottager, as "The Ruined Cottage" made so painfully clear. Much of Wordsworth's poem rests on the initial establishment of this bold image of contradiction, on the analogous one hinted at in the subtitle's date, and on the relation between them which the poem subtly encourages us to make. It was, of course, a relation which Wordsworth himself made explicit in his *Letter to the Bishop of Llandaff*.

But like "The Ruined Cottage," "Tintern Abbey" 's method is to replace an image and landscape of contradiction with one dominated by "the power / Of harmony" (48–9). So in 1798 he observes the ruined abbey and its environs "with an eye made quiet" by such power. He sees not "the landscape [of] a blind man's eye" (25) — not the place of conflict and contradiction which he now associates with his own "blind" jacobinism of 1793 — but an earlier, more primal landscape which he explicitly associates with his childhood. This last is the landscape which does not fill the eye of the mind with external and soulless images, but with "forms of beauty" (24) through which we can "see into the life of things" (50), to penetrate the surface of a landscape to reach its indestructible heart and meaning:

> a sense sublime
> Of something far more deeply interfused,
> Whose dwelling is the light of setting suns,
> And the round ocean, and the living air,
> And the blue sky, and in the mind of man,
> A motion and a spirit, that impels
> All thinking things, all objects of all thought,
> And rolls through all things.   (96–103)

This famous passage defines Wordsworth's sense of "the life of things" which lies beneath the external "forms of beauty." The lines have transcended ordinary description altogether, however, and replaced what might have been a picture *in* the mind (of a ruined abbey) with a picture *of* the mind: a picture, that is — as the pun on the preposition makes clear — of the "mind" in its act of generating itself within an external landscape. Wordsworth narrates that act of replacement in four magnificent lines of verse:

> And now, with gleams of half-extinguish'd thought,
> With many recognitions dim and faint,
> And somewhat of a sad perplexity,
> The picture of the mind revives again.   (59–62)

The abbey associated with 1793 fades, as in a palimpsest, and in its disappearing outlines we begin to discern not a material reality but a process, or power, exercising itself in an act of sympathy which is its most characteristic feature. No passage in Wordsworth better conveys the actual moment when a spiritual displacement occurs—when the light and appearances of sense fade into an immaterial plane of reality, the landscape of Wordsworth's emotional needs.

That Wordsworth was himself well aware of what his poem was doing is clear from the conclusion, where he declares himself to be a "worshipper of Nature" (153) rather than a communicant in some visible church. Whereas these fade and fall to ruin, the abbey of the mind suffers no decay, but passes from sympathetic soul to sympathetic soul—here, through all the phases of Wordsworth's own changing life, and thence from him to Dorothy as well, whose mind:

> Shall be a mansion for all lovely forms,
> Thy memory be as a dwelling-place
> For all sweet sounds and harmonies; oh! then
> If solitude, or fear, or pain, or grief,
> Should be thy portion, with what healing thoughts
> Of tender joy wilt thou remember me,
> And these my exhortations!   (140–46)

Dorothy is, of course, the reader's surrogate just as Tintern Abbey's ruins appear, on the one hand, as a visible emblem of everything that is transitory, and on the other as an emotional focus of all that is permanent.

At the poem's end we are left only with the initial scene's simplest natural forms: "these steep woods and lofty cliffs, / And this green pastoral landscape" (158–9). Everything else has been erased—the abbey, the beggars and displaced vagrants, all that civilized culture creates and destroys, gets and spends. We are not permitted to remember 1793 and the turmoil of the French Revolution, neither its 1793 hopes nor—what is more to the point for Wordsworth—the subsequent ruin of those hopes. Wordsworth displaces

all that into a spiritual economy where disaster is self-consciously transformed into the threat of disaster ("*If* this / Be but a vain belief," 50–51; my italics), and where that threat, fading into a further range of self-conscious anticipation, suddenly becomes a focus not of fear but of hope. For the mind has triumphed over its times.

Thus the poem concludes in what appears to be an immense gain, but what is in reality the deepest and most piteous loss. Between 1793 and 1798 Wordsworth lost the world merely to gain his own immortal soul. The greatness of this great poem lies in the clarity and candor with which it dramatizes not merely this event, but the structure of this event.

This part of my argument can be briefly concluded. The processes of elision which I have been describing reach their notorious and brilliant apogee in the "Intimations Ode," a work which has driven the philologically inclined critic to despair. In this poem all contextual points of reference are absorbed back into the poem's intertextual structure. The famous "pansy at my feet," the one tree of many, the timely utterance: readers have sought long and in vain to specify the references of these passages. Perhaps we glimpse a metaphoric afterimage of the Bastille in "Shades of the prison-house"—but perhaps not. The poem generalizes—we now like to say mythologizes—all its conflicts, or rather resituates those conflicts out of a socio-historical context and into an ideological one. "We in thought will join your throng." This is the famous process of internalization which is at once the ode's central problem and its final solution as well.

The problem is clearly presented in stanza IV when Wordsworth acknowledges his belief that "all the earth is gay" (29):

> Oh evil day! if I were sullen
> While Earth herself is adorning,
>   This sweet May-morning,
> And the Children are culling
>   On every side,
> In a thousand valleys far and wide,
> Fresh flowers; while the sun shines warm,
> And the Babe leaps up on his Mother's arm:—
>   I hear, I hear, with joy I hear!   (42–50)

The pattern in the first four stanzas is to set a contrast between all that Wordsworth can "hear," which the poem associates with his belief in and feelings of universal joy, and all that Wordsworth can and cannot see. These latter things, which Wordsworth associates initially with loss, induce in him a sense of fear and anxiety. The contrast establishes a distinction between a world of the indefinite and the unseen on the one hand, and a world of visible particulars on the other. "The things which I have seen I now can see no more"; the catalogue in stanza II is itself not a record of immediacies, but a recitation of generalities recalled from particular past experiences, as the very heterogeneous character of the items shows. And the unadorned presentation of these memory-mediated particulars explains that the flight of the visionary gleam is a function of the loss of immediacy.

In short, the poem's problem emerges when Wordsworth recognizes that his sense of a universal joy—his insight into the life of things—has resulted in his loss of the concrete and particular:

> —But there's a Tree, of many, one,
> A single Field which I have looked upon.
> Both of them speak of something that is gone:
> The Pansy at my feet
> Doth the same tale repeat.   (51–5)

Scholars who have labored to identify that tree and the "single field," and to locate the spot where Wordsworth observed the pansy, have followed the poet's own futile quest. These things are gone, and Wordsworth fears—despite his own reiterated convictions—that their departure will signal the passage of "the glory and the dream" as well.

As "The Ruined Cottage" and "Tintern Abbey" have already shown, the disappearance of such particulars occurred as part of a strategy of displacement. But where these earlier poems involved dramatizations and enactments of the strategy's discovery, the "Intimations Ode" is a study of its character and, finally, a justification and embodiment of its operations. The ode begins with a fearful sense that the immediate and concrete experience has disappeared into the mists of consciousness and memory. It concludes, however, with the reiterated conviction that

> The thought of our past years in me doth breed
> Perpetual benediction.   (134–5)

Immediacy is "fugitive" and impermanent, but not so the consciousness of all that is fugitive. Wordsworth therefore lifts a final "song of thanks and praise" for the activity of displacement itself, for the moments of loss. In the ode, objective history has disappeared. The poem annihilates its history, biographical and socio-historical alike, and replaces these particulars with a record of pure consciousness. The paradox of the work is that it embodies an immediate and concrete experience of that most secret and impalpable of all human acts: the transformation of fact into idea, and of experience into ideology.

Its pathos is a function of that paradox. For Wordsworth's poem does not actually transcend the evils it is haunted by, it merely occupies them at the level of consciousness. That Wordsworth's is as well a false consciousness needs scarcely to be said, nor is it an indictment of the poem's greatness that this should be the case. The work completes and perfects the tragic losses of Wordsworth's life and times. Had he merely "yielded up moral questions in despair" (*Prelude* XI, 305) his case would have been pitiful. Wordsworth went on to struggle further with those problems and to arrive at what he believed was their solution. What he actually discovered was no more than his own desperate need for a solution. The reality of that need mirrored a cultural one that was much greater and more widespread. Wordsworth transformed both of these realities into illusions. The process began with the displacement of the problem inwardly, but when he went on to conceptualize his need, as we observe in the ode, the pity of Wordsworth's situation approaches tragic proportions. Indeed, it is a very emblem of the tragedy of his epoch, for in that conceptualization Wordsworth imprisoned his true voice of feeling within the bastille of his consciousness. Wordsworth made a solitude and he called it peace.

Poetry like Wordsworth's belongs to what Hans Enzensberger has called "The Consciousness Industry"[5]—a light industry, if the pun be permitted, which Wordsworth and the other Romantics helped to found, and which they sought to preserve free of cultural contamination. The futility of this effort is apparent in the curricula of our educational institutions. When we read and study Wordsworth we always do so within a certain institutional framework—for good and ill alike. Because we must come to grips with this social dimension of "Wordsworth's poetry," one word more remains to be said.

"Like a planet revolving around an absent sun, an ideology is made out of what it does not mention; it exists because there are things which must not be spoken of."[6] These remarks are a latter-day version of a recurrent truth. From Wordsworth's vantage, an ideology is born out of things which (literally) *cannot* be spoken of. So the "Immortality Ode" is crucial for us because it speaks about ideology from the point of view and in the context of its origins. If Wordsworth's poetry elides history, we observe in this "escapist" or "reactionary" move its own self-revelation. It is a rare, original, and comprehensive record of the birth and character of a particular ideology — in this case, one that has been incorporated into our academic programs. The idea that poetry, or even consciousness, can set one free of the ruins of history and culture is the grand illusion of every Romantic poet. This idea continues as one of the most important shibboleths of our culture, especially — and naturally — at its higher levels.

Wordsworth stands to his later history as a poetic tale stands to its forms of worship. To his earlier history he stands as a prophet in his own country. Understanding this historical distinction is an imperative of literary criticism, for it is a distinction which enables poetry to be read as part of a society and its culture — without at the same time being absorbed by those structures. It is a distinction, as well, which Blake observed when he differentiated "men" from what he wittily called "the states" which they passed through. Indeed, when criticism begins to set poetry "free" in this manner — that is to say, when criticism restores poetry to its historical determinations — it will have begun to set itself "free" as well. The works of the Romantic Period are not in bondage to themselves: they survive in the valley of their saying, where they speak their truths (including the errors of their truths). Rather, they have been mastered by a critical history which has come to possess them in the name of various Romanticisms. Swingle's acute sense of this event leads him to seek a non-ideological approach to Romantic works. But this move is futile, not merely because ideology is a central (as opposed to a "supporting") factor in Romantic works, but also because it is a central factor in the criticism of Romantic works. The issue now is whether critics shall be able to distinguish themselves and their works from the "states" which they too inhabit and serve.

Notes

1. In a recent series of papers I have tried to demonstrate the practical methods that are involved in a critical project of this sort. See "The Text, the Poem, and the Problem of Historical Method," *New Literary History* 12 (1981), 269–88; "The Meaning of the Ancient Mariner," *Critical Inquiry* 8 (Autumn, 1981), 35–67; "The Anachronism of George Crabbe," *English Literary History* 48 (1981), 555–72; "Christina Rossetti: A New Edition and a Revaluation," *Victorian Studies* 23 (Winter, 1980), 237–54; "Shall These Bones Live?" *Text* 1 (not yet published); and two essays which will be published shortly, "Tennyson and the Histories of Criticism" (to appear in *Review)* and "Textual and Bibliographical Studies and Their Meaning for Literary Criticism" (to appear in a collection of essays by various hands).

2. My text for this poem is James Butler's critical edition, *The Ruined Cottage and The Pedlar* (Ithaca, N.Y., 1979). The most comprehensive discussion of the poem can be found in Jonathan Wordsworth, *The Music of Humanity* (London, 1969).

3. *Ibid.*, 4.

4. Marjorie Levinson, "Insight and Oversight: A Reading of 'Tintern Abbey,'" unpublished manuscript essay.

5. See Hans Magnus Enzensberger, *The Consciousness Industry: On Literature, Politics, and the Media* (New York, 1974).

6. Pierre Machery, *A Theory of Literary Production*, trans. Geoffrey Wall (London, 1978), 132.

Personal Property: Exchange Value and the Female Self in *The Awakening*

Margit Stange

Poststructural in its focus on the "construction of the self-owning female self" and historicist in its placing of Chopin's novel in the context of late-nineteenth-century feminism, Margit Stange's essay reflects as well the influence of the new historicism and the new economic criticism with its emphasis on exchange value and the circulation of power: "Chopin's dramatization of female self-ownership demonstrates the central importance of the ideology of women's value in exchange to contemporary notions of female selfhood." Looking to Thorstein Veblen rather than to Marx and drawing on the work of Catherine Gallagher and Walter Benn Michaels, Stange makes little use of the traditional Marxist distinctions between base and superstructure or between exchange value and use value. In her economic analysis, "exchange"—the circulation of value, of signs, of power—is the key term. "Like Adèle, the photograph concretizes erotic value that is both publicly produced and privately owned. The erotic availability and desirability of the actor whose photograph 'anyone might possess' is a product of reproduction and circulation, as Edna's own kisses are incited by and followed by the circulation of the object." Stange agrees with Sandra Gilbert and Cynthia Griffin Wolff in finding the dinner party scene central to the novel, but she reads it in very different terms: "The dinner dramatizes the richness of [Edna's] market-determined transformations: ceremonial drink, invention, queen, luxurious gift. To say that it is her 'birthday' is to say that her self is born through exchange and consists of these multiple signs which circulate in the market." Even Edna's death figures in the same economic terms: "Edna seizes the most extreme prerogatives of this self-ownership, withholding herself from motherhood by withholding herself from life and thus giving herself in a maternal dissolution." A historical reading, to be sure, but one very different from traditional literary history.

In the beginning of *The Awakening,* New Orleans stockbroker Léonce Pontellier, staying with his wife, Edna, at an exclusive Creole family resort, surveys Edna as she walks up from the beach in the company of her summer flirtation, Robert Lebrun. " 'You are burnt beyond recognition' [Léonce says], looking at his wife as one looks at a valuable piece of personal property which has suffered some damage."[1] Léonce's comment is the reader's introduction to Edna, whose search for self is the novel's subject.[2] To take Léonce's hyperbole — "you are burnt beyond recognition" — as literally as Léonce takes his role as Edna's "owner" is to be introduced to an Edna who exists as a recognizable individual in reference to her status as valuable property. This status appears to determine Edna's perception of herself: in response to Léonce's anxiety, Edna makes her first self-examination in this novel about a heroine who is "beginning to realize her position in the universe as a human being, and to recognize her relations as an individual to the world within and about her" (15). Edna, having been told "you are burnt beyond recognition,"

held up her hands, strong, shapely hands, and surveyed them critically, drawing up her lawn sleeves above the wrists. This reminded her of her rings, which she had given to her husband before leaving for the beach. She silently reached out to him, and he, understanding, took the rings from his vest pocket and dropped them into her open palm. She slipped them upon her fingers. (4)

In the context of the property system in which Edna exists as a sign of value, Edna's body is detachable and alienable from her own viewpoint: the hands and wrists are part of the body yet can be objectified, held out and examined as if they belonged to someone else — as indeed, in some sense that Léonce insists upon very literally, they do belong to someone else. Edna's perception of her own body is structured by the detachability of the hand and arm as signs of Léonce's ownership of her. Her hands also suggest the possibility of being an owner herself when they make the proprietary gesture of reaching out for the rings that Léonce obediently drops into the palm (this gesture of Edna's contrasts with a bride's conventional passive reception of the ring). The hands are the organs of appropriation; Elizabeth Cady Stanton, in a speech on female rights given in 1892, argued that "to deny [to woman] the rights of property is like cutting off the hands."[3] In having

Edna put on the rings herself (a gesture Edna will again perform at a moment when she decisively turns away from her domestic role), Chopin suggests that the chief item of property owned by the proprietary Edna is Edna herself. Thus the opening scene foreshadows the turning point of the plot at which Edna, deciding to leave Léonce's house, resolves "never again to belong to another than herself" (80).

"Self-ownership" was a central project of feminist reformers of the second half of the nineteenth century. In the lexicon of late nineteenth-century women's rights reformers and feminist free love advocates, the term *self-ownership,* when applied to women, had a specific sexual meaning. First popularized by Lucinda Chandler in the 1840s and widely used by the feminist reformers who followed her, self-ownership signified the wife's right to refuse to have sex with her husband. According to Chandler, the practice of self-ownership would mean that "the woman . . . has control over her own person, independent of the desires of her husband."[4] Self-ownership was closely linked with "voluntary motherhood" and thus became a program for putting woman in control of sex and reproduction. "Self-ownership," writes historian William Leach, "meant that woman, not man, would decide when, where, and how the sexual act would be performed. . . . It also meant that woman, not man, would determine when children would be conceived and how many."[5] Self-ownership became central to feminist ideology of the second half of the century. According to Linda Gordon, by the mid-seventies, advocacy of so-called voluntary motherhood — woman's "right to choose when to be pregnant" — was shared by "the whole feminist community."[6]

This feminist community, in contradiction of its advocacy of choice and control for women, was unanimously opposed to the use of birth control devices. This opposition was shared by suffragists, moral reformers, and free love advocates alike. Various kinds of contraceptive technology were accessible to middle-class women. However, as historian Gordon notes, nineteenth-century birth control practice was determined by ideology rather than the availability of technology. In the prevailing ideology of even the most radical feminist reformers, motherhood was an inextricable part of female sexuality.[7] Why did feminists, whose goal was to win for women the civil and proprietary rights that would make them equal to men, choose to deny women the freedom to have sex without pregnancy? As Gordon points out, the linkage of self-ownership with reproduction certainly reflects the reality of many women's lives, which were dominated by multiple births and the attendant realities of risk, disease, and pain.[8] Some of the resistance to birth control technology, Gordon suggests, was motivated by material conditions: birth control devices, by separating sex from reproduction, appeared to threaten the family structure that provided most middle-class women their only social standing and economic security.[9] But even among those reformers who were not concerned with upholding the family (free love advocates and nonmarrying career women, for example), there was a strong resistance to contraception—a resistance that amounts to a refusal to separate motherhood from female sexuality.

To put voluntary motherhood practiced without birth control devices at the center of self-ownership is to make motherhood central to a woman's life and identity. The capacity to bear children is the sexual function that most dramatically distinguishes the sexual lives—and the day-do-day lives—of women from those of men. The ban on contraceptive technology enforces a lived distinction between male and female sexuality: without effective contraception, sex for a woman always means sex *as* a woman because it means a potential pregnancy. The opposition to contraceptive technology (as well as the idealization of motherhood of which it is a part) reflects a commitment to the sexualization of female identity. Through the practice of self-ownership, this differentiated sexuality with motherhood at its core becomes the possession that a woman makes available or withholds in order to demonstrate self-ownership. To ask why the feminist reformers opposed contraceptive technology is, then, to ask how motherhood functions in the construction of the self-owning female self. In making motherhood a central possession of the self, the feminists were defining that self as sexual and as female. The possession of this sexualized self through self-ownership amounts to the exercise of a right to alienate (confirmed by a right to withhold). This selfhood, then, consists of the alienation of female sexuality in a market. Charlotte Perkins Gilman, in her 1899 critique of this sexual market, attacked it as a market in which "he is . . . the demand . . . she is the supply."[10] The feminists' opposition to birth control technology reflects a commitment to this market: underlying their construction of female selfhood is the ideology of woman's sexual value in exchange.

Chopin's dramatization of female self-ownership demonstrates the central importance of the ideology of woman's value in exchange to contemporary notions of female selfhood. If, as Stanton declares in the speech on female selfhood quoted above, "in discussing the rights of woman, we are to consider, first, what belongs to her as an individual," what Edna Pontellier considers as her property is, first, her body.[11] Her body is both what she owns and what she owns with. She begins to discover a self by uncovering her hands and "surveying them critically" with her eyes, thus making an appropriative visual assessment of herself as a proprietary being. Her hands and eyes will serve her in her "venture" into her "work" of sketching and painting (54–55). Thus her hands, by remaining attached (and not cut off like those of the woman who is denied the rights of property), serve her visual appropriation of the world and provide the first object of this appropriation: her own body.

Edna's hands appear in two states: naked and sunburned, and ringed. In the first state, they are conventionally "unrecognizable" as signs of her status as Léonce's wife. Sunburned hands, by indicating the performance of outdoor labor, would nullify Edna's "value" as a sign of Léonce's wealth. In the terminology of Thorstein Veblen's turn-of-the-century analysis of the ownership system, Edna is an item of "conspicuous consumption" that brings "reputability" (a degree of status) to Léonce. Such status-bearing wealth must be surplus wealth: useful articles do not serve to advertise the owner's luxurious freedom from need. Edna must, then, appear to be surplus—she must appear to perform no useful labor.[12] The rings—showy, luxurious, useless items of conspicuous consumption *par excellence*—restore her status as surplus. Yet this status is also constituted by the sight of her hands without the rings: the significance of the sunburned hands quickly collapses into the significance of the ringed hands when the sunburned, naked hands "remind" both Léonce and Edna of the ringed, value-bearing hands. And Edna's sunburn is directly constitutive of her "value," for it results from her conspicuous, vicarious consumption of leisure on Léonce's behalf (what Veblen calls "vicarious leisure"): she has been enjoying a holiday at the respectable, luxurious resort frequented by Léonce's Creole circle.

Thus Edna's hands appear in their naked and exposed state as a reminder of Léonce's property interests while they also, in this state, suggest an identity and proprietary interests of her own. The appropriative survey of the female body as a sign of male ownership continues to engage Edna: her visual fascination fastens on the hands and body of her friend Adèle Ratignolle, whose "excessive physical charm" at first attracts Edna (15). Edna "like[s] to sit and gaze at her fair companion." She watches Adèle at her domestic labors. "Never were hands more exquisite than [Adèle's], and it was a joy to look at them when she threaded her needle or adjusted her gold thimble . . . as she sewed away on the little night drawers" (10). Here, the hands are the organs of labor—but again, gender determines possessive status. Adèle's hands are perfectly white because she always wears dogskin gloves with gauntlets (16). The femininity of the laboring hands, their luxuriously aesthetic and spectacular quality, conspicuously signifies that the value of Adèle's labor does not stem from production for use: Edna "[can]not see the use" of Adèle's labor (16). Adèle's laboring hands signify her consecration to her "role" within the family, and they are marked with the gold of a thimble as Edna's are marked with the gold of a ring.

In their white, "exquisite" beauty, Adèle's hands are stably—organically—signs of her status as wealth. When Adèle jokes "with excessive naiveté" about the fear of making her husband jealous, "that made them all laugh. The right hand jealous of the left! . . . But for that matter, the Creole husband is never jealous; with him the gangrene passion is one which has become dwarfed by disuse" (12). (This ownership is not reciprocal: the question of jealousy pertains only to the husband; the wife's jealous, proprietary interest in her husband is not evoked.) Adèle's entire presence is a reminder of the property system in which woman is a form of surplus wealth whose value exists in relation to exchange. A woman of "excessive physical charm," Adèle is luxuriously draped in "pure white, with a fluffiness of ruffles that became her. The draperies and fluttering things which she wore suited her rich, luxuriant beauty" (15–16). Her body is as rich, white, and ornamental as her clothes: she appears "more beautiful than ever" in a negligee that leaves her arms "almost wholly bare" and "expose[s] the rich, melting curves of her white throat" (55).

In her rich and elaborate yet revealing clothing, Adèle is excessively covered while her body, already a sign of wealth, makes such coverings redundant. Adèle appears as a concretized *feme covert*. Under the Napoleonic Code which was still in force in Louisiana in the 1890s, wives were legally identical with their husbands; being in *coverture,* they had no separate legal or proprietary identity and could not own property in their own right.[13] Adèle's beauty is her conspicuousness as a form of wealth: her looks are describable by "no words . . . save the old ones that have served so often to picture the bygone heroine of romance." These words—"gold," "sapphires," "cherries or some other delicious crimson fruit"—construct femininity as tangible property. The value of the woman is emphatically defined as social wealth that exists as an effect of the public circulation of the tropes— "the old [words] that have served so often"—that identify her as beautiful. Her beauty is the product and representation of its own circulation. Adèle's "excessive physical charm" is a kind of currency that makes her the "embodiment of every womanly grace and charm" (10).

It is in public display that Adèle's beauty manifests itself. The sight of woman as social wealth is the starting point of Edna's self-seeking. "Mrs. Pontellier liked to sit and gaze at her fair companion as she might look upon a faultless Madonna" (12). An amateur artist, Edna finds such "joy" in looking at Adèle that she wants to "try herself on Madame Ratignolle" (13). Adèle, "seated there like some sensuous Madonna, with the gleam of the fading day enriching her splendid color" (13), appears to Edna as a particularly "tempting subject" of a sketch. This sketch becomes the second sight that Edna "surveys critically" (the first being her hands); finding that it "[bears] no resemblance to Madame Ratignolle" (and despite the fact that it is "a fair enough piece of work, and satisfying in many ways"), Edna enforces her proprietary rights in regard to the sketch as she smudges it and "crumple[s] the paper between her hands" (13). Edna is inspired to make another try when she visits Adèle at home in New Orleans and finds her again at her ornamental domestic labor (Adèle is unnecessarily sorting her husband's laundry). "Madame Ratignolle looked more beautiful than ever there at home. . . . 'Perhaps I shall be able to paint your picture some day,' said Edna. . . . 'I believe I ought to work again' " (55). The sight of Adèle at home inspires Edna to do the work that will help her get out of the home. Later she will leave Léonce and support herself on the income from her art and from a legacy of her mother's.

In her insistence on owning her own property and supporting herself, Edna is a model of the legal opposite of the *feme covert*—she is the *feme sole*. Thus Chopin connects her to the Married Women's Property Acts, property law reforms instituted in the latter part of the century that gave married women varying rights of ownership. Edna comes from "old Presbyterian Kentucky stock" (66). Kentucky belonged to the block of states with the most advanced separation of property in marriage. In fact, Kentucky had the most advanced Married Women's Property Act in the nation, granting married women not only the right to own separate property and make contracts, but the right to keep their earnings.[14]

Thus Chopin connects Edna to the feminist drive for women's property rights. Elizabeth Cady Stanton, in her speech on female selfhood quoted above, makes possessive individualism the first consideration among women's rights: "In discussing the rights of woman, we are to consider, first, what belongs to her as an individual."[15] Chopin suggests that what a woman owns in owning herself is her sexual exchange value. The *feme covert,* in being both property and the inspiration to own, allows Edna to be a *feme sole*. The self she owns can be owned — is property — because it is recognizable as social wealth. Adèle, who concretizes the status of the woman and mother as domestic property, makes visible to Edna the female exchange value that constitutes a self to own. Thus Edna's possessive selfhood looks "back" to the chattel form of marriage, valorizing (in a literal sense) the woman as property. In Adèle, the "bygone heroine," Edna finds the capital which she invests to produce her market selfhood.

The way that Edna owns herself by owning her value in exchange is a form of voluntary motherhood: "Edna had once told Madame Ratignolle that she would never sacrifice herself for her children, or for any one. Then had followed a rather heated argument." In this argument Edna "explains" to Adèle, "I would give my life for my children; but I wouldn't give myself." Adèle's answer is, "a woman who would give her life for her children could do no more than that. . . . I'm sure I couldn't do more than that." Withholding nothing, Adèle cannot conceive of giving more than she already gives. Edna cannot at first identify what it is she has chosen to withhold:

"I wouldn't give myself. I can't make it more clear; . . . it's only something which . . . is revealing itself to me" (48).

The self at first exists in the presumption of the right to withhold oneself as a mother. But Edna, like the feminist advocates of self-ownership, soon determines that voluntary motherhood means withholding herself sexually. After her first successful swim (during which she experiences a moment of self-support and the absolute solitariness of death), she stays on the porch, refusing Léonce's repeated orders and entreaties to come inside to bed (32). Later Edna stops sleeping with her husband altogether, so that Léonce complains to the family doctor, "she's making it devilishly uncomfortable for me . . . She's got some sort of notion in her head concerning the eternal rights of women; and—you understand—we meet in the morning at the breakfast table" (65). It is by withholding herself sexually, then, that Edna exercises the "eternal rights of women" in insisting that she has a self and that she owns that self.

The freedom to withhold oneself has its complement in the freedom to give oneself. No longer sleeping with—or even living with—her husband, Edna declares herself free to have sex with whomever she chooses. She tells Robert, "I am no longer one of Mr. Pontellier's possessions to dispose of or not. I give myself where I choose" (107). Edna supposes that her self-giving is chosen because she has presumed the choice of not giving—she has made her motherhood voluntary. Adèle, in contrast, is the mother who never withholds and thus cannot choose but to give. Will and intention seem to be with Edna, whereas Adèle exercises no will (and has no self). Yet Adèle's giving is not an involuntary and therefore selfless reflex, but a consciously and intentionally developed identity. Adèle is Grand Isle's greatest exponent of the "role" of "mother-woman," a role that is produced through deliberate public staging (10). First presented to Edna as a beautiful vision of the "Madonna," Adèle produces her maternity through public discourse. Her children are "thoughts" brought out in speech: Adèle "thinks" (out loud) of "a fourth one" and, after giving birth to it, implores Edna, in a phrase that Edna will not be able to get out of her mind, to "think of the children, oh think of them" (110).

"Madame Ratignolle had been married seven years. About every two years she had a baby. At that time she . . . was beginning to think of a fourth one.

She was always talking about her 'condition.' Her 'condition' was in no way apparent, and no one would have known a thing about it but for her persistence in making it the subject of conversation" (11). Adèle produces her "role" of "mother-woman" by thinking and provoking thought, but it is impossible to determine whether Adèle thinks about getting pregnant; whether, that is, she practices self-ownership and voluntary motherhood by withholding herself from sex. The two-year intervals between her pregnancies might result from chance, or they might represent intentional spacing that keeps Adèle in or nearly in the "condition" that provides her identity. This ambiguity characterizes the "condition" of motherhood that Adèle is "always" producing for herself. Motherhood is a "role" and therefore consciously produced and paraded. Yet the intention and will that are used to stage the role conflict with its content, for the role of mother demands selflessness: the mother-women of Grand Isle "efface themselves as individuals" (10). Motherhood is never voluntary or involuntary. If motherhood is a social role that Adèle intentionally inhabits, it is also a condition that she can never actually choose, since intending to become pregnant cannot make her so. Thus, motherhood has a kind of built-in selflessness that is dramatically expressed in the scene when Adèle, who is usually in control of her presence, becomes pathetically hysterical and paranoic during labor and childbirth. Here, Adèle's intentional embrace of motherhood gets its force from the unwilled nature of the "torture" that it attempts to appropriate. Hardly able to speak after her ordeal in childbirth, Adèle whispers in an "exhausted" voice, "think of the children, Edna" (109).[16]

Adèle and Edna embody the two poles of motherhood: Adèle is the "mother-woman" and Edna is "not a mother-woman" (15, 10). The axis of motherhood gives Edna her original sense of identity. What makes her "not a mother-woman" is her refusal to "give" herself for her children. Unlike Adèle, Edna does not embrace the role. Her motherhood seems arbitrary, externally imposed and unwilled, "a responsibility which she had blindly assumed." She is "fond of her children in an uneven, impulsive way. She [will] sometimes gather them passionately to her heart; she [will] sometimes forget them" (20). Her "half-remembered" experience of childbirth is an "ecstasy" and a "stupor" (109, 108). Edna's refusal to

give herself as a mother, rather than making her the controller and proprietor of her life, entails the passivity of thoughtlessness. In refusing to be a mother-woman she absents herself from the motherhood that is thus all the more arbitrarily thrust upon her.

Indeed, Edna is inescapably a mother. Motherhood is what Edna withholds and thus she, too, is essentially a "mother-woman." Adèle's presence is a provocation and reminder of the self-constituting function of motherhood. Adèle's selflessness is an inducement to Edna to identify a self to give. For Edna, who "become[s] herself" by "daily casting aside that fictitious self which we assume like a garment with which to appear before the world" (57), the friendship with Adèle is "the most obvious . . . influence" in the loosening of Edna's "mantle of reserve" (57, 14–15). The Creole community recognizes no private sphere. Adèle's sexual and reproductive value is already located in the sphere of public exchange (or, the public is already like the private: the Creoles are like "one big family") (11). In this Creole openness, Edna is inspired to resituate her sexual exchange value in an economy of public circulation.

"The candor of [Adèle's] whole existence, which every one might read," is part of a Creole lack of prudery that allows for the open circulation of stories about sex and childbirth. With "profound astonishment" Edna reads "in secret and solitude" a book that "had gone the rounds" and was openly discussed at table. "Never would Edna Pontellier forget the shock with which she heard Madame Ratignolle relating to old Monsieur Farival the harrowing story of one of her *accouchements*, withholding no intimate detail. She was growing accustomed to like shocks, but she could not keep the mounting color back from her cheeks" (11). The candor of Adèle's motherhood provokes blushes that simultaneously constitute Edna's reserve and "give her away" to the public. Her body, whether sunburned or blushing, is red from an exposure that privatizes and valorizes that body as her domestic, private attributes—sexuality, modesty, reproduction—are manifested as social value.

Adèle has nothing to hide because her body underneath her clothes is manifestly social wealth. Her bareness is as ornamentally "beautiful" as her ornamented, clothed self. The reserved, private, domestic self of Adèle reveals itself to Edna as the valuable product of circulation, and this revelation prompts Edna to explore her own possessive privacy. She becomes aware of having "thoughts and emotions which never voiced themselves. They belonged to her and were her own" (48). Her erotic longings belong in this category. "Edna often wondered at one propensity which sometimes had inwardly disturbed her without causing any outward show or manifestation on her part" (18). This is a propensity to become silently infatuated with various men. These "silent" possessions of the self are owned in a way most clearly illustrated in the story of Edna's greatest infatuation, whose object was a "great tragedian."

> The picture of the tragedian stood enframed upon her desk. Anyone may possess the portrait of a tragedian without exciting suspicion or comment. (This was a sinister reflection which she cherished.) In the presence of others she expressed admiration for his exalted gifts, as she handed the photograph around and dwelt upon the fidelity of the likeness. When alone she sometimes picked it up and kissed the cold glass passionately. (19)

Edna's comment upon the fidelity of the likeness recapitulates the book's opening, in which Léonce's anxiety about Edna's lapse from recognizability, and his restoration of her recognizability via the wedding rings, consists of a discourse that constantly remembers and reinscribes her as a sign of him in his proprietary office. Her "fidelity" in this marital, possessive sense is her recognizability as such a sign. Edna's photograph is to Edna as Edna is to Léonce. It represents her possessive identity, her selfhood as an owner (thus there is a mirrorlike quality in the "cold glass" which shows her herself kissing herself). The photograph embodies and reflects Edna's erotic desire for the tragedian. It objectifies her sexuality in an image that is handed around, praised for its "fidelity," and kissed in private.

Like Adèle, the photograph concretizes erotic value that is both publicly produced and privately owned. The erotic availability and desirability of the actor whose photograph "anyone might possess" is a product of reproduction and circulation, as Edna's own kisses are incited by and followed by the circulation of the object. The mode of owning it is "handing it around" while she praises the "fidelity" of the likeness. That is, she assumes an individual possessive relationship to the photograph only in the context of its possession by any number of other owners, whose possession produces the "sinister reflection" of her own possessive, cherishing privacy. But

Edna's position as an owner is not that of Adèle's husband—or of her own. Edna gives up possession in order to have this possessive relationship. In praising the "fidelity of the likeness" she does not praise its likeness to her but emphasizes that the photograph represents and thus "belongs to" its original—a man whose inaccessibility makes her infatuation "hopeless." Edna can see her photograph as property only by seeing it as male property—just as her own hands, in their function as signs of Léonce's ownership of her, appear detachable and therefore ownable. Yet the absence of Edna in what the photograph represents allows her to imagine a possessive self that is somehow hidden and concealed—and therefore her own. Alone with her photograph, she imagines it circulating. Circulating it, she is able to imagine being secretly alone with it. In her ownership of the photograph, Edna establishes her possessive relationship to her sexuality.

"I am no longer one of Mr. Pontellier's possessions to dispose of or not. I give myself where I choose," says Edna to Robert (106–107). She has withheld herself from her husband in order to give herself. Instead of being property "to dispose of or not," she intends to be property that is necessarily disposed of. The forms of value in which Edna exchanges herself are the duties and functions of the woman and wife—female sexual service, motherhood, and the performance of wifely domestic/social amenities. Edna reprivatizes and reserves this value by giving up her social and domestic duties as the lady of the house, by moving out of the impressive family home into a private domestic space, the "pigeon house" (91), and by withholding sex from her husband. This reserved self is what she gives away at her "grand dinner," when she launches her sexual exchange value into wider circulation.

> Whatever came, she had resolved never again to belong to another than herself. "I shall give a grand dinner before I leave the old house!" Edna exclaimed. (80)

At the dinner, the "glittering circlet" of Edna's wedding ring (57) is now her crown.

> "Something new, Edna?" exclaimed Miss Mayblunt, with lorgnette directed toward a magnificent cluster of diamonds that sparkled, that almost sputtered, in Edna's hair. . . .

"... a present from my husband.... I may as well admit that this is my birthday.... In good time I expect you to drink my health. Meanwhile, I shall ask you to begin with this cocktail, composed ... by my father in honor of Sister Janet's wedding."
(86)

Her wedding rings had "sparkled," but the tiara (a conventional adornment of the "young matron") "sputters." This dinner marks the exploding of the intramarriage market, in which she repeatedly sells herself to the same man, into the public market, in which she circulates as the owner of her own sexual exchange value. In its very conception, the dinner collapses the private and public: "though Edna had spoken of the dinner as a very grand affair, it was in truth a very small affair and very select" (85). The absent beloved, Robert, is represented by Victor, his flirtatious younger brother. Flanking Edna are representatives of two modes of the market in sex value: Arobin, the gambler and playboy, represents adulterous and extramarital serial liaisons, while Monsieur Ratignolle enjoys the quasi-organic bond of Creole marriage.

The wealth of the Pontellier household is conspicuously displayed and offered to the guests. On the table "there were silver and gold ... and crystal which glittered like the gems which the women wore" (86). The women, like the accoutrements, are presented as forms of wealth, and Edna is the queen among them. In her diamond crown, she both embodies and reigns over Léonce's riches. This dinner at which, like all women under exogamy, she leaves "the old house" is a version of the woman-giving potlatch, the marriage feast at which the father gives away the virgin daughter. The cocktail "composed" by the father for the daughter Janet's wedding is explicitly compared by Edna's lover Arobin to the gift of Edna herself: "It might not be amiss to start out by drinking the Colonel's health in the cocktail which he composed, on the birthday of the most charming of women—the daughter whom he invented" (87). Edna is thus the gift not just of Léonce, who makes her into a form of wealth by marking her as value, but of her father, too; that is, she is a bride. As a bride, she is an invention—man-made, brought into the world for, by, and on the occasion of the staging of ownership in the conspicuous consumption of a wedding/potlatch.

An "invention," Edna is thoroughly representational. As a sign of value she is hailed as a sign of her father's wealth of inventiveness in making signs/wealth. The dinner dramatizes the richness of her market-determined transformations: ceremonial drink, invention, queen, luxurious gift. To say it is her "birthday" is to say that her self is born through exchange and consists of these multiple signs which circulate in the market. What Edna wears marks her as value:

> The golden shimmer of Edna's satin gown spread in rich folds on either side of her. There was a soft fall of lace encircling her shoulders. It was the color of her skin, without the glow, the myriad living tints that one may sometimes discover in vibrant flesh. There was something in her attitude, in her whole appearance ... which suggested the regal woman, the one who rules, who looks on, who stands alone. (88)

The gold of her dress makes reference to the value in which she is robed. The lace "encircling" her shoulders refers to the skin which at the novel's opening effects Edna's transformation into "surplus." It is as if the lace is an extra skin—a conspicuously surplus skin—which in its decorative insubstantiality mirrors the meaning of Edna's skin. But the lace is not a true mirror. It points out the superior capacity of the "real" skin to change, to have "myriad tints" which allow it to be continually dissolved and recreated as a sign of value.

Edna as a sign of value is the referent of all the surrounding signs of value. She sits at the head of the table in her crown like "the regal woman, the one who rules, ... who stands alone," as if she were the principle (and principal) of value that reigns over all its manifestations—the gold, silver, crystal, gems, and delicacies. Now Edna is like Adèle, the regal woman who has the "grace and majesty which queens are ... supposed to possess" (14). And like Adèle, who is tortured and "exhausted" by childbirth, Edna experiences the complement of regal power in the exhausted passivity that overcomes her after the dinner, when the celebration of private wealth moves into the realization of value through the ceremonial enactment of breakage and loss.

Edna leaves the Pontellier house with Arobin, who pauses outside the door of the "old house" to break off a spray of jessamine, enacting this defloration. He offers it to Edna: "No; I don't want anything," she answers. Emptied, she says she feels as if "something inside of me had snapped." This metaphorical defloration empties Edna of the erotic desire whose ownership constitutes her selfhood. Edna's shoulders are bare of the encircling lace and Arobin caresses them. Edna is passive, but Arobin feels the "respònse of her flesh," which, in its consecration to value, embodies the sexuality that is created in circulation. Now, after Edna's ceremonial "self-giving," this eroticism no longer constitutes a sensation that Edna can appropriate as her own desire (91).

The loss of the self in maternal bloodshedding is enacted at the end of the dinner when the ceremony changes from a potlatch to a sacred, sacrificial rite. The desirous Mrs. Highcamp crowns Victor with a garland of yellow and red roses, effecting his magical transformation into a bacchanalian "vision of Oriental beauty." One of the transfixed guests mutters Swinburne under his breath: "There was a graven image of Desire / Painted with red blood on a ground of gold." This "graven image," like Edna's photograph, reflects her desire. Victor publicly sings the secret song that expresses the production of Edna's "private" desire as a suspicious reflection of circulation, *si tu savais ce que tes yeux me disent* ("if you knew what your eyes are saying to me") (90). She reacts with such consternation that she breaks her wine glass, and the contents—either red or gold, like the roses and the graven image—flow over Arobin and Mrs. Highcamp. Arobin has consecrated the evenings drinks as analogues of Edna, who has invited the guests to "drink her health"—that is, drink *her*—on her "birthday." In involuntarily shattering the glass, which, like the "cold glass" covering the photo, contains a possessive reflection of her value, Edna shatters the "mantle of reserve," symbolically releasing the maternal blood that constitutes her value.

The maternal quality of her self-giving—its involuntary and selfless aspects—overwhelms Edna again some time after the potlatch when, just as she is about to "give" herself to Robert, Edna is called away to witness Adèle enduring the agonies of childbirth. The sight of Adèle's "torture" overwhelms Edna (as does Adèle's exhausted plea to "think of the children"), leaving her "stunned and speechless" (109–111). When she returns to her little house, Robert is gone forever. Deprived of the chance to "give" herself to her desire, she spends the night thinking of her children. Later, she walks to the beach from which she will swim to her death "not thinking of these things" (113). Withholding herself

from motherhood, insisting on her right to refuse to "sacrifice" herself for her children, Edna owns herself. In the logic of self-ownership and voluntary motherhood, motherhood is itself the ground on which woman claims ownership of her sexual value. Edna seizes the most extreme prerogatives of this self-ownership, withholding herself from motherhood by withholding herself from life and thus giving herself in a maternal dissolution.

Edna's death in the ocean dramatizes the self-ownership rhetoric of Elizabeth Cady Stanton. Stanton argues that "self-sovereignty" is the existential birthright of both women and men, for every human being "launched on the sea of life" is unique and "alone." But women's self-sovereignty specifically denotes sexual self-determination.[17] And women—that is, mothers—earn a special presumptive self-sovereignty: "alone [woman] goes to the gates of death to give life to every man that is born into the world; no one can share her fears, no one can mitigate her pangs; and if her sorrow is greater than she can bear, alone she passes beyond the gates into the vast unknown."[18] At the moment of extreme maternal giving, the moment when motherhood takes her life, the woman owns her self by withholding herself from motherhood.

Notes

Note: I would like to thank Catherine Gallagher and Walter Benn Michaels for their help with this essay at several stages of its composition. I am also grateful to David Lloyd, Tricia Moran, Lora Romero, and Lyn Wardley, who read this essay in draft and made helpful suggestions.

1. Kate Chopin, *The Awakening,* ed. Margaret Culley (New York: Norton, 1976), p. 4. All further references are given in the text and refer to this edition.

2. Many critics who have discussed the search for selfhood in *The Awakening* argue that Chopin opposes selfhood to socially imposed feminine roles that entail passivity, relative identity, and other-centeredness. See, for example, Per Seyersted, *Kate Chopin: A Critical Biography* (Baton Rouge: Louisiana University Press, 1969) and Margaret Culley, "Edna Pontellier: 'A Solitary Soul,'" in *The Awakening,* ed. Culley, pp. 224–228. Susan Rosowski and Cynthia Griffin Wolff

argue that Chopin depicts the difficulty of resisting the infantilizing, fantasy-prone narcissism encouraged by the feminine role in order to achieve autonomy in the realm of the real. See Susan Rosowski, "The Novel of Awakening," *Genre* 12 (Fall 1979): 313–332, and Cynthia Griffin Wolff, "Thanatos and Eros: Kate Chopin's *The Awakening*," *American Quarterly* 25 (October 1973): 449–471. Sandra M. Gilbert locates the achievement of selfhood outside of the existing, male-dominated social order. Chopin's heroine, Gilbert argues, achieves symbolic "rebirth" by departing for a mythical matriarchal realm. See Sandra M. Gilbert, "Introduction: The Second Coming of Aphrodite," in *The Awakening and Selected Stories by Kate Chopin*, ed. Sandra M. Gilbert (New York: Penguin Books, 1984), pp. 7–33.

3. Elizabeth Cady Stanton, "The Solitude of Self," in Ellen Carol Dubois, ed., *Elizabeth Cady Stanton, Susan B. Anthony: Correspondence, Writings, Speeches* (New York: Schocken, 1981), p. 249. In this speech Stanton gave in 1892 on the occasion of her resignation from the presidency of the suffrage movement, Stanton argued for full civil rights for woman on the grounds of her aloneness and existential "self-sovereignty." In its argument and rhetoric, this speech of Stanton's is strikingly similar to Chopin's presentation of female selfhood (*The Awakening*'s original title was *A Solitary Soul*). Like the self Chopin's heroine discovers, Stanton's self is an absolute, possessive self whose metaphorical situation is that of a lone individual "on a solitary island" or "launched on the sea of life" (247–248). In Stanton and in Chopin, female subjectivity and women's rights are grounded in absolute selfhood. For an account of early English feminists' commitment to absolute selfhood, see Catherine Gallagher, "Embracing the Absolute: The Politics of the Female Subject in Seventeenth-Century England," *Genders* 1 (Spring 1988): 24–39.

4. Lucinda Chandler, "Motherhood," *Woodhull and Claflin's Weekly*, May 13, 1871. Quoted in William Leach, *True Love and Perfect Union: The Feminist Reform of Sex and Society* (London: Routledge and Kegan Paul, 1981), p. 89. Leach sees the drive for women's property rights as an attempt to codify self-ownership through property law. He writes,

"Chandler believed so strongly in the principle of self-ownership that she wanted it fixed in the law; she joined the moral educationists of Washington in an attempt to repeal the law of couverture in the District of Columbia and to give every woman the 'legal . . . custody and control of her person in wifehood to govern according to her wisdom and instincts the maternal office and protect her child . . . from the dangers of selfish passion, alcoholism and vice'" (89).

5. Ibid.

6. Linda Gordon, *Woman's Body, Woman's Right: Birth Control in America* (New York: Penguin Books, 1974), p. 109. On voluntary motherhood, see Gordon, *Woman's Body*, chap. 5, "Voluntary Motherhood: The Beginnings of the Birth Control Movement," pp. 95–115. William Leach writes, "by the 1870s, self-ownership . . . had become the stock in trade of feminist thinking on birth control" (Leach, *True Love*, p. 92). Daniel Scott Smith notes that "the theme of the wife's right to control her body and her fertility was not uncommon" in Victorian American. Smith quotes Henry C. Wright as follows: "it is a woman's right, not her privilege, to control the surrender of her person; she should have pleasure or not allow access unless she wanted a child." Henry C. Wright, *Marriage and Parentage* (Boston: Bela Marsh, 1853), pp. 252–255, quoted in Daniel Scott Smith, "Family Limitation Sexual Control and Domestic Feminism in Victorian America," in *Clio's Consciousness Raised*, ed. Lois Banner and Mary Hartman (New York, 1974), pp. 119–136, 129. Smith also quotes Dido Lewis on the advocacy of the Moral Education Society for the right "of a wife to be her own person, and her sacred right to deny her husband if need be; and to decide how often and when she should become a mother." Dido Lewis, *Chastity, or Our Secret Sins* (New York: Canfield Publishing Company, 1888), p. 18, quoted in Smith, "Family Limitation," p. 129.

7. Gordon, *Woman's Body*, pp. 106–111.

8. Ibid., pp. 109–111.

9. Ibid., p. 110.

10. Charlotte Perkins Gilman, *Women and Economics: The Economic Factor between Men and Women as a Factor in Social Evolution*, ed. Carl Degler (New York: Harper and Row, 1966), p. 86. For

a twentieth-century critique of the market in woman, see Gayle Rubin, "The Traffic in Women: Notes on the 'Political Economy' of Sex" in Rayna R. Reiter, ed., *Toward an Anthropology of Women* (New York: Monthly Review Press, 1975, 157–210), p. 177.

11. Stanton, "The Solitude of Self," p. 247.

12. Thorstein Veblen, *The Theory of the Leisure Class: An Economic Study in the Evolution of Institutions* (New York: Macmillan Company, 1899). Veblen argues that the purpose of the ownership of personal property is to achieve social status (or "reputability"); all property is a version of that original property whose "usefulness" was to serve as a trophy marking the "prepotence," or social superiority, of the trophy's owner (23, 29). Objects that are appropriated for use do not cause reputability or prepotence to accrue to their possessors, and such objects are not owned in the conventional sense but instead subject to "use-appropriation" (23). Ownership, and the reputable self it produces, exists only when the community has reached a point of social and economic organization that allows for the production of a surplus. The first form taken by this "margin worth fighting for" is woman. The original form of ownership was the ownership of women by men. Veblen's account depends upon the idea that woman is already property, for the first ownership came about when the men of one tribe stole the women of another tribe in order to hold them as trophies (20, 23). To be a woman, then, is to be an object of exchange, a social product, surplus. In Veblen's famous characterization of the contemporary domestic ownership system, the bourgeois wife advertises her status as surplus in her role as the chief item of household property as she earns "reputability" for her husband through vicarious consumption and by performing vicarious leisure (usually in the form of nonproductive domestic and social functions) (65–67). This reading of Veblen suggests that ownership and the male selfhood it constitutes are produced by and reflect not the self but others, whose ever-shifting perceptions and positions create and destroy the effect of reputability and thus of selfhood. Surplus is a product of social/economic organization; to own (surplus) is thus to establish a mediated relationship with the world. Like Veblen, Chopin pokes fun at the figure of the male owner whose relationship to the world is thus mediated. In the opening pages of *The Awakening*, Léonce rather ridiculously governs himself according to his notions of property rights; for example, he grants the caged birds the right to sing because they are owned by Mme. Lebrun and grants himself the right to retreat to "his own cottage" (3). The surplus and mediating character of personal property is manifested in the woman's femininity. While femininity reflects the oppressive system that makes woman property, for Edna, the unstable, nonessential, and representative character of her status as Léonce's property becomes suggestive of the possibility of a self-determination that paradoxically remains within the bounds of the male ownership system: she can herself put her wedding rings on or take them off.

13. Margaret Culley, "The Context of *The Awakening*," in *The Awakening*, ed. Culley, p. 118.

14. Leach, *True Love*, p. 175.

15. Stanton, "The Solitude of Self," p. 247.

16. Motherhood (which includes the abstention from motherhood) is thus a form of a speculative risk taking. The intention to become a mother is the kind of "weak" intention that Walter Benn Michaels connects with "acts that take place in the market, such as speculating in commodities." See chapter 7, "Action and Accident: Photography and Writing," in Walter Benn Michaels, *The Gold Standard and the Logic of Naturalism: American Literature at the Turn of the Century* (Berkeley: University of California Press, 1987), p. 237. Michaels argues that for the self in the market, "self-possession" and "self-interest" are grounded in "the possibility of intention and action coming apart" (244, 241). My discussion of the logic of voluntary motherhood—like Michaels's own example of Lily Bart as a self-speculating self—emphasizes that this self-interest is gendered. For women, self-speculation is sexual; that is to say that sexuality is the content of the female self in the market. Contrary to what Michaels claims, Lily is "a victim of patriarchal capitalism" in a way that the male entrepreneurs in the novel are not (240). The "voluntariness" of female self-speculation is merely an effect of the commodity system, which constructs value along the

polarities of accessibility and rarity. The woman cannot choose whether to speculate or what to speculate in; by being a woman she is already sexually at risk. The speculative risk taken by Lily Bart in the marriage market includes the risk of withholding sexual accessibility from the market—a risk that results in her death (complete with hallucinated motherhood). "Voluntary motherhood" concretizes female self-speculation as the risk of pregnancy—which is the risk of life—and points to the enforced nature of female self-speculation by identifying all women as mothers.

17. Ellen Carol Dubois writes, "everywhere [Stanton] lectured, she held parlor meetings of women only on 'marriage and maternity.' . . . Her central point was that women ought to be able to control their own sexual lives, a right which she called 'individual' or 'self' sovereignty." Ellen Carol Dubois, Introduction in Stanton, *Elizabeth Cady Stanton*, p. 95.

18. Ibid., pp. 248, 251.

Ode: Intimations of Immortality from Recollections of Early Childhood

William Wordsworth

The Child is father of the Man;
And I could wish my days to be
Bound each to each by natural piety.[1]

I

There was a time when meadow, grove, and stream
The earth, and every common sight,

To me did seem
Apparelled in celestial light,
The glory and the freshness of a dream.   5
It is not now as it hath been of yore;—
Turn wheresoe'er I may,
By night or day,
The things which I have seen I now can see no more.

II

The Rainbow comes and goes,   10
And lovely is the Rose,
The Moon doth with delight

---

[1]The final lines from Wordsworth's "My Heart Leaps Up." When first published, the poem had only "Ode" as its title and carried an epigraph from Virgil's "Fourth Eclogue": *"Paulo maiora canamus"* (Let us sing a rather more exalted [theme]).

Look round her when the heavens are bare,
    Waters on a starry night
    Are beautiful and fair;   15
The sunshine is a glorious birth;
But yet I know, where'er I go,
That there hath past away a glory from the earth.

III

Now, while the birds thus sing a joyous song,
    And while the young lambs bound   20
        As to the tabor's sound,
To me alone there came a thought of grief:
A timely utterance gave that thought relief,
        And I again am strong:
The cataracts blow their trumpets from the steep;   25
No more shall grief of mine the season wrong;
I hear the Echoes through the mountains throng,
The Winds come to me from the fields of sleep,
        And all the earth is gay;
          Land and sea   30
    Give themselves up to jollity,
        And with the heart of May
    Doth every Beast keep holiday; —
        Thou Child of Joy,
Shout round me, let me hear thy shouts, thou happy Shepherd boy! 35

IV

Ye blessèd Creatures, I have heard the call
    Ye to each other make; I see
The heavens laugh with you in your jubilee;
    My heart is at your festival,
        My head hath its coronal,   40
The fulness of your bliss, I feel — I feel it all.
        Oh evil day! if I were sullen
        While Earth herself is adorning,
          This sweet May-morning,
        And the Children are culling   45
          On every side,
        In a thousand valleys far and wide,
        Fresh flowers; while the sun shines warm,
And the Babe leaps up on his Mother's arm: —
        I hear, I hear, with joy I hear!   50
        —But there's a Tree, of many, one,
A single Field which I have looked upon,
Both of them speak of something that is gone:
        The Pansy at my feet
        Doth the same tale repeat: 55
Whither is fled the visionary gleam?
Where is it now, the glory and the dream?

V

Our birth is but a sleep and a forgetting:
The Soul that rises with us, our life's Star,
    Hath had elsewhere its setting,   60
    And cometh from afar:

Not in entire forgetfulness,
And not in utter nakedness,
But trailing clouds of glory do we come
From God, who is our home: 65
Heaven lies about us in our infancy!
Shades of the prison-house begin to close
Upon the growing Boy,
But He beholds the light, and whence it flows,
He sees it in his joy;   70

The Youth, who daily farther from the east
Must travel, still is Nature's Priest,
And by the vision splendid
Is on his way attended;
At length the Man perceives it die away,   75
And fade into the light of common day.

VI

Earth fills her lap with pleasures of her own;
Yearnings she hath in her own natural kind,
And, even with something of a Mother's mind,
And no unworthy aim,   80
The homely Nurse doth all she can
To make her Foster-child, her Inmate Man,
Forget the glories he hath known,
And that imperial palace whence he came.

VII

Behold the Child among his new-born blisses,   85
A six years' Darling of a pigmy size!
See, where 'mid work of his own hand he lies,
Fretted by sallies of his mother's kisses,
With light upon him from his father's eyes!
See, at his feet, some little plan or chart,   90
Some fragment from his dream of human life,
Shaped by himself with newly-learned art;
A wedding or a festival,
A mourning or a funeral;
And this hath now his heart,   95
And unto this he frames his song:
Then will he fit his tongue
To dialogues of business, love, or strife;
But it will not be long
Ere this be thrown aside,   100
And with new joy and pride
The little Actor cons another part;
Filling from time to time his "humorous stage"
With all the Persons, down to palsied Age,
That Life brings with her in her equipage;   105
As if his whole vocation
Were endless imitation.

VIII

Thou, whose exterior semblance doth belie
Thy Soul's immensity;

Thou best Philosopher, who yet dost keep 110
Thy heritage, thou Eye among the blind,
That, deaf and silent, read'st the eternal deep,
Haunted for ever by the eternal mind, —
     Mighty Prophet! Seer blest!
     On whom those truths do rest, 115
Which we are toiling all our lives to find,
In darkness lost, the darkness of the grave;
Thou, over whom thy Immortality
Broods like the Day, a Master o'er a Slave,
A Presence which is not to be put by; 120
Thou little Child, yet glorious in the might
Of heaven-born freedom on thy being's height,
Why with such earnest pains dost thou provoke
The years to bring the inevitable yoke,
Thus blindly with thy blessedness at strife? 125
Full soon thy Soul shall have her earthly freight,
And custom lie upon thee with a weight,
Heavy as frost, and deep almost as life!

           IX
     O joy! that in our embers
     Is something that doth live, 130
     That nature yet remembers
     What was so fugitive!
The thought of our past years in me doth breed
Perpetual benediction: not indeed
For that which is most worthy to be blest; 135
Delight and liberty, the simple creed
Of Childhood, whether busy or at rest,
With new-fledged hope still fluttering in his breast: —
     Not for these I raise
     The song of thanks and praise; 140
     But for those obstinate questionings
     Of sense and outward things,
     Fallings from us, vanishings;
     Blank misgivings of a Creature
Moving about in worlds not realised, 145
High instincts before which our mortal Nature
Did tremble like a guilty Thing surprised:
     But for those first affections,
     Those shadowy recollections,
     Which, be they what they may, 150
Are yet the fountain-light of all our day,
Are yet a master-light of all our seeing;
     Uphold us, cherish, and have power to make
Our noisy years seem moments in the being
Of the eternal Silence: truths that wake, 155
     To perish never:
Which neither listlessness, nor mad endeavour,
     Nor Man nor Boy,
Nor all that is at enmity with joy,
Can utterly abolish or destroy. 160
     Hence in a season of calm weather
     Though inland far we be,

Our Souls have sight of that immortal sea
      Which brought us hither,
        Can in a moment travel thither,   165
And see the Children sport upon the shore,
And hear the mighty waters rolling evermore.

               X
Then sing, ye Birds, sing, sing a joyous song!
      And let the young Lambs bound
        As to the tabor's sound!   170
We in thought will join your throng,
      Ye that pipe and ye that play,
      Ye that through your hearts to-day
      Feel the gladness of the May!

What though the radiance which was once so bright   175
Be now for ever taken from my sight,
   Though nothing can bring back the hour
Of splendour in the grass, of glory in the flower;
      We will grieve not, rather find
      Strength in what remains behind;   180
      In the primal sympathy
      Which having been must ever be;
      In the soothing thoughts that spring
      Out of human suffering;
      In the faith that looks through death,   185
In years that bring the philosophic mind.

              XI
And O, ye Fountains, Meadows, Hills, and Groves,
Forebode not any severing of our loves!
Yet in my heart of hearts I feel your might;
I only have relinquished one delight   190
To live beneath your more habitual sway.
I love the Brooks which down their channels fret,
Even more than when I tripped lightly as they;
The innocent brightness of a new-born Day
        Is lovely yet;   195
The Clouds that gather round the setting sun
Do take a sober colouring from an eye
That hath kept watch o'er man's mortality;
Another race hath been, and other palms are won.
   Thanks to the human heart by which we live,   200
   Thanks to its tenderness, its joys, and fears,
   To me the meanest flower that blows can give
   Thoughts that do often lie too deep for tears.

The Awakening

Kate Chopin

I

A green and yellow parrot, which hung in a cage outside the door, kept repeating over and over: *"Allez vous-en! Allez vous-en! Sapristi!* That's all right!"

He could speak a little Spanish, and also a language which nobody understood, unless it was the mocking-bird that hung on the other side of the door, whistling his fluty notes out upon the breeze with maddening persistence.

Mr. Pontellier, unable to read his newspaper with any degree of comfort, arose with an expression and an exclamation of disgust. He walked down the gallery and across the narrow "bridges" which connected the Lebrun cottages one with the other. He had been seated before the door of the main house. The parrot and the mocking-bird were the property of Madame Lebrun, and they had the right to make all the noise they wished. Mr. Pontellier had the privilege of quitting their society when they ceased to be entertaining.

He stopped before the door of his own cottage, which was the fourth one from the main building and next to the last. Seating himself in a wicker rocker which was there, he once more applied himself to the task of reading the newspaper. The day was Sunday; the paper was a day old. The Sunday papers had not yet reached Grand Isle. He was already acquainted with the market reports, and he glanced restlessly over the editorials and bits of news which he had not had time to read before quitting New Orleans the day before.

Mr. Pontellier wore eye-glasses. He was a man of forty, of medium height and rather slender build; he stooped a little. His hair was brown and straight, parted on one side. His beard was neatly and closely trimmed.

Once in a while he withdrew his glance from the newspaper and looked about him. There was more noise than ever over at the house. The main building was called "the house," to distinguish it from the cottages. The chattering and whistling birds were still at it. Two young girls, the Farival twins, were playing a duet from "Zampa" upon the piano. Madame Lebrun was bustling in and out, giving orders in a high key to a yard-boy whenever she got inside the house, and directions in an equally high voice to a dining-room servant whenever she got outside. She was a fresh, pretty woman, clad always in white with elbow sleeves. Her starched skirts crinkled as she came and went. Farther down, before one of the cottages, a lady in black was walking demurely up and down, telling her beads. A good many persons of the *pension* had gone over to the *Chênière Caminada* in Beaudelet's lugger to hear mass. Some young people were out under the wateroaks playing croquet. Mr. Pontellier's two children were there—sturdy little fellows of four and five. A quadroon nurse followed them about with a far-away, meditative air.

This is the original text of *The Awakening,* first published in April 1899.

Mr. Pontellier finally lit a cigar and began to smoke, letting the paper drag idly from his hand. He fixed his gaze upon a white sunshade that was advancing at snail's pace from the beach. He could see it plainly between the gaunt trunks of the water-oaks and across the stretch of yellow camomile. The gulf looked far away, melting hazily into the blue of the horizon. The sunshade continued to approach slowly. Beneath its pink-lined shelter were his wife, Mrs. Pontellier, and young Robert Lebrun. When they reached the cottage, the two seated themselves with some appearance of fatigue upon the upper step of the porch, facing each other, each leaning against a supporting post.

"What folly! to bathe at such an hour in such heat!" exclaimed Mr. Pontellier. He himself had taken a plunge at daylight. That was why the morning seemed long to him.

"You are burnt beyond recognition," he added, looking at his wife as one looks at a valuable piece of personal property which has suffered some damage. She held up her hands, strong, shapely hands, and surveyed them critically, drawing up her lawn sleeves above the wrists. Looking at them reminded her of her rings, which she had given to her husband before leaving for the beach. She silently reached out to him, and he, understanding, took the rings from his vest pocket and dropped them into her open palm. She slipped them upon her fingers; then clasping her knees, she looked across at Robert and began to laugh. The rings sparkled upon her fingers. He sent back an answering smile.

"What is it?" asked Pontellier, looking lazily and amused from one to the other. It was some utter nonsense; some adventure out there in the water, and they both tried to relate it at once. It did not seem half so amusing when told. They realized this, and so did Mr. Pontellier. He yawned and stretched himself. Then he got up, saying he had half a mind to go over to Klein's hotel and play a game of billiards.

"Come go along, Lebrun," he proposed to Robert. But Robert admitted quite frankly that he preferred to stay where he was and talk to Mrs. Pontellier.

"Well, send him about his business when he bores you, Edna," instructed her husband as he prepared to leave.

"Here, take the umbrella," she exclaimed, holding it out to him. He accepted the sunshade, and lifting it over his head descended the steps and walked away.

"Coming back to dinner?" his wife called after him. He halted a moment and shrugged his shoulders. He felt in his vest pocket; there was a ten-dollar bill there. He did not know; perhaps he would return for the early dinner and perhaps he would not. It all depended upon the company which he found over at Klein's and the size of "the game." He did not say this, but she understood it, and laughed, nodding good-by to him.

Both children wanted to follow their father when they saw him starting out. He kissed them and promised to bring them back bonbons and peanuts.

II

Mrs. Pontellier's eyes were quick and bright; they were a yellowish brown, about the color of her hair. She had a way of turning them swiftly upon an object and holding them there as if lost in some inward maze of contemplation or thought.

Her eyebrows were a shade darker than her hair. They were thick and almost horizontal, emphasizing the depth of her eyes. She was rather handsome than beautiful. Her face was captivating by reason of a certain frankness of expression and a contradictory subtle play of features. Her manner was engaging.

Robert rolled a cigarette. He smoked cigarettes because he could not afford cigars, he said. He had a cigar in his pocket which Mr. Pontellier had presented him with, and he was saving it for his after-dinner smoke.

This seemed quite proper and natural on his part. In coloring he was not unlike his companion. A clean-shaved face made the resemblance more pronounced than it would otherwise have been. There rested no shadow of care upon his open countenance. His eyes gathered in and reflected the light and languor of the summer day.

Mrs. Pontellier reached over for a palm-leaf fan that lay on the porch and began to fan herself, while Robert sent between his lips light puffs from his cigarette. They chatted incessantly: about the things around them; their amusing adventure out in the water — it had again assumed its entertaining aspect; about the wind, the trees, the people who had gone to the Chênière; about the children playing croquet under the oaks, and the Farival twins, who were now performing the overture to "The Poet and the Peasant."

Robert talked a good deal about himself. He was very young, and did not know any better. Mrs. Pontellier talked a little about herself for the same reason. Each was interested in what the other said. Robert spoke of his intention to go to Mexico in the autumn, where fortune awaited him. He was always intending to go to Mexico, but some way never got there. Meanwhile he held on to his modest position in a mercantile house in New Orleans, where an equal familiarity with English, French and Spanish gave him no small value as a clerk and correspondent.

He was spending his summer vacation, as he always did, with his mother at Grand Isle. In former times, before Robert could remember, "the house" had been a summer luxury of the Lebruns. Now, flanked by its dozen or more cottages, which was always filled with exclusive visitors from the *Quartier Français*," it enabled Madame Lebrun to maintain the easy and comfortable existence which appeared to be her birthright.

Mrs. Pontellier talked about her father's Mississippi plantation and her girlhood home in the old Kentucky blue-grass country. She was an American woman, with a small infusion of French which seemed to have been lost in dilution. She read a letter from her sister, who was away in the East, and who had engaged herself to be married. Robert was interested, and wanted to know what manner of girls the sisters were, what the father was like, and how long the mother had been dead.

When Mrs. Pontellier folded the letter it was time for her to dress for the early dinner.

"I see Léonce isn't coming back," she said, with a glance in the direction whence her husband had disappeared. Robert supposed he was not, as there were a good many New Orleans club men over at Klein's.

When Mrs. Pontellier left him to enter her room, the young man descended the steps and strolled over toward the croquet players, where, during the half-hour before dinner, he amused himself with the little Pontellier children, who were very fond of him.

III

It was eleven o'clock that night when Mr. Pontellier returned from Klein's hotel. He was in an excellent humor, in high spirits, and very talkative. His entrance awoke his wife, who was in bed and fast asleep when he came in. He talked to her while he undressed, telling her anecdotes and bits of news and gossip that he had gathered during the day.

From his trousers pockets he took a fistful of crumpled bank notes and a good deal of silver coin, which he piled on the bureau indiscriminately with keys, knife, handkerchief, and whatever else happened to be in his pockets. She was overcome with sleep, and answered him with little half utterances.

He thought it very discouraging that his wife, who was the sole object of his existence, evinced so little interest in things which concerned him, and valued so little his conversation.

Mr. Pontellier had forgotten the bonbons and peanuts for the boys. Notwithstanding he loved them very much, and went into the adjoining room where they slept to take a look at them and make sure that they were resting comfortably. The result of his investigation was far from satisfactory. He turned and shifted the youngsters about in bed. One of them began to kick and talk about a basket full of crabs.

Mr. Pontellier returned to his wife with the information that Raoul had a high fever and needed looking after. Then he lit a cigar and went and sat near the open door to smoke it.

Mrs. Pontellier was quite sure Raoul had no fever. He had gone to bed perfectly well, she said, and nothing had ailed him all day. Mr. Pontellier was too well acquainted with fever symptoms to be mistaken. He assured her the child was consuming at that moment in the next room.

He reproached his wife with her inattention, her habitual neglect of the children. If it was not a mother's place to look after children, whose on earth was it? He himself had his hands full with his brokerage business. He could not be in two places at once; making a living for his family on the street, and staying at home to see that no harm befell them. He talked in a monotonous, insistent way.

Mrs. Pontellier sprang out of bed and went into the next room. She soon came back and sat on the edge of the bed, leaning her head down on the pillow. She said nothing, and refused to answer her husband when he questioned her. When his cigar was smoked out he went to bed, and in half a minute he was fast asleep.

Mrs. Pontellier was by that time thoroughly awake. She began to cry a little, and wiped her eyes on the sleeve of her *peignoir*. Blowing out the candle, which her husband had left burning, she slipped her bare feet into a pair of satin *mules* at the foot of the bed and went out on the porch, where she sat down in the wicker chair and began to rock gently to and fro.

It was then past midnight. The cottages were all dark. A single faint light gleamed out from the hallway of the house. There was no sound abroad except the hooting of an old owl in the top of a wateroak, and the everlasting voice of the sea, that was not uplifted at that soft hour. It broke like a mournful lullaby upon the night.

The tears came so fast to Mrs. Pontellier's eyes that the damp sleeve of her *peignoir* no longer served to dry them. She was holding the back of her chair with one hand; her loose sleeve had slipped almost to the shoulder of her uplifted arm. Turning, she thrust her face, steaming and wet, into the bend of her arm, and she went on crying there, not caring any longer to dry her face, her eyes, her arms. She could not have told why she was crying. Such experiences as the foregoing were not uncommon in her married life. They seemed never before to have weighed much against the abundance of her husband's kindness and a uniform devotion which had come to be tacit and self-understood.

An indescribable oppression, which seemed to generate in some unfamiliar part of her consciousness, filled her whole being with a vague anguish. It was like a shadow, like a mist passing across her soul's summer day. It was strange and unfamiliar; it was a mood. She did not sit there inwardly upbraiding her husband, lamenting at Fate, which had directed her footsteps to the path which they had taken. She was just having a good cry all to herself. The mosquitoes made merry over her, biting her firm, round arms and nipping at her bare insteps.

The little stinging, buzzing imps succeeded in dispelling a mood which might have held her there in the darkness half a night longer.

The following morning Mr. Pontellier was up in good time to take the rockaway which was to convey him to the steamer at the wharf. He was returning to the city to his business, and they would not see him again at the Island till the coming Saturday. He had regained his composure, which seemed to have been somewhat impaired the night before. He was eager to be gone, as he looked forward to a lively week in Carondelet Street.

Mr. Pontellier gave his wife half of the money which he had brought away from Klein's hotel the evening before. She liked money as well as most women, and accepted it with no little satisfaction.

"It will buy a handsome wedding present for Sister Janet!" she exclaimed, smoothing out the bills as she counted them one by one.

"Oh! we'll treat Sister Janet better than that, my dear," he laughed, as he prepared to kiss her good-by.

The boys were tumbling about, clinging to his legs, imploring that numerous things be brought back to them. Mr. Pontellier was a great favorite, and ladies, men, children, even nurses, were always on hand to say good-by to him. His wife stood smiling and waving, the boys shouting, as he disappeared in the old rockaway down the sandy road.

A few days later a box arrived for Mrs. Pontellier from New Orleans. It was from her husband. It was filled with *friandises*, with luscious and toothsome bits — the finest of fruits, *patés*, a rare bottle or two, delicious syrups, and bonbons in abundance.

Mrs. Pontellier was always very generous with the contents of such a box; she was quite used to receiving them when away from home. The *patés* and fruit were brought to the dining-room; the bonbons were passed around. And the ladies, selecting with dainty and discriminating fingers and a little greedily, all declared that Mr. Pontellier was the best husband in the world. Mrs. Pontellier was forced to admit that she knew of none better.

IV

It would have been a difficult matter for Mr. Pontellier to define to his own satisfaction or any one else's wherein his wife failed in her duty toward their children. It was something which he felt rather than perceived, and he never voiced the feeling without subsequent regret and ample atonement.

If one of the little Pontellier boys took a tumble whilst at play, he was not apt to rush crying to his mother's arms for comfort; he would more likely pick himself up, wipe the water out of his eyes and the sand out of his mouth, and go on playing. Tots as they were, they pulled together and stood their ground in childish battles with doubled fists and uplifted voices, which usually prevailed against the other mother-tots. The quadroon nurse was looked upon as a huge encumbrance, only good to button up waists and panties and to brush and part hair; since it seemed to be a law of society that hair must be parted and brushed.

In short, Mrs. Pontellier was not a mother-woman. The mother-women seemed to prevail that summer at Grand Isle. It was easy to know them, fluttering about with extended, protecting wings when any harm, real or imaginary, threatened their precious brood. They were women who idolized their children, worshiped their husbands, and esteemed it a holy privilege to efface themselves as individuals and grow wings as ministering angels.

Many of them were delicious in the rôle; one of them was the embodiment of every womanly grace and charm. If her husband did not adore her, he was a brute, deserving of death by slow torture. Her name was Adèle Ratignolle. There are no words to describe her save the old ones that have served so often to picture the bygone heroine of romance and the fair lady of our dreams. There was nothing subtle or hidden about her charms; her beauty was all there, flaming and apparent: the spun-gold hair that comb nor confining pin could restrain; the blue eyes that were like nothing but sapphires; two lips that pouted, that were so red one could only think of cherries or some other delicious crimson fruit in looking at them. She was growing a little stout, but it did not seem to detract an iota from the grace of every step, pose, gesture. One would not have wanted her white neck a mite less full or her beautiful arms more slender. Never were hands more exquisite than hers, and it was a joy to look at them when she threaded her needle or adjusted her gold thimble to her taper middle finger as she sewed away on the little night-drawers or fashioned a bodice or a bib.

Madame Ratignolle was very fond of Mrs. Pontellier, and often she took her sewing and went over to sit with her in the afternoons. She was sitting there the afternoon of the day the box arrived from New Orleans. She had possession of the rocker, and she was busily engaged in sewing upon a diminutive pair of night-drawers.

She had brought the pattern of the drawers for Mrs. Pontellier to cut out — a marvel of construction, fashioned to enclose a baby's body so effectually that only two small eyes might look out from the garment, like an Eskimo's. They were designed for winter wear, when treacherous drafts came down chimneys and insidious currents of deadly cold found their way through key-holes.

Mrs. Pontellier's mind was quite at rest concerning the present material needs of her children, and she could not see the use of anticipating and making winter night garments the subject of her summer meditations. But she did not want to appear unamiable and uninterested, so she had brought forth newspapers, which she spread upon the floor of the gallery, and under Madame Ratignolle's directions she had cut a pattern of the impervious garment.

Robert was there, seated as he had been the Sunday before, and Mrs. Pontellier also occupied her former position on the upper step, leaning listlessly against the post. Beside her was a box of bonbons, which she held out at intervals to Madame Ratignolle.

That lady seemed at a loss to make a selection, but finally settled upon a stick of nougat, wondering if it were not too rich; whether it could possibly hurt her. Madame Ratignolle had been married seven years. About every two years she had a baby. At that time she had three babies, and was beginning to think of a fourth one. She was always talking about her "condition." Her "condition" was in no way apparent, and no one would have known a thing about it but for her persistence in making it the subject of conversation.

Robert started to reassure her, asserting that he had known a lady who had subsisted upon nougat during the entire — but seeing the color mount into Mrs. Pontellier's face he checked himself and changed the subject.

Mrs. Pontellier, though she had married a Creole, was not thoroughly at home in the society of Creoles; never before had she been thrown so intimately among them. There were only Creoles that summer at Lebrun's. They all new each other, and felt like one large family, among whom existed the most amicable relations. A characteristic which distinguished them and which impressed Mrs. Pontellier most forcibly was their entire absence of prudery. Their freedom of expression was at first incomprehensible to her, though she had no difficulty in reconciling it with a lofty chastity which in the Creole woman seems to be inborn and unmistakable.

Never would Edna Pontellier forget the shock with which she heard Madame Ratignolle relating to old Monsieur Farival the harrowing story of one of her *accouchements*, withholding no intimate detail. She was growing accustomed to like shocks, but she could not keep the mounting color back from her cheeks. Oftener than once her coming had interrupted the droll story with which Robert was entertaining some amused group of married women.

A book had gone the rounds of the *pension*. When it came her turn to read it, she did so with profound astonishment. She felt moved to read the book in secret and solitude, though none of the others had done so — to hide it from view at the sound of approaching footsteps. It was openly criticized and freely discussed at table. Mrs. Pontellier gave over being astonished, and concluded that wonders would never cease.

V

They formed a congenial group sitting there that summer afternoon — Madame Ratignolle sewing away, often stopping to relate a story or incident with much expressive gesture of her perfect hands; Robert and Mrs. Pontellier sitting idle, exchanging occasional words, glances or smiles which indicated a certain advanced stage of intimacy and *camaraderie.*

He had lived in her shadow during the past month. No one thought anything of it. Many had predicted that Robert would devote himself to Mrs. Pontellier when he arrived. Since the age of fifteen, which was eleven years before, Robert each summer at Grand Isle had constituted himself the devoted attendant of some fair dame or damsel. Sometimes it was a young girl, again a widow; but as often as not it was some interesting married woman.

For two consecutive seasons he lived in the sunlight of Mademoiselle Duvigné's presence. But she died between summers; then Robert posed as an inconsolable, prostrating himself at the feet of Madame Ratignolle for whatever crumbs of sympathy and comfort she might be pleased to vouchsafe.

Mrs. Pontellier liked to sit and gaze at her fair companion as she might look upon a faultless Madonna.

"Could any one fathom the cruelty beneath that fair exterior?" murmured Robert. "She knew that I adored her once, and she let me adore her. It was 'Robert, come; go; stand up; sit down; do this; do that; see if the baby sleeps; my thimble, please, that I left God knows where. Come and read Daudet to me while I sew.'"

"*Par example!* I never had to ask. You were always there under my feet, like a troublesome cat."

"You mean like an adoring dog. And just as soon as Ratignolle appeared on the scene, then it *was* like a dog. '*Passez! Adieu! Allez vous-en!*'"

"Perhaps I feared to make Alphonse jealous," she interjoined, with excessive naïveté. That made them all laugh. The right hand jealous of the left! The heart jealous of the soul! But for that matter, the Creole husband is never jealous; with him the gangrene passion is one which has become dwarfed by disuse.

Meanwhile Robert, addressing Mrs. Pontellier, continued to tell of his one time hopeless passion for Madame Ratignolle; of sleepless nights, of consuming flames till the very sea sizzled when he took his daily plunge. While the lady at the needle kept up a little running, contemptuous comment:

"*Blagueur — farceur — gros bête va!*"

He never assumed his serio-comic tone when alone with Mrs. Pontellier. She never knew precisely what to make of it; at that moment it was impossible for her to guess how much of it was jest and what proportion was earnest. It was understood that he had often spoken words of love to Madame Ratignolle, without any thought of being taken seriously. Mrs. Pontellier was glad he had not assumed a similar rôle toward herself. It would have been unacceptable and annoying.

Mrs. Pontellier had brought her sketching materials, which she sometimes dabbled with in an unprofessional way. She liked the dabbling. She felt in it satisfaction of a kind which no other employment afforded her.

She had long wished to try herself on Madame Ratignolle. Never had that lady seemed a more tempting subject than at that moment, seated there like some sensuous Madonna, with the gleam of the fading day enriching her splendid color.

Robert crossed over and seated himself upon the step below Mrs. Pontellier, that he might watch her work. She handled her brushes with a certain ease and freedom which came, not from long and close acquaintance with them, but from a natural aptitude. Robert followed her work with close attention, giving forth little ejaculatory expressions of appreciation in French, which he addressed to Madame Ratignolle.

"*Mais ce n'est pas mal! Elle s'y connait, elle a de la force, oui.*"

During his oblivious attention he once quietly rested his head against Mrs. Pontellier's arm. As gently she repulsed him. Once again he repeated the offense. She could not but believe it to be thoughtlessness on his part; yet that was no reason she should submit to it. She did not remonstrate, except again to repulse him quietly but firmly. He offered no apology.

The picture completed bore no resemblance to Madame Ratignolle. She was greatly disappointed to find that it did not look like her. But it was a fair enough piece of work, and in many respects satisfying.

Mrs. Pontellier evidently did not think so. After surveying the sketch critically she drew a broad smudge of paint across its surface, and crumpled the paper between her hands.

The youngsters came tumbling up the steps, the quadroon following at the respectful distance which they required her to observe. Mrs. Pontellier made them carry her paints and things into the house. She sought to detain them for a little talk and some pleasantry. But they were greatly in earnest. They had only come to investigate the contents of the bonbon box. They accepted without murmuring what she chose to give them, each holding out two chubby hands scoop-like, in the vain hope that they might be filled; and then away they went.

The sun was low in the west, and the breeze soft and languorous that came up from the south, charged with the seductive odor of the sea. Children, freshly befurbeloved, were gathering for their games under the oaks. Their voices were high and penetrating.

Madame Ratignolle folded her sewing, placing thimble, scissors and thread all neatly together in the roll, which she pinned securely. She complained of faintness. Mrs. Pontellier flew for the cologne water and a fan. She bathed Madame Ratignolle's face with cologne, while Robert plied the fan with unnecessary vigor.

The spell was soon over, and Mrs. Pontellier could not help wondering if there were not a little imagination responsible for its origin, for the rose tint had never faded from her friend's face.

She stood watching the fair woman walk down the long line of galleries with the grace and majesty which queens are sometimes supposed to possess. Her little ones ran to meet her. Two of them clung about her white skirts, the third she took from its nurse and with a thousand endearments bore it along in her own fond, encircling arms. Though, as everybody well knew, the doctor had forbidden her to lift so much as a pin!

"Are you going bathing?" asked Robert of Mrs. Pontellier. It was not so much a question as a reminder.

"Oh, no," she answered, with a tone of indecision. "I'm tired; I think not." Her glance wandered from his face away toward the Gulf, whose sonorous murmur reached her like a loving but imperative entreaty.

"Oh, come!" he insisted. "You mustn't miss your bath. Come on. The water must be delicious; it will not hurt you. Come."

He reached up for her big, rough straw hat that hung on a peg outside the door, and put it on her head. They descended the steps, and walked away together toward the beach. The sun was low in the west and the breeze was soft and warm.

VI

Edna Pontellier could not have told why, wishing to go to the beach with Robert, she should in the first place have declined, and in the second place have followed in obedience to one of the two contradictory impulses which impelled her.

A certain light was beginning to dawn dimly within her,—the light which, showing the way, forbids it.

At the early period it served but to bewilder her. It moved her to dreams, to thoughtfulness, to the shadowy anguish which had overcome her the midnight when she had abandoned herself to tears.

In short, Mrs. Pontellier was beginning to realize her position in the universe as a human being, and to recognize her relations as an individual to the world within and about her. This may seem like a ponderous weight of wisdom to descend upon the soul of a young woman of twenty-eight—perhaps more wisdom than the Holy Ghost is usually pleased to vouchsafe to any woman.

But the beginning of things, of a world especially, is necessarily vague, tangled, chaotic, and exceedingly disturbing. How few of us ever emerge from such beginning! How many souls perish in its tumult!

The voice of the sea is seductive; never ceasing, whispering, clamoring, murmuring, inviting the soul to wander for a spell in abysses of solitude; to lose itself in mazes of inward contemplation.

The voice of the sea speaks to the soul. The touch of the sea is sensuous, enfolding the body in its soft, close embrace.

VII

Mrs. Pontellier was not a woman given to confidences, a characteristic hitherto contrary to her nature. Even as a child she had lived her own small life all within herself. At a very early period she had apprehended instinctively the dual life—that outward existence which conforms, the inward life which questions.

That summer at Grand Isle she began to loosen a little the mantle of reserve that had always enveloped her. There may have been—there must have been—influences, both subtle and apparent, working in their several ways to induce her to do this; but the most obvious was the influence of Adèle Ratignolle. The excessive physical charm of the Creole had first attracted her, for Edna had a sensuous susceptibility to beauty. Then the candor of the woman's whole existence, which every one might read, and which formed so striking a contrast to her own habitual reserve—this might have furnished a link. Who can tell what metals the gods use in forging the subtle bond which we call sympathy, which we might as well call love.

The two women went away one morning to the beach together, arm in arm, under the huge white sunshade. Edna had prevailed upon Madame Ratignolle to leave the children behind, though she could not induce her to relinquish a diminutive roll of needlework, which Adèle begged to be allowed to slip into the depths of her pocket. In some unaccountable way they had escaped from Robert.

The walk to the beach was no inconsiderable one, consisting as it did of a long, sandy path, upon which a sporadic and tangled growth that bordered it on either side made frequent and unexpected inroads. There were acres of yellow camomile reaching out on either hand. Further away still, vegetable gardens abounded, with frequent small plantations of orange or lemon trees intervening. The dark green clusters glistened from afar in the sun.

The women were both of goodly height, Madame Ratignolle possessing the more feminine and matronly figure. The charm of Edna Pontellier's physique stole insensibly upon you. The lines of her body were long, clean and symmetrical; it was a body which occasionally fell into splendid poses; there was no suggestion of the trim, stereotyped fashion-plate about it. A casual and indiscriminating observer, in passing, might not cast a second glance upon the figure. But with more feeling and discernment he would have recognized the noble beauty of its modeling, and the graceful severity of poise and movement, which made Edna Pontellier different from the crowd.

She wore a cool muslin that morning—white, with a waving vertical line of brown running through it; also a white linen collar and the big straw hat which she had taken from the peg outside the door. The hat rested any way on her yellow-brown hair, that waved a little, was heavy, and clung close to her head.

Madame Ratignolle, more careful of her complexion, had twined a gauze veil about her head. She wore dogskin gloves, with gauntlets that protected her wrists. She was dressed in pure white, with a fluffiness of ruffles that became her. The draperies and fluttering things which she wore suited her rich, luxuriant beauty as a greater severity of line could not have done.

There were a number of bath-houses along the beach, of rough but solid construction, built with small, protecting galleries facing the water. Each house consisted of two compartments, and each family at Lebrun's possessed a compartment for itself, fitted out with all the essential paraphernalia of the bath and whatever other conveniences the owners might desire. The two women had no intention of bathing; they had just strolled down to the beach for a walk and to be alone and near the water. The Pontellier and Ratignolle compartments adjoined one another under the same roof.

Mrs. Pontellier had brought down her key through force of habit. Unlocking the door of her bath-room she went inside, and soon emerged, bringing a rug, which she spread upon the floor of the gallery, and two huge hair pillows covered with crash, which she placed against the front of the building.

The two seated themselves there in the shade of the porch, side by side, with their backs against the pillows and their feet extended. Madame Ratignolle removed her veil, wiped her face with a rather delicate handkerchief, and fanned herself with the fan which she always carried suspended somewhere about her person by a long, narrow ribbon. Edna removed her collar and opened her dress at the throat. She took the fan from Madame Ratignolle and began to fan both herself and her companion. It was very warm, and for a while they did nothing but exchange remarks about the heat, the sun, the glare. But there was a breeze blowing, a choppy, stiff wind that whipped the water into froth. It fluttered the skirts of the two women and kept them for a while engaged in adjusting, readjusting, tucking in, securing hairpins and hat-pins. A few persons were sporting some distance away in the water. The beach was very still of human sound at that hour. The lady in black was reading her morning devotions on the porch of a neighboring bath-house. Two young lovers were exchanging their hearts' yearnings beneath the children's tent, which they had found unoccupied.

Edna Pontellier, casting her eyes about, had finally kept them at rest upon the sea. The day was clear and carried the gaze out as far as the blue sky went; there were a few white clouds suspended idly over the horizon. A lateen sail was visible in the direction of Cat Island, and others to the south seemed almost motionless in the far distance.

"Of whom—of what are you thinking?" asked Adèle of her companion, whose countenance she had been watching with a little amused attention, arrested by the absorbed expression which seemed to have seized and fixed every feature into a statuesque repose.

"Nothing," returned Mrs. Pontellier, with a start, adding at once: "How stupid! But it seems to me it is the reply we make instinctively to such a question. Let me see," she went on, throwing back her head and narrowing her fine eyes till they shone like two vivid points of light. "Let me see. I was really not conscious of thinking of anything; but perhaps I can retrace my thoughts."

"Oh! never mind!" laughed Madame Ratignolle. "I am not quite so exacting. I will let you off this time. It is really too hot to think, especially to think about thinking."

"But for the fun of it," persisted Edna. "First of all, the sight of the water stretching so far away, those motionless sails against the blue sky, made a delicious picture that I just wanted to sit and look at. The hot wind beating in my face made me think—without any connection that I can trace—of a summer day in Kentucky, of a meadow that seemed as big as the ocean to the very little girl walking through the grass, which was higher than her waist. She threw out her arms as if swimming when she walked, beating the tall grass as one strikes out in the water. Oh, I see the connection now!"

"Where were you going that day in Kentucky, walking through the grass?"

"I don't remember now. I was just walking diagonally across a big field. My sun-bonnet obstructed the view. I could see only the stretch of green before me, and I felt as if I must walk on forever, without coming to the end of it. I don't remember whether I was frightened or pleased. I must have been entertained."

"Likely as not it was Sunday," she laughed; "and I was running away from prayers, from the Presby-

terian service, read in a spirit of gloom by my father that chills me yet to think of."

"And have you been running away from prayers ever since, *ma chère?*" asked Madame Ratignolle, amused.

"No! oh, no!" Edna hastened to say. "I was a little unthinking child in those days, just following a misleading impulse without question. On the contrary, during one period of my life religion took a firm hold upon me; after I was twelve and until—until—why, I suppose until now, though I never thought much about it—just driven along by habit. But do you know," she broke off, turning her quick eyes upon Madame Ratignolle and leaning forward a little so as to bring her face quite close to that of her companion, "sometimes I feel this summer as if I were walking through the green meadow again; idly, aimlessly, unthinking and unguided."

Madame Ratignolle laid her hand over that of Mrs. Pontellier, which was near her. Seeing that the hand was not withdrawn, she clasped it firmly and warmly. She even stroked it a little, fondly, with the other hand, murmuring in an undertone, *"Pauvre chérie."*

The action was at first a little confusing to Edna, but she soon lent herself readily to the Creole's gentle caress. She was not accustomed to an outward and spoken expression of affection, either in herself or in others. She and her younger sister, Janet, had quarreled a good deal through force of unfortunate habit. Her older sister, Margaret, was matronly and dignified, probably from having assumed matronly and housewifely responsibilities too early in life, their mother having died when they were quite young. Margaret was not effusive; she was practical. Edna had had an occasional girl friend, but whether accidentally or not, they seemed to have been all of one type—the self-contained. She never realized that the reserve of her own character had much, perhaps everything, to do with this. Her most intimate friend at school had been one of rather exceptional intellectual gifts, who wrote fine-sounding essays, which Edna admired and strove to imitate; and with her she talked and glowed over the English classics, and sometimes held religious and political controversies.

Edna often wondered at one propensity which sometimes had inwardly disturbed her without causing any outward show or manifestation on her part. At a very early age—perhaps it was when she traversed the ocean of waving grass—she remembered that she had been passionately enamored of a dignified and sad-eyed cavalry officer who visited her father in Kentucky. She could not leave his presence when he was there, nor remove her eyes from his face, which was something like Napoleon's, with a lock of black hair falling across the forehead. But the cavalry officer melted imperceptibly out of her existence.

At another time her affections were deeply engaged by a young gentleman who visited a lady on a neighboring plantation. It was after they went to Mississippi to live. The young man was engaged to be married to the young lady, and they sometimes called upon Margaret, driving over of afternoons in a buggy. Edna was a little miss, just merging into her teens; and the realization that she herself was nothing, nothing, nothing to the engaged young man was a bitter affliction to her. But he, too, went the way of dreams.

She was a grown young woman when she was overtaken by what she supposed to be the climax of her fate. It was when the face and figure of a great tragedian began to haunt her imagination and stir her senses. The persistence of the infatuation lent it an aspect of genuineness. The hopelessness of it colored it with the lofty tones of a great passion.

The picture of the tragedian stood enframed upon her desk. Any one may possess the portrait of a tragedian without exciting suspicion or comment. (This was a sinister reflection which she cherished.) In the presence of others she expressed admiration for his exalted gifts, as she handed the photograph around and dwelt upon the fidelity of the likeness. When alone she sometimes picked it up and kissed the cold glass passionately.

Her marriage to Léonce Pontellier was purely an accident, in this respect resembling many other marriages which masquerade as the decrees of Fate. It was in the midst of her secret great passion that she met him. He fell in love, as men are in the habit of doing, and pressed his suit with an earnestness and an ardor which left nothing to be desired. He pleased her; his absolute devotion flattered her. She fancied there was a sympathy of thought and taste between them, in which fancy she was mistaken. Add to this the violent opposition of her father and her sister Margaret to her marriage with a Catholic, and we need seek no further for the motives which led her to accept Monsieur Pontellier for her husband.

The acme of bliss, which would have been a marriage with the tragedian, was not for her in this world.

As the devoted wife of a man who worshiped her, she felt she would take her place with a certain dignity in the world of reality, closing the portals forever behind her upon the realm of romance and dreams.

But it was not long before the tragedian had gone to join the cavalry officer and the engaged young man and a few others; and Edna found herself face to face with the realities. She grew fond of her husband, realizing with some unaccountable satisfaction that no trace of passion or excessive and fictitious warmth colored her affection, thereby threatening its dissolution.

She was fond of her children in an uneven, impulsive way. She would sometimes gather them passionately to her heart; she would sometimes forget them. The year before they had spent part of the summer with their grandmother Pontellier in Iberville. Feeling secure regarding their happiness and welfare, she did not miss them except with an occasional intense longing. Their absence was a sort of relief, though she did not admit this, even to herself. It seemed to free her of a responsibility which she had blindly assumed and for which Fate had not fitted her.

Edna did not reveal so much as all this to Madame Ratignolle that summer day when they sat with faces turned to the sea. But a good part of it escaped her. She had put her head down on Madame Ratignolle's shoulder. She was flushed and felt intoxicated with the sound of her own voice and the unaccustomed taste of candor. It muddled her like wine, or like a first breath of freedom.

There was the sound of approaching voices. It was Robert, surrounded by a troop of children, searching for them. The two little Pontelliers were with him, and he carried Madame Ratignolle's little girl in his arms. There were other children beside, and two nurse-maids followed, looking disagreeable and resigned.

The women at once rose and began to shake out their draperies and relax their muscles. Mrs. Pontellier threw the cushions and rug into the bath-house. The children all scampered off to the awning, and they stood there in a line, gazing upon the intruding lovers, still exchanging their vows and sighs. The lovers got up, with only a silent protest, and walked slowly away somewhere else.

The children possessed themselves of the tent, and Mrs. Pontellier went over to join them.

Madame Ratignolle begged Robert to accompany her to the house; she complained of cramp in her limbs and stiffness of the joints. She leaned drag-gingly upon his arm as they walked.

VIII

"Do me a favor, Robert," spoke the pretty woman at his side, almost as soon as she and Robert had started on their slow, homeward way. She looked up in his face, leaning on his arm beneath the encircling shadow of the umbrella which he had lifted.

"Granted; as many as you like," he returned, glancing down into her eyes that were full of thought-fulness and some speculation.

"I only ask for one; let Mrs. Pontellier alone."

"*Tiens!*" he exclaimed with a sudden, boyish laugh. "*Voilà que Madame Ratignolle est jalouse!*"

"Nonsense! I'm in earnest; I mean what I say. Let Mrs. Pontellier alone."

"Why?" he asked; himself growing serious at his companion's solicitation.

"She is not one of us; she is not like us. She might make the unfortunate blunder of taking you seriously."

His face flushed with annoyance, and taking off his soft hat he began to beat it impatiently against his leg as he walked. "Why shouldn't she take me seri-ously?" he demanded sharply. "Am I a comedian, a clown, a jack-in-the-box? Why shouldn't she? You Creoles! I have no patience with you! Am I always to be regarded as a feature of an amusing programme? I hope Mrs. Pontellier does take me seriously. I hope she has discernment enough to find in me something besides the *blagueur*. If I thought there was any doubt—"

"Oh, enough, Robert!" she broke into his heated outburst. "You are not thinking of what you are say-ing. You speak with about as little reflection as we might expect from one of those children down there playing in the sand. If your attentions to any married women here were ever offered with any intention of being convincing, you would not be the gentleman we all know you to be, and you would be unfit to as-sociate with the wives and daughters of the people who trust you."

Madame Ratignolle had spoken what she believed to be the law and the gospel. The young man shrugged his shoulders impatiently.

"Oh! well! That isn't it," slamming his hat down vehemently upon his head. "You ought to feel that such things are not flattering to say to a fellow."

"Should our whole intercourse consist of an ex-change of compliments? *Ma foi!*"

"It isn't pleasant to have a woman tell you—" he went on, unheedingly, but breaking off suddenly: "Now if I were like Arobin—you remember Alcée Arobin and that story of the consul's wife at Biloxi?" And he related the story of Alcée Arobin and the con-sul's wife; and another about the tenor of the French Opera, who received letters which should never have been written; and still other stories, grave and gay, till Mrs. Pontellier and her possible propensity for taking young men seriously was apparently forgotten.

Madame Ratignolle, when they had regained her cottage, went in to take the hour's rest which she considered helpful. Before leaving her, Robert begged her pardon for the impatience—he called it rudeness—with which he had received her well-meant caution.

"You made one mistake, Adèle," he said, with a light smile; "there is no earthly possibility of Mrs. Pontellier ever taking me seriously. You should have warned me against taking myself seriously. Your ad-vice might then have carried some weight and given me subject for some reflection. *Au revoir*. But you look tired," he added, solicitously. "Would you like a cup of bouillon? Shall I stir you a toddy? Let me mix you a toddy with a drop of Angostura."

She acceded to the suggestion of bouillon, which was grateful and acceptable. He went himself to the kitchen, which was a building apart from the cot-tages and lying to the rear of the house. And he himself brought her the golden-brown bouillon, in a dainty Sèvres cup, with a flaky cracker or two on the saucer.

She thrust a bare, white arm from the curtain which shielded her open door, and received the cup from his hands. She told him he was a *bon garçon*, and she meant it. Robert thanked her and turned away toward "the house."

The lovers were just entering the grounds of the *pension*. They were leaning toward each other as the wateroaks bent from the sea. There was not a parti-cle of earth beneath their feet. Their heads might have been turned upside-down, so absolutely did they tread upon blue ether. The lady in black, creep-ing behind them, looked a trifle paler and more jaded than usual. There was no sign of Mrs. Pontel-lier and the children. Robert scanned the distance for any such apparition. They would doubtless remain away till the dinner hour. The young man ascended to his mother's room. It was situated at the top of the house, made up of odd angles and a queer, sloping ceiling. Two broad dormer windows looked out toward the Gulf, and as far across it as a man's eye might reach. The furnishings of the room were light, cool, and practical.

Madame Lebrun was busily engaged at the sewing-machine. A little black girl sat on the floor, and with her hands worked the treadle of the machine. The Creole woman does not take any chances which may be avoided of imperiling her health.

Robert went over and seated himself on the broad sill of one of the dormer windows. He took a book from his pocket and began energetically to read it, judging by the precision and frequency with which he turned the leaves. The sewing-machine made a resounding clatter in the room; it was of a ponderous, bygone make. In the lulls, Robert and his mother exchanged bits of desultory conversation.

"Where is Mrs. Pontellier?"

"Down at the beach with the children."

"I promised to lend her the Goncourt. Don't forget to take it down when you go; it's there on the bookshelf over the small table." Clatter, clatter, clatter, bang! for the next five or eight minutes.

"Where is Victor going with the rockaway?"

"The rockaway? Victor?"

"Yes; down there in front. He seems to be getting ready to drive away somewhere."

"Call him." Clatter, clatter!

Robert uttered a shrill, piercing whistle which might have been heard back at the wharf.

"He won't look up."

Madame Lebrun flew to the window. She called "Victor!" She waved a handkerchief and called again. The young fellow below got into the vehicle and started the horse off at a gallop.

Madame Lebrun went back to the machine, crimson with annoyance. Victor was the younger son and brother—*a tête montée*, with a temper which invited violence and a will which no ax could break.

"Whenever you say the word I'm ready to thrash any amount of reason into him that he's able to hold."

"If your father had only lived!" Clatter, clatter, clatter, clatter, bang! It was a fixed belief with Madame Lebrun that the conduct of the universe and all things pertaining thereto would have been manifestly of a more intelligent and higher order had

not Monsieur Lebrun been removed to other spheres during the early years of their married life.

"What do you hear from Montel?" Montel was a middle-aged gentleman whose vain ambition and desire for the past twenty years had been to fill the void which Monsieur Lebrun's taking off had left in the Lebrun household. Clatter, clatter, bang, clatter!

"I have a letter somewhere," looking in the machine drawer and finding the letter in the bottom of the work-basket. "He says to tell you he will be in Vera Cruz the beginning of next month"—clatter, clatter!—"and if you still have the intention of joining him"—bang! clatter, clatter, bang!

"Why didn't you tell me so before, mother? You know I wanted—" Clatter, clatter, clatter!

"Do you see Mrs. Pontellier starting back with the children? She will be in late to luncheon again. She never starts to get ready for luncheon till the last minute." Clatter, clatter! "Where are you going?"

"Where did you say the Goncourt was?"

IX

Every light in the hall was ablaze; every lamp turned as high as it could be without smoking the chimney or threatening explosion. The lamps were fixed at intervals against the wall, encircling the whole room. Some one had gathered orange and lemon branches, and with these fashioned graceful festoons between. The dark green of the branches stood out and glistened against the white muslin curtains which draped the windows, and which puffed, floated, and flapped at the capricious will of a stiff breeze that swept up from the Gulf.

It was Saturday night a few weeks after the intimate conversation held between Robert and Madame Ratignolle on their way from the beach. An unusual number of husbands, fathers, and friends had come down to stay over Sunday; and they were being suitably entertained by their families, with the material help of Madame Lebrun. The dining tables had all been removed to one end of the hall, and the chairs ranged about in rows and in clusters. Each little family group had had its say and exchanged its domestic gossip earlier in the evening. There was now an apparent disposition to relax; to widen the circle of confidences and give a more general tone to the conversation.

Many of the children had been permitted to sit up beyond their usual bedtime. A small band of them were lying on their stomachs on the floor looking at the colored sheets of the comic papers which Mr. Pontellier had brought down. The little Pontellier boys were permitting them to do so, and making their authority felt.

Music, dancing, and a recitation or two were the entertainments furnished, or rather, offered. But there was nothing systematic about the programme, no appearance of prearrangement nor even premeditation.

At an early hour in the evening the Farival twins were prevailed upon to play the piano. They were girls of fourteen, always clad in the Virgin's colors, blue and white, having been dedicated to the Blessed Virgin at their baptism. They played a duet from "Zampa," and at the earnest solicitation of every one present followed it with the overture to "The Poet and the Peasant."

"*Allez vous-en! Sapristi!*" shrieked the parrot outside the door. He was the only being present who possessed sufficient candor to admit that he was not listening to these gracious performances for the first time that summer. Old Monsieur Farival, grandfather of the twins, grew indignant over the interruption and insisted upon having the bird removed and consigned to regions of darkness. Victor Lebrun objected; and his decrees were as immutable as those of Fate. The parrot fortunately offered no further interruption to the entertainment, the whole venom of his nature apparently having been cherished up and hurled against the twins in the one impetuous outburst.

Later a young brother and sister gave recitations, which every one present had heard many times at winter evening entertainments in the city.

A little girl performed a skirt dance in the center of the floor. The mother played her accompaniments and at the same time watched her daughter with greedy admiration and nervous apprehension. She need have had no apprehension. The child was mistress of the situation. She had been properly dressed for the occasion in black tulle and black silk tights. Her little neck and arms were bare, and her hair, artificially crimped, stood out like fluffy black plumes over her head. Her poses were full of grace, and her little black-shod toes twinkled as they shot out and upward with a rapidity and suddenness which were bewildering.

But there was no reason why every one should not dance. Madame Ratignolle could not, so it was she who gaily consented to play for the others. She

played very well, keeping excellent waltz time and infusing an expression into the strains which was indeed inspiring. She was keeping up her music on account of the children, she said; because she and her husband both considered it a means of brightening the home and making it attractive.

Almost every one danced but the twins, who could not be induced to separate during the brief period when one or the other should be whirling around the room in the arms of a man. They might have danced together, but they did not think of it.

The children were sent to bed. Some went submissively; others with shrieks and protests as they were dragged away. They had been permitted to sit up till after the ice-cream, which naturally marked the limit of human indulgence.

The ice-cream was passed around with cake— gold and silver cake arranged on platters in alternate slices; it had been made and frozen during the afternoon back of the kitchen by two black women, under the supervision of Victor. It was pronounced a great success—excellent if it had only contained a little less vanilla or a little more sugar, if it had been frozen a degree harder, and if the salt might have been kept out of portions of it. Victor was proud of his achievement, and went about recommending it and urging every one to partake of it to excess.

After Mrs. Pontellier had danced twice with her husband, once with Robert, and once with Monsieur Ratignolle, who was thin and tall and swayed like a reed in the wind when he danced, she went out on the gallery and seated herself on the low windowsill, where she commanded a view of all that went on in the hall and could look out toward the Gulf. There was a soft effulgence in the east. The moon was coming up, and its mystic shimmer was casting a million lights across the distant, restless water.

"Would you like to hear Mademoiselle Reisz play?" asked Robert, coming out on the porch where she was. Of course Edna would like to hear Mademoiselle Reisz play; but she feared it would be useless to entreat her.

"I'll ask her," he said. "I'll tell her that you want to hear her. She likes you. She will come." He turned and hurried away to one of the far cottages, where Mademoiselle Reisz was shuffling away. She was dragging a chair in and out of her room, and at intervals objecting to the crying of a baby, which a nurse in the adjoining cottage was endeavoring to put to sleep. She was a disagreeable little woman, no longer young, who had quarreled with almost every one, owing to a temper which was self-assertive and a disposition to trample upon the rights of others. Robert prevailed upon her without any too great difficulty.

She entered the hall with him during a lull in the dance. She made an awkward, imperious little bow as she went in. She was a homely woman, with a small weazened face and body and eyes that glowed. She had absolutely no taste in dress, and wore a batch of rusty black lace with a bunch of artificial violets pinned to the side of her hair.

"Ask Mrs. Pontellier what she would like to hear me play," she requested of Robert. She sat perfectly still before the piano, not touching the keys, while Robert carried her message to Edna at the window. A general air of surprise and genuine satisfaction fell upon every one as they saw the pianist enter. There was a settling down, and a prevailing air of expectancy everywhere. Edna was a trifle embarrassed at being thus singled out for the imperious little woman's favor. She would not dare to choose, and begged that Mademoiselle Reisz would please herself in her selections.

Edna was what she herself called very fond of music. Musical strains, well rendered, had a way of evoking pictures in her mind. She sometimes liked to sit in the room of mornings when Madame Ratignolle played or practiced. One piece which that lady played Edna had entitled "Solitude." It was a short, plaintive, minor strain. The name of the piece was something else, but she called it "Solitude." When she heard it there came before her imagination the figure of a man standing beside a desolate rock on the seashore. He was naked. His attitude was one of hopeless resignation as he looked toward a distant bird winging its flight away from him.

Another piece called to her mind a dainty young woman clad in an Empire gown, taking mincing dancing steps as she came down a long avenue between tall hedges. Again, another reminded her of children at play, and still another of nothing on earth but a demure lady stroking a cat.

The very first chords which Mademoiselle Reisz struck upon the piano sent a keen tremor down Mrs. Pontellier's spinal column. It was not the first time she had heard an artist at the piano. Perhaps it was the first time she was ready, perhaps the first time her being was tempered to take an impress of the abiding truth.

She waited for the material pictures which she thought would gather and blaze before her imagination. She waited in vain. She saw no pictures of solitude, of hope, of longing, or of despair. But the very passions themselves were aroused within her soul, swaying it, lashing it, as the waves daily beat upon her splendid body. She trembled, she was choking, and the tears blinded her.

Mademoiselle had finished. She arose, and bowing her stiff, lofty bow, she went away, stopping for neither thanks nor applause. As she passed along the gallery she patted Edna upon the shoulder.

"Well, how did you like my music?" she asked. The young woman was unable to answer; she pressed the hand of the pianist convulsively. Mademoiselle Reisz perceived her agitation and even her tears. She patted her again upon the shoulder as she said:

"You are the only one worth playing for. Those others? Bah!" and she went shuffling and sidling on down the gallery toward her room.

But she was mistaken about "those others." Her playing had aroused a fever of enthusiasm. "What passion!" "What an artist!" "I have always said no one could play Chopin like Mademoiselle Reisz!" "That last prelude! *Bon Dieu!* It shakes a man!"

It was growing late, and there was a general disposition to disband. But some one, perhaps it was Robert, thought of a bath at that mystic hour and under that mystic moon.

X

At all events Robert proposed it, and there was not a dissenting voice. There was not one but was ready to follow when he led the way. He did not lead the way, however, he directed the way; and he himself loitered behind with the lovers, who had betrayed a disposition to linger and hold themselves apart. He walked between them, whether with malicious or mischievous intent was not wholly clear, even to himself.

The Pontelliers and Ratignolles walked ahead; the women leaning upon the arms of their husbands. Edna could hear Robert's voice behind them, and could sometimes hear what he said. She wondered why he did not join them. It was unlike him not to. Of late he had sometimes held away from her for an entire day, redoubling his devotion upon the next and the next, as though to make up for hours that had been lost. She missed him the days when some pretext served to take him away from her, just as one misses the sun on a cloudy day without having thought much about the sun when it was shining.

The people walked in little groups toward the beach. They talked and laughed; some of them sang. There was a band playing down at Klein's hotel, and the strains reached them faintly, tempered by the distance. There were strange, rare odors abroad — a tangle of the sea smell and of weeds and damp, new-plowed earth, mingled with the heavy perfume of a field of white blossoms somewhere near. But the night sat lightly upon the sea and the land. There was no weight of darkness; there were no shadows. The white light of the moon had fallen upon the world like the mystery and the softness of sleep.

Most of them walked into the water as though into a native element. The sea was quiet now, and swelled lazily in broad billows that melted into one another and did not break except upon the beach in little foamy crests that coiled back like slow, white serpents.

Edna had attempted all summer to learn to swim. She had received instructions from both the men and women; in some instances from the children. Robert had pursued a system of lessons almost daily; and he was nearly at the point of discouragement in realizing the futility of his efforts. A certain ungovernable dread hung about her when in the water, unless there was a hand near by that might reach out and reassure her.

But that night she was like the little tottering, stumbling, clutching child, who of a sudden realizes its powers, and walks for the first time alone, boldly and with over-confidence. She could have shouted for joy. She did shout for joy, as with a sweeping stroke or two she lifted her body to the surface of the water.

A feeling of exultation overtook her, as if some power of significant import had been given her to control the working of her body and her soul. She grew daring and reckless, overestimating her strength. She wanted to swim far out, where no woman had swum before.

Her unlooked-for achievement was the subject of wonder, applause, and admiration. Each one congratulated himself that his special teachings had accomplished this desired end.

"How easy it is!" she thought. "It is nothing," she said aloud; "why did I not discover before that it was nothing. Think of the time I have lost splashing about like a baby!" She would not join the groups in their sports and bouts, but intoxicated with her newly conquered power, she swam out alone.

She turned her face seaward to gather in an impression of space and solitude, which the vast expanse of water, meeting and melting with the moonlit sky, conveyed to her excited fancy. As she swam she seemed to be reaching out for the unlimited in which to lose herself.

Once she turned and looked toward the shore, toward the people she had left there. She had not gone any great distance — that is, what would have been a great distance for an experienced swimmer. But to her unaccustomed vision the stretch of water behind her assumed the aspect of a barrier which her unaided strength would never be able to overcome.

A quick vision of death smote her soul, and for a second of time appalled and enfeebled her senses. But by an effort she rallied her staggering faculties and managed to regain the land.

She made no mention of her encounter with death and her flash of terror, except to say to her husband, "I thought I should have perished out there alone."

"You were not so very far, my dear; I was watching you," he told her.

Edna went at once to the bath-house, and she had put on her dry clothes and was ready to return home before the others had left the water. She started to walk away alone. They all called to her and shouted to her. She waved a dissenting hand, and went on, paying no further heed to their renewed cries which sought to detain her.

"Sometimes I am tempted to think that Mrs. Pontellier is capricious," said Madame Lebrun, who was amusing herself immensely and feared that Edna's abrupt departure might put an end to the pleasure.

"I know she is," assented Mr. Pontellier; "sometimes, not often."

Edna had not traversed a quarter of the distance on her way home before she was overtaken by Robert.

"Did you think I was afraid?" she asked him, without a shade of annoyance.

"No; I knew you weren't afraid."

"Then why did you come? Why didn't you stay out there with the others?"

"I never thought of it."

"Thought of what?"

"Of anything. What differences does it make?"

"I'm very tired," she uttered, complainingly.

"I know you are."

"You don't know anything about it. Why should you know? I never was so exhausted in my life. But it isn't unpleasant. A thousand emotions have swept through me to-night. I don't comprehend half of them. Don't mind what I'm saying; I am just thinking aloud. I wonder if I shall ever be stirred again as Mademoiselle Reisz's playing moved me to-night. I wonder if any night on earth will ever again be like this one. It is like a night in a dream. The people about me are like some uncanny, half-human beings. There must be spirits abroad to-night."

"There are," whispered Robert. "Didn't you know this was the twenty-eighth of August?"

"The twenty-eighth of August?"

"Yes. On the twenty-eighth of August, at the hour of midnight, and if the moon is shining—the moon must be shining—a spirit that has haunted these shores for ages rises up from the Gulf. With its own penetrating vision the spirit seeks some one mortal worthy to hold him company, worthy of being exalted for a few hours into realms of the semi-celestials. His search has always hitherto been fruitless, and he has sunk back, disheartened, into the sea. But to-night he found Mrs. Pontellier. Perhaps he will never wholly release her from the spell. Perhaps she will never again suffer a poor, unworthy earthling to walk in the shadow of her divine presence."

"Don't banter me," she said, wounded at what appeared to be his flippancy. He did not mind the entreaty, but the tone with its delicate note of pathos was like a reproach. He could not explain; he could not tell her that he had penetrated her mood and understood. He said nothing except to offer her his arm, for, by her own admission, she was exhausted. She had been walking alone with her arms hanging limp, letting her white skirts trail along the dewy path. She took his arm, but she did not lean upon it. She let her hand lie listlessly, as though her thoughts were elsewhere—somewhere in advance of her body, and she was striving to overtake them.

Robert assisted her into the hammock which swung from the post before her door out to the trunk of a tree.

"Will you stay out here and wait for Mr. Pontellier?" he asked.

"I'll stay out here. Good-night."

"Shall I get you a pillow?"

"There's one here," she said, feeling about, for they were in the shadow.

"It must be soiled; the children have been tumbling it about."

"No matter." And having discovered the pillow, she adjusted it beneath her head. She extended herself in the hammock with a deep breath of relief. She was not a supercilious or an overdainty woman. She was not much given to reclining in the hammock, and when she did so it was with no cat-like suggestion of voluptuous ease, but with a beneficent repose which seemed to invade her whole body.

"Shall I stay with you till Mr. Pontellier comes?" asked Robert, seating himself on the outer edge of one of the steps and taking hold of the hammock rope which was fastened to the post.

"If you wish. Don't swing the hammock. Will you get my white shawl which I left on the window-sill over at the house?"

"Are you chilly?"

"No; but I shall be presently."

"Presently?" he laughed. "Do you know what time it is? How long are you going to stay out here?"

"I don't know. Will you get the shawl?"

"Of course I will," he said, rising. He went over to the house, walking along the grass. She watched his figure pass in and out of the strips of moonlight. It was past midnight. It was very quiet.

When he returned with the shawl she took it and kept it in her hand. She did not put it around her.

"Did you say I should stay till Mr. Pontellier came back?"

"I said you might if you wished to."

He seated himself again and rolled a cigarette, which he smoked in silence. Neither did Mrs. Pontellier speak. No multitude of words could have been more significant than those moments of silence, or more pregnant with the first-felt throbbings of desire.

When the voices of the bathers were heard approaching, Robert said good-night. She did not answer him. He thought she was asleep. Again she watched his figure pass in and out of the strips of moonlight as he walked away.

XI

"What are you doing out here, Edna? I thought I should find you in bed," said her husband, when he discovered her lying there. He had walked up with

Madame Lebrun and left her at the house. His wife did not reply.

"Are you asleep?" he asked, bending down close to look at her.

"No." Her eyes gleamed bright and intense, with no sleepy shadows, as they looked into his.

"Do you know it is past one o'clock? Come on," and he mounted the steps and went into their room.

"Edna!" called Mr. Pontellier from within, after a few moments had gone by.

"Don't wait for me," she answered. He thrust his head through the door.

"You will take cold out there," he said, irritably. "What folly is this? Why don't you come in?"

"It isn't cold; I have my shawl."

"The mosquitoes will devour you."

"There are no mosquitoes."

She heard him moving about the room; every sound indicating impatience and irritation. Another time she would have gone in at his request. She would, through habit, have yielded to his desire; not with any sense of submission or obedience to his compelling wishes, but unthinkingly, as we walk, move, sit, stand, go through the daily treadmill of the life which has been portioned out to us.

"Edna, dear, are you not coming in soon?" he asked again, this time fondly, with a note of entreaty.

"No; I am going to stay out here."

"This is more than folly," he blurted out. "I can't permit you to stay out there all night. You must come in the house instantly."

With a writhing motion she settled herself more securely in the hammock. She perceived that her will had blazed up, stubborn and resistant. She could not at that moment have done other than denied and resisted. She wondered if her husband had ever spoken to her like that before, and if she had submitted to his command. Of course she had; she remembered that she had. But she could not realize why or how she should have yielded, feeling as she then did.

"Léonce, go to bed," she said. "I mean to stay out here. I don't wish to go in, and I don't intend to. Don't speak to me like that again; I shall not answer you."

Mr. Pontellier had prepared for bed, but he slipped on an extra garment. He opened a bottle of wine, of which he kept a small and select supply in a buffet of his own. He drank a glass of the wine and went out on the gallery and offered a glass to his wife. She did not wish any. He drew up the rocker, hoisted his slippered feet on the rail, and proceeded to smoke a cigar. He smoked two cigars; then he went inside and drank another glass of wine. Mrs. Pontellier again declined to accept a glass when it was offered to her. Mr. Pontellier once more seated himself with elevated feet, and after a reasonable interval of time smoked some more cigars.

Edna began to feel like one who awakens gradually out of a dream, a delicious, grotesque, impossible dream, to feel again the realities pressing into her soul. The physical need for sleep began to overtake her; the exuberance which had sustained and exalted her spirit left her helpless and yielding to the conditions which crowded her in.

The stillest hour of the night had come, the hour before dawn, when the world seems to hold its breath. The moon hung low, and had turned from silver to copper in the sleeping sky. The old owl no longer hooted, and the wateroaks had ceased to moan as they bent their heads.

Edna arose, cramped from lying so long and still in the hammock. She tottered up the steps, clutching feebly at the post before passing into the house.

"Are you coming in, Léonce?" she asked, turning her face toward her husband.

"Yes, dear," he answered, with a glance following a misty puff of smoke. "Just as soon as I have finished my cigar."

XII

She slept but a few hours. They were troubled and feverish hours, disturbed with dreams that were intangible, that eluded her, leaving only an impression upon her half-awakened senses of something unattainable. She was up and dressed in the cool of the early morning. The air was invigorating and steadied somewhat her faculties. However, she was not seeking refreshment or help from any source, either external or from within. She was blindly following whatever impulse moved her, as if she had placed herself in alien hands for direction, and freed her soul of responsibility.

Most of the people at this early hour were still in bed and asleep. A few, who intended to go over to the *Chênière* for mass, were moving about. The lovers, who had laid their plans the night before, were already strolling toward the wharf. The lady in black, with her Sunday prayer-book, velvet and gold-clasped, and her Sunday silver beads, was following them at no great distance. Old Monsieur Farival was up, and was more than half inclined to do anything that suggested itself. He put on his big straw hat, and taking his umbrella from the stand in the hall, followed the lady in black, never overtaking her.

The little negro girl who worked Madame Lebrun's sewing-machine was sweeping the galleries with long, absent-minded strokes of the broom. Edna sent her up into the house to awaken Robert.

"Tell him I am going to the *Chênière*. The boat is ready; tell him to hurry."

He had soon joined her. She had never sent for him before. She had never asked for him. She had never seemed to want him before. She did not appear conscious that she had done anything unusual in commanding his presence. He was apparently equally unconscious of anything extraordinary in the situation. But his face was suffused with a quiet glow when he met her.

They went together back to the kitchen to drink coffee. There was no time to wait for any nicety of service. They stood outside the window and the cook passed them their coffee and a roll, which they drank and ate from the window-sill. Edna said it tasted good. She had not thought of coffee nor of anything. He told her he had often noticed that she lacked forethought.

"Wasn't it enough to think of going to the *Chênière* and waking you up?" she laughed. "Do I have to think of everything? — as Léonce says when he's in a bad humor. I don't blame him; he'd never be in a bad humor if it weren't for me."

They took a short cut across the sands. At a distance they could see the curious procession moving toward the wharf — the lovers, shoulder to shoulder, creeping; the lady in black, gaining steadily upon them; old Monsieur Farival, losing ground inch by inch, and a young barefooted Spanish girl, with a red kerchief on her head and a basket on her arm, bring up the rear.

Robert knew the girl, and he talked to her a little in the boat. No one present understood what they said. Her name was Mariequita. She had a round, sly, piquant face and pretty black eyes. Her hands were small, and she kept them folded over the handle of her basket. Her feet were broad and coarse. She did not strive to hide them. Edna looked at her feet, and noticed the sand and slime between her brown toes.

Beaudelet grumbled because Mariequita was there, taking up so much room. In reality he was annoyed at having old Monsieur Farival, who considered himself the better sailor of the two. But he would not quarrel with so old a man as Monsieur Farival, so he quarreled with Mariequita. The girl was deprecatory at one moment, appealing to Robert. She was saucy the next, moving her head up and down, making "eyes" at Robert and making "mouths" at Beaudelet.

The lovers were all alone. They saw nothing, they heard nothing. The lady in black was counting her beads for the third time. Old Monsieur Farival talked incessantly of what he knew about handling a boat, and of what Beaudelet did not know on the same subject.

Edna liked it all. She looked Mariequita up and down, from her ugly brown toes to her pretty black eyes, and back again.

"Why does she look at me like that?" inquired the girl of Robert.

"Maybe she thinks you are pretty. Shall I ask her?"

"No. Is she your sweetheart?"

"She's a married lady, and has two children."

"Oh! well! Francisco ran away with Sylvano's wife, who had four children. They took all his money and one of the children and stole his boat."

"Shut up!"

"Does she understand?"

"Oh, hush!"

"Are those two married over there — leaning on each other?"

"Of course not," laughed Robert.

"Of course not," echoed Mariequita, with a serious, confirmatory bob of the head.

The sun was high up and beginning to bite. The swift breeze seemed to Edna to bury the sting of it into the pores of her face and hands. Robert held his umbrella over her.

As they went cutting sidewise through the water, the sails bellied taut, with the wind filling and overflowing them. Old Monsieur Farival laughed sardonically at something as he looked at the sails, and Beaudelet swore at the old man under his breath.

Sailing across the bay to the *Chênière Caminada*, Edna felt as if she were being borne away from some anchorage which had held her fast, whose chains had been loosening — had snapped the night before when the mystic spirit was abroad, leaving her free to drift whithersoever she chose to set her sails. Robert spoke to her incessantly; he no longer noticed Mariequita. The girl had shrimps in her bamboo basket. They were covered with Spanish moss. She beat the moss down impatiently, and muttered to herself sullenly.

"Let us go to Grande Terre to-morrow?" said Robert in a low voice.

"What shall we do there?"

"Climb up the hill to the old fort and look at the little wriggling gold snakes, and watch the lizards sun themselves."

She gazed away toward Grande Terre and thought she would like to be alone there with Robert, in the sun, listening to the ocean's roar and watching the slimy lizards writhe in and out among the ruins of the old fort.

"And the next day or the next we can sail to the Bayou Brulow," he went on.

"What shall we do there?"

"Anything — cast bait for fish."

"No; we'll go back to Grande Terre. Let the fish alone."

"We'll go wherever you like," he said. "I'll have Tonie come over and help me patch and trim my boat. We shall not need Beaudelet nor any one. Are you afraid of the pirogue?"

"Oh, no."

"Then I'll take you some night in the pirogue when the moon shines. Maybe your Gulf spirit will whisper to you in which of these islands the treasures are hidden — direct you to the very spot, perhaps."

"And in a day we should be rich!" she laughed. "I'd give it all to you, the pirate gold and every bit of treasure we could dig up. I think you would know how to spend it. Pirate gold isn't a thing to be hoarded or utilized. It is something to squander and throw to the four winds, for the fun of seeing the golden specks fly."

"We'd share it, and scatter it together," he said. His face flushed.

They all went together up to the quaint little Gothic church of Our Lady of Lourdes, gleaming all brown and yellow with paint in the sun's glare.

Only Beaudelet remained behind, tinkering at his boat, and Mariequita walked away with her basket of shrimps, casting a look of childish ill-humor and reproach at Robert from the corner of her eye.

XIII

A feeling of oppression and drowsiness overcame Edna during the service. Her head began to ache, and the lights on the altar swayed before her eyes. Another time she might have made an effort to regain her composure; but her one thought was to quit the stifling atmosphere of the church and reach the open air. She arose, climbing over Robert's feet with a muttered apology. Old Monsieur Farival, flurried, curious, stood up, but upon seeing that Robert had followed Mrs. Pontellier, he sank back into his seat. He whispered an anxious inquiry of the lady in black, who did not notice him or reply, but kept her eyes fastened upon the pages of her velvet prayer-book.

"I felt giddy and almost overcome," Edna said, lifting her hands instinctively to her head and pushing her straw hat up from her forehead. "I couldn't have stayed through the service." They were outside in the shadow of the church. Robert was full of solicitude.

"It was folly to have thought of going in the first place, let alone staying. Come over to Madame Antoine's: you can rest there." He took her arm and led her away, looking anxiously and continuously down into her face.

How still it was, with only the voice of the sea whispering through the reeds that grew in the salt-water pools! The long line of little gray, weather-beaten houses nestled peacefully among the orange trees. It must always have been God's day on that low, drowsy island, Edna thought. They stopped, leaning over a jagged fence made of sea-drift, to ask for water. A youth, a mild-faced Acadian, was drawing water from the cistern, which was nothing more than a rusty buoy, with an opening on one side, sunk in the ground. The water which the youth handed to them in a tin pail was not cold to taste, but it was cool to her heated face, and it greatly revived and refreshed her.

Madame Antoine's cot was at the far end of the village. She welcomed them with all the native hospitality, as she would have opened her door to let the sunlight in. She was fat, and walked heavily and clumsily across the floor. She could speak no English, but when Robert made her understand that the lady who accompanied him was ill and desired to rest, she was all eagerness to make Edna feel at home and to dispose of her comfortably.

The whole place was immaculately clean, and the big, four-posted bed, snow-white, invited one to repose. It stood in a small side room which looked out across a narrow grass plot toward the shed, where there was a disabled boat lying keel upward.

Madame Antoine had not gone to mass. Her son Tonie had, but she supposed he would soon be back, and she invited Robert to be seated and wait for him. But he went and sat outside the door and smoked. Madame Antoine busied herself in the large front room preparing dinner. She was boiling mullets over a few red coals in the huge fireplace.

Edna, left alone in the little side room, loosened her clothes, removing the greater part of them. She bathed her face, her neck and arms in the basin that stood between the windows. She took off her shoes and stockings and stretched herself in the very center of the high, white bed. How luxurious it felt to rest thus in a strange, quaint bed, with its sweet country odor of laurel lingering about the sheets and mattress! She stretched her strong limbs that ached a little. She ran her fingers through her loosened hair for a while. She looked at her round arms as she held them straight up and rubbed them one after the other, observing closely, as if it were something she saw for the first time, the fine, firm quality and texture of her flesh. She clasped her hands easily above her head, and it was thus she fell asleep.

She slept lightly at first, half awake and drowsily attentive to the things about her. She could hear Madame Antoine's heavy, scraping tread as she walked back and forth on the sanded floor. Some chickens were clucking outside the windows, scratching for bits of gravel in the grass. Later she half heard the voices of Robert and Tonie talking under the shed. She did not stir. Even her eyelids rested numb and heavily over her sleepy eyes. The voices went on—Tonie's slow, Acadian drawl, Robert's quick, soft, smooth French. She understood French imperfectly unless directly addressed, and the voices were only part of the other drowsy, muffled sounds lulling her senses.

When Edna awoke it was with the conviction that she had slept long and soundly. The voices were hushed under the shed. Madame Antoine's step was no longer to be heard in the adjoining room. Even the chickens had gone elsewhere to scratch and cluck. The mosquito bar was drawn over her; the old woman had come in while she slept and let down the bar. Edna arose quietly from the bed, and looking between the curtains of the window, she saw by the slanting rays of the sun that the afternoon was far advanced. Robert was out there under the shed, reclining in the shade against the sloping keel of the overturned boat. He was reading from a book. Tonie was no longer with him. She wondered what had become of the rest of the party. She peeped out at him two or three times as she stood washing herself in the little basin between the windows.

Madame Antoine had laid some coarse, clean towels upon a chair, and had placed a box of *poudre de riz* within easy reach. Edna dabbed the powder upon her nose and cheeks as she looked at herself closely in the little distorted mirror which hung on the wall above the basin. Her eyes were bright and wide awake and her face glowed.

When she had completed her toilet she walked into the adjoining room. She was very hungry. No one was there. But there was a cloth spread upon the table that stood against the wall, and a cover was laid for one, with a crusty brown loaf and a bottle of wine beside the plate. Edna bit a piece from the brown loaf, tearing it with her strong, white teeth. She poured some of the wine into the glass and drank it down. Then she went softly out of doors, and plucking an orange from the low-hanging bough of a tree, threw it at Robert, who did not know she was awake and up.

An illumination broke over his whole face when he saw her and joined her under the orange tree.

"How many years have I slept?" she inquired. "The whole island seems changed. A new race of beings must have sprung up, leaving only you and me as past relics. How many ages ago did Madame Antoine and Tonie die? and when did our people from Grand Isle disappear from the earth?"

He familiarly adjusted a ruffle upon her shoulder.

"You have slept precisely one hundred years. I was left here to guard your slumbers; and for one hundred years I have been out under the shed reading a book. The only evil I couldn't prevent was to keep a broiled fowl from drying up."

"If it has turned to stone, still will I eat it," said Edna, moving with him into the house. "But really, what has become of Monsieur Farival and the others?"

"Gone hours ago. When they found that you were sleeping they thought it best not to awake you. Any way, I wouldn't have let them. What was I here for?"

"I wonder if Léonce will be uneasy!" she speculated, as she seated herself at table.

"Of course not; he knows you are with me," Robert replied, as he busied himself among sundry pans and covered dishes which had been left standing on the hearth.

"Where are Madame Antoine and her son?" asked Edna.

"Gone to Vespers, and to visit some friends, I believe. I am to take you back in Tonie's boat whenever you are ready to go."

He stirred the smoldering ashes till the broiled fowl began to sizzle afresh. He served her with no mean repast, dripping the coffee anew and sharing it with her. Madame Antoine had cooked little else than the mullets, but while Edna slept Robert had foraged the island. He was childishly gratified to discover her appetite, and to see the relish with which she ate the food which he had procured for her.

"Shall we go right away?" she asked, after draining her glass and brushing together the crumbs of the crusty loaf.

"The sun isn't as low as it will be in two hours," he answered.

"The sun will be gone in two hours."

"Well, let it go; who cares!"

They waited a good while under the orange trees, till Madame Antoine came back, panting, waddling, with a thousand apologies to explain her absence. Tonie did not dare to return. He was shy, and would not willingly face any woman except his mother.

It was very pleasant to stay there under the orange trees, while the sun dipped lower and lower, turning the western sky to flaming copper and gold. The shadows lengthened and crept out like stealthy, grotesque monsters across the grass.

Edna and Robert both sat upon the ground — that is, he lay upon the ground beside her, occasionally picking at the hem of her muslin gown.

Madame Antoine seated her fat body, broad and squat, upon a bench beside the door. She had been talking all the afternoon, and had wound herself up to the story-telling pitch.

And what stories she told them! But twice in her life she had left the *Chênière Caminada*, and then for the briefest span. All her years she had squatted and waddled there upon the island, gathering legends of the Baratarians and the sea. The night came on, with the moon to lighten it. Edna could hear the whispering voices of dead men and the click of muffled gold.

When she and Robert stepped into Tonie's boat, with the red lateen sail, misty spirit forms were prowling in the shadows and among the reeds, and upon the water were phantom ships, speeding to cover.

XIV

The youngest boy, Etienne, had been very naughty, Madame Ratignolle said, as she delivered him into the hands of his mother. He had been unwilling to go to bed and had made a scene; whereupon she had taken charge of him and pacified him as well as she could. Raoul had been in bed and asleep for two hours.

The youngster was in his long white nightgown, that keep tripping him up as Madame Ratignolle led him along by the hand. With the other chubby fist he rubbed his eyes, which were heavy with sleep and ill humor. Edna took him in her arms, and seating herself in the rocker, began to coddle and caress him, calling him all manner of tender names, soothing him to sleep.

It was not more than nine o'clock. No one had yet gone to bed but the children.

Léonce had been very uneasy at first, Madame Ratignolle said, and had wanted to start at once for the *Chênière*. But Monsieur Farival had assured him that his wife was only overcome with sleep and fatigue, that Tonie would bring her safely back later in the day; and he had been thus dissuaded from crossing the bay. He had gone over to Klein's, looking up some cotton broker whom he wished to see in regard to securities, exchanges, stocks, bonds, or something of the sort, Madame Ratignolle did not remember what. He said he would not remain away late. She herself was suffering from heat and oppression, she said. She carried a bottle of salts and a large fan. She would not consent to remain with Edna, for Monsieur Ratignolle was alone, and he detested above all things to be left alone.

When Etienne had fallen asleep Edna bore him into the back room, and Robert went and lifted the mosquito bar that she might lay the child comfortably in his bed. The quadroon had vanished. When they emerged from the cottage Robert bade Edna goodnight.

"Do you know we have been together the whole livelong day, Robert — since early this morning?" she said at parting.

"All but the hundred years when you were sleeping. Good-night."

He pressed her hand and went away in the direction of the beach. He did not join any of the others, but walked alone toward the Gulf.

Edna stayed outside, awaiting her husband's return. She had no desire to sleep or to retire; nor did she feel like going over to sit with the Ratignolles, or to join Madame Lebrun and a group whose animated voices reached her as they sat in conversation before the house. She let her mind wander back over her stay at Grand Isle; and she tried to discover wherein this summer had been different from any and every other summer of her life. She could only realize that she herself—her present self—was in some way different from the other self. That she was seeing with different eyes and making the acquaintance of new conditions in herself that colored and changed her environment, she did not yet suspect.

She wondered why Robert had gone away and left her. It did not occur to her to think he might have grown tired of being with her the livelong day. She was not tired, and she felt that he was not. She regretted that he had gone. It was so much more natural to have him stay when he was not absolutely required to leave her.

As Edna waited for her husband she sang low a little song that Robert had sung as they crossed the bay. It began with "Ah! *Si tu savais,*" and every verse ended with "*si tu savais.*"

Robert's voice was not pretentious. It was musical and true. The voice, the notes, the whole refrain haunted her memory.

XV

When Edna entered the dining-room one evening a little late, as was her habit, an unusually animated conversation seemed to be going on. Several persons were talking at once, and Victor's voice was predominating, even over that of his mother. Edna had returned late from her bath, had dressed in some haste, and her face was flushed. Her head, set off by her dainty white gown, suggested a rich, rare blossom. She took her seat at table between old Monsieur Farival and Madame Ratignolle.

As she seated herself and was about to begin to eat her soup, which had been served when she entered the room, several persons informed her simultaneously that Robert was going to Mexico. She laid her spoon down and looked about her bewildered.

He had been with her, reading to her all the morning, and had never even mentioned such a place as Mexico. She had not seen him during the afternoon; she had heard some one say he was at the house, upstairs with his mother. This she had thought nothing of, though she was surprised when he did not join her later in the afternoon, when she went down to the beach.

She looked across at him, where he sat beside Madame Lebrun, who presided. Edna's face was a blank picture of bewilderment, which she never thought of disguising. He lifted his eyebrows with the pretext of a smile as he returned her glance. He looked embarrassed and uneasy.

"When is he going?" she asked every one in general, as if Robert were not there to answer for himself.

"To-night!" "This very evening!" "Did you ever!" "What possesses him!" were some of the replies she gathered, uttered simultaneously in French and English.

"Impossible!" she exclaimed. "How can a person start off from Grand Isle to Mexico at a moment's notice, as if he were going over to Klein's or to the wharf or down to the beach?"

"I said all along I was going to Mexico; I've been saying so for years!" cried Robert, in an excited and irritable tone, with the air of a man defending himself against a swarm of stinging insects.

Madame Lebrun knocked on the table with her knife handle.

"Please let Robert explain why he is going, and why he is going to-night," she called out. "Really, this table is getting to be more and more like Bedlam every day, with everybody talking at once. Sometimes—I hope God will forgive me—but positively, sometimes I wish Victor would lose the power of speech."

Victor laughed sardonically as he thanked his mother for her holy wish, of which he failed to see the benefit to anybody, except that it might afford her a more ample opportunity and license to talk herself.

Monsieur Farival thought that Victor should have been taken out in mid-ocean in his earliest youth and drowned. Victor thought there would be more logic in thus disposing of old people with an established claim for making themselves universally obnoxious. Madame Lebrun grew a trifle hysterical; Robert called his brother some sharp, hard names.

"There's nothing much to explain, mother," he said; though he explained, nevertheless — looking chiefly at Edna — that he could only meet the gentleman whom he intended to join at Vera Cruz by taking such and such a steamer, which left New Orleans on such a day; that Beaudelet was going out with his lugger-load of vegetables that night, which gave him an opportunity of reaching the city and making his vessel in time.

"But when did you make up your mind to all this?" demanded Monsieur Farival.

"This afternoon," returned Robert, with a shade of annoyance.

"At what time this afternoon?" persisted the old gentleman, with nagging determination, as if he were cross-questioning a criminal in a court of justice.

"At four o'clock this afternoon, Monsieur Farival," Robert replied, in a high voice and with a lofty air, which reminded Edna of some gentleman on the stage.

She had forced herself to eat most of her soup, and now she was picking the flaky bits of a *court bouillon* with her fork.

The lovers were profiting by the general conversation on Mexico to speak in whispers of matters which they rightly considered were interesting to no one but themselves. They lady in black had once received a pair of prayer-beads of curious workmanship from Mexico, with very special indulgence attached to them, but she had never been able to ascertain whether the indulgence extended outside the Mexican border. Father Fochel of the Cathedral had attempted to explain it; but he had not done so to her satisfaction. And she begged that Robert would interest himself, and discover, if possible, whether she was entitled to the indulgence accompanying the remarkably curious Mexican prayer-beads.

Madame Ratignolle hoped that Robert would exercise extreme caution in dealing with the Mexicans, who, she considered, were a treacherous people, unscrupulous and revengeful. She trusted she did them no injustice in thus condemning them as a race. She had known personally but one Mexican, who made and sold excellent tamales, and whom she would have trusted implicitly, so soft-spoken was he. One day he was arrested for stabbing his wife. She never knew whether he had been hanged or not.

Victor had grown hilarious, and was attempting to tell an anecdote about a Mexican girl who served chocolate one winter in a restaurant in Dauphine Street. No one would listen to him but old Monsieur Farival, who went into convulsions over the droll story.

Edna wondered if they had all gone mad, to be talking and clamoring at that rate. She herself could think of nothing to say about Mexico or the Mexicans.

"At what time do you leave?" she asked Robert.

"At ten," he told her. "Beaudelet wants to wait for the moon."

"Are you all ready to go?"

"Quite ready. I shall only take a hand-bag, and shall pack my trunk in the city."

He turned to answer some question put to him by his mother, and Edna, having finished her black coffee, left the table.

She went directly to her room. The little cottage was close and stuffy after leaving the outer air. But she did not mind; there appeared to be a hundred different things demanding her attention indoors. She began to set the toilet-stand to rights, grumbling at the negligence of the quadroon, who was in the adjoining room putting the children to bed. She gathered together stray garments that were hanging on the backs of chairs, and put each where it belonged in closet or bureau drawer. She changed her gown for a more comfortable and commodious wrapper. She rearranged her hair, combing and brushing it with unusual energy. Then she went in and assisted the quadroon in getting the boys to bed.

They were very playful and inclined to talk — to do anything but lie quiet and go to sleep. Edna sent the quadroon away to her supper and told her she need not return. Then she sat and told the children a story. Instead of soothing it excited them, and added to their wakefulness. She left them in heated argument, speculating about the conclusion of the tale which their mother promised to finish the following night.

The little black girl came in to say that Madame Lebrun would like to have Mrs. Pontellier go and sit with them over at the house till Mr. Robert went away. Edna returned answer that she had already undressed, that she did not feel quite well, but perhaps she would go over to the house later. She started to dress again, and got as far advanced as to remove her *peignoir*. But changing her mind once more she resumed the *peignoir*, and went outside and sat down before her door. She was overheated and irritable, and fanned herself energetically for a while. Madame Ratignolle came down to discover what was the matter.

"All that noise and confusion at the table must have upset me," replied Edna, "and moreover, I hate shocks and surprises. The idea of Robert starting off in such a ridiculously sudden and dramatic way! As if it were a matter of life and death! Never saying a word about it all morning when he was with me."

"Yes," agreed Madame Ratignolle. "I think it was showing us all — you especially — very little consideration. It wouldn't have surprised me in any of the others; those Lebruns are all given to heroics. But I must say I should never have expected such a thing from Robert. Are you not coming down? Come on, dear; it doesn't look friendly."

"No," said Edna, a little sullenly. "I can't go to the trouble of dressing again; I don't feel like it."

"You needn't dress; you look all right; fasten a belt around your waist. Just look at me!"

"No," persisted Edna; "but you go on. Madame Lebrun might be offended if we both stayed away."

Madame Ratignolle kissed Edna good-night, and went away, being in truth rather desirous of joining in the general animated conversation which was still in progress concerning Mexico and the Mexicans.

Somewhat later Robert came up, carrying his hand-bag.

"Aren't you feeling well?" he asked.

"Oh, well enough. Are you going right away?"

He lit a match and looked at his watch. "In twenty minutes," he said. The sudden and brief flare of the match emphasized the darkness for a while. He sat down upon a stool which the children had left out on the porch.

"Get a chair," said Edna.

"This will do," he replied. He put on his soft hat and nervously took it off again, and wiping his face with his handkerchief, complained of the heat.

"Take the fan," said Edna, offering it to him.

"Oh, no! Thank you. It does no good; you have to stop fanning some time, and feel all the more uncomfortable afterward."

"That's one of the ridiculous things which men always say. I have never known one to speak otherwise of fanning. How long will you be gone?"

"Forever, perhaps. I don't know. It depends upon a good many things."

"Well, in case it shouldn't be forever, how long will it be?"

"I don't know."

"This seems to me perfectly preposterous and uncalled for. I don't like it. I don't understand your motive for silence and mystery, never saying a word to me about it this morning." He remained silent, not offering to defend himself. He only said, after a moment:

"Don't part from me in an ill-humor. I never knew you to be out of patience with me before."

"I don't want to part in any ill-humor," she said. "But can't you understand? I've grown used to seeing you, to having you with me all the time, and your action seems unfriendly, even unkind. You don't even offer an excuse for it. Why, I was planning to be together, thinking of how pleasant it would be to see you in the city next winter."

"So was I," he blurted. "Perhaps that's the —" He stood up suddenly and held out his hand. "Good-by, my dear Mrs. Pontellier; good-by. You won't — I hope you won't completely forget me." She clung to his hand, striving to detain him.

"Write to me when you get there, won't you, Robert?" she entreated.

"I will, thank you. Good-by."

How unlike Robert! The merest acquaintance would have said something more emphatic than "I will, thank you; good-by," to such a request.

He had evidently already taken leave of the people over at the house, for he descended the steps and went to join Beaudelet, who was out there with an oar across his shoulder waiting for Robert. They walked away in the darkness. She could only hear Beaudelet's voice; Robert had apparently not even spoken a word of greeting to his companion.

Edna bit her handkerchief convulsively, striving to hold back and to hide, even from herself as she would have hidden from another, the emotion which was troubling — tearing — her. Her eyes were brimming with tears.

For the first time she recognized anew the symptoms of infatuation which she had felt incipiently as a child, as a girl in her earliest teens, and later as a young woman. The recognition did not lessen the reality, the poignancy of the revelation by any suggestion or promise of instability. The past was nothing to her; offered no lesson which she was willing to heed. The future was a mystery which she never attempted to penetrate. The present alone was significant; was hers, to torture her as it was doing then with the biting conviction that she had lost that which she had held, that she had been denied that which her impassioned, newly awakened being demanded.

XVI

"Do you miss your friend greatly?" asked Mademoiselle Reisz one morning as she came creeping up behind Edna, who had just left her cottage on her way to the beach. She spent much of her time in the water since she had acquired finally the art of swimming. As their stay at Grand Isle drew near its close, she felt that she could not give too much time to a diversion which afforded her the only real pleasurable moments that she knew. When Mademoiselle Reisz came and touched her upon the shoulder and spoke to her, the woman seemed to echo the thought which was ever in Edna's mind; or, better, the feeling which constantly possessed her.

Robert's going had some way taken the brightness, the color, the meaning out of everything. The conditions of her life were in no way changed, but her whole existence was dulled, like a faded garment which seems to be no longer worth wearing. She sought him everywhere—in others whom she induced to talk about him. She went up in the mornings to Madame Lebrun's room, braving the clatter of the old sewing-machine. She sat there and chatted at intervals as Robert had done. She gazed around the room at the pictures and photographs hanging upon the wall, and discovered in some corner an old family album, which she examined with the keenest interest, appealing to Madame Lebrun for enlightenment concerning the many figures and faces which she discovered between its pages.

There was a picture of Madame Lebrun with Robert as a baby, seated in her lap, a round-faced infant with a fist in his mouth. The eyes alone in the baby suggested the man. And that was he also in kilts, at the age of five, wearing long curls and holding a whip in his hand. It made Edna laugh, and she laughed, too, at the portrait in his first long trousers; while another interested her, taken when he left for college, looking thin, long-faced, with eyes full of fire, ambition and great intentions. But there was no recent picture, none which suggested the Robert who had gone away five days ago, leaving a void and wilderness behind him.

"Oh, Robert stopped having his pictures taken when he had to pay for them himself! He found wiser use for his money, he says," explained Madame Lebrun. She had a letter from him, written before he left New Orleans. Edna wished to see the letter, and Madame Lebrun told her to look for it either on the table or the dresser, or perhaps it was on the mantelpiece.

The letter was on the bookshelf. It possessed the greatest interest and attraction for Edna; the envelope, its size and shape, the post-mark, the handwriting. She examined every detail of the outside before opening it. There were only a few lines, setting forth that he would leave the city that afternoon, that he had packed his trunk in good shape, that he was well, and sent her his love and begged to be affectionately remembered to all. There was no special message to Edna except a postscript saying that if Mrs. Pontellier desired to finish the book which he had been reading to her, his mother would find it in his room, among other books there on the table. Edna experienced a pang of jealousy because he had written to his mother rather than to her.

Every one seemed to take for granted that she missed him. Even her husband, when he came down the Saturday following Robert's departure, expressed regret that he had gone.

"How do you get on without him, Edna?" he asked.

"It's very dull without him," she admitted. Mr. Pontellier had seen Robert in the city, and Edna asked him a dozen questions or more. Where had they met? On Carondelet Street, in the morning. They had gone "in" and had a drink and a cigar together. What had they talked about? Chiefly about his prospects in Mexico, which Mr. Pontellier thought were promising. How did he look? How did he seem—grave, or gay, or how? Quite cheerful, and wholly taken up with the idea of his trip, which Mr. Pontellier found altogether natural in a young fellow about to seek fortune and adventure in a strange, queer country.

Edna tapped her foot impatiently, and wondered why the children persisted in playing in the sun when they might be under the trees. She went down and led them out of the sun, scolding the quadroon for not being more attentive.

It did not strike her as in the least grotesque that she should be making of Robert the object of conversation and leading her husband to speak of him. The sentiment which she entertained for Robert in no way resembled that which she felt for her husband, or had ever felt, or ever expected to feel. She had all her life long been accustomed to harbor thoughts and emotions which never voiced themselves. They had never taken the form of struggles. They belonged to her and were her own, and she entertained the conviction that she had a right to them and that they concerned no one but herself. Edna had once told Madame Ratignolle that she would never sacrifice herself for her children, or for any one. Then had followed a rather heated argument; the two women did not appear to understand each other or to be talking the same language. Edna tried to appease her friend, to explain.

"I would give up the unessential; I would give my money, I would give my life for my children; but I wouldn't give myself. I can't make it more clear; it's only something which I am beginning to comprehend, which is revealing itself to me."

"I don't know what you would call the essential, or what you mean by the unessential," said Madame Ratignolle, cheerfully; "but a woman who would give her life for her children could do no more than that—your Bible tells you so. I'm sure I couldn't do more than that."

"Oh, yes you could!" laughed Edna.

She was not surprised at Mademoiselle Reisz's question the morning that lady, following her to the beach, tapped her on the shoulder and asked if she did not greatly miss her young friend.

"Oh, good morning, Mademoiselle; is it you? Why, of course I miss Robert. Are you going down to bathe?"

"Why should I go down to bathe at the very end of the season when I haven't been in the surf all summer," replied the woman, disagreeably.

"I beg your pardon," offered Edna, in some embarrassment, for she should have remembered that Mademoiselle Reisz's avoidance of the water had furnished a theme for much pleasantry. Some among them thought it was on account of her false hair, or the dread of getting the violets wet, while others attributed it to the natural aversion for water sometimes believed to accompany the artistic temperament. Mademoiselle offered Edna some chocolates in a paper bag, which she took from her pocket, by way of showing that she bore no ill feeling. She habitually ate chocolates for their sustaining quality; they contained much nutriment in small compass, she said. They saved her from starvation, as Madame Lebrun's table was utterly impossible; and no one save so impertinent a woman as Madame Lebrun could

think of offering such food to people and requiring them to pay for it.

"She must feel very lonely without her son," said Edna, desiring to change the subject. "Her favorite son, too. It must have been quite hard to let him go."

Mademoiselle laughed maliciously.

"Her favorite son! Oh, dear! Who could have been imposing such a tale upon you? Aline Lebrun lives for Victor, and for Victor alone. She has spoiled him into the worthless creature he is. She worships him and the ground he walks on. Robert is very well in a way, to give up all the money he can earn to the family, and keep the barest pittance for himself. Favorite son, indeed! I miss the poor fellow myself, my dear. I liked to see him and to hear him about the place—the only Lebrun who is worth a pinch of salt. He comes to see me often in the city. I like to play to him. That Victor! hanging would be too good for him. It's a wonder Robert hasn't beaten him to death long ago."

"I thought he had great patience with his brother," offered Edna, glad to be talking about Robert, no matter what was said.

"Oh! he thrashed him well enough a year or two ago," said Mademoiselle. "It was about a Spanish girl, whom Victor considered that he had some sort of claim upon. He met Robert one day talking to the girl, or walking with her, or bathing with her, or carrying her basket—I don't remember what;—and he became so insulting and abusive that Robert gave him a thrashing on the spot that has kept him comparatively in order for a good while. It's about time he was getting another."

"Was her name Mariequita?" asked Edna.

"Mariequita—yes, that was it; Mariequita. I had forgotten. Oh, she's a sly one, and a bad one, that Mariequita!"

Edna looked down at Mademoiselle Reisz and wondered how she could have listened to her venom so long. For some reason she felt depressed, almost unhappy. She had not intended to go into the water; but she donned her bathing suit, and left Mademoiselle alone; seated under the shade of the children's tent. The water was growing cooler as the season advanced. Edna plunged and swam about with an abandon that thrilled and invigorated her. She remained a long time in the water, half hoping that Mademoiselle Reisz would not wait for her.

But Mademoiselle waited. She was very amiable during the walk back, and raved much over Edna's appearance in her bathing suit. She talked about music. She hoped that Edna would go to see her in the city, and wrote her address with the stub of a pencil on a piece of card which she found in her pocket.

"When do you leave?" asked Edna.

"Next Monday; and you?"

"The following week," answered Edna, adding, "It has been a pleasant summer, hasn't it, Mademoiselle?"

"Well," agreed Mademoiselle Reisz, with a shrug, "rather pleasant, if it hadn't been for the mosquitoes and the Farival twins."

XVII

The Pontelliers possessed a very charming home on Esplanade Street in New Orleans. It was a large, double cottage, with a broad front veranda, whose round, fluted columns supported the sloping roof. The house was painted a dazzling white; the outside shutters, or jalousies, were green. In the yard, which was kept scrupulously neat, were flowers and plants of every description which flourishes in South Louisiana. Within doors the appointments were perfect after the conventional type. The softest carpets and rugs covered the floors; rich and tasteful draperies hung at doors and windows. There were paintings, selected with judgment and discrimination, upon the walls. The cut glass, the silver, the heavy damask which daily appeared upon the table were the envy of many women whose husbands were less generous than Mr. Pontellier.

Mr. Pontellier was very fond of walking about his house examining its various appointments and details, to see that nothing was amiss. He greatly valued his possessions, chiefly because they were his, and derived genuine pleasure from contemplating a painting, a statuette, a rare lace curtain—no matter what—after he had bought it and placed it among his household goods.

On Tuesday afternoons—Tuesday being Mrs. Pontellier's reception day—there was a constant stream of callers—women who came in carriages or in the street cars, or walked when the air was soft and distance permitted. A light-colored mulatto boy, in dress coat and bearing a diminutive silver tray for the reception of cards, admitted them. A maid, in white fluted cap, offered the callers liqueur, coffee, or chocolate, as they might desire. Mrs. Pontellier, attired in a handsome reception gown, remained in the drawing-room the entire afternoon receiving her visitors. Men sometimes called in the evening with their wives.

This had been the programme which Mrs. Pontellier had religiously followed since her marriage, six years before. Certain evenings during the week she and her husband attended the opera or sometimes the play.

Mr. Pontellier left his home in the mornings between nine and ten o'clock, and rarely returned before half-past six or seven in the evening—dinner being served at half-past seven.

He and his wife seated themselves at table one Tuesday evening, a few weeks after their return from Grand Isle. They were alone together. The boys were being put to bed; the patter of their bare, escaping feet would be heard occasionally, as well as the pursuing voice of the quadroon, lifted in mild protest and entreaty. Mrs. Pontellier did not wear her usual Tuesday reception gown; she was in ordinary house dress. Mr. Pontellier, who was observant about such things, noticed it, as she served the soup and handed it to the boy in waiting.

"Tired out, Edna? Whom did you have? Many callers?" he asked. He tasted his soup and began to season it with pepper, salt, vinegar, mustard—everything within reach.

"There were a good many," replied Edna, who was eating her soup with evident satisfaction. "I found their cards when I got home; I was out."

"Out!" exclaimed her husband, with something like genuine consternation in his voice as he laid down the vinegar cruet and looked at her through his glasses. "Why, what could have taken you out on Tuesday? What did you have to do?"

"Nothing. I simply felt like going out, and I went out."

"Well, I hope you left some suitable excuse," said her husband, somewhat appeased, as he added a dash of cayenne pepper to the soup.

"No, I left no excuse. I told Joe to say I was out, that was all."

"Why, my dear, I should think you'd understand by this time that people don't do such things; we've got to observe *les convenances* if we ever expect to get on and keep up with the procession. If you felt that you had to leave home this afternoon, you should have left some suitable explanation for your absence.

"This soup is really impossible; it's strange that woman hasn't learned yet to make a decent soup.

Any free-lunch stand in town serves a better one. Was Mrs. Belthrop here?"

"Bring the tray with the cards, Joe. I don't remember who was here."

The boy retired and returned after a moment, bringing the tiny silver tray, which was covered with ladies' visiting cards. He handed it to Mrs. Pontellier.

"Give it to Mr. Pontellier," she said.

Joe offered the tray to Mr. Pontellier, and removed the soup.

Mr. Pontellier scanned the names of his wife's callers, reading some of them aloud, with comments as he read.

" 'The Misses Delasidas.' I worked a big deal in futures for their father this morning; nice girls; it's time they were getting married. 'Mrs. Belthrop.' I tell you what it is, Edna; you can't afford to snub Mrs. Belthrop. Why, Belthrop could buy and sell us ten times over. His business is worth a good, round sum to me. You'd better write her a note. 'Mrs. James Highcamp.' Hugh! the less you have to do with Mrs. Highcamp, the better. 'Madame Laforcé.' Came all the way from Carrolton, too, poor old soul. 'Miss Wiggs,' 'Mrs. Eleanor Boltons.' " He pushed the cards aside.

"Mercy!" exclaimed Edna, who had been fuming. "Why are you taking the thing so seriously and making such a fuss over it?"

"I'm not making any fuss over it. But it's just such seeming trifles that we've got to take seriously; such things count."

The fish was scorched. Mr. Pontellier would not touch it. Edna said she did not mind a little scorched taste. The roast was in some way not to his fancy, and he did not like the manner in which the vegetables were served.

"It seems to me," he said, "we spend money enough in this house to procure at least one meal a day which a man could eat and retain his self-respect."

"You used to think the cook was a treasure," returned Edna, indifferently.

"Perhaps she was when she first came; but cooks are only human. They need looking after, like any other class of persons that you employ. Suppose I didn't look after the clerks in my office, just let them run things their own way; they'd soon make a nice mess of me and my business."

"Where are you going?" asked Edna, seeing that her husband arose from table without having eaten a morsel except a taste of the highly-seasoned soup.

"I'm going to get my dinner at the club. Good night." He went into the hall, took his hat and stick from the stand, and left the house.

She was somewhat familiar with such scenes. They had often made her very unhappy. On a few previous occasions she had been completely deprived of any desire to finish her dinner. Sometimes she had gone into the kitchen to administer a tardy rebuke to the cook. Once she went to her room and studied the cookbook during an entire evening, finally writing out a menu for the week, which left her harassed with a feeling that, after all, she had accomplished no good that was worth the name.

But that evening Edna finished her dinner alone, with forced deliberation. Her face was flushed and her eyes flamed with some inward fire that lighted them. After finishing her dinner she went to her room, having instructed the boy to tell any other callers that she was indisposed.

It was a large, beautiful room, rich and picturesque in the soft, dim light which the maid had turned low. She went and stood at an open window and looked out upon the deep tangle of the garden below. All the mystery and witchery of the night seemed to have gathered there amid the perfumes and the dusky and tortuous outlines of flowers and foliage. She was seeking herself and finding herself in just such sweet, half-darkness which met her moods. But the voices were not soothing that came to her from the darkness and the sky above the stars. They jeered and sounded mournful notes without promise, devoid even of hope. She turned back into the room and began to walk to and fro down its whole length, without stopping, without resting. She carried in her hands a thin handkerchief, which she tore into ribbons, rolled into a ball, and flung from her. Once she stopped, and taking off her wedding ring, flung it upon the carpet. When she saw it lying there, she stamped her heel upon it, striving to crush it. But her small boot heel did not make an indenture, not a mark upon the little glittering circlet.

In a sweeping passion she seized a glass vase from the table and flung it upon the tiles of the hearth. She wanted to destroy something. The crash and clatter were what she wanted to hear.

A maid, alarmed at the din of breaking glass, entered the room to discover what was the matter.

"A vase fell upon the hearth," said Edna. "Never mind; leave it till morning."

"Oh! you might get some of the glass in your feet, ma'am," insisted the young woman, picking up bits of the broken vase that were scattered upon the carpet. "And here's your ring, ma'am, under the chair."

Edna held out her hand, and taking the ring, slipped it upon her finger.

XVIII

The following morning Mr. Pontellier, upon leaving for his office, asked Edna if she would not meet him in town in order to look at some new fixtures for the library.

"I hardly think we need new fixtures, Léonce. Don't let us get anything new; you are too extravagant. I don't believe you ever think of saving or putting by."

"The way to become rich is to make money, my dear Edna, not to save it," he said. He regretted that she did not feel inclined to go with him and select new fixtures. He kissed her good-by, and told her she was not looking well and must take care of herself. She was unusually pale and very quiet.

She stood on the front veranda as he quitted the house, and absently picked a few sprays of jessamine that grew upon a trellis near by. She inhaled the odor of the blossoms and thrust them into the bosom of her white morning gown. The boys were dragging along the banquette a small "express wagon," which they had filled with blocks and sticks. The quadroon was following them with little quick steps, having assumed a fictitious animation and alacrity for the occasion. A fruit vender was crying his wares in the street.

Edna looked straight before her with a self-absorbed expression upon her face. She felt no interest in anything about her. The street, the children, the fruit vender, the flowers growing there under her eyes, were all part and parcel of an alien world which had suddenly become antagonistic.

She went back into the house. She had thought of speaking to the cook concerning her blunders of the previous night; but Mr. Pontellier had saved her that disagreeable mission, for which she was so poorly fitted. Mr. Pontellier's arguments were usually convincing with those whom he employed. He left home feeling quite sure that he and Edna would sit down that evening, and possibly a few subsequent evenings, to a dinner deserving of the name.

Edna spent an hour or two in looking over some of her old sketches. She could see their shortcomings and defects, which were glaring in her eyes. She tried to work a little, but found she was not in the humor. Finally she gathered together a few of the sketches — those which she considered the least discreditable; and she carried them with her when, a little later, she dressed and left the house. She looked handsome and distinguished in her street gown. The tan of the seashore had left her face, and her forehead was smooth, white, and polished beneath her heavy, yellow-brown hair. There were a few freckles on her face, and a small, dark mole near the under lip and one on the temple, half-hidden in her hair.

As Edna walked along the street she was thinking of Robert. She was still under the spell of her infatuation. She had tried to forget him, realizing the inutility of remembering. But the thought of him was like an obsession, ever pressing itself upon her. It was not that she dwelt upon details of their acquaintance, or recalled in any special or peculiar way his personality; it was his being, his existence, which dominated her thought, fading sometimes as if it would melt into the mist of the forgotten, reviving again with an intensity which filled her with an incomprehensible longing.

Edna was on her way to Madame Ratignolle's. Their intimacy, begun at Grand Isle, had not declined, and they had seen each other with some frequency since their return to the city. The Ratignolles lived at no great distance from Edna's home, on the corner of a side street, where Monsieur Ratignolle owned and conducted a drug store which enjoyed a steady and prosperous trade. His father had been in the business before him, and Monsieur Ratignolle stood well in the community and bore an enviable reputation for integrity and clear-headedness. His family lived in commodious apartments over the store, having an entrance on the side within the *porte cochère*. There was something which Edna thought very French, very foreign, about their whole manner of living. In the large and pleasant salon which extended across the width of the house, the Ratignolles entertained their friends once a fortnight with a *söirée musicale*, sometimes diversified by cardplaying. There was a friend who played upon the 'cello. One brought his flute and another his violin, while there were some who sang and a number who performed upon the piano with various degrees of taste and agility. The Ratignolles' *soirées musicales* were widely known, and it was considered a privilege to be invited to them.

Edna found her friend engaged in assorting the clothes which had returned that morning from the laundry. She at once abandoned her occupation upon seeing Edna, who had been ushered without ceremony into her presence.

"'Cité can do it as well as I; it is really her business," she explained to Edna, who apologized for interrupting her. And she summoned a young black woman, whom she instructed, in French, to be very careful in checking off the list which she handed her. She told her to notice particularly if a fine linen handkerchief of Monsieur Ratignolle's, which was missing last week, had been returned; and to be sure to set to one side such pieces as required mending and darning.

Then placing an arm around Edna's waist, she led her to the front of the house, to the salon, where it was cool and sweet with the odor of great roses that stood upon the hearth in jars.

Madame Ratignolle looked more beautiful than ever there at home, in a negligé which left her arms almost wholly bare and exposed the rich, melting curves of her white throat.

"Perhaps I shall be able to paint your picture some day," said Edna with a smile when they were seated. She produced the roll of sketches and started to unfold them. "I believe I ought to work again. I feel as if I wanted to be doing something. What do you think of them? Do you think it worth while to take it up again and study some more? I might study for a while with Laidpore."

She knew that Madame Ratignolle's opinion in such a matter would be next to valueless, that she herself had not alone decided, but determined; but she sought the words of praise and encouragement that would help her to put heart into her venture.

"Your talent is immense, dear!"

"Nonsense!" protested Edna, well pleased.

"Immense, I tell you," persisted Madame Ratignolle, surveying the sketches one by one, at close range, then holding them at arm's length, narrowing her eyes, and dropping her head on one side. "Surely, this Bavarian peasant is worthy of framing; and this basket of apples! never have I seen anything more lifelike. One might almost be tempted to reach out a hand and take one."

Edna could not control a feeling which bordered upon complacency at her friend's praise, even realizing, as she did, its true worth. She retained a few of the sketches, and gave all the rest to Madame Ratig-

nolle, who appreciated the gift far beyond its value and proudly exhibited the pictures to her husband when he came up from the store a little later for his midday dinner.

Mr. Ratignolle was one of those men who are called the salt of the earth. His cheerfulness was unbounded, and it was matched by his goodness of heart, his broad charity, and common sense. He and his wife spoke English with an accent which was only discernible through its un-English emphasis and a certain carefulness and deliberation. Edna's husband spoke English with no accent whatever. The Ratignolles understood each other perfectly. If ever the fusion of two human beings into one has been accomplished on this sphere it was surely in their union.

As Edna seated herself at table with them she thought, "Better a dinner of herbs," though it did not take her long to discover that it was no dinner of herbs, but a delicious repast, simple, choice, and in every way satisfying.

Monsieur Ratignolle was delighted to see her, though he found her looking not so well as at Grand Isle, and he advised a tonic. He talked a good deal on various topics, a little politics, some city news and neighborhood gossip. He spoke with an animation and earnestness that gave an exaggerated importance to every syllable he uttered. His wife was keenly interested in everything he said, laying down her fork the better to listen, chiming in, taking the words out of his mouth.

Edna felt depressed rather than soothed after leaving them. The little glimpse of domestic harmony which had been offered her, gave her no regret, no longing. It was not a condition of life which fitted her, and she could see in it but an appalling and hopeless ennui. She was moved by a kind of commiseration for Madame Ratignolle,—a pity for that colorless existence which never uplifted its possessor beyond the region of blind contentment, in which no moment of anguish ever visited her soul, in which she would never have the taste of life's delirium. Edna vaguely wondered what she meant by "life's delirium." It had crossed her thought like some unsought, extraneous impression.

XIX

Edna could not help but think that it was very foolish, very childish, to have stamped upon her wedding ring and smashed the crystal vase upon the tiles. She was visited by no more outbursts, moving her to such futile expedients. She began to do as she liked and to feel as she liked. She completely abandoned her Tuesdays at home, and did not return the visits to those who had called upon her. She made no ineffectual efforts to conduct her household *en bonne ménagère,* going and coming as it suited her fancy, and, so far as she was able, lending herself to any passing caprice.

Mr. Pontellier had been a rather courteous husband so long as he met a certain tacit submissiveness in his wife. But her new and unexpected line of conduct completely bewildered him. It shocked him. Then her absolute disregard for her duties as a wife angered him. When Mr. Pontellier became rude, Edna grew insolent. She had resolved never to take another step backward.

"It seems to me the utmost folly for a woman at the head of a household, and the mother of children, to spend in an atelier days which would be better employed contriving for the comfort of her family."

"I feel like painting," answered Edna. "Perhaps I shan't always feel like it."

"Then in God's name paint! but don't let the family go to the devil. There's Madame Ratignolle; because she keeps up her music, she doesn't let everything else go to chaos. And she's more a musician than you are a painter."

"She isn't a musician, and I'm not a painter. It isn't on account of painting that I let things go."

"On account of what, then?"

"Oh! I don't know. Let me alone; you bother me."

It sometimes entered Mr. Pontellier's mind to wonder if his wife were not growing a little unbalanced mentally. He could see plainly that she was not herself. That is, he could not see that she was becoming herself and daily casting aside that fictitious self which we assume like a garment with which to appear before the world.

Her husband let her alone as she requested, and went away to his office. Edna went up to her atelier — a bright room in the top of the house. She was working with great energy and interest, without accomplishing anything, however, which satisfied her even in the smallest degree. For a time she had the whole household enrolled in the service of art. The boys posed for her. They thought it amusing at first, but the occupation soon lost its attractiveness when they discovered that it was not a game arranged es-

pecially for their entertainment. The quadroon sat for hours before Edna's palette, patient as a savage, while the house-maid took charge of the children, and the drawing-room went undusted. But the house-maid, too, served her term as model when Edna perceived that the young woman's back and shoulders were molded on classic lines, and that her hair, loosened from its confining cap, became an inspiration. While Edna worked she sometimes sang low the little air, "*Ah! si tu savais!*"

It moved her with recollections. She could hear again the ripple of the water, the flapping sail. She could see the glint of the moon upon the bay, and could feel the soft, gusty beating of the hot south wind. A subtle current of desire passed through her body, weakening her hold upon the brushes and making her eyes burn.

There were days when she was very happy without knowing why. She was happy to be alive and breathing, when her whole being seemed to be one with the sunlight, the color, the odors, the luxuriant warmth of some perfect Southern day. She liked then to wander alone into strange and unfamiliar places. She discovered many a sunny, sleepy corner, fashioned to dream in. And she found it good to dream and to be alone and unmolested.

There were days when she was unhappy, she did not know why,—when it did not seem worth while to be glad or sorry, to be alive or dead; when life appeared to her like a grotesque pandemonium and humanity like worms struggling blindly toward inevitable annihilation. She could not work on such a day, nor weave fancies to stir her pulses and warm her blood.

XX

It was during such a mood that Edna hunted up Mademoiselle Reisz. She had not forgotten the rather disagreeable impression left upon her by their last interview; but she nevertheless felt a desire to see her — above all, to listen while she played upon the piano. Quite early in the afternoon she started upon her quest for the pianist. Unfortunately she had mislaid or lost Mademoiselle Reisz's card, and looking up her address in the city directory, she found that the woman lived on Bienville Street, some distance away. The directory which fell into her hands was a year or more old, however, and upon reaching the number indicated, Edna discovered that the house was occupied by a respectable family of mulattoes who had *chambres garnies* to let. They had been living there for six months, and knew absolutely nothing of a Mademoiselle Reisz. In fact, they knew nothing of any of their neighbors; their lodgers were all people of the highest distinction, they assured Edna. She did not linger to discuss class distinctions with Madame Pouponne, but hastened to a neighboring grocery store, feeling sure that Mademoiselle would have left her address with the proprietor.

He knew Mademoiselle Reisz a good deal better than he wanted to know her, he informed his questioner. In truth, he did not want to know her at all, or anything concerning her — the most disagreeable and unpopular woman who ever lived in Bienville Street. He thanked heaven she had left the neighborhood, and was equally thankful that he did not know where she had gone.

Edna's desire to see Mademoiselle Reisz had increased tenfold since these unlooked-for obstacles had arisen to thwart it. She was wondering who could give her the information she sought, when it suddenly occurred to her that Madame Lebrun would be the one most likely to do so. She knew it was useless to ask Madame Ratignolle, who was on the most distant terms with the musician, and preferred to know nothing concerning her. She had once been almost as emphatic in expressing herself upon the subject as the corner grocer.

Edna knew that Madame Lebrun had returned to the city, for it was the middle of November. And she also knew where the Lebruns lived, on Chartres Street.

Their home from the outside looked like a prison, with iron bars before the door and lower windows. The iron bars were a relic of the old *régime,* and no one had ever thought of dislodging them. At the side was a high fence enclosing the garden. A gate or door opening upon the street was locked. Edna rang the bell at this side garden gate, and stood upon the banquette, waiting to be admitted.

It was Victor who opened the gate for her. A black woman, wiping her hands upon her apron, was close at his heels. Before she saw them Edna could hear them in altercation, the woman — plainly an anomaly — claiming the right to be allowed to perform her duties, one of which was to answer the bell.

Victor was surprised and delighted to see Mrs. Pontellier, and he made no attempt to conceal either his astonishment or his delight. He was a dark-browed, good-looking youngster of nineteen, greatly resembling his mother, but with ten times her impetuosity. He instructed the black woman to go at once and inform Madame Lebrun that Mrs. Pontellier desired to see her. The woman grumbled a refusal to do part of her duty when she had not been permitted to do it all, and started back to her interrupted task of weeding the garden. Whereupon Victor administered a rebuke in the form of a volley of abuse, which, owing to its rapidity and incoherence, was all but incomprehensible to Edna. Whatever it was, the rebuke was convincing, for the woman dropped her hoe and went mumbling into the house.

Edna did not wish to enter. It was very pleasant there on the side porch, where there were chairs, a wicker lounge, and a small table. She seated herself, for she was tired from her long tramp; and she began to rock gently and smooth out the folds of her silk parasol. Victor drew up his chair beside her. He at once explained that the black woman's offensive conduct was all due to imperfect training, as he was not there to take her in hand. He had only come up from the island the morning before, and expected to return next day. He stayed all winter at the island; he lived there, and kept the place in order and got things ready for the summer visitors.

But a man needed occasional relaxation, he informed Mrs. Pontellier, and every now and again he drummed up a pretext to bring him to the city. My! but he had had a time of it the evening before! He wouldn't want his mother to know, and he began to talk in a whisper. He was scintillant with recollections. Of course, he couldn't think of telling Mrs. Pontellier all about it, she being a woman and not comprehending such things. But it all began with a girl peeping and smiling at him through the shutters as he passed by. Oh! but she was a beauty! Certainly he smiled back, and went up and talked to her. Mrs. Pontellier did not know him if she supposed he was one to let an opportunity like that escape him. Despite herself, the youngster amused her. She must have betrayed in her look some degree of interest or entertainment. The boy grew more daring, and Mrs. Pontellier must have found herself, in a little while, listening to a highly colored story but for the timely appearance of Madame Lebrun.

That lady was still clad in white, according to her custom of the summer. Her eyes beamed an effusive welcome. Would not Mrs. Pontellier go inside?

Would she partake of some refreshment? Why had she not been there before? How was that dear Mr. Pontellier and how were those sweet children? Had Mrs. Pontellier ever known such a warm November?

Victor went and reclined on the wicker lounge behind his mother's chair, where he commanded a view of Edna's face. He had taken her parasol from her hands while he spoke to her, and he now lifted it and twirled it above him as he lay on his back. When Madame Lebrun complained that it was *so* dull coming back to the city; that she saw *so* few people now; that even Victor, when he came up from the island for a day or two, had *so* much to occupy him and engage his time; then it was that the youth went into contortions on the lounge and winked mischievously at Edna. She somehow felt like a confederate in crime, and tried to look severe and disapproving.

There had been but two letters from Robert, with little in them, they told her. Victor said it was really not worth while to go inside for the letters, when his mother entreated him to go in search of them. He remembered the contents, which in truth he rattled off very glibly when put to the test.

One letter was written from Vera Cruz and the other from the City of Mexico. He had met Montel, who was doing everything toward his advancement. So far, the financial situation was no improvement over the one he had left in New Orleans, but of course the prospects were vastly better. He wrote of the City of Mexico, the buildings, the people and their habits, the conditions of life which he found there. He sent his love to the family. He inclosed a check to his mother, and hoped she would affectionately remember him to all his friends. That was about the substance of the two letters. Edna felt that if there had been a message for her, she would have received it. The despondent frame of mind in which she had left home began again to overtake her, and she remembered that she wished to find Mademoiselle Reisz.

Madame Lebrun knew where Mademoiselle Reisz lived. She gave Edna the address, regretting that she would not consent to stay and spend the remainder of the afternoon, and pay a visit to Mademoiselle Reisz some other day. The afternoon was already well advanced.

Victor escorted her out upon the banquette, lifted her parasol, and held it over her while he walked to the car with her. He entreated her to bear in mind that the disclosures of the afternoon were strictly confidential. She laughed and bantered him a little, remembering too late that she should have been dignified and reserved.

"How handsome Mrs. Pontellier looked!" said Madame Lebrun to her son.

"Ravishing!" he admitted. "The city atmosphere has improved her. Some way she doesn't seem like the same woman."

XXI

Some people contended that the reason Mademoiselle Reisz always chose apartments up under the roof was to discourage the approach of beggars, peddlars and callers. There were plenty of windows in her little front room. They were for the most part dingy, but as they were nearly always open it did not make so much difference. They often admitted into the room a good deal of smoke and soot; but at the same time all the light and air that there was came through them. From her windows could be seen the crescent of the river, the masts of ships and the big chimneys of the Mississippi steamers. A magnificent piano crowded the apartment. In the next room she slept, and in the third and last she harbored a gasoline stove on which she cooked her meals when disinclined to descend to the neighboring restaurant. It was there also that she ate, keeping her belongings in a rare old buffet, dingy and battered from a hundred years of use.

When Edna knocked at Mademoiselle Reisz's front room door and entered, she discovered that person standing beside the window, engaged in mending or patching an old prunella gaiter. The little musician laughed all over when she saw Edna. Her laugh consisted of a portion of the face and all the muscles of the body. She seemed strikingly homely, standing there in the afternoon light. She still wore the shabby lace and the artificial bunch of violets on the side of her head.

"So you remembered me at last," said Mademoiselle. "I had said to myself, 'Ah, bah! she will never come.'"

"Did you want me to come?" asked Edna with a smile.

"I had not thought much about it," answered Mademoiselle. The two had seated themselves on a little bumpy sofa which stood against the wall. "I am glad, however, that you came. I have the water boiling back there, and was just about to make some coffee. You will drink a cup with me. And how is *la belle dame?* Always handsome! always healthy! always contented!" She took Edna's hand between her strong wiry fingers, holding it loosely without warmth, and executing a sort of double theme upon the back and palm.

"Yes," she went on; "I sometimes thought: 'She will never come. She promised as those women in society always do, without meaning it. She will not come.' For I really don't believe you like me, Mrs. Pontellier."

"I don't know whether I like you or not," replied Edna, gazing down at the little woman with a quizzical look.

The candor of Mrs. Pontellier's admission greatly pleased Mademoiselle Reisz. She expressed her gratification by repairing forthwith to the region of the gasoline stove and rewarding her guest with the promised cup of coffee. The coffee and the biscuit accompanying it proved very acceptable to Edna, who had declined refreshment at Madame Lebrun's and was now beginning to feel hungry. Mademoiselle set the tray which she brought in upon a small table near at hand, and seated herself once again on the lumpy sofa.

"I have had a letter from your friend," she remarked, as she poured a little cream into Edna's cup and handed it to her.

"My friend?"

"Yes, your friend Robert. He wrote to me from the City of Mexico."

"Wrote to *you?*" repeated Edna in amazement, stirring her coffee absently.

"Yes, to me. Why not? Don't stir all the warmth out of your coffee; drink it. Though the letter might as well have been sent to you; it was nothing but Mrs. Pontellier from beginning to end."

"Let me see it," requested the young woman, entreatingly.

"No; a letter concerns no one but the person who writes it and the one to whom it is written."

"Haven't you just said it concerned me from beginning to end?"

"It was written about you, not to you. 'Have you seen Mrs. Pontellier? How is she looking?' he asks. 'As Mrs. Pontellier says,' or 'as Mrs. Pontellier once said.' 'If Mrs. Pontellier should call upon you, play for her that Impromptu of Chopin's, my favorite. I heard it here a day or two ago, but not as you play it. I should like to know how it affects her,' and so on,

as if he supposed we were constantly in each other's society."

"Let me see the letter."

"Oh, no."

"Have you answered it?"

"No."

"Let me see the letter."

"No, and again, no."

"Then play the Impromptu for me."

"It is growing late; what time do you have to be home?"

"Time doesn't concern me. Your question seems a little rude. Play the Impromptu."

"But you have told me nothing of yourself. What are you doing?"

"Painting!" laughed Edna. "I am becoming an artist. Think of it!"

"Ah! an artist! You have pretensions, Madame."

"Why pretensions? Do you think I could not become an artist?"

"I do not know you well enough to say. I do not know your talent or your temperament. To be an artist includes much; one must possess many gifts—absolute gifts—which have not been acquired by one's own effort. And, moreover, to succeed, the artist must possess the courageous soul."

"What do you mean by the courageous soul?"

"Courageous, *ma foi!* The brave soul. The soul that dares and defies."

"Show me the letter and play for me the Impromptu. You see that I have persistence. Does that quality count for anything in art?"

"It counts with a foolish old woman whom you have captivated," replied Mademoiselle, with her wriggling laugh.

The letter was right there at hand in the drawer of the little table upon which Edna had just placed her coffee cup. Mademoiselle opened the drawer and drew forth the letter, the topmost one. She placed it in Edna's hands, and without further comment arose and went to the piano.

Mademoiselle played a soft interlude. It was an improvisation. She sat low at the instrument, and the lines of her body settled into ungraceful curves and angles that gave it an appearance of deformity. Gradually and imperceptibly the interlude melted into the soft opening minor chords of the Chopin Impromptu.

Edna did not know when the Impromptu began or ended. She sat in the sofa corner reading Robert's letter by the fading light. Mademoiselle had glided from the Chopin into the quivering lovenotes of Isolde's song, and back again to the Impromptu with its soulful and poignant longing.

The shadows deepened in the little room. The music grew strange and fantastic—turbulent, insistent, plaintive and soft with entreaty. The shadows grew deeper. The music filled the room. It floated out upon the night, over the housetops, the crescent of the river, losing itself in the silence of the upper air.

Edna was sobbing, just as she had wept one midnight at Grand Isle when strange, new voices awoke in her. She arose in some agitation to take her departure. "May I come again, Mademoiselle?" she asked at the threshold.

"Come whenever you feel like it. Be careful; the stairs and landing are dark; don't stumble."

Mademoiselle reentered and lit a candle. Robert's letter was on the floor. She stooped and picked it up. It was crumpled and damp with tears. Mademoiselle smoothed the letter out, restored it to the envelope, and replaced it in the table drawer.

XXII

One morning on his way into town Mr. Pontellier stopped at the house of his old friend and family physician, Doctor Mandelet. The Doctor was a semi-retired physician, resting, as the saying is, upon his laurels. He bore a reputation for wisdom rather than skill—leaving the active practice of medicine to his assistants and younger contemporaries—and was much sought for in matters of consultation. A few families, united to him by bonds of friendship, he still attended when they required the services of a physician. The Pontelliers were among these.

Mr. Pontellier found the Doctor reading at the open window of his study. His house stood rather far back from the street, in the center of a delightful garden, so that it was quiet and peaceful at the old gentleman's study window. He was a great reader. He stared up disapprovingly over his eye-glasses as Mr. Pontellier entered, wondering who had the temerity to disturb him at that hour of the morning.

"Ah, Pontellier! Not sick, I hope. Come and have a seat. What news do you bring this morning?" He was quite portly, with a profusion of gray hair, and small blue eyes which age had robbed of much of their brightness but none of their penetration.

"Oh! I'm never sick, Doctor. You know that I come of tough fiber—of that old Creole race of Pontelliers

that dry up and finally blow away. I came to consult—no, not precisely to consult—to talk to you about Edna. I don't know what ails her."

"Madame Pontellier not well?" marveled the Doctor. "Why, I saw her—I think it was a week ago—walking along Canal Street, the picture of health, it seemed to me."

"Yes, yes; she seems quite well," said Mr. Pontellier, leaning forward and whirling his stick between his two hands; "but she doesn't act well. She's odd, she's not like herself. I can't make her out, and I thought perhaps you'd help me."

"How does she act?" inquired the doctor.

"Well, it isn't easy to explain," said Mr. Pontellier, throwing himself back in his chair. "She lets the housekeeping go to the dickens."

"Well, well; women are not all alike, my dear Pontellier. We've got to consider—"

"I know that; I told you I couldn't explain. Her whole attitude—toward me and everybody and everything—has changed. You know I have a quick temper, but I don't want to quarrel or be rude to a woman, especially my wife; yet I'm driven to it, and feel like ten thousand devils after I've made a fool of myself. She's making it devilishly uncomfortable for me," he went on nervously. "She's got some sort of notion in her head concerning the eternal rights of women; and—you understand—we meet in the morning at the breakfast table."

The old gentleman lifted his shaggy eyebrows, protruded his thick nether lip, and tapped the arms of his chair with his cushioned fingertips.

"What have you been doing to her, Pontellier?"

"Doing! *Parbleu!*"

"Has she," asked the Doctor, with a smile, "has she been associating of late with a circle of pseudo-intellectual women—super-spiritual superior beings? My wife has been telling me about them."

"That's the trouble," broke in Mr. Pontellier, "she hasn't been associating with any one. She has abandoned her Tuesdays at home, has thrown over all her acquaintances, and goes tramping about by herself, moping in the street-cars, getting in after dark. I tell you she's peculiar. I don't like it; I feel a little worried over it."

This was a new aspect for the Doctor. "Nothing hereditary?" he asked, seriously. "Nothing peculiar about her family antecedents, is there?"

"Oh, no, indeed! She comes of sound old Presbyterian Kentucky stock. The old gentleman, her father,

I have heard, used to atone for his week-day sins with his Sunday devotions. I know for a fact, that his race horses literally ran away with the prettiest bit of Kentucky farming land I ever laid eyes upon. Margaret—you know Margaret—she has all the Presbyterianism undiluted. And the youngest is something of a vixen. By the way, she gets married in a couple of weeks from now."

"Send your wife up to the wedding," exclaimed the Doctor, foreseeing a happy solution. "Let her stay among her own people for a while; it will do her good."

"That's what I want her to do. She won't go to the marriage. She says a wedding is one of the most lamentable spectacles on earth. Nice thing for a woman to say to her husband!" exclaimed Mr. Pontellier, fuming anew at the recollection.

"Pontellier," said the Doctor, after a moment's reflection, "let your wife alone for a while. Don't bother her, and don't let her bother you. Woman, my dear friend, is a very peculiar and delicate organism—a sensitive and highly organized woman, such as I know Mrs. Pontellier to be, is especially peculiar. It would require an inspired psychologist to deal successfully with them. And when ordinary fellows like you and me attempt to cope with their idiosyncrasies the result is bungling. Most women are moody and whimsical. This is some passing whim of your wife, due to some cause or causes which you and I needn't try to fathom. But it will pass happily over, especially if you let her alone. Send her around to see me."

"Oh! I couldn't do that; there'd be no reason for it," objected Mr. Pontellier.

"Then I'll go around and see her," said the Doctor. "I'll drop in to dinner some evening *en bon ami*."

"Do! by all means," urged Mr. Pontellier. "What evening will you come? Say Thursday. Will you come Thursday?" he asked, rising to take his leave.

"Very well; Thursday. My wife may possibly have some engagement for me Thursday. In case she has, I shall let you know. Otherwise, you may expect me."

Mr. Pontellier turned before leaving to say:

"I am going to New York on business very soon. I have a big scheme on hand, and want to be on the field proper to pull the ropes and handle the ribbons. We'll let you in on the inside if you say so, Doctor," he laughed.

"No, I thank you, my dear sir," returned the Doctor. "I leave such ventures to you younger men with the fever of life still in your blood."

"What I wanted to say," continued Mr. Pontellier, with his hand on the knob; "I may have to be absent a good while. Would you advise me to take Edna along?"

"By all means, if she wishes to go. If not, leave her here. Don't contradict her. The mood will pass, I assure you. It may take a month, two, three months—possibly longer, but it will pass; have patience."

"Well, good-by, *à jeudi*," said Mr. Pontellier, as he let himself out.

The Doctor would have liked during the course of conversation to ask, "Is there any man in the case?" but he knew his Creole too well to make such a blunder as that.

He did not resume his book immediately, but sat for a while meditatively looking out into the garden.

XXIII

Edna's father was in the city, and had been with them several days. She was not very warmly or deeply attached to him, but they had certain tastes in common, and when together they were companionable. His coming was in the nature of a welcome disturbance; it seemed to furnish a new direction for her emotions.

He had come to purchase a wedding gift for his daughter, Janet, and an outfit for himself in which he might make a creditable appearance at her marriage. Mr. Pontellier had selected the bridal gift, as every one immediately connected with him always deferred to his taste in such matters. And his suggestions on the question of dress—which too often assumes the nature of a problem—were of inestimable value to his father-in-law. But for the past few days the old gentleman had been upon Edna's hands, and in his society she was becoming acquainted with a new set of sensations. He had been a colonel in the Confederate army, and still maintained, with the title, the military bearing which had always accompanied it. His hair and mustache were white and silky, emphasizing the rugged bronze of his face. He was tall and thin, and wore his coats padded, which gave a fictitious breadth and depth to his shoulders and chest. Edna and her father looked very distinguished together, and excited a good deal of notice during their perambulations. Upon his arrival she began by introducing him to her atelier and making a sketch of him. He took the whole matter very seriously. If her talent had been ten-fold greater than it was, it would not have surprised him, convinced as he was that he had bequeathed to all of his daughters the germs of a masterful capability, which only depended upon their own efforts to be directed toward successful achievement.

Before her pencil he sat rigid and unflinching, as he had faced the cannon's mouth in days gone by. He resented the intrusion of the children, who gaped with wondering eyes at him, sitting so stiff up there in their mother's bright atelier. When they drew near he motioned them away with an expressive action of foot, loath to disturb the fixed lines of his countenance, his arms, or his rigid shoulders.

Edna, anxious to entertain him, invited Mademoiselle Reisz to meet him, having promised him a treat in her piano playing; but Mademoiselle declined the invitation. So together they attended a *soirée musicale* at the Ratignolles'. Monsieur and Madame Ratignolle made much of the Colonel, installing him as the guest of honor and engaging him at once to dine with them the following Sunday, or any day which he might select. Madame coquetted with him in the most captivating and naïve manner, with eyes, gestures, and a profusion of compliments, till the Colonel's old head felt thirty years younger on his padded shoulders. Edna marveled, not comprehending. She herself was almost devoid of coquetry.

There were one or two men whom she observed at the *soirée musicale*; but she would never have felt moved to any kittenish display to attract their notice — to any feline or feminine wiles to express herself toward them. Their personality attracted her in an agreeable way. Her fancy selected them, and she was glad when a lull in the music gave them an opportunity to meet her and talk with her. Often on the street the glance of strange eyes had lingered in her memory, and sometimes had disturbed her.

Mr. Pontellier did not attend these *soirées musicales*. He considered them *bourgeois*, and found more diversion at the club. To Madame Ratignolle he said the music dispensed at her *soirées* was too "heavy," too far beyond his untrained comprehension. His excuse flattered her. But she disapproved of Mr. Pontellier's club, and she was frank enough to tell Edna so.

"It's a pity Mr. Pontellier doesn't stay home more in the evenings. I think you would be more — well, if you don't mind my saying it — more united, if he did."

"Oh! dear no!" said Edna, with a blank look in her eyes. "What should I do if he stayed home? We wouldn't have anything to say to each other."

She had not much of anything to say to her father, for that matter; but he did not antagonize her. She discovered that he interested her, though she realized that he might not interest her long; and for the first time in her life she felt as if she were thoroughly acquainted with him. He kept her busy serving him and ministering to his wants. It amused her to do so. She would not permit a servant or one of the children to do anything for him which she might do herself. Her husband noticed, and thought it was the expression of a deep filial attachment which he had never suspected.

The Colonel drank numerous "toddies" during the course of the day, which left him, however, imperturbed. He was an expert at concocting strong drinks. He had even invented some, to which he had given fantastic names, and for whose manufacture he required diverse ingredients that it devolved upon Edna to procure for him.

When Doctor Mandelet dined with the Pontelliers on Thursday he could discern in Mrs. Pontellier no trace of that morbid condition which her husband had reported to him. She was excited and in a manner radiant. She and her father had been to the race course, and their thoughts when they seated themselves at table were still occupied with the events of the afternoon, and their talk was still of the track. The Doctor had not kept pace with turf affairs. He had certain recollections of racing in what he called "the good old times" when the Lecompte stables flourished, and he drew upon this fund of memories so that he might not be left out and seem wholly devoid of the modern spirit. But he failed to impose upon the Colonel, and was even far from impressing him with this trumped-up knowledge of bygone days. Edna had staked her father on his last venture, with the most gratifying results to both of them. Besides, they had met some very charming people, according to the Colonel's impressions. Mrs. Mortimer Merriman and Mrs. James Highcamp, who were there with Alcée Arobin, had joined them and had enlivened the hours in a fashion that warmed him to think of.

Mr. Pontellier himself had no particular leaning toward horseracing, and was even rather inclined to discourage it as a pastime, especially when he considered the fate of that blue-grass farm in Kentucky. He endeavored, in a general way, to express a particular disapproval, and only succeeded in arousing the ire and opposition of his father-in-law. A pretty dispute followed, in which Edna warmly espoused her father's cause and the Doctor remained neutral.

He observed his hostess attentively from under his shaggy brows, and noted a subtle change which had transformed her from the listless woman he had known into a being who, for the moment, seemed palpitant with the forces of life. Her speech was warm and energetic. There was no repression in her glance or gesture. She reminded him of some beautiful, sleek animal waking up in the sun.

The dinner was excellent. The claret was warm and the champagne was cold, and under their beneficent influence the threatened unpleasantness melted and vanished with the fumes of the wine.

Mr. Pontellier warmed up and grew reminiscent. He told some amusing plantation experiences, recollections of old Iberville and his youth, when he hunted 'possum in company with some friendly darky; thrashed the pecan trees, shot the grosbec, and roamed the woods and fields in mischievous idleness.

The Colonel, with little sense of humor and of the fitness of things, related a somber episode of those dark and bitter days, in which he had acted a conspicuous part and always formed a central figure. Nor was the Doctor happier in his selection, when he told the old, ever new and curious story of the waning of a woman's love, seeking strange, new channels, only to return to its legitimate source after days of fierce unrest. It was one of the many little human documents which had been unfolded to him during his long career as a physician. The story did not seem especially to impress Edna. She had one of her own to tell, of a woman who paddled away with her lover one night in a pirogue and never came back. They were lost amid the Baratarian Islands, and no one ever heard of them or found trace of them from that day to this. It was a pure invention. She said that Madame Antoine had related it to her. That, also, was an invention. Perhaps it was a dream she had had. But every glowing word seemed real to those who listened. They could feel the hot breath of the Southern night; they could hear the long sweep of the pirogue through the glistening moonlit water, the beating of birds' wings, rising startled from among the reeds in the saltwater pools; they could see the faces of the lovers, pale, close together, rapt in oblivious forgetfulness, drifting into the unknown.

The champagne was cold, and its subtle fumes played fantastic tricks with Edna's memory that night.

Outside, away from the glow of the fire and the soft lamplight, the night was chill and murky. The Doctor doubled his old-fashioned cloak across his breast as he strode home through the darkness. He knew his fellow-creatures better than most men; knew that inner life which so seldom unfolds itself to unanointed eyes. He was sorry he had accepted Pontellier's invitation. He was growing old, and beginning to need rest and an imperturbed spirit. He did not want the secrets of other lives thrust upon him.

"I hope it isn't Arobin," he muttered to himself as he walked. "I hope to heaven it isn't Alcée Arobin."

XXIV

Edna and her father had a warm, and almost violent dispute upon the subject of her refusal to attend her sister's wedding. Mr. Pontellier declined to interfere, to interpose either his influence or his authority. He was following Doctor Mandelet's advice, and letting her do as she liked. The Colonel reproached his daughter for her lack of filial kindness and respect, her want of sisterly affection and womanly consideration. His arguments were labored and unconvincing. He doubted if Janet would accept any excuse— forgetting that Edna had offered none. He doubted if Janet would ever speak to her again, and he was sure Margaret would not.

Edna was glad to be rid of her father when he finally took himself off with his wedding garments and his bridal gifts, with his padded shoulders, his Bible reading, his "toddies" and ponderous oaths.

Mr. Pontellier followed him closely. He meant to stop at the wedding on his way to New York and endeavor by every means which money and love could devise to atone somewhat for Edna's incomprehensible action.

"You are too lenient, too lenient by far, Léonce," asserted the Colonel. "Authority, coercion are what is needed. Put your foot down good and hard; the only way to manage a wife. Take my word for it."

The Colonel was perhaps unaware that he had coerced his own wife into her grave. Mr. Pontellier had a vague suspicion of it which he thought it needless to mention at that late day.

Edna was not so consciously gratified at her husband's leaving home as she had been over the departure of her father. As the day approached when he was to leave her for a comparatively long stay, she grew melting and affectionate, remembering his many acts of consideration and his repeated expressions of an ardent attachment. She was solicitous about his health and his welfare. She bustled around, looking after his clothing, thinking about heavy underwear, quite as Madame Ratignolle would have done under similar circumstances. She cried when he went away, calling him her dear, good friend, and she was quite certain she would grow lonely before very long and go to join him in New York.

But after all, a radiant peace settled upon her when she at last found herself alone. Even the children were gone. Old Madame Pontellier had come herself and carried them off to Iberville with their quadroon. The old madame did not venture to say she was afraid they would be neglected during Léonce's absence; she hardly ventured to think so. She was hungry for them—even a little fierce in her attachment. She did not want them to be wholly "children of the pavement," she always said when begging to have them for a space. She wished them to know the country, with its streams, its fields, its woods, its freedom, so delicious to the young. She wished them to taste something of the life their father had lived and had known and loved when he, too, was a little child.

When Edna was at last alone, she breathed a big, genuine sigh of relief. A feeling that was unfamiliar but very delicious came over her. She walked all through the house, from one room to another, as if inspecting it for the first time. She tried the various chairs and lounges, as if she had never sat and reclined upon them before. And she perambulated around the outside of the house, investigating, looking to see if windows and shutters were secure and in order. The flowers were like new acquaintances; she approached them in a familiar spirit, and made herself at home among them. The garden walks were damp, and Edna called to the maid to bring out her rubber sandals. And there she stayed, and stooped, digging around the plants, trimming, picking dead, dry leaves. The children's little dog came out, interfering, getting in her way. She scolded him, laughed at him, played with him. The garden smelled so good and looked so pretty in the afternoon sunlight. Edna plucked all the bright flowers she could find, and went into the house with them, she and the little dog.

Even the kitchen assumed a sudden interesting character which she had never before perceived. She went in to give directions to the cook, to say that the butcher would have to bring much less meat, that they would require only half their usual quantity of bread, of milk and groceries. She told the cook that she herself would be greatly occupied during Mr. Pontellier's absence, and she begged her to take all thought and responsibility of the larder upon her own shoulders.

That night Edna dined alone. The candelabra, with a few candles in the center of the table, gave all the light she needed. Outside the circle of light in which she sat, the large dining-room looked solemn and shadowy. The cook, placed upon her mettle, served a delicious repast—a luscious tenderloin broiled à point. The wine tasted good; the marron glacé seemed to be just what she wanted. It was so pleasant, too, to dine in a comfortable peignoir.

She thought a little sentimentally about Léonce and the children, and wondered what they were doing. As she gave a dainty scrap or two to the doggie, she talked intimately to him about Etienne and Raoul. He was beside himself with astonishment and delight over these companionable advances, and showed his appreciation by his little quick, snappy barks and a lively agitation.

Then Edna sat in the library after dinner and read Emerson until she grew sleepy. She realized that she had neglected her reading, and determined to start anew upon a course of improving studies, now that her time was completely her own to do with as she liked.

After a refreshing bath, Edna went to bed. And as she snuggled comfortably beneath the eiderdown a sense of restfulness invaded her, such as she had not known before.

XXV

When the weather was dark and cloudy Edna could not work. She needed the sun to mellow and temper her mood to the sticking point. She had reached a stage when she seemed to be no longer feeling her way, working, when in the humor, with sureness and ease. And being devoid of ambition, and striving not toward accomplishment, she drew satisfaction from the work in itself.

On rainy or melancholy days Edna went out and sought the society of the friends she had made at Grand Isle. Or else she stayed indoors and nursed a mood with which she was becoming too familiar for her own comfort and peace of mind. It was not despair; but it seemed to her as if life were passing by, leaving its promise broken and unfulfilled. Yet there were other days when she listened, was led on and deceived by fresh promises which her youth held out to her.

She went again to the races, and again. Alcée Arobin and Mrs. Highcamp called for her one bright afternoon in Arobin's drag. Mrs. Highcamp was a worldly but unaffected, intelligent, slim, tall blonde woman in the forties, with an indifferent manner and blue eyes that stared. She had a daughter who served her as a pretext for cultivating the society of young men of fashion. Alcée Arobin was one of them. He was a familiar figure at the race course, the opera, the fashionable clubs. There was a perpetual smile in his eyes, which seldom failed to awaken a corresponding cheerfulness in any one who looked into them and listened to his good-humored voice. His manner was quiet, and at times a little insolent. He possessed a good figure, a pleasing face, not overburdened with depth of thought or feeling; and his dress was that of the conventional man of fashion.

He admired Edna extravagantly, after meeting her at the races with her father. He had met her before on other occasions, but she had seemed to him unapproachable until that day. It was at his instigation that Mrs. Highcamp called to ask her to go with them to the Jockey Club to witness the turf event of the season.

There were possibly a few track men out there who knew the race horse as well as Edna, but there was certainly none who knew it better. She sat between her two companions as one having authority to speak. She laughed at Arobin's pretensions, deplored Mrs. Highcamp's ignorance. The race horse was a friend and intimate associate of her childhood. The atmosphere of the stables and the breath of the blue grass paddock revived in her memory and lingered in her nostrils. She did not perceive that she was talking like her father as the sleek geldings ambled in review before them. She played for very high stakes, and fortune favored her. The fever of the game flamed in her cheeks and eyes, and it got into her blood and into her brain like an intoxicant. People turned their heads to look at her, and more than one lent an attentive ear to her utterances, hoping thereby to secure the elusive but ever-desired "tip." Arobin caught the contagion of excitement which drew him to Edna like a magnet. Mrs. Highcamp remained, as usual, unmoved, with her indifferent stare and uplifted eyebrows.

Edna stayed and dined with Mrs. Highcamp upon being urged to do so. Arobin also remained and sent away his drag.

The dinner was quiet and uninteresting, save for the cheerful efforts of Arobin to enliven things. Mrs. Highcamp deplored the absence of her daughter from the races, and tried to convey to her what she had missed by going to the "Dante reading" instead of joining them. The girl held a geranium leaf up to her nose and said nothing, but looked knowing and noncommittal. Mr. Highcamp was a plain, bald-headed man, who only talked under compulsion. He was unresponsive. Mrs. Highcamp was full of delicate courtesy and consideration toward her husband. She addressed most of her conversation to him at table. They sat in the library after dinner and read the evening papers together under the droplight; while the younger people went into the drawing-room near by and talked.

Miss Highcamp played some selections from Grieg upon the piano. She seemed to have apprehended all of the composer's coldness and none of his poetry. While Edna listened she could not help wondering if she had lost her taste for music.

When the time came for her to go home, Mr. Highcamp grunted a lame offer to escort her, looking down at his slippered feet with tactless concern. It was Arobin who took her home. The car ride was long, and it was late when they reached Esplanade Street. Arobin asked permission to enter for a second to light his cigarette — his match safe was empty. He filled his match safe, but did not light his cigarette until he left her, after she had expressed her willingness to go to the races with him again.

Edna was neither tired nor sleepy. She was hungry again, for the Highcamp dinner, though of excellent quality, had lacked abundance. She rummaged in the larder and brought forth a slice of Gruyère and some crackers. She opened a bottle of beer which she found in the ice-box. Edna felt extremely restless and excited. She vacantly hummed a fantastic tune as she poked at the wood embers on the hearth and munched a cracker.

She wanted something to happen—something, anything; she did not know what. She regretted that she had not made Arobin stay a half hour to talk over the horses with her. She counted the money she had won. But there was nothing else to do, so she went to bed, and tossed there for hours in a sort of monotonous agitation.

In the middle of the night she remembered that she had forgotten to write her regular letter to her husband; and she decided to do so next day and tell him about her afternoon at the Jockey Club. She lay wide awake composing a letter which was nothing like the one which she wrote next day. When the maid awoke her in the morning Edna was dreaming of Mr. Highcamp playing the piano at the entrance of a music store on Canal Street, while his wife was saying to Alcée Arobin, as they boarded an Esplanade Street car:

"What a pity that so much talent has been neglected! but I must go."

When, a few days later, Alcée Arobin again called for Edna in his drag, Mrs. Highcamp was not with him. He said they would pick her up. But as that lady had not been apprised of his intention of picking her up, she was not at home. The daughter was just leaving the house to attend the meeting of a branch Folk Lore Society, and regretted that she could not accompany them. Arobin appeared nonplused, and asked Edna if there were any one else she cared to ask.

She did not deem it worth while to go in search of any of the fashionable acquaintances from whom she had withdrawn herself. She thought of Madame Ratignolle, but knew that her fair friend did not leave the house, except to take a languid walk around the block with her husband after nightfall. Mademoiselle Reisz would have laughed at such a request from Edna. Madame Lebrun might have enjoyed the outing, but for some reason Edna did not want her. So they went alone, she and Arobin.

The afternoon was intensely interesting to her. The excitement came back upon her like a remittent fever. Her talk grew familiar and confidential. It was no labor to become intimate with Arobin. His manner invited easy confidence. The preliminary stage of becoming acquainted was one which he always endeavored to ignore when a pretty and engaging woman was concerned.

He stayed and dined with Edna. He stayed and sat beside the wood fire. They laughed and talked; and before it was time to go he was telling her how different life might have been if he had known her years before. With ingenuous frankness he spoke of what a wicked, ill-disciplined boy he had been, and impulsively drew up his cuff to exhibit upon his wrist the scar from a saber cut which he had received in a duel outside of Paris when he was nineteen. She touched his hand as she scanned the red cicatrice on the inside of his white wrist. A quick impulse that was somewhat spasmodic impelled her fingers to close in a sort of clutch upon his hand. He felt the pressure of her pointed nails in the flesh of his palm.

She arose hastily and walked toward the mantel.

"The sight of a wound or scar always agitates and sickens me," she said. "I shouldn't have looked at it."

"I beg your pardon," he entreated, following her; "it never occurred to me that it might be repulsive."

He stood close to her, and the effrontery in his eyes repelled the old, vanishing self in her, yet drew all her awakening sensuousness. He saw enough in her face to impel him to take her hand and hold it while he said his lingering good night.

"Will you go to the races again?" he asked.

"No," she said. "I've had enough of the races. I don't want to lose all the money I've won, and I've got to work when the weather is bright, instead of—"

"Yes; work; to be sure. You promised to show me your work. What morning may I come up to your atelier? To-morrow?"

"No!"

"Day after?"

"No, no."

"Oh, please don't refuse me! I know something of such things. I might help you with a stray suggestion or two."

"No. Good night. Why don't you go after you have said good night? I don't like you," she went on in a high, excited pitch, attempting to draw away her hand. She felt that her words lacked dignity and sincerity, and she knew that he felt it.

"I'm sorry you don't like me. I'm sorry I offended you. How have I offended you? What have I done? Can't you forgive me?" And he bent and pressed his lips upon her hands as if he wished never more to withdraw them.

"Mr. Arobin," she complained, "I'm greatly upset by the excitement of the afternoon; I'm not myself.

My manner must have misled you in some way. I wish you to go, please." She spoke in a monotonous, dull tone. He took his hat from the table, and stood with eyes turned from her, looking into the dying fire. For a moment or two he kept an impressive silence.

"Your manner has not misled me, Mrs. Pontellier," he said finally. "My own emotions have done that. I couldn't help it. When I'm near you, how could I help it? Don't think anything of it, don't bother, please. You see, I go when you command me. If you wish me to stay away, I shall do so. If you let me come back, I—oh! you will let me come back?"

He cast one appealing glance at her, to which she made no response. Alcée Arobin's manner was so genuine that it often deceived even himself.

Edna did not care to think whether it were genuine or not. When she was alone she looked mechanically at the back of her hand which he had kissed so warmly. Then she leaned her head down on the mantelpiece. She felt somewhat like a woman who in a moment of passion is betrayed into an act of infidelity, and realizes the significance of the act without being wholly awakened from its glamour. The thought was passing vaguely through her mind, "What would he think?"

She did not mean her husband; she was thinking of Robert Lebrun. Her husband seemed to her now like a person whom she had married without love as an excuse.

She lit a candle and went up to her room. Alcée Arobin was absolutely nothing to her. Yet his presence, his manners, the warmth of his glances, and above all the touch of his lips upon her hand had acted like a narcotic upon her.

She slept a languorous sleep, interwoven with vanishing dreams.

XXVI

Alcée Arobin wrote Edna an elaborate note of apology, palpitant with sincerity. It embarrassed her; for in a cooler, quieter moment it appeared to her absurd that she should have taken his action so seriously, so dramatically. She felt sure that the significance of the whole occurrence had lain in her own self-consciousness. If she ignored his note it would give undue importance to a trivial affair. If she replied to it in a serious spirit it would still leave in his mind the impression that she had in a susceptible moment yielded to his influence. After all, it was no great matter to have one's hand kissed. She was provoked

at his having written the apology. She answered in as light and bantering a spirit as she fancied it deserved, and said she would be glad to have him look in upon her at work whenever he felt the inclination and his business gave him the opportunity.

He responded at once by presenting himself at her home with all his disarming naïveté. And then there was scarcely a day which followed that she did not see him or was not reminded of him. He was prolific in pretexts. His attitude became one of good-humored subservience and tacit adoration. He was ready at all times to submit to her moods, which were as often kind as they were cold. She grew accustomed to him. They became intimate and friendly by imperceptible degrees, and then by leaps. He sometimes talked in a way that astonished her at first and brought the crimson into her face; in a way that pleased her at last, appealing to the animalism that stirred impatiently within her.

There was nothing which so quieted the turmoil of Edna's senses as a visit to Mademoiselle Reisz. It was then, in the presence of that personality which was offensive to her, that the woman, by her divine art, seemed to reach Edna's spirit and set it free.

It was misty, with heavy, lowering atmosphere, one afternoon, when Edna climbed the stairs to the pianist's apartments under the roof. Her clothes were dripping with moisture. She felt chilled and pinched as she entered the room. Mademoiselle was poking at a rusty stove that smoked a little and warmed the room indifferently. She was endeavoring to heat a pot of chocolate on the stove. The room looked cheerless and dingy to Edna as she entered. A bust of Beethoven, covered with a hood of dust, scowled at her from the mantelpiece.

"Ah! here comes the sunlight!" exclaimed Mademoiselle, rising from her knees before the stove. "Now it will be warm and bright enough; I can let the fire alone."

She closed the stove door with a bang, and approaching, assisted in removing Edna's dripping mackintosh.

"You are cold; you look miserable. The chocolate will soon be hot. But would you rather have a taste of brandy? I have scarcely touched the bottle which you brought me for my cold." A piece of red flannel was wrapped around Mademoiselle's throat; a stiff neck compelled her to hold her head on one side.

"I will take some brandy," said Edna, shivering as she removed her gloves and overshoes. She drank the liquor from the glass as a man would have done.

Then flinging herself upon the uncomfortable sofa she said, "Mademoiselle, I am going to move away from my house on Esplanade Street."

"Ah!" ejaculated the musician, neither surprised nor especially interested. Nothing ever seemed to astonish her very much. She was endeavoring to adjust the bunch of violets which had become loose from its fastening in her hair. Edna drew her down upon the sofa, and taking a pin from her own hair, secured the shabby artificial flowers in their accustomed place.

"Aren't you astonished?"

"Passably. Where are you going? to New York? to Iberville? to your father in Mississippi? where?"

"Just two steps away," laughed Edna, "in a little four-room house around the corner. It looks so cozy, so inviting and restful, whenever I pass by; and it's for rent. I'm tired looking after that big house. It never seemed like mine, anyway—like home. It's too much trouble. I have to keep too many servants. I am tired bothering with them."

"That is not your true reason, *ma belle*. There is no use in telling me lies. I don't know your reason, but you have not told me the truth." Edna did not protest or endeavor to justify herself.

"The house, the money that provides for it, are not mine. Isn't that enough reason?"

"They are your husband's," returned Mademoiselle, with a shrug and a malicious elevation of the eyebrows.

"Oh! I see there is no deceiving you. Then let me tell you: It is a caprice. I have a little money of my own from my mother's estate, which my father sends me by driblets. I won a large sum this winter on the races, and I am beginning to sell my sketches. Laidpore is more and more pleased with my work; he says it grows in force and individuality. I cannot judge of that myself, but I feel that I have gained in ease and confidence. However, as I said, I have sold a good many through Laidpore. I can live in the tiny house for little or nothing, with one servant. Old Celestine, who works occasionally for me, says she will come stay with me and do my work. I know I shall like it, like the feeling of freedom and independence."

"What does your husband say?"

"I have not told him yet. I only thought of it this morning. He will think I am demented, no doubt. Perhaps you think so."

Mademoiselle shook her head slowly. "Your reason is not yet clear to me," she said.

Neither was it quite clear to Edna herself; but it unfolded itself as she sat for a while in silence. In-

stinct had prompted her to put away her husband's bounty in casting off her allegiance. She did not know how it would be when he returned. There would have to be an understanding, an explanation. Conditions would some way adjust themselves, she felt; but whatever came, she had resolved never again to belong to another than herself.

"I shall give a grand dinner before I leave the old house!" Edna exclaimed. "You will have to come to it, Mademoiselle. I will give you everything that you like to eat and to drink. We shall sing and laugh and be merry for once." And she uttered a sigh that came from the very depths of her being.

If Mademoiselle happened to have received a letter from Robert during the interval of Edna's visits, she would give her the letter unsolicited. And she would seat herself at the piano and play as her humor prompted her while the young woman read the letter.

The little stove was roaring; it was red-hot, and the chocolate in the tin sizzled and sputtered. Edna went forward and opened the stove door, and Mademoiselle rising, took a letter from under the bust of Beethoven and handed it to Edna.

"Another! so soon!" she exclaimed, her eyes filled with delight. "Tell me, Mademoiselle, does he know that I see his letters?"

"Never in the world! He would be angry and would never write to me again if he thought so. Does he write to you? Never a line. Does he send you a message? Never a word. It is because he loves you, poor fool, and is trying to forget you, since you are not free to listen to him or to belong to him."

"Why do you show me his letters, then?"

"Haven't you begged for them? Can I refuse you anything? Oh! you cannot deceive me," and Mademoiselle approached her beloved instrument and began to play. Edna did not at once read the letter. She sat holding it in her hand, while the music penetrated her whole being like an effulgence, warming and brightening the dark places of her soul. It prepared her for joy and exultation.

"Oh!" she exclaimed, letting the letter fall to the floor. "Why did you not tell me?" She went and grasped Mademoiselle's hands up from the keys. "Oh! unkind! malicious! Why did you not tell me?"

"That he was coming back? No great news, *ma foi*. I wonder he did not come long ago."

"But when, when?" cried Edna, impatiently. "He does not say when."

"He says 'very soon.' You know as much about it as I do; it is all in the letter."

"But why? Why is he coming? Oh, if I thought—" and she snatched the letter from the floor and turned the pages this way and that way, looking for the reason, which was left untold.

"If I were young and in love with a man," said Mademoiselle, turning on the stool and pressing her wiry hands between her knees as she looked down at Edna, who sat on the floor holding the letter, "it seems to me he would have to be some *grand esprit*; a man with lofty aims and ability to reach them; one who stood high enough to attract the notice of his fellow-men. It seems to me if I were young and in love I should never deem a man of ordinary caliber worthy of my devotion."

"Now it is you who are telling lies and seeking to deceive me, Mademoiselle; or else you have never been in love, and know nothing about it. Why," went on Edna, clasping her knees and looking up into Mademoiselle's twisted face, "do you suppose a woman knows why she loves? Does she select? Does she say to herself: 'Go to! Here is a distinguished statesman with presidential possibilities; I shall proceed to fall in love with him.' Or, 'I shall set my heart upon this musician, whose fame is on every tongue?' Or, 'This financier, who controls the world's money markets?'"

"You are purposely misunderstanding me, *ma reine*. Are you in love with Robert?"

"Yes," said Edna. It was the first time she had admitted it, and a glow overspread her face, blotching it with red spots.

"Why?" asked her companion. "Why do you love him when you ought not to?"

Edna, with a motion or two, dragged herself on her knees before Mademoiselle Reisz, who took the glowing face between her two hands.

"Why? Because his hair is brown and grows away from his temples; because he opens and shuts his eyes, and his nose is a little out of drawing; because he has two lips and a square chin, and a little finger which he can't straighten from having played baseball too energetically in his youth. Because—"

"Because you do, in short," laughed Mademoiselle. "What will you do when he comes back?" she asked.

"Do? Nothing, except feel glad and happy to be alive."

She was already glad and happy to be alive at the mere thought of his return. The murky, lowering sky, which had depressed her a few hours before, seemed bracing and invigorating as she splashed through the streets on her way home.

She stopped at a confectioner's and ordered a huge box of bonbons for the children in Iberville. She slipped a card in the box, on which she scribbled a tender message and sent an abundance of kisses.

Before dinner in the evening Edna wrote a charming letter to her husband, telling him of her intention to move for a while into the little house around the block, and to give a farewell dinner before leaving, regretting that he was not there to share it, to help her out with the menu and assist her in entertaining the guests. Her letter was brilliant and brimming with cheerfulness.

XXVII

"What is the matter with you?" asked Arobin that evening. "I never found you in such a happy mood." Edna was tired by that time, and was reclining on the lounge before the fire.

"Don't you know the weather prophet has told us we shall see the sun pretty soon?"

"Well, that ought to be reason enough," he acquiesced. "You wouldn't give me another if I sat here all night imploring you." He sat close to her on a low tabouret, and as he spoke his fingers lightly touched the hair that fell a little over her forehead. She liked the touch of his fingers through her hair, and closed her eyes sensitively.

"One of these days," she said, "I'm going to pull myself together for a while and think—try to determine what character of a woman I am; for, candidly, I don't know. By all the codes which I am acquainted with, I am a devilishly wicked specimen of the sex. But some way I can't convince myself that I am. I must think about it."

"Don't. What's the use? Why should you bother thinking about it when I can tell you what manner of woman you are." His finger strayed occasionally down to her warm, smooth cheeks and firm chin, which was growing a little full and double.

"Oh, yes! You will tell me that I am adorable; everything that is captivating. Spare yourself the effort."

"No; I shan't tell you anything of the sort, though I shouldn't be lying if I did."

"Do you know Mademoiselle Reisz?" she asked irrelevantly.

"The pianist? I know her by sight. I've heard her play."

"She says queer things sometimes in a bantering way that you don't notice at the time and you find yourself thinking about afterward."

"For instance?"

"Well, for instance, when I left her to-day, she put her arms around me and felt my shoulder blades, to see if my wings were strong, she said. 'The bird that would soar above the level plain of tradition and prejudice must have strong wings. It is a sad spectacle to see the weaklings bruised, exhausted, fluttering back to earth.'"

"Whither would you soar?"

"I'm not thinking of any extraordinary flights. I only half comprehend her."

"I've heard she's partially demented," said Arobin.

"She seems to me wonderfully sane," Edna replied.

"I'm told she's extremely disagreeable and unpleasant. Why have you introduced her at a moment when I desired to talk of you?"

"Oh! talk of me if you like," cried Edna, clasping her hands beneath her head; "but let me think of something else while you do."

"I'm jealous of your thoughts to-night. They're making you a little kinder than usual; but some way I feel as if they were wandering, as if they were not here with me." She only looked at him and smiled. His eyes were very near. He leaned upon the lounge with an arm extended across her, while the other hand still rested upon her hair. They continued silently to look into each other's eyes. When he leaned forward and kissed her, she clasped his head, holding his lips to hers.

It was the first kiss of her life to which her nature had really responded. It was a flaming torch that kindled desire.

XXVIII

Edna cried a little that night after Arobin left her. It was only one phase of the multitudinous emotions which had assailed her. There was with her an overwhelming feeling of irresponsibility. There was the shock of the unexpected and the unaccustomed. There was her husband's reproach looking at her from the external things around her which he had provided for her external existence. There was Robert's reproach making itself felt by a quicker,

fiercer, more overpowering love, which had awakened within her toward him. Above all, there was understanding. She felt as if a mist had been lifted from her eyes, enabling her to look upon and comprehend the significance of life, that monster made up of beauty and brutality. But among the conflicting sensations which assailed her, there was neither shame nor remorse. There was a dull pang of regret because it was not the kiss of love which had inflamed her, because it was not love which had held this cup of life to her lips.

XXIX

Without even waiting for an answer from her husband regarding his opinion or wishes in the matter, Edna hastened her preparations for quitting her home on Esplanade Street and moving into the little house around the block. A feverish anxiety attended her every action in that direction. There was no moment of deliberation, no interval of repose between the thought and its fulfillment. Early upon the morning following those hours passed in Arobin's society, Edna set about securing her new abode and hurrying her arrangements for occupying it. Within the precincts of her home she felt like one who has entered and lingered within the portals of some forbidden temple in which a thousand muffled voices bade her be gone.

Whatever was her own in the house, everything which she had acquired aside from her husband's bounty, she caused to be transported to the other house, supplying simple and meager deficiencies from her own resources.

Arobin found her with rolled sleeves, working in company with the house-maid when he looked in during the afternoon. She was splendid and robust, and had never appeared handsomer than in the old blue gown, with a red silk handkerchief knotted at random around her head to protect her hair from the dust. She was mounted upon a high step-ladder, unhooking a picture from the wall when he entered. He had found the front door open, and had followed his ring by walking in unceremoniously.

"Come down!" he said. "Do you want to kill yourself?" She greeted him with affected carelessness, and appeared absorbed in her occupation.

If he had expected to find her languishing, reproachful, or indulging in sentimental tears, he must have been greatly surprised.

He was no doubt prepared for any emergency, ready for any one of the foregoing attitudes, just as he bent himself easily and naturally to the situation which confronted him.

"Please come down," he insisted, holding the ladder and looking up at her.

"No," she answered; "Ellen is afraid to mount the ladder. Joe is working over at the 'pigeon house'—that's the name Ellen gives it, because it's so small and looks like a pigeon house—and some one has to do this."

Arobin pulled off his coat, and expressed himself ready and willing to tempt fate in her place. Ellen brought him one of her dust-caps, and went into contortions of mirth, which she found it impossible to control, when she saw him put it on before the mirror as grotesquely as he could. Edna herself could not refrain from smiling when she fastened it at his request. So it was he who in turn mounted the ladder, unhooking pictures and curtains, and dislodging ornaments as Edna directed. When he had finished he took off his dust-cap and went out to wash his hands.

Edna was sitting on the tabouret, idly brushing the tips of a feather duster along the carpet when he came in again.

"Is there anything more you will let me do?" he asked.

"That is all," she answered. "Ellen can manage the rest." She kept the young woman occupied in the drawing-room, unwilling to be left alone with Arobin.

"What about the dinner?" he asked; "the grand event, the *coup d'état?*"

"It will be day after to-morrow. Why do you call it the '*coup d'état*'? Oh! it will be very fine; all my best of everything—crystal, silver and gold, Sèvres, flowers, music, and champagne to swim in. I'll let Léonce pay the bills. I wonder what he'll say when he sees the bills."

"And you ask me why I call it a *coup d'état?*" Arobin had put on his coat, and he stood before her and asked if his cravat was plumb. She told him it was, looking no higher than the tip of his collar.

"When do you go to the 'pigeon house'?—with all due acknowledgment to Ellen."

"Day after to-morrow, after the dinner. I shall sleep there."

"Ellen, will you very kindly get me a glass of water?" asked Arobin. "The dust in the curtains, if you

will pardon me for hinting such a thing, has parched my throat to a crisp."

"While Ellen gets the water," said Edna, rising, "I will say good-by and let you go. I must get rid of this grime, and I have a million things to do and think of."

"When shall I see you?" asked Arobin, seeking to detain her, the maid having left the room.

"At the dinner, of course. You are invited."

"Not before?—not to-night or to-morrow morning or to-morrow noon or night? or the day after morning or noon? Can't you see yourself, without my telling you, what an eternity it is?"

He had followed her into the hall and to the foot of the stairway, looking up at her as she mounted with her face half turned to him.

"Not an instant sooner," she said. But she laughed and looked at him with eyes that at once gave him courage to wait and made it torture to wait.

XXX

Though Edna had spoken of the dinner as a very grand affair, it was in truth a very small affair and very select, in so much as the guests invited were few and were selected with discrimination. She had counted upon an even dozen seating themselves at her round mahogany board, forgetting for the moment that Madame Ratignolle was to the last degree *souffrante* and unpresentable, and not foreseeing that Madame Lebrun would send a thousand regrets at the last moment. So there were only ten, after all, which made a cozy, comfortable number.

There were Mr. and Mrs. Merriman, a pretty, vivacious little woman in the thirties; her husband, a jovial fellow, something of a shallow-pate, who laughed a good deal at other people's witticisms, and had thereby made himself extremely popular. Mrs. Highcamp had accompanied them. Of course, there was Alcée Arobin; and Mademoiselle Reisz had consented to come. Edna had sent her a fresh bunch of violets with black lace trimmings for her hair. Monsieur Ratignolle brought himself and his wife's excuses. Victor Lebrun, who happened to be in the city, bent upon relaxation, had accepted with alacrity. There was a Miss Mayblunt, no longer in her teens, who looked at the world through lorgnettes and with the keenest interest. It was thought and said that she was intellectual; it was suspected of her that she wrote under a *nom de guerre*. She had come with a gentleman by the name of Gouvernail, connected with one of the daily papers, of whom nothing special could be said, except that he was observant and seemed quiet and inoffensive. Edna herself made the tenth, and at half-past eight they seated themselves at table, Arobin and Monsieur Ratignolle on either side of their hostess.

Mrs. Highcamp sat between Arobin and Victor Lebrun. Then came Mrs. Merriman, Mr. Gouvernail, Miss Mayblunt, Mr. Merriman, and Mademoiselle Reisz next to Monsieur Ratignolle.

There was something extremely gorgeous about the appearance of the table, an effect of splendor conveyed by a cover of pale yellow satin under strips of lace-work. There were wax candles in massive brass candelabra, burning softly under yellow silk shades; full, fragrant roses, yellow and red, abounded. There were silver and gold, as she had said there would be, and crystal which glittered like the gems which the women wore.

The ordinary stiff dining chairs had been discarded for the occasion and replaced by the most commodious and luxurious which could be collected throughout the house. Mademoiselle Reisz, being exceedingly diminutive, was elevated upon cushions, as small children are sometimes hoisted at table upon bulk volumes.

"Something new, Edna?" exclaimed Miss Mayblunt, with lorgnette directed toward a magnificent cluster of diamonds that sparkled, that almost sputtered, in Edna's hair, just over the center of her forehead.

"Quite new; 'brand' new, in fact; a present from my husband. It arrived this morning from New York. I may as well admit that this is my birthday, and that I am twenty-nine. In good time I expect you to drink my health. Meanwhile, I shall ask you to begin with this cocktail, composed—would you say 'composed'?" with an appeal to Miss Mayblunt—"composed by my father in honor of Sister Janet's wedding."

Before each guest stood a tiny glass that looked and sparkled like a garnet gem.

"Then, all things considered," spoke Arobin, "it might not be amiss to start out by drinking the Colonel's health in the cocktail which he composed, on the birthday of the most charming of women—the daughter whom he invented."

Mr. Merriman's laugh at this sally was such a genuine outburst and so contagious that it started the dinner with an agreeable swing that never slackened.

Miss Mayblunt begged to be allowed to keep her cocktail untouched before her, just to look at. The color was marvelous! She could compare it to nothing she had ever seen, and the garnet lights which it emitted were unspeakably rare. She pronounced the Colonel an artist, and stuck to it.

Monsieur Ratignolle was prepared to take things seriously: the *mets*, the *entre-mets*, the service, the decorations, even the people. He looked up from his pompono and inquired of Arobin if he were related to the gentleman of that name who formed one of the firm of Laitner and Arobin, lawyers. The young man admitted that Laitner was a warm personal friend, who permitted Arobin's name to decorate the firm's letterheads and to appear upon a shingle that graced Perdido Street.

"There are so many inquisitive people and institutions abounding," said Arobin, "that one is really forced as a matter of convenience these days to assume the virtue of an occupation if he has it not."

Monsieur Ratignolle stared a little, and turned to ask Mademoiselle Reisz if she considered the symphony concerts up to the standard which had been set the previous winter. Mademoiselle Reisz answered Monsieur Ratignolle in French, which Edna thought a little rude, under the circumstances, but characteristic. Mademoiselle had only disagreeable things to say of the symphony concerts, and insulting remarks to make of all the musicians of New Orleans, singly and collectively. All her interest seemed to be centered upon the delicacies placed before her.

Mr. Merriman said that Mr. Arobin's remark about inquisitive people reminded him of a man from Waco the other day at the St. Charles Hotel—but as Mr. Merriman's stories were always lame and lacking point, his wife seldom permitted him to complete them. She interrupted him to ask if he remembered the name of the author whose book she had bought the week before to send to a friend in Geneva. She was talking "books" with Mr. Gouvernail and trying to draw from him his opinion upon current literary topics. Her husband told the story of the Waco man privately to Miss Mayblunt, who pretended to be greatly amused and to think it extremely clever.

Mrs. Highcamp hung with languid but unaffected interest upon the warm and impetuous volubility of her left-hand neighbor, Victor Lebrun. Her attention was never for a moment withdrawn from him after seating herself at table; and when he turned to Mrs. Merriman, who was prettier and more vivacious than Mrs. Highcamp, she waited with easy indifference for an opportunity to reclaim his attention. There was the occasional sound of music, of mandolins, sufficiently removed to be an agreeable accompaniment rather than an interruption to the conversation. Outside the soft, monotonous splash of a fountain could be heard; the sound penetrated into the room with the heavy odor of jessamine that came through the open windows.

The golden shimmer of Edna's satin gown spread in rich folds on either side of her. There was a soft fall of lace encircling her shoulder. It was the color of her skin, without the glow, the myriad living tints that one may sometimes discover in vibrant flesh. There was something in her attitude, in her whole appearance when she leaned her head against the high-backed chair and spread her arms, which suggested the regal woman, the one who rules, who looks on, who stands alone.

But as she sat there amid her guests, she felt the old ennui overtaking her; the hopelessness which so often assailed her, which came upon her like an obsession, like something extraneous, independent of volition. It was something which announced itself; a chill breath that seemed to issue from some vast cavern wherein discords wailed. There came over her the acute longing which always summoned into her spiritual vision the presence of the beloved one, overpowering her at once with a sense of the unattainable.

The moments glided on, while a feeling of good fellowship passed around the circle like a mystic cord, holding and binding these people together with jest and laughter. Monsieur Ratignolle was the first to break the pleasant charm. At ten o'clock he excused himself. Madame Ratignolle was waiting for him at home. She was *bien souffrante,* and she was filled with vague dread, which only her husband's presence could allay.

Mademoiselle Reisz arose with Monsieur Ratignolle, who offered to escort her to the car. She had eaten well; she had tasted the good rich wines, and they must have turned her head, for she bowed pleasantly to all as she withdrew from table. She kissed Edna upon the shoulder, and whispered: *"Bonne nuit, ma reine; soyez sage."* She had been a little bewildered upon rising, or rather, descending

from her cushions, and Monsieur Ratignolle gallantly took her arm and led her away.

Mrs. Highcamp was weaving a garland of roses, yellow and red. When she had finished the garland, she laid it lightly upon Victor's black curls. He was reclining far back in the luxurious chair, holding a glass of champagne to the light.

As if a magician's wand had touched him, the garland of roses transformed him into a vision of Oriental beauty. His cheeks were the color of crushed grapes, and his dusky eyes glowed with a languishing fire.

"Sapristi!" exclaimed Arobin.

But Mrs. Highcamp had one more touch to add to the picture. She took from the back of her chair a white silken scarf, with which she had covered her shoulders in the early part of the evening. She draped it across the boy in graceful folds, and in a way to conceal his black, conventional evening dress. He did not seem to mind what she did to him, only smiled, showing a faint gleam of white teeth, while he continued to gaze with narrowing eyes at the light through his glass of champagne.

"Oh! to be able to paint in color rather than in words!" exclaimed Miss Mayblunt, losing herself in a rhapsodic dream as she looked at him.

" 'There was a graven image of Desire
Painted with red blood on a ground of gold.' "

murmured Gouvernail, under his breath.

The effect of the wine upon Victor was to change his accustomed volubility into silence. He seemed to have abandoned himself to a reverie, and to be seeing pleasing visions in the amber bead.

"Sing," entreated Mrs. Highcamp. "Won't you sing to us?"

"Let him alone," said Arobin.

"He's posing," offered Mr. Merriman; "let him have it out."

"I believe he's paralyzed," laughed Mrs. Merriman. And leaning over the youth's chair, she took the glass from his hand and held it to his lips. He sipped the wine slowly, and when he had drained the glass she laid it upon the table and wiped his lips with her little filmy handkerchief.

"Yes, I'll sing for you," he said, turning in his chair toward Mrs. Highcamp. He clasped his hands behind his head, and looking up at the ceiling began to hum a little, trying his voice like a musician tuning an instrument. Then, looking at Edna, he began to sing:

"Ah! si tu savais!"

"Stop!" she cried, "don't sing that. I don't want you to sing it," and she laid her glass so impetuously and blindly upon the table as to shatter it against a carafe. The wine spilled over Arobin's legs and some of it trickled down upon Mrs. Highcamp's black gauze gown. Victor had lost all idea of courtesy, or else he thought his hostess was not in earnest, for he laughed and went on:

"Ah! si tu savais
Ce que tes yeux me disent" —

"Oh! you mustn't! you mustn't," exclaimed Edna, and pushing back her chair she got up, and going behind him placed her hand over his mouth. He kissed the soft palm that pressed upon his lips.

"No, no, I won't, Mrs. Pontellier. I didn't know you meant it," looking up at her with caressing eyes. The touch of his lips was like a pleasing sting to her hand. She lifted the garland of roses from his head and flung it across the room.

"Come, Victor; you've posed long enough. Give Mrs. Highcamp her scarf."

Mrs. Highcamp undraped the scarf from about him with her own hands. Miss Mayblunt and Mr. Gouvernail suddenly conceived the notion that it was time to say good night. And Mr. and Mrs. Merriman wondered how it could be so late.

Before parting from Victor, Mrs. Highcamp invited him to call upon her daughter, who she knew would be charmed to meet him and talk French and sing French songs with him. Victor expressed his desire and intention to call upon Miss Highcamp at the first opportunity which presented itself. He asked if Arobin were going his way. Arobin was not.

The mandolin players had long since stolen away. A profound stillness had fallen upon the broad, beautiful street. The voices of Edna's disbanding guests jarred like a discordant note upon the quiet harmony of the night.

XXXI

"Well?" questioned Arobin, who had remained with Edna after the others had departed.

"Well," she reiterated, and stood up, stretching her arms, and feeling the need to relax her muscles after having been so long seated.

"What next?" he asked.

"The servants are all gone. They left when the musicians did. I have dismissed them. The house has to be closed and locked, and I shall trot around to the pigeon house, and shall send Celestine over in the morning to straighten things up."

He looked around, and began to turn out some of the lights.

"What about upstairs?" he inquired.

"I think it is all right; but there may be a window or two unlatched. We had better look; you might take a candle and see. And bring me my wrap and hat on the foot of the bed in the middle room."

He went up with the light, and Edna began closing doors and windows. She hated to shut in the smoke and the fumes of the wine. Arobin found her cape and hat, which he brought down and helped her to put on.

When everything was secured and the lights put out, they left through the front door, Arobin locking it and taking the key, which he carried for Edna. He helped her down the steps.

"Will you have a spray of jessamine?" he asked, breaking off a few blossoms as he passed.

"No; I don't want anything."

She seemed disheartened, and had nothing to say. She took his arm, which he offered her, holding up the weight of her satin train with the other hand. She looked down, noticing the black line of his leg moving in and out so close to her against the yellow shimmer of her gown. There was the whistle of a railway train somewhere in the distance, and the midnight bells were ringing. They met no one in their short walk.

The "pigeon house" stood behind a locked gate, and a shallow *parterre* that had been somewhat neglected. There was a small front porch, upon which a long window and the front door opened. The door opened directly into the parlor; there was no side entry. Back in the yard was a room for servants, in which old Celestine had been ensconced.

Edna had left a lamp burning low upon the table. She had succeeded in making the room look habitable and homelike. There were some books on the table and a lounge near at hand. On the floor was a fresh matting, covered with a rug or two; and on the walls hung a few tasteful pictures. But the room was filled with flowers. These were a surprise to her. Arobin had sent them, and had had Celestine distribute them during Edna's absence. Her bedroom was adjoining, and across a small passage were the dining-room and kitchen.

Edna seated herself with every appearance of discomfort.

"Are you tired?" he asked.

"Yes, and chilled, and miserable. I feel as if I had been wound up to a certain pitch — too tight — and something inside of me had snapped." She rested her head against the table upon her bare arm.

"You want to rest," he said, "and to be quiet. I'll go; I'll leave you and let you rest."

"Yes," she replied.

He stood up beside her and smoothed her hair with his soft, magnetic hand. His touch conveyed to her a certain physical comfort. She could have fallen quietly asleep there if he had continued to pass his hand over her hair. He brushed the hair upward from the nape of her neck.

"I hope you will feel better and happier in the morning," he said. "You have tried to do too much in the past few days. The dinner was the last straw; you might have dispensed with it."

"Yes," she admitted; "it was stupid."

"No, it was delightful; but it has worn you out." His hand had strayed to her beautiful shoulders, and he could feel the response of her flesh to his touch. He seated himself beside her and kissed her lightly upon the shoulder.

"I thought you were going away," she said, in an uneven voice.

"I am, after I have said good night."

"Good night," she murmured.

He did not answer, except to continue to caress her. He did not say good night until she had become supple to his gentle, seductive entreaties.

XXXII

When Mr. Pontellier learned of his wife's intention to abandon her home and take up her residence elsewhere, he immediately wrote her a letter of unqualified disapproval and remonstrance. She had given reasons which he was unwilling to acknowledge as adequate. He hoped she had not acted upon her rash impulse; and he begged her to consider first, foremost, and above all else, what people would say. He was not dreaming of scandal when he uttered this warning; that was a thing which would never have entered into his mind to consider in connection with his wife's name or his own. He was simply thinking of his financial integrity. It might get noised about that the Pontelliers had met with reverses, and were forced to conduct their *ménage* on a humbler scale than heretofore. It might do incalculable mischief to his business prospects.

But remembering Edna's whimsical turn of mind of late, and foreseeing that she had immediately acted upon her impetuous determination, he grasped the situation with his usual promptness and handled it with his well-known business tact and cleverness.

The same mail which brought to Edna his letter of disapproval carried instructions — the most minute instructions — to a well-known architect concerning the remodeling of his home, changes which he had long contemplated, and which he desired carried forward during his temporary absence.

Expert and reliable packers and movers were engaged to convey the furniture, carpets, pictures — everything movable, in short — to places of security. And in an incredibly short time the Pontellier house was turned over to the artisans. There was to be an addition — a small snuggery; there was to be frescoing, and hardwood flooring was to be put into such rooms as had not yet been subjected to this improvement.

Furthermore, in one of the daily papers appeared a brief notice to the effect that Mr. and Mrs. Pontellier were contemplating a summer sojourn abroad, and that their handsome residence on Esplanade Street was undergoing sumptuous alterations, and would not be ready for occupancy until their return. Mr. Pontellier had saved appearances!

Edna admired the skill of his maneuver, and avoided any occasion to balk his intentions. When the situation as set forth by Mr. Pontellier was accepted and taken for granted, she was apparently satisfied that it should be so.

The pigeon house pleased her. It at once assumed the intimate character of a home, while she herself invested it with a charm which it reflected like a warm glow. There was with her a feeling of having descended in the social scale, with a corresponding sense of having risen in the spiritual. Every step which she took toward relieving herself from obligations added to her strength and expansion as an individual. She began to look with her own eyes; to see and to apprehend the deeper undercurrents of life. No longer was she content to "feed upon opinion" when her own soul had invited her.

After a little while, a few days, in fact, Edna went up and spent a week with her children in Iberville. They were delicious February days, with all the summer's promise hovering in the air.

How glad she was to see the children! She wept for very pleasure when she felt their little arms clasping her; their hard, ruddy cheeks pressed against her own glowing cheeks. She looked into their faces with hungry eyes that could not be satisfied with looking. And what stories they had to tell their mother! About the pigs, the cows, the mules! About riding to the mill behind Gluglu; fishing back in the lake with their Uncle Jasper; picking pecans with Lidie's little black brood, and hauling chips in their express wagon. It was a thousand times more fun to haul real chips for old lame Susie's real fire than to drag painted blocks along the banquette on Esplanade Street!

She went with them herself to see the pigs and the cows, to look at the darkies laying the cane, to thrash the pecan trees, and catch fish in the back lake. She lived with them a whole week long, giving them all of herself, and gathering and filling herself with their young existence. They listened, breathless, when she told them the house in Esplanade Street was crowded with workmen, hammering, nailing, sawing, and filling the place with clatter. They wanted to know where their bed was; what had been done with their rocking-horse; and where did Joe sleep, and where had Ellen gone, and the cook? But, above all, they were fired with a desire to see the little house around the block. Was there any place to play? Were there any boys next door? Raoul, with pessimistic foreboding, was convinced that there were only girls next door. Where would they sleep, and where would papa sleep? She told them the fairies would fix it all right.

The old Madame was charmed with Edna's visit, and showered all manner of delicate attention upon her. She was delighted to know that the Esplanade Street house was in a dismantled condition. It gave her the promise and pretext to keep the children indefinitely.

It was with a wrench and a pang that Edna left her children. She carried away with her the sound of their voices and the touch of their cheeks. All along the journey homeward their presence lingered with her like the memory of a delicious song. But by the time she had regained the city the song no longer echoed in her soul. She was again alone.

XXXIII

It happened sometimes when Edna went to see Mademoiselle Reisz that the little musician was absent, giving a lesson or making some small necessary household purchase. The key was always left in a secret hiding-place in the entry, which Edna knew. If Mademoiselle happened to be away, Edna would usually enter and wait for her return.

When she knocked at Mademoiselle Reisz's door one afternoon there was no response; so unlocking the door, as usual, she entered and found the apartment deserted, as she had expected. Her day had been quite filled up, and it was for a rest, for a refuge and to talk about Robert, that she sought out her friend.

She had worked at her canvas—a young Italian character study—all the morning, completing the work without the model; but there had been many interruptions, some incident to her modest housekeeping, and others of a social nature.

Madame Ratignolle had dragged herself over, avoiding the too public thoroughfares, she said. She complained that Edna had neglected her much of late. Besides, she was consumed with curiosity to see the little house and the manner in which it was conducted. She wanted to hear all about the dinner party; Monsieur Ratignolle had left *so* early. What had happened after he left? The champagne and grapes which Edna sent over were *too* delicious. She has so little appetite; they had refreshed and toned her stomach. Where on earth was she going to put Mr. Pontellier in that little house, and the boys? And then she made Edna promise to go to her when her hour of trial overtook her.

"At any time—any time of the day or night, dear," Edna assured her.

Before leaving Madame Ratignolle said:

"In some way you seem to me like a child, Edna. You seem to act without a certain amount of reflection which is necessary in this life. That is the reason I want to say you mustn't mind if I advise you to be a little careful while you are living here alone. Why don't you have some one come and stay with you? Wouldn't Mademoiselle Reisz come?"

"No; she wouldn't wish to come, and I shouldn't want her always with me."

"Well, the reason—you know how evil-minded the world is—someone was talking of Alcée Arobin visiting you. Of course, it wouldn't matter if Mr. Arobin had not such a dreadful reputation. Monsieur Ratignolle was telling me that his attentions alone are considered enough to ruin a woman's name."

"Does he boast of his successes?" asked Edna, indifferently, squinting at her picture.

"No, I think not. I believe he is a decent fellow as far as that goes. But his character is so well known among the men. I shan't be able to come back and see you; it was very, very imprudent to-day."

"Mind the step!" cried Edna.

"Don't neglect me," entreated Madame Ratignolle; "and don't mind what I said about Arobin, or having some one to stay with you."

"Of course not," Edna laughed. "You may say anything you like to me." They kissed each other good-by. Madame Ratignolle had not far to go, and Edna stood on the porch a while watching her walk down the street.

Then in the afternoon Mrs. Merriman and Mrs. Highcamp had made their "party call." Edna felt that they might have dispensed with the formality. They had also come to invite her to play *vingt-et-un* one evening at Mrs. Merriman's. She was asked to go early, to dinner, and Mr. Merriman or Mr. Arobin would take her home. Edna accepted in a half-hearted way. She sometimes felt very tired of Mrs. Highcamp and Mrs. Merriman.

Late in the afternoon she sought refuge with Mademoiselle Reisz, and stayed there alone, waiting for her, feeling a kind of repose invade her with the very atmosphere of the shabby, unpretentious little room.

Edna sat at the window, which looked out over the housetops and across the river. The window frame was filled with pots of flowers, and she sat and picked the dry leaves from a rose geranium. The day was warm, and the breeze which blew from the river was very pleasant. She removed her hat and laid it on the piano. She went on picking the leaves and digging around the plants with her hat pin. Once she thought she heard Mademoiselle Reisz approaching. But it was a young black girl, who came in, bringing a small bundle of laundry, which she deposited in the adjoining room, and went away.

Edna seated herself at the piano, and softly picked out with one hand the bars of a piece of music which lay open before her. A half-hour went by. There was the occasional sound of people going and coming in the lower hall. She was growing interested in her occupation of picking out the aria, when there was a second rap at the door. She vaguely wondered what these people did when they found Mademoiselle's door locked.

"Come in," she called, turning her face toward the door. And this time it was Robert Lebrun who presented himself. She attempted to rise; she could not have done so without betraying the agitation which mastered her at sight of him, so she fell back upon the stool, only exclaiming, "Why, Robert!"

He came and clasped her hand, seemingly without knowing what he was saying or doing.

"Mrs. Pontellier! How do you happen — oh! how well you look! Is Mademoiselle Reisz not here? I never expected to see you."

"When did you come back?" asked Edna in an unsteady voice, wiping her face with her handkerchief. She seemed ill at ease on the piano stool, and he begged her to take the chair by the window. She did so, mechanically, while he seated himself on the stool.

"I returned day before yesterday," he answered, while he leaned his arm on the keys, bringing forth a crash of discordant sound.

"Day before yesterday!" she repeated, aloud; and went on thinking to herself, "day before yesterday," in a sort of an uncomprehending way. She had pictured him seeing her at the very first hour, and he had lived under the same sky since day before yesterday; while only by accident had he stumbled upon her. Mademoiselle must have lied when she said "Poor fool, he loves you."

"Day before yesterday," she repeated, breaking off a spray of Mademoiselle's geranium; "then if you had not met me here today you wouldn't — when — that is, didn't you mean to come and see me?"

"Of course, I should have gone to see you. There have been so many things —" he turned the leaves of Mademoiselle's music nervously. "I started in at once yesterday with the old firm. After all there is as much chance for me here as there was there — that is, I might find it profitable some day. The Mexicans were not very congenial."

So he had come back because the Mexicans were not congenial; because business was as profitable here as there; because of any reason, and not because he cared to be near her. She remembered the day she sat on the floor, turning the pages of his letter, seeking the reason which was left untold.

She had not noticed how he looked — only feeling his presence; but she turned deliberately and observed him. After all, he had been absent but a few months, and was not changed. His hair — the color or hers — waved back from his temples in the same way as before. His skin was not more burned than it had been at Grand Isle. She found in his eyes, when he looked at her for one silent moment, the same tender caress, with an added warmth and entreaty which had not been there before—the same glance which had penetrated to the sleeping places of her soul and awakened them.

A hundred times Edna had pictured Robert's return, and imagined their first meeting. It was usually at her home, whither he had sought her out at once. She always fancied him expressing or betraying in some way his love for her. And here, the reality was that they sat ten feet apart, she at the window, crushing geranium leaves in her hand and smelling them, he twirling around on the piano stool, saying:

"I was very much surprised to hear of Mr. Pontellier's absence; it's a wonder Mademoiselle Reisz did not tell me; and your moving—mother told me yesterday. I should think you would have gone to New York with him, or to Iberville with the children, rather than be bothered here with housekeeping. And you are going abroad, too, I heard. We shan't have you at Grand Isle next summer; it won't seem—do you see much of Mademoiselle Reisz? She often spoke of you in the few letters she wrote."

"Do you remember that you promised to write to me when you went away?" A flush overspread his whole face.

"I couldn't believe that my letters would be of any interest to you."

"That is an excuse; it isn't the truth." Edna reached for her hat on the piano. She adjusted it, sticking the hat pin through the heavy coil of hair with some deliberation.

"Are you not going to wait for Mademoiselle Reisz?" asked Robert.

"No; I have found when she is absent this long, she is liable not to come back till late." She drew on her gloves, and Robert picked up his hat.

"Won't you wait for her?" asked Edna.

"Not if you think she will not be back till late," adding, as if suddenly aware of some discourtesy in his speech, "and I should miss the pleasure of walking home with you." Edna locked the door and put the key back in its hiding-place.

They went together, picking their way across muddy streets and sidewalks encumbered with the cheap display of small tradesmen. Part of the distance they rode in the car, and after disembarking, passed the Pontellier mansion, which looked broken and half torn asunder. Robert had never known the house, and looked at it with interest.

"I never knew you in your home," he remarked.

"I am glad you did not."

"Why?" She did not answer. They went on around the corner, and it seemed as if her dreams were coming true after all, when he followed her into the little house.

"You must stay and dine with me, Robert. You see I am all alone, and it is so long since I have seen you. There is so much I want to ask you."

She took off her hat and gloves. He stood irresolute, making some excuse about his mother who expected him; he even muttered something about an engagement. She struck a match and lit the lamp on the table; it was growing dusk. When he saw her face in the lamp-light, looking pained, with all the soft lines gone out of it, he threw his hat aside and seated himself.

"Oh! you know I want to stay if you will let me!" he exclaimed. All the softness came back. She laughed, and went and put her hand on his shoulder.

"This is the first moment you have seemed like the old Robert. I'll go tell Celestine." She hurried away to tell Celestine to set an extra plate. She even sent her off in search of some added delicacy which she had not thought of for herself. And she recommended great care in dripping the coffee and having the omelet done to a proper turn.

When she reentered, Robert was turning over magazines, sketches, and things that lay upon the table in great disorder. He picked up a photograph, and exclaimed:

"Alcée Arobin! What on earth is this picture doing here?"

"I tried to make a sketch of his head one day," answered Edna, "and he thought the photograph might help me. It was at the other house. I thought it had been left there. I must have packed it up with my drawing materials."

"I should think you would give it back to him if you have finished with it."

"Oh! I have a great many such photographs. I never think of returning them. They don't amount to anything." Robert kept on looking at the picture.

"It seems to me—do you think his head worth drawing? Is he a friend of Mr. Pontellier's? You never said you knew him."

"He isn't a friend of Mr. Pontellier's; he's a friend of mine. I always knew him—that is, it is only of late that I know him pretty well. But I'd rather talk about you, and know what you have been seeing and doing and feeling out there in Mexico." Robert threw aside the picture.

"I've been seeing the waves and the white beach of Grand Isle; the quiet, grassy street of the *Chênière;* the old fort at Grande Terre. I've been working like a machine, and feeling like a lost soul. There was nothing interesting."

She leaned her head upon her hand to shade her eyes from the light.

"And what have you been seeing and doing and feeling all these days?" he asked.

"I've been seeing the waves and the white beach of Grand Isle; the quiet, grassy street of the *Chênière Caminada;* the old sunny fort at Grand Terre. I've been working with little more comprehension than a machine and still feeling like a lost soul. There was nothing interesting."

"Mrs. Pontellier, you are cruel," he said, with feeling, closing his eyes and resting his head back in the chair. They remained in silence till old Celestine announced dinner.

XXXIV

The dining-room was very small. Edna's round mahogany would have almost filled it. As it was there was but a step or two from the little table to the kitchen, to the mantel, the small buffet, and the side door that opened out on the narrow brick-paved yard.

A certain degree of ceremony settled upon them with the announcement of dinner. There was no return to personalities. Robert related incidents of his sojourn in Mexico, and Edna talked of events likely to interest him, which had occurred during his absence. The diner was of ordinary quality, except for the few delicacies which she had sent out to purchase. Old Celestine, with a bandana *tignon* twisted about her head, hobbled in and out, taking a personal interest in everything; and she lingered occasionally to talk patois with Robert, whom she had known as a boy.

He went out to a neighboring cigar stand to purchase cigarette papers, and when he came back he found that Celestine had served the black coffee in the parlor.

"Perhaps I shouldn't have come back," he said. "When you are tired of me, tell me to go."

"You never tire me. You must have forgotten the hours and hours at Grand Isle in which we grew accustomed to each other and used to being together."

"I have forgotten nothing at Grand Isle," he said, not looking at her, but rolling a cigarette. His tobacco pouch, which he laid upon the table, was a fantastic embroidered silk affair, evidently the handiwork of a woman.

"You used to carry your tobacco in a rubber pouch," said Edna, picking up the pouch and examining the needlework.

"Yes; it was lost."

"Where did you buy this one? In Mexico?"

"It was given to me by a Vera Cruz girl; they are very generous," he replied, striking a match and lighting his cigarette.

"They are very handsome, I suppose, those Mexican women; very picturesque, with their black eyes and their lace scarfs."

"Some are; others are hideous. Just as you find women everywhere."

"What was she like—the one who gave you the pouch? You must have known her very well."

"She was very ordinary. She wasn't of the slightest importance. I knew her well enough."

"Did you visit at her house? Was it interesting? I should like to know and hear about the people you met, and the impressions they made on you."

"There are some people who leave impressions not so lasting as the imprint of an oar upon the water."

"Was she such a one?"

"It would be ungenerous for me to admit that she was of that order and kind." He thrust the pouch back in his pocket, as if to put away the subject with the trifle which had brought it up.

Arobin dropped in with a message from Mrs. Merriman, to say that the card party was postponed on account of the illness of one of her children.

"How do you do, Arobin?" said Robert, rising from the obscurity.

"Oh! Lebrun. To be sure! I heard yesterday you were back. How did they treat you down in Mexique?"

"Fairly well."

"But not well enough to keep you there. Stunning girls, though, in Mexico. I thought I should never get away from Vera Cruz when I was down there a couple of years ago."

"Did they embroider slippers and tobacco pouches and hatbands and things for you?" asked Edna.

"Oh! my! no! I didn't get so deep in their regard. I fear they made more impression on me than I made on them."

"You were less fortunate than Robert, then."

"I am always less fortunate than Robert. Has he been imparting tender confidences?"

"I've been imposing myself long enough," said Robert, rising, and shaking hands with Edna. "Please convey my regards to Mr. Pontellier when you write."

He shook hands with Arobin and went away.

"Fine fellow, that Lebrun," said Arobin when Robert had gone. "I never heard you speak of him."

"I knew him last summer at Grand Isle," she replied. "Here is that photograph of yours. Don't you want it?"

"What do I want with it? Throw it away." She threw it back on the table.

"I'm not going to Mrs. Merriman's," she said. "If you see her, tell her so. But perhaps I had better write. I think I shall write now, and say that I am sorry her child is sick, and tell her not to count on me."

"It would be a good scheme," acquiesced Arobin. "I don't blame you; stupid lot!"

Edna opened the blotter, and having procured paper and pen, began to write the note. Arobin lit a cigar and read the evening paper, which he had in his pocket.

"What is the date?" she asked. He told her.

"Will you mail this for me when you go out?"

"Certainly." He read to her little bits out of the newspaper, while she straightened things on the table.

"What do you want to do?" he asked, throwing aside the paper. "Do you want to go out for a walk or a drive or anything? It would be a fine night to drive."

"No; I don't want to do anything but just be quiet. You go away and amuse yourself. Don't stay."

"I'll go away if I must; but I shan't amuse myself. You know that I only live when I am near you."

He stood up to bid her good night.

"Is that one of the things you always say to women?"

"I have said it before, but I don't think I ever came so near meaning it," he answered with a smile. There were no warm lights in her eyes; only a dreamy, absent look.

"Good night. I adore you. Sleep well," he said, and he kissed her hand and went away.

She stayed alone in a kind of reverie—a sort of stupor. Step by step she lived out every instant of the time she had been with Robert after he had entered Mademoiselle Reisz's door. She recalled his words, his looks. How few and meager they had been for her hungry heart! A vision—a transcendently seductive vision of a Mexican girl arose before her. She writhed with a jealous pang. She wondered when he would come back. He had not said he would come back. She had been with him, had heard his voice and touched his hand. But some way he had seemed nearer to her off there in Mexico.

XXXV

The morning was full of sunlight and hope. Edna could see before her no denial—only the promise of excessive joy. She lay in bed awake, with bright eyes full of speculation. "He loves you, poor fool." If she could but get that conviction firmly fixed in her mind, what mattered about the rest? She felt she had been childish and unwise the night before in giving herself over to despondency. She recapitulated the motives which no doubt explained Robert's reserve. They were not insurmountable; they would not hold if he really loved her; they could not hold against her own passion, which he must come to realize in time. She pictured him going to his business that morning. She even saw how he was dressed; how he walked down one street, and turned the corner of another; saw him bending over his desk, talking to people who entered the office, going to his lunch, and perhaps watching for her on the street. He would come to her in the afternoon or evening, sit and roll his cigarette, talk a little, and go away as he had done the night before. But how delicious it would be to have him there with her! She would have no regrets, nor seek to penetrate his reserve if he still chose to wear it.

Edna ate her breakfast only half dressed. Her maid brought her a delicious printed scrawl from Raoul, expressing his love, asking her to send him some bonbons, and telling her they had found that morning ten tiny white pigs all lying in a row beside Lidie's big white pig.

A letter also came from her husband, saying he hoped to be back early in March, and then they would get ready for that journey abroad which he had promised her so long, which he felt now fully able to afford; he felt able to travel as people should, without any thought of small economies—thanks to his recent speculations in Wall Street.

Much to her surprise she received a note from Arobin, written at midnight from the club. It was to say good morning to her, to hope she had slept well, to assure her of his devotion, which he trusted she in some faintest manner returned.

All these letters were pleasing to her. She answered the children in a cheerful frame of mind, promising them bonbons, and congratulating them upon their happy find of the little pigs.

She answered her husband with friendly evasiveness,—not with any fixed design to mislead him, only because all sense of reality had gone out of her life; she had abandoned herself to Fate, and awaited the consequences with indifference.

To Arobin's note she made no reply. She put it under Celestine's stove-lid.

Edna worked several hours with much spirit. She saw no one but a picture dealer, who asked her if it were true that she was going abroad to study in Paris.

She said possibly she might, and he negotiated with her for some Parisian studies to reach him in time for the holiday trade in December.

Robert did not come that day. She was keenly disappointed. He did not come the following day, nor the next. Each morning she awoke with hope, and each night she was a prey to despondency. She was tempted to seek him out. But far from yielding to the impulse, she avoided any occasion which might throw her in his way. She did not go to Mademoiselle Reisz's nor pass by Madame Lebrun's, as she might have done if he had still been in Mexico.

When Arobin, one night, urged her to drive with him, she went—out to the lake, on the Shell Road. His horses were full of mettle, and even a little unmanageable. She liked the rapid gait at which they spun along, and the quick, sharp sound of the horse's hoofs on the hard road. They did not stop anywhere to eat or to drink. Arobin was not needlessly imprudent. But they ate and they drank when they regained Edna's little dining-room—which was comparatively early in the evening.

It was late when he left her. It was getting to be more than a passing whim with Arobin to see her and be with her. He had detected the latent sensuality, which unfolded under his delicate sense of her nature's requirements like a torpid, torrid, sensitive blossom.

There was no despondency when she fell asleep that night; nor was there hope when she awoke in the morning.

XXXVI

There was a garden out in the suburbs; a small, leafy corner, with a few green tables under the orange trees. An old cat slept all day on the stone step in the sun, and an old *mulatresse* slept her idle hours away in her chair at the open window, till some one happened to knock on one of the green tables. She had

milk and cream cheese to sell, and bread and butter. There was no one who could make such excellent coffee or fry a chicken so golden brown as she.

The place was too modest to attract the attention of people of fashion, and so quiet as to have escaped the notice of those in search of pleasure and dissipation. Edna had discovered it accidentally one day when the high-board gate stood ajar. She caught sight of a little green table, blotched with the checkered sunlight that filtered through the quivering leaves overhead. Within she had found the slumbering *mulatresse,* the drowsy cat, and glass of milk which reminded her of the milk she had tasted in Iberville.

She often stopped there during her perambulations; sometimes taking a book with her, and sitting an hour or two under the trees when she found the place deserted. Once or twice she took a quiet dinner there alone, having instructed Celestine beforehand to prepare no dinner at home. It was the last place in the city where she would have expected to meet any one she knew.

Still she was not astonished when, as she was partaking of a modest dinner late in the afternoon, looking into an open book, stroking the cat, which had made friends with her—she was not greatly astonished to see Robert come in at the tall garden gate.

"I am destined to see you only by accident," she said, shoving the cat off the chair beside her. He was surprised, ill at ease, almost embarrassed at meeting her thus so unexpectedly.

"Do you come here often?" he asked.

"I almost live here," she said.

"I used to drop in very often for a cup of Catiche's good coffee. This is the first time since I came back."

"She'll bring you a plate, and you will share my dinner. There's always enough for two—even three." Edna had intended to be indifferent and as reserved as he when she met him; she had reached the determination by a laborious train of reasoning, incident to one of her despondent moods. But her resolve melted when she saw him before her, seated there beside her in the little garden, as if a designing Providence had led him into her path.

"Why have you kept away from me, Robert?" she asked, closing the book that lay open upon the table.

"Why are you so personal, Mrs. Pontellier? Why do you force me to idiotic subterfuges?" he exclaimed with sudden warmth. "I suppose there's no use telling you I've been very busy, or that I've been sick, or that

I've been to see you and not found you at home. Please let me off with any one of these excuses."

"You are the embodiment of selfishness," she said. "You save yourself something—I don't know what—but there is some selfish motive, and in sparing yourself you never consider for a moment what I think, or how I feel your neglect and indifference. I suppose this is what you would call unwomanly; but I have got into a habit of expressing myself. It doesn't matter to me, and you may think me unwomanly if you like."

"No; I only think you cruel, as I said the other day. Maybe not intentionally cruel; but you seem to be forcing me into disclosures which can result in nothing; as if you would have me bare a wound for the pleasure of looking at it, without the intention or power of healing it."

"I'm spoiling your dinner, Robert; never mind what I say. You haven't eaten a morsel."

"I only came in for a cup of coffee." His sensitive face was all disfigured with excitement.

"Isn't this a delightful place?" she remarked. "I am so glad it has never actually been discovered. It is so quiet, so sweet, here. Do you notice there is scarcely a sound to be heard? It's so out of the way; and a good walk from the car. However, I don't mind walking. I always feel so sorry for women who don't like to walk; they miss so much—so many rare little glimpses of life; and we women learn so little of life on the whole.

"Catiche's coffee is always hot. I don't know how she manages it, here in the open air. Celestine's coffee gets cold bringing it from the kitchen to the dining-room. Three lumps! How can you drink it so sweet? Take some of the cress with your chop; it's so biting and crisp. Then there's the advantage of being able to smoke with your coffee out here. Now, in the city—aren't you going to smoke?"

"After a while," he said, laying a cigar on the table.

"Who gave it to you?" she laughed.

"I bought it. I suppose I'm getting reckless; I bought a whole box." She was determined not to be personal again and make him uncomfortable.

The cat made friends with him, and climbed into his lap when he smoked his cigar. He stroked her silky fur, and talked a little about her. He looked at Edna's book, which he had read; and he told her the end, to save her the trouble of wading through it, he said.

Again he accompanied her back to her home; and it was after dusk when they reached the little "pigeon house." She did not ask him to remain, which he was grateful for, as it permitted him to stay without the discomfort of blundering through an excuse which he had no intention of considering. He helped her to light the lamp; then she went into her room to take off her hat and to bathe her face and hands.

When she came back Robert was not examining the pictures and magazines as before; he sat off in the shadow, leaning his head back on the chair as if in a reverie. Edna lingered a moment beside the table, arranging the books there. Then she went across the room to where he sat. She bent over the arm of his chair and called his name.

"Robert," she said, "are you asleep?"

"No," he answered, looking up at her.

She leaned over and kissed him—a soft, cool, delicate kiss, whose voluptuous sting penetrated his whole being—then she moved away from him. He followed, and took her in his arms, just holding her close to him. She put her hand up to his face and pressed his cheek against her own. The action was full of love and tenderness. He sought her lips again. Then he drew her down upon the sofa beside him and held her hand in both of his.

"Now you know," he said, "now you know what I have been fighting against since last summer at Grand Isle; what drove me away and drove me back again."

"Why have you been fighting against it?" she asked. Her face glowed with soft lights.

"Why? Because you were not free; you were Léonce Pontellier's wife. I couldn't help loving you if you were ten times his wife; but so long as I went away from you and kept away I could help telling you so." She put her free hand up to his shoulder, and then against his cheek, rubbing it softly. He kissed her again. His face was warm and flushed.

"There in Mexico I was thinking of you all the time, and longing for you."

"But not writing to me," she interrupted.

"Something put into my head that you cared for me; and I lost my senses. I forgot everything but a wild dream of your some way becoming my wife."

"Your wife!"

"Religion, loyalty, everything would give way if only you cared."

"Then you must have forgotten that I was Léonce Pontellier's wife."

"Oh! I was demented, dreaming of wild, impossible things, recalling men who had set their wives free, we have heard of such things."

"Yes, we have heard of such things."

"I came back full of vague, mad intentions. And when I got here—"

"When you got here you never came near me!" She was still caressing his cheek.

"I realized what a cur I was to dream of such a thing, even if you had been willing."

She took his face between her hands and looked into it as if she would never withdraw her eyes more. She kissed him on the forehead, the eyes, the cheeks, and the lips.

"You have been a very, very foolish boy, wasting your time dreaming of impossible things when you speak of Mr. Pontellier setting me free! I am no longer one of Mr. Pontellier's possessions to dispose of or not. I give myself where I choose. If he were to say, 'Here, Robert, take her and be happy; she is yours,' I should laugh at you both."

His face grew a little white. "What do you mean?" he asked.

There was a knock at the door. Old Celestine came in to say that Madame Ratignolle's servant had come around the back way with a message that Madame had been taken sick and begged Mrs. Pontellier to go to her immediately.

"Yes, yes," said Edna, rising; "I promised. Tell her yes—to wait for me. I'll go back with her."

"Let me walk over with you," offered Robert.

"No," she said; "I will go with the servant." She went into her room to put on her hat, and when she came in again she sat once more upon the sofa beside him. He had not stirred. She put her arms about his neck.

"Good-by, my sweet Robert. Tell me good-by." He kissed her with a degree of passion which had not before entered into his caress, and strained her to him.

"I love you," she whispered, "only you; no one but you. It was you who awoke me last summer out of a life-long, stupid dream. Oh! you have made me so unhappy with your indifference. Oh! I have suffered, suffered! Now you are here we shall love each other, my Robert. We shall be everything to each other. Nothing else in the world is of any consequence. I must go to my friend; but you will wait for me? No matter how late; you will wait for me, Robert?"

"Don't go; don't go! Oh! Edna, stay with me," he pleaded. "Why should you go? Stay with me, stay with me."

"I shall come back as soon as I can; I shall find you here." She buried her face in his neck, and said good-by again. Her seductive voice, together with his great love for her, had enthralled his senses, had deprived him of every impulse but the longing to hold her and keep her.

XXXVII

Edna looked in at the drug store. Monsieur Ratignolle was putting up a mixture himself, very carefully, dropping a red liquid into a tiny glass. He was grateful to Edna for having come; her presence would be a comfort to his wife. Madame Ratignolle's sister, who had always been with her at such trying times, had not been able to come up from the plantation, and Adèle had been inconsolable until Mrs. Pontellier so kindly promised to come to her. The nurse had been with them at night for the past week, as she lived a great distance away. And Dr. Mandelet had been coming and going all afternoon. They were then looking for him any moment.

Edna hastened upstairs by a private stairway that led from the rear of the store to the apartments above. The children were all sleeping in a back room. Madame Ratignolle was in the salon, whither she had strayed in her suffering impatience. She sat on the sofa, clad in an ample white *peignoir,* holding a handkerchief tight in her hand with a nervous clutch. Her face was drawn and pinched, her sweet blue eyes haggard and unnatural. All her beautiful hair had been drawn back and plaited. It lay in a long braid on the sofa pillow, coiled like a golden serpent. The nurse, a comfortable looking *Griffe* woman in white apron and cap, was urging her to return to her bedroom.

"There is no use, there is no use," she said at once to Edna. "We must get rid of Mandelet; he is getting too old and careless. He said he would be here at half-past seven; now it must be eight. See what time it is, Joséphine."

The woman was possessed of a cheerful nature, and refused to take any situation too seriously, especially a situation with which she was so familiar. She urged Madame to have courage and patience. But Madame only set her teeth hard into her under lip, and Edna saw the sweat gather in beads on her white forehead. After a moment or two she uttered a profound sigh and wiped her face with the handkerchief rolled in a ball. She appeared exhausted. The nurse gave her a fresh handkerchief, sprinkled with cologne water.

"This is too much!" she cried. "Mandelet ought to be killed! Where is Alphonse? Is it possible I am to be abandoned like this—neglected by every one?"

"Neglected, indeed!" exclaimed the nurse. Wasn't she there? And here was Mrs. Pontellier leaving, no doubt, a pleasant evening at home to devote to her? And wasn't Monsieur Ratignolle coming that very instant through the hall? And Joséphine was quite sure she had heard Doctor Mandelet's coupé. Yes, there it was, down at the door.

Adèle consented to go back to her room. She sat on the edge of the little low couch next to her bed.

Doctor Mandelet paid no attention to Madame Ratignolle's upbraidings. He was accustomed to them at such times, and was too well convinced of her loyalty to doubt it.

He was glad to see Edna, and wanted her to go with him into the salon and entertain him. But Madame Ratignolle would not consent that Edna should leave her for an instant. Between agonizing moments, she chatted a little, and said it took her mind off her sufferings.

Edna began to feel uneasy. She was seized with a vague dread. Her own like experiences seemed far away, unreal, and only half remembered. She recalled faintly an ecstasy of pain, the heavy odor of chloroform, a stupor which had deadened sensation, and an awakening to find a little new life to which she had given being, added to the great unnumbered multitude of souls that come and go.

She began to wish she had not come; her presence was not necessary. She might have invented a pretext for staying away; she might even invent a pretext now for going. But Edna did not go. With an inward agony, with a flaming, outspoken revolt against the ways of Nature, she witnessed the scene of torture.

She was still stunned and speechless with emotion when later she leaned over her friend to kiss her and softly say good-by. Adèle, pressing her cheek, whispered in an exhausted voice: "Think of the children, Edna. Oh think of the children! Remember them!"

XXXVIII

Edna still felt dazed when she got outside in the open air. The Doctor's coupé had returned for him and stood before the *porte cochère*. She did not wish to enter the coupé, and told Doctor Mandelet she would walk; she was not afraid, and would go alone. He directed his carriage to meet him at Mrs. Pontellier's, and he started to walk home with her.

Up—away up, over the narrow street between the tall houses, the stars were blazing. The air was mild and caressing, but cool with the breath of spring and the night. They walked slowly, the Doctor with a heavy, measured tread and his hands behind him; Edna, in an absent-minded way, as she had walked one night at Grand Isle, as if her thoughts had gone ahead of her and she was striving to overtake them

"You shouldn't have been there, Mrs. Pontellier," he said. "That was no place for you. Adèle is full of whims at such times. There were a dozen women she might have had with her, unimpressionable women. I felt that it was cruel, cruel. You shouldn't have gone."

"Oh, well!" she answered, indifferently. "I don't know that it matters after all. One has to think of the children some time or other; the sooner the better."

"When is Léonce coming back?"

"Quite soon. Some time in March."

"And you are going abroad?"

"Perhaps—no, I am not going. I'm not going to be forced into doing things. I don't want to go abroad. I want to be let alone. Nobody has any right—except children, perhaps—and even then, it seems to me—or it did seem—" She felt that her speech was voicing the incoherency of her thoughts, and stopped abruptly.

"The trouble is," sighed the Doctor, grasping her meaning intuitively, "that youth is given up to illusions. It seems to be a provision of Nature; a decoy to secure mothers for the race. And Nature takes no account of moral consequences, of arbitrary conditions which we create, and which we feel obliged to maintain at any cost."

"Yes," she said. "The years that are gone seem like dreams—if one might go on sleeping and dreaming—but to wake up and find—oh! well! perhaps it is better to wake up after all, even to suffer, rather than to remain a dupe to illusions all one's life."

"It seems to me, my dear child," said the Doctor at parting, holding her hand, "you seem to me to be in trouble. I am not going to ask for your confidence. I will only say that if ever you feel moved to give it to me, perhaps I might help you. I know I would understand, and I tell you there are not many who would—not many, my dear."

"Some way I don't feel moved to speak of things that trouble me. Don't think I am ungrateful or that I don't appreciate your sympathy. There are periods of despondency and suffering which take possession of me. But I don't want anything but my own way.

That is wanting a good deal, of course, when you have to trample upon the lives, the hearts, the prejudices of others—but no matter—still, I shouldn't want to trample upon the little lives. Oh! I don't know what I'm saying, Doctor. Good night. Don't blame me for anything."

"Yes, I will blame you if you don't come and see me soon. We will talk of things you never have dreamt of talking about before. It will do us both good. I don't want you to blame yourself, whatever comes. Good night, my child."

She let herself in at the gate, but instead of entering she sat upon the step of the porch. The night was quiet and soothing. All the tearing emotion of the last few hours seemed to fall away from her like a somber, uncomfortable garment, which she had but to loosen to be rid of. She went back to that hour before Adèle had sent for her; and her senses kindled afresh in thinking of Robert's words, the pressure of his arms, and the feeling of his lips upon her own. She could picture at that moment no greater bliss on earth than possession of the beloved one. His expression of love had already given him to her in part. When she thought that he was there at hand, waiting for her, she grew numb with the intoxication of expectancy. It was so late; he would be asleep perhaps. She would awaken him with a kiss. She hoped he would be asleep that she might arouse him with her caresses.

Still, she remembered Adèle's voice whispering, "Think of the children; think of them." She meant to think of them; that determination had driven into her soul like a death wound—but not to-night. To-morrow would be time to think of everything.

Robert was not waiting for her in the little parlor. He was nowhere at hand. The house was empty. But he had scrawled on a piece of paper that lay in the lamplight:

"I love you. Good-by—because I love you."

Edna grew faint when she read the words. She went and sat on the sofa. Then she stretched herself out there, never uttering a sound. She did not sleep. She did not go to bed. The lamp sputtered and went out. She was still awake in the morning, when Celestine unlocked the kitchen door and came in to light the fire.

XXXIX

Victor, with hammer and nails and scraps of scantling, was patching a corner of one of the galleries. Mariequita sat near by, dangling her legs, watching him work, and handing him nails from the tool-box. The sun was beating down upon them. The girl had covered her head with her apron folded into a square pad. They had been talking for an hour or more. She was never tired of hearing Victor describe the dinner at Mrs. Pontellier's. He exaggerated every detail, making it appear a veritable Lucullean feast. The flowers were in tubs, he said. The champagne was quaffed from huge golden goblets. Venus rising from the foam could have presented no more entrancing a spectacle than Mrs. Pontellier, blazing with beauty and diamonds at the head of the board, while the other women were all of them youthful houris, possessed of incomparable charms.

She got it into her head that Victor was in love with Mrs. Pontellier, and he gave her evasive answers, framed so as to confirm her belief. She grew sullen and cried a little, threatening to go off and leave him to his fine ladies. There were a dozen men crazy about her at the Chênière; and since it was the fashion to be in love with married people, why, she could run away any time she liked to New Orleans with Célina's husband.

Célina's husband was a fool, a coward, and a pig, and to prove it to her, Victor intended to hammer his head into a jelly the next time he encountered him. This assurance was very consoling to Mariequita. She dried her eyes, and grew cheerful at the prospect.

They were still talking of the dinner and the allurements of city life when Mrs. Pontellier herself slipped around the corner of the house. The two youngsters stayed dumb with amazement before what they considered to be an apparition. But it was really she in flesh and blood, looking tired and a little travel-stained.

"I walked up from the wharf," she said, "and heard the hammering. I supposed it was you, mending the porch. It's a good thing. I was always tripping over those loose planks last summer. How dreary and deserted everything looks!"

It took Victor some little time to comprehend that she had come in Beaudelet's lugger, and she had come alone, and for no purpose but to rest.

"There's nothing fixed up yet, you see. I'll give you my room; it's the only place."

"Any corner will do," she assured him.

"And if you can stand Philomel's cooking," he went on, "though I might try to get her mother while you are here. Do you think she would come?" turning to Mariequita.

Mariequita thought that perhaps Philomel's mother might come for a few days, and money enough.

Beholding Mrs. Pontellier make her appearance, the girl had at once suspected a lovers' rendezvous. But Victor's astonishment was so genuine, and Mrs. Pontellier's indifference so apparent, that the disturbing notion did not lodge long in her brain. She contemplated with the greatest interest this woman who gave the most sumptuous dinners in America, and who had all the men in New Orleans at her feet.

"What time will you have dinner?" asked Edna. "I'm very hungry; but don't get anything extra."

"I'll have it ready in little or no time," he said, bustling and packing away his tools. "You may go to my room to brush up and rest yourself. Mariequita will show you."

"Thank you," said Edna. "But, do you know, I have a notion to go down to the beach and take a good wash and even a little swim, before dinner?"

"The water is too cold!" they both exclaimed. "Don't think of it."

"Well, I might go down and try—dip my toes in. Why, it seems to me the sun is hot enough to have warmed the very depths of the ocean. Could you get me a couple of towels? I'd better go right away, so as to be back in time. It would be a little too chilly if I waited till this afternoon."

Mariequita ran over to Victor's room, and returned with some towels, which she gave to Edna.

"I hope you have fish for dinner," said Edna, as she started to walk away; "but don't do anything extra if you haven't."

"Run and find Philomel's mother," Victor instructed the girl. "I'll go to the kitchen and see what I can do. By Gimminy! Women have no consideration! She might have sent me word."

Edna walked on down to the beach rather mechanically, not noticing anything special except that the sun was hot. She was not dwelling upon any particular train of thought. She had done all the thinking which was necessary after Robert went away, when she lay awake upon the sofa till morning.

She had said over and over to herself: "To-day it is Arobin; to-morrow it will be some one else. It makes no difference to me, it doesn't matter about Léonce Pontellier—but Raoul and Etienne!" She understood now clearly what she had meant long ago when she said to Adèle Ratignolle that she would give up the unessential, but she would never sacrifice herself for her children.

Despondency had come upon her there in the wakeful night, and had never lifted. There was no one thing in the world that she desired. There was no human being whom she wanted near her except Robert; and she even realized that the day would come when he, too, and the thought of him would melt out of her existence, leaving her alone. The children appeared before her like antagonists who had overcome her; who had overpowered and sought to drag her into the soul's slavery for the rest of her days. But she knew a way to elude them. She was not thinking of these things when she walked down to the beach.

The water of the Gulf stretched out before her, gleaming with the million lights of the sun. The voice of the sea is seductive, never ceasing, whispering, clamoring, murmuring, inviting the soul to wander in abysses of solitude. All along the white beach, up and down, there was no living thing in sight. A bird with a broken wing was beating the air above, reeling, fluttering, circling disabled down, down to the water.

Edna had found her old bathing suit still hanging, faded, upon its accustomed peg.

She put it on, leaving her clothing in the bathhouse. But when she was there beside the sea, absolutely alone, she cast the unpleasant, pricking garments from her, and for the first time in her life she stood naked in the open air, at the mercy of the sun, the breeze that beat upon her, and the waves that invited her.

How strange and awful it seemed to stand naked under the sky! how delicious! She felt like some newborn creature, opening its eyes in a familiar world that it had never known.

The foamy wavelets curled up to her white feet, and coiled like serpents about her ankles. She walked out. The water was chill, but she walked on. The water was deep, but she lifted her white body and reached out with a long, sweeping stroke. The touch of the sea is sensuous, enfolding the body in its soft, close embrace.

She went on and on. She remembered the night she swam far out, and recalled the terror that seized her at the fear of being unable to regain the shore. She did not look back now, but went on and on, thinking of the blue-grass meadow that she had traversed when a little child, believing that it had no beginning and no end.

Her arms and legs were growing tired.

She thought of Léonce and the children. They were a part of her life. But they need not have thought that they could possess her, body and soul. How Mademoiselle Reisz would have laughed, perhaps sneered, if she knew! "And you call yourself an artist! What pretensions, Madame! The artist must possess the courageous soul that dares and defies."

Exhaustion was pressing upon and overpowering her.

"Good-by—because I love you." He did not know; he did not understand. He would never understand. Perhaps Doctor Mandelet would have understood if she had seen him—but it was too late; the shore was far behind her, and her strength was gone.

She looked into the distance, and the old terror flamed up for an instant, then sank again. Edna heard her father's voice and her sister Margaret's. She heard the barking of an old dog that was chained to the sycamore tree. The spurs of the cavalry officer clanged as he walked across the porch. There was the hum of bees, and the musky odor of pinks filled the air.

INDEX